# OXFORD Learner's French Dictionary

Project management

Nicholas Rollin
Joanna Brough

Editors

Isabelle Stables-Lemoine
Mary O'Neill
Pat Bulhosen
Alain Nogaret
Gabrielle Goldet
Amanda Leigh

Consultants

Danièle Bourdais
Sue Finnie

Great Clarendon Street, Oxford OX2 6DP

Oxford University Press is a department of the University of Oxford.
It furthers the University's objective of excellence in research, scholarship, and education by publishing worldwide in

Oxford New York

Auckland Cape Town Dar es Salaam Hong Kong Karachi
Kuala Lumpur Madrid Melbourne Mexico City Nairobi
New Delhi Shanghai Taipei Toronto

With offices in

Argentina Austria Brazil Chile Czech Republic France Greece
Guatemala Hungary Italy Japan Poland Portugal Singapore
South Korea Switzerland Thailand Turkey Ukraine Vietnam



First published 2006



British Library Cataloguing in Publication Data

Data available

ISBN: 978-0-19-911371-2

3 5 7 9 10 8 6 4 2

Printed in Italy by Legoprint

# Contents

# Introduction

This bilingual dictionary has been specifically written for students of French – from those just starting out all the way up to those preparing for exams. It presents essential information in a format designed to be clear and easy to consult. There are two main sections: French–English and English–French. These sections are divided by a central section in full colour.

**TIP** To help you find words quickly, the first word on each page is printed top left and the last word on the page is printed top right.

## French–English

Look up French words – listed alphabetically – to find their meaning in English. When a word has more than one meaning, make sure you choose the one that is most relevant.

**TIP** Look at the number after a verb you look up and find that number in the verb table: it shows the endings for that verb.

## English–French

Look up English words – listed alphabetically – to find out how to say them in French. When you find the French word, the entry will tell you whether it is masculine (masc) or feminine (fem). To choose the right word and use it properly, make sure you read through the examples provided.

**TIP** To find out more about the French translation that you are given, look it up on the French-English side of the dictionary afterwards.

## Colour section

In the colour section you will find reference material such as: verb tables for regular verbs and most common irregular verbs, key vocabulary (grouped by theme to help you in your oral exam: Leisure and holidays, Careers and future plans, etc.), classroom language, useful phrases (e.g. days, months, dates, time); sample letters with key opening and closing phrases; email and text messaging vocabulary; a sample CV and hints for job applications.

# Get to know your dictionary

## User-friendly layout

- **Two-colour layout**
  Headwords (words you are looking up) are in blue for easy identification.
- **Easy to navigate**
  The alphabet runs down the side of each page indicating what letter you are looking at, and whether you are on the French–English or English–French side of the dictionary:

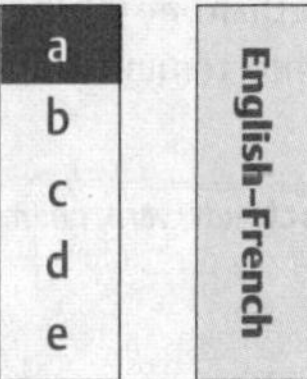


- **Symbols explained**
  The key symbols and *être* symbols are explained along the bottom of every other page.

  ♪ indicates key words    Ⓔ means the verb takes être to form the perfect

## Clear entries

- **Parts of speech written out in full**
  *Noun*, *verb*, *adjective*, *adverb*, *conjunction*, *preposition* or *determiner* are all written out clearly after the headword:

  **calmement** *adverb*
  **calmly**

- **Gender of nouns doubly clear**
  Both the definite (or if appropriate, the indefinite) article and the abbreviations *masc* and *fem* are used on both sides of the dictionary to make it clear whether a word is masculine or feminine.

  ♪ **balcony** *noun*
  le **balcon** *masc*

  ♪ le **balcon** *masc noun*

Other abbreviations used are:

| | | | |
|---|---|---|---|
| *masc* | masculine | *fem* | feminine |
| *pl* | plural | *adj* | adjective |
| *adv* | adverb | *prep* | preposition |
| *conj* | conjunction | *excl* | exclamation |

- **All variations shown**
  Both the masculine and feminine singular, and the masculine and feminine plural forms of adjectives are usually shown:

  **central** *masc adjective*, **centrale** *fem*, **centraux** *masc pl*, **centrales** *fem pl*

  ♪ **beautiful** *adjective*
  **beau** *masc*, **bel** *masc*, **belle** *fem*, **beaux** *masc pl*, **belles** *fem pl*

- **Pointers to other parts of speech**
  Where a word can do more than one job (be a noun *and* a verb, for example), a helpful pointer reminds students to check other parts of speech:

  ♪ **back** *adjective* ▷ see **back** *adv, verb, noun*

## Extra help with verbs

- **Heavy-duty verbs**
  Common verbs are given special treatment in tinted panels:

  ♪ **aller** *verb* Ⓔ [7] ▷ see **aller** *noun*
  **1 to go**
  **Je vais à Paris.** I'm going to Paris.
  **Je vais chez le boulanger.** I'm going to the baker's.

- **Verb tables in centre section** (*see* **Introduction**)
  The centre section contains full conjugations for regular *-er*, *-ir* and *-re* verbs plus the most common irregular verbs.
- **Links to verb tables**
  On both sides of the dictionary, each French verb is followed by a number linking it to the central verb tables:

  to **baptize** *verb*
  **baptiser [1]**

  **chatouiller** *verb* **[1]**
  **to tickle**

- **Use of *to* before a verb**
  On the English–French side of the dictionary, English verbs are preceded by *to* (see above).
- **Conjugations with *être***
  A symbol reminds you that this particular verb is conjugated with *être* in the perfect tense:
  se **cacher** *reflexive verb* Ⓔ
  **to hide**
- **Irregular forms of verbs**
  If you look up past participles and non-infinitive forms of a verb, you are cross-referenced to the relevant headword:

  **a** *verb* ▷ **avoir**

## Extra help with difficult points of French

- **Help with grammar and spelling**

  'Word tips' give extra help with tricky grammatical points and reminders on how French spelling is different from English:

> **WORD TIP** Adjectives never have capitals in French, even for nationality or regional origin.

- **Typical problematic areas**

  Extra help is given with traditionally problematic areas, such as agreement in French:

**by** *preposition*

**5** (*with myself, yourself, etc*) **tout seul** *masc*, **toute seule** *fem*
**by yourself** tout seul (*boy, man*), toute seule (*girl, woman*)
**I was by myself.** J'étais tout seul (*boy speaking*), J'étais toute seule (*girl speaking*).
**She did it by herself.** Elle l'a fait toute seule.

- **False friends**

  False friends are shown on the French–English side of the dictionary:

> **WORD TIP** *actuel* does not mean *actual* in English; for the meaning of *actual* ▷ **vrai**

## Language in context – example sentences

- **Thousands of example sentences**

  Thousands of examples of 'real language' at an appropriate level for the age group, progressing from simpler to more complex sentences:

to **phone** *verb* ▷ see **phone** *noun*
**1 téléphoner [1]**
**while I was phoning** pendant que je téléphonais
**It's quicker to phone.** Ça va plus vite de téléphoner.
**Phone up and ask for information.** Téléphone et demande-leur des renseignements.

- **Correctly punctuated**

  All example sentences are correctly punctuated with capital letters and full stops (see above).

## Additional features

- **Core vocabulary highlighted**
  All the key curriculum note words secondary school pupils need are highlighted with a key to help you prepare for your exams.

  le **manteau** *masc noun*, les **manteaux** *plural*
  **coat**

- **Colour section**
  This full-colour central section will help you communicate in both written and spoken French.

- **Mini-infos**
  Boxed notes provide interesting cultural information throughout the A–Z text:

**Cycling**

**The *Tour de France* cycle race takes place in France every summer. The 4,000 kilometre route changes every year but always finishes in Paris. The previous day's winner wears a special yellow jersey.**

- **Language functions covered**
  Exam syllabus language functions, such as requests/demands, are covered within example sentences:

  le **café** *masc noun*

  1. **coffee**
     **prendre un café** to have a coffee
     **Vous prendrez un café?** Would you like a coffee? (*formal*)
     **Tu veux prendre un café?** Do you want a coffee? (*informal*)
  2. **cafe**
     **aller au café** to go to the cafe
     **Leila va au café tous les midis.** Leila goes to the cafe every lunchtime.

  - le **café au lait** white coffee
  - le **café-crème** white coffee
  - le **café en grains** coffee beans
  - le **café instantané** instant coffee
  - le **café moulu** ground coffee
  - le **café soluble** instant coffee
  - le **café-tabac** cafe (*where you can buy cigarettes and stamps*)

# Aa

**a** *verb* ▷ **avoir**

♪ **à** *preposition*

**1 at**
**à la maison** at home
**à l'école** at school
**au marché** at the market
**à deux heures** at two o'clock
**À quelle heure?** At what time?

**2 in**
**à Londres** in London
**à la campagne** in the country
**au printemps** in the spring
**assis au soleil** sitting in the sun

**3 to**
**aller à Paris** to go to Paris
**aller aux États-Unis** to go to the United States
**Donnez l'argent à Julie.** Give the money to Julie.

**4** (*showing how*) **à vélo** by bike
**Tu viens à vélo?** Are you coming by bike?
**aller à pied** to go on foot

**5 with**
**une fille aux yeux bleus** a girl with blue eyes
**le garçon aux lunettes** the boy with glasses

**6** (*in distances*) **à trois kilomètres d'ici** three kilometres from here
**à quelques mètres de la route** a few metres from the road
**à 100 kilomètres de Paris** 100 kilometres from Paris

**7** (*showing ownership*) **Ce bracelet est à Natalie.** This bracelet belongs to Natalie.
**À qui est ce portable?** Whose is this mobile?
**C'est à moi.** It's mine.

**8** (*showing where*) **à côté de** beside
**à droite** on the right
**à gauche** on the left
**à l'étranger** abroad

**9** (*in notices, etc*) **'À vendre'** 'For sale'
**'Vélos à louer'** 'Bicycles for hire'

**WORD TIP** *à + le* gives *au*; *à + les* gives *aux*.

**abandonner** *verb* **[1]**

**1 to give up**
**Elle a abandonné les maths.** She has given up maths.

**2 to abandon**
**un enfant abandonné** an abandoned child

un **abat-jour** *masc noun*
**lampshade**

un **abattoir** *masc noun*
**slaughterhouse**

**abattre** *verb* **[21]**

**1 to shoot down** (*a person*)
**2 to slaughter** (*an animal*)
**3 to demolish** (*a building*)
**4 to cut down** (*a tree*)

une **abbaye** *fem noun*
**abbey**
**l'abbaye de Westminster** Westminster Abbey

un **abbé** *masc noun*
**priest**

une **abeille** *fem noun*
**bee**

**abîmer** *verb* **[1]**

**1 to damage**
**2 to ruin**
**La grêle a abîmé les raisins.** The hail has ruined the grapes.

s'**abîmer** *reflexive verb* ❷

**1 to get damaged**
**2 to go bad** (*fruit, meat, etc*)

**abolir** *verb* **[2]**
**to abolish**

**abominable** *masc & fem adjective*
**abominable**

une **abondance** *fem noun*
**Il y a des fruits en abondance.** There's plenty of fruit.

un **abonné** *masc noun*, une **abonnée** *fem*
▷ see **abonné** *adj*

**1 season ticket holder** (*for bus, train, etc*)
**2 subscriber** (*to a magazine*)

**abonné** *masc adjective*, **abonnée** *fem*
▷ see **abonné** *noun*

**1** **être abonné** to have a season ticket
**2** **être abonné** to have a subscription

un **abonnement** *masc noun*

**1 subscription**
**2 season ticket**

s'**abonner** *reflexive verb* ❷ **[1]**
**s'abonner à quelque chose** to subscribe to something
**Je m'abonne à un magazine de musique rock.** I subscribe to a rock music magazine.

**abord** *masc noun*

**1** ▷ **d'abord**
**2** **les abords** the surrounding area

♪ indicates key words

**abordable** *masc & fem adjective*
1 **affordable** (*prices*)
2 **approachable** (*person*)

**aborder** *verb* [1]
1 **to tackle** (*a problem*)
2 **to approach** (*a person*)

**aboutir** *verb* [2]
1 **aboutir à quelque chose** to lead to something
2 **aboutir à** to end up in
**Nous avons abouti à Rennes.** We ended up in Rennes.

**aboyer** *verb* [39]
**to bark**

**abrégé** *masc adjective*, **abrégée** *fem*
**abridged**
**la version abrégée** the abridged version

une **abréviation** *fem noun*
**abbreviation**

un **abri** *masc noun*
1 **shelter**
**trouver un abri** to take shelter
2 **shed**
3 **être à l'abri de quelque chose** to be sheltered from something
**Nous étions à l'abri du vent.** We were sheltered from the wind.

♪ un **abricot** *masc noun*
**apricot**

un **abricotier** *masc noun*
**apricot tree**

**abriter** *verb* [1]
**to shelter**

s'**abriter** *reflexive verb* ⓔ
**to take shelter**

**abrupt** *masc adjective*, **abrupte** *fem*
1 **steep** (*slope, path, etc*)
2 **abrupt** (*in manner, tone*)

**abrutir** *verb* [2]
1 **to deafen**
2 **to stupefy** (*from work, heat, etc*)

une **absence** *fem noun*
**absence**
**pendant mon absence** while I was away

♪ **absent** *masc adjective*, **absente** *fem*
1 **être absent** to be out, to be away
**Je serai absent pendant une heure.** I'll be out for an hour.
2 **absent** (*from school, work*)
**Elle était absente hier.** She was absent yesterday.

s'**absenter** *reflexive verb* ⓔ [1]
**to go away**
**Elle s'est absentée pendant deux jours.** She was away for two days.

**absolu** *masc adjective*, **absolue** *fem*
**absolute**

♪ **absolument** *adverb*
**absolutely**

**absorbant** *masc adjective*, **absorbante** *fem*
1 **absorbing** (*book, story*)
2 **absorbent** (*cloth*)

**absorber** *verb* [1]
1 **to absorb**
2 **to take** (*food, drink*)

**absurde** *masc & fem adjective*
**absurd**

l'**absurdité** *fem noun*
1 **absurdity** (*of a situation*)
2 **des absurdités** nonsense
**Il dit des absurdités.** He's talking nonsense.

l'**abus** *masc noun*
**abuse**
**l'abus d'alcool** alcohol abuse

**abuser** *verb* [1]
1 **abuser de quelque chose** to misuse
**abuser de l'alcool** to drink too much (*regularly*)
2 **abuser de ta gentillesse** to take advantage of your kindness

**abusif** *masc adjective*, **abusive** *fem*
1 **excessive**
2 **unfair**

l'**acajou** *masc noun*
**mahogany**

**accablant** *masc adjective*, **accablante** *fem*
**overwhelming**

un **accélérateur** *masc noun*
**accelerator**

l'**accélération** *fem noun*
**acceleration**

**accélérer** *verb* [24]
1 **to speed up** (*a process*)
2 **to accelerate** (*in a car*)

♪ un **accent** *masc noun*
1 **accent**
**un accent étranger** a foreign accent
2 **accent** (*in French spelling*)
**Ça s'écrit avec ou sans accent?** Is it spelt with or without an accent?
- un **accent aigu** acute accent (*as in é*)
- un **accent grave** grave accent (*as in è*)
- un **accent circonflexe** circumflex (*as in ê*)

ⓔ means the verb takes être to form the perfect

**accentuer** *verb* **[1]**
**to stress**

**accepter** *verb* **[1]**
1 **to accept**
**J'ai accepté son invitation.** I accepted her invitation.
2 **accepter de faire quelque chose** to agree to do something
**Elle a accepté de m'aider.** She agreed to help me.

un **accès** *masc noun*
1 **access**
**'Accès interdit'** 'No entry'
2 **outburst**
**un accès de colère** an outburst of rage

**accessible** *masc & fem adjective*
1 **accessible** (*place*)
**C'est un livre accessible.** It's an easy book to read.
2 **affordable**
**des prix accessibles** affordable prices

un **accessoire** *masc noun*
**accessory**
- les **accessoires** fashion accessories

♪ un **accident** *masc noun*
1 **accident**
**un accident de la route** a road accident
**avoir un accident** to have an accident
2 **hitch**
**Il y a eu un petit accident.** There's been a slight hitch.

**accidenté** *masc adjective*, **accidentée** *fem*
1 **injured**
2 **damaged**
3 **uneven**
**'Chaussée accidentée'** 'Uneven road surface'

un **accompagnateur** *masc noun*, une **accompagnatrice** *fem*
1 **tourist guide**
2 **courier** (*for package holidays*)
3 **accompanying adult** (*with a child*)
4 **accompanist** (*for a singer*)

♪ **accompagner** *verb* **[1]**
1 **to accompany**
**Je t'accompagne.** I'll go with you., I'll come with you.
**Je t'accompagne jusqu'à chez toi.** I'll see you home.
2 **accompagné de quelqu'un** accompanied by somebody
**Elle est partie accompagnée de son frère.** She left accompanied by her brother.
3 **to accompany** (*on the piano*)

**accomplir** *verb* **[2]**
**to carry out** (*a task, a project*)

♪ un **accord** *masc noun*
1 **agreement**
2 **d'accord** all right
**Je suis d'accord.** I agree.
**Je ne suis pas d'accord avec Odile.** I don't agree with Odile.
**être d'accord pour faire quelque chose** to agree to do something
**Paul est d'accord pour venir avec nous.** Paul's agreed to come with us.
**se mettre d'accord** to come to an agreement
**Ils se sont mis d'accord sur le prix.** They agreed on the price.

un **accordéon** *masc noun*
**accordeon**

**accorder** *verb* **[1]**
1 **to grant** (*permission*)
2 **to tune** (*an instrument*)

s'**accorder** *reflexive verb* Ⓔ
**to agree**
**Nous nous sommes accordés sur le prix.** We agreed on the price.

un **accotement** *masc noun*
**verge** (*beside a road*)

**accoucher** *verb* **[1]**
**to give birth**

**accoutumé** *masc adjective*, **accoutumée** *fem*
1 **usual**
2 **être accoutumé à quelque chose** to be accustomed to something

s'**accoutumer** *reflexive verb* Ⓔ **[1]**
**s'accoutumer à faire quelque chose** to get used to doing something
**On s'accoutume à se lever tôt.** You get used to getting up early.

**accro** *masc & fem adjective*
(*informal*) **être accro de quelque chose** to be hooked on something
**Il est complètement accro de la télé.** He's completely hooked on the telly.

un **accroc** *masc noun*
1 **tear** (*in clothes*)
2 **hitch**
**sans accrocs** without a hitch

**accrocher** *verb* **[1]**
**to hang**
**accrocher un tableau au mur** to hang a picture on the wall

s'**accrocher** *reflexive verb* ⓔ **[1]**
**s'accrocher à quelque chose** to hold on to something

s'**accroupir** *reflexive verb* ⓔ **[2]**
**to crouch (down)**, **to squat**

un **accueil** *masc noun*
**1 welcome**
**un accueil chaleureux** a warm welcome
**2 reception desk**
**Madame Martin est priée de se présenter à l'accueil.** Would Mrs Martin please go to the reception desk.

**accueillir** *verb* **[35]**
**1 to welcome**
**être bien accueilli** to be given a warm welcome
**être accueilli par quelque chose** to be greeted with something
**Ils sont accueillis par des acclamations.** They are greeted with cheers.
**2 to receive** (*guests, visitors*)

**accumuler** *verb* **[1]**
**to collect**

s'**accumuler** *reflexive verb* ⓔ
**to pile up** (*leaves, problems, etc*)

une **accusation** *fem noun*
**accusation**

un **accusé de réception** *masc noun*
**recorded delivery**
**envoyer une lettre avec accusé de réception** to send a letter by recorded delivery

**accuser** *verb* **[1]**
**to accuse**
**accuser quelqu'un d'avoir fait quelque chose** to accuse somebody of doing something
**Il m'a accusé d'avoir volé son stylo.** He accused me of stealing his pen.

s'**acharner** *reflexive verb* ⓔ **[1]**
**s'acharner à faire quelque chose** to keep on doing something
**Ils s'acharnent à la taquiner.** They keep on teasing her.

un **achat** *masc noun*
**purchase**

**acheter** *verb* **[16]**
**1 to buy**
**Je vais acheter du pain.** I'm going to buy some bread.
**2 acheter quelque chose pour quelqu'un** to buy somebody something
**Il m'a acheté un cadeau.** He bought me a present.
**Qu'est-ce que tu lui achètes?** What are you buying for him?
**3 acheter quelque chose à quelqu'un** to buy something from somebody
**C'est Lisa qui m'a acheté le portable.** Lisa bought my mobile from me.

un **acheteur** *masc noun*, une **acheteuse** *fem*
**buyer**

**achever** *verb* **[50]**
**1 to finish** (*an assignment*)
**2 to finish off** (*to kill*)

**acide** *masc & fem adjective* ▷ see **acide** *noun*
**sharp**, **sour** (*taste*)

un **acide** *masc noun* ▷ see **acide** *adj*
**acid**

l'**acier** *masc noun*
**steel**

l'**acné** *fem noun*
**acne**

une **acoustique** *fem noun*
**acoustics**

**acquérir** *verb* **[17]**
**to acquire**

un & une **acrobate** *masc & fem noun*
**acrobat**

l'**acrobatie** *fem noun*
**acrobatics**

un **acte** *masc noun*
**1 act**
**2 deed** (*legal document*)

un **acteur** *masc noun*
**actor**

**actif** *masc adjective*, **active** *fem*
**active**
**la vie active** working life

une **action** *fem noun*
**1 action**
**un film d'action** an action film
**une bonne action** a good deed
**2 effect**

**activement** *adverb*
**actively**

**activer** *verb* **[1]**
**to speed up** (*a process, work*)

s'**activer** *reflexive verb* ⓔ
**to hurry up**
**Il faudrait s'activer là!** We'd better hurry up!

une **activité** *fem noun*
**activity**
- une **activité professionelle** occupation



ⓔ means the verb takes être to form the perfect

♪ un **actrice** *fem noun*
**actress**

♪ l'**actualité** *fem noun*
1 **les actualités** news
**regarder les actualités à la télévision** to watch the news on television
2 **current affairs**
**s'intéresser à l'actualité** to be interested in current affairs

**actuel** *masc adjective*, **actuelle** *fem*
**present**
**la situation actuelle** the present situation
**le monde actuel** today's world

**WORD TIP** *actuel* does not mean *actual* in English; for the meaning of *actual* ▷ **vrai**

**actuellement** *adverb*
**at present**

**WORD TIP** *actuellement* does not mean *actually* in English; for the meaning of *actually* ▷ **fait** *masc noun*

**adapté** *masc adjective*, **adaptée** *fem*
1 **suitable**
**des vêtements adaptés aux climats chauds** clothes suitable for a warm climate
2 **adjusted**
**une élève bien adaptée** a well-adjusted student
3 **adapted** (*for the cinema, TV, theatre*)

**adapter** *verb* [1]
**to adapt**

s'**adapter** *reflexive verb* ❷
**s'adapter à quelque chose** to get used to something
**Nous nous sommes adaptés à la situation.** We've got used to the situation.

un **additif** *masc noun*
**additive**

♪ une **addition** *fem noun*
1 **bill** (*in a restaurant*)
**L'addition, s'il vous plaît.** Can I have the bill please?
2 **addition** (*in arithmetic*)

**additionner** *verb* [1]
**to add up**

**adhésif** *masc adjective*, **adhésive** *fem*
**adhesive** (*tape, etc*)

un **adieu** *masc noun*, les **adieux** *pl*
**goodbye**, **farewell** (*for ever*)

un **adjectif** *masc noun*
(*Grammar*) **adjective**

un **adjoint** *masc noun*, une **adjointe** *fem*
1 **assistant**
2 **deputy**

**admettre** *verb* [11]
1 **to admit**
**Il faut admettre qu'ils ont raison.** You have to admit that they're right.
2 **to allow in** (*dogs, children, etc*)
**Les chiens ne sont pas admis.** Dogs are not allowed in.
3 **to suppose**
**Admettons que la France gagne.** Let's suppose that France wins.

une **administration** *fem noun*
**administration**

l'**admiration** *fem noun*
**admiration**

**admirer** *verb* [1]
**to admire**

une **adolescence** *fem noun*
**adolescence**

♪ un **adolescent** *masc noun*, une **adolescente** *fem*
▷ see **adolescent** *adj*
**teenager**, **adolescent**

♪ **adolescent** *masc adjective*, **adolescente** *fem* ▷ see **adolescent** *noun*
**teenage**, **adolescent**

**adopter** *verb* [1]
**to adopt**

**adoptif** *masc adjective*, **adoptive** *fem*
**adopted**
**un enfant adoptif** an adopted child

une **adoption** *fem noun*
**adoption**

**adorable** *masc & fem adjective*
**adorable**

**adorer** *verb* [1]
**to love**, **to adore**

♪ une **adresse** *fem noun*
1 **address**
**Quelle est ton adresse?** What's your address?
**Vous vous êtes trompé d'adresse.** You've got the wrong address.
2 **skill**
**Elle fait ça avec beaucoup d'adresse.** She does that very skilfully.
3 **speech**
• une **adresse électronique** email address

**adresser** *verb* [1]
1 **adresser une lettre** to address a letter
2 **adresser une lettre à quelqu'un** to send somebody a letter
3 **adresser la parole à quelqu'un** to speak to somebody ⏩

Elle ne m'adresse jamais la parole. She never speaks to me.

s'**adresser** *reflexive verb* ⓔ

1 s'adresser à to enquire at
Adressez-vous à la réception. Enquire at reception.

2 s'adresser à quelqu'un to be aimed at somebody
Le film s'adresse aux adolescents. The film is aimed at teenagers.

**adroit** *masc adjective*, **adroite** *fem*
**skilful**

**adulte** *masc & fem adjective*
▷ see **adulte** *noun*
**adult**

un **adulte** *masc & fem noun* ▷ see **adulte** *adj*
**adult**

un **adverbe** *masc noun*
(*Grammar*) **adverb**

un & une **adversaire** *masc & fem noun*
**opponent**

**adverse** *masc & fem adjective*
**opposing**

l'**aération** *fem noun*
**ventilation**

l'**aérobic** *masc noun*
**aerobics**
faire de l'aérobic to do aerobics

une **aérogare** *fem noun*
**terminal** (*in an airport*)

l'**aéroglisseur** *masc noun*
**hovercraft**

l'**aéronautique** *fem noun*
**aeronautics**

un **aéroport** *masc noun*
**airport**
à l'aéroport at the airport, to the airport

un **aérosol** *masc noun*
**aerosol**

une **affaire** *fem noun*
▷ see **affaires** *plural fem noun*

1 **business**
une sale affaire a nasty business

2 **matter**
C'est une autre affaire. That's another matter.

3 **affair** (*scandal*)

4 **bargain**
Ça, c'est une affaire! That's a real bargain!

les **affaires** *plural fem noun*
▷ see **affaire** *fem noun*

1 **business**
les affaires business
un homme d'affaires a businessman
une femme d'affaires a businesswoman
un voyage d'affaires a business trip

2 **business** (*personal information*)
Occupe-toi de tes affaires! Mind your own business!

3 **belongings**
Tu peux laisser tes affaires dans la chambre. You can leave your things in the bedroom.

**affamé** *masc adjective*, **affamée** *fem*
**starving**

**affamer** *verb* [1]
**to starve**

**affecter** *verb* [1]
**to affect**

l'**affection** *fem noun*
**affection**

**affectueusement** *adverb*
**affectionately**

**affectueux** *masc adjective*, **affectueuse** *fem*
**affectionate**

une **affiche** *fem noun*

1 **poster**
mettre des affiches to put posters up

2 **notice**

**afficher** *verb* [1]

1 **to put up** (*posters, pictures*)
'Défense d'afficher' 'Stick no bills'

2 **to display** (*on a computer screen*)

**affliger** *verb* [52]
**to distress**

**affligeant** *masc adjective*, **affligeante** *fem*
**distressing, pathetic**

une **affluence** *fem noun*
**crowds** (*at busy times in shops, streets*)
aux heures d'affluence at peak times

**affoler** *verb* [1]
affoler quelqu'un to send somebody into a panic

s'**affoler** *reflexive verb* ⓔ
**to panic**
Ne t'affole pas. Don't panic.

**affreux** *masc adjective*, **affreuse** *fem*

1 **dreadful**
un accident affreux a dreadful accident
Le temps était affreux. The weather was dreadful.



ⓔ means the verb takes être to form the perfect

2 **hideous**
une couleur affreuse a hideous colour

**afin** *preposition*
1 afin de faire quelque chose in order to do something
afin de travailler ensemble in order to work together
2 afin que ... so that ...
Je lui ai écrit afin qu'il ne se sente pas abandonné. I wrote to him so that he wouldn't feel so neglected.

**africain** *masc adjective*, **africaine** *fem*
▷ see **Africain** *noun*
**African**

un **Africain** *masc noun*, une **Africaine** *fem*
▷ see **africain** *adj*
**African**

l'**Afrique** *fem noun*
**Africa**

**agaçant** *masc adjective*, **agaçante** *fem*
**annoying**

**agacer** *verb* [61]
**to annoy**
Ça m'agace! That gets on my nerves!

♪ un **âge** *masc noun*
**age**
à l'âge de cinq ans at the age of five
Quel âge as-tu? How old are you?
Il a l'âge de mon père. He's the same age as my father.
Elle a l'âge de voyager seule. She's old enough to travel on her own.

♪ **âgé** *masc adjective*, **âgée** *fem*
1 **old**
les personnes âgées old people
2 âgé de aged
une femme âgée de trente ans a woman aged thirty

♪ une **agence** *fem noun*
1 **agency**
2 **branch** (*of a bank*)
- une **agence de voyages** travel agent's
- une **agence immobilière** estate agent's

un **agenda** *masc noun*
**diary**

♪ un **agent** *masc noun*
1 **official**
2 **agent**
- un **agent commercial** sales rep

♪ un **agent de police** *masc noun*, une **agente de police** *fem*
**police officer**

**aggraver** *verb* [1]
**to make worse**
aggraver la situation to make things worse

s'**aggraver** *reflexive verb* ❷
**to get worse**
La situation s'aggrave. Things are getting worse.

**agir** *verb* [2]
1 **to act, to take action**
Il faut agir. We've got to act.
2 **to behave**
agir comme un idiot to behave like an idiot

s'**agir** *reflexive verb* ❷
s'agir de quelque chose to be about something
De quoi s'agit-il? What's it about?
Il s'agit de ton frère. It's about your brother.

l'**agitation** *fem noun*
1 **hustle and bustle**
2 **unrest**
3 **restlessness**

**agité** *masc adjective*, **agitée** *fem*
1 **restless**
2 **rough** (*sea*)
3 **bustling** (*street*)

**agiter** *verb* [1]
**to shake**
agiter la main to wave your hand

♪ un **agneau** *masc noun*, les **agneaux** *pl*
**lamb**

une **agrafe** *fem noun*
1 **staple**
2 **hook** (*in clothes*)

**agrafer** *verb* [1]
1 **to staple**
2 **to fasten**

une **agrafeuse** *fem noun*
**stapler**

**agrandir** *verb* [2]
1 **to enlarge** (*a photo*)
2 **to extend** (*a house*)

un **agrandissement** *masc noun*
1 **enlargement** (*of a photo*)
2 **extension** (*of a house*)

♪ **agréable** *masc & fem adjective*
**pleasant, nice**

**agréer** *verb* [32]
1 **to agree to**
2 **Veuillez agréer l'expression de mes sentiments respectueux. Yours faithfully, Yours sincerely,**

**WORD TIP** A typical ending for a formal letter.

**agresser** *verb* [1]
1 **to attack**
2 **to mug**
**Il a été agressé dans le parking.** He was mugged in the car park.
**se faire agresser** to get mugged

un **agresseur** *masc noun*
**attacker**

**agressif** *masc adjective*, **agressive** *fem*
**aggressive**

une **agression** *fem noun*
1 **attack**
2 **mugging**

l'**agressivité** *fem noun*
**aggressiveness**

**agricole** *masc & fem adjective*
**agricultural**

un **agriculteur** *masc noun*, une **agricultrice** *fem*
**farmer**

**ai** *verb* ▷ **avoir**

une **aide** *fem noun*
▷ see **aide** *masc & fem noun*
1 **help**
**avec l'aide de Claire** with Claire's help
**à l'aide de quelque chose** with the help of something
**à l'aide d'un ordinateur** with the help of a computer
**venir à l'aide de quelqu'un** to help somebody
**Ils sont venus à notre aide.** They helped us.
2 **aid** *(to a person, country)*

un & une **aide** *masc & fem noun*
▷ see **aide** *fem noun*
1 **assistant**
2 **helper**

**aider** *verb* [1]
1 **to help**
**Est-ce que je peux t'aider?** Would you like some help?
**Aide-moi.** Help me.
**aider quelqu'un à faire quelque chose** to help somebody to do something
**Il m'a aidé à faire mes devoirs.** He helped me do my homework.
2 **to give aid to** *(a person, a country)*

un **aigle** *masc & fem noun*
**eagle**

un **aiglefin** *masc noun*
**haddock**

**aigre** *masc & fem adjective*
1 **sour** *(taste)*
2 **sharp** *(tone)*

**aigu** *masc adjective*, **aiguë** *fem*
1 **high-pitched** *(sound)*
2 **acute** *(very bad)*
**une douleur aiguë** acute pain

une **aiguille** *fem noun*
1 **needle**
2 **hand** *(on a watch)*
**dans le sens des aiguilles d'une montre** clockwise

un **aiguilleur du ciel** *masc noun*, une **aiguilleuse du ciel** *fem*
**air traffic controller**

un **ail** *masc noun*
**garlic**
**à l'ail** with garlic

une **aile** *fem noun*
**wing**

**ailleurs** *adverb*
1 **somewhere else**
**partout ailleurs** everywhere else
**nulle part ailleurs** nowhere else
2 **d'ailleurs** besides

**aimable** *masc & fem adjective*
**kind, nice**
**Vous êtes très aimable.** That's very kind of you.
**Ils ne sont pas du tout aimables.** They're really not very nice.

un **aimant** *masc noun*
**magnet**

**aimer** *verb* [1]
1 **to like**
**Est-ce que tu aimes les fraises?** Do you like strawberries?
**J'aime le poisson.** I like fish.
**J'aime ça!** I like it!
**aimer faire quelque chose** to like doing something
**Elle aime aller au cinéma.** She likes going to the cinema.
**Elle aimerait aller au cinéma.** She'd like to go to the cinema.
**J'ai toujours aimé aller à la plage.** I've always liked going to the beach.
2 **aimer mieux** to prefer
**J'aime mieux les fraises que les framboises.** I prefer strawberries to raspberries
**J'aimerais mieux aller au cinéma.** I'd rather go to the cinema.
3 **to love**
**Je t'aime.** I love you.
4 **aimer bien** to like
**Je t'aime bien.** I like you.
**J'aime bien les frites.** I like chips.

On aime bien faire du camping. We like going camping.
Elle aimerait bien un portable. She would like a mobile phone.
J'aimerais bien savoir. I'd like to know.

s'**aimer** *reflexive verb* ⓔ
1 **to love each other**
2 **to like each other**
Ils ne s'aiment pas beaucoup. They don't like each other much.

♪ **aîné** *masc adjective*, **aînée** *fem*
▷ see **aîné** *noun*
1 **elder**, **older** (*of two*)
leur fils aîné their elder son
2 **eldest**, **oldest** (*of more than two*)
ma sœur aînée my eldest sister

♪ un **aîné** *masc noun*, une **aînée** *fem*
▷ see **aîné** *adj*
l'aîné the eldest, the oldest (*boy*)
l'aînée the eldest, the oldest (*girl*)

**ainsi** *adverb*
1 **so, thus**
C'est ainsi que l'on fait. That's the way you do it.
2 **in this way**
3 ainsi que as well as, along with

un **aïoli** *masc noun*
**garlic mayonnaise**

♪ un **air** *masc noun*
1 **air**
en plein air in the open air
2 avoir l'air ... to look ...
Le gâteau a l'air bon. The cake looks good.
Chloë a l'air très fatiguée. Chloë looks very tired.
3 avoir l'air de to look like
Il a l'air d'un policier. He looks like a policeman.
4 avoir l'air de faire quelque chose to look as if you are doing something
Il a l'air de comprendre. He looks as if he understands.
5 (*saying how*) d'un air ..., d'un air méfiant suspiciously
Elle souriait d'un air heureux. She was smiling happily
6 **tune**
l'air d'une chanson the tune of a song
- un **air bag**® airbag (*in a car*)

une **aire** *fem noun*
**area** (*for an activity*)
- une **aire de jeu** playground
- une **aire de pique-nique** picnic area
- une **aire de repos** motorway rest area
- une **aire de services** motorway service station

l'**aise** *fem noun*
1 être à l'aise to be at ease
être à l'aise avex tout le monde to be at ease with everybody
2 être mal à l'aise to feel uneasy
J'étais vraiment mal à l'aise. I felt really uneasy.

une **aisselle** *fem noun*
**armpit**

**ajouter** *verb* [1]
**to add**
Ajoutez un œuf. Add an egg.
Ajoutez du sucre. Add some sugar.

une **alarme** *fem noun*
**alarm**
sonner l'alarme to sound the alarm

un **album** *masc noun*
**album**
- un **album de bandes dessinées** comic book
- un **album de photos** photograph album
- un **album de timbres** stamp album

l'**alcool** *masc noun*
**alcohol**

**alcoolique** *masc & fem noun*
**alcoholic**
C'est un alcoolique. He's an alcoholic.

**alcoolisé** *masc adjective*, **alcoolisée** *fem*
une boisson alcoolisée an alcoholic drink
une boisson non alcoolisée a soft drink

un **alcootest** *masc noun*
**Breathalyzer**®

les **alentours** *plural masc noun*
1 **surrounding area**
2 aux alentours de Paris in the area around Paris

l'**algèbre** *fem noun*
**algebra**

l'**Algérie** *fem noun*
**Algeria**

**algérien** *masc adjective*, **algérienne** *fem*
▷ see **Algérien** *noun*
**Algerian**

un **Algérien** *masc noun*, une **Algérienne** *fem* ▷ see **algérien** *adj*
**Algerian** (*person*)

les **algues** *plural fem noun*
**seaweed**

un **aliment** *masc noun*
**food**

French–English

a b c d e f g h i j k l m n o p q r s t u v w x y z

**alimentaire** *masc & fem adjective*
des produits alimentaires food products
l'industrie alimentaire the food industry

l'**alimentation** *fem noun*
1 **groceries**
2 **diet**

une **allée** *fem noun*
**path, drive**

l'**Allemagne** *fem noun*
**Germany**

**allemand** *masc adjective*, **allemande** *fem* ▷ see **Allemand** *noun*
**German**

un **Allemand** *masc noun*, une **Allemande** *fem* ▷ see **allemand** *adj*
1 **German** (*person*)
2 l'allemand *masc* German (*the language*)

**aller** *verb* Ⓔ **[7]** ▷ see **aller** *noun*
1 **to go**
**Je vais à Paris.** I'm going to Paris.
**Je vais chez le boulanger.** I'm going to the baker's.
**Elle n'est pas allée à l'école jeudi.** She didn't go to school on Thursday.
**Hier nous sommes allés au cinéma.** Yesterday we went to the cinema.
**Où vas-tu?** Where are you going?
**Où va-t-elle demain?** Where is she going tomorrow?
**Ne va pas si vite.** Don't go so fast.
**Allons en ville.** Let's go into town.
**Allons-y!** Let's go!
**Vas-y, demande au professeur.** Go on, ask the teacher.
2 (*to say how you are, etc*) **Comment ça va?**, **Ça va?** How are you?
**Ça va bien.** I'm fine.
**Ça ne va pas du tout.** I'm really not well.
**Ça va mieux.** I feel better.
**Comment va ta mère?** How's your mother?
**Elle va bien.** She's fine.
**Tout va bien.** Everything's fine.
**Qu'est-ce qui ne va pas?** What's wrong?
3 (*to say something will happen*) **Je vais sortir avec Julien ce soir.** I'm going out with Julien this evening.
**Il va chercher les CD.** He's going to get the CDs.
**Elle ne va pas oublier.** She's not going to forget.
4 **to suit**
**Cette robe te va bien.** That dress suits you.
**Est-ce que jeudi te va?** Does Thursday suit you?

s'**en aller** *reflexive verb* Ⓔ
**to leave**
**Je m'en vais!** I'm off!
**Va-t-en!** Go away! (*to one person*)
**Allez-vous-en** Go away! (*to two or more people*)

un **aller** *masc noun* ▷ see **aller** *verb*
1 **outward journey**
2 **away match**

un **aller retour** *masc noun*
**return ticket**
**Un aller retour pour Tours, s'il vous plaît.** A return ticket to Tours, please.

un **aller simple** *masc noun*
**single ticket**
**Avignon aller simple, s'il vous plaît.** A single to Avignon, please.

**allergique** *masc & fem adjective*
**être allergique à quelque chose** to be allergic to something
**Elle est allergique aux chats.** She's allergic to cats.

une **alliance** *fem noun*
1 **wedding ring**
2 **alliance**

un **allié** *masc noun*, une **alliée** *fem*
**ally**

**allô** *exclamation*
**hello** (*when answering a phone*)

une **allocation** *fem noun*
**benefit**
- l'**allocation chômage** unemployment benefit
- les **allocations familiales** family allowance

**allonger** *verb* **[52]**
1 **to lengthen** (*a dress*)
2 **to extend** (*a holiday, a journey*)

s'**allonger** *reflexive verb* Ⓔ
**to lie down**

**allumer** *verb* **[1]**
1 **to light**
**allumer le feu** to light the fire
2 **to switch on**
**allumer la télé** to switch on the TV
3 **to switch on the lights**

une **allumette** *fem noun*
**match**

une **allure** *fem noun*
1 **speed**
**à toute allure** at top speed
2 **appearance** (*of a person*)

Ⓔ means the verb takes être to form the perfect

𝄞 **alors** *adverb*
1 **so**
**Alors, comment ça va?** So how are you?
**Je suis en retard. Et alors?** I'm late. So what?
2 **alors que** while
**alors qu'elle faisait ses devoirs** while she was doing her homework
3 **then, at that time**
**Elle travaillait alors à Paris.** She was working in Paris then.

une **alouette** *fem noun*
**skylark**

**Alpes** *plural fem noun*
**les Alpes** the Alps

𝄞 un **alphabet** *masc noun*
**alphabet**

**alphabétique** *masc & fem adjective*
**alphabetical**
**par ordre alphabétique** in alphabetical order

𝄞 l'**alpinisme** *masc noun*
**mountaineering**

**alsacien** *masc adjective*, **alsacienne** *fem*
▷ see **Alsacien** *noun*
**from Alsace, Alsatian**

**WORD TIP** Adjectives never have capitals in French, even for nationality or regional origin.

un **Alsacien** *masc noun*, une **Alsacienne** *fem* ▷ see **alsacien** *adj*
**Alsatian** *(person from Alsace)*

**alternatif** *masc adjective*, **alternative** *fem*
**alternative**

une **altitude** *fem noun*
**altitude**

l'**aluminium** *masc noun*
**aluminium**

une **amande** *fem noun*
1 **almond**
2 **kernel** *(stone of a fruit)*

un **amant** *masc noun*
**lover**

**amateur** *masc & fem adjective*
▷ see **amateur** *noun*
**amateur**
**C'est une photographe amateur.** She's an amateur photographer.

un **amateur** *masc noun* ▷ see **amateur** *adj*
**enthusiast**
**un amateur de musique** a music lover

une **ambassade** *fem noun*
**embassy**
**l'ambassade de France** the French Embassy

un **ambassadeur** *masc noun*
**ambassador**

une **ambiance** *fem noun*
**atmosphere**
**une bonne ambiance** a good atmosphere

**ambitieux** *masc adjective*, **ambitieuse** *fem*
**ambitious**

𝄞 une **ambition** *fem noun*
**ambition**

𝄞 une **ambulance** *fem noun*
**ambulance**

un **ambulancier** *masc noun*, une **ambulancière** *fem*
**ambulance driver**

une **amélioration** *fem noun*
**improvement**

**améliorer** *verb* **[1]**
**to improve**

s'**améliorer** *reflexive verb*
**to get better, to improve**

**aménagé** *masc adjective*, **aménagée** *fem*
1 **equipped** *(kitchen, etc)*
2 **converted** *(attic, loft)*

**aménager** *verb* **[52]**
1 **to convert, to do up** *(a building, a room)*
2 **to develop** *(an area)*
3 **to improve** *(a road, a road system)*

une **amende** *fem noun*
**fine**
**une amende de 500 euros** a 500-euro fine

**amener** *verb* **[50]**
1 **to bring**
**Elle a amené son cousin.** She brought her cousin.
**Tu amènes ton frère?** Are you bringing your brother?
2 **to take**
**amener un enfant à l'école** to take a child to school

**amer** *masc adjective*, **amère** *fem*
**bitter**

**américain** *masc adjective*, **américaine** *fem* ▷ see **Américain** *noun*
**American**

**WORD TIP** Adjectives never have capitals in French, even for nationality or regional origin.

un **Américain** *masc noun*, une **Américaine** *fem* ▷ see **américain** *adj*
1 **American** *(person)*
2 **l'américain** American English

l'**Amérique** *fem noun*
**America**

**WORD TIP** Countries and regions in French take *le*, *la* or *les*.

l'**ameublement** *masc noun*
**furniture**

un **ami** *masc noun*, une **amie** *fem*
**friend**
un ami à moi a friend of mine
une amie à Lisa a friend of Lisa's
se faire des amis to make friends
Je me suis fait quelques amis. I've made some friends.

**amical** *masc adjective*, **amicale** *fem*, **amicaux** *masc pl*, **amicales** *fem pl*
▶ see **amicale** *noun*
**friendly**

une **amicale** *fem noun* ▷ see **amical** *adj*
**association**

**amicalement** *adverb*
1 **in a friendly way**
2 Amicalement, Odile Best wishes, Odile (*informal letter ending*)

l'**amitié** *fem noun*
1 **friendship**
2 Amitiés, Hélène Love, Hélène (*informal letter ending*)

l'**amour** *masc noun*
**love**
- l'**amour-propre** self-esteem

**amoureux** *masc adjective*, **amoureuse** *fem*
**in love**
être amoureux de quelqu'un to be in love with somebody
Elle était amoureuse de lui. She was in love with him.
Il est amoureux d'elle. He is in love with her.

un **amphithéâtre** *masc noun*
1 **amphitheatre**
2 **lecture theatre** (*in a university*)

**ample** *masc & fem adjective*
1 **loose-fitting** (*clothes*)
2 **ample** (*amount*)

une **ampleur** *fem noun*
1 **size** (*of a problem*)
2 **scope** (*of a project*)

un **ampli** *masc noun*
(*informal*) **amplifier**

un **amplificateur** *masc noun*
**amplifier**

une **ampoule** *fem noun*
1 **light bulb**
2 **blister**
J'ai une ampoule au pied. I've got a blister on my foot.

**amusant** *masc adjective*, **amusante** *fem*
1 **funny**
2 **entertaining**

un **amuse-gueule** *masc noun*
des amuse-gueule nibbles (*crisps, nuts, etc*)

**amuser** *verb* **[1]**
1 **to amuse**
Ça l'amuse de faire des grimaces. He enjoys pulling faces.
2 **to entertain**
amuser les gens dans la rue to entertain people in the street

s'**amuser** *reflexive verb* ⓔ
1 **to play**
Ils s'amusent dans le jardin. They're playing in the garden.
2 **to have a good time**
On s'est bien amusé. We had a really good time.
Amuse-toi bien! Have fun! (*to one person*)
Amusez-vous bien! Have fun! (*to two or more people*)

un **an** *masc noun*
**year**
Elle a dix ans. She's ten (years old).
le Nouvel An the New Year
le jour de l'an New Year's Day
tous les ans every year

un **analgésique** *masc noun*
**analgesic, painkiller**

une **analyse** *fem noun*
**analysis**
- une **analyse de sang** blood test

un **ananas** *masc noun*
**pineapple**

l'**anatomie** *fem noun*
**anatomy**

un & une **ancêtre** *masc & fem noun*
**ancestor**

un **anchois** *masc noun*
**anchovy**

**ancien** *masc adjective*, **ancienne** *fem*
1 **old**
une maison ancienne an old house
une table ancienne an antique table
2 **former**
l'ancien président the former president
mon ancienne école my old school

**WORD TIP** *ancien*, after a noun, means *old* or *ancient*. *ancien*, before a noun, means *former*.



ⓔ means the verb takes être to form the perfect

une **ancre** *fem noun*
**anchor**

un **âne** *masc noun*
**donkey**

un **ange** *masc noun*
**angel**

une **angine** *fem noun*
**throat infection**
avoir une angine to have a throat infection

♪ **anglais** *masc adjective*, **anglaise** *fem*
▷ see **Anglais** *noun*
**English**
un mot anglais an English word
la cuisine anglaise English cooking

**WORD TIP** Adjectives never have capitals in French, even for nationality or regional origin.

♪ un **Anglais** *masc noun*, une **Anglaise** *fem*
▷ see **anglais** *adj*
1 **Englishman**, **Englishwoman**
les Anglais the English
2 l'anglais *masc* English (*the language*)

**WORD TIP** Languages never have capitals in French.

un **angle** *masc noun*
1 **angle**
2 **corner**
à l'angle de la rue at the corner of the street
• un **angle droit** right angle

♪ l'**Angleterre** *fem noun*
**England**
en Angleterre in England
aller en Angleterre to go to England

**WORD TIP** Countries and regions in French take *le*, *la* or *les*.

**Anglo-Normande** *masc & fem adjective*
les îles Anglo-Normandes the Channel Islands

**anglophone** *masc & fem adjective*
**English-speaking**

une **angoisse** *fem noun*
**anxiety**

**angoissé** *masc adjective*, **angoissée** *fem*
**anxious**

une **anguille** *fem noun*
**eel**

**anguleux** *masc adjective*, **anguleuse** *fem*
**bony**

un **animal** *masc noun*, les **animaux** *pl*
**animal**

un **animateur** *masc noun*, une **animatrice** *fem*
1 **group leader**
2 **organizer** (*of a festival, conference*)
3 **presenter** (*in radio, TV*)

l'**animation** *fem noun*
1 **liveliness, life**
Il y a beaucoup d'animation dans le quartier le soir. There's a lot going on in the area at night.
2 **organization** (*of a group, a programme*)

**animé** *masc adjective*, **animée** *fem*
1 **lively** (*person, discussion*)
2 **busy** (*street, market*)
des rues animées busy streets

**animer** *verb* **[1]**
1 **to run** (*a course*)
2 **to lead** (*a group*)
3 **to present** (*a programme*)
4 **to liven up** (*a party*)

s'**animer** *reflexive verb* ⓔ
1 **to liven up**
2 **to come to life**
**Le quartier s'anime dès huit heures.** The area comes to life after eight o'clock.

l'**anis** *masc noun*
**aniseed**

un **anneau** *masc noun*, les **anneaux** *pl*
**ring**

♪ une **année** *fem noun*
**year**
l'année prochaine next year
l'année dernière last year
les années 90 the nineties
une année bissextile a leap year
Bonne année! Happy New Year!

une **annexe** *fem noun*
1 **appendix** (*of a book*)
2 **annexe** (*of a building*)

♪ un **anniversaire** *masc noun*
1 **birthday**
fêter son anniversaire to celebrate your birthday
Bon anniversaire!, Joyeux anniversaire! Happy Birthday!
2 **anniversary**
• un **anniversaire de mariage** wedding anniversary

une **annonce** *fem noun*
1 **advertisement**
les petites annonces the small ads (*in a newspaper*)
2 **announcement** (*of results, an event*)
3 **sign**

French–English

**annoncer** *verb* **[61]**
**1 to announce**
**2 to forecast**
Ils annoncent de la neige pour demain. Snow is forecast for tomorrow.

un **annuaire** *masc noun*
**directory**
- un **annuaire téléphonique** telephone directory

**annuel** *masc adjective*, **annuelle** *fem*
**yearly**

**annuler** *verb* **[1]**
**to cancel**
Le match a été annulé. The match has been cancelled.

**anonyme** *masc & fem adjective*
**anonymous**

un **anorak** *masc noun*
**anorak**

l'**anorexie** *fem noun*
**anorexia**

l'**Antarctique** *masc noun*
**the Antarctic**

une **antenne** *fem noun*
**1 aerial** (*for a radio, TV*)
**2 antenna** (*of an insect, radio mast*)
- une **antenne parabolique** satellite dish

un **antibiotique** *masc noun*
**antibiotic**
prendre des antibiotiques to be on antibiotics

**anticiper** *verb* **[1]**
**to foresee** (*a change*)

un **antidépresseur** *masc noun*
**antidepressant**

l'**antigel** *masc noun*
**antifreeze**

**antillais** *masc adjective*, **antillaise** *fem*
▷ see **Antillais** *noun*
**West Indian**

un **Antillais** *masc noun*, une **Antillaise** *fem*
▷ see **antillais** *adj*
**West Indian** (*person*)

les **Antilles** *plural fem noun*
**the West Indies**

une **antilope** *fem noun*
**antelope**

**antiquaire** *masc & fem noun*
**antique dealer**

une **antiquité** *fem noun*
**antique**

**antiseptique** *masc & fem adjective*
▷ see **antiseptique** *noun*
**antiseptic**

un **antiseptique** *masc noun*
▷ see **antiseptique** *adj*
**antiseptic**

**antiterroriste** *masc & fem adjective*
**antiterrorist**

un **antivol** *masc noun*
**1 lock** (*on a bike, motorcycle*)
**2 steering lock** (*in a car*)

**anxieux** *masc adjective*, **anxieuse** *fem*
**anxious**

**août** *masc noun*
**August**
en août, au mois d'août in August

**WORD TIP** Months of the year and days of the week start with small letters in French.

**apercevoir** *verb* **[66]**
**to catch sight of**

s'**apercevoir** *reflexive verb* ⓔ
s'apercevoir de quelque chose to notice something
Elle s'est aperçue de mon absence. She noticed my absence.
s'apercevoir que ... to notice that ...
Je m'aperçois que la clé est sur la porte. I notice that the key is in the door.

un **aperçu** *masc noun*
**1 insight**
**2 glimpse**

un **apéritif** *masc noun*
**drink** (*usually alcoholic, before a meal*)

**aplatir** *verb* **[2]**
**1 to flatten**
**2 to smooth out**

une **apostrophe** *fem noun*
**apostrophe**

**apparaître** *verb* **[57]**
**1 to appear**
**2 to seem**

un **appareil** *masc noun*
**1 device, appliance**
**2 telephone**
Qui est à l'appareil? Who's calling, please?
C'est Paul à l'appareil. It's Paul speaking.
- un **appareil (dentaire)** brace (*for teeth*)
- un **appareil photo** camera
- un **appareil photo numérique** digital camera

**apparemment** *adverb*
**apparently**



ⓔ means the verb takes être to form the perfect

une **apparence** *fem noun*
**appearance** (*seen from outside*)
**se fier aux apparences** to judge by appearances

**apparent** *masc adjective*, **apparente** *fem*
1 **obvious**
2 **apparent**
**sans raison apparente** for no apparent reason

une **apparition** *fem noun*
**appearance** (*when something or somebody becomes visible*)
**l'apparition des boutons** the appearance of spots
**Il a fait son apparition très tard.** He turned up very late.

un **appartement** *masc noun*
**flat, apartment**

**appartenir** *verb* **[81]**
**appartenir à quelqu'un** to belong to somebody
**Ces chaussures m'appartiennent.** These shoes belong to me.
**Est-ce que ce stylo t'appartient?** Is this pen yours?

un **appel** *masc noun*
1 **call, appeal**
**un appel d'aide** a call for help
**Ils ont lancé un appel à la radio.** They made an appeal on the radio.
2 **faire appel à quelqu'un** to appeal to somebody
3 **faire l'appel** to take the register (*in class*)
• un **appel (téléphonique)** telephone call

♂ **appeler** *verb* **[18]**
1 **to call**
**Ils l'ont appelé Hassan.** They called him Hassan.
2 **to phone**
**Appelle-moi ce soir.** Phone me this evening.
3 **to call**
**appeler un taxi** to call a taxi

s'**appeler** *reflexive verb* ⓔ
**to be called**
**Il s'appelle Romain.** He's called Romain.
**Comment t'appelles-tu?, Tu t'appelles comment?** What's your name?
**Je m'appelle Marie.** My name is Marie.

un **appendice** *masc noun*
**appendix** (*part of the body*)

l'**appendicite** *fem noun*
**appendicitis**

**appétissant** *masc adjective*, **appétissante** *fem*
**appetizing**

un **appétit** *masc noun*
**appetite**
**Bon appétit!** Enjoy your meal. (*said to others at table*)

**applaudir** *verb* **[2]**
**to applaud**

les **applaudissements** *plural masc noun*
**applause**

l'**application** *fem noun*
1 **care and attention**
**Elle a écrit la lettre avec beaucoup d'application.** She wrote the letter with great care.
2 **application** (*of a law, rule*)

**appliquer** *verb* **[1]**
**to apply**

s'**appliquer** *reflexive verb* ⓔ
1 **to apply yourself**
**Il s'applique mieux cette année.** He's applying himself more this year.
2 **s'appliquer à quelqu'un** to apply to somebody
**Le règlement ne s'applique pas à vous.** The rule doesn't apply to you.

♂ **apporter** *verb* **[1]**
**to bring**
**Apporte-moi mon cahier.** Bring me my note book.

♂ **apprécier** *verb* **[1]**
1 **to appreciate** (*food, music, help*)
**Il a apprécié la blague.** He liked the joke.
2 **to like** (*a person*)

**appréhender** *verb* **[1]**
1 **to arrest**
2 **to dread**

un **apprenant** *masc noun*, une **apprenante** *fem*
**learner**

♂ **apprendre** *verb* **[64]**
1 **to learn**
**apprendre à parler français** to learn to speak French
2 **to hear**
**J'ai appris que tu vas partir.** I hear you're leaving.
3 **to teach**
**apprendre quelque chose à quelqu'un** to teach somebody something
**Elle leur apprend le français.** She's teaching them French.
**apprendre à faire quelque chose à** ▸▸

quelqu'un to teach somebody something
**Elle leur apprend à conduire.** She's teaching them to drive.

un **apprentissage** *masc noun*
**apprenticeship**
**Il va en apprentissage.** He's going to do an apprenticeship.

une **approche** *fem noun*
**approach**

**approcher** *verb* [1]
1 **to approach**
**Les vacances approchent.** The holidays are approaching.
**Nous approchons de Rouen.** We're approaching Rouen.
2 **approcher quelqu'un** to go up to somebody
3 **to move (something) closer**
**approcher quelque chose de quelque chose** to move something closer to something
**Approche ta chaise de la table.** Move your chair closer to the table.

s'**approcher** *reflexive verb* Ⓔ
**to get close**
**Je m'approche un peu pour mieux voir.** I'm getting closer to see better.
**s'approcher de quelque chose** to get close to something
**Ne t'approche pas de ce chien, il mord.** Don't go near that dog, he bites.

**approuver** *verb* [1]
1 **to approve of**
2 **to give approval to** (*officially*)

un **appui** *masc noun*
**support**

**appuyer** *verb* [41]
1 **appuyer sur quelque chose** to press something
**Appuie sur le bouton.** Press the button.
2 **to lean**
**appuyer quelque chose contre quelque chose** to lean something against something

**après** *adverb* ▷ see **après** *prep*
**afterwards, later**
**peu après** shortly afterwards
**une heure après** an hour later
**longtemps après** a long time later

**après** *preposition* ▷ see **après** *adv*
1 **after**
**après dix heures** after ten o'clock
**après l'école** after school
2 **après avoir fait quelque chose** after doing something
**Après avoir mangé, j'ai écouté des CD.** After eating, I listened to some CDs.
**Après être rentrée, elle s'est couchée.** After she got home, she went to bed.

**après-demain** *adverb*
**the day after tomorrow**

un & une **après-midi** *masc & fem noun*
**afternoon**
**cet après-midi** this afternoon
**demain après-midi** tomorrow afternoon
**hier après-midi** yesterday afternoon
**tous les après-midi** every afternoon

un **après-rasage** *masc noun*
**aftershave**

une **aptitude** *fem noun*
**aptitude**

l'**aquarelle** *fem noun*
**watercolours** (*method of painting*)
**une aquarelle** a watercolour (painting)

un **aquarium** *masc noun*
1 **fish tank**
2 **aquarium**

**arabe** *masc & fem adjective*
▷ see **Arabe** *noun*
1 **Arab**
2 **Arabic** (*numeral, text*)

un & une **Arabe** *masc & fem noun*
▷ see **arabe** *adj*
1 **Arab** (*a person*)
2 **l'arabe** *masc* **Arabic** (*the language*)

une **araignée** *fem noun*
**spider**

un **arbitre** *masc noun*
**referee**

un **arbre** *masc noun*
**tree**
• un **arbre généalogique** family tree

un **arbuste** *masc noun*
**bush**

un **arc** *masc noun*
1 **arch**
2 **bow** (*for arrows*)
• un **arc-en-ciel** rainbow

l'**archéologie** *fem noun*
**archeology**

un & une **archéologue** *masc & fem noun*
**archeologist**

un **archevêque** *masc noun*
**archbishop**

un & une **architecte** *masc & fem noun*
**architect**

Ⓔ means the verb takes être to form the perfect

l'**Arctique** *masc noun*
**the Arctic**

une **ardoise** *fem noun*
**slate**

une **arène** *fem noun*
1 **arena**
2 **bullring**

une **arête** *fem noun*
**fishbone**

♪ l'**argent** *masc noun*
1 **money**
**dépenser de l'argent** to spend money
**retirer de l'argent à la banque** to take money out of the bank
2 **silver**
**une chaîne en argent** a silver chain
- l'**argent de poche** pocket money

l'**argile** *fem noun*
**clay**

l'**argot** *masc noun*
**slang**

l'**arithmétique** *fem noun*
**arithmetic**

une **arme** *fem noun*
**weapon**
- une **arme à feu** firearm

une **armée** *fem noun*
**army**
- l'**armée de l'air** air force
- l'**armée de terre** army

♪ une **armoire** *fem noun*
1 **wardrobe**
2 **cupboard**

un **arobase** *masc noun*
**at**, @ (*in email addresses*)
**un arobase** an at-sign
**jean-point-dupont-arobase-mondecom-point-com** jean-dot-dupont-at-mondecom-dot-com

les **aromates** *plural masc noun*
**herbs and spices**

l'**aromathérapie** *fem noun*
**aromatherapy**

**aromatisé** *masc adjective*, **aromatisée** *fem*
**flavoured**

un **arôme** *masc noun*
1 **flavouring**, **flavour**
**arôme fraise** strawberry flavour
**à l'arôme de vanille** vanilla-flavoured
2 **aroma** (*smell*)

**arracher** *verb* **[1]**
1 **arracher quelque chose à quelqu'un** to snatch something from somebody
**Elle m'a arraché mon porte-monnaie.** She snatched my purse from me.
2 **to rip out**
**J'ai arraché les pages de mon journal.** I ripped the pages out of my diary.
3 **to pull up** (*weeds, vegetables*)

un **arrangement** *masc noun*
**arrangement**

**arranger** *verb* **[52]**
1 **to arrange** (*flowers*)
2 **to sort out** (*a problem*)
**Cela ne va pas arranger les choses.** That's not going to help things.
3 **to repair** (*a watch*)
4 **to suit**
**Si ça t'arrange, on peut partir d'ici.** If it suits you better, we can leave from here.

s'**arranger** *reflexive verb* ❷
1 **to get better** (*weather, situation*)
**Ça va s'arranger.** It'll sort itself out.
2 **s'arranger avec quelqu'un** to sort it out with somebody
**Tu t'arranges avec Jean.** Sort it out with Jean.
**s'arranger avec quelqu'un pour faire quelque chose** to arrange with somebody to do something
**Elle s'est arrangée avec Julie pour aller en ville.** She's arranged with Julie to go into town.

une **arrestation** *fem noun*
**arrest**

♪ un **arrêt** *masc noun*
1 **stop**
**au prochain arrêt** at the next stop
2 **sans arrêt** non-stop
**Ils bavardent sans arrêt.** They chat away non-stop.
- un **arrêt de bus** bus stop

♪ **arrêter** *verb* **[1]**
1 **to arrest** (*a suspect*)
2 **to stop**
**arrêter la voiture** to stop the car
3 **to switch off** (*an engine, a machine*)
4 **arrêter de faire quelque chose** to stop doing something
**Il a arrêté de fumer.** He's stopped smoking.
**Elle n'arrête pas de travailler.** She doesn't stop working.

s'**arrêter** *reflexive verb* ⓔ
**to stop**
On va s'arrêter à la boulangerie. We'll stop at the baker's.

les **arrhes** *plural fem noun*
**deposit**

**arrière** *masc & fem adjective*
▷ see **arrière** *noun*
**back**
la porte arrière the back door

un **arrière** *masc noun* ▷ see **arrière** *adj*
**back**
à l'arrière in the back *(of a car)*
regarder en arrière to look back
rester en arrière to stay back
- un **arrière-goût** after-taste
- une **arrière-grand-mère** great-grandmother
- un **arrière-grand-père** great-grandfather
- les **arrière-grands-parents** great-grandparents
- les **arrière-petits-enfants** great-grandchildren

une **arrivée** *fem noun*
**arrival**

𝄞 **arriver** *verb* ⓔ [1]
1 **to arrive**
arriver à Londres to arrive in London
Je suis arrivé à cinq heures. I arrived at five o'clock.
Ils arrivent à quelle heure? What time do they arrive?
J'arrive! I'm coming!
2 **to happen**
L'accident est arrivé hier. The accident happened yesterday.
Qu'est-ce qui arrive? What's happening?
Ça m'est arrivé aussi. That happened to me too.
3 arriver à faire quelque chose to be able to do something
Est-ce que tu arrives à voir? Can you see?
Je n'arrive pas à tourner la clef. I can't turn the key.

**arrogant** *masc adjective*, **arrogante** *fem*
**arrogant**

un **arrondissement** *masc noun*
**arrondissement** *(a numbered area of a large French-speaking city)*
dans le neuvième arrondissement in the ninth arrondissement

**arroser** *verb* [1]
1 **to water**
arroser les plantes to water the plants
2 **to celebrate** *(with drinks)*
On va arroser l'anniversaire de mon frère. We're going to have a few drinks to celebrate my brother's birthday.

un **arrosoir** *masc noun*
**watering can**

l'**art** *masc noun*
**art**

une **artère** *fem noun*
1 **artery**
2 **arterial road**
3 **main road**

un **artichaut** *masc noun*
**artichoke**

𝄞 un **article** *masc noun*
1 **article** *(in a newspaper)*
2 **item** *(on sale)*
les articles de toilette toiletries
3 **article** *(in grammar: un, une; le, la, les)*
- l'**article défini** definite article *(le, la, les)*
- l'**article indéfini** indefinite article *(un, une)*

une **articulation** *fem noun*
**joint** *(of elbow, knee)*

**artificiel** *masc adjective*, **artificielle** *fem*
**artificial**

un **artisan** *masc noun*
**craftsman**

**artisanal** *masc adjective*, **artisanale** *fem*, **artisanaux** *masc pl*, **artisanales** *fem pl*
1 **traditional** *(skill, craft)*
une foire artisanale a craft fair
de fabrication artisanale made by traditional methods
2 **home-made** *(food)*
biscuits artisanaux home-made biscuits

un & une **artiste** *masc & fem noun*
1 **artist**
2 **performer**

un **as** *masc noun* ▷ see **as** *verb*
**ace**

**as** *verb* ▷ see **as** *noun* ▷ **avoir**

𝄞 un **ascenseur** *masc noun*
**lift**
prendre l'ascenseur to take the lift

**asiatique** *masc & fem adjective*
**Asian**

l'**Asie** *fem noun*
**Asia**
aller en Asie to go to Asia

un **asile** *masc noun*
1 **refuge**

2 **asylum**
l'asile politique political asylum
le droit d'asile the right of asylum

un **aspect** *masc noun*
1 **aspect** (*of a problem*)
2 **appearance** (*of a person, thing*)
3 **side**

les **asperges** *plural fem noun*
**asparagus**

⚷ un **aspirateur** *masc noun*
**vacuum cleaner**
passer l'aspirateur to do the vacuuming

⚷ une **aspirine** *fem noun*
**aspirin**

**assaisonner** *verb* [1]
**to season**

un **assassin** *masc noun*, une **assassine** *fem*
**murderer**

l'**assassinat** *masc noun*
**murder**

**assassiner** *verb* [1]
**to murder**

une **assemblée** *fem noun*
1 **meeting**
2 **assembly** (*in politics*)

**assembler** *verb* [1]
**to assemble** (*a kit, a machine*)

s'**assembler** *reflexive verb* ❷
**to gather** (*people, crowds*)

s'**asseoir** *reflexive verb* ❷ [20]
**to sit down**
s'asseoir sur une chaise to sit down on a chair
Assieds-toi. Take a seat.
Asseyez-vous. Do sit down. (*polite form*) ▷ **assis**

⚷ **assez** *adverb*
1 **enough**
Elle ne mange pas assez. She doesn't eat enough.
Est-ce que tu dors assez? Are you getting enough sleep?
2 assez de enough (*of something*)
assez de pain enough bread
Il y a assez de verres. There are enough glasses.
Il n'y a pas assez d'argent. There isn't enough money.
3 **enough**
Est-ce que l'eau est assez chaude? Is the water hot enough?
Il n'est pas assez fort pour porter la valise. He's not strong enough to carry the suitcase.
4 **quite**
assez joli quite pretty
Je la vois assez souvent. I see her quite often.
5 (*informal*) J'en ai assez! I've had enough!

⚷ une **assiette** *fem noun*
**plate**
- une **assiette plate** dinner plate
- une **assiette creuse** soup plate
- une **assiette à soupe** soup plate

⚷ **assis** *masc adjective*, **assise** *fem*
être assis to be sitting
Elle était assise dans un fauteuil. She was sitting in an armchair.

une **assistance** *fem noun*
1 **audience**
2 **assistance** (*help*)

un **assistant** *masc noun*, une **assistante** *fem*
**assistant**

**assister** *verb* [1]
1 assister à quelque chose to attend something, to be at (*an event*)
J'ai assisté à leur mariage. I was at their wedding.
2 **to help**
3 **to aid** (*a country, etc*)

une **association** *fem noun*
**association**

un **associé** *masc noun*, une **associée** *fem*
**associate, partner**

s'**associer** *reflexive verb* ❷
1 s'associer à un groupe to join a group
2 s'associer pour faire quelque chose to join forces to do something

**assommer** *verb* [1]
1 assommer quelqu'un to knock somebody out
2 (*informal*) assommer quelqu'un to bore somebody stiff
Ça m'assomme de rester ici! I'm bored stiff staying here!

**assorti** *masc adjective*, **assortie** *fem*
1 **matching**
2 **assorted** (*chocolates, etc*)

un **assortiment** *masc noun*
**assortment, selection**

**assumer** *verb* [1]
assumer la responsabilité de quelque chose to take responsibility for something
assumer une fonction to hold a position

**l'assurance** *fem noun*
1 **confidence**
**prendre de l'assurance** to gain confidence
**avec assurance** confidently
2 **insurance**
• une **assurance maladie** health insurance
• une **assurance voyage** travel insurance

**assuré** *masc adjective*, **assurée** *fem*
1 **confident**
2 **insured**

**assurer** *verb* **[1]**
1 **to assure**
**Je vous assure que c'est vrai.** I assure you it's true.
2 **to insure**
3 **to provide** *(a service)*
4 **to carry out** *(a task)*

**s'assurer** *reflexive verb* ⓔ
**to make sure**

un **astérisque** *masc noun*
**asterisk**

**asthmatique** *masc & fem adjective*
**asthmatic**

un **asthme** *masc noun*
**asthma**

un **asticot** *masc noun*
**maggot**

l'**astrologie** *fem noun*
**astrology**

un & une **astrologue** *masc & fem noun*
**astrologer**

un & une **astronome** *masc & fem noun*
**astronomer**

l'**astronomie** *fem noun*
**astronomy**

l'**astuce** *fem noun*
1 **cleverness**
2 **craftiness, shrewdness**
3 **une astuce** a trick *(for getting something)*

**astucieux** *masc adjective*, **astucieuse** *fem*
1 **clever**
2 **crafty**

un **atelier** *masc noun*
1 **workshop**
2 **studio** *(of an artist, sculptor)*
3 **work group**

un & une **athée** *masc & fem noun*
**atheist**

**Athènes** *noun*
**Athens**

un & une **athlète** *masc & fem noun*
**athlete**

l'**athlétisme** *masc noun*
**athletics**
**faire de l'athlétisme** to do athletics

l'**Atlantique** *masc noun*
**l'Atlantique** the Atlantic

un **atlas** *masc noun*
**atlas**

l'**atmosphère** *fem noun*
**atmosphere**

**atomique** *masc & fem adjective*
**atomic**

un **atout** *masc noun*
1 **advantage**
2 **trump card**
**C'est atout pique.** Spades are trumps.

**atroce** *masc & fem adjective*
**dreadful, terrible**

une **atrocité** *fem noun*
**atrocity**

**attachant** *masc adjective*, **attachante** *fem*
**lovable**

une **attache** *fem noun*
1 **tie**
2 **attaches familiales** family ties
3 **string**
4 **strap**

**attacher** *verb* **[1]**
**to tie**
**attacher ses cheveux** to tie your hair back
**Attachez vos ceintures.** Fasten your seatbelts.

s'**attacher** *reflexive verb* ⓔ
**to stick** *(to a pot, a table)*
**La sauce s'attache à la poêle.** The sauce is sticking to the pan.

**attaquer** *verb* **[1]**
**to attack**

**atteindre** *verb* **[60]**
1 **to reach, to get to**
**La temperature atteint 35° à midi.** The temperature reaches 35° at midday.
2 **to achieve** *(an aim, a goal)*

**atteint** *masc adjective*, **atteinte** *fem*
**être atteint par quelque chose** to be affected by something
**les pays atteints par le désastre** the countries affected by the disaster

**attendant** *in phrase*
**en attendant** meanwhile, in the meantime



ⓔ means the verb takes être to form the perfect

𝄞 **attendre** *verb* **[3]**

**1 to wait for**
J'attends le bus. I'm waiting for the bus.
Je t'attends dehors. I'll wait for you outside.

**2 to expect**
attendre un bébé to be expecting a baby
J'attends le médecin. I'm expecting the doctor.

**3 to wait**
Tu peux attendre deux minutes? Can you wait two minutes?

s'**attendre** *reflexive verb* ❺
s'attendre à quelque chose to expect something
Je ne m'attendais pas aux cadeaux. I wasn't expecting the presents.

**WORD TIP** *attendre* does not mean *attend* in English; for the meaning of *attend* ▷ **assister**.

un **attentat** *masc noun*
**1 attack**
un attentat à la bombe a bomb attack
**2 assassination attempt**

une **attente** *fem noun*
**wait**
une attente de vingt minutes a twenty-minute wait

**attentif** *masc adjective*, **attentive** *fem*
**1 attentive**
**2 careful**

𝄞 l'**attention** *fem noun*
**1 attention**
Attention! Watch out!
Attention au chien! Beware of the dog!
faire attention to pay attention
Fais attention à l'annonce. Pay attention to the announcement.
Ne fais pas attention à Pierre. Don't take any notice of Pierre.
**2** faire attention à quelque chose to watch out for something
Faites attention aux pickpockets! Watch out for pickpockets!

un **atterrissage** *masc noun*
**landing**
• un **atterrissage en catastrophe** crash landing

**attirant** *masc adjective*, **attirante** *fem*
**attractive**

**attirer** *verb* **[1]**
**to attract**
Il a essayé d'attirer mon attention. He tried to attract my attention.

s'**attirer** *reflexive verb* ❺
s'attirer des ennuis to make trouble for yourself

une **attitude** *fem noun*
**attitude**

une **attraction** *fem noun*
**attraction**
les attractions touristiques the tourist attractions

**attraper** *verb* **[1]**
**to catch** *(a ball, a cold)*

**attrayant** *masc adjective*, **attrayante** *fem*
**attractive**

**attrister** *verb* **[1]**
**to sadden**

**au** ▷ **à**

l'**aube** *fem noun*
**dawn**
à l'aube at dawn

𝄞 une **auberge** *fem noun*
**inn**
• une **auberge de jeunesse** youth hostel

une **aubergine** *fem noun*
**aubergine**

**aucun** *masc adjective*, **aucune** *fem*
▷ see **aucun** *pron*
**no**
en aucun cas under no circumstances
sans aucun doute without any doubt
Elle n'a aucun talent. She has no talent.
Je n'ai eu aucune nouvelle de Laura. I haven't had any news from Laura.

**WORD TIP** *ne* or *n'* is used with *aucun* or *aucune* when there is a verb.

**aucun**, **aucune** *pronoun* ▷ see **aucun** *adj*
**1** *(for a masc noun)* **none**
Aucun d'entre eux n'est venu. None of them came.
Aucun des deux n'est venu. Neither of the two came.
Je ne connais aucun de tes amis. I don't know any of your friends.
**2** *(for a fem noun)* **none**
Aucune d'entre elles n'est venue. None of them came.
Aucune des cartes n'est pour moi. None of the cards is for me.
Je ne connais aucune de tes amies. I don't know any of your friends.

**WORD TIP** *ne* or *n'* is used with *aucun* or *aucune* when there is a verb.

**au-delà de** *preposition*
**beyond**
**au-delà de cette limite** beyond that limit

**au-dessous** *adverb*
1 **underneath**
2 **below**
**Il habite l'étage au-dessous.** He lives on the floor below.
3 **au-dessous de** underneath, below
**au-dessous de la table** underneath the table
**Elle habite l'étage au-dessous de chez nous.** She lives on the floor below us.

**au-dessus** *adverb*
1 **above**
**C'est à l'étagère au-dessus.** It's on the shelf above.
2 **au-dessus de** above
**au-dessus de ma tête** above my head

**audiovisuel** *masc adjective*, **audiovisuelle** *fem*
**audiovisual**

un **auditeur** *masc noun*, une **auditrice** *fem*
**listener** (*to radio*)

une **augmentation** *fem noun*
**increase**
**l'augmentation des prix** the increase in prices

**augmenter** *verb* [1]
1 **to raise**
2 **to go up**

**aujourd'hui** *adverb*
**today**
**Nous sommes lundi aujourd'hui.** Today is Monday.

**auparavant** *adverb*
1 **before**
2 **previously**

**auprès de** *preposition*
1 **beside, next to**
2 **to** (*when talking to someone*)
**se plaindre auprès du professeur** to complain to the teacher

**auquel** *pronoun*
**to whom**
**le garçon auquel je parle** the boy I'm talking to, the boy to whom I'm talking

**WORD TIP** *auquel* becomes *à laquelle* for a fem singular noun, *auxquels* for a masc plural noun, and *auxquelles* for a fem plural noun.

**aura**, **aurai**, **auras**, **aurez**, **aurons**, **auront** *verb* ▷ **avoir**

**au revoir** *exclamation*
**goodbye**

**aussi** *adverb*
1 **also, too**
**Moi aussi.** Me too.
**J'ai aussi invité ton frère.** I also invited your brother.
2 (*in comparisons*) **aussi ... que** as ... as
**Mon panier est aussi lourd que le tien.** My basket is as heavy as yours.
3 **aussi bien que** as well as
**les enfants aussi bien que les adultes** children as well as adults

**aussitôt** *adverb*
**immediately**
**aussitôt que possible** as soon as possible

l'**Australie** *fem noun*
**Australia**
**être en Australie** to be in Australia
**aller en Australie** to go to Australia

**WORD TIP** Countries and regions in French take *le*, *la* or *les*.

**australien** *masc adjective*, **australienne** *fem* ▷ see **Australien** *noun*
**Australian**

**WORD TIP** Adjectives never have capitals in French, even for nationality or regional origin.

un **Australien** *masc noun*, une **Australienne** *fem*
▷ see **australien** *adj*
**Australian**

**autant** *adverb*
1 **as much, so much**
**Je n'ai jamais mangé autant.** I've never eaten so much.
2 **autant que** as much as, as many as
**Tu en as autant que moi.** You have as much as I have., You have as many as I have.
3 **autant de ... que** as much ... as, as many ... as
**Elle a autant d'argent que toi.** She has as much money as you do.
**Tu as autant de problèmes que moi.** You have as many problems as I do.

un **auteur** *masc noun*
**author**

une **auto** *fem noun*
**car**

un **autobus** *masc noun*
**bus**

un **autocar** *masc noun*
**coach**

**autocollant** *masc adjective*, **autocollante** *fem*
**self-adhesive**

une **auto-école** *fem noun*
**driving school**

un **automate** *masc noun*
**robot**

**automatique** *masc & fem adjective*
**automatic**

l'**automne** *masc noun*
**autumn**
en automne in autumn

**automobile** *masc & fem adjective*
▷ see **automobile** *noun*
l'industrie automobile the car industry

♁ une **automobile** *fem noun*
▷ see **automobile** *adj*
**car**

**automobiliste** *masc & fem noun*
**motorist**

un **autoradio** *masc noun*
**car radio**

une **autorisation** *fem noun*
1 **permission**
**avoir l'autorisation de faire quelque chose** to have permission to do something
**Ils ont l'autorisation de sortir.** They have permission to go out.
2 **permit**

**autoriser** *verb* [1]
1 **to authorize**
2 **autoriser quelqu'un à faire quelque chose** to allow somebody to do something
**Mes parents m'autorisent à sortir le weekend.** My parents allow me to go out at weekends.

une **autorité** *fem noun*
**authority**

♁ une **autoroute** *fem noun*
**motorway**
• une **autoroute à péage** toll motorway

♁ l'**auto-stop** *masc noun*
**hitchhiking**
faire de l'auto-stop to hitchhike

un **auto-stoppeur** *masc noun*, une **auto-stoppeuse** *fem*
**hitchhiker**

♁ **autour** *adverb*
1 **around**
**un lac avec des arbres tout autour** a lake with trees all around it
2 **autour de** round, around
**Nous étions assis autour de la table.** We were sitting around the table.

♁ **autre** *masc & fem adjective* ▷ see **autre** *pron*
1 **other**
l'autre jour the other day
2 **un autre, une autre** another
un autre film another film
3 **quelqu'un d'autre** somebody else
**personne d'autre** nobody else

♁ **autre** *pronoun* ▷ see **autre** *adj*
1 **un autre, une autre** another one
**Donne-moi un autre.** Give me another one.
2 **les autres** the others
**Où sont les autres?** Where are the others?

♁ **autrefois** *adverb*
**in the past**
**Autrefois là il y avait une épicerie.** In the past there was a grocer's shop there.

**autre part** *adverb*
**somewhere else**

l'**Autriche** *fem noun*
**Austria**

**autrichien** *masc adjective*, **autrichienne** *fem* ▷ see **Autrichien** *noun*
**Austrian**

un **Autrichien** *masc noun*, une **Autrichienne** *fem*
▷ see **autrichien** *adj*
**Austrian**

une **autruche** *fem noun*
**ostrich**

**aux** *preposition*

**WORD TIP** *aux is formed by à + les* ▷ **à** *preposition*

**auxquelles** *pronoun*
**to whom**
**les filles auxquelles je parlais** the girls I was talking to, the girls to whom I was talking

**auxquels** *pronoun*
**to whom**
**les garçons auxquels je parlais** the boys I was talking to, the boys to whom I was talking

une **avalanche** *fem noun*
**avalanche**

**avaler** *verb* [1]
1 **to swallow**
2 **to inhale**

une **avance** *fem noun*
1 **advance**
2 **lead**
**avoir deux buts d'avance** to have a two-goal lead
3 **en avance** early
**Je suis arrivé dix minutes en avance.** I arrived ten minutes early. ▸▸

4 à l'avance in advance
Il faut réserver à l'avance. You must book in advance.

**avancer** *verb* [61]
1 **to move forward**
2 **avancer quelque chose** to bring something forward
**Ils ont avancé le match.** They brought the match forward.
3 **to be fast** (*watches, clocks*)
**Ma montre avance de cinq minutes.** My watch is five minutes fast.

**avant** *masc & fem adjective* ▷ see **avant** *adv, noun, prep*
**front** (*set, wheel*)

**avant** *adverb* ▷ see **avant** *adj, noun, prep*
1 **before**
**longtemps avant** a long time before
**la semaine d'avant** the week before
2 **en avant** forward

l'**avant** *masc noun* ▷ see **avant** *adj, adv, prep*
1 **front**
**à l'avant** in the front (*of a car*)
2 **forward** (*in football, etc*)

**avant** *preposition* ▷ see **avant** *adj, adv, noun*
1 **before**
**avant Noël** before Christmas
**avant six heures** before six o'clock
2 **avant de faire quelque chose** before doing something
**Je vais lui téléphoner avant de partir.** I'll phone her before I leave.

un **avantage** *masc noun*
**advantage**

**avantageux** *masc adjective*, **avantageuse** *fem*
**advantageous**

**avant-dernier** *masc adjective*, **avant-dernière** *fem*
**last but one**

**avant-hier** *adverb*
**the day before yesterday**
**Nous sommes arrivés avant-hier.** We arrived the day before yesterday.

**avec** *preposition*
**with**
**avec Chloé** with Chloé
**avec un couteau** with a knife
**Avec ça?** Anything else? (*in a shop*)

l'**avenir** *masc noun*
**future**
**à l'avenir** in the future

une **aventure** *fem noun*
**adventure**

une **avenue** *fem noun*
**avenue**

une **averse** *fem noun*
**shower**
**Des averses sont à craindre en soirée.** Showers are to be expected in the evening.

**avertir** *verb* [2]
1 **to inform**
2 **to warn**

un **avertissement** *masc noun*
**warning**

**aveugle** *masc & fem adjective*
**blind**

**avez** *verb* ▷ **avoir**

l'**aviation** *fem noun*
1 **aviation**
2 **air force**

un **avion** *masc noun*
**aeroplane**
**par avion** by airmail
**aller à Paris en avion** to fly to Paris, to go to Paris by air

un **aviron** *masc noun*
1 **rowing**
**faire de l'aviron** to row
2 **oar**

un **avis** *masc noun*
1 **opinion**
**à mon avis** in my opinion
**changer d'avis** to change your mind
**Elle a changé d'avis.** She's changed her mind.
2 **notice**

un **avocat** *masc noun*, une **avocate** *fem*
1 **lawyer**
2 **avocado** (*fruit*)

l'**avoine** *fem noun*
**oats**

**avoir** *verb* [5]
1 **to have, to have got**
**Elle a un vélo.** She has a bike., She's got a bike.
**Je n'ai pas d'argent.** I don't have any money.
**Nous avons un chien.** We have a dog.
**As-tu des frères et sœurs?** Do you have brothers and sisters?
2 (*talking about age*) **to be**
**Élodie a douze ans.** Élodie's twelve.
**Quel âge a Pierre?** How old is Pierre?
**quand j'avais cinq ans** when I was five
3 (*to say you're cold, hot, etc*) **to be**
**J'ai chaud.** I'm hot.
**J'ai froid.** I'm cold.

Ils ont très froid. They're very cold.
J'ai mal. It hurts.
avoir mal à la tête to have a headache

**4** (*to say you're hungry, thirsty, etc*) **to be**
Est-ce que tu as faim? Are you hungry?
Je n'ai pas faim. I'm not hungry.
J'ai vraiment soif. I'm really thirsty.

**5** il y a there is, there are
Il y a une femme à la porte. There's a woman at the door.
Il y avait trois livres sur la table. There were three books on the table.
Il n'y a pas de temps. There's no time.
Qu'est-ce qu'il y a? What's the matter?

**WORD TIP** However many there are, French always uses *il y + a, il y + avait, etc.*

**6** (*to say ago*) il y a un an a year ago
il y a huit jours a week ago

**7** (*Used with the past participle (usually ending -é -i or -u) to form the **have** and **had** tenses.*)
J'ai perdu mon stylo. I have lost my pen.
J'ai vu ta mère hier. I saw your mother yesterday.
Ils avaient déjà parlé avec le prof. They had already spoken to the teacher.

**WORD TIP** You will find phrases using avoir at entries like *besoin, envie, lieu, raison* and *tort.*

**avons** *verb* ▷ **avoir**

un **avortement** *masc noun*
**abortion**

**avouer** *verb* **[1]**
**to admit, to confess**

♪ **avril** *masc noun*
**April**
en avril, au mois d'avril in April

**WORD TIP** Months of the year and days of the week start with small letters in French.

***avril***

Le premier avril, à l'école, on colle des poissons en papier dans le dos des profs ! On fait des farces. On dit: « Poisson d'avril ! » Les médias aussi font des farces.

# B b

le **baby-foot** *masc noun*
**table football**
une partie de baby-foot a game of table football

**baby-sitting** *masc noun*
**baby-sitting**

♪ le **bac** *masc noun*
**1** (*informal*) **baccalaureate** ▷ See **baccalauréat** for examples.
**2** **tub**
- le **bac blanc** mock baccalaureate
- le **bac à glace** ice tray

♪ le **baccalauréat** *masc noun*
**baccalaureate** (*exam taken by French secondary school students at 17-18, which leads to higher education*)
réussir au baccalauréat to pass the baccalaureate
être reçu au baccalauréat to pass the baccalaureate
Je vais passer le baccalauréat. I'm going to sit the baccalaureate.
Il a échoué au baccalauréat. He failed the baccalaureate.

le **badaud** *masc noun*, la **badaude** *fem*
**1** **passerby**
**2** **onlooker** (*watching out of curiosity*)

le **baffle** *masc noun*
**speaker** (*on a music system*)

♪ le **bagage** *masc noun*
un bagage a piece of luggage
des bagages luggage
Où sont tes bagages? Where's your luggage?
Je dois faire mes bagages. I've got to pack.
- le **bagage à main** hand luggage

la **bagarre** *fem noun*
**fight**

se **bagarrer** *reflexive verb* Ⓔ **[1]**
**to fight**
Ils se bagarrent toujours. They're always fighting.

la **bagnole** *fem noun*
(*informal*) **car**

la **bague** *fem noun*
**ring**

♪ la **baguette** *fem noun*
**1** **baguette** (*French bread stick*)
**2** **stick** (*of wood*)
**3** **drumstick**
**4** **chopstick**
- la **baguette magique** magic wand

les **Bahamas** *plural fem noun*
les îles Bahamas the Bahamas, the Bahama Islands

la **baie** *fem noun*
1 **bay** (*on the coast*)
2 **berry**

la **baignade** *fem noun*
**swimming**
"Baignade interdite" 'No swimming'

se **baigner** *reflexive verb* Ⓔ **[1]**
**to go for a swim**
**Je suis allé me baigner.** I went for a swim.
**Allons nous baigner!** Let's go for a swim!

la **baignoire** *fem noun*
**bath**

**bâiller** *verb* **[1]**
**to yawn**

le **bain** *masc noun*
1 **bath**
**un bain moussant** a bubble bath
**prendre un bain** to have a bath
2 (*in swimming*)
**le grand bain** the main pool
**le petit bain** the learners' pool

le **baiser** *masc noun*
**kiss**
**Bons baisers** Love and kisses (*letter ending*)

la **baisse** *fem noun*
**fall**
**être en baisse** to be falling
**La température est en baisse.** The temperature is falling.

**baisser** *verb* **[1]**
**to lower**
**baisser le store** to lower the blind
**baisser les prix** to reduce prices
**Tu peux baisser la lumière?** Can you turn down the lights?

se **baisser** *reflexive verb* Ⓔ
**to bend down**

le **bal** *masc noun*
1 **dance**
**un bal populaire** a dance (or disco)
**Il y aura un bal populaire le 14 juillet.** There will be a dance on July 14.
2 **ball** (*a formal dance*)

la **balade** *fem noun*
1 **walk**
2 **cycle ride**
3 **drive**
**faire une balade à la campagne** to go for a drive in the country

se **balader** *reflexive verb* Ⓔ **[1]**
1 **to go for a walk**
**Je vais me balader au bord du lac.** I'm going for a walk by the lake.
2 **to go for a cycle ride**
3 **to go for a drive**
**Ils se baladent en Écosse.** They're driving round Scotland.

le **baladeur** *masc noun*
**personal stereo**

le **balai** *masc noun*
**brush** (*for sweeping*)
**passer le balai** to sweep the floor

la **balance** *fem noun* ▷ see **Balance** *noun*
**scales**
• la **balance de cuisine** kitchen scales

la **Balance** *fem noun* ▷ see **balance** *noun*
**Libra**
**Emilie est Balance.** Emilie is a Libra.

**WORD TIP** Signs of the zodiac do not take an article: *un* or *une*.

**balancer** *verb* **[61]**
1 **to swing** (*your arms, legs, etc*)
2 (*informal*) **to chuck**, **to throw**
**Arrête de balancer des cailloux!** Stop throwing stones!
3 (*informal*) **to throw out**
**J'ai balancé mes vieux vêtements.** I threw out my old clothes.

la **balançoire** *fem noun*
1 **swing**
2 **seesaw**

**balayer** *verb* **[59]**
1 **to sweep**
**balayer la cuisine** to sweep the kitchen
2 **to sweep up**
**balayer les miettes** to sweep up the crumbs

la **balayeuse** *fem noun*
**roadsweeper** (*a machine*)

**balbutier** *verb* **[1]**
**to mumble**

le **balcon** *masc noun*
1 **balcony**
**Le balcon donne sur la rue.** The balcony looks onto the street.
2 **circle** (*in a theatre*)

la **baleine** *fem noun*
**whale**

la **balle** *fem noun*
1 **ball**
**une balle de tennis** a tennis ball
**jouer à la balle** to play ball
2 **bullet**

la **ballerine** *fem noun*
**ballerina**

le **ballet** *masc noun*
**ballet**

♪ le **ballon** *masc noun*
1 **ball**
un ballon de football a football
jouer au ballon to play ball
2 **balloon** (*for parties, decoration*)
3 (*informal*) **Breathalyzer®**

le **ball-trap** *masc noun*
**clay pigeon shooting**

**balnéaire** *masc & fem adjective*
**seaside**

le **bambou** *masc noun*
**bamboo**

**banal** *masc adjective*, **banale** *fem* **banals** *masc pl* **banales** *fem pl*
**ordinary**
une histoire peu banale an unusual story

♪ la **banane** *fem noun*
1 **banana**
un kilo de bananes a kilo of bananas
2 **bumbag**

le **banc** *masc noun*
**bench**

la **bande** *fem noun*
1 **group**
une bande de jeunes a group of young people
2 **gang**
une bande de criminels a gang of criminals
3 **strip** (*of fabric, paper*)
4 **tape** (*for recordings*)
On va faire une bande démo. We're going to make a demo tape.
5 **bandage**
- la **bande-annonce** trailer (*for a film*)
- la **bande d'arrêt d'urgence** hard shoulder (*on motorway*)

le **bandeau** *masc noun*, les **bandeaux** *pl*
1 **headband**
2 **blindfold**

la **bande dessinée** *fem noun*
1 **comic strip**
2 **comic book**

mini-info **bande dessinée**
La bande dessinée (BD) a son musée et son festival à Angoulême.

la **bande rugueuse** *fem noun*
**rumble strip** (*on motorway*)

la **bande sonore** *fem noun*
1 **rumble strip** (*on motorway*)
2 **soundtrack** (*of film*)

le **bandit** *masc noun*
**bandit**

le **banditisme** *masc noun*
**crime** (*as an activity*)

♪ la **banlieue** *fem noun*
1 la banlieue the suburbs
2 une banlieue a suburb
un train de banlieue a commuter train
J'habite dans la banlieue de Leeds. I live in the suburbs of Leeds.

♪ la **banque** *fem noun*
1 **bank**
aller à la banque to go to the bank
Elle a 950 euros sur son compte en banque. She has 950 euros in the bank.
2 **banking**
Je voudrais travailler dans une banque. I'd like to work in banking.

le **banquet** *masc noun*
**banquet**

la **banquette** *fem noun*
1 **wall seat** (*in a cafe, restaurant*)
2 **seat** (*in a car, bus, train*)

le **banquier** *masc noun*, la **banquière** *fem*
**banker**

le **baptême** *masc noun*
**christening**

**baptiser** *verb* [1]
1 **to christen**
2 **to name**
3 **to nickname**

♪ le **bar** *masc noun*
1 **bar** (*place for drinking*)
le bar au coin de la rue the bar on the corner
2 **bar** (*the counter*)
On va prendre un pot au bar. We're going to have a drink at the bar.

la **baraque** *fem noun*
(*informal*) **house**

la **Barbade** *fem noun*
**Barbados**
à la Barbade in Barbados
aller à la Barbade to go to Barbados

**barbadien** *masc adjective*, **barbadienne** *fem* ▷ see **Barbadien** *noun*
**Barbadian**

le **Barbadien** *masc noun*, la **Barbadienne** *fem* ▷ see **barbadien** *adj*
**Barbadian**

**barbant** *masc adjective*, **barbante** *fem adjective*
**boring**
C'est barbant, les maths. Maths is a drag.

la **barbe** *fem noun*
1 **beard**
Mon père porte une barbe. My dad has a beard.
2 **drag**
Quelle barbe! What a drag!
• la **barbe à papa** candyfloss

le **barbecue** *masc noun*
**barbecue**
On va faire un barbecue ce soir. We're going to have a barbecue this evening.

**barbouiller** *verb* [1]
1 **to smear**
J'avais la figure barbouillée de chocolat. I had chocolate all over my face.
2 **to daub**
un mur barbouillé de slogans a wall daubed with slogans

**barbu** *masc adjective*, **barbue** *fem*
▷ see **barbu** *noun*
**bearded**

le **barbu** *masc noun* ▷ see **barbu** *adj*
un barbu a bearded man

la **barmaid** *fem noun*
**barmaid**

le **barman** *masc noun*
**barman**

le **baromètre** *masc noun*
**barometer**

la **barque** *fem noun*
**rowing boat**
faire une promenade en barque to go for a boat ride

la **barquette** *fem noun*
**tub**, **container**
une barquette de frites a portion of chips (*sold in a plastic container*)
une barquette de fraises a punnet of strawberries

le **barrage** *masc noun*
1 **dam**
2 **roadblock**

la **barre** *fem noun*
**bar**
une barre de fer an iron bar
une barre de chocolat a chocolate bar

le **barreau** *masc noun*, les **barreaux** *pl*
**bar**
Il y a des barreaux sur les fenêtres. There are bars on the windows.

**barrer** *verb* [1]
1 **to block**
'Route barrée' 'Road closed'
2 **to cross out**
barrer trois mots to cross out three words

se **barrer** *reflexive verb* ⓔ
**to push off**, **to leave**
Je me barre! I'm off!

la **barrette** *fem noun*
**hairslide**

la **barrière** *fem noun*
1 **fence**
2 **gate**

le **bar-tabac** *masc noun*, les **bars-tabac** *pl*
**cafe** (*selling cigarettes, tobacco, stamps*)

**bas** *masc adjective*, **basse** *fem*
▷ see **bas** *adv, noun*
**low**
un prix bas a low price
une température basse a low temperature
Ils vendent des CD à bas prix. They sell CDs at a low price.

**bas** *adverb* ▷ see **bas** *adj, noun*
1 **low**
plus bas lower down
2 en bas downstairs
La salle de bains est en bas. The bathroom is downstairs.
3 en bas at the bottom
Les notes sont marquées en bas de la page. The marks are written at the bottom of the page.

le **bas** *noun masc* ▷ see **bas** *adj, adv*
1 **bottom** (*the lowest part of something*)
le bas de la liste the bottom of the list
au bas de l'escalier at the bottom of the stairs
2 les bas stockings

le **bas-côté** *masc noun*
**verge** (*on the roadside*)

la **bascule** *fem noun*
1 **weighing machine**
2 **seesaw**
3 **rocker**
un fauteuil à bascule a rocking chair

**basculer** *verb* [1]
**to topple over**
faire basculer quelqu'un to knock somebody off balance

la **base** *fem noun*
**1 basis**
une bonne base pour faire quelque chose a good basis for doing something
**2 base**
un plat à base de riz a rice-based dish
**3** de base basic
les ingrédients de base the basic ingredients
• la **base de données** database

le **base-ball** *masc noun*
**baseball**
jouer au base-ball to play baseball

**baser** *verb* **[1]**
**to base**
être basé sur quelque chose to be based on something

le **basilic** *masc noun*
**basil**

le **basket** *masc noun*
**1 basketball**
jouer au basket to play basketball
**2 trainer**
acheter des baskets to buy some trainers

le **basketteur** *masc noun*, la **basketteuse** *fem*
**basketball player**

**basque** *masc & fem adjective*
▷ see **Basque** *noun*
**Basque**
le Pays basque the Basque Country

un & une **Basque** *masc & fem noun*
▷ see **basque** *adj*
**1 Basque** (*person*)
**2** le basque Basque (*the language*)

**basse** *fem adjective* ▷ see **basse** *noun* ▷ **bas**

la **basse** *fem noun* ▷ see **basse** *fem adj*
**bass** (*in music*)

♪ le **bassin** *masc noun*
**1 pond**
**2 pelvis**

la **bassine** *fem noun*
**bowl**

le & la **bassiste** *masc & fem noun*
**bassist**

la **bataille** *fem noun*
**1 battle**
la bataille de Normandie the Battle of Normandie (*in 1944*)
**2 a card game** (*like beggar-my-neighbour*)
**3** en bataille in a mess
Elle a les cheveux en bataille. Her hair is in a mess.

♪ le **bateau** *masc noun*, les **bateaux** *pl*
**boat, ship**
faire du bateau to go boating
Je vais faire du bateau en Corse. I'm going sailing in Corsica.
Nous y allons en bateau. We're going there by boat.
• le **bateau à moteur** motorboat
• le **bateau de plaisance** pleasure boat
• le **bateau-mouche** sight-seeing boat
• le **bateau pneumatique** rubber dinghy
• le **bateau à voile** sailing boat

**bâti** *masc adjective*, **bâtie** *fem*
**built**
un homme bien bâti a well-built man

♪ le **bâtiment** *masc noun*
**1** un bâtiment a building
les vieux bâtiments du centre-ville the old buildings in the town centre
**2** le bâtiment the building trade
Son père travaille dans le bâtiment. His father works in the building trade.

**bâtir** *verb* **[2]**
**to build**

la **bâtisse** *fem noun*
**building**

le **bâton** *masc noun*
**stick**
• le **bâton de ski** ski pole

le **bâtonnet** *masc noun*
**stick** (*small in size*)
• le **bâtonnet de poisson** fish finger

la **batte** *fem noun*
**bat** (*for cricket, baseball*)

la **batterie** *fem noun*
**1 battery** (*for a car*)
**2 drum kit**
être à la batterie to be on drums (*in a band*)
• la **batterie de cuisine** pots and pans

le **batteur** *masc noun*
**1 drummer**
**2 whisk**
• le **batteur électrique** (electric) mixer

**battre** *verb* **[21]**
**1 to beat** (*in a competition*)
Nous allons les battre. We're going to beat them.
Nicole m'a battu au tennis. Nicole beat me at tennis.
**2 to beat** (*causing pain*)
battre quelqu'un to beat somebody
**3 to beat** (*in cooking*)
battre les œufs to beat the eggs
battre la crème to whip the cream ▸▸

**4 to clap**
**battre des mains** to clap your hands
**5 to beat**
**Mon cœur battait fort.** My heart was beating like mad.
**6 to bang**
**La porte bat.** The door's banging.

se **battre** *reflexive verb* Ⓔ
**to fight**
**Ils n'arrêtent pas de se battre.** They're always fighting.
**Je me suis battu avec mon frère.** I fought with my brother.

**bavard** *masc adjective*, **bavarde** *fem*
**talkative**
**Paul est trop bavard.** Paul talks too much.

**bavarder** *verb* **[1]**
**to chat**
**J'aime bavarder avec mes copains.** I like chatting with my friends.
**Arrêtez de bavarder.** Stop chattering.

la **bavure** *fem noun*
**1 smudge** (*of ink, paint*)
**2 blunder**

le **bazar** *masc noun*
**1 general store**
**2** (*informal*) **mess**
**C'est le bazar dans ma chambre!** My bedroom's a complete mess!

**BCBG** *abbreviation*
(*= bon chic, bon genre*) **chic and stylish**

la **B.D.** *invariable fem noun*
(*= bande dessinée*) **comic book**
**ma collection de B.D.** my comic book collection
**lire les B.D.** to read comic books ▷ bande dessinée

**beau** *masc adjective*, **bel** *masc*, **belle** *fem*, **beaux** *masc pl*, **belles** *fem pl*
**1 beautiful, lovely**
**un beau bébé** a beautiful baby
**une belle maison** a beautiful house
**un bel instrument** a beautiful instrument
**un bel homme** a handsome man
**de beaux vêtements** lovely clothes
**2** (*talking of the weather*) **Il fait beau.** It's a lovely day.
**Il fait moins beau qu'hier.** It's not as nice as yesterday.

**WORD TIP** *bel* is used before words beginning with *a, e, i, o, u* and silent *h*.

**beaucoup** *adverb*
**1 a lot**
**Je lis beaucoup.** I read a lot.
**20 euros, c'est beaucoup.** 20 euros, that's a lot.
**J'aime beaucoup les jeux d'ordinateur.** I like computer games a lot.
**J'ai beaucoup aimé le film.** I enjoyed the film a lot.
**2** (*when you use ne ... pas, etc*) **not ... much**
**Camille ne parle pas beaucoup.** Camille doesn't talk much.
**Il n'aime pas beaucoup la viande.** He doesn't like meat very much.
**3 beaucoup de** a lot of
**beaucoup de jeux** a lot of games
**Il a beaucoup d'argent.** He has a lot of money.
**Il y avait beaucoup de gens au cinéma.** There were a lot of people at the cinema.
**J'ai beaucoup de choses à faire.** I've got a lot of things to do.
**Il n'a pas beaucoup d'amis.** He doesn't have many friends.
**Est-ce que tu as beaucoup de devoirs à faire?** Do you have a lot of homework to do?
**Non, je n'en ai pas beaucoup.** No, I don't have much.
**4** (*expressions with beaucoup*)
**beaucoup plus** much more
**beaucoup moins** much less
**beaucoup trop** far too much
**beaucoup trop court** far too short
**beaucoup plus rapide** much faster
**beaucoup mieux** much better
**Yasmina va beaucoup mieux.** Yasmina is feeling much better.

le **beau-fils** *masc noun*, les **beaux-fils** *pl*
**1 son-in-law**
**2 stepson**

le **beau-frère** *masc noun*, les **beaux-frères** *pl*
**brother-in-law**

le **beau-père** *masc noun*, les **beaux-pères** *pl*
**1 father-in-law**
**2 stepfather**

la **beauté** *fem noun*
**beauty**

les **beaux-arts** *plural masc noun*
**fine arts** (*a subject to study*)
**l'école des beaux-arts** art school

les **beaux-parents** *plural masc noun*
**parents-in-law**

le **bébé** *masc noun*
**baby**
**s'occuper du bébé** to look after the baby

Ⓔ means the verb takes être to form the perfect

a **b** c d e f g h i j k l m n o p q r s t u v w x y z

le **bec** *masc noun*
**beak**

la **bêche** *fem noun*
**spade**

**bégayer** *verb* **[59]**
**to stammer**

**beige** *masc & fem adjective*
**beige**

le **beignet** *masc noun*
**1 fritter**
**2 doughnut**

**bel** *masc adjective* ▷ **beau**

la **belette** *fem noun*
**weasel**

♪ **belge** *masc & fem adjective* ▷ see **Belge** *noun*
**Belgian**

**WORD TIP** Adjectives never have capitals in French, even for nationality or regional origin.

♪ un & une **Belge** *masc & fem noun*
▷ see **belge** *adj*
**Belgian** (*person*)
les Belges the Belgians

la **Belgique** *fem noun*
**Belgium**
en Belgique in Belgium
aller en Belgique to go to Belgium

**WORD TIP** Countries or regions in French take *le*, *la* or *les*.

le **bélier** *masc noun* ▷ see **Bélier** *noun*
**ram**

**Bélier** *masc noun* ▷ see **bélier** *noun*
**Aries**
Je suis Bélier. I'm an Aries.

**WORD TIP** Signs of the zodiac do not take an article: *un* or *une*.

**belle** *fem adjective* ▷ **beau**

la **belle** *fem noun*
ma belle darling (*said to a girl*)

la **belle-famille** *fem noun*
**in-laws**

la **belle-fille** *fem noun*, les **belles-filles** *pl*
**1 daughter-in-law**
**2 stepdaughter**

♪ la **belle-mère** *fem noun*, les **belles-mères** *pl*
**1 mother-in-law**
**2 stepmother**

la **belle-sœur** *fem noun*, les **belles-sœurs** *pl*
**sister-in-law**

le **bénéfice** *masc noun*
**profit**
faire un bénéfice de 10.000 euros to make a profit of 10,000 euros

**bénévole** *masc & fem adjective*
▷ see **bénévole** *noun*
**voluntary, unpaid**

le & la **bénévole** *masc & fem noun*
▷ see **bénévole** *adj*
**voluntary worker**

la **benne** *fem noun*
**skip** (*for rubbish*)

la **béquille** *fem noun*
**crutch**
marcher avec des béquilles to walk on crutches

le **berceau** *masc noun*, les **berceaux** *pl*
**cradle**

**bercer** *verb* **[61]**
**to rock** (*a baby*)

le **béret** *masc noun*
**beret**

la **berge** *fem noun*
**bank** (*of a river, canal*)

le **berger** *masc noun*, **bergère** *fem*
**shepherd**
• le **berger allemand** German shepherd

♪ le **besoin** *masc noun*
**need**
avoir besoin de quelque chose to need something
J'ai besoin de 10 euros. I need 10 euros.
avoir besoin de faire quelque chose to need to do something
J'ai besoin de faire une pause. I need to take a break.
Tu n'as pas besoin de téléphoner. You don't need to phone.

le **bétail** *masc noun*
**1 livestock** (*farm animals*)
**2 cattle**

**bête** *masc & fem adjective* ▷ see **bête** *noun*
**stupid**

♪ la **bête** *fem noun* ▷ see **bête** *adj*
**animal**

la **bêtise** *fem noun*
**1** faire une bêtise to do something stupid
Il fait toujours des bêtises. He's always doing stupid things.
**2** la bêtise stupidity

le **béton** *masc noun*
**concrete**

la **bétonnière** *fem noun*
**cement mixer**

la **betterave** la **betterave rouge** *fem noun*
**beetroot**

le & la **beur** *masc & fem noun*
**young person of North African origin**

♪ le **beurre** *masc noun*
**butter**
**une tartine de beurre et de confiture** a slice of bread and butter with jam

**beurrer** *verb* [1]
**to butter**

le **bibelot** *masc noun*
**ornament**

le **biberon** *masc noun*
**baby's bottle**

la **Bible** *fem noun*
(*Religion*) **the Bible**

le & la **bibliothécaire** *masc & fem noun*
**librarian**

♪ la **bibliothèque** *fem noun*
1 **library**
**emprunter des livres à la bibliothèque** to borrow books from the library
2 **bookcase**

le **bic®** *masc noun*
**un stylo bic®** a Biro®

la **biche** *fem noun*
**doe**

♪ la **bicyclette** *fem noun*
**bicycle**
**faire de la bicyclette** to cycle, to go cycling

♪ le **bidet** *masc noun*
**bidet** (*part of a bathroom suite*)

**bidon** *invariable adjective* ▷ see **bidon** *noun*
(*informal*) **false, phoney**
**une adresse bidon** a false address
**Son histoire est bidon!** His story's rubbish!

le **bidon** *masc noun* ▷ see **bidon** *adj*
1 **can** (*for paint, petrol*)
2 **drum** (*larger, for oil*)

le **bidonville** *masc noun*
**shanty town**

le **bidule** *masc noun*
(*informal*) **whatsit, thingamajig**

♪ **bien** *invariable adjective* ▷ see **bien** *adv, noun*
1 **good, nice**
**des gens bien** nice people
**C'est bien!** That's good!
**Ce sera bien de revoir mes copains.** It'll be nice to see my friends again.
2 **well**
**Je me sens vraiment bien ce matin.** I feel really good this morning.
**Pauline ne se sent pas très bien.** Pauline isn't feeling very well.
3 **nice, comfortable**
**On est bien ici.** It's very comfortable here.
**On est très bien dans ce fauteuil.** This chair's really comfortable.

♪ **bien** *adverb* ▷ see **bien** *adj, noun*
1 **well**
**Elle chante bien.** She sings well.
**Bien joué!** Well done!
**J'aime mon bifteck bien cuit.** I like my steak well done.
**Elle est bien habillée.** She is well dressed.
2 **aller bien** to be well
**Tu vas bien?** Are you well?
**Je vais très bien, merci.** I'm very well, thanks.
3 **aller bien à quelqu'un** to suit somebody
**Ça me va?** Does it suit me?
**Le blouson te va bien.** The jacket suits you.
4 **bien se passer** to go well
**Ça se passe bien.** Things are going well.
**Alors, la fête s'est bien passée?** So, did the party go well?
5 **bien vouloir quelque chose** not to mind something
**Je voudrais bien de la confiture.** I wouldn't mind some jam.
**Tu veux de l'eau? Oui, je veux bien.** Would you like some water? Yes please.
6 **bien vouloir faire quelque chose** to be happy to do something
**Il veut bien t'aider.** He's happy to help you.
**Je veux bien le faire.** I'm happy to do it.
7 **very, really**
**bien triste** very sad
**J'espère bien!** I really hope so!
8 **at least**
**Il a bien 20 ans.** He's at least 20.
**Ça vaut bien 100 euros.** It's worth 100 euros at least.
9 **much** (*with a following adjective*)
**bien mieux** much better
**bien plus chaud** much hotter
10 **bien de** many, a great deal of
**bien des gens** many people
**Elle s'est donnée bien du mal.** She went to a great deal of trouble.

le **bien** *masc noun* ▷ see **bien** *adj, adv*
1 **good**
le bien et le mal good and evil
**Ça te fera du bien.** That'll do you good.
2 **possession**
tous leurs biens all their possessions
- **bien entendu** of course
- le **bien-être** well-being

**bien que** *conjunction*
**although**
**Bien qu'il soit petit, il est assez fort.**
Although he is small, he is quite strong.

**WORD TIP** *bien que* is followed by a verb in the subjunctive.

**bien sûr** *adverb*
**of course**
**Bien sûr que oui!** Of course!
**Bien sûr que je viens!** Of course I'm coming!

♂ **bientôt** *adverb*
**soon**
**À bientôt!** See you soon! (*when saying goodbye, in a letter, etc*)

♂ le **bienvenu** *noun masc*, la **bienvenue** *fem* ▷ see **bienvenue** *fem*
**welcome**
**Soyez le bienvenu!** Welcome! (*to a boy*)
**Soyez la bienvenue!** Welcome! (*to a girl*)

♂ la **bienvenue** *fem noun* ▷ see **bienvenu** *masc*
**welcome**
**Bienvenue!** Welcome!
souhaiter la bienvenue à quelqu'un to welcome somebody
**Allons leur souhaiter la bienvenue.** Let's go and welcome them.

♂ la **bière** *fem noun*
**beer**
boire de la bière to drink beer
**Trois bières, s'il vous plaît!** Three beers, please!
- la **bière blonde** lager
- la **bière brune** brown ale

♂ le **bifteck** *masc noun*
**steak**

la **bifurcation** *fem noun*
**fork** (*in a road*)

le **bijou** *masc noun*, les **bijoux** *pl*
un bijou a piece of jewellery
des bijoux jewellery

la **bijouterie** *fem noun*
**jeweller's (shop)**

le **bijoutier** *masc noun*, la **bijoutière** *fem*
**jeweller**

le **bilan** *masc noun*
1 **balance sheet** (*in accounts*)
2 faire le bilan de quelque chose to assess something
**'Tremblement de terre, bilan: 1000 morts'**
'1,000 dead in earthquake' (*in a headline*)

**bilingue** *masc & fem adjective*
**bilingual**

le **billard** *masc noun*
1 **billiards**
jouer au billard to play billiards
2 **billiard table**
- le **billard américain** pool
- le **billard anglais** snooker

la **bille** *fem noun*
1 **marble**
jouer aux billes to play marbles
2 **billiard ball**

♂ le **billet** *masc noun*
1 **note**
un billet de banque a banknote
un billet de cent euros a hundred-euro note
2 **ticket**
un billet de train a train ticket

le **billion** *masc noun*
**billion**

**bio** *invariable adjective*
(*informal*) **organic**
les produits bio organic produce

la **biochimie** *fem noun*
**biochemistry**

la **biographie** *fem noun*
**biography**

♂ la **biologie** *fem noun*
**biology**

**biologique** *masc & fem adjective*
1 **biological**
2 **organic** (*agriculture, food*)

le & la **biologiste** *masc & fem noun*
**biologist**

le **bip** *masc noun*
**beep**
**Parlez après le bip sonore.** Speak after the tone (*on an answering machine*)

la **biscotte** *fem noun*
**continental toast**

♂ le **biscuit** *masc noun*
**biscuit**

la **bise** *fem noun*
1 (*informal*) **kiss**
faire la bise à quelqu'un to kiss somebody on the cheek (*when saying hello, good-bye*)
Fais-moi la bise! Give me a kiss!
Grosses bises Lots of love (*in an informal letter*)
2 **north wind** (*a cold wind*)

**bise**

Pour dire bonjour ou au revoir à la famille et aux amis, les Français font des bises : une, deux, trois ou quatre, ça dépend des gens et des régions!

le **bistro**, **bistrot** *masc noun*
**bistro**, **cafe**

**bizarre** *masc & fem adjective*
**strange**
C'est vraiment bizarre. It's really strange.

la **blague** *fem noun*
1 (*informal*) **joke**
Sans blague! No joking!
2 (*informal*) **trick**
Je lui ai fait une blague. I played a trick on him/her.

**blaguer** *verb* **[1]**
(*informal*) **to joke**

le **blaireau** *masc noun*, les **blaireaux** *pl*
1 **badger**
2 **shaving brush**

**blâmer** *verb* **[1]**
1 **to criticize**
2 **to blame**

**blanc** *masc adjective*, **blanche** *fem*
▷ see **blanc** *noun*, **Blanc** *noun*
1 **white**
des chaussures blanches white shoes
2 **blank**
une feuille blanche a blank sheet of paper

le **blanc** *masc noun* ▷ see **blanc** *adj*, **Blanc** *noun*
1 **white**
peint en blanc painted white
2 **blank space**
laisser un blanc to leave a blank space
3 **breast** (*of chicken, etc*)
un blanc de poulet a chicken breast
• le **blanc d'œuf** egg white

un **Blanc** *masc noun* ▷ see **blanc** *adj, noun*
**white man**
les Blancs white people

**WORD TIP** Names of peoples take a capital in French.

**blanche** *fem adjective* ▷ **blanc**

une **Blanche** *fem noun*
**white woman**
▷ **Blanc**

**blanchir** *verb* **[2]**
**to whiten**

la **blanchisserie** *fem noun*
**laundry**

le **blé** *masc noun*
**wheat**

**blessé** *masc adjective*, **blessée** *fem*
▷ see **blessé** *noun*
**injured**

le **blessé** *masc noun*, la **blessée** *fem*
▷ see **blessé** *adj*
**injured person**

**blesser** *verb* **[1]**
**to injure**
**Elle a été blessée dans l'accident.** She was injured in the accident.

se **blesser** *reflexive verb* Ⓔ
**to hurt yourself**
Il s'est blessé. He hurt himself.
Elle s'est blessée à la main. She hurt her hand.

la **blessure** *fem noun*
1 **injury**
2 **wound**

**bleu** *masc adjective*, **bleue** *fem*
▷ see **bleu** *noun*
**blue**
bleu clair light blue
bleu foncé dark blue
peint en bleu painted blue
une veste bleu marine a navy blue jacket

le **bleu** *masc noun* ▷ see **bleu** *adj*
1 **blue**
**Le bleu est ma couleur préférée.** Blue is my favourite colour.
2 **bruise**
**J'ai un bleu sur le bras.** I've got a bruise on my arm.

le **bloc** *masc noun*
1 **block** (*of concrete, etc*)
2 **pad** (*for notes, letters*)
un bloc de papier à lettres a writing pad
• les **bloc-notes** notepad

**blond** *masc adjective*, **blonde** *fem*
**fair-haired**
la fille blonde the fair-haired girl
J'ai les cheveux blonds. I've got fair hair.

Ⓔ means the verb takes être to form the perfect

**bloqué** *masc adjective*, **bloquée** *fem*
1 **blocked** (*road*)
2 **jammed** (*mechanism*)
3 **stuck** (*car*)

**bloquer** *verb* **[1]**
1 **to block** (*a road*)
2 **to jam** (*a mechanism*)

la **blouse** *fem noun*
**overall** (*to protect clothes*)

♂ le **blouson** *masc noun*
**jacket**
un blouson en jean a denim jacket
un blouson en cuir a leather jacket

le **blue-jean** *masc noun*
**jeans**
J'ai acheté un blue-jean. I bought a pair of jeans.

la **bobine** *fem noun*
**reel**

le **bocal** *masc noun*, les **bocaux** *pl*
**jar**

♂ le **bœuf** *masc noun*
1 **beef**
Est-ce que tu aimes le bœuf? Do you like beef?
2 **bullock**

**bof** *exclamation*
(*informal*) **'C'était bien hier?' — 'Bof!'** 'Did you have a good time yesterday?' — 'Nothing special.'

le **bohémien** *masc noun*, la **bohémienne** *fem*
**gypsy**

♂ **boire** *verb* **[22]**
**to drink**
Vous voulez boire quelque chose? Would you like something to drink?
Je boirais bien un jus d'orange. I'd really like an orange juice.

♂ le **bois** *masc noun*
1 **wood** (*the material*)
une table en bois a wooden table
2 **wood** (*of trees*)
se promener dans les bois to take a walk in the woods

♂ la **boisson** *fem noun*
**drink**
une boisson fraîche a cold drink
Et comme boisson? What would you like to drink? (*in a restaurant*)

♂ la **boîte** *fem noun*
1 **tin**
une boîte de sardines a tin of sardines
2 **box**
une boîte d'allumettes a box of matches
3 (*informal*) **club**
aller en boîte to go out to a club
On va en boîte ce soir. We're going out to a club tonight.
- la **boîte de conserve** tin, can
- la **boîte de dialogue** dialog box (*on the computer screen*)
- la **boîte d'envoi** outbox (*in email*)
- la **boîte aux lettres** post box
- la **boîte de nuit** nightclub
- la **boîte de réception** intray (*in email*)
- la **boîte de vitesses** gearbox

♂ le **bol** *masc noun*
1 **bowl**
un bol de riz a bowl of rice
2 en avoir ras le bol (*informal*) to be fed up

**bombarder** *verb* **[1]**
1 **to bombard**
2 **to bomb**

la **bombe** *fem noun*
1 **bomb**
2 **spray** (*aerosol*)
une bombe de peinture paint spray

♂ **bon** *masc adjective*, **bonne** *fem*
▷ see **bon** *adv, excl, noun*
1 **good**
un bon repas a good meal
J'ai de bonnes copines. I've got good friends.
C'est bon pour la santé. It's good for your health.
être bon en quelque chose to be good at something
Max est bon en français. Max is good at French.
2 **right**
le bon numéro the right number
la bonne adresse the right address
C'est bon. It's OK, It's fine.
3 **valid**
Mon ticket est bon. My ticket is valid.

♂ **bon** *adverb* ▷ see **bon** *adj, excl, noun*
sentir bon to smell good
Ça sent bon! That smells good!
Il fait bon aujourd'hui. It's a nice day today.
Il fait bon chez moi. It's lovely and warm at my house.

♂ **bon** *exclamation* ▷ see **bon** *adj, adv, noun*
1 Bon! Right!
Bon, on y va? Right, shall we go?
Ah bon? Really?
2 (*in greetings and wishes*) **Bonne année!** Happy New Year! ▸▸

Bon anniversaire! Happy birthday!
Bon appétit! Enjoy your meal!
Bonne chance! Good luck!
Bonne journée! Have a nice day!
Bonne nuit! Good night!
Bon retour! Safe journey back!
Bon voyage! Have a nice trip!

♪ le **bon** *noun masc* ▷ see **bon** *adj, adv, excl*
1 **voucher**
2 **pour de bon** for good
**partir pour de bon** to go away for good

**bonne heure** *in phrase*
**de bonne heure** early
**Demain, il faudra se lever de bonne heure.** Tomorrow we'll have to get up early.

**bon marché** *invariable adjective*
**cheap**
**des vêtements bon marché** cheap clothes

le **bon sens** *masc noun*
**common sense**

♪ le **bonbon** *masc noun*
**sweet**
**un bonbon à la menthe** a mint

la **bonbonne** *fem noun*
**une bonbonne de gaz** a gas cylinder

le **bond** *masc noun*
**jump**
**se lever d'un bond** to jump to your feet

**bondé** *masc adjective*, **bondée** *fem*
**crowded**
**un bus bondé d'étudiants** a bus packed with students

**bondir** *verb* **[2]**
**to jump**
**bondir de joie** to jump for joy

le **bonheur** *masc noun*
1 **happiness**
**Je vous souhaite beaucoup de bonheur.** I wish you every happiness.
2 **pleasure**
**avoir le bonheur de faire quelque chose** to have the pleasure of doing something

le **bonhomme de neige** *masc noun*, les **bonshommes de neige** *pl*
**snowman**

♪ **bonjour** *greeting*
1 **hello**
2 **good morning**
3 **good afternoon**

**WORD TIP** You can use *bonjour* at most times of the day.

**bonne** *fem adjective* ▷ **bon**

le **bonnet** *masc noun*
**(woolly) hat**

♪ **bonsoir** *greeting*
1 **good evening**
2 **good night**

la **bonté** *fem noun*
**kindness**

le **boom** *masc noun*
**boom** (*a time of prosperity*)

♪ le **bord** *masc noun*
1 **edge** (*of a table, cliff*)
2 **rim** (*of a glass, cup, vase*)
3 **side** (*of a road*)
**au bord de la route** at the side of the road
4 **au bord de la mer** at the seaside
5 **bank** (*of a lake, river, stream*)
**les bords de la Loire** the banks of the Loire
6 **à bord** on board
**Il y a 300 passagers à bord de l'avion.** There are 300 passengers on board the plane.
**Bienvenue à bord!** Welcome aboard!

**bordeaux** *invariable adjective*
**maroon**
**une jupe bordeaux** a maroon skirt

**border** *verb* **[1]**
**to edge**
**une route bordée d'arbres** a tree-lined road
**un mouchoir bordé de dentelle** a handkerchief edged with lace

la **bordure** *fem noun*
1 **border** (*of fabric, flowers*)
2 **edge** (*of a road, a path*)
3 **en bordure de** on the edge of

la **borne** *fem noun*
1 **kilometre marker** (*like a milestone*)
2 **bollard**

la **bosse** *fem noun*
**bump**

**bosser** *verb* **[1]**
(*informal*) **to work**
**Elle bosse tard le soir.** She works late into the evening.

**botanique** *masc & fem adjective*
▷ see **botanique** *noun*
**les jardins botaniques** the botanic gardens

la **botanique** *fem noun*
▷ see **botanique** *adj*
**botany**

♪ la **botte** *fem noun*
1 **boot** (*shoe*)
**des bottes de cuir** leather boots
2 **bale** (*of hay, straw*)

3 **bunch** (*of carrots, radishes*)

la **bottine** *fem noun*
**ankle boot**

le **bouc** *masc noun*
**billy goat**

♪ la **bouche** *fem noun*
**mouth**
- le **bouche-à-bouche** mouth-to-mouth resuscitation
- la **bouche d'égout** manhole

la **bouchée** *fem noun*
**mouthful**

**boucher** *verb* **[1]** ▷ see **boucher** *noun*
1 **to cork** (*a bottle*)
2 **to fill** (*a hole, a gap, a crack, etc*)

se **boucher** *reflexive verb* ❷
**to get blocked up**
se boucher le nez to hold your nose

♪ le **boucher** *masc noun*, la **bouchère** *fem* ▷ see **boucher** *verb*
**butcher**
aller chez le boucher to go to the butcher's

la **boucherie** *fem noun*
**butcher's (shop)**

le **bouchon** *masc noun*
1 **cork** (*for a wine bottle*)
2 **screw-cap** (*for a bottle of water*)
3 **traffic jam**
un bouchon sur la A-10 a traffic jam on the A-10 motorway

la **boucle** *fem noun*
1 **buckle** (*of a belt*)
2 **curl** (*in your hair*)

**bouclé** *masc adjective*, **bouclée** *fem*
**curly**
Elle a les cheveux bouclés. She has curly hair.

la **boucle d'oreille** *fem noun*
**earring**
porter des boucles d'oreille to wear earrings

le **Bouddha** *masc noun*
**Buddha**

le **bouddhisme** *masc noun*
**Buddhism**

**WORD TIP** Use a small letter for names of religions in French.

**bouder** *verb* **[1]**
**to sulk**

le **boudin** *masc noun*
**black pudding**

la **boue** *fem noun*
**mud**

la **bouée** *fem noun*
1 **rubber ring**
2 **buoy**
- la **bouée de sauvetage** lifebelt

**boueux** *masc adjective*, **boueuse** *fem*
**muddy**

la **bouffe** *fem noun*
(*informal*) **food, grub**

la **bouffée** *fem noun*
une bouffée d'air frais a breath of fresh air

le **bougeoir** *masc noun*
**candlestick**

**bouger** *verb* **[52]**
**to move**
Ne bougez plus! Stay still! (*to people when taking a photo*)

la **bougie** *fem noun*
1 **candle** (*on a cake*)
2 **spark plug** (*in a car engine*)

la **bouillabaisse** *fem noun*
**Mediterranean fish soup** (*made with fish and vegetables*)

**bouillant** *masc adjective*, **bouillante** *fem*
**boiling**
faire cuire à l'eau bouillante cook in boiling water

**bouillir** *verb* **[23]**
1 **to boil** (*in cooking*)
faire bouillir le lait to boil the milk
2 (*to get angry*) Ça me fait bouillir! It makes me mad!

la **bouilloire** *fem noun*
**kettle**

le **bouillon** *masc noun*
**stock** (*made with meat, fish, or vegetables*)
- le **bouillon-cube** stock cube

la **bouillotte** *fem noun*
**hot-water bottle**

♪ le **boulanger** *masc noun*, la **boulangère** *fem*
**baker**

la **boulangerie** *fem noun*
**bakery**
acheter du pain à la boulangerie to buy bread at the baker's

la **boulangerie-pâtisserie** *fem noun*
**bakery** (*selling bread, pastries, cakes, etc*)

la **boule** *fem noun*
1 **boule**
jouer aux boules to play boules ▸▸

**2 scoop** (*of ice-cream*)
Vous voulez combien de boules? How many scoops would you like?
- la **boule de neige** snowball

le **bouleau** *masc noun*, les **bouleaux** *pl*
**birch tree**

la **boulette** *fem noun*
**pellet**
- la **boulette de viande** meatball

le **boulevard** *masc noun*
**boulevard**
- le **boulevard périphérique** ring road

**bouleverser** *verb* **[1]**
**1 to shatter**, **to overwhelm**
être bouleversé par une mauvaise nouvelle to be shattered by bad news
**2 to disrupt** (*a schedule, plans*)

le **boulot** *masc noun*
**1** (*informal*) **work**
C'est un boulot immense. It's a huge amount of work.
**2** (*informal*) **job**
Elle a un nouveau boulot. She has a new job.

le **bouquet** *masc noun*
**bunch** (*of flowers or herbs*)

le **bouquin** *masc noun*
(*informal*) **book**

le **bourdon** *masc noun*
**bumblebee**

le **bourg** *masc noun*
**1 market town**
**2 village**

**bourgeois** *masc adjective*, **bourgeoise** *fem* ▷ see **bourgeois** *noun*
**middle-class**

le **bourgeois** *masc noun*, la **bourgeoise** *fem* ▷ see **bourgeois** *adj*
**middle-class person**

le **bourgeon** *masc noun*
**bud** (*on a tree*)

la **Bourgogne** *fem noun*
**Burgundy**

**WORD TIP** Countries or regions in French take *le*, *la* or *les*.

**bourré** *masc adjective*, **bourrée** *fem*
**1** bourré de crammed with
bourré de monde packed (*with people*)
**2** (*informal*) **drunk**

**bourrer** *verb* **[1]**
**to cram**

la **bourse** *fem noun*
**1 purse**
**2 grant** (*for studies*)
**3** la Bourse the stock exchange

**bousculer** *verb* **[1]**
**1 to bump into**
Quelqu'un m'a bousculé. Someone bumped into me.
**2 to rush**

la **boussole** *fem noun*
**compass**

le **bout** *masc noun*
**1 end**
Il est resté jusqu'au bout. He stayed until the end.
au bout de at the end of
Julien habite tout au bout de la rue. Julien lives right at the end of the street.
**2 tip** (*of nose, finger, tongue*)
**3 piece**
un bout de pain a piece of bread
un petit bout de fromage a little bit of cheese
des bouts de papier scraps of paper
**4** au bout de after
au bout d'une demi-heure after half an hour

la **bouteille** *fem noun*
**bottle**
une bouteille de lait a milk bottle
de l'eau en bouteille bottled water
- la **bouteille d'oxygène** oxygen cylinder

la **boutique** *fem noun*
**shop**
une boutique hors taxes a duty-free shop

le **bouton** *masc noun*
**1 button** (*on clothes, machines*)
Appuie sur le bouton! Press the button!
**2 spot** (*on your skin*)
Ça me donne des boutons. It brings me out in spots.
**3 bud** (*of a flower*)
- le **bouton d'or** buttercup

la **boxe** *fem noun*
**boxing**

le **boxeur** *masc noun*
**boxer**

le **bracelet** *masc noun*
**1 bracelet**
**2 bangle**
- le **bracelet-montre** wristwatch

le **brancard** *masc noun*
**stretcher**

**branché** *masc adjective*, **branchée** *fem*
(*informal*) **trendy**

la **branche** *fem noun*
**branch** (*of a tree*)

**brancher** *verb* **[1]**
**1 to plug in** (*an iron, a television*)
**2 to connect** (*electricity, telephone, computer*)

♪ le **bras** *masc noun*
**arm**
- le **bras de fer** arm wrestling

la **brasse** *fem noun*
**breaststroke**
- la **brasse papillon** butterfly (stroke)
- la **brasse coulée** racing breaststroke

la **brasserie** *fem noun*
**1 brasserie**
**2 brewery**

**brave** *masc & fem adjective*
**1 nice**
**Ce sont de braves gens.** They're nice people.
**2 brave**

**bravo** *exclamation*
**bravo, well done**
**Bravo, tes notes sont excellentes!** Well done, your marks are excellent!

le **break** *masc noun*
**estate car**

la **brebis** *fem noun*
**ewe**

**bref** *masc adjective*, **brève** *fem*
**1 short** (*vowel, sound*)
**en bref** in short
**2 brief** (*story, visit*)
**dans les plus brefs délais** as soon as possible

le **Brésil** *masc noun*
**Brazil**

**brésilien** *masc adjective*, **brésilienne** *fem*
▷ see **Brésilien** *noun*
**Brazilian**

le **Brésilien** *masc noun*, la **Brésilienne** *fem*
▷ see **brésilien** *adj*
**1 Brazilian**
**2** le brésilien Brazilian Portuguese (*the language*)

la **Bretagne** *fem noun*
**Brittany**

**WORD TIP** Countries or regions in French take *le*, *la* or *les*.

la **bretelle** *fem noun*
**1 strap** (*of a dress, a swimsuit*)
**2 des bretelles braces**
**3 slip road** (*of a motorway*)

**breton** *masc adjective*, **bretonne** *fem*
▷ see **Breton** *noun*
**Breton**

**WORD TIP** Adjectives never have capitals in French, even for nationality or regional origin.

le **Breton** *masc noun*, la **Bretonne** *fem*
▷ see **breton** *adj*
**1 Breton** (*person from Brittany*)
**2** le breton Breton (*language*)

le **brevet** *masc noun*
**certificate**
- le **brevet des collèges** certificate of general education (*taken at around 15 at the end of study in a collège*)
- le **brevet de secourisme** first aid certificate

♪ le **bricolage** *masc noun*
**DIY**

**bricoler** *verb* **[1]**
**to do DIY**

le **bricoleur** *masc noun*, la **bricoleuse** *fem*
**DIY enthusiast**

**brièvement** *adverb*
**briefly**

**brillamment** *adverb*
**brilliantly**

**brillant** *masc adjective*, **brillante** *fem*
**1 shiny** (*hair, shoes*)
**2 bright** (*eyes*)
**3 brilliant** (*pupil, result*)

♪ **briller** *verb* **[1]**
**to shine**
**faire briller ses chaussures** to polish your shoes

la **brindille** *fem noun*
**twig**

la **brioche** *fem noun*
**brioche**

la **brique** *fem noun*
**1 brick**
**2 carton** (*of fruit juice, milk*)

le **briquet** *masc noun*
**lighter**

la **brise** *fem noun*
**breeze**

**briser** *verb* **[1]**
**to break**

♪ **britannique** *masc & fem adjective*
▷ see **Britannique** *noun*
**British**

**WORD TIP** Adjectives never have capitals in French, even for nationality or regional origin.

♪ le & la **Britannique** *masc & fem noun*
▷ see **britannique** *adj*
**Briton**
les Britanniques the British

la **brocante** *fem noun*
1 **second-hand shop**
2 **flea market**

la **broche** *fem noun*
1 **brooch**
2 **spit** *(for roasting)*
faire cuire un poulet à la broche to spit-roast a chicken

la **brochette** *fem noun*
1 **skewer**
2 **kebab**
une brochette de viande a meat kebab

♪ la **brochure** *fem noun*
1 **booklet**
2 **brochure**

les **brocolis** *plural*
**broccoli**

**broder** *verb* **[1]**
**to embroider**

la **broderie** *fem noun*
**embroidery**
des broderies embroidery

la **bronchite** *fem noun*
**bronchitis**
avoir une bronchite to have bronchitis

le **bronzage** *masc noun*
**suntan**

♪ **bronzer** *verb* **[1]**
1 **to tan**
Je bronze facilement. I tan easily.
2 **to sunbathe**

♪ la **brosse** *fem noun*
**brush**
- la **brosse à cheveux** hairbrush
- la **brosse à dents** toothbrush

**brosser** *verb* **[1]**
**to brush**

se **brosser** *reflexive verb* ❷
se brosser les dents to brush your teeth

la **brouette** *fem noun*
**wheelbarrow**

♪ le **brouillard** *masc noun*
**fog**
Il y a du brouillard ce matin. It's foggy this morning.

le **brouillon** *masc noun*
**draft** *(of a letter, a document, etc)*

la **bru** *fem noun*
**daughter-in-law**

le **brugnon** *masc noun*
**nectarine**

♪ le **bruit** *masc noun*
1 **noise**
entendre un bruit to hear a noise
le bruit de la circulation the noise of the traffic
Vous faites trop de bruit. You're making too much noise.
2 **rumour**
Le bruit court qu'elle a un petit copain. They say she's got a boyfriend.

**brûlant** *masc adjective*, **brûlante** *fem*
1 **boiling hot** *(tea, coffee)*
2 **burning hot** *(oven, sand)*

le **brûlé** *masc noun*
un goût de brûlé a burnt taste
Ça sent le brûlé. There's a smell of burning.

**brûler** *verb* **[1]**
**to burn**
Attention, ça brûle! Careful, it's very hot!

se **brûler** *reflexive verb* ❷
**to burn yourself**
Pierre s'est brûlé. Pierre burnt himself.
Elle s'est brûlée. She's burnt herself.
Je me suis brûlé la main. I burnt my hand.

la **brûlure** *fem noun*
**burn**

la **brume** *fem noun*
**mist**
la brume matinale early morning mist

♪ **brun** *masc adjective*, **brune** *fem*
1 **dark** *(hair)*
2 **dark-haired**
Moi, je suis brune et Sylvie est blonde. I'm dark-haired and Sylvie is blonde.
3 **brown** *(eyes, skin, fur)*
J'ai les yeux bruns. I've got brown eyes.

le **brushing** *masc noun*
**blow-dry**
se faire un brushing to have a blow-dry.

**brut** *masc adjective*, **brute** *fem*
1 **raw** *(material)*
2 **crude** *(oil)*
3 **gross** *(income)*

❷ means the verb takes être to form the perfect

4 **dry** (*champagne, cider*)

**brutal** *masc adjective*, **brutale** *fem*, **brutaux** *masc pl*, **brutales** *fem pl*
1 **sudden** (*pain, death*)
2 **violent** (*shock, attack*)
3 **brutal** (*words*)

**Bruxelles** *noun*
**Brussels** (*capital of Belgium*)

**bruyant** *masc adjective*, **bruyante** *fem*
1 **noisy**
2 **loud** (*music*)

la **bruyère** *fem noun*
**heather**

**bu** *verb* ▷ **boire**

la **bûche** *fem noun*
**log**
- la **bûche de Noël** Yuletide log

le **budget** *masc noun*
**budget**

♪ le **buffet** *masc noun*
1 **sideboard**
2 **buffet** (*food*)

le **buisson** *masc noun*
**bush**

**buissonnière** *fem adjective*
faire l'école buissonnière to play truant

la **Bulgarie** *fem noun*
**Bulgaria**

la **bulle** *fem noun*
**bubble**

♪ le **bulletin** *masc noun*
1 **bulletin**
un bulletin d'information a news bulletin
2 **report**
un bulletin scolaire a school report
3 **certificate**
un bulletin de naissance a birth certificate
- le **bulletin de notes** school report

♪ le **bureau** *masc noun*, les **bureaux** *pl*
1 **desk**
Elle est à son bureau. She's at her desk.
2 **office**
aller au bureau to go to the office
Ma mère travaille dans un bureau. My mother works in an office.
3 **study** (*at home*)
L'ordinateur se trouve dans le bureau. The computer is in the study.
- le **bureau de change** bureau de change
- le **bureau des objets trouvés** lost property office
- le **bureau de poste** post office
- le **bureau de tabac** tobacconist's
- le **bureau de tourisme** tourist information office

la **bureaucratie** *fem noun*
**bureaucracy**

♪ le **bus** *masc noun*
**bus**
prendre le bus to take the bus
Allons-y en bus. Let's go there by bus.

la **buse** *fem noun*
**buzzard**

le **buste** *masc noun*
**bust**

le **but** *masc noun*
1 **aim** (*objective*)
2 **goal** (*in football, hockey*)
marquer un but to score a goal

**buvable** *masc & fem adjective*
**drinkable**

le **buvard** *masc noun*
**blotter**
du papier buvard blotting paper

la **buvette** *fem noun*
**bar** (*at a dance, village fair, etc*)

**buvez**, **buvons** *verb* ▷ **boire**

# C c

**c'** *abbreviation: ce*

**WORD TIP** *ce* becomes *c'* before a word beginning with *e-* or *é-*. ▷ **ce** *pronoun*

♪ **ça** *pronoun* ▷ **see ça** *adv*
1 Ça va? How are you?
Comment ça va? How are you?
Ça va bien, merci. I'm fine, thanks.
2 **that**
Donne-moi ça! Give me that!
Je n'aime pas ça! I don't like that!
Ça, c'est un moineau. That's a sparrow.
C'est ça. That's right.
Ça y est, j'ai terminé mes devoirs! That's it, I've finished my homework! ▸▸

**3 it**
**Ça ne fait rien.** It doesn't matter.
**Ça dépend.** It depends.
**Ça me fait mal.** It hurts.
**Ça me va!** It fits me.
**Dix heures, ça me va.** 10 o'clock suits me.

**WORD TIP** *ça* is the informal version of ▷ **cela**.

**çà** *adverb* ▷ **see ça** *pron*
**çà et là** here and there

la **cabane** *fem noun*
**hut**
**une cabane dans le jardin** a hut in the garden

le **cabillaud** *masc noun*
**cod**

la **cabine** *fem noun*
1 **cabin** (*on a ship*)
2 **cab** (*on a lorry*)
3 **cubicle**, **changing room** (*at the swimming pool*)
- la **cabine de douche** shower cubicle
- la **cabine d'essayage** fitting room
- la **cabine téléphonique** telephone box

le **cabinet** *masc noun*
▷ **see cabinets** *pl masc noun*
1 **office** (*solicitor's*)
2 **surgery** (*doctor's, dentist's*)
- le **cabinet médical** medical practice

les **cabinets** *plural masc noun*
▷ **see cabinet** *noun*
**toilet**

le **câble** *masc noun*
1 **cable**
**un câble électrique** an electric cable
2 **cable TV**
**J'aimerais avoir le câble.** I'd like to have cable TV.

**câblé** *masc adjective*, **câblée** *fem*
**être câblé** to have cable TV
**Nous sommes câblés.** We have cable TV.

**cabosser** *verb* [1]
**to dent**

la **cacahuète** *fem noun*
**peanut**
- les **cacahuètes grillées** roasted peanuts

le **cacao** *masc noun*
**cocoa**

**cache-cache** *invariable masc noun*
**jouer à cache-cache** to play hide and seek

**caché** *masc adjective*, **cachée** *fem*
**hidden**

le **cachemire** *masc noun*
**cashmere**

le **cache-nez** *invariable masc noun*
**(thick) scarf**

le **cache-pot** *invariable masc noun*
**flowerpot holder**

**cacher** *verb* [1]
**to hide**
**cacher quelque chose** to hide something
**J'ai caché mon journal intime.** I hid my diary.

se **cacher** *reflexive verb* ⓔ
**to hide**
**Elle s'est cachée dans le cagibi.** She hid in the store cupboard.

le **cachet** *masc noun*
**tablet**
- le **cachet d'aspirine** aspirin
- le **cachet de la poste** postmark

la **cachette** *fem noun*
1 **hiding place**
2 **en cachette** secretly
**Il lui téléphone en cachette.** He phones her secretly.

le **cachot** *masc noun*
**dungeon**

le **cactus** *masc noun*
**cactus**

le **cadavre** *masc noun*
**corpse**, **body**

le **caddie**® *masc noun*
**shopping trolley**

le **cadeau** *masc noun*, les **cadeaux** *pl*
1 **present**
**un cadeau d'anniversaire** a birthday present
**les cadeaux de Noël** Christmas presents
**faire un cadeau à quelqu'un** to give somebody a present
**J'ai fait un cadeau au professeur.** I gave a present to the teacher.
**faire cadeau de quelque chose à quelqu'un** to give somebody something
**Il m'a fait cadeau de son portable.** He gave me his mobile.
2 **du papier cadeau** wrapping paper
**Je vous fais un paquet-cadeau?** Shall I gift-wrap it for you?

le **cadenas** *masc noun*
**padlock**

la **cadence** *fem noun*
**rhythm**

ⓔ means the verb takes être to form the perfect

♪ **cadet** *masc adjective*, **cadette** *fem*
▷ see **cadet** *noun*
**1 younger**
mon frère cadet my younger brother
**2 youngest**
ma sœur cadette my youngest sister

♪ le **cadet** *masc noun*, la **cadette** *fem*
▷ see **cadet** *adj*
**younger child, youngest child**
Le cadet, c'est Antoine. Antoine's the youngest.

le **cadran** *masc noun*
**1 face** (*of a watch, a clock*)
**2 dial** (*on a speedometer*)
- le **cadran solaire** sundial

le **cadre** *masc noun*
**1 frame** (*of a picture, a window, a bicycle*)
**2 surroundings** (*of a place*)
**3 executive** (*in business*)
un cadre supérieur à la banque a senior executive at the bank

le **cafard** *masc noun*
**1 cockroach**
**2 depression**
avoir le cafard to be down in the dumps
J'ai un peu le cafard aujourd'hui. I'm a bit down in the dumps today.
donner le cafard à quelqu'un to get somebody down
Cette pluie me donne le cafard! This rain is getting me down!

♪ le **café** *masc noun*
**1 coffee**
prendre un café to have a coffee
Vous prendrez un café? Would you like a coffee? (*formal*)
Tu veux prendre un café? Do you want a coffee? (*informal*)
**2 cafe**
aller au café to go to the cafe
Leila va au café tous les midis. Leila goes to the cafe every lunchtime.
- le **café au lait** white coffee
- le **café-crème** white coffee
- le **café en grains** coffee beans
- le **café instantané** instant coffee
- le **café moulu** ground coffee
- le **café soluble** instant coffee
- le **café-tabac** cafe (*where you can buy cigarettes and stamps*)

la **caféine** *fem noun*
**caffeine**

la **cafétéria** *fem noun*
**cafeteria**

♪ la **cafetière** *fem noun*
**1 coffee pot**
**2 coffee maker**
une cafetière électrique a coffee machine

la **cage** *fem noun*
**cage**

le **cageot** *masc noun*
**crate**

le **cagibi** *masc noun*
**store cupboard**

la **cagnotte** *fem noun*
**1 kitty** (*of money*)
**2 jackpot** (*in a lottery*)

la **cagoule** *fem noun*
**balaclava** (*winter hat for children*)

♪ le **cahier** *masc noun*
**notebook**
- le **cahier d'appel** register
- le **cahier de brouillon** roughbook
- le **cahier de correspondance** school diary (*recording marks for parent-teacher meetings*)
- le **cahier d'exercices** exercise book
- le **cahier de textes** homework diary

la **caille** *fem noun*
**quail** (*a smal game bird*)

**cailler** *verb* **[1]**
**1 to curdle** (*milk*)
**2** (*informal*) **to be freezing**
Ça caille ici! It's freezing here!

le **caillou** *masc noun*, les **cailloux** *pl*
**stone**
jeter des cailloux to throw stones

♪ la **caisse** *fem noun*
**1 till, cash register**
**2 checkout**
Je dois passer à la caisse. I've got to go to the checkout.
**3 crate** (*for fruit, vegetables*)
- la **caisse à outils** toolbox
- la **caisse d'épargne** savings bank

le **caissier** *masc noun*, la **caissière** *fem*
**checkout assistant**

le **cake** *masc noun*
**fruit cake**

la **calamité** *fem noun*
**disaster**

**calcaire** *masc & fem adjective*
▷ see **calcaire** *noun*
eau calcaire hard water
L'eau ici est très calcaire. The water here is very hard.

le **calcaire** *masc noun* ▷ see **calcaire** *adj*
**1 limestone** (*the rock*)
**2 fur** (*inside a kettle*)

le **calcium** *masc noun*
**calcium**

le **calcul** *masc noun*
**1 arithmetic**
Elle est bonne en calcul. She's good at arithmetic.
**2 calculation**
faire des calculs to do some calculations
J'ai fait des calculs avant d'acheter le CD. I did some calculations before I bought the CD.
• le **calcul mental** mental arithmetic

la **calculatrice** *fem noun*
**pocket calculator**

**calculer** *verb* **[1]**
**to calculate**

la **calculette** *fem noun*
**pocket calculator**

**calé** *masc adjective*, **calée** *fem*
(*informal*) **clever**
Elle est calée en maths. She's clever at maths.

le **caleçon** *masc noun*
**1 boxer shorts**
**2 leggings**

le **calembour** *masc noun*
**pun, play on words**

le **calendrier** *masc noun*
**calendar**

**caler** *verb* **[1]**
**1** caler quelque chose to wedge something in place
**2 to stall**
La voiture a calé. The car stalled.

le **calibre** *masc noun*
**1 grade** (*of eggs, fruit, vegetables*)
**2 calibre** (*of a gun*)

**câlin** *masc adjective*, **câline** *fem*
▷ see **câlin** *noun*
**affectionate**

le **câlin** *masc noun* ▷ see **câlin** *adj*
**cuddle**
faire un câlin à quelqu'un to give somebody a cuddle
Fais un calin à ta grand-mère! Give your gran a cuddle!
Fais-moi un câlin! Give me a cuddle! (*said to a child, friend or family member*)

**câliner** *verb* **[1]**
**to cuddle**

**calmant** *masc adjective*, **calmante** *fem*
▷ see **calmant** *noun*
**soothing**

le **calmant** *masc noun* ▷ see **calmant** *adj*
**sedative**

le **calmar** *masc noun*
**squid**

♪ **calme** *masc & fem adjective*
▷ see **calme** *noun*
**calm, quiet**
D'habitude, Chloë est assez calme. Chloë is usually quite calm.

♪ le **calme** *masc noun* ▷ see **calme** *adj*
**peace and quiet**

**calmement** *adverb*
**calmly**

**calmer** *verb* **[1]**
**1** calmer quelqu'un to calm somebody down
Va te promener. Ça va te calmer. Go for a walk. That will calm you down.
**2 to ease**
L'aspirine a calmé la douleur. The aspirin eased the pain.

se **calmer** *reflexive verb* ⓔ
**to calm down**
Calme-toi! Calm down!

la **calorie** *fem noun*
**calorie**

le **calque** *masc noun*
un calque a tracing
du papier-calque tracing paper

le **calvados** *masc noun*
**calvados** (*apple brandy made in Normandy*)

♪ le & la **camarade** *masc & fem noun*
**friend**
mes camarades de classe my classmates

♪ le **cambriolage** *masc noun*
**burglary**
Il y a eu un cambriolage. There's been a burglary.

**cambrioler** *verb* **[1]**
être cambriolé to be burgled
La maison a été cambriolée hier soir. The house was burgled last night.
se faire cambrioler to be burgled
Les voisins se sont fait cambrioler. The neighbours were burgled.

le **cambrioleur** *masc noun*, la **cambrioleuse** *fem*
**burglar**

la **caméra** *fem noun*
**cine-camera**

ⓔ means the verb takes être to form the perfect

le **caméscope** *masc noun*
**camcorder**

♪ le **camion** *masc noun*
**truck, lorry**

le **camion-citerne** *masc noun*
**tanker lorry**

la **camionnette** *fem noun*
**van**

le **camionneur** *masc noun*
**lorry driver, truck driver**

le **camp** *masc noun*
**camp**

**campagnard** *masc adjective*, **campagnarde** *fem*
**country**
**les fêtes campagnardes** country fairs

♪ la **campagne** *fem noun*
1 **country**
**vivre à la campagne** to live in the country
**J'aimerais vivre à la campagne.** I'd like to live in the country.
**La campagne est jolie par ici.** The countryside round here is pretty.
2 **campaign** (*for a war, an election*)
**La campagne électorale a commencé.** The election campaign has started.

♪ **camper** *verb* **[1]**
**to camp**

♪ le **campeur** *masc noun*, la **campeuse** *fem*
**camper**

♪ le **camping** *masc noun*
1 **camping**
**faire du camping** to go camping
**Nous faisons du camping en Bretagne.** We're camping in Brittany.
2 **campsite**
**Nous cherchons le camping.** We're looking for the campsite.
**Le camping était complet.** The campsite was full.

- le **camping-car** camper van
- le **camping-gaz**® camping stove

le **Canada** *masc noun*
**Canada**
**habiter au Canada.** to live in Canada.
**Marie va au Canada.** Marie's going to Canada.

**WORD TIP** Countries and regions in French take *le*, *la* or *les*.

**canadien** *masc adjective*, **canadienne** *fem*
▷ see **Canadien** *noun*
**Canadian**
**Julie est canadienne.** Julie is Canadian.

**WORD TIP** Adjectives never have capitals in French, even for nationality or regional origin.

le **Canadien** *masc noun*, la **Canadienne** *fem* ▷ see **canadien** *adj*
**Canadian**

le **canal** *masc noun*, les **canaux** *pl*
**canal**

♪ le **canapé** *masc noun*
**sofa**

le **canapé-lit** *masc noun*, les **canapés-lits** *pl*
**sofa bed**

♪ le **canard** *masc noun*
**duck**

le **canari** *masc noun*
**canary**

le **cancer** *masc noun* ▷ see **Cancer** *noun*
**cancer**
**avoir un cancer** to have cancer
**Elle a un cancer du sein.** She has breast cancer.

le **Cancer** *masc noun* ▷ see **cancer** *noun*
**Cancer**
**Lucien est Cancer.** Lucien's a Cancer.

**WORD TIP** Signs of the zodiac do not take an article: *un* or *une*.

le **candidat** *masc noun*, la **candidate** *fem*
1 **candidate** (*in an election, an exam*)
**les candidats à l'examen** the exam candidates
2 **applicant** (*for a job*)
**se porter candidat à un poste** to apply for a post
3 **contestant**
**J'étais candidate à un jeu-concours à la télévision.** I was a contestant in a TV gameshow.

la **candidature** *fem noun*
**application** (*for a job*)
**poser sa candidature à un poste** to apply for a job
**J'ai posé ma candidature pour un emploi de vacances.** I've applied for a summer job.

le **caneton** *masc noun*
**duckling**

la **canette** *fem noun*
1 **une canette de bière** a small bottle of beer
2 **can** (*of beer, soft drink*)

le **canevas** *masc noun*
**tapestry work**

le **caniche** *masc noun*
**poodle**

la **canicule** *fem noun*
1 **scorching heat**
**sortir en pleine canicule** to go out in the scorching heat
2 **heatwave**

le **canif** *masc noun*
**penknife**

le **caniveau** *masc noun*, les **caniveaux** *pl*
**gutter**

la **canne** *fem noun*
**walking stick**
- la **canne à pêche** fishing rod
- la **canne à sucre** sugar cane

la **cannelle** *fem noun*
**cinnamon**

la **cannette** *fem noun*
**can** (*for drinks*)

le **canoë** *masc noun*
1 **canoe**
2 **faire du canoë** to go canoeing
**J'ai fait du canoë sur la rivière.** I went canoeing on the river.

le **canon** *masc noun*
1 **gun**
2 **barrel** (*of a gun*)
3 **cannon**
**On peut voir les vieux canons au musée.** You can see the old cannons in the museum.

le **canot** *masc noun*
**small boat**, **dinghy**
- le **canot pneumatique** inflatable dinghy
- le **canot de sauvetage** lifeboat

la **cantatrice** *fem noun*
**opera singer**

la **cantine** *fem noun*
**canteen**
**manger à la cantine** to have school dinners
**Je déteste manger à la cantine.** I hate school dinners.
**Nous mangeons à la cantine tous les jours.** We have school dinners every day.

le **caoutchouc** *masc noun*
**rubber**
**des gants en caoutchouc** rubber gloves
**des bottes en caoutchouc** wellington boots

le **cap** *masc noun*
1 **cape** (*a headland*)
**le cap Horn** Cape Horn
2 **course** (*of a ship*)
**changer le cap** to change course
**mettre le cap sur l'ouest** to head west

**capable** *masc & fem adjective*
**capable**
**être capable de faire quelque chose** to be capable of doing something
**Je suis bien capable de courir un marathon.** I'm quite capable of running a marathon.

la **capacité** *fem noun*
1 **ability**
2 **capacity**
**la capacité de mémoire d'un ordinateur** the memory capacity of a computer

la **cape** *fem noun*
**cape**, **cloak**
**un film de cape et d'épée** a swashbuckler

le **capitaine** *masc noun*
**captain**
**le capitaine des pompiers** the chief fire officer

**capital** *masc adjective*, **capitale** *fem*, **capitaux** *masc pl*, **capitales** *fem pl*
▷ see **capital** *noun*
1 **major**
**Cette information est d'une importance capitale.** This piece of information is of major importance.
2 **key**
**un chapitre capital du roman** a key chapter in the novel
3 **la peine capitale** capital punishment

le **capital** *masc noun*, les **capitaux** *pl*
▷ see **capital** *adj*
**capital** (*in finance*)

la **capitale** *fem noun*
**capital city**
**Paris est la capitale de la France.** Paris is the capital of France.

le **capot** *masc noun*
**bonnet** (*of a car*)

la **câpre** *fem noun*
**caper**
**une sauce aux câpres** a caper sauce

le **caprice** *masc noun*
1 **whim**
2 **tantrum**
**faire un caprice** to throw a tantrum
**Elle fait souvent des caprices.** She often throws tantrums.

le **Capricorne** *masc noun*
**Capricorn**
Daniel est Capricorne. Daniel's a Capricorn.

**WORD TIP** Signs of the zodiac do not take an article: *un* or *une*.

la **capsule** *fem noun*
1 **cap**, **top** (*of a bottle*)
2 **capsule**
une capsule spatiale a space capsule

**capter** *verb* [1]
1 **to receive** (*TV channel, programme*)
On capte combien de chaînes ici? How many channels can you receive here?
2 **capter l'attention de quelqu'un** to catch somebody's attention
Il essaie de capter l'attention des filles. He's trying to catch the girls' attention.

le **captif** *masc noun*, la **captive** *fem*
**captive**

**captivant** *masc adjective*, **captivante** *fem*
1 **fascinating** (*person*)
2 **gripping** (*book, film, story*)

la **captivité** *fem noun*
**captivity**
en captivité in captivity
Ce lion a été né en captivité. This lion was born in captivity.

**capturer** *verb* [1]
**to capture**

la **capuche** *fem noun*
**hood** (*on a jacket*)

le **capuchon** *masc noun*
**top**, **cap** (*of a pen*)

la **capucine** *fem noun*
**nasturtium**

♪ **car** *conjunction* ▷ see **car** *noun*
**because**

♪ le **car** *masc noun* ▷ see **car** *conj*
**coach**, **bus**
en car by coach
Nous allons voyager en car. We're going to travel by coach.
• le **car de ramassage scolaire** school bus

la **carabine** *fem noun*
**rifle**

le **caractère** *masc noun*
1 **nature**
avoir bon caractère to be good-natured
avoir mauvais caractère to be bad-tempered
Ce cheval a mauvais caractère. This horse is bad-tempered.
2 **character**
Leur maison a beaucoup de caractère. Their house has a lot of character.
3 **character** (*in print*)
écrit en gros caractères written in large print

**caractéristique** *masc & fem adjective*
▷ see **caractéristique** *noun*
**characteristic**

la **caractéristique** *fem noun*
▷ see **caractéristique** *adj*
**characteristic**

♪ la **carafe** *fem noun*
**carafe**, **jug** (*for wine, water*)

les **Caraïbes** *plural fem noun*
les îles Caraïbes the Caribbean Islands
habiter aux Caraïbes. to live in the Caribbean.
Je vais aux Caraïbes. I'm going to the Caribbean.

le **carambolage** *masc noun*
**pile-up**
Il y a eu un carambolage sur l'autoroute. There was a pile-up on the motorway.

le **caramel** *masc noun*
1 **caramel** (*in ice cream, cakes*)
du caramel caramel
un dessert au caramel a toffee-flavoured dessert
2 **toffee** (*a sweet*)
un caramel a toffee

♪ la **caravane** *fem noun*
**caravan**

le **carbone** *masc noun*
1 **carbon**
2 **carbon paper**

**carbonisé** *masc adjective*, **carbonisée** *fem*
**burnt** (*to cinders*)

le **carburant** *masc noun*
**fuel**

le **carburateur** *masc noun*
**carburettor** (*in an engine*)

la **carcasse** *fem noun*
**carcass**

**cardiaque** *masc & fem adjective*
une crise cardiaque a heart attack
Il est cardiaque. He has a heart condition.

le **cardinal** *masc noun*, les **cardinaux** *pl*
1 (*Religion*) **cardinal**
2 **cardinal number**

le **carême** *masc noun*
(*Religion*) **Lent**

**caresser** *verb* [1]
**to stroke** (*an animal*)
Je peux le caresser? Can I stroke him?

la **cargaison** *fem noun*
**cargo**

la **caricature** *fem noun*
**caricature**

le & la **caricaturiste** *masc & fem noun*
**cartoonist**

la **carie** *fem noun*
1 la carie dentaire tooth decay
2 **hole** (*in a tooth*)
J'ai une carie. I've got a hole in my tooth.

le **carillon** *masc noun*
1 **bell** (*of a church*)
2 **chimes** (*of a clock, a door*)

**caritatif** *masc adjective*, **caritative** *fem*
**charitable**
une association caritative a charity

le **carnaval** *masc noun*
**carnival**
le carnaval de Nice the Nice carnival
**On se déguise pour le carnaval.** We dress up for the carnival.

le **carnet** *masc noun*
1 **notebook**
2 **book** (*of tickets, stamps*)
- le **carnet de chèques** chequebook
- le **carnet de correspondance** school diary
- le **carnet de notes** school report
- le **carnet de timbres** book of stamps

mini-info **carnet (de correspondance)**

Les élèves ont un carnet de correspondance pour les communications école-parents. Il y a des informations générales sur l'école. On note les absences, les retards, les problèmes, les rendez-vous, etc.

la **carotte** *fem noun*
**carrot**
les carottes râpées grated carrots

la **carpe** *fem noun*
**carp** (*fish*)

**carré** *masc adjective*, **carrée** *fem*
▷ see **carré** *noun*
**square**
un écran carré a square screen
un mètre carré a square metre

le **carré** *masc noun* ▷ see **carré** *adj*
**square**
- le **carré d'agneau** rack of lamb
- le **carré de chocolat** piece of chocolat

le **carreau** *masc noun*, les **carreaux** *pl*
1 **floor tile**
2 **wall tile**
3 **window pane**
faire les carreaux to clean the windows
4 une chemise à carreaux a checked shirt
du tissu à carreaux checked fabric
du papier à carreaux squared paper
5 **diamonds** (*in cards*)
la reine de carreau the queen of diamonds

le **carrefour** *masc noun*
**crossroads, junction**
**Au carrefour, tournez à droite.** Turn right at the crossroads.

le **carrelage** *masc noun*
**tiled floor**
**Le carrelage est sale.** The floor is dirty.
**Il y a du carrelage dans la salle de bains.** There are tiles in the bathroom.

le **carrelet** *masc noun*
**plaice**

**carrément** *adverb*
**completely**
être carrément fou to be completely mad
**C'est carrément malhonnête.** It's downright dishonest.

la **carrière** *fem noun*
1 **career**
une carrière de médecin a career as a doctor
faire carrière to make a career
**J'aimerais faire carrière dans le journalisme.** I'd like to make a career in journalism.
2 **quarry**

la **carrosserie** *fem noun*
**bodywork** (*of a car*)
un atelier de carrosserie a body repair workshop

le **cartable** *masc noun*
**schoolbag, satchel**
**J'ai oublié mon cartable.** I forgot my schoolbag.

la **carte** *fem noun*
1 **card** (*for greetings*)
**Il m'a envoyé une carte.** He sent me a card.
2 **playing card**
un jeu de cartes a pack of cards
**J'ai horreur des jeux de cartes.** I hate card games.
**Nous jouons aux cartes.** We're playing cards.
3 **map**
**Regardons la carte.** Let's look at the map.

4 **menu** (*with dishes priced separately*)
manger à la carte to eat à la carte
Nous mangeons toujours à la carte. We always eat à la carte. ▷ **menu**

- la **carte d'abonnement** season ticket
- la **carte d'adhérent** membership card
- la **carte d'anniversaire** birthday card
- la **carte bancaire** bank card
- la **carte bleue** credit card (*used only in France*)
- la **carte de crédit** credit card
- la **carte d'embarquement** boarding card
- la **carte grise** logbook (*for a car*)
- la **carte de fidelité** loyalty card
- la **carte d'identité** identity card
- la **carte à jouer** playing card
- la **carte à mémoire** smart card
- la **carte postale** postcard
- la **carte à puce** chip and pin card
- la **carte routière** roadmap
- la **carte de séjour** resident's permit
- la **carte SIM** SIM card
- la **carte de téléphone** phonecard
- la **carte des vins** wine list
- la **carte de visite** business card
- la **carte de vœux** greetings card

le **carton** *masc noun*
1 **cardboard**
une chemise en carton a cardboard folder
2 **cardboard box**
Il faut beaucoup de cartons quand on déménage. You need a lot of cardboard boxes when you move house.

la **cartouche** *fem noun*
**cartridge**
une cartouche d'encre an ink cartridge

le **cas** *masc noun*
1 **case**
trois cas de rougeole three cases of measles
en tout cas in any case, at any rate
En tout cas, ce n'était pas moi! In any case, it wasn't me!
2 en aucun cas on no account
3 au cas où just in case.
Je prends mon manteau, au cas où. I'm taking my coat, just in case.

la **cascade** *fem noun*
1 **waterfall**
2 **stunt** (*in a film*)

le **cascadeur** *masc noun*, la **cascadeuse** *fem*
1 **stuntman**
2 **stuntwoman**

**cascher** *invariable masc & fem adjective*
(*Religion*) **kosher**

la **case** *fem noun*
1 **square** (*on a board game*)
2 **box** (*in a form*)
Cochez la bonne case. Tick the correct box.
3 **hut** (*for living in*)

**casier** *masc noun*
1 **pigeonhole** (*for post*)
2 **locker** (*for belongings*)
3 **rack** (*for storage*)
un casier à bouteilles a bottle rack

le **casino** *masc noun*
**casino**

le **casque** *masc noun*
1 **crash helmet**
2 **headphones**

la **casquette** *fem noun*
**cap**
- la **casquette de base-ball** baseball cap

le **casse-croûte** *invariable masc noun*
**snack**

le **casse-noisettes** *invariable masc noun*
**nutcracker**

**casse-pieds** *invariable masc & fem adjective*
être casse-pieds (*informal*) to be a pain in the neck
Elle est un peu casse-pieds! She's a bit of a pain!

♪ **casser** *verb* [1]
**to break**
Qui a cassé la tasse? Who broke the cup?
C'est Pierre qui l'a cassée. Pierre broke it.

se **casser** *reflexive verb* ⓔ
**to break**
Tout d'un coup, la branche s'est cassée. All of a sudden, the branch broke.
se casser la jambe to break your leg
Elle s'est cassé la jambe au ski. She broke her leg skiing.

♪ la **casserole** *fem noun*
**saucepan**

le **casse-tête** *invariable masc noun*
**brainteaser**

♪ la **cassette** *fem noun*
**cassette, tape**
- la **cassette vidéo** video cassette

♪ le **cassis** *masc noun*
**blackcurrant**

le **cassoulet** *masc noun*
**oven-baked beans** (*with meat and sausage*)

le **castor** *masc noun*
**beaver**

le **catalogue** *masc noun*
**catalogue**

la **catastrophe** *fem noun*
**disaster**, **catastrophe**

le **catch** *masc noun*
**wrestling**

le **catcheur** *masc noun*, la **catcheuse** *fem*
**wrestler**

la **catégorie** *fem noun*
**category**

la **cathédrale** *fem noun*
**cathedral**
la cathédrale de Chartres Chartres Cathedral

le **catholicisme** *masc noun*
**(Roman) Catholicism**

**catholique** *masc & fem adjective*
▷ see **catholique** *noun*
**(Roman) Catholic**

le & la **catholique** *masc & fem noun*
▷ see **catholique** *adj*
**(Roman) Catholic**

le **cauchemar** *masc noun*
**nightmare**
**Quel cauchemar!** What a nightmare!
**faire un cauchemar** to have a nightmare
**J'ai fait un cauchemar cette nuit.** I had a nightmare last night.

la **cause** *fem noun*
1 **cause**
**la cause de l'accident** the cause of the accident
2 **à cause de** because of
**Nous avons perdu à cause de lui.** We lost because of him.
3 **reason**
**la cause de la réunion** the reason for the meeting
4 **cause**
**une bonne cause** a good cause

**causer** *verb* [1]
1 **to cause**
**causer un accident** to cause an accident
**La canicule a causé une centaine de morts.** The heatwave caused about a hundred deaths.
2 (*informal*) **to talk**, **to chat**

la **caution** *fem noun*
1 **deposit**
**verser une caution** to pay a deposit
**Il faut verser une caution pour louer un vélo.** You have to pay a deposit to hire a bicycle.
2 **bail**
**libéré sous caution** released on bail

le **cavalier** *masc noun*, la **cavalière** *fem*
**rider**

la **cave** *fem noun*
**cellar**
**Il y a une cave au sous-sol.** There is a cellar in the basement.

le **caveau** *masc noun*, les **caveaux** *pl*
**vault** (*of a church*)

la **caverne** *fem noun*
**cave**

le **CD** *masc noun*, les **CD** *pl*
**CD**

**ce** *masc adjective*, **cet** *masc*, **cette** *fem*, **ces** *masc & fem pl* ▷ see **ce** *pron*
1 **this**
**ce magasin** this shop
**cet acteur** this actor
**cet hôpital** this hospital
**ce couteau-ci** this knife (*right here*)
**Ce stylo ne marche pas.** This pen doesn't work.
2 **this**
**cette semaine** this week
**cette actrice** this actress
**Je n'aime pas cette image.** I don't like that picture.
3 **that**
**Ce DVD est cassé.** That DVD's broken.
**Passe-moi cette assiette-là.** Pass me that plate (*over there*).
4 **cette nuit** last night, tonight
**J'ai mal dormi cette nuit.** I didn't sleep well last night.
**Tu vas bien dormir cette nuit.** You'll sleep well tonight.

**WORD TIP** *ce* is used before masc nouns in the singular. *cet* is used before masc nouns beginning with *a, e, i, o, u* or *silent h*. *cette* is used with fem nouns in the singular. ▷ **ces**

**ce**, **c'** *pronoun* ▷ see **ce** *adj*
1 **it**, **that**, **this**
**C'est vrai?** Is that true?
**Non, ce n'est pas vrai.** No, it's not true.
**Ce n'était pas une bonne idée.** That wasn't a good idea.
**Qui est-ce?** Who is it?
**C'est moi.** It's me.
**Qu'est-ce que c'est?** What is it?
**C'est un MP3.** It's an MP3.
**C'est la première maison à gauche.** It's the first house on the left.
2 **he**, **she**, **they**
**C'est un médecin.** He's a doctor.

C'est une infirmière. She's a nurse.
Ce sont mes copains. They're my friends.
3 ce qui what
Mange ce qui reste. Eat what's left.
C'est ce qui énerve Laura. That's what annoys Laura.
4 ce que, ce qu' what
Prends ce que tu veux. Take what you want.
Je ne sais pas ce qu'on dit en français. I don't know what they say in French.
5 C'est tout ce qui reste. That's all that's left.
Prends tout ce que tu veux. Take whatever you want.

**WORD TIP** *ce* becomes *c'* before a word beginning with *e-*. *ce que* becomes *ce qu'* before *a, e, i, o, u*. *ce qui* never changes. ▷ **cet, cette**

**ceci** *pronoun*
**this**
Ceci n'est pas à moi. This is not mine.

la **cécité** *fem noun*
**blindness**

**céder** *verb* **[24]**
1 **to give in**
Mes parents n'ont pas cédé. My parents didn't give in.
céder à quelqu'un to give in to somebody
Ils cèdent toujours à mon petit frère. They always give in to my little brother.
2 **to give up** (*a seat, a share*)
Il a cédé sa place. He gave up his seat.
'Cédez le passage' 'Give way' (*road sign*)

♪ le **cédérom** *masc noun*
**CD-ROM**

la **cédille** *fem noun*
**cedilla** (*the letter ç*)

le **cèdre** *masc noun*
**cedar**

♪ la **ceinture** *fem noun*
1 **belt**
J'aime mieux la ceinture rouge. I like the red belt better.
Elle est ceinture noire de judo. She's got a black belt in judo.
2 **waist**
J'avais de l'eau jusqu'à la ceinture. I was up to my waist in water.
- la **ceinture de sauvetage** lifebelt

la **ceinture de sécurité** *fem noun*
**seatbelt**
Attachez vos ceintures de sécurité. Fasten your seatbelts.

**cela** *pronoun*
**that, this, it**
Cela change tout. That changes everything.
Cela ne fait rien. It doesn't matter.
Cela ne me concerne pas. That doesn't concern me.
Il y a un an de cela. That was one year ago.

**WORD TIP** *cela* is the formal form of ▷ **ça.**

la **célébration** *fem noun*
**celebration**

♪ **célèbre** *masc & fem adjective*
**famous**
quelques personnages célèbres some famous people

**célébrer** *verb* **[24]**
**to celebrate**

le **céleri** *masc noun*
**celery**
- le **céleri-rémoulade** grated celeriac in a mayonnaise dressing

♪ **célibataire** *masc & fem adjective*
▷ see **célibataire** *noun*
**single, unmarried**
Il est toujours célibataire. He's still single.

♪ le & la **célibataire** *masc & fem noun*
▷ see **célibataire** *adj*
1 **bachelor**
2 **single woman**

**celle** *pronoun*

**WORD TIP** This is the fem form of ▷ **celui.**

**celle-ci** *pronoun*

**WORD TIP** This is the fem form of ▷ **celui-ci.**

**celle-là** *pronoun*

**WORD TIP** This is the fem form of ▷ **celui-là.**

**celles** *pronoun*

**WORD TIP** This is the fem form of ▷ **ceux.**

**celles-ci** *pronoun*

**WORD TIP** This is the fem form of ▷ **ceux-ci.**

**celles-là** *pronoun*

**WORD TIP** This is the fem form of ▷ **ceux-là.**

la **cellule** *fem noun*
1 **(prison) cell**
2 **cell** (*in biology and medicine*)

**celui, celle** *pronoun*
1 (*for a masc singular noun*) **the one**
Quel portable? Celui qui est sur la table. Which mobile ? The one on the table.
2 (*for a fem singular noun*) **the one**
Quelle bague? Celle qui est dans la vitrine. Which ring? The one in the shop window.

**celui-ci**, **celle-ci** *pronoun*
1 (*for a masc singular noun*) **this one**
Quel CD? Prends celui-ci. Which CD? Take this one.
2 (*for a fem singular noun*) **this one**
Quelle veste? Prends celle-ci. Which jacket? Take this one.

**celui-là**, **celle-là** *pronoun*
1 (*for a masc singular noun*) **that one**
Quel pull? Je préfère celui-là. Which sweater? I prefer that one.
2 (*for a fem singular noun*) **that one**
Quelle jupe? Je préfère celle-là. Which skirt? I prefer that one.

la **cendre** *fem noun*
**ash**

le **cendrier** *masc noun*
**ashtray**

**Cendrillon** *fem noun*
**Cinderella**

**censé** *masc adjective*, **censée** *fem*
être censé faire quelque chose to be supposed to do something
Je suis censé rentrer après le cours. I'm supposed to go home after the class.
Nous sommes censés faire nos devoirs. We're supposed to do our homework.

**cent** *number* ▷ see **cent** *noun*
**a hundred**, **one hundred**
trois cents personnes three hundred people
deux cent cinquante personnes two hundred and fifty people

**WORD TIP** *cent* does not take *-s* when it is followed by another number.

le **cent** *masc noun* ▷ see **cent** *number*
**cent** (*in euros and dollars*)

la **centaine** *fem noun*
une centaine de personnes about a hundred people
plusieurs centaines de personnes several hundred people
des centaines de lettres hundreds of letters

le **centenaire** *masc noun*
**centenary**

le & la **centième** *number*
**hundredth**

le **centime** *masc noun*
1 **cent** (*one hundredth of a euro*)
2 **centime** (*one hundredth of the former French currency, the franc*)

le **centimètre** *masc noun*
1 **centimetre**
un centimètre carré a square centimetre
un centimètre cube a cubic centimetre
2 **tape measure**

**central** *masc adjective*, **centrale** *fem*, **centraux** *masc pl*, **centrales** *fem pl* ▷ see **central, centrale** *noun*
**central**

le **central** *masc noun*, les **centraux** *pl* ▷ see **central** *adj*
- le **central téléphonique** telephone exchange

la **centrale** *fem noun* ▷ see **central** *adj*
**power station**
une centrale nucléaire a nuclear power station

**centraliser** *verb* **[1]**
**to centralize**

le **centre** *masc noun*
**centre**
au centre de in the centre of
un marché au centre du village a market in the centre of the village
- le **centre aéré** day centre (*for children*)
- le **centre commercial** shopping centre, mall
- le **centre de loisirs** leisure centre
- le **centre sportif** sports centre

le **centre-ville** *masc noun*
**town centre**, **city centre**
Le 46 va au centre-ville. The number 46 bus goes to the town centre.
Julien habite au centre-ville. Julien lives in the town centre.

**cependant** *adverb*
**however**

le **cercle** *masc noun*
**circle**
en cercle in a circle

le **cercueil** *masc noun*
**coffin**

la **céréale** *fem noun*
1 **cereal**, **grain**
2 des céréales cereal
Je mange des céréales au petit déjeuner. I have cereal for breakfast.

la **cérémonie** *fem noun*
**ceremony**

le **cerf** *masc noun*
**stag**

le **cerf-volant** *masc noun*
**kite**
**jouer au cerf-volant** to fly a kite

♪ la **cerise** *fem noun*
**cherry**
**J'adore la confiture aux cerises.** I love cherry jam.

le **cerisier** *masc noun*
**cherry tree**

♪ **certain** *masc adjective*, **certaine** *fem*
▷ see **certains** *pron*
1 **certain**
**un certain nombre d'élèves** a certain number of students
**une certaine personne** a certain person
2 **some**
**dans certains pays** in some countries
**certaines personnes** some people
3 **certain, sure**
**être certain que ...** to be certain that ...
**Il est certain que c'était Sophie.** He's certain it was Sophie.
**être certain d'avoir fait quelque chose** to be sure that you've done something
**Est-ce que tu es certaine d'avoir fermé la fenêtre?** Are you sure you closed the window?
**Oui, j'en suis certaine.** Yes, I'm sure I did.

♪ **certains, certaines** *pronoun*
▷ see **certain** *adj*
**some**
**certains de mes copains** some of my friends
**certaines de mes copines** some of my girlfriends

**certainement** *adverb*
1 **most probably**
**Nicolas arrivera certainement en retard.** Nicolas will most probably be late.
2 **certainly**
**Je n'irai certainement pas!** I certainly won't be going!
3 **of course**
**Je peux t'emprunter ton stylo? Mais certainement!** May I borrow your pen? Of course!

**certes** *adverb*
**admittedly**

le **certificat** *masc noun*
**certificate**
**un certificat médical** a medical certificate

**certifier** *verb* [1]
**to certify**

le **cerveau** *masc noun*, les **cerveaux** *pl*
**brain**
**C'est le cerveau de la classe!** He's the brains of the class.

♪ **ces** *plural masc adjective*
1 **these**
**Léa m'a acheté ces fleurs.** Léa bought me these flowers.
2 **those**
**Ces livres que je t'ai prêtés, où sont-ils?** Those books I lent you, where are they?

♪ le **CES** *masc noun*
(*= Collège d'enseignement secondaire*)
**secondary school**

**cesse** *fem noun*
**sans cesse** all the time
**Antoine sourit sans cesse.** Antoine smiles all the time.

**cesser** *verb* [1]
**to stop**
**Francine a cessé le piano.** Francine has stopped her piano lessons.
**cesser de faire quelque chose** to stop doing something
**Elle a cessé de fumer.** She's stopped smoking.

le **cessez-le-feu** *invariable masc noun*
**ceasefire**

♪ **c'est-à-dire** *phrase*
1 **that is ..., that's to say ...** (*when you want to make something clearer*)
**Mes amis, c'est-à-dire Pierre, Anita, Julie, Rashid ...** My friends, that's Pierre, Anita, Julie, Rashid, ...
**Elle est rédactrice, c'est-à-dire qu'elle écrit des articles pour un journal.** She's an editor, that's to say she writes articles for a newspaper.
2 **well, actually**
**'Tu n'en veux pas?' — 'C'est-à-dire que je suis au régime.'** 'You don't want any?' — 'Well, actually I'm on a diet.'

**cet** *masc adjective*

**WORD TIP** *ce* becomes *cet* before a word beginning with *a, e, i, o, u* or silent *h*. ▷ **ce**

**cette** *fem adjective*

**WORD TIP** *ce* becomes *cette* before a fem singular word. ▷ **ce**

**ceux, celles** *pronoun*
**the ones**
**'Quels DVD?' — 'Ceux qui sont sur la table.'** 'Which DVDs?' — 'The ones on the table.' (*DVD is masc plural, so replaced by ceux*)
**'Quelles vidéos?' — 'Celles que tu m'as** ▸▸



French-English
a b c d e f g h i j k l m n o p q r s t u v w x y z

prêtées hier.' 'Which videos?' — 'The ones you lent me yesterday.' (*vidéos is fem plural, so replaced by celles*) ▷ **celui**

**ceux-ci**, **celles-ci** *pronoun*
**these ones**

**ceux-là**, **celles-là** *pronoun*
**those ones**

le **chacal** *masc noun*
**jackal**

& **chacun**, **chacune** *pronoun*
1 (*for masc nouns in the singular*) **each**
**Ils ont chacun un billet.** They each have a ticket.
2 (*for fem nouns in the singular*) **each**
**Elles ont chacune un maillot de bain.** They each have a swimsuit.
3 **everyone**
**comme chacun sait ...** as everyone knows ...
**Chacun son tour!** Wait your turn!

le **chagrin** *masc noun*
**grief**

& la **chaîne** *fem noun*
1 **chain**
2 **channel** (*on TV*)
**C'est sur quelle chaîne?** What channel is it on?
- la **chaîne hi-fi** hi-fi system
- la **chaîne laser** CD player
- la **chaîne stéréo** stereo system

la **chair** *fem noun*
1 **flesh** (*of fruit, fish*)
2 **meat** (*of chicken*)
- la **chair de poule** goose pimples
- la **chair à saucisses** sausage meat

& la **chaise** *fem noun*
**chair**
**Il n'y a pas assez de chaises.** There aren't enough chairs.

le **châle** *masc noun*
**shawl**

le **chalet** *masc noun*
**chalet**

la **chaleur** *fem noun*
**heat**, **warmth**
**Quelle chaleur!** It's sweltering!

**chaleureux** *masc adjective*, **chaleureuse** *fem*
**warm** (*hospitable, friendly*)
**un accueil chaleureux** a warm welcome

& la **chambre** *fem noun*
1 **bedroom**
**Je reste dans ma chambre.** I'm staying in my bedroom.
2 **room** (*in a hotel, etc*)
**une chambre pour une personne** a single room
**une chambre pour deux personnes** a double room
**Il ne reste plus de chambres.** There are no rooms left.
- la **chambre d'amis** spare bedroom
- la **chambre de commerce** chamber of commerce
- les **chambres d'hôte** bed and breakfast

le **chameau** *masc noun*, les **chameaux** *pl*
**camel**

& le **champ** *masc noun*
**field**
**se promener dans les champs** to go for a walk in the fields
- le **champ de bataille** battlefield
- le **champ de courses** racetrack

le **champagne** *masc noun*
**champagne** (*the drink*)

la **Champagne** *masc noun*
**the Champagne region** (*in north-east France*)

**WORD TIP** Countries and regions in French take *le*, *la* or *les*.

& le **champignon** *masc noun*
1 **mushroom**
**Je n'aime pas les champignons.** I don't like mushrooms.
2 **fungus** (*skin infection*)
- le **champignon de Paris** button mushroom

& le **champion** *masc noun*, la **championne** *fem*
**champion**
**le champion d'Europe** the European champion
**une championne de ski** a skiing champion

le **championnat** *masc noun*
**championship**

& la **chance** *fem noun*
**luck**
**un coup de chance** a stroke of luck
**Bonne chance!** Good luck!
**Pas de chance!** Bad luck!
**avoir de la chance** to be lucky
**Tu as de la chance de vivre ici!** You're lucky to live here!
**J'ai eu la chance de les voir en concert.** I was lucky enough to be able to see them in

concert.
ne pas avoir de chance to be unlucky
Elle n'a pas eu de chance. She was unlucky.

le **chancelier** *masc noun*
**chancellor**

le **chandail** *masc noun*
**jumper** (*woolly and thick*)

le **chandelier** *masc noun*
1 **candlestick**
2 **candelabra** (*for several candles*)

le **change** *masc noun*
**exchange rate**
▷ See **bureau de change**

**changeant** *masc adjective*, **changeante** *fem*
**changeable**

le **changement** *masc noun*
**change**
• le **changement climatique** climate change

♂ **changer** *verb* **[52]**
1 **to change**
**Tu n'as pas changé.** You haven't changed.
**J'ai beaucoup changé.** I've changed a lot.
2 **to change** (*money*)
**On peut changer jusqu'à 1 000 euros.** You can change up to 1,000 euros.
**Je voudrais changer 100 livres sterling en euros.** I'd like to change 100 pounds into euros.
3 **changer quelque chose** to change something
**Ils n'ont pas changé les draps.** They haven't changed the sheets.
**Tu sais changer un bébé?** Can you change a baby's nappy?
4 **changer quelque chose pour** to exchange something for (*something else*)
**J'ai changé les bottes pour une paire de chaussures.** I've exchanged the boots for a pair of shoes.
5 **changer quelque chose, quelqu'un en ...** to turn something, somebody into a ...
**Harry l'a changé en rat.** Harry turned him into a rat.
6 **changer de** to change (*by switching*)
**Je dois changer de chaussures.** I've got to change my shoes.
**Elle a changé de place avec Nicole.** She changed places with Nicole.
**Il faut changer de train.** You have to change trains.
**changer d'avis** to change your mind
**J'ai changé d'avis.** I've changed my mind.
**changer d'adresse** to change address
**Nous avons changé d'adresse.** We've changed our address.

se **changer** *reflexive verb* Ⓔ
**to get changed**
**Va te changer.** Go and get changed.
**Nous nous sommes changés après le match.** We got changed after the match.

♂ la **chanson** *fem noun*
**song**
**ma chanson préférée** my favourite song
**une chanson populaire** a popular song
**une chanson pour enfants** a children's song
**C'est une vedette de la chanson.** She's a singing star.
**Je voudrais faire carrière dans la chanson.** I'd like to have a career as a singer.

le **chant** *masc noun*
1 **singing**
**une leçon de chant** a singing lesson
2 **song** (*of a bird, an instrument*)
• le **chant choral** choral singing
• le **chant de Noël** Christmas carol

le **chantage** *masc noun*
**blackmail**

♂ **chanter** *verb* **[1]**
**to sing**
**chanter juste** to sing in tune
**chanter quelque chose à quelqu'un** to sing something for somebody
**Tu me chantes quelque chose?** Will you sing something for me?
**Non, j'ai peur de chanter faux.** No, I'm afraid I'll sing out of tune.

♂ le **chanteur** *masc noun*, la **chanteuse** *fem*
**singer**

le **chantier** *masc noun*
1 **building site**
2 (*informal*) **mess**
**Quel chantier!** What a mess!

**chantonner** *verb* **[1]**
**to hum**

le **chaos** *masc noun*
**chaos**

**chaotique** *masc & fem adjective*
**chaotic**

♂ le **chapeau** *masc noun*, les **chapeaux** *pl*
1 **hat**
2 (*informal*) **Chapeau!** Well done!
• le **chapeau melon** bowler hat

la **chapelle** *fem noun*
**chapel**

le **chapiteau** *masc noun*, les **chapiteaux** *pl*
1 **marquee**
2 **big top** (*in a circus*)

le **chapitre** *masc noun*
**chapter**

**chaque** *masc & fem adjective*
**each**, **every**
Chaque été, nous allons à la plage. Every summer we go to the beach.
Chaque candidat porte un numéro. Each candidate has a number.
À chaque fois, c'est la même chose! It's the same thing every time!

le **char** *masc noun*
1 **tank** (*for battle*)
2 **carnival float**

la **charade** *fem noun*
**riddle**

le **charbon** *masc noun*
**coal**
• le **charbon de bois** charcoal

la **charcuterie** *fem noun*
1 **pork butcher's** (*selling pork, ham, sausages and bacon as well as salads and prepared dishes*)
le rayon charcuterie the delicatessen counter (*at a supermarket*)
J'ai acheté le rôti de porc à la charcuterie. I bought the pork joint at the delicatessen.
2 **pork products** (*ham, salami, pâté, etc*)
une assiette de charcuterie a plate of assorted cold pork meats

le **charcutier** *masc noun*, la **charcutière** *fem*
**pork butcher**

le **chardon** *masc noun*
**thistle**

la **charge** *fem noun*
1 **load** (*a burden*)
2 **responsibility**
avoir la charge de faire quelque chose to be responsible for doing something
J'avais la charge de distribuer les livres. I was responsible for giving out the books.

**charger** *verb* **[52]**
1 **to load** (*goods, luggage*)
charger quelque chose dans quelque chose to load something into something
J'ai chargé le programme dans l'ordinateur. I loaded the program into the computer.
2 **charger quelqu'un de faire quelque chose** to give somebody the job of doing something
Il m'a chargé d'acheter les pizzas. He gave me the job of buying the pizzas.
Nous sommes chargés de faire l'enquête. Our job is to do the survey.
3 **to charge** (*a battery*)

le **chariot** *masc noun*
1 **trolley** (*in a supermarket*)
2 **wagon** (*horse-drawn*)

la **charité** *fem noun*
**charity**

**charmant** *masc adjective*, **charmante** *fem*
**charming**
un endroit charmant au bord de la mer a charming place by the sea
C'est une petite fille charmante. She's a delightful little girl.
Ils sont partis sans nous? C'est charmant! They've left without us? How charming!

le **charme** *masc noun*
1 **charm**
Odile a beaucoup de charme. Odile has lots of charm.
faire du charme to turn on the charm
Regarde, Jean-Marie fait du charme! Look, Jean-Marie's turning on the charm!
2 **spell**
tomber sous le charme de quelqu'un to fall under somebody's spell
Pierre est tombé sous le charme d'Élodie. Pierre's fallen under Élodie's spell.

**charmer** *verb* **[1]**
**to charm**

la **charnière** *fem noun*
**hinge**

le **charpentier** *masc noun*
**carpenter**

la **charrette** *fem noun*
**cart**

la **charrue** *fem noun*
**plough**

la **charte** *fem noun*
**charter**

**charter** *invariable masc & fem adjective*
un vol charter a charter flight

la **chasse** *fem noun*
**hunting**, **shooting** (*with a gun*)
une manifestation contre la chasse a demonstration against hunting
• la **chasse au trésor** treasure hunt

la **chasse d'eau** *fem noun*
**(toilet) flush**
tirer la chasse to flush the toilet

le **chasse-neige** *invariable masc noun*
**snowplough**

**chasser** *verb* [1]
1 **to hunt**, **to shoot** (*with a gun*)
2 **chasser quelqu'un** to chase somebody away
**Le chien nous a chassés.** The dog chased us away.
**chasser quelqu'un de quelque part** to drive somebody out of somewhere
**On a chassé les musiciens du métro.** They've driven the buskers out of the underground.

le **chasseur** *masc noun*
**hunter**

♪ le **chat** *masc noun*
1 **cat**
**Je n'ai pas de chat.** I don't have a cat.
2 **tom cat**
3 **jouer à chat** to play tag
**Les petits jouent à chat pendant la récréation.** The little children play tag at break.
**C'est toi le chat!** You're it!
4 (*Internet, mobile phones*) **chat** (*pronounced as in English*)

la **châtaigne** *fem noun*
**sweet chestnut**

le **châtaignier** *masc noun*
**sweet chestnut tree**

♪ **châtain** *masc & fem adjective*
**brown** (*hair*)
**Il est châtain.** He has brown hair.
**Elle a les cheveux châtains.** She has brown hair.

**WORD TIP** *châtain* has no feminine form.

♪ **château** *masc noun*, les **châteaux** *pl*
1 **castle**
**le château de Warwick** Warwick Castle
2 **manor** (*large country house*)
3 **palace**
**le château de Versailles** the palace of Versailles
**les châteaux de la Loire** the châteaux of the Loire Valley
- le **château d'eau** water tower

**chatouiller** *verb* [1]
**to tickle**

le **chatroom** *masc noun*
**chatroom**

la **chatte** *fem noun*
**female cat**

♪ **chaud** *masc adjective*, **chaude** *fem*
1 **hot**, **warm**
**du lait chaud** hot milk
**des chaussettes chaudes** warm socks
2 **avoir chaud** to be hot
**J'ai chaud.** I'm hot.
**Elle a trop chaud.** She's too hot.
3 **faire chaud** to be hot
**Il fait chaud ici.** It's hot here.
**Il ne fait pas très chaud.** It's not very warm.
4 **tenir chaud à quelqu'un** to keep somebody warm
**Ce pull me tient chaud.** This jumper's keeping me warm.

la **chaudière** *fem noun*
**boiler**

♪ le **chauffage** *masc noun*
**heating**
**mettre le chauffage** to put on the heating
- le **chauffage central** central heating

le **chauffe-eau** *invariable masc noun*
**water heater**

**chauffer** *verb* [1]
1 **to heat**, **to heat up**
**être bien chauffé** to be well heated
**La maison n'est pas bien chauffée.** The house isn't well heated.
**faire chauffer quelque chose** to heat something up
**Je fais chauffer la sauce.** I'm heating the sauce up.
2 **to warm**
**chauffer les assiettes** to warm the plates

♪ le **chauffeur** *masc noun*
1 **driver**
**Mon frère est chauffeur de taxi.** My brother is a taxi driver.
2 **chauffeur** (*of a limousine*) (***Une chauffeuse** exists, but it's a type of chair rather than a female driver!*)

la **chaumière** *fem noun*
**thatched cottage**

la **chaussée** *fem noun*
**roadway**

♪ la **chaussette** *fem noun*
**sock**
**des chaussettes blanches** white socks

le **chausson** *masc noun*
**slipper**
- le **chausson aux pommes** apple turnover
- le **chausson de danse** ballet shoe

ℰ la **chaussure** *fem noun*
**shoe**
**faire les magasins de chaussures** to go around the shoe shops

**chauve** *masc & fem adjective*
**bald**

la **chauve-souris** *fem noun*, les **chauves-souris** *pl*
**bat**

**chavirer** *verb* **[1]**
**to capsize**
**faire chavirer un bateau** to capsize a boat

ℰ le **chef** *masc noun*
1 **leader** (*of a group, a political party*)
2 **head** (*of a company*)
3 **boss**
**C'est le chef.** He's the boss.
- le **chef de classe** class monitor
- le **chef de cuisine** chef
- le **chef-d'œuvre** masterpiece
- le **chef d'orchestre** conductor

ℰ le **chemin** *masc noun*
1 **country lane**, **path**
2 **way**
**en chemin** on the way
**sur le chemin du collège** on the way to the school
**sur le chemin du retour** on the way back
**demander son chemin à quelqu'un** to ask somebody the way
**Demandons notre chemin au policier!** Let's ask the policeman the way!
**indiquer le chemin à quelqu'un** to tell somebody the way
**Pourriez-vous m'indiquer le chemin de la gare, s'il vous plaît?** Could you tell me the way to the train station, please? (*polite form.*)
**perdre son chemin** to lose your way
**Nous avons perdu notre chemin.** We lost our way.
**se tromper de chemin** to go the wrong way
**Je me suis trompé de chemin.** I went the wrong way.
- le **chemin de fer** railway

la **cheminée** *fem noun*
1 **chimney**
2 **fireplace**
3 **mantlepiece**

le **cheminot** *masc noun*
**railway worker**

ℰ la **chemise** *fem noun*
1 **shirt**
**une chemise à manches courtes** a short-sleeved shirt
2 **folder** (*for homework, papers*)
**une chemise en plastique** a plastic folder
- la **chemise de nuit** nightdress

ℰ le **chemisier** *masc noun*
**blouse**

le **chêne** *masc noun*
1 **oak tree**
2 **oak**
**une table en chêne massif** a solid oak table

le **chenil** *masc noun*
1 **dog kennel** (*for one dog*)
2 **kennels** (*for housing dogs*)

la **chenille** *fem noun*
**caterpillar**

ℰ le **chèque** *masc noun*
**cheque**
**un chèque à l'ordre de M. Dubois** a cheque payable to M. Dubois
**faire un chèque** to write a cheque
**Je vous fais un chèque de 100 euros.** I'll write you a cheque for 100 euros.
- le **chèque de voyage** traveller's cheque

le **chéquier** *masc noun*
**chequebook**

ℰ **cher** *masc adjective*, **chère** *fem*
▷ see **cher** *adv*
1 **dear**
**Chère Anne** Dear Anne (*informally to a girl*)
**Cher Monsieur** Dear Sir (*formally to a man*)
2 **expensive**
**C'est trop cher.** It's too expensive.
**Un euro pour un sandwich, ce n'est pas cher!** A sandwich for one euro! That's really reasonable.
**À Londres la vie est plus chère.** In London the cost of living is higher.

**cher** *adverb* ▷ see **cher** *adj*
**coûter cher** to be expensive
**Les jeux électroniques coûtent cher.** Computer games are expensive.

ℰ **chercher** *verb* **[1]**
1 **chercher quelque chose** to look for something
**Qu'est-ce que tu cherches?** What are you looking for?
**Je cherche mes lunettes.** I'm looking for my glasses.
**Vous cherchez quelqu'un?** Are you looking for someone?
**Je cherchais le professeur.** I was looking for the teacher.
2 **chercher quelque chose dans** to look something up in (*a dictionary, the phone book*)
**J'ai cherché le nom dans l'annuaire.** I looked the name up in the phone book.

Cherchez le mot dans le dictionnaire. Look up the word in the dictionary.

3 **aller chercher** to go and get (*somebody or something*)
**Va chercher le médecin!** Go and get the doctor!
**Je vais chercher des verres.** I'll fetch some glasses.

4 **to pick up**
**Il est venu nous chercher à l'école.** He came and picked us up from school.
**On vient me chercher.** I'm being picked up.

5 **chercher à faire quelque chose** to try to do something
**Je cherche à comprendre, c'est tout.** I'm just trying to understand, that's all.

le **chercheur** *masc noun*, la **chercheuse** *fem*
**researcher**
**Elle est chercheuse dans un laboratoire.** She's a researcher in a laboratory.

le **chéri** *masc noun*, la **chérie** *fem*
**darling**

**chérir** *verb* [2]
**to cherish**

♪ le **cheval** *masc noun*, les **chevaux** *pl*

1 **horse**
**un garçon à cheval** a boy on horseback
**monter à cheval** to ride a horse
**J'aime monter à cheval.** I love riding horses.

2 **horseriding**
**faire du cheval** to go horseriding
**Elle fait du cheval tous les dimanches.** She goes horseriding every Sunday.

- le **cheval à bascule** rocking horse
- le **cheval de trait** carthorse

le **chevet** *masc noun*

1 **bedhead**
**une lampe de chevet** a bedside lamp
**L'infirmière est restée à mon chevet.** The nurse stayed at my bedside.

2 **bedside table**

♪ le **cheveu** *masc noun*, les **cheveux** *pl*

1 **un cheveu** a hair

2 **les cheveux** hair
**Il a les cheveux blonds.** He has blond hair.
**Elle s'est fait couper les cheveux.** She's had her hair cut.

3 **Adrien a un cheveu sur la langue.** Adrien has a lisp.

la **cheville** *fem noun*
**ankle**
**J'ai une entorse à la cheville.** I've got a sprained ankle.

la **chèvre** *fem noun* ▷ see **chèvre** *masc noun*
**goat**

le **chèvre** *masc noun* ▷ see **chèvre** *fem noun*
**goat's cheese**

le **chèvrefeuille** *masc noun*
**honeysuckle**

le **chevreuil** *masc noun*

1 **roe deer**

2 **venison**

♪ **chez** *preposition*

1 **at**
**être chez quelqu'un** to be at somebody's (house)
**Camille est chez sa grand-mère.** Camille is at her grandmother's.
**Je suis chez moi.** I'm at home.
**Il sera chez lui.** He'll be at home.
**Elle est chez le coiffeur.** She's at the hairdresser's.
**Chez Maxipop, on trouve des CD bon marché.** At Maxipop's, you can get cheap CDs.
**Fais comme chez toi.** Make yourself at home.

2 **to**
**aller chez quelqu'un** to go to somebody's (place)
**Viens chez moi.** Come round to my place.
**Je vais chez Léa ce soir.** I'm going to Léa's this evening.
**Je rentre chez moi.** I'm going home.
**Elle est rentrée chez elle.** She's gone home.
**aller chez Harrods** to go to Harrods
**Va chez le boulanger.** Go to the baker's.
**Je dois aller chez le dentiste demain.** I've got to go to the dentist's tomorrow.

3 **chez moi** in my family
**Chez eux, on dîne à six heures.** In their family, they eat at six o'clock.

♪ **chic** *invariable masc & fem adjective*

1 **chic, well-dressed**
**Marine est toujours très chic.** Marine is always very chic.

2 **nice**
**C'est chic de ta part.** It's really nice of you.

3 **Chic alors!** (*informal*) Cool!

la **chicorée** *fem noun*

1 **curly endive** (*for salads*)

2 **chicory powder** (*in hot drinks or added to coffee*)

♪ le **chien** *masc noun*
**dog**
**J'ai toujours voulu un chien.** I've always wanted a dog.
**'Chien Méchant!'** 'Beware of the Dog!' ▸▸

French–English

a b c d e f g h i j k l m n o p q r s t u v w x y z

- le **chien d'aveugle** guide dog
- le **chien de berger** sheepdog
- le **chien de garde** guard dog

la **chienne** *fem noun*
**bitch**

le **chiffon** *masc noun*
1 **rag**
une poupée de chiffons a rag doll
2 **duster**
un chiffon humide a damp cloth

♪ le **chiffre** *masc noun*
**figure**
un numéro à cinq chiffres a five-figure number
Donne-moi un chiffre entre zéro et neuf! Give me a number between zero and nine!
- le **chiffre arabe** Arabic numeral
- le **chiffre romain** Roman numeral

le **chignon** *masc noun*
**bun**
Elle a un chignon. She wears her hair in a bun.

♪ la **chimie** *fem noun*
**chemistry**
Alice est bonne en chimie. Alice is good at chemistry.
La chimie est ma matière préférée. Chemistry is my favourite subject.

**chimique** *masc & fem adjective*
**chemical**

le **chimpanzé** *masc noun*
**chimpanzee**

la **Chine** *fem noun*
**China**

**chinois** *masc adjective*, **chinoise** *fem*
▷ see **Chinois** *noun*
**Chinese**

le **Chinois** *masc noun*, la **Chinoise** *fem*
▷ see **chinois** *adj*
1 **Chinese man, Chinese woman**
les Chinois the Chinese
2 le chinois *masc* Chinese (*the language*)

le **chiot** *masc noun*
**puppy**

♪ les **chips** *plural fem noun*
**crisp**
un paquet de chips a packet of crisps

**chirurgical** *masc adjective*, **chirurgicale** *fem*, **chirurgicaux** *masc pl*, **chirurgicales** *fem pl*
**surgical**
une intervention chirurgicale an operation

la **chirurgie** *fem noun*
**surgery**
- la **chirurgie au laser** laser surgery

le **chirurgien** *masc noun*, la **chirurgienne** *fem*
**surgeon**
- le **chirurgien-dentiste** dental surgeon

le **choc** *masc noun*
**shock**
Ça m'a fait un choc. It gave me a shock.

♪ le **chocolat** *masc noun*
**chocolate**
un gâteau au chocolat a chocolate cake
une tablette de chocolat a bar of chocolate
une boîte de chocolats a box of chocolates
Au petit déjeuner, les enfants prennent un bol de chocolat. For breakfast children have a bowl of hot chocolate.
- le **chocolat blanc** white chocolate
- le **chocolat chaud** hot chocolate
- le **chocolat à croquer** plain chocolate
- le **chocolat au lait** milk chocolate
- le **chocolat noir** plain chocolate
- le **chocolat en poudre** drinking chocolate

le **chœur** *masc noun*
1 **choir** (*professional*)
2 **chorus** (*in an opera, a piece of music*)
chanter en chœur to sing in a chorus

♪ **choisir** *verb* **[2]**
**to choose**
Choisis une couleur! Choose a colour!
choisir de faire quelque chose to choose to do something
Nous avons choisi de manger chinois. We chose to eat Chinese.
choisir quelqu'un comme to choose somebody as
J'ai choisi Romain comme partenaire. I chose Romain as my partner.
Pizza ou pâtes - c'est à toi de choisir. Pizza or pasta - it's up to you.

♪ le **choix** *masc noun*
1 **choice**
Il y a un grand choix de DVD. There's a wide choice of DVDs.
C'est un bon choix. It's a good choice.
'Fromage ou dessert au choix' 'A choice of cheese or dessert' (*on a menu*)
2 **de choix** choice (*high quality*)
des produits de premier choix top quality products

♪ le **chômage** *masc noun*
**unemployment**
le chômage des jeunes youth unemployment

a b c d e f g h i j k l m n o p q r s t u v w x y z

être au chômage to be unemployed
Il est au chômage depuis janvier. He's been unemployed since January.
mettre quelqu'un au chômage to make somebody redundant
L'usine a mis 500 ouvriers au chômage. The factory made 500 workers redundant.

le **chômeur** *masc noun*, la **chômeuse** *fem*
**unemployed person**
On doit aider les chômeurs. We must help the unemployed.

la **chope** *fem noun*
**beer mug**

**choquer** *verb* [1]
**to shock**
Ça m'a vraiment choqué. I was really shocked by that.

la **chorale** *fem noun*
**choir** (*amateur*)

le & la **choriste** *masc & fem noun*
1 **choir member**, **chorister**
les choristes the choir
2 **member of a chorus** (*in an opera*)
les choristes the chorus

♪ la **chose** *fem noun*
**thing**
les choses qui m'intéressent the things that interest me
J'ai plusieurs choses à te dire. I've got several things to tell you.
Je prends la même chose. I'll have the same.
Tiens, j'ai pensé à une chose. Hang on, I've just thought of something.
Parlons d'autre chose! Let's talk about something else.
Ce sont des choses qui arrivent. These things happen.

♪ le **chou** *masc noun*, les **choux** *pl*
**cabbage**
- le **chou de Bruxelles** Brussels sprout
- le **chou à la crème** cream puff

le **chouchou** *masc noun*, la **chouchoute** *fem* ▷ see **chouchou** *masc noun*
**teacher's pet**
Cédric est le chouchou de la prof. Cédric is the teacher's pet.

le **chouchou** *masc noun*
▷ see **chouchou** *masc noun*
**scrunchie**

la **choucroute** *fem noun*
**sauerkraut** (*pickled cabbage served with different types of sausage, ham and bacon*)

♪ **chouette** *masc & fem adjective, exclamation*
▷ see **chouette** *noun*
1 (*informal*) **great**
Chouette! Great!
C'est chouette! That's great!
Leur maison est très chouette. Their house is really lovely.
2 (*informal*) **nice** (*person*)
C'est vraiment chouette de ta part! It's really nice of you!
Il est chouette avec nous. He's nice to us.

♪ la **chouette** *fem noun*
▷ see **chouette** *adj, excl*
**owl**

le **chou-fleur** *masc noun*, les **choux-fleurs** *pl*
**cauliflower**

**chrétien** *masc adjective*, **chrétienne** *fem*
▷ see **chrétien** *noun*
**Christian**

le **chrétien** *masc noun*, la **chrétienne** *fem*
▷ see **chrétien** *adj*
**Christian**

**WORD TIP** Adjectives and nouns of religion start with a small letter in French.

le **christianisme** *masc noun*
**Christianity**

**WORD TIP** Use *le* or *la* before the name of a religion in French.

le **chrome** *masc noun*
**chromium**

**chronique** *masc & fem adjective*
▷ see **chronique** *noun*
**chronic**

la **chronique** *fem noun*
▷ see **chronique** *adj*
1 **column** (*by a journalist in a newspaper*)
2 **(radio) programme**

le **chronomètre** *masc noun*
**stopwatch**

le **chrysanthème** *masc noun*
**chrysanthemum**

**chuchoter** *verb* [1]
**to whisper**
chuchoter quelque chose à l'oreille de quelqu'un to whisper something in somebody's ear
Elle m'a chuchoté quelques mots à l'oreille. She whispered a few words in my ear.

**chut** *exclamation*
**shh!**

French-English

la **chute** *fem noun*
**1** **fall**
**Il a fait une chute de cinq mètres.** He fell five metres.
**2** **fall**, **drop** (*in price, value, temperature*)
**Il y aura une chute de température.** There will be a drop in temperature.
- la **chute de neige** snowfall
- la **chute de pluie** rainfall

**chuter** *verb* **[1]**
**to fall**, **to drop**

**Chypre** *fem noun*
**Cyprus**
**Anita va à Chypre.** Anita's going to Cyprus.

**WORD TIP** Unlike other names of countries, *Chypre* does not take *le* or *la*.

**-ci** *suffix*
**ce côté-ci** this side
**ce mois-ci** this month
**ces timbres-ci** these stamps
**ces jours-ci** these last few days

**WORD TIP** *-ci* is attached to a noun for emphasis. Compare with *-là*.

la **cible** *fem noun*
**target**

la **ciboulette** *fem noun*
**de la ciboulette** chives

la **cicatrice** *fem noun*
**scar**

**ci-contre** *adverb*
**opposite**

**ci-dessous** *adverb*
**below**

**ci-dessus** *adverb*
**above**

le **cidre** *masc noun*
**cider**

le **ciel** *masc noun*, les **cieux** *pl*
**1** **sky**
**dans le ciel** in the sky
**2** **heaven**
**au ciel** in heaven

la **cigale** *fem noun*
**cicada** (*type of insect*)

le **cigare** *masc noun*
**cigar**

la **cigarette** *fem noun*
**cigarette**

la **cigogne** *fem noun*
**stork**

**ci-joint** *masc adjective*, **ci-jointe** *fem*
▷ see **ci-joint** *adv*
**enclosed** (*in a letter*), **attached** (*to an email*)
**la facture ci-jointe** the enclosed invoice

**ci-joint** *adverb* ▷ see **ci-joint** *adj*
**enclosed**, **attached**
**Veuillez trouver ci-joint une facture.** Please find enclosed an invoice.

le **cil** *masc noun*
**eyelash**

le **ciment** *masc noun*
**cement**

le **cimetière** *masc noun*
**1** **cemetery**
**2** **churchyard**, **graveyard**
- le **cimetière de voitures** scrapyard

le & la **cinéaste** *masc & fem noun*
**film director**

le **ciné-club** *masc noun*
**film club**

le **cinéma** *masc noun*
**1** **cinema**
**aller au cinéma** to go to the cinema
**Je vais au cinéma avec mes copains.** I go to the cinema with my friends.
**2** (*informal*) **play-acting**
**Arrête ton cinéma!** Stop that nonsense!

***cinéma***
Deux Français, les frères Lumière, ont inventé le 'cinématographe' en 1895.

le & la **cinéphile** *masc & fem noun*
**cinema enthusiast**

**cinglé** *masc adjective*, **cinglée** *fem*
(*informal*) **crazy**

**cinq** *number*
**five**
**Lucie a cinq ans.** Lucie's five.
**À cinq heures, je pars.** I'm leaving at five o'clock.
**Le cinq avril, c'est mon anniversaire.** The fifth of April is my birthday.
**Ça fait cinq euros.** That's five euros.

la **cinquantaine** *fem noun*
**une cinquantaine** about fifty
**une cinquantaine de personnes** about fifty people
**Elle a la cinquantaine.** She is about fifty.

**cinquante** *number*
**fifty**

**cinquantième** *number*
**fiftieth**

**cinquième** *masc & fem adjective*
▷ see **cinquième** *masc noun, fem noun*
**fifth**
C'est la cinquième fois qu'elle gagne. It's the fifth time she's won.

le **cinquième** *masc noun*
▷ see **cinquième** *adj, fem noun*
**fifth** (*in a series*)
J'habite au cinquième. I live on the fifth floor.

la **cinquième** *fem noun*
▷ see **cinquième** *adj, masc noun*
**the equivalent of Year 8** (*in a French collège*)
Aurélie est en cinquième. Aurélie is in year 8.

le **cintre** *masc noun*
**(clothes) hanger**

le **cirage** *masc noun*
**shoe polish**

la **circonférence** *fem noun*
**circumference**

le **circonflexe** *masc noun*
un accent circonflexe a circumflex accent (*as on â, ê, î, ô, û*)

la **circonstance** *fem noun*
**circumstance**

le **circuit** *masc noun*
1 **circuit** (*on an athletics track*)
2 **tour** (*in tourism*)
3 un circuit électrique an electrical circuit

**circulaire** *masc & fem adjective*
▷ see **circulaire** *fem noun*
**circular**

la **circulaire** *fem noun* ▷ see **circulaire** *adj*
**circular** (*leaflet*)

♪ la **circulation** *fem noun*
1 **traffic**
Il y a beaucoup de circulation ce soir. There's a lot of traffic this evening.
2 **circulation**
la circulation du sang blood circulation

**circuler** *verb* [1]
1 **to run** (*providing a transport service*)
Ce train ne circule pas le dimanche. That train doesn't run on Sundays.
2 **to get around**
Elle circule à vélo. She gets around by bike.
Circulez, s'il vous plaît! Move along please!
3 **to circulate** (*blood, air*)

la **cire** *fem noun*
**wax**
les personnages en cire the wax models

**cirer** *verb* [1]
**to polish**

♪ le **cirque** *masc noun*
**circus**
Les enfants adorent aller au cirque. Children love going to the circus.

les **ciseaux** *plural masc noun*
**scissors**
une paire de ciseaux a pair of scissors

le **citadin** *masc noun*, la **citadine** *fem*
**city dweller**

la **citation** *fem noun*
**quotation**

la **cité** *fem noun*
1 **city, town**
2 **housing estate**
les cités de banlieue suburban housing estates (*typically tower blocks*)
une cité universitaire a university hall of residence

**citer** *verb* [1]
**to quote**

la **citerne** *fem noun*
**tank**

le **citoyen** *masc noun*, la **citoyenne** *fem*
**citizen**

♪ le **citron** *masc noun*
**lemon**
du jus de citron lemon juice
une tarte au citron a lemon tart
- le **citron givré** lemon sorbet (*served inside a lemon*)
- un **citron pressée** freshly squeezed lemon juice
- le **citron vert** lime

la **citronnade** *fem noun*
**lemonade** (*not fizzy*)

le **citronnier** *masc noun*
**lemon tree**

la **citrouille** *fem noun*
**pumpkin**

le **civet** *masc noun*
**stew**

**civil** *masc adjective*, **civile** *fem*
▷ see **civil** *noun*
1 **civilian** (*life, authorities, clothes*)
2 **un mariage civil** a civil wedding (*as opposed to a church wedding*)

French–English

le **civil** *masc noun* ▷ see **civil** *adj*
**civilian**
**un soldat en civil** a soldier in civilian clothes
**un policier en civil** a plain-clothes policeman
**Que fait-il dans le civil?** What does he do in civilian life?

la **civilisation** *fem noun*
**civilization**

**civique** *masc & fem adjective*
**civic**
**l'éducation civique** civics (*equivalent to PHSE*)

**clair** *masc adjective*, **claire** *fem* ▷ see **clair** *adv*
1 **light**
**bleu clair** light blue
**J'aimerais mieux une couleur plus claire.** I'd prefer a lighter colour.
**La chambre est très claire.** The bedroom is very light.
2 **clear** (*sky, water, idea*)
**Le temps est clair aujourd'hui.** It's a clear day today.
**Elle a été très claire sur ce point.** She was very clear on this point.

**clair** *adverb* ▷ see **clair** *adj*
1 **clearly**
**Je n'arrive pas à voir clair.** I can't see clearly.
2 **faire clair** to get light
**Il fait clair très tôt.** It gets light very early.

le **clair de lune** *masc noun*
**moonlight**

**clairement** *adverb*
**clearly**

le **clapier** *masc noun*
**rabbit hutch**

la **claque** *fem noun*
**slap**

**claqué** *masc adjective*, **claquée** *fem*
(*informal*) **exhausted**, **whacked out**

**claquer** *verb* [1]
1 **to slam**
**Il a claqué la porte.** He slammed the door.
2 (*informal*) **to spend**, **to blow**
**J'ai claqué mon argent de poche en jeux vidéo.** I blew all my pocket money on video games.

**clarifier** *verb* [1]
**to clarify**

la **clarinette** *fem noun*
**clarinet**
**Jean-Marc joue de la clarinette.** Jean-Marc plays the clarinet.

la **clarté** *fem noun*
1 **light** (*in a room*)
2 **clarity** (*of water, speech*)

la **classe** *fem noun*
1 **class** (*the year, the form*)
**en classe** in class
**Elle est dans ma classe à l'école.** She's in my class (or year) at school.
**Tu es dans quelle classe cette année?** What form are you in this year?
**Je redouble ma classe.** I'm repeating the year.
**Denise est la première de la classe.** Denise is top of the class.
2 **school**, **lesson**
**le soir après la classe** in the evening after school
**aller en classe** to go to school
**Je ne suis pas allé en classe hier.** I didn't go to school yesterday.
**avoir classe** to have school
**Nous n'avons pas classe demain.** We don't have school tomorrow.
**Il n'y aura pas classe ce matin.** There'll be no lesson this morning.
**faire classe** to teach
**C'est Mme Petit qui fera classe.** Mme Petit will be teaching.
3 **classroom**
**Notre classe est située près du laboratoire.** Our classroom is next to the laboratory.
4 **class** (*category*)
**voyager en première classe** to travel first class
**voyager en classe touriste** to travel in economy class
5 **les classes sociales** the social classes
- la **classe de mer** school trip to the seaside
- la **classe de neige** school skiing trip
- la **classe verte** school field trip

le **classement** *masc noun*
1 **classification** (*of objects, books, animals*)
2 **ranking** (*in sports*)
**le classement par équipe** team ranking
3 **grading** (*of students, employees*)
4 **filing** (*of documents*)

**classer** *verb* [1]
1 **to classify** (*objects, books, animals*)
2 **to grade** (*students, employees*)
3 **to file** (*documents, archives*)

le **classeur** *masc noun*
1 **ring binder**, **folder**
2 **filing cabinet**

a b c d e f g h i j k l m n o p q r s t u v w x y z

**classique** *masc & fem adjective*
1 **classical**
Je préfère la musique classique. I prefer classical music.
2 **classic**
La question classique - Qu'est-ce que tu veux faire plus tard? The classic question - What do you want to be when you grow up?
C'est classique! That's typical!

♪ le **clavier** *masc noun*
**keyboard**
- le **clavier numérique** keypad (*on a telephone*)

♪ la **clé** *fem noun*
1 **key**
fermer quelque chose à clé to lock something
Je ferme toujours la porte de ma chambre à clé. I always lock my bedroom door.
2 **spanner**
3 **clef** (*in music*)
la clé de sol the treble clef
la clé de fa the bass clef

la **clef** ▷ **clé**

la **clémentine** *fem noun*
**clementine**

le **clic** *masc noun*
**click** (*of a mouse*)
en un seul clic with a click (of the mouse)
Tu peux fermer le programme en un seul clic. You can close the program with one click.

♪ le **client** *masc noun*, la **cliente** *fem*
1 **customer**
2 **client**
3 **guest** (*of a hotel*)

la **clientèle** *fem noun*
**customers**

**cligner** *verb* [1]
1 cligner des yeux to blink
Le soleil m'a fait cligner des yeux. The sunshine made me blink.
2 cligner de l'œil to wink
Il n'arrête pas de me cligner de l'œil! He keeps winking at me!

le **clignotant** *masc noun*
**indicator** (*on a vehicle*)
mettre le clignotant to indicate (*when driving*)

**clignoter** *verb* [1]
**to flash**

♪ le **climat** *masc noun*
**climate**
un climat doux a mild climate
J'adore le climat chaud de Provence. I love the hot climate of Provence.

la **climatisation** *fem noun*
**air-conditioning**

**climatisé** *masc adjective*, **climatisée** *fem*
**air-conditioned**

le **clin d'œil** *masc noun*
1 **wink**
faire un clin d'œil à quelqu'un to wink at somebody
Son copain m'a fait un clin d'œil. His friend winked at me.
2 **en un clin d'œil in a flash**
Ils ont disparu en un clin d'œil. They disappeared in a flash.

la **clinique** *fem noun*
**private hospital**
- la **clinique vétérinaire** veterinary clinic

le **clip** *masc noun*
1 **pop video**
2 **clip-on (earring)**

**cliquer** *verb* [1]
cliquer sur quelque chose to click on something (*using the mouse*)
Clique deux fois sur l'icône. Double-click on the icon.
Il faut cliquer sur l'image en appuyant sur le bouton droit de la souris. You have to right-click on the image.

**cliqueter** *verb* [48]
1 **to jingle** (*coins, keys*)
2 **to rattle** (*chains*)

le **clochard** *masc noun*, la **clocharde** *fem*
1 **tramp**
2 **bag lady**

la **cloche** *fem noun*
1 **bell**
2 (*informal*) **idiot**
Quelle cloche! What an idiot!

le **clocher** *masc noun* ▷ see **clocher** *verb*
1 **church tower**
2 **steeple**

**clocher** *verb* [1] ▷ see **clocher** *noun*
(*informal*) Ça cloche! It's not quite right.
Il y a quelque chose qui cloche. There's something wrong.

la **cloison** *fem noun*
1 **partition wall**
2 **movable screen**

French-English

le **cloître** *masc noun*
**cloister**

le **clonage** *masc noun*
**cloning**

le **clone** *masc noun*
**clone**

**clos** *masc adjective*, **close** *fem*
**closed**

la **clôture** *fem noun*
**1 fence** (*around a field*)
**2 closing** (*of shops, offices*)

le **clou** *masc noun*
**1 nail** (*for attaching, hanging*)
**2 les clous** pedestrian crossing (*once marked by studs in the street*)
**traverser la rue dans les clous** to cross at the pedestrian crossing
• le **clou de girofle** clove

**clouer** *verb* **[1]**
**clouer quelque chose** to nail something down
**Il cloue le couvercle sur la caisse.** He's nailing down the lid of the crate.
**clouer quelqu'un au sol** to pin somebody down
**Le catcheur a cloué son adversaire au sol.** The wrestler pinned his opponent down.

le **clown** *masc noun*
**clown**
**faire le clown** to clown about
**Omar n'arrête pas de faire le clown en classe.** Omar's always clowning about in class.

le **club** *masc noun*
**club**
**un club de foot** a football club
**Je fais partie d'un club sportif.** I'm in a sports club.

le **cobaye** *masc noun*
**guinea pig**

le **coca** *masc noun*
**Coke®** (*short for Coca-Cola®*)
**Tu veux du coca?** Would you like some Coke®?
**Je voudrais un coca, s'il vous plaît.** I'd like a Coke® please.

la **cocaïne** *fem noun*
**cocaine**

la **coccinelle** *fem noun*
**ladybird**

**cocher** *verb* **[1]**
**to tick**
**Cochez la bonne case.** Tick the correct box.

**cochon** *masc adjective*, **cochonne** *fem*
▷ see **cochon** *noun*
(*informal*) **dirty** (*joke, story*)

le **cochon** *masc noun* ▷ see **cochon** *adj*
**pig**
• le **cochon d'Inde** guinea pig

le **cocktail** *masc noun*
**1 cocktail**
**2 cocktail party**

le **cocorico** *masc noun*
**cock-a-doodle-do**

la **cocotte** *fem noun*
**1 casserole**
**du bœuf à la cocotte** beef casserole
**2 hen** (*in baby talk*)
**3 ma cocotte** sweetheart (*said with affection to someone*)
**4 une cocotte en chocolat** chocolate hen (*eaten at Easter*)
• la **cocotte-minute®** pressure cooker

le **code** *masc noun*
**code**
**en code** in code
**des messages en code** coded messages
**J'ai déchiffré le code.** I cracked the code.
• le **code confidentiel (d'identification)** PIN number
• le **code postal** postcode
• le **code de la route** the highway code

les **codes** *plural masc noun*
**dipped headlights**

le **cœur** *masc noun*
**1 heart**
**avoir mal au cœur** to feel sick
**J'ai souvent mal au cœur en voiture.** I often feel car sick.
**2 par cœur** by heart
**apprendre quelque chose par cœur** to learn something by heart
**Il faut apprendre ces paroles par cœur.** You've got to learn these words by heart.
**savoir quelque chose par cœur** to know something by heart
**Je le savais par cœur.** I knew it by heart.
**3 hearts** (*in card games*)
**le roi de cœur** the king of hearts

le **coffre** *masc noun*
**1 chest**
**un coffre au trésor** a treasure chest
**un coffre à jouets** a toy box
**2 safe** (*for valuables*)
**3 boot**
**Mettez les valises dans le coffre.** Put the suitcases in the boot.
• le **coffre-fort** safe (*for valuables*)

**cogner** *verb* **[1]**
1 **to knock, to bang**
**On a cogné à la porte.** Somebody banged on the door.
**Il cognait du poing sur la table.** He was banging his fist on the table.
2 (*informal*) **to hit**
**Ce boxeur cogne dur.** This boxer hits hard.

se **cogner** *reflexive verb* ⓔ
**to bump into something, to bang something**
**Il s'est cogné contre le mur.** He bumped into the wall.
**Elle s'est cognée contre le mur.** She bumped into the wall.
**Je me suis cogné au genou.** I got a bang on my knee.
**Annie s'est cogné la tête contre la table.** Annie bumped her head on the table.

**coiffé** *masc adjective*, **coiffée** *fem*
**Tu es bien coiffée aujourd'hui.** Your hair looks really nice today.
**Je suis vraiment mal coiffé.** My hair's really untidy.

**coiffer** *verb* **[1]**
**coiffer quelqu'un** to do somebody's hair
**C'est toujours Pauline qui me coiffe.** Pauline always does my hair. (*at hair stylist's*)

se **coiffer** *reflexive verb* ⓔ
**to do your hair**
**Je n'ai pas eu le temps de me coiffer.** I didn't have time to do my hair.

♪ le **coiffeur** *masc noun*, la **coiffeuse** *fem*
▷ see **coiffeuse** *fem noun*
**hairdresser**
**Je déteste aller chez le coiffeur.** I hate going to the hairdresser's.

♪ la **coiffeuse** *fem noun* ▷ see **coiffeur** *masc noun*
**dressing table**

la **coiffure** *fem noun*
1 **hairdressing**
**apprendre la coiffure** to train to be a hairdresser
2 **hairstyle**
**Tu as changé de coiffure.** You've changed your hairstyle.

♪ le **coin** *masc noun*
1 **corner**
**un coin de table** a corner of the table
**le coin de la rue** the corner of the street
**au coin** in the corner
**Ça se trouve au coin de la rue.** It's on the corner of the street.
**Allons nous asseoir au coin du feu!** Let's sit down by the fire!
**Il étudie dans son coin.** He's working in his own little corner.
2 **area** (*a district*)
**Tu habites dans le coin?** Do you live in the area?
**Je vais au café du coin.** I go to the local cafe.
**Les gens du coin sont sympas.** The locals are nice.

**coincé** *masc adjective*, **coincée** *fem*
**stuck**
**Le tiroir est coincé.** The drawer is stuck.
**J'étais coincé dans un embouteillage.** I was stuck in a traffic jam.

**coincer** *verb* **[61]**
1 **to wedge** (*a door*)
**Trouve quelque chose pour coincer la porte!** Find something to wedge the door!
2 **to jam** (*a drawer, a zip, a key*)
**J'ai coincé la clé dans la serrure.** I jammed the key in the lock.

se **coincer** *reflexive verb* ⓔ
1 **to get stuck**
**Ma fermeture s'est coincée.** My zip's got stuck.
2 **Estelle s'est coincé le doigt dans la porte.** Estelle jammed her finger in the door.

la **coïncidence** *fem noun*
**coincidence**

le **col** *masc noun*
1 **collar** (*of a shirt*)
2 **neck** (*of a vase, bottle*)
3 **pass** (*in the mountains*)

la **colère** *fem noun*
**anger**
**être en colère contre quelq'un** to be angry with somebody
**Il est très en colère contre toi.** He's very angry with you.
**mettre quelqu'un en colère** to make somebody angry
**Ça me met toujours en colère.** That always makes me angry.
**se mettre en colère** to get angry
**Il se met en colère quand on bavarde en cours.** He gets angry when people chat in class.

le **colin** *masc noun*
**hake**

la **colique** *fem noun*
**diarrhoea**

le **colis** *masc noun*
**parcel**



French-English
a b c d e f g h i j k l m n o p q r s t u v w x y z

**collant** *masc adjective*, **collante** *fem*
▷ see **collant** *noun*
**sticky**

ꟹ le **collant** *masc noun* ▷ see **collant** *adj*
un collant a pair of tights
un collant noir a pair of black tights

la **colle** *fem noun*
1 **glue**
2 **detention** (*at school*)
une heure de colle an hour's detention

la **collecte** *fem noun*
**collection** (*of money*)

la **collection** *fem noun*
**collection**

**collectionner** *verb* **[1]**
**to collect** (*comics, stamps, cards, etc*)

le **collectionneur** *masc noun*, la **collectionneuse** *fem*
**collector**

ꟹ le **collège** *masc noun*
**secondary school** (*French students spend their first 4 years of secondary education in the CES. There,* ***la sixième, la cinquième, la quatrième*** *and* ***la troisième*** *are the equivalent of years 7, 8, 9 and 10 of the British system. Students then go on to* ***le lycée*** *for 3 years:* ***la seconde, la première*** *and* ***la terminale*** *at the end of which they sit* ***le baccalauréat****.*)

le **collégien** *masc noun*, la **collégienne** *fem*
**schoolboy** (*at secondary school*), **schoolgirl** (*at secondary school*)

le & la **collègue** *masc & fem noun*
**colleague**

**coller** *verb* **[1]**
1 **to stick** (*a photo, a stamp*)
**Ils ont collé des affiches sur les murs.** They stuck posters on the walls.
**J'ai collé la photo dans mon cahier.** I stuck the photo in my exercise book.
2 **to glue** (*paper, wood*)
3 **to be sticky**
**J'ai les doigts qui collent.** I have sticky fingers.
4 **to press**
**Il collait son nez contre la vitre.** He was pressing his nose against the window.
5 **coller quelqu'un** to give somebody detention
**On m'a collé pour bavardage.** I got detention for talking in class.
6 (*informal*) **se faire coller** to fail (*an exam*)
**Il s'est fait coller en chimie.** He failed chemistry.

le **collier** *masc noun*
1 **necklace**
2 **collar** (*for a pet*)

ꟹ la **colline** *fem noun*
**hill**

la **collision** *fem noun*
**collision**

la **colombe** *fem noun*
**dove**

le **colonel** *masc noun*
**colonel**

la **colo** *fem noun*
(*informal*) **holiday camp** (*for children*)
aller en colo to go to a holiday camp

ꟹ la **colonie** *fem noun*
**colony**
• la **colonie de vacances** holiday camp (*for children*)

la **colonne** *fem noun*
**column**
• la **colonne vertébrale** spine

le **colorant** *masc noun*
**colouring** (*for hair, food*)

**coloré** *masc adjective*, **colorée** *fem*
1 **coloured**
des dessins très colorés brightly-coloured drawings
2 **colourful** (*crowd, life*)

**colorer** *verb* **[1]**
**to colour**

**colorier** *verb* **[1]**
**to colour in**

le **coloris** *masc noun*
**colour** (*within a range of clothes on sale*)
**Existe en plusieurs coloris.** Available in several colours.

le **combat** *masc noun*
**fighting**
• un **combat de boxe** a boxing match

le **combattant** *masc noun*, la **combattante** *fem*
un ancien combattant a war veteran

**combattre** *verb* **[21]**
**to fight**

ꟹ **combien** *adverb* ▷ see **combien** *noun*
1 **how much?**
**C'est combien?** How much is it?
**Ça coûte combien?** How much does it cost?
**Je vous dois combien?** How much do I owe you?
**Tu pèses combien?** How much do you weigh?

Tu en veux combien? How much do you want?

2 **how many?**
Tu en veux combien? How many do you want?
Combien sont-elles? How many of them are there?

3 combien de how much, how many
Combien de fois dois-je le répéter? How many times do I have to repeat it?
Combien de chaises faut-il? How many chairs do we need?
Tu as besoin de combien d'argent? How much money do you need?

4 combien de temps how long
Tu as mis combien de temps? How long did it take you?

5 combien de kilomètres how far
C'est à combien de kilomètres d'ici? How far is it from here?

♪ le & la **combien** *invariable masc & fem noun* ▷ see **combien** *adv*

1 (*about dates*) Nous sommes le combien aujourd'hui? What's the date today?
Vous arrivez le combien? What date are you coming?

2 (*about shoe sizes*) Tu chausses du combien? What shoe size do you take?

3 (*about positions in a race, a class*) Elle est la combien en classe? Where is she in the class?
Vous êtes arrivés les combien à la course? Where did you come in the race?

la **combinaison** *fem noun*

1 **combination** (*of a padlock, safe*)

2 **overalls**

3 **petticoat**

- la **combinaison de ski** ski suit
- la **combinaison de plongée** wetsuit

le **combiné** *masc noun*
**receiver** (*of a telephone*)

le **comble** *masc noun*

1 le comble de the height of
le comble du luxe the height of luxury

2 Ça c'est le comble! That's the last straw!

la **comédie** *fem noun*

1 **comedy**

2 (*informal*) **to-do**
Quelle comédie! What a to-do!

- la **comédie musicale** musical

le **comédien** *masc noun*, la **comédienne** *fem*

1 **actor**

2 **actress**

**comestible** *masc & fem adjective*
**edible**

**comique** *masc & fem adjective*
▷ see **comique** *noun*
**funny**

le **comique** *masc noun* ▷ see **comique** *adj*
**comic, comedian**

le **comité** *masc noun*
**committee**

le **commandant** *masc noun*

1 **major** (*in the army*)

2 **squadron leader** (*in the air force*)

- le **commandant en chef** commander-in-chief

la **commande** *fem noun*

1 **order**
sur commande to order

2 **command** (*on the computer*)

♪ **commander** *verb* **[1]**

1 **to order** (*at the restaurant, cafe*)
Avez-vous commandé? Have you ordered?
Nous n'avons pas encore commandé. We haven't ordered yet.
J'ai commandé un steak-frites. I've ordered steak and chips.

2 **to be in charge**
Ce n'est pas toi qui commandes. You're not in charge.

♪ **comme** *conjunction* ▷ see **comme** *adv*

1 **like**
J'ai une montre comme la tienne. I have a watch like yours.
Marion est comme moi, elle adore les chevaux. Marion's like me, she loves horses.
Tiens-le comme ça! Hold it like this!
Je n'ai jamais vu un château comme celui-là. I've never seen a castle like that.

2 **as**
Comme tu veux! As you wish!
Je ferai comme toi. I'll do as you do.
Comme d'habitude, ils sont en retard. As usual, they're late.

3 **as** (*at the time when*)
Comme je fermais la porte, j'ai glissé. As I was closing the door, I slipped.

4 **as, since**
Comme je suis malade, je dois rester au lit. As I'm ill, I've got to stay in bed.
Comme il fait beau, on va se promener. As it's nice, we're going for a walk.

5 **as a**
Adam travaille comme serveur. Adam works as a waiter. ▸▸

Qu'est-ce qu'il y a comme dessert? What's for dessert?

6 **comme si** as if
**Fais comme si tu ne l'as pas vue.** Act as if you haven't seen her.

7 **comme il faut** properly, correctly
**faire quelque chose comme il faut** to do something properly
**Elle s'habille comme il faut.** She dresses properly.

**comme** *adverb* ▷ see **comme** *conj*
**Comme il est gentil!** He's so nice!
**Comme c'est gentil!** That's so kind of you!
**Comme c'est beau!** It's so beautiful!
**Comme il fait chaud!** It's so hot!
**Comme tu as grandi!** You've grown so much!

le **commencement** *masc noun*
**beginning, start**

♪ **commencer** *verb* **[61]**
1 **to begin, to start**
**Le film a déjà commencé.** The film has already started.
2 **commencer à faire quelque chose** to start to do something
**Elle a commencé à faire ses devoirs.** She's started to do her homework.
**Je commence à comprendre.** I'm beginning to understand.
**Il commence à pleuvoir.** It's starting to rain.

♪ **comment** *adverb*
1 **how**
**Comment vas-tu?** How are you?
**Comment va ta mère?** How's your mother?
**Comment as-tu fait ce gâteau?** How did you make this cake?
**Je ne sais pas comment le faire.** I don't know how to do it.
**Comment ça va?** How are things?
2 **what**
**Elle est comment leur maison?** What's their house like?
**Comment t'appelles-tu?** What's your name?
**Il s'appelle comment, ton frère?** What's your brother's name?
3 **pardon?, excuse me?**
**Comment? Pouvez-vous répéter, s'il vous plaît?** Pardon? Could you repeat please?

le **commentaire** *masc noun*
1 **comment**
**faire des commentaires désagréables** to make nasty comments
2 **commentary** *(on TV, radio)*

**commenter** *verb* **[1]**
**commenter quelque chose** to comment on something *(on a poem, a text)*

♪ le **commerçant** *masc noun*, la **commerçante** *fem*
**shopkeeper**

le **commerce** *masc noun*
1 **shop**
**Il y a beaucoup de commerces par ici.** There are a lot of shops around here.
2 **business**
**un commerce d'import-export** an import-export business
**Je fais des études de commerce.** I'm doing business studies.
3 **trade**
**le commerce mondial** world trade

**commercial** *masc adjective*, **commerciale** *fem*, **commerciaux** *masc pl*, **commerciales** *fem pl*
**commercial**
• le **centre commercial** shopping centre

**commettre** *verb* **[11]**
1 **commettre une erreur** to make a mistake
**J'ai commis une erreur.** I made a mistake.
2 **commettre un crime** to commit a crime
**Il a commis un crime.** He committed a crime.

♪ le **commissariat de police** *masc noun*
**police station**

la **commission** *fem noun*
1 **committee**
2 **commission** *(money paid for a service)*
3 **errand**
**faire une commission pour quelqu'un** to run an errand for somebody
4 **les commissions** the shopping
**faire les commissions** to do the shopping
**Qui fait les commissions?** Who's doing the shopping?

♪ **commode** *masc & fem adjective*
▷ see **commode** *noun*
1 **convenient**
**La télécommande, c'est bien commode.** The remote control is very convenient.
2 **easy**
**L'étagère est commode à monter.** The bookshelf is easy to assemble.
**Pour aller chez toi, ce n'est pas commode.** It's not easy to get to your house.
3 **easy-going** *(person)*
**Le professeur est assez commode.** The teacher's quite easy-going.

♪ la **commode** *fem noun*
▷ see **commode** *adj*
**chest of drawers**

**commun** *masc adjective*, **commune** *fem*
1 **common**
**Nous avons des amis communs.** We have friends in common.
**C'est une faute commune.** It's a common mistake.
2 **shared**
**La piscine est commune aux deux hôtels.** The pool is shared by both hotels.
3 **en commun** jointly, together
**les transports en commun** public transport
**faire quelque chose en commun** to do something together
**Nous faisons un exposé en commun.** We're doing a presentation together.
**avoir quelque chose en commun** to have something in common
**Ils n'ont rien en commun.** They have nothing in common.

la **communauté** *fem noun*
**community**

la **communication** *fem noun*
**communication**
• la **communication téléphonique** telephone call

la **communion** *fem noun*
**communion**

**communiquer** *verb* **[1]**
1 **to communicate**
2 **communiquer quelque chose à quelqu'un** to pass something on to somebody
**Je lui ai communiqué la nouvelle.** I passed the news on to him.

le **communisme** *masc noun*
**communism**

**communiste** *masc & fem adjective*
▷ see **communiste** *noun*
**communist**

le & la **communiste** *masc & fem noun*
▷ see **communiste** *adj*
**communist**

**compact** *masc adjective*, **compacte** *fem*
1 **dense** *(fog)*
2 **compact** *(soil)*
**un disque compact** a compact disc, a CD
**J'ai acheté deux disques compacts.** I bought two compact discs.

la **compagnie** *fem noun*
1 **company, firm**
**une compagnie d'assurances** an insurance company
2 **company**
**tenir compagnie à quelqu'un** to keep somebody company
**Tiens-moi compagnie!** Keep me company!
**Elle m'a tenu compagnie.** She kept me company.
• la **compagnie aérienne** airline

le **compagnon** *masc noun*
**companion**

**comparable** *masc & fem adjective*
**comparable**

la **comparaison** *fem noun*
**comparison**
**faire la comparaison** to compare
**si on fait la comparaison** if you compare them

**comparatif** *masc adjective*, **comparative** *fem*
**comparative**

**comparé** *masc adjective*, **comparée** *fem*
**comparé à** compared to
**Comparé à mes copains, je n'ai pas beaucoup grandi.** Compared to my friends, I haven't grown very much.

**comparer** *verb* **[1]**
**to compare**
**Tu me compares toujours à mes copines.** You're always comparing me with my friends.

♪ le **compartiment** *masc noun*
**compartment**
**le compartiment non fumeurs** the non-smoking compartment

le **compas** *masc noun*
**compass**

**compatir** *verb* **[2]**
**to sympathize**

la **compensation** *fem noun*
**compensation**

**compenser** *verb* **[1]**
**to compensate for**

la **compétence** *fem noun*
1 **ability**
2 **skill, competence**
**Il a de bonnes compétences en informatique.** He has good computing skills.

**compétent** *masc adjective*, **compétente** *fem*
**competent**
**une cavalière compétente** a competent horse rider
**être compétent en quelque chose** to be ⏩

competent at something
**Il est compétent en calcul mental.** He's competent at mental arithmetics.

**compétitif** *masc adjective*, **compétitive** *fem*
**competitive**

la **compétition** *fem noun*
**competition**
**Je participe à une compétition de natation.** I'm taking part in a swimming competition.

**complémentaire** *masc & fem adjective*
**further**
**pour toute information complémentaire** for further information

**complet** *masc adjective*, **complète** *fem*
▷ see **complet** *noun*
1 **complete** (*silence, success, revision, list*)
**Elle a la série complète des Tintins.** She's got the complete series of Tintin books.
2 **comprehensive**
**un guide complet sur le MP3** a comprehensive guide to the MP3
3 **full** (*camp site, train, car park*)
**'Complet'** 'No Vacancies'
**Toutes les chambres d'hôtes sont complètes.** All the B&Bs are full.
4 **wholemeal** (*bread, flour, pasta*)
**le pain complet** wholemeal bread

le **complet** *masc noun* ▷ see **complet** *adj*
**suit**

**complètement** *adverb*
**completely**

**compléter** *verb* **[24]**
1 **to complete**
2 **to fill in** (*a form*)

**complexe** *masc & fem adjective*
▷ see **complexe** *noun*
**complex**

le **complexe** *masc noun*
▷ see **complexe** *adj*
**complex**
**Ça me donne un complexe.** I'm getting a complex about it.

la **complication** *fem noun*
**complication**

le & la **complice** *masc & fem noun*
**accomplice**

le **compliment** *masc noun*
**compliment**
**faire des compliments à quelqu'un** to compliment somebody
**On m'a fait des compliments sur ma robe.** People complimented me on my dress.

**compliqué** *masc adjective*, **compliquée** *fem*
**complicated**
**Ça devient compliqué!** It's getting complicated!

**compliquer** *verb* **[1]**
**to complicate**

le **complot** *masc noun*
**plot**

le **comportement** *masc noun*
**behaviour**

**comporter** *verb* **[1]**
1 **to include** (*notes, bibliography*)
2 **to be made up of**
**Le mot de passe comporte des chiffres et des lettres.** The password is made up of numbers and letters.

se **comporter** *reflexive verb* Ⓔ
**to behave**
**Il se comporte comme un enfant.** He's behaving like a child.

**composé** *masc adjective*, **composée** *fem*
1 **être composé de** to be made up of
**L'équipe est composée de filles et de garçons.** The team is made up of boys and girls.
2 **une salade composée** a mixed salad

**composer** *verb* **[1]**
1 **to make up**
**les gaz qui composent l'air** the gases that make up the air
2 **to put together** (*a menu, a programme*)
**Eric a composé des pages web.** Eric has put together some web pages.
3 **to compose** (*music*)
4 **composer un numéro (de téléphone)** to dial a (telephone) number
**Composez le 00 44 pour le Royaume Uni.** Dial 00 44 for the United Kingdom.

se **composer** *reflexive verb* Ⓔ
**se composer de** to be made up of
**Le comité se compose de cinq personnes.** The committee is made up of five people.

le **compositeur** *masc noun*, la **compositrice** *fem*
**composer**

la **composition** *fem noun*
**composition**

**composter** *verb* **[1]**
**to punch** (*a ticket*)
**N'oubliez pas de composter votre billet.** Remember to punch your ticket. (*at the machines in train stations and on buses in France. It is an offence not to.*)

Ⓔ means the verb takes être to form the perfect

la **compote** *fem noun*
**stewed fruit**
- la **compote de pommes** apple puree

**compréhensible** *masc & fem adjective*
**understandable**

**compréhensif** *masc adjective*, **compréhensive** *fem*
**understanding** (*sympathetic*)

la **compréhension** *fem noun*
**comprehension**
un test de compréhension a comprehension test

♪ **comprendre** *verb* **[64]**
1 **to understand**
**Est-ce que tu comprends l'allemand?** Do you understand German?
**Je ne comprends pas la question.** I don't understand the question.
**Elle n'a rien compris.** She didn't understand anything.
**Je comprends ce que tu veux dire.** I know what you mean.
**J'ai mal compris.** I misunderstood.
2 **to include**
**Le prix du billet comprend une boisson.** A drink is included in the price of the ticket.

se **comprendre** *reflexive verb* ❷
1 **to understand each other**
**Ils se comprennent bien.** They understand each other well.
2 **to be understandable**
**Ça se comprend.** That's understandable.

♪ le **comprimé** *masc noun*
**tablet**

♪ **compris** *masc adjective*, **comprise** *fem*
1 **included**
**service compris** service included
**non compris** not included
**Les boissons ne sont pas comprises.** Drinks are not included.
2 **tout compris** all inclusive
**un séjour au ski tout compris** an all-inclusive ski holiday
**Ça fait 100 euros tout compris.** It's 100 euros all in.
3 **y compris** including
**tout le monde y compris les enfants** everybody including the children

le **compromis** *masc noun*
**compromise**

la **comptabilité** *fem noun*
1 **accountancy**
**Elle fait des études de comptabilité.** She's studying accountancy.
2 **accounting**
**Mon père travaille dans la comptabilité.** My father works in accounting.
3 **accounts** (*of a business*)

le & la **comptable** *masc & fem noun*
**accountant**

le **compte** *masc noun*
1 **count** (*a calculation*)
**faire le compte de quelque chose** to count up something (*things, people*)
**On a fait le compte de nos CD.** We counted up our CDs.
2 **amount** (*of money*)
**Le compte est bon.** That's the right amount.
3 **account** (*in a bank*)
**ouvrir un compte** to open an account
**J'ai cent livres sur mon compte.** I have a hundred pounds in my account.
4 **tenir compte de quelque chose** to take something into account
**Il faut tenir compte de ces conseils.** We need to take this advice into account.
5 **se rendre compte de quelque chose** to realize something
**Il ne se rend pas compte du danger.** He doesn't realize the danger.
**Je me suis rendu compte que j'avais oublié mes clés.** I realized that I had forgotten my keys.
6 **en fin de compte** in the end, all things considered
**En fin de compte, il avait raison.** In the end, he was right.
- le **compte bancaire** bank account
- le **compte d'épargne** savings account
- le **compte rendu** report

♪ **compter** *verb* **[1]**
1 **to count**
**Compte les visiteurs.** Count the visitors.
2 **to count** (*to be valid*)
**Est-ce que ça compte?** Does that count?
**Ça ne compte pas.** That doesn't count.
3 **compter faire quelque chose** to intend to do something
**Je compte acheter un lecteur DVD.** I intend to buy a DVD player.
4 **compter sur quelqu'un** to count on somebody
**Elle compte sur moi pour l'aider.** She's counting on me to help her.

le **compteur** *masc noun*
**meter** (*to measure gas, water, speed*)
- le **compteur de vitesse** speedometer

la **comptine** *fem noun*
**nursery rhyme**

le **comptoir** *masc noun*
1 **bar** (*in a cafe*)
2 **counter** (*in a shop*)

**concentré** *masc adjective*, **concentrée** *fem*
**concentrated**
• le **concentré de tomate** tomato puree

se **concentrer** *reflexive verb* Ⓔ **[1]**
**to concentrate**
**Concentre-toi.** Concentrate.
**Je me concentre sur le film.** I'm concentrating on the film.

la **conception** *fem noun*
**design** (*of a product*)

**concernant** *preposition*
1 **concerning**
**des informations concernant l'école** some information concerning the school
2 **as regards, with regard to**
**Concernant la sortie de demain, il n'y a pas de changements.** There are no changes with regard to tomorrow's trip.

**concerner** *verb* **[1]**
**to concern**
**Cela ne me concerne pas.** This doesn't concern me.
**En ce qui me concerne, je préfère rester ici.** As far as I'm concerned, I'd rather stay here.

♪ le **concert** *masc noun*
**concert**
**Je suis allé à un concert de reggae hier soir.** I went to a reggae concert last night.
**Le groupe est en concert le 25 juin à Bercy.** The band is playing at Bercy on June 25.
• le **concert de rock** rock concert

le & la **concessionnaire** *masc & fem noun*
**agent, dealer** (*for motor vehicles*)

♪ le & la **concierge** *masc & fem noun*
**caretaker**
**Je laisserai la clé chez la concierge.** I'll leave the key with the caretaker.

**conclure** *verb* **[25]**
**to conclude**

la **conclusion** *fem noun*
**conclusion**

le **concombre** *masc noun*
**cucumber**

le **concours** *masc noun*
1 **competition**
**un concours de gymnastique** a gymnastics competition
**Je l'ai gagné à un concours sur le net.** I won it in an Internet competition.
2 **competitive examination** (*for a school place, job*)
**Il faut passer un concours.** You have to sit an exam.

**concret** *masc adjective*, **concrète** *fem*
1 **concrete** (*real*)
2 **practical** (*person, mind*)

la **concurrence** *fem noun*
**competition** (*between people*)
**Il y a beaucoup de concurrence.** There's a lot of competition.

le **concurrent** *masc noun*, la **concurrente** *fem*
**competitor**

**condamner** *verb* **[1]**
**to sentence** (*a criminal*)

la **condition** *fem noun*
1 **condition**
**Le VTT est en bonne condition.** The mountain bike is in good condition
**Il est en bonne condition physique.** He's fit.
2 **à condition que** provided that
**Tu peux sortir à condition que tu me préviennes d'abord.** You can go out provided you tell me beforehand.
**à condition de** provided that
**Tu peux emprunter mon vélo à condition de me le rendre.** You can borrow my bike provided you give it back to me.
3 **à une condition** on one condition
**Il veut bien aider, mais à une condition ...** He's happy to help but on one condition ...

le **conditionnel** *masc noun*
**conditional tense**

**conditionner** *verb* **[1]**
1 **to package** (*products, goods*)
2 **to condition** (*a person, an animal*)

le **conducteur** *masc noun*, la **conductrice** *fem*
**driver**

♪ **conduire** *verb* **[26]**
1 **to drive** (*a vehicle*)
**J'apprends à conduire.** I'm learning to drive.
**Il m'a conduit à la gare.** He drove me to the station.
2 **to take** (*a person*)
**Je vous conduis à votre chambre.** I'll take you to your room.

se **conduire** *reflexive verb* Ⓔ
**to behave**
**Elle s'est bien conduite à l'enterrement.** She handled herself well at the funeral.

Ⓔ means the verb takes être to form the perfect

la **conduite** *fem noun*
1 **behaviour**
une mauvaise conduite bad behaviour
2 **driving**
En France, la conduite à droite est obligatoire. In France, you must drive on the right.
3 **riding** (*on motorbike*)
4 **driving test**
Demain, je passe la conduite. Tomorrow I'm taking my driving test.
• la **conduite accompagnée** driving (*accompanied by a qualified driver*)

la **confection** *fem noun*
**clothing industry**

la **conférence** *fem noun*
1 **lecture**
2 **conference**

se **confesser** *reflexive verb* Ⓔ **[1]**
**to go to confession**

la **confiance** *fem noun*
1 **trust**
faire confiance à quelqu'un to trust somebody
Fais-moi confiance! Trust me!
Je te fais confiance. I trust you.
Je n'ai pas trop confiance en lui. I don't really trust him.
2 **confidence** (*in your ability*)
la confiance en soi self-confidence
avoir confiance en soi to be self-confident
Elle a beaucoup de confiance en elle. She is very self-confident.

**confiant** *masc adjective*, **confiante** *fem*
**confident**

la **confidence** *fem noun*
**secret**
faire des confidences à quelqu'un to confide in somebody
Je lui ai fait des confidences. I confided in her.
Elle me fait souvent des confidences sur Paul. She often confides in me about Paul.

**confier** *verb* **[1]**
confier quelque chose à quelqu'un to entrust something to somebody
Je peux te confier mon portable? Can I leave my mobile with you?

se **confier** *reflexive verb* Ⓔ
se confier à quelqu'un to confide in somebody
Il s'est confié à son ami. He confided in his friend.

la **confirmation** *fem noun*
**confirmation**

**confirmer** *verb* **[1]**
**to confirm**

♪ la **confiserie** *fem noun*
1 **sweet shop**
2 **confectionery**

**confisquer** *verb* **[1]**
**to confiscate**
On a confisqué mon portable. My mobile was confiscated.

**confit** *masc adjective*, **confite** *fem*
les fruits confits crystallized fruits

♪ la **confiture** *fem noun*
**jam**
• la **confiture d'abricots** apricot jam
• la **confiture d'oranges** marmalade

le **conflit** *masc noun*
**conflict**

**confondre** *verb* **[69]**
1 confondre quelque chose to get something mixed up
confondre 'malle' et 'mâle' to confuse 'malle' with 'mâle'
Je confonds toujours les noms. I always get the names mixed up.
2 confondre quelqu'un avec quelqu'un to mistake somebody for somebody
On me confond souvent avec ma jumelle. People often mistake me for my twin sister.

le **confort** *masc noun*
**comfort**
un appartement tout confort a flat with all mod cons
aimer son confort to like your home comforts

♪ **confortable** *masc & fem adjective*
**comfortable**
Le canapé n'est pas confortable. The sofa is uncomfortable.

la **confrontation** *fem noun*
**confrontation**

**confus** *masc adjective*, **confuse** *fem*
1 **confused** (*muddled*)
2 **embarrassed**

la **confusion** *fem noun*
1 **confusion** (*disorder*)
2 **embarrassment**
être rouge de confusion to be blushing with embarrassment

♪ le **congé** *masc noun*
1 **holiday** (*from work*)
son jour de congé his/her day off
Elle est en congé aujourd'hui. She's on holiday today.
Mes parents prennent une semaine de ▸▸

congé. My parents are taking a week's holiday.
2 **leave**
**en congé de maladie** on sick leave

♪ le **congélateur** *masc noun*
**freezer**

**congeler** *verb* [45]
**to freeze**

la **congestion** *fem noun*
**congestion**

le **congrès** *masc noun*
**conference**

le **conifère** *masc noun*
**conifer**

le **conjoint** *masc noun*, la **conjointe** *fem*
**spouse** (*husband or wife*)

la **conjonctivite** *fem noun*
**conjunctivitis**

la **conjugaison** *fem noun*
**conjugation**

la **connaissance** *fem noun*
1 **knowledge**
**tes connaissances en français** your knowledge of French
2 **acquaintance**
**une nouvelle connaissance** a new acquaintance
**faire la connaissance de quelqu'un** to meet somebody
**J'ai fait sa connaissance à Paris.** I met him/her in Paris.
**Nous avons déjà fait connaissance.** We've already met.
3 **consciousness**
**perdre connaissance** to lose consciousness
**J'ai failli perdre connaissance.** I almost lost consciousness.

♪ **connaître** *verb* [27]
1 **to know**
**connaître quelqu'un** to know somebody
**Est-ce que tu connais Emma?** Do you know Emma?
**Je la connais depuis trois ans.** I've known her for three years.
**Je ne connais pas Londres.** I don't know London.
**C'est une actrice très connue.** She's a very well-known actor.
2 **to meet**
**Il a connu ma tante à Jersey.** He met my aunt in Jersey.

**WORD TIP** Compare with *savoir* which means to know *facts* and to know *how to do something*.

se **connaître** *reflexive verb* ⓔ
1 **to know each other**
**On se connaît.** We know each other.
2 **to meet**
**Nous nous sommes connus en vacances.** We met on holiday.
3 **s'y connaître en quelque chose** to know all about something
**Tu t'y connais en informatique?** Do you know anything about computers?
**Je ne m'y connais pas du tout.** I know absolutely nothing about them.

**connecter** *verb* [1]
**to connect**
**être connecté** to be on line (*on a computer*)

se **connecter** *reflexive verb* ⓔ
**to get on line** (*on a computer*)
**Je me connecte à Internet et j'écoute de la musique.** I get on line and listen to music.

la **connexion** *fem noun*
**connection**

**connu** *masc adjective*, **connue** *fem*
**well-known**
**une chanteuse très connue** a very well-known singer

**consacrer** *verb* [1]
**to devote**
**Elle consacre tout son temps libre à la lecture.** She devotes all her spare time to reading.

**consciemment** *adverb*
**consciously**

la **conscience** *fem noun*
1 **conscience**
**avoir mauvaise conscience** to have a guilty conscience
**J'ai un peu mauvaise conscience.** I have a slightly guilty conscience.
2 **avoir conscience de quelque chose** to be aware of something
**Il n'a pas conscience du danger.** He's not aware of the danger.

**consciencieux** *masc adjective*, **consciencieuse** *fem*
**conscientious**

**conscient** *masc adjective*, **consciente** *fem*
1 **aware**
**être conscient de quelque chose** to be aware of something
**Je suis consciente du problème.** I'm aware of the problem.
2 **conscious** (*lucid*)
**rester conscient** to remain conscious

le **conseil** *masc noun*

**1 advice**
un conseil a piece of advice
donner un conseil à quelqu'un to give someone a piece of advice
Je te donne un conseil. Ne dis rien. I'd advise you to say nothing.

**2** des conseils advice
suivre les conseils de quelqu'un to follow somebody's advice
Je n'ai pas suivi tes conseils. I didn't follow your advice.

**3 council** (*a gathering of people*)

- le **conseil de classe** staff meeting (*for staff teaching a particular class*)
- le **conseil de famille** family meeting (*to discuss a subject, problem*)

le **conseiller** *masc noun*, la **conseillère** *fem* ▷ see **conseiller** *verb*
**adviser**

- le **conseiller d'éducation** supervisor (*with a disciplinary role in French schools*)
- le **conseiller d'orientation** careers adviser

**conseiller** *verb* **[1]** ▷ see **conseiller** *noun*

**1 to advise**
conseiller à quelqu'un de faire quelque chose to advise somebody to do something
Je te conseille de parler au professeur. I advise you to talk to the teacher.

**2 to recommend**
Pouvez-vous me conseiller un dentiste? Could you recommend a dentist for me?

le **consentement** *masc noun*
**consent** (*agreement*)

**consentir** *verb* **[58]**
consentir à faire quelque chose to agree to do something
Ils consentent à partir demain. They agree to leave tomorrow.

la **conséquence** *fem noun*

**1 consequence**
**2** en conséquence consequently

**conséquent** *masc adjective*, **conséquente** *fem*

**1 substantial**
une somme d'argent conséquente a substantial amount of money

**2** par conséquent therefore, consequently

le **conservateur** *masc noun*, la **conservatrice** *fem*
▷ see **conservateur** *masc noun*

**1 conservative**
un parti politique conservateur a conservative political party

**2 curator** (*in a museum*)

le **conservateur** *masc noun*
▷ see **conservateur** *noun*
**(food) preservative**

la **conservation** *fem noun*

**1 conservation** (*of wildlife, heritage*)
**2** lait longue conservation long-life milk

la **conserve** *fem noun*

**1** les conserves canned food
les légumes en conserve canned vegetables.

**2 preserve** (*home-made jam, pickle*)
des conserves de tomates tomato preserves

**conserver** *verb* **[1]**
**to keep**
J'ai conservé tous mes vieux cahiers. I've kept all my old copybooks.
'À conserver au frais' 'Keep in a cool place'

se **conserver** *reflexive verb* ❷
**to keep**
Ce fromage se conserve bien. This cheese keeps well.

**considérable** *masc & fem adjective*
**considerable**

**considérablement** *adverb*
**considerably**

la **considération** *fem noun*
**consideration**

**considérer** *verb* **[24]**
**to consider**
considérer quelqu'un comme to consider somebody to be
Je l'ai considéré comme un frère. I considered him to be like a brother.

♂ la **consigne** *fem noun*

**1 left luggage office**
On a laissé les sacs à dos à la consigne. We left the rucksacks at the left luggage office.

**2 deposit** (*on a returnable bottle*)

**3 instructions**
les consignes à suivre en cas d'incendie what to do in the event of a fire

- la **consigne automatique** left-luggage lockers

**consistant** *masc adjective*, **consistante** *fem*
**substantial**
un repas consistant a substantial meal

**consister** *verb* **[1]**
consister en to consist of, to consist in
Le village consiste en quelques maisons et une église. The village consists of a few houses and a church.

la **console** *fem noun*
**games console**
**J'aime jouer sur une console.** I like playing on a games console.

le **consommateur** *masc noun*, la **consommatrice** *fem*
1 **consumer**
2 **customer** *(in a cafe)*

la **consommation** *fem noun*
1 **consumption** *(of fuel, electricity)*
2 **drink** *(at a cafe, bar)*
**regler les consommations** to pay for the drinks
**pousser à la consommation** to encourage people to drink more *(negative sense)*

**consommer** *verb* **[1]**
1 **to use** *(fuel)*
2 **to eat** *(meat, fish)*
**Ils ne consomment pas de viande.** They don't eat meat.
3 **to have a drink** *(in a cafe)*

la **consonne** *fem noun*
**consonant** *(any letter except a, e, i, o, u)*

la **conspiration** *fem noun*
**conspiracy**

**conspirer** *verb* **[1]**
**to conspire**, **to plot**

**constamment** *adverb*
**constantly**

**constant** *masc adjective*, **constante** *fem*
**constant**

**constater** *verb* **[1]**
**to notice**

**constipé** *masc adjective*, **constipée** *fem*
**constipated**

la **construction** *fem noun*
**construction**
**Le gymnase est en construction.** The sports hall is under construction.

**construire** *verb* **[26]**
**to build**
**Il adore construire des maquettes.** He loves building models.
**faire construire quelque chose** to have something built
**Ils font construire une maison de vacances.** They're having a holiday home built.

le **consul** *masc noun*
**consul**

le **consulat** *masc noun*
**consulate**

la **consultation** *fem noun*
1 **consultation** *(with a doctor, an expert)*
2 **surgery hours**
**Elle est actuellement en consultation.** She's with a patient at the moment.

**consulter** *verb* **[1]**
1 **to consult** *(a doctor, an expert)*
2 **to check**
**Allez consulter l'horaire.** Go and check the timetable.
3 **to hold surgery** *(doctors)*

le **contact** *masc noun*
1 **contact**
**prendre contact avec quelqu'un** to contact somebody
**Je prendrai contact avec Mélanie.** I'll contact Melanie.
**rester en contact avec quelqu'un** to keep in touch with somebody
**Je ne suis pas restée en contact avec elle.** I didn't keep in touch with her.
**Restons en contact.** Let's stay in touch.
2 **mettre le contact** to switch on the ignition
**couper le contact** to switch off the ignition

**contacter** *verb* **[1]**
**to contact**

**contagieux** *masc adjective*, **contagieuse** *fem*
**infectious**

la **contamination** *fem noun*
**contamination**

**contaminer** *verb* **[1]**
**to contaminate**

le **conte** *masc noun*
**tale**, **story**
• le **conte de fées** fairy tale

**contempler** *verb* **[1]**
1 **to look at** *(a picture)*
2 **to contemplate** *(a scene)*

**contemporain** *masc adjective*, **contemporaine** *fem*
**contemporary**

le **conteneur** *masc noun*
**container**

**contenir** *verb* **[77]**
1 **to contain**
**'Ne contient pas de sucre'** 'Does not contain sugar'
2 **to hold** *(a certain amount)*
**La boîte contient jusqu'à cent CD.** The box holds up to one hundred CDs.

ℓ **content** *masc adjective*, **contente** *fem*
**pleased**, **glad**, **happy**
**Il n'est pas content.** He's not happy.
**être content de quelque chose** to be pleased with something

Je suis très contente de ma nouvelle chambre. I'm very pleased with my new room.
Ils étaient contents de me voir. They were pleased to see me.

**contenter** *verb* **[1]**
**to satisfy**

se **contenter** *reflexive verb* ⓔ
se contenter de faire quelque chose to content yourself with doing something
Je dois me contenter de rester à la maison. I've got to content myself with staying at home.

le **contenu** *masc noun*
**contents**
Le contenu de la caisse pèse 20 kg. The contents of the crate weigh 20kg.

**contesté** *masc adjective*, **contestée** *fem*
**controversial**

**contester** *verb* **[1]**
1 **to challenge** (*an authority*)
2 **to question** (*a need, a decision*)

le **contexte** *masc noun*
**context**

le **continent** *masc noun*
**continent**

**continu** *masc adjective*, **continue** *fem*
**continuous**

la **continuation** *fem noun*
**continuation**

♪ **continuer** *verb* **[1]**
**to continue, to go on with**
Je peux continuer mon histoire? Can I go on with my story?
Continue! Go on!
continuer à faire, de faire quelque chose to go on doing something
Elle a continué à parler. She went on talking.
Je vais continuer de faire du dessin. I'm going to continue drawing.

le **contour** *masc noun*
**outline**

**contourner** *verb* **[1]**
**to go round** (*an obstacle*)

le **contraceptif** *masc noun*
**contraceptive**

la **contraception** *fem noun*
**contraception**

le **contractuel** *masc noun*, la **contractuelle** *fem*
**traffic warden**

la **contradiction** *fem noun*
**contradiction**

**contradictoire** *masc & fem adjective*
**contradictory**

**contraindre** *verb* **[31]**
**to force**

**contraire** *masc & fem adjective*
▷ see **contraire** *noun*
**opposite**
Il est allé dans le sens contraire. He went in the opposite direction.

le **contraire** *masc noun*
▷ see **contraire** *adj*
1 le contraire the opposite
C'est le contraire de ce que je pensais. It's the opposite of what I thought.
2 au contraire on the contrary

**contrairement** *adverb*
1 **contrary to**
Contrairement à ce qu'il nous a dit ... Contrary to what he told us ...
2 **unlike**
Contrairement à Raphaël, j'aime la techno. Unlike Raphaël, I like techno music.

**contrariant** *masc adjective*, **contrariante** *fem*
**annoying**

**contrarier** *verb* **[1]**
1 **to upset**
Je suis contrarié parce que j'ai perdu mon appareil photo. I'm upset because I've lost my camera.
2 **to annoy**
C'est ce qui me contrarie. That's what annoys me.

le **contraste** *masc noun*
**contrast**

**contraster** *verb* **[1]**
**to contrast**

le **contrat** *masc noun*
**contract**

la **contravention** *fem noun*
1 **parking ticket**
2 **speeding ticket**

♪ **contre** *preposition* ▷ see **contre** *adv, noun*
1 **against**
contre le mur against the wall
être contre quelque chose to be against something
Je suis tout à fait contre cette idée. I'm totally against this idea.
jouer contre quelqu'un to play against somebody ▸▸

Dimanche, on joue contre Valbonne. On Sunday we play against Valbonne.
2 **versus**
C'est Lyon contre Marseille. It's Lyons versus Marseilles.
3 échanger quelque chose contre to exchange something for (*something else*)
J'ai échangé ma console de jeux contre un lecteur DVD. I exchanged my games console for a DVD player.
4 par contre on the other hand
Il ne téléphone pas, par contre il envoie des textos. He doesn't phone. On the other hand, he sends text messages.

**contre** *adverb* ▷ see **contre** *noun, prep*
'Que penses-tu de l'idée?' — 'Je suis contre.' 'What do you think of the idea?' — 'I'm against it.'
Moi, je n'ai rien contre. I have nothing against it.

le **contre** *masc noun* ▷ see **contre** *adv, prep*
le pour et le contre the pros and cons (*points for and against*)

la **contrebande** *fem noun*
1 **smuggling**
2 **smuggled goods**

la **contrebasse** *fem noun*
**double bass**

**contredire** *verb* **[47]**
**to contradict**

la **contrefaçon** *fem noun*
1 **forgery** (*a signature, banknote, painting*)
Méfiez-vous des contrefaçons! Beware of forgeries!
2 **counterfeit** (*money*)
3 **pirated copy** (*of DVD, video*)

le **contremaître** *masc noun*
**foreman**

la **contremaîtresse** *fem noun*
**supervisor**

le **contreplaqué** *masc noun*
**plywood**

le & la **contribuable** *masc & fem noun*
**taxpayer**

**contribuer** *verb* **[1]**
contribuer à quelque chose to contribute to something
Natalie contribue au débat. Natalie contributes to the discussion.

la **contribution** *fem noun*
**contribution**
apporter sa contribution à quelque chose to make your contribution to something
Chacun peut apporter sa contribution à la tâche. Everyone can make their contribution to the task.

le **contrôle** *masc noun*
1 **control**
2 **test** (*at school*)
J'ai un contrôle de français lundi. I've got a French test on Monday.
- le **contrôle des billets** ticket inspection
- le **contrôle continu** continuous assessment
- le **contrôle d'identité** identity check
- le **contrôle des naissances** birth control
- le **contrôle des passeports** passport control
- le **contrôle de police** police check

**contrôler** *verb* **[1]**
1 **to control** (*a country, an organisation*)
2 **to check** (*a ticket, somebody's identity*)

le **contrôleur** *masc noun*, la **contrôleuse** *fem*
**ticket inspector**
- le **contrôleur aérien** air traffic controller

**controversé** *masc adjective*, **controversée** *fem*
**controversial**
une décision controversée a controversial decision

**convaincant** *masc adjective*, **convaincante** *fem*
**convincing**

**convaincre** *verb* **[79]**
1 **to convince**
Elle n'est pas convaincue. She's not convinced.
2 **to persuade**
Je les ai convaincus d'acheter un ordinateur. I persuaded them to buy a computer.

**convenable** *masc & fem adjective*
1 **suitable** (*place, clothes*)
2 **decent** (*salary, housing, meal*)
3 **proper** (*behaviour*)

**convenir** *verb* **[81]**
1 convenir à to suit, to be suitable for
Est-ce que dix heures te convient? Does ten o'clock suit you?
Ça me convient mieux. That suits me better.
Le film ne convient pas aux enfants. The film isn't suitable for children.
2 convenir de faire quelque chose to agree to do something
Nous avons convenu de travailler ensemble. We agreed to work together.

la **convention** *fem noun*
1 **agreement**
2 **convention**

la **conversation** *fem noun*
**conversation**
**faire de la conversation** to make conversation

**convertir** *verb* **[2]**
**to convert**

la **conviction** *fem noun*
**conviction**
**avoir la conviction que...** to be convinced that...
**J'ai la conviction que Leila va gagner.** I am convinced that Leila will win.

le & la **convive** *masc & fem noun*
**guest** *(at a meal, a party)*

**convivial** *masc adjective*, **conviviale** *fem*, **conviviaux** *masc pl*, **conviviales** *fem pl*
1 **friendly**
**une atmosphère conviviale** a friendly atmosphere
2 **user-friendly**
**un jeu d'ordinateur très convivial** a user-friendly computer game

le **convoi** *masc noun*
**convoy**
**'Convoi Exceptionnel'** 'Abnormal Load' *(on truck)*

**convoquer** *verb* **[1]**
1 **to invite** *(to a meeting)*
2 **to summon, to call**
**J'ai été convoqué au bureau du directeur.** I was called to the headmaster's office.

**coopératif** *masc adjective*, **coopérative** *fem*
**cooperative**

la **coopération** *fem noun*
**cooperation**

la **coopérative** *fem noun*
**cooperative** *(a business)*

**coopérer** *verb* **[24]**
**to cooperate**

les **coordonnées** *plural fem noun*
**address and telephone number**
**Je te donnerai mes coordonnées.** I'll give you my address and telephone number.

**coordonner** *verb* **[1]**
**to coordinate**

♂ le **copain** *masc noun*
1 **mate, friend**
**Je sors avec les copains.** I'm going out with my mates.
2 **boyfriend**
**Elle est partie en vacances avec son copain.** She's gone on holiday with her boyfriend.

la **copie** *fem noun*
1 **copy** *(of something)*
**Tu peux me faire une copie de ce logiciel?** Can you make me a copy of this software?
**Ce serait une copie pirate!** That would be a pirate copy!
2 **image** *(of somebody)*
**C'est la copie conforme de son père.** He's the spitting image of his father.
3 **paper** *(an exam script or written exercise)*
**Elle ramasse les copies déjà.** She's already collecting the papers.
**J'ai rendu une copie blanche.** I handed in a blank sheet of paper.
**Elle aura un tas de copies à corriger.** She's going to have a pile of marking to do.

**copier** *verb* **[1]**
**to copy**

**copier-coller** *verb* **[1]**
**to cut and paste**
**Copiez-collez la liste!** Cut and paste the list!

**copieux** *masc adjective*, **copieuse** *fem*
**hearty**
**un petit déjeuner copieux** a hearty breakfast

♂ la **copine** *fem noun*
1 **mate, friend** *(female)*
**Je sors avec les copines.** I'm going out with my mates.
2 **girlfriend**
**Il est parti en vacances avec sa copine.** He's gone on holiday with his girlfriend.

le **coq** *masc noun*
**cockerel**

la **coque** *fem noun*
1 **hull** *(of a boat)*
2 **shell** *(of a nut)*
3 **un œuf à la coque** a soft-boiled egg

le **coquelicot** *masc noun*
**poppy**

la **coqueluche** *fem noun*
**whooping-cough**

**coquet** *masc adjective*, **coquette** *fem*
1 **être coquet** to like to look good
**Paul est coquet.** Paul likes to look good.
**C'est une petite fille coquette.** She likes to look pretty. ▸▸

2 **pretty** (*village, house*)
un petit coin coquet de la Bretagne a pretty little spot in Brittany

le **coquetier** *masc noun*
**eggcup**

le **coquillage** *masc noun*
1 **shellfish**
À la mer, on mange des coquillages. At the seaside, we eat shellfish.
2 **seashell**
J'aime ramasser des coquillages. I like collecting seashells.

la **coquille** *fem noun*
1 **shell** (*of an egg, a nut, a shellfish*)
2 **misprint**
- la **coquille Saint-Jacques** scallop

**coquin** *masc adjective*, **coquine** *fem*
**cheeky** (*child*)

le **cor** *masc noun*
**horn** (*musical instrument*)

le **corail** *masc noun*, **coraux** *pl*
**coral**

le **Coran** *masc noun*
(*Religion*) le Coran the Koran

le **corbeau** *masc noun*, les **corbeaux** *pl*
**crow**

la **corbeille** *fem noun*
**basket**
- la **corbeille à papier** wastepaper basket
- la **corbeille à linge** linen basket

le **corbillard** *masc noun*
**hearse**

la **corde** *fem noun*
1 **rope**
2 **string** (*of a racket, bow, guitar*)
- la **corde à linge** clothes line
- la **corde à sauter** skipping rope

**cordial** *masc adjective*, **cordiale** *fem*, **cordiaux** *masc pl*, **cordiales** *fem pl*
**warm, cordial**

**cordialement** *adverb*
1 **warmly**
2 Cordialement à vous Yours sincerely (*formal ending to a letter*)

la **cordonnerie** *fem noun*
**shoe repair shop**

le **cordonnier** *masc noun*
**shoe repairer**
aller chez le cordonnier to go to the shoe repair shop

la **corne** *fem noun*
**horn**

la **cornemuse** *fem noun*
**bagpipes**
jouer de la cornemuse to play the bagpipes

le **cornet** *masc noun*
**cone** (*for ice cream*)
une glace en cornet an ice-cream cone
- le **cornet de frites** a box of chips (*in cardboard box*)

la **corniche** *fem noun*
1 **cornice** (*on a building*)
2 la (route de) corniche the coastal road

le **cornichon** *masc noun*
**gherkin**

la **Cornouailles** *fem noun*
**Cornwall**
en Cornouailles in Cornwall

**WORD TIP** Countries and regions in French take *le*, *la* or *les*.

le **corps** *masc noun*
**body**
le corps humain the human body

**correct** *masc adjective*, **correcte** *fem*
1 **correct**
La réponse est correcte. The answer is correct.
2 **reasonable**
à un prix correct at a reasonable price
Le repas était tout à fait correct. The meal was quite good.
3 **proper** (*behaviour*)

**correctement** *adverb*
1 **correctly**
Il faut remplir le formulaire correctement. You have to fill in the form correctly.
2 **properly**
savoir se conduire correctement to know how to behave properly
3 **reasonably well**
manger correctement to eat reasonably well

le **correcteur orthographique** *masc noun*
**spell checker**

la **correction** *fem noun*
1 **correction**
J'ai quelques corrections à faire dans ma dissertation. I've got some corrections to make to my essay.
2 **marking** (*of an exam paper*)
La prof n'a pas fini ses corrections. The teacher hasn't finished marking the papers.
3 **good manners**
manquer de correction to have no manners

4 **hiding**
recevoir une bonne correction to get a good hiding

♪ la **correspondance** *fem noun*
1 **letters, correspondence**
**Elle a fini sa correspondance pour aujourd'hui.** She's finished writing letters for today.
**Je fais signer mon carnet de correspondance tous les jours.** I get my school diary signed every day.
2 **mail order**
**acheter quelque chose par correspondance** to buy something by mail order
**Quelquefois, j'achète des vêtements par correspondance.** I sometimes buy clothes by mail order.
3 **connection** *(in air, rail travel)*
**les vols en correspondance** connecting flights
**J'ai raté ma correspondance.** I missed my connection.

♪ le **correspondant** *masc noun*, la **correspondante** *fem*
**penfriend**
**Ma correspondante habite à Nice.** My penfriend lives in Nice.

**correspondre** *verb* **[3]**
**to correspond**

la **corrida** *fem noun*
**bullfight**

**corriger** *verb* **[52]**
1 **to correct** *(a mistake)*
2 **to mark** *(school work, exam papers)*
**Elle est en train de corriger ses copies.** She's doing her marking.

**corse** *masc & fem adjective* ▷ see **Corse** *noun*
**Corsican**

**WORD TIP** Adjectives never have capitals in French, even for nationality or regional origin.

la **Corse** *fem noun* ▷ see **corse** *adj*
1 **Corsica**
**Nous allons en Corse.** We're going to Corsica.
2 le & la **Corsican** *(person from Corsica)*

**WORD TIP** Countries and regions in French take *le, la* or *les.*

la **corvée** *fem noun*
1 **chore**
2 **C'est la corvée!** It's a real drag!

les **cosmétiques** *plural masc noun*
**cosmetics**

**costaud** *masc adjective*, **costaude** *fem*
**strong, sturdy**

♪ le **costume** *masc noun*
1 **suit**
**Il a mis un costume cravate.** He wore a suit and tie.
2 **costume** *(for dressing up, in film)*
**Les costumes d'époque sont superbes.** The period costumes are superb.

la **côte** *fem noun*
1 **coast**
2 **hill, slope**
**Il faut monter la côte à vélo.** We have to cycle up the hill.
3 **rib**
**Elle s'est cassé une côte.** She broke a rib.
4 **chop**
**des côtes de porc grillées** grilled pork chops
5 **côte à côte** side by side
**Ils galopaient côte à côte.** They were cantering side by side.
- **la côte d'agneau** lamb chop
- **la Côte d'Azur** French Riviera
- **la côte de bœuf** rib of beef

le **côté** *masc noun*
1 **side**
**Mettez ça de l'autre côté.** Put that on the other side.
**de l'autre côté de** on the other side of
**Ils habitent de l'autre côté de la rue.** They live on the other side of the street.
2 **way** *(direction)*
**De quel côté vas-tu?** Which way are you going?
3 **d'un côté** on the one hand
**d'un autre côté** on the other hand
**D'un côté j'aime le ski ...** On the one hand I love skiing ...
**... d'un autre côté je déteste le froid.** ... on the other hand I hate the cold.
4 **à côté** nearby
**Mon frère habite à côté.** My brother lives nearby.
5 **à côté de** next to, beside
**Mets-toi à côté de Romain.** Go and sit beside Romain.
**Elle était assise à côté de moi.** She was sitting next to me.
6 **mettre quelque chose de côté** to put something aside
**J'ai mis de l'argent de côté pour m'acheter ce blouson.** I put some money aside to buy that jacket.

la **côtelette** *fem noun*
**chop**
- la **côtelette de porc** pork chop

la **cotisation** *fem noun*
**subscription** (*to an association, a club*)

♪le **coton** *masc noun*
1 **cotton**
un pull en coton a cotton jumper
2 **cotton wool**
du coton some cotton wool
**Passe-moi un coton.** Give me a piece of cotton wool.
3 (*informal*) **une question plutôt coton** a rather tricky question

♪le **cou** *masc noun*
**neck**

le **couchage** *masc noun*
**sleeping arrangements**
**une villa avec couchage pour douze** a villa sleeping twelve people
- le **sac de couchage** sleeping bag

**couchant** *masc adjective*
**le soleil couchant** the setting sun
**au soleil couchant** at sunset

la **couche** *fem noun*
1 **layer**
2 **coat** (*of paint*)
3 **nappy**
- la **couche d'ozone** ozone layer

♪**coucher** *verb* **[1]**
1 **to sleep**
**Nous allons toutes coucher chez Sophie.** We're all sleeping at Sophie's house.
2 **coucher un enfant** to put a child to bed
**J'arrive à 7 heures et je couche les enfants.** I arrive at 7 and I put the children to bed.

se **coucher** *reflexive verb* Ⓔ
1 **to go to bed**
**Elle s'est couchée tôt.** She went to bed early.
**Je ne me couche jamais avant dix heures.** I never go to bed before ten o'clock.
2 **to lie down**
**Il va se coucher dans son panier.** He goes and lies down in his basket.
- le **coucher de soleil** sunset

♪la **couchette** *fem noun*
**berth** (*on a train or boat*)
**une cabine avec deux couchettes** a two-berth cabin

le **coucou** *masc noun*
1 **cuckoo**
2 **cowslip**

♪le **coude** *masc noun*
**elbow**

**coudre** *verb* **[28]**
**to sew**
**J'ai cousu un bouton à ma chemise.** I sewed a button onto my shirt.

la **couette** *fem noun*
1 **duvet, continental quilt**
2 **des couettes** bunches (*hairstyle*)

**couler** *verb* **[1]**
1 **to flow**
2 **J'ai le nez qui coule.** I've got a runny nose.
**Il va faire couler un bain.** He's going to run a bath.
3 **to sink** (*a boat*)

♪la **couleur** *fem noun*
**colour**
**De quelle couleur sont ses yeux?** What colour are his eyes?
**une couleur peu commune** an unusual colour

la **couleuvre** *fem noun*
**grass snake**

les **coulisses** *plural fem noun*
**wings** (*in a theatre*)

le **couloir** *masc noun*
**corridor**
- le **couloir d'autobus** bus lane

♪le **coup** *masc noun*
1 **blow, knock**
**un coup à la tête** a blow to the head
**J'ai entendu un coup à la porte.** I heard a knock on the door.
**Il a reçu un coup dans l'estomac.** He was hit in the stomach.
2 **time**
**à tous les coups** every time
**Elle me dit ça à tous les coups.** She says that to me every time.
**Ce coup-ci, je ne le raterai pas.** This time I won't miss it.
**Il a eu son permis du premier coup.** He passed his driving test first time.
**Il a bu son verre d'un seul coup.** He emptied his glass in one go.
3 **tenir le coup** to hold out (*keep going*)
**Je ne tiens plus le coup!** I can't go on any longer!
4 (*informal*) **boire un coup** to have a drink
**On va boire un coup.** We're going to have a drink.
5 **donner un coup de balai** to sweep the floor
**Il donne un coup de balai à la cuisine.** He's sweeping the kitchen floor.

**6** sur le coup at first
Sur le coup, il a été très surpris. At first, he was very surprised.
**7** tout d'un coup, tout à coup all of a sudden
Tout d'un coup, l'alarme a sonné. All of a sudden, the bell rang.
- le **coup de chance** stroke of luck
- le **coup de feu** (gun)shot

le **coup de fil** *masc noun*
**phone call**
passer un coup de fil to make a phone call
passer un coup de fil à quelqu'un to phone somebody
Je te passe un coup de fil demain. I'll phone you tomorrow.

le **coup franc** *masc noun*
**free kick** (*in football*)

le **coup de main** *masc noun*
donner un coup de main à quelqu'un to give somebody a hand
Tu peux me donner un coup de main? Can you give me a hand?
Je te donne un coup de main pour ranger. I'll give you a hand tidying up.

le **coup d'œil** *masc noun*
**glance**
jeter un coup d'œil à quelque chose to have a quick look at something
Je peux jeter un coup d'œil à tes photos? Can I have a quick look at your pictures?

le **coup de peinture** *masc noun*
**lick of paint**

♪ le **coup de pied** *masc noun*
**kick**
donner un coup de pied à quelqu'un to kick somebody
Il lui a donné un coup de pied. He kicked her.

le **coup de poing** *masc noun*
**punch**
donner un coup de poing à quelqu'un to punch somebody

♪ le **coup de soleil** *masc noun*
attraper un coup de soleil to get sunburnt
J'ai attrapé un coup de soleil à la plage. I got sunburnt on the beach.

♪ le **coup de téléphone** *masc noun*
**phone call**
Je peux faire un coup de téléphone? Can I make a phone call?

le **coup de tonnerre** *masc noun*
**clap of thunder**
J'ai entendu des coups de tonnerre. I heard thunder.

le **coup de vent** *masc noun*
**gust of wind**

le & la **coupable** *masc & fem noun*
▷ see **coupable** *adj*
**culprit**

**coupable** *masc & fem adjective*
▷ see **coupable** *noun*
**guilty**

la **coupe** *fem noun*
**1** **cup** (*a trophy*)
**2** **haircut**
- la **Coupe du Monde** World Cup

♪ **couper** *verb* **[1]**
**1** **to cut**
J'ai coupé le tissu en trois morceaux. I've cut the material into three pieces.
**2** **to cut down**
Cet arbre est trop haut. Il faut le couper. The tree is too high. It must be cut down.
**3** **to turn off** (*the gas, the electricity*)
Ils ont coupé l'électricité pour faire des réparations. They turned off the electricity in order to carry out repairs.
**4** **to cut off** (*a telephone line*)
On a coupé le téléphone. The phone's been cut off.
**5** couper l'appétit à quelqu'un to spoil somebody's appetite
Ça m'a coupé l'appétit. It spoilt my appetite.
**6** couper la parole à quelqu'un to interrupt somebody
Excuse-moi, je t'ai coupé la parole. Sorry, I interrupted you.

se **couper** *reflexive verb* ❷
**1** **to cut yourself**
Elle s'est coupée. She cut herself.
Elle s'est coupé le doigt. She cut her finger.
**2** se faire couper les cheveux to have your hair cut
Elle s'est fait couper les cheveux. Have you had your hair cut?
Demain je me fais couper les cheveux. Tomorrow I'm having my hair cut.

le **couple** *masc noun*
**couple**

le **couplet** *masc noun*
**verse** (*of song*)

la **coupure** *fem noun*
**cut**
J'ai eu une coupure au menton. I got a cut on my chin.
- la **coupure de courant** power cut

♪ indicates key words

la **cour** *fem noun*
1 **school playground**
2 **inner courtyard** (*of an apartment block*)
3 **court** (*of a king, queen*)
4 **law court**

le **courage** *masc noun*
1 **courage**, **bravery**
2 **energy**
**avoir le courage de faire quelque chose** to have the energy to do something
**Je n'ai pas le courage de travailler tard.** I haven't got the energy to work late.
3 **Allons, courage!** Come on, don't lose heart!
**Bon courage!** Good luck!

**courageux** *masc adjective*, **courageuse** *fem*
**brave**

**couramment** *adverb*
**fluently**
**Il parle couramment le français.** He speaks fluent French.

**courant** *masc adjective*, **courante** *fem*
▷ see **courant** *noun*
1 **common** (*word, activity*)
**C'est devenu très courant chez les jeunes.** It's become very common among young people.
**C'est un problème courant.** It's a common problem.
2 **le français courant** standard French

le **courant** *masc noun* ▷ see **courant** *adj*
1 **current** (*in sea, river*)
2 **electricity**
**On a coupé le courant.** The electricity has been cut off.
**Il y a une panne de courant.** There's a power cut.
3 **être au courant de quelque chose** to know about something
**Est-ce que ta sœur est au courant?** Does your sister know?
**Elle n'est pas encore au courant.** She doesn't know yet.
**Tiens-moi au courant.** Keep me posted.
• le **courant d'air** draught

la **courbe** *fem noun*
**curve**

**courber** *verb* **[1]**
**to bend**

le **coureur** *masc noun*, la **coureuse** *fem*
**runner** (*athlete*)

la **courge** *fem noun*
**marrow** (*the vegetable*)

la **courgette** *fem noun*
**courgette**

**courir** *verb* **[29]**
1 **to run**
**Estelle court vite.** Estelle runs fast.
**J'ai traversé la rue en courant.** I ran across the street.
2 **courir un risque** to run a risk
**Nous courons un gros risque.** We're running a big risk.
**C'est un risque à courir.** It's a risk you have to take.

la **couronne** *fem noun*
**crown**

le **courriel** *masc noun*
**email**

le **courrier** *masc noun*
1 **post**, **mail**
**Je n'ai pas eu de courrier.** I didn't get any post.
**Le courrier est en retard ce matin.** The post is late this morning.
2 **letter**
**un courrier de confirmation** a letter of confirmation
• le **courrier électronique** electronic mail, email

le **cours** *masc noun*
1 **class**, **lesson**
**le cours de français** the French lesson
**Je vais suivre des cours d'espagnol.** I'm going to go to Spanish classes.
**Nous n'avons pas cours le mercredi après-midi.** We don't have lessons on Wednesday afternoons.
2 **course** (*of events*)
**au cours de** in the course of
**au cours de l'été** during the summer
• le **cours particulier** private lesson

la **course** *fem noun*
1 **race**
**On fait la course?** Shall we have a race?
2 **running** (*in athletics*)
3 **une course à faire** an errand
**J'ai une course à faire.** I've got to get something.

les **courses** *plural fem noun*
**shopping**
**faire des courses** to go shopping
**On fait les courses le samedi.** We do the shopping on Saturdays.
• les **courses hippiques** horse-racing

♪ **court** *masc adjective*, **courte** *fem*
▷ see **court** *noun*
**short**
une jupe très courte a very short skirt
Ce chemin-là est plus court. That way is shorter.
- le **court-circuit** short-circuit
- le **court-métrage** short film

♪ le **court** *masc noun* ▷ see **court** *adj*
**court** (*for tennis, squash, etc*)
- le **court de tennis** tennis court

**couru** *verb* ▷ **courir**

♪ le **cousin** *masc noun*, la **cousine** *fem*
**cousin**
mon cousin germain my first cousin
C'est ma cousine préférée. She's my favourite cousin.

le **coussin** *masc noun*
**cushion**

le **coût** *masc noun*
**cost**
- le **coût de la vie** cost of living

♪ le **couteau** *masc noun*, les **couteaux** *pl*
**knife**
- le **couteau à pain** breadknife

♪ **coûter** *verb* [1]
**to cost**
Ça coûte combien? How much is it?, How much does it cost?
Ça coûte dix euros. It's ten euros.
Cette voiture nous a coûté mille livres. This car cost us a thousand pounds.
coûte que coûte at all costs
coûter cher to be expensive
Est-ce que ça t'a coûté cher? Was it expensive?
Ça ne m'a pas coûté cher. It wasn't expensive.

la **coutume** *fem noun*
**custom**
une coutume très ancienne a very old custom

la **couture** *fem noun*
1 **dressmaking**
2 **sewing** (*activity, piece of sewing*)
faire de la couture to sew
J'ai de la couture à faire. I have some sewing to do.
3 **seam**
La couture se défait. The seam is coming apart.

le **couturier** *masc noun*
**fashion designer**

la **couturière** *fem noun*
**dressmaker**

le **couvent** *masc noun*
**convent**

le **couvercle** *masc noun*
1 **lid**
2 **screwtop**

♪ **couvert** *masc adjective*, **couverte** *fem*
▷ see **couvert** *noun*
1 **covered**
un marché couvert a covered market
la piscine couverte the indoor swimming-pool
2 couvert de quelque chose covered with something
Le sommet de la montagne est couvert de neige. The summit is covered with snow.
3 **overcast**, **cloudy**
Le temps est couvert. The weather is overcast.

♪ le **couvert** *masc noun* ▷ see **couvert** *adj*
1 **place setting**
un repas de 10 couverts a meal for 10
Mets le couvert, s'il te plaît. Lay the table please.
2 les couverts the cutlery
Il manque les couverts. The knives and forks aren't on the table.

♪ la **couverture** *fem noun*
1 **blanket**
2 **cover** (*of a book*)

le **couvre-lit** *masc*, les **couvre-lits** *pl*
**bedspread**

**couvrir** *verb* [30]
**to cover**

se **couvrir** *reflexive verb* ⓔ
1 **to wrap up**
Couvre-toi bien, il fait très froid! Wrap up well, it's freezing!
2 **to cloud over**
Ça s'est couvert dans l'après-midi. It clouded over in the afternoon.
3 se couvrir de quelque chose to be covered with something
L'arbre se couvre de fleurs. The tree is covered with blooms.
4 se couvrir de ridicule to make a laughing stock of yourself

le **crabe** *masc noun*
**crab**

**cracher** *verb* [1]
**to spit**

le **crachin** *masc noun*
**drizzle**

la **craie** *fem noun*
**chalk**

**craindre** *verb* **[31]**
**to be afraid of**

la **crainte** *fem noun*
**fear**

la **crampe** *fem noun*
**cramp**
une crampe à la jambe a cramp in your leg

le **crâne** *masc noun*
**skull**
J'ai mal au crâne. (*informal*) I've got a headache.

**crâner** *verb* **[1]**
(*informal*) **to show off**

le **crapaud** *masc noun*
**toad**

le **craquement** *masc noun*
**creak**

**craquer** *verb* **[1]**
1 **to split**
Ma jupe a craqué. My skirt split at the seams.
2 **to creak**
Le plancher craque. The floor creaks.
3 (*informal*) **to crack up** (*because of pressure*)
Je vais craquer! I'm going to crack up!
J'ai craqué, alors je l'ai acheté. I just couldn't resist it, so I bought it.
4 **craquer pour quelqu'un** to fall in love with somebody
Elle a craqué pour lui. She fell in love with him.

la **crasse** *fem noun*
**filth**

la **cravate** *fem noun*
**tie**

le **crawl** *masc noun*
**crawl**
Je sais bien nager le crawl. I can do the crawl well.

le **crayon** *masc noun*
**pencil**

**créatif** *masc adjective*, **créative** *fem*
**creative**

la **création** *fem noun*
**creation**

la **créativité** *fem noun*
**creativity**

la **crèche** *fem noun*
1 **crèche, day nursery**
2 **nativity scene** (*as a Christmas decoration*)

le **crédit** *masc noun*
1 **credit**
2 **funds**
- le **crédit immobilier** mortgage

**créer** *verb* **[32]**
**to create**

la **crème** *fem noun*
**cream**
- la **crème anglaise** custard
- la **crème caramel** crème caramel
- la **crème Chantilly** whipped cream
- la **crème solaire** sun cream

la **crémerie** *fem noun*
**shop selling dairy products**

**crémeux** *masc adjective*, **crémeuse** *fem*
**creamy**

la **crêpe** *fem noun*
**pancake**
Ils font sauter des crêpes. They're tossing pancakes.

la **crêperie** *masc noun*
**shop or stall selling** *crêpes*

le **crépon** *masc noun*
**crêpe paper**

le **crépuscule** *masc noun*
**twilight**

le **cresson** *masc noun*
**watercress**

**creuser** *verb* **[1]**
**to dig** (*a hole*)

se **creuser** *reflexive verb* Ⓔ
1 **to widen** (*of a gap, differences between people*)
2 (*informal*) **se creuser la cervelle** to rack your brains
Je me suis creusé la cervelle pour trouver une solution. I've been racking my brains to find a solution.

**creux** *masc adjective*, **creuse** *fem*
▷ see **creux** *noun*
1 **hollow**
2 **une assiette creuse** a soup plate

le **creux** *masc noun* ▷ see **creux** *adj*
1 **hollow, dip**
2 (*informal*) **J'ai un petit creux.** I've got the munchies.

la **crevaison** *fem noun*
**puncture**

**crevant** *masc adjective*, **crevante** *fem*
(*informal*) **exhausting**
Mélanie a eu une journée crevante. Mélanie's had an exhausting day.

Ⓔ means the verb takes être to form the perfect

♪ **crevé** *masc adjective*, **crevée** *fem*
1 **burst**
un pneu crevé a burst tyre, a puncture
2 (*informal*) **knackered**

**crever** *verb* **[50]**
1 **to burst** (*a bubble, balloon*)
**Le paquet de chips a crevé.** The bag of crisps burst open.
2 **to get a puncture**
**Nous avons crevé en route.** We got a puncture on the way.
3 (*informal*) **to die**
**Je crève de faim!** I'm starving!
**Elle crève de chaud.** She's boiling hot.

la **crevette** *fem noun*
**prawn**

le **cri** *masc noun*
**cry, shout**

**criard** *masc adjective*, **criarde** *fem*
**garish** (*colour*)

le **cric** *masc noun*
**(car) jack**

le **cricket** *masc noun*
**cricket**
**Il joue au cricket le dimanche.** He plays cricket on Sundays.

♪ **crier** *verb* **[1]**
**to shout**
**Ne crie pas!** Don't shout!
**Ils crient de joie.** They're shouting for joy.
**J'ai crié de douleur.** I cried out in pain.
**Ce n'est pas la peine de crier.** There's no point in shouting.

le **crime** *masc noun*
1 **crime**
2 **murder**

**criminel** *masc adjective*, **criminelle** *fem*
▷ see **criminel** *noun*
**criminal**
**des activités criminelles** criminal activities

le **criminel** *masc noun*, la **criminelle** *fem*
▷ see **criminel** *adj*
1 **criminal**
2 **murderer**

la **crinière** *fem noun*
**mane**

le **criquet** *masc noun*
**grasshopper**

la **crise** *fem noun*
1 **crisis**
2 **attack** (*of an illness*)
3 (*informal*) **fit** (*of rage*)
**piquer une crise** to have a fit
**Mes parents ont failli piquer une crise.** My parents nearly had a fit.
- la **crise cardiaque** heart attack
- la **crise de foie** indigestion
- la **crise de nerfs** hysterics

le **cristal** *masc noun*, les **cristaux** *pl*
**crystal**

le **critère** *masc noun*
**criterion** (*for assessing, judging*)
**les critères** criteria

**critique** *masc & fem adjective*
▷ see **critique** *noun*
**critical**

la **critique** *fem noun* ▷ see **critique** *adj*
**criticism**

**critiquer** *verb* **[1]**
**to criticize**

la **Croatie** *fem noun*
**Croatia**

le **croche-pied** *masc noun*, les **croche-pieds** *pl*
**faire un croche-pied à quelqu'un** (*informal*) to trip somebody up
**Quelqu'un m'a fait un croche-pied.** Someone tripped me up.

le **crochet** *masc noun*
1 **hook** (*for hanging up*)
2 **detour**
**J'ai fait un crochet par la boulangerie.** I made a detour via the bakery.
3 **crochet** (*way of knitting*)
**Elle se fait un poncho au crochet.** She's crocheting a poncho for herself.

le **crocodile** *masc noun*
**crocodile**

♪ **croire** *verb* **[33]**
**to think**
1 **croire que ...** to think that ...
**Je crois qu'il est parti.** I think he's left.
**Tu crois que c'est trop tard?** Do you think it's too late?
**Je ne crois pas.** I don't think so.
**Je crois que oui.** I think so.
2 **to believe**
**Je ne peux pas le croire.** I can't believe it.
3 **croire à quelque chose** to believe in something
**Kevin croit aux fantômes.** Kevin believes in ghosts.
**Je n'y crois pas.** I don't believe in them.
4 **croire en** to believe in
**Je n'en croyais pas mes yeux!** I couldn't believe my eyes!

**croiser** *verb* **[1]**
**1 to cross** (*arms, legs*)
**Elle s'asseoit les jambes croisées.** She's sitting with her legs crossed.
**Ne croisez pas les bras.** Don't fold your arms.
**Je croise les doigts!** I'll keep my fingers crossed!
**2 croiser quelqu'un** to bump into somebody
**J'ai croisé Odile devant la banque.** I bumped into Odile outside the bank.

se **croiser** *reflexive verb* ⓔ
**to cross**
**Nos lettres se sont croisées.** Our letters crossed in the post.
**Les routes se croisent dans un kilomètre.** The roads cross a kilometre from here.

la **croisière** *fem noun*
**cruise**

la **croissance** *fem noun*
**growth**

♪ le **croissant** *masc noun*
**croissant**
**On mange des croissants au beurre pour le petit déjeuner.** We have croissants for breakfast.
- le **croissant aux amandes** almond croissant

**croître** *verb* **[34]**
**to grow**

la **croix** *fem noun*
**cross**
- la **Croix-Rouge** Red Cross

**croquant** *masc adjective*, **croquante** *fem*
**crunchy**

le **croque-monsieur** *invariable masc noun*
**toasted ham and cheese sandwich**

le **croque-mort** *masc noun*
(*informal*) **undertaker**

**croquer** *verb* **[1]**
**to crunch** (*an apple*)
**un biscuit qui croque** a crunchy biscuit
**J'ai croqué dans la pomme.** I took a bite of the apple.

le **croquis** *masc noun*
**sketch** (*a drawing*)

la **crotte** *fem noun*
**dropping**
**des crottes de souris** mouse droppings
**des crottes de chien** dog mess

**croustillant** *masc adjective*, **croustillante** *fem*
**crispy**

la **croûte** *fem noun*
**1 crust** (*of bread*)
**2 rind** (*of cheese*)
**3 scab** (*on a cut*)

le **croûton** *masc noun*
**crouton** (*for salads, soups*)

la **croyance** *fem noun*
**belief**

**cru** *verb* ▷ **see cru** *adj* ▷ **croire**

**cru** *masc adjective*, **crue** *fem* ▷ **see cru** *verb*
**1 raw** (*meat, vegetables*)
**2 uncooked** (*pastry*)
**3 crude** (*language*)

la **cruauté** *fem noun*
**cruelty**
**Ils ont été traités avec beaucoup de cruauté.** They were cruelly treated.

la **cruche** *fem noun*
**(large) jug**

♪ les **crudités** *plural fem noun*
**raw vegetables and salads** (*served as a starter*)

**cruel** *masc adjective*, **cruelle** *fem*
**cruel**

le **crustacé** *masc noun*
**shellfish**

la **crypte** *fem noun*
**crypt**

**Cuba** *fem noun*
**Cuba**

**WORD TIP** Unlike other names of countries, *Cuba* does not take *le* or *la*.

**cubain** *masc adjective*, **cubaine** *fem* ▷ **see Cubain** *noun*
**Cuban**

le **Cubain** *masc noun*, la **Cubaine** *fem* ▷ **see cubain** *adj*
**Cuban**

**cube** *masc & fem adjective* ▷ **see cube** *noun*
**cubic**
**un mètre cube** a cubic metre

le **cube** *masc noun* ▷ **see cube** *adj*
**cube**

**cueillir** *verb* **[35]**
**to pick** (*fruit, flowers*)
**On va cueillir des fraises.** We're going strawberry-picking.

♪ la **cuiller** *fem noun*
**1 spoon**
**2 spoonful**

la **cuillère** *fem noun* ▷ **cuiller**



ⓔ means the verb takes être to form the perfect

la **cuillerée** *fem noun*
**spoonful**

♪ le **cuir** *masc noun*
**leather**
une blouson en cuir a leather jacket
- le **cuir chevelu** scalp

**cuire** *verb* **[36]**
1 **to cook**
Ça cuit. It's cooking.
faire cuire du riz to cook some rice
Faire cuire les légumes à la poêle. Fry the vegetables.
2 **to bake** (*bread*)
On cuit les pommes de terre au four. You bake the potatoes in the oven.
3 **to roast** (*meat*)

♪ la **cuisine** *fem noun*
1 **kitchen**
2 **cooking**
faire la cuisine to cook, to do the cooking
Mon père aime faire la cuisine. My dad likes cooking.
C'est moi qui fait la cuisine ce soir. I'm doing the cooking tonight.
3 **food**
Je n'aime pas la cuisine chinoise. I don't like Chinese food.

**cuisiner** *verb* **[1]**
**to cook**

le **cuisinier** *masc noun*, la **cuisinière** *fem*
▷ see **cuisinière** *fem noun*
**cook**
Elle est cuisinière. She's a cook.

♪ la **cuisinière** *fem noun*
▷ see **cuisinier** *noun*
**cooker**
- la **cuisinière à gaz** gas cooker
- la **cuisinière électrique** electric cooker

la **cuisse** *fem noun*
**thigh**
- la **cuisse de poulet** chicken leg

♪ **cuit** *masc adjective*, **cuite** *fem*
**cooked**
bien cuit well done (*meat*)
trop cuit overcooked
pas assez cuit undercooked

le **cuivre** *masc noun*
**copper**
- le **cuivre jaune** brass

le **culot** *masc noun*
(*informal*) **cheek**
Elle a du culot! She's got a nerve!

la **culotte** *fem noun*
une (petite) culotte knickers

la **culpabilité** *fem noun*
**guilt**

le **cultivateur** *masc*, la **cultivatrice** *fem*
**farmer**

**cultivé** *masc adjective*, **cultivée** *fem*
**cultivated** (*well educated*)

**cultiver** *verb* **[1]**
1 **to grow** (*plants, vegetables*)
2 **to cultivate** (*a field*)

se **cultiver** *reflexive verb* Ⓔ
**to broaden your general knowledge**

la **culture** *fem noun*
1 **farming**
une région de grande culture a large-scale farming region
2 **growing** (*of crops*)
la culture du blé wheat growing
de culture biologique organically produced
3 **crop** (*the harvest*)
4 **culture** (*of a society, country*)
5 **general knowledge**
Il a une bonne culture générale. His general knowledge is good.

**culturel** *masc adjective*, **culturelle** *fem*
**cultural**

le **culturisme** *masc noun*
**bodybuilding**

la **cure** *fem noun*
**course of treatment**

le **curé** *masc noun*
**parish priest**

le **cure-dent** *invariable masc noun*
**toothpick**

se **curer** *reflexive verb* Ⓔ **[1]**
se curer les ongles to clean your nails
Arrête de te curer le nez! Stop picking your nose!

**curieux** *masc adjective*, **curieuse** *fem*
1 **strange, odd**
par une curieuse coïncidence by a strange coincidence
C'est curieux, je pensais avoir éteint la télé. That's odd, I thought I switched the TV off.
2 **curious**
Je suis curieux de voir leur réaction. I'm curious to see their reaction.
Il est trop curieux. He's nosy.
Elle est curieuse d'apprendre tout sur les animaux. She's keen to learn everything about animals.

la **curiosité** *fem noun*
**curiosity**

French–English

♂ le **curseur** *masc noun*
**cursor**

la **cuve** *fem noun*
**vat, tank**

la **cuvette** *fem noun*
**bowl**
la cuvette des wc the toilet bowl

le **CV** *masc noun*
**CV, curriculum vitae**

le **cybercafé** *masc noun*
**Internet cafe**
Où est-ce qu'il y a un cybercafé? Where can I find an Internet cafe?

le & la **cybernaute** *masc & fem noun*
**web surfer, cybernaut**

**cyclable** *masc & fem adjective*
une piste cyclable a cycle track

le **cycle** *masc noun*
**cycle**

♂ le **cyclisme** *masc noun*
**cycling**
faire du cyclisme to go cycling

♂ le & la **cycliste** *masc & fem noun*
**cyclist**
un short de cycliste cycling shorts

le **cyclone** *masc noun*
**hurricane**

le **cygne** *masc noun*
**swan**

le **cylindre** *masc noun*
**cylinder**

**cynique** *masc & fem adjective*
**cynical**

le **cyprès** *masc noun*
**cypress (tree)**

# D d

**d'** *abbreviation: de*

**WORD TIP** *de* becomes *d'* before a word beginning with *a, e, i, o, u, y* or *silent h.* ▷ **de** *determiner, preposition*

♂ **d'abord** *adverb*
1 **first**
Je vais d'abord faire du café. I'll make some coffee first.
tout d'abord first of all
2 **at first**
J'ai d'abord cru qu'il était français. I thought at first that he was French.

♂ **d'accord** *adverb*
'D'accord!' 'All right!'
être d'accord to agree
Je suis d'accord avec toi. I agree with you.

le **daim** *masc noun*
1 **suede**
des chaussures en daim suede shoes
2 **fallow deer**

la **dalle** *fem noun*
1 **paving slab**
2 J'ai la dalle! I'm starving!

**daltonien** *masc adjective*, **daltonienne** *fem*
**colour-blind**

♂ la **dame** *fem noun* ▷ see **dames** *pl*
1 **lady**
la vieille dame the old lady
2 **queen** (*in cards, chess*)

les **dames** *plural fem noun* ▷ see **dame** *fem noun*
**draughts**
On joue aux dames? Shall we play draughts?

le **Danemark** *masc noun*
**Denmark**

le **danger** *masc noun*
**danger**

♂ **dangereux** *masc adjective*, **dangereuse** *fem*
1 **dangerous**
'Baignade dangereuse.' 'Caution: no swimming.'
2 **hazardous**

**danois** *masc adjective*, **danoise** *fem* ▷ see **Danois** *noun*
**Danish**

le **Danois** *masc noun*, la **Danoise** *fem* ▷ see **danois** *adj*
1 **Dane** (*person*)
2 le danois Danish (*the language*)



ⓔ means the verb takes être to form the perfect

**dans** *preposition*

1 **in**
**Mon sac est dans la voiture.** My bag is in the car.
**J'arrive dans cinq minutes.** I'm coming in five minutes.

2 **into**
**Il a sauté dans la piscine.** He jumped into the swimming pool.

3 **on** (*the plane, train*)
**Monte vite dans le train!** Quickly get on the train!

4 **out of**
**Prends 10 euros dans mon porte-monnaie!** Take 10 euros out of my purse!

la **danse** *fem noun*

1 **dance**
2 **dancing**
• la **danse classique** ballet

**danser** *verb* [1]
**to dance**

le **danseur** *masc noun*, la **danseuse** *fem*
**dancer**

**d'après** *preposition*

1 **according to**
**d'après le ministre** according to the minister
**d'après moi** in my opinion

2 **based on**
**un film d'après le roman de Flaubert** a film based on the novel by Flaubert

3 **in the style of**
**un tableau d'après Degas** a painting in the style of Degas

la **date** *fem noun*
**date**
**la date d'aujourd'hui** today's date
**date et lieu de naissance** date and place of birth
**À quelle date pars-tu en vacances?** When do you go on holiday?
• la **date limite de vente** sell-by date
• la **date de naissance** date of birth

la **datte** *fem noun*
**date** (*fruit*)

le **dauphin** *masc noun*
**dolphin**

**davantage** *adverb*

1 **more**
**Puis-je avoir davantage d'argent de poche?** May I have more pocket money?

2 **longer**
**Alice peut rester davantage.** Alice can stay longer.

**de, d', du, des** *preposition*
▷ see **de** *determiner*

1 (*For expressions such as* ***de bonne heure, de la part de, de rien, de temps en temps*** *etc, see the entries for* ***heure, part, rien, temps*** *etc.*)

2 **of**
**un verre de limonade** a glass of lemonade
**une boîte d'allumettes** a box of matches

3 (*talking about who something belongs to*)
**le nom du chat** the cat's name
**le père de Marie** Marie's father
**la porte de la classe** the classroom door

4 **from**
**Isabelle vient de Paris.** Isabelle comes from Paris.
**Elle rentre du bureau à six heures.** She comes home from the office at six o'clock.

5 **de ... à ...** from ... to ...
**de Paris à Lourdes** from Paris to Lourdes
**du 2 au 8 mai** from 2 to 8 May

6 **by**
**Ce livre est de Jeanne Bourrin.** This book is by Jeanne Bourrin.

7 **with**
**Daniel écrit de la main gauche.** Daniel writes with his left hand.

8 (*with quantity, duration, age, etc*)
**un livre de 250 pages** a 250-page book
**un stage de 2 mois** a 2-month training course
**Elle a une fille de 9 ans.** She has a nine-year-old daughter.

9 **made from**
**une table de bois** a wooden table

10 **about**
**Ils parlent de football.** They are talking about football.

**WORD TIP** *de* becomes *d'* before *a, e, i, o, u, y* or *silent h*; *de + le* becomes *du*; *de + les* becomes *des*.

**de, de la, du, des** *determiner* ▷ see **de** *prep*

1 **some**
**du chocolat** (some) chocolate
**Veux-tu de l'eau?** Would you like some water?

2 **any**
**Je n'ai pas de chocolat.** I don't have any chocolate.
**Il n'a pas de gants.** He hasn't got any gloves.
**Est-ce qu'il y a du lait?** Is there any milk?

3 **Nous avons des pommes et des oranges.** We have apples and oranges.
**Annie et Martin sont des amis à moi.** Annie and Martin are friends of mine. ▸▸

Elle ne boit jamais de vin. She never drinks wine.

**WORD TIP** *de + le becomes du; de + les becomes des.*

le **dé** *masc noun*
**dice**
Lance le dé! Throw the dice!

**déballer** *verb* **[1]**
**to unpack**

le **débardeur** *masc noun*
**vest top**

**débarquer** *verb* **[1]**
1 **to disembark** (*passengers*)
2 **to land** (*soldiers*)
3 (*informal*) **to turn up**
Elle a débarqué chez moi. She turned up at my place.

le **débarras** *masc noun*
1 **junk room**
2 (*informal*) 'Annick est partie.' — 'Bon débarras!' 'Annick has gone.' — 'Good riddance!'

**débarrasser** *verb* **[1]**
1 **to clear** (*the table*)
2 **to clear out** (*a room*)

se **débarrasser** *reflexive verb* Ⓔ
se débarrasser de quelque chose to get rid of something

le **débat** *masc noun*
**debate**

**débattre** *verb* **[21]**
1 **to discuss** (*an issue*)
2 **to negotiate** (*a price*)
'Prix à débattre' 'Price negotiable'

se **débattre** *reflexive verb* Ⓔ
**to struggle** (*in a fight*)

**débile** *masc & fem adjective*
(*informal*)
1 **stupid**
Tu es débile ou quoi? Are you stupid or something?
2 **crazy**
C'est complètement débile! That's completely crazy!

**déblayer** *verb* **[59]**
**to clear** (*a road*)

**débordé** *masc adjective*, **débordée** *fem*
être débordé to be up to your eyes in work

le **débordement** *masc noun*
1 **overflowing** (*of a river*)
2 **flood** (*of insults*)

**déborder** *verb* **[1]**
1 **to overflow** (*river*)
2 déborder de quelque chose to overflow with something
Ses yeux débordaient de larmes. His eyes were overflowing with tears.

le **débouché** *masc noun*
**job opportunity**

**déboucher** *verb* **[1]**
1 **to uncork** (*a bottle*)
2 **to unblock** (*a drain, a pipe*)
3 déboucher sur quelque chose to lead onto something (*a street*)

**déboussoler** *verb* **[1]**
(*informal*) **to confuse**

**debout** *adverb*
1 **standing**
les personnes debout the people standing
Je suis resté debout toute la journée. I've been on my feet all day.
être, se tenir debout to stand
Tiens-toi debout près de la porte! Stand next to the door!
se mettre debout to stand up
Tout le monde s'est mis debout. Everybody stood up.
2 **upright**
Mets le verre debout! Stand the glass upright!
3 **up** (*out of bed*)
Je suis debout à six heures tous les jours. I'm up at six every day.

**débrancher** *verb* **[1]**
1 **to unplug** (*an iron, a television set*)
2 **to disconnect** (*the electricity, gas, water, telephone*)

le **débris** *masc noun*
1 **fragment** (*of glass*)
2 **piece of wreckage**
dans les débris de sa voiture in the wreckage of her car

se **débrouiller** *reflexive verb* Ⓔ **[1]**
**to manage**
Je peux me débrouiller tout seul. I can manage by myself.
Je me débrouille en français. I can get by in French.
Débrouille-toi! Get on with it!

le **début** *masc noun*
**beginning**, **start**
le début des vacances the beginning of the holidays
au début to start with, at first
Au début, je n'aimais pas la prof. At first I didn't like the teacher.
du début jusqu'à la fin from start to finish



Ⓔ means the verb takes être to form the perfect

On commencera début mars. We'll start at the beginning of March.

le **débutant** *masc noun*, la **débutante** *fem*
**beginner**

**débuter** *verb* **[1]**
**to begin, to start**

**décaféiné** *masc adjective*, **décaféinée** *fem*
**decaffeinated**

le **décalage horaire** *masc noun*
**time difference** (*between time zones*)
À son retour, il a mal supporté le décalage horaire. When he came back, he suffered from jet-lag.

**décaler** *verb* **[1]**
**to move** (*forward or back*)

**décapotable** *masc & fem adjective*
une voiture décapotable a convertible (car)

le **décapsuleur** *masc noun*
**bottle opener**

**décéder** *verb* **[24]**
**to die**
Jean-Paul est décédé en novembre. Jean-Paul died in November.
Marie-Thérèse est décédée en novembre. Marie-Thérèse died in November.

♪ **décembre** *masc noun*
**December**
en décembre, au mois de décembre in December

**WORD TIP** Months of the year and days of the week start with small letters in French.

la **décennie** *fem noun*
**decade**

**décent** *masc adjective*, **décente** *fem*
**decent**

la **déception** *fem noun*
**disappointment**

le **décès** *masc noun*
**death**

**décevant** *masc adjective*, **décevante** *fem*
**disappointing**

**décevoir** *verb* **[66]**
**to disappoint**

**WORD TIP** *Décevoir* does not mean *deceive* in English; for the meaning of *deceive* ▷ **tromper**.

la **décharge** *fem noun*
**(public) rubbish tip**

**décharger** *verb* **[52]**
**to unload**

se **déchausser** *reflexive verb* ❷ **[1]**
**to take your shoes off**

les **déchets** *plural masc noun*
**waste**
- les **déchets nucléaires** nuclear waste

**déchiffrer** *verb* **[1]**
**to decipher**

**déchirant** *masc adjective*, **déchirante** *fem*
**heart-rending** (*cry, story*)

**déchirer** *verb* **[1]**
1 **to tear**
2 **to tear up** (*a cheque, a piece of work*)
3 **to tear out** (*pages*)
4 **to tear off** (*wrapping paper*)

se **déchirer** *reflexive verb* ❷
**to tear, to rip**
Morgane s'est déchiré un muscle en tombant. Morgane tore a muscle when she fell.

**décidé** *masc adjective*, **décidée** *fem*
1 **determined** (*person*)
Laurie est décidée à gagner. Laurie is determined to win.
2 **settled** (*decision*)
C'est décidé, je l'achète. It's settled, I'm buying it.

**décidément** *adverb*
**really**
Décidément, il n'a pas de chance! He really is unlucky!

♪ **décider** *verb* **[1]**
**to decide**
décider de faire quelque chose to decide to do something

se **décider** *reflexive verb* ❷
**to make up your mind**
se décider à faire quelque chose to decide to do something

la **décimale** *fem noun*
**decimal**

la **décision** *fem noun*
**decision**
Il est temps de prendre une décision. It's time to make a decision.

la **déclaration** *fem noun*
1 **statement** (*to the press*)
2 **declaration** (*of love, war*)

**déclarer** *verb* **[1]**
**to declare**

**déclencher** *verb* **[1]**
1 **to cause** (*an explosion, a reaction*)
2 **to set off** (*an alarm*)

le **déclic** *masc noun*
**click** (*of a camera*)

**décliner** *verb* **[1]**
**to decline** *(an invitation)*

le **décollage** *masc noun*
**take-off** *(of a plane)*

**décoller** *verb* **[1]**
1 **to take off** *(planes)*
2 **to peel off** *(stickers)*

se **décoller** *reflexive verb* ⓔ
**to peel off**

le **décolleté** *masc noun*
**neckline** *(of a sweater, a dress)*

se **décolorer** *reflexive verb* ⓔ **[1]**
**to bleach** *(hair, material)*
**se faire décolorer les cheveux** to have your hair bleached
**Magali s'est fait décolorer les cheveux.** Magali had her hair bleached.

les **décombres** *plural masc noun*
**rubble**

**décongeler** *verb* **[45]**
**to defrost**

**déconseillé** *masc adjective*, **déconseillée** *fem*
**not recommended**
**'Déconseillé pour les enfants'** 'Not recommended for children'

**déconseiller** *verb* **[1]**
**déconseiller à quelqu'un de faire quelque chose** to advise somebody not to do something

**décontracté** *masc adjective*, **décontractée** *fem*
1 **relaxed** *(person, body)*
2 **laid-back** *(person, attitude)*
3 **casual** *(clothes)*

se **décontracter** *reflexive verb* ⓔ **[1]**
**to relax**
**Essaie de te décontracter!** Try to relax!

le **décor** *masc noun*
1 **decor** *(of a room)*
2 **setting** *(the surroundings outside)*
3 **set** *(at the theatre)*

le **décorateur** *masc noun*, la **décoratrice** *fem*
**interior designer**

**décoratif** *masc adjective*, **décorative** *fem*
1 **ornamental**
2 **decorative**

la **décoration** *fem noun*
1 **decoration**
2 **interior design**

**décorer** *verb* **[1]**
**to decorate**

**découper** *verb* **[1]**
1 **to cut out** *(a picture, an article)*
2 **to carve** *(meat)*

**décourager** *verb* **[52]**
**to discourage**

la **découverte** *fem noun*
**discovery**

**découvrir** *verb* **[30]**
**to discover**

§ **décrire** *verb* **[38]**
**to describe**

§ **décrocher** *verb* **[1]**
1 **to pick up the receiver** *(of a telephone)*
2 **to take down** *(a picture, curtains)*

§ **déçu** *masc adjective*, **déçue** *fem*
**disappointed**
**Nous sommes tous très déçus.** We're all very disappointed.

**dedans** *adverb*
**inside**

**déduire** *verb* **[26]**
1 **to deduce** *(a consequence)*
2 **to deduct** *(a sum of money)*
**Tu peux déduire 10 euros du prix total.** You may deduct 10 euros from the total price.

la **déesse** *fem noun*
**goddess**

**défaire** *verb* **[10]**
1 **to undo** *(a tie, a belt, a parcel)*
2 **to untie** *(laces, shoes)*
3 **to unpack** *(a suitcase)*

la **défaite** *fem noun*
**defeat**

le **défaut** *masc noun*
1 **fault** *(of a person)*
2 **defect** *(in a product)*

**défavorisé** *masc adjective*, **défavorisée** *fem*
**underprivileged**

**défectueux** *masc adjective*, **défectueuse** *fem*
**faulty**
**une prise défectueuse** a faulty plug

**défendre** *verb* **[3]**
1 **to forbid**
**défendre à quelqu'un de faire quelque chose** to forbid somebody to do something
2 **to defend**



ⓔ means the verb takes être to form the perfect

se **défendre** *reflexive verb* ⓔ
**to defend oneself**
**Ne te laisse pas insulter, défends-toi!** Don't let them abuse you, stand up for yourself!

♪ **défendu** *masc adjective*, **défendue** *fem*
**forbidden**
**Il est défendu de boire de l'alcool.** It is forbidden to drink alcohol.

♪ la **défense** *fem noun*
1 **defence** (*against an aggressor*)
2 **protection**
**la défense de l'environnement** the protection of the environment
3 (*in signs*) **'Défense de fumer'** 'No smoking' **'Défense d'entrer'** 'No entry'
4 **tusk** (*of an elephant*)

le **défi** *masc noun*
**challenge**
**lancer un défi à quelqu'un** to challenge somebody

le **défilé** *masc noun*
1 **parade** (*in a fête, a carnival*)
2 **march** (*of demonstrators*)
3 **stream** (*of visitors*)
• le **défilé de mode** fashion show

**défiler** *verb* **[1]**
1 **to parade**
2 **to march** (*demonstrators, soldiers*)
3 **to scroll down** (*the text on a computer screen*)

**définir** *verb* **[2]**
**to define**

la **définition** *fem noun*
**definition**

**définitivement** *adverb*
**for good**
**Vanessa est définitivement éliminée.** Vanessa is eliminated for good.

**défoncer** *verb* **[61]**
**to smash in** (*a door*)

**déformer** *verb* **[1]**
1 **to bend out of shape** (*a piece of metal*)
2 **to stretch** (*a garment, shoes*)
3 **to distort** (*a picture*)

se **défouler** *reflexive verb* ⓔ **[1]**
1 **to let off steam**
**Il se défoule sur son vélo.** He lets off steam riding his bike.
2 **to unwind**
**La télé, ça me défoule.** The TV helps me to unwind.
3 **se défouler sur quelqu'un** to take it out on somebody
**Il se défoule toujours sur sa petite sœur.** He always takes it out on his little sister.

**dégagé** *masc adjective*, **dégagée** *fem*
1 **clear** (*sky, view, way*)
2 **casual** (*attitude*)

**dégager** *verb* **[52]**
1 **to free** (*something trapped*)
2 **to clear** (*a desk, the road, the way*)

les **dégâts** *plural masc noun*
**damage**
**faire des dégâts** to cause damage

**dégeler** *verb* **[45]**
**to thaw**

**dégénérer** *verb* **[24]**
1 **to degenerate**
2 **to get out of hand**

**dégivrer** *verb* **[1]**
1 **to defrost** (*a fridge*)
2 **to de-ice** (*a windscreen, a lock*)

**dégonfler** *verb* **[1]**
**to let down** (*a tyre, an airbed*)

**dégouliner** *verb* **[1]**
**to trickle**

**dégourdi** *masc adjective*, **dégourdie** *fem*
**smart**
**C'est un gamin dégourdi.** He's a smart kid.

♪ **dégoûtant** *masc adjective*, **dégoûtante** *fem* ▷ see **dégoûté** *adj*
1 **filthy**
**Tes mains sont dégoûtantes.** Your hands are filthy.
2 **disgusting**
**Cette histoire est dégoûtante.** This story is disgusting.

**dégoûté** *masc adjective*, **dégoûtée** *fem* ▷ see **dégoûtant** *adj*
**disgusted**
**être dégoûté de quelque chose** to have had enough of something

**dégoûter** *verb* **[1]**
1 **to disgust**
2 **dégoûter quelqu'un de quelque chose** to put somebody off something
**Ça m'a dégoûté du poisson.** That put me off fish.

**dégrader** *verb* **[1]**
**to damage** (*a site, a monument*)

se **dégrader** *reflexive verb* ⓔ
**to deteriorate**

**dégraisser** *verb* **[1]**
**to dry-clean**

♪ le **degré** *masc noun*
**degree**
**Il fait 20 degrés aujourd'hui.** It's 20 degrees today.

**dégringoler** *verb* **[1]**
(*informal*) **to tumble down**

**déguisé** *masc adjective*, **déguisée** *fem*
1 **in fancy dress**
2 **Valentin est déguisé en punk.** Valentin is dressed up as a punk.
**une soirée déguisée** a fancy-dress party
3 **disguised** (*in order to deceive*)

**déguiser** *verb* **[1]**
**to disguise**

se **déguiser** *reflexive verb* Ⓔ
**to dress up**
**Il s'est déguisé en Père Noël.** He dressed up as Father Christmas.

la **dégustation** *fem noun*
**tasting**

**déguster** *verb* **[1]**
1 **to savour, to enjoy**
2 **to taste** (*wine, cheese*)

**dehors** *adverb*
1 **outside**
**Je t'attends dehors.** I'll wait for you outside.
2 **en dehors de** apart from
**En dehors de la salade, tout est prêt.** Everything's ready apart from the salad.
3 **Dehors!** Get out!

**déjà** *adverb*
1 **already**
**Tu pars déjà?** Are you leaving already?
**Il a déjà fini ses devoirs.** He's already finished his homework.
2 **before**
**Tu es déjà venu ici?** Have you been here before?
**Je t'ai déjà dit de ne pas faire ça!** I told you before not to do that!

le **déjeuner** *masc noun*
▷ see **déjeuner** *verb*
**lunch**
**la pause du déjeuner** lunch break
**C'est l'heure du déjeuner.** It's lunchtime.
**Après déjeuner, je vais à la piscine.** After lunch I'm going swimming.

**déjeuner** *verb* **[1]** ▷ see **déjeuner** *noun*
1 **to have lunch**
**Nous déjeunons à une heure.** We have lunch at one o'clock.
2 **to have breakfast**

**délacer** *verb* **[61]**
**to undo** (*shoes*)

le **délai** *masc noun*
1 **period of time allowed**
**Tu as un délai de deux jours pour me rendre mon vélo.** You have two days to return my bicycle.
2 **wait**
**dans les plus brefs délais** as soon as possible
**Il y a deux semaines de délai pour la livraison d'un ordinateur.** There is a two-week wait for the delivery of a computer.
3 **extra time**
**J'ai besoin d'un délai, je ne peux pas payer maintenant.** I need extra time, I can't pay now.

**WORD TIP** *délai* does not mean *delay* in English; for the meaning of *delay* ▷ **retard**

se **délecter** *reflexive verb* Ⓔ **[1]**
**se délecter de quelque chose** to enjoy something thoroughly

le **délégué** *masc noun*, la **déléguée** *fem*
**delegate** (*at a conference*)
• le **délégué de classe** student representative

**délibéré** *masc adjective*, **délibérée** *fem*
**deliberate**

**délibérer** *verb* **[24]**
**to discuss**

**délicat** *masc adjective*, **délicate** *fem*
1 **delicate**
2 **thoughtful** (*person, gesture*)

le **délice** *masc noun*, les **délices** *pl*
**delight**
**C'est un vrai délice!** It's absolutely delicious!

**délicieux** *masc adjective*, **délicieuse** *fem*
**delicious**

la **délinquance** *fem noun*
**crime** (*illegal activities*)

le **délinquant** *masc noun*, la **délinquante** *fem*
**offender**

**délirant** *masc adjective*, **délirante** *fem*
(*informal*) **crazy**

le **délire** *masc noun*
1 (*informal*) **madness**
2 **frenzy**

**délirer** *verb* **[1]**
(*informal*) **to be crazy**

le **délit** *masc noun*
**crime, criminal offence**

**délivrer** *verb* **[1]**
**to free**

**déloyal** *masc adjective*, **déloyale** *fem*, **déloyaux** *masc pl*, **déloyales** *fem pl*
**disloyal**

le **deltaplane** *masc noun*
**hang-glider**
faire du deltaplane to go hang-gliding

le **déluge** *masc noun*
**downpour**

♪ **demain** *adverb*
**tomorrow**
**À demain!** See you tomorrow!
**Elle arrive après-demain.** She's coming the day after tomorrow.
**Nous partirons demain en huit.** We'll be leaving a week tomorrow.

la **demande** *fem noun*
1 **request**
**à la demande générale** by popular request
2 **demand**
**l'offre et la demande** supply and demand
3 **application**
**J'ai fait une demande d'inscription à l'université de Bristol.** I've applied for a place at Bristol university.
**'Demandes d'emplois'** 'Situations wanted'

**demandé** *masc adjective*, **demandée** *fem*
**très demandé** very popular

♪ **demander** *verb* **[1]**
1 **to ask for**
**Il faut demander de l'aide.** We need to ask for help.
**demander quelque chose à quelqu'un** to ask somebody (for) something
**Demande de l'argent à ton père!** Ask your father for some money!
**Il m'a demandé ton adresse.** He asked me for your address.
2 **demander à quelqu'un de faire quelque chose** to ask somebody to do something
**Elle m'a demandé de mettre la table.** She asked me to lay the table.

se **demander** *reflexive verb* ⓔ
**to wonder**
**Je me demande ce qu'elle est en train de faire.** I wonder what she's doing.

le **demandeur** *masc noun*, la **demandeuse** *fem*
**applicant**
- le **demandeur d'asile** asylum-seeker
- le **demandeur d'emploi** job-seeker

la **démangeaison** *fem noun*
**itch**

**démanger** *verb* **[52]**
**Ça me démange.** It's itchy.

le **démaquillant** *masc noun*
**make-up remover**

la **démarche** *fem noun*
1 **walk** (*the way you walk*)
**Il a une démarche bizarre.** He has a funny walk.
2 **step**
**faire des démarches** to take steps
**Nous avons fait des démarches pour obtenir une classe plus grande.** We took steps to obtain a larger classroom.

**démarrer** *verb* **[1]**
1 **to start**
**La voiture ne veut pas démarrer.** The car won't start.
2 **to drive off** (*driver*)
3 **to start up** (*a project*)

le **démarreur** *masc noun*
**starter** (*in a car*)

**démêler** *verb* **[1]**
**to untangle**

le **déménagement** *masc noun*
1 **house move**
**C'est mon premier déménagement.** It's my first house move.
2 **removal**
**une société de déménagement** a removals firm

**déménager** *verb* **[52]**
1 **to move (house)**
**Bernard déménage à Rennes.** Bernard is moving to Rennes.
2 **to move out**
**Nous déménageons la semaine prochaine.** We're moving out next week.

le **déménageur** *masc noun*, la **déménageuse** *fem*
**removal man, removal woman**

la **déménageuse** *fem noun*
**removal van**

**dément** *masc adjective*, **démente** *fem*
**crazy**

**démentir** *verb* **[53]**
**to deny** (*an accusation, information*)

**démesuré** *masc adjective*, **démesurée** *fem*
**excessive**

la **demeure** *fem noun*
**residence**

**demeurer** *verb* **[1]**
**to reside**
**Hugo demeure 9 avenue Manet.** Hugo resides at 9 avenue Manet.

French-English

𝄞 **demi** *masc adjective*, **demie** *fem*
▷ see **demi** *masc noun*, **demie** *fem noun*
1 **half**
2 une demi-pomme half an apple
une demi-bouteille half a bottle
3 et demi, et demie and a half
un mètre et demi one and a half metres
deux millions et demi de personnes two and a half million people
une heure et demie an hour and a half
Elle a trois ans et demi. She's three and a half.
Il est trois heures et demie It's half past three.
• le **demi-frère** half-brother
• la **demi-sœur** half-sister

𝄞 le **demi** *masc noun*
▷ see **demi** *adj*, **demie** *fem noun*
**half** *(litre, of beer)*

le **demi-cercle** *masc noun*
**semicircle**

la **demi-douzaine** *fem noun*
**half a dozen**

la **demie** *fem noun*
▷ see **demi** *adj, masc noun*
**half-hour**
à la demie on the half-hour

**demi-écrémé** *masc adjective*, **demi-écrémée** *fem*
**semi-skimmed**

le **demi-frère** *masc noun*
**half brother**

la **demi-finale** *fem noun*
**semifinal**

la **demi-heure** *fem noun*
une demi-heure half an hour
toutes les demi-heures every half hour

la **demi-journée** *fem noun*
**half a day**

le **demi-litre** *masc noun*
**half a litre**

la **demi-pension** *fem noun*
**half board**

le & la **demi-pensionnaire** *masc & fem noun*
**pupil who eats school lunches**

**demi-sel** *invariable adjective*
**slightly salted**

la **demi-sœur** *fem noun*
**half-sister**

la **démission** *fem noun*
**resignation**

**démissionner** *verb* **[1]**
**to resign**

**demi-tarif** *invariable adjective*
**half-price**
un billet demi-tarif a half-price ticket

le **demi-tour** *masc noun*
**a U-turn**
Il faut faire demi-tour. We have to turn back.

le & la **démocrate** *masc & fem noun*
▷ see **démocrate** *adj*
**democrat**

**démocrate** *masc & fem adjective*
▷ see **démocrate** *noun*
**democratic**

la **démocratie** *fem noun*
**democracy**

**démocratique** *masc & fem adjective*
**democratic**

**démodé** *masc adjective*, **démodée** *fem*
**old-fashioned**

la **demoiselle** *fem noun*
**young lady**
• la **demoiselle d'honneur** bridesmaid

**démolir** *verb* **[2]**
**to demolish**

la **démolition** *fem noun*
**demolition**

le **démon** *masc noun*
**demon**

la **démonstration** *fem noun*
1 **demonstration** *(of a product, appliance)*
2 **display** *(of strength, courage)*

**démonter** *verb* **[1]**
1 **to take apart** *(a piece of furniture, a model)*
2 **to take down** *(a tent)*

**démontrer** *verb* **[1]**
**to demonstrate**

**dénoncer** *verb* **[61]**
**to denounce**

se **dénoncer** *reflexive verb* ⓔ
**to give yourself up** *(culprit)*

le **dénouement** *noun*
**ending, dénouement** *(of a film, book)*

**dénouer** *verb* **[1]**
**to undo**

**dense** *masc & fem adjective*
**dense**

a b c d e f g h i j k l m n o p q r s t u v w x y z



ⓔ means the verb takes être to form the perfect

la **densité** *fem noun*
**density**

𝄞 la **dent** *fem noun*
**tooth**
**avoir mal aux dents** to have toothache
**Kevin a mal aux dents.** Kevin has toothache.
- la **dent de lait** milk tooth
- la **dent de sagesse** wisdom tooth

**dentaire** *masc & fem adjective*
**dental**

**dentelé** *masc adjective*, **dentelée** *fem*
1 **indented** *(coast)*
2 **serrated** *(paper, blade)*
3 **perforated** *(stamp)*

la **dentelle** *fem noun*
**lace**

le **dentier** *masc noun*
**dentures**
**Ma grand-mère a un dentier.** My grandmother has dentures.

𝄞 le **dentifrice** *masc noun*
**toothpaste**

𝄞 le & la **dentiste** *masc & fem noun*
**dentist**
**Jérémy est chez le dentiste.** Jérémy is at the dentist's.

le **déodorant** *masc noun*
**deodorant**

le **dépannage** *masc noun*
**repair**
**le service de dépannage** the breakdown service
**un véhicule de dépannage** a breakdown vehicle

**dépanner** *verb* **[1]**
1 **to repair**
2 **dépanner quelqu'un** to repair somebody's car
3 *(informal)* **dépanner quelqu'un** to help somebody out

la **dépanneuse** *fem noun*
**breakdown truck**

𝄞 le **départ** *masc noun*
1 **departure**
**Je t'appellerai avant mon départ.** I'll phone you before I leave.
2 **start** *(of a race)*
3 **au départ** at first, to start with
**Au départ, j'ai eu peur.** At first I was scared.

𝄞 le **département** *masc noun*
**department**
- les **départements et territoires d'outre-mer DOM-TOM** French overseas departments and territories

***département***

La France a 95 départements, numérotés par ordre alphabétique (excepté autour de Paris). Il y a aussi quatre départements loin de la France : la Guadeloupe, la Martinique, la Guyane et la Réunion.

**dépassé** *masc adjective*, **dépassée** *fem*
1 **outdated** *(style)*
2 **overwhelmed** *(person)*

**dépasser** *verb* **[1]**
1 **to overtake** *(a vehicle, a competitor)*
2 **to exceed** *(a weight, a temperature)*
3 **to go past** *(a place)*
4 **Ça me dépasse!** It's beyond me!

𝄞 se **dépêcher** *reflexive verb* Ⓔ **[50]**
**to hurry up**
**Dépêche-toi!** Hurry up!

la **dépendance** *fem noun*
1 **dependence** *(of a country, a person)*
2 **outbuilding**

**dépendre** *verb* **[3]**
1 **dépendre de quelque chose** to depend on something
**Ça dépend (de l'heure).** It depends (on the time).
2 **dépendre de quelqu'un** to be dependent on somebody

𝄞 **dépenser** *verb* **[1]**
**to spend**

les **dépenses** *plural fem noun*
1 **expenses**
2 **spending**

**dépensier** *masc adjective*, **dépensière** *fem*
**extravagant**

**dépilatoire** *masc & fem adjective*
**une crème dépilatoire** a hair-removing cream

le **dépit** *masc noun*
**en dépit de** in spite of

**déplacé** *masc adjective*, **déplacée** *fem*
**out of place**

le **déplacement** *masc noun*
**trip**
**les frais de déplacement** travel expenses

**déplacer** *verb* **[61]**
**to move**

se **déplacer** *reflexive verb* ⓔ
**to travel**

**déplaire** *verb* **[62]**
**Le film lui a déplu.** He didn't like the film.
**Ça ne me déplairait pas de visiter la Chine.** I wouldn't mind visiting China.

**déplaisant** *masc adjective*, **déplaisante** *fem*
**unpleasant**

le **dépliant** *masc noun*
**leaflet**

**déplier** *verb* **[1]**
**to unfold**

**déposer** *verb* **[1]**
1 **to put down** (*luggage*)
2 **to dump** (*rubbish*)
3 **to drop off**
4 **déposer un chèque** to pay in a cheque

le **dépôt** *masc noun*
1 **warehouse**
2 **deposit** (*of money*)
• le **dépôt d'ordures** rubbish tip

la **dépression** *fem noun*
**depression**
**Sa sœur fait de la dépression.** Her sister suffers from depression.
• la **dépression nerveuse** nervous breakdown

**déprimant** *masc adjective*, **déprimante** *fem*
**depressing**

**déprimer** *verb* **[1]**
1 **to depress**
2 **to be depressed**

**depuis** *adverb* ▷ see **depuis** *prep*
**since**
**Je n'ai pas revu Frédéric depuis.** I haven't seen Frédéric since.

**depuis** *preposition* ▷ see **depuis** *adv*
1 **since**
**depuis vendredi** since Friday
**Je suis à Paris depuis le 2 janvier.** I've been in Paris since 2 January.
**J'habite à Londres depuis avril.** I've been living in London since April.
**Depuis leur dispute, ils ne se parlent plus.** Since they had an argument, they haven't spoken to each other.
2 **for**
**Elle habite à Londres depuis cinq ans.** She's lived in London for five years.
**Je le connais depuis longtemps.** I've known him for a long time.
3 **Depuis quand...?, Depuis combien de temps...?** How long...?
**Depuis quand es-tu à Paris?** How long have you been in Paris?
**Tu es là depuis combien de temps?** How long have you been here?

**WORD TIP** In French, *depuis* refers to a state which is still going on, so use the present tense rather than the perfect tense.

le **député** *masc noun*
**deputy** (*the French equivalent of a member of Parliament*)

**déranger** *verb* **[52]**
**to disturb**
**'Ne pas déranger'** 'Do not disturb'
**Excusez-moi de vous déranger!** Sorry to bother you!
**Est-ce que cela vous dérange si j'ouvre la fenêtre?** Do you mind if I open the window?
**Cela ne me dérange pas du tout.** I don't mind at all.

**déraper** *verb* **[1]**
1 **to skid** (*car, motorbike*)
2 **to get out of control** (*discussion*)

**dérisoire** *masc & fem adjective*
**trivial**
**Je l'ai acheté pour une somme dérisoire.** I bought it for next to nothing.

le **dériveur** *masc noun*
**sailing dinghy**

le & la **dermatologue** *masc & fem noun*
**dermatologist**

**dernier** *masc adjective*, **dernière** *fem* ▷ see **dernier** *noun*
1 **last**
**jeudi dernier** last Thursday
**la semaine dernière** last week
**l'année dernière** last year
**Le dernier train part à minuit.** The last train leaves at midnight.
2 **latest**
**leur dernier album** their latest album
**les dernières nouvelles** the latest news
**ces derniers temps** recently
3 **en dernier** last
**Il est arrivé en dernier.** He arrived last.

le **dernier** *masc noun*, la **dernière** *fem noun* ▷ see **dernier** *adj*
**last**
**C'est le dernier qui me reste.** It's my last one.
**Martin est le dernier de la classe.** Martin is bottom of the class.
**Angeline est la petite dernière.** Angeline is the youngest child.



ⓔ means the verb takes être to form the perfect

**dernièrement** *adverb*
**recently**

**dérouler** *verb* **[1]**
**to unroll**

se **dérouler** *reflexive verb* Ⓔ
**to take place**
**L'histoire se déroule au dix-huitième siècle.** The story takes place in the eighteenth century.
**Ça s'est très bien déroulé.** It went very well.

**déroutant** *masc adjective*, **déroutante** *fem*
**puzzling**

♂ **derrière** *adverb* ▷ see **derrière** *noun, prep*
**behind**
**Le prof est juste derrière.** The teacher is just behind.
**Ne poussez pas derrière!** Stop pushing at the back!

♂ le **derrière** *masc noun* ▷ see **derrière** *adv, prep*
1 **back** (*of an object, a house*)
2 (*informal*) **bottom, backside**

♂ **derrière** *preposition* ▷ see **derrière** *adv, noun*
**behind**
**derrière la porte** behind the door

**des** *determiner*
**some, any**

**WORD TIP** *des* is formed by *de + les* ▷ **de** *determiner, preposition*

**dès** *preposition*
1 **from**
**dès l'âge de cinq ans** from the age of five
2 **dès que** as soon as
**Dès que j'arrive, je t'envoie un SMS.** As soon as I arrive, I'll send you a text.

**désagréable** *masc & fem adjective*
**unpleasant**

le **désastre** *masc noun*
**disaster**

le **désavantage** *masc noun*
**disadvantage**

♂ **descendre** *verb* **[3]**
1 Ⓔ **to come down** (*from upstairs*)
**Je descends dans une seconde!** I'll be down in a second!
2 Ⓔ **to get out** (*of a bus, train*)
**Il est descendu à Dijon.** He got off at Dijon.
3 **descendre de quelque chose** Ⓔ to come from something
**Clara descend d'une famille d'émigrés italiens.** Clara comes from a family of Italian emigrants.
4 **to get down** (*an object from storage*)
**Elle a descendu ma valise.** She got my case down.
5 **to take, bring downstairs** (*an object*)
**Je vais descendre mes bagages.** I'm going to bring down my luggage.
6 **to go down** (*the stairs*)
**Il a descendu l'escalier.** He went down the stairs.

**WORD TIP** When you say *what you get down, take down, go down* etc, use *avoir* in the perfect tense in French.

la **descente** *fem noun*
**descent**
**À la descente du bus...** When you get off the bus...

**descriptif** *masc adjective*, **descriptive** *fem*
**descriptive**

♂ la **description** *fem noun*
**description**
**faire une description de quelque chose** to give a description of something
**Faites une description de ta maison.** Give a description of your home.

le **désert** *masc noun* ▷ see **désert** *adj*
**desert**

**désert** *masc adjective*, **déserte** *fem* ▷ see **désert** *noun*
**deserted**
**une île déserte** a desert island

**désespéré** *masc adjective*, **désespérée** *fem*
1 **desperate** (*attempt*)
2 **in despair** (*a person*)
3 **hopeless** (*situation*)

**désespérer** *verb* **[24]**
**to despair, to give up hope**
**Ne vous désespèrez pas!** Don't give up hope!
**Ils désespèrent de l'avenir.** They despair of the future.

le **désespoir** *masc noun*
**despair**

♂ **déshabiller** *verb* **[1]**
**to undress** (*a child, a doll*)

se **déshabiller** *reflexive verb* Ⓔ
1 **to get undressed**
2 **to take your coat off**

le **déshérité** *masc noun*, la **déshéritée** *fem*
**les déshérités** the underprivileged

**déshydraté** *masc adjective*, **déshydratée** *fem*
**dehydrated**

**désigner** *verb* [1]
**1** **to refer to**
**2** **to choose**

le **désinfectant** *masc noun*
**disinfectant**

le **désir** *masc noun*
**wish**, **desire**

**désirer** *verb* [1]
**to want**
Que désirez-vous? What would you like?

**désobéir** *verb* [2]
**1** **to be disobedient**
**2** désobéir à quelqu'un to disobey somebody

**désobéissant** *masc adjective*, **désobéissante** *fem*
**disobedient**

**désobligeant** *masc adjective*, **désobligeante** *fem*
**unpleasant**

le **désodorisant** *masc noun*
**air freshener**

**désolé** *masc adjective*, **désolée** *fem*
**sorry**
Désolé, c'est fermé! Sorry, we're closed!
Je suis désolé de te déranger. I'm sorry to bother you.

**désopilant** *masc adjective*, **désopilante** *fem*
**hilarious**

**désordonné** *masc adjective*, **désordonnée** *fem*
**untidy**

le **désordre** *masc noun*
**1** **mess**
être en désordre to be in a mess (*room*)
**2** **disorder**

**désorganisé** *masc adjective*, **désorganisée** *fem*
**disorganized**

**désorienté** *masc adjective*, **désorientée** *fem*
**confused**

**désormais** *adverb*
**from now on**

**desquels**, **desquelles** *pronoun*
**of which**
Les vacances ont duré dix jours au cours desquels nous avons fait du kayak. The holidays lasted ten days during which we went canoeing.

**WORD TIP** *de + lesquels* becomes *desquels*; *de + lesquelles* becomes *desquelles*.

**dessécher** *verb* [24]
**to dry out**
Le froid dessèche la peau. The cold dries your skin out.

se **dessécher** *reflexive verb* ⓔ
**to dry out**
J'ai des cheveux fins qui se dessèchent facilement. My hair is fine and dries out easily.

**desserrer** *verb* [1]
**to loosen**

le **dessert** *masc noun*
**dessert**, **pudding**
Comme dessert Estelle a pris une glace. For dessert Estelle had an ice cream.

**desservir** *verb* [58]
**1** **to call at** (*trains*)
**2** **to clear** (*the table*)

le **dessin** *masc noun*
**1** **drawing**, **art**
un dessin a drawing
Marie fait du dessin. Marie is drawing.
**2** **design**
le dessin de la voiture the design of the car
- le **dessin animé** cartoon (*on TV*)
- le **dessin humoristique** cartoon (*in newspaper*)

**dessiner** *verb* [1]
**to draw**
Nous dessinons au crayon. We are drawing in pencil.

**dessous** *adverb* ▷ see **dessous** *noun*
**underneath**
Soulève la pierre, la clé est dessous. Lift the stone, the key is underneath.

le **dessous** *masc noun* ▷ see **dessous** *adv*
**1** **underside**
le dessous du pied the sole of the foot
**2** les voisins du dessous the neighbours below
**3** les dessous underwear
**4** en dessous underneath
Mets-le en dessous. Put it underneath.
Il me faut la taille en dessous. I need the next size down.
**5** en dessous de below
30 degrés en dessous de zéro 30 degrees below zero
- le **dessous-de-plat** table mat (*for a dish*)

**dessus** *adverb* ▷ see **dessus** *noun*
**on top**
un gâteau avec des fraises dessus a cake with strawberries on top
Prends celui du dessus. Take the top one.

le **dessus** *masc noun* ▷ see **dessus** *adv*
1 **top**
le dessus du carton the top of the box
2 les voisins du dessus the neighbours above
3 en dessus above
• le **dessus-de-lit** bedspread

le **destin** *masc noun*
**fate, destiny**

le & la **destinataire** *masc & fem noun*
**addressee**

♪ la **destination** *fem noun*
**destination**
le train à destination de Nice the train for Nice

**destiner** *verb* [1]
être destiné à quelque chose to be intended for something

le **détachant** *masc noun*
**stain remover**

**détacher** *verb* [1]
1 **to untie** (*a horse*)
2 **to undo** (*a knot*)
3 **to tear off** (*a cheque*)
4 **to remove**
5 **to remove the stains from** (*clothes*)

se **détacher** *reflexive verb* Ⓔ
1 **to break loose** (*horse*)
2 **to come out**

le **détail** *masc noun*
1 **detail**
en détail in detail
2 **retail**
Il achète au détail. He buys retail.

**détecter** *verb* [1]
**to detect**

le **détective** *masc noun*
**detective**

**déteindre** *verb* [60]
1 **to fade**
2 **to run** (*in the wash*)

**détendre** *verb* [3]
1 **to be relaxing**
2 **to calm**

se **détendre** *reflexive verb* Ⓔ
**to relax**

**détendu** *masc adjective*, **détendue** *fem*
**relaxed**

**détenir** *verb* [81]
1 **to keep** (*objects*)
2 **to detain** (*a criminal*)

la **détente** *fem noun*
**relaxation**

le **détenu** *masc noun*, la **détenue** *fem*
**prisoner**

le **détergent** *masc noun*
**detergent**

se **détériorer** *reflexive verb* Ⓔ [1]
**to deteriorate**

le **déterminant** *masc noun*
(*Grammar*) **determiner**

**WORD TIP** In French these are *un, une, des* and *le, la, les*. In English they are *a, an* and *the*.

la **détermination** *fem noun*
**determination**

**détestable** *masc & fem adjective*
**appalling**

♪ **détester** *verb* [1]
**to hate**
Karine déteste faire la vaisselle. Karine hates doing the dishes.

le **détour** *masc noun*
**detour**
Nous allons faire un détour par Lille. We'll make a detour via Lille.

le **détournement** *masc noun*
un détournement d'avion a hijacking

**détourner** *verb* [1]
1 **to divert** (*somebody's attention, the traffic*)
2 Leila essaie de détourner la conversation. Leila is trying to change the subject.
3 **to hijack**
4 **to look away**

les **détritus** *plural masc noun*
**rubbish**

**détruire** *verb* [26]
**to destroy**

la **dette** *fem noun*
**debt**

le **deuil** *masc noun*
1 **bereavement**
2 **mourning**
Yasmina est en deuil de sa grand-mère. Yasmina is in mourning for her grandmother.

♪ **deux** *number*
1 **two**
deux enfants two children
Elle a deux ans. She's two.
Il est deux heures. It's two o'clock.
2 deux fois twice
une fois sur deux fifty percent of the time
Laurie s'entraîne un jour sur deux. Laurie trains every other day.
3 **second**
(*in dates*) le deux juin the second of June ▸▸

**4 both**
**les deux frères** both brothers
**tous les deux, toutes les deux** both
**Ils sont malades tous les deux.** They're both ill (*males or mixed group*).
**Toutes les deux sont malades.** They're both ill (*females only*).
- le **deux-points** (*Grammar*) colon

**deuxième** *masc & fem adjective*
**second**
**une deuxième fois** a second time
**Nelly habite au deuxième (étage).** Nelly lives on the second floor.

**deuxièmement** *adverb*
**secondly**

**dévaliser** *verb* [1]
1 **to rob** (*a bank*)
2 **to raid** (*the fridge*)

**devant** *adverb* ▷ see **devant** *noun, prep*
**Assieds-toi devant!** Sit in the front! (*in a car*)
**Si tu cherches le cinéma, tu te trouves juste devant.** If you're looking for the cinema, you're standing just in front of it.
**Tu es trop lent, je passe devant.** You're too slow, I'll go ahead of you.

le **devant** *masc noun* ▷ see **devant** *adv, prep*
**front**
**Regarde ton T-shirt, il y a une tache sur le devant.** Look at your T-shirt, there is a stain on the front.

**devant** *preposition* ▷ see **devant** *adv, noun*
1 **in front of**
**Elle était devant moi dans la queue.** She was in front of me in the queue.
**Il l'a dit devant ses parents.** He said it in front of his parents.
2 **outside**
**Je t'attendrai devant la bibliothèque.** I will wait for you outside the library.
3 **ahead of**
**Julien est loin devant nous.** Julien is a long way ahead of us.

le **développement** *masc noun*
**development**
**les pays en voie de développement** developing countries

**développer** *verb* [1]
**to develop**

se **développer** *reflexive verb* Ⓔ
1 **to expand**
2 **to become widespread**

**devenir** *verb* [81]
**to become**
**Il est devenu célèbre.** He's become famous.
**Philippe voudrait devenir avocat.** Philippe would like to be a lawyer.
**Elle est devenue infirmière.** She went into nursing.
**Elle est devenue toute pâle.** She went really pale.

**déverser** *verb* [1]
1 **to pour** (*liquid*)
2 **to dump** (*rubbish, chemicals*)

la **déviation** *fem noun*
**diversion**

**deviner** *verb* [1]
**to guess**
**Devine qui vient nous voir?** Guess who's coming to see us?

la **devinette** *fem noun*
**riddle**

le **devis** *masc noun* ▷ see **devises** *pl noun*
**quote, estimate**

les **devises** *plural fem noun*
▷ see **devis** *masc noun*
**(foreign) currency**

**dévisser** *verb* [1]
**to unscrew**

le **devoir** *masc noun* ▷ see **devoir** *verb*
1 **test**
**On a un devoir de physique la semaine prochaine.** We have a physics test next week.
2 **homework**
**Je fais mes devoirs.** I'm doing my homework.
**At-tu fini ton devoir de maths?** Have you finished your maths homework?
3 **duty**

**devoir** *verb* [8] ▷ see **devoir** *noun*
1 **to owe**
**Alexandre me doit vingt euros.** Alexandre owes me twenty euros.
**Je vous dois combien?** How much do I owe you?
2 **to have to, must**
**Je dois partir à dix heures.** I have to leave at ten o'clock.
3 **must** (*in guessing*)
**Tu dois être fatigué.** You must be tired.
**Elle doit avoir quarante ans.** She must be forty.
**Yves a dû oublier.** Yves must have forgotten.



Ⓔ means the verb takes être to form the perfect

4 (*in recommendations*) **Tu devrais reviser davantage.** You ought to revise more. **Malaurie aurait dû partir.** Malaurie should have left.
5 **to be supposed to**
**Éric doit le voir demain.** Éric is supposed to see him tomorrow.

**dévoué** *masc adjective*, **dévouée** *fem*
**devoted**

se **dévouer** *reflexive verb* ⓔ **[1]**
**se dévouer à quelque chose** to devote oneself to something

♪ **d'habitude** *adverb*
**usually**
**D'habitude Chloë va au lit à 8 heures du soir.** Usually Chloë goes to bed at 8 pm.

le **diabète** *masc noun*
**diabetes**

**diabétique** *masc & fem adjective*
**diabetic**

le **diable** *masc noun*
**devil**

le **diabolo** *masc noun*
**fruit cordial and lemonade**
**un diabolo menthe** a mint cordial and lemonade

le **diagnostic** *masc noun*
**diagnosis**

**diagnostiquer** *verb* **[1]**
**to diagnose**

**diagonal** *masc adjective*, **diagonale** *fem*, **diagonaux** *masc pl*, **diagonales** *fem pl*
▷ see **diagonale** *noun*
**diagonal**

la **diagonale** *fem noun* ▷ see **diagonal** *adj*
**diagonal**
**en diagonale** diagonally

le **diagramme** *masc noun*
**graph**

le **dialogue** *masc noun*
**dialogue**

le **diamant** *masc noun*
**diamond**

le **diamètre** *masc noun*
**diameter**

la **diapositive** *fem noun*
**slide** (*in photography*)

la **diarrhée** *fem noun*
**diarrhoea**

le **dico** *masc noun*
(*informal*) **dictionary**
▷ short for **dictionnaire**

le **dictateur** *masc noun*
**dictator**

la **dictature** *fem noun*
**dictatorship**

**dicter** *verb* **[1]**
**to dictate**

le **dictionnaire** *masc noun*
**dictionary**

le **dicton** *masc noun*
**saying**

le **diesel** *masc noun*
**diesel**

**diététique** *masc & fem adjective*
▷ see **diététique** *noun*
**dietary**
**des produits diététiques** health food

la **diététique** *fem noun*
▷ see **diététique** *adj*
**un magasin de diététique** a health-food shop

le **dieu** *masc noun*, les **dieux** *pl*
▷ see **Dieu** *masc noun*
**god**

**Dieu** *masc noun* ▷ see **dieu** *masc noun*
**God**

♪ la **différence** *fem noun*
1 **difference**
**Vois-tu la différence?** Can you see the difference?
2 **à la différence de** unlike
**À la différence de Louis, Maxime aime la musique classique.** Unlike Louis, Maxime likes classical music.

le **différend** *masc noun*
**disagreement**

♪ **différent** *masc adjective*, **différente** *fem*
1 **different**
**Ce mot a des sens différents.** This word has different senses.
**Elle est vraiment différente de sa sœur.** She's really different from her sister.
2 **various, different**
**différentes personnes** various people, different people

♪ **difficile** *masc & fem adjective*
1 **difficult, hard**
**difficile à faire** difficult to do
**Leur maison est difficile à trouver.** Their house is difficult to find.
**C'est difficile à imaginer.** It's hard to imagine.
2 **hard to please**
**Je me demande si Éliza va aimer mon** ▸▸



French-English
a b c d e f g h i j k l m n o p q r s t u v w x y z

cadeau, elle est si difficile. I wonder if Éliza will like my present, she's so hard to please.

**difficilement** *adverb*
**with difficulty**

la **difficulté** *fem noun*
**difficulty**
avoir de la difficulté à faire quelque chose to have difficulty in doing something
faire des difficultés to raise objections

**diffuser** *verb* [1]
1 **to broadcast** (*a programme*)
2 **to distribute** (*a magazine*)

**digérer** *verb* [24]
**to digest**

le **digestif** *masc noun*
**(after-dinner) liqueur**

la **digestion** *fem noun*
**digestion**

**digital** *masc adjective*, **digitale** *fem*, **digitaux** *masc pl*, **digitales** *fem pl*
**digital**

**digne** *masc & fem adjective*
1 **dignified** (*person, silence*)
2 **worthy**
digne de confiance trustworthy

la **dignité** *fem noun*
**dignity**

la **digue** *fem noun*
**sea wall**

le **dilemme** *masc noun*
**dilemma**

**diligent** *masc adjective*, **diligente** *fem*
**diligent**

**diluer** *verb* [1]
1 **to dilute**
2 **to thin** (*paint*)

♪ le **dimanche** *masc noun*
1 **Sunday**
Nous sommes dimanche aujourd'hui. It's Sunday today.
dimanche dernier last Sunday
dimanche prochain next Sunday
2 **on Sunday**
Je t'appellerai dimanche soir. I'll ring you on Sunday evening.
3 le dimanche on Sundays
fermé le dimanche closed on Sundays
4 tous les dimanches every Sunday

**WORD TIP** Months of the year and days of the week start with small letters in French.

la **dimension** *fem noun*
1 **dimension**
un objet à trois dimensions a three-dimensional object
prendre les dimensions de quelque chose to measure something
2 **size**
Cette glace existe en plusieurs dimensions. This mirror comes in several sizes.

**diminuer** *verb* [1]
1 **to reduce** (*a quantity, the cost, the duration*)
2 **to decrease**
3 **to go down** (*candle, fever*)

la **dinde** *fem noun*
**turkey** (*the female bird, the meat*)

le **dindon** *masc noun*
**turkey** (*the male bird*)

♪ le **dîner** *masc noun* ▷ see **dîner** *verb*
**dinner**
C'est l'heure du dîner. It's dinner time.
Qu'est-ce qu'on mange pour dîner? What's for dinner?
Elle prépare le dîner. She's getting dinner ready.
Nous prenons le dîner à 19 h 30. We have dinner at 7.30 pm.

**dîner** *verb* [1] ▷ see **dîner** *noun*
**to have dinner**
Viens dîner chez nous ce soir. Come to dinner with us this evening.

**dingue** *masc & fem adjective*
(*informal*) **crazy**

le **dinosaure** *masc noun*
**dinosaur**

le & la **diplomate** *masc & fem noun*
**diplomat**

♪ le **diplôme** *masc noun*
1 **qualification, diploma**
Quels diplômes faut-il pour devenir vétérinaire? Which qualifications do you need to be a vet?
2 **(university) degree**
Marine a un diplôme d'architecte. Marine has a degree in architecture.
3 **certificate**
un diplôme de secouriste a first aid certificate

**diplômé** *masc adjective*, **diplômée** *fem*
**qualified**
une infirmière diplômée a qualified nurse
Anthony est diplômé en droit. Anthony has a degree in law.

♪ **dire** *verb* [9]
1 **to say**
**Qu'est-ce qu'elle a dit?** What did she say?
**Comment dit-on 'gourmand' en anglais?** How do you say 'gourmand' in English?
2 **to tell**
**dire quelque chose à quelqu'un** to tell somebody something
**J'ai dit à Anne que tu l'appellerais.** I told Anne you'd ring her.
**dire à quelqu'un de faire quelque chose** to tell somebody to do something
**Je leur ai dit de venir à cinq heures.** I told them to come at five o'clock.
**dire la vérité** to tell the truth
**dire des mensonges** to tell lies
**dire l'heure** to tell the time
3 **to think**
**Qu'en dis-tu?** What do you think?
**On dirait que Léa me déteste.** You'd think that Léa hated me.
**On dirait qu'il va pleuvoir.** It looks like rain.
4 **Ça ne me dit rien.** I don't feel like it.
5 **vouloir dire quelque chose** to mean something
**Qu'est-ce que ça veut dire?** What does it mean?
6 **à vrai dire** actually
**À vrai dire, je préfère ne pas y aller.** Actually, I prefer not to go.

se **dire** *verb reflexive* ê
1 **to tell oneself**
**Je me dis souvent ...** I often tell myself ...
2 **to claim to be**
3 **to say**
**Ça se dit comment 'l'ordinateur' en allemand?** How do you say 'the computer' in German?
**Ça ne se dit pas.** You can't say that.

♪ **direct** *masc adjective*, **directe** *fem*
1 **direct**
**un vol direct** a direct flight
2 (*in broadcasting*) **en direct de ...** live from ...

**directement** *adverb*
1 **straight**
**Je rentre directement à la maison.** I'm going straight home.
2 **directly**

♪ le **directeur** *masc noun*, la **directrice** *fem*
1 **director**
2 **manager**
3 **head** (*of a school*)

le **directeur général** *masc noun*, la **directrice générale** *fem*
**managing director**

♪ la **direction** *fem noun*
1 **direction**
**en direction de** towards, in the direction of
**Nous sommes dans la bonne direction.** We are heading the right way.
**Fahrid s'est trompé de direction.** Fahrid went in the wrong direction.
**Demande la direction de la gare!** Ask for directions to the station!
**Pouvez-vous m'indiquer la direction du musée, s'il vous plaît?** Could you please tell me the way to the museum?
2 **management**
**'Changement de direction'** 'Under new management'
3 **steering** (*of a vehicle*)

le **dirigeant** *masc noun*, la **dirigeante** *fem*
**leader**

**diriger** *verb* [52]
1 **to manage**
2 **to direct** (*an operation*)
3 **to steer** (*a vehicle*)
4 **to conduct** (*an orchestra*)

se **diriger** *reflexive verb* ê
**se diriger vers quelque chose** to make for something
**Flore s'est dirigée vers la porte.** Flore made for the door.

**discerner** *verb* [1]
**to make out** (*a shape, an object*)

la **discipline** *fem noun*
1 **discipline**
2 **subject** (*of study*)

**discipliner** *verb* [1]
**to control**

le **disco** *masc noun*
**disco music**

♪ la **discothèque** *fem noun*
1 **club, disco**
**Samedi soir, nous allons à la discothèque.** On Saturday evening we are going clubbing.
2 **music library**

le **discours** *masc noun*
**speech**

**discret** *masc adjective*, **discrète** *fem*
1 **discreet**
2 **subtle**

la **discrimination** *fem noun*
**discrimination**

la **discussion** *fem noun*
**discussion**

**discutable** *masc & fem adjective*
**questionable**

**discuter** *verb* [1]
1 **to talk**
**On peut discuter tranquillement chez moi.** We can talk in peace at my house.
2 **discuter de quelque chose** to discuss something
**Nous allons discuter du pour et du contre.** We are going to discuss the pros and cons.
**On va en discuter demain.** We'll discuss it tomorrow.
3 **discuter avec quelqu'un** to talk to somebody
**Mes parents ont discuté avec la directrice.** My parents talked to the headmistress.
4 **to argue**
**Ça se discute.** It's arguable.

**disparaître** *verb* [27]
1 **to disappear**
**Mes clés ont encore disparu.** My keys have disappeared again.
**Disparaissez!** Out of my sight!
2 **to go**
**Ma douleur à l'épaule a disparu.** My shoulder pain has gone.
3 **to come out** (*stain*)
4 **faire disparaître quelque chose** to remove something
5 **to die**
6 **to die out** (*traditions, customs*)

la **disparition** *fem noun*
1 **disappearance**
2 **une espèce en voie de disparition** an endangered species

**disparu** *masc adjective*, **disparue** *fem*
▷ see **disparu** *noun*
1 **missing**
**la petite fille disparue depuis deux semaines** the little girl who has been missing for two weeks
2 **lost**
**la civilisation disparue des Mayas** the lost civilisation of the Mayas
3 **dead**
**mille personnes disparues en mer** one thousand people lost at sea
4 **extinct**
**une espèce disparue** an extinct species

le **disparu** *masc noun*, la **disparue** *fem*
▷ see **disparu** *adj*
1 **missing person**
2 **les disparus** the dead

**dispenser** *verb* [1]
1 **to give**
2 **dispenser quelqu'un de quelque chose** to excuse somebody from something
**Amélie est dispensée de gym.** Amélie is excused from gymnastics.

**disperser** *verb* [1]
1 **to scatter**
2 **to break up** (*a crowd, a demonstration*)

se **disperser** *reflexive verb* Ⓔ
**to break up**
**La foule s'est dispersée.** The crowd broke up.

**disponible** *masc & fem adjective*
**available**

**disposé** *masc adjective*, **disposée** *fem*
1 **arranged**
2 **être disposé à faire quelque chose** to be willing to do something

**disposer** *verb* [1]
1 **to arrange**
**Le prof a disposé les tables en cercle.** The teacher arranged the tables in a circle.
2 **disposer de quelque chose** to have something (at your disposal)
**L'école dispose d'une piscine.** The school has a swimming pool at its disposal.

le **dispositif** *masc noun*
**device**

la **disposition** *fem noun*
1 **arrangement**
**la disposition de l'appartement** the layout of the flat
2 **disposal**
**à votre disposition** at your disposal

la **dispute** *fem noun*
**argument**

**disputé** *masc adjective*, **disputée** *fem*
1 **contested**
2 **controversial**

**disputer** *reflexive verb* Ⓔ [1]
**se faire disputer** (*informal*) to get told off
**Mon père me dispute pour tout.** My father tells me off all the time.

se **disputer** *reflexive verb* Ⓔ
1 **to argue**
**Ils se sont disputés.** They had an argument.
2 **se disputer quelque chose** to fight over something
**Les deux chiens se disputaient le jouet.** The two dogs were fighting over the toy.

**disqualifier** *verb* [1]
**to disqualify**



Ⓔ means the verb takes être to form the perfect

♪ le **disque** *masc noun*
1 **record**
passer un disque to play a record
2 **(computer) disk**
3 **discus**
le lancer du disque the discus
• le **disque compact** compact disc, CD
• le **disque dur** hard disk (*of a computer*)

♪ la **disquette** *fem noun*
**diskette, floppy disk**

la **dissertation** *fem noun*
**essay**

**dissimuler** *verb* [1]
**to conceal**

**dissocier** *verb* [1]
**to separate**

le **dissolvant** *masc noun*
1 **nail polish remover**
2 **solvent**

**dissoudre** *verb* [67]
**to dissolve**

**dissuader** *verb* [1]
1 dissuader quelqu'un de faire quelque chose to put somebody off doing something
La pluie l'a dissuadée de sortir. The rain put her off going out.
2 **to deter**
pour dissuader les voleurs in order to deter thieves

♪ la **distance** *fem noun*
1 **distance**
une distance de cinq kilomètres a distance of five kilometres
C'est à quelle distance d'ici? How far is it from here?
l'enseignement à distance distance learning
2 **gap**
Elles sont nées à deux mois de distance. They were born two months apart.

**distant** *masc adjective*, **distante** *fem*
**distant**
distant de far away from
un village distant de trois kilomètres a village three kilometres away

la **distillerie** *fem noun*
**distillery**

**distinct** *masc adjective*, **distincte** *fem*
1 **distinct**
2 **clear** (*voice*)
Il s'exprime de façon distincte. He speaks clearly.

la **distinction** *fem noun*
**distinction**

**distingué** *masc adjective*, **distinguée** *fem*
**distinguished**

**distinguer** *verb* [1]
1 **to distinguish between**
J'ai du mal à distinguer les jumeaux. I find it hard to tell the twins apart.
2 **to distinguish**
Ce qui distingue Laura de Claire, c'est ... What distinguishes Laura from Claire is ...
3 **to make out**
Nous distinguons un bateau à l'horizon. We can make out a boat on the horizon.

la **distraction** *fem noun*
1 **entertainment, leisure**
On a besoin d'un peu de distraction. We need a bit of entertainment.
Sa distraction favorite est le jeu vidéo. Her favourite way of relaxing is to play video games.
2 **absent-mindedness**

**distraire** *verb* [78]
1 **to entertain**
2 **to distract**

se **distraire** *reflexive verb* ©
**to enjoy yourself**

**distrait** *masc adjective*, **distraite** *fem*
**absent-minded**

**distribuer** *verb* [1]
1 **to distribute, to give out**
Maeva distribue les cahiers. Maeva is distributing the exercise books.
distribuer les cartes to deal (the cards)
2 **to deliver** (*the mail*)
3 **to award** (*the prizes*)

le **distributeur** *masc noun*
**distributor**
• le **distributeur automatique** vending machine
• le **distributeur de billets** cash dispenser
• le **distributeur de tickets** ticket machine

la **distribution** *fem noun*
1 **distribution**
2 **delivery** (*of mail*)
3 **cast** (*of a play*)
• la **distribution des prix** prizegiving

**divers** *masc adjective*, **diverse** *fem*
**various**

**divertir** *verb* [2]
**to entertain**

se **divertir** *reflexive verb* Ⓔ
**to enjoy oneself**
**Nous nous sommes bien divertis.** We really enjoyed ourselves.

**divertissant** *masc adjective*, **divertissante** *fem*
**amusing, entertaining**

**diviser** *verb* **[1]**
**to divide**

la **division** *fem noun*
**division**

le **divorce** *masc noun*
**divorce**

♪ **divorcé** *masc adjective*, **divorcée** *fem*
**divorced**
**Mes parents sont divorcés.** My parents are divorced.

**divorcer** *verb* **[61]**
**to get divorced**
**Ses parents ont divorcé.** Her parents got divorced.

♪ **dix** *number*
**ten**
**Elle a dix ans.** She's ten.
**Il est dix heures.** It's ten o'clock.
**le dix juillet** the tenth of July

♪ **dix-huit** *number*
**eighteen**
**Il a dix-huit ans.** He's eighteen.
**à dix-huit heures** at six p.m.
**On a un rendez-vous le dix-huit.** We have an appointment on the eighteenth.

♪ **dixième** *masc & fem adjective*
**tenth**

♪ **dix-neuf** *number*
**nineteen**
**Elle a dix-neuf ans.** She's nineteen.
**à dix-neuf heures** at seven p.m.

♪ **dix-sept** *number*
**seventeen**
**Elle a dix-sept ans.** She's seventeen.
**à dix-sept heures** at five p.m.

♪ la **dizaine** *fem noun*
**ten**
**une dizaine de personnes** about ten people

♪ **d'occasion** *adverb*
**secondhand**
**Je l'ai acheté d'occasion.** I bought it secondhand.
**C'est une voiture d'occasion.** It's a secondhand car.

♪ le **docteur** *masc noun*
**doctor**

le **document** *masc noun*
**document**

le **documentaire** *masc noun*
**documentary**

le & la **documentaliste** *masc & fem noun*
**(school) librarian**

la **documentation** *fem noun*
**1 information, material**
**Voici une documentation sur la région.** Here is some information about the area.
**2 research**

se **documenter** *reflexive verb* Ⓔ **[1]**
**se documenter sur quelque chose** to gather information on something

le **dodo** *masc noun*
(*baby talk*) **Fais dodo!** Go to sleep!
**Au dodo!** Off to bed!

♪ le **doigt** *masc noun*
**finger**
**Levez le doigt!** Put your hand up!
**le bout des doigts** the fingertips
**se couper le doigt** to cut your finger
**Clara s'est coupé le doigt.** Clara cut her finger.
- le **doigt de pied** toe

le **domaine** *masc noun*
**1 estate** (*area of land*)
**2 field** (*area of interest*)

le **dôme** *masc noun*
**dome**

le & la **domestique** *masc & fem noun*
**servant**

♪ le **domicile** *masc noun*
**place of residence**
**à domicile** at home
**livraison à domicile** home delivery
**Elle travaille à domicile.** She works from home.
**Ils ont changé de domicile.** They moved.

**dominant** *masc adjective*, **dominante** *fem*
**1 dominant** (*colour, character*)
**2 main** (*idea, theme*)

**dominer** *verb* **[1]**
**1 to dominate**
**2 to rule**
**3 to be in the lead**

se **dominer** *verb reflexive* Ⓔ
**to control oneself**

**dominicain** *masc adjective*, **dominicaine** *fem*
**Dominican**
**la République dominicaine** the Dominican Republic

le **domino** *masc noun*
**domino**
**jouer aux dominos** to play dominoes

♪ le **dommage** *masc noun*
1 **C'est dommage.** It's a pity.
**C'est dommage qu'elle n'y soit pas allée.** It's a pity she didn't go.
2 **les dommages** damage
**causer des dommages à quelque chose** to damage something

**dompter** *verb* [1]
**to tame**

les **DOM-TOM**
(= *départements et territoires d'outre-mer*)
(*French overseas departments and territories*)

le **don** *masc noun*
1 **donation**
2 **gift**, **talent**
**Elle a un don pour les langues.** She has a gift for languages.
**avoir le don de faire quelque chose** to have a talent for doing something

♪ **donc** *conjunction*
**so, therefore**
**La voiture est tombée en panne, ils ont donc pris le train.** The car broke down so they took the train.

**donné** *masc adjective*, **donnée** *fem*
▷ see **donnée** *noun*
1 **given**
**à un endroit donné** in a given place
**Deux euros, c'est donné!** Two euros, it's a bargain!
2 **étant donné** given
**Étant donné les circonstances ...** Given the circumstances ...
**Étant donné qu'il pleut, je ne crois pas qu'il viendra.** Given that it's raining, I don't think he'll come.

la **donnée** *fem noun* ▷ see **donné** *adj*
1 **fact**
2 **les données** data
**les données informatiques** computer data

♪ **donner** *verb* [1]
1 **to give**
**donner quelque chose à quelqu'un** to give somebody something
**Elle m'a donné dix euros.** She gave me ten euros.
**Donne-moi ton adresse.** Give me your address.
2 **donner à boire à quelqu'un** to give somebody something to drink
**Tu me donnes à boire, s'il te plaît, j'ai soif.** Give me something to drink please, I'm thirsty.
3 **to give away**
**Il a donné tous ses livres.** He gave away all his books.
4 **donner sur quelque chose** to overlook something
**Ma chambre donne sur la mer.** My bedroom overlooks the sea.

se **donner** *reflexive verb* ❷
**se donner à quelque chose** to devote yourself to something
**Perrine se donne toute entière à la peinture.** Perrine is devoting herself entirely to her painting.

♪ **dont** *relative pronoun*
1 **whose**
**la fille dont la mère est française** the girl whose mother is French
**une personne dont j'ai oublié le nom** a person whose name I've forgotten
2 **of which**
**six verres dont l'un est cassé** six glasses, one of which is broken
3 **of whom**
**dix élèves, dont cinq ont moins de dix ans** ten pupils, of whom five are under ten
4 **la maison dont je parle** the house I'm talking about
**le bébé dont je m'occupe** the baby I look after

**doré** *masc adjective*, **dorée** *fem*
**golden**

**dorénavant** *adverb*
**from now on**

♪ **dormir** *verb* [37]
**to sleep**
**Elle dort.** She's asleep.
**Tu as bien dormi?** Did you sleep well?
**Cindy va dormir chez moi.** Cindy's going to spend the night at my house.
**Clément a envie de dormir.** Clément is sleepy.

♪ le **dortoir** *masc noun*
**dormitory**

♪ le **dos** *masc noun*
**back**
**Elle me tournait le dos.** She had her back to me.
**Signe au dos du chèque.** Sign on the back of the cheque.
**avoir mal au dos** to have backache
**Lucile a mal au dos.** Lucile has backache.

le **dosage** *masc noun*
**amount**

la **dose** *fem noun*
1 **dose**
2 **measure**

le **dossier** *masc noun*
1 **file**
2 **application form**
3 **project** (*at school*)
4 **back** (*of a chair*)
• le **dossier médical** medical records

♂ la **douane** *fem noun*
la douane customs
**Il faut passer à la douane.** We need to go through customs.

♂ le **douanier** *masc noun*, la **douanière** *fem noun*
**customs officer**

**double** *masc & fem adjective*
▷ see **double** *noun*
**double**
**une chambre double** a double room
**une rue à double sens** a two-way street
**en double exemplaire** in duplicate
**Camille a la double nationalité.** Camille has dual nationality.

le **double** *masc noun* ▷ see **double** *adj*
1 **double**
le double (de) twice as much, twice as many
**Arnaud gagne le double de moi.** Arnaud earns twice as much as I do.
**Leur jardin fait le double du nôtre.** Their garden is twice as big as ours.
**100 est le double de 50.** 100 is twice 50.
2 **copy**
**Tu envoies l'original et tu gardes le double.** You send the original and you keep the copy.

**doublé** *masc adjective*, **doublée** *fem*
1 **lined** (*coat*)
2 **dubbed** (*film*)

♂ **doubler** *verb* [1]
1 **to double**
2 **to overtake**
3 **to line** (*a coat*)
4 **to dub** (*a film*)

la **doublure** *fem noun*
1 **lining** (*of a coat*)
2 **double** (*of an actor*)

**douce** *fem adjective* ▷ **doux**

♂ **doucement** *adverb*
1 **gently**
**Doucement, tu me fais mal!** Gently please, you're hurting me!
2 **slowly**
**La vieille dame marche doucement.** The old lady walks slowly.
3 **quietly**
**Ferme la porte tout doucement!** Shut the door very quietly!

la **douceur** *fem noun*
1 **softness**
2 **gentleness**
3 **mildness** (*of weather*)

♂ la **douche** *fem noun*
**shower**
**Nelly prend une douche.** Nelly is having a shower.
**Djamila est sous la douche.** Djamila is in the shower.

se **doucher** *reflexive verb* Ⓔ [1]
**to have a shower**
**Delphine se douche.** Delphine is having a shower.

**doué** *masc adjective*, **douée** *fem*
**gifted, talented**
**être doué en quelque chose** to have a talent for something
**Raphaël est doué en musique.** Raphaël has a talent for music
**être doué pour quelque chose** to have a gift for something
**Gwenaëlle est douée pour la danse classique.** Gwenaëlle has a gift for ballet.

**douillet** *masc adjective*, **douillette** *fem*
1 **soft** (*person*)
2 **cosy** (*bed, apartment*)

la **douleur** *fem noun*
1 **pain**
**J'ai une douleur dans le coude.** I've got a pain in my elbow.
**un médicament contre la douleur** a painkiller
2 **grief**

**douloureux** *masc adjective*, **douloureuse** *fem*
**painful**

le **doute** *masc noun*
1 **doubt**
**J'ai des doutes.** I have my doubts.
2 **sans doute** probably

**douter** *verb* [1]
**to doubt**
**douter de quelque chose** to have doubts about something
**Il doutait de son amitié.** He had doubts about his friendship.

se **douter** *reflexive verb* ⓔ
1 **se douter de quelque chose** to think you know something
**Je me doute de sa réponse.** I think I know his reply.
**Je m'en doutais.** I thought as much.
2 **se douter que ...** to suspect that ...
**Il se doutait bien que ce serait difficile à faire.** He suspected that it would be hard to do.

**douteux** *masc adjective*, **douteuse** *fem*
1 **doubtful**
2 **dubious** (*taste, piece of information*)

**Douvres** *noun*
**Dover**

♪ **doux** *masc adjective*, **douce** *fem*
1 **soft**
**Elle a la peau douce.** She has soft skin.
2 **gentle** (*person, expression*)
3 **mild** (*weather*)
4 **sweet** (*cider*)

♪ la **douzaine** *fem noun*
**dozen**
**une douzaine d'œufs** a dozen eggs

♪ **douze** *number*
**twelve**
**Elle a douze ans.** She's twelve.
**le douze juillet** the twelfth of July

♪ **douzième** *masc & fem adjective*
**twelfth**

la **dragée** *fem noun*
**sugared almond**

**draguer** *verb* [1]
(*informal*) **draguer quelqu'un** to chat somebody up
**se faire draguer** to get chatted up

**dramatique** *masc & fem adjective*
1 **tragic**
**Ce n'est pas dramatique si ...** It's not the end of the world if ...
2 **dramatic**
**l'art dramatique** drama

le **drame** *masc noun*
1 **tragedy**
**un drame de famille** a family tragedy
2 **drama**
**un drame en trois actes** a three-act play

♪ le **drap** *masc noun*
**sheet**
- le **drap de bain** bath towel

le **drapeau** *masc noun*, les **drapeaux** *pl*
**flag**

**dresser** *verb* [1]
1 **to train** (*an animal*)
2 **to put up** (*a tent*)
3 **to draw up** (*a list*)

se **dresser** *reflexive verb* ⓔ
**to stand up**

♪ la **drogue** *fem noun*
**drug**
**la drogue** drugs
- les **drogues douces** soft drugs
- les **drogues dures** hard drugs

**droguer** *verb* [1]
**to drug**

se **droguer** *reflexive verb* ⓔ
**to take drugs**

la **droguerie** *fem noun*
**hardware shop**

**droit** *masc adjective*, **droite** *fem*
▷ see **droit** *adv, noun*
1 **straight**
**une ligne droite** a straight line
2 **right**
**ma main droite** my right hand
3 **un angle droit** a right angle

**droit** *adverb* ▷ see **droit** *adj, noun*
**straight**
**droit devant** straight ahead
**Continuez tout droit.** Carry straight on.

♪ le **droit** *masc noun* ▷ see **droit** *adj, adv*
1 **right**
**Je connais mes droits.** I know my rights.
**les droits de l'homme** human rights
2 **avoir le droit de faire quelque chose** to be allowed to do something
**Je n'ai pas le droit de sortir ce soir.** I'm not allowed to go out tonight.
3 **avoir le droit de faire quelque chose** to have the right to do something
**J'ai le droit de savoir.** I have a right to know.
4 **avoir droit à quelque chose** to be entitled to something
**Vous avez droit à une boisson chacun.** You're allowed one drink each.
5 **le droit** law
**un étudiant en droit** a law student
6 **fee**
**les droits d'inscription** the enrolment fees

la **droite** *fem noun*
1 **right**
**à droite** on the right
**l'élève de droite** the pupil on the right
**tourner à droite** to turn right
**En France, on roule à droite.** In France, you drive on the right.
**à ta droite, sur ta droite** on your right ▸▸

2 la droite the right (*in politics*)
3 une droite a straight line (*in maths*)

**droitier** *masc adjective*, **droitière** *fem*
**right-handed**

**drôle** *masc & fem adjective*
1 **funny**
une histoire drôle a funny story
2 **odd**
un drôle de film an odd film
C'est drôle qu'elle n'ait pas appelé. It's odd she hasn't phoned.

**drôlement** *adverb*
(*informal*) **really**
C'était drôlement bon! It was really good!

**du** *determiner* ▷ see **dû** *verb*
**some, any**
*de* + *le* becomes *du*. ▷ **de**

**dû**, **due**, **dus** *verb* ▷ **devoir**

le **duc** *masc noun*
**duke**

la **duchesse** *fem noun*
**duchess**

la **dune** *fem noun*
**dune**

le **duo** *masc noun*
**duet**

le **duplex** *masc noun*
**maisonette**

**duquel** *pronoun*
le mur au-dessus duquel il a sauté the wall over which he jumped
18 ans, c'est l'âge à partir duquel on peut voter. You can vote from the age of 18.

**WORD TIP** *de* + *lequel* becomes *duquel*. *duquel* becomes *de laquelle* when it is used for a fem singular noun, *desquels* when it is used for a masc plural noun, and *desquelles* when it is used for a fem plural noun. ▷ **dont**.

**dur** *masc adjective*, **dure** *fem* ▷ see **dur** *adv*
1 **hard**
Cette boîte est dure à ouvrir. This box is hard to open.
2 **tough** (*meat*)
La viande est un peu dure. The meat is a bit tough.
3 **difficult, hard**
L'exercice de maths est vraiment dur. The maths exercise is really hard.
4 **harsh** (*criticism, voice, climate*)
Ses parents ont été durs avec elle. Her parents were harsh with her.

**dur** *adverb* ▷ see **dur** *adj*
**hard**
Marc travaille dur. Marc works hard.

**durant** *preposition*
1 **for**
des années durant for years
2 **during**
durant la partie during the game
durant les deux derniers mois during the last two months

**durcir** *verb* [2]
1 **to harden**
Le beurre durcit au frigidaire. The butter hardens in the fridge.
2 **to set**
La colle n'a pas encore durci. The glue hasn't set yet.

se **durcir** *reflexive verb* Ⓔ
1 **to harden**
2 **to become harsher**

la **durée** *fem noun*
**length**
La durée du spectacle est de trois heures. The length of the show is three hours.
pendant toute la durée des vacances for the duration of the holidays

**durement** *adverb*
**harshly**

**durer** *verb* [1]
1 **to last**
Ça ne durera pas. It won't last.
La grève a duré deux semaines. The strike lasted two weeks.
2 **to go on**
durer pendant trois mois to go on for three months
Cela fait dix ans que ça dure. It's been going on for ten years.
3 **to run**
L'exposition dure du 2 au 20 juin. The exhibition runs from the 2nd to the 20th of June.

la **dureté** *fem noun*
1 **hardness**
2 **toughness**
3 **difficulty**

le **duvet** *masc noun*
**sleeping bag**

le **DVD** *invariable masc noun*
**DVD**
J'ai une centaine de DVD. I've got about a hundred DVDs.

**dynamique** *masc & fem adjective*
**dynamic**

**dyslexique** *masc & fem adjective*
**dyslexic**

Ⓔ means the verb takes être to form the perfect

# E e

♪ l'**eau** *fem noun*
**water**
un verre d'eau a glass of water
de l'eau du robinet some tap water
'Eau potable.' 'Drinking water.'
'Eau non potable.' 'Not drinking water.'
- l'**eau de Javel** bleach
- l'**eau de toilette** eau de toilette (perfume)
- l'**eau gazeuse** sparkling mineral water
- l'**eau minérale** mineral water
- l'**eau plate** still mineral water

**ébaucher** *verb* [1]
**1 to sketch**
**2 to outline**

un & une **ébéniste** *masc & fem noun*
**cabinet maker**

**éblouir** *verb* [2]
**to dazzle**

**éblouissant** *masc adjective*, **éblouissante** *fem*
**dazzling**

un **éboueur** *masc noun*
**refuse collector**

**ébouillanter** *verb* [1]
**to scald**

**ébranler** *verb* [1]
**to shake, to rattle**

l'**ébullition** *fem noun*
**boiling point**

une **écaille** *fem noun*
**1 scale** (*of a fish, a reptile*)
**2 tortoiseshell**

s'**écailler** *reflexive verb* ❻ [1]
**to flake**

un **écart** *masc noun*
**1 gap**
un écart de 10 mètres a 10-metre gap
**2 swerve**
faire un écart to swerve
**3 difference** (*in prices, temperatures*)
**4** à l'écart de away from
**5 lapse**
faire des écarts to allow oneself the occasional treat

**écarté** *masc adjective*, **écartée** *fem*
**1 remote**
un village écarté a remote village
**2** les jambes écartées with legs apart
**3** les bras écartés with arms outstretched

**écarter** *verb* [1]
**1 to move apart**
écarter les rideaux to open the curtains
**2 to move aside** (*things or people in the way*)

s'**écarter** *reflexive verb* ❻
**to move back, to move out of the way**

un **échafaudage** *masc noun*
**scaffolding**

une **échalote** *fem noun*
**shallot**

♪ un **échange** *masc noun*
**exchange**
faire un échange en France to go to France on an exchange
en échange (de) in exchange (for), in return (for)

**échanger** *verb* [52]
**to exchange, to swap**

un **échangeur** *masc noun*
**(motorway) interchange**

un **échantillon** *masc noun*
**sample**

**échapper** *verb* [1]
échapper à quelque chose, quelqu'un to escape from something, somebody
**Ils ont réussi à échapper à la police.** They managed to escape from the police.

s'**échapper** *reflexive verb* ❻
**to escape**
**Ils se sont échappés.** They escaped.

une **écharde** *fem noun*
**splinter**

une **écharpe** *fem noun*
**scarf**

une **échasse** *fem noun*
**stilt**

un **échec** *masc noun*
**failure**

♪ les **échecs** *plural masc noun*
**chess**
jouer aux échecs to play chess

une **échelle** *fem noun*
**1 ladder**
monter à une échelle to climb up a ladder
**2 scale** (*of a map, a scale model*)

un **échelon** *masc noun*
**1 rung** (*of a ladder*)
**2 grade** (*in a company, an organization*)

un **échiquier** *masc noun*
**chessboard**

un **écho** *masc noun*
1 **echo**
2 des échos rumours

une **échographie** *fem noun*
**(medical) scan**
passer une échographie to have a scan

**échouer** *verb* [1]
1 **to fail**
échouer à quelque chose to fail something
2 **to run aground**

**éclabousser** *verb* [1]
**to splash, to spatter**

un **éclair** *masc noun*
**flash of lightning**
- un **éclair au chocolat** chocolate eclair

l'**éclairage** *masc noun*
**lighting**

un & une **éclairagiste** *masc & fem noun*
**lighting engineer**

une **éclaircie** *fem noun*
**sunny interval**

**éclairer** *verb* [1]
**to light (up)**

un **éclat** *masc noun*
1 **splinter of glass**
2 **brightness, sparkle**
3 **splendour**
- un **éclat de rire** roar of laughter

**éclatant** *masc adjective*, **éclatante** *fem*
**brilliant** (*colours*)

**éclater** *verb* [1]
1 **to burst** (*balloons, tyres*)
2 **to shatter** (*bottles, bulbs*)
3 **to break out** (*war, fighting*)
4 (*with emotions*) éclater de rire to burst out laughing
éclater en sanglots to burst into tears

une **éclipse** *fem noun*
**eclipse**

une **écluse** *fem noun*
**lock** (*on a canal, a river*)

**écœurant** *masc adjective*, **écœurante** *fem*
1 **sickly**
2 **revolting**

**écœurer** *verb* [1]
**to make (somebody) feel sick**

une **école** *fem noun*
**school**
aller à l'école to go to school
- une **école de conduite** driving school
- une **école de langues** language school
- une **école maternelle** (state) nursery school (*age 2 to 6*)
- une **école primaire** primary school (*age 6 to 11*)

un **écolier** *masc noun*, une **écolière** *fem*
**schoolchild**

l'**écologie** *fem noun*
**ecology**

**écologique** *masc & fem adjective*
1 **ecological**
2 **environmentally friendly**

un & une **écologiste** *masc & fem noun*
**ecologist**

un **économe** *masc noun*
▷ see **économe** *adjective*
**vegetable peeler**

**économe** *masc & fem adjective*
▷ see **économe** *noun*
**economical**

l'**économie** *fem noun*
1 **economy**
2 **economics**
faire des études d'économie to study economics
3 les économies savings
Je vais faire des économies. I'm going to save up.

**économique** *masc & fem adjective*
1 **economical**
2 **economic**

**économiser** *verb* [1]
**to save**
économiser l'énergie to save energy

un & une **économiste** *masc & fem noun*
**economist**

l'**écorce** *fem noun*
1 **bark** (*of a tree*)
2 **peel** (*of an orange, a lemon*)

s'**écorcher** *reflexive verb* ⓔ [1]
**to graze yourself**
Chloë s'est écorché la main. Chloë grazed her hand.

une **écorchure** *fem noun*
**graze**

**écossais** *masc adjective*, **écossaise** *fem*
▷ see **écossais** *masc noun* **Écossais** *masc & fem noun*
1 **Scottish**
2 **tartan**

**WORD TIP** Adjectives never have capitals in French, even for nationality or regional origin.

un **écossais** *masc noun* ▷ see **écossais** *adj*
**Écossais** *noun*
**tartan** (*the cloth*)

♪ un **Écossais** *masc noun*, une **Écossaise** *fem*
▷ see **écossais** *masc noun, adj*
**Scotsman**, **Scotswoman**, **Scot**
les Écossais the Scots

♪ l'**Écosse** *fem noun*
**Scotland**
habiter en Écosse to live in Scotland
aller en Écosse to go to Scotland

**WORD TIP** Countries and regions in French take *le*, *la* or *les*.

**écourter** *verb* **[1]**
**to shorten**

♪ **écouter** *verb* **[1]**
**to listen to**
**Dans la voiture, j'écoute la radio.** In the car, I listen to the radio.
**Écoute-moi.** Listen to me.

un **écouteur** *masc noun*
1 **receiver** (*on a telephone*)
2 **headphones**

♪ un **écran** *masc noun*
1 **screen**

**écrasant** *masc adjective*, **écrasante** *fem*
1 **crushing**, **overwhelming**
2 **sweltering**

**écraser** *verb* **[1]**
1 **to crush**
2 **to squash**
3 écraser une cigarette to stub out a cigarette
4 se faire écraser to get run over
**Mon chien s'est fait écraser.** My dog got run over.

s'**écraser** *reflexive verb* Ⓔ
**to crash**

**écrémé** *masc adjective*, **écrémée** *fem*
**skimmed**
le lait écrémé skimmed milk
le lait demi-écrémé semi-skimmed milk

une **écrevisse** *fem noun*
**crayfish**

♪ **écrire** *verb* **[38]**
**to write**
**Elle m'a écrit une lettre.** She wrote me a letter.
**J'écris mes cartes postales.** I'm writing my postcards.

s'**écrire** *reflexive verb* Ⓔ
1 **to write to each other**
**Ils s'écrivent tous les jours.** They write to each other every day.
2 **to be spelled**
**Le mot s'écrit avec un accent.** The word is spelled with an accent.
**Comment ça s'écrit?** How do you spell it?

**écrit** *masc adjective*, **écrite** *fem*
▷ see **écrit** *noun*
**written**

un **écrit** *masc noun* ▷ see **écrit** *adj*
1 **(piece of) writing**
2 **written paper** (*of an exam*)
3 à l'écrit, par écrit in writing

une **écriture** *fem noun*
1 **handwriting**
2 **writing** (*on a page*)

un **écrivain** *masc noun*
**writer**

**WORD TIP** A female writer is also *un* écrivain.

un **écrou** *masc noun*
**nut** (*screwed onto a bolt*)

s'**écrouler** *reflexive verb* Ⓔ **[1]**
**to collapse**
s'écrouler de rire (*informal*) to be doubled up laughing

l'**écume** *fem noun*
1 **foam**, **froth**
2 **scum** (*on a liquid*)

un **écureuil** *masc noun*
**squirrel**

une **écurie** *fem noun*
**stable**

l'**eczéma** *masc noun*
**eczema**

**EDF** *fem noun*
(= *Électricité de France*) (*French electricity company*)

**Édimbourg** *noun*
**Edinburgh**

**éditer** *verb* **[1]**
**to publish**

un **éditeur** *masc noun*, une **éditrice** *fem*
**publisher**

l'**édition** *fem noun*
1 l'édition publishing
2 **edition**
• une **édition de poche** paperback edition

l'**édredon** *masc noun*
**eiderdown**

un **éducateur** *masc noun*, une **éducatrice** *fem*
**teacher**, **youth worker**

**éducatif** *masc adjective*, **éducative** *fem*
**educational**

l'**éducation** *fem noun*
**education**
• l'**éducation physique** physical education, PE

**éduquer** *verb* [1]
1 **to educate**
2 **to bring up** (*a child*)

**effacer** *verb* [61]
**to rub out**, **to erase**

un **effaceur** *masc noun*
**correction pen**

**effarant** *masc adjective*, **effarante** *fem*
**amazing**, **alarming**

**effarer** *verb* [1]
**to alarm**

**effectivement** *adverb*
**indeed** (*showing agreement*)
**'Tu as oublié ton maillot.' — 'Ah oui, effectivement!'** 'You've left your swimsuit behind.' — 'Oh yes, so I have!'

**effectuer** *verb* [1]
**to carry out** (*a change, repairs*)

un **effet** *masc noun*
1 **effect**
**Ça n'a aucun effet.** It has no effect.
2 **en effet** indeed (*showing agreement*)
**'Il fait très froid.' — 'Oui, en effet.'** 'It's very cold.' — 'Yes, it is, isn't it?'

**efficace** *masc & fem adjective*
1 **efficient**
**Elle est très efficace.** She's very efficient.
2 **effective**
**C'est un remède très efficace.** It's a very effective remedy.

l'**efficacité** *fem noun*
1 **efficiency**
**Il est connu pour son efficacité.** He's known for his efficiency.
2 **effectiveness**

s'**effondrer** *reflexive verb* Ⓔ [1]
**to collapse**

s'**efforcer** *reflexive verb* Ⓔ [61]
**s'efforcer de faire quelque chose** to try hard to do something

un **effort** *masc noun*
**effort**
**faire l'effort de faire quelque chose** to make the effort to do something
**J'ai fait l'effort d'y aller.** I made the effort to go.

**effrayant** *masc adjective*, **effrayante** *fem*
**frightening**

**effrayer** *verb* [59]
**to frighten**

l'**effroi** *masc noun*
**terror**

**effronté** *masc adjective*, **effrontée** *fem*
**cheeky**

**effroyable** *masc & fem adjective*
**dreadful**

**égal** *masc adjective*, **égale** *fem*, **égaux** *masc pl*, **égales** *fem pl* ▷ see **égal** *noun*
1 **equal**
**une distance égale** an equal distance
**des quantités égales** equal quantities
**être égal à** to be equal to
2 **être égal à quelqu'un** to be all the same to somebody
**Ça m'est égal.** I don't mind., I don't care.
**'Tu veux aller au cinéma?' — 'Ça m'est égal.'** 'Do you want to go to the cinema?' — 'I don't mind.'

un **égal** *masc noun*, une **égale** *fem* les **égaux** *masc pl* les **égales** *fem pl* ▷ see **égal** *adj*
**equal**

**également** *adverb*
**also**

**égaler** *verb* [1]
**to equal**
**Trois plus cinq égalent huit.** Three plus five equals eight.

**égaliser** *verb* [1]
**to equalize**

l'**égalité** *fem noun*
**equality**

l'**égard** *masc noun*
1 **à l'égard de** towards, regarding
**à mon égard** towards me
2 **à cet égard** in this respect

**égaré** *masc adjective*, **égarée** *fem*
**stray**, **lost**

**égarer** *verb* [1]
**to mislay**

s'**égarer** *reflexive verb* Ⓔ
**to get lost**

**égayer** *verb* [59]
1 **to brighten up**
2 **to cheer up**



Ⓔ means the verb takes être to form the perfect

♂ une **église** *fem noun*
**church**
aller à l'église to go to church

l'**égoïsme** *masc noun*
**selfishness**

**égoïste** *masc & fem adjective*
**selfish**

un **égout** *masc noun*
**sewer**

**égoutter** *verb* [1]
1 **to drain** (*vegetables*)
2 **to strain** (*pasta*)
3 **to drip**

une **égratignure** *fem noun*
**scratch**

l'**Égypte** *fem noun*
**Egypt**

♂ **eh bien** *exclamation*
**well**
Eh bien, ça me fait plaisir de te revoir. Well, it's nice to see you again.

s'**élancer** *reflexive verb* Ⓔ [61]
**to dash**

**élargir** *verb* [2]
**to widen**

**élastique** *masc & fem adjective*
▷ see **élastique** *noun*
1 **elastic**
2 **elasticated**

un **élastique** *masc noun*
▷ see **élastique** *adj*
1 **rubber band**
2 **elastic**

un **électeur** *masc noun*, une **électrice** *fem*
**voter**

♂ une **élection** *fem noun*
**election**

un **électricien** *masc noun*, une **électricienne** *fem*
**electrician**

♂ l'**électricité** *fem noun*
**electricity**

**électrique** *masc & fem adjective*
1 **electric**
2 **electrical**

l'**électroménager** *masc noun*
**domestic appliances**

**électronique** *masc & fem adjective*
▷ see **électronique** *noun*
**electronic**

l'**électronique** *fem noun*
▷ see **électronique** *adj*
**electronics**

♂ **élégant** *masc adjective*, **élégante** *fem*
**elegant**

un **élément** *masc noun*
1 **element**
2 **part, section** (*to be assembled*)

**élémentaire** *masc & fem adjective*
**basic, elementary**

un **éléphant** *masc noun*
**elephant**

l'**élevage** *masc noun*
1 **farming** (*of cattle, pigs, sheep*)
2 **farm**

**élevé** *masc adjective*, **élevée** *fem*
**high**
une note élevée a high mark

♂ un & une **élève** *masc & fem noun*
**student, pupil**

**élever** *verb* [50]
1 élever un enfant to bring up a child
2 **to breed** (*animals*)
3 élever la voix to raise one's voice

s'**élever** *reflexive verb* Ⓔ
1 **to rise** (*temperatures*)
2 s'élever à quelque chose to amount to something
La facture s'élève à cinq cents euros. The bill amounts to five hundred euros.

un **éleveur** *masc noun*, une **éleveuse** *fem*
**breeder**

**éliminer** *verb* [1]
1 **to eliminate, to get rid of**
2 **to eliminate, to knock out**
3 **to rule out** (*a possibility, an option*)

**élire** *verb* [51]
**to elect**

♂ **elle** *pronoun*
1 (*as the subject of the verb*) **she**
Elle parle bien français. She speaks French well.
2 (*for a fem singular noun*) **it**
'Où est ma tasse?' — 'Elle est sur la table.' 'Where's my cup?' — 'It's on the table.'
3 **her** (*as opposed to anybody else*)
C'est elle. It's her.
chez elle at her house
Je pense à elle. I'm thinking of her.
4 (*for emphasis*) **she**
C'est elle qui me l'a dit. She's the one who told me.
Elle et moi sommes très copines. She ▸▸

and I are good friends.
**Elle, elle n'est jamais contente!** She's never happy!
5 (*after prepositions like* **avec** *or* **sans** *and in comparisons*) **her**
**Paul est avec elle.** Paul's with her.
**Je suis plus grande qu'elle.** I'm taller than her.
6 **à elle** hers (*belonging to her*)
**Ce sont des amis à elle.** They're friends of hers.

**elle-même** *pronoun*
1 **herself**
**Elle a tout fait elle-même.** She did everything herself.
**'Madame Dubois?' — 'Elle-même.'** 'Madame Dubois?' — 'Speaking.'
2 (*for fem things*) **itself**
**La chanson elle-même est bien mais je n'aime pas ce groupe.** The song itself is good but I don't like that group.

**elles** *fem plural pronoun*
1 (*for female people and things as the subject*) **they**
**Elles habitent tout près.** They live near here.
**Mes chaussures! Elles sont ruinées!** My shoes! They're ruined!
2 (*after prepositions like* **avec** *or* **sans** *and in comparisons*) **them**
**Je reste avec elles.** I'm staying with them.
**Tu es plus sympa qu'elles.** You're nicer than them.
3 **à elles** theirs (*belonging to them*)
**Le voiture rouge est à elles.** The red car is theirs.
4 **chez elles** at their house

**elles-mêmes** *pronoun*
(*for female people and objects*) **themselves**

**éloigné** *masc adjective*, **éloignée** *fem*
**distant**
**éloigné du centre-ville** far from the town centre
**la maison la plus éloignée** the house furthest away

s'**éloigner** *reflexive verb* Ⓔ **[1]**
**to move away**
**Ne t'éloigne pas trop.** Don't go too far away.
**s'éloigner de quelque chose** to move away from something
**Le ferry s'éloignait de la côte.** The ferry was moving away from the coast.

l'**Élysée** *masc noun*
**the Élysée Palace** (*the official residence of the French President*)

l'**email**, **e-mail** *masc noun*
**email**

l'**émail** *masc noun*
**enamel**

**WORD TIP** *émail* does not mean *email* in English; for the meaning of *email* ▷ **courrier électronique, courriel, email**.

l'**emballage** *masc noun*
**wrapping**

**emballer** *verb* **[1]**
1 **to wrap, to pack**
2 (*informal*) **emballer quelqu'un** to fill somebody with enthusiasm
**Le film ne m'emballe pas.** I'm not keen on the film.

s'**emballer** *reflexive verb* Ⓔ **[1]**
1 **to bolt** (*horses*)
2 (*informal*) **s'emballer pour quelque chose** to become enthusiastic about something
**Ne t'emballe pas!** Don't get carried away!

l'**embarquement** *masc noun*
**boarding**

**embarquer** *verb* **[1]**
1 **to board**
2 (*informal*) **to go off with**
**Qui a embarqué la télécommande?** Who's gone off with the remote?

s'**embarquer** *reflexive verb* Ⓔ
**s'embarquer pour l'Amérique** to set sail for America

un **embarras** *masc noun*
1 **embarrassment**
2 **dilemma**
**être dans l'embarras** to have money problems
3 **avoir l'embarras du choix** to be spoilt for choice

**embarrassé** *masc adjective*, **embarrassée** *fem*
1 **embarrassed**
2 **cluttered**

**embarrasser** *verb* **[1]**
1 **to embarrass**
2 **to clutter up**

**embaucher** *verb* **[1]**
**to take on** (*an employee*)

**embêtant** *masc adjective*, **embêtante** *fem*
**annoying**

**embêter** *verb* **[1]**
**to annoy**

s'**embêter** *reflexive verb* ❷
**1 to be bored**
**On ne s'embête pas ici.** There's plenty going on here.
**2 to worry**
**Ne t'embête pas pour ça.** Don't worry about it.
**3 to bother**
**Est-ce que ça t'embête?** Does it bother you?

♪ un **embouteillage** *masc noun*
**traffic jam**

**embrasser** *verb* **[1]**
**1 to kiss**
**2** *(in greetings)* **Je t'embrasse.** Lots of love. *(in letters)*
**Salut, je t'embrasse.** Take care, bye. *(in phone calls)*

un **embrayage** *masc noun*
**clutch** *(in a vehicle)*

une **émeraude** *fem noun*
**emerald**

**émerger** *verb* **[52]**
**to emerge**

une **émeute** *fem noun*
**riot**

♪ une **émission** *fem noun*
**programme**
**On a regardé une émission à la télé.** We watched a programme on TV.
**Qu'est-ce qu'il y a comme émission?** What programmes are on?

**emménager** *verb* **[52]**
**to move in** *(to a flat, a house)*

**emmener** *verb* **[50]**
**to take**
**Il m'emmène au cinéma.** He's taking me to the cinema.
**Tu veux que je t'emmène?** Would you like a lift?

**émotif** *masc adjective*, **émotive** *fem*
**emotional**

une **émotion** *fem noun*
**emotion**

**émouvant** *masc adjective*, **émouvante** *fem*
**moving**

s'**emparer** *reflexive verb* ❷ **[1]**
**s'emparer de quelque chose** to seize something

**empêcher** *verb* **[1]**
**1 to prevent, to stop**
**empêcher quelqu'un de faire quelque chose** to stop somebody from doing something
**Rien ne t'empêche d'essayer.** There's nothing to stop you trying.
**2 Elle n'a pas pu s'empêcher de rire.** She couldn't help laughing.

un **empereur** *masc noun*
**emperor**

**empiler** *verb* **[1]**
**to pile up**

**empirer** *verb* **[1]**
**to get worse**

♪ un **emplacement** *masc noun*
**1 pitch** *(for a tent)*
**Est-ce qu'il reste des emplacements?** Are there any pitches left?
**2 site** *(for a building)*

♪ un **emploi** *masc noun*
**1 job**
**Il cherche un emploi.** He's looking for a job.
**Après mes examens, je vais trouver un emploi.** After my exams, I'm going to find a job.
**2 use**
**le mode d'emploi** instructions for use
• un **emploi du temps** timetable *(at school)*

♪ un **employé** *masc noun*, une **employée** *fem*
**employee**

**employer** *verb* **[39]**
**1 to employ**
**2 to use**

un **employeur** *masc noun*, une **employeuse** *fem*
**employer**

**empoisonné** *masc adjective*, **empoisonnée** *fem*
**poisoned**

**empoisonner** *verb* **[1]**
**to poison**

**emporter** *verb* **[1]**
**1 to take away**
**Ils ont emporté le vieux frigo.** They took away the old fridge.
**'Plats à emporter'** 'Takeaway meals'
**2 se laisser emporter** to get carried away
**Je me suis laissé emporter.** I got carried away.
**3 to sweep away**
**Ils ont été emportés par le courant.** They were swept away by the current.

une **empreinte** *fem noun*
**footprint**
• une **empreinte digitale** fingerprint

French–English

a b c d e f g h i j k l m n o p q r s t u v w x y z

**emprisonner** *verb* **[1]**
**to imprison**

un **emprunt** *masc noun*
**loan**
- un **emprunt-logement** mortgage

**emprunter** *verb* **[1]**
**to borrow**
**emprunter de l'argent** to borrow money
**emprunter quelque chose à quelqu'un** to borrow something from somebody
**Je peux t'emprunter ta montre?** Can I borrow your watch?

l'**EMT** *noun fem*
(*= Éducation manuelle et technique*) **Design and Technology, DT**

**ému** *masc adjective*, **émue** *fem*
**moved**

**en** *preposition* ▷ see **en** *pron*
1 **in**
**en été** in summer
**en avril** in April
**une chanson en français** a song in French
**habillé en noir** dressed in black
**J'étais en pyjama.** I was in my pyjamas.
**Elle habite en Écosse.** She lives in Scotland.
2 **into**
**aller en ville** to go into town
**traduire en anglais** to translate into English
3 **to**
**aller en Italie** to go to Italy
**rentrer en Angleterre** to return to England
4 **by**
**en avion** by plane
5 **made of**
**une table en bois** a wooden table
**une jupe en jean** a denim skirt
6 **en vacances** on holiday
**en voyage d'affaires** on a business trip
7 **Elle s'est brûlée en repassant sa chemise.** She burned herself (while) ironing her shirt.

**WORD TIP** *en* followed by any verb ending in *-ant* shows one action taking place at the same time as another.

**en** *pronoun* ▷ see **en** *prep*
1 (*in general statements*) **some**
**Tu veux des pièces d'un euro? J'en ai.** You want 1 euro coins? I've got some.
**Du beurre? Il y en a dans le frigo.** Butter? There's some in the fridge.
**Des biscuits? Je crois qu'il en reste.** Biscuits? I think there are some left.
2 (*in negative statements and in simple questions*) **any**
**Je n'en veux pas.** I don't want any.
**Est-ce que tu en as?** Do you have any?
**Est-ce qu'il en reste?** Is there any left?
3 **of it**, **of them** (*en is often not translated*)
**Tu en as combien?** How much (of it) do you have?, How many (of them) do you have?
**Elle en a quatre.** She's got four.
**'Qui a un stylo?' — 'J'en ai un.'** 'Who's got a pen?' — 'I've got one.'
4 **it**, **about it** (*referring to something known about*)
**Elle m'en a parlé.** She told me about it.
**Ne m'en parle pas!** Don't even talk to me about it!
**Je m'en souviens très bien.** I remember it very well.
**Est-ce que tu en as besoin?** Do you need it?

un **encadrement** *masc noun*
1 **frame**
2 **framing**

**encadrer** *verb* **[1]**
**to frame**

**enceinte** *fem adjective*
▷ see **enceinte** *noun*
**pregnant**
**Elle est enceinte de six mois.** She's six months pregnant.

une **enceinte** *fem noun* ▷ see **enceinte** *adj*
1 **surrounding wall**
2 **compound**
3 **loudspeaker**

l'**encens** *masc noun*
**incense**

**encercler** *verb* **[1]**
1 **to surround**
2 **to circle** (*when filling in a questionnaire*)

**enchanté** *masc adjective*, **enchantée** *fem*
1 **delighted**
2 (*in introductions*) **Enchanté.** Pleased to meet you (*boy speaking*).
**Enchantée.** Pleased to meet you (*girl speaking*).
**'Anaïs, je te présente mes parents.' — 'Enchantée.'** 'Anaïs, this is my Mum and Dad.' — 'Pleased to meet you.'
3 **enchanted**

une **enchère** *fem noun*
**bid** (*in an auction*)
**une vente aux enchères** an auction

**encombrant** *masc adjective*,
**encombrante** *fem*
**cumbersome**

**encombrer** *verb* **[1]**
1 **to clutter up**
2 **to obstruct**

♪ **encore** *adverb*
1 **still**
Elle est encore au supermarché. She's still at the supermarket.
Il reste encore du poulet. There's still some chicken left.
2 pas encore not yet
Ce n'est pas encore prêt. It's not ready yet.
Il n'est pas encore rentré. He hasn't come home yet.
3 **again**
Je l'ai encore oublié. I've forgotten it again.
C'est encore moi! It's me again!
4 **more**
encore un peu a little more
encore une fois one more time
attendre encore une semaine to wait for another week
5 **even**
encore mieux even better
encore pire even worse

**encourageant** *masc adjective*, **encourageante** *fem*
**encouraging**

l'**encouragement** *masc noun*
**encouragement**

**encourager** *verb* [52]
1 **to encourage**
2 **to cheer on** (*a team*)

l'**encre** *fem noun*
**ink**

l'**encyclopédie** *fem noun*
**encyclopedia**

l'**endive** *fem noun*
**chicory**

**endommager** *verb* [52]
**to damage**

**endormi** *masc adjective*, **endormie** *fem*
**asleep**
J'étais à moitié endormi. I was half asleep.

**endormir** *verb* [37]
endormir quelqu'un to send somebody to sleep (*literally*)

s'**endormir** *reflexive verb* ⓔ
**to fall asleep, to go to sleep**
Je n'arrive pas à m'endormir. I can't get to sleep.

♪ un **endroit** *masc noun*
1 **place**
un drôle d'endroit a strange place
2 **the right side** (*of a garment*)
3 à l'endroit the right way up (*for parcels, crates*)

l'**énergie** *fem noun*
**energy**

**énergique** *masc & fem adjective*
**energetic**

**énervé** *masc adjective*, **énervée** *fem*
**irritated, annoyed**

**énerver** *verb* [1]
**to irritate, to annoy**
Ça m'énerve! This is getting on my nerves!

s'**énerver** *reflexive verb* ⓔ
**to get annoyed**
Ne t'énerve pas! Calm down!

l'**enfance** *fem noun*
**childhood**

♪ un & une **enfant** *masc & fem noun*
**child**
• un & une **enfant unique** only child

**enfantin** *masc adjective*, **enfantine** *fem*
1 **easy**
2 **childish**

l'**enfer** *masc noun*
**hell**

**enfermer** *verb* [1]
1 **to shut up**
2 **to lock up** (*your property, valuables*)

s'**enfermer** *reflexive verb* ⓔ
**to shut yourself up**

**enfiler** *verb* [1]
1 **to put on** (*clothes*)
2 enfiler une aiguille to thread a needle

♪ **enfin** *adverb*
1 **at last**
J'ai enfin fini. I've finished at last.
2 **finally**
Elle a enfin réussi. She finally succeeded.
3 **for heaven's sake**
Mais enfin, qu'est-ce qui se passe? Oh for heaven's sake, what's happening?

**enflé** *masc adjective*, **enflée** *fem*
**swollen**

une **enflure** *fem noun*
**swelling**

**enfoncer** *verb* [61]
1 **to push in** (*a nail, a pin*)
2 **to break down** (*a door*)

s'**enfoncer** *reflexive verb* ⓔ
s'enfoncer dans quelque chose to sink into something
Mes pieds s'enfoncent dans la neige. My feet are sinking into the snow.

**enfreindre** *verb* [2]
**to disobey**

un **engagement** *masc noun*
**commitment**

**engager** *verb* **[52]**
**1 to take on** (*an employee*)
**2** engager la conversation to strike up a conversation

s'**engager** *reflexive verb* ⓔ
s'engager à faire quelque chose to promise to do something

une **engelure** *fem noun*
**chilblain**

un **engin** *masc noun*
**device**

**engourdi** *masc adjective*, **engourdie** *fem*
**numb**

s'**engourdir** *reflexive verb* ⓔ **[2]**
**to go numb**

l'**engrais** *masc noun*
**fertilizer**

**engueuler** *verb* **[1]**
(*informal*) **to tell off**
Elle nous engueule tout le temps. She's always telling us off.
se faire engueuler to get a telling off
Je me suis fait engueuler. I got a telling off.

s'**engueuler** *reflexive verb* ⓔ **[1]**
**to have a row**
Je me suis engueulée avec ma copine. I've had a row with my friend.

**énième** *masc & fem adjective*
**umpteenth**
pour la énième fois for the umpteenth time

une **énigme** *fem noun*
**riddle**

**enivrer** *verb* **[1]**
enivrer quelqu'un to make somebody drunk

s'**enivrer** *reflexive verb* ⓔ
**to get drunk**

un **enlèvement** *masc noun*
**kidnapping**

**enlever** *verb* **[50]**
**1 to take off** (*a garment*)
Enlève tes baskets. Take your trainers off.
**2 to remove, to take away**
enlever une tache to remove a stain
Tu peux enlever les assiettes. You can take away the plates.
**3 to kidnap**

**enneigé** *masc adjective*, **enneigée** *fem*
**1 snowy**
**2 snow-covered**
une route enneigée a snow-covered road

un **ennemi** *masc noun*, une **ennemie** *fem*
**enemy**

l'**ennui** *masc noun*
**1 boredom**
**2 problem**
avoir des ennuis to have problems

**ennuyé** *masc adjective*, **ennuyée** *fem*
**1 bored**
**2 embarrassed**

**ennuyer** *verb* **[41]**
**1 to bore**
Le film m'a vraiment ennuyé. I found the film really boring.
**2 to bother**
Je t'ennuie? Am I bothering you?

s'**ennuyer** *reflexive verb* ⓔ
**to be bored, to get bored**
s'ennuyer à mourir to be bored stiff
On s'ennuie ici. It's boring here.
On ne s'ennuie pas! We're having fun!

**ennuyeux** *masc adjective*, **ennuyeuse** *fem*
**1 boring**
une émission ennuyeuse a boring programme
**2 annoying**
Ça, c'est vraiment ennuyeux. That's a real nuisance.

**énorme** *masc & fem adjective*
**huge**

**énormément** *adverb*
**1 tremendously**
**2** énormément de quelque chose masses of something
J'ai énormément de choses à faire. I've got masses of things to do.

une **enquête** *fem noun*
**1 investigation**
**2 inquiry**
**3 survey**

un **enregistrement** *masc noun*
**1 recording**
**2 check-in** (*at an airport*)

**enregistrer** *verb* **[1]**
**1 to record**
**2 to register**
**3 to check in** (*at an airport*)
enregistrer ses bagages to check in your luggage

s'**enregistrer** *reflexive verb* ⓔ **[1]**
**to record oneself** (*on an audio tape*)



ⓔ means the verb takes être to form the perfect

**enregistreur DVD** *masc noun*
**DVD recorder**

**enrhumer** *verb* **[1]**
**être enrhumé** to have a cold

s'**enrhumer** *reflexive verb* **Ⓔ**
**to catch a cold**
**Je me suis enrhumé.** I caught a cold.

**enrichir** *verb* **[2]**
1 **to make rich**
2 **to enrich**

**enrichissant** *masc adjective*, **enrichissante** *fem*
**rewarding**

**enrouler** *verb* **[1]**
**to wind**

♪ un **enseignant** *masc noun*, une **enseignante** *fem*
**teacher**

une **enseigne** *fem noun*
**sign**
- une **enseigne lumineuse** neon sign

l'**enseignement** *masc noun*
1 **teaching**
2 **education**

**enseigner** *verb* **[1]**
**to teach**

♪ **ensemble** *adverb* ▷ see **ensemble** *noun*
**together**
**Ils sont toujours ensemble.** They're still together.

un **ensemble** *masc noun*
▷ see **ensemble** *adv*
1 **outfit**
2 **l'ensemble de** the whole of
**l'ensemble des élèves dans la classe** all the students in the class
3 **dans l'ensemble** on the whole

♪ **ensoleillé** *masc adjective*, **ensoleillée** *fem*
**sunny**

**ensommeillé** *masc adjective*, **ensommeillée** *fem*
**sleepy**

♪ **ensuite** *adverb*
**then**

**entamer** *verb* **[1]**
**to start** (*when eating, drinking or opening something*)
**On entame le dessert?** Shall we start eating dessert?

**entasser** *verb* **[1]**
**to pile up**

♪ **entendre** *verb* **[3]**
1 **to hear**
**Je n'entends rien.** I can't hear a thing.
2 **J'ai entendu dire que ...** I've heard that ...

s'**entendre** *reflexive verb* **Ⓔ**
**s'entendre bien** to get on well
**Je m'entends très bien avec eux.** I get on very well with them.
**Je ne m'entends pas avec mon frère.** I don't get on with my brother.

**entendu** *exclamation*
1 **okay, fine**
2 **bien entendu** of course

une **entente** *fem noun*
1 **understanding**
2 **agreement**

un **enterrement** *masc noun*
**funeral, burial**

**enterrer** *verb* **[1]**
**to bury**

**entêté** *masc adjective*, **entêtée** *fem*
**stubborn**

s'**entêter** *reflexive verb* **Ⓔ [1]**
**to be stubborn**

l'**enthousiasme** *masc noun*
**enthusiasm**

s'**enthousiasmer** *reflexive verb* **Ⓔ [1]**
**to get enthusiastic**

**enthousiaste** *masc & fem adjective*
**enthusiastic**

**entier** *masc adjective*, **entière** *fem*
1 **whole**
**le monde entier** the whole world
2 **Je n'ai pas lu sa lettre en entier.** I haven't read his letter right through.
3 **le lait entier** full-fat milk

**entièrement** *adverb*
**completely, totally**
**entièrement gratuit** completely free of charge
**Je suis entièrement d'accord avec vous.** I totally agree with you.

une **entorse** *fem noun*
**sprain**

♪ **entouré** *masc adjective*, **entourée** *fem*
1 **entouré de** surrounded by
**Elle est entourée d'amis.** She's surrounded by friends.
2 **être bien entouré** to be well looked after

French–English

**entourer** *verb* **[1]**
**to surround**
**les vignobles qui entourent le village** the vineyards surrounding the village
**entourer de** to surround with
**entourer d'un cercle la bonne réponse** to circle the correct answer

un **entracte** *masc noun*
**interval** *(at the theatre)*

l'**entraînement** *masc noun*
1 **training** *(in sport)*
2 **practice**

**entraîner** *verb* **[1]**
1 **to lead to**
2 **to take**
3 **to train**
4 **to drag along**

s'**entraîner** *reflexive verb* Ⓔ
**to train**

♪ **entre** *preposition*
1 **between**
**entre la porte et la fenêtre** between the door and the window
**un match entre la France et l'Italie** a match between France and Italy
2 **among**
**entre eux** among themselves
3 **l'un d'entre eux, l'une d'entre elles** one of them
**L'une d'entre elles monte à cheval.** One of them goes horse-riding.

♪ une **entrecôte** *fem noun*
**steak**

une **entrée** *fem noun*
1 **entrance**
**billets à l'entrée** tickets at the door
2 **hall(way)**
3 **admission**
**entrée gratuite** free admission
4 **starter**, **first course**
**Qu'est-ce que tu prends en entrée?** What are you having as a starter?

un **entremets** *masc noun*
**flan**, **cream dessert**

un **entrepôt** *masc noun*
**warehouse**

**entreprendre** *verb* **[64]**
1 **to undertake** *(work)*
2 **to start** *(a task)*

une **entreprise** *fem noun*
**firm**, **business**

♪ **entrer** *verb* **[1]**
1 **to go in**
**entrer dans un magasin** to go into a shop
**entrer à l'hôpital** to go into hospital
2 **to come in**
**entrer dans une pièce** to come into a room
**Entrez!** Come in!

**entre-temps** *adverb*
**meanwhile**

**entretenir** *verb* **[81]**
1 **to maintain** *(a building, a car)*
2 **to look after** *(plants, clothes)*
3 **to support** *(a family)*

un **entretien** *masc noun*
1 **interview**
**L'entretien s'est bien passé.** The interview went well.
2 **discussion**
**avoir un entretien avec le professeur** to have a discussion with the teacher
3 **upkeep**
**l'entretien de la maison** the upkeep of the house

une **entrevue** *fem noun*
**interview**

**entrouvert** *masc adjective*, **entrouverte** *fem*
**ajar**, **half-open**

**envahir** *verb* **[2]**
**to invade**

une **enveloppe** *fem noun*
**envelope**
- une **enveloppe matelassée** padded envelope

**envelopper** *verb* **[1]**
**to wrap up**

l'**envers** *masc noun* ▷ see **envers** *prep*
1 **wrong side** *(of fabric, of knitting)*
2 **à l'envers** upside down, inside out, back to front

**envers** *preposition* ▷ see **envers** *noun*
**towards**, **to**

♪ l'**envie** *fem noun*
1 **urge**
**avoir envie de faire quelque chose** to want to do something, to feel like doing something
**Tu as envie d'aller au cinéma?** Do you feel like going to the cinema?
2 **avoir envie de quelque chose** to feel like something
**J'ai envie d'une glace.** I feel like an ice cream.



Ⓔ means the verb takes être to form the perfect

**3 envy**
Tu me fais envie. You're making me envious.

**envier** *verb* **[1]**
**to envy**

**envieux** *masc adjective*, **envieuse** *fem*
**envious**

♪ **environ** *adverb*
**about**
environ trente personnes about thirty people

l'**environnement** *masc noun*
**environment**

les **environs** *plural masc noun*
**surroundings**
J'habite aux environs de Londres. I live near London.

**envisager** *verb* **[52]**
envisager de faire quelque chose to plan to do something
Qu'est-ce que vous envisagez de faire? What are you planning to do?

un **envoi** *masc noun*
**1 dispatch**
**2 consignment**

s'**envoler** *reflexive verb* Ⓔ **[1]**
**to fly away**

♪ **envoyer** *verb* **[40]**
**to send**
envoyer quelque chose à quelqu'un to send somebody something
Elle m'a envoyé une carte. She sent me a card.
Elle m'a envoyé chercher les verres. She sent me to get the glasses.

♪ **épais** *masc adjective*, **épaisse** *fem*
**thick**
une tranche épaisse a thick slice

l'**épaisseur** *fem noun*
**thickness**

l'**épargne** *fem noun*
**savings**
un compte d'épargne a savings account

**épatant** *masc adjective*, **épatante** *fem*
(*informal*) **great**
C'était vraiment épatant! It was really great!

♪ une **épaule** *fem noun*
**shoulder**

une **épaulette** *fem noun*
**1 shoulder strap**
**2 shoulder pad**

une **épave** *fem noun*
**wreck**

une **épée** *fem noun*
**sword**

**épeler** *verb* **[18]**
**to spell**

un **épi** *masc noun*
**ear** (*of corn*)
• un **épi de maïs** corn cob

une **épice** *fem noun*
**spice**

**épicé** *masc adjective*, **épicée** *fem*
**spicy, hot**

une **épicerie** *fem noun*
**grocer's (shop)**

♪ un **épicier** *masc noun*, une **épicière** *fem*
**grocer**

une **épidémie** *fem noun*
**epidemic**

l'**épilepsie** *fem noun*
**epilepsy**

**épiler** *verb* **[1]**
une pince à épiler tweezers

s'**épiler** *reflexive verb* Ⓔ
s'épiler les sourcils to pluck your eyebrows
s'épiler les jambes to shave your legs (*or use wax or cream to remove hair*)

les **épinards** *plural masc noun*
**spinach**

une **épine** *fem noun*
**thorn**

**épineux** *masc adjective*, **épineuse** *fem*
**prickly**

une **épingle** *fem noun*
**pin**
• une **épingle de sûreté** safety pin

**épingler** *verb* **[1]**
**to pin**

**éplucher** *verb* **[1]**
**to peel**

une **éponge** *fem noun*
**1 sponge**
**2 towelling**

**éponger** *verb* **[52]**
**1 to mop up**
**2 to sponge**

une **époque** *fem noun*
**time**
à cette époque-là at that time

une **épouse** *fem noun*
**wife**

**épouser** *verb* [1]
**to marry**

**épouvantable** *masc & fem adjective*
**dreadful**

un **épouvantail** *masc noun*
**scarecrow**

l'**épouvante** *fem noun*
**terror**
un film d'épouvante a horror film

**épouvanter** *verb* [1]
**to terrify**

un **époux** *masc noun*
**husband**

une **épreuve** *fem noun*
1 **test**
2 **exam**
l'épreuve de français the French exam
3 **event** (*in athletics*)
4 **ordeal**

**éprouver** *verb* [1]
**to feel**, **to experience**

une **éprouvette** *fem noun*
**test tube**

l'**EPS** *fem noun*
(*= Éducation physique et sportive*) **PE**

**épuisant** *masc adjective*, **épuisante** *fem*
**exhausting**

**épuisé** *masc adjective*, **épuisée** *fem*
1 **exhausted**, **worn out**
Je suis épuisé. I'm worn out.
2 **out of stock**

**épuiser** *verb* [1]
**to wear out**

l'**équateur** *masc noun*
**equator**

**équestre** *masc & fem adjective*
un centre équestre a riding school

l'**équilibre** *masc noun*
**balance**
perdre l'équilibre to lose your balance

**équilibré** *masc adjective*, **équilibrée** *fem*
**balanced**
une alimentation équilibrée a balanced diet

un **équipage** *masc noun*
**crew**

une **équipe** *fem noun*
**team**
Je voudrais faire partie de l'équipe. I'd like to join the team.

**équipé** *masc adjective*, **équipée** *fem*
1 **equipped**
2 une cuisine équipée a fitted kitchen

un **équipement** *masc noun*
**equipment**

les **équipements** *plural masc noun*
**facilities**
- les **équipements sportifs** sports facilities

l'**équitation** *fem noun*
**(horse-)riding**
faire de l'équitation to go horse-riding

**équivalent** *masc adjective*, **équivalente** *fem*
**equivalent**

un **érable** *masc noun*
**maple tree**
le sirop d'érable maple syrup

**errer** *verb* [1]
**to wander**, **to roam**

une **erreur** *fem noun*
**mistake**
par erreur by mistake

**es** *verb* ▷ **être**

un **escabeau** *masc noun*
**stepladder**

l'**escalade** *fem noun*
**rock-climbing**

un **escalier** *masc noun*
1 **stairs**
dans l'escalier on the stairs
2 **staircase**
- un **escalier de secours** emergency staircase
- un **escalier mécanique** escalator
- un **escalier roulant** escalator

un **escargot** *masc noun*
**snail**

l'**esclavage** *masc noun*
**slavery**

un & une **esclave** *masc & fem noun*
**slave**

l'**escrime** *fem noun*
**fencing**
faire de l'escrime to do fencing

un **escroc** *masc noun*
**crook**, **swindler**

**escroquer** *verb* [1]
**to swindle**

l'**escroquerie** *fem noun*
**swindle**

un **espace** *masc noun*
1 **space**
2 **(outer) space**
- un **espace de loisirs** leisure complex
- les **espaces verts** open spaces (*in cities*)

**espacer** *verb* **[61]**
**to space out**

un **espadon** *masc noun*
**swordfish**

l'**Espagne** *fem noun*
**Spain**

**espagnol** *masc adjective*, **espagnole** *fem* ▷ see **Espagnol** *noun*
**Spanish**

un **Espagnol** *masc noun*, une **Espagnole** *fem* ▷ see **espagnol** *adj*
1 **Spaniard** (*person*)
les Espagnols the Spanish
2 l'espagnol Spanish (*the language*)

une **espèce** *fem noun*
1 **sort**
une espèce de sauce épicée a sort of spicy sauce
2 **species**
une espèce très rare a very rare species
3 **en espèces** in cash
4 (*showing annoyance*) **Espèce d'idiot!** You idiot!

♪ **espérer** *verb* **[24]**
**to hope**
J'espère que tu vas mieux. I hope you're feeling better.
espérer faire quelque chose to hope to do something
Ils espèrent pouvoir venir. They're hoping to be able to come.
J'espère qu'elle n'a pas oublié. I hope she hasn't forgotten.
J'espère bien! I certainly hope so!
J'espère que non! I hope not!

**espiègle** *masc & fem adjective*
**mischievous**

un **espion** *masc noun*, une **espionne** *fem noun*
**spy**

l'**espionnage** *masc noun*
**spying, espionage**

**espionner** *verb* **[1]**
**to spy on**

un **espoir** *masc noun*
**hope**

l'**esprit** *masc noun*
1 **mind**
Ça ne m'est pas venu à l'esprit. It didn't cross my mind.
2 **wit**
avoir de l'esprit to be witty
- l'**esprit d'équipe** team spirit

un **esquimau**® *masc noun*, les **esquimaux** *pl*
**ice lolly**

un **Esquimau** *masc noun*, les **Esquimaux** *pl*
**Eskimo, Inuit**

une **esquisse** *fem noun*
**sketch** (*in drawing*)

**esquisser** *verb* **[1]**
**to sketch**

un **essai** *masc noun*
1 **trial** (*of a new model of car, plane*)
2 **test** (*in a laboratory*)
3 **attempt**

un **essaim** *masc noun*
**swarm**

♪ **essayer** *verb* **[59]**
1 **to try**
Tiens, est-ce que tu veux essayer? Here, do you want to try?
essayer de faire quelque chose to try to do something
J'ai essayé de t'appeler. I tried to phone you.
Essaie de la convaincre. Try to persuade her.
2 **to try on**
essayer une robe to try on a dress
3 **to test**

♪ l'**essence** *fem noun*
1 **petrol**
2 **essential oil**
- l'**essence sans plomb** unleaded petrol

**essentiel** *masc adjective*, **essentielle** *fem* ▷ see **essentiel** *noun*
**essential**

l'**essentiel** *masc noun* ▷ see **essentiel** *adj*
**main thing**
L'essentiel, c'est de participer. The main thing is to take part.

**essentiellement** *adverb*
1 **mainly**
2 **essentially**

l'**essorage** *masc noun*
**spin-dry**

French-English

**essorer** *verb* [1]
**to spin-dry**

une **essoreuse** *fem noun*
**spin-drier**

**essoufflé** *masc adjective*, **essoufflée** *fem*
**out of breath**

un **essuie-glace** *masc noun*
**windscreen wiper**

un **essuie-tout** *masc noun*
**(paper) kitchen towel**

**essuyer** *verb* [41]
**to wipe**
essuyer le plancher to wipe the floor
J'ai essuyé la vaisselle. I did the drying-up.

s'**essuyer** *reflexive verb* ⓔ
s'essuyer les mains to dry your hands

**est** *adjective* ▷ see **est** *noun, verb*
1 **east**
2 **eastern**

l'**est** *masc noun* ▷ see **est** *adj, verb*
**east**
l'est de Paris the east of Paris
dans l'est de la France in the east of France
l'Europe de l'Est Eastern Europe

**est** *verb* ▷ see **est** *adj, noun* ▷ **être**

**est-ce que** *phrase*
Est-ce qu'il pleut? Is it raining?
Est-ce que Julie est partie? Has Julie left?
Où est-ce qu'il habite? Where does he live?

une **esthéticienne** *fem noun*
**beautician**

l'**estime** *fem noun*
**respect**

**estimer** *verb* [1]
1 **to think**
J'estime qu'ils ont raison. I think that they're right.
2 **to think highly of** (*a person*)
3 **to value**
faire estimer un tableau to have a painting valued

**estival** *masc adjective*, **estivale** *fem*, **estivaux** *masc pl*, **estivales** *fem pl*
**summer**

un **estivant** *masc noun*, une **estivante** *fem*
**summer visitor**

l'**estomac** *masc noun*
**stomach**
avoir mal à l'estomac to have stomachache

l'**Estonie** *fem noun*
**Estonia**

une **estrade** *fem noun*
**platform**

l'**estragon** *masc noun*
**tarragon** (*the herb*)

**et** *conjunction*
**and**

**établir** *verb* [2]
1 **to establish**
2 **to draw up** (*a plan, a document*)

s'**établir** *reflexive verb* ⓔ
**to settle**
Ils se sont établis en France. They settled in France.

un **établissement** *masc noun*
1 **institution**
2 **organization**

un **étage** *masc noun*
**floor**
au premier étage on the first floor
au dernier étage on the top floor
à l'étage upstairs

une **étagère** *fem noun*
1 **shelf**
2 **set of shelves**

l'**étain** *masc noun*
1 **tin**
2 **pewter**

un **étalage** *masc noun*
**window display**

**étaler** *verb* [1]
1 **to spread**
2 **to spread out**
3 **to roll out** (*pastry*)

**étanche** *masc & fem adjective*
1 **watertight**
2 **waterproof**

un **étang** *masc noun*
**pond**

une **étape** *fem noun*
1 **stage**
la dernière étape de la course the last stage of the race
2 **stopping place**
faire étape to stop off
On a fait étape à Rouen. We stopped off in Rouen.

l'**état** *masc noun* ▷ see **état** *masc noun*
1 **state** (*of an object*)
en mauvais état in a bad state
en bon état in good condition
en état de marche in working order



ⓔ means the verb takes être to form the perfect

2 **state** (*of a person*)
**être dans tous ses états** to be in a state
**être en état de faire quelque chose** to be in a fit state to do something
**Elle n'est pas en état de passer l'examen.** She's not in a fit state to take the exam.

♪ un **état** *masc noun* ▷ see **état** *masc noun*
**state, State**

les **États-Unis** *plural masc noun*
**les États-Unis** the United States
**aux États-Unis** in the United States, to the United States

**WORD TIP** Countries and regions in French take *le, la* or *les.*

l'**été** *masc noun* ▷ see **été** *verb*
**summer**
**en été** in summer
**l'été dernier** last summer
**l'été prochain** next summer

**été** *verb* ▷ see **été** *noun* ▷ **être**

**éteindre** *verb* **[60]**
1 **to turn off, to switch off** (*the lights, the TV*)
2 **to put out** (*a fire, a cigarette*)

s'**éteindre** *reflexive verb* ⓔ
**to go out**

**éteint** *masc adjective*, **éteinte** *fem*
**extinct** (*volcano*)

**étendre** *verb* **[3]**
1 **to stretch out** (*your arms or legs*)
**Étendez les bras.** Stretch out your arms.
2 **to spread out**
**J'ai étendu ma serviette.** I spread my towel out.
3 **étendre le linge** to hang out the washing

s'**étendre** *reflexive verb* ⓔ
1 **s'étendre sur le canapé** to stretch out on the sofa
2 **to stretch**
3 **to spread, to expand**

**éternel** *masc adjective*, **éternelle** *fem*
**eternal**

l'**éternité** *fem noun*
**eternity**

un **éternuement** *masc noun*
**sneeze**

**éternuer** *verb* **[1]**
**to sneeze**

**êtes** *verb* ▷ **être**

une **ethnie** *fem noun*
**ethnic group**

**ethnique** *masc & fem adjective*
**ethnic**

**étinceler** *verb* **[18]**
**to sparkle, to twinkle**

une **étincelle** *fem noun*
**spark**

une **étiquette** *fem noun*
1 **label**
2 **l'étiquette** etiquette

**étirer** *verb* **[1]**
**to stretch**

une **étoffe** *fem noun*
**fabric**

♪ une **étoile** *fem noun*
**star**
**un hôtel trois étoiles** a three-star hotel
**dormir à la belle étoile** to sleep out in the open
- une **étoile filante** shooting star

**étoilé** *masc adjective*, **étoilée** *fem*
**starry**

♪ **étonnant** *masc adjective*, **étonnante** *fem*
1 **surprising**
2 **astonishing**

l'**étonnement** *masc noun*
1 **surprise**
2 **astonishment**

**étonner** *verb* **[1]**
**to surprise**
**Ça ne m'étonne pas du tout.** That doesn't surprise me at all.

s'**étonner** *reflexive verb* ⓔ
**to be surprised**

**étouffant** *masc adjective*, **étouffante** *fem*
**stifling**

**étouffer** *verb* **[1]**
1 **to stifle**
2 **to suffocate**

s'**étouffer** *reflexive verb* ⓔ
**to choke**
**s'étouffer de rire** to be choking with laughter

l'**étourderie** *fem noun*
1 **absent-mindedness**
2 **une étourderie** a careless mistake

**étourdi** *masc adjective*, **étourdie** *fem*
▷ see **étourdi** *noun*
**scatterbrained, absent-minded**

un **étourdi** *masc noun*, une **étourdie** *fem*
▷ see **étourdi** *adj*
**scatterbrain**

**étourdir** *verb* [2]
**to daze, to stun**

un **étourneau** *masc noun*
**starling**

**étrange** *masc & fem adjective*
**strange**

**étranger** *masc adjective*, **étrangère** *fem*
▷ see **étranger** *nouns*
**foreign**
un pays étranger a foreign country
les mœurs étrangères foreign customs

un **étranger** *masc noun*, une **étrangère** *fem* ▷ see **étranger** *adj, noun*
1 **foreigner**
2 **stranger**

l'**étranger** *masc noun* ▷ see **étranger** *adj, noun*
à l'étranger abroad
aller à l'étranger to go abroad

**étrangler** *verb* [1]
1 **to strangle**
2 **to choke**

un **être** *masc noun* ▷ see **être** *verb*
**being**
• un **être humain** human being

**être** *verb* [6] ▷ see **être** *noun*
1 **to be**
**Je suis le frère de Jean.** I'm Jean's brother.
**Nous sommes dans la cuisine.** We're in the kitchen.
**Elle est malade.** She's ill.
**Le jardin n'est pas grand.** The garden isn't big.
**Qui est-ce?** Who is it?
**Où sont-ils?** Where are they?
**C'est moi.** It's me.
2 **to be** (*talking about what you do for a living*)
**être professeur** to be a teacher
**Elle est infirmière.** She's a nurse.
3 **être à quelqu'un** to belong to somebody, to be somebody's
**Ce livre est à Paul.** This book is Paul's.
**Ce livre est à moi.** This book is mine.
**Le stylo n'est pas à elle.** The pen isn't hers.
4 **to be** (*telling the time*)
**Il est 6 heures.** It's 6 o'clock.
**Il était tard.** It was late.
**Il n'est même pas midi.** It's not even midday.
5 **to be** (*talking about the date*)
**Nous sommes le 7 mars.** It's the 7th of March (today).
**Quelle date sommes-nous?** What's the date today?
6 (*used with some verbs to form past tenses: for a list of these, see the centre pages*)
**Je suis allé à Paris.** I went to Paris.
**Elle est tombée dans l'escalier.** She fell down the stairs.
**Nous sommes rentrés à 7 heures.** We got home at 7 o'clock.
7 (*used to form the passive*)
**Ses robes sont faites par sa mère.** Her dresses are made by her mother.
8 ▷ **est-ce que**

**étroit** *masc adjective*, **étroite** *fem*
1 **narrow**
**une veste aux manches étroites** a jacket with narrow sleeves
2 **close**

**étroitement** *adverb*
**closely**

l'**étude** *fem noun*
1 **study**
**L'étude a été réalisée par notre classe.** Our class carried out the study.
2 **les études** studies
**faire des études** to be a student
**faire des études de médecine** to study medicine
3 **study period**
**J'ai une heure d'étude.** I've got an hour's study period.

un **étudiant** *masc noun*, une **étudiante** *fem*
**student** (*at university*)

**étudier** *verb* [1]
**to study**

un **étui** *masc noun*
**case** (*for spectacles, small items*)

**eu** *verb* ▷ **avoir**

un **euro** *masc noun*
**euro**
**L'euro est divisé en cents.** The euro is divided into cents.

l'**Europe** *fem noun*
**Europe**
**en Europe** in Europe, to Europe
**les pays de l'Europe** the countries of Europe

**WORD TIP** Countries and regions in French take *le*, *la* or *les*.

**européen** *masc*, **européenne** *fem*
**European**

**WORD TIP** Adjectives never have capitals in French, even for nationality or regional origin.

l'**euthanasie** *fem noun*
**euthanasia**

**eux** *pronoun*
1 (*for males after prepositions like* ***avec*** *or* ***sans*** *and in comparisons*) **them**
**Je suis parti sans eux.** I left without them.
**Tu es plus grand qu'eux.** You're taller than them.
2 **à eux** theirs (*belonging to them*)
**Jean et Paul sont des amis à eux.** Jean and Paul are friends of theirs.
**La voiture n'est pas à eux.** The car isn't theirs.
3 (*for emphasis*) **they**
**Eux, ils sont parfaitement contents.** They are perfectly happy.
**Ce sont eux qui me l'ont dit.** They're the ones who told me.
4 **chez eux** at their house

**eux-mêmes** *pronoun*
(*for males and male objects*) **themselves**

**évacuer** *verb* **[1]**
**to evacuate**

s'**évader** *reflexive verb* Ⓔ **[1]**
**to escape**

**évaluer** *verb* **[1]**
**to assess**

s'**évanouir** *reflexive verb* Ⓔ **[2]**
**to faint**
**Je me suis évanoui.** I fainted.

s'**évaporer** *reflexive verb* Ⓔ **[1]**
**to evaporate**

l'**évasion** *fem noun*
**escape**
**une tentative d'évasion** an attempt to escape

**éveillé** *masc adjective*, **éveillée** *fem*
1 **awake**
**rester éveillé** to stay awake
2 **alert**

**éveiller** *verb* **[1]**
1 **to arouse** (*somebody's curiosity, suspicion*)
2 **to awaken** (*somebody's interest*)

♂ un **événement** *masc noun*
**event**
**C'est l'événement de l'année.** It's the big event of the year.

un **éventail** *masc noun*
**fan** (*for staying cool*)

une **éventualité** *fem noun*
**possibility**

**éventuel** *masc adjective*, **éventuelle** *fem*
**possible**

**éventuellement** *adverb*
1 **possibly**
**David vient et Manon aussi éventuellement.** David's coming and possibly Manon too.
2 **if necessary**
**Éventuellement, on contacte les parents.** If necessary, we contact the parents.

**WORD TIP** *éventuellement* does not mean *eventually* in English; for the meaning of *eventually* ▷ **finalement**

un **évêque** *masc noun*
**bishop**

**évidemment** *adverb*
**of course**
**Elle est arrivée en retard, évidemment.** She arrived late, of course.
**'Tu vois, je suis au courant.' — 'Évidemment!'** 'You see, I know all about it.' — 'So I see!'

l'**évidence** *fem noun*
1 **être en évidence** to be clearly visible
**Ne laisse pas tes affaires en évidence comme ça.** Don't leave your things around like that for people to see.
2 **de toute évidence** clearly
**De toute évidence il a oublié de venir.** He's clearly forgotten to come.

**évident** *masc adjective*, **évidente** *fem*
**obvious**
**C'est évident.** It's obvious.
**Ce n'est pas évident.** (*informal*) It's not that easy.

♂ un **évier** *masc noun*
**sink**

**éviter** *verb* **[1]**
1 **to avoid**
**Il m'évite, j'en suis sûr.** He's avoiding me, I'm sure of it.
**éviter de faire quelque chose** to avoid doing something
**J'évite de manger tard le soir.** I avoid eating late at night.
2 **éviter à quelqu'un de faire quelque chose** to save somebody having to do something
**Ça t'évitera de sortir.** That'll save you having to go out.

**évolué** *masc adjective*, **évoluée** *fem*
**advanced**

**évoluer** *verb* [1]
1 **to develop**
Nous ne savons pas comment la situation va évoluer. We do not know how the situation will develop.
2 **to progress**
**L'informatique évolue très rapidement.** Computer science progresses very rapidly.
3 **to change**
**Les choses ont évolué depuis.** Things have changed since.

l'**évolution** *fem noun*
1 **development**
2 **progress**
3 **evolution**

**exact** *masc adjective*, **exacte** *fem*
1 **correct**
C'est exact. That's absolutely right.
2 **exact, precise**
le chiffre exact the exact figure

**exactement** *adverb*
**exactly**

**exagéré** *masc adjective*, **exagérée** *fem*
1 **exaggerated**
2 **excessive**

**exagérer** *verb* [24]
1 **to exaggerate**
2 **to go too far**
Là, tu exagères! You're going too far now!

♪ un **examen** *masc noun*
**exam**
passer un examen to sit an exam
réussir à un examen to pass an exam
échouer à un examen to fail an exam
- un **examen blanc** mock exam
- un **examen médical** medical examination

un **examinateur** *masc noun*, une **examinatrice** *fem*
**examiner**

**examiner** *verb* [1]
**to examine**

**exaspérant** *masc adjective*, **exaspérante** *fem*
**exasperating**

**exaspérer** *verb* [24]
**to exasperate**

l'**excellence** *fem noun*
**excellence**

♪ **excellent** *masc adjective*, **excellente** *fem*
**excellent**

un & une **excentrique** *masc & fem noun*
**eccentric**

**excepté** *preposition*
**except**

une **exception** *fem noun*
1 **exception**
faire une exception to make an exception
2 à l'exception de except for
**tout le monde, à l'exception des parents** everybody, except for the parents

**exceptionnel** *masc adjective*, **exceptionnelle** *fem*
1 **exceptional**
2 **special**

**exceptionnellement** *adverb*
**exceptionally**

l'**excès** *masc noun*
**excess**
- l'**excès de vitesse** speeding

**excessif** *masc adjective*, **excessive** *fem*
**excessive**

**excessivement** *adverb*
**excessively**
**Il est excessivement timide.** He's incredibly shy.

**excitant** *masc adjective*, **excitante** *fem*
▷ see **excitant** *noun*
**exciting**

un **excitant** *masc noun* ▷ see **excitant** *adj*
**stimulant**

l'**excitation** *fem noun*
**excitement**

**excité** *masc adjective*, **excitée** *fem*
1 **frenzied**
2 **over-excited**
3 **thrilled**

s'**exciter** *reflexive verb* Ⓔ [1]
1 **to get excited**
2 **to get wound up**

une **exclamation** *fem noun*
**exclamation**

s'**exclamer** *reflexive verb* Ⓔ [1]
**to exclaim**

**exclu** *masc adjective*, **exclue** *fem*
**excluded**
se sentir exclu to feel left out
**Elle se sent exclue.** She feels left out.

**exclusif** *masc adjective*, **exclusive** *fem*
**exclusive**

♪ une **excursion** *fem noun*
**excursion, trip**
faire une excursion to go on an outing





a b c d e f g h i j k l m n o p q r s t u v w x y z

une **excuse** *fem noun*
1 des excuses an apology
Je vous dois des excuses. I owe you an apology.
2 **excuse**
Ce n'est pas une excuse. That's no excuse.

♪ **excuser** *verb* [1]
**to forgive**
Excusez-moi! Sorry!
Excusez-moi de vous déranger. Sorry to disturb you.

s'**excuser** *reflexive verb* ⓔ
**to apologize**
Je m'excuse. I'm sorry.
Je m'excuse d'être en retard. Sorry I'm late.

**exécuter** *verb* [1]
1 **to execute**
2 **to carry out** (*a task, work*)

un **exemplaire** *masc noun*
**copy**

♪ un **exemple** *masc noun*
**example**
par exemple for example
donner l'exemple to set an example
J'ai suivi l'exemple de Julien. I followed Julien's example.

**exercer** *verb* [61]
1 **to exercise** (*a right*)
2 **to practise** (*an art, a profession*)
3 **to exert** (*authority, pressure*)

s'**exercer** *reflexive verb* ⓔ
1 **to practise** (*as a musician*)
2 **to train** (*as an athlete*)

l'**exercice** *masc noun*
**exercise**
faire de l'exercice to get some exercise

**exhiber** *verb* [1]
1 **to show off** (*possessions, wealth etc*)
2 **to display**

un **exhibitionniste** *masc noun*
**flasher**

**exigeant** *masc adjective*, **exigeante** *fem*
**demanding**

**exiger** *verb* [52]
1 **to demand**
2 **to require**

l'**exil** *masc noun*
**exile** (*far from home*)

un **exilé** *masc noun*, une **exilée** *fem*
**exile** (*a person*)

l'**existence** *fem noun*
**existence**

**exister** *verb* [1]
**to exist**

**exotique** *masc & fem adjective*
**exotic**

l'**expansion** *fem noun*
1 **expansion**
2 **growth**

**expédier** *verb* [1]
**to send (off)**

un **expéditeur** *masc noun*, une **expéditrice** *fem*
**sender**

une **expédition** *fem noun*
**expedition**

une **expérience** *fem noun*
1 **experience**
avoir de l'expérience to be experienced
2 **experiment**
faire une expérience to carry out an experiment

**expérimenté** *masc adjective*, **expérimentée** *fem*
**experienced**

un **expert** *masc noun*
**expert**

**WORD TIP** A female expert is also *un* expert.

♪ une **explication** *fem noun*
**explanation**
demander des explications to ask for an explanation

**explicite** *masc & fem adjective*
**explicit**

♪ **expliquer** *verb* [1]
**to explain**
Explique-moi comment faire. Explain to me how it's done.
J'ai du mal à expliquer. I find it hard to explain.
expliquer quelque chose à quelqu'un to explain something to somebody
Elle ne m'a rien expliqué. She didn't explain anything to me.

un **exploit** *masc noun*
1 **achievement**
2 **feat**

**exploiter** *verb* [1]
1 **to exploit** (*a person*)
2 **to use, to make use of** (*resources, talents*)

**explorer** *verb* [1]
**to explore**

**exploser** *verb* **[1]**
**to explode, to blow up**
faire exploser un bâtiment to blow up a building

**explosif** *masc adjective*, **explosive** *fem*
**explosive**

une **explosion** *fem noun*
**1 explosion**
**2 boom**

un **export** *masc noun*
**export**

un **exportateur** *masc noun*, une **exportatrice** *fem*
**exporter**

l'**exportation** *fem noun*
**export**

**exporter** *verb* **[1]**
**to export**

**exposé** *masc adjective*, **exposée** *fem*
▷ see **exposé** *noun*
**1 exposed**
**2 on display**

un **exposé** *masc noun* ▷ see **exposé** *adj*
**talk, presentation**

**exposer** *verb* **[1]**
**1 to exhibit**
**2 to expose**
**3 to explain**

une **exposition** *fem noun*
**exhibition**

**exprès** *adjective* ▷ see **exprès** *adv*
**special delivery**
envoyer un paquet en exprès to send a package special delivery

**exprès** *adverb* ▷ see **exprès** *adj*
**1 deliberately**
faire quelque chose exprès to do something deliberately
Tu l'as fait exprès. You did it on purpose.
Je ne l'ai pas fait exprès. I didn't mean to do it.
**2 specially**
Je suis venu exprès pour te voir. I've come specially to see you.

un **express** *masc noun*
**1 fast train**
**2 espresso coffee**

une **expression** *fem noun*
**expression**

**exprimer** *verb* **[1]**
**to express**

s'**exprimer** *reflexive verb* ⓔ
**to express yourself**
Je m'exprime mal. I'm expressing myself badly.

**expulser** *verb* **[1]**
**1 to evict**
**2 to expel**

**exquis** *masc adjective*, **exquise** *fem*
**exquisite, delightful**

l'**extase** *fem noun*
**ecstasy**

**extensif** *masc adjective*, **extensive** *fem*
**extensive**

une **extension** *fem noun*
**extension**

**extérieur** *masc adjective*, **extérieure** *fem*
▷ see **extérieur** *noun*
**1 outside**
**2 outer**

l'**extérieur** *masc noun* ▷ see **extérieur** *adj*
**1 outside**
à l'extérieur outside
**2 exterior**

un **externat** *masc noun*
**day school**

un & une **externe** *masc & fem noun*
**day pupil**

un **extincteur** *masc noun*
**fire extinguisher**

l'**extinction** *fem noun*
**extinction**
en voie d'extinction in danger of extinction

**extra** *adjective*
(*informal*) **great, fantastic**

l'**extraction** *fem noun*
**1 extraction**
**2 mining**

**extraire** *verb* **[78]**
**1 to extract**
**2 to mine**

un **extrait** *masc noun*
**extract**

♪ **extraordinaire** *masc & fem adjective*
**extraordinary, amazing**

un & une **extra-terrestre** *masc & fem noun*
**alien, extra-terrestrial**

**extravagant** *masc adjective*, **extravagante** *fem*
**1 eccentric**
**2 extravagant**

un **extrême** *masc noun*
**extreme**

**extrêmement** *adverb*
**extremely**

l'**Extrême-Orient** *masc noun*
l'Extrême-Orient the Far East

une **extrémité** *fem noun*
1 **end** (*of a line, a road*)
2 **tip** (*of your finger, a stick*)
3 **edge** (*of a town or an area in general*)

# F f

**F** *abbreviation*
(*= franc*) franc (*the currency of Switzerland*)

le **fabricant** *masc noun*
**manufacturer**

la **fabrication** *fem noun*
**manufacture**
**une voiture de fabrication française** a car made in France

**fabriquer** *verb* [1]
1 **to make**
**des meubles fabriqués en France** furniture made in France
**André fabrique une boîte en bois.** André is making a wooden box.
2 (*informal*) **to do**
**Qu'est-ce que tu fabriques?** What are you doing?

**fabuleux** *masc adjective*, **fabuleuse** *fem*
1 **fabulous**
**une fortune fabuleuse** a fabulous fortune
2 **mythical**
**La licorne est un animal fabuleux.** The unicorn is a mythical animal.

la **fac** *fem noun*
(*informal*) **uni**, **university**
**Rémy ira en fac l'année prochaine.** Rémy will go to university next year.
**Audrey est en fac d'anglais.** Audrey is doing a degree in English.

♪ la **face** *fem noun*
1 **face**
**face à face** face to face
**Il est tombé face contre terre.** He fell flat on his face.
2 **side**
**la face d'un disque** the side of a record
**Examinons la question sous toutes ses faces.** Let's examine the issue from all angles.
3 **en face** opposite
**en face de l'école** opposite the school
**la maison d'en face** the house opposite
**le magasin en face de chez nous** the shop opposite our house
**Quentin est assis en face d'Elsa.** Quentin is sitting opposite Elsa.
4 **face à** facing
**face à la mer** facing the sea
**Mon bureau est face à la porte.** My desk is facing the door.
**Face aux nombreuses difficultés, il abandonne son projet.** Faced with many difficulties, he's giving up his project.
5 (*when you toss a coin*) **Pile ou face?** Heads or tails?

♪ **fâché** *masc adjective*, **fâchée** *fem*
**angry**, **upset**
**Est-ce que tu es fâché?** Are you angry? (*to a boy*)
**Est-ce que tu es fâchée?** Are you angry? (*to a girl*)
**Elle est fâchée contre moi.** She's angry with me.

se **fâcher** *reflexive verb* Ⓔ [1]
1 **to get angry**
**Ne te fâche pas, je vais le recoller!** Don't get angry, I'll glue it back on.
**se fâcher contre quelqu'un** to get angry with somebody
**Elle s'est fâchée contre moi.** She got angry with me.
2 **se fâcher avec quelqu'un** to fall out with somebody
**Olivier s'est fâché avec Pierre.** Olivier has fallen out with Pierre.

♪ **facile** *adjective*
1 **easy**
**C'est facile.** It's easy.
**C'est facile à comprendre.** It's easy to understand.
2 **easy-going**
**Amandine a un caractère facile.** Amandine is easy-going.

**facilement** *adverb*
**easily**

la **facilité** *fem noun*
**easiness**

**faciliter** *verb* **[1]**
**to make things easier**
**Ton aide va nous faciliter les choses.** Your help will make things easier for us.

la **façon** *fem noun*
1 **way**
**d'une façon extraordinaire** in an extraordinary way
**Il y a plusieurs façons de le faire.** There are several ways of doing it.
**De quelle façon est-il tombé?** How did he fall?
**En voilà une façon d'étudier!** What a way to study!
**Je n'aime pas la façon dont il me parle.** I don't like the way he speaks to me.
2 **de toute façon** anyway
**De toute façon, ce n'est pas mon problème.** Anyway, it isn't my problem.
3 **des façons** manners, behaviour
**Je n'aime pas ses façons.** I don't like his manners.
**En voilà des façons!** That's no way to behave!
**faire des façons** to stand on ceremony
**Ne fais pas tant de façons!** Don't stand on ceremony!
**Non merci, sans façons!** No thank you, really!

**façonner** *verb* **[1]**
1 **to make**
**Il façonne des objets en bois.** He makes things in wood.
2 **to shape** *(clay, stone)*

le **facteur** *masc noun*, la **factrice** *fem*
1 **postman**
**Est-ce que le facteur est passé?** Has the postman been?
2 **postwoman**

la **facture** *fem noun*
**bill**
**la facture d'électricité** the electricity bill

**facultatif** *masc adjective*, **facultative** *fem*
**optional**

la **faculté** *fem noun*
**faculty**

**fade** *masc & fem adjective*
**bland**
**La sauce est un peu fade.** The sauce is a bit bland.

**faible** *masc & fem adjective* ▷ **see faible** *noun*
**weak, faint**
**une voix faible** a faint voice
**une classe très faible** a very weak class
**des résultats faibles en maths** poor results in maths
**Élisa est faible en chimie.** Élisa is weak in chemistry.
**Elle est encore très faible après son opération.** She's still very weak after her operation.

un **faible** *masc noun* ▷ **see faible** *adj*
**avoir un faible pour quelqu'un** to have a soft spot for someone
**Elle a un faible pour le prof d'anglais.** She has a soft spot for the English teacher.
**avoir un faible pour quelque chose** to have a weakness for something
**J'ai un faible pour le chocolat.** I have a weakness for chocolate.

la **faiblesse** *fem noun*
**weakness**

**faiblir** *verb* **[2]**
**to weaken**

la **faïence** *fem noun*
**earthenware**
**une tasse en faïence** an earthenware cup

**faillir** *verb* **[42]**
**faillir faire** *(to say something nearly happened)*
**J'ai failli tomber.** I nearly fell.
**Elle a failli gagner.** She nearly won.
**Il a failli rater le train.** He nearly missed the train.

la **faillite** *fem noun*
**bankruptcy**
**faire faillite** to go bankrupt
**La société Dupont a fait faillite.** The Dupont company went bankrupt.

la **faim** *fem noun*
**hunger**
**Je meurs de faim!** I'm dying of hunger.
**Ces gâteaux me donnent faim.** Those cakes make me feel hungry.
**avoir faim** to be hungry
**Les enfants ont très faim.** The children are very hungry.
**Elle n'a plus faim.** She's had enough to eat.

**fainéant** *masc adjective*, **fainéante** *fem*
**lazy**

**faire** *verb* **[10]**
1 **to make**
**faire un gâteau** to make a cake
**faire du bruit** to make a noise
**faire une erreur** to make a mistake
**faire son lit** to make your bed
**Faites comme chez vous!** Make yourselves at home!
2 **to do**
**Il fait ses devoirs.** He's doing his homework.

**Qu'est-ce que tu fais?** What are you doing?
**Fais comme tu veux!** Do as you like!
**Je fais de mon mieux.** I'm doing my best.
**faire du français** to do French
**Ils font du français.** They do French.

3 **to play** (*sports, music, an instrument*)
**Camille fait du piano.** Camille plays the piano.
**Sophie et Inès font de la clarinette.** Sophie and Inès play the clarinet.
**Oscar fait du football.** Oscar plays football.

4 **to dial**, **to press**
**Appelez le numéro suivant et puis faire le 2.** Call the following number and then press 2.

5 (*in sums, measurements*) **2 plus 2 font 4.** 2 plus 2 make 4.
**Ça fait 10 euros.** That's 10 euros.
**Elle fait 1,65 m.** She's 1.65m tall.

6 (*talking about the weather*) **Il fait beau.** It's a nice day.
**Quel temps fait-il?** What's the weather like?
**Il fait froid.** It's cold.
**Il fait chaud.** It's hot.
**Il fait beau en été ici.** The weather's nice here in summer.

7 (*saying how long something takes*) **Ça fait 10 minutes.** That's 10 minutes.
**Ça fait une heure que j'attends.** I've been waiting for an hour.

8 (*talking about distances, journeys*) **On a fait 10 kilomètres à pied.** We walked 10 kilometres.
**Ils ont fait le Maroc à cheval.** They travelled around Morocco on horseback.
**Cette année nous faisons les châteaux de la Loire.** This year we are visiting the châteaux along the Loire.

9 (*to imitate*) **faire le clown** to act the clown
**Mon chien fait le mort.** My dog's pretending to be dead.

10 **to look**
**Ça fait joli.** It looks pretty.
**Il fait vieux.** He looks old.

11 (*to cause*) **L'accident a fait 10 morts.** 10 people died in the accident.
**Ça ne fait rien.** It doesn't matter.

12 (*asking what's happened to something*)
**Qu'as-tu fait de mes clés?** What have you done with my keys?

13 **faire faire quelque chose** to have something done
**Elle a fait réparer son vélo.** She had her bike repaired.
**J'ai fait tondre le chien.** I've had the dog clipped.

14 **faire + infinitive**
**Je fais bouillir de l'eau pour le café.** I'm boiling some water for the coffee.
**Elle fait cuire des frites.** She's cooking chips.

**WORD TIP** *faire* is used with many nouns to say 'to do' an activity, e.g. *faire du bricolage, faire du camping, faire la cuisine*. You can work out the translation from the meaning of the noun. These examples give: to do DIY, to go camping, to cook.

se **faire** *reflexive verb* ⓔ

1 **to make**
**se faire des amis** to make friends
**se faire un thé** to make yourself a cup of tea

2 **to do**
**Ça ne se fait pas.** You don't do that.

3 **se faire faire quelque chose** to have something done
**se faire couper les cheveux** to have one's hair cut
**Il s'est fait faire des mèches.** He's had highlights done.
**Anne s'est fait voler son sac.** Anne had her bag stolen.

4 **se faire + infinitive** to be + past participle
**Luc se fait gronder.** Luc is being scolded.
**Le chat s'est fait écraser.** The cat's been run over.

5 **s'en faire** to worry
**Ne t'en fais pas pour moi!** Don't worry about me!

6 **se faire à quelque chose, quelqu'un** to get used to something, somebody
**Claire se fait bien à son nouveau maître.** Claire is getting used to her new teacher.
**Je ne m'y fais pas.** I can't get used to it.

le **faire-part** *invariable masc noun*
**announcement** (*of a birth, a wedding, etc*)

**fais** *verb* ▷ **faire**

le **faisan** *masc noun*
**pheasant**

**faisons** *verb* ▷ **faire**

le **fait** *masc noun* ▷ **see fait** *verb*

1 **fact**
**C'est un fait.** It's a fact.
**Le fait est que ça ne marche pas.** The fact is that it doesn't work.

2 **en fait** actually
**En fait je l'ai vu hier.** In fact I saw him yesterday.

3 **au fait** by the way
**Au fait, as-tu fermé la porte à clé?** By the way, did you lock the door?

4 **event**
**des faits réels** real-life events ⏩

**5 point**
Il est allé droit au fait. He went straight to the point.
**6 tout à fait** absolutely
C'est tout à fait vrai. It's absolutely true.
- le **fait d'actualité** news item
- le **fait divers** small news item

**fait** *verb* ▷ see **fait** *noun*
(*in expressions*) **un travail bien fait** a job well done
**C'est mal fait.** It's badly designed.
**un fromage bien fait** a ripe cheese
**'Il a été puni.' — 'C'est bien fait, je l'avais prévenu.'** 'He's been punished.' — 'Serves him right, I warned him.'

**faites** *verb* ▷ **faire**

la **falaise** *fem noun*
**cliff**

**fallait** *verb* ▷ **falloir**

**falloir** *impersonal verb* **[43]**
**1** (*to say something must be done*) **Il faut le faire.** You must do it., It has to be done.
**Il ne faut pas faire ça.** You mustn't do that.
**Il ne fallait pas faire ça.** You shouldn't have done that.
**Il faudra partir à six heures.** We'll have to leave at six o'clock.
**Il faudrait téléphoner à ta grand-mère.** You should phone your grandmother.
**2** (*to say something is needed*) **Il me faut un stylo.** I need a pen.
**Il leur faut une voiture.** They need a car.
**Il nous faut 100 euros.** We need 100 euros.
**Il faut 100 grammes de beurre pour cette recette.** We need 100 grams of butter for this recipe.
**Qu'est-ce qu'il te faut?** What do you need?
**3** (*to say the time needed to do something*) **Il faut une heure pour aller de Tours à Blois.** It takes an hour to go from Tours to Blois.
**Il nous a fallu deux ans pour finir la maison.** It took two years to finish the house.
**4 il faut que... + subjunctive** I, you, she, he, etc, must, ought to ...
**Il faut que tu viennes.** You must come., You have to come., You ought to come.
**5 comme il faut** properly
**Il le fait comme il faut.** He does it properly.
**Marche comme il faut!** Walk properly

**WORD TIP** *falloir* is only used with *il*.

**famé** *masc adjective*, **famée** *fem*
**un quartier mal famé** a rough area

**fameux** *masc adjective*, **fameuse** *fem*
**1 excellent**
**Ton rôti était fameux.** Your roast was excellent.
**2 famous**
**les fameuses grottes de Lascaux** the famous caves at Lascaux

**familial** *masc adjective*, **familiale** *fem*, **familiaux** *masc pl*, **familiales** *fem pl*
**family**
**la vie familiale** family life

se **familiariser** *reflexive verb* Ⓔ **[1]**
**se familiariser avec quelque chose** to become familiar with something
**Je me suis familiarisé avec mon nouvel ordinateur.** I've become familiar with my new computer.
**Les filles se sont familiarisées avec leur nouvelle école.** The girls have got used to their new school.

la **familiarité** *fem noun*
**familiarity**

**familier** *masc adjective*, **familière** *fem*
**familiar**
**un endroit familier** a familiar place

♪ la **famille** *fem noun*
**1 family**
**la famille Leprêtre** the Leprêtre family
**un déjeuner en famille** a family lunch
**une famille nombreuse** a large family
**une famille monoparentale** a single-parent family
**2 relatives**
**J'ai de la famille à Dijon.** I have relatives in Dijon.
**Elle rentre dans sa famille tous les week-ends.** She goes home every weekend.

**fanatique** *masc & fem noun*
**fanatic**

**fané** *masc adjective*, **fanée** *fem*
**withered**

la **fanfare** *fem noun*
**brass band**

la **fantaisie** *fem noun*
**1 imagination**
**un enfant plein de fantaisie** a child full of original ideas
**2 des bijoux fantaisie** costume jewellery

**fantastique** *masc & fem adjective*
**fantastic**

le **fantôme** *masc noun*
**ghost**



Ⓔ means the verb takes être to form the perfect

la **farce** *fem noun*
1 **practical joke**
**Elle a fait une farce à son oncle.** She played a practical joke on her uncle.
2 **stuffing** *(for a chicken, a turkey)*

**farci** *masc adjective*, **farcie** *fem*
**stuffed** *(in cooking)*
**des tomates farcies** stuffed tomatoes

**farcir** *verb* [2]
**to stuff** *(a chicken, a turkey)*

le **fard à paupières** *masc noun*
**eye shadow**

le **fardeau** *masc noun*, les **fardeaux** *plural*
**burden**

**farfelu** *masc adjective*, **farfelue** *fem*
**bizarre**, **weird**
**C'est un type farfelu.** He's a bizarre bloke.
**Elle a toujours des idées farfelues.** She always has weird ideas.

la **farine** *fem noun*
**flour**

**fascinant** *masc adjective*, **fascinante** *fem*
**fascinating**
**Son histoire était fascinante.** His story was fascinating.

la **fascination** *fem noun*
**fascination**

**fasciner** *verb* [1]
**to fascinate**
**Ça me fascine.** I find that fascinating.

le **fascisme** *masc noun*
**fascism**

le **fast-food** *masc noun*
1 **fast food restaurant**
**Antoine connaît tous les fast-foods du coin.** Antoine knows all the local fast food restaurants.
2 **fast food**
**Tatiana est une peu ronde car elle ne mange que du fast-food.** Tatiana is a bit plump because she only eats fast food.

**fastidieux** *masc adjective*, **fastidieuse** *fem*
**tedious**
**un travail fastidieux** tedious work

**fatal** *masc adjective*, **fatale** *fem*
1 **inevitable**
**Un accident était fatal.** An accident was bound to happen.
2 **fatal**
**des coups fatals** fatal blows

la **fatalité** *fem noun*
**fate**

**fatigant** *masc adjective*, **fatigante** *fem*
1 **tiring**
**un travail fatigant** a tiring job
2 **tiresome**
**Arrête, tu es fatigante!** Stop it, you're so tiresome!
3 **boring**
**Il est fatigant avec ses histoires.** He's boring with his stories.

la **fatigue** *fem noun*
**tiredness**

♪ **fatigué** *masc adjective*, **fatiguée** *fem*
**tired**
**Je suis fatigué.** I'm tired *(boy speaking)*.
**Je suis fatiguée.** I'm tired *(girl speaking)*.
**Tu as l'air fatigué.** You look tired.

**fatiguer** *verb* [1]
1 **to tire (somebody) out**
**La promenade m'a fatigué.** The walk tired me out.
2 **to strain** *(your eyes)*

se **fatiguer** *reflexive verb* ©
**to get tired**
**Elle se fatigue vite.** She gets tired quickly .

le **faubourg** *masc noun*
**suburb**
**les faubourgs de Marseille** the suburbs of Marseilles

**fauché** *masc adjective*, **fauchée** *fem*
*(informal)* **broke**
**Je suis fauché, je ne peux pas aller au cinéma.** I'm broke, I can't go to the cinema.

**faucher** *verb* [1]
1 **to mow** *(hay)*
2 *(informal)* **to pinch**
**On m'a fauché mon vélo.** Somebody's pinched my bike.

le **faucon** *masc noun*
**falcon**

**faudra**, **faudrait** *verb* ▷ **falloir**

se **faufiler** *reflexive verb* © [1]
**Diane se faufile entre deux spectateurs.** Diane is squeezing between two spectators.

la **faune** *fem noun*
**wildlife**
- la **faune marine** marine life

**fausse** *fem adjective* ▷ **faux**

**faussement** *adverb*
**wrongly**

**fausser** *verb* [1]
1 **to distort**
2 **to bend**

**faut** *verb* ▷ **falloir**

**la faute** *fem noun*
1 **mistake, error**
**une faute d'orthographe** a spelling mistake
**J'ai fait deux fautes dans la dictée.** I made two mistakes in the dictation.
2 **fault**
**C'est ma faute.** It's my fault.
**C'est de ma faute.** It's my fault.
**C'est la faute de Sophie.** It's Sophie's fault.
**C'est de la faute de Jacques.** It's Jacques' fault.
3 **sans faute** without fail
**À demain, sans faute.** See you tomorrow, without fail.
4 **faute de** for lack of
**Le projet n'a pas abouti, faute de temps.** The project didn't come off for lack of time.
**Faute de mieux, je le prendrai.** For want of anything better, I'll take it.

**le fauteuil** *masc noun*
1 **armchair**
2 **seat** *(in a cinema, a theatre)*
- le **fauteuil à bascule** rocking chair
- le **fauteuil roulant** wheelchair

**fautif** *masc adjective*, **fautive** *fem*
**guilty**
**C'est son frère qui est fautif.** Her brother is guilty.

**fauve** *masc & fem adjective* ▷ **see fauve** *noun*
**tawny**

le **fauve** *masc noun* ▷ **see fauve** *adj*
1 **wild animal**
2 **big cat**

**faux** *adverb* ▷ **see faux** *adj, noun*
**out of tune**
**Nicolas chante faux.** Nicolas sings out of tune.

**le faux** *masc noun* ▷ **see faux** *adj, adv*
**fake, forgery**
**Ce billet de 50 euros est un faux.** This 50-euro note is a forgery.

**faux** *masc adjective*, **fausse** *fem* ▷ **see faux** *adv, noun*
1 **wrong**
**Ton résultat est faux.** Your result's wrong.
2 **untrue**
**C'est faux, ça ne s'est pas passé ainsi.** That's not true, it didn't happen like that.
3 **false**
**une fausse barbe** a false beard
4 **imitation**
**C'est un faux diamant.** It's an imitation diamond.
- le **faux ami** false friend *(A French word, spelt the same in English, but with a different meaning.)*
- le **faux-filet** sirloin

la **faveur** *fem noun*
**favour**

**favorable** *masc & fem adjective*
**favourable**

**favori** *masc adjective*, **favorite** *fem*
**favourite**
**C'est mon groupe favori.** It's my favourite pop band.

**favoriser** *verb* **[1]**
**to favour**

**le fax** *masc noun*
1 **fax**
**Je vous envoie un fax.** I'm sending you a fax.
2 **fax machine**
**L'imprimante est aussi un fax.** The printer is also a fax machine.

**fédéral** *masc adjective*, **fédérale** *fem*, **fédéraux** *masc pl*, **fédérales** *fem pl*
**federal**

la **fédération** *fem noun*
**federation**

la **fée** *fem noun*
**fairy**

**féerique** *masc & fem adjective*
**magical**

**feignant** *masc adjective*, **feignante** *fem*
*(informal)* **lazy**

**fêler** *verb* **[1]**
**to crack**

se **fêler** *reflexive verb* Ⓔ
**to crack**

**les félicitations** *plural fem noun*
**congratulations**
**Tu as eu ton bac. Félicitations!** You passed your baccalaureat. Congratulations!

**féliciter** *verb* **[1]**
**to congratulate**

la **fêlure** *fem noun*
**crack**

la **femelle** *fem noun*
**female** *(of a species)*
**La femelle du merle est brune.** The female blackbird is brown.

**féminin** *masc adjective*, **féminine** *fem* ▷ **see féminin** *noun*
1 **female**
**le sexe féminin** the female sex
2 **feminine**
**Elle est très féminine.** She's very feminine.

Ⓔ means the verb takes être to form the perfect

**Cet ensemble est très féminin.** This outfit is very feminine.

3 **women's**
**la presse féminine** women's magazines
**les questions féminines** women's issues

le **féminin** *masc noun* ▷ see **féminin** *adj*
(*Grammar*) **feminine**
**au féminin** in the feminine
**'Boulangère' est le féminin de 'boulanger.'** 'Boulangère' is the feminine for 'boulanger.'

le & la **féministe** *masc & fem noun*
**feminist**

✓ la **femme** *fem noun*
1 **woman**
**C'est une femme très cultivée.** She's a very educated woman
2 **wife**
**la femme de David** David's wife
- la **femme d'affaires** businesswoman
- la **femme au foyer** housewife
- la **femme de ménage** cleaning lady

**fendre** *verb* [3]
1 **to chop**
**Il fend du bois pour faire du feu.** He's chopping wood to make a fire.
2 **to crack** (*a wall, a vase*)
3 **fendre le cœur à quelqu'un** to break somebody's heart
**Ses pleurs me fendent le cœur.** Her tears break my heart.

✓ la **fenêtre** *fem noun*
**window**
**Ouvre la fenêtre!** Open the window!
**Il regarde par la fenêtre.** He's looking out of the window.

la **fente** *fem noun*
1 **slit**
**une jupe avec une fente** a skirt with a slit
2 **slot**
**Mets une pièce d'un euro dans la fente.** Put a one-euro coin in the slot.
3 **crack**
**Il y a une fente dans le mur.** There is a crack in the wall.

le **fer** *masc noun*
**iron**
- le **fer à cheval** horseshoe
- le **fer forgé** wrought iron
- le **fer à repasser** iron (*for clothes*)

✓ **férié** *masc adjective*, **fériée** *fem*
**un jour férié** a public holiday
**Demain c'est férié.** Tomorrow is a public holiday.

**ferme** *masc & fem adjective*
▷ see **ferme** *noun*
**firm**
**un matelas ferme** a firm mattress
**une voix ferme** a firm voice

✓ la **ferme** *fem noun* ▷ see **ferme** *adj*
1 **farm**
**Pendant les vacances je travaille dans une ferme.** During the holidays I work on a farm.
2 **farmhouse**
**Nous passons nos vacances dans une ferme du Limousin.** We spend our holidays in a farmhouse in the Limousin.
- la **ferme éolienne** windfarm

✓ **fermé** *masc adjective*, **fermée** *fem*
**closed**
**Le magasin est fermé le dimanche.** The shop is closed on Sundays.
**Les volets sont fermés.** The shutters are closed.
**Le robinet est mal fermé.** The tap is not properly turned off.

**fermenter** *verb* [1]
**to ferment**

✓ **fermer** *verb* [1]
1 **to close, to shut**
**Il ferme la porte.** He shuts the door.
**Il a fermé les yeux.** He closed his eyes.
**Je ferme la porte à clé.** I lock the door.
2 **to turn off** (*the tap, the water, etc*)
**N'oublie pas de fermer le gaz.** Don't forget to turn off the gas.
3 **to do up** (*clothes, shoes*)
**Ferme ton manteau, il fait froid!** Do your coat up, it's cold!
4 **to close down**
**On a fermé l'usine.** They closed down the factory.

se **fermer** *reflexive verb* Ⓔ
**to close** (*by itself*)
**La porte s'est fermée.** The door closed.

✓ la **fermeture** *fem noun*
1 **closing**
**les heures de fermeture** closing times
2 **fastening** (*on a garment*)
- la **fermeture annuelle** annual close-down (*of businesses for holidays*)
- la **fermeture éclair**® zip

**fermier** *masc adjective*, **fermière** *fem*
▷ see **fermier** *noun*
**farm, farm-produced**
**des produits fermiers** farm produce
**un poulet fermier** a free-range chicken

French-English

a b c d e **f** g h i j k l m n o p q r s t u v w x y z

♪ le **fermier** *masc noun*, la **fermière** *fem*
▷ see **fermier** *adj*
**1** **farmer**
**Mon oncle et ma tante sont fermiers en Normandie.** My uncle and aunt are farmers in Normandy.
**2** **la fermière** the farmer's wife

le **fermoir** *masc noun*
**clasp**

**féroce** *masc & fem adjective*
**fierce**
**un examinateur féroce** a fierce examiner
**une bête féroce** a fierce animal
**un appétit féroce** a terrific appetite

la **ferraille** *fem noun*
**scrap metal**

**ferroviaire** *masc & fem adjective*
**rail, railway**
**le réseau ferroviaire** the rail network

**fertile** *masc & fem adjective*
**fertile**

la **fertilité** *fem noun*
**fertility**

la **fesse** *fem noun*
**buttock**
**les fesses** your bottom

le **festin** *masc noun*
**feast**
**Nous avons fait un festin.** We had a feast.

le **festival** *masc noun*
**festival**
**un festival de folk** a folk music festival

♪ la **fête** *fem noun*
**1** **public holiday**
**les fêtes de Pâques** Easter
**sauf dimanches et fêtes** except Sundays and public holidays
**les fêtes de fin d'année** the end-of-year festive season
**2** **party**
**Estelle fait une fête pour son anniversaire.** Estelle is having a party for her birthday.
**faire la fête** to party
**Ils ont fait la fête tout le week-end.** The've been partying all weekend.
**3** **fête, fair**
**Il y a la fête au village.** There's a fair in the village.
**une fête de la musique** a music festival
**4** **saint's name day** (*In France every day has a saint and many people celebrate their saint's day.*)
**La fête de Sophie est le 23 mai.** Sophie's saint's day is 23 May.
- la **fête foraine** funfair
- la **fête des Mères** Mother's Day (*in France on the last Sunday in May*)
- la **fête nationale** Bastille Day (*14 July*)
- la **fête des Pères** Father's Day

**fêter** *verb* **[1]**
**to celebrate**
**Elle vient de fêter ses 18 ans.** She's just celebrated her eighteenth birthday.

♪ le **feu** *masc noun*, les **feux** *plural*
**1** **fire**
**Il jette les vieux cartons au feu.** He's throwing the old boxes onto the fire.
**faire du feu** to light a fire
**Faisons du feu dans la cheminée.** Let's light a fire in the fireplace.
**prendre feu** to catch fire
**La poêle a pris feu.** The frying pan caught fire.
**éteindre le feu** to put the fire out
**Les pompiers ont éteint le feu.** The firemen have put the fire out.
**mettre le feu à quelque chose** to set fire to something
**Ils ont mis le feu à la grange.** They set fire to the barn.
**2** (*as a warning*) **Au feu!** Fire!
**3** **light** (*in road signals*)
**le feu rouge** red light
**le feu vert** green light
**les feux de signalisation** the traffic lights
**4** **heat** (*when cooking*)
**Faites cuire à feu doux.** Cook on a gentle heat.

le **feu d'artifice** *masc noun*
**1** **firework**
**2** **firework display**
**le feu d'artifice du 14 juillet** the firework display on 14 July

le **feuillage** *masc noun*
**foliage**

la **feuille** *fem noun*
**1** **leaf**
**2** **une feuille de papier** a sheet of paper
**une feuille double** a double sheet of paper

**feuilleté** *masc adjective*, **feuilletée** *fem*
▷ see **feuilleté** *noun*
**la pâte feuilletée** puff pastry

le **feuilleté** *masc noun* ▷ see **feuilleté** *adj*
**savoury pasty**

**feuilleter** *verb* **[48]**
**to leaf through**
**Elle feuillette des magazines en attendant.** She's leafing through magazines as she waits.

♪ le **feuilleton** *masc noun*
1 **serial**
2 **soap opera** (*on television*)

le **feutre** *masc noun*
1 **felt**
2 **un feutre** a felt-tip pen

la **fève** *fem noun*
1 **broad bean**
2 **small figurine** (*in a Twelfth Night cake*)
▷ galette des Rois

♪ **février** *masc noun*
**February**
**en février, au mois de février** in February
**Fin février nous allons au ski.** In late February we're going skiing.

**WORD TIP** Months of the year and days of the week start with small letters in French.

**fiable** *masc & fem adjective*
**reliable**

les **fiançailles** *plural fem noun*
**engagement** (*to be married*)
**la bague de fiançailles** the engagement ring
**Les fiançailles d'Aurélie et Boris auront lieu le 2 juin.** Aurélie's and Boris's engagement will take place on 2 June.

♪ le **fiancé** *masc noun*, la **fiancée** *fem*
1 **fiancé** (*man*)
2 **fiancée** (*woman*)

se **fiancer** *reflexive verb* **Ⓔ [61]**
**to get engaged**
**Arthur et Joséphine se sont fiancés hier.** Arthur and Joséphine got engaged yesterday.

la **fibre** *fem noun*
**fibre**

**ficeler** *verb* **[18]**
**to tie up**

la **ficelle** *fem noun*
1 **string**
2 **thin baguette** (*French bread*)

♪ la **fiche** *fem noun*
1 **form**
**remplir une fiche** to fill in a form
2 **index card**
**Pour mes révisions, je fais des fiches.** When I revise, I fill in index cards.
• la **fiche d'inscription** registration form

**ficher** *verb* **[1]**
1 **ficher quelqu'un** to open a file on somebody
**Le cambrioleur est fiché à la police.** The burglar is on the police files.
2 (*informal*) **to do**
**Qu'est-ce que tu fiches?** What on earth are you doing?
3 (*informal*) **to put**
**Fiche ce vieux pull à la poubelle!** Put this old jumper in the bin!
4 **ficher la paix à quelqu'un** to leave somebody alone
**Fiche-moi la paix!** Leave me alone!

se **ficher** *reflexive verb* **Ⓔ**
(*informal*) **se ficher de quelqu'un** to make fun of somebody
**Ne te fiche pas de lui!** Don't make fun of him!
**Je m'en fiche!** I don't care!
**se ficher de ce que quelqu'un fait** not to care less about what somebody does
**Elle se fiche bien de ce qu'il pense.** She couldn't care less what he thinks.

le **fichier** *masc noun*
**file** (*for documents*)

**fichu** *masc adjective*, **fichue** *fem*
(*informal*) **done for**
**Ma voiture est fichue.** My car's done for.
**S'il me pose des questions, je suis fichu.** If he asks me any questions, I'm done for.

la **fiction** *fem noun*
**fiction**

**fidèle** *masc & fem adjective*
1 **faithful**
**Malgré tout, elle est restée fidèle à son mari.** In spite of everything she stayed faithful to her husband.
2 **loyal**
**un consommateur fidèle à une marque** a customer loyal to a brand

**fier** *masc adjective*, **fière** *fem*
**proud**

se **fier** *reflexive verb* **Ⓔ [1]**
**se fier à** to trust
**Je me fie à Thomas pour nous montrer le chemin.** I trust Thomas to show us the way.

la **fierté** *fem noun*
**pride**

la **fièvre** *fem noun*
**fever**
**avoir de la fièvre** to have a temperature

la **figue** *fem noun*
**fig**

le **figuier** *masc noun*
**fig tree**

la **figure** *fem noun*
1 **face**
2 **figure** (*in maths*)
**une figure géométrique** geometric figure

**figurer** *verb* **[1]**
**to be, to appear**
**Ton nom ne figure pas sur la liste.** Your name isn't on the list.

se **figurer** *reflexive verb* ⓔ
**to imagine**
**Tu te figures que je vais payer.** And you imagine I'm going to pay.
**Figure-toi qu'il a eu son permis de conduire!** He passed his driving test, can you imagine!

le **fil** *masc noun*
1 **thread**
**du fil à coudre** sewing thread
2 **wire, flex** (*of a telephone, an electrical appliance*)
- le **fil de fer** wire
- le **fil de fer barbelé** barbed wire

la **file** *fem noun*
1 **queue**
**Il y a une longue file devant le cinéma.** There's a long queue in front of the cinema.
2 **lane** (*on a road*)
**Reste dans la file de gauche!** Stay in the left-hand lane!
3 **à la file** in a row
**Ils ont regardé trois DVD à la file.** They watched three DVDs in a row.
- la **file d'attente** queue
- la **file indienne** single file

**filer** *verb* **[1]**
1 **to speed along**
2 (*informal*) **to pass on**
**Elle m'a filé deux CD.** She passed on two CDs to me.

le **filet** *masc noun*
1 **net**
**un filet de pêche** a fishing net
2 **fillet**
**un filet de poisson** a fish fillet

♪ la **fille** *fem noun*
1 **girl**
**une petite fille** a little girl
**une jeune fille** a young woman
2 **daughter**
**C'est la fille du directeur.** She's the headmaster's daughter.

la **fillette** *fem noun*
**little girl**

le **filleul** *masc noun*
**godson**

la **filleule** *fem noun*
**goddaughter**

♪ le **film** *masc noun*
**film**
- le **film d'animation** cartoon
- le **film d'épouvante** horror film
- le **film policier** thriller

**filmer** *verb* **[1]**
**to film**

♪ le **fils** *masc noun*
**son**

le **filtre** *masc noun*
**filter**

**filtrer** *verb* **[1]**
**to filter**

♪ **fin** *masc adjective*, **fine** *fem* ▷ **see fin** *noun*
1 **fine**
**du sable fin** fine sand
2 **thin**
**une tranche fine** a thin slice
3 **slender**
**Elle a la taille fine.** She has a slender waist.

♪ la **fin** *fem noun* ▷ **see fin** *adj*
**end**
**à la fin** in the end
**à la fin du film** at the end of the film
**en fin de journée** at the end of the day
**sans fin** endless
**Je commence fin juillet.** I'm starting at the end of July.

les **fines herbes** *plural fem noun*
**mixed herbs**

**final** *masc adjective*, **finale** *fem*, **finaux** *masc pl*, **finales** *fem pl* ▷ **see finale** *noun*
**final**

la **finale** *fem noun* ▷ **see final** *adj*
**final** (*in a competition*)

**finalement** *adverb*
1 **in the end, finally**
**Finalement nous avons choisi la rouge.** In the end we chose the red one.
2 **after all**
**Finalement c'est une bonne idée.** After all, it's a good idea.

la **finance** *fem noun*
**finance**

**financer** *verb* **[61]**
**to finance**



ⓔ means the verb takes être to form the perfect

**finir** *verb* **[2]**
1 **to finish, to end**
**Le film finit à dix heures.** The film finishes at ten o'clock.
2 **finir quelque chose** to finish something
**J'ai fini le roman.** I've finished the novel.
**As-tu fini tes devoirs?** Have you finished your homework?
**Qui veut finir le gâteau?** Who wants to finish the cake?
**J'ai fini le sucre.** I've used up the sugar.
3 **finir de faire quelque chose** to finish doing something
**J'ai fini de faire ma valise.** I've finished packing.
4 **finir par faire quelque chose** to end up doing something
**Il a fini par aller à Paris.** He ended up going to Paris.

**finlandais** *masc adjective*, **finlandaise** *fem*
▷ see **Finlandais** *noun*
**Finnish**

le **Finlandais** *masc noun*, la **Finlandaise** *fem* ▷ see **finlandais** *adj*
**Finn**

la **Finlande** *fem noun*
**Finland**

le **finnois** *masc noun*
**Finnish** (*the language*)

la **firme** *fem noun*
**firm**

le **fisc** *masc noun*
**tax office**

la **fissure** *fem noun*
**crack**

**fixe** *masc & fem adjective*
1 **fixed**
**une idée fixe** a fixed idea
**un menu à prix fixe** a fixed-price menu
**Nous mangeons à heures fixes.** We eat at set times.
2 **permanent**
**un emploi fixe** a permanent job

**fixer** *verb* **[1]**
1 **to fix** (*to attach*)
**Il fixe un cadre au mur.** He's fixing a frame on the wall.
2 **to set** (*a date, a price*)
**Il a fixé la date de la rencontre au samedi 2 mai.** He's set the date for the match for Saturday 2 May.
3 **to stare at**
**Pourquoi me fixe-t-il ainsi?** Why is he staring at me like that?

le **flacon** *masc noun*
**(small) bottle**

**flamand** *masc adjective*, **flamande** *fem*
▷ see **Flamand** *noun*
**Flemish**

**WORD TIP** Adjectives never have capitals in French, even for nationality or regional origin.

le **Flamand** *masc noun*, la **Flamande** *fem*
▷ see **flamand** *adjective*
1 **Fleming** (*Dutch-speaking Belgian*)
2 **le flamand** Flemish (*the language*)

le **flamant** *masc noun*
**flamingo**

**flamber** *verb* **[1]**
1 **to blaze** (*fires*)
2 **to rocket** (*prices*)

la **flamme** *fem noun*
**flame**

le **flan** *masc noun*
**custard tart**

**WORD TIP** *flan* does not mean *flan* in English; for the meaning of *flan* ▷ **tarte**.

le **flanc** *masc noun*
**side** (*of a person, an animal*)

**flâner** *verb* **[1]**
**to stroll**

la **flaque** *fem noun*
**une flaque d'eau** a puddle

le **flash** *masc noun*
1 **flash** (*on a camera*)
2 **news headlines**
**le flash de midi** the news headlines at midday (*on the radio*)

**flatter** *verb* **[1]**
**to flatter**

**flatteur** *masc adjective*, **flatteuse** *fem*
**flattering**

la **flèche** *fem noun*
1 **arrow**
2 **road sign, arrow**
**Suivez la flèche.** Follow the arrow.
3 **spire**
**les flèches de la cathédrale de Chartres** the spires of Chartres cathedral

la **fléchette** *fem noun*
**dart**
**une partie de fléchettes** a game of darts

**fléchir** *verb* **[2]**
1 **to bend**
**Fléchis les genoux!** Bend your knees!
2 **to weaken**
**Sa détermination fléchit.** His determination is weakening.

la **fleur** *fem noun*
**flower**
**un tissu à fleurs** a flower-patterned fabric
**un cerisier en fleur** a cherry-tree in blossom

**fleuri** *masc adjective*, **fleurie** *fem*
1 **flowery**, **with lots of flowers**
**du tissu fleuri** flowery material
2 **Ton jardin est très fleuri.** You've got lots of flowers in your garden.

**fleurir** *verb* [2]
1 **to flower**
**Le rosier fleurit.** The rose is flowering.
**Le pommier fleurit.** The apple tree is coming into blossom.
2 **to flourish**
**Le commerce fleurit.** Business is flourishing.

le & la **fleuriste** *masc & fem noun*
**florist**

le **fleuve** *masc noun*
**river** (*that reaches the sea, e.g. la Seine, la Loire, etc*)

**flexible** *masc & fem adjective*
**flexible**

le **flic** *masc noun*
(*informal*) **policeman**, **cop**

le **flipper** *masc noun*
**pinball machine**

**flirter** *verb* [1]
**to flirt**

le **flocon** *masc noun*
**flake**
- le **flocon de neige** snowflake
- les **flocons d'avoine** porridge oats

**floral** *masc adjective*, **florale** *fem*, **floraux** *masc pl*, **florales** *fem pl*
**floral**

la **flotte** *fem noun*
**fleet** (*of ships*)

**flotter** *verb* [1]
1 **to float**
**Une bouteille flotte à la surface du lac.** A bottle is floating on the lake.
2 **to fly**
**Le drapeau flotte au vent.** The flag is flying in the wind.
3 (*informal*) **to rain**
**Et voilà, il flotte!** There you are, it's raining!

**flou** *masc adjective*, **floue** *fem*
1 **blurred**
**une image floue** a blurred image
2 **vague**
**Ses projets sont un peu flous.** Her plans are a bit vague.

**fluide** *masc & fem adjective*
**fluid**

**fluo** *invariable masc & fem adjective*
(*informal*) **fluorescent**
**du vert fluo** fluorescent green

le **fluor** *masc noun*
**fluorine**
**du dentifrice au fluor** fluoride toothpaste

**fluorescent** *masc adjective*, **fluorescente** *fem*
**fluorescent**

la **flûte** *fem noun*
**flute**
**Elle joue de la flûte.** She plays the flute.
- la **flûte à bec** recorder
- la **flûte à champagne** flute
- la **flûte traversière** flute

**focaliser** *verb* [1]
**to focus**

la **foi** *fem noun*
**faith**

le **foie** *masc noun*
**liver**
**une crise de foie** a bout of indigestion
**J'ai une crise de foie.** I have indigestion,

le **foin** *masc noun*
**hay**

la **foire** *fem noun*
**fair**

la **fois** *fem noun*
1 **time**
**une fois** once
**deux fois** twice
**trois fois** three times
**plusieurs fois** several times
**la première fois** the first time
**trois fois plus grand** three times as big
**Trois fois dix font trente.** Tree times ten is thirty.
2 **à la fois** at the same time, at once
**trois à la fois** three at a time
3 **une fois que** once
**Une fois que j'aurai pris une douche ...** Once I've had a shower ...
**Une fois j'ai vu ...** I once saw...
4 **à chaque fois** whenever, each time
**À chaque fois que nous sortons, nous fermons la porte à clé.** Whenever we go out, we lock the door.
5 (*to begin stories*) **Il était une fois...** Once upon a time...

la **folie** *fem noun*
**madness**
C'est de la folie! It's madness!

le **folk** *masc noun*
**folk music**

la **folle** *fem noun, adjective* ▷ **fou**

♪ **foncé** *masc adjective*, **foncée** *fem*
**dark**
**des couleurs foncées** dark colours
**le bleu foncé** dark blue
**J'ai les cheveux bruns foncés.** I have dark brown hair.

**foncer** *verb* **[61]**
(*informal*) **to rush**
**Ils ont foncé vers la porte.** They rushed for the door.

la **fonction** *fem noun*
1 **function**
2 **post, job**
**une voiture de fonction** a company car
**Le nouveau directeur prend ses fonctions en septembre.** The new head is taking up his post in September.
- la **fonction publique** civil service

**fonctionnaire** *masc & fem noun*
**civil servant**

le **fonctionnement** *masc noun*
**working**
**Je ne comprends pas le fonctionnement de cette machine.** I don't understand how this machine works.

**fonctionner** *verb* **[1]**
**to work**

♪ le **fond** *masc noun*
1 **bottom**
**au fond du lac** at the bottom of the lake
**au fond de la bouteille** at the bottom of the bottle
2 **back**
**au fond du tiroir** at the back of the drawer
**au fond de la classe** at the back of the classroom
3 **end**
**au fond du couloir** at the end of the corridor
4 **background**
**sur fond blanc** on a white background
**de la musique de fond** background music
5 **au fond, dans le fond** in fact
**Au fond, c'est assez simple.** In fact it's quite easy.
- le **fond de teint** foundation (*make-up*)

**fondamental** *masc adjective*, **fondamentale** *fem*, **fondamentaux** *masc pl*, **fondamentales** *fem pl*
**basic, fundamental**

le **fondateur** *masc noun*, la **fondatrice** *fem*
**founder**

la **fondation** *fem noun*
1 **founding** (*of a hospital, a college, etc*)
2 **les fondations** the foundations (*of a building*)

**fonder** *verb* **[1]**
1 **to found**
**Mon oncle a fondé une association.** My uncle has founded an association.
2 **to base**
**Ses conclusions sont fondées sur des faits.** His conclusions are based on facts.

**fondre** *verb* **[3]**
1 **to melt**
**Le beurre fond au soleil.** The butter is melting in the sun.
2 **to dissolve**
**Le sucre fond dans l'eau.** Sugar dissolves in water.
3 **fondre en larmes** to burst into tears
**L'histoire était si triste qu'elle fondit en larmes.** The story was so sad that she burst into tears.

**fondu** *masc adjective*, **fondue** *fem*
**melted**

**font** *verb* ▷ **faire**

la **fontaine** *fem noun*
**fountain**
**Alice boit à la fontaine.** Alice is drinking from the fountain.

la **fonte** *fem noun*
1 **cast iron**
**une poêle en fonte** a cast-iron frying pan
2 **melting** (*of metal, ice*)
3 **thaw** (*of ice, snow*)

le **foot** *masc noun*
**football**
**un match de foot** a football match
**Ludivine joue au foot.** Ludivine plays football.

♪ le **football** *masc noun*
**football**
**Je joue au football après l'école.** I play football after school.
**Il aime regarder le football à la télé.** He likes watching football on TV.

le **footballeur** *masc noun*, la **footballeuse** *fem*
**footballer**

le **footing** *masc noun*
**jogging**
**Je fais du footing tous les matins.** I go jogging every morning.

**forain** *masc adjective*, **foraine** *fem*
**un marchand forain** a stallkeeper
**une fête foraine** a funfair

la **force** *fem noun*
1 **strength**
**la force de caractère** strength of character
**Il reprend des forces après sa maladie.** He's getting his strength back after his illness.
**Suzanne est à bout de forces.** Suzanne is feeling drained.
**avoir de la force** to be strong
**Tu as assez de force pour le faire.** You're strong enough to do it.
**avoir la force de faire quelque chose** to have the strength to do something
**Je n'ai pas la force de sortir ce soir.** I haven't got the strength to go out tonight.
2 **force**
**de force** by force
**Ils sont entrés de force dans la maison.** They entered the house by force.
3 **à force de faire quelque chose** by doing something
**À force d'économiser, elle a pu s'acheter son portable.** By saving very hard, she was able to buy her mobile.
4 **les forces de l'ordre** the police
**les forces armées** the armed forces

**forcément** *adverb*
1 **inevitably**
**Il y a forcément une solution.** There has to be a solution.
2 **pas forcément** not necessarily

**forcer** *verb* **[61]**
**to force**
**Les cambrioleurs ont forcé la porte.** The burglars forced the door.
**forcer quelqu'un à faire quelque chose** to force somebody to do something
**Sa mère le force à manger des épinards.** His mother forces him to eat spinach.

se **forcer** *reflexive verb* Ⓔ
**to force yourself**
**se forcer à faire quelque chose** to make yourself do something
**Je me force à boire un litre d'eau tous les jours.** I make myself drink one litre of water a day.

♪ la **forêt** *fem noun*
**forest**

le **forfait** *masc noun*
1 **fixed price**
**Il est payé au forfait.** He's paid a fixed rate.
2 **package**
**un forfait tout compris** an all-inclusive package
3 **withdrawal** (*of a player, a team in a competition*)
**déclarer forfait** to withdraw
**Notre équipe a déclaré forfait.** Our team withdrew.
4 **(serious) crime**
**Il a été condamné à 25 ans de prison pour son forfait.** He was sentenced to 25 years' prison for his crime.

le **forgeron** *masc noun*
**blacksmith**

la **formalité** *fem noun*
**formality**

le **format** *masc noun*
1 **format** (*of a disquette, a newspaper*)
2 **size** (*of a sheet of paper, a photo*)

♪ la **formation** *fem noun*
**training**
**Elle a une formation d'infirmière.** She's a trained nurse.
- la **formation continue** continuing education
- la **formation professionnelle** vocational training

la **forme** *fem noun*
1 **shape**
**une sucette en forme de lapin** a lolly in the shape of a rabbit
2 **form**
**dans sa forme actuelle** in its present form
**J'aime la musique sous toutes ses formes.** I like all kinds of music.
3 **en forme** in form
**David est en forme.** David's on form.
**Tu as l'air en pleine forme.** You're looking in great shape.

**formel** *masc adjective*, **formelle** *fem*
1 **formal**
2 **categorical**
**un refus formel** a categorical refusal
**Elle a dit 100 euros, je suis formel.** She said 100 euros, I'm positive about it.
3 **strict**
**un ordre formel** a strict order

**formellement** *adverb*
**strictly**
**formellement interdit** strictly forbidden



Ⓔ means the verb takes être to form the perfect

**former** *verb*[1]
1 **to form**
**Formez un cercle!** Form a circle!
**Ils ont formé une deuxième équipe.** They formed a second team.
**Nous formons une famille très unie.** We are a close-knit family.
2 **to train**
**Ici on forme des programmeurs.** They train programmers here.

♪ **formidable** *masc & fem adjective*
(*informal*) **great, fantastic**
**Le film était formidable.** The film was fantastic.
**Le baby-sitter est formidable avec mon petit frère.** The babysitter's wonderful with my little brother.

le **formulaire** *masc noun*
**form**
**Nous devons remplir un formulaire pour nous inscrire.** We have to fill in a form to enrol.

la **formule** *fem noun*
1 **formula**
**la formule un** Formula One (*in car racing*)
2 **expression** (*in language*)
**une formule toute faite** a set expression

♪ **fort** *masc adjective*, **forte** *fem*
▷ **see fort** *adv*
1 **strong**
**Nadia est très forte.** Nadia's very strong.
**Ton café est trop fort.** Your coffee's too strong.
2 **être fort en quelque chose** to be good at something
**Olivier est fort en maths.** Olivier's good at maths.
3 **stout**
**une jeune fille un peu forte** a girl on the stout side

**fort** *adverb* ▷ **see fort** *adj*
1 **extremely**
**C'était fort bon.** It was extremely good.
2 **hard**
**Ce boxeur frappe fort.** This boxer hits hard.
3 **loudly**
**Il chante fort.** He sings loudly.
**Parle plus fort!** Speak louder!

la **forteresse** *fem noun*
**fortress**

le **fortifiant** *masc noun*
**tonic**

**fortifier** *verb*[1]
1 **to strengthen**
**Ce shampooing fortifie les cheveux.** This shampoo strengthens your hair.
**Le sport, ça fortifie.** Sport makes you strong.
2 **to fortify** (*a city, a port, etc*)

**fortuit** *masc adjective*, **fortuite** *fem*
**accidental**

la **fortune** *fem noun*
1 **fortune**
**les grandes fortunes** big fortunes
**Ce tableau vaut une fortune.** This painting is worth a fortune.
**faire fortune** to make a fortune
**Il a fait fortune au Japon.** He made his fortune in Japan.
2 **de fortune** makeshift
**un lit de fortune** a makeshift bed

le **fossé** *masc noun*
1 **ditch**
**Sa voiture est allée dans le fossé.** His car went into the ditch.
2 **moat** (*around a castle*)
3 **gap**
**le fossé qui sépare les riches et les pauvres** the gap between the rich and the poor

la **fossette** *fem noun*
**dimple**

♪ **fou** *masc adjective*, **folle** *fem* ▷ **see fou** *noun*
1 **mad**
**Il devient fou.** He's going mad.
2 **crazy, amazing**
**On a passé une soirée folle.** We had an amazing evening.
3 **huge**
**Ils ont un succès fou.** They're having a huge success.
**Il y a un monde fou.** There are masses of people.
4 **être fou de quelque chose** to be mad about something
**Il est fou de musique ska.** He's mad about ska music.

le **fou** *masc noun*, la **folle** *fem* ▷ **see fou** *adj*
**madman, madwoman**
**Un fou m'a doublé dans un virage.** A madman overtook me on a bend.
**Elle travaille comme une folle.** She works like mad.

la **foudre** *fem noun*
**lightning**
**un arbre frappé par la foudre** a tree struck by lightning

le **fouet** *masc noun*
**1 whip**
**2 whisk** (*for eggs, cream, etc*)
**un fouet électrique** an electric whisk

**fouetter** *verb* **[1]**
**1 to whip**
**2 to whisk** (*eggs, cream*)
**Pour faire une omelette, fouette trois œufs.** To make an omelette, whisk three eggs.
**la crème fouettée** whipped cream

la **fougère** *fem noun*
**1 fern**
**2 bracken**
**Le chevreuil disparut dans les fougères.** The deer disappeared in the bracken.

la **fouille** *fem noun*
**search**

**fouiller** *verb* **[1]**
**1 to search**
**La police a fouillé la maison.** The police searched the house.
**J'ai été fouillé à l'aéroport.** I was searched at the airport.
**2 fouiller dans quelque chose** to rummage through something
**Tu as fouillé dans mon sac à main.** You've rummaged through my handbag.

le **fouillis** *masc noun*
**mess** (*in a room*)
**ranger le fouillis dans la cuisine** to tidy up the mess in the kitchen

le **foulard** *masc noun*
**scarf**
- le **foulard islamique** Muslim headscarf

la **foule** *fem noun*
**1 crowd**
**Anaïs s'est perdue dans la foule.** Anaïs got lost in the crowd.
**venir en foule à** to flock to
**Les fans sont venus en foule au concert.** The fans flocked to the concert.
**2 une foule de quelque chose** lots of something
**Il m'a posé une foule de questions.** He asked me lots of questions.

le **four** *masc noun*
**oven**
**à four moyen** in a medium oven
**un poulet au four** a roast chicken
**des légumes cuits au four** baked vegetables
**mettre quelque chose au four** to put something in the oven
**Mamie a mis le gâteau au four.** Granny put the cake in the oven.
- le **four à micro-ondes** microwave oven

la **fourche** *fem noun*
**fork**

la **fourchette** *fem noun*
**fork**

le **fourgon** *masc noun*
**van**

la **fourgonnette** *fem noun*
**(small) van**

la **fourmi** *fem noun*
**1 ant**
**Il y a des fourmis partout.** There are ants everywhere.
**2 avoir des fourmis** to have pins and needles
**Je suis restée assise trop longtemps, maintenant j'ai des fourmis dans les jambes.** I've been sitting down too long, now I've got pins and needles in my legs.

**fourmiller** *verb* **[1]**
**fourmiller de quelque chose** to be swarming with something
**La ville fourmille de touristes.** The town is swarming with tourists.

le **fourneau** *masc noun*, les **fourneaux** *plural*
**stove**

la **fournée** *fem noun*
**batch** (*of cakes, bread*)

**fournir** *verb* **[2]**
**to supply**
**fournir quelqu'un en quelque chose** to supply somebody with something
**Mes voisins me fournissent en légumes frais.** My neighbours supply me with fresh vegetables.

le **fournisseur** *masc noun*
**supplier**

les **fournitures** *plural fem noun*
**stationery**
- les **fournitures de bureau** office stationery
- les **fournitures scolaires** school stationery

**WORD TIP** *fournitures* does not mean *furniture* in English; for the meaning of *furniture* ▷ **meuble**.

**fourré** *masc adjective*, **fourrée** *fem*
**1 filled**
**un gâteau fourré au chocolat** a cake with a chocolate filling
**2 fur-lined**
**des bottes fourrées** fur-lined boots

la **fourrure** *fem noun*
1 **fur**
un manteau de fourrure a fur coat
de la fausse fourrure imitation fur
2 **coat** (*of animals*)

♪ le **foyer** *masc noun*
1 **home**
rester au foyer to stay at home
une femme au foyer a housewife
2 **household**
La majorité des foyers disposent d'un micro-ordinateur. The majority of households have a PC.
3 **hostel**
un foyer d'étudiants a student's hostel
4 **club**
un foyer de jeunes a youth club
5 **fireplace**

le **fracas** *masc noun*
**crash** (*noise*)

**fracasser** *verb* **[1]**
**to smash, to break to pieces**

la **fraction** *fem noun*
**fraction**

la **fracture** *fem noun*
**fracture**
une fracture de la cheville a fractured ankle

**fracturer** *verb* **[1]**
1 **to fracture**
un os fracturé a fractured bone
2 **to break**
Les voleurs ont fracturé le coffre-fort. The thieves broke open the safe.

♪ **fragile** *masc & fem adjective*
1 **fragile**
Ne touche pas, c'est fragile! Don't touch, it's fragile!
2 **frail, delicate**
une vieille dame fragile a frail old lady
Il a l'estomac fragile. He has a delicate stomach.
Mon oncle a le cœur fragile. My uncle has a weak heart.
Il a une santé fragile. He has poor health.

le **fragment** *masc noun*
**fragment**

**fraîche** *fem* ▷ **frais**

la **fraîcheur** *fem noun*
1 **coolness**
la fraîcheur de la cave the coolness of the cellar
2 **freshness** (*of food*)

♪ **frais** *masc adjective*, **fraîche** *fem*
▷ **see frais** *adv, noun*
1 **cool, cold**
un matin frais a chilly morning
2 **cool**
une boisson fraîche a cool drink
3 **fresh**
du pain frais fresh bread
des nouvelles fraîches fresh news
'Peinture Fraîche' 'Wet Paint'

♪ **frais** *adverb* ▷ **see frais** *adj, noun*
Il fait frais ce soir. It's cool tonight.
'Servir frais' 'Serve chilled'

♪ le **frais** *masc noun* ▷ **see frais** *adj, adv*
1 (*about food*) À conserver au frais. Keep in a cool place.
J'ai mis du jus d'orange au frais. I put some orange juice to cool.
2 **prendre le frais** to get some fresh air
Il y a trop de fumée ici, je vais prendre le frais. It's too smoky in here, I'm going to get some fresh air.
3 **les frais** expenses, costs
les frais de déplacement travelling expenses
les frais de publicité advertising costs

♪ la **fraise** *fem noun*
**strawberry**
une glace à la fraise a strawberry ice cream
• la **fraise des bois** wild strawberry

♪ la **framboise** *fem noun*
**raspberry**
un yaourt à la framboise a raspberry yoghurt

**franc** *masc adjective*, **franche** *fem*
▷ **see franc** *noun*
**frank**

le **franc** *masc noun* ▷ **see franc** *adj*
**franc** (*the currency of Switzerland; name of the currencies used in France, Belgium and Luxembourg until replaced by the euro; 100 French francs = 15.24 euros*)
L'euro a remplacé le franc en 2002. The euro replaced the franc in 2002.

♪ **français** *masc adjective*, **française** *fem*
▷ **see Français** *noun*
**French**
un film français a French film
la cuisine française French cooking

**WORD TIP** Adjectives never have capitals in French, even for nationality or regional origin.

♪ le **Français** *masc noun*, la **Française** *fem*
▷ **see français** *adj*
1 **Frenchman**
2 **Frenchwoman** ▸▸

♪ indicates key words

3 les Français the French
4 le français French (*language*)
**J'apprends le français.** I'm learning French.
**Laura parle très bien français.** Laura speaks very good French.

**WORD TIP** Languages never have capitals in French.

♪ la **France** *fem noun*
**France**
**Mon amie habite en France.** My friend lives in France.
**Nous allons en France pour nos vacances.** We go to France for our holidays.

**WORD TIP** Countries and regions in French take *le*, *la* or *les*.

**franche** *fem* ▷ **franc**

**franchement** *adverb*
1 **frankly**
**Franchement, je ne le crois pas.** Frankly, I don't believe him.
2 **really**
**Le film était franchement nul.** The film was really awful.

**franchir** *verb* [2]
**to cross**
**Le coureur franchit la ligne d'arrivée.** The runner is crossing the finishing line.
**Le cheval a franchi l'obstacle.** The horse has cleared the fence.

la **franchise** *fem noun*
1 **frankness**
**en toute franchise** quite frankly
2 **franchise**
**un magasin en franchise** a franchise (*shop, business, etc*)

**francophone** *masc & fem adjective*
**French-speaking**
**les pays francophones** French-speaking countries

la **frange** *fem noun*
**fringe**

le **frangin** *masc noun*, la **frangine** *fem* (*informal*)
1 **brother**
2 **sister**

la **frangipane** *fem noun*
**almond cream**

le **franglais** *masc noun*
**Franglais** (*a mixture of French and English, eg footing = jogging*)

♪ **frapper** *verb* [1]
1 **to hit**
**Il a frappé son chien.** He hit his dog.
**une région frappée par le chômage** an area hit by unemployment
**La Louisiane a été frappée par un terrible ouragan.** Louisiana was hit by a terrible hurricane.
2 **to knock**
**frapper à la porte** to knock at the door
**On a frappé.** There was a knock on the door.
**frapper dans ses mains** to clap your hands
3 **être frappé par quelque chose** to be struck by something
**J'ai été frappé par sa timidité.** I was struck by his shyness.
**Ça m'a beaucoup frappé.** That made a big impression on me.
4 **to chill** (*wine*)

la **fraude** *fem noun*
1 **fraud**
**la fraude informatique** computer fraud
2 **cheating** (*in an exam*)

**fredonner** *verb* [1]
**to hum**

le **freezer** *masc noun*
**freezer compartment** (*in a fridge*)

**WORD TIP** *freezer* does not mean *freezer* in English; for the meaning of *freezer* ▷ **congélateur**.

le **frein** *masc noun*
**brake**
**les freins** the brakes
**le frein à main** the handbrake

♪ **freiner** *verb* [1]
1 **to brake**
**La voiture a freiné trop tard.** The car braked too late.
2 **to slow down** (*on skis, skates*)
**Freine un peu ou tu vas tomber!** Slow down a bit or you'll fall over!

**frêle** *masc & fem adjective*
**frail**

le **frelon** *masc noun*
**hornet**

**frémir** *verb* [2]
1 **to shudder**
**Cette idée me fait frémir.** This idea makes me shudder.
2 **to simmer**
**Laisser frémir pendant 5 minutes.** Simmer for 5 minutes.

le **frêne** *masc noun*
**ash tree**

**fréquemment** *adverb*
**frequently**, **often**

la **fréquence** *fem noun*
**frequency**

**fréquenté** *masc adjective*, **fréquentée** *fem*
1 **popular**
**un café très fréquenté** a very popular cafe
2 **un quartier mal fréquenté** a rough area

**fréquenter** *verb* [1]
1 **to see** (*people*)
**Nous fréquentons beaucoup les Tournier.** We see the Tourniers a lot.
2 **to go often to** (*a beach, a cafe, a restaurant*)
**Didier fréquente le restaurant du coin.** Didier often goes to the local restaurant.
3 **to go to** (*a school, a church*)
**Elle fréquente l'école Sainte Marie.** She goes to Saint Mary's (school).

♪le **frère** *masc noun*
**brother**
**C'est mon petit frère.** He's my little brother.

les **friandises** *plural fem noun*
**sweet things**
**À ma fête d'anniversaire, on a mangé beaucoup de friandises.** At my birthday party we ate a lot of sweet things.

le **fric** *masc noun*
(*informal*) **money**

**frictionner** *verb* [1]
**to rub**

le **frigidaire®** *masc noun*
**fridge**

♪le **frigo** *masc noun*
(*informal*) **fridge**
**La soupe est au frigo.** The soup is in the fridge.

**frileux** *masc adjective*, **frileuse** *fem*
**être frileux** to feel the cold
**Je ne suis pas frileuse.** I don't feel the cold.

la **frime** *fem noun*
(*informal*) **C'est de la frime!** It's all show!

**frimer** *verb* [1]
(*informal*) **to show off**

le **frimeur** *masc noun*, la **frimeuse** *fem*
(*informal*) **show-off**
**C'est un vrai frimeur.** He's a real show-off.

les **fringues** *plural fem noun*
(*informal*) **clothes**

**fripé** *masc adjective*, **fripée** *fem*
**crumpled**
**Ma jupe est toute fripée.** My skirt is all crumpled.

**frire** *verb* [74]
**faire frire quelque chose** to fry something
**Il faut d'abord faire frire les oignons.** First you've got to fry the onions.

**frisé** *masc adjective*, **frisée** *fem*
▷ see **frisée** *noun*
1 **curly**
**des cheveux frisés** curly hair
2 **curly-haired**
**un petit garçon frisé** a curly-haired little boy

la **frisée** *fem noun* ▷ see **frisé** *adj*
**curly endive**, **frisée** (*a type of lettuce*)

**friser** *verb* [1]
**to curl**

le **frisson** *masc noun*
**shiver**
**avoir des frissons** to shiver
**J'ai froid, j'ai des frissons.** I'm cold, I'm shivering.

**frissonner** *verb* [1]
1 **to shiver**
**Elle a beaucoup de fièvre et elle frissone.** She's got a high temperature and she's shivering.
2 **to shudder**
**Il frissonnait d'horreur.** He was shuddering with horror.

**frit** *masc adjective*, **frite** *fem*
**fried**
**du poisson frit** fried fish

♪la **frite** *fem noun*
**chip**, **French fry**
**un steak frites** steak and chips

la **friture** *fem noun*
1 **frying**
2 **une friture de poissons** fried fish, whitebait

♪**froid** *masc adjective*, **froide** *fem*
▷ see **froid** *noun*
1 **cold**
**de l'eau froide** cold water
2 **cold**, **cool**
**La maîtresse est très froide avec les parents.** The teacher is very cold towards the parents.
**Nous avons eu un accueil froid.** We had a cool welcome.

♪ le **froid** *masc noun* ▷ see **froid** *adj*
**1 cold**
**Je n'aime pas le froid.** I don't like the cold.
**avoir froid** to be cold (*person*)
**Elle a froid.** She's cold.
**J'ai froid aux mains.** My hands are cold.
**2 faire froid** to be cold (*weather*)
**Il fait froid aujourd'hui.** It's cold today.
**3 prendre froid** to catch a chill
**Il a pris froid au parc.** He caught a chill at the park.

**froidement** *adverb*
**coldly**

la **froideur** *fem noun*
**coldness**

**froisser** *verb* **[1]**
**1 to crease**
**Il a froissé son pantalon.** He creased his trousers.
**2 to hurt** (*upset*)
**Ta plaisanterie l'a froissé.** Your joke hurt him.

se **froisser** *reflexive verb* Ⓔ
**1 to crease**
**La soie se froisse facilement.** Silk creases easily.
**2 to take offence**
**Ne te froisse pas, c'était seulement pour rire!** Don't take offence, it was only a joke!
**3 to strain** (*a muscle*)

**frôler** *verb* **[1]**
**to brush against**

♪ le **fromage** *masc noun*
**cheese**

***fromage***

Les Français mangent le plus de fromage au monde : 23 kg par personne par an!

la **fromagerie** *fem noun*
**1 cheese shop**
**le rayon fromagerie du supermarché** the supermarket's cheese counter
**2 dairy**
**Pendant les vacances je travaille à la fromagerie.** During the holidays I work at the dairy.

le **froment** *masc noun*
**wheat**

**froncer** *verb* **[61]**
**froncer les sourcils** to frown

le **front** *masc noun*
**1 forehead**
**2 faire front à quelque chose** to face up to something
**Il fait front à ses problèmes.** He's facing up to his problems.
**3 faire front contre quelque chose** to make a stand against something
**Nous faisons front contre le racisme.** We're making a stand against racism.

la **frontière** *fem noun*
**border**
**passer la frontière** to cross the border
**Nous avons passé la frontière à Bâle.** We crossed the border at Basle.

**frotter** *verb* **[1]**
**1 to rub**
**Frotte-moi le dos!** Rub my back!
**2 to scrub**
**Elle frotte le plancher.** She's scrubbing the floor.

se **frotter** *reflexive verb* Ⓔ
**to rub**
**Estelle se frotte les yeux.** Estelle is rubbing her eyes.
**Le chat aime se frotter contre mes jambes.** The cat likes rubbing against my legs.

♪ le **fruit** *masc noun*
**les fruits** fruit
**Il faut acheter des fruits.** We need to buy some fruit.
**un fruit** a piece of fruit
**Veux-tu un fruit?** Would you like some fruit?
- les **fruits de mer** seafood

**fruité** *masc adjective*, **fruitée** *ajective fem*
**fruity**

**frustrant** *masc adjective*, **frustrante** *fem*
**frustrating**

**frustré** *masc adjective*, **frustrée** *fem*
**frustrated**

la **fugue** *fem noun*
**1 une adolescente en fugue** a runaway teenager
**faire une fugue** to run away
**Juliette a fait une fugue.** Juliette has run away.
**2** (*Music*) **fugue**
**une fugue de Bach** a fugue by Bach

**fuir** *verb* **[44]**
**1 to run away, to flee**
**2 fuir quelque chose, quelqu'un** to run away from something, somebody
**La vedette a voulu fuir les journalistes.** The star tried to run away from the journalists.
**3 to leak**
**La bouilloire fuit.** The kettle's leaking.

la **fuite** *fem noun*
1 **flight**
**la fuite du fugitif** the escape of the fugitive
**la fuite des cerveaux** the brain drain
2 **prendre la fuite** to flee
**L'automobiliste a pris la fuite après l'accident.** The motorist fled after the accident.
3 **leak**
**une fuite de gaz** a gas leak
**Il y a une fuite dans le tuyau.** There is a leak in the hosepipe.

**fulgurant** *masc adjective*, **fulgurante** *fem*
**dazzling**

**fumé** *masc adjective*, **fumée** *fem*
▷ see **fumée** *noun*
**smoked**
**du saumon fumé** smoked salmon

la **fumée** *fem noun* ▷ see **fumé** *adj*
**smoke**

♪ **fumer** *verb* [1]
1 **to smoke**
**Je ne fume pas.** I don't smoke.
2 **fumer une cigarette** to smoke a cigarette
**Elle fume la cigarette.** She smokes.
**Mon père fume la pipe.** My father smokes a pipe.

**WORD TIP** Use *la pipe, la cigarette* to say what kind of smoker a person is.

le **fumeur** *masc noun*, la **fumeuse** *fem*
**smoker**
**un zone non-fumeurs** a no-smoking area

le **fumier** *masc noun*
**manure**

le & la **funambule** *masc & fem noun*
**tightrope walker**

**funèbre** *masc & fem adjective*
1 **funeral**
**les pompes funèbres** the undertaker's
2 **gloomy**
**une voix funèbre** a gloomy voice

les **funérailles** *plural fem noun*
**funeral**

le **funiculaire** *masc noun*
**funicular**

**fur et à mesure** *adverb*
1 **au fur et à mesure** as you go along
**Je corrige les erreurs au fur et à mesure.** I correct the mistakes as I go along.
2 **au fur et à mesure que** as
**Au fur et à mesure que les années passent, Nicolas devient plus tolérant.** As the years go by, Nicolas's becoming more tolerant.

le **furet** *masc noun*
**ferret**

la **fureur** *fem noun*
1 **rage, fury**
**un accès de fureur** an outburst of rage
**la fureur des combats** the fury of the fighting
2 **frenzy**
**avec fureur** frenziedly
3 **faire fureur** to be all the rage
**Cette chanson fait fureur en ce moment.** This song is all the rage at the moment.

**furibond** *masc adjective*, **furibonde** *fem*
**furious**

**furieusement** *adverb*
**furiously**

**furieux** *masc adjective*, **furieuse** *fem*
**furious**
**être furieux contre quelqu'un** to be furious with somebody
**Elle est furieuse contre son copain.** She's furious with her boyfriend.

le **fusain** *masc noun*
**charcoal** (*for drawing*)

le **fuseau** *masc noun*, les **fuseaux** *pl*
**ski pants**
• le **fuseau horaire** time zone

la **fusée** *fem noun*
**rocket**

le **fusible** *masc noun*
**fuse**

le **fusil** *masc noun*
**gun, rifle**
**un coup de fusil** a gun shot

**fusiller** *verb* [1]
**to shoot** (*to execute*)

**fusionner** *verb* [1]
**to merge**

le **fût** *masc noun*
**cask, barrel**
**un fût de vin** a cask of wine

**futé** *masc adjective*, **futée** *fem*
1 **crafty**
**Émilie est une petite fille futée.** Émilie is a crafty little girl.
2 **clever**
**Il n'est pas très futé.** He isn't very clever.

**futur** *masc adjective*, **future** *fem*
▷ see **futur** *noun*
**future**
**le futur président** the future president
**son futur mari** her husband-to-be

le **futur** *masc noun* ▷ see **futur** *adj*
1 **future**
dans un futur proche in the near future
Ce sont nos projets pour le futur. These are our future plans.
2 (*Grammar*) **future**

# G g

**gâcher** *verb* [1]
1 **to waste** (*food*)
2 **to spoil** (*fun*)

la **gaffe** *fem noun*
(*informal*)
1 **blunder**
Aurore a fait une gaffe. Aurore has done something stupid.
2 faire gaffe to watch out

le **gagnant** *masc noun*, la **gagnante** *fem*
**winner**

♪ **gagner** *verb* [1]
1 **to win**
Il a gagné! He's won!
Elles ont gagné le match. They won the match.
2 **to earn**
Elle gagne bien sa vie. She makes a good living.
3 gagner du temps to save time

**gai** *masc adjective*, **gaie** *fem*
**cheerful**

la **galerie** *fem noun*
**gallery**
• la **galerie marchande** shopping arcade

le **galet** *masc noun*
**pebble**

la **galette** *fem noun*
1 **biscuit**
2 **pancake** (*savoury*)
3 **round flat cake or loaf**
• la **galette des Rois** Twelfth Night cake

mini-info **galette**

Le 6 janvier, c'est l'Épiphanie. On mange une galette des Rois, un gâteau rond et plat avec une fève. Si on a la fève, on est roi ou reine. On met une couronne en papier !

♪ **Galles** *noun*
le pays de Galles Wales

**WORD TIP** Countries and regions in French take *le*, *la* or *les*.

♪ **gallois** *masc adjective*, **galloise** *fem*
▷ see **Gallois** *noun*
**Welsh**

**WORD TIP** Adjectives never have capitals in French, even for nationality or regional origin.

♪ le **Gallois** *masc noun*, la **Galloise** *fem*
▷ see **gallois** *adj*
1 **Welshman**, **Welshwoman**
les Gallois the Welsh
2 le gallois Welsh (*the language*)
Je parle gallois. I speak Welsh.

**WORD TIP** Languages never have capitals in French.

**galoper** *verb* [1]
1 **to canter** (*horses*)
2 **to gallop** (*horses*)
3 **to dash around** (*people*)

le **gamin** *masc noun*, la **gamine** *fem*
(*informal*) **kid**

la **gamme** *fem noun*
1 **range** (*of products*)
2 **scale** (*in music*)

♪ le **gant** *masc noun*
**glove**

♪ le **garage** *masc noun*
**garage**

♪ le & la **garagiste** *masc & fem noun*
1 **garage owner**
2 **motor mechanic**

la **garantie** *fem noun*
**guarantee**

**garantir** *verb* [2]
**to guarantee**

♪ le **garçon** *masc noun*
1 **boy**
2 **young man**
3 **bachelor**
4 **waiter**

le & la **garde** *masc & fem noun*
1 **guard**
2 **nurse**
3 être de garde to be on duty
la pharmacie de garde the duty chemist's

4 **mettre quelqu'un en garde** to warn somebody
**prendre garde** to be careful

♪ **garder** *verb* **[1]**
1 **to keep**
**Est-ce que tu peux garder mon sac?** Can you keep my bag for me?
**Il t'a gardé une place.** He's kept you a seat.
**Pour garder la forme ...** To keep healthy...
2 **to keep on**
**Elle a gardé son manteau.** She kept her coat on.
3 **to look after**
**Audrey garde les enfants ce soir.** Audrey is looking after the children this evening.
4 **to guard**
**Le chien garde la maison.** The dog guards the house.

se **garder** *reflexive verb* Ⓔ
**to keep** (*food*)

la **garderie** *fem noun*
**day nursery**

la **garde-robe** *fem noun*
**wardrobe**

le **gardien** *masc noun*, la **gardienne** *fem*
1 **security guard**
2 **caretaker** (*in a hotel*)
3 **attendant** (*in a museum*)
4 **warder** (*in a prison*)
- le **gardien de but** goalkeeper
- le **gardien de la paix** policeman

♪ la **gare** *fem noun*
**(railway) station**
- la **gare routière** coach station

**garer** *verb* **[1]**
**to park** (*a car*)

se **garer** *reflexive verb* Ⓔ
**to park**

**garnir** *verb* **[2]**
1 **to decorate** (*a cake*)
2 **to garnish** (*meat*)
3 **to stock** (*shelves*)

la **garniture** *fem noun*
1 **side dish**
2 **filling** (*for a sandwich*)
3 **topping** (*for a pizza*)
4 **trimming** (*for clothes*)

le **gars** *masc noun*
(*informal*) **guy**

la **Gascogne** *fem noun*
**Gascony**

**WORD TIP** Countries and regions in French take *le*, *la* or *les*.

**gaspiller** *verb* **[1]**
**to waste**

♪ le **gâteau** *masc noun*, les **gâteaux** *plural*
**cake**
- le **gâteau au chocolat** chocolate cake

**gâter** *verb* **[1]**
**to spoil**

se **gâter** *reflexive verb* Ⓔ
**to go bad**

♪ **gauche** *masc & fem adjective*
▷ see **gauche** *noun*
**left**
**sa main gauche** his left hand

♪ la **gauche** *fem noun* ▷ see **gauche** *adj*
1 **left**
**à gauche** on the left
**tournez à gauche** turn left
**à ma gauche, sur ma gauche** on my left
2 **la gauche** the Left (*in politics*)

**gaucher** *masc adjective*, **gauchère** *fem*
**left-handed**

la **gaufre** *fem noun*
**waffle**

le **gaz** *invariable masc noun*
**gas**
**le chauffage au gaz** gas central heating

**gazeux** *masc adjective*, **gazeuse** *fem*
**fizzy**
**eau gazeuse** sparkling mineral water

le **gazole** *masc noun*
**diesel (oil)**

le **gazon** *masc noun*
**lawn**

le **géant** *masc noun*, **géante** *fem*
**giant**

le **gel** *masc noun*
1 **frost**
2 **gel**

**gelé** *masc adjective*, **gelée** *fem*
▷ see **gelée** *noun*
**frozen**

la **gelée** *fem noun* ▷ see **gelé** *adj*
1 **jelly**
2 **frost**

♪ **geler** *verb* **[45]**
**to freeze**
**Il gèle dehors.** It's freezing outside.

les **Gémeaux** *plural masc noun*
**Gemini** (*sign of the Zodiac*)
Yasmina est Gémeaux. Yasmina is a Gemini.

**WORD TIP** Signs of the zodiac do not take an article: *un* or *une*.

**gémir** *verb* **[2]**
**to moan**

**gênant** *masc adjective*, **gênante** *fem*
1 **annoying** (*noise, person*)
2 **awkward** (*situation*)

la **gencive** *fem noun*
**gum** (*part of your mouth*)

le **gendarme** *masc noun*
**policeman**

la **gendarmerie** *fem noun*
**police station**
• la **gendarmerie nationale** (French) national police force

le **gendre** *masc noun*
**son-in-law**

la **gêne** *fem noun*
1 **embarrassment**
sans aucune gêne without a hint of embarrassment
2 **discomfort** (*physical*)
3 **inconvenience**

**gêné** *masc adjective*, **gênée** *fem*
**embarrassed**

**gêner** *verb* **[1]**
1 **to bother**
Ça te gêne si je mets la radio? Do you mind if I put the radio on?
2 **to embarrass**
Ça me gêne. It's embarrassing.
3 **to block** (*traffic*)

**général** *masc adjective*, **générale** *fem*, **généraux** *masc pl*, **générales** *fem pl*
▷ see **général** *noun*
**general**
en général in general, generally

le **général** *masc noun*, les **généraux** *plural*
▷ see **général** *adj*
**general**
le général Dubois General Dubois

**généralement** *adverb*
**generally**

la **génération** *fem noun*
**generation**

**généreux** *masc adjective*, **généreuse** *fem*
**generous**

la **générosité** *fem noun*
**generosity**

la **génétique** *fem noun*
**genetics**

**Genève** *noun*
**Geneva**

**génial** *masc adjective*, **géniale** *fem*, **géniaux** *masc pl*, **géniales** *fem pl*
**brilliant**

le **génie** *masc noun*
1 **genius**
2 **engineering**

le **genou** *masc noun*, les **genoux** *plural*
**knee**
être à genoux to be kneeling
Elle est à genoux. She's kneeling.
se mettre à genoux to kneel down
Mettez-vous à genoux! Kneel down!

le **genre** *masc noun*
**kind**
Quel genre de livre aimes-tu lire? What kind of book do you like to read?
• le **genre humain** mankind

les **gens** *plural masc noun*
**people**
beaucoup de gens a lot of people

**gentil** *masc adjective*, **gentille** *fem*
1 **kind, nice**
Elle est très gentille. She's really nice.
C'est très gentil de ta part. It's very kind of you.
2 **good**
Sois gentil! Be good!

la **gentillesse** *fem noun*
**kindness**

**gentiment** *adverb*
1 **nicely**
2 **kindly**

la **géographie** *fem noun*
**geography**

la **géologie** *fem noun*
**geology**

le **gérant** *masc noun*, la **gérante** *fem*
**manager, manageress**

**gérer** *verb* **[24]**
1 **to manage**
2 **to run** (*a country*)
3 **to handle** (*a problem*)

**germain** *masc adjective*, **germaine** *fem*
un cousin germain a first cousin

le **geste** *masc noun*
**gesture**

la **gestion** *fem noun*
**management**

la **gifle** *fem noun*
**slap**

**gifler** *verb* [1]
**to slap**

**gigantesque** *masc & fem adjective*
**gigantic**

le **gigaoctet** *masc noun*
**gigabyte**

le **gigot** *masc noun*
**leg of lamb**

le **gilet** *masc noun*
1 **cardigan**
2 **waistcoat**
• le **gilet de sauvetage** life-jacket

le **gingembre** *masc noun*
**ginger**

la **girafe** *fem noun*
**giraffe**

le **gitan** *masc noun*, la **gitane** *fem*
**gipsy**

♪ le **gîte**, **gîte rural** *masc noun*
**self-catering cottage**

♪ la **glace** *fem noun*
1 **ice cream**
2 **ice**
3 **mirror**
se regarder dans la glace to look at yourself in the mirror
4 **window** (*in a car*)
Peux-tu baisser ta glace? Can you open your window?

**glacé** *masc adjective*, **glacée** *fem*
1 **icy cold**
2 du thé glacé iced tea

le **glaçon** *masc noun*
**ice cube**

**glissant** *masc adjective*, **glissante** *fem*
**slippery**

♪ **glisser** *verb* [1]
1 **to slip**
Attention, ça glisse! Be careful, it's slippery!
2 **to slide**
Il a glissé une lettre sous la porte. He slid a letter under the door.

**global** *masc adjective*, **globale** *fem*, **globaux** *masc pl*, **globales** *fem pl*
**total**

la **gloire** *fem noun*
**glory**

**glorieux** *masc adjective*, **glorieuse** *fem*
**glorious**

**gluant** *masc adjective*, **gluante** *fem*
1 **sticky** (*pasta, rice*)
2 **slimy** (*fish*)

le **goal** *masc noun*
**goalkeeper**

le **gobelet** *masc noun*
**cup**

la **godasse** *fem noun*
(*informal*) **shoe**

**gogo** *adverb*
(*informal*) à gogo as much as you like
pizza à gogo as much pizza as you can eat

le **golf** *masc noun*
1 **golf**
jouer au golf to play golf
2 **golf course**

la **gomme** *fem noun*
**rubber**

**gommer** *verb* [1]
**to rub out**

**gonfler** *verb* [1]
1 **to pump up** (*tyres*)
2 **to blow up** (*a balloon*)

♪ la **gorge** *fem noun*
1 **throat**
J'ai mal à la gorge. I've got a sore throat.
2 **gorge**

la **gorgée** *fem noun*
**sip**

le **gorille** *masc noun*
**gorilla**

♪ le & la **gosse** *masc & fem noun*
(*informal*) **kid**

le **goudron** *masc noun*
**tar**

la **gourde** *fem noun*
**bottle** (*made of plastic, metal*)

**gourmand** *masc adjective*, **gourmande** *fem*
1 **greedy**
Il est gourmand. He loves his food.
2 un repas gourmand a gourmet meal

la **gourmandise** *fem noun*
**greed**

la **gousse d'ail** *fem noun*
**clove of garlic**

French–English

le **goût** *masc noun*
1 **taste**
**Cette eau a un goût de citron.** The water tastes of lemon.
**de bon goût** in good taste
**chacun ses goûts** each to their own
2 **flavour**
**un yaourt au goût vanille** a vanilla-flavoured yoghurt
3 **liking**
**à mon goût** for my liking

le **goûter** *masc noun* ▷ see **goûter** *verb*
1 **afternoon snack**
2 **children's party**
**le goûter d'anniversaire de Camille** Camille's birthday party

**goûter** *verb* [1] ▷ see **goûter** *noun*
1 **to taste, to try**
**Je peux goûter?** May I taste it?
2 **goûter à** to taste, to try
**Il n'a même pas goûté au foie gras.** He didn't even try the foie gras.
3 **to have a mid-afternoon snack**
**Aujourd'hui les enfants ont goûté au parc.** Today the children had their mid-afternoon snack in the park.

la **goutte** *fem noun*
**drop**
**goutte à goutte** drop by drop

le **gouvernement** *masc noun*
**government**

**gouverner** *verb* [1]
**to rule**

la **goyave** *fem noun*
**guava**

la **grâce** *fem noun*
1 **grace**
2 **grâce à** thanks to

**gracieux** *masc adjective*, **gracieuse** *fem*
**graceful**

le **grade** *masc noun*
**rank**

les **gradins** *plural masc noun*
**terraces** (*in a stadium*)

**graduel** *masc adjective*, **graduelle** *fem*
**gradual**

le **grain** *masc noun*
1 **grain, corn**
2 **du poivre en grains** peppercorns
**du café en grains** coffee beans
- le **grain de raisin** grape
- le **grain de sable** grain of sand

la **graine** *fem noun*
**seed**

la **graisse** *fem noun*
**fat**

la **grammaire** *fem noun*
**grammar**

le **gramme** *masc noun*
**gramme**

**grand** *adverb* ▷ see **grand** *adj*
**wide**
**La porte était grande ouverte.** The door was wide open.
**Ouvre grand la bouche!** Open your mouth wide!
**Ouvre grand tes oreilles!** Listen carefully!

**grand** *masc adjective*, **grande** *fem* ▷ see **grand** *adv*
1 **big**
**une grande maison** a big house
**C'est ma grande sœur.** She's my big sister.
2 **tall**
**un grand arbre** a tall tree
**Ton frère est très grand.** Your brother's very tall.
**Elle est plus grande que moi.** She's taller than me.
3 **long**
**un grand voyage** a long journey
4 **great**
**un grand artiste** a great artist
**un grand ami** a great friend
5 **old**
**Manon est assez grande pour sortir seule.** Manon is old enough to go out on her own.
6 **main**
**les grandes lignes** main (railway) lines
- la **grande personne** grown-up
- la **grande surface** hypermarket

**grand-chose** *pronoun*
**much**
**pas grand-chose** not much
**Il ne reste pas grand-chose.** There's not much left.

la **Grande-Bretagne** *fem noun*
**Great Britain**

**WORD TIP** Countries and regions in French take *le*, *la* or *les*.

la **grandeur** *fem noun*
**size**
**grandeur nature** life-size

**grandir** *verb* [2]
**to grow, to grow up**

♪ la **grand-mère** *fem noun*, les **grands-mères** *plural*
**grandmother**

♪ le **grand-père** *masc noun*, les **grands-pères** *plural*
**grandfather**

♪ les **grands-parents** *plural masc noun*
**grandparents**

la **grange** *fem noun*
**barn**

le & la **graphiste** *masc & fem noun*
**graphic designer**

la **grappe** *fem noun*
**bunch**
- la **grappe de raisin** bunch of grapes

♪ **gras** *masc adjective*, **grasse** *fem*
▷ see **gras** *noun*
1 **fatty**
40% de matières grasses 40% fat (*on cheese or yoghurt label*)
2 **oily**, **greasy**
une peau grasse oily skin

♪ le **gras** *masc noun* ▷ see **gras** *adj*
1 **fat**
2 **grease**

le **gratte-ciel** *invariable masc noun*
**skyscraper**

**gratter** *verb* [1]
1 **to scratch**
Est-ce que tu peux me gratter le dos? Can you scratch my back?
2 **to itch**
Ça me gratte partout. I'm itching all over.

se **gratter** *reflexive verb* ⓔ
**to scratch**

♪ **gratuit** *masc adjective*, **gratuite** *fem*
**free**
Le concert est gratuit. The concert's free.
'Entrée gratuite' 'Admission free'

**gratuitement** *adverb*
1 **free**
2 **for nothing** (*without payment*)

**grave** *masc & fem adjective*
1 **serious**
un grave accident a serious accident
un blessé grave a seriously injured person
Ce n'est pas grave. It doesn't matter.
2 **deep**
une voix grave a deep voice

**gravement** *adverb*
**seriously**
Elle est gravement malade. She's seriously ill.

le **gré** *masc noun*
contre son gré against his will
de plein gré willingly
de bon gré gladly

**grec** *masc adjective*, **grecque** *fem*
▷ see **Grec** *noun*
**Greek**

le **Grec** *masc noun* la **Grecque** *fem*
▷ see **grec** *adj*
1 **Greek** (*person*)
2 le grec Greek (*the language*)

la **Grèce** *fem noun*
**Greece**

la **grêle** *fem noun*
**hail**

**grelotter** *verb* [1]
**to shiver**

la **grenade** *fem noun*
1 **grenade**
2 **pomegranate**

la **grenadine** *fem noun*
**grenadine** (*pomegranate cordial*)

le **grenier** *masc noun*
**attic**
au grenier in the attic

la **grenouille** *fem noun*
**frog**
les cuisses de grenouille frogs' legs

la **grève** *fem noun*
1 **strike**
une grève des trains a train strike
Le métro est en grève. The underground's on strike.
faire grève to strike
2 **shore**

le & la **gréviste** *masc & fem noun*
**striker**

**grièvement** *adverb*
**seriously**
grièvement blessé seriously injured

la **griffe** *fem noun*
**claw**

**griffonner** *verb* [1]
**to scribble**

la **grillade** *fem noun*
**grilled meat**
une grillade de porc a pork steak

le **grillage** *masc noun*
**wire netting**

la **grille** *fem noun*
1 **metal gate**
2 **railings**

**grillé** *masc adjective*, **grillée** *fem*
1 **grilled**
2 **toasted**
du pain grillé toast
3 **roasted** (*nuts*)
des cacahuètes grillées roasted peanuts

le **grille-pain** *invariable masc noun*
**toaster**

**griller** *verb* [1]
1 **to grill**
2 **to toast**

la **grimace** *fem noun*
**grimace**
faire des grimaces à quelqu'un to make faces at somebody

**grimper** *verb* [1]
**to climb**
Elle aime grimper aux arbres. She likes climbing trees.

**grincer** *verb* [61]
**to creak**
La porte grince. The door creaks.

**grincheux** *masc adjective*, **grincheuse** *fem*
**grumpy**

la **grippe** *fem noun*
**flu**
avoir la grippe to have flu
Aurélie a la grippe. Aurélie has flu.
• la **grippe aviaire** bird flu

**gris** *masc adjective*, **grise** *fem*
**grey**

la **grisaille** *fem noun*
**dull overcast weather**

**grogner** *verb* [1]
1 **to grumble**
2 **to growl** (*dog*)

**gronder** *verb* [1]
1 **to tell off**
Ses parents l'ont grondé. His parents told him off.
se faire gronder to get a telling-off
Brice s'est fait gronder. Brice got told off.
2 **to rumble** (*thunder, cannons*)

**gros** *masc adjective*, **grosse** *fem*
1 **big**
un gros problème a big problem
des grosses larmes big tears
2 **fat**
un gros monsieur a fat man
3 **bad**
un gros rhume a bad cold
4 **heavy**
un gros fumeur a heavy smoker
5 **en gros roughly**
En gros, nous sommes une vingtaine.
Roughly there are about twenty of us.
• le **gros lot** jackpot
• le **gros mot** swear word

la **groseille** *fem noun*
**redcurrant**
• la **groseille à maquereau** gooseberry

**grosse** *fem adjective* ▷ **gros**

la **grossesse** *fem noun*
**pregnancy**

la **grosseur** *fem noun*
1 **size**
deux oranges de la même grosseur two oranges of the same size
2 **lump**
Il a une grosseur dans le cou. He has a lump in his neck.

**grossier** *masc adjective*, **grossière** *fem*
1 **rude**
David est grossier. David is rude.
2 **crude**
un travail grossier a crude piece of work
une erreur grossière a bad mistake

**grossir** *verb* [2]
1 **to enlarge** (*photo*)
2 **to put on weight**
Annie a grossi de dix kilos. Annie put on ten kilos.

**grosso modo** *adverb*
**roughly**

**grotesque** *masc & fem adjective*
**ridiculous**

la **grotte** *fem noun*
**cave**

le **groupe** *masc noun*
**group**
un groupe de lycéens a group of secondary school students
en groupe in a group
travailler en groupes de deux to work in pairs
• le **groupe sanguin** blood group

**grouper** *verb* [1]
**to group**

se **grouper** *reflexive verb* ê
1 **to gather**
2 **to form a group**

la **grue** *fem noun*
**crane**

le **guépard** *masc noun*
**cheetah**

la **guêpe** *fem noun*
**wasp**

**guère** *adverb*
ne ... guère ... hardly
Je ne l'ai guère vu depuis Noël. I've hardly seen him since Christmas.

**guérir** *verb* **[2]**
1 **to cure**
Le médecin l'a guéri. The doctor cured him.
2 **to get better**
J'espère que tu vas vite guérir. I hope you'll get better soon.

la **guérison** *fem noun*
**recovery** (*from an illness, an injury*)

**Guernesey** *fem noun*
**Guernsey** (*in the Channel Islands*)

**WORD TIP** Unlike other names of islands, *Guernesey* does not take *le* or *la*.

la **guerre** *fem noun*
**war**
en guerre at war
la Deuxième Guerre mondiale the Second World War

**guetter** *verb* **[1]**
**to watch out for**

la **gueule** *fem noun*
1 **mouth** (*of an animal*) (*considered rude if used for a person*)
2 (*informal*) faire la gueule to sulk
Elle fait la gueule. She's sulking.

**gueuler** *verb* **[1]**
(*informal*) **to yell**

⚷ le **guichet** *masc noun*
1 **ticket office** (*in a station*)
2 **box office** (*in a theatre*)
3 **counter, window** (*in a bank*)
• le **guichet automatique** cashpoint

⚷ le **guide** *masc noun*
**guide**

**guider** *verb* **[1]**
**to guide**

le **guidon** *masc noun*
**handlebars**

les **guillemets** *plural masc noun*
**quotations marks**
entre guillemets in quotation marks (*usually « ... » in French*)

la **guirlande** *fem noun*
1 **garland**
2 **tinsel**
• la **guirlande électrique** fairy lights
• la **guirlande en papier** paper chain

la **guitare** *fem noun*
**guitar**
jouer de la guitare to play the guitar

le & la **guitariste** *masc & fem noun*
**guitarist**

la **gym** *fem noun*
**gymnastics, PE**

⚷ le **gymnase** *masc noun*
**gym**

la **gymnastique** *fem noun*
1 **gymnastics**
2 **exercises**

# Hh

**habile** *masc & fem adjective*
**clever**
Elle est habile de ses mains. She's clever with her hands.

**habillé** *masc adjective*, **habillée** *fem*
1 **dressed**
2 **smart** (*dress, suit*)

**habiller** *verb* **[1]**
**to dress** (*a child*)

s'**habiller** *reflexive verb* ❷
**to get dressed**
Habille-toi vite! Get dressed quick!

un **habitant** *masc noun*, une **habitante** *fem*
**inhabitant**

une **habitation** *fem noun*
**house**
• une **habitation à loyer modéré HLM** council flat

⚷ **habiter** *verb* **[1]**
**to live**
Ils habitent Paris., Ils habitent à Paris. They live in Paris.
Nous habitons en Angleterre. We live in England.

une **habitude** *fem noun*
1 **habit**
une mauvaise habitude a bad habit
2 d'habitude usually
3 comme d'habitude as usual
4 avoir l'habitude de faire quelque chose to be used to doing something
J'ai l'habitude de travailler le soir. I tend to work in the evening.

**habitué** *masc adjective*, **habituée** *fem*
être habitué à quelque chose to be used to something
Nous sommes habitués aux bruits de la rue. We are used to the noise from the street.

**habituel** *masc adjective*, **habituelle** *fem*
**usual**

s'**habituer** *reflexive verb* Ⓔ [1]
s'habituer à quelque chose to get used to something
Il s'est habitué à sa nouvelle école. He got used to his new school.

**haché** *masc adjective*, **hachée** *fem*
1 **chopped**
2 **minced**
un bifteck haché a burger (*without the bun*)

le **hachis Parmentier** *masc noun*
**shepherd's pie**

le **haddock** *masc noun*
**smoked haddock**

la **haie** *fem noun*
**hedge**

la **haine** *fem noun*
**hatred**

**haïr** *verb* [46]
**to hate**

**Haïti** *masc noun*
**Haiti**
en Haïti in Haiti

**WORD TIP** Unlike other names of countries, *Haiti* does not take *le* or *la*.

**haïtien** *masc adjective*, **haïtienne** *fem*
▷ see **Haïtien** *noun*
**Haitian**

le **Haïtien** *masc noun*, la **Haïtienne** *fem*
▷ see **haïtien** *adj*
**Haitian**

l'**haleine** *fem noun*
**breath**
hors d'haleine out of breath

le **hall** *masc noun*
**entrance hall**

les **halles** *plural fem noun*
**covered market**

la **halte** *fem noun*
**stop**
Halte! Stop!

l'**haltérophilie** *fem noun*
**weightlifting**

le **hamster** *masc noun*
**hamster**

la **hanche** *fem noun*
**hip**

le **handball** *masc noun*
**handball**
jouer au handball to play handball

le **handicap** *masc noun*
**handicap**

un **handicapé** *masc noun*, une **handicapée** *fem*
**disabled person**
les handicapés the disabled

**harceler** *verb* [45]
**to harass**

le **hareng** *masc noun*
**herring**
• le **hareng saur** smoked herring

le **haricot** *masc noun*
**bean**
• le **haricot blanc** haricot bean
• le **haricot vert** French bean

une **harmonie** *fem noun*
**harmony**

la **harpe** *fem noun*
**harp**

le **hasard** *masc noun*
1 **chance**
par hasard by chance
2 au hasard at random
3 à tout hasard just in case

la **hâte** *fem noun*
**haste**
à la hâte hastily

la **hausse** *fem noun*
**increase, rise**
une hausse des prix a rise in prices

**hausser** *verb* [1]
1 **to raise**
2 hausser les épaules to shrug your shoulders

♂ **haut** *masc adjective*, **haute** *fem*
▷ see **haut** *adv, noun*
**high**
**un immeuble haut de 50 étages** a block of flats 50 storeys high

♂ **haut** *adverb* ▷ see **haut** *adj, noun*
**high**
**Voir plus haut.** See above (*in a book*).

♂ le **haut** *masc noun* ▷ see **haut** *adj, adv*
1 **top**
**le haut du mur** the top of the wall
**J'ai acheté un haut.** I bought a top.
2 **L'arbre fait 10 mètres de haut.** The tree is 10 metres high.
3 **en haut** upstairs
4 **en haut de** at the top of

le **hautbois** *masc noun*
**oboe**
**Luc joue du hautbois.** Luc plays the oboe.

la **hauteur** *fem noun*
1 **height**
**Quelle est la hauteur de la porte?** How high is the door?
2 **le saut en hauteur** high jump (*the sport*)
3 **hill**

le **haut-parleur** *masc noun*
**loudspeaker**

un **hebdomadaire** *masc noun*
**weekly magazine**

♂ un **hébergement** *masc noun*
1 **accommodation**
2 **hosting**
**l'hébergement de site Internet** website hosting

**héberger** *verb* [52]
1 **to put up** (*a guest for the night*)
2 **to host** (*a website*)

**hein** *exclamation*
(*informal*) **what?, eh?**

**hélas** *exclamation*
**unfortunately**

♂ l'**herbe** *fem noun*
1 **grass**
2 **herb**
• les **herbes de Provence** mixed herbs

le **hérisson** *masc noun*
**hedgehog**

un **héritage** *masc noun*
**inheritance**

**hériter** *verb* [1]
**to inherit**
**hériter de quelque chose** to inherit something

**hermétique** *masc & fem adjective*
**airtight**

l'**héroïne** *fem noun*
1 **heroine**
2 **heroin** (*the drug*)

le **héros** *masc noun*
**hero**

une **hésitation** *fem noun*
**hesitation**

**hésiter** *verb* [1]
**to hesitate**
**Nous hésitons entre ...** We can't decide between ...

♂ une **heure** *fem noun*
1 **hour**
**une demi-heure** half an hour
**une heure et demie** an hour and a half
**toutes les heures** every hour
**à l'heure** per hour
2 **time**
**Quelle heure est-il?** What time is it?
**C'est l'heure de...** It's time for...
**à huit heures du matin** at eight o'clock in the morning
**à six heures et demie** at half past six
**à deux heures moins le quart** at quarter to two
**À quelle heure te lèves-tu demain?** What time are you getting up tomorrow?
3 **à l'heure** on time
4 **de bonne heure** early
5 **tout à l'heure** (*in a while*) later, (*a moment ago*) earlier
**À tout à l'heure!** See you later!

**heureusement** *adverb*
**fortunately**

♂ **heureux** *masc adjective*, **heureuse** *fem*
1 **happy**
**Elle est heureuse d'être ici.** She's happy to be here.
2 **pleased**
**Je suis heureux que Grégory soit guéri** I am pleased that Grégory is better (*boy speaking*).
**Je suis heureuse que Grégory soit guéri** I am pleased that Grégory is better (*girl speaking*).
3 **lucky**
**un heureux gagnant** a lucky winner

**heurter** *verb* **[1]**
**to hit**

un **hexagone** *masc noun*
1 **hexagon**
2 l'Hexagone France (*French journalists often refer to France as **l'Hexagone** as it has a six-sided shape on the map*)

le **hibou** *masc noun*, les **hiboux** *plural*
**owl**

**hier** *adverb*
**yesterday**
hier matin yesterday morning
hier soir last night
avant-hier the day before yesterday

la **hi-fi** *invariable fem noun*
**hi-fi**

**hippique** *masc & fem adjective*
**equestrian**
un club hippique a riding school

une **hirondelle** *fem noun*
**swallow**

une **histoire** *fem noun*
1 **history**
l'histoire de France French history
2 **story**
l'histoire de ma vie the story of my life
3 **matter**
une histoire de famille a family matter
4 faire des histoires to make a fuss
Il fait toujours des histoires. He's always making a fuss.
• l'**histoire-géo** history and geography (*school subject*)

**historique** *masc & fem adjective*
**historic**

le **hit-parade** *masc noun*
**charts** (*in pop music*)

l'**hiver** *masc noun*
**winter**
en hiver in winter

un **HLM** *invariable masc & fem noun*
(*= habitation à loyer modéré*) **un logement HLM** a council flat
les HLM council housing

**hocher** *verb* **[1]**
1 hocher la tête to shake your head (*in disagreement*)
2 hocher la tête to nod (*in agreement*)

le **hockey** *masc noun*
**hockey**
jouer au hockey to play hockey
• le **hockey sur glace** ice hockey

**hollandais** *masc adjective*, **hollandaise** *fem* ▷ see **Hollandais** *noun*
**Dutch**

le **Hollandais** *masc noun*, la **Hollandaise** *fem* ▷ see **hollandais** *adj*
1 **Dutchman, Dutchwoman**
les Hollandais the Dutch
2 l'hollandais Dutch (*the language*)

la **Hollande** *fem noun*
**Holland**

le **homard** *masc noun*
**lobster**

**homéopathique** *masc & fem adjective*
**homeopathic**

un **hommage** *masc noun*
**tribute**

un **homme** *masc noun*
1 **mankind**
2 **human being**
3 **man**
l'homme de la rue the man in the street

**homosexuel** *masc adjective*, **homosexuelle** *fem*
**homosexual**

la **Hongrie** *fem noun*
**Hungary**

**hongrois** *masc adjective*, **hongroise** *fem* ▷ see **Hongrois** *noun*
**Hungarian**

le **Hongrois** *masc noun*, la **Hongroise** *fem noun* ▷ see **hongrois** *adj*
1 **Hungarian** (*person*)
2 l'hongrois Hungarian (*the language*)

**honnête** *masc & fem adjective*
**honest**

**honnêtement** *adverb*
**honestly**

l'**honnêteté** *fem noun*
**honesty**

un **honneur** *masc noun*
**honour**

**honorer** *verb* **[1]**
**to honour**

la **honte** *fem noun*
1 **shame**
avoir honte de quelque chose to be ashamed of something
2 **disgrace**

**honteux** *masc adjective*, **honteuse** *fem*
**disgraceful**

♪ un **hôpital** *masc noun*
**hospital**
être à l'hôpital to be in hospital

le **hoquet** *masc noun*
**hiccup**
avoir le hoquet to have hiccups

♪ un **horaire** *masc noun*
1 **timetable**
les horaires de train the train timetable
2 **hours**
les horaires du travail the working hours

un **horizon** *masc noun*
**horizon**

**horizontal** *masc adjective*, **horizontale** *fem*, **horizontaux** *masc pl*, **horizontales** *fem pl*
**horizontal**

une **horloge** *fem noun*
**clock**

une **horreur** *fem noun*
1 **horror**
Quelle horreur! How awful!
2 **avoir horreur de quelque chose** to hate something
Nina a horreur des épinards. Nina hates spinach.

**horrifier** *verb* **[1]**
**to horrify**

♪ **hors** *preposition*
hors de outside
Hors d'ici! Get out of here!
les boutiques hors taxes the duty-free shops
- le **hors-d'œuvre** starter (*to a meal*)
- **hors-jeu** offside (*in sports*)
- **hors service** out of order

**hospitalier** *masc adjective*, **hospitalière** *fem*
un centre hospitalier a hospital

l'**hospitalité** *fem noun*
**hospitality**

l'**hostilité** *fem noun*
**hostility**

un **hôte** *masc noun* ▷ see **hôte** *masc & fem noun*
**host**

un & une **hôte** *masc & fem noun*
▷ see **hôte** *masc noun*
**guest**
- un **hôte payant** paying guest

♪ un **hôtel** *masc noun*
**hotel**
**Nous passons deux nuits à l'hôtel.** We are spending two nights in a hotel.
- un **hôtel de ville** town hall

♪ une **hôtesse** *fem noun*
1 **hostess**
2 **receptionist**
- une **hôtesse de l'air** flight attendant

la **housse** *fem noun*
**cover** (*for a chair*)
- la **housse de couette** duvet cover

le **houx** *masc noun*
**holly**

♪ un **hovercraft** *masc noun*
**hovercraft**

♪ une **huile** *fem noun*
**oil**
des sardines à l'huile sardines in vegetable oil
- l'**huile d'olive** olive oil

♪ **huit** *number*
1 **eight**
Paul a huit ans. Paul's eight.
le huit juillet the eighth of July
2 huit jours a week

**huitième** *masc & fem adjective*
**eighth**

une **huître** *fem noun*
**oyster**

**humain** *masc adjective*, **humaine** *fem*
1 **human**
2 **humane**

une **humeur** *fem noun*
**mood**
**Il est de bonne humeur.** He's in a good mood.
**Elle est de mauvaise humeur.** She's in a bad mood.
**être d'humeur à faire quelque chose** to be in the mood to do something

**humide** *masc & fem adjective*
**damp**

l'**humidité** *fem noun*
1 **damp**
2 **humidity** (*of climate*)



French-English
a b c d e f g h i j k l m n o p q r s t u v w x y z

French-English

**humoristique** *masc & fem adjective*
**humorous**
un dessin humoristique a cartoon

l'**humour** *masc noun*
**humour**
avec humour humorously
avoir de l'humour to have a sense of humour

**hurler** *verb* [1]
1 **to yell**
2 **to howl**
3 hurler de rire to roar with laughter

la **hutte** *fem noun*
**hut**

**hydratant** *masc adjective*, **hydratante** *fem*
**moisturizing**

l'**hygiène** *fem noun*
**hygiene**
une bonne hygiène de vie a healthy lifestyle

**hygiénique** *masc & fem adjective*
**hygienic**

un **hymne** *masc noun*
**hymn**
- un **hymne national** national anthem

un **hypermarché** *masc noun*
**hypermarket**

# I i

un **iceberg** *masc noun*
**iceberg**

**ici** *adverb*
1 **here**
**Il y a trop de monde ici.** There are too many people here.
**Suivez-moi, c'est par ici.** Follow me, it's this way.
2 **jusqu'ici** so far, as far as this
**Jusqu'ici, il a fait beau.** So far the weather's been good.
**Les bus ne viennent pas jusqu'ici.** The buses don't come this far.

une **icône** *fem noun*
**icon**

**idéal** *masc adjective*, **idéale** *fem*, **idéaux** *masc pl*, **idéales** *fem pl*
**ideal**

une **idée** *fem noun*
**idea**
**Quelle bonne idée!** What a good idea!
**Je n'ai aucune idée.** I've got no idea.

**identifier** *verb* [1]
**to identify**

**identique** *masc & fem adjective*
**identical**

une **identité** *fem noun*
**identity**

**idiot** *masc adjective*, **idiote** *fem*
▷ see **idiot** *noun*
**stupid**
**C'est vraiment idiot!** It's really stupid!

un **idiot** *masc noun*, une **idiote** *fem*
▷ see **idiot** *adj*
**idiot**
**Ne fais pas l'idiot!** Don't fool around!

l'**igname** *fem noun*
**yam**

l'**ignorance** *fem noun*
**ignorance**

**ignorant** *masc adjective*, **ignorante** *fem*
**ignorant**

**ignorer** *verb* [1]
1 **not to know**
**J'ignore leur adresse.** I don't know their address.
2 **to ignore**
**Ils l'ont ignorée.** They ignored her.

**il** *pronoun*
1 (*as the subject of the verb*) **he**
**'Où est Robert?' - 'Il est dans la cuisine.'** 'Where's Robert?' - 'He's in the kitchen.'
**Il parle bien français.** He speaks French well.
2 (*for masc things*) **it**
**'Où est mon sac?' - 'Il est sur la chaise.'** 'Where's my bag?' - 'It's on the chair.'
3 (*to talk about weather, time, and with verbs like pleuvoir, falloir*) **it**
**Il pleut.** It's raining.
**Il faut attendre.** We must wait.
**Il fait beau.** It's sunny.
▷ **il y a**

une **île** *fem noun*
**island**
les îles Anglo-normandes the Channel Islands
l'île Maurice Mauritius

**illégal** *masc adjective*, **illégale** *fem*, **illégaux** *masc pl*, **illégales** *fem pl*
**illegal**

**illimité** *masc adjective*, **illimitée** *fem*
**unlimited**

**illisible** *masc & fem adjective*
**illegible**

l'**illumination** *fem noun*
**floodlighting**
- les **illuminations de Noël** Christmas lights

**illuminer** *verb* [1]
**to floodlight**

une **illusion** *fem noun*
**illusion**
Elle se fait des illusions. She's fooling herself.

une **illustration** *fem noun*
**illustration**

**illustré** *masc adjective*, **illustrée** *fem*
▷ see **illustré** *adjective*
**illustrated**

un **illustré** *masc noun* ▷ see **illustré** *adj*
**comic** (*magazine*)

**illustrer** *verb* [1]
**to illustrate**

♪ **ils** *pronoun*
(*for male people and things as the subject*) **they**
Ils sont en vacances. They're on holiday.
Mes baskets! Ils sont ruinés! My trainers! They're ruined!

**WORD TIP** *ils* is used for people when you talk about males and females together.

♪ **il y a** *phrase*
**there is, there are**
Il y a une fête ce soir. There's a party tonight.
Il y a beaucoup de gens. There are lots of people. ▷ **avoir**

♪ une **image** *fem noun*
**picture**
une vraie image a true picture

**imaginaire** *masc & fem adjective*
**imaginary**

l'**imagination** *fem noun*
**imagination**
avoir de l'imagination to be imaginative

**imaginer** *verb* [1]
1 **to imagine**
Je n'arrive pas à l'imaginer. I can't imagine it.
2 **to suppose**
Elle va appeler, j'imagine. I suppose she'll phone.

**imbattable** *masc & fem adjective*
**unbeatable**

**imbécile** *masc & fem adjective*
▷ see **imbécile** *noun*
**idiotic**

un & une **imbécile** *masc & fem noun*
▷ see **imbécile** *adj*
**fool**

une **imitation** *fem noun*
**imitation**

**imiter** *verb* [1]
**to imitate**

**immangeable** *masc & fem adjective*
**inedible**

l'**immatriculation** *fem noun*
**registration** (*of a car*)

**immédiat** *masc adjective*, **immédiate** *fem*
**immediate**
dans l'immédiat for the time being

♪ **immédiatement** *adverb*
**immediately**

**immense** *masc & fem adjective*
**huge**

♪ un **immeuble** *masc noun*
1 **block of flats**
2 **building**
un immeuble de six étages a six-storey building
- un **immeuble de bureaux** office block

l'**immigration** *fem noun*
**immigration**

un **immigré** *masc noun*, une **immigrée** *fem*
**immigrant**

**immobile** *masc & fem adjective*
**motionless**

**immobilier** *masc adjective*, **immobilière** *fem*
un agent immobilier an estate agent

**immobiliser** *verb* [1]
**to immobilize**

**immoral** *masc adjective*, **immorale** *fem*, **immoraux** *masc pl*, **immorales** *fem pl*
**immoral**

**immuniser** *verb* **[1]**
**to immunize**

un **impact** *masc noun*
**impact**

**impair** *masc adjective*, **impaire** *fem*
**odd**
un nombre impair an odd number

**imparfait** *masc adjective*, **imparfaite** *fem*
▷ see **imparfait** *noun*
**imperfect**

l'**imparfait** *masc noun*
▷ see **imparfait** *adj*
(*Grammar*) **imperfect**
à l'imparfait in the imperfect

une **impasse** *fem noun*
**dead end**

l'**impatience** *fem noun*
**impatience**

**impatient** *masc adjective*, **impatiente** *fem*
**impatient**

s'**impatienter** *reflexive verb* ⓔ **[1]**
**to lose patience**
Ils commencent à s'impatienter. They're getting impatient.

**impeccable** *masc & fem adjective*
1 **perfect**
2 **spotless**
L'appartement est impeccable. The flat's spotless.
3 **brilliant**
'On a rendez-vous au café à midi.' — 'Impeccable!' 'We're meeting in the cafe at twelve.' —'Brilliant!'

un **imper** *masc noun* (*informal*)
**raincoat, mac**

l'**impératif** *masc noun*
(*Grammar*) **imperative**
à l'impératif in the imperative

une **impératrice** *fem noun*
**empress**

une **imperfection** *fem noun*
**defect**

♪ un **imperméable** *masc noun*
**raincoat**

**impertinent** *masc adjective*, **impertinente** *fem*
**cheeky**

**impliquer** *verb* **[1]**
1 **to mean**
Cela implique que ... This means that ...
2 être impliqué dans quelque chose to be involved in something

**impoli** *masc adjective*, **impolie** *fem*
**rude**

l'**importance** *fem noun*
**importance**
Ça n'a pas d'importance. It doesn't matter.

♪ **important** *masc adjective*, **importante** *fem*
1 **important**
des événements importants important events
Ce n'est pas important. It's not important.
Il est important de savoir que ... It's important to know that ...
2 **considerable**
un nombre important d'élèves a considerable number of students
Il y aura des retards importants. There will be considerable delays.
3 **sizeable**
C'est une ville importante. It's a sizeable city.

les **importations** *plural fem noun*
**imports**

**importer** *verb* **[1]**
1 **to import** (*goods*)
2 **to matter**
'Lequel veux-tu?' - 'N'importe!'
'Which one do you want?' - 'It doesn't matter!' ▷ **n'importe**

**imposer** *verb* **[1]**
1 **to impose**
2 imposer à quelqu'un de faire quelque chose to make somebody do something

♪ **impossible** *masc & fem adjective*
▷ see **impossible** *noun*
**impossible**

♪ l'**impossible** *masc noun*
▷ see **impossible** *adj*
faire l'impossible to do your utmost
Nous ferons l'impossible pour les contacter. We'll do our utmost to contact them.

un **impôt** *masc noun*
**tax**

**imprécis** *masc adjective*, **imprécise** *fem*
**vague**

une **impression** *fem noun*
**impression**
ma première impression my first impression
Elle a fait très bonne impression. She made a very good impression.



ⓔ means the verb takes être to form the perfect

**impressionnant** *masc adjective*, **impressionante** *fem*
**impressive**

**impressionner** *verb* **[1]**
**to impress**

**imprévisible** *masc & fem adjective*
**unpredictable**

**imprévu** *masc adjective*, **imprévue** *fem*
**unexpected**

♂ une **imprimante** *fem noun*
**printer** (*for a computer*)
• une **imprimante laser** laser printer

**imprimé** *masc adjective*, **imprimée** *fem*
▷ see **imprimé** *noun*
**printed** (*fabrics, letters*)

un **imprimé** *masc noun* ▷ see **imprimé** *adj*
**form** (*to be filled in*)

**imprimer** *verb* **[1]**
**to print**

**improviser** *verb* **[1]**
**to improvise**

l'**improviste** *masc noun*
à l'improviste unexpectedly

**imprudent** *masc adjective*, **imprudente** *fem*
1 **careless**
un conducteur imprudent a careless driver
2 **rash**

**impuissant** *masc adjective*, **impuissante** *fem*
**helpless**

**impulsif** *masc adjective*, **impulsive** *fem*
**impulsive**

**inacceptable** *masc & fem adjective*
**unacceptable**

**inaccessible** *masc & fem adjective*
**inaccessible**

**inachevé** *masc adjective*, **inachevée** *fem*
**unfinished**

**inadapté** *masc adjective*, **inadaptée** *fem*
**unsuitable**

**inaperçu** *masc adjective*, **inaperçue** *fem*
passer inaperçu to go unnoticed

**inattendu** *masc adjective*, **inattendue** *fem*
**unexpected**
une visite inattendue an unexpected visit

l'**inattention** *fem noun*
**lack of attention**
une faute d'inattention a careless mistake

**inaugurer** *verb* **[1]**
1 **to open** (*an exhibition, a new building*)
2 **to unveil** (*a monument*)

**incassable** *masc & fem adjective*
**unbreakable**

un & une **incendiaire** *masc & fem noun*
**arsonist**

♂ une **incendie** *masc noun*
**fire**
**L'incendie a détruit l'église.** The fire destroyed the church.

**incertain** *masc adjective*, **incertaine** *fem*
1 **uncertain**
**Le résultat est toujours incertain.** The result is still uncertain.
2 **unsettled** (*weather*)

un **incident** *masc noun*
**incident**

**inciter** *verb* **[1]**
1 **to encourage**
**inciter quelqu'un à faire quelque chose** to encourage somebody to do something
2 **inciter à la haine** to stir up hatred

**inclure** *verb* **[25]**
1 **to include**
2 **to enclose**

**inclus** *masc adjective*, **incluse** *fem*
**including**
**jusqu'à samedi inclus** up to and including Saturday
**Il y aura trente invités, enfants inclus.** There will be thirty guests, including children.

**incollable** *masc & fem adjective*
le riz incollable easy-cook rice

**incolore** *masc & fem adjective*
**colourless**

**incommode** *masc & fem adjective*
1 **awkward**
2 **uncomfortable**

**incompétent** *masc adjective*, **incompétente** *fem*
**incompetent**

**incompréhensible** *masc & fem adjective*
**incomprehensible**

l'**inconditionnel** *masc noun*
l'**inconditionnelle** *fem*
**devotee, fan**
**C'est un inconditionnel du jazz.** He's a real jazz fan.

**inconfortable** *masc & fem adjective*
**uncomfortable**

**inconnu** *masc adjective*, **inconnue** *fem*
▷ see **inconnu** *noun*
**unknown**
Elle m'est inconnue. I don't know her.

un **inconnu** *masc noun*, une **inconnue** *fem*
▷ see **inconnu** *adj*
**stranger**

**inconsciemment** *adverb*
**unconsciously**

**inconscient** *masc adjective*, **inconsciente** *fem*
1 **unthinking**
2 **unconscious** (*in a faint*)

**incontournable** *masc & fem adjective*
**unavoidable**
C'est un fait incontournable. It's an undeniable fact.

un **inconvénient** *masc noun*
**drawback**
Il y a plusieurs inconvénients. There are several drawbacks.

**incorporer** *verb* [1]
**to blend in** (*ingredients*)
Incorporez les œufs au mélange. Blend the eggs into the mixture.

**incorrect** *masc adjective*, **incorrecte** *fem*
1 **incorrect**
2 **rude**, **impolite**

**incroyable** *masc & fem adjective*
**incredible**
une coïncidence incroyable an incredible coincidence

**inculper** *verb* [1]
inculper quelqu'un de quelque chose to charge somebody with something
Elle a été inculpée de vol. She was charged with theft.

l'**Inde** *fem noun*
**India**

**indécis** *masc adjective*, **indécise** *fem*
1 **undecided**
2 **indecisive**

**indemne** *masc & fem adjective*
**unharmed**
sortir indemne to escape unharmed

l'**indemnisation** *fem noun*
**compensation**

**indemniser** *verb* [1]
**to compensate**
demander à être indemnisé to demand compensation

**indépendamment** *adverb*
**independently**

l'**indépendance** *fem noun*
**independence**

**indépendant** *masc adjective*, **indépendante** *fem*
1 **independent**
2 **separate** (*kitchen, bathroom*)

un **index** *masc noun*
1 **index**
2 **forefinger**

un **indicateur** *masc noun*
1 **timetable** (*for trains, coaches*)
2 **street directory**
3 **un panneau indicateur a road sign**
- un **indicateur de pression** pressure gauge
- un **indicateur des départs** departures board

un **indicatif** *masc noun*
1 **dialling code**
Quel est l'indicatif pour l'Angleterre? What's the dialling code for England?
L'indicatif pour la Grande Bretagne est 44. The dialling code for Britain is 44.
2 **theme tune**
3 (*Grammar*) **indicative**

les **indications** *plural fem noun*
**directions**

un **indice** *masc noun*
**clue**

**indien** *masc adjective*, **indienne** *fem*
▷ see **Indien** *noun*
**Indian**

**Indien** *masc noun*, **Indienne** *fem*
▷ see **indien** *adj*
**Indian**

**indifférent** *masc adjective*, **indifférente** *fem*
**indifferent**

un & une **indigène** *masc & fem noun*
**native**
les indigènes the locals

une **indigestion** *fem noun*
**indigestion**

**indigne** *masc & fem adjective*
1 **unworthy**
2 **disgraceful**

s'**indigner** *reflexive verb* Ⓔ [1]
**to be outraged**

**indiqué** *masc adjective*, **indiquée** *fem*
**recommended**
Ce n'est pas très indiqué. It's not a very good idea.



Ⓔ means the verb takes être to form the perfect

**indiquer** *verb* [1]
**to point out, to show**
Pouvez-vous m'indiquer la gare? Can you show me the way to the station?

**indirect** *masc adjective*, **indirecte** *fem*
**indirect**

**indiscret** *masc adjective*, **indiscrète** *fem*
1 **indiscreet**
2 **nosy**

**indispensable** *masc & fem adjective*
**essential**
les vêtements indispensables essential clothing

**indisposé** *masc adjective*, **indisposée** *fem*
**unwell**

un **individu** *masc noun*
**individual**
C'est un drôle d'individu. He's strange.

**individuel** *masc adjective*, **individuelle** *fem*
1 **individual**
2 **separate**
une chambre individuelle a single room

**indolore** *masc & fem adjective*
**painless**

**indulgent** *masc adjective*, **indulgente** *fem*
**lenient**

**industrialisé** *masc adjective*, **industrialisée** *fem*
les pays industrialisés the industrialized countries

♪ une **industrie** *fem noun*
**industry**
l'industrie du spectacle the entertainment industry

**industriel** *masc adjective*, **industrielle** *fem*
**industrial**

**inédit** *masc adjective*, **inédite** *fem*
1 **unpublished**
2 **new**
un spectacle inédit a totally new show

**inefficace** *masc & fem adjective*
1 **inefficient** (*worker*)
2 **ineffective** (*cure*)

**inégal** *masc adjective*, **inégale** *fem*, **inégaux** *masc pl*, **inégales** *fem pl*
1 **uneven**
2 **unequal**

**inévitable** *masc & fem adjective*
1 **inevitable**
2 **unavoidable**
C'était inévitable. It was bound to happen.

**inexact** *masc adjective*, **inexacte** *fem*
1 **incorrect**
2 **inaccurate**

**inexpérimenté** *masc adjective*, **inexpérimentée** *fem*
**inexperienced**

un **infarctus** *masc noun*
**heart attack**

**infect** *masc adjective*, **infecte** *fem*
**revolting**
Le repas était infect! The meal was revolting!

**infecter** *verb* [1]
**to infect**

s'**infecter** *reflexive verb* ❷
**to go septic**

une **infection** *fem noun*
**infection**

**inférieur** *masc adjective*, **inférieure** *fem*
1 **lower**
des prix inférieurs à la moyenne lower-than-average prices
2 **smaller**
la taille inférieure the smaller size
3 **inferior, worse**
des produits de qualité inférieure poorer-quality products

**infernal** *masc adjective*, **infernale** *fem*, **infernaux** *masc pl*, **infernales** *fem pl*
**frightful, dreadful**

**infini** *masc adjective*, **infinie** *fem*
**infinite**

l'**infinitif** *masc noun*
(*Grammar*) **infinitive**

**infirme** *masc & fem adjective*
▷ see **infirme** *noun*
**disabled**
Est-il infirme? Does he have a disability?

un & une **infirme** *masc & fem noun*
▷ see **infirme** *adj*
**disabled person**

une **infirmerie** *fem noun*
**medical room** (*in a school*)

♪ un **infirmier** *masc noun*, une **infirmière** *fem*
**nurse**

l'**infirmité** *fem noun*
**disability**

**inflammable** *masc & fem adjective*
**flammable**

l'**inflation** *fem noun*
**inflation**

une **influence** *fem noun*
**influence**

**influencer** *verb* [61]
**to influence**

un **informaticien** *masc noun*, une **informaticienne** *fem*
**computer scientist**

♪ les **informations** *plural fem noun*
**the news**
les informations de midi the mid-day news

♪ **informatique** *masc & fem adjective*
▷ see **informatique** *noun*
**computer**
un système informatique a computer system

♪ l'**informatique** *fem noun*
▷ see **informatique** *adj*
**computer science, IT**

**informatiser** *verb* [1]
**to computerize**

**informer** *verb* [1]
**to inform**

s'**informer** *reflexive verb* Ⓔ
**to find out**
Je peux m'informer si tu veux. I can find out if you like.

les **infos** *plural fem noun*
**the news** (*on TV or radio*)

une **infusion** *fem noun*
**herbal tea**

l'**ingénierie** *fem noun*
**engineering**

♪ un & une **ingénieur** *masc noun*
**engineer**
faire des études d'ingénieur to study engineering

**ingénieux** *masc adjective*, **ingénieuse** *fem*
**ingenious**

**ingrat** *masc adjective*, **ingrate** *fem*
**ungrateful**

un **ingrédient** *masc noun*
**ingredient**

**inhabité** *masc adjective*, **inhabitée** *fem*
**uninhabited**

**inhabituel** *masc adjective*, **inhabituelle** *fem*
**unusual**

un **inhalateur** *masc noun*
**inhaler**

**inhumain** *masc adjective*, **inhumaine** *fem*
**inhuman**

une **initiale** *fem noun*
**initial** (*for your name*)

une **initiation** *fem noun*
**introduction** (*to a new place, skill*)
une initiation à la salsa an introduction to salsa dancing
une journée d'initiation an introductory day (*on a course*)

une **initiative** *fem noun*
**initiative**

**initier** *verb* [1]
**1** initier quelqu'un à quelque chose to introduce somebody to something (*a new skill*)
**2** **to initiate** (*a plan, an idea, a change*)

s'**initier** *reflexive verb* Ⓔ
s'initier à quelque chose to learn about something
Elle s'initie à la photo. She's starting to learn photography.

**injecter** *verb* [1]
**to inject**

une **injection** *fem noun*
**injection**

une **injure** *fem noun*
**insult**

**injurier** *verb* [1]
injurier quelqu'un to swear at somebody
Il m'a injurié. He swore at me.

**injuste** *masc & fem adjective*
**unfair**

**innocent** *masc adjective*, **innocente** *fem*
**innocent**

**innombrable** *masc & fem adjective*
**countless**

**innover** *verb* [1]
**to break new ground**

**inoccupé** *masc adjective*, **inoccupée** *fem*
**empty**

une **inondation** *fem noun*
**flood**
des inondations flooding

**inonder** *verb* [1]
**to flood**

**inoubliable** *masc & fem adjective*
**unforgettable**

**inouï** *masc adjective*, **inouïe** *fem*
**incredible**

l'**inox** *masc noun*
**stainless steel**
une casserole en inox a stainless steel sauce pan

**inoxydable** *masc & fem adjective*
l'acier inoxydable stainless steel

♪ **inquiet** *masc adjective*, **inquiète** *fem*
**anxious, worried**
Nous étions inquiets pour toi. We were worried about you.

**inquiétant** *masc adjective*, **inquiétante** *fem*
**worrying**

♪ **inquiéter** *verb* **[24]**
**to worry**
Ça m'inquiète un peu. It worries me.

s'**inquiéter** *reflexive verb* ⓔ
**to worry, to be worried**
Elle va s'inquiéter si nous sommes en retard. She'll worry if we're late.
Ne t'inquiète pas! Don't worry!

une **inquiétude** *fem noun*
**anxiety**

**insatisfait** *masc adjective*, **insatisfaite** *fem*
**dissatisfied**

une **inscription** *fem noun*
**enrolment** (*for a course, in a school*)

**inscrire** *verb* **[38]**
1 **to enrol** (*someone for a course, school*)
Elle m'a inscrit pour l'examen. She's entered me for the exam.
2 **to register** (*someone for university*)

s'**inscrire** *reflexive verb* ⓔ
**to enrol**
s'inscrire au club de foot to join the football club
Je me suis inscrit au cours de poterie. I've enrolled on the pottery course.

♪ un **insecte** *masc noun*
**insect**

**insérer** *verb* **[24]**
1 **to insert**
2 **to integrate** (*into a community*)

l'**insertion** *fem noun*
1 **insertion** (*of an advertisement in a paper*)
2 **integration** (*into a new community*)
l'insertion des jeunes dans la société the integration of young people into society

**insignifiant** *masc adjective*, **insignifiante** *fem*
**insignificant**

**insister** *verb* **[1]**
**to insist** (*on doing something*)
Elle insiste pour être vue. She insists on being seen.
Il faut insister. Keep on trying.

une **insolation** *fem noun*
**sunstroke**
attraper une insolation to get sunstroke

**insoutenable** *masc & fem adjective*
**unbearable**

**inspecter** *verb* **[1]**
**to inspect**

un **inspecteur** *masc noun*, une **inspectrice** *fem*
**inspector**

une **inspection** *fem noun*
**inspection**
- l'**inspection académique** the local education authority

l'**inspiration** *fem noun*
**inspiration**

**inspirer** *verb* **[1]**
1 **to inspire**
2 Ça ne m'inspire pas. That doesn't appeal to me.
3 **to breathe in**
Inspire fort! Breathe in deeply!

s'**inspirer** *reflexive verb* ⓔ
s'inspirer de quelqu'un, quelque chose to be inspired by somebody, something
Il s'est inspiré de Picasso. He was inspired by Picasso.

**instable** *masc & fem adjective*
**unstable**
Il fait un temps instable. The weather's unsettled.

l'**installation** *fem noun*
1 **installation** (*of central heating, a washing machine, etc*)
2 **move** (*to a house, a town*)
avant son installation à Paris before he moved to Paris
- les **installations sportives** sports facilities

**installer** *verb* **[1]**
1 **to install** (*central heating, a dishwasher*)
2 **to connect up** (*gas, electricity, a phone*)

s'**installer** *reflexive verb* ⓔ
**to settle, to settle in**
Je me suis installée dans ma nouvelle maison. I settled into my new house.
On va s'installer au soleil. We're going to sit in the sun.
Installez-vous. Please sit down.

un **instant** *masc noun*
**moment**
dans un instant in a moment
pour l'instant for the moment



French-English

a b c d e f g h i j k l m n o p q r s t u v w x y z

French–English

**instantané** *masc adjective*, **instantanée** *fem*
**instant**
une réaction instantanée an instant reaction

l'**instinct** *masc noun*
**instinct**

un **institut** *masc noun*
**institute**
- l'**institut de beauté** beautician's

♪ un **instituteur** *masc noun*, une **institutrice** *fem*
**primary school teacher**

une **institution** *fem noun*
1 **institution**
2 **private school**

une **institutrice** *fem noun* ▷ **instituteur**

un **instructeur** *masc noun*, une **instructrice** *fem*
**instructor**

l'**instruction** *fem noun*
**education**
- l'**instruction civique** civics, citizenship studies

♪ les **instructions** *plural fem noun*
**instructions**
suivre les instructions to follow the instructions
- les **instructions de lavage** washing instructions

**instruire** *verb* **[26]**
**to teach, to train**

s'**instruire** *reflexive verb* ⓔ
**to learn**

**instruit** *masc adjective*, **instruite** *fem*
**educated**

♪ un **instrument** *masc noun*
1 **instrument**
un instrument de mesure a measuring instrument
2 jouer d'un instrument to play an instrument
- un **instrument de musique** musical instrument
- les **instruments de bord** controls (*on a plane*)

une **insuffisance** *fem noun*
**shortage**

**insuffisant** *masc adjective*, **insuffisante** *fem*
1 **insufficient**
2 **inadequate**
C'est insuffisant. It's not good enough.

**insultant** *masc adjective*, **insultante** *fem*
**insulting**

une **insulte** *fem noun*
**insult**

**insulter** *verb* **[1]**
**to insult**

**insupportable** *masc & fem adjective*
**unbearable**
Je la trouve insupportable. I can't stand her.

**intact** *masc adjective*, **intacte** *fem*
**intact**

**intégral** *masc adjective*, **intégrale** *fem*, **intégraux** *masc pl*, **intégrales** *fem pl*
▷ see **intégrale** *noun*
**complete** (*unedited, uncut*)

l'**intégrale** *fem noun* ▷ see **intégral** *adj*
**complete works** (*usually music*)
l'intégrale des Beatles the complete Beatles' collection

**intellectuel** *masc adjective*, **intellectuelle** *fem*
▷ see **intellectuel** *noun*
**intellectual**

un **intellectuel** *masc noun*, une **intellectuelle** *fem*
▷ see **intellectuel** *adj*
**intellectual**

l'**intelligence** *fem noun*
**intelligence**

♪ **intelligent** *masc adjective*, **intelligente** *fem*
**clever**, **intelligent**

l'**intendance** *fem noun*
**administration** (*in a school*)

**intense** *masc & fem adjective*
**intense**

**intensif** *masc adjective*, **intensive** *fem*
**intensive**

une **intention** *fem noun*
**intention**
avoir l'intention de faire quelque chose to mean to do something
J'avais l'intention d'y aller mais ... I meant to go but ...

une **interdiction** *fem noun*
**ban**
'Interdiction de fumer' 'No smoking'

**interdire** *verb* **[47]**
**to forbid**
interdire à quelqu'un de faire quelque chose to forbid somebody to do something



ⓔ means the verb takes être to form the perfect

On nous a interdit de quitter la cour. We were not allowed to leave the playground.

♪ **interdit** *masc adjective*, **interdite** *fem*
1 **forbidden**
'Entrée interdite' 'No entry'
'Stationnement interdit' 'No parking'
Le film est interdit aux moins de 18 ans. The film has got an 18 certificate.
2 **banned** (*by censor*)

♪ **intéressant** *masc adjective*, **intéressante** *fem* ▷ see **intéressant** *noun*
1 **interesting**
une ville très intéressante a very interesting town
2 **attractive** (*financially*)
une offre intéressante an attractive offer
à un prix intéressant at a good price

l'**intéressant** *masc noun*, l'**intéressante** *fem* ▷ see **intéressant** *adj*
faire l'intéressant to show off

♪ **intéressé** *masc adjective*, **intéressée** *fem* ▷ see **intéressé** *noun*
1 **interested**
être intéressé par quelque chose to be interested in something
J'ai toujours été intéressé par les animaux. I've always been interested in animals.
2 **attentive**
Ils étaient peu intéressés. They weren't very attentive.

♪ un **intéressé** *masc noun*, une **intéressée** *fem* ▷ see **intéressé** *adj*
**person concerned**

♪ **intéresser** *verb* **[1]**
**to interest**
Tout les intéresse à cet âge. Everything interests them at that age.

s'**intéresser** *reflexive verb* ⓔ
s'intéresser à quelque chose to be interested in something
Elle s'intéresse beaucoup à l'informatique. She's very interested in computing.

l'**intérêt** *masc noun*
1 **interest**
2 avoir intérêt à faire quelque chose to had better do something
Tu as intérêt à le dire à Faiza. You'd better tell Faiza.

**intérieur** *masc adjective*, **intérieure** *fem* ▷ see **intérieur** *noun*
**inside**, **internal**
le côté intérieur the inside

♪ un **intérieur** *masc noun* ▷ see **intérieur** *adj*
**inside**, **interior**
l'intérieur du placard the inside of the cupboard
'Où est-elle?' - 'À l'intérieur' 'Where is she?' - 'Inside.' (*in the house*)

**intermédiaire** *masc & fem adjective* ▷ see **intermédiaire** *noun*
**intermediate**
Avez-vous la taille intermédiaire? Do you have the size in between?

un & une **intermédiaire** *masc & fem noun* ▷ see **intermédiaire** *adj*
**go-between**

un **internat** *masc noun*
**boarding school**

♪ **international** *masc adjective*, **internationale** *fem*, **internationaux** *masc pl*, **internationales** *fem pl*
**international**
un concours international an international competition

**interne** *masc & fem adjective* ▷ see **interne** *noun*
**internal**

un & une **interne** *masc & fem noun* ▷ see **interne** *adj*
**boarder** (*in a school*)

l'**Internet** *masc noun*
l'Internet the Internet
sur Internet on the Internet

**Internet**

Les sites Internet français finissent par « .fr » (point f r)

**interpeller** *verb* **[1]**
1 **to call out to**
2 **to question** (*by police*)

un **interphone** *masc noun*
**entry phone**

un & une **interprète** *masc & fem noun*
1 **actor** (*in the theatre*)
2 **performer**, **soloist** (*in music*)
3 **interpreter**

**interpréter** *verb* **[24]**
1 **to perform** (*a theatre role, a piece of music*)
2 **to sing** (*a song*)
3 **to interpret** (*a language, a remark*)
Il l'a mal interprété. He took it the wrong way.

l'**interrogatif** *masc noun*
(*Grammar*) **interrogative**
à l'interrogatif in the interrogative

une **interrogation** *fem noun*
1 **test** (*at school*)
2 **questioning**

**interroger** *verb* [52]
1 **to question**
interroger quelqu'un sur quelque chose to ask somebody about something
Il m'a interrogé sur mon séjour en France. He asked me about my stay in France.
2 **to test** (*at school*)

**interrompre** *verb* [69]
**to interrupt**
interrompre quelqu'un to interrupt somebody

un **interrupteur** *masc noun*
**switch**

une **interruption** *fem noun*
1 **interruption**
2 sans interruption without stopping

un **intervalle** *masc noun*
1 **interval** (*a gap between things, events*)
2 dans l'intervalle in the meantime

**intervenir** *verb* [81]
**to intervene**

une **intervention** *fem noun*
1 **intervention** (*by the police, army*)
2 **operation** (*by a surgeon*)

une **interview** *fem noun*
**interview** (*on TV, radio, for a magazine*)

un **intestin** *masc noun*
**intestine**

**intime** *masc & fem adjective*
**intimate**
un journal intime personal diary

**intimider** *verb* [1]
**to intimidate**

l'**intimité** *fem noun*
**intimacy**
dans l'intimité in private

**intolérable** *masc & fem adjective*
**intolerable**

**intolérant** *masc adjective*, **intolérante** *fem*
**intolerant**

l'**intoxication** *fem noun*
**poisoning**
• l'**intoxication alimentaire** food poisoning

**intoxiquer** *verb* [1]
**to poison**

une **intrigue** *fem noun*
**plot** (*of a play, a novel*)

une **introduction** *fem noun*
**introduction**

**introduire** *verb* [26]
**to introduce**

s'**introduire** *reflexive verb* Ⓔ
s'introduire dans quelque chose to get into something
Un cambrioleur s'est introduit dans l'appartement. A burglar got into the flat.

un **intrus** *masc noun*, une **intruse** *fem*
**intruder**

l'**intuition** *fem noun*
**intuition**

**inusable** *masc & fem adjective*
**hard-wearing**

**WORD TIP** *inusable* does not mean *unusable* in English; for the meaning of *unusable* ▷ **inutilisable**.

**inutile** *masc & fem adjective*
**pointless**
Il est inutile de l'appeler. There's no point phoning him.
Inutile de dire que ... Needless to say ...

**inutilisable** *masc & fem adjective*
**unusable**

un & une **invalide** *masc & fem noun*
**disabled person**

une **invasion** *fem noun*
**invasion**

**inventer** *verb* [1]
**to invent**

une **invention** *fem noun*
**invention**

**inverse** *masc & fem adjective*
▷ see **inverse** *noun*
**opposite**
en sens inverse in the opposite direction
dans l'ordre inverse in reverse order

l'**inverse** *masc noun* ▷ see **inverse** *adj*
l'inverse the opposite
L'inverse est vrai. The opposite is true.

une **investigation** *fem noun*
**investigation**

un **investissement** *masc noun*
**investment**

**invisible** *masc & fem adjective*
**invisible**

une **invitation** *fem noun*
**invitation**



Ⓔ means the verb takes être to form the perfect

un **invité** *masc noun*, une **invitée** *fem*
**guest**
**Nous avons des invités ce soir.** We've got visitors this evening.

♪ **inviter** *verb* **[1]**
**to invite**
**Ils l'ont invité à dîner.** They invited him to dinner.
**On a été invités chez eux.** They invited us home.

**involontaire** *masc & fem adjective*
**unintentional**

**invraisemblable** *masc & fem adjective*
**unlikely**
**une explication invraisemblable** an unlikely explanation

**ira, irai, iraient, irais, irait, iras** *verb* ▷ **aller**

♪ **irlandais** *masc adjective*, **irlandaise** *fem*
▷ see **Irlandais** *noun*
**Irish**

**WORD TIP** Adjectives never have capitals in French, even for nationality or regional origin.

♪ un **Irlandais** *masc noun*, une **Irlandaise** *fem* ▷ see **irlandais** *adj*
1 **Irishman, Irishwoman**
**les Irlandais** the Irish
2 **l'irlandais** Irish (*the language*)

**WORD TIP** Languages never have capitals in French.

♪ l'**Irlande** *fem noun*
**Ireland**
**en Irlande** in Ireland
**aller en Irlande** to go to Ireland
• **l'Irlande du Nord** Northern Ireland

**WORD TIP** Countries and regions in French take *le, la* or *les*.

l'**ironie** *fem noun*
**irony**

**ironique** *masc & fem adjective*
**ironic**

**irons, iront** *verb* ▷ **aller**

**irréel** *masc adjective*, **irréelle** *fem*
**unreal**

**irrégulier** *masc adjective*, **irrégulière** *fem*
**irregular**

**irrésistible** *masc & fem adjective*
**irresistible**

**irresponsable** *masc & fem adjective*
**irresponsible**

**irritable** *masc & fem adjective*
**irritable**

l'**irritation** *fem noun*
**irritation**

**irriter** *verb* **[1]**
**to irritate**
**Cela m'irrite.** That makes me cross.

**islamique** *masc & fem adjective*
**Islamic**

**WORD TIP** Adjectives and nouns of religion start with a small letter in French.

l'**isolation** *fem noun*
**insulation**
• **l'isolation acoustique** soundproofing

**isolé** *masc adjective*, **isolée** *fem*
**remote** (*place*)

**isoler** *verb* **[1]**
1 **to insulate** (*a room, a building*)
2 **to isolate** (*a sick person, a prisoner*)

l'**Israël** *masc noun*
**Israel**

**israélien** *masc adjective*, **israélienne** *fem*
▷ see **Israélien** *noun*
**Israeli**

**Israélien** *masc noun*, **Israélienne** *fem*
▷ see **israélien** *adj*
**Israeli**

une **issue** *fem noun*
**exit**
• **une issue de secours** emergency exit

l'**Italie** *fem noun*
**Italy**

**italien** *masc adjective*, **italienne** *fem*
▷ see **Italien** *noun*
**Italian**

un **Italien** *masc noun*, une **Italienne** *fem*
▷ see **italien** *adj*
1 **Italian** (*person*)
2 **l'italien** Italian (*the language*)

un **itinéraire** *masc noun*
**route** (*of a journey*)

**itinérant** *masc adjective*, **itinérante** *fem*
**travelling**

l'**ivoire** *masc noun*
**ivory**

**ivre** *masc & fem adjective*
**drunk**

l'**ivresse** *fem noun*
**drunkenness**

un & une **ivrogne** *masc & fem noun*
**drunkard**

# J j



**j'** *abbreviation: je* ▷ **je** *pronoun*

**WORD TIP** *je* becomes *j'* before a word beginning with *a, e, i, o, u* or *silent h.*

la **jacinthe** *fem noun*
**hyacinth**

la **jalousie** *fem noun*
**jealousy**

**jaloux** *masc adjective*, **jalouse** *fem*
**jealous**
**Elle est jalouse de mes résultats d'examen.** She's jealous of my exam results.

**jamaïquain** *masc adjective*, **jamaïquaine** *fem* ▷ **see jamaïquain** *noun*
**Jamaican**

un **Jamaïquain** *masc noun*, une **Jamaïquaine** *fem* ▷ **see jamaïquain** *adj*
**Jamaican** (*person*)

la **Jamaïque** *fem noun*
**Jamaica**

𝄞 **jamais** *adverb*
1 **never**
**Elle ne fume jamais.** She never smokes.
**On ne sait jamais.** You never know.
**Jamais plus!** Never again! ▷ **ne**.
2 **ever**
**plus grand que jamais** bigger than ever
**si jamais il pleut** if by any chance it rains
**Si jamais tu viens à Londres, passe me voir.** If you're ever in London, come and see me.
**à jamais** forever

𝄞 la **jambe** *fem noun*
**leg**
**Sandrine s'est cassé la jambe à la patinoire.** Sandrine broke her leg at the ice rink.

𝄞 le **jambon** *masc noun*
**ham**
**un jambon beurre** a ham sandwich (*with buttered bread*)
- le **jambon blanc** cooked ham
- le **jambon de pays** cured raw ham

𝄞 **janvier** *masc noun*
**January**
**en janvier, au mois de janvier** in January
**un mois de janvier pluvieux** a rainy January

**WORD TIP** Months of the year and days of the week start with small letters in French.

le **Japon** *masc noun*
**Japan**

**japonais** *masc adjective*, **japonaise** *fem* ▷ **see Japonais** *noun*
**Japanese**

un **Japonais** *masc noun*, une **Japonaise** *fem* ▷ **see japonais** *adj*
1 **Japanese** (*person*)
**les Japonais** the Japanese
2 **le japonais** Japanese (*language*)

𝄞 le **jardin** *masc noun*
**garden**
**Patrick est dans le jardin.** Patrick's in the garden.
**une chaise de jardin** a garden chair
- le **jardin anglais** landscape garden
- le **jardin d'enfants** kindergarten
- le **jardin à la française** formal garden
- le **jardin potager** vegetable garden
- le **jardin public** park

le **jardinage** *masc noun*
**gardening**
**Mon grand-père fait le jardinage.** My grandpa does the gardening.

le **jardinier** *masc noun*, la **jardinière** *fem*
**gardener**

la **jardinière** *fem noun*
**(large) plant pot**
- la **jardinière de légumes** mixed vegetables

le **jaune** *masc noun* ▷ **see jaune** *adj*
**yellow**
- le **jaune d'œuf** egg-yolk

𝄞 **jaune** *masc & fem adjective* ▷ **see jaune** *noun*
**yellow**
**une robe jaune** a yellow dress

la **jaunisse** *fem noun*
**jaundice**

**Javel** *noun*
**l'eau de Javel** bleach

le **jazz** *masc noun*
**jazz**
**J'aime le jazz.** I like jazz.

**je, j'** *pronoun*
**I**
**Je me lève à huit heures.** I get up at eight.
**J'habite à Lyon.** I live in Lyons.

**WORD TIP** *je* becomes *j'* before *a, e, i, o, u* or *silent h.*

le **jean** *masc noun*
1 **(pair of) jeans**
**J'ai acheté un jean.** I've bought a pair of jeans.
2 **denim**
**une jupe en jean** a denim skirt

le **jet** *masc noun*
**jet** *(of water, steam)*
**les jets d'eau de Versailles** the fountains at Versailles

**jetable** *masc & fem adjective*
**disposable**
**Je me sers d'un appareil photo jetable.** I use a disposable camera.

la **jetée** *fem noun*
**jetty**

♪ **jeter** *verb* **[48]**
1 **to throw**
**Ne jette pas de cailloux!** Do not throw stones!
2 **to throw away**
**J'ai jeté ces vieilles chaussures.** I've thrown away those old shoes.
3 **jeter un coup d'œil** to have a look
**Est-ce que tu peux jeter un coup d'œil à ce blog?** Can you have a look at this blog?

le **jeton** *masc noun*
1 **counter** *(for a board game)*
2 **token** *(for a machine)*

le **jeu** *masc noun*, les **jeux** *plural*
1 **le jeu** play
**Les enfants apprennent par le jeu.** Children learn through play.
2 **un jeu** a game
**On va faire un jeu!** Let's play a game!
**gagner par trois jeux à deux** to win by three games to two
**les Jeux Olympiques** the Olympic Games
3 **game show** *(on TV)*
4 **gambling**
5 **acting**
• le **jeu-concours** competition

♪ le **jeudi** *masc noun*
1 **Thursday**
**Nous sommes jeudi aujourd'hui.** It's Thursday today.
**jeudi prochain** next Thursday
**jeudi dernier** last Thursday
2 **on Thursday**
**Je l'ai vu jeudi soir.** I saw him on Thursday evening.
3 **le jeudi** on Thursdays
**'Fermé le jeudi'** 'Closed on Thursdays'
4 **tous les jeudis** every Thursday

**WORD TIP** Months of the year and days of the week start with small letters in French.

le **jeu de cartes** *masc noun*
1 **pack of cards**
2 **game of cards**

le **jeu électronique** *masc noun*
**computer game**

♪ le & la **jeune** *masc & fem noun*
▷ see **jeune** *adj*
**young person**
**une émission destinée aux jeunes** a programme aimed at young people

♪ **jeune** *masc & fem adjective* ▷ see **jeune** *noun*
1 **young**
**un jeune homme** a young man
**une jeune femme** a young woman
**une jeune fille** a girl
2 **younger**
**ma jeune sœur** my younger sister
3 **new**
**un jeune diplômé** a new graduate
**une jeune avocate** a newly-qualified lawyer
**les jeunes mariés** the newly-weds

la **jeunesse** *fem noun*
1 **young people**
**la jeunesse d'aujourd'hui** young people today
2 **youth**
**dans ma jeunesse** in my youth

le **jeu vidéo** *masc noun*
**video game**

un **job** *masc noun*
**job**
**J'ai un job (d'été).** I have a summer job.

le **jogging** *masc noun*
1 **faire du jogging** to go jogging
**Il fait du jogging pour se maintenir en forme.** He goes jogging to keep fit.
2 **un jogging** a track-suit

la **joie** *fem noun*
**joy**

**joindre** *verb* **[49]**
1 **to get hold of**
**Je n'ai pas pu la joindre.** I wasn't able to get hold of her.
2 **to enclose** *(in a letter, a parcel)*
3 **to put together**
**les pieds joints** feet together

se **joindre** *reflexive verb* ⓔ
**se joindre à quelqu'un** to join somebody
**Tout le monde se joint à moi pour te souhaiter un bon anniversaire.** Everybody joins me in wishing you happy birthday.

**joli** *masc adjective*, **jolie** *fem*
**pretty**

**jongler** *verb* [1]
**to juggle**

le **jongleur** *masc noun*, la **jongleuse** *fem*
**juggler**

la **jonquille** *fem noun*
**daffodil**

la **joue** *fem noun*
**cheek**

**jouer** *verb* [1]
1 **to play**
**Elle joue avec le chien.** She's playing with the dog.
**À toi de jouer!** Your go!
**Bien joué!** Well done!
2 **jouer à quelque chose** to play something (*a sport, a game*)
**On va jouer au foot.** We're going to play football.
3 **jouer de quelque chose** to play something (*an instrument*)
**Sophie joue du cor d'harmonie.** Sophie plays the French horn.
**Il joue du Chopin.** He's playing some Chopin.
4 (*in a film, play*) **Elle joue mal.** She can't act.
**Il joue bien dans ce film.** He's really good in this film.
**Il joue le rôle d'Octave.** He plays the part of Octave.
**Maxime joue dans 'Othello.'** Maxime is performing in 'Othello.'
**On joue 'Le Parrain' au cinéma du coin.** The local cinema is showing 'The Godfather.'
**Au Théâtre de la Ville on joue 'Le Tartuffe.'** The Théâtre de la Ville is putting on 'Tartuffe.'
5 **to gamble**
**Il joue au casino.** He gambles at the casino.
**Mon oncle joue aux courses.** My uncle bets on horses at the races.

le **jouet** *masc noun*
**toy**

le **joueur** *masc noun*, la **joueuse** *fem*
▷ see **joueur** *adj*
**player**

**joueur** *masc adjective*, **joueuse** *fem*
▷ see **joueur** *noun*
**playful**
**Les chiots sont joueurs.** Puppies are playful.

le **jour** *masc noun*
1 **day**
**les jours de la semaine** the days of the week
**trois jours plus tard** three days later
**tous les jours** every day
**le jour où** the day when
**un de ces jours** one of these days
**dans huit jours** in a week
**dans quinze jours** in two weeks
**au jour le jour** one day at a time
**Quel jour on est?** What day is it today?
2 **être à jour** to be up to date
**Le calendrier n'est pas à jour.** The schedule is not up to date.
**mettre quelque chose à jour** to bring something up to date
**Elle doit mettre à jour son journal intime.** She must bring her diary up to date.
3 **de nos jours** nowadays
**De nos jours, ils sont assez fréquents.** Nowadays they are quite common.
4 **daylight**
**Il fait jour.** It's daylight.
**en plein jour** in broad daylight
**jour et nuit** night and day
- le **jour de l'an** New Year's Day
- le **jour férié** public holiday
- le **jour ouvrable** working day

le **journal** *masc noun*, les **journaux** *plural*
1 **newspaper**
**Mon père lit le journal tous les jours.** My father reads the newspaper every day.
**Le matin, je distribue les journaux.** In the mornings I do a paper round.
**le journal du soir** the evening paper
2 **news**
**le journal de vingt heures** the eight o'clock news (*on TV, radio*)
- le **journal intime** diary
- le **journal télévisé** news (*on television*)

le **journalisme** *masc noun*
**journalism**

le & la **journaliste** *masc & fem noun*
**journalist**

la **journée** *fem noun*
**day**
**toute la journée** all day, the whole day
**Il est payé à la journée.** He's paid by the day.

**joyeux** *masc adjective*, **joyeuse** *fem*
**happy**
**Joyeux Anniversaire** Happy Birthday
**Joyeux Noël** Merry Christmas

le **judaïsme** *masc noun*
**Judaism**

**WORD TIP** Adjectives and nouns of religion start with a small letter in French.

**judicieux** *masc adjective*, **judicieuse** *fem*
**sensible**
un choix judicieux a wise choice

le **judo** *masc noun*
**judo**

le **juge** *masc noun*
**judge**
- le **juge d'instruction** examining magistrate
- le **juge de ligne** line judge (*in tennis*)
- le **juge de touche** linesman (*in football, rugby*)

le **jugement** *masc noun*
**judgement**

**juger** *verb* **[52]**
**1 to judge**
**Il ne faut pas juger sur les apparences.** You mustn't judge by appearances.
**2 to consider**
**Ils ont jugé l'exercice trop difficile.** They considered the exercise too difficult.
**Elle a jugé bon de partir tôt.** She considered it a good idea to leave early.

le **juif** *masc noun*, la **juive** *fem* ▷ see **juif** *adj*
**Jew**

**WORD TIP** Adjectives and nouns of religion start with a small letter in French.

**juif** *masc adjective*, **juive** *fem* ▷ see **juif** *noun*
**Jewish**

♪ **juillet** *masc noun*
**July**
**en juillet, au mois de juillet** in July
**le quatorze juillet** Bastille Day

**WORD TIP** Months of the year and days of the week start with small letters in French.

**mini-info juillet**

Le 14 Juillet est la fête nationale en France. C'est l'anniversaire de la Révolution française en 1789. Il y a des défilés militaires, des bals et des feux d'artifice.

♪ **juin** *masc noun*
**June**
**en juin, au mois de juin** in June
**J'aime le mois de juin.** I like June.

**WORD TIP** Months of the year and days of the week start with small letters in French.

♪ le **jumeau** *masc noun*, la **jumelle** *fem*, les **jumeaux** *plural*
**twin**
**des vrais jumeaux** identical twins

♪ **jumeler** *verb* **[18]**
**to twin** (*towns*)
**Oxford est jumelé avec Grenoble.** Oxford is twinned with Grenoble.

♪ la **jumelle** *fem noun* ▷ jumeau

les **jumelles** *plural fem noun*
**binoculars**

la **jument** *fem noun*
**mare**

la **jungle** *fem noun*
**jungle**

♪ la **jupe** *fem noun*
**skirt**

le **jupon** *masc noun*
**petticoat**

**jurer** *verb* **[1]**
**to swear**

**juridique** *masc & fem adjective*
**legal**
**le système juridique** the legal system

le **jury** *masc noun*
**1 jury**
**2 board of examiners**

♪ le **jus** *masc noun*
**1 juice**
**un jus d'orange** an orange juice
**2 juices**
**le jus de viande** the meat juices
- le **jus de fruit** fruit juice

♪ **jusque** *preposition*
**1 as far as** (*a place*)
**Ce train va jusqu'à Paris.** This train goes as far as Paris.
**Nous avons marché jusqu'au lac.** We walked as far as the lake.
**Il m'a accompagné jusque chez moi.** He took me all the way home.
**Jusqu'où va le train?** How far does the train go?
**2 until**
**Elle reste jusqu'en avril.** She's staying until April.
**Jusqu'à quand reste-t-il?** How long is he staying for?
**jusqu'à présent, jusqu'ici** until now
**3 jusqu'à ce que** until
**On peut aller jouer jusqu'à ce qu'on nous appelle pour le dîner.** We can go and play until we are called for dinner.

**juste** *masc & fem adjective* ▷ see **juste** *adv*
**1 fair**
**Ce n'est pas juste!** It's not fair!
**2 right**
**le mot juste** the right word ▸▸

Ce que tu dis est juste. What you say is right.
J'ai tout juste. I've got everything right.

3 **correct**
Mon calcul est juste. My sum is correct.
As-tu l'heure juste? Have you got the correct time?

4 **in tune**
Ton piano est juste. Your piano's in tune.

5 **tight**
Mon T-shirt est trop juste. My T-shirt's too tight.
Une heure pour visiter le château, c'est un peu juste. An hour to visit the château is a bit tight.

6 **valid**
Ta remarque est juste. Your comment is valid.
Il dit des choses justes. He's making some valid points.

**juste** *adverb* ▷ see **juste** *adj*

1 **just**
juste à temps just in time
Il vient tout juste d'arriver. He's only just arrived.
La poste est juste après la boulangerie. The post office is just after the bakery.
C'est juste ce qui me faut. That's just what I need.

2 **in tune**
Elle chante juste. She sings in tune.

**justement** *adverb*

1 **precisely**
C'est justement ce qu'il faut faire. That's precisely what you should do.

2 **just**
Je parlais justement de toi. I was just talking about you.

3 **correctly**
Comme elle a dit très justement... As she so rightly said...

la **justesse** *fem noun*

1 **correctness**
avec justesse correctly

2 **de justesse** only just
Il a eu son avion, mais de justesse. He caught his plane but only just.
J'ai eu mon examen de justesse. I passed my exam but only just.

la **justice** *fem noun*
**justice**

**justifier** *verb* [1]
**to justify**

**juteux** *masc adjective*, **juteuse** *fem*
**juicy**

**juvénile** *masc & fem adjective*
**youthful**

# Kk

**kaki** *invariable adjective*
**khaki**
une casquette kaki a khaki cap

le **kangourou** *masc noun*
**kangaroo**

le **karaté** *masc noun*
**karate**

le **karting** *masc noun*
**go-karting**
On va faire du karting. We're going go-karting.

**kascher** *invariable adjective*
**kosher**

la **kermesse** *fem noun*
**fête**
La kermesse de l'école a lieu le 22 juin. The school fête will take place on 22 June.

le **ketchup** *masc noun*
**ketchup**

**kidnapper** *verb* [1]
**to kidnap**

le **kidnappeur** *masc noun*, la **kidnappeuse** *fem*
**kidnapper**

le **kilo** *masc noun*
**kilo**
deux kilos de pommes two kilos of apples
J'ai pris trois kilos. I've put on three kilos.
C'est trois euros le kilo. It's three euros a kilo.

le **kilogramme** *masc noun*
**kilogram**

le **kilométrage** *masc noun*
**mileage**

le **kilomètre** *masc noun*
**kilometre**
**à dix kilomètres d'ici** ten kilometres from here
**Paris est à combien de kilomètres de Dijon?** How many kilometres is it from Paris to Dijon?
**Elle a combien de kilomètres votre voiture?** What's the mileage on your car?

le & la **kinésithérapeute** *masc & fem noun*
**physiotherapist**

la **kinésithérapie** *fem noun*
**physiotherapy**

♪ le **kiosque** *masc noun*
**kiosk**

le **kiwi** *masc noun*
**kiwi** (*the bird and the fruit*)

le **klaxon**® *masc noun*
**horn** (*on a car*)

**klaxonner** *verb* [1]
**to beep the horn** (*in a car*)

le **kleenex**® *masc noun*
**tissue**

**km** *abbreviation* ▷ short for **kilomètre**
**km/h**, **kph** (*kilometres per hour*)

**KO** *invariable adjective*
1 **mettre quelqu'un KO** to knock somebody out
**Youssef a mis Arnaud KO.** Youssef knocked Arnaud out.
2 **Je suis KO.** I'm whacked. (*informal*)

le **koala** *masc noun*
**koala bear**

le **kraft** *masc noun*
**le papier kraft** brown paper

le **K-way**® *masc noun*
**windcheater**

# Ll

**l'** *abbreviation: le or la*
▷ **le, la** *determiner, pronoun*

**WORD TIP** *le* or *la* becomes *l'* before a word beginning with *a, e, i, o, u* or *silent h.*

♪ **la, l'** *fem determiner* ▷ **see la** *pron*
1 (*with singular fem nouns*) **the**
**la voiture** the car
**l'école** the school
**l'habitude** the habit
2 (*with parts of the body* **la** *is translated by* **my, your, his, her,** *etc*) **Je lui ai serré la main.** I shook his hand.
**Le chien s'est cassé la patte.** The dog broke its leg.
3 (**la** *is often not translated*) **la lutte pour la justice** the fight for justice.
**J'adore la glace.** I love ice cream.
**C'est la maison d'Annie.** That's Annie's house.

**WORD TIP** *la* becomes *l'* before *a, e, i, o, u* or *silent h.* ▷ **le, les.**

♪ **la, l'** *pronoun* ▷ **see la** *determiner*
1 (*as direct object for a female*) **her**
**Je la connais bien.** I know her well.
**Je l'ai aidé.** I helped her.
2 (*for a fem direct object*) **it**
**Attention à la tasse! Tu vas la casser.** Mind the cup! You'll break it!

**WORD TIP** *la* becomes *l'* before *a, e, i, o, u* or *silent h.* ▷ **le, les.**

♪ **là** *adverb*
1 **here**
**Danielle n'est pas là.** Danielle's not here.
2 **there**
**Est-ce que Paul est là?** Is Paul there?
3 **when**
**C'est là que j'ai pensé à toi.** That's when I thought of you.
4 **where**
**C'est là que nous habitons.** That's where we live.
5 **then**
**Et là, elle s'est mise à hurler.** And then, she started screaming.
6 (*for emphasis*) **cette maison-là** that house
**ces gens-là** those people
**à ce moment-là** at that moment
**dans ce cas-là** in that case

**WORD TIP** *-là* is attached to a noun for emphasis. Compare with *-ci*, meaning *this* or *these.*

♪ **là-bas** *adverb*
1 **there**
**Qu'est-ce que vous avez fait là-bas?** What did you do there? ▸▸

**2** **over there**
Notre maison est là-bas. Our house is over there.

le **labo** *masc noun*
(*informal*) **lab**

le **laboratoire** *masc noun*
**laboratory**
- le **laboratoire de langues** language laboratory

♪ le **lac** *masc noun*
**lake**
le lac Léman Lake Geneva

**lacer** *verb* **[61]**
lacer ses chaussures to do up your shoes

le **lacet** *masc noun*
**lace**
des chaussures à lacets lace-up shoes

**lâche** *masc & fem adjective*
**1** **cowardly**
Samuel est lâche. Samuel's a coward.
**2** **loose** (*belt, rope, knot*)

**lâcher** *verb* **[1]**
**1** **lâcher quelqu'un** to let go of somebody
Lâche-moi! Let go of me!
**2** **to drop**
Elle a lâché son sac. She dropped her bag.

la **lâcheté** *fem noun*
**cowardliness**

**là-dedans** *adverb*
**in there**, **in here**
Qu'est-ce qu'il y a là-dedans? What's in there?
Je mettrai l'argent là-dedans. I'll put the money in here.
Il n'y a rien là-dedans. There's nothing in there.

**là-dessous** *adverb*
**under here**, **under there**
Viens voir là-dessous! Come and look under here!
Les chaussures sont là-dessous. The shoes are under there.

**là-dessus** *adverb*
**1** **on here**, **on there**
Monte là-dessus! Climb on here!
Ne laisse pas tes livres là-dessus, c'est mouillé. Don't leave your books on there, it's wet.
**2** **about it**, **on it**
Ils sont d'accord là-dessus. They agree about it.
Est-ce qu'il a dit quelque chose là-dessus? Did he say anything about it?
J'ai un livre là-dessus. I've got a book about it.

**là-haut** *adverb*
**1** **up there**, **up here**
Il est là-haut dans l'arbre. He's up there in the tree.
Viens là-haut, il fait plus frais. Come up here, it's cooler.
**2** **upstairs**
Nathalie est là-haut. Nathalie's upstairs.

♪ **laid** *masc adjective*, **laide** *fem*
**ugly**

la **laideur** *fem noun*
**ugliness**

♪ la **laine** *fem noun*
**wool**
un pull en laine a woollen jumper
acheter de la laine to buy some wool
- la **laine vierge** pure new wool

**laïque** *masc & fem adjective*
**non-denominational**

la **laisse** *fem noun*
**lead**

♪ **laisser** *verb* **[1]**
**1** **to leave**
J'ai laissé mon portable chez toi. I've left my mobile at your house.
Tu peux laisser ta valise ici. You can leave your case here.
Bon, je vous laisse. Right, I must go.
**2** **laisser quelqu'un faire quelque chose** to let somebody do something
Laisse-le parler! Let him speak!
Laisse-moi t'aider. Let me help you.
**3** **to leave** (*till later*)
J'ai laissé mes devoirs pour demain. I've left my homework till tomorrow.

se **laisser** *reflexive verb* Ⓔ
**to put up with**
Il se laisse insulter. He puts up with being insulted.

le **laisser-aller** *invariable masc noun*
**carelessness**

♪ le **lait** *masc noun*
**milk**
un café au lait a white coffee
- le **lait demi-écrémé** semi-skimmed milk
- le **lait écrémé** skimmed milk
- le **lait entier** whole milk

**laitier** *masc adjective*, **laitière** *fem*
les produits laitiers dairy products

la **laitue** *fem noun*
**lettuce**

Ⓔ means the verb takes être to form the perfect

la **lame** *fem noun*
**blade**
- la **lame de rasoir** razor blade

**lamentable** *masc & fem adjective*
**awful**

le **lampadaire** *masc noun*
**1 standard lamp**
**2 street lamp**

♪ la **lampe** *fem noun*
**lamp**
- la **lampe de chevet** bedside lamp
- la **lampe de poche** torch

la **lance** *fem noun*
**spear**

le **lancement** *masc noun*
**launch** (*of a film, a product, a spacecraft*)

**lancer** *verb* **[61]**
**1 to throw**
**Arrêtez de lancer des cailloux!** Stop throwing stones!
**lancer quelque chose à quelqu'un** to throw something to somebody
**Il m'a lancé le ballon.** He threw the ball to me.
**2 to launch** (*a product, a spacecraft*)

le **landau** *masc noun*
**pram**

la **lande** *fem noun*
**moor**

**WORD TIP** *lande* does not mean *land* in English; for the meaning of *land* ▷ **terre, terrain**.

le **langage** *masc noun*
**language**
- le **langage de programmation** programming language

la **langouste** *fem noun*
**crayfish**

♪ la **langue** *fem noun*
**1 tongue**
**Il m'a tiré la langue.** He stuck his tongue out at me.
**2 language**
**les pays de langue française** French-speaking countries
- la **langue étrangère** foreign language
- les **langues vivantes** modern languages

la **lanière** *fem noun*
**strap**

♪ le **lapin** *masc noun*
**1 rabbit**
**2 sweetheart**
**Ça va mon petit lapin?** Are you all right, sweetheart?

la **laque** *fem noun*
**hairspray**

**laquelle** *pronoun* ▷ **lequel**

le **lard** *masc noun*
**streaky bacon**

les **lardons** *plural masc noun*
**diced bacon**

♪ **large** *masc & fem adjective* ▷ **see large** *noun*
**wide**
**un large couloir** a wide corridor
**Le fleuve est large de cinquante mètres.** The river is fifty metres wide.
**avoir les idées larges** to be broadminded

**WORD TIP** *large* does not mean *large* in English; for the meaning of *large* ▷ **grand**.

le **large** *masc noun* ▷ **see large** *adj*
**1 faire un mètre de large** to be a metre wide
**Ça fait dix mètres de large.** It's ten metres wide.
**2 open sea**

**largement** *adverb*
**C'est largement suffisant.** That's more than enough.
**J'ai largement le temps.** I've got plenty of time.

la **largeur** *fem noun*
**width**
**Le ruban fait deux centimètres de largeur.** The ribbon is two centimetres wide.

la **larme** *fem noun*
**tear**
**en larmes** in tears
**Elle avait les larmes aux yeux.** She had tears in her eyes.
**fondre en larmes** to burst into tears

la **laryngite** *fem noun*
**laryngitis**

les **lasagnes** *plural fem noun*
**lasagna**

le **laser** *masc noun*
**laser**
**un spectacle laser** a laser show

se **lasser** *reflexive verb* Ⓔ **[1]**
**se lasser de quelque chose** to get tired of something
**Je me lasse de cette musique.** I'm getting tired of this musique.

la **lassitude** *fem noun*
**tiredness**

le **lauréat** *masc noun*, la **lauréate** *fem*
**winner**
**un lauréat du prix Nobel** a Nobel Prize winner

French–English

le **laurier** *masc noun*
**laurel**

**lavable** *masc & fem adjective*
**washable**
lavable en machine machine-washable

♪ le **lavabo** *masc noun*
**washbasin**

le **lavage** *masc noun*
1 **washing** (*of floor, clothes*)
2 **wash programme** (*on a washing-machine*)

la **lavande** *fem noun*
**lavender**

le **lave-linge** *invariable masc noun*
**washing machine**

♪ **laver** *verb* [1]
**to wash, to clean**
**Il lave la voiture.** He's washing the car.
**J'ai lavé le carrelage.** I cleaned the floor.

se **laver** *reflexive verb* ⓔ
**to wash**
**Je vais me laver.** I'm going to have a wash.
**Elle se lave la tête.** She's washing her hair.

la **laverie** *fem noun*
**launderette**

♪ le **lave-vaisselle** *invariable masc noun*
**dishwasher**

**WORD TIP** *lave-vaisselle* never changes in the plural.

♪ **le** *masc determiner*, **l'** ▷ **see le** *pron*
1 (*with singular masc nouns*) **the**
le chat the cat
l'homme the man
2 (*with parts of the body* **le** *is translated by* **my, your,** *his, her, etc*)
**Je me suis brûlé le doigt.** I burnt my finger.
3 (*le is often not translated*) **J'aime le chocolat.** I love chocolate.
**pendant le déjeuner** during lunch
**le vélo d'Isabelle** Isabelle's bicycle
4 **a, an**
**cinq euros le kilo** five euros a kilo

**WORD TIP** *le* becomes *l'* before *a, e, i, o, u* or *silent h.* ▷ **le, les.**

♪ **le, l'** *pronoun* ▷ **see le** *determiner*
1 (*as direct object for a male*) **him**
**Je le connais.** I know him.
**Je l'ai vu hier soir.** I saw him last night.
2 (*for a masc direct object*) **it**
**Tu vois le couteau? Donne-le-moi.** Do you see that knife? Give it to me.
**Mon vélo? Il l'a déjà emprunté.** My bike? He's already borrowed it.
3 (*le is often not translated*)
**Je le sais.** I know.
**Il me l'a dit.** He told me.

**WORD TIP** *le* becomes *l'* before *a, e, i, o, u* or *silent h.* ▷ **la, les.**

**lécher** *verb* [24]
**to lick**
**se lécher les doigts** to lick your fingers

le **lèche-vitrines** *invariable masc noun*
**faire du lèche-vitrines** to go window-shopping

la **leçon** *fem noun*
**lesson**

le **lecteur** *masc noun*, la **lectrice** *fem*
1 **reader**
2 **foreign language assistant** (*at a school, university*)
- le **lecteur de cassettes** cassette player
- le **lecteur DVD** DVD player
- le **lecteur de disquettes** floppy disk drive
- le **lecteur laser** CD player

♪ la **lecture** *fem noun*
**reading**
**J'aime la lecture.** I like reading.

**WORD TIP** *lecture* does not mean *lecture* in English; for the meaning of *lecture* ▷ **conférence**.

**légal** *masc adjective*, **légale** *fem*, **légaux** *masc pl*, **légales** *fem pl*
**legal**

la **légende** *fem noun*
1 **legend**
2 **caption** (*for a picture*)
3 **key** (*to a map*)

♪ **léger** *masc adjective*, **légère** *fem*
1 **light**
**une veste légère** a light jacket
2 **weak**
**un café léger** a weak coffee
3 **slight**
**un léger retard** a slight delay
**une légère différence** a slight difference

**légèrement** *adverb*
1 **lightly**
**légèrement parfumé** lightly perfumed
2 **slightly**
**Il est légèrement blessé.** He's slightly hurt.

la **légèreté** *fem noun*
**lightness**

les **législatives** *plural fem noun*
**general election**

♪ le **légume** *masc noun*
**vegetable**
- les **légumes secs** pulses (*beans, peas, lentils*)
- les **légumes verts** green vegetables

a b c d e f g h i j k **l** m n o p q r s t u v w x y z



ⓔ means the verb takes être to form the perfect

*le* **lendemain** *masc noun*
**le lendemain** the next day
**le lendemain matin** the next morning
**Marc est arrivé le lendemain.** Marc arrived the next day.
**C'était le lendemain de l'accident.** It was the day after the accident.

*lent* *masc adjective*, **lente** *fem*
**slow**
**Ce film est trop lent.** This film is too slow.

**lentement** *adverb*
**slowly**

la **lenteur** *fem noun*
**slowness**

la **lentille** *fem noun*
1 **lens**
**Elle porte des lentilles.** She wears contact lenses.
2 **lentil**
**la soupe aux lentilles** lentil soup
- les **lentilles de contact** contact lenses

le **léopard** *masc noun*
**leopard**

**lequel** *masc pronoun*, **laquelle** *fem*, **lesquels** *masc pl*, **lesquelles** *fem pl*
1 (*in questions*) **which one**
**'J'adore cette veste!' — 'Laquelle?'** 'I just love that jacket!' — 'Which one?'
**'Passe-moi les verres.' — 'Lesquels?'** 'Pass me the glasses.' — 'Which ones?'
**Lequel des deux chevaux préfères-tu?** Which of the two horses do you prefer?
2 (*after prepositions like* ***avec, dans***) **which, whom**
**l'immeuble dans lequel ils habitaient** the block of flats which they were living in
**les gens chez lesquels je passe mes vacances** the people with whom I spend my holidays
**la dame avec laquelle je discutais** the lady I was talking to

**les** *determiner* ▷ see **les** *pron*
1 (*with plural nouns*) **the**
**les enfants** the children
2 (*with parts of the body* ***les*** *is translated by* ***my, your, his, her,*** *etc*)
**Elle se lave les cheveux.** She's washing her hair.
3 (***les*** *is often not translated*) **les cousins d'Amélie** Amélie's cousins
**J'aime bien les nouilles.** I like noodles.
**Les Français roulent à droite.** The French drive on the right .
▷ **la** and **le**.

**les** *pronoun* ▷ see **les** *determiner*
1 (*as direct object for people*) **them**
**Je les connais bien.** I know them well.
**Aide-les!** Help them!
**Mes parents les ont aidés.** My parents helped them.
2 (*for a plural direct object*) **them**
**Les billets - où est-ce que tu les as mis?** The tickets - where did you put them?
**Donne-les-moi.** Give them to me.
▷ **le** and **la**.

**lesquels**, **lesquelles** *pronoun* ▷ **lequel**

la **lessive** *fem noun*
1 **washing**
**mettre la lessive à sécher** to put the washing out to dry
2 **washing powder**, **washing liquid**
**Je n'ai plus de lessive.** I've run out of washing powder.

*la* **lettre** *fem noun*
1 **letter** (*postal*)
**J'ai écrit une lettre à ma correspondante.** I wrote a letter to my penpal.
2 **letter** (*in the alphabet*)
**en lettres majuscules** in capital letters
3 **les lettres** arts (*at university*)
- la **lettre majuscule** capital letter
- la **lettre minuscule** small letter, lower-case letter
- la **lettre de motivation** covering letter

**leur** *masc & fem adjective*, **leurs** *pl* ▷ see **leur** *pron*
**their**
**C'est leur nouvelle maison.** It's their new house.
**Leurs voisins sont sympathiques.** Their neighbours are nice.

**WORD TIP** *leur*, adjective, takes *-s* with plural nouns.

**leur** *pronoun* ▷ see **leur** *adj*
1 (*as indirect object*) **(to) them**
**Elle leur a expliqué le problème.** She explained the problem to them.
**Nous leur envoyons de l'argent.** We send money to them.
**Donne-leur un coup de main.** Give them a hand.

**WORD TIP** *leur*, pronoun, never changes.

2 **le leur, la leur, les leurs** theirs
**C'est notre jardin, et ça, c'est le leur.** That's our garden and that's theirs.
**Ça, c'est votre maison, et ça, c'est la leur.** That's your house and that's theirs.
**Nous avons appelé nos parents et ils ont** ▸▸

appelé les leurs. We phoned our parents and they phoned theirs.

**WORD TIP** Choose *le leur, la leur, les leurs* according to whether the noun referred to is masc, fem, plural.

**lever** *verb* **[50]** ▷ see **lever** *noun*
**to raise**
lever les bras to raise your arms (*in gym*)
lever la main to put your hand up (*in class*)
lever les yeux to look up
Il a levé les yeux. He looked up.

se **lever** *reflexive verb* Ⓔ
1 **to get up**
Je me lève à sept heures. I get up at seven o'clock.
Nous nous sommes levés tôt. We got up early.
2 **to stand up**
Levez-vous! Stand up!
3 **to rise**
Le soleil va se lever. The sun is about to rise.

le **lever** *masc noun* ▷ see **lever** *verb*
au lever du soleil at sunrise

le **levier** *masc noun*
**lever**

la **lèvre** *fem noun*
**lip**

le **lévrier** *masc noun*
**greyhound**

le **lexique** *masc noun*
**word list**

le **lézard** *masc noun*
**lizard**

la **liaison** *fem noun*
1 **love affair**
2 **link**
une liaison aérienne an air link
3 **contact**
une liaison radio a radio contact
4 **connection** (*on telephone*)
La liaison est mauvaise. It's a bad line.
• la **liaison satellite** satellite link

la **libellule** *fem noun*
**dragonfly**

la **libération** *fem noun*
1 **release**
la libération des otages the release of the hostages
2 **liberation**
la libération de la ville the liberation of the city
• la **Libération** the Liberation (*the end of the German occupation in 1944*)
• la **libération des femmes** women's liberation

**libérer** *verb* **[24]**
1 **to set free** (*a prisoner, a hostage*)
2 **to vacate** (*a hotel room, a flat*)

se **libérer** *reflexive verb* Ⓔ
**to free yourself**
Le renard s'est libéré du piège. The fox freed itself from the trap.
Je ne peux pas me libérer ce week-end. I can't get away this weekend.

la **liberté** *fem noun*
**freedom, liberty**
la Statue de la liberté the Statue of Liberty
être en liberté to be free

le & la **libraire** *masc & fem noun*
**bookseller**

la **librairie** *fem noun*
**bookshop**

**WORD TIP** *librairie* does not mean *library* in English; for the meaning of *library* ▷ **bibliothèque**.

• la **librairie-papeterie** bookseller's and stationer's shop

**libre** *masc & fem adjective*
1 **free**
Est-ce que cette place est libre? Is this seat free?
Il n'y a plus de places libres. There are no free seats left.
Je suis libre le week-end prochain. I'm free next weekend.
2 **available**
Avez-vous une chambre libre? Do you have a room available?

**librement** *adverb*
**freely**

le **libre-service** *masc noun*
**self-service** (*shop, restaurant*)

la **licence** *fem noun*
**degree**
une licence de chimie a chemistry degree

**WORD TIP** *licence* does not mean *licence* in English; for the meaning of *licence* ▷ **permis**.

**licencier** *verb* **[1]**
licencier quelqu'un to make somebody redundant
Ils licencient du personnel. They are making staff redundant.

le **lien** *masc noun*
1 **link**
établir des liens avec des villes françaises to create links with French towns
2 **link**
suivre les liens follow the links

a b c d e f g h i j k l m n o p q r s t u v w x y z



Ⓔ means the verb takes être to form the perfect

le **lierre** *masc noun*
**ivy**

♪ le **lieu** *masc noun*, les **lieux** *plural*
1 **place**
**un lieu public** a public place
**le lieu de travail** the workplace
2 **en premier lieu** in the first place
**En premier lieu, je n'ai pas d'argent et en plus ...** In the first place, I've got no money and what's more ...
3 **avoir lieu** to take place
**Le festival aura lieu en juin.** The festival will take place in June.
4 **au lieu de faire quelque chose** instead of doing something
**Au lieu de prendre le bus, il est parti à pied.** Instead of taking the bus, he went off on foot.
5 **les lieux** the premises

le **lieutenant** *masc noun*
**lieutenant**

le **lièvre** *masc noun*
**hare**

le **lifting** *masc noun*
**face-lift**

♪ la **ligne** *fem noun*
1 **line**
**une ligne droite** a straight line
2 **line**
**la ligne Paris-Dijon** the Paris-Dijon line
3 **cable**
**une ligne électrique** an electric cable
4 **(telephone) line**
**Restez en ligne, s'il vous plaît!** Hold the line please!
5 **figure**
**pour garder la ligne** to keep your figure, to stay slim
6 **fishing line**
7 (*Computers*) **en ligne** online
**Je l'ai commandé en ligne.** I ordered it online.
- la **ligne d'arrivée** finishing line

le **lilas** *invariable masc noun*
**lilac**

la **limace** *fem noun*
**slug**

la **lime** *fem noun*
**file** (*for metal, wood*)

**WORD TIP** *lime* does not mean *lime* in English; for the meaning of *lime* ▷ **citron vert**.

- la **lime à ongles** nail file

la **limite** *fem noun*
1 **border** (*between countries*)
2 **boundary** (*of a village, town*)
3 **limit**
**Sa patience a des limites.** There are limits to his, her patience.
4 **sans limites** endless
**Ils ont une énergie sans limites.** They have endless energy.
5 **dans la limite de quelque chose** within the limits of something
**dans la limite du possible** as far as possible
6 **maximum**
**la vitesse limite** the maximum speed
- la **limite d'âge** age limit

**limiter** *verb* [1]
**to limit**
**limiter une recherche** to limit a computer search

se **limiter** *reflexive verb* ❷
**to limit yourself**

♪ la **limonade** *fem noun*
**lemonade**

le **lin** *masc noun*
**linen**

♪ le **linge** *masc noun*
1 **linen**
**du linge sale** dirty linen
**le linge de maison** household linen
2 **washing**
**J'ai du linge à laver.** I've got some washing to do.
3 **underwear**
**changer de linge** to change your underwear
- le **linge de corps** underwear

la **lingerie** *fem noun*
**lingerie**

le **lion** *masc noun* ▷ **see Lion** *noun*
**lion**

le **Lion** *masc noun* ▷ **see lion** *noun*
**Leo**
**Nicolas est Lion.** Nicolas is a Leo.
**Les Lions sont généreux.** Leos are generous.

**WORD TIP** Signs of the zodiac do not take an article: *un* or *une*.

la **lionne** *fem noun*
**lioness**

la **liqueur** *fem noun*
**liqueur**

la **liquidation** *fem noun*
**clearance sale** (*in a shop*)
**'Liquidation totale'** 'Everything must go'

**liquide** *masc & fem adjective*
▷ **see liquide** *noun*
**liquid**

French-English
a b c d e f g h i j k l m n o p q r s t u v w x y z

le **liquide** *masc noun* ▷ **see liquide** *adj*
1 **liquid**
2 **cash**
**payer en liquide** to pay cash

**lire** *verb* **[51]**
**to read**
**Lis le texte.** Read the text.
**Elle sait lire en français.** She can read French.
**Elle nous lisait des histoires.** She used to read us stories.

**lis** *verb* ▷ **lire**

**lisible** *masc & fem adjective*
**legible**

**lisse** *masc & fem adjective*
**smooth**

la **liste** *fem noun*
**list**
**la liste des courses** the shopping list
**faire une liste** to make a list
**faire la liste de quelque chose** to make a list of something
**J'ai fait la liste des invités.** I've made a guest list.
- la **liste d'attente** waiting list

le **lit** *masc noun* ▷ **see lit** *verb*
**bed**
**une chambre à deux lits** a twin room
**Je vais au lit à 20 heures.** I go to bed at 10 p.m.
**Tu n'as pas encore fait ton lit.** You haven't made your bed yet.
- le **lit à une place** single bed
- le **lit à deux places** double bed

**lit** *verb* ▷ **see lit** *noun* ▷ **lire**

la **literie** *fem noun*
**bedding**

la **litière** *fem noun*
**litter**
- la **litière pour chat** cat litter

le **litre** *masc noun*
**litre**
**un litre de jus d'orange** a litre of orange juice

**littéralement** *adverb*
**literally**

la **littérature** *fem noun*
**literature**

la **livraison** *fem noun*
**delivery**
**Ils font des livraisons à domicile.** They do home deliveries.

le **livre** *masc noun* ▷ **see livre** *fem noun*
**book**
**un livre pour enfants** a children's book
- le **livre de cuisine** cookery book
- le **livre de poche** paperback
- le **livre scolaire** school book

la **livre** *fem noun* ▷ **see livre** *masc noun*
1 **pound**
**la livre sterling** the pound sterling
**Ça coûte une livre.** It costs a pound.
**Il a gagné mille livres.** He won a thousand pounds.
2 **half a kilo** (*half a kilo or 500 grammes*)
**une livre de cerises** half a kilo of cherries

**livrer** *verb* **[1]**
1 **to deliver**
**livrer quelque chose à quelqu'un** to deliver something to somebody
**Le facteur nous a livré un colis.** The postman delivered a parcel to us.
2 **to hand over**
**Il a été livré à la police.** He was handed over to the police.

se **livrer** *reflexive verb* ⓔ
**to surrender**

le **livret** *masc noun*
**booklet**
- le **livret de famille** family record book (*with dates of births, marriages and deaths*)
- le **livret scolaire** school report book

**local** *masc adjective*, **locale** *fem*, **locaux** *masc pl*, **locales** *fem pl* ▷ **see local** *noun*
**local**
**un journal local** a local newspaper
**à minuit heure locale** at midnight, local time

le **local** *masc noun*, les **locaux** *plural* ▷ **see local** *adj*
**place** (*usually a building*)
**des locaux commerciaux** business premises
**dans les locaux du lycée** on school premises

**localement** *adverb*
**locally**

le & la **locataire** *masc & fem noun*
1 **tenant**
2 **lodger**

la **location** *fem noun*
1 **renting**
**un appartement de location** a rented flat
**être en location** to live in rented accommodation



ⓔ means the verb takes être to form the perfect

2 **hire**, **rental**
la location de DVD DVD rental
**C'est une voiture de location.** It's a hire car.
3 **reservation** (*of theatre seats*)

**WORD TIP** *location* does not mean *location* in English; for the meaning of *location* ▷ **endroit**.

la **locomotive** *fem noun*
**engine**, **locomotive**

la **loge** *fem noun*
1 **(caretaker's) lodge** (*in a block of flats*)
2 **dressing-room** (*for actors*)
3 **box** (*for theatregoers*)

le **logement** *masc noun*
1 **accommodation**
**chercher un logement** to look for accommodation
2 **flat**
**un logement au deuxième étage** a flat on the second floor
3 **housing**
**la crise du logement** the housing crisis

♪ **loger** *verb* **[52]**
**to stay**
**Nous logeons à l'auberge de jeunesse.** We're staying at the youth hostel.
**loger chez quelqu'un** to stay at somebody's house
**Pour l'instant, elle loge chez nous.** For the moment, she's staying at our house.

le **logiciel** *masc noun*
1 **software**
2 **(computer) program**
• le **logiciel antivirus** antivirus software
• le **logiciel de jeux** games program

**logique** *masc & fem adjective*
**logical**

la **loi** *fem noun*
**law**
**enfreindre la loi** to break the law

♪ **loin** *adverb*
1 **far**
**C'est un peu loin.** It's a bit far.
**Ce n'est pas loin d'ici.** It's not far from here.
**10 kilomètres, c'est loin!** 10 kilometres is a long way!
**Elle habite trop loin de chez moi.** She lives too far away from me.
**Le cinéma est plus loin.** The cinema is further on.
2 **far off** (*in time*)
**Mon anniversaire n'est pas très loin.** My birthday isn't far off.
**Les vacances sont encore loin.** The holidays are still a long way off.
**Il n'est pas loin de midi.** It's almost midday.
3 **de loin** by far
**C'est de loin le plus cher.** It's by far the most expensive.
4 **au loin** in the distance
**On voit la mer tout au loin.** You can see the sea far away in the distance.
5 **de loin** from a long way off

**lointain** *masc adjective*, **lointaine** *fem*
**distant**

♪ les **loisirs** *plural masc noun*
1 **spare time**
**Pendant mes loisirs je vais en ville avec mes copines.** In my spare time I go to town with my (girl) friends.
2 **leisure activities**
**Le club propose de nombreux loisirs.** The club offers lots of leisure activities.

le **Londonien** *masc noun*, la **Londonienne** *fem*
**Londoner**

**Londres** *noun*
**London**

♪ **long** *masc adjective*, **longue** *fem*
▷ see **long** *noun*
**long**
**un long silence** a long silence
**une longue vie** a long life
**la rue la plus longue de Paris** the longest street in Paris
**une chemise à manches longues** a long-sleeved shirt
**être long d'un mètre** to be a metre long
**La pièce est longue de quatre mètres.** The room is four metres long.

♪ le **long** *masc noun* ▷ see **long** *adj*
1 **faire un mètre de long** to be a metre long
**Ça fait cinq mètres de long.** It's five metres long.
2 **le long de quelque chose** along something
**Il marche le long de la route.** He's walking along the road.
3 **tout le long de quelque chose** all the way through something
**tout le long du voyage** all the way through the journey
**Elle a dormi tout le long du film.** She slept all the way through the film.

♪ **longtemps** *adverb*
**(for) a long time**
**Ça va prendre longtemps.** It will take a long time.
**Elle travaille ici depuis longtemps.** She's been working here for a long time.
**Ils ne se sont pas vus depuis longtemps.** They haven't seen each other for ages. ▸▸

Ça fait longtemps qu'on ne s'est pas téléphoné! It's ages since we've phoned each other!
Il y a longtemps que j'y suis allé. I went there a long time ago.
Tu peux le garder plus longtemps. You can keep it for longer.
longtemps après a long time afterwards

**longuement** *adverb*
**for a long time**

la **longueur** *fem noun*
1 **length**
De quelle longueur est le bateau? How long is the boat?
faire des longueurs to swim lengths
le saut en longueur the long jump
2 traîner en longueur to go on forever
Le film traîne en longueur. The film goes on forever.
Il y a des longueurs dans le film. The film tends to drag.

**lorsque**, **lorsqu'** *conjunction*
**when**
Lorsque j'étais petite ... When I was a little girl...
Lorsqu'il est arrivé ... When he arrived...

**WORD TIP** *lorsque* becomes *lorsqu'* before *a, e, i, o, u* or *silent h.*

le **lot** *masc noun*
1 **batch**
un lot de trente cahiers a batch of thirty exercise books
un lot de trois boîtes a pack of three cans
2 **prize**
le gros lot the jackpot

**WORD TIP** *lot* does not mean *lot* in English; for the meaning of *a lot of* ▷ **beaucoup**.

la **loterie** *fem noun*
1 **lottery**
2 **raffle**

la **lotion** *fem noun*
**lotion**

le **lotissement** *masc noun*
**housing estate**

le **loto** *masc noun*
**lottery**

la **lotte** *fem noun*
**monkfish**

la **louche** *fem noun* ▷ see **louche** *adj*
**ladle**

**louche** *masc & fem adjective*
▷ see **louche** *noun*
**fishy, odd**
un type louche a fishy-looking guy

**louer** *verb* **[1]**
1 **to let** (*a house, a flat*)
Ils louent leur maison. They let their house.
'À louer' 'To let', 'To rent'
2 **to rent**
Nous avons loué un appartement à la plage. We rented a flat by the beach.
3 **to hire** (*a car, a bike, a boat*)
Peut-on louer des vélos? Is it possible to hire bicycles?
4 **to praise**
Le professeur a loué toute la classe. The teacher praised the whole class.

le **loup** *masc noun*
**wolf**

la **loupe** *fem noun*
**magnifying glass**

**louper** *verb* **[1]**
1 (*informal*) **to miss** (*a train, an opportunity, a person*)
2 (*informal*) **to fail** (*an exam, a test*)

**lourd** *masc adjective*, **lourde** *fem*
1 **heavy**
Ta valise est très lourde. Your case is very heavy.
Le repas était un peu lourd. The meal was a bit heavy.
2 **muggy**
Il fait lourd aujourd'hui. It's muggy today.
3 **serious**
une lourde erreur a serious mistake
4 **annoying**
Tu es vraiment lourd! You're a real pest!

la **loutre** *fem noun*
**otter**

**loyal** *masc adjective*, **loyale** *fem*, **loyaux** *masc pl*, **loyales** *fem pl*
**faithful**

la **loyauté** *fem noun*
**loyalty**

le **loyer** *masc noun*
**rent**
Le loyer est de 700 euros par mois. The rent is 700 euros a month.

**lu** *verb* ▷ **lire**

la **lucarne** *fem noun*
**skylight**

la **luge** *fem noun*
**sledge**

**lugubre** *masc & fem adjective*
**gloomy**

**lui** *pronoun*
1 **him** (*as opposed to anybody else*)
**C'est lui.** It's him.
**chez lui** at his house
**Elle pense à lui.** She's thinking of him.
2 (*as indirect object for a male*) **(to) him**
**Pierre est vexé, qu'est-ce que tu lui as dit?** Pierre's upset, what did you say to him?
**Je lui ai envoyé un texto.** I sent him a text message.
**Où est le livre que je lui ai prêté?** Where's the book I lent him?
**Donne-lui quelque chose à boire!** Give him something to drink!
3 (*as indirect object for a female*) **(to) her**
**Nadine est vexée, qu'est-ce que tu lui as dit?** Nadine's upset, what did you say to her?
**Je lui ai envoyé un e-mail.** I sent her an email.
**Donne-lui un pull!** Give her a jumper!
4 (*as indirect object for animals*) **(to) it**
**Ce chat a peur. Qu'est-ce que tu lui as fait?** That cat's afraid. What did you do to it?
**Donne-lui de l'eau!** Give it some water!
5 (*for emphasis*) **he**
**C'est lui qui me l'a dit.** He's the one who told me.
**Lui et moi sommes très copains.** He and I are good friends.
**Elle aime le cinéma mais lui préfère le théâtre.** She likes the cinema but he prefers the theatre.
**Lui, il n'est jamais content!** He's never happy!
6 (*after prepositions like* ***avec*** *or* ***sans*** *and in comparisons*) **him**
**Daniel joue avec lui.** Daniel plays with him.
**Oscar est plus grand que lui.** Oscar is taller than him.
7 **à lui** his (*belonging to him*)
**Ce sont des amis à lui.** They're friends of his.

**lui-même** *pronoun*
1 **himself**
**Il l'a fait lui-même.** He did it himself.
**'Monsieur Dubois?' - 'Lui-même.'** 'Monsieur Dubois?' - 'Speaking.'
2 (*for masc things*) **itself**
**Le tableau lui-même ne vaut rien.** The painting itself is worth nothing.

la **lumière** *fem noun*
**light**

**lumineux** *masc adjective*, **lumineuse** *fem*
**luminous**
**un panneau lumineux** an electronic display board

le **lunch** *masc noun*
**buffet** (*lunch, supper*)

le **lundi** *masc noun*
1 **Monday**
**lundi dernier** last Monday
**lundi prochain** next Monday
**On est lundi aujourd'hui.** It's Monday today.
2 **on Monday**
**Appelle-moi lundi.** Ring me on Monday.
**À lundi!** See you on Monday!
3 **le lundi** on Mondays
**La boulangerie est fermée le lundi.** The bakery is closed on Mondays.
4 **tous les lundis** every Monday
**Tous les lundis, j'ai un cours de danse.** Every Monday I have a dance class.

**WORD TIP** Months of the year and days of the week start with small letters in French.

la **lune** *fem noun*
**moon**
• la **lune de miel** honeymoon

les **lunettes** *plural fem noun*
**glasses**
**mettre ses lunettes** to put on your glasses
**porter des lunettes** to wear glasses
• les **lunettes de natation** swimming goggles
• les **lunettes de soleil** sunglasses

la **lutte** *fem noun*
1 **fight**
**la lutte contre la drogue** the fight against drugs
**la lutte pour la justice** the fight for justice
2 **wrestling**

**lutter** *verb* **[1]**
**to fight**

le **luxe** *masc noun*
**luxury**
**une voiture de luxe** a luxury car

le **Luxembourg** *masc noun*
**Luxembourg**
**au Luxembourg** in Luxembourg

**WORD TIP** Countries and regions in French take: *le, la* or *les.*

**luxueux** *masc adjective*, **luxueuse** *fem*
**luxurious**

le **lycée** *masc noun*
**secondary school** (*for students aged 15-18, leading to the* ***baccalauréat*** *exam*)
• le **lycée professionnel** vocational school

le **lycéen** *masc noun*, la **lycéenne** *fem*
**secondary school student**

# M m



**M.** *abbreviation*
(= *Monsieur*) **Mister**
M. Dupont Mr Dupont ▷ **Monsieur**

**m'** *abbreviation: me* ▷ **me** *pronoun*

**WORD TIP** *me* becomes *m'* before a word beginning with *a, e, i, o, u* or *silent h*.

♂ **ma** *fem adjective*
**my**
▷ **mon**

les **macaronis** *plural masc noun*
**macaroni**

**mâcher** *verb* **[1]**
**to chew**

le **machin** *masc noun*
(*informal*) **thing, whatsit**
Qu'est-ce que c'est que ce machin? What's this thing?

la **machine** *fem noun*
**machine**
Mon T-shirt se lave en machine. My T-shirt is machine-washable.
- la **machine à écrire** typewriter
- la **machine à laver** washing machine
- la **machine à sous** fruit machine

la **mâchoire** *fem noun*
**jaw**

**mâchonner** *verb* **[1]**
**to chew**

le **maçon** *masc noun*
1 **builder**
2 **bricklayer**

♂ **madame** *fem noun*, **mesdames** *plural*
1 Madame Jones Ms Jones, Mrs Jones
2 Madame, ... Dear Madam, ... (*in a letter*)
3 Bonsoir, madame. Good evening. (*When greeting a woman you don't know well, add 'Madame' or 'Mademoiselle' to the greeting.*)

♂ **mademoiselle** *fem noun*, **mesdemoiselles** *plural*
**Miss, Ms**
▷ **Madame**

♂ le **magasin** *masc noun*
**shop**
un grand magasin a department store
faire les magasins to go shopping
Sara travaille dans un magasin. Sara works in a shop.

♂ le **magazine** *masc noun*
**magazine**

**maghrébin** *masc adjective*, **maghrébine** *fem* ▷ see **Maghrébin** *noun*
**North African**

un **Maghrébin** *masc noun*, une **Maghrébine** *fem*
▷ see **maghrébin** *adj*
**North African** (*person*)

le **magicien** *masc noun*, la **magicienne** *fem*
**magician**

la **magie** *fem noun*
**magic**

**magique** *masc & fem adjective*
1 **magic**
2 **magical**

**magistral** *masc adjective*, **magistrale** *fem*, **magistraux** *masc pl*, **magistrales** *fem pl*
un cours magistral a lecture (*at university*)

**magnétique** *masc & fem adjective*
**magnetic**

♂ le **magnétophone** *masc noun*
**tape recorder**

♂ le **magnétoscope** *masc noun*
**video recorder**

♂ **magnifique** *masc & fem adjective*
**splendid**

♂ **mai** *masc noun*
**May**
en mai, au mois de mai in May
le premier mai May Day
fin mai late May

**WORD TIP** Months of the year and days of the week start with small letters in French.

♂ **maigre** *masc & fem adjective*
1 **thin, skinny**
2 **lean** (*meat*)
3 **low-fat** (*cheese*)

**maigrir** *verb* **[2]**
**to lose weight**
**Lisa a maigri de deux kilos.** Lisa's lost two kilos.

le **mail** *masc noun*
**email**
**Audrey m'a envoyé un mail.** Audrey sent me an email.

♂ le **maillot** *masc noun*
1 **shirt** (*in football, rugby*)

2 **jersey** (*in cycling*)
**le maillot jaune** the yellow jersey (*worn by the leader in the Tour de France*)
- le **maillot de bain** swimsuit, swimming trunks
- le **maillot de corps** vest

♪ la **main** *fem noun*
**hand**
**avoir quelque chose à la main** to have something in your hand
**Qu'est-ce que tu as à la main?** What have you got in your hand?
**serrer la main à quelqu'un** to shake hands with somebody
**Le gagnant sert la main du perdant.** The winner shakes hands with the loser.
**se serrer la main** to shake hands
**Nous nous sommes serré la main.** We shook hands.
**se donner la main** to hold hands
**Anna et Djamel se donnaient la main.** Anna and Djamel were holding hands.
**donner un coup de main à quelqu'un** to give somebody a hand
**Tu veux un coup de main?** Do you want a hand?
**fait à la main, fait main** handmade
- la **main-d'œuvre** labour

♪ **maintenant** *adverb*
1 **now**
**à partir de maintenant** from now on
2 **nowadays**
**Maintenant presque tout le monde a un portable.** Nowadays nearly everybody has a mobile phone.

**maintenir** *verb* [81]
1 **to maintain**
2 **to keep**
3 **to stand by**
**Je maintiens ce que j'ai dit.** I stand by what I said.

le **maire** *masc noun*
**mayor**

la **mairesse** *fem noun*
**mayoress**

♪ la **mairie** *fem noun*
1 **town hall**
2 **town council, city council** (*the administration*)

♪ **mais** *conjunction*
**but**
**Mais oui.** Yes of course.
**Mais non.** Of course not.

le **maïs** *masc noun*
1 **maize**
2 **sweetcorn**
3 **un épi de maïs** corn on the cob

♪ la **maison** *fem noun*
1 **house** (*building*)
**une maison individuelle** a detached house
2 **home** (*where you live*)
**rester à la maison** to stay at home
**Il pleut, je reste à la maison.** It's raining, I'm staying at home.
**rentrer à la maison** to go home
**C'est l'heure de rentrer à la maison.** It's time to go home.
- la **maison de retraite** old people's home
- la **maison des jeunes** youth club

le **maître** *masc noun*, la **maîtresse** *fem*
**teacher** (*in a primary school*)
**Maîtresse!** Please, miss!
- le **maître-nageur** swimming instructor, pool attendant

la **maîtresse** *fem noun*
**lover**
▷ **maître**

la **maîtrise** *fem noun*
1 **skill**
**la maîtrise du pianiste** the pianist's skill
2 **command**
**une bonne maîtrise de la langue française** a good command of the French language
3 **master's degree**
**une maîtrise de langues modernes** a master's in modern languages
- la **maîtrise de soi** self-control

**maîtriser** *verb* [1]
1 **to control**
**Les pompiers ont maîtrisé les flammes.** The firefighters brought the flames under control.
2 **to master**
**Il a maîtrisé la langue française.** He's mastered the French language.

se **maîtriser** *reflexive verb* ⓔ
**to have self-control**

**majestueux** *masc adjective*, **majestueuse** *fem*
**majestic**

**majeur** *masc adjective*, **majeure** *fem*
▷ see **majeur** *noun*
1 **major**
**la majeure partie des Français** the majority of French people
2 **être majeur** to be over 18

**majeur** *masc noun* ▷ see **majeur** *adj*
**middle finger**

la **majorité** *fem noun*
**majority**

la **majuscule** *fem noun*
**capital (letter)**
en majuscules in capital letters
une R majuscule a capital R

✆ le **mal** *masc noun*, les **maux** *plural*
▷ see **mal** *adj, adv*
1 **pain**, **ache**
**Luc a mal à la tête.** Luc has a headache.
**faire mal** to hurt
**Ça fait mal.** It hurts.
**faire mal à quelqu'un** to hurt somebody
**Aïe! Tu me fais mal!** Ouch! you're hurting me!
**se faire mal** to hurt yourself
**Benoît s'est fait mal.** Benoît hurt himself.
2 **avoir du mal à faire quelque chose** to have difficulty in doing something
**J'ai du mal à comprendre ce qu'il dit.** I have difficulty in understanding what he says.
**se donner du mal pour faire quelque chose** to go to a lot of trouble to do something
**Elle s'est donné beaucoup de mal pour contacter tout le monde.** She went to a lot of trouble to contact everybody.
3 **harm**
**Il n'y a pas de mal.** No harm done.
4 **evil**
**le bien et le mal** good and evil
- le **mal de dents** toothache
- le **mal de mer** seasickness
- le **mal de tête** headache
- le **mal des transports** motion sickness
- le **mal du pays** homesickness

✆ **mal** *invariable adjective* ▷ see **mal** *adv, noun*
1 **wrong**
2 **pas mal** not bad
3 **pas mal de** quite a lot of
**On a pas mal de devoirs.** We've got quite a lot of homework.

**WORD TIP** *mal* never changes.

✆ **mal** *adverb* ▷ see **mal** *adj, noun*
**badly**
**Ça va mal.** It's going badly.
**C'est un enfant mal élevé.** He's a badly brought up child.
**Je t'entends mal.** I can't hear you very well.
**Je me sens mal.** I don't feel well.
**Cette machine fonctionne mal.** This machine doesn't work.

✆ le & la **malade** *masc & fem noun*
▷ see **malade** *adj*
**patient**

✆ **malade** *masc & fem adjective*
▷ see **malade** *noun*
1 **ill**, **sick**
**tomber malade** to fall ill
**Marie est tombée malade.** Marie has fallen ill.
2 **crazy**
**Tu es malade! Ne fais pas ça!** You're crazy! Don't do that!

la **maladie** *fem noun*
1 **illness**
2 **disease**

la **maladresse** *fem noun*
1 **clumsiness**
2 **blunder**

**maladroit** *masc adjective*, **maladroite** *fem*
**clumsy**

le **malaise** *masc noun*
1 **feeling of faintness**
**avoir un malaise** to feel faint, to pass out
2 **créer un malaise** to make people feel uncomfortable

la **malchance** *fem noun*
**bad luck**

le **mâle** *masc noun* ▷ see **mâle** *adj*
**male**

**mâle** *masc & fem adjective* ▷ see **mâle** *noun*
**male**

la **malédiction** *fem noun*
**curse**

le **malentendu** *masc noun*
**misunderstanding**

le **malfaiteur** *masc noun*
**criminal**

**malgré** *preposition*
1 **in spite of**
**malgré le froid** in spite of the cold
2 **malgré tout** all the same
**Mais malgré tout nous avons décidé d'y aller.** But we decided to go all the same.

le **malheur** *masc noun*
**misfortune**
**porter malheur** to be bad luck
**Ne passe pas là-dessous, ça porte malheur!** Don't walk under there, it's bad luck!

✆ **malheureusement** *adverb*
**unfortunately**

✆ le **malheureux** *masc noun*, la **malheureuse** *fem*
▷ see **malheureux** *adj*
**Le malheureux, il a tout perdu.** Poor man, he lost everything.

La malheureuse, elle a beaucoup souffert. Poor woman, she suffered a lot.

♪ **malheureux** *masc adjective*, **malheureuse** *fem*
▷ see **malheureux** *noun*
1 **unhappy** (*feeling*)
avoir l'air malheureux to look unhappy
Cet enfant a l'air malheureux. This child looks unhappy.
2 **unfortunate** (*choice, decision*)
un choix malheureux an unfortunate choice

**malhonnête** *masc & fem adjective*
**dishonest**

la **malice** *fem noun*
**mischief**

**WORD TIP** *malice* does not mean *malice* in English; for the meaning of *malice* ▷ **malveillance**.

**malicieux** *masc adjective*, **malicieuse** *fem*
**mischievous**

**WORD TIP** *malicieux* does not mean *malicious* in English; for the meaning of *malicious* ▷ **malveillant**.

**malin** *masc adjective*, **maligne** *fem*
1 **clever** (*person*)
Ce n'était pas très malin. That wasn't very clever.
2 **malignant** (*tumour*)

la **malle** *fem noun*
**trunk**

**malodorant** *masc adjective*, **malodorante** *fem*
**smelly**

**malpoli** *masc adjective*, **malpolie** *fem*
**rude**

**malpropre** *masc & fem adjective*
**dirty**

**malsain** *masc adjective*, **malsaine** *fem*
**unhealthy**

**maltraiter** *verb* **[1]**
**to ill-treat**
les enfants maltraités battered children

la **malveillance** *fem noun*
**malice**

**malveillant** *masc adjective*, **malveillante** *fem*
**malicious**

♪ la **maman** *fem noun*
**mum, mummy**

la **mamie** *fem noun*
**grandma, granny**

le **mammifère** *masc noun*
**mammal**

**manager** *verb* **[52]**
**to manage**

le **manageur** *masc noun*
**manager**

le **manche** *masc noun* ▷ see **manche** *fem noun*
**handle** (*of a tool*)

la **manche** *fem noun* ▷ see **manche** *masc noun*
1 **sleeve**
à manches courtes short-sleeved
sans manches sleeveless
2 **round** (*of a game*)
3 **leg** (*of a football match*)

♪ la **Manche** *fem noun*
la Manche the Channel
le tunnel sous la Manche the Channel Tunnel

la **mandarine** *fem noun*
**mandarin orange**

le **manège** *masc noun*
1 **merry-go-round**
2 **riding school**

la **manette** *fem noun*
**lever**
- la **manette de jeu** joystick

**mangeable** *masc & fem adjective*
**edible**

♪ **manger** *verb* **[52]**
**to eat**
Qu'est-ce qu'on va manger? What shall we have to eat?
J'ai déjà mangé. I've already eaten.
J'ai assez mangé. I've had enough.
Ce soir, on mange chinois. Tonight we'll have a Chinese meal.
donner à manger à quelqu'un to feed someone
As-tu donné à manger au chien? Have you fed the dog?
faire à manger to cook
Qu'est-ce que tu fais à manger pour midi? What are you cooking for lunch?
manger au restaurant to go out for a meal
Il a invité son père à manger au restaurant. He invited his father out for a meal.

la **mangue** *fem noun*
**mango**

le & la **maniaque** *masc & fem noun*
▷ see **maniaque** *adj*
1 **fusspot**
2 (*informal*) **fanatic**
Valérian est un maniaque du foot. Valérian is football mad.

French–English

**maniaque** *masc & fem adjective*
▷ see **maniaque** *noun*
**fussy**

la **manie** *fem noun*
1 **habit**
2 **mania**

**manier** *verb* [1]
**to handle**

la **manière** *fem noun*
1 **way**
**à ma manière** my way
**une manière plus facile** an easier way
**de cette manière** like this, like that
**d'une autre manière** in another way
**d'une certaine manière** in a way
2 **de toute manière** in any case
3 **les manières** manners
**les bonnes manières** good manners

le **manifestant** *masc noun*, la **manifestante** *fem*
**demonstrator**

la **manifestation** *fem noun*
**demonstration**
**une manifestation contre le racisme** a demonstration against racism

**manifester** *verb* [1]
**to demonstrate, to take part in a demonstration**

le **manioc** *masc noun*
**cassava**

**manipuler** *verb* [1]
1 **to handle**
2 **to manipulate**

le **mannequin** *masc noun*
1 **fashion model**
2 **dummy** (*in a shop window*)

le **manque** *masc noun*
**le manque de** the lack of, the shortage of

**manqué** *masc adjective*, **manquée** *fem*
1 **failed**
**un acteur manqué** a failed actor
2 **missed**
**une occasion manquée** a missed opportunity

♪ **manquer** *verb* [1]
1 **to be missing**
**Il manque trois fourchettes.** There are three forks missing.
**manquer de quelque chose** to lack something
**Il manque d'ambition.** He lacks ambition.
2 (*a person, a place you like*) **manquer à quelqu'un** to miss somebody or something
**Tu me manques.** I miss you.
**Londres leur manque.** They miss London.
3 (*a train, a bus, etc*) **manquer quelque chose** to miss something
**Elle a manqué son train.** She missed her train.
**J'ai manqué le début.** I missed the beginning.
4 **manquer de faire quelque chose, manquer faire quelque chose** to almost do something
**Il a manqué de tomber dans la piscine.** He almost fell into the pool.
**Ella a manqué se faire écraser par un bus.** Ella almost got run over by a bus.

♪ le **manteau** *masc noun*, les **manteaux** *plural*
**coat**

le **manuel** *masc noun* ▷ see **manuel** *adj*
1 **manual**
2 **textbook**
• le **manuel scolaire** school book

**manuel** *masc adjective*, **manuelle** *fem*
▷ see **manuel** *noun*
**manual**

la **manufacture** *fem noun*
**factory**

le **manuscrit** *masc noun*
▷ see **manuscrit** *adj*
**manuscript**

**manuscrit** *masc adjective*, **manuscrite** *fem* ▷ see **manuscrit** *noun*
**handwritten**

le **maquereau** *masc noun*, les **maquereaux** *plural*
**mackerel**

la **maquette** *fem noun*
**scale model**
**une maquette d'avion** a model aeroplane

♪ le **maquillage** *masc noun*
**make-up**

se **maquiller** *reflexive verb* Ⓔ [1]
1 **to put make-up on**
**Attends-moi, je me maquille.** Wait for me, I'm just putting some make-up on.
2 **to wear make-up**
**Aurélie n'a pas le droit de se maquiller.** Aurélie is not allowed to wear make-up.

le **marais** *masc noun*
**marsh**

le **marathon** *masc noun*
**marathon**



Ⓔ means the verb takes être to form the perfect

le **marbre** *masc noun*
**marble**
**une cheminée en marbre** a marble fireplace

♂ le **marchand** *masc noun*, la **marchande** *fem*
1 **shopkeeper**
2 **stallholder** (*on a market*)
3 **merchant**
• le **marchand de fruits et légumes** greengrocer
• le **marchand de journaux** newsagent

**marchander** *verb* [1]
**to haggle (over)**

la **marchandise** *fem noun*
**goods**

la **marche** *fem noun*
1 **walking** (*for exercise, to get from one place to another*)
**la marche à pied** walking
**faire de la marche** to go walking
2 **march** (*in the army*)
**une marche pour la paix** a peace march
3 **step** (*on a staircase, ladder, bus, train*)
**Attention à la marche!** Mind the step!
4 **en marche** running (*an engine*), on (*TV sets, radios*)
**Le moteur est en marche.** The engine is running.
**La télévision est en marche.** The TV is on.
**mettre en marche quelque chose** to start something
**Peux-tu mettre la machine à laver en marche?** Can you start the washing-machine?
**en état de marche** in working order

la **marche arrière** *masc noun*
**reverse**

le **marchepied** *masc noun*
**step** (*on a train*)

♂ le **marché** *masc noun*
1 **market**
**le marché aux fleurs** the flower market
**aller au marché** to go to market
**Je vais au marché tous les dimanches matin.** I go to market every Sunday morning.
2 **deal**
3 **bon marché** cheap
**Elle l'a acheté bon marché.** She bought it cheap.
• le **marché aux puces** flea market
• le **marché de l'emploi** job market

♂ **marcher** *verb* [1]
1 **to walk**
**On va marcher jusqu'au parc.** We'll walk as far as the park.
**marcher sur quelque chose** to tread on something
**Tu as marché sur mes lunettes.** You trod on my glasses.
2 **to march** (*in the army*)
3 **to work** (*machines*)
**Le lecteur DVD ne marche pas.** The DVD player doesn't work.
4 (*informal*) **Et ton boulot, ça marche?** And how's the job going?
5 (*informal*) **to fall for it**
**Tu vas voir, elle marche à tous les coups.** You'll see, she falls for it every time.
**faire marcher quelqu'un** to pull somebody's leg
**Je te faisais marcher.** I was pulling your leg.

♂ le **mardi** *masc noun*
1 **Tuesday**
**On est mardi aujourd'hui.** It's Tuesday today.
**mardi prochain** next Tuesday
**mardi dernier** last Tuesday
2 **on Tuesday**
3 **le mardi** on Tuesdays
**C'est fermé le mardi.** It's closed on Tuesdays.
4 **tous les mardis** every Tuesday
• le **mardi gras** Shrove Tuesday

**WORD TIP** Months of the year and days of the week start with small letters in French.

la **mare** *fem noun*
**pond**

**WORD TIP** *mare* does not mean *mare* (female horse) in English; for the meaning of *mare* ▷ **jument**.

le **marécage** *masc noun*
**swamp**

♂ la **marée** *fem noun*
**tide**
**à marée haute** at high tide
**à marée basse** at low tide
**La marée monte.** The tide's coming in.
**La marée descend.** The tide's going out.
• la **marée noire** oil slick

la **margarine** *fem noun*
**margarine**

la **marge** *fem noun*
1 **margin**
2 **en marge de** on the fringe of
**Il vit en marge de la société.** He lives on the fringes of society.

♪ le **mari** *masc noun*
**husband**

♪ le **mariage** *masc noun*
1 **marriage**
2 **wedding**
le jour de leur mariage their wedding day

**Marianne** *fem noun*
**Marianne** (*a female figure representing the French Republic in statues, paintings and on the standard French stamp*)

♪ le **marié** *masc noun*, la **mariée** *fem*
▷ see **marié** *adj*
1 **bridegroom**
2 **bride**
3 les mariés the bride and groom
les jeunes mariés the newly-weds

**marié** *masc adjective*, **mariée** *fem*
▷ see **marié** *noun*
**married**

**marier** *verb* [1]
**to marry somebody** (*person who carries out ceremony*)
le prêtre qui les a mariés the priest who married them

se **marier** *reflexive verb* Ⓔ
**to get married** (*bride and groom*)
Ils se sont mariés à Londres. They got married in London.
se marier avec quelqu'un to marry somebody
Frank s'est marié avec Rita. Frank married Rita.
Rita s'est mariée avec Frank. Rita married Frank.

le **marin** *masc noun* ▷ see **marin** *adj*
**sailor**

**marin** *masc adjective*, **marine** *fem*
▷ see **marin** *noun*
**sea**
l'air marin the sea air

**marine** *invariable adjective*
▷ see **marine** *noun*
bleu marine navy blue

**marine** *fem noun* ▷ see **marine** *adj*
**navy**

la **marionnette** *fem noun*
**puppet**

la **marmelade** *fem noun*
la marmelade d'oranges amères orange marmalade

la **marmite** *fem noun*
**cooking pot**

**marmonner** *verb* [1]
**to mutter, to mumble**

le **Maroc** *masc noun*
**Morocco**

**marocain** *masc adjective*, **marocaine** *fem*
▷ see **Marocain** *noun*
**Moroccan**

un **Marocain** *masc noun*, une **Marocaine** *fem* ▷ see **marocain** *adj*
**Moroccan** (*person*)

la **maroquinerie** *fem noun*
1 **leather shop**
2 **leather goods**

**marquant** *masc adjective*, **marquante** *fem*
**memorable**

♪ la **marque** *fem noun*
1 **brand** (*of a product*)
une marque de nourriture pour chats a brand of cat food
2 **make** (*of appliances, cars, etc*)
C'est une marque de voiture bien connue. It's a well-known make of sports car.
3 **mark**
une marque sur le mur a mark on the wall
• la **marque déposée** registered trademark

**marquer** *verb* [1]
1 **to write down**
J'ai marqué ton nom sur la liste. I've written down your name on the list.
2 **to score**
Il a marqué deux buts. He scored two goals.
3 **to be significant**
Le 14 juillet 1789 est une date qui a marqué dans l'histoire de France. July 14th 1789 is a significant date in French history.

le **marqueur** *masc noun*
**marker pen**

la **marraine** *fem noun*
**godmother**

**marrant** *masc adjective*, **marrante** *fem*
(*informal*) **funny**

**marre** *adverb*
en avoir marre (*informal*) to be fed up
J'en ai marre. I'm fed up.

se **marrer** *reflexive verb* Ⓔ [1]
(*informal*)
1 **to have a great time**
On s'est bien marrés chez Jonathan. We had a great time at Jonathan's.
2 **to have a good laugh**
Pourquoi tu te marres? Why are you laughing?

Ⓔ means the verb takes être to form the perfect

♪ le **marron** *masc noun* ▷ see **marron** *adj*
1 **(sweet) chestnut**
2 **(horse) chestnut**

♪ **marron** *invariable adjective*
▷ see **marron** *noun*
**brown**
des chaussures marron brown shoes
marron clair light brown
marron foncé dark brown

**WORD TIP** *marron* never changes.

le **marronnier** *masc noun*
**chestnut tree**

♪ **mars** *masc noun*
**March**
en mars, au mois de mars in March

**WORD TIP** Months of the year and days of the week start with small letters in French.

la **Marseillaise** *fem noun*
**the Marseillaise** (*the French national anthem*)

le **marteau** *masc noun*, les **marteaux** *plural*
1 **hammer**
2 **doorknocker**

**martyrisé** *masc adjective*, **martyrisée** *fem*
un enfant martyrisé a battered child

la **mascotte** *fem noun*
**mascot**

le **masculin** *masc noun* ▷ see **masculin** *adj*
(*Grammar*) **masculine**
au masculin in the masculine

**masculin** *masc adjective*, **masculine** *fem*
▷ see **masculin** *noun*
1 **male**
2 **men's**
3 **masculine**

le **masque** *masc noun*
**mask**

le **massacre** *masc noun*
1 **massacre**
2 (*informal*) **botch**

**massacrer** *verb* [1]
**to massacre**

le **massage** *masc noun*
**massage**

la **masse** *fem noun*
1 **mass**
2 **une masse de** (*informal*) **a lot of**
J'ai une masse de choses à faire. I've got a lot of things to do.
(*informal*) 'Tu as aimé ce film?' — 'Pas des masses!' 'Did you like the film?' — 'Not much!'

**masser** *verb* [1]
**to massage**

se **masser** *reflexive verb* ❻
**to assemble**

**massif** *masc adjective*, **massive** *fem*
1 **solid**
2 **massive**

les **mass media** *plural masc noun*
**the mass media**

**mastiquer** *verb* [1]
1 **to chew**
2 **to putty** (*a window*)
3 **to fill** (*a crack*)

**mat** *masc adjective*, **mate** *fem*
**matt**
le papier mat matt paper

le **mât** *masc noun*
1 **mast**
2 **pole**

♪ le **match** *masc noun*
**match**
un match de foot a football match
un match nul a draw
faire match nul to draw
Levallois a fait match nul contre Bourg-la-Reine. Levallois drew against Bourg-la-Reine.

- le **match aller** first leg
- le **match amical** friendly match
- le **match à domicile** home match
- le **match à l'extérieur** away match

le **matelas** *masc noun*
**mattress**

- le **matelas pneumatique** air bed

**matelassé** *masc adjective*, **matelassée** *fem*
**quilted**

le **matelot** *masc noun*
**sailor**

les **matériaux** *plural masc noun*
**materials**

le **matériel** *masc noun*
**equipment**
le matériel de sport sports equipment

**maternel** *masc adjective*, **maternelle** *fem*
▷ see **maternelle** *noun*
1 **motherly**
2 **maternal**
mon grand-père maternel my grandfather on my mother's side of the family

la **maternelle** *fem noun*
▷ see **maternelle** *adj*
**(state) nursery school** (*for French children aged between 2 and 6*)

la **maternité** *fem noun*
1 **motherhood**
2 **pregnancy**
le congé de maternité maternity leave
3 **maternity unit**

♪ les **mathématiques** *plural fem noun*
**mathematics**

le **matheux** *masc noun*, la **matheuse** *fem*
(*informal*) **maths genius**

les **maths** *plural fem noun*
**maths**

♪ la **matière** *fem noun*
1 **subject**
**Ma matière préférée, c'est l'histoire.** My favourite subject is history.
2 **material**
• les **matières grasses** fat (*in food*)
• la **matière première** raw material

♪ le **matin** *masc noun*
**morning**
**À quelle heure te lèves-tu le matin?** What time do you get up in the morning?
à six heures du matin at six o'clock in the morning
du matin au soir from morning till night
de bon matin early in the morning

**matinal** *masc adjective*, **matinale** *fem*, **matinaux** *masc pl*, **matinales** *fem pl*
1 **morning**
mon jogging matinal my morning jog
2 être matinal to be an early riser

la **matinée** *fem noun*
1 **morning**
au cours de la matinée during the morning
2 **matinée**
**Nous allons voir la pièce en matinée.** We're going to see a matinée.
3 faire la grasse matinée to have a lie-in
**Le week-end mes parents font la grasse matinée.** At the weekend my parents have a lie-in.

le **matou** *masc noun*
**tomcat**

**matrimonial** *masc adjective*, **matrimoniale** *fem*, **matrimoniaux** *masc pl*, **matrimoniales** *fem pl*
une agence matrimoniale a marriage bureau

la **maturité** *fem noun*
**maturity**

**maudire** *verb* [9]
**to curse**

**maussade** *masc & fem adjective*
1 **sullen**
2 **dull**

♪ **mauvais** *masc adjective*, **mauvaise** *fem*
▷ see **mauvais** *adv*
1 **bad**
une mauvaise expérience a bad experience
**Le temps est mauvais.** The weather is bad.
**Rosie est mauvaise en physique.** Rosie is bad at physics.
2 **wrong** (*not correct*)
le mauvais numéro the wrong number
3 **poor**
une mauvaise éducation a poor education
de mauvais résultats poor results
4 **nasty** (*vicious*)
un mauvais rhume a nasty cold
5 **not well, unwell**
**Elle a mauvaise mine.** She doesn't look well.
• la **mauvaise herbe** weed

♪ **mauvais** *adverb* ▷ **see mauvais** *adj*
1 sentir mauvais to smell
**Ce chien sent mauvais.** This dog smells.
2 **Il fait mauvais.** The weather is bad.

les **maux** *plural masc noun* ▷ **mal**

le **maximum** *masc noun*
▷ see **maximum** *adj*
**maximum**
faire le maximum to do your utmost

**maximum** *masc & fem adjective*
▷ see **maximum** *noun*
**maximum**

la **mayonnaise** *fem noun*
**mayonnaise**

le **mazout** *masc noun*
**fuel oil**

**me**, **m'** *pronoun*
1 (*as a direct object*) **me**
**Elle me déteste.** She hates me.
**Il m'a vu.** He saw me.
2 (*as an indirect object*) **(to) me**
**Elle ne me parle jamais.** She never speaks to me.
**Il va m'expliquer tout ça.** He's going to explain all that to me.
**Elle m'a donné son adresse.** She gave me her address.
**Il me l'a donné.** He gave it to me.
3 (*with reflexive verbs*) **myself**
**Je me lève à sept heures.** I get up at seven o'clock.

Je me brosse les dents. I brush my teeth.
Je me suis blessé. I hurt myself.

4 (*with reflexive verbs*) **(for) myself**
Je me fais une salade. I'm making a salad for myself.
Je me suis acheté un cadeau. I bought myself a present.

**WORD TIP** *me* becomes *m'* before *a, e, i, o, u* or *silent h.*

le **mec** *masc noun*
(*informal*) **guy**

♪ le **mécanicien** *masc noun*, la **mécanicienne** *fem*
1 **mechanic**
2 **train driver**

la **mécanique** *fem noun*
▷ see **mécanique** *adj*
**mechanics**

**mécanique** *masc & fem adjective*
▷ see **mécanique** *noun*
1 **mechanical**
2 **clockwork**

**WORD TIP** *mécanique* does not mean *mechanic* in English; for the meaning of *mechanic* ▷ **mécanicien**.

le **mécanisme** *masc noun*
**mechanism**

**méchamment** *adverb*
**nastily**

la **méchanceté** *fem noun*
**nastiness**

♪ **méchant** *masc adjective*, **méchante** *fem*
1 **nasty**
2 **spiteful**
3 **vicious**
'Chien méchant' 'Beware of the dog'

la **mèche** *fem noun*
1 **lock** (*of hair*)
2 **wick** (*of a candle*)

**méconnaissable** *masc & fem adjective*
**unrecognizable**

**mécontent** *masc adjective*, **mécontente** *fem*
**dissatisfied**

le **mécontentement** *masc noun*
1 **dissatisfaction**
2 **displeasure**

la **médaille** *fem noun*
1 **medal**
2 **medallion**
3 **name tag**

♪ le **médecin** *masc noun*
**doctor**
aller chez le médecin to go to the doctor's
Je dois aller chez le médecin. I must go to the doctor's.
• le **médecin généraliste** general practitioner

♪ la **médecine** *fem noun*
**medicine**
faire des études de médecine to go to medical school
• les **médecines douces** alternative medicine

les **médias** *plural masc noun*
**the media**

la **médiathèque** *fem noun*
**multimedia library**

**médical** *masc adjective*, **médicale** *fem*, **médicaux** *masc pl*, **médicales** *fem pl*
**medical**

♪ le **médicament** *masc noun*
**drug, medicine**

**médiéval** *masc adjective*, **médiévale** *fem*, **médiévaux** *masc pl*, **médiévales** *fem pl*
**medieval**

**médiocre** *masc & fem adjective*
**second-rate, poor**

**médire** *verb* **[9]**
**to criticize**

la **méditation** *fem noun*
**meditation**

**méditer** *verb* **[1]**
**to meditate**

la **Méditerranée** *fem noun*
**the Mediterranean**

**méditerranéen** *masc adjective*, **méditerranéenne** *fem*
**Mediterranean**

la **méduse** *fem noun*
**jellyfish**

le **méfait** *masc noun*
**crime**

la **méfiance** *fem noun*
**suspicion**

**méfiant** *masc adjective*, **méfiante** *fem*
**suspicious**

se **méfier** *reflexive verb* ❸ **[1]**
Méfie-toi! Watch out!
se méfier de quelqu'un not to trust somebody ▸▸



French–English
a b c d e f g h i j k l m n o p q r s t u v w x y z

Tu dois te méfier de lui. You mustn't trust him.

le **mégaoctet** *masc noun*
**megabyte**

le **mégot** *masc noun*
**cigarette end**

le **meilleur** *masc noun* ▷ see **meilleur** *adj*
**best**
**le meilleur des deux** the better of the two
**C'est le meilleur.** It's the best one.

**meilleur** *masc adjective*, **meilleure** *fem* ▷ see **meilleur** *noun*
1 **better**
**Le climat est bien meilleur au sud.** The climate's much better in the south.
**meilleur que** better than
**Ton gâteau est meilleur que le mien.** Your cake's better than mine.
2 **best**
**C'est ma meilleure amie.** She's my best friend.
**André est le meilleur nageur de la classe.** André is the best swimmer in the class.
**meilleurs vœux** best wishes

le **mél** *masc noun*
**email address**

le **mélange** *masc noun*
**mixture**

**mélanger** *verb* **[52]**
1 **to mix**
**Mélange le sucre et le beurre.** Mix the sugar and the butter.
2 **to mix up**
**J'ai mélangé les dates.** I got the dates mixed up.

la **mêlée** *fem noun*
**scrum**

**mêler** *verb* **[1]**
**to mix**

se **mêler** *reflexive verb* ⓔ
1 **se mêler à quelque chose** to get mixed up with something
**Il s'est mêlé à une affaire douteuse.** He got mixed up in some shady business.
**se mêler à quelqu'un** to mingle with somebody
**Elle s'est mêlée aux invités.** She mingled with the guests.
2 **se mêler de quelque chose** to meddle in something
**Mêle-toi de tes affaires!** Mind your own business!

la **mélodie** *fem noun*
**melody**

le **melon** *masc noun*
**melon**

le **membre** *masc noun*
1 **member**
2 **limb**

**même** *masc & fem adjective* ▷ see **même** *adv*
1 **same**
**Inès a le même anniversaire que toi.** Inès has the same birthday as you.
**en même temps** at the same time
2 **tout de même, quand même** all the same
**Tout de même tu pourrais faire un effort.** All the same you could try harder.

**même** *adverb* ▷ see **même** *adj*
**even**
**Il n'a même pas demandé.** He didn't even ask.

la **mémé** *fem noun*
(*informal*) **granny**

la **mémoire** *fem noun*
**memory**
**Rosalie a de la mémoire.** Rosalie has a good memory.
**Mon ordinateur a une mémoire de 3 gigaoctets.** My computer has a 3-gigabyte memory.

**mémoriser** *verb* **[1]**
**to memorize**

la **menace** *fem noun*
**threat**

**menacer** *verb* **[61]**
**to threaten**

le **ménage** *masc noun*
**housework**
**faire le ménage** to do the cleaning
**Marie fait le ménage tous les lundis.** Marie does the cleaning every Monday.
**une femme de ménage** a cleaning lady

**ménager** *verb* **[52]** ▷ see **ménager** *adj*
**ménager quelqu'un** to treat somebody gently
**Il ménage son vieux grand-père.** He's treating his old grandfather gently.
**ménager quelque chose** to be careful with something
**Ménage ma vieille voiture!** Be careful with my old car!

se **ménager** *reflexive verb* ⓔ
**to take it easy**
**Elle doit se ménager après son opération.** She must take it easy after her surgery.

**ménager** *masc adjective*, **ménagère** *fem*
▷ see **ménager** *verb*
**household**
les travaux ménagers housework

la **ménagère** *fem noun*
**house-wife**

le **mendiant** *masc noun*, la **mendiante** *fem*
**beggar**

**mendier** *verb* [1]
**to beg**

**mener** *verb* [50]
1 **to lead**
**Elle mène son cheval par la bride.** She's leading her horse by the reins.
**mener à quelque chose** to lead to something
**Les disputes ne mènent à rien.** Arguments don't lead anywhere.
2 **to run**
**Il mène une société.** He runs a company.

la **méningite** *fem noun*
**meningitis**

les **menottes** *plural fem noun*
**handcuffs**

le **mensonge** *masc noun*
**lie**
**dire des mensonges** to tell lies
**Vincent adore dire des mensonges.** Vincent loves telling lies.

la **mensualité** *fem noun*
**monthly payment**

**mensuel** *masc adjective*, **mensuelle** *fem*
**monthly**

**mental** *adjective masc*, **mentale** *fem*, **mentaux** *masc pl*, **mentales** *fem pl*
**mental**

la **mentalité** *fem noun*
**mentality**

le **menteur** *masc noun*, la **menteuse** *fem*
▷ see **menteur** *adj*
**liar**

**menteur** *masc adjective*, **menteuse** *fem*
▷ see **menteur** *noun*
**untruthful**

la **menthe** *fem noun*
**mint**
**un bonbon à la menthe** a mint

la **mention** *fem noun*
1 **mention** (*in conversation*)
2 **grade** (*in exams, a degree*)
**Elle a eu son bac avec mention bien.** She got a grade B plus in her baccalaureate.

**mentionner** *verb* [1]
**to mention**

**mentir** *verb* [53]
**to lie**
**mentir à quelqu'un** to lie to somebody
**Il ne faut pas me mentir.** You musn't lie to me.

♪ le **menton** *masc noun*
**chin**

♪ le **menu** *masc noun* ▷ see **menu** *adj*
**menu**
**le menu du jour** today's menu
**Qu'est-ce qu'il y a au menu?** What's on the menu?
**Je prends le menu à 20 euros.** I'll have the 20 euro menu.

mini-info ***menu***

Les restaurants français ont une carte et des menus à prix fixe, avec entrée, plat principal et dessert. Avant le dessert, on mange souvent une salade verte et du fromage.

♪ **menu** *masc adjective*, **menue** *fem*
▷ see **menu** *noun*
1 **slight** (*person*)
2 **tiny** (*feet, steps*)

la **menuiserie** *fem noun*
**joinery**

le **menuisier** *masc noun*
**joiner**

le **mépris** *masc noun*
**contempt**

**mépriser** *verb* [1]
**to despise**

♪ la **mer** *fem noun*
**sea**
**au bord de la mer** at the seaside
**aller à la mer** to go to the seaside
**Ce week-end, nous allons à la mer.** This weekend we're going to the seaside.
- la **mer du Nord** the North Sea
- la **mer des Antilles** the Caribbean (Sea)

la **mercerie** *fem noun*
**haberdashery**

♪ **merci** *exclamation*
**thank you, thanks**
**merci beaucoup, merci bien** thank you very much
**Merci de m'avoir rappelé.** Thank you for calling me back.

♪ le **mercredi** *masc noun*
1 **Wednesday**
**On est mercredi aujourd'hui.** It's Wednesday today. ▸▸



French-English
a b c d e f g h i j k l m n o p q r s t u v w x y z

mercredi prochain next Wednesday
mercredi dernier last Wednesday
2 **on Wednesday**
3 le mercredi on Wednesdays
C'est fermé le mercredi. It's closed on Wednesdays.
tous les mercredis every Wednesday
• le **mercredi des Cendres** Ash Wednesday

**WORD TIP** Months of the year and days of the week start with small letters in French.

♪ la **mère** *fem noun*
**mother**
la mère de Sophie Sophie's mother

**mini-info** ***mère***
En France, la fête des Mères est le dernier dimanche de mai.

la **merguez** *invariable fem noun*
**spiced beef sausage**

**méridional** *adjective masc*, **méridionale** *fem*, **méridionaux** *masc pl*, **méridionales** *fem pl*
**southern**

la **meringue** *fem noun*
**meringue**

la **mérite** *fem noun*
**merit**

**mériter** *verb* [1]
**to deserve**

le **merlan** *masc noun*
**whiting**

le **merle** *masc noun*
**blackbird**

la **merveille** *fem noun*
1 **wonder**
Ton gâteau est une vraie merveille. Your cake's absolutely wonderful.
2 à merveille wonderfully
Tout a marché à merveille. Everything went like a dream.
se porter à merveille to be in excellent health
Mamie se porte à merveille. Granny is in excellent health.

♪ **merveilleux** *masc adjective*, **merveilleuse** *fem*
**marvellous**

**mes** *masc & fem plural adjective* ▷ **mon**

♪ **mesdames** *plural fem noun* ▷ **madame**

**mesdemoiselles** *plural fem noun* ▷ **mademoiselle**

**mesquin** *masc adjective*, **mesquine** *fem*
**petty**

le **message** *masc noun*
**message**

le **messager** *masc noun*, la **messagère** *fem*
**messenger**

la **messe** *fem noun*
**mass** (*religious service*)

♪ **messieurs** *plural masc noun* ▷ **monsieur**

la **mesure** *fem noun*
1 **measurement**
un costume fait sur mesure a made-to-measure suit
2 **measure**
prendre des mesures pour faire quelque chose to take measures to do something
3 être en mesure de faire quelque chose to be in a position to do something
Nous ne sommes pas en mesure de vous aider. We are not in a position to help you.

**mesurer** *verb* [1]
**to measure**

**met** *verb: present tense* ▷ **mettre**

le **métal** *masc noun*, les **métaux** *plural*
**metal**

**métallique** *masc & fem adjective*
**metallic**

**métallisé** *masc adjective*, **métallisée** *fem*
**metallic**
bleu métallisé metallic blue

♪ la **météo** *fem noun*
**weather forecast**

la **méthode** *fem noun*
1 **method**
2 **manual, tutor**
une méthode de clarinette a clarinet tutor

le **métier** *masc noun*
**job**
Pour moi, le métier idéal, c'est journaliste. My ideal job is a journalist.

♪ le **mètre** *masc noun*
1 **metre**
Ça fait deux mètres. This is two metres long.
2 **metre rule**
Passe-moi le mètre! Pass me the metre rule!

**métrique** *masc & fem adjective*
**metric**

♪ le **métro** *masc noun*
**underground**
une station de métro an underground station

**mets** *verb* ▷ **mettre**

le **metteur en scène** *masc noun*
**director**

**mettre** *verb* [11]
1 **to put**
**Il met les pieds sur la table.** He puts his feet on the table.
**Où as-tu mis le sel?** Where have you put the salt?
2 **to put on**
**Je mets mon manteau.** I'm putting my coat on.
3 **to wear**
**Mon père ne met jamais de cravate.** My father never wears a tie.
4 **to turn on** (*the radio, the television, the heating*)
**J'ai mis le chauffage.** I've turned the heating on.
5 **mettre le couvert** to lay the table
**J'ai mis le couvert dans la cuisine.** I've laid the table in the kitchen.
6 **mettre quelqu'un en colère** to make somebody angry
**Elle met souvent sa mère en colère.** She often makes her mother angry.
7 **to take**
**J'ai mis trois heures pour le faire.** It took me three hours to do it.

se **mettre** *reflexive verb* Ⓔ
1 **to put yourself** (*standingor sitting*)
**Mets-toi devant la fenêtre!** Go over to the window!
**se mettre debout** to stand up
**Nous nous mettons debout quand elle arrive.** We stand up when she arrives.
2 **se mettre à faire quelque chose** to start to do something
**Estelle s'est mise à chanter.** Estelle started to sing.

**meublé** *masc adjective*, **meublée** *fem*
**furnished**

le **meuble** *masc noun*
**piece of furniture**
**des meubles** furniture

le **meurtre** *masc noun*
**murder**

le **meurtrier** *masc noun*, la **meurtrière** *fem* ▷ **see meurtrier** *adj*
**murderer**

**meurtrier** *masc adjective*, **meurtrière** *fem* ▷ **see meurtrier** *noun*
**deadly**

**mexicain** *masc adjective*, **mexicaine** *fem* ▷ **see Mexicain** *noun*
**Mexican**

un **Mexicain** *masc noun*, une **Mexicaine** *fem* ▷ **see mexicain** *adj*
**Mexican** (*person*)

**Mexico** *noun*
**Mexico City**

le **Mexique** *masc noun*
**Mexico**

**mi-** *prefix*
1 **half-**
**mi-anglais, mi-français** half-English, half-French
2 **mid-**
**à la mi-février** in mid-February

le **mi-bas** *invariable masc noun*
**knee sock**

le **micro** *masc noun*
**microphone**

le **microbe** *masc noun*
**germ**

le **micro-ondes** *invariable masc noun*
**microwave**

le **micro-ordinateur** *masc noun*
**microcomputer**

le **microscope** *masc noun*
**microscope**

le **midi** *masc noun* ▷ **see Midi** *masc noun*
1 **midday, noon**
**Il est midi vingt.** It's twenty past twelve.
2 **lunchtime**
**Je fais mes courses à midi.** I do my shopping in my lunch hour.

le **Midi** *masc noun* ▷ **see midi** *masc noun*
**le Midi** the South of France

le **miel** *masc noun*
**honey**

le **mien** *masc pronoun*, la **mienne** *fem*, les **miens** *masc pl*, les **miennes** *fem pl*
**mine**
**Tu n'as pas ta moto? On va prendre la mienne.** You don't have your motorbike? We'll take mine.
**'À qui sont ces chaussures?' — 'Ce sont les miennes.'** 'Whose shoes are these?' - 'They're mine.'
**Puis-je t'emprunter ton vélo? Le mien est chez moi.** Can I borrow your bike? Mine's at home.
**'Est-ce que ces chaussures sont à Natalie?' — 'Non, ce sont les miennes.'** 'Are these shoes Natalie's?' — 'No, they're mine.'

**WORD TIP** The article and pronoun change in French when they refer to fem and plural nouns.

la **miette** *fem noun*
**crumb**

♪ **mieux** *invariable adjective* ▷ see **mieux** *adv, noun*
1 **better**
**C'est mieux comme ça.** It's better like that.
**de mieux en mieux** better and better
2 **best**
**C'est le rouge que j'aime le mieux.** I like the red one best., I prefer the red one.

**WORD TIP** *mieux* never changes.

♪ **mieux** *adverb* ▷ see **mieux** *adj, noun*
**better**
**Tu la connais mieux que moi.** You know her better than I do.
**Je me sens mieux.** I feel better.
**Mon père va mieux maintenant.** My father's better now.

♪ le **mieux** *masc noun* ▷ see **mieux** *adj, adv*
**Le mieux est de revenir.** The best thing is to come back.
**au mieux** at best, at least
**Fais de ton mieux!** Do your best!

♪ **mignon** *masc adjective*, **mignonne** *fem*
**sweet**

la **migraine** *fem noun*
**migraine**

**mijoter** *verb* [1]
**to simmer**

♪ le **milieu** *masc noun*, les **milieux** *plural*
1 **middle**
**au milieu de la journée** in the middle of the day
**au beau milieu du déjeuner** right in the middle of lunch
2 **environment**
**le milieu familial** the home environment
**en milieu urbain** in a town
**en milieu rural** in the country
3 **background**
**Il vient d'un milieu pauvre.** He comes from a poor background.

le **militaire** *masc noun* ▷ see **militaire** *adj*
**serviceman**

**militaire** *masc & fem adjective* ▷ see **militaire** *noun*
**military**
**le service militaire** military service

♪ **mille** *number*
**a thousand**
**mille personnes** a thousand people
**deux mille personnes** two thousand people

le **millefeuille** *masc noun*
**millefeuille** (*small layered cake made of puff pastry filled with custard and cream*)

le **millénaire** *masc noun*
**millennium**

le **mille-pattes** *invariable masc noun*
**centipede**

le **milliard** *masc noun*
**billion**

le & la **milliardaire** *masc & fem noun*
**multimillionaire**

le **millier** *masc noun*
**thousand**
**des milliers d'euros** thousands of euros

le **milligramme** *masc noun*
**milligramme**

le **millimètre** *masc noun*
**millimetre**

♪ le **million** *masc noun*
**million**
**deux millions d'euros** two million euros

le & la **millionnaire** *masc & fem noun*
**millionaire**

le & la **mime** *masc & fem noun*
**mime artist**

**mimer** *verb* [1]
1 **to mime**
2 **to mimic**

**minable** *masc & fem adjective*
(*informal*)
1 **pathetic**
**Ses plaisanteries sont minables.** Her jokes are pathetic.
2 **crummy**
**un film minable** a crummy film

♪ **mince** *masc & fem adjective*
1 **thin**
**une mince tranche de viande** a thin slice of meat
2 **slim**
**Elle est mince.** She's slim.
3 (*informal*) **Mince alors!** Oh bother!

la **minceur** *fem noun*
1 **thinness**
2 **slimness**

la **mine** *fem noun*
1 **appearance**
**Elle a bonne mine.** She looks well.
**Tu as mauvaise mine.** You don't look well.
2 **expression**
**Il a une mine réjouie.** He has a cheerful expression.

Pourquoi fais-tu cette mine? Why are you pulling that face?
3 **mine** (*for coal, diamonds, etc*)
4 **pencil lead**

**minéral** *masc adjective*, **minérale** *fem*, **minéraux** *masc pl*, **minérales** *fem pl*
▷ see **minéral** *noun*
**mineral**
eau minérale mineral water

le **minéral** *masc noun*, les **minéraux** *plural*
▷ see **minéral** *adj*
**mineral**

**mineur** *masc adjective*, **mineure** *fem*
▷ see **mineur** *noun*
1 **under 18**
Elle est mineure. She's under 18.
2 **minor**
un problème mineur a minor problem

le **mineur** *masc noun*, la **mineure** *fem*
▷ see **mineur** *adj*
1 **person under 18, minor**
2 **miner** (*working in a mine*)

la **mini-jupe** *fem noun*
**mini-skirt**

**minimal** *masc adjective*, **minimale** *fem*, **minimaux** *masc pl*, **minimales** *fem pl*
**minimal**

**minimiser** *verb* [1]
**to minimize**

le **minimum** *masc noun*
▷ see **minimum** *adj*
**minimum**
au minimum at the very least

**minimum** *masc & fem adjective*
▷ see **minimum** *noun*
**minimum**
l'âge minimum the minimum age

le **ministère** *masc noun*
**ministry**

**WORD TIP** *ministère* does not mean *minister* in English; for the meaning of *minister* ▷ **ministre**

le **ministre** *masc noun*
**minister**

le **Minitel®** *masc noun*
(*Minitel is an online data service; users can access many kinds of information, including telephone directories*)

la **minorité** *fem noun*
**minority**

le **minou** *masc noun*
**pussycat**

♪ **minuit** *masc noun*
**midnight**
à minuit at midnight

**WORD TIP** minuit doesn't take the determiner *le*.

**minuscule** *masc & fem adjective*
▷ see **minuscule** *noun*
**tiny**

la **minuscule** *fem noun*
▷ see **minuscule** *adj*
**small letter** (*not a capital letter*)
en miniscules in small letters
une T miniscule a small T

♪ la **minute** *fem noun*
**minute**
dans dix minutes in ten minutes
Attends une minute! Wait a minute!

**minutieux** *masc adjective*, **minutieuse** *fem*
1 **meticulous**
un travail minutieux a meticulous work
2 **detailed**
une étude minutieuse a detailed study

la **mirabelle** *fem noun*
**small yellow plum**

le **miracle** *masc noun*
**miracle**
par miracle miraculously

**miraculeux** *masc adjective*, **miraculeuse** *fem*
**miraculous**

♪ le **miroir** *masc noun*
**mirror**

**mis** *verb: past participle* ▷ **mettre**

**miser** *verb* [1]
**to bet**

**misérable** *masc & fem adjective*
**poor**

**WORD TIP** *misérable* does not mean *miserable* in English; for the meaning of *miserable* ▷ **malheureux**

la **misère** *fem noun*
**extreme poverty**

**WORD TIP** *misère* does not mean *misery* in English; for the meaning of *misery* ▷ **souffrance**

le **missile** *masc noun*
**missile**

le & la **missionnaire** *masc & fem noun*
**missionary**

le **mistral** *masc noun*
**mistral** (*a strong cold north wind which blows down the Rhône valley to the Mediterranean*)

French–English
a b c d e f g h i j k l m n o p q r s t u v w x y z

♂ le **mi-temps** *invariable masc noun*
▷ see **mi-temps** *fem noun*
**part-time job**
**travailler à mi-temps** to work part-time
**La prof de gym travaille à mi-temps.** The PE teacher works part-time.

**WORD TIP** *mi-temps* never changes.

♂ la **mi-temps** *invariable fem noun*
▷ see **mi-temps** *masc noun*
**half-time** (*in a match*)
**à la mi-temps** at half-time

**WORD TIP** *mi-temps* never changes.

**miteux** *masc adjective*, **miteuse** *fem*
1 **seedy**
2 **shabby**

la **mitraillette** *fem noun*
**submachine gun**

le **mi-trimestre** *masc noun*
**half term**

**mixer** *verb*[1]
**to mix**

♂ **mixte** *masc & fem adjective*
1 **coeducational**
**une école mixte** a coeducational school
2 **mixed**
**une équipe mixte** a mixed team

**Mlle** *abbreviation*
(*= Mademoiselle*) **Miss**
**Mlle Dupont** Miss Dupont
▷ **Mademoiselle**

**Mme** *abbreviation*
(*= Madame*) **Ms, Mrs**
**Mme Dupont** Mrs Dupont, Ms Dupont ▷ **Madame**

**mobile** *masc & fem adjective*
▷ see **mobile** *noun*
1 **mobile**
2 **loose** (*pages, etc*)

le **mobile** *masc noun* ▷ **see mobile** *adj*
1 **motive**
**le mobile du crime** the motive for the crime
2 **mobile**

le **mobilier** *masc noun*
**furniture**

la **mobylette** *fem noun*
**moped**

♂ **moche** *masc & fem adjective*
1 (*informal*) **ugly**
**Ce nouvel immeuble est vraiment moche.** This new block of flats is really ugly.
2 (*informal*) **awful**, **nasty**
**Le temps est moche ce matin.** The weather is awful this morning.
**C'est moche de dire ça!** That's a nasty thing to say!

la **mode** *fem noun* ▷ **see mode** *masc noun*
**fashion**
**être à la mode** to be fashionable
**La mini-jupe est à la mode.** The miniskirt is fashionable.

le **mode** *masc noun* ▷ **see mode** *fem noun*
**way**, **mode**
**le mode de vie** the way of life
• le **mode d'emploi** instructions for use

le **modèle** *masc noun*
1 **example**
2 **model**, **size**
3 **style** (*of clothing*)
**Ce modèle existe en plusieurs coloris.** This style is available in several colours.

**modéré** *masc adjective*, **modérée** *fem*
**moderate**

♂ **moderne** *masc & fem adjective*
**modern**

**moderniser** *verb*[1]
**to modernize**

**modeste** *masc & fem adjective*
1 **modest** (*person, house*)
2 **humble** (*family, origin*)

la **modestie** *fem noun*
**modesty**

**modifier** *verb*[1]
**to change**

la **moelle** *fem noun*
**marrow** (*of bone*)

**moelleux** *masc adjective*, **moelleuse** *fem*
1 **soft** (*towel, bed*)
2 **mellow** (*wine*)

les **mœurs** *plural fem noun*
1 **customs**
2 **morals**

♂ **moi** *pronoun*
1 **me** (*as opposed to anybody else*)
**Allo, c'est moi.** Hello, it's me.
**'J'ai froid.' — 'Moi pas.'** 'I'm cold.' — 'I'm not.'
**Elle pense à moi.** She's thinking of me.
**chez moi** at my house
2 (*after prepositions like* **avec** *or* **sans** *and in comparisons*) **me**
**Tu viens avec moi?** Are you coming with me?
**C'est pour moi.** It's for me.
**Elle est plus grande que moi.** She's taller than me.

Camille travaille plus que moi. Camille works harder than me.
3 **à moi** mine (*belonging to me*)
**C'est à moi, ça?** Is that mine?
**C'est un ami à moi.** He's a friend of mine.
**Ce DVD n'est pas à moi.** This DVD is not mine.
4 **I** (*for emphasis*)
**Moi, je reste ici.** I'm staying here.
**Alex et moi, nous partons en vacance.** Alex and I are going on holiday.
**C'est moi qui ai payé.** I'm the one who paid.
**C'est à moi de jouer.** It's my turn to play.

**moi-même** *pronoun*
**myself**
**Je l'ai fait moi-même.** I did it myself.

**moindre** *masc & fem adjective*
**slightest**
**Je n'en ai pas la moindre idée.** I haven't the slightest idea.

le **moine** *masc noun*
**monk**

le **moineau** *masc noun*, les **moineaux** *plural*
**sparrow**

♪ **moins** *preposition* ▷ see **moins** *adv*
1 **minus**
**Sept moins deux égale cinq.** Seven minus two equals five.
2 **Il est dix heures moins cinq.** It's five to ten.

♪ **moins** *adverb* ▷ see **moins** *prep*
1 **less**
**de moins en moins** less and less
**Tu as moins d'argent que moi.** You've got less money than I have.
**Il est moins grand que son frère.** He's shorter than his brother.
2 **le moins** the least
**C'est le parfum caramel que j'aime le moins.** I like the caramel flavour the least.
3 **le moins, la moins, les moins** the least
**le moins difficile** the least difficult
**la moins jolie** the least pretty
**le moins gros** the smallest
**les jeunes et les moins jeunes** the young and the not so young
4 **de moins** less, fewer
**Le voyage dure deux heures de moins en voiture.** The journey takes two hours less by car.
**Il y a 100 candidats de moins.** There are 100 fewer candidates.
5 **moins de** less, fewer
**moins de beurre** less butter
**moins de voitures** fewer cars
6 **moins... moins...** the less... the less
**Moins on travaille, moins on a envie de travailler.** The less you work, the less you feel like working.
7 **au moins** at least
**Au moins, il s'est excusé.** At least he apologized.
8 **du moins** at least
**Du moins, c'est ce qu'il m'a dit.** At least, that's what he told me.
9 **à moins que** unless
**à moins qu'elle soit malade** unless she's ill

♪ le **mois** *masc noun*
**month**
**au mois de mai** in May
**le mois dernier** last month
**le mois prochain** next month
**Il reçoit 100€ d'argent de poche par mois.** He gets €100 pocket money a month.

le **moisi** *masc noun* ▷ see **moisi** *adj*
**mould**

**moisi** *masc adjective*, **moisie** *fem* ▷ see **moisi** *noun*
**mouldy**

**moisir** *verb* [2]
**to go mouldy**

la **moisson** *fem noun*
**harvest**

**moite** *masc & fem adjective*
1 **sweaty**
**J'ai les mains moites.** I've got sweaty hands.
2 **muggy**
**Il y a une chaleur moite.** It's muggy.

♪ la **moitié** *fem noun*
1 **half**
**la moitié d'une pomme** half an apple
**la moitié d'entre eux** half of them
2 **à moitié** half
**à moitié vide** half empty

**moitié-moitié** *adverb*
**half-and-half**
**On partage moitié-moitié.** We go halves.

la **molaire** *fem noun*
**molar**

**molle** *fem adjective* ▷ **mou**

le **mollet** *masc noun*
**calf** (*of the leg*)

le & la **môme** *masc & fem noun*
(*informal*) **kid**

♪ le **moment** *masc noun*
1 **moment**
**Un moment, s'il vous plaît.** Just a moment, please.
**en ce moment** at the moment
**pour le moment** for the moment
2 **time**
**Elle a attendu un bon moment.** She waited for some time.
**par moments** at times
3 **À ce moment-là, on a frappé à la porte.** Just then, there was a knock on the door.
**au moment où...** just when...

**mon** *masc adjective*, **ma** *fem*, **mes** *masc & fem plural*
**my**
**mon frère** my brother
**ma sœur** my sister
**mes amis** my friends
**mes yeux** my eyes

♪ la **monarchie** *fem noun*
**monarchy**

le **monastère** *masc noun*
**monastery**

le **monde** *masc noun*
1 **world**
2 **people**
**Il y a beaucoup de monde.** There are a lot of people.
**peu de monde** not many people
**tout le monde** everybody

**mondial** *masc adjective*, **mondiale** *fem*, **mondiaux** *masc pl*, **mondiales** *fem pl*
1 **world**
**la Seconde Guerre mondiale** the Second World War
2 **worldwide**
**un problème mondial** a worldwide issue

la **monétique** *fem noun*
**electronic banking**

le **moniteur** *masc noun*, la **monitrice** *fem*
1 **instructor** (*in sports, driving*)
**un moniteur de ski** a ski instructor
2 **group leader** (*at a camp*)
3 (*Computers*) **monitor**

♪ la **monnaie** *fem noun*
1 **currency**
**La monnaie de l'Angleterre est la livre sterling.** The English currency is the pound sterling.
2 **une pièce de monnaie** a coin
3 **change**
**Je n'ai pas de monnaie.** I don't have any change.

**monotone** *masc & fem adjective*
**monotonous**

♪ **monsieur** *masc noun*, **messieurs** *plural*
1 **Monsieur Leprêtre** Mr Leprêtre
**Bonjour monsieur.** Good morning. (*When greeting a man you don't know well, add 'Monsieur' to the greeting.*)
2 **Monsieur, ...** Dear Sir, ... (*in a letter*)
3 **man**
**un grand monsieur** a tall man

le **monstre** *masc noun*
**monster**

**monstrueux** *masc adjective*, **monstrueuse** *fem*
**monstrous**

le **mont** *masc noun*
**mountain**
**le mont Blanc** Mont Blanc

♪ la **montagne** *fem noun*
1 **mountain**
**la montagne** the mountains
**à la montagne** in the mountains
2 **une montagne de** a mountain of
**Il y a une montagne de formulaires à remplir.** There is a mountain of forms to fill in.
- **les montagnes russes** roller coaster

**montagneux** *masc adjective*, **montagneuse** *fem*
**mountainous**

le **montant** *masc noun* ▷ see **montant** *adj*
**sum**

**montant** *masc adjective*, **montante** *fem* ▷ see **montant** *noun*
1 **rising**
**la marée montante** the rising tide
2 **des chaussures montantes** ankle boots

la **montée** *fem noun*
1 **way up**, **ascent**
**la montée de la côte** the way up the hill
2 **hill**
**Elle habite en haut de la montée.** She lives at the top of the hill.
3 **rise**
**la montée des prix du pétrole** the rise in oil prices

♪ **monter** *verb* [1]
1 **to go up**, **to come up**
**monter l'escalier** to go or come up the stairs
**monter la colline** to go up the hill
2 **monter quelque chose** to take something up (*from downstairs*)



ⓔ means the verb takes être to form the perfect

Je vais monter ta valise. I'll take your case up.
**3 to assemble** (*a kit*)
**4 to put up** (*a tent*)
**5 monter dans quelque chose** Ⓔ to get on something (*a bus, a train, etc*)
**Il est monté dans le train.** He got on the train.
**6 monter sur quelque chose** Ⓔ to get on something (*a bike, a horse*)
**Monte sur ton vélo!** Get on your bicycle!
**Elle est monté sur le tabouret.** She climbed onto the stool.
**7** Ⓔ **to rise** (*prices*)
Les prix ont monté. Prices have risen.
**8 monter à cheval** to ride a horse
**Arnaud apprend à monter à cheval.** Arnaud is learning to ride a horse.

**WORD TIP** When you say what you *go up, take up, assemble, put up* etc, use *avoir* in the perfect tense.

la **montgolfière** *fem noun*
**hot-air balloon**

la **montre** *fem noun*
**watch**

**montrer** *verb* **[1]**
**to show**

la **monture** *fem noun*
**frames** (*of glasses*)

𝄞 le **monument** *masc noun*
**1 monument**
**2 historic building**
- le **monument aux morts** war memorial

se **moquer** *reflexive verb* Ⓔ **[1]**
**1 se moquer de quelqu'un** to make fun of somebody
**Tout le monde s'est moqué de moi.** Everybody made fun of me.
**2 se moquer de quelque chose** not to care about something
**Je m'en moque.** I couldn't care less.

la **moquette** *fem noun*
**fitted carpet**

**moqueur** *masc adjective*, **moqueuse** *fem*
**mocking**

**moral** *masc adjective*, **morale** *fem*, **moraux** *masc pl*, **morales** *fem pl*
▷ see **moral** *noun*
**1 moral**
**2 mental**

le **moral** *masc noun* ▷ see **moral** *adj*
**morale**
**Les élèves ont mauvais moral.** The pupils' morale is low.
**Je n'ai pas le moral.** I'm feeling really down.

la **morale** *fem noun*
**1 moral**
**la morale de la fable** the moral of the fable
**La prof lui a fait la morale.** The teacher gave him a lecture.
**2 morality**

la **moralité** *fem noun*
**moral**
**Je n'ai pas travaillé mes maths. Moralité: j'ai eu une mauvaise note au contrôle.** I didn't work on my maths. The moral is: I got a bad mark in the test.

le **morceau** *masc noun*, **les morceaux** *pl*
**piece, bit**
**un morceau de sucre** a sugar lump
**un morceau de piano** a piano piece

**mordre** *verb* **[3]**
**to bite**

**mordu** *masc adjective*, **mordue** *fem*
▷ see **mordu** *noun*
**être mordu de quelque chose** to be mad about something
**Olivier est mordu de snowboard.** Olivier is mad about snowboarding.

le **mordu** *masc noun*, *la*, **mordue** *fem*
▷ see **mordu** *adj*
(*informal*) **fanatic**

**morne** *masc & fem adjective*
**1 gloomy**
**2 dismal, dreary**

la **morsure** *fem noun*
**bite**

𝄞 **mort** *masc adjective*, **morte** *fem*
▷ see **mort** *masc & fem nouns*
**dead**

𝄞 le **mort** *masc noun*, la **morte** *fem*
▷ see **mort** *adj, fem noun*
**1 dead man**
**2 dead woman**
**3 les morts** the dead

𝄞 la **mort** *fem noun* ▷ see **mort** *adj, masc noun*
**death**
- la **mort-aux-rats** rat poison

**mortel** *masc adjective*, **mortelle** *fem*
**1 deadly**
**un champignon mortel** a deadly poisonous mushroom
**2 fatal**
**un coup mortel** a fatal blow
**3 deadly boring**
**Cette soirée est mortelle.** This party is deadly boring.

French-English

la **morue** *fem noun*
1 **cod**
2 **salt cod**

la **mosaïque** *fem noun*
**mosaic**

**Moscou** *noun*
**Moscow**

la **mosquée** *fem noun*
**mosque**

le **mot** *masc noun*
1 **word**
**mot à mot** word for word
**en quelques mots** in a few words
**Nous ne parlons pas un mot d'italien.** We don't speak a word of Italian.
**dire un mot à quelqu'un** to have a word with somebody
**Attends une minute, j'ai un mot à te dire.** Wait a minute, I'd like a word with you.
2 **note**
**Il a laissé un mot sur la table.** He left a note on the table.
- le **mot de passe** password
- les **mots croisés** crossword

le **motard** *masc noun*, la **motarde** *fem*
(*informal*) **motorcyclist**

le **moteur** *masc noun*
**engine**

le **motif** *masc noun*
1 **motive**
2 **pattern**
**un tissu à motifs géométriques** a material with a geometric pattern

**motiver** *verb* **[1]**
**to motivate**

la **moto** *fem noun*
**motorbike**
**Je suis venu à moto.** I came by motorbike.

le & la **motocycliste** *masc & fem noun*
**motorcyclist**

la **motte** *fem noun*
1 **lump**
2 **slab**

**mou** *masc adjective*, **molle** *fem*
1 **soft**
2 **listless**

la **mouche** *fem noun*
**fly**

se **moucher** *reflexive verb* Ⓔ **[1]**
**to blow your nose**
**Mouche-toi et arrête de renifler!** Blow your nose and stop sniffing!

le **moucheron** *masc noun*
**midge**

le **mouchoir** *masc noun*
**handkerchief**
- le **mouchoir en papier** tissue

la **moue** *fem noun*
**pout**
**faire la moue** to pout

la **mouette** *fem noun*
**seagull**

la **moufle** *fem noun*
**mitten**

**mouillé** *masc adjective*, **mouillée** *fem*
**wet**

**mouiller** *verb* **[1]**
**to wet**

se **mouiller** *reflexive verb* Ⓔ
**to get wet**

**moulant** *masc adjective*, **moulante** *fem*
**tight-fitting**
**un jean moulant** tight-fitting jeans

le **moule** *masc noun* ▷ **see moule** *fem noun*
1 **mould** (*for modelling*)
2 **tin** (*for baking*)
- le **moule à cake** loaf tin
- le **moule à gâteau** cake tin
- le **moule à tarte** flan dish

la **moule** *fem noun* ▷ **see moule** *masc noun*
**mussel**

**mouler** *verb* **[1]**
**to mould**

le **moulin** *masc noun*
**mill**
- le **moulin à poivre** pepper mill
- le **moulin à vent** windmill

**mourir** *verb* Ⓔ **[54]**
**to die**
**Elle est morte en février.** She died in February.
**mourir de quelque chose** to die of something
**Mon grand-père est mort d'un cancer.** My grandfather died of cancer.
**Je meurs de faim!** I'm starving!

**moussant** *masc adjective*, **moussante** *fem*
**foaming**

la **mousse** *fem noun*
1 **foam** (*in the bath*), **lather** (*on soap*), **froth** (*on milk, coffee*)
2 **foam** (*for mattresses, etc*)
**un matelas de mousse** a foam mattress
3 **moss**
4 **mousse** (*food*)

Ⓔ means the verb takes être to form the perfect

- la **mousse au chocolat** chocolate mousse
- la **mousse à raser** shaving foam

**mousser** *verb* [1]
**to foam**

**mousseux** *masc adjective*, **mousseuse** *fem*
du vin mousseux sparkling wine

la **moustache** *fem noun*
**moustache**

le **moustique** *masc noun*
**mosquito**

♪ la **moutarde** *fem noun*
**mustard**

♪ le **mouton** *masc noun*
1 **sheep**
2 **mutton**
**un ragoût de mouton** a mutton stew

le **mouvement** *masc noun*
1 **movement**
2 **bustle**
3 **impulse, reaction**
**Mon premier mouvement a été de refuser.** My first impulse was to refuse.
4 **action**
**un mouvement de grève** industrial action

**mouvementé** *masc adjective*, **mouvementée** *fem*
**hectic, eventful**
**J'ai eu une semaine mouvementée.** I've had a hectic week.

♪ le **moyen** *masc noun* ▷ **see moyen** *adj*
1 **means, way**
**un moyen de transport** a means of transport
2 **les moyens** the means (*enough money*)
**Je n'ai pas les moyens de m'acheter un ordinateur.** I can't afford to buy a computer.

♪ **moyen** *masc adjective*, **moyenne** *fem* ▷ **see moyen** *noun*
1 **medium**
**un poids moyen** a medium weight
2 **medium-sized**
**une école de taille moyenne** a medium-sized school
3 **average**
**la température moyenne** the average temperature
- le **Moyen Âge** Middle Ages

la **moyenne** *fem noun*
1 **average**
**en moyenne** on average
2 **half marks, 50%**
**J'ai eu la moyenne à mon devoir de maths.** I got 50% for my maths test.

le **Moyen-Orient** *masc noun*
**Middle East**

**muet** *masc adjective*, **muette** *fem*
1 **dumb**
**Sasha est sourd et muet.** Sasha is deaf and dumb.
2 **silent**
**le cinéma muet** silent movies

**multiple** *masc & fem adjective*
**multiple**

la **multiplication** *fem noun*
1 **multiplication**
2 **increase**

**multiplier** *verb* [1]
1 **to multiply**
**Dix multiplié par cinq égale cinquante.** Ten multiplied by five equals fifty.
2 **to increase**
**Le club multiplie le nombre de ses adhérents.** The club is increasing the number of its members.

se **multiplier** *reflexiver verb* ⓔ
**to increase**
**Les accidents se multiplient.** The accidents are on the increase.

**municipal** *masc adjective*, **municipale** *fem*, **municipaux** *masc pl*, **municipales** *fem pl*
1 **local, town**
**le conseil municipal** the town council
**les élections municipales** the local elections
2 **municipal**
**la bibliothèque municipale** the municipal library

la **municipalité** *fem noun*
1 **municipality**
2 **town council**

les **munitions** *plural fem noun*
**ammunition**

**mûr** *masc adjective*, **mûre** *fem*
1 **ripe**
2 **mature**
**l'âge mûr** middle age

♪ le **mur** *masc noun*
**wall**

la **muraille** *fem noun*
**wall**
**la Grande Muraille de Chine** the Great Wall of China

la **mûre** *fem noun*
**blackberry**

**mûrir** *verb* **[2]**
**1 to ripen**
**2 to mature** (*people, wines*)

le **murmure** *masc noun*
**murmur**

**murmurer** *verb* **[1]**
**to murmur**

la **muscade** *fem noun*
**nutmeg**

le **muscle** *masc noun*
**muscle**

**musclé** *masc adjective*, **musclée** *fem*
**muscular**

la **musculation** *fem noun*
**bodybuilding**

le **museau** *masc noun*, les **museaux** *plural*
**muzzle** (*of a dog*)

♪ le **musée** *masc noun*
**1 museum**
le musée des sciences the science museum
**2 art gallery**
un musée d'art contemporain a modern art gallery

**musical** *adjective masc*, **musicale** *fem*, **musicaux** *masc pl*, **musicales** *fem pl*
**musical**

♪ le **musicien** *masc noun*, la **musicienne** *fem*
**musician**

# N n

la **nage** *fem noun*
**swimming**
**Ils ont traversé la fleuve à la nage.** They swam across the river.

♪ **nager** *verb* **[52]**
**to swim**
Je sais nager. I can swim.

le **nageur** *masc noun*, la **nageuse** *fem*
**swimmer**

**naïf** *masc adjective*, **naïve** *fem*
**naïve**

le **nain** *masc noun*, la **naine** *fem*
**dwarf**

♪ la **musique** *fem noun*
**music**
J'aime la musique classique. I like classical music.
**mettre de la musique** to put some music on
**Lorsque j'étudie, je mets de la musique.** When I study, I put some music on.

**musulman** *masc adjective*, **musulmane** *fem* ▷ see **musulman** *noun*
**Muslim**

le **musulman** *masc noun*, la **musulmane** *fem* ▷ see **musulman** *adj*
**Muslim** (*person*)

**WORD TIP** Adjectives and nouns of religion start with a small letter in French.

**mutuel** *masc adjective*, **mutuelle** *fem*
**mutual**

**myope** *masc & fem adjective*
**short-sighted**

le **mystère** *masc noun*
**mystery**

♪ **mystérieux** *masc adjective*, **mystérieuse** *fem*
**mysterious**

**mystifier** *verb* **[1]**
**to fool**

**mystique** *masc & fem adjective*
**mystical**

le **mythe** *masc noun*
**myth**

♪ la **naissance** *fem noun*
**birth**
lieu de naissance place of birth

♪ **naître** *verb* Ⓔ **[55]**
**to be born**
**Je suis né à Londres en 1990.** I was born in London in 1990 (*boy speaking*).
**Je suis née en Écosse le 11 mars.** I was born in Scotland on 11th March (*girl speaking*).

la **nana** *fem noun*
(*informal*) **girl**

♪ la **nappe** *fem noun*
**tablecloth**

la **narine** *fem noun*
**nostril**



Ⓔ means the verb takes être to form the perfect

**natal** *masc adjective*, **natale** *fem*
**native**
ma ville natale my home town

la **natalité** *fem noun*
le taux de natalité the birth rate

♪ la **natation** *fem noun*
**swimming**
faire de la natation to go swimming
• une **leçon de natation** a swimming lesson

**natif** *masc adjective*, **native** *fem*
**native**

la **nation** *fem noun*
**nation**
les Nations unies the United Nations

**national** *masc adjective*, **nationale** *fem*, **nationaux** *masc pl*, **nationales** *fem pl*
**national**
une route nationale a main road

**nationaliser** *verb* **[1]**
**to nationalize**

la **nationalité** *fem noun*
**nationality**
la double nationalité dual nationality
acquérir la nationalité française to become a French citizen

la **nativité** *fem noun*
**Nativity**

la **natte** *fem noun*
**1** **plait** (*of hair*)
**2** **mat**

**nature** *invariable adjective*
▷ see **nature** *noun*
**plain**
yaourt nature plain yoghurt
un thé nature tea without milk or sugar

la **nature** *fem noun* ▷ see **nature** *adj*
**nature**

**naturel** *masc adjective*, **naturelle** *fem*
▷ see **naturel** *noun*
**natural**

♪ **naturel** *masc noun* ▷ see **naturel** *adj*
**1** **nature** (*of a person*)
**2** **au naturel plain** (*food*)
riz au naturel plain rice

**naturellement** *adverb*
**1** **of course**
**Naturellement, il a oublié.** Of course, he forgot.
**2** **naturally**
**Ses cheveux bouclent naturellement.** Her hair is naturally curly.

**nautique** *masc & fem adjective*
faire du ski nautique to go water-skiing
Club Nautique de la Baule la Baule Sailing Club

la **nausée** *fem noun*
**nausea**
avoir **[5]** la nausée to feel sick
J'ai la nausée. I feel sick.

le **navet** *masc noun*
**1** **turnip**
**2** **flop** (*film, event, etc*)

la **navette** *fem noun*
**shuttle** (*bus*)
faire la navette to commute

le **navigateur** *masc noun*
(*Computers*) **browser**

**naviguer** *verb* **[1]**
**1** **to sail** (*in a boat*)
**2** (*Computers*) **to surf**
naviguer sur le Web to surf the Web

le **navire** *masc noun*
**ship**
• le **navire-citerne** oil tanker

**navré** *masc adjective*, **navrée** *fem*
**sorry**
Je suis vraiment navré. I'm very sorry.

♪ **ne**, **n'** *adverb*
**1** ne ... pas not
**Je ne veux pas le faire.** I don't want to do it.
**Je n'aime pas le lait.** I don't like milk.
**2** ne ... jamais never
**Je ne vais jamais au marché.** I never go to the market.
**3** ne ... que only
**Je n'ai que dix euros.** I only have ten euros.
**4** ne ... plus no longer
**Elle n'habite plus à Cardiff.** She no longer lives in Cardiff.
**5** ne ... rien not ... anything, nothing
**Il ne mange rien.** He doesn't eat anything.
**Elle ne s'intéresse à rien.** She's not interested in anything.
**6** ne ... personne not ... anybody, nobody
**Il n'y a personne.** There's nobody there.
**Personne n'a compris.** Nobody understood.

**WORD TIP** *ne* becomes *n'* before *a, e, i, o, u* or *silent h*. *ne* goes before the verb, and *pas, que, jamais* etc come after it.

**né** *masc adjective*, **née** *fem*
**born**

**néanmoins** *adverb*
**nevertheless**
Il est néanmoins vrai que ... Nevertheless, it's true that ...

**nécessaire** *masc & fem adjective*
**necessary**
Est-ce qu'il est nécessaire de réserver? Is it necessary to book?

la **nécessité** *fem noun*
**necessity**
Le téléphone mobile est devenu une nécessité. A mobile phone has become a necessity.

la **nectarine** *fem noun*
**nectarine**

**néerlandais** *masc adjective*, **néerlandaise** *fem*
▷ see **Néerlandais** *noun*
**Dutch**

un **Néerlandais** *masc noun*, une **Néerlandaise** *fem*
▷ see **néerlandais** *adj*
1 **Dutch** (*person*)
2 le néerlandais Dutch (*language*)

**négatif** *masc adjective*, **négative** *fem*
▷ see **négatif** *noun*
**negative**

le **négatif** *masc noun* ▷ see **négatif** *adj*
**negative** (*of a photo*)

**négligé** *masc adjective*, **négligée** *fem*
**scruffy**

**négligent** *masc adjective*, **négligente** *fem*
**careless**

**négliger** *verb* [52]
**to neglect**
Il a négligé de le faire. He didn't bother to do it.

le **négociant** *masc noun*, la **négociante** *fem*
**merchant**

**négocier** *verb* [1]
négocier avec quelqu'un to negotiate with someone

la **neige** *fem noun*
**snow**

**neiger** *verb* [52]
**to snow**
Il neige. It's snowing.

le **néon** *masc noun*
**neon**

**néo-zélandais** *masc adjective*, **néo-zélandaise** *fem*
▷ see **Néo-Zélandais** *noun*
**from** *or* **of New Zealand**

**WORD TIP** Adjectives never have capitals in French, even for nationality or regional origin.

un **Néo-Zélandais** *masc noun*, une **Néo-Zélandaise** *fem*
▷ see **néo-zélandais** *adj*
**New Zealander**

le **nerf** *masc noun*
**nerve**
Elle me tape sur les nerfs! She's getting on my nerves!

**nerveux** *masc adjective*, **nerveuse** *fem*
**nervous**

**n'est-ce pas?** *adverb*
Il fait froid ce soir, n'est-ce pas? It's cold this evening, isn't it?
Il habite à Paris, n'est-ce pas? He lives in Paris, doesn't he?
Tu as déjà mangé, n'est-ce pas? You've already eaten, haven't you?

**WORD TIP** *n'est-ce pas* is translated by *isn't it, don't you, haven't you* etc according to subject of the sentence coming before it.

**net** *masc adjective*, **nette** *fem*
1 **clear** (*picture, etc*)
2 **net** (*in weights, prices, etc*)
3 **distinct** (*improvement*)

**nettement** *adverb*
**much**
C'est nettement meilleur. It's much better.

le **nettoyage** *masc noun*
**cleaning**
- le **nettoyage à sec** dry cleaning

**nettoyer** *verb* [39]
**to clean**

**neuf** *masc adjective*, **neuve** *fem*
▷ see **neuf** *number*
**new**
C'est tout neuf. It's brand new.
une voiture toute neuve a brand new car

**WORD TIP** *neuf* always means just bought, just made etc.

♪ **neuf** *number* ▷ see **neuf** *adj*
**nine**
**Il est neuf heures du matin.** It's nine o'clock in the morning.
**Julie a neuf ans.** Julie's nine.
**le neuf juillet** the ninth of July

**neuvième** *masc & fem adjective*
▷ see **neuvième** *noun*
**ninth**
**au neuvième étage** on the ninth floor

la **neuvième** *fem noun*
▷ see **neuvième** *adj*
**year 4**
**Pierre est en neuvième.** Pierre is in year 4.

**neutre** *masc & fem adjective*
**neutral**

♪ le **neveu** *masc noun*, **neveux** *pl*
**nephew**

♪ le **nez** *masc noun*
**nose**
**J'ai le nez bouché.** I have a blocked nose.
**Tu saignes du nez.** Your nose is bleeding.

**ni** *conjunction*
**ni ... ni ...** neither ... nor
**ni lui ni son frère** neither he nor his brother
**Ni Françoise ni Andrée ne le sait.** Neither Françoise nor Andrée knows.

la **niche** *fem noun*
1 **kennel** (*for a dog*)
2 **niche** (*for a statue, etc*)

le **nid** *masc noun*
**nest**

♪ la **nièce** *fem noun*
**niece**

**nier** *verb* **[1]**
**to deny**

**n'importe** *adverb*
1 **either**, **it doesn't matter**
**'Tu veux une aile ou une cuisse?' — 'N'importe.'** 'Do you want a wing or a leg?' — 'Either will do.'
2 **n'importe qui** anybody
**N'importe qui peut le faire.** Anybody can do it.
**On ne peut pas demander à n'importe qui.** We can't ask just anybody.
3 **n'importe quoi** anything
**Je ferai n'importe quoi pour t'aider.** I'll do anything to help you.
4 **n'importe quand** any time
**Tu peux m'appeler n'importe quand.** You can ring me any time.
5 **n'importe comment** any how
**Tu peux les ranger n'importe comment.** You can put them away any old how.
6 **n'importe où** anywhere (you like)
**Asseyez-vous n'importe où.** Sit down anywhere you like.

le **niveau** *masc noun*, **niveaux** *plural*
**level**
**au même niveau** at the same level
• le **niveau de vie** standard of living

les **noces** *plural fem noun*
**wedding**
• les **noces d'argent** silver wedding anniversary
• les **noces d'or** golden wedding anniversary

**nocif** *masc adjective*, **nocive** *fem*
**harmful**

**nocturne** *masc & fem adjective*
▷ see **nocturne** *noun*
**nocturnal**

la **nocturne** *fem noun* ▷ see **nocturne** *adj*
**late-night opening** (*of shops*)

♪ le **Noël** *masc noun*
**Christmas**
**à Noël** at Christmas
**Joyeux Noël!** Merry Christmas!

le **nœud** *masc noun*
**knot**
**faire un nœud** to tie a knot

♪ **noir** *masc adjective*, **noire** *fem*
▷ see **noir** *noun*
1 **black**
**un chapeau noir** a black hat
2 **dark**
**Il fait noir.** It's dark.

♪ le **noir** *masc noun* ▷ see **noir** *adj*
1 **black**
**Elle s'habille toujours en noir.** She always wears black.
2 **dark**
**J'ai peur du noir.** I'm scared of the dark.

♪ un **Noir** *masc noun*, une **Noire** *fem*
1 **black man**
2 **black woman**
3 **les Noirs** black people

**WORD TIP** Names of peoples take a capital in French.

**noircir** *verb* **[2]**
**to blacken**

la **noisette** *fem noun*
**hazelnut**



French–English
a b c d e f g h i j k l m n o p q r s t u v w x y z

la **noix** *fem noun*
1 **walnut**
2 **small amount**
une noix de beurre a knob of butter
- la **noix de cajou** cashew nut
- la **noix de coco** coconut

le **nom** *masc noun*
1 **name**
2 au nom de on behalf of
au nom de la famille Dupont on behalf of the Dupont family
- le **nom de famille** surname
- le **nom de jeune fille** maiden name

le **nombre** *masc noun*
**number**
un bon nombre de a good many
Le nombre de victimes s'élève à 13. The number of dead is 13.

**nombreux** *masc adjective*, **nombreuse** *fem*
**many**
de nombreuses personnes many people
Ils étaient nombreux. There were a lot of them.
Une famille nombreuse a big family

le **nombril** *masc noun*
**navel**

**nommer** *verb* [1]
1 **to name**
On l'a nommé Alex. They named him Alex.
2 **to appoint** (*to a job*)

**non** *adverb*
1 **no**
Elle a dit non. She said no.
2 non seulement not only
3 non loin de not far from
4 non plus neither
moi non plus me neither
5 (*with nouns, adjectives*) un non-fumeur a non-smoker
eau non potable water not suitable for drinking

**nord** *invariable adjective* ▷ see **nord** *noun*
1 **north**
le côté nord the north side
2 **northern**
la région nord the northern area

**WORD TIP** *nord* never changes.

le **nord** *masc noun* ▷ see **nord** *adj*
**north**
le nord de la France northern France
le vent du nord the north wind
Je suis du nord. I'm from the north.
J'habite dans le nord (de l'Ecosse). I live in the north (of Scotland).
La Belgique est au nord de la France. Belgium is to the north of France.

**nord-américain** *masc adjective*, **nord-américaine** *fem* ▷ see **Nord-américain** *noun*
**North American**

le **Nord-Américain** *masc noun*, la **Nord-Américaine** *fem* ▷ see **nord-américain** *adj*
**North American**

le **nord-est** *masc noun*
**north-east**
le nord-est de l'Angleterre north-east England

le **nord-ouest** *masc noun*
**north-west**
le nord-ouest du Pays de Galles north-west Wales

**normal** *masc adjective*, **normale** *fem*, **normaux** *masc pl*, **normales** *fem pl*
**normal**
un enfant normal a normal child
C'est normal. There's nothing unusual about it.

**normalement** *adverb*
1 **normally**
Normalement, je la vois tous les jours. Normally, I see her every day.
2 **according to plan**
Normalement, elle doît être à Newcastle. If things have gone according to plan, she should be in Newcastle.

**normand** *masc adjective*, **normande** *fem* ▷ see **Normand** *noun*
**of** *or* **from Normandy**
la côte normande the Normandy coast

**WORD TIP** Adjectives never have capitals in French, even for nationality or regional origin.

un **Normand** *masc noun*, une **Normande** *fem* ▷ see **normand** *adj*
**a person from Normandy**

la **Normandie** *fem noun*
**Normandy**
en Normandie in Normandy

**WORD TIP** Countries and regions in French take *le*, *la* or *les*.

la **Norvège** *fem noun*
**Norway**

**norvégien** *masc adjective*, **norvégienne** *fem* ▷ see **Norvégien** *noun*
**Norwegian**

un **Norvégien** *masc noun*, une **Norvégienne** *fem* ▷ see **norvégien** *adj*
**Norwegian**

✓ **nos** *plural masc & fem adjective*
**our**
nos amis français our French friends
nos idées our ideas

**WORD TIP** Use *nos* for *our* with plural French nouns. ▷ **notre**

le **notaire** *masc noun*
**lawyer**, **notary** (*dealing with property sales, wills, etc*)

**notamment** *adverb*
**especially**

✓ la **note** *fem noun*
1 **bill**
**La note, s'il vous plaît.** Can I have the bill please?
2 **mark**
**J'ai eu une bonne note en allemand.** I got a good mark in German.
3 **note**
**prendre des notes** to take notes

**noter** *verb* **[1]**
1 **to write down**
C'est bien noté? Have you got that?
2 **to notice** (*something unusual*)

la **notion** *fem noun*
**idea**
des notions basic knowledge
**J'ai des notions d'espagnol.** I have a basic knowledge of Spanish.

✓ **notre** *masc & fem adjective*, **nos** *pl*
**our**
notre professeur our teacher
notre voiture our car

**WORD TIP** Use *notre* for *our* with singular French nouns. ▷ **nos**

✓ le **nôtre** *masc pronoun*, la **nôtre** *fem*, les **nôtres** *pl*
**ours**
un pays comme le nôtre a country like ours
**Cette voiture, c'est la nôtre.** This car is ours.
**'Ces photos sont à vous?' — 'Oui, ce sont les nôtres.'** 'Are these photos yours?' — 'Yes, they're ours.'

**WORD TIP** The article and pronoun change in French when they refer to fem and plural nouns.

**nouer** *verb*
**to tie**
nouer ses cheveux to tie one's hair back

les **nouilles** *plural fem noun*
**noodles**

la **nourrice** *fem noun*
1 **childminder**
2 **babysitter**

**nourrir** *verb* **[2]**
nourrir de quelque chose to feed on something
bien nourri well-fed
mal nourri undernourished

la **nourriture** *fem noun*
**food**
la nourriture et la boisson food and drink

✓ **nous** *pronoun*
1 (*as the subject of the verb*) **we**
**Nous apprenons le français.** We're learning French.
**Nous allons au cinéma ce soir.** We're going to the cinema tonight. ▷ **on**
2 (*after prepositions like* **avec**, **contre** *and in comparisons*) **us**
**Viens avec nous.** Come with us.
**Ils sont plus âgés que nous.** They're older than us.
3 (*as a direct object*) **us**
**Elle nous aide.** She helps us.
**Elle nous a aidés.** She helped us.
4 (*as an indirect object*) **to us, us**
**Elle nous a parlé longtemps.** She spoke to us for a long time.
**Elle nous a donné son adresse.** She gave us her address.
**Elle nous achète des cadeaux.** She buys us presents.
5 **à nous** ours
**Ce sont des amis à nous.** They're friends of ours.
**La voiture n'est pas à nous.** The car is not ours.
6 (*with reflexive verbs*) **Nous nous levons à sept heures.** We get up at seven o'clock.
7 **for ourselves, ourselves**
**Nous nous ferons quelque chose à manger.** We'll make ourselves something to eat.
8 **chez nous** at our house

**nous-mêmes** *pronoun*
**ourselves**
**Nous l'avons fait nous-mêmes.** We did it ourselves.

French-English

**nouveau** *masc adjective*, **nouveaux** *masc pl*, **nouvel** *masc sing*, **nouvelle** *fem*, **nouvelles** *fem*
1 **new** (*new or different to the speaker*)
mon nouveau sac my new bag
mon nouvel appartement my new flat
2 à nouveau, de nouveau again
Elle l'a fait à nouveau. She did it again

**WORD TIP** Masculine *nouveau* becomes *nouvel* before a vowel or silent *h*.

la **nouveauté** *fem noun*
1 **novelty** (*something new*)
2 **new release** (*single, CD, etc*)

le **Nouvel An** *masc noun*
**New Year**
fêter le Nouvel An to celebrate New Year

une **nouvelle** *fem noun*
1 une nouvelle a piece of news
J'ai une bonne nouvelle! I've got good news!
2 **short story**
une nouvelle de Sagan a Sagan short story
3 les nouvelles the news (*on TV, radio*)
4 des nouvelles news
As-tu des nouvelles de lui? Have you any news of him?
Nous n'avons pas de nouvelles pour l'instant. We have no news for the moment.

la **Nouvelle-Zélande** *fem noun*
**New Zealand**

**WORD TIP** Countries and regions in French take *le, la* or *les*.

la **Nouvelle Calédonie** *fem noun*
**New Caledonia** (*French island territory in the Pacific*)

le **novembre** *masc noun*
**November**
en novembre, au mois de novembre in November

**WORD TIP** Months of the year and days of the week start with small letters in French.

**novembre**

Le 1er novembre, c'est la Toussaint, la fête des morts. Les Français ne travaillent pas. Beaucoup vont au cimetière en famille. Ils mettent des chrysanthèmes sur les tombes familiales.

le **noyau** *masc noun*, **noyaux** *pl*
1 **stone** (*in fruit*)
2 **nucleus** (*in an atom*)

le **noyer** *masc noun* ▷ see **noyer** *verb*
**walnut tree**

**noyer** *verb* [39] ▷ see **noyer** *noun*
**to drown**

se **noyer** *reflexive verb* Ⓔ
**to drown**
Il s'est noyé. He drowned.

**nu** *masc adjective*, **nue** *fem*
1 **naked**
2 **bare** (*feet, walls*)

le **nuage** *masc noun*
**cloud**

**nuageux** *masc adjective*, **nuageuse** *fem*
**cloudy**
un ciel nuageux a cloudy sky

**nucléaire** *masc & fem adjective*
**nuclear**
l'énergie nucléaire nuclear power
une centrale nucléaire a nuclear power station

**nuisible** *masc & fem adjective*
**harmful**

la **nuit** *fem noun*
1 **night**
cette nuit last night, tonight
dans la nuit in the night
toute la nuit all night
toutes les nuits every night
2 **dark**
Il fait nuit. It's getting dark.
La nuit tombe à sept heures. It gets dark at seven o'clock.

**nul** *masc adjective*, **nulle** *fem*
1 (*informal*) **awful**
Le film était nul. The film was awful.
Je suis nul en histoire. I'm hopeless at history.
2 (*Sport*) un match nul a draw

**nulle part** *adverb*
**nowhere**
Je ne trouve nulle part mon portable. I can't find my mobile anywhere.

le **numéro** *masc noun*
**number**
Ils habitent au numéro cinq. They live at number five.

le **nu-pied** *masc noun*
**open sandal**

**nutritif** *masc adjective*, **nutritive** *fem*
**nutritious**
valeur nutritive nutritional value

le **nylon** *masc noun*
**nylon**

# O o

une **oasis** *invariable fem noun*
**oasis**

**obéir** *verb* [2]
**Manon, tu dois obéir.** Manon, you must do as you're told.
**obéir à quelqu'un** to obey somebody

**obéissant** *masc adjective*, **obéissante** *fem adj*
**obedient**

un **objectif** *masc noun*
**objective**

une **objection** *fem noun*
**objection**

un **objet** *masc noun*
1 **object**
**un objet volant non identifié** an unidentified flying object
2 **subject** (*of a debate, criticism, inquiry*)
• les **objets trouvés**
**lost property**

**obligatoire** *masc & fem adjective*
**compulsory**

**obligé** *masc adjective*, **obligée** *fem*
**être obligé de faire quelque chose** to have to do something
**Léa est obligée de rester.** Léa must stay.

**obliger** *verb* [52]
**obliger quelqu'un à faire quelque chose** to force somebody to do something
**La grève m'a obligé à rester chez moi.** The strike forced me to stay at home.

**obscur** *masc adjective*, **obscure** *fem*
**dark**
**une pièce obscure** a dark room

l'**obscurité** *fem noun*
**darkness**
**dans l'obscurité** in the dark
**Il a peur de l'obscurité.** He's afraid of the dark.

**obséder** *verb* [24]
**to obsess**
**être obsédé par quelque chose** to be obsessed by something
**Elle est obsédée par son travail.** She's obsessed by her work.

les **obsèques** *plural fem noun*
**funeral**

une **observation** *fem noun*
**comment**
**faire des observations sur quelque chose** to make comments on something
**Ils ont fait des observations sur mon exposé.** They made comments on my talk.

**observer** *verb* [1]
1 **to watch**
**Elle nous observait de loin.** She was watching us from a distance.
2 **to observe** (*rules*)
**observer le règlement de l'école** to observe the school rules

une **obsession** *fem noun*
**obsession**

un **obstacle** *masc noun*
**obstacle**

**obstiné** *masc adjective*, **obstinée** *fem*
**stubborn**

**obtenir** *verb* [77]
**to get**

**occasionner** *verb* [1]
**to cause** (*an accident*)

l'**occident** *masc noun*
**l'Occident** the West (*Europe & America, etc*)

**occidental** *masc adjective*, **occidentale** *fem*, **occidentaux** *masc pl*, **occidentales** *fem pl*
**western**

une **occupation** *fem noun*
1 **occupation**
**Mon occupation préférée c'est la causette.** My favourite occupation is chatting on the Internet.
2 **l'Occupation** the Occupation (*France 1940-1944*)

**occupé** *masc adjective*, **occupée** *fem*
1 **busy**
**Elle est occupée en ce moment.** She's busy at the moment.
2 **engaged** (*telephones, toilets*)
**Ça sonne occupé.** It's engaged.
3 **taken**
**Cette place est occupée.** This seat is taken.
4 **occupied** (*by an army*)

**occuper** *verb* [1]
1 **to take up**
**L'armoire occupe trop de place.** The wardrobe takes up too much room.
2 **to occupy**
**Les grévistes occupent les locaux.** The strikers are occupying the premises. ▸▸

Il occupe la troisième place du classement. He's third in the ranking.

3 **to keep busy**
Ses maquettes d'avion l'occupent tout le week-end. His model aeroplanes keep him busy all weekend.

s'**occuper** *reflexive verb* Ⓔ
1 s'occuper de quelque chose to deal with something, to see to something
Je vais m'occuper du dîner. I'll go and see to dinner.
Je m'en occupe. I'll see to it.
2 s'occuper de quelqu'un to look after somebody
Ce soir, je m'occupe de ma petite sœur. The evening I am looking after my little sister.
Est-ce qu'on s'occupe de vous? Are you being served? (*in shops*)

un **océan** *masc noun*
**ocean**
• l'**océan Atlantique** the Atlantic Ocean
• l'**océan Pacifique** the Pacific Ocean

un **octet** *masc noun*
(*Computers*) **byte**

**octobre** *masc noun*
**October**
en octobre, au mois d'octobre in October

**WORD TIP** Months of the year and days of the week start with small letters in French.

un & une **oculiste** *masc & fem noun*
**eye specialist**

une **odeur** *fem noun*
1 **smell**
une bonne odeur a nice smell
des odeurs de cuisine cooking smells
2 **scent** (*of flowers, etc*)

♪ un **œil** *masc noun*, les **yeux** *plural*
**eye**
Il a les yeux bleus. He has blue eyes.

♪ un **œuf** *masc noun*
**egg**
un œuf à la coque a boiled egg
un œuf dur a hard-boiled egg
un œuf mollet a soft-boiled egg
un œuf sur le plat a fried egg
des œufs brouillés scrambled eggs
une œuf de Pâques Easter egg

une **œuvre** *fem noun*
**work**
les œuvres complètes de Flaubert the complete works of Flaubert
• une **œuvre d'art** a work of art

**offenser** *verb* [1]
**to offend**

s'**offenser** *reflexive verb* Ⓔ
**to take offence**

♪ un **office** *masc noun*
1 **office**
2 un office religieux a religious service
• l'**office du tourisme** tourist information office

**officiel** *masc adjective*, **officielle** *fem*
**official**

un **officier** *masc noun*
**officer**

une **offre** *fem noun*
1 **offer**
2 'Offres d'emploi' 'Situations Vacant' (*in the small ads*)

**offrir** *verb* [56]
1 **to offer**
offrir quelque chose à quelqu'un to offer somebody something
Il nous a offert à boire. He offered us a drink.
Elle a offert de nous aider. She offered to help us.
2 **to give**
Elle m'a offert une montre. She gave me a watch.
3 **to buy**
Je t'offre un DVD. I'll buy you a DVD.

s'**offrir** *reflexive verb* Ⓔ
s'offrir quelque chose to treat yourself to something
Je vais m'offrir un nouveau jeu électronique. I'm going to treat myself to a new computer game.

une **oie** *fem noun*
**goose**

♪ un **oignon** *masc noun*
1 **onion**
une soupe à l'oignon an onion soup
2 **bulb**
un oignon de tulipe a tulip bulb

♪ un **oiseau** *masc noun*, les **oiseaux** *plural*
**bird**
• un **oiseau de proie** bird of prey

une **olive** *fem noun*
**olive**
l'huile d'olive olive oil

un **olivier** *masc noun*
**olive tree**

**olympique** *masc & fem adjective*
**Olympic**



Ⓔ means the verb takes être to form the perfect

**ombragé** *masc adjective*, **ombragée** *fem*
**shaded** (*from the sun*)

une **ombre** *fem noun*
1 **shade**
à l'ombre in the shade
2 **shadow**
• une **ombre à paupières** eyeshadow

une **ombrelle** *fem noun*
**sun umbrella**

une **omelette** *fem noun*
**omelette**
une omelette aux champignons a mushroom omelette

**omettre** *verb* **[11]**
**to omit, to leave out**
**Il n'omet aucun détail.** He leaves nothing out.
**omettre de faire quelque chose** to fail to do something
**Elle a omis de saluer la directrice.** She failed to greet the headmistress.

**on** *pronoun*
1 **we** (*more informal than* ***nous***)
**On va au cinéma.** We're going to the cinema.
2 **you**
**De la terrasse, on voit la mer.** From the terrace you can see the sea.
3 (*when you don't say exactly who*) **On t'appelle.** Someone's calling you.
**On m'a dit que ...** I've been told that ...
**On a volé leur voiture.** Their car's been stolen.
**En France, on aime beaucoup le fromage.** In France people love cheese.

♪ un **oncle** *masc noun*
**uncle**
**Oncle Didier est prof de tennis.** Uncle Didier is a tennis coach.

une **onde** *fem noun*
**radio wave**

une **ondée** *fem noun*
**shower** (*of rain*)

un **ongle** *masc noun*
**nail**
se faire les ongles to do your nails
**Je me suis coupé les ongles.** I've cut my nails.
• un **ongle de pied** toenail

l'**ONU** *noun fem*
(*= Organisation des Nations unies*) **UN, United Nations**

**onze** *number*
**eleven**
**Mélanie a onze ans.** Mélanie is eleven.
le onze mai the eleventh of May

**WORD TIP** Use the definite article *le* in front of *onze*, rather than *l'*.

**onzième** *masc & fem adjective*
**eleventh**
au onzième étage on the eleventh floor
la onzième fois the eleventh time

un **opéra** *masc noun*
**opera**

un **opérateur** *masc noun*, une **opératrice** *fem*
**operator**

une **opération** *fem noun*
1 **operation**
2 **calculation** (*in maths*)

**opérer** *verb* **[24]**
**to operate on**
opérer quelqu'un to operate on somebody
**On l'a opéré d'un cancer à la gorge.** He was operated on for throat cancer.
se faire opérer to have an operation
**Il s'est fait opéré du foie.** He's had a liver operation.

♪ une **opinion** *fem noun*
**opinion**

**opposé** *masc adjective*, **opposée** *fem*
1 **opposite**
dans le sens opposé in the opposite direction
2 **opposed**
être opposé à quelque chose to be opposed to something
**Nous sommes opposés à cette idée.** We are opposed to this idea.

**opposer** *verb* **[1]**
**Le match de samedi oppose les Anglais et les Français.** The Saturday match brings the English and the French head to head.

s'**opposer** *reflexive verb* ⓔ
s'opposer à quelque chose to oppose something
**Ils s'opposent à tous les changements.** They oppose all the changes.

une **opposition** *fem noun*
**opposition**

**opter** *verb* **[1]**
**to opt**

un **opticien** *masc noun*, une **opticienne** *fem*
**optician**
Elle est opticienne. She's an optician.

**optimiste** *masc & fem adjective*
**optimistic**
de façon optimiste optimistically

une **option** *fem noun*
**option**
Elle a pris l'option informatique pour son examen. She took computing as an optional subject for her exam.

l'**or** *masc noun* ▷ see **or** *conj*
**gold**
une montre en or a gold watch
des cheveux d'or golden hair
une occasion en or a golden opportunity

**or** *conjunction* ▷ see **or** *noun*
**and yet**
Tu m'as dit que tu étais là or personne ne t'a vu. You told me you were there, and yet nobody saw you.

un **orage** *masc noun*
**storm**, **thunderstorm**

**orageux** *masc adjective*, **orageuse** *fem*
**stormy**

**oral** *masc adjective*, **orale** *fem*, **oraux** *masc pl*, **orales** *fem pl* ▷ see **oral** *noun*
1 **oral**
une épreuve orale an oral exam
2 administrer par voie orale to be taken orally (*medicine*)

un **oral** *masc noun*, les **oraux** *plural* ▷ see **oral** *adj*
**oral (exam)**
l'oral de français the French oral
- un **oral de rattrapage** a resit oral (*taken when a written exam is failed*)

**orange** *invariable masc & fem adjective* ▷ see **orange** *noun*
**orange**
des cubes orange orange cubes

**WORD TIP** *orange* never changes.

une **orange** *fem noun* ▷ see **orange** *adj*
**orange**
- une **orange givrée** orange sorbet
- une **orange pressée** freshly squeezed orange juice

un **orchestre** *masc noun*
1 **orchestra**
un orchestre de chambre a chamber orchestra
2 **band**
un orchestre de jazz a jazz band

**ordinaire** *masc & fem adjective* ▷ see **ordinaire** *noun*
1 **ordinary**
une journée ordinaire an ordinary day
un repas ordinaire an average meal
2 **usual**
sa gentillesse ordinaire her usual kindness

l'**ordinaire** *masc noun* ▷ see **ordinaire** *adj*
sortir de l'ordinaire to be out of the ordinary
Ce film sort de l'ordinaire. This film is out of the ordinary.

un **ordinateur** *masc noun*
**computer**

une **ordonnance** *fem noun*
**prescription**

**ordonné** *masc adjective*, **ordonnée** *fem*
**tidy**

**ordonner** *verb* [1]
**to order**
ordonner à quelqu'un de faire quelque chose to order somebody to do something
Le prof nous a ordonné de nous taire. The teacher ordered us to keep quiet.

un **ordre** *masc noun*
1 **order**, **command**
2 **order**
par ordre alphabétique in alphabetical order
mettre de l'ordre to tidy up
Je dois mettre de l'ordre dans mon atelier. I must tidy up my workshop.

les **ordures** *plural fem noun*
**rubbish**
les ordures ménagères household rubbish
mettre quelque chose aux ordures to put something in the bin

une **oreille** *fem noun*
**ear**

un **oreiller** *masc noun*
**pillow**

les **oreillons** *plural masc noun*
**mumps**

un **organe** *masc noun*
**organ** (*of the body*)

**organique** *masc & fem adjective*
**organic**

un **organisateur** *masc noun*, une **organisatrice** *fem*
**organizer**

une **organisation** *fem noun*
**organization**

**organiser** *verb* [1]
**to organize**

s'**organiser** *reflexive verb* Ⓔ
**to get organized**

un & une **organiste** *masc & fem noun*
**organist**

l'**orge** *fem noun*
**barley**

un **orgue** *masc noun*
**organ**
**Il joue de l'orgue.** He plays the organ.

**orgueilleux** *masc adjective*, **orgueilleuse** *fem*
**proud**

l'**Orient** *masc noun*
**l'Orient** the East (*Asia, etc*)

**oriental** *masc adjective*, **orientale** *fem*, **orientaux** *masc pl*, **orientales** *fem pl*
1 **eastern**
**la côte orientale** the eastern coast
2 **oriental**
**les langues orientales** oriental languages

l'**orientation** *fem noun*
1 **le sens de l'orientation** a good sense of direction
2 **l'orientation professionnelle** careers advice (*for students*)
3 **orienteering** (*the sport*)

s'**orienter** *reflexive verb* Ⓔ [1]
1 **to get one's bearings**
2 **s'orienter vers quelque chose** to turn towards something
**Mathis s'oriente vers les langues.** Mathis is going in for languages.

**originaire** *masc & fem adjective*
**native**
**Elle est originaire d'Afrique.** She's from Africa.
**Gabriel est originaire de La Baule.** Gabriel comes from La Baule.

**original** *masc adjective*, **originale** *fem*, **originaux** *masc pl*, **originales** *fem pl*
**original**
**Le film est en version originale.** The film is in its foreign language version.

l'**origine** *fem noun*
1 **origin**
**Elle est d'origine écossaise.** She's Scottish.
2 **à l'origine** originally

un **orphelin** *masc noun*, une **orpheline** *fem*
**orphan**

un **orphelinat** *masc noun*
**orphanage**

un **orteil** *masc noun*
**toe**
**le gros orteil** the big toe

l'**orthographe** *fem noun*
**spelling**

un **os** *masc noun*
**bone**

**oser** *verb* [1]
**to dare**
**Je n'ose pas y aller.** I daren't go there.

un **otage** *masc noun*
**hostage**
**être pris en otage** to be taken hostage
**Les journalistes ont été pris en otage.** The journalists were taken hostage.

**ôter** *verb* [1]
**to take off**
**Je vais ôter ma veste.** I'll take off my jacket.
**Ôte tes pieds du canapé!** Take your feet off the sofa!

une **otite** *fem noun*
**earache**

♪ **ou** *conjunction*
1 **or**
**Veux-tu une glace ou un fruit?** Would you like an ice cream or fruit?
**Tu viens ou pas?** Are you coming or not?
2 **ou ... ou ...** either ... or ...
**Il est ou dans ma chambre ou dans le salon.** It's either in my bedroom or in the sitting-room.
3 **ou bien** or else
**On peut se retrouver au cinéma ou bien chez moi.** We can meet at the cinema or else at my place.

♪ **où** *adverb, pronoun*
1 **where**
**Où es-tu?** Where are you?
**Où vont-ils?** Where are they going?
**Ton frère habite où?** Where does your brother live?
**le quartier où elle habite** the area where she lives
**la ville d'où il vient** the town he comes from ⏩

Par où tu passes pour aller au lycée? Which way do you go to school?

2 **when, that**
le jour où je suis arrivé the day I arrived
Il est à l'âge où il peut sortir avec ses copains. He's at the age when he can go out with his friends.

l'**ouate** *fem noun*
**cotton wool**

**oublier** *verb* [1]
1 **to forget**
Elle oublie souvent d'éteindre la lumière. She often forgets to turn off the light.
2 **to leave**
Il a oublié ses clefs chez Jérôme. He's left his keys at Jérôme's.

**ouest** *invariable adjective* ▷ see **ouest** *noun*
1 **west**
la côte ouest the west coast
2 **western**
la frontière ouest the western border

**WORD TIP** *ouest* never changes.

l'**ouest** *masc noun* ▷ see **ouest** *adj*
**west**
un vent d'ouest a westerly wind
Versailles est à l'ouest de Paris. Versailles is west of Paris.
La Bretagne se situe dans l'ouest de la France. Brittany is in the west of France.
l'Ouest the West
J'habite dans l'Ouest. I live in the West.
l'Europe de l'Ouest Western Europe

**ouf** *exclamation*
**phew!**

**oui** *adverb*
**yes**
Il a dit oui. He said yes.
'Est-ce qu'elle vient?' — 'Je crois que oui.' 'Is she coming?' — 'I think so.'

un **ouragan** *masc noun*
**hurricane**

un **ours** *masc noun*
**bear**

**ours**

Il y a des ours bruns dans les Pyrénées mais ils sont rares.

un **outil** *masc noun*
**tool**

**outré** *masc adjective*, **outrée** *fem*
**outraged**

**outre-Manche** *adverb*
**on the other side of the Channel, in Britain**

**outre-mer** *adverb*
**overseas**

**ouvert** *masc adjective*, **ouverte** *fem*
1 **open**
Laisse la fenêtre ouverte. Leave the window open.
'Ouvert le dimanche' 'Open on Sundays'
2 **on**
Elle a laissé le robinet ouvert. She left the tap on.

une **ouverture** *fem noun*
**opening**
les heures d'ouverture opening hours
l'ouverture d'un nouveau supermarché the opening of a new supermarket

un **ouvre-boîtes** *invariable masc noun*
**tin-opener**

un **ouvre-bouteilles** *invariable masc noun*
**bottle-opener**

un **ouvrier** *masc noun*, une **ouvrière** *fem*
**worker**

**ouvrir** *verb* [30]
1 **to open**
Elle a ouvert la porte. She opened the door.
Ouvre vite la lettre! Open your letter quick!
2 **to turn on**
Jessica ouvre le robinet. Jessica is turning the tap on.

s'**ouvrir** *reflexive verb* ⓔ
Ça s'ouvre comment? How do you open it?
Sa valise s'est ouverte dans l'aéroport. His case came open in the airport.

**ovale** *adjective*
**oval**

une **overdose** *fem noun*
**overdose**
une overdose d'héroïne an overdose of heroine

un **ovni** *noun masc*
(= *objet volant non identifié*) **UFO, unidentified flying object**

l'**oxygène** *masc noun*
**oxygen**

l'**ozone** *fem noun*
**ozone**



ⓔ means the verb takes être to form the perfect

# P p

le **Pacifique** *masc noun*
le Pacifique the Pacific

♪ la **page** *fem noun*
**page**
à la première page on the first page
- la **page d'accueil** home page
- la **page Web** web page

la **paie** *fem noun*
**pay, wages**

le **paiement** *masc noun*
**payment**

la **paille** *fem noun*
**straw**

♪ le **pain** *masc noun*
1 **bread**
du pain frais newly baked bread
une tranche de pain a slice of bread
2 un pain a loaf of bread
un petit pain a roll
- le **pain au chocolat** pastry with chocolate chips
- le **pain complet** wholemeal bread
- le **pain grillé** toast
- le **pain de mie** sandwich loaf
- le **pain de seigle** rye bread

**pair** *masc adjective*, **paire** *fem*
▷ see **pair** *noun*
**even** (*number*)

le **pair** *masc noun* ▷ see **pair** *adj*
au pair au pair
une jeune fille au pair an au pair girl

la **paire** *fem noun*
**pair**
une paire de chaussures a pair of shoes

la **paix** *fem noun*
**peace**
faire la paix avec quelqu'un to make peace with somebody
Elle veut faire la paix avec son voisin. She wants to make peace with her neighbour.

la **Pakistan** *fem noun*
**Pakistan**

**pakistanais** *masc adjective*, **pakistanaise** *fem*
▷ see **Pakistanais** *noun*
**Pakistani**

un **Pakistanais** *masc noun*, une **Pakistanaise** *fem noun*
▷ see **pakistanais** *adj*
**Pakistani**

le **palais** *masc noun*
**palace**
- le **palais de justice** law courts
- le **palais des sports** stadium

♪ **pâle** *masc & fem adjective*
**pale**
le bleu pâle pale blue

la **Palestine** *fem noun*
**Palestine**

le **palier** *masc noun*
**landing** (*on a staircase*)

**pâlir** *verb* **[2]**
1 **to turn pale**
2 **to fade**

la **palme** *fem noun*
**flipper** (*for swimming*)

le **palmier** *masc noun*
**palm tree**

**palpitant** *masc adjective*, **palpitante** *fem*
**thrilling**
une aventure palpitante a thrilling adventure

le **pamplemousse** *masc noun*
**grapefruit**

le **panaché** *masc noun*
**shandy**

la **pancarte** *fem noun*
1 **notice, sign**
2 **placard**

**pané** *masc adjective*, **panée** *fem*
**coated in breadcrumbs**
une escalope panée an escalope coated in breadcrumbs

♪ le **panier** *masc noun*
1 **basket**
2 **basket** (*in basketball*)
Éva a marqué un panier. Éva scored a basket.
- le **panier à linge** linen basket

la **panique** *fem noun*
**panic**
Pas de panique! Don't panic!

**paniquer** *verb* **[1]**
**to panic**

♪ la **panne** *fem noun*
**breakdown** (*of cars, machines*)
être en panne d'essence to run out of petrol
La voiture est en panne. The car's ▸▸

French-English

broken down.
**Je suis tombé en panne dans l'embouteillage.** I broke down in the traffic jam.
- la **panne de courant** power cut

le **panneau** *masc noun*, les **panneaux** *plural*
**sign**
- le **panneau d'affichage** notice board
- le **panneau publicitaire** billboard
- le **panneau solaire** solar panel

le **panorama** *masc noun*
**view, panorama**

le **pansement** *masc noun*
1 **plaster** (*for a cut*)
2 **dressing** (*for a wound*)

le **pantalon** *masc noun*
**trousers**
**un pantalon neuf** a new pair of trousers
**Où est mon pantalon?** Where are my trousers?
**deux pantalons** two pairs of trousers
**un pantalon en velours côtelé** a pair of cords

la **panthère** *fem noun*
**panther**

la **pantoufle** *fem noun*
**slipper**

le **paon** *masc noun*
**peacock**

le **papa** *masc noun*
**Dad, Daddy**

la **papaye** *fem noun*
**pawpaw**

le **pape** *masc noun*
**pope**

la **papeterie** *fem noun*
**stationer's shop**

le **papi** *masc noun*
**grandpa, granddad**

le **papier** *masc noun*
1 **paper**
**une feuille de papier** a sheet of paper
2 **les papiers** identity papers
**Vos papiers, s'il vous plaît!** Your identity papers, please!
- le **papier à lettres** writing paper
- le **papier cadeau** wrapping paper
- le **papier hygiénique** toilet paper
- le **papier peint** wallpaper
- les **papiers d'identité** identity papers

le **papillon** *masc noun*
**butterfly**

le **paquebot** *masc noun*
**liner**

**Pâques** *masc noun*
**Easter**
**à Pâques** at Easter
**un œuf de Pâques** an Easter egg
**le lundi de Pâques** Easter Monday

le **paquet** *masc noun*
1 **packet**
**un paquet de sucre** a packet of sugar
2 **parcel**
3 **bundle** (*of clothes, papers*)

le **paquet-cadeau** *masc noun*, les **paquets-cadeaux** *plural*
**gift-wrapped present**

**par** *preposition*
1 (*saying how*) **by**
**passer par Rennes** to go by Rennes
**payer par chèque** to pay by cheque
**envoyer quelque chose par la poste** to send something by post
**Entre par le garage!** Come in through the garage!
2 (*giving reasons for*) **par ennui** out of boredom
**par vengeance** out of revenge
3 (*saying where*) **par endroits** in places
**Il a jeté quelque chose par la fenêtre.** He threw something out of the window.
4 (*saying how many*) **50 euros par personne** 50 euros per person
**deux fois par semaine** twice a week
**deux par deux** two by two
5 (*in expressions*) **par accident** by accident
**par hasard** by chance
6 **par contre** on the other hand

le **parachute** *masc noun*
**parachute**

le & la **parachutiste** *masc & fem noun*
**parachutist**

le **paradis** *masc noun*
**heaven**

le **paragraphe** *masc noun*
**paragraph**

**paraître** *verb* **[57]**
1 **to seem**
**Il paraît qu'il est parti.** It seems that he's gone.
2 **to appear**
**paraître en public** to appear in public
3 **to come out** (*to be published*)
**Le roman va paraître en juin.** The novel is coming out in June.
4 **paraît-il** apparently
**Elle est à Nice, paraît-il.** She's in Nice, apparently.



Ⓔ means the verb takes être to form the perfect

**parallèle** *masc & fem adjective*
**parallel**
La rue Balzac est parallèle à la rue Renoir. Rue Balzac is parallel to rue Renoir.

**paralysé** *masc adjective*, **paralysée** *fem*
**paralyzed**
Il est paralysé des jambes. He's paralyzed in both legs.

le **parapente** *masc noun*
1 **paraglider**
2 **paragliding**
faire du parapente to go paragliding

♪ le **parapluie** *masc noun*
**umbrella**

le **parasol** *masc noun*
**parasol**

le **parc** *masc noun*
1 **park**
Je vais au parc. I'm going to the park.
2 **grounds** (*of a large house, a château*)
• le **parc d'attractions** amusement park

♪ **parce que** *conjunction*
**because**
Elle ne vient pas parce qu'elle est malade. She isn't coming because she's ill.

**par-ci** *adverb*
par-ci par-là here and there

le **parcmètre** *masc noun*
**parking meter**

**parcourir** *verb* [29]
**to travel around**
J'ai parcouru l'Europe. I travelled around Europe.

le **parcours** *masc noun*
1 **route** (*of a bus, a traveller*)
2 **course** (*of a race*)

**par-dessous** *adverb*
**underneath**
La barrière est trop haute, je passe par-dessous. The fence is too high, I'm going underneath.

**par-dessus** *adverb, preposition*
▷ see **pardessus** *noun*
1 **on top**
une couverture et un édredon par-dessus a blanket and an eiderdown on top
2 **over**
Il a sauté par-dessus. He jumped over it.
Elle a sauté par-dessus le ruisseau. She jumped over the stream.

♪ le **pardessus** *masc noun* ▷ see **par-dessus** *adv, prep*
**overcoat**

♪ le **pardon** *masc noun*
1 **sorry** (*apologizing*)
Pardon! Sorry!
2 **sorry**, **excuse me** (*asking for something*)
Pardon monsieur, pouvez-vous me dire où se trouve le cinéma? Excuse me, could you tell me where the cinema is?

**pardonner** *verb* [1]
1 (*interrupting politely*) Pardonnez-moi, mais ... Excuse me, but ...
2 **to forgive**
Je ne lui pardonnerai jamais son erreur. I'll never forgive him for his mistake.

**pare-balles** *masc & fem adjective*
**bullet-proof**
un gilet pare-balles a bullet-proof vest

le **pare-brise** *invariable masc noun*
**windscreen**

le **pare-chocs** *invariable masc noun*
**bumper** (*on a car*)

**pareil** *masc adjective*, **pareille** *fem*
1 **the same**
C'est toujours pareil. It's always the same.
Nos chaussures sont presque pareilles. Our shoes are almost the same.
2 **such**
Je n'ai jamais dit une chose pareille. I never said any such thing.

♪ le **parent** *masc noun*
1 **parent**
mes parents my parents
2 **relation**
mes parents et amis my friends and relations

la **parenthèse** *fem noun*
**bracket**
entre parenthèses in brackets

la **paresse** *fem noun*
**laziness**

♪ **paresseux** *masc adjective*, **paresseuse** *fem*
**lazy**

**parfait** *masc adjective*, **parfaite** *fem*
**perfect**

**parfaitement** *adverb*
**perfectly**
Tu le sais parfaitement! You know that perfectly well!

♪ **parfois** *adverb*
**sometimes**

♪ le **parfum** *masc noun*
1 **perfume, scent**
**Elle porte du parfum.** She's wearing perfume.
2 **flavour**
**Pour la glace, quel parfum veux-tu?** What flavour ice cream would you like?

**parfumé** *masc adjective*, **parfumée** *fem*
1 **flavoured**
**parfumé au citron** a lemon-flavoured
2 **fragrant**
3 **scented**

la **parfumerie** *fem noun*
**perfume shop**

le **pari** *masc noun*
**bet**
**faire un pari** to make a bet

**parier** *verb* [1]
**to bet**
**Je te parie 5 euros que les bleus gagneront.** I bet you 5 euros the French team will win.
**Je te parie qu'il ne viendra pas.** I bet you he won't come.

**parisien** *masc adjective*, **parisienne** *fem*
▷ see **Parisien** *noun*
**Parisian, Paris**
**la vie parisienne** Parisian life
**un restaurant parisien** a Paris restaurant

le **Parisien** *masc noun*, la **Parisienne** *fem*
▷ see **parisien** *adj*
**Parisian**

♪ le **parking** *masc noun*
**car park**

le **Parlement** *masc noun*
**Parliament**
**le Parlement européen** the European Parliament

♪ **parler** *verb* [1]
1 **to speak**
**parler (le) français** to speak French
**Jules parle avec Juliette.** Jules is speaking to Juliette.
**parler à quelqu'un** to speak to somebody, to talk to somebody
**Elle parle à mon prof de maths.** She's talking to my maths teacher.
**parler de quelque chose, quelqu'un** to talk about something, somebody
**Parle-moi de tes vacances!** Tell me about your holidays!
**Grégoire parle beaucoup de toi.** Grégoire talks a lot about you.
**Je dois te parler de ton frère.** I must talk to you about your brother.
2 **to speak, to talk**
**parler en italien** to speak in Italian
**Il parle très vite.** He talks very fast.
3 **parler de quelque chose** to be about something (*books, films, articles*)

se **parler** *reflexive verb* Ⓔ
**to talk to each other**
**Ils se parlent.** They are talking to each other.
**Ils ne se parlent plus.** They aren't on speaking terms any more.

♪ **parmi** *preposition*
**among**
**parmi les élèves** among the pupils
**Je dois choisir parmi tous ces CD.** I must choose from all those CDs.

la **parole** *fem noun*
1 **word**
**Il n'a pas dit une parole.** He didn't say a word.
2 **promise**
**Elle viendra, elle m'a donné sa parole.** She'll come, she promised.
**Elle a tenu sa parole, elle est venue.** She kept her word, she's come.
3 **les paroles** the lyrics (*of a song*)
4 (*the opportunity to speak*) **prendre la parole** to speak
**C'est à toi de prendre la parole.** It's your turn to speak.

le **parquet** *masc noun*
**wooden floor**

le **parrain** *masc noun*
1 **godfather**
2 **sponsor** (*of a project, a candidate, a child*)

**parrainer** *verb* [1]
**to sponsor**
**Nous parrainons un enfant d'un orphelinat étranger.** We sponsor a child in a foreign orphanage.

**parsemer** *verb* [50]
**to sprinkle**

la **part** *fem noun*
1 **share**
**Il a payé sa part.** He paid his share.
**Elle a fait sa part du travail.** She did her share of the work.
**faire part de quelque chose à quelqu'un** to tell somebody about something
**Elle m'a fait part de ses projets.** She told me about her plans.
2 **portion** (*of pie, pizza*)
3 **side**
**de toutes parts** from all sides

4 **de la part de quelqu'un** for somebody, on somebody's behalf
**Dis-lui bonjour de ma part!** Say hello to him for me!
**C'est de la part de qui?** Who's calling?

**partager** *verb* **[52]**
1 **to share** (*belongings, food, ideas*)
**Elle partage ses magazines avec Camille.** She shares her magazines with Camille.
2 **to divide**
**Je partage mon temps entre l'école et le sport.** I divide my time between school and football.

le & la **partenaire** *masc & fem noun*
**partner**

le **parterre** *masc noun*
**flower bed**

le **parti** *masc noun*
**party** (*in politics*)
**le parti communiste** the communist party

la **participation** *fem noun*
**participation**

le **participe** *masc noun*
(*Grammar*) **participle**
**le participe passé** the past participle
**le participe présent** the present participle

**participer** *verb* **[1]**
1 **to participate**, **to take part**
**Nous participons à la manifestation.** We're taking part in the demonstration.
2 **participer à quelque chose** to contribute to something

**particulier** *masc adjective*, **particulière** *fem*
1 **private**
**une voiture particulière** a private car
**en particulier** in private
2 **special**
**un signe particulier** a special feature
**en particulier** especially
**Il aime tous les sports, en particulier le foot.** He likes all sports, especially football.
3 **particular**, **specific**

**particulièrement** *adverb*
**especially**

la **partie** *fem noun*
1 **part**
**la première partie** the first part
**les parties du corps** the parts of the body
2 **en partie** partly
**C'est en partie de ta faute.** It's partly your fault.
3 **faire partie de quelque chose** to be part of something
**Anne-Laure fait partie de la famille.** Anne-Laure's one of the family.
4 **game**
**Tu as gagné la partie.** You've won the game.

♪ **partir** *verb* **Ⓔ [58]**
1 **to leave**, **to go**
**Manon part.** Manon is leaving.
**Elle est partie en Italie.** She's gone to Italy.
**Nous partons en vacances.** We're going away on holiday.
2 **to start**
**Le chemin part de l'église.** The path starts at the church.
**Je suis parti à huit heures.** I started out at eight o'clock.
3 **to come out**, **to come off**
**La tache ne part pas.** The stain's not coming out.
**L'étiquette est partie.** The label's come off.
4 **à partir de** from
**à partir de lundi** from Monday onwards
**à partir d'ici** from here onwards

la **partition** *fem noun*
**score** (*in music*)

♪ **partout** *adverb*
1 **everywhere**
**J'ai cherché partout.** I've looked everywhere.
**Ça se trouve un peu partout.** You can find it almost anywhere.
2 (*Sport*) **trois buts partout** three goals all

**parvenir** *verb* **Ⓔ [81]**
1 **parvenir à** to reach
**Ma lettre lui est parvenue.** My letter's reached him.
2 **parvenir à faire quelque chose** to manage to do something
**Il est parvenu à ouvrir la porte.** He managed to open the door.

♪ **pas** *adverb* ▷ **see pas** *noun*
1 (*with* **ne** *to make verbs negative*) **not**
**Je ne suis pas grande.** I am not tall.
**Je n'ai pas de stylo.** I don't have a pen.
**Il n'y a pas de café.** There isn't any coffee.
**Ils n'ont pas le téléphone.** They're not on the phone.
2 (*without* **ne**) **not**
**C'est lui qui paie, pas moi.** He's paying, not me.
**Tu viens ou pas?** Are you coming or not?
**une radio pas chère** a cheap radio
3 (*in expressions*) **pas du tout** not at all
**pas mal** not bad
**Pas de chance!** Bad luck!

le **pas** *masc noun* ▷ see **pas** *adv*
1 **step** (*in walking*)
2 **footprint**
3 **footstep**

**passable** *masc & fem adjective*
1 **quite good**
'Comment était le film?' — 'Passable.'
'How was the film?' — 'Quite good.'
2 **fair** (*as a mark at school*)

le **passage** *masc noun*
1 **traffic**
2 **crossing**
le passage en ferry the ferry crossing
'Passage interdit' 'No through traffic'
3 **way**
Je peux te prendre au passage. I can pick you up on my way.
Dégagez le passage! Clear the way!
4 **passage** (*in a book*)
- le **passage à niveau** level crossing
- le **passage pour piétons** pedestrian crossing
- le **passage protégé** pedestrian crossing
- le **passage souterrain** subway (*under a road*)

**passager** *masc adjective*, **passagère** *fem*
▷ see **passager** *noun*
**temporary**

le **passager** *masc noun*, la **passagère** *fem*
▷ see **passager** *adj*
**passenger**

le **passant** *masc noun*, la **passante** *fem*
**passer-by**

**passé** *masc adjective*, **passée** *fem*
▷ see **passé** *noun*
**past**
l'an passé last year
Il est dix heures passées. It's past ten o'clock.

le **passé** *masc noun* ▷ see **passé** *adj*
1 **past**
2 (*Grammar*) **past tense**
Mets cette phrase au passé. Put this sentence into the past tense.
- le **passé composé** present perfect
- le **passé simple** past historic

le **passe-partout** *invariable masc noun*
**master key**

♂ le **passeport** *masc noun*
**passport**
Je dois renouveler mon passeport. I must renew my passport.

♂ **passer** *verb* [1]
1 Ⓔ **to pass, to get through**
On ne peut pas passer. We can't get past.
laisser passer quelqu'un, quelque chose to let somebody, something through
Laisse-le passer! Let him through!
2 Ⓔ **to go past**
Elle regarde passer les trains. She's watching the trains go by.
3 Ⓔ **to drop in, to call by**
Pierre est passé ce matin. Pierre dropped in this morning.
passer prendre quelqu'un, quelque chose to pick somebody, something up
Je passerai te prendre à huit heures. I'll pick you up at eight.
4 Ⓔ **passer à** to go to
Le client passe à la caisse. The customer is going to the checkout.
5 Ⓔ **passer par** to go through
Je passe par le parc. I go through the park.
Par où tu passes? Which way do you go?
6 Ⓔ **to pass**
Le temps passe vite. Time passes quickly.
7 Ⓔ (*in school*) **passer en** to move up to
Ludovic passe en quatrième. Ludovic is moving up to year 9.
8 Ⓔ **to be on, to be showing**
Qu'est-ce qu'on passe comme film au cinéma? What's on at the cinema?
9 **to spend** (*time*)
J'ai passé deux jours à Paris. I spent two days in Paris.
passer son temps à faire quelque chose to spend your time doing something
Le weekend, il passe son temps à faire du cheval. At weekends, he spends his time horse-riding.
10 **to lend** (*a book, a video, etc*)
Aurélie m'a passé son vélo. Aurélie lent me her bike.
11 **to pass on** (*a cold, flu, information*)
Tu m'as passé ton rhume. You've given me your cold.
passer quelque chose à quelqu'un to pass somebody something (*sauce, glasses*)
Passe-moi le sel, si'l te plaît. Pass me the salt, please.
12 **to cross** (*a bridge*)
Le camion a passé le pont. The lorry has crossed the bridge.
13 **to take** (*a test, an exam*)
Demain, je passe le permis de conduire. Tomorrow I'm taking my driving test.
14 **to put (somebody) through** (*on the telephone*)
Je vous passe le responsable. I'll put you through to the manager.
Pouvez-vous me passer Djamila, s'il vous



Ⓔ means the verb takes être to form the perfect

plaît? Could you put me through to Djamila please?
**15** (*in expressions*) **passer l'aspirateur** to vacuum
**passer le chiffon** to dust

**WORD TIP** Use *passer* with *être* in the perfect tense with verbs of movement, showing films, etc; in other words, when the verb has no object. Use *passer* with *avoir* in the perfect tense of verbs to do with spending (time), lending, giving or crossing (a bridge), etc, when the verb has an object.

se **passer** *reflexive verb* ❹
**1 to happen**
**Qu'est-ce qui se passe?** What's happening?
**Ça s'est passé à Londres.** It happened in London.
**2 to take place**
**Le film se passe au début du siècle.** The film takes place at the beginning of the century.
**3 to go**
**Mon entretien s'est bien passé.** My interview went well.
**Comment se sont passées tes vacances?** How did your holidays go?
**4 se passer de quelque chose** to do without something
**Il peut se passer de son vélo.** He can do without his bike.

la **passerelle** *fem noun*
**footbridge**

♪ le **passe-temps** *invariable masc noun*
**hobby, pastime**
**Qu'est-ce que tu as comme passe-temps?** What hobbies do you have?
**Quel est ton passe-temps préféré?** What's your favourite pastime?
**Comme passe-temps, je fais de la danse.** My hobby is ballet.

**WORD TIP** *passe-temps* does not change.

**passif** *masc adjective*, **passive** *fem* ▷ see **passif** *noun*
**passive**

le **passif** *masc noun* ▷ see **passif** *adj*
(*Grammar*) **passive**

la **passion** *fem noun*
**passion**

♪ **passionnant** *masc adjective*, **passionnante** *fem*
**exciting**
**une idée passionnante** an exciting idea

**passionné** *masc adjective*, **passionnée** *fem* ▷ see **passionné** *noun*
**keen**
**C'est une musicienne passionnée.** She's a keen musician.
**Marion est passionnée de chevaux.** Marion is very keen on horses.

le **passionné** *masc noun*, la **passionnée** *fem* ▷ see **passionné** *adj*
**enthusiast**
**un passionné de théâtre** a theatre enthusiast

la **passoire** *fem noun*
**1 sieve** (*for flour*)
**2 colander** (*for vegetables, pasta*)
**3 strainer** (*for tea leaves*)

la **pastille** *fem noun*
**pastille**
**des pastilles pour la gorge** throat sweets

la **patate** *fem noun*
(*informal*) **potato**, **spud**
• la **patate douce** sweet potato

la **pâte** *fem noun*
**1 pastry**
**la pâte feuilletée** puff pastry
**2 batter**
**la pâte à crêpes** pancake batter
**3 dough**
**la pâte à pain** bread dough
**4 les pâtes** pasta
• le **pâte à modeler** Plasticine®

le **pâté** *masc noun*
**1 pâté**
**un sandwich au pâté de foie** a liver pâté sandwich
**2 un pâté de maisons** a block of houses

la **patience** *fem noun*
**patience**
**Il faut prendre patience, ça ne sera pas long.** Be patient, it won't be long.

le **patient** *masc noun*, la **patiente** *fem*
**patient**

**patienter** *verb* [1]
**to wait**
**Patientez, s'il vous plaît!** Please hold the line! (*telephoning*)

le **patin** *masc noun*
**skate**

le **patin à glace** *masc noun*
**1 ice skate**
**2 ice skating**
**faire du patin à glace** to go ice skating

le **patin à roulettes** *masc noun*
**1 roller skate**
**2 roller skating**

le **patinage** *masc noun*
**skating**
• le **patinage artistique** figure skating

**patiner** *verb* **[1]**
**to skate**

le **patineur** *masc noun*, la **patineuse** *fem*
**skater**

♪ la **patinoire** *fem noun*
**ice rink**

♪ la **pâtisserie** *fem noun*
1 **cake shop, pâtisserie**
2 **pastry-making, baking**
3 **cake**

la **patrie** *fem noun*
**homeland**

le **patron** *masc noun*, la **patronne** *fem*
1 **boss**
2 **owner**
**Elle est la patronne du restaurant.** She's the owner of the restaurant.

**patronner** *verb* **[1]**
**to sponsor**

la **patrouille** *fem noun*
**patrol**

la **patte** *fem noun*
1 **leg** (*of an animal*)
2 **paw**

la **paume** *fem noun*
**palm** (*of the hand*)

**paumer** *verb* **[1]**
(*informal*) **to lose**

la **paupière** *fem noun*
**eyelid**

la **pause** *fem noun*
**break**
**la pause café** the coffee break
**la pause déjeuner** the lunch break
**Faisons une pause!** Let's take a break!

♪ **pauvre** *masc & fem adjective*
▷ see **pauvre** *noun*
**poor**
**a poor family** une famille pauvre
**un vocabulaire pauvre** a poor vocabulary

♪ le & la **pauvre** *masc & fem noun*
▷ see **pauvre** *adj*
**poor man, poor woman**
**les pauvres** the poor

♪ la **pauvreté** *fem noun*
**poverty**

le **pavé** *masc noun*
**cobblestone**

le **pavillon** *masc noun*
**detached house**
**un pavillon de banlieue** a house in the suburbs

**payant** *masc adjective*, **payante** *fem*
**not free** (*of a show, an event*)
**un parking payant** a car park where you pay

la **paye** *fem noun*
**wages, pay**

♪ **payer** *verb* **[59]**
1 **to pay** (*a bill, a person*)
**C'est moi qui paie.** I'm paying.
**J'ai payé le gaz.** I paid the gas bill.
**payer quelqu'un** to pay somebody
**La femme de ménage est payée à l'heure.** The cleaning lady is paid by the hour.
2 **payer quelque chose** to pay for something
**Il a payé le repas.** He paid for the meal.
3 (*informal*) **payer quelque chose à quelqu'un** to buy somebody something
**Je te paie un verre.** I'll buy you a drink.

♪ le **pays** *masc noun*
1 **country**
2 **region**
**des fruits du pays** locally produced fruit
- le **pays d'accueil** host country
- le **pays en voie de développement** developing country

le **paysage** *masc noun*
**landscape**

♪ le **paysan** *masc noun*, la **paysanne** *fem*
**farmer**

les **Pays-Bas** *plural masc noun*
**the Netherlands**

♪ le **Pays de Galles** *masc noun*
**Wales**

**WORD TIP** Countries and regions in French take *le, la* or *les.*

le **PC** *masc noun*
**PC, personal computer**

♪ le **péage** *masc noun*
1 **toll**
**une autoroute à péage** toll motorway
2 **tollbooth**
**On arrive au péage.** Here we are at the tollbooths.

♪ la **peau** *fem noun*, les **peaux** *plural*
1 **skin**
**Tu as une peau de pêche.** You have very soft skin.
2 **peel** (*of an orange, a lemon*)

♪ la **pêche** *fem noun*
1 **peach**
2 **fishing**
**la pêche au saumon** salmon fishing
**la pêche à la ligne** angling
**On va à la pêche.** We're going fishing.

le **péché** *masc noun*
**sin**

**pêcher** *verb* **[1]** ▷ see **pêcher** *noun*
**1 to fish for** (*trout, salmon, other fish*)
**2 to catch**
**Denise a pêché une truite.** Denise caught a trout.

le **pêcher** *masc noun* ▷ see **pêcher** *verb*
**peach tree**

le **pêcheur** *masc noun*
**fisherman**

**pédagogique** *masc & fem adjective*
**educational**

la **pédale** *fem noun*
**pedal**

**pédaler** *verb* **[1]**
**to pedal**

le **pédalo**® *masc noun*
**pedalo, pedal boat**

♪ le **peigne** *masc noun*
**comb**

**peigner** *verb* **[1]**
**to comb** (*somebody's hair*)

se **peigner** *reflexive verb* Ⓔ
**to comb your hair**

le **peignoir** *masc noun*
**bathrobe**

**peindre** *verb* **[60]**
**to paint**
**Ils peignent les bancs en vert.** They're painting the benches green.

la **peine** *fem noun*
**1 trouble, effort**
**Elle a eu beaucoup de peine à trouver un logement.** She had a lot of trouble finding somewhere to live.
**Ce n'est pas la peine.** It's not worth the trouble.
**se donner de la peine pour faire quelque chose** to go to the trouble of doing something
**Elle s'est donné de la peine pour organiser cette sortie.** She went to a lot of trouble to organize this outing.
**prendre la peine de faire quelque chose** to take the trouble to do something
**Il n'a même pas pris la peine d'appeler.** He didn't even take the trouble to ring.
**2 sorrow, grief**
**Il a de la peine.** He's feeling sad.
**3 à peine** hardly, scarcely
**Je le connais à peine.** I hardly know him.
**Il était à peine cinq heures.** It was barely five o'clock.
**4 penalty**
**une peine de prison** a prison sentence
• la **peine de mort** death penalty

le **peintre** *masc noun*
**painter**
• le **peintre en bâtiment** painter and decorator

le **peintre-décorateur** *masc noun*, les **peintres-décorateurs** *plural*
**interior decorator**

la **peinture** *fem noun*
**1 paint**
**de la peinture blanche** white paint
**'Peinture fraîche'** 'Wet paint'
**2 painting**
**faire de la peinture** to paint
**3 paintwork**
**4 une peinture** a painting
**une peinture de Bacon** a painting by Bacon

le **pèlerin** *masc noun*
**pilgrim**

le **pèlerinage** *masc noun*
**pilgrimage**

la **pelle** *fem noun*
**1 shovel**
**2 spade** (*toy*)
**3 dustpan**
**le balai et la pelle** dustpan and brush
• la **pelle mécanique** mechanical digger

♪ la **pellicule** *fem noun*
**1 film** (*for a camera*)
**une pellicule couleur** a colour film
**2 les pellicules** dandruff

la **pelouse** *fem noun*
**lawn**
**'Pelouse interdite'** 'Keep off the grass'

la **peluche** *fem noun*
**soft toy**
**les jouets en peluche** soft toys

**pencher** *verb* **[1]**
**to tilt**
**Le tableau penche du côté gauche** The picture's tilting to the left.

se **pencher** *reflexive verb* Ⓔ
**to lean out**
**se pencher par la fenêtre** to lean out of the window
**Penche-toi et ramasse mes clés!** Bend down and pick up my keys!

♪ **pendant** *preposition*
**1 for**
**pendant longtemps** for a long time
**J'ai attendu pendant deux heures.** I waited for two hours. ▸▸

French-English

a b c d e f g h i j k l m n o **p** q r s t u v w x y z

French–English

**Pendant combien de temps as-tu habité au Pays de Galles?** How long have you lived in Wales?
**Il a plu pendant toutes les vacances.** It rained throughout the holiday.
2 **during**
**pendant l'hiver** during the winter
3 **pendant que** while
**Ils s'amusent pendant que je travaille.** They play while I work.

le **pendentif** *masc noun*
**pendant**

la **penderie** *fem noun*
**wardrobe**

**pendre** *verb* **[3]**
**pendre quelque chose** to hang something up
**Elle a pendu la clé au clou.** She hung the key on the nail.

la **pendule** *fem noun*
**clock**

**pénétrer** *verb* **[24]**
1 **pénétrer dans** to enter, to get into
**Un voleur a pénétré dans le bureau.** A thief got into the office.
2 **to seep into** (*water, wax*)
3 **to get to the bottom of** (*a mystery*)

**pénible** *masc & fem adjective*
1 **difficult**
**une situation pénible** a difficult situation
**un travail pénible** hard work
2 **tiresome** (*person*)
**Il est pénible avec ses jeux vidéo.** He's so tiresome with his video games.

la **péniche** *fem noun*
**barge**

le **pénis** *masc noun*
**penis**

la **pensée** *fem noun*
1 **thought**
2 **pansy** (*flower*)

**penser** *verb* **[1]**
1 **to think**
**Je pense que tu as raison.** I think you're right.
**Oui, je pense.** Yes, I think so.
**Je ne pense pas.** I don't think so.
2 **penser faire quelque chose** to intend to do something
**Nous pensons partir le soir.** We're intending to leave this evening.
3 **penser à quelque chose** to remember something
**J'ai pensé à prendre mes affaires de gym.** I remembered to take my PE kit.
4 **penser à quelque chose** to think about something
**À quoi penses-tu?** What are you thinking about?
**Je pense aux enfants d'Afrique.** I'm thinking about the children in Africa.
5 **faire penser quelqu'un à quelque chose, à quelqu'un** to remind somebody of something, somebody
**Cette chanson me fait penser à ta mère.** This song reminds me of your mother.
**faire penser quelqu'un à faire quelque chose** to remind somebody to do something
**Fais-moi penser à acheter du pain.** Remind me to buy some bread.

la **pension** *fem noun*
1 (*in hotels*) **la pension complète** full board
**la demi-pension** half board
2 **boarding house**
3 **pension** (*in retirement*)
4 **boarding school**
• la **pension de famille** family hotel

le & la **pensionnaire** *masc & fem noun*
**boarder**

le **pensionnat** *masc noun*
**boarding school**

la **pente** *fem noun*
**slope**
**Le jardin est en pente.** The garden is on a slope.

la **Pentecôte** *fem noun*
**Whitsun**

le **pépin** *masc noun*
1 **pip** (*in fruit*)
2 (*informal*) **little problem**
**J'ai eu un pépin avec ma mobylette.** I had a little problem with my moped.

**perçant** *masc adjective*, **perçante** *fem*
1 **penetrating**
**un regard perçant** a penetrating look
**le froid perçant** the biting cold
2 **shrill**
**un cri perçant** a shrill scream

**percer** *verb* **[61]**
**percer un trou dans le mur** to make a hole in the wall
**Karine s'est fait percer les oreilles.** Karine had her ears pierced.

la **perceuse** *fem noun*
**drill**

le **perdant** *masc noun*, la **perdante** *fem*
**loser**

a b c d e f g h i j k l m n o p q r s t u v w x y z

**perdre** *verb* [3]
1 **to lose**
**L'équipe de Pierre a perdu.** Pierre's team lost.
2 **perdre quelque chose** to lose something
**Sophie a perdu son appareil-photo.** Sophie lost her camera.
3 **perdre du temps** to waste time
**Nous avons perdu beaucoup de temps dans la queue.** We wasted a lot of time in the queue.

se **perdre** *reflexive verb* ⓔ
**to get lost**
**Arthur s'est perdu dans l'hypermarché.** Arthur got lost in the hypermarket.

la **perdrix** *invariable fem noun*
**partridge**

**perdu** *masc adjective*, **perdue** *fem*
**lost**
**un enfant perdu** a lost child
**Je suis perdu.** I'm lost.
**C'est du temps perdu.** It's a waste of time.
**un chien perdu** a stray dog

le **père** *masc noun*
**father**
**le père Noël** Father Christmas, Santa Claus

**périmé** *masc adjective*, **périmée** *fem*
1 **out-of-date**
**une carte périmée** an out-of-date card
2 **Ce paquet de biscuit est périmé.** This packet of biscuits has passed its sell-by date.

la **période** *fem noun*
**period**

le **périphérique** *masc noun*
**ring road**

la **perle** *fem noun*
1 **pearl**
2 **bead**

la **permanence** *fem noun*
1 **en permanence** permanently, all the time
2 **service**
**'Permanence de 8 h à 19 h'** 'Open from 8 am to 7 pm'
3 **study period**
**J'ai permanence le lundi de 10 h à 11 h.** I have a study period on Mondays from 10 to 11 am.

**permanent** *masc adjective*, **permanente** *fem*
1 **permanent** (*job, exhibition*)
2 **continuous**
**cinéma permanent de 13 h à 23 h** continuous film performances from 1 to 11 pm

**permettre** *verb* [11]
**Permettez-moi de vous aider!** Let me help you!
**Il n'est pas permis d'utiliser son portable au lycée.** You aren't allowed to use your mobile at school.
**permettre à quelqu'un de faire quelque chose** to let somebody to do something
**Ses parents lui permettent de sortir en boîte.** Her parents let her to go clubbing.
**Il a permis à son frère de l'accompagner.** He let his brother come with him.

se **permettre** *reflexive verb* ⓔ
**to afford**
**Il peut se permettre d'aller au cinéma toutes les semaines.** He can afford to go to the cinema every week.

le **permis** *masc noun*
**permit**
**Il vous faut un permis.** You need a permit.
- le **permis de conduire** driving licence
- le **permis de pêche** fishing permit
- le **permis de séjour** residence permit

la **permission** *fem noun*
1 **permission**
**J'ai la permission de venir après l'école.** I have permission to come after school.
2 **leave** (*from the army*)

le **perroquet** *masc noun*
**parrot**

la **perruche** *fem noun*
**budgie**

la **persécution** *fem noun*
**persecution**

**persévérer** *verb* [24]
**to persevere**

le **persil** *masc noun*
**parsley**

le **personnage** *masc noun*
1 **character** (*in a book, a film, etc*)
**les personnages principaux du film** the main characters in the film
2 **person**
**un personnage célèbre** a famous person

la **personnalité** *fem noun*
1 **personality**
**une forte personnalité** a strong personality
2 **important person**
**Il y avait des personnalités dans l'avion.** There were important people in the plane.

la **personne** *fem noun*
▷ see **personne** *pron*
**person**
**les grandes personnes** the adults ▸▸

French–English

a b c d e f g h i j k l m n o p q r s t u v w x y z

les personnes âgées the elderly
en personne in person
Une seule personne est venue. Only one person came.

**personne** *pronoun* ▷ see **personne** *noun*
1 **nobody**
Personne ne veut jouer au foot. Nobody wants to play football.
2 **anybody**
Je n'ai vu personne. I didn't see anybody.
Je ne l'ai dit à personne. I didn't tell anybody

**WORD TIP** Remember to use *ne* before *personne* in a sentence that contains a verb: *Je n'ai vu personne.* ▷ **ne**.

**personnel** *masc adjective*, **personnelle** *fem* ▷ see **personnel** *noun*
**personal**

le **personnel** *masc noun*
▷ see **personnel** *adj*
**staff**

**personnellement** *adverb*
**personally**

la **perspective** *fem noun*
1 **perspective**
un dessin en perspective a perspective drawing
2 **view**
Du sommet, la perspective est magnifique. From the top the view is magnificent.
3 **prospect**
Elle a la perspective d'une bonne situation. She has the prospect of a good job.

**persuader** *verb* [1]
1 **to persuade**
persuader quelqu'un de faire quelque chose to persuade somebody to do something
Je l'ai persuadé de revenir. I persuaded him to come back.
2 être persuadé que ... to be sure that ...
Il est persuadé qu'elle le déteste. He's sure that she hates him.

la **perte** *fem noun*
1 **loss**
la perte de son portefeuille the loss of his wallet
2 **waste**
une perte de temps a waste of time

**perturber** *verb* [1]
**to disrupt**

le **pèse-personne** *fem noun*
**bathroom scales**

**peser** *verb* [50]
**to weigh**
Je pèse 60 kilos. I weigh 60 kilos.

**pessimiste** *masc & fem adjective*
**pessimistic**

le **pétale** *masc noun*
**petal**

la **pétanque** *fem noun*
**bowls**

le **pétard** *masc noun*
**firework**

**pétillant** *masc adjective*, **pétillante** *fem*
**sparkling** (*wine, mineral water*)

le **petit** *masc noun*, la **petite** *fem*
▷ see **petit** *adj*
1 **little boy**, **little girl**, **child**
2 les petits the children

**petit** *adjective masc*, **petite** *fem*
▷ see **petit** *noun*
1 **little**, **small**
un petit garçon a little boy
une petite fille a little girl
une petite maison a small house
une toute petite maison a tiny house
Thibault est petit pour son âge. Thibault is small for his age.
2 **short**
une petite promenade a short walk
3 petit à petit little by little
- le **petit ami** boyfriend
- la **petite amie** girlfriend
- la **petite annonce** small ad
- le **petit déjeuner** breakfast
- la **petite-fille** granddaughter
- le **petit- fils** grandson
- les **petits-enfants** grandchildren
- les **petits pois** garden pea

le **pétrole** *masc noun*
**oil**
le pétrole brut crude oil

**WORD TIP** *pétrole* does not mean *petrol* in English; for the meaning of *petrol* ▷ **essence**.

le **pétrolier** *masc noun*
**oil tanker**

**peu** *adverb*
1 **not much, not many**
Camille mange peu. Camille doesn't eat much.
Il gagne très peu. He earns very little.
2 **not very**
peu intéressant not very interesting
peu réaliste unrealistic
3 peu de not much, not many
Il reste peu de temps. There's not much

time left.
**Peu d'élèves le savent.** Few pupils know that.
**4 un peu** a little, a bit
**Mange un peu!** Eat a little!
**Parle un peu plus fort!** Speak a little louder!
**5 un peu de quelque chose** a little of something
**Il reste un peu de café.** There's a little coffee left.
**Tu vas un peu plus vite.** You're going a bit faster.
**6 à peu près** about
**à peu près mille personnes** about a thousand people
**7 peu à peu** little by little

le **peuple** *masc noun*
**people**

♪ la **peur** *fem noun*
**fear**
**avoir peur de quelque chose** to be afraid of something
**Nadine a peur des souris.** Nadine's afraid of mice.
**faire peur à quelqu'un** to frighten somebody
**Tu m'as fait peur!** You gave me a fright!

**peut** *verb* ▷ **pouvoir**

♪ **peut-être** *adverb*
**perhaps, maybe**
**Elle a peut-être oublié.** Perhaps she's forgotten.
**'Tu viens ce soir?' — 'Peut-être.'** 'Are you coming tonight?' — 'Maybe.'

**peuvent**, **peux** *verb* ▷ **pouvoir**

le **phare** *masc noun*
**1 lighthouse**
**2 headlight** (*of a car*)

♪ la **pharmacie** *fem noun*
**1 chemist's, pharmacy**
**2 medicine cabinet**
**3 pharmacy** (*at university*)

le **pharmacien** *masc noun*, la **pharmacienne** *fem*
**chemist, pharmacist**

le **phénomène** *masc noun*
**phenomenon, happening**

la **philosophie** *fem noun*
**philosophy**

le **phoque** *masc noun*
**seal**

la **photo** *fem noun*
**1 photo, photograph**
**une photo d'identité** a passport photo
**prendre quelqu'un, quelque chose en photo** to take a photograph of somebody, something
**2 photography**

la **photocopie** *fem noun*
**photocopy**

**photocopier** *verb* **[1]**
**to photocopy**

la **photocopieuse** *fem noun*
**photocopier**

le & la **photographe** *masc & fem noun*
**photographer**

la **photographie** *fem noun*
**1 photography** (*as a hobby, a subject*)
**2 photograph**
**la photographie de la classe** the class photograph

**photographier** *verb* **[1]**
**to photograph**

le **photomaton®** *masc noun*
**photo booth**

♪ la **phrase** *fem noun*
**sentence**

**physique** *masc & fem adjective*
▷ see **physique** *noun*
**physical**

♪ la **physique** *fem noun* ▷ see **physique** *adj*
**physics** (*as subject*)
**J'étudie la physique.** I study physics.

le & la **pianiste** *masc & fem noun*
**pianist**

le **piano** *masc noun*
**piano**
**Je joue du piano.** I play the piano.

le **pichet** *masc noun*
**jug**

♪ la **pièce** *fem noun*
**1 room**
**un appartement de quatre pièces** a four-roomed flat (*excluding kitchen and bathroom*)
**2 coin**
**une pièce de deux euros** a two-euro coin
**3 play**
**une pièce de Feydeau** a Feydeau play
**4 bit, piece**
**les pièces d'un puzzle** the pieces of a jigsaw
**5 item**
**dix euros (la) pièce** ten euros each
- la **pièce d'identité** identification (*e.g. a passport, identity card*)
- la **pièce de rechange** spare part
- la **pièce de théâtre** play
- la **pièce jointe** attachment, enclosure

ℰ le **pied** *masc noun*
1 **foot**
J'y vais à pied. I'm going on foot.
2 **foot**, **bottom**
au pied du lit at the foot of the bed
3 **le pied de la table** the table leg
4 (*when swimming*) **J'ai pied.** I can touch the bottom.
Je n'ai pas pied. I'm out of my depth.

le **piège** *masc noun*
**trap**
être pris au piège to be trapped

**piéger** *verb* **[15]**
1 **to trap**
2 **to booby-trap**

la **pierre** *fem noun*
**stone**
une maison de pierre a stone house

ℰ le **piéton** *masc noun*, la **piétonne** *fem*
**pedestrian**

**piétonnier** *masc adjective*, **piétonnière** *fem*
**pedestrian**
une rue piétonnière a pedestrianized street

la **pieuvre** *fem noun*
**octopus**

le **pigeon** *masc noun*
**pigeon**

la **pile** *fem noun* ▷ see **pile** *adv*
1 **battery**
2 **pile** (*of clothes, magazines*)
3 **tails** (*when tossing a coin*)
Pile ou face? Heads or tails?

**pile** *adverb* ▷ see **pile** *noun*
(*informal*) **à dix heures pile** at ten o'clock on the dot
**On a commencé pile à l'heure.** We started dead on time.

le **pilote** *masc noun*
**pilot**
- le **pilote de course** racing driver

**piloter** *verb* **[1]**
**to fly** (*a plane*)

ℰ la **pilule** *fem noun*
**pill**
**la pilule (contraceptive)** the (contraceptive) pill
**la pilule du lendemain** the morning-after pill

le **piment** *masc noun*
**chilli**

le **pin** *masc noun*
**pine tree**

la **pince** *fem noun*
1 une pince a pair of pliers
2 **pincer** (*of a crab*)
- la **pince à épiler** tweezers
- la **pince à linge** clothes peg

le **pinceau** *masc noun*, les **pinceaux** *plural*
**paintbrush**

la **pincée** *fem noun*
**pinch** (*of salt, spice*)

**pincer** *verb* **[61]**
**to pinch** (*a person*)

le **pingouin** *masc noun*
**penguin**

le **ping-pong** *masc noun*
**ping-pong**

la **pintade** *fem noun*
**guinea fowl**

le **pion** *masc noun*
▷ see **pion** *masc & fem noun*
1 **counter** (*in board games*)
2 **pawn** (*in chess*)
3 **piece** (*in draughts*)

le **pion** *masc noun*, la **pionne** *fem noun*
▷ see **pion** *masc noun*
(*informal*) **supervisor** (*in schools*)

la **pipe** *fem noun*
**pipe**

**piquant** *masc adjective*, **piquante** *fem*
**spicy** (*food, sauce*)

le **pique** *masc noun*
**spades** (*in cards*)
le trois de pique the three of spades

le **pique-nique** *masc noun*
**picnic**

**pique-niquer** *verb* **[1]**
**to have a picnic**

**piquer** *verb* **[1]**
1 **to sting**
**J'ai été piqué par une guêpe.** I've been stung by a wasp.
2 **to bite**
**Il a été piqué par des moustiques.** He's been bitten by mosquitoes.
3 (*informal*) **to pinch**
**On m'a piqué mon stylo.** Somebody's pinched my pen.

se **piquer** *reflexive verb* ⓔ
**to prick yourself**
**Je me suis piqué le doigt.** I've pricked my finger.





ⓔ means the verb takes être to form the perfect

la **piqûre** *fem noun*
1 **injection**
**faire une piqûre à quelqu'un** to give somebody an injection
2 **bite** (*of a mosquito*)
3 **sting** (*of a wasp, nettles*)
4 **prick** (*of a thorn, a pin*)

le **pirate** *masc noun*
**pirate**
- le **pirate de l'air** hijacker (*of a plane*)
- le **pirate informatique** computer hacker

**pire** *masc & fem adjective* ▷ **see pire** *noun*
1 **worse**
**C'est bien pire.** It's much worse.
**pire que** worse than
**C'est pire que ça!** It's worse than that!
2 **worst**
**le pire mensonge** the worst lie

le **pire** *masc noun* ▷ **see pire** *adj*
**le pire** the worst
**Nous craignons le pire.** We fear the worst.

♪ la **piscine** *fem noun*
**swimming pool**
**la piscine couverte** the indoor swimming pool

la **pistache** *fem noun*
**pistachio**

la **piste** *fem noun*
1 **trail** (*escapee's, animal's*)
2 **track** (*for racing, sport*)
3 **piste, trail** (*in skiing*)
4 **runway** (*for planes*)
- la **piste cyclable** cycle lane

le **pistolet** *masc noun*
**pistol**

la **pitié** *fem noun*
**pity**
**J'ai eu pitié du mendiant.** I felt sorry for the beggar.

**pittoresque** *masc & fem adjective*
**picturesque**

la **pizza** *fem noun*
**pizza**

la **pizzeria** *fem noun*
**pizzeria**

♪ le **placard** *masc noun*
**cupboard**

**WORD TIP** *placard* does not mean *placard* in English; for the meaning of *placard* ▷ **pancarte**.

♪ la **place** *fem noun*
1 **place**
**remettre les livres à leur place** to put the books back in their place
2 **à la place de quelqu'un** instead of somebody
**Il y est allé à ma place.** He went instead of me.
3 **square**
**la place du village** the village square
**la place Rouge** Red Square
4 **space, room**
**Il y a assez de place pour deux.** There's enough room for two.
5 **seat** (*in a theatre, a cinema, a train, a bus*)
6 **space** (*to park*)
**une place de parking** a parking space
7 **place** (*in ranking, grading*)
**en troisième place** in third place
8 **job**
**Faustine a une bonne place dans cette société.** Faustine has a good job with this firm.

**placer** *verb* [61]
1 **to place**
2 **to seat** (*a person*)
**On m'a placé à côté de Louis.** I was put next to Louis.

♪ le **plafond** *masc noun*
**ceiling**

**WORD TIP** *plafond* does not mean *platform* in English; for the meaning of *platform* ▷ **quai**.

♪ la **plage** *fem noun*
**beach**
**une plage de sable** a sandy beach
**des vacances à la plage** holidays by the sea
**On va à la plage.** We're going to the beach.

la **plaie** *fem noun*
**wound**

**plaindre** *verb* [31]
**to feel sorry for**
**Je te plains.** I'm sorry for you.

se **plaindre** *reflexive verb* ⓔ
**to complain**
**Je ne me plains pas.** I'm not complaining.
**se plaindre de quelque chose à quelqu'un** to complain about something to somebody
**Elle s'est plainte de la cantine au responsable.** She complained to the manager about the canteen.

la **plaine** *fem noun*
**plain**

la **plainte** *fem noun*
**complaint**
**porter plainte contre quelqu'un** to make a complaint about somebody
**Il a porté plainte contre le directeur.** He's made a complaint about the headmaster.

French–English

**plaire** *verb* [62]
1 La couleur me plaît. I like the colour.
La chambre vous plaît? Do you like your room?
Le film a beaucoup plu à Jean. Jean liked the film a lot.
2 s'il te plaît please (*informal*)
s'il vous plaît please (*formal*)
Deux billets, s'il vous plaît. Two tickets, please.

**plaisanter** *verb* [1]
**to joke**
Je l'ai dit en plaisantant. I said it as a joke.

la **plaisanterie** *fem noun*
**joke**

le **plaisir** *masc noun*
**pleasure**
le plaisir de chanter the pleasure of singing
'Vous venez avec nous?' — 'Oui, avec plaisir.' 'Are you coming with us?' — 'Yes, I'd love to.'
faire plaisir à quelqu'un to please somebody

le **plan** *masc noun*
1 **map** (*of a town, an underground system*)
le plan du Métro the map of the Metro
2 **plan**
un plan d'action an action plan
le plan du bâtiment the plan of the building
• le **plan d'eau** artificial lake (*for water sports, etc*)

la **planche** *fem noun*
**plank**
• la **planche à repasser** ironing board
• la **planche à roulettes** skateboard

la **planche à voile** *fem noun*
1 **windsurfing board**
2 **windsurfing**
faire de la planche à voile to go windsurfing

le **plancher** *masc noun*
**floor**

**planer** *verb* [1]
**to glide**

la **planète** *fem noun*
**planet**

la **plante** *fem noun*
**plant**

**planter** *verb* [1]
1 **to plant** (*a tree, a shrub, a plant*)
2 **to hammer in** (*a nail*)
3 **to pitch** (*a tent*)

se **planter** *reflexive verb* Ⓔ
(*informal*) **to get it wrong**
Je me suis planté dans ma division. I got my division wrong.

le **plaquage** *masc noun*
1 **tackle**
2 **tackling** (*in football*)

la **plaque** *fem noun*
1 **patch** (*of damp, ice*)
2 **sheet** (*of metal, glass*)
• la **plaque d'immatriculation** car number plate

**plaqué** *masc adjective*, **plaquée** *fem*
plaqué or gold-plated
plaqué argent silver-plated

la **plaquette** *fem noun*
1 **bar** (*of chocolate*)
2 **pack** (*of butter*)

le **plastique** *masc noun*
**plastic**
un sac en plastique a plastic bag

**plat** *masc adjective*, **plate** *fem*
▷ see **plat** *noun*
1 **flat**
un pays plat a flat country
des chaussures plates flat shoes
2 l'eau plate still water

le **plat** *masc noun* ▷ see **plat** *adj*
1 **dish** (*large plate*)
2 **dish** (*food*)
un plat froid a cold dish
Le steak-frites est mon plat préféré. Steak and chips is my favourite dish.
3 **course** (*of a meal*)
le plat principal the main course
• le **plat cuisiné** cooked dish
• le **plat du jour** dish of the day

le **plateau** *masc noun*, les **plateaux** *plural*
1 **tray**
2 **plateau**

la **plate-bande** *fem noun*, les **plates-bandes** *pl*
**flower bed**

le **plâtre** *masc noun*
**plaster**
avoir une jambe dans le plâtre to have a leg in plaster.

**plein** *masc adjective*, **pleine** *fem*
▷ see **plein** *noun*
1 **full**
Le sac est plein. The bag is full.
Élia est pleine de vie. Élia's full of life.
un T-shirt plein de taches a T-shirt covered



Ⓔ means the verb takes être to form the perfect

with stains
**un emploi à plein temps** a full-time job
2 **en pleine nuit** in the middle of the night
**en plein centre-ville** right in the middle of town
**en plein air** outdoors

le **plein** *masc noun* ▷ see **plein** *adj*
**faire le plein** to fill up (*the fuel tank*)
**Le plein, s'il vous plaît.** Fill her up, please.

♪ **pleurer** *verb* **[1]**
**to cry**
**Il fait toujours pleurer sa petit sœur.** He always makes his little sister cry.

**pleut** *verb* ▷ **pleuvoir**

♪ **pleuvoir** *verb* **[63]**
**to rain**
**Il pleut.** It's raining.
**Il a plu cette nuit.** It rained last night.

le **pli** *masc noun*
1 **fold**
2 **pleat**
3 **crease** (*in trousers*)

**plier** *verb* **[1]**
1 **to fold**
2 **to bend** (*your arm, your leg*)

le **plomb** *masc noun*
1 **lead**
**de l'essence sans plomb** unleaded petrol
2 **fuse**
**Les plombs ont sauté.** The fuses have blown.

le **plombage** *masc noun*
**filling** (*in a tooth*)

le **plombier** *masc noun*
**plumber**

la **plongée** *fem noun*
**diving**
**faire de la plongée** to go diving

le **plongeoir** *masc noun*
**diving board**

**plonger** *verb* **[52]**
**to dive**

le **plongeur** *masc noun*, la **plongeuse** *fem*
1 **diver**
2 **washer-up**

**plu** *verb* ▷ **plaire, pleuvoir**

♪ la **pluie** *fem noun*
**rain**
**un jour de pluie** a rainy day
**des pluies violentes** heavy showers

la **plume** *fem noun*
1 **feather**
2 **nib** (*of a pen*)

la **plupart** *invariable fem noun*
**la plupart de** most
**la plupart des gens** most people
**la plupart d'entre eux** most of them
**la plupart du temps** most of the time

le **pluriel** *masc noun*
**plural**
**au pluriel** in the plural

♪ **plus** *adverb*
1 **plus de** more
**Voulez-vous un peu plus de fromage?** Would you like a little more cheese?
2 **plus de** more than
**Il y avait plus de cent personnes.** There were more than a hundred people.
3 (*in comparisons*) **plus que** more than
**Sa chambre est plus grande que la mienne.** Her bedroom is bigger than mine.
**Le film est plus intéressant que le livre.** The film's more interesting than the book.
4 (*to form a superlative*) **le plus rapide** the fastest
**le plus joli** the prettiest
5 **plus ... plus ...** the more ... the more ...
**Plus je gagne, plus je dépense.** The more I earn the more I spend.
6 **en plus** more
**Il nous faut trois côtelettes en plus.** We need three more chops.
7 **de plus** more
**trois chaises de plus** three more chairs
**une fois de plus** once more
8 **de plus en plus** more and more
**Elle travaille de plus en plus.** She works more and more.
**Il fait de plus en plus chaud.** It's getting hotter and hotter.
9 **plus ou moins** more or less
**La classe est plus ou moins propre.** The classroom's more or less clean.
10 **le plus** the most
**C'est lui qui gagne le plus.** He earns the most.
11 (*to form a negative*) **ne ... plus** not any more
**Elle n'habite plus ici.** She doesn't live here any more.
**Il n'y a plus de lait.** There's no milk left.
12 (*in sums*) **plus**, **add**
**Deux plus trois égalent cinq.** Two plus three is five.

♪ **plusieurs** *invariable plural adjective*
**several**
**Plusieurs personnes sont intéressées.** Several people are interested. ➤➤

French–English

a b c d e f g h i j k l m n o p q r s t u v w x y z

Il y en a plusieurs. There are several of them.

**WORD TIP** *plusieurs* does not change.

**plutôt** *adverb*
1 (*giving preferences*) **rather**, **instead**
**Je préfère envoyer un SMS plutôt que téléphoner.** I'd rather text than phone.
**Viens plutôt demain!** Come tomorrow instead!
2 (*somewhat*) **rather**, **quite**
**Elle est plutôt maigre.** She's rather thin.
**Le repas était plutôt bon.** The meal was quite good.
**C'est plutôt bien.** It's pretty good.

**pluvieux** *masc adjective*, **pluvieuse** *fem*
**rainy**

le **pneu** *masc noun*
**tyre**
**le pneu avant** the front tyre

la **poche** *fem noun*
**pocket**
**l'argent de poche** pocket money
**un livre de poche** a paperback
**Tu es parti avec seulement 50 euros en poche?** You went away with only 50 euros on you?

le **poêle** *masc noun* ▷ see **poêle** *fem noun*
**stove** (*for heating*)

la **poêle** *fem noun* ▷ see **poêle** *masc noun*
**frying pan**

le **poème** *masc noun*
**poem**

la **poésie** *fem noun*
**poetry**

le **poète** *masc noun*
**poet**

le **poids** *masc noun*
**weight**
**prendre du poids** to put on weight
**La prof a pris un peu de poids.** The teacher has put on some weight.
**perdre du poids** to lose weight
**Gilles a perdu du poids.** Gilles lost weight.
- le **poids lourd** lorry, truck

la **poignée** *fem noun*
1 **handful**
**une poignée de cailloux** a handful of pebbles
2 **handle**
**la poignée du sac** the handle of the door
- la **poignée de main** handshake

le **poignet** *masc noun*
**wrist**

le **poil** *masc noun*
**hair**
**un poil** a hair
**Le chat perd ses poils.** The cat's moulting.

**poilu** *masc adjective*, **poilue** *fem*
**hairy**

le **poing** *masc noun*
**fist**
**un coup de poing** a punch
**Elle a tapé du poing sur la table.** She banged her fist on the table.

le **point** *masc noun* ▷ see **pointe** *fem noun*
1 **point** (*in general*)
**un point de rencontre** a meeting point
2 **être sur le point de faire quelque chose** to be just about to do something
**J'étais sur le point de t'appeler.** I was on the point of phoning you.
3 **dot**
**le point sur le 'i'** the dot on the 'i'
4 **full stop**
5 **point** (*in scores*)
**six points contre sept** six points to seven
6 **mark** (*in a test*)
7 **stitch** (*in sewing, knitting*)
8 **à point** just in time
**Tu es arrivé à point.** You arrived just in time.
9 (*for food*) **un steak cuit à point** a medium rare steak
**un brie à point** a ready-to-eat brie
- le **point cardinal** compass point
- le **point chaud** trouble spot
- le **point de départ** starting point
- le **point d'exclamation** exclamation mark
- le **point d'interrogation** question mark
- le **point noir** blackhead
- le **point de vue** point of view
- le **point-virgule** semi-colon

la **pointe** *fem noun* ▷ see **point** *masc noun*
1 **point**
**la pointe d'un couteau** the point of a knife
**sur la pointe des pieds** on tip-toe
2 **tip**
**la pointe de l'aiguille** the tip of the needle
3 (*showing extremes*) **une vitesse de pointe de 250 km/h** a top speed of 250 kph
**les heures de pointe** the rush hour, peak time
**les technologies de pointe** advanced technologies
**un système audio à la pointe du progrès** a state-of-the-art sound system
4 **touch** (*a small quantity*)
**une pointe d'ail** a touch of garlic

le **pointillé** *masc noun*
**dotted line**

**pointu** *masc adjective*, **pointue** *fem*
**pointed**

♂ la **pointure** *fem noun*
**size** (*of shoes*)
Quelle pointure fais-tu?, Quelle est ta pointure? What size do you take?

♂ la **poire** *fem noun*
**pear**

le **poireau** *masc noun*, les **poireaux** *plural*
**leek**

le **poirier** *masc noun*
**pear tree**

le **pois** *masc noun*
1 **pea**
2 **à pois spotted**
un tissu à pois a spotted fabric
• le **pois chiche** chick pea

le **poison** *masc noun*
**poison**

♂ le **poisson** *masc noun*
**fish**
J'aime le poisson. I like fish.

le **poisson d'avril** *masc noun*
**April fool**
Il m'a fait un poisson d'avril. He played an April fool trick on me.

la **poissonnerie** *fem noun*
**fishmonger's**

le **poissonnier** *masc noun*, la **poissonnière** *fem*
**fishmonger**

le **poisson rouge** *masc noun*
**goldfish**

les **Poissons** *plural masc noun*
**Pisces** (*sign of the Zodiac*)
Odile est Poissons. Odile is Pisces.

**WORD TIP** Signs of the zodiac do not take an article: *un* or *une*.

♂ la **poitrine** *fem noun*
1 **chest**
2 **bust**
Quel est votre tour de poitrine? What is your bust size?

♂ le **poivre** *masc noun*
**pepper**

le **poivrier** *masc noun*
**pepper pot**

le **poivron** *masc noun*
**pepper** (*to eat as a vegetable*)

le **poker** *masc noun*
**poker**

le **pôle** *masc noun*
**pole**
le pôle Nord the North Pole
le pôle Sud the South Pole

♂ **poli** *masc adjective*, **polie** *fem*
**polite**
Tu dois être poli avec ta grand-mère. You must be polite to your grandmother.

la **police** *fem noun*
1 **police**
Ma tante est dans la police. My aunt is in the police.
Pour appeler la police, faire le 17. To call the police, dial 17.
2 **policy**
une police d'assurance an insurance policy

**policier** *masc adjective*, **policière** *fem*
▷ see **policier** *noun*
un chien policier a police dog
une enquête policière a police investigation

le **policier** *masc noun* ▷ see **policier** *adj*
**police officer**
une femme policier a woman police officer

la **politesse** *fem noun*
**politeness**

le **politicien** *masc noun*, la **politicienne** *fem*
**politician**

**politique** *masc & fem adjective*
▷ see **politique** *noun*
1 **political**
2 **un homme politique a politician**

la **politique** *fem noun* ▷ see **politique** *adj*
1 **politics**
2 **policy**
la politique étrangère foreign policy

♂ **polluer** *verb* [1]
**to pollute**

**pollué** *masc adjective*, **pollué** *fem*
**polluted**

la **pollution** *fem noun*
**pollution**

le **polo** *masc noun*
**polo shirt**

la **Pologne** *fem noun*
**Poland**

**polonais** *masc adjective*, **polonaise** *fem* ▷ see **Polonais** *noun*
**Polish**

un **Polonais** *masc noun*, une **Polonaise** *fem* ▷ see **polonais** *adj*
1 **Pole**
2 le polonais Polish (*the language*)

la **pommade** *fem noun*
**ointment**

♪ la **pomme** *fem noun*
**apple**
- la **pomme de pin** pine cone
- la **pomme de terre** potato
- les **pommes frites** chips

le **pommier** *masc noun*
**apple tree**

la **pompe** *fem noun*
**pump**
- la **pompe à essence** petrol pump

♪ les **pompes funèbres** *plural fem noun*
**undertaker's**

♪ le **pompier** *masc noun*
**fire fighter**

le & la **pompiste** *masc & fem noun*
**petrol pump attendant**

la **ponctuation** *fem noun*
**punctuation**

**ponctuel** *masc adjective*, **ponctuelle** *fem*
**punctual**

le **poney** *masc noun*
**pony**

♪ le **pont** *masc noun*
1 **bridge**
2 **deck** (*of a ship*)
3 **long weekend holiday** (*to extend a public holiday*)
faire le pont to have a long weekend
**Comme le 14 juillet est tombé un mardi, nous avons fait le pont.** As July 14th fell on a Tuesday, we had a long weekend.

**populaire** *masc & fem adjective*
1 **working-class** (*housing, area, etc*)
2 **popular** (*art, writing*)
3 **folk**

la **population** *fem noun*
**population**

♪ le **porc** *masc noun*
1 **pig**
2 **pork**
un rôti de porc a pork roast

la **porcelaine** *fem noun*
**china, porcelain**

la **porcherie** *fem noun*
**pigsty**

♪ le **port** *masc noun*
1 **port**
2 **harbour**
- le **port de plaisance** marina

**portable** *masc & fem adjective* ▷ see **portable** *noun*
**portable**
**un ordinateur portable** a laptop computer

le **portable** *masc noun* ▷ see **portable** *adj*
1 **mobile** (*phone*)
2 **laptop** (*computer*)

le **portail** *masc noun*
**gate**

**portatif** *masc adjective*, **portative** *fem*
**portable** (*computer*)

♪ la **porte** *fem noun*
1 **door** (*of a house, etc*)
la porte d'entrée the front door
2 **gate** (*in an airport*)
**la porte numéro douze** gate number twelve
3 **mettre quelqu'un à la porte** to sack somebody

le **porte-bagages** *masc noun*
**luggage rack**

le **porte-clés** *masc noun*
**key-ring**

♪ le **portefeuille** *masc noun*
**wallet**

le **portemanteau** *masc noun*, les **portemanteaux** *plural*
1 **coat rack**
2 **coat hanger**

le **portemine** *masc noun*
**propelling pencil**

♪ le **porte-monnaie** *masc noun*
**purse**

le **porte-parole** *masc noun*
**spokesperson**

♪ **porter** *verb* **[1]**
1 **to carry**
**porter un sac** to carry a bag
2 **to take**
**porter quelque chose quelque part** to take something somewhere
**Je porte un paquet à la poste.** I'm taking a parcel to the post office.
3 **to wear**
**Elle portait un jean délavé.** She was wearing faded jeans.

se **porter** *reflexive verb* Ⓔ
Je me porte bien. I'm well.
Elle se porte mal. She's unwell

le **porteur** *masc noun*, la **porteuse** *fem*
**porter**

la **portière** *fem noun*
**door** (*of a car*)

la **portion** *fem noun*
1 **portion**
2 **helping** (*of food*)

**portoricain** *masc adjective*, **portoricaine** *fem* ▷ see **Portoricain** *noun*
**Puerto Rican**

un **Portoricain** *masc noun*, une **Portoricaine** *fem*
▷ see **portoricain** *adj*
**Puerto Rican** (*person*)

**Porto Rico** *fem noun*
**Puerto Rico**

**WORD TIP** Unlike other names of islands, *Porto Rico* does not take *le* or *la*.

le **portrait** *masc noun*
**portrait**

**portugais** *masc adjective*, **portugaise** *fem*
▷ see **Portugais** *noun*
**Portuguese**

un **Portugais** *masc noun*, une **Portugaise** *fem* ▷ see **portugais** *adj*
1 **Portuguese** (*person*)
2 **le portugais Portuguese** (*the language*)

le **Portugal** *masc noun*
**Portugal**

♪ **poser** *verb* **[1]**
1 **to put down**
**Il a posé sa tasse sur la table.** He put his cup down on the table.
2 **to plant** (*a bomb*)
3 **to put up** (*posters*)
4 **poser un problème à quelqu'un** to pose a problem for somebody
**Ça ne pose pas de problème.** That's no problem.
5 **poser une question à quelqu'un** to ask somebody a question
**J'ai une question à te poser.** I have a question to ask you.

**positif** *masc adjective*, **positive** *fem*
**positive**

la **position** *fem noun*
**position**

**posséder** *verb* **[24]**
**to own**

la **possibilité** *fem noun*
1 **possibility**
2 **opportunity**

♪ **possible** *masc & fem adjective*
1 **possible**
**aussi grand que possible** as big as possible
**le moins possible** as little as possible
**dès que possible** as soon as possible
**Ce n'est pas possible!** That's not possible!
2 **potential**
**Ils sont de possibles candidats.** They are potential candidates.

♪ la **poste** *fem noun* ▷ see **poste** *masc noun*
**post office**
**mettre quelque chose à la poste** to post something
**J'ai mis ta lettre à la poste.** I posted your letter.

***poste***

Les boîtes aux lettres de la Poste sont rectangulaires et jaunes.

♪ le **poste** *masc noun* ▷ see **poste** *fem noun*
1 **job, post**
**un poste de secrétaire** a job as a secretary
**Le poste d'assistante est vacant.** The post of assistant is vacant.
2 **set** (*TV, radio*)
3 **extension** (*on a telephone system*)
**Mon numéro de poste est le 3641.** My extension number is 3641.
**Le poste 578, s'il vous plaît.** Extension 578, please.
- le **poste à essence** petrol station
- le **poste de police** police station

le **poster** *masc noun*
**poster**

le **pot** *masc noun*
1 **jar**
**un pot de confiture** a jar of jam
2 **carton**
**un pot de crème** a carton of cream
3 **tin**
**un pot de peinture** a tin of paint
4 **prendre un pot** to have a drink
**Tu viens prendre un pot avec nous?** Are you coming for a drink with us?

**WORD TIP** *pot* does not mean *pot* (for cooking) in English; for the meaning of *pot* ▷ **casserole**.

**potable** *masc & fem adjective*
**eau potable** drinking water
**non potable** unsuitable for drinking



French–English
a b c d e f g h i j k l m n o p q r s t u v w x y z

le **potage** *masc noun*
**soup**
**potage aux légumes** vegetable soup

le **potager** *masc noun*
**vegetable garden**

le **pot-au-feu** *masc noun*
**boiled beef with vegetables**

le **poteau** *masc noun*, les **poteaux** *plural*
1 **post** (*a stake*)
le poteau d'arrivée the finishing post
2 **goalpost**
- le **poteau indicateur** signpost

la **poterie** *fem noun*
1 **pottery**
**Aesha fait de la poterie.** Aesha does pottery.
2 **piece of pottery**
**Ils vendent des poteries.** They sell pottery.

le **pou** *masc noun*, les **poux** *pl*
**louse**

la **poubelle** *fem noun*
**bin**, **dustbin**
**mettre quelque chose à la poubelle** to throw something in the bin
**Je l'ai mis à la poubelle.** I threw it in the bin.

le **pouce** *masc noun*
1 **thumb**
2 **inch**

la **poudre** *fem noun*
**powder**
**du lait en poudre** powdered milk

le **poulain** *masc noun*
**foal**

la **poule** *fem noun*
**hen**

le **poulet** *masc noun*
**chicken**
**du poulet rôti** roast chicken
- le **poulet d'élevage** battery chicken
- le **poulet fermier** free-range chicken

le **pouls** *masc noun*
**pulse**
**prendre le pouls de quelqu'un** to take somebody's pulse
**Le médecin a pris mon pouls.** The doctor took my pulse.

le **poumon** *masc noun*
**lung**

la **poupée** *fem noun*
**doll**
- la **poupée mannequin** Barbie® doll

**pour** *preposition*
1 **for**
**un cadeau pour Laure** a present for Laure
**un billet pour Calais** a ticket for Calais
**le train pour Londres** the train for London
**Ce sera prêt pour samedi?** Will it be ready for Saturday?
**être pour quelque chose** to be in favour of something
**Je suis pour l'équipe bleue.** I support the blue team.
2 **to**, **in order to**
**pour faire quelque chose** in order to do something
**Je suis là pour t'aider.** I'm here to help you.
**Pour aller à la poste, prenez le bus.** To get to the post office, take the bus.
3 **pour ne pas faire quelque chose** so as not to do something
**Je me lève tôt pour ne pas rater mon bus.** I get up early so as not to miss my bus.
4 **pour que ...** so that ...
**Je te le dis pour que tu comprennes.** I'm telling you so that you understand.

le **pourboire** *masc noun*
**tip**
**J'ai donné un pourboire à la serveuse.** I tipped the waitress.

le **pour cent** *masc noun*
**per cent**
**vingt pour cent** twenty per cent

le **pourcentage** *masc noun*
**percentage**

**pourquoi** *adverb*
**why**
**Pourquoi est-ce que tu ris?** Why are you laughing?
**Pourquoi ont-ils refusé?** Why did they refuse?
**Je veux savoir pourquoi.** I want to know why.
**Pourquoi pas?** Why not?

**pourri** *masc adjective*, **pourrie** *fem*
**rotten**
**des légumes pourris** rotten vegetables

**pourrir** *verb* **[2]**
**to go bad** (*food*)

**poursuivre** *verb* **[75]**
1 **to chase** (*a person, an animal*)
2 **to continue** (*a task, efforts, studies*)
**poursuivre son chemin** to continue on your way
**J'aimerais poursuivre mes études en France.** I would like to continue my studies in France.

**pourtant** *adverb*
1 **though**
**Et pourtant c'est vrai.** It's true though.
**Il faut pourtant leur dire.** We have to tell them though.
2 **yet**
**Et pourtant ça aurait pu être bien.** And yet it could have been good.

**pourvu que** *conjunction*
1 **providing (that), as long as**
**pourvu que tu reviennes samedi** providing that you come back on Saturday
2 **let's hope (that)**
**Pourvu qu'il ne pleuve pas!** Let's hope that it doesn't rain!

**WORD TIP** *Pourvu que* is followed by a verb in the subjunctive.

♪ **pousser** *verb* **[1]**
1 **to push**
**Elle a poussé la porte.** She pushed the door.
**'Poussez'** 'Push'
2 **pousser quelqu'un à faire quelque chose** to encourage somebody to do something
**Ils m'ont poussé à participer au concours.** They encouraged me to enter the competition.
3 **pousser un cri** to cry out
**J'ai entendu quelqu'un pousser des cris.** I heard somebody cry out.
4 **to grow** (*child, hair, plant*)
**Les fraises poussent bien.** The strawberries are growing well.

se **pousser** *reflexive verb* ❷
**to move over**
**Pousse-toi!** Move over!

la **poussette** *fem noun*
**pushchair**

la **poussière** *fem noun*
**dust**
**être couvert de poussière** to be covered in dust
**Le bâtiment tombe en poussière.** The building is crumbling away.

la **poutre** *fem noun*
**beam** (*in a ceiling*)

**pouvez** *verb* ▷ **pouvoir**

le **pouvoir** *masc noun* ▷ see **pouvoir** *verb*
1 **power**
**après dix ans au pouvoir** after ten years in power
**des pouvoirs surnaturels** supernatural powers
**avoir le pouvoir de faire quelque chose** to have the power to do something
**Ils ont le pouvoir de tout changer.** They have the power to change everything.
2 **les pouvoirs publics** the authorities

♪ **pouvoir** *verb* **[12]** ▷ see **pouvoir** *noun*
**can**
**Je peux le faire.** I can do it.
**Je ne peux pas l'ouvrir.** I can't open it.
**Est-ce que tu peux m'aider?** Can you help me?
**Vous pourriez m'indiquer la gare, s'il vous plaît?** Could you tell me where the station is, please?
**Ils ne pouvaient pas téléphoner avant.** They couldn't phone before.
**Je n'ai pas pu réserver.** I wasn't able to book.
**Elle aurait pu nous le dire.** She could have told us.
**Puis-je parler à Julien, s'il vous plaît?** May I speak to Julien, please?
**Tu peux toujours essayer.** There's no harm in trying.

**WORD TIP** Use *puis-je* and *vous pourriez* to ask polite questions.

**pouvons** *verb* ▷ **pouvoir**

la **prairie** *fem noun*
1 **meadow**
2 **la prairie** the prairies (*in the US*)

**pratique** *masc & fem adjective*
▷ see **pratique** *noun*
**practical, useful**
**C'est un petit sac pratique.** It's a handy little bag.
**des renseignements pratiques** useful information

la **pratique** *fem noun* ▷ see **pratique** *adj*
1 **practice**
2 **practical experience**
**Il manque de pratique.** He lacks practical experience.

**pratiquement** *adverb*
**practically**
**C'est pratiquement fini.** It's practically finished.

**pratiquer** *verb* **[1]**
1 **to play, to do** (*a sport, a hobby*)
**Elle pratique plusieurs sports.** She plays several sports.
**Je pratique le yoga.** I do yoga.
2 **to practise** (*a language*)
**J'aurai la possibilité de pratiquer mon français.** I'll be able to practise my French.

le **pré** *masc noun*
**meadow**

**préalable** *masc & fem adjective*
**prior** (*permission, notice*)

la **précaution** *fem noun*
**precaution**
**par précaution** as a precaution
**prendre ses précautions** to take precautions

**précédent** *masc adjective*, **précédente** *fem*
**previous**

**précieux** *masc adjective*, **précieuse** *fem*
**precious**, **valuable**
**une pierre précieuse** a precious stone
**des renseignements précieux** very valuable information

le **précipice** *masc noun*
**precipice**

la **précipitation** *fem noun*
1 **haste**
**avec précipitation** in a hurry
2 **les précipitations** rainfall
**de fortes précipitations** heavy rainfall

se **précipiter** *reflexive verb* ❷ **[1]**
**to rush**
**Ils se sont précipités vers la porte.** They rushed for the door.
**se précipiter pour faire quelque chose** to rush to do something
**Je me suis précipité pour les aider.** I rushed to help them.

**précis** *masc adjective*, **précise** *fem*
1 **precise** (*time, person, etc*)
**à deux heures précises** at two o'clock exactly
2 **accurate** (*watch, instrument*)

**précisément** *adverb*
**precisely**

**préciser** *verb* **[1]**
1 **to specify** (*a place, a date, a figure*)
**On n'a pas précisé la date.** They haven't specified the date.
2 **to explain**
**Pouvez-vous préciser comment?** Could you explain exactly how?

la **précision** *fem noun*
1 **precision**
**faire quelque chose avec précision** to do something accurately
2 **detail**
**Voici quelques précisions sur le voyage.** Here are some details about the journey.

la **préfecture** *fem noun*
**prefecture** (*France is divided into 96 départements, which are roughly equivalent to British counties. The local prefecture is responsible for the day-to-day administration of each of these départements.*)
• la **préfecture de police** (local) police headquarters

**préférable** *masc & fem adjective*
**preferable**

♪ **préféré** *masc adjective*, **préférée** *fem*
**favourite**
**Ma matière préférée, c'est le français.** My favourite subject is French.

♪ la **préférence** *fem noun*
1 **preference**
**Les pâtes ou les nouilles, je n'ai pas de préférence.** Pasta or noodles, I don't have a preference.
2 **de préférence** preferably
**Je prends le train de préférence.** I prefer to take the train.

♪ **préférer** *verb* **[24]**
**to prefer**
**préférer quelque chose à quelque chose d'autre** to prefer something to something else
**Elle préfère le poisson à la viande.** She prefers fish to meat.
**C'est comme tu préfères.** Whatever you prefer.
**préférer faire quelque chose** to prefer to do something
**Je préfère aller à l'école à pied.** I prefer to walk to school.
**Aller au cinéma? Non, je préfère rester ici.** Go to the cinema? No, I'd rather stay here.
**Marie préfère danser plutôt que de nager.** Marie prefers dancing to swimming.

le **préfet** *masc noun*
**prefect** (*an official in charge of the administration of a French* **département**)
▷ **préfecture**
• le **préfet de police** chief of police

le **préjugé** *masc noun*
**prejudice**
**les préjugés raciaux** racial prejudice
**être plein de préjugés** to be very prejudiced

♪ **premier** *masc adjective*, **première** *fem*
▷ **see premier** *noun*, **première** *fem*
1 **first**
**le premier immeuble à droite** the first apartment block on the right
**au premier étage** on the first floor
**la première fois** the first time
**le premier juin** the first of June
2 **top** (*in ranking*)
**de première qualité** top quality



❷ means the verb takes être to form the perfect

être premier en biologie to be top in biology

♪le **premier** *masc noun*, la **première** *fem*
▷ see **premier** *adj*, **première** *fem noun*

1 **first**
Elle est toujours la première à parler. She's always the first to speak.
Nous étions les premiers à partir. We were the first to leave.
être le premier de la classe to be top of the class

2 en premier first
C'est Pierre qui est arrivé en premier. Pierre arrived first.

la **première** *fem noun*
▷ see **première** *adj, noun*

1 **première** (*of a film, a play*)
une première mondiale a world first (*inventions, achievements, etc*)

2 voyager en première to travel first-class

3 (*Education*) **Year 12** (*French equivalent*)
J'entre en première cette année. I'm going into Year 12 this year.

**premièrement** *adverb*
**firstly**

♪le **premier ministre** *masc noun*
**prime minister**

♪**prendre** *verb* **[64]**

1 **to take**
Je vais prendre un taxi. I'm going to take a taxi.
J'ai pris ce DVD à la bibliothèque. I got this DVD out of the library.
Je dois prendre de l'argent au distributeur. I need to get money from the cash dispenser.

2 prendre quelque chose à quelqu'un to take something from somebody
Elle a pris de l'argent à ses parents. She took money from her parents.
Qui m'a pris mon vélo? Who's taken my bike?

3 **to have** (*something to eat, drink*)
Je prends une bière. I'll have a beer.
Qu'est-ce que tu prends? What would you like?

4 **to bring**
Je vais prendre mon parapluie. I'm going to bring my umbrella.

5 passer prendre quelqu'un to pick somebody up
Je passerai te prendre à dix heures. I'll pick you up at ten.

♪le **prénom** *masc noun*
**first name**

les **préparatifs** *plural masc noun*
**preparations**
les préparatifs du voyage the preparations for the journey

la **préparation** *fem noun*
**preparation**

♪**préparer** *verb* **[1]**
**to prepare** (*a room, a meal, a lesson*)
Je vais préparer les légumes. I'll go and prepare the vegetables.
Guillaume prépare le dîner. Guillaume's getting dinner ready.
Je prépare mes examens. I'm working for my exams.
Est-ce que tu as préparé tes affaires pour le matin? Have you got your things ready for the morning?
• les **plats préparés** ready-to-eat meals

se **préparer** *reflexive verb* ⓔ
**to get ready**
Je vais me préparer pour partir. I'll get ready to leave.
Prépare-toi! Get ready!
se préparer à quelque chose to prepare for something
Je me prépare aux examens. I'm preparing for the exams.

la **préposition** *fem noun*
(*Grammar*) **preposition**

♪**près** *adverb*

1 **nearby**
La poste est tout près. The post office is quite close.

2 près de near
près de la gare near the station
près d'ici near here

3 près de nearly, almost
près de mille euros nearly a thousand euros

4 de près closely
Elle regarde l'écran de près. She's looking closely at the screen.

5 à peu près about
à peu près deux heures about two hours
Ça coûte à peu près dix euros. It costs about ten euros.

la **présence** *fem noun*
**presence**
en présence d'une grande foule in front of a large crowd

**présent** *masc adjective*, **présente** *fem*
▷ see **présent** *noun*
**present**
Présent! Present! (*at roll-call*)
Toute la famille était présente. The whole family was there.

le **présent** *masc noun* ▷ see **présent** *adj*
1 (*Grammar*) **present (tense)**
au présent in the present
2 à présent now

le **présentateur** *masc noun*, la **présentatrice** *fem*
1 **presenter** (*of a programme*)
2 **newsreader**

la **présentation** *fem noun*
**presentation** (*of work, ideas, food*)
une présentation de mode a fashion show
faire les présentations to do the introductions

**présenter** *verb* [1]
1 **to introduce** (*people*)
Je vous présente mon père. This is my father.
Alain, je te présente Raphaël. Alain, this is Raphaël.
2 **to show** (*a ticket, a pass, a document*)
Il faut présenter votre passeport. You must show your passport.
3 **to present** (*a programme, a show*)

se **présenter** *reflexive verb* ⓔ
1 **to make yourself known**
En arrivant, présentez-vous à la réception. When you arrive, make yourself known in reception.
2 se présenter à quelqu'un to introduce yourself to somebody
Il s'est présenté à la classe. He introduced himself to the class.

le **préservatif** *masc noun*
**condom**

la **préservation** *fem noun*
1 **preservation** (*of heritage*)
2 **conservation** (*of buildings, sites*)

le **président** *masc noun*
▷ see **présidente** *fem noun*
1 **president**
2 **chairman**
• le **président de la République** president of France

la **présidente** *fem noun*
▷ see **président** *masc noun*
1 **president**
2 **chairwoman**

les **présidentielles** *plural fem noun*
**presidential elections**

**presque** *adverb*
1 **nearly**
Ils sont presque toujours là. They're nearly always there.
J'ai presque fini. I've nearly finished.
2 presque pas de hardly any
Il ne reste presque pas de lait. There's hardly any milk left.
3 presque rien hardly anything
Il n'a presque rien fait. He's done next to nothing.

la **presse** *fem noun*
la presse the press, the newspapers
Que dit la presse? What do the papers say?

**pressé** *masc adjective*, **pressée** *fem*
1 être pressé to be in a hurry
Elle avait l'air pressée. She looked as if she was in a hurry.
2 **urgent**
Ce n'est pas pressé. It's not urgent.

**presser** *verb* [1]
1 **to squeeze** (*an orange, a lemon*)
2 **to be urgent**
Ça ne presse pas. It's not urgent.

se **presser** *reflexive verb* ⓔ
**to hurry**

le **pressing** *masc noun*
**dry cleaner's**

la **pression** *fem noun*
1 **pressure**
sous pression pressurized
faire pression sur quelqu'un to put pressure on somebody
2 (*informal*) **draught beer**
un demi pression a half of draught beer

le **prestidigitateur** *masc noun*, la **prestidigitatrice** *fem*
**conjurer**

**prêt** *masc adjective*, **prête** *fem*
▷ see **prêt** *noun*
**ready**
Le dîner est prêt! Dinner's ready!
Tout était prêt pour la fête. Everything was ready for the party.
Vous êtes prêts à partir? Are you ready to leave?

le **prêt** *masc noun* ▷ see **prêt** *adj*
**loan**

le **prêt-à-porter** *masc noun*
**ready-to-wear clothes**

**prétendre** *verb* [3]
**to claim**
Elle prétend que ce n'est pas de sa faute. She claims it's not her fault.

**WORD TIP** *prétendre* does not mean *pretend* in English: for the meaning of *pretend* see *faire semblant* ▷ **semblant**.

ⓔ means the verb takes être to form the perfect

**prêter** *verb* [1]
1 **to lend**
**prêter quelque chose à quelqu'un** to lend somebody something
**Je te prêterai mon vélo.** I'll lend you my bike.
**Elle ne veut pas me prêter de l'argent.** She doesn't want to lend me any money.
2 **prêter attention à quelqu'un** to pay attention to somebody

le **prétexte** *masc noun*
**excuse**

le **prêtre** *masc noun*
**priest**

la **preuve** *fem noun*
1 **proof**
**fournir des preuves** to provide proof
**Il est jaloux, la preuve c'est qu'il refuse de me parler.** He won't speak to me. That proves that he's jealous.
2 **faire preuve de quelque chose** to show something
**Ils ont fait preuve de beaucoup de courage.** They showed a lot of courage.

**prévenir** *verb* [81]
1 **to tell**, **to warn**
**Ils arrivent toujours sans nous prévenir.** They always turn up without warning us.
**Elle ne m'a pas prévenu qu'elle partait.** She never told me she was leaving.
2 **to call** (*the police, a doctor, etc*)
**Quelqu'un a dû prévenir la police.** Somebody must have called the police.

la **prévention** *fem noun*
**prevention**
- la **prévention routière** road safety

la **prévision** *fem noun*
**forecast**, **forecasting**
**faire des prévisions** to make forecasts
- les **prévisions météorologiques** weather forecast

**prévoir** *verb* [65]
1 **to predict**
**Qui aurait pu prévoir ce désastre?** Who could have predicted that disaster?
2 **to plan** (*a journey, an arrangement*)
**Ça s'est passé, comme prévu.** It took place, as planned.
3 **Tout a été prévu.** Everything's been taken care of.
4 **Le départ est prévu pour huit heures.** Departure is scheduled for eight o'clock.
5 **to allow for** (*in your calculations*)
**Prévoyez 10 euros pour le taxi.** Allow 10 euros for the taxi.

**prier** *verb* [1]
1 **to pray**
2 **prier quelqu'un de faire quelque chose** to ask somebody to do something
**Les clients sont priés de ne pas fumer.** Customers are kindly requested not to smoke.
3 **Je vous en prie.** You're welcome, Don't mention it.
**'Merci beaucoup.' — 'Je vous en prie.'** 'Thank you very much.' — 'You're welcome.'

la **prière** *fem noun*
1 **prayer**
2 (*on signs*) **'Prière de fermer la porte'** 'Please close the door'

& **primaire** *masc & fem adjective*
**primary**

la **prime** *fem noun*
1 **bonus**
2 **free gift**

le **prince** *masc noun*
**prince**
**le prince Harry** Prince Harry

la **princesse** *fem noun*
**princess**
**la princesse Stéphanie** Princess Stephanie

& **principal** *masc adjective*, **principale** *fem*, **principaux** *masc pl*, **principales** *fem pl*
**principal**
**un des principaux pays industrialisés** one of the main industrialized countries

le **principe** *masc noun*
1 **principle**
2 **en principe** as a rule
**En principe je rentre à six heures.** As a rule I get back at six.
3 **en principe** in theory
**En principe tout le monde a été informé.** In theory, everybody's been informed.

& le **printemps** *masc noun*
**spring**
**au printemps** in (the) spring

la **priorité** *fem noun*
1 **priority**
**Les enfants ont la priorité.** Children take priority.
2 **right of way**
**'Vous n'avez pas la priorité'** 'You do not have right of way' (*road sign*)

French-English

**pris** *masc adjective*, **prise** *fem*
▷ see **pris** *verb*
1 **busy**
**Je suis très prise ce matin.** I'm very busy this morning.
2 **taken**
**Toutes les places sont prises.** All the seats are taken.
3 **être pris de quelque chose** to be overcome with something
**La foule était prise de panique.** The crowd was overcome with panic.

**pris** *verb* ▷ see **pris** *adj* ▷ **prendre**

la **prise** *fem noun*
1 **(wall) socket** (*for electrical appliances*)
2 **plug** (*for electricity*)
3 **capture** (*in war, etc*)
- la **prise de courant** power point
- la **prise de sang** blood test
- la **prise multiple** adaptor plug

la **prison** *fem noun*
**prison**

le **prisonnier** *masc noun*, la **prisonnière** *fem*
**prisoner**

♪ **privé** *masc adjective*, **privée** *fem*
▷ see **privé** *noun*
1 **private**
**'Propriété privée'** 'Private property'
2 **être privé de quelque chose** to be without something
**Nous sommes privés d'électricité.** We're without any electricity.

♪ le **privé** *masc noun* ▷ see **privé** *adj*
1 **private sector** (*of the economy, etc*)
2 **en privé** in private

**priver** *verb* [1]
1 **priver quelqu'un de quelque chose** to deprive somebody of something
**Le conflit les prive d'aide.** They conflict deprives them of aid.
2 **être privé de sortie** to be grounded
**On m'a privé de sortie pendant une semaine.** I've been grounded for a week.

se **priver** *reflexive verb* Ⓔ
**se priver de quelque chose** to do without something
**Il va falloir se priver de vacances.** We'll have to do without our holidays.

**privilégier** *verb* [1]
1 **to favour** (*a person*)
2 **to give priority to** (*a task, a problem*)

♪ le **prix** *masc noun*
1 **price**
**Quel est le prix des places?** What price are the seats?
**Le prix a augmenté.** The price has gone up.
**Vous me faites un prix?** Can you give me a discount?
**C'est hors de prix.** It's extremely expensive.
2 **à tout prix** at all costs
3 **prize**
**le prix pour la meilleure traduction** the prize for the best translation

**probable** *masc & fem adjective*
**likely**
**C'est peu probable.** It's unlikely.

**probablement** *adverb*
**probably**

♪ le **problème** *masc noun*
**problem**
**Sans problème!** No problem!

le **procédé** *masc noun*
**process**

le **procès** *masc noun*
1 **trial**
2 **lawsuit**

**WORD TIP** *procès* does not mean *process* in English; for the meaning of *process* ▷ **procédé**.

la **procession** *fem noun*
**procession**

♪ **prochain** *masc adjective*, **prochaine** *fem*
**next**
**la prochaine fois** the next time
**le mois prochain** next month
**jeudi prochain** next Thursday
**À la prochaine!** See you soon!

**prochainement** *adverb*
**soon**

♪ **proche** *masc & fem adjective*
1 **near**
**La ville la plus proche est Valence.** The nearest town is Valence.
**Leur maison est proche de Nice.** Their house is near Nice.
2 **close**
**C'est un de mes amis les plus proches.** He's one of my closest friends.

le **Proche-Orient** *masc noun*
**le Proche-Orient** the Middle East



Ⓔ means the verb takes être to form the perfect

les **proches** *plural masc noun*
**close family and friends**

se **procurer** *reflexive verb* Ⓔ **[1]**
**se procurer quelque chose** to get something
**se procurer le dernier exemplaire** to get hold of the last copy

le **producteur** *masc noun*, la **productrice** *fem*
**producer**
**les pays producteurs de pétrole** the oil-producing countries

la **production** *fem noun*
**production**

**produire** *verb* **[26]**
**to produce**

se **produire** *reflexive verb* Ⓔ
**to happen**
**Je me demande ce qui va se produire.** I wonder what's going to happen.
**Ça s'est produit au mois de mai.** It happened in May.

♪ le **produit** *masc noun*
**product**
- les **produits biologiques** organic produce
- les **produits congelés** frozen foods
- les **produits de beauté** beauty products
- les **produits d'entretien** household products
- les **produits laitiers** dairy products

le **prof** *masc noun*
(*informal*) **teacher**
**notre prof de français** our French teacher

♪ le **professeur** *masc noun*
1 **teacher**
**Elle est professeur de physique.** She's a physics teacher.
2 **university professor**

la **profession** *fem noun*
**profession**, **occupation**

**professionnel** *masc adjective*, **professionnelle** *fem*
**professional**

le **profil** *masc noun*
**profile**

le **profit** *masc noun*
1 **profit**
**les profits de la société** the company's profits
**vendre quelque chose à profit** to sell something at a profit
2 **au profit de quelque chose** in aid of something
**au profit des sans-abri** in aid of the homeless
3 **tirer profit de quelque chose** to profit from something

**profiter** *verb* **[1]**
**profiter de quelque chose** to take advantage of something
**J'ai profité des soldes pour m'acheter un PC.** I took advantage of the sales to buy myself a PC.
**Profite bien de tes vacances!** Make the most of your holiday!

**profond** *masc adjective*, **profonde** *fem*
1 **deep**
**un trou profond de 3 mètres** a hole three metres deep
2 **la France profonde** provincial France

la **profondeur** *fem noun*
**depth**
**La piscine a une profondeur de 3 mètres.** The swimming pool is 3 metres deep.
**Ils ont étudié la question en profondeur.** They've studied the issue in depth.

le **programmateur** *masc noun*
1 **timer**
2 **programme selector** (*on an appliance*)

♪ le **programme** *masc noun*
1 **programme** (*for a concert, a match*)
**Ce n'est pas au programme.** It's not on the programme.
2 **program** (*for a computer*)
3 **syllabus**
**le programme de maths** the maths syllabus

**programmer** *verb* **[1]**
1 **to schedule** (*TV, radio programmes*)
2 (*Computers*) **to program**

le **programmeur** *masc noun*, la **programmeuse** *fem*
(*Computers*) **programmer**

le **progrès** *masc noun*
**progress**
**les progrès de l'informatique** the advances in computer science
**faire des progrès** to make progress
**J'ai fait des progrès en maths.** I've made progress in maths.

**progresser** *verb* **[1]**
1 **to progress**
2 **to make progress**

le **projecteur** *masc noun*
1 **floodlight**
2 **spotlight**
3 **projector**

French–English

a b c d e f g h i j k l m n o p q r s t u v w x y z

le **projet** *masc noun*
1 **plan**
**mes projets pour l'été** my plans for the summer
**Quels sont tes projets pour l'avenir?** What plans do you have for the future?
**Il a encore deux films en projet.** He's planning two more films.
2 **project**
**participer à un projet** to take part in a project
**un projet pour construire un barrage** a project to build a dam
• le **projet de loi** government bill (*not yet law*)

**projeter** *verb* **[48]**
1 **to throw**
**Le choc l'a projeté de sa voiture.** The impact hurled him out of his car.
2 **to show** (*a film, slides*)
3 **to cast** (*a shadow*)
4 **projeter de faire quelque chose** to plan to do something
**Je projette de faire le tour du monde.** I'm planning to go round the world.

la **prolongation** *fem noun*
1 **continuation** (*of a conflict*)
2 **extension** (*of a show, a performance*)
3 (*Sport*) **extra time**
**jouer les prolongations** to go into extra time

**prolongé** *masc adjective*, **prolongée** *fem*
**lengthy**

**prolonger** *verb* **[52]**
1 **to prolong** (*a trip, a holiday*)
**Elle a prolongé ses vacances.** She's prolonged her holidays.
2 **to continue** (*a course of treatment*)

se **prolonger** *reflexive verb* ⓔ
**to go on** (*situation, meeting, show*)
**Le spectacle s'est prolongé jusqu'à 23 h.** The show went on till 11 p.m.

la **promenade** *fem noun*
1 **walk**
**une promenade en voiture** a drive
**une promenade à vélo** a bike ride
**une promenade en bateau** a boat trip
**faire une promenade** to go for a walk
2 **promenade** (*on the seafront*)

**promener** *verb* **[50]**
**to take for a walk** (*a child, a dog*)
**Je dois promener le chien.** I must take the dog for a walk.

se **promener** *reflexive verb* ⓔ
**to go for a walk**
**Ils sont sortis se promener.** They've gone out for a walk.
**se promener en voiture** to go for a drive
**se promener à vélo** to go for a bike ride

la **promesse** *fem noun*
**promise**
**tenir sa promesse** to keep your promise
**Il m'a fait une promesse.** He made me a promise.

**promettre** *verb* **[11]**
**to promise**
**promettre de faire quelque chose** to promise to do something
**Il a promis de téléphoner ce soir.** He promised to ring this evening.
**promettre à quelqu'un de faire quelque chose** to promise somebody you'll do something
**J'ai promis à ma mère de lui écrire souvent.** I promised my mother I would write to her often.

la **promotion** *fem noun*
1 **special offer**
**être en promotion** to be on special offer
**Les fraises sont en promotion.** Strawberries are on special offer.
2 **promotion** (*at work*)
**avoir une promotion** to be promoted

le **pronom** *masc noun*
(*Grammar*) **pronoun**

**prononcer** *verb* **[61]**
1 **to pronounce** (*a word, a name*)
**facile à prononcer** easy to pronounce
2 **to make** (*a speech*)

se **prononcer** *reflexive verb* ⓔ
**to be pronounced**
**Ça se prononce comment?** How do you pronounce it?
**Le 't' de 'mont' ne se prononce pas.** You don't pronounce the 't' in 'mont'.

la **prononciation** *fem noun*
**pronunciation**

la **propagande** *fem noun*
**propaganda**

la **proportion** *fem noun*
**proportion**

le **propos** *masc noun*
1 **intention**
2 **à propos** by the way
**À propos, est-ce que tu l'as appelé?** By the way, did you ring him?
3 **à propos de** about
**Il n'a rien dit à propos de son père.** He didn't say anything about his father.

**proposer** *verb* **[1]**
1 **proposer quelque chose à quelqu'un** to suggest something to somebody
**Je leur ai proposé une petite promenade.** I suggested we went for a little walk.
2 **proposer quelque chose à quelqu'un** to offer somebody something
**On lui a proposé un poste de technicien.** She has been offered a job as a technician.

la **proposition** *fem noun*
**offer**

♪ **propre** *masc & fem adjective*
1 **clean** (*after the noun*)
**une chemise propre** a clean shirt
**des vêtements propres** clean clothes
2 **own** (*before the noun*)
**ma propre voiture** my own car
**ses propres paroles** her own words
**leurs propres enfants** their own children

**WORD TIP** *propre* does not mean *proper* in English; for the meaning of *proper* ▷ **correct**

**proprement** *adverb*
1 **properly**
**Mange proprement!** Eat properly!
2 **à proprement parler** strictly speaking

la **propreté** *fem noun*
**cleanliness**

le & la **propriétaire** *masc & fem noun*
1 **owner** (*of a building, a business*)
2 **landlord**, **landlady** (*of a rented house*)

la **propriété** *fem noun*
**property**
**'Propriété privée'** 'Private property'

le **prospectus** *masc noun*
**leaflet**

**prospère** *masc & fem adjective*
**prosperous**

le **prostitué** *masc noun*, la **prostituée** *fem*
1 **male prostitute**
2 **prostitute**

**protecteur** *masc adjective*, **protectrice** *fem*
**protective**
**une crème protectrice** protective cream

la **protection** *fem noun*
**protection**
**des lunettes de protection** protective goggles

**protéger** *verb* **[15]**
**to protect**
**pour protéger l'environnement** to protect the environment
**Ils se sentent protégés.** They feel protected.

se **protéger** *reflexive verb* ❷
**se protéger de quelque chose** to protect yourself from something
**Je me protège du soleil.** I'm protecting myself from the sun.

le **protestant** *masc noun*, la **protestante** *fem*
(*Religion*) **Protestant**

la **protestation** *fem noun*
**protest**
**un mouvement de protestation** a protest movement

**protester** *verb* **[1]**
**to protest**
**protester contre quelque chose** to protest against something
**Ils protestent contre le racisme.** They're protesting against racism.

**prouver** *verb* **[1]**
**to prove**
**Ça ne prouve rien.** That doesn't prove anything.

la **provenance** *fem noun*
**origin**
**du fromage en provenance de France** cheese from France
**le train en provenance de Lyon** the train arriving from Lyon

**provençal** *masc adjective*, **provençale** *fem*, **provençaux** *masc pl*, **provençales** *fem pl*
**from Provence, Provençal**

**WORD TIP** Adjectives never have capitals in French, even for nationality or regional origin.

**provenir** *verb* **[81]**
**provenir de** to come from
**Ce fromage provient de Normandie.** This cheese is from Normandy.

le **proverbe** *masc noun*
**proverb**

la **province** *fem noun*
**province**
**une ville de province** a provincial town
**Ils habitent en province.** They live in the provinces.

la **provision** *fem noun*
1 **supply**
**faire provision de quelque chose** to stock up on something
**Nous avons fait provision de charbon.** We've stocked up on coal.
2 **des provisions** food
**Maman est partie prendre des provisions.** Mum's gone off shopping for food.

**provisoire** *masc & fem adjective*
**temporary**

**provoquer** *verb* [1]
1 **to cause**
**provoquer un accident** to cause an accident
**provoquer une discussion** to spark off a discussion
2 **provoquer quelqu'un** to provoke somebody
**Il aime bien provoquer.** He likes to be provoking.

la **proximité** *fem noun*
**nearness**
**avec des magasins à proximité** with shops close by
**à proximité de quelque chose** near something
**un hôtel à proximité de l'autoroute** a hotel near the motorway

**prudemment** *adverb*
**carefully**

la **prudence** *fem noun*
**caution**
**Conduisez avec prudence!** Drive carefully!

**prudent** *masc adjective*, **prudente** *fem*
1 **careful**
**Soyez prudents par mauvais temps!** Be careful in bad weather!
2 **sensible**
**Il est plus prudent de réserver.** It's more sensible to book.
**Ce n'est pas prudent d'y aller seul.** It's not sensible to go there alone.

♪ la **prune** *fem noun*
**plum**

**WORD TIP** *prune* does not mean *prune* in English; for the meaning of *prune* ▷ **pruneau**.

le **pruneau** *masc noun*, les **pruneaux** *plural*
**prune**

le **prunier** *masc noun*
**plum tree**

le & la **psychanalyste** *masc & fem noun*
**psychoanalyst**

le & la **psychiatre** *masc & fem noun*
**psychiatrist**

la **psychologie** *fem noun*
**psychology**

le & la **psychologue** *masc & fem noun*
**psychologist**

**pu** *verb* ▷ **pouvoir**

la **pub** *fem noun*
1 (*informal*) **advertising**
2 **ad**, **advertisement**

**WORD TIP** *pub* does not mean *pub* in English; for the meaning of *pub* ▷ **bar**.

♪ **public** *masc adjective*, **publique** *fem* ▷ see **public** *noun*
**public**
**dans un lieu public** in a public place
**une école publique** a state school

♪ le **public** *masc noun* ▷ see **public** *adj*
1 **public**
**en public** in public
**des produits grand public** consumer products
**ouvert au public** open to the public
**'Interdit au public'** 'No entry'
2 **audience**, **spectators**
3 **fans** (*of a singer, etc*)

**publicitaire** *masc & fem adjective*
**une annonce publicitaire** a commercial (*on TV*)
**une campagne publicitaire** an advertising campaign

♪ la **publicité** *fem noun*
1 **advertising**
**travailler dans la publicité** to work in advertising
**faire de la publicité** to advertise
**un coup de publicité** a publicity stunt
2 **advertisement** (*in the press, on TV, etc*)
**une bonne publicité** a good advert

**publier** *verb* [1]
**to publish**

la **puce** *fem noun*
1 **une carte à puce** a smart card
2 **flea**
**un marché aux puces** a fleamarket
• la **puce électronique** microchip

**puer** *verb* [1]
**to stink**

♪ **puis** *adverb*
**then**
**Nous allons à Cannes, puis à Nice.** We're going to Cannes, then Nice.

**puisque** *conjunction*
**since**
**Puisqu'il pleut, je vais prendre le bus.** Since it's raining I'll take the bus.

la **puissance** *fem noun*
**power** (*force, country*)

**puissant** *masc adjective*, **puissante** *fem*
**powerful**

le **puits** *masc noun*
**well**

♪ le **pull**, le **pull-over** *masc noun*
**jumper**

le **pulvérisateur** *masc noun*
**spray** (*for perfume, etc*)

la **punaise** *fem noun*
1 **drawing-pin**
2 **bug** (*insect*)

**punir** *verb* **[2]**
**to punish**
Toute la classe est punie. The whole class is being punished.

la **punition** *fem noun*
**punishment**

**pur** *masc adjective*, **pure** *fem*
1 **pure** (*uncontaminated*)
un shampooing très doux, très pur an ultra-mild, ultra-pure shampoo
un croissant pur beurre an all-butter croissant
2 **sheer**, **utter**
C'est de la folie pure. It's sheer madness.

la **purée** *fem noun*
**purée**
purée de tomates tomato purée

le **puzzle** *masc noun*
**jigsaw puzzle**

le **PV** *masc noun*
**parking ticket**

♪ le **pyjama** *masc noun*
**(pair of) pyjamas**

la **pyramide** *fem noun*
**pyramid**

les **Pyrénées** *plural fem noun*
les Pyrénées the Pyrenees

# Qq

♪ **qu'est-ce que** *phrase*
Qu'est-ce que ... ? What ... ?
Qu'est-ce que c'est? What's that?
Qu'est-ce que tu as trouvé? What have you found?
Qu'est-ce qu'il y a? What's the matter?

**WORD TIP** *qu'est-ce que* becomes *qu'est-ce qu'* before *a*, *e*, *i*, *o*, *u* and *silent h*.

♪ **qu'est-ce qui** *phrase*
Qu'est-ce qui ...? What ...?
Qu'est-ce qui fait ce bruit? What's making that noise?

**WORD TIP** The spelling of *qui* never changes, even before a vowel.

♪ le **quai** *masc noun*
1 **platform**
Le train à destination de Paris va arriver au quai numéro trois. The train for Paris is about to arrive at platform three.
2 **quay** (*for boats*)
3 **bank** (*of a river*)

**qualifié** *masc adjective*, **qualifiée** *fem*
1 **qualified**
2 **skilled**

**qualifier** *verb* **[1]**
**to qualify**

se **qualifier** *reflexive verb* ⓔ
**to qualify**
L'équipe s'est qualifiée pour la finale. The team has qualified for the final.

la **qualité** *fem noun*
**quality**
de première qualité top quality fruit
Jean a des qualités de leader. Jean has leadership qualities.

♪ **quand** *adverb, conjunction*
**when**
quand j'étais en France when I was in France
Quand est-ce que ton frère arrive? When does your brother arrive?
Quand tu auras dix-sept ans, tu pourras apprendre à conduire. When you're seventeen you'll be able to learn to drive.

**WORD TIP** When *quand* refers to the future, use the future tense and not the present as in English.
▷ **depuis**

**quand même** *adverb*
**all the same**
Il pleut mais je vais sortir quand même. It's raining but I'm going to go out all the same.

**quant à** *preposition*
**as for**
Quant à moi, je reste. As for me, I'm staying here.

la **quantité** *fem noun*
**amount**
**une petite quantité d'alcool** a small amount of alcohol

la **quarantaine** *fem noun*
**about forty**
**une quarantaine de personnes** about forty people
**Il approche la quarantaine.** He'll soon be forty.

**quarante** *number*
**forty**

le **quart** *masc noun*
1 **quarter** (*in time*)
**un quart d'heure** a quarter of an hour
**midi moins le quart** a quarter to twelve
**sept heures et quart** a quarter past seven
**Ça a duré une heure et quart.** It lasted an hour and a quarter.
2 **quarter** (*fraction*)
**le quart du gâteau** a quarter of the cake
**un quart d'eau minérale** a quarter-litre bottle of mineral water
**les trois quarts du paquet** three quarters of the packet
- le **quart de finale** quarter-final

le **quartier** *masc noun*
**area** (*of a town*)
**un quartier résidentiel** a residential area
**les gens du quartier** the local people

**WORD TIP** *quartier* does not mean *quarter* in English; for the meaning of *quarter* ▷ **quart**.

**quasi** *adverb*
**almost**
**quasi parfait** almost perfect

**quasiment** *adverb*
**practically**
**C'est quasiment neuf.** It's practically new.

**quatorze** *number*
**fourteen**
**Céline a quatorze ans.** Céline's fourteen.

**quatre** *number*
**four**
**le quatre mars** the fourth of March

**quatre-vingt-dix** *number*
**ninety**
**quatre-vingt-dix-neuf** ninety-nine

**quatre-vingts** *number*
**eighty**
**quatre-vingt-trois** eighty-three
**quatre-vingt-seize** ninety-six

**WORD TIP** The *-s* of *vingts* is omitted when another number follows.

**quatrième** *masc & fem adjective*
▷ see **quatrième** *masc noun, fem noun*
**fourth**
**au quatrième étage** on the fourth floor

le **quatrième** *masc noun*
▷ see **quatrième** *adj, fem noun*
**fourth floor**

la **quatrième** *fem noun*
▷ see **quatrième** *adj, masc noun*
**Year 9** (*in French schools*)

**que**, **qu'** *adverb, conjunction, pronoun*
1 **that** (*often omitted in English*)
**Elle dit que c'est vrai.** She says (that) it's true.
**Je sais qu'il y habite.** I know (that) he lives there.
2 (*in comparisons*) **than, as**
**plus ... que** more ... than
**Anaïs est plus grande que Marie.** Anaïs is taller than Marie.
**aussi...que** as...as
**Elle est aussi grande que moi.** She's as tall as me.
**moins ... que** not as ... as
**Elle est moins grande que toi.** She's not as tall as you.
3 **ne ... que** only
**Je n'ai que dix euros.** I've only got ten euros. ▷ **ne**
4 (*connecting two phrases*) **that, which, whom** (*often omitted in English*)
**le livre que je lis en ce moment** the book (that) I'm reading at the moment
**la chemise qu'il a achetée** the shirt (which) he bought
5 (*in questions*) **what**
**Que veut-il?** What does he want?
**Je ne sais pas ce qu'il veut.** I don't know what he wants.
6 (*in exclamations*) **how**
**Que tu as grandi!** How you've grown!

**WORD TIP** *que* becomes *qu'* before *a, e, i, o, u, y* or *silent h.*

le **Québec** *masc noun*
**le Québec** Quebec

**WORD TIP** Countries and regions in French take *le, la* or *les.*

**québécois** *masc adjective*, **québécoise** *fem* ▷ see **Québécois** *noun*
**from Quebec, Quebecker**

**WORD TIP** Adjectives never have capitals in French, even for nationality or regional origin.

un **Québécois** *masc noun*, une **Québécoise** *fem* ▷ see **québécois** *adj*
1 **French Canadian**, **Quebecker**
les Québécois the French Canadians
2 le québecois Canadian French (*the language*)

**WORD TIP** Languages never have capitals in French.

♪ **quel** *masc adjective*, **quelle** *fem*
1 (*in questions*) **which**, **what**
**Quel livre lis-tu?** Which book are you reading?
**Quelle voiture avez-vous?** Which car do you have?
**Quels DVD as-tu achetés?** What DVDs did you buy?
**Quelles langues est-ce que tu étudies?** What languages are you studying?
2 (*in exclamations*) **what**
**Quel beau temps!** What lovely weather!
**Quelle coïncidence!** What a coincidence!

**quelle** *fem adjective* ▷ **quel**

♪ **quelque** *adjective*
**some**
**J'ai passé quelque temps en France.** I have spent some time in France.
**Nous habitons ici depuis quelque temps.** We've been living here for some time.

♪ **quelque chose** *pronoun*
1 **something**
**Il faut manger quelque chose.** You must eat something.
**J'ai quelque chose à te dire.** I have something to tell you.
2 **quelque chose de** + *adjective* something + adjective
**quelque chose de nouveau** something new
3 **anything**
**Est-ce que tu as vu quelque chose?** Did you see anything?

♪ **quelquefois** *adverb*
**sometimes**

**quelque part** *adverb*
1 **somewhere**
**J'ai laissé la clé quelque part dans le bureau.** I left the key somewhere in the office.
2 **anywhere**
**Est-ce que tu as vu mes lunettes quelque part?** Have you seen my glasses anywhere?

**quelques** *plural adjective*
1 **some**
**Je vais te donner quelques cerises.** I'll give you some cherries.
2 **a few**
**Il reste quelques fraises.** There are a few strawberries left.

**quelqu'un** *pronoun*
1 **somebody**
**Quelqu'un a appelé pour toi.** Somebody rang for you.
2 **anybody**
**Il y a quelqu'un?** Is there anybody there?
**Est-ce que quelqu'un t'a aidé?** Did anybody help you?

**quelques-uns** *plural masc pronoun*, **quelques-unes** *pl fem*
**some**
**quelques-uns des enfants** some of the children
**Les cerises sont bonnes. Prends-en quelques-unes!** The cherries are good. Have some!

**WORD TIP** Use *quelques-unes* for a fem plural noun.

**quels** *plural masc adjective*, **quelles** *pl fem* ▷ **quel**

la **querelle** *fem noun*
**quarrel**

♪ la **question** *fem noun*
1 **question**
**Elle n'a pas répondu à mes questions.** She didn't answer my questions.
**Il me pose toujours des questions difficiles.** He always asks me difficult questions.
2 **matter**, **question**
**C'est une question de goût.** It's a matter of taste.
**C'est hors de question.** It's out of the question.
**Pas question!** No way!

le **questionnaire** *masc noun*
**questionnaire**

**questionner** *verb* **[1]**
**to question** (*in an interview*)
**On l'a questionné à propos des émeutes.** He was questioned about the riots.

la **queue** *fem noun*
1 **tail**
**la queue du chat** the cat's tail
2 **queue**
**faire la queue** to queue
3 **la queue du train** the rear of the train
• la **queue de cheval** ponytail

♪ **qui** *pronoun*
1 (*in questions*) **who**
**Qui vient ce soir?** Who's coming this evening? ⏩

**Qui voulez-vous voir?** Who do you want to see?
**De qui parles-tu?** Who are you talking about?
**C'est pour qui?** Who's it for?

2 (*connecting two phrases*) **who, that**
**la personne qui m'a téléphoné** the person who phoned me
**Voilà le chien qui a mordu Victor.** That's the dog that bit Victor.

3 **à qui ... ?** whose ... ?
**À qui est ce pull?** Whose is this jumper?
**Je ne sais pas à qui c'est.** I don't know whose it is.

**WORD TIP** The spelling of *qui* never changes.

la **quiche** *fem noun*
**quiche**

la **quincaillerie** *fem noun*
**hardware shop**

la **quinzaine** *fem noun*
1 **about fifteen**
**une quinzaine d'enfants** about fifteen children
2 **fortnight**
**une quinzaine de jours** a fortnight

**quinze** *number*
1 **fifteen**
**le quinze juillet** the fifteenth of July
**Romaine a quinze ans.** Romaine is fifteen.
2 **quinze jours** two weeks
**tous les quinze jours** every two weeks

**quitter** *verb* **[1]**
1 **to leave** (*a place, a person, etc*)
**Elle quitte le bureau à cinq heures.** She leaves the office at five.
**Elle l'a quitté il y a deux ans.** She left him two years ago.
2 (*on the telephone*) **Ne quittez pas.** Hold the line.
3 (*Computers*) **to quit**

**quoi** *pronoun*
1 **what** (*in questions*)
**Quoi encore?** What now?
**Quoi de neuf?** What's new?
**Pour quoi faire?** What for?
**À quoi penses-tu?** What are you thinking about?
2 (*in expressions*) **Il n'y a pas de quoi se fâcher.** There's no reason to get angry.
**'Merci.' — 'Il n'y a pas de quoi.'** 'Thank you.' — 'Don't mention it.'

**quoique** *conjunction*
**although, though**
**Quoique petit, il est assez fort.** Although he's small, he's quite strong.

**quotidien** *masc adjective*, **quotidienne** *fem* ▷ see **quotidien** *masc noun*
**daily**
**la vie quotidienne** daily life

le **quotidien** *masc noun*
▷ see **quotidien** *adj*
**daily newspaper**

# R r

le **rabais** *masc noun*
**discount**
**Je l'ai acheté au rabais.** I bought it at a discount.

**raccompagner** *verb* **[1]**
**raccompagner quelqu'un chez soi** to see somebody home
**Je te raccompagne chez toi.** I'll see you home.

le **raccourci** *masc noun*
**shortcut**

**raccrocher** *verb* **[1]**
**to hang up** (*on the phone*)

la **race** *fem noun*
1 **race**
**la race humaine** the human race
2 **breed**
**différentes races de chien** different breeds of dogs

**racheter** *verb* **[16]**
1 **to buy more** (*bread, paper*)
2 **racheter quelque chose à quelqu'un** to buy something from somebody
**Il m'a racheté mon vélo.** He bought my bike from me.

la **racine** *fem noun*
**root**

**raciste** *masc & fem adjective*
▷ see **raciste** *noun*
**racist** (*remark*)

**raciste** *masc & fem noun*
▷ see **raciste** *adjective*
**racist**

**raconter** *verb* **[1]**
**to tell** (*a story*)

le **radar** *masc noun*
**radar**

le **radeau** *masc noun*, les **radeaux** *plural*
**raft**

le **radiateur** *masc noun*
**radiator**

ℰ la **radio** *fem noun*
1 **radio**
**Il a entendu la nouvelle à la radio.** He heard the news on the radio.
2 **radio station**
3 **X-ray**
**passer une radio** to have an X-ray
• le **radio-réveil** clock radio

le **radis** *masc noun*
**radish**

**raffoler** *verb* **[1]**
(*informal*) **raffoler de quelque chose** to be mad about something
**Je ne raffole pas des huîtres.** I'm not mad about oysters.

**rafraîchir** *verb* **[2]**
**to cool (down)**
**La pluie a rafraîchi l'atmosphère.** The rain cooled the atmosphere.

se **rafraîchir** *reflexive verb* ⓔ
**to get cooler** (*weather*)

le **rafraîchissement** *masc noun*
1 **refreshment**
2 **drop in temperature**

le **rafting** *masc noun*
**(white water) rafting**

la **rage** *fem noun*
1 **rabies**
2 **être fou de rage** to be hopping mad
• la **rage de dents** raging toothache

le **ragoût** *masc noun*
**stew**

**raide** *masc & fem adjective*
1 **stiff** (*body*)
2 **straight** (*hair*)
3 **steep** (*slope*)

la **raie** *fem noun*
1 **parting** (*in your hair*)
2 **skate** (*the fish*)

le **rail** *masc noun*
**rail** (*for trains*)

ℰ le **raisin** *masc noun*
**grapes**
**une grappe de raisin** a bunch of grapes
**un grain de raisin** a grape

**WORD TIP** *raisin* does not mean *raisin* in English; for the meaning of *raisin* ▷ **raisin sec**

• le **raisin de Corinthe** currant
• le **raisin sec** raisin

ℰ la **raison** *fem noun*
1 **reason**
**pour cette raison** for this reason
**pour raisons de santé** for health reasons
2 **avoir raison** to be right
**Cette fois, tu as raison.** This time, you're right.

**raisonnable** *masc & fem adjective*
**sensible**

le **raisonnement** *masc noun*
**reasoning**

**rajouter** *verb* **[1]**
**to add** (*ingredients*)

**ralentir** *verb* **[2]**
**to slow down**

le **ralentisseur** *masc noun*
**speed hump**

**râler** *verb* **[1]**
(*informal*) **to moan**

le **râleur** *masc noun*, la **râleuse** *fem*
**moaner**

la **rallonge** *fem noun*
**extension lead**

**rallumer** *verb* **[1]**
**to put back on again** (*light, heating*)

le **ramassage** *masc noun*
**collection**

**ramasser** *verb* **[1]**
1 **to pick up** (*papers, books*)
2 **to pick** (*fruit*)
3 **to collect** (*chestnuts, shells*)
4 **to collect in** (*books, homework*)

la **rame** *fem noun*
1 **oar**
2 **train**
**une rame de métro** an underground train

le **rameau** *masc noun*, les **rameaux** *plural*
**branch**
**les Rameaux, le dimanche des Rameaux** Palm Sunday

**ramener** *verb* **[50]**
1 **ramener quelqu'un (en voiture)** to give somebody a lift home
**Tu veux que je te ramène?** Do you want me to give you a lift home? ⏩

2 **to take back**
**ramener des livres à la bibliothèque** to take books back to the library

**ramer** *verb* **[1]**
**to row**

la **rampe** *fem noun*
1 **bannister**
2 **ramp**

la **rançon** *fem noun*
**ransom**

la **rancune** *fem noun*
**resentment**

la **randonnée** *fem noun*
**hike**
**faire une randonnée pédestre** to go on a hike (*on public footpaths*)
**faire une randonnée à cheval** to go pony-trekking
**une randonnée à vélo** a long-distance bike ride

le **randonneur** *masc noun*, la **randonneuse** *fem*
1 **hiker**
2 **touring cyclist**

le **rang** *masc noun*
**row**

la **rangée** *fem noun*
**row** (*of chairs, houses*)

**ranger** *verb* **[52]**
1 **to put away**
**ranger la vaisselle** to put away the dishes
2 **to tidy**
**Je vais ranger ma chambre.** I'm going to tidy my room.
3 **to arrange**
**rangé par ordre alphabétique** arranged alphabetically

**râper** *verb* **[1]**
**to grate** (*cheese*)

**rapide** *masc & fem adjective*
▷ see **rapide** *noun*
1 **fast**
**Le guépard est l'animal le plus rapide.** The cheetah is the fastest animal.
2 **quick**
**une réaction rapide** a quick reaction

le **rapide** *masc noun* ▷ **see rapide** *adj*
1 **express train**
2 **rapids**

**rapidement** *adverb*
**quickly**

le **rappel** *masc noun*
1 **reminder** (*for a bill*)
2 **booster** (*vaccination*)

**rappeler** *verb* **[18]**
1 **to remind**
**Rappelle-moi de passer à la vidéothèque!** Remind me to go to the videolibrary!
**Ça me rappelle mes vacances.** It reminds me of my holidays.
2 **to ring back** (*on the phone*)
**Je rappellerai plus tard.** I'll ring back later.

se **rappeler** *reflexive verb* Ⓔ
**to remember**
**Je me rappelle qu'elle avait les cheveux longs.** I remember she had long hair.
**Je ne me rappelle plus.** I can't remember.

le **rapport** *masc noun*
1 **connection**
2 **relations**
**des rapports amicaux** friendly relations
**avoir des rapports sexuels** to have sex
3 **report**
**un rapport officiel** an official report
4 **par rapport à quelque chose** compared with something
**Il fait très beau par rapport à hier.** The weather is very good compared with yesterday.

**rapporter** *verb* **[1]**
1 **to bring back**
2 **to bring in money**

**rapprocher** *verb* **[1]**
1 **to move something closer**
**Je rapproche mon bureau de la fenêtre.** I'm moving my desk closer to the window.
2 **to bring together** (*different people, different countries*)

se **rapprocher** *reflexive verb* Ⓔ
**to get closer**
**Elle s'est rapprochée de la table.** She moved closer to the table.

la **raquette** *fem noun*
1 **racket** (*for tennis*)
2 **bat** (*for ping-pong*)

**rare** *masc & fem adjective*
**rare**
**une fleur rare** a rare flower

**rarement** *adverb*
**rarely**

**ras** *masc adjective*, **rase** *fem* ▷ **see ras** *adv*
1 **short** (*hair, fur*)
**un chien à poil ras** a short-haired dog
2 **à ras bord** to the brim
3 (*informal*) **en avoir ras le bol de quelque chose, quelqu'un** to be fed up with

Ⓔ means the verb takes être to form the perfect

something, somebody
J'en ai ras le bol! I'm fed up with it!

**ras** *adverb* ▷ see **ras** *adj*
**short**
des cheveux coupés ras close-cropped hair

**raser** *verb* [1]
**to shave**
Il a rasé sa barbe. He's shaved off his beard.

se **raser** *reflexive verb* ⓔ
**to shave**
se raser les jambes to shave your legs

le **rasoir** *masc noun*
**razor**

le **rassemblement** *masc noun*
**rally** (*for peace, support, etc.*)

**rassembler** *verb* [1]
**to gather (together)**

se **rassembler** *reflexive verb* ⓔ
**to gather**
Ils se sont rassemblés pour l'écouter. They all gathered to listen to him.

**rassis** *masc adjective*, **rassise** *fem*
**stale** (*bread*)

**rassurer** *verb* [1]
**to reassure**
Ça me rassure! That puts my mind at rest!

se **rassurer** *reflexive verb* ⓔ
**to reassure yourself**
Rassure-toi, tout se passera bien! Don't worry, it'll be fine!

le **rat** *masc noun*
**rat**

le **râteau** *masc noun*, les **râteaux** *plural*
**rake**

**rater** *verb* [1]
1 **to fail** (*an exam, a driving test*)
2 **to miss** (*a bus, a train, a plane*)

la **RATP** *fem noun*
(*= Régie autonome des transports parisiens*)
(*transport network serving the Île-de-France region around Paris*)

**rattacher** *verb* [1]
**to fasten again** (*a seatbelt, a belt*)

**rattraper** *verb* [1]
1 **to catch up with** (*a person*)
Ils nous rattraperont. They'll catch up with us.
2 **to make up for** (*lost time*)
rattraper son retard en to catch up in (*a school subject*)
J'ai rattrapé mon retard en français. I've caught up in French.
3 **to catch** (*a ball*)

se **rattraper** *reflexive verb* ⓔ
**to make up for it**
J'ai très peu joué cet été mais je vais me rattraper. I've played very little this summer but I'll make up for it.

la **rature** *fem noun*
**crossing-out**

♪ **ravi** *masc adjective*, **ravie** *fem*
**delighted**
Je suis ravi de vous voir. I'm delighted to see you (*boy speaking*).
Je suis ravie de vous avoir rencontré. I'm delighted to have met you (*girl speaking*).

le **ravisseur** *masc noun*, la **ravisseuse** *fem*
**kidnapper**

**rayé** *masc adjective*, **rayée** *fem*
**striped** (*fabric*)

**rayer** *verb* [59]
1 **to cross out** (*a mistake*)
2 **to scratch** (*a surface*)

♪ le **rayon** *masc noun*
1 **department** (*in a department store*)
le rayon jouets the toy department
2 **section** (*in a supermarket*)
3 **ray**
les rayons X X-rays
4 **radius**
dans un rayon de deux kilomètres within a two-kilometre radius
5 **shelf**

la **rayure** *fem noun*
1 **stripe**
2 **scratch**

le **réacteur** *masc noun*
1 **jet engine**
2 un réacteur nucléaire a nuclear reactor

la **réaction** *fem noun*
**reaction**

**réagir** *verb* [2]
**to react**

le **réalisateur** *masc noun*, la **réalisatrice** *fem*
**director** (*of a film, a TV programme*)

la **réalisation** *fem noun*
1 **carrying out** (*of a plan, a project*)
2 **production** (*of a film, a radio or TV programme*)

**réaliser** *verb* [1]
1 **to carry out** (*a project*)
2 **to fulfil** (*a dream*)
3 **to make** (*a film*)

**réaliste** *masc & fem adjective*
**realistic**

la **réalité** *fem noun*
**reality**

la **réanimation** *fem noun*
**resuscitation**
**le service de réanimation** the intensive care unit

le & la **rebelle** *masc & fem noun*
**rebel**

**rebondir** *verb* **[2]**
**to bounce**

le **rebord** *masc noun*
**edge** (*of a bathtub*)
- le **rebord de fenêtre** windowsill

**récemment** *adverb*
**recently**

♪ **récent** *masc adjective*, **récente** *fem*
**recent**

♪ la **réception** *fem noun*
1 **welcome**
**une réception enthousiaste** an enthousiastic welcome
2 **reception desk**
**Demandez la clé à la réception.** Ask for the key at the reception desk.
3 **reception** (*party*)

le & la **réceptionniste** *masc & fem noun*
**receptionist**

♪ la **recette** *fem noun*
**recipe**
**la recette du gâteau au chocolat** the recipe for chocolate cake

♪ **recevoir** *verb* **[66]**
1 **to receive**, **to get**
**J'ai reçu ta lettre.** I received your letter.
**Il a reçu ton message.** He got your message.
2 **to welcome** (*a visitor, a guest*)
3 **to entertain** (*to invite people round*)
4 **to see** (*a patient, a client*)
5 **être reçu à un examen** to pass an exam
**Il va être reçu au bac.** He'll pass the baccalaureat.
**Elle a été reçue première à l'examen.** She came top in the exam.

le **rechange** *masc noun*
**de rechange** spare
**des vêtements de rechange** spare clothes

la **recharge** *fem noun*
**refill**

le **réchaud** *masc noun*
**stove**

**réchauffer** *verb* **[1]**
1 **to heat up** (*food*)
2 **to warm up** (*hands, feet*)

se **réchauffer** *reflexive verb* ⓔ
1 **to warm up**
2 **to get warmer** (*weather*)

le **réchauffement de la planète** *masc noun*
**global warming**

la **recherche** *fem noun*
1 **research**
2 **être à la recherche de quelque chose** to be looking for something

**rechercher** *verb* **[1]**
**to look for** (*a person, a job*)

le **récipient** *masc noun*
**container**

**réciproque** *masc & fem adjective*
**mutual**

le **récit** *masc noun*
**story**

la **récitation** *fem noun*
**text** (*often a poem that schoolchildren learn off by heart*)
**J'ai appris ma récitation.** I've learnt my text off by heart.

**réciter** *verb* **[1]**
**to recite**

la **réclamation** *fem noun*
**complaint**
**une lettre de réclamation** a letter of complaint

♪ la **réclame** *fem noun*
1 **advertisement**
**une réclame pour du parfum** an advertisement for perfume
2 **en réclame** on (special) offer (*at supermarket*)

**réclamer** *verb* **[1]**
**to demand**
**Ils réclament trois jours de plus de vacances.** They're demanding three more days' holiday.

la **récolte** *fem noun*
1 **harvest**
2 **crop**

**récolter** *verb* **[1]**
1 **to harvest** (*wheat, corn*)
2 **to collect** (*money*)
3 (*informal*) **to get** (*a fine*)

la **recommandation** *fem noun*
**recommendation**



ⓔ means the verb takes être to form the perfect

**recommandé** *masc adjective*, **recommandée** *fem*
**registered** (*letter*)
**envoyer une lettre sous pli recommandé** to send a letter by registered post

♂ **recommander** *verb* [1]
1 **to advise**
**Je te recommande de ne rien dire.** I advise you to say nothing.
2 **to recommend**
**Pourrais-tu recommander un bon restaurant?** Could you recommend a good restaurant?

**recommencer** *verb* [61]
1 **to do again**
**Ne recommence pas!** Don't do it again!
**Je recommence ma lettre, j'ai fait trop de fautes.** I'm writing my letter again, I've made too many mistakes.
2 **recommencer quelque chose à zéro** to start something again from scratch
3 **to start again**
**Les cours recommencent en octobre.** The classes start again in October.
**Ça recommence!** Here we go again!

♂ la **récompense** *fem noun*
**reward**
**En récompense, j'ai eu un billet gratuit.** As a reward, I got a free ticket.

**récompenser** *verb* [1]
**to reward**

se **réconcilier** *reflexive verb* Ⓔ [1]
**to make up** (*after a row*)
**se réconcilier avec quelqu'un** to make it up with somebody
**Zoé s'est réconciliée avec Marine.** Zoé made it up with Marine.

**réconfortant** *masc adjective*, **réconfortante** *fem*
**comforting**

**reconnaissable** *masc & fem adjective*
**recognizable**

la **reconnaissance** *fem noun*
**gratitude**

**reconnaissant** *masc adjective*, **reconnaissante** *fem*
**grateful**

**reconnaître** *verb* [27]
1 **to recognize**
**Je ne l'ai pas reconnue.** I didn't recognize her.
2 **to admit**
**Il faut reconnaître que c'est difficile.** You have to admit that it's difficult.

**reconstruire** *verb* [26]
**to rebuild**

**recopier** *verb* [1]
**to copy out**

le **record** *masc noun*
**record**
**un record mondial** a world record
**Il a battu le record du 75 mètres à l'école.** He broke the school record for the 75 metres.

**recouvrir** *verb* [30]
**to cover**

♂ la **récréation** *fem noun*
**break**
**à la récréation** at break

le **rectangle** *masc noun*
**rectangle**

**rectangulaire** *masc & fem adjective*
**rectangular**

**rectifier** *verb* [1]
**to correct**

♂ le **reçu** *masc noun* ▷ see **reçu** *verb*
**receipt**
**Vous avez encore le reçu?** Do you still have the receipt?

♂ **reçu** *verb* ▷ see **reçu** *noun* ▷ **recevoir**

le **recueil** *masc noun*
**collection** (*of poems, essays*)

**reculer** *verb* [1]
1 **to move back**
2 **to reverse** (*in a car*)

**reculons** *adverbial phrase*
**à reculons** backwards

**récupérer** *verb* [24]
1 **to get back** (*something borrowed*)
2 **to fetch**
3 **to recover** (*from an illness*)

**recycler** *verb* [1]
**to recycle**
**Nous recyclons aussi les bouteilles en plastique.** We recycle plastic bottles too.

la **rédaction** *fem noun*
**essay**
**J'ai eu une bonne note à ma rédaction.** I got a good mark for my essay.

**redemander** *verb* [1]
1 **to ask again**
**Tu devrais redemander.** You should ask again.
2 **to ask for more**
**Il faut qu'on redemande des cahiers.** We'll have to ask for more exercise books.

**redescendre** *verb* Ⓔ **[3]**
1 **to go back down**
**Elle est redescendue à la cave.** She went back down to the cellar.
2 **to come back down** (*from somewhere further north*)
3 **to bring back down** (*from upstairs*)

**rédiger** *verb* **[52]**
**to write** (*an article*)

**redonner** *verb* **[1]**
**to give again**
**Je leur ai redonné mon adresse.** I gave them my address again

**redoubler** *verb* **[1]**
**to repeat a year** (*at school*)

**redresser** *verb* **[1]**
1 **to straighten** (*picture, teeth*)
2 **to rectify** (*an error*)

se **redresser** *reflexive verb* Ⓔ
**to straighten up**

♂ la **réduction** *fem noun*
1 **reduction**
**une réduction du nombre d'étudiants** a reduction in the number of students
2 **discount**
**une réduction de 20%** a 20% discount
**faire une réduction à quelqu'un** to give somebody a discount
**Ils font une réduction de 30% aux étudiants.** They give students a 30% discount.
3 **concession**
**une réduction pour les moins de 15 ans** a concession for the under-15s

**réduire** *verb* **[68]**
**to cut** (*prices, taxes*)
**à prix réduit** cut-price

la **rééducation** *fem noun*
**physiotherapy**

**réel** *masc adjective*, **réelle** *fem*
**real**

**réellement** *adverb*
**really**

**refaire** *verb* **[10]**
1 **to redo**
**Je dois refaire mon devoir de maths.** I have to redo my maths homework.
2 **to make more**
**Je refais du café.** I'm making some more coffee.

la **référence** *fem noun*
**reference**
**la date de référence** the date of reference
**faire référence à quelque chose** to refer to something
**Il fait référence à l'article du journal.** He's referring to the newspaper article.

**réfléchi** *masc adjective*, **réfléchie** *fem*
**reflexive** (*verb*)

**réfléchir** *verb* **[2]**
1 **to think**
**Réfléchis bien avant d'accepter.** Think carefully before accepting.
**Ça fait réfléchir.** It makes you think.
2 **réfléchir à quelque chose** to think about something
**J'ai réfléchi à ta question.** I've thought about your question.

le **reflet** *masc noun*
1 **reflection**
**regarder son reflet dans l'eau** to look at your reflection in the water
2 **des cheveux aux reflets blonds** hair with blond highlights

**refléter** *verb* **[24]**
**to reflect**

le **réflexe** *masc noun*
1 **reflex**
**J'ai de bons réflexes.** I've got good reflexes.
2 **reaction**
**Mon premier réflexe a été de crier.** My first reaction was to shout.

la **réflexion** *fem noun*
1 **thought**
**Réflexion faite, je n'irai pas.** On second thoughts, I won't go.
2 **comment**, **remark**
**faire des réflexions** to make remarks

le **refrain** *masc noun*
**chorus**

le **réfrigérateur** *masc noun*
**refrigerator**

**refroidir** *verb* **[2]**
1 **to cool down**
2 **to get cold**
**La soupe va refroidir!** The soup will get cold!

le **refuge** *masc noun*
1 **refuge**
2 **mountain hut** (*for climbers*)
3 **animal sanctuary**
4 **traffic island**

le **réfugié** *masc noun*, la **réfugiée** *fem*
**refugee**

se **réfugier** *reflexive verb* Ⓔ **[1]**
**to take refuge**



Ⓔ means the verb takes être to form the perfect

le **refus** *masc noun*
**refusal**

**refuser** *verb* **[1]**
1 **to refuse**
**refuser de faire quelque chose** to refuse to do something
**Elle a refusé de répondre.** She refused to answer.
2 **to turn down** (*an application for a job*)

**regagner** *verb* **[1]**
**to get back to**
**Il a regagné la plage.** He got back to the beach.

le **régal** *masc noun*
**feast** (*delicious meal*)

se **régaler** *reflexive verb* ❷ **[1]**
**Je me régale.** It's delicious.
**se régaler avec quelque chose** to enjoy something thoroughly
**On s'est régalé avec les festivals de musique.** We thoroughly enjoyed the music festivals.

le **regard** *masc noun*
**look**
**Il jette un regard rapide à sa montre.** He takes a quick look at his watch.

♂ **regarder** *verb* **[1]**
1 **to look at**
**Je regarde la carte.** I'm looking at the map.
2 **to look in** (*the phone book, the dictionary*)
**On a regardé dans le dictionnaire.** We looked in the dictionary.
3 **to watch** (*the TV*)
**Tu veux regarder le film?** Do you want to watch the film?
4 **to look**
**Regarde!** Look!
**regarder par la fenêtre** to look out of the window
5 **to concern**
**Cela ne nous regarde pas.** That doesn't concern us.
**Ça ne te regarde pas.** That's none of your business.

se **regarder** *reflexive verb* ❷
1 **to look at yourself**
**Il se regarde dans la glace.** He's looking at himself in the mirror.
2 **to look at each other**
3 **to face each other** (*buildings*)

la **régate** *fem noun*
**regatta**

le **régime** *masc noun*
1 **diet**
**un régime sans sel** a salt-free diet
**Je fais un régime.** I'm on a diet.
2 **bunch** (*of bananas*)
3 **regime**

♂ la **région** *fem noun*
**region**, **area**
**la région parisienne** the Paris region
**les vins de la région** the local wines
**visiter la région** to visit the area
**la Région Aquitaine** the Aquitaine Region
(*Une région is a large French administrative region made up of smaller areas called **départements**.*)

**régional** *masc adjective*, **régionale** *fem*, **régionaux** *masc pl*, **régionales** *fem pl*
**regional**

le **registre** *masc noun*
**register**

**réglable** *masc & fem adjective*
**adjustable**

la **règle** *fem noun*
1 **ruler**
2 **rule**
**les règles du jeu** the rules of the game
**En règle générale...** As a general rule...
3 **en règle** in order (*valid*)
**Mes papiers sont tous en règle.** My papers are all in order.
4 **les règles** period (*menstruation*)
• les **règles de sécurité** safety regulations

♂ le **règlement** *masc noun*
1 **rules**
**C'est contraire au règlement de l'école.** It's against the school rules.
2 **payment**
**un mode de règlement** a method of payment
3 **settlement** (*after a dispute*)

**régler** *verb* **[24]**
1 **to pay** (*a bill, a debt*)
**Vous réglez comment, monsieur?** How would you like to pay, sir?
2 **to sort out** (*details, a problem*)
3 **to adjust** (*the height, the width*)

la **réglisse** *fem noun*
**liquorice**

le **règne** *masc noun*
**reign**

**régner** *verb* **[24]**
**to reign**

le **regret** *masc noun*
**regret**
sans regret with no regrets
Mille regrets. I'm terribly sorry.

**regretter** *verb* **[1]**
**1 to be sorry**
Je regrette, elle est partie. I'm sorry, she's left.
regretter de faire quelque chose to be sorry to do something
Je regrette de ne pas pouvoir t'aider. I'm sorry I can't help you.
**2 to regret** *(a decision)*
Je ne regrette rien. I have no regrets.
**3 to miss**
Elle regrette la vie à Paris. She misses life in Paris.

**regrouper** *verb* **[1]**
**to group together**

se **regrouper** *reflexive verb* Ⓔ
**to gather**

la **régularité** *fem noun*
**regularity**

**régulier** *masc adjective*, **régulière** *fem*
**regular**
un vol régulier a scheduled flight

**régulièrement** *adverb*
**regularly**

le **rein** *masc noun*
**1 kidney**
**2** avoir mal aux reins to have backache

♪ la **reine** *fem noun*
**queen**
la reine Élisabeth Queen Elizabeth

**rejeter** *verb* **[48]**
**to reject**

**rejoindre** *verb* **[49]**
**1 to meet up with**
Je vous rejoins dans la cour. I'll meet you in the playground.
**2 to catch up with**
**3 to join** *(other people, a group, a movement)*

se **rejoindre** *reflexive verb* Ⓔ
**1 to meet up** *(people)*
**2 to merge** *(motorways, lanes)*

**rejouer** *verb* **[1]**
**to replay**

**relâcher** *verb* **[1]**
**1 to loosen** *(a grip, a hold)*
**2 to set free** *(a hostage, an animal)*

le **relais** *masc noun*
**1** prendre le relais to take over
Il a pris le relais au volant. He took over the driving.
**2 relay race**

**relatif** *masc adjective*, **relative** *fem*
**relative**

la **relation** *fem noun*
**1 connection**
en relation avec in connection with
**2 acquaintance**
une relation de mon frère an acquaintance of my brother's
**3 relationship**
Il n'a pas de bonnes relations avec son père. He hasn't got a good relationship with his father.
**4** les relations publiques public relations, PR

**WORD TIP** *Relation* does not mean *relation* in English; for the meaning of *relation* ▷ **famille**.

**relativement** *adverb*
**relatively**

**relax** *invariable masc & fem adjective*
**1** *(informal)* **laid back** *(person)*
**2 casual** *(party, event)*

**relaxer** *verb* **[1]**
**to relax**

le **relevé** *masc noun*
faire le relevé de quelque chose to make a list of something
On a fait le relevé des dépenses. We made a list of the expenses.
- le **relevé de compte** bank statement
- le **relevé de notes** school report

**relever** *verb* **[50]**
**1 to raise**
**2** relever la tête to look up
**3 to notice** *(details, mistakes)*
**4 to read** *(the meter)*

se **relever** *reflexive verb* Ⓔ
**to pick yourself up** *(after a fall)*

**relier** *verb* **[1]**
**1 to link**
Un canal relie Brest à Nantes. A canal links Brest to Nantes.
**2 to join up**
Relie les points! Join up the dots!

**religieux** *masc adjective*, **religieuse** *fem*
▷ see **religieux** *noun*
**religious**

le **religieux** *masc noun*, la **religieuse** *fem*
▷ see **religieux** *adj*
**1 monk**
**2 nun**





Ⓔ means the verb takes être to form the perfect

la **religion** *fem noun*
**religion**

**relire** *verb* [51]
**to reread**

**remarié** *masc adjective*, **remariée** *fem*
**remarried**

**remarquable** *masc & fem adjective*
**remarkable**
**des progrès remarquables** remarkable progress

la **remarque** *fem noun*
1 **remark**
**une remarque déplaisante** an nasty remark
2 **comment**
**Il y a des remarques dans la marge.** There are some comments in the margin.

♪ **remarquer** *verb* [1]
1 **to notice**
**Il n'a rien remarqué.** He didn't notice anything.
**J'ai remarqué qu'elle est arrivée en retard.** I noticed she arrived late.
2 **se faire remarquer** to draw attention to yourself
**Il n'aime pas se faire remarquer.** He doesn't like to draw attention to himself.
3 **faire remarquer quelque chose à quelqu'un** to point something out to somebody
**Elle nous a fait remarquer que c'était trop tard.** She pointed out to us that it was too late.
4 **Remarque, moi ça m'est égal!** Mind you, it's all the same to me!

**rembobiner** *verb* [1]
**to rewind** (*a tape*)

le **remboursement** *masc noun*
**refund**

**rembourser** *verb* [1]
1 **to pay back**
**Je te rembourserai demain.** I'll pay you back tomorrow.
2 **to refund the price of** (*a ticket, a purchase*)
3 **to give a refund**
**Ce magasin ne rembourse pas.** This shop doesn't give refunds.
**se faire rembourser** to get a refund

le **remède** *masc noun*
**remedy**

le **remerciement** *masc noun*
**thanks**
**tous mes remerciements** many thanks
**une lettre de remerciement** a thank-you letter

**remercier** *verb* [1]
1 **to thank**
**Je voudrais remercier tous mes amis.** I would like to thank all my friends.
**Je vous remercie.** Thank you.
2 **remercier quelqu'un d'avoir fait quelque chose** to thank somebody for doing something
**Il nous a remerciés de l'avoir aidé.** He thanked us for helping him.

**remettre** *verb* [11]
1 **to put back**
**Il a remis la photo sur la table.** He put the photo back on the table.
2 **to put back on** (*a sweater, a jacket*)
3 **to wear again** (*an item of clothing*)
4 **remettre quelque chose à quelqu'un** to hand something over to somebody
**Pouvez-vous me remettre les clés demain?** Can you hand over the keys to me tomorrow?
5 **to put off** (*a meeting, a trip*)
**Ils ont remis la réunion à jeudi.** They've put the meeting off until Thursday.

se **remettre** *reflexive verb* ⓔ
**to start again**
1 **Charlène s'est remise au piano.** Charlène's started playing the piano again.
**Il se remet à pleuvoir.** It's starting to rain again.
2 **se remettre de quelque chose** to recover from something
**Elle ne s'est pas remise de sa chute.** She hasn't recovered from her fall.

la **remise** *fem noun*
1 **handing out** (*of awards*)
**la remise des prix** prizegiving
2 **discount**
**une remise de 20% sur les CD** a 20% discount on CDs
3 **garden shed**

le **remonte-pente** *masc noun*, les **remonte-pentes** *plural*
**ski lift**

**remonter** *verb* [1]
1 ⓔ **to go back up**
**Natalie est remontée dans sa chambre.** Natalie's gone back up to her room.
2 ⓔ **to come back up** (*from somewhere further south*)
3 ⓔ **to get back in**
**Ils sont remontés dans le car.** They got back into the coach.
4 **to take back up** (*upstairs*) ▸▸

**5** **to put up** *(in an overhead section)*
**Il a remonté sa valise au filet.** He put his case up in the luggage rack.
**6** **remonter la pente** to go back up the hill
**7** **remonter le moral à quelqu'un** to cheer somebody up
**Ses blagues m'ont remonté le moral.** His jokes cheered me up.

**WORD TIP** When you say what you *take back up, put back up* etc, use *avoir* in the perfect tense.

le **remords** *masc noun*
**remorse**

la **remorque** *fem noun*
**trailer** *(for a car)*

le **remplaçant** *masc noun*, la **remplaçante** *fem*
**1** **replacement** *(for another person)*
**2** **supply teacher**

**remplacer** *verb* **[61]**
**1** **to stand in for** *(a person)*
**2** **to replace**
**Il faut remplacer les piles.** You need to replace the batteries.

**remplir** *verb* **[2]**
**1** **to fill**
**remplir quelque chose de quelque chose** to fill something with something
**Il a rempli ses poches de bonbons.** He filled his pockets with sweets.
**La salle était remplie de jeunes.** The hall was full of young people.
**2** **to fill in** *(a form, a questionnaire)*
**Je dois remplir un formulaire d'inscription.** I have to fill in a registration form.
**3** **to carry out** *(a duty, a role)*
**Elle remplit bien son rôle de déléguée de classe.** She carries out her role as class rep well.

**remporter** *verb* **[1]**
**to win** *(a competition)*

le **remue-ménage** *invariable masc noun*
**commotion**

le **remue-méninges** *invariable masc noun*
**brainstorming**

**remuer** *verb* **[1]**
**1** **to move** *(your head, your hand)*
**Le chien remuait la queue.** The dog was wagging its tail.
**2** **to shake** *(a branch, a tree)*
**3** **to stir** *(a sauce, a coffee)*
**4** **to toss** *(a salad)*
**5** **to upset** *(a person)*

**rémunérer** *verb* **[24]**
**1** **to pay** *(a person)*
**2** **to pay for** *(work)*

le **renard** *masc noun*
**fox**

la **rencontre** *fem noun*
**1** **meeting**
**Elle est venue à ma rencontre.** She came to meet me.
**2** *(Sport)* **match**
**la rencontre entre la France et l'Allemagne** the match between France and Germany

**rencontrer** *verb* **[1]**
**1** **to meet** *(a person)*
**Je l'ai rencontré en 1999.** I met him in 1999.
**2** **to play** *(an opponent, a team)*
**3** **rencontrer des amis** to make new friends

**WORD TIP** If you mean *to meet up with existing friends* ▷ **retrouver**.

se **rencontrer** *reflexive verb* Ⓔ
**to meet**
**Nous nous sommes rencontrés à Londres.** We met in London.

le **rendez-vous** *invariable masc noun*
**1** **appointment**
**prendre rendez-vous** to make an appointment
**J'ai pris rendez-vous avec ton professeur.** I made an appointment with your teacher.
**Claire a rendez-vous chez le dentiste.** Claire's got a dentist's appointment.
**2** **donner rendez-vous à quelqu'un** to arrange to meet somebody
**Il m'a donné rendez-vous au café.** He arranged to meet me at the cafe.
**3** **date**
**Oscar a rendez-vous avec sa copine.** Oscar's got a date with his girlfriend.

se **rendormir** *reflexive verb* Ⓔ **[37]**
**to go back to sleep**

**rendre** *verb* **[3]**
**1** **to give back**
**Je te rendrai ton pull demain.** I'll give you back your sweater tomorrow.
**2** **to make**
**rendre quelqu'un heureux** to make somebody happy
**3** **to hand in** *(homework)*
**Elle rend ses devoirs en retard.** She hands her homework in late.
**4** **rendre visite à quelqu'un** to pay somebody a visit
**André a rendu visite à son oncle.** André paid his uncle a visit.
**5** **to be sick**
**Il rend toujours sur le bateau.** He always

gets sick on the boat.
**J'ai envie de rendre.** I feel sick.

se **rendre** *reflexive verb* Ⓔ

1 **to go**
**Je me rends au Québec.** I'm going to Quebec.
2 **to give yourself up**
**Ils se sont rendus à la police.** They gave themselves up to the police.
3 **se rendre compte de quelque chose** to realize something
**Je me suis rendu compte que j'avais oublié mon sac.** I realized I had forgotten my bag.

**renifler** *verb* [1]
**to sniff**

le **renne** *masc noun*
**reindeer**

**renommé** *masc adjective*, **renommée** *fem*
**famous**

**renoncer** *verb* [61]

1 **to give up**
**C'est trop difficile, je renonce!** It's too difficult, I give up!
2 **renoncer à quelque chose** to give something up
**Nous avons reconcé à notre projet de visiter le Japon.** We gave up our plans to visit Japan.

**renouveler** *verb* [18]
**to renew** (*a passport, a subscription*)

**rénover** *verb* [1]

1 **to renovate** (*a house*)
2 **to restore** (*furniture*)

♂ le **renseignement** *masc noun*

1 **un renseignement** a piece of information
**un renseignement utile** a useful piece of information
2 **des renseignements** information
**Je cherche des renseignements.** I'm looking for information.
**On va demander des renseignements au bureau de tourisme.** We'll ask for information at the tourist office.
**Adressez-vous aux renseignements!** Ask at the information desk!
3 (*for phone numbers*) **les renseignements** directory enquiries

**renseigner** *verb* [1]

1 **renseigner quelqu'un** to give somebody information
**La brochure vous renseigne sur les horaires.** The brochure gives you timetable information.
**être bien renseigné sur quelque chose** to be well-informed about something

se **renseigner** *reflexive verb* Ⓔ
**to find out**
**Je vais me renseigner au bureau de tourisme.** I'm going to find out at the tourist office.

**rentable** *masc & fem adjective*
**profitable**

♂ la **rentrée** *fem noun*
**la rentrée (des classes)** the start of the new school year

♂ **rentrer** *verb* [1]

1 Ⓔ **to get home**
**Il est tard, je rentre.** It's late, I'm going home.
**Maman rentre à dix-huit heures.** Mum will be home at six.
2 Ⓔ **to get back**
**Ils rentrent de Paris jeudi.** They'll be back from Paris on Thursday.
**On rentre le 6 septembre.** We're going back to school on 6 September.
3 Ⓔ **to come in**
**Rentrez!** Do go in!
4 Ⓔ **rentrer dans quelque chose** to go into something
**Rentre dans mon bureau!** Go into my office!
**Elles sont rentrées dans un magasin.** They've gone into a shop.
5 Ⓔ **rentrer dans quelque chose** to crash into something
**La voiture est rentrée dans un mur.** The car crashed into a wall.
6 Ⓔ **to get into**
**Il ne rentre plus dans son pantalon.** He can't get into his trousers any more.
7 **rentrer quelque chose** to bring something in (*from outside*)
**Rentre les chaises, il pleut!** Bring the chairs in, it's raining!
**Papa a rentré la voiture au garage.** Dad put the car in the garage.

**WORD TIP** When you say what you *bring in* etc, use *avoir* in the perfect tense.

**renverser** *verb* [1]

1 **to knock over** (*a glass, a vase*)
2 **être renversé par une voiture** to be knocked down by a car
**Antoine a été renversé par une voiture.** Antoine was knocked down by a car.
3 **to spill** (*your drink*)

**renvoyer** *verb* **[40]**
1 **to send back**
**Je renvoie le colis.** I'm sending the parcel back.
**On m'a renvoyé à l'hôpital.** They sent me back to hospital.
2 **to throw back** (*a ball*)
3 **to dismiss** (*an employee*)

la **réouverture** *fem noun*
**reopening**

**répandu** *masc adjective*, **répandue** *fem*
**widespread**

la **réparation** *fem noun*
**repair**

**réparer** *verb* **[1]**
**to repair**
**Je fais réparer ma moto.** I'm having my motorbike repaired.

**repartir** *verb* Ⓔ **[58]**
1 **to go off again**
**Les enfants sont déjà repartis.** The children have already gone off again.
2 **to go again**
**Je suis reparti chez moi.** I went home again.
3 **repartir à zéro** to start from scratch
**Ils ont déménagé en Corse et sont repartis à zéro.** They moved to Corsica and started from scratch.

**répartir** *verb* **[2]**
**to share out** (*tasks, roles*)

♪ le **repas** *masc noun*
**meal**
**à l'heure des repas** at mealtimes
**le repas de midi** lunch
**le repas du soir** the evening meal
**le repas de Noël** the Christmas dinner
**le repas de noces** the wedding banquet

le **repassage** *masc noun*
**ironing**

**repasser** *verb* **[1]**
1 **to drop in again**
**Il va repasser demain.** He'll drop in again tomorrow.
2 **to iron**
**une planche à repasser** an ironing board
3 **to resit** (*an exam*)
4 **to replay** (*a video*)

**repeindre** *verb* **[60]**
**to repaint**

le **repère** *masc noun*
**landmark**

**repérer** *verb* **[24]**
1 (*informal*) **to spot** (*a mistake*)
2 **to locate** (*a place*)

le **répertoire** *masc noun*
**notebook** (*with a thumb index*)
**un répertoire d'adresses** an address book

♪ **répéter** *verb* **[24]**
1 **to repeat**
**Pourriez-vous répéter, s'il vous plaît?** Could you repeat please?
2 **to rehearse** (*a play*)
**On répète le vendredi soir.** We rehearse on Friday evenings.
3 **to practise** (*a piece of music*)

se **répéter** *reflexive verb* Ⓔ
1 **to repeat yourself**
2 **to happen again**
**Espérons que cela ne se répétera pas.** Let's hope it doesn't happen again.

la **répétition** *fem noun*
1 **rehearsal**
2 **repetition**
• **la répétition générale** dress rehearsal

**replier** *verb* **[1]**
**to fold up** (*a map, a brochure*)

le **répondeur** *masc noun*
**answering machine**

♪ **répondre** *verb* **[3]**
1 **to answer**
**Léa n'a pas répondu.** Léa didn't answer.
2 **répondre à quelqu'un** to answer somebody
**Il m'a parlé mais je ne lui ai pas répondu.** He spoke to me but I didn't answer him.
3 **répondre à quelque chose** to answer something
**Elle a répondu à ma question.** She answered my question.
**Je vais répondre à sa lettre.** I'm going to reply to her letter.
4 **to answer back**

♪ la **réponse** *fem noun*
**answer**
**la bonne réponse** the right answer
**en réponse à ta question** in answer to your question

le **reportage** *masc noun*
1 **report**
**un reportage sur la drogue** a report on drugs
2 **(news) story**

le **reporter** *masc noun* ▷ see **reporter** *verb*
**reporter**
**une femme reporter** a woman reporter

**reporter** *verb* **[1]** ▷ see **reporter** *noun*
**to postpone**
**On a reporté le match à jeudi.** The match has been postponed until Thursday.

**WORD TIP** *reporter* does not mean *to report* in English; for the meaning of *to report* ▷ **signaler**.

le **repos** *masc noun*
**rest**
**dix jours de repos** ten days' rest

♪ **reposer** *verb* **[1]**
**reposer quelque chose** to put something back down
**Elle a reposé l'assiette sur la table.** She put the plate back down on the table.

se **reposer** *reflexive verb* Ⓔ
**to have a rest**
**J'ai besoin de me reposer.** I need a rest.
**Repose-toi bien!** Have a good rest!

**repousser** *verb* **[1]**
1 **to grow back**
2 **to push back** (*a heavy object, a crowd*)
3 **to postpone** (*a match*)

**reprendre** *verb* **[64]**
1 **to have some more** (*food, drink*)
2 **to take back**
**Je reprends mes CD.** I'm taking back my CDs.
3 **to start again**
**L'école reprend en septembre.** School starts again in September.
4 **reprendre le travail** to go back to work
**Ils reprennent le travail lundi.** They go back to work on Monday.
5 **reprendre la route** to set off again

le **représentant** *masc noun*, la **représentante** *fem*
**sales rep**

la **représentation** *fem noun*
**performance** (*of a play*)
**'Prochaine représentation à 20 heures'** 'Next performance 8 pm'

**représenter** *verb* **[1]**
1 **to depict** (*a scene, a landscape*)
2 **to represent** (*a team, a company*)

**réprimer** *verb* **[1]**
**to suppress**

la **reprise** *fem noun*
1 **resumption** (*of work, discussions*)
2 **rerun** (*of a play, a film*)
3 **repeat** (*of a broadcast*)
4 **à plusieurs reprises** on several occasions

le **reproche** *masc noun*
**criticism**
**Il m'a fait des reproches.** He criticized me.

**reprocher** *verb* **[1]**
1 **to criticize** (*people*)
**Elle lui a reproché sa paresse.** She criticized him for his laziness.
**reprocher à quelqu'un de faire quelque chose** to criticize somebody for doing something
**Il a reproché à son fils de ne pas travailler.** He criticized his son for not working.
2 **to criticize** (*things*)
**Que reproches-tu à ma lettre?** What's wrong with my letter?

se **reprocher** *reflexive verb* Ⓔ
**to blame yourself**

la **reproduction** *fem noun*
**reproduction**

**reproduire** *verb* **[26]**
1 **to reproduce**
2 **to breed** (*animals*)

se **reproduire** *reflexive verb* Ⓔ
1 **to happen again**
2 **to breed**

**républicain** *masc adjective*, **républicaine** *fem*
**republican**

la **république** *fem noun*
**republic**
**la République française** the French Republic

***république***

La France est une république et a un président, pas de roi ou reine.

**répugnant** *masc adjective*, **répugnante** *fem*
**revolting**

la **réputation** *fem noun*
**reputation**

le **requin** *masc noun*
**shark**

le **RER** *masc noun*
(*= Réseau express régional*) (*the suburban rail and metro network serving Paris*)

le **réseau** *masc noun*, les **réseaux** *plural*
**network**

♪ la **réservation** *fem noun*
**reservation**

la **réserve** *fem noun*
1 **stock**
**J'ai deux bouteilles de Coca en réserve.** I've put aside two bottles of Coke.
2 **reserve** *(for birds, animals)*
**une réserve ornithologique** a bird sanctuary

**réservé** *masc adjective*, **réservée** *fem*
**reserved**

**réserver** *verb* [1]
1 **to reserve, to book**
**J'ai réservé deux places pour ce soir.** I've booked two seats for this evening.
2 **to put aside** *(some food for somebody)*
3 **to keep** *(for a special occasion)*
**Elle réserve le grand vin pour Noël.** She's keeping the really good wine for Christmas.
4 **to have in store**
**Je lui réserve une surprise.** I've got a surprise in store for her.

le **réservoir** *masc noun*
1 **tank**
2 **reservoir**
- le **réservoir à essence** petrol tank

la **résidence** *fem noun*
1 **residence**
**une résidence secondaire** a holiday home
2 **apartment block**
- la **résidence universitaire** hall of residence

le **résident** *masc noun*, la **résidente** *fem*
**resident**

**résidentiel** *masc adjective*, **résidentielle** *fem*
**residential**

**résistant** *masc adjective*, **résistante** *fem*
▷ see **résistant** *noun*
**tough**

le **résistant** *masc noun*, la **résistante** *fem*
▷ see **résistant** *adj*
**Resistance fighter** *(in France during World War II)*

**résister** *verb* [1]
**to resist**
**Je n'ai pas pu résister alors je l'ai acheté.** I couldn't resist so I bought it.
**Il faut résister aux tyrans.** You've got to stand up to bullies.
**résister à quelque chose** to withstand something *(a force, an explosion, a storm)*
**Les arbres n'ont pas résisté à la tempête.** The trees couldn't withstand the storm.

**résolu** *masc adjective*, **résolue** *fem*
1 **determined**
2 **resolved** *(sorted out)*

**résoudre** *verb* [67]
**to solve** *(a problem)*

se **résoudre** *reflexive verb* Ⓔ
**se résoudre à faire quelque chose** to make up your mind to do something

le **respect** *masc noun*
**respect**

**respecter** *verb* [1]
**to respect**

**respectueux** *masc adjective*, **respectueuse** *fem*
**respectful**

la **respiration** *fem noun*
**breathing**
**retenir sa respiration** to hold your breath

**respirer** *verb* [1]
**to breathe**
**Respirez!** Breathe in!
**Respirez bien fort!** Take a deep breath!

la **responsabilité** *fem noun*
**responsibility**

**responsable** *masc & fem adjective*
▷ see **responsable** *noun*
**responsible**
**être responsable de quelque chose** to be responsible for something
**Il est responsable de l'incendie.** He's responsible for the fire.

le & la **responsable** *masc & fem noun*
▷ see **responsable** *adj*
1 **person in charge**
**Je voudrais parler au responsable.** I'd like to speak to the person in charge.
2 **person responsible**
**les responsables de la catastrophe** those responsible for the disaster
- le **responsable de classe** class rep

la **ressemblance** *fem noun*
1 **likeness**
**un portrait d'une grande ressemblance** a very good likeness
2 **similarity**

**ressembler** *verb* [1]
**ressembler à quelqu'un** to look like somebody
**Elle ressemble beaucoup à sa mère.** She looks very like her mother.
**Cela ressemble à du bois.** It looks like wood.

se **ressembler** *reflexive verb* Ⓔ
**to be alike**

le **ressentiment** *masc noun*
**resentment**

**resserrer** *verb* [1]
**to tighten** (*a knot, a screw*)

se **resserrer** *reflexive verb* Ⓔ
**to move closer together**
Resserrez-vous un peu! Squeeze up a bit!

**resservir** *verb* [58]
1 **to give another helping**
2 **to be used again**
Ça peut toujours resservir! It can always be used again!

se **resservir** *reflexive verb* Ⓔ
**to help yourself to more**

le **ressort** *masc noun*
**spring** (*in a bed, a chair*)

**ressortir** *verb* Ⓔ [58]
**to go out again**

la **ressource** *fem noun*
1 **resource**
des ressources énergétiques energy resources
2 les ressources resources (*income*)

le **restaurant** *masc noun*
**restaurant**
manger au restaurant to go out for a meal
• le **restaurant rapide** fast-food restaurant

la **restauration** *fem noun*
1 **catering**
2 **restoration**
• la **restauration rapide** fast-food industry

**restaurer** *verb* [1]
**to restore**

le **reste** *masc noun*
1 le reste the rest
le reste du temps the rest of the time
2 les restes the leftovers
les restes du poulet the leftover chicken

♪ **rester** *verb* Ⓔ [1]
1 **to stay**
Reste ici, je reviens! Stay here, I'll be back!
Camille est restée à la maison. Camille stayed at home.
2 **to remain**
3 rester debout to remain standing
Je préfère rester debout. I prefer to stand.
4 rester assis to remain seated
Elle est restée assise toute la journée. She's been sitting down all day.
Reste tranquille! Keep still!
Hier, je suis resté sans manger. I didn't have anything to eat yesterday.
5 **to be left**
Il reste du fromage. There's some cheese left.
Il nous reste combien d'argent? How much money have we got left?
Il ne reste pas beaucoup à faire. There's not much left to do.

la **restriction** *fem noun*
**restriction**

♪ le **résultat** *masc noun*
**result**
les résultats des examens the exam results
Il a de bons résultats à l'école. He gets good marks at school.

le **résumé** *masc noun*
**summary**
en résumé to sum up

**résumer** *verb* [1]
**to sum up**

**rétablir** *verb* [2]
**to restore**

se **rétablir** *reflexive verb* Ⓔ
**to recover** (*after an illness*)

**retaper** *verb* [1]
**to do up** (*a house*)

♪ le **retard** *masc noun*
1 **delay**
un retard d'une heure sur notre vol an hour's delay on our flight
sans retard without delay
2 avoir du retard to be late
Excusez mon retard! I'm sorry I'm late!
Ils sont arrivés avec trois heures de retard. They arrived three hours late.
3 être en retard to be late
Il est en retard pour rendre ses devoirs. He's late handing in his homework.

**retarder** *verb* [1]
1 **to hold up**
Le mauvais temps nous a retardés. The bad weather held us up.
être retardé to be delayed
Le train était retardé. The train was delayed.
2 **to put off**
Il a retardé son départ. He put off his departure.
3 **to be slow**
Je retarde de cinq minutes. My watch is five minutes slow.

**retenir** *verb* [77]
1 **to keep**
Je ne vous retiendrai pas longtemps. I won't keep you long. ▸▸

2 **to hold up** (*to delay*)
Elle a été retenue au bureau. She was held up at the office.
3 **retenir son souffle** to hold your breath
4 **to book** (*seats*)
5 **to remember**
Je ne retiens jamais leur adresse. I can never remember their address.

se **retenir** *reflexive verb* ⓔ
**to stop yourself**
Je n'ai pas pu me retenir de pleurer. I couldn't stop myself from crying.

la **retenue** *fem noun*
**detention**
être en retenue to be in detention

la **réticence** *fem noun*
**reluctance**

**retirer** *verb* [1]
1 **to take off**
D'abord, je retire ma veste. I'm taking my jacket off first.
2 **to take out**
Attends, je vais retirer les arêtes! Wait, I'll take out the bones!
retirer de l'argent to take money out (*of a bank account*)
J'ai retiré 300 euros. I took out 300 euros.
3 **to take away**
Ils lui ont retiré son permis. They took his licence away from him.

le **retour** *masc noun*
1 **return**
un billet aller-retour a return ticket
dès mon retour as soon as I get back
2 être de retour to be back
Elle sera de retour vers onze heures. She'll be back about eleven.

**retourner** *verb* [1]
1 ⓔ **to go back**
Elle est retournée à l'école. She went back to school.
2 **to turn over** (*a steak, a pancake*)

**WORD TIP** When you say what you *turn over* etc, use *avoir* in the perfect tense.

la **retraite** *fem noun*
**retirement**
Mon oncle est à la retraite. My uncle is retired.
prendre sa retraite to retire
une maison de retraite an old people's home

le **retraité** *masc noun*, la **retraitée** *fem*
**pensioner**

**rétrécir** *verb* [2]
**to shrink**

**retrousser** *verb* [1]
1 **to roll up** (*your sleeves*)
2 **to hitch up** (*your skirt*)

**retrouver** *verb* [1]
1 **to find**
As-tu retrouvé ton sac? Did you find your bag?
2 **to meet** (*friends*)
Je te retrouve à la sortie. I'll meet you at the exit.

se **retrouver** *reflexive verb* ⓔ
1 **to meet**
On se retrouve devant la patinoire? Shall we meet outside the ice rink?
Nous nous retrouverons à Noël. We'll see each other again at Christmas.
2 **to end up**
On s'est retrouvé chez Karim. We ended up at Karim's place.
3 **to find your way around**
Je n'arrive jamais à me retrouver dans Londres. I can never find my way around London.

le **rétroviseur** *masc noun*
**rearview mirror**

la **réunion** *fem noun*
1 **meeting**
Elle est en réunion. She's in a meeting.
La réunion aura lieu à 20 h 30. The meeting will take place at 8.30 pm.
2 **gathering**
On fait une réunion de famille. We're having a family gathering.
3 **reunion**

se **réunir** *reflexive verb* ⓔ [2]
**to meet**
Nous nous réunissons entre amis. We're having a get-together with friends.

**réussi** *masc adjective*, **réussie** *fem*
**successful**
une expérience réussie a successful experiment
Ta soirée était très réussie. Your party was a success.

**réussir** *verb* [2]
1 **to succeed**
J'espère qu'elle va réussir. I hope she'll succeed.
2 **to pass**
réussir un examen to pass an exam
3 **to be successful**
4 réussir à faire quelque chose to manage to do something



ⓔ means the verb takes être to form the perfect

J'ai réussi à les persuader. I managed to persuade them.
**5** **réussir à quelqu'un** to do somebody good (*food, holiday, rest*)

la **réussite** *fem noun*
**success**

**réutilisable** *masc & fem adjective*
**reusable**

la **revanche** *fem noun*
**1** **return match**
**2** **revenge**
**prendra sa revanche sur quelqu'un** to get your revenge on somebody
**3** **en revanche** on the other hand
**Je déteste les légumes, en revanche j'adore les fruits.** I hate vegetables, but I love fruit.

le **rêve** *masc noun*
**dream**
**J'ai fait un rêve.** I had a dream.
**la moto de mes rêves** my dream motorbike
**Mon rêve, c'est d'avoir un poney.** My dream is to have a pony.

le **réveil** *masc noun*
**alarm clock**

♪ **réveiller** *verb* **[1]**
**réveiller quelqu'un** to wake somebody up
**Elle m'a réveillé à sept heures.** She woke me at seven.
**Nicolas est réveillé.** Nicolas is awake.

se **réveiller** *reflexive verb* Ⓔ
**to wake up**
**D'habitude, je me réveille à sept heures.** I usually wake up at seven.

le **réveillon** *masc noun*
**le réveillon du Nouvel An** the New Year's Eve celebrations

***réveillon***

Un réveillon, c'est un repas de fête, tard le soir. Les Français font deux réveillons: le 24 décembre pour Noël et le 31 décembre pour le Nouvel An.

**réveillonner** *verb* **[1]**
**1** **to celebrate Christmas Eve**
**2** **to see the New Year in**

le **revenant** *masc noun*, la **revenante** *fem*
**ghost**

**revendre** *verb* **[3]**
**to sell**

**revenir** *verb* Ⓔ **[81]**
**1** **to come back**
**Elles sont revenues très tard.** They came back very late.
**Je reviens de Montréal le 5 mai.** I'm back from Montréal on 5 May.
**2** **to come to**
**Ça revient à quinze euros.** That comes to fifteen euros.
**3** **revenir de quelque chose** to get over something
**Elle est revenue de ses frayeurs.** She got over her fright.
**Je n'en reviens pas!** I can't get over it!
**4** **faire revenir** to brown (*onions, meat*)

le **revenu** *masc noun*
**income**

**rêver** *verb* **[1]**
**1** **to dream**
**Elle rêve de devenir pilote.** She dreams of becoming a pilot.
**2** **to daydream**

le **réverbère** *masc noun*
**street lamp**

le **revers** *masc noun*
**1** **back**
**d'un revers de la main** with the back of your hand
**le revers de la médaille** the other side of the coin
**2** **lapel** (*on a jacket*)
**3** **turn-up** (*on trousers*)
**4** **cuff** (*on a sleeve*)
**5** **backhand** (*in tennis*)

**réviser** *verb* **[1]**
**1** **to revise** (*for an exam*)
**2** **to service** (*a car, a machine*)

la **révision** *fem noun*
**1** **revision** (*for exams*)
**2** **service** (*for a car*)

**revoir** *verb* **[13]**
**1** **to see again**
**Et nous ne l'avons jamais revue.** And we never saw her again.
**2** **to revise** (*for an exam*)
**3** **to go over** (*a lesson*)
**Cette leçon est à revoir.** You need to go over this lesson again.
**4** **au revoir** goodbye

la **révolte** *fem noun*
**1** **revolt**
**2** **rebellion**

**révolter** *verb* **[1]**
**to appal**

se **révolter** *reflexive verb* Ⓔ
**to rebel**

la **révolution** *fem noun*
**revolution**

**révolutionner** *verb* **[1]**
**to revolutionize**

le **revolver** *masc noun*
**revolver**

**revouloir** *verb* **[14]**
(*informal*) **to have a second helping of**

la **revue** *fem noun*
**magazine**
une revue scientifique a scientific journal

♪ le **rez-de-chaussée** *invariable masc noun*
**ground floor**
La réception est au rez-de-chaussée. Reception is on the ground floor.

**RF** *fem noun*
(*= République française*) **French Republic**

se **rhabiller** *verb reflexive* ❺ **[1]**
**to put your clothes on again**

le **Rhin** *masc noun*
le Rhin the Rhine (*the river*)

le **rhinocéros** *masc noun*
**rhinoceros**

la **rhubarbe** *fem noun*
**rhubarb**

le **rhum** *masc noun*
**rum**

♪ le **rhume** *masc noun*
**cold**
J'ai attrapé un rhume. I've caught a cold.
- le **rhume de cerveau** head cold
- le **rhume des foins** hay fever

**ri** *verb* ▷ **rire**

**ricaner** *verb* **[1]**
**to snigger**

♪ **riche** *masc & fem adjective*
1 **well-off, rich**
Sa famille est très riche. Her family is very rich.
Nous ne sommes pas très riches. We're not very well-off.
2 **rich** (*food*)
C'est riche en vitamines. It's rich in vitamins.

la **richesse** *fem noun*
1 **wealth**
2 **les richesses naturelles** natural resources

la **ride** *fem noun*
**wrinkle** (*on your skin*)

♪ le **rideau** *masc noun*, les **rideaux** *plural*
**curtain**

**ridicule** *masc & fem adjective*
**ridiculous**
C'est totalement ridicule! That's completely ridiculous!
Tu as l'air ridicule. You look silly.

♪ un **rien** *masc noun* ▷ **see rien** *pron*
**little thing**
Elle se met à hurler pour un rien. She starts shouting at the slightest thing.
en un rien de temps in next to no time

♪ **rien** *pronoun* ▷ **see rien** *noun*
1 **nothing**
Ce n'est rien. It's nothing.
Il ne reste plus rien. There's nothing left.
Rien n'a changé. Nothing's changed.
Je n'ai rien vu. I didn't see anything.
'Qu'est-ce qu'elle a dit?' — 'Rien.' 'What did she say?' — 'Nothing.'
Il n'y a rien d'autre à manger. There's nothing else to eat.
2 **rien que** just
'Que reste-t-il à faire?' — 'Rien que la vaisselle.' 'What's left to do?' — 'Just the washing-up.'
3 (*in expressions*) **rien du tout** nothing at all
**rien de bon** nothing good
'Merci.' — 'De rien.' 'Thank you.' — 'You're welcome.'
Ça ne fait rien. It doesn't matter.
4 **Je n'y arrive pas, il n'y a rien à faire!** I can't do it, it's no good!

**WORD TIP** Remember to use *ne* before *rien* in a sentence that contains a verb: *Ce n'est rien.* ▷ **ne**

**rigoler** *verb* **[1]**
(*informal*)
1 **to laugh**
Elle rigole tout le temps. She's always laughing.
2 **to have a good time**
Nous avons bien rigolé. We had a great time.
3 **to be joking**

**rigolo** *masc adjective*, **rigolote** *fem*
(*informal*) **funny**

**rigoureux** *masc adjective*, **rigoureuse** *fem*
1 **rigorous** (*checks*)
2 **strict** (*discipline*)
3 **harsh** (*winter, climate*)

les **rillettes** *plural fem noun*
les rillettes de porc potted pork

la **rime** *fem noun*
**rhyme**

**rimer** *verb* **[1]**
**to rhyme**

**rincer** *verb* **[61]**
**to rinse**



❺ means the verb takes être to form the perfect

se **rincer** *reflexive verb* ⓔ
**to rinse**
se rincer les cheveux to rinse your hair

♪ le **rire** *masc noun* ▷ **see rire** *verb*
**laughter**
un rire a laugh
J'ai entendu des rires. I heard laughter.

♪ **rire** *verb* **[68]** ▷ **see rire** *noun*
1 **to laugh**
J'ai bien ri. I laughed a lot.
Louis nous fait rire. Louis makes us laugh.
Il n'y a pas de quoi rire. It's not funny.
2 **to have fun**
On va bien rire. We're going to have a lot of fun.
3 **to joke**
C'était pour rire. It was meant as a joke.

le **risque** *masc noun*
**risk**
J'ai pris un risque. I took a risk.
un risque d'incendie a fire hazard

**risqué** *masc adjective*, **risquée** *fem*
**risky**

**risquer** *verb* **[1]**
1 **to risk** (*your life*)
Vas-y, tu ne risques rien! Go ahead, it's quite safe!
2 Tu risques de te brûler. You might burn yourself.

le **rivage** *masc noun*
**shore**

le **rival** *masc noun*, la **rivale** *fem*, les **rivaux** *masc pl*, les **rivales** *fem pl*
**rival**

la **rive** *fem noun*
1 **bank** (*of a river*)
la Rive gauche the Left Bank (*With the Seine in Paris and other rivers, the left bank is the side of the river as you face downstream.*)
2 **shore** (*by the sea*)

♪ la **rivière** *fem noun*
**river**
Elle se baigne dans la rivière. She swims in the river.

♪ le **riz** *masc noun*
**rice**
du gâteau de riz rice pudding
- le **riz cantonais** egg fried rice
- le **riz au lait** rice pudding

la **RN** *fem noun*
(*= route nationale*) **A road**

♪ la **robe** *fem noun*
**dress**
une robe d'été a summer dress
- la **robe de chambre** dressing gown
- la **robe de mariée** wedding dress
- la **robe du soir** evening dress

♪ le **robinet** *masc noun*
**tap**
l'eau du robinet tap water
ouvrir le robinet to turn the tap on
fermer le robinet to turn the tap off

le **robot** *masc noun*
**robot**
- le **robot ménager** food processor

la **roche** *fem noun*
**rock**

le **rocher** *masc noun*
**rock** (*large boulder*)

le **rock** *masc noun*
**rock** (*music*)

**rôder** *verb* **[1]**
**to prowl**

les **rognons** *plural masc noun*
**kidneys** (*for cooking*)

le **roi** *masc noun*
**king**
le roi Charles King Charles
la fête des Rois Twelfth Night
les Rois mages the Three Wise Men

le **rôle** *masc noun*
**role**

le **roller** *masc noun*
1 **roller-skate**
2 **roller-skating**
faire du roller to go roller-skating

**romain** *masc adjective*, **romaine** *fem*
**Roman**

♪ le **roman** *masc noun*
**novel**
- le **roman policier** detective story
- le **roman d'amour** love story

le **romancier** *masc noun*, la **romancière** *fem*
**novelist**

**romantique** *masc & fem adjective*
**romantic**

le **romarin** *masc noun*
**rosemary**

**rompre** *verb* **[69]**
**to split up** (*couples, bands*)
rompre avec quelqu'un to break up with somebody
Anne a rompu avec son copain. Anne's broken up with her boyfriend.

French-English

la **ronce** *fem noun*
**bramble**

**rond** *masc adjective*, **ronde** *fem*
▷ see **rond** *noun*
1 **round** (*shape, table*)
2 **plump** (*person*)

♪ le **rond** *masc noun* ▷ see **rond** *adj*
**circle**
s'asseoir en rond to sit in a circle

la **rondelle** *fem noun*
1 **slice** (*of salami, cucumber, lemon*)
2 **washer** (*for a tap, a screw*)

♪ le **rond-point** *masc noun*, les **ronds-points** *plural*
**roundabout**
Au rond-point, prenez à gauche! Turn left at the roundabout!

**ronfler** *verb* [1]
**to snore**

**ronger** *verb* [52]
**to gnaw**

se **ronger** *reflexive verb* ❷
se ronger les ongles to bite your nails

**ronronner** *verb* [1]
**to purr**

le **rosbif** *masc noun*
**roast beef**

♪ **rose** *masc & fem adjective* ▷ see **rose** *noun*
**pink**
une chemise rose pâle a pale pink shirt

♪ la **rose** *fem noun* ▷ see **rose** *adj*
**rose**

le **rosé** *masc noun*
**rosé (wine)**

la **rosée** *fem noun*
**dew**

le **rosier** *masc noun*
**rosebush**

le **rossignol** *masc noun*
**nightingale**

♪ le **rôti** *masc noun*
1 **roast**
du rôti de bœuf roast beef
2 **joint** (*of pork, beef*)

**rôtir** *verb* [2]
**to roast**
le poulet rôti roast chicken

**roucouler** *verb* [1]
**to coo**

la **roue** *fem noun*
1 **wheel**
la roue de secours the spare wheel
2 **cartwheel** (*in gymnastics*)

♪ **rouge** *masc & fem adjective*
▷ see **rouge** *noun*
**red**
tes chaussettes rouges your red socks
le feu rouge the red light

♪ le **rouge** *masc noun* ▷ see **rouge** *adjective*
1 **red**
Le rouge ne me va pas. Red doesn't suit me.
2 **red traffic light**
Il est passé au rouge. He jumped the lights.
Le feu est passé au rouge. The light changed to red.
3 **red wine**
- le **rouge-gorge** robin
- le **rouge à lèvres** lipstick

la **rougeur** *fem noun*
**redness**

**rougir** *verb* [2]
**to blush**

la **rouille** *fem noun*
**rust**

**rouillé** *masc adjective*, **rouillée** *fem*
**rusty**

**rouiller** *verb* [1]
**to go rusty**

la **roulade** *fem noun*
**roll** (*in sports*)

**roulant** *masc adjective*, **roulante** *fem*
un fauteuil roulant a wheelchair

le **rouleau** *masc noun*, les **rouleaux** *plural*
**roll**
un rouleau d'essuie-tout a roll of kitchen towel
- le **rouleau à pâtisserie** rolling pin

♪ **rouler** *verb* [1]
1 **to go**
Le train roule très vite. The train's going very fast.
2 **to drive**
Nous avons roulé toute la nuit. We drove all night.
En France on roule à droite. In France people drive on the right.
3 **to roll**
Le ballon a roulé dans le caniveau. The ball rolled into the gutter.
4 **to roll up** (*a carpet, a sleeping bag, a newspaper*)
5 (*informal*) **to cheat**

la **Roumanie** *fem noun*
**Romania**
vivre en Roumanie to live in Romania
aller en Roumanie to go to Romania

**rousse** *fem adjective* ▷ **roux**

❷ means the verb takes être to form the perfect

a b c d e f g h i j k l m n o p q r s t u v w x y z

♪ la **route** *fem noun*
1 **road**
**une grande route** a main road
**la route de Caen** the road to Caen
**un accident de la route** a road accident
**C'est à trois heures de route d'ici.** It's three hours' drive from here.
2 **route**
**changer de route** to change your route
3 **way**
**être sur la bonne route** to be heading the right way
**prendre une autre route** to go a different way
**La route est longue.** It's a long way.
**en route, en cours de route** on the way (*during a journey*)
**Nous sommes en route pour Nice.** We're on our way to Nice.
**se mettre en route** to set off
**Il est l'heure de se mettre en route.** It's time to set off.
**Bonne route!** Safe journey!
- la **route à quatre voies** dual carriageway
- la **route départementale** secondary road, B road
- la **route nationale** A road

**routier** *masc adjective*, **routière** *fem*
▷ see **routier** *noun*
**road**
**le transport routier** road transport

le **routier** *masc noun* ▷ see **routier** *adj*
**lorry driver**

la **routine** *fem noun*
**routine**

♪ **roux** *masc adjective*, **rousse** *fem*
**ginger**
**un chat roux** a ginger cat
**un petit garçon roux** a little red-haired boy

**royal** *masc adjective*, **royale** *fem*, **royaux** *masc pl*, **royales** *fem pl*
**royal**

le **royaume** *masc noun*
**kingdom**

le **Royaume-Uni** *masc noun*
**United Kingdom**

**WORD TIP** Countries and regions in French take *le, la* or *les.*

le **ruban** *masc noun*
**ribbon**
- le **ruban adhésif** sticky tape

la **rubéole** *fem noun*
**German measles**

la **ruche** *fem noun*
**beehive**

**rudement** *adverb*
(*informal*) **really**
**rudement bon** really tasty

♪ la **rue** *fem noun*
**street**
**une rue piétonne** a pedestrian street

le **rugby** *masc noun*
**rugby**
**jouer au rugby** to play rugby

le **rugbyman** *masc*, les **rugbymen** *pl*
**rugby player**

la **ruine** *fem noun*
**ruin**
**un château en ruine** a ruined castle

**ruiner** *verb* [1]
**to ruin**

le **ruisseau** *masc noun*, les **ruisseaux** *pl*
**stream**

la **rumeur** *fem noun*
**rumour**

le **rumsteck** *masc noun*
**rump steak**

la **rupture** *fem noun*
**break-up** (*of a relationship*)

**rural** *masc adjective*, **rurale** *fem*, **ruraux** *masc pl*, **rurales** *fem pl*
**country**
**la vie rurale** country life

la **ruse** *fem noun*
**trick**
**les ruses du métier** the tricks of the trade

**rusé** *masc adjective*, **rusée** *fem*
**crafty**

**russe** *masc & fem adjective* ▷ see **Russe** *noun*
**Russian**
**un avion russe** a Russian plane

un **Russe** *masc noun*, une **Russe** *fem*
▷ see **russe** *adjective*
1 **Russian** (*person*)
**les Russes** the Russians
2 **Russian** (*the language*)
**Je parle russe.** I speak Russian.

la **Russie** *fem noun*
**Russia**
**Moscou est en Russie.** Moscow is in Russia.
**Cet été, je pars en Russie.** This summer I'm going to Russia.

le **rythme** *masc noun*
**1 rhythm**
un rythme lent a slow rhythm
**2 pace**
travailler à son propre rythme to work at your own pace

# S s

**s'** *abbreviation: se or si* ▷ **se** *reflexive pronoun,* **si** *conjunction*

**WORD TIP** *se* becomes *s'* before a word beginning with *a, e, i, o, u* or *silent h.*

**sa** *fem adjective* ▷ **son**

le **sable** *masc noun*
**sand**

**sablé** *masc adjective,* **sablée** *fem*
▷ see **sablé** *noun*
la pâte sablée shortcrust pastry

le **sablé** *masc noun* ▷ see **sablé** *adj*
**shortbread biscuit**

le **sac** *masc noun*
**1 bag**
un sac de sucre a bag of sugar
**2 sack**
un sac de charbon a sack of coal
- le **sac à dos** rucksack
- le **sac à main** handbag
- le **sac de couchage** sleeping bag

le **sachet** *masc noun*
**sachet**
un sachet de thé a teabag

la **sacoche** *fem noun*
**1 bag**
**2 pannier** (*for a bike*)

**sacré** *masc adjective,* **sacrée** *fem*
**1** (*informal*) un sacré problème a hell of a problem
Il a un sacré culot! He's got a hell of a nerve!
**2 sacred**

le **sacrifice** *masc noun*
**sacrifice**

**sacrifier** *verb* **[1]**
**to sacrifice**

**sage** *masc & fem adjective*
**1 good, well-behaved**
Alors les filles, soyez sages! Right, girls! Be good!
**2 sensible, wise**
Ce n'est pas sage de sortir en ton état. It's not wise to go out in your state.
- la **sage-femme** midwife

la **sagesse** *fem noun*
**wisdom**
une dent de sagesse a wisdom tooth

le **Sagittaire** *masc noun*
**Sagittarius**
Jean-Marc est Sagittaire. Jean-Marc is a Sagittarius.

**WORD TIP** Signs of the zodiac do not take an article: *un* or *une.*

**saignant** *masc adjective,* **saignante** *fem*
**rare** (*beef*)

**saigner** *verb* **[1]**
**to bleed**
Je saigne du nez. I've got a nosebleed.

**sain** *masc adjective,* **saine** *fem*
**healthy**
une alimentation saine a healthy diet

**saint** *masc adjective,* **sainte** *fem*
▷ see **saint** *noun*
**holy**
le Saint-Esprit the Holy Spirit
le vendredi saint Good Friday

le **saint** *masc noun,* la **sainte** *fem*
▷ see **saint** *adj*
**saint**

la **Saint-Jean** *fem noun*
**Midsummer's Day** (*June 24th*)

la **Saint-Sylvestre** *fem noun*
**New Year's Eve**

la **Saint-Valentin** *fem noun*
**St Valentine's Day**

**sais** *verb* ▷ **savoir** *verb*

**saisir** *verb* **[2]**
**1 to grab**
**2** saisir l'occasion to seize the opportunity
**3 to understand**
Je n'ai pas tout à fait saisi ... I didn't completely understand ...
**4 to catch, to hear**
Je n'ai pas saisi votre nom. I didn't catch your name.

♪ la **saison** *fem noun*
**season**
la haute saison the high season

**sait** *verb* ▷ **savoir** *verb*

la **salade** *fem noun*
1 **lettuce**
2 **salad**
une salade de fruits a fruit salad

le **salaire** *masc noun*
**salary, wages**

le **salami** *masc noun*
**salami**

le **salarié** *masc noun*, la **salariée** *fem*
**salaried employee**

♪ **sale** *masc & fem adjective*
1 **dirty** (*when after a noun*)
avoir les mains sales to have dirty hands
2 (*informal*) **horrible** (*when before a noun*)
Quel sale temps! What horrible weather!

♪ **salé** *masc adjective*, **salée** *fem*
1 **salty**
2 **savoury**
des petits gâteaux salés savoury biscuits

la **saleté** *fem noun*
**dirt**

**salir** *verb* [2]
salir quelque chose to get something dirty
Tu vas salir ta robe. You'll get your dress dirty.

se **salir** *reflexive verb* ⓔ
**to get dirty**
Les enfants se sont salis. The children got dirty.

la **salive** *fem noun*
**saliva**

♪ la **salle** *fem noun*
1 **dining-room** (*in a restaurant*)
2 **hall**
3 **auditorium** (*in a theatre, a cinema*)
- la **salle à manger** dining room
- la **salle d'attente** waiting room
- la **salle d'eau** shower room
- la **salle de bains** bathroom
- la **salle de classe** classroom
- la **salle de jeux** games room
- la **salle d'embarquement** departure lounge
- la **salle de séjour** living room

♪ le **salon** *masc noun*
1 **sitting room**
dans le salon in the sitting room
2 **living-room suite**
3 **trade fair**
4 **salon**
un salon de coiffure a hair salon

la **salopette** *fem noun*
1 **dungarees**
2 **overalls**

**saluer** *verb* [1]
1 **to say hello to**
Je l'ai salué. I said hello to him.
saluer quelqu'un de la main to wave at somebody
Elle l'a salué de la main. She waved at him.
2 **to say goodbye to**

♪ **salut** *greeting*
**Hi!**

♪ le **samedi** *masc noun*
1 **Saturday**
samedi dernier last Saturday
samedi prochain next Saturday
Nous sommes samedi aujourd'hui. It's Saturday today.
2 **on Saturday**
Viens me voir samedi. Come and see me on Saturday.
À samedi! See you on Saturday!
3 le samedi on Saturdays
'Fermé le samedi' 'Closed on Saturdays'
4 tous les samedis every Saturday
Tous les samedis, je vais à la patinoire. Every Saturday I go to the skating rink.

**WORD TIP** Months of the year and days of the week start with small letters in French.

le **SAMU** *masc noun*
(*= Service d'assistance médicale d'urgence*) **ambulance service**

la **sandale** *fem noun*
**sandal**

♪ le **sandwich** *masc noun*
**sandwich**
un sandwich au jambon a ham sandwich

la **sandwicherie** *fem noun*
**snack bar**

♪ le **sang** *masc noun*
**blood**
être en sang to be covered in blood
- le **sang-froid** calm, composure

le **sanglier** *masc noun*
**wild boar**

le **sanglot** *masc noun*
**sob**
éclater en sanglots to burst into tears

la **sanisette**® *fem noun*
**automatic public toilet**

**sanitaire** *masc & fem adjective*
▷ see **sanitaire** *noun*
**health**
les conditions sanitaires sanitary conditions

le **sanitaire** *masc noun* ▷ see **sanitaire** *adj*
les sanitaires the toilet block (*in a campsite*)

**sans** *preposition*
**without**
un café sans sucre a coffee with no sugar
Ils sont partis sans nous. They left without us.
Avec ou sans glaçons? With or without ice?
sans faire quelque chose without doing something
Il prend mes affaires sans me demander. He takes my things without asking me.
Ne sors pas sans le dire à Papa. Don't go out without telling Dad.

le & la **sans-abri** *masc & fem noun*
**homeless person**
les sans-abri the homeless

le & la **sans-emploi** *masc & fem noun*
**unemployed person**

la **santé** *fem noun*
1 **health**
être en bonne santé to be in good health
2 À votre santé! Cheers!

le **sapeur-pompier** *masc noun*
**firefighter**
les sapeurs-pompiers the fire brigade

le **sapin** *masc noun*
**fir tree**
un sapin de Noël a Christmas tree

le **sarcasme** *masc noun*
**sarcasm**

la **sardine** *fem noun*
**sardine**

le **satellite** *masc noun*
**satellite**

le **satin** *masc noun*
**satin**

la **satisfaction** *fem noun*
**satisfaction**

**satisfaire** *verb* **[10]**
**to satisfy**

**satisfaisant** *masc adjective*, **satisfaisante** *fem*
1 **satisfactory**
une réponse satisfaisante a satisfactory answer
2 **satisfying**
une expérience très satisfaisante a very satisfying experience

**satisfait** *masc adjective*, **satisfaite** *fem*
1 **satisfied**
être satisfait de quelque chose to be satisfied with something
Êtes-vous satisfait de votre repas? Are you satisfied with your meal?
2 avoir l'air satisfait to look pleased

la **sauce** *fem noun*
1 **sauce**
2 **gravy**

la **saucisse** *fem noun*
**sausage**

le **saucisson** *masc noun*
**sausage**

**sauf** *preposition*
1 **except**
tous les jours sauf le lundi every day except Monday
sauf quand il pleut except when it rains
2 sauf si unless
C'est tout, sauf s'il y a des questions? That's all, unless there are any questions?
3 sauf que except that
Tout va bien, sauf que ta cousine n'est pas encore arrivée. Everything's fine, except that your cousin hasn't arrived yet.

le **saule** *masc noun*
**willow**

le **saumon** *masc noun*
**salmon**
du saumon fumé some smoked salmon

**saupoudrer** *verb* **[1]**
**to sprinkle**

le **saut** *masc noun*
**jump**
- le **saut à la perche** pole vault
- le **saut à l'élastique** bungee jumping
- le **saut en hauteur** high jump
- le **saut en longueur** long jump

**sauter** *verb* **[1]**
1 **to jump**
Elle a sauté dans un taxi. She jumped into a taxi.
sauter quelque chose to jump over something
Pierre a sauté la barrière. Pierre jumped over the gate.
sauter de quelque chose to jump out of something
J'ai sauté du lit. I jumped out of bed.
2 sauter à la corde to skip (*with a rope*)

**3 to skip** (*a class, a page*)
**Nous avons sauté trois pages.** We've skipped three pages.
**4 faire sauter quelque chose to blow something up**
**Les terroristes ont fait sauter l'avion.** The terrorists blew up the plane.

la **sauterelle** *fem noun*
**grasshopper**

**sauvage** *masc & fem adjective*
**1 wild**
**les animaux sauvages** wild animals
**2 savage**
**3 unsociable**

**sauvegarder** *verb* **[1]**
**1 to save** (*on a computer*)
**J'ai sauvegardé tous mes fichiers.** I've saved all my files.
**2 to back up** (*a file*)

**sauver** *verb* **[1]**
**to save**
**sauver la vie à quelqu'un** to save somebody's life
**Vous m'avez sauvé la vie.** You saved my life.

se **sauver** *reflexive verb* ❷
**1 to run away**
**2 Je me sauve!** (*informal*) I'm off!

le **sauvetage** *masc noun*
**1 rescue**
**le sauvetage en montagne** mountain rescue
**2 life-saving**

**savent**, **savez** *verb* ▷ **savoir** *verb*

le **savoir** *masc noun* ▷ see **savoir** *verb*
**knowledge**
- le **savoir-faire** know-how

♂ **savoir** *verb* **[70]** ▷ see **savoir** *noun*
**1 to know**
**savoir que ...** to know (that) ...
**Je sais que Paul habite à Londres.** I know that Paul lives in London.
**Je ne savais pas qu'elle était médecin.** I didn't know she was a doctor.
**Le sais-tu?** Did you know?
**Je n'en sais rien.** I know nothing about it.
**2 savoir faire quelque chose to know how to do something**
**Je sais faire du ski.** I know how to ski.
**Il est important de savoir lire et écrire.** It's important to be able to read and write.
**Tu sais jouer du piano?** Can you play the piano?
**Il ne savait pas nager.** He couldn't swim.

**WORD TIP** *savoir* is used for knowing facts or how to do things. For knowing people or places, use *connaître*.

♂ le **savon** *masc noun*
**soap**

la **savonnette** *fem noun*
**bar of soap**

**savons** *verb* ▷ **savoir** *verb*

**savoureux** *masc adjective*, **savoureuse** *fem*
**tasty**

le **scandale** *masc noun*
**scandal**
**C'est un scandale!** It's outrageous!

**scandinave** *masc & fem adjective* ▷ see **Scandinave** *noun*
**Scandinavian**

le & la **Scandinave** *masc & fem noun* ▷ see **scandinave** *adj*
**Scandinavian**

la **Scandinavie** *fem noun*
**Scandinavia**

**scanner** *verb* **[1]**
**to scan** (*a document*)

le **scanneur** *masc noun*
**1 scanner** (*for scanning documents*)
**2 scan** (*in medical check*)
**passer un scanneur** to have a scan

le **scarabée** *masc noun*
**beetle**

le & la **scénariste** *masc & fem noun*
**scriptwriter**

la **scène** *fem noun*
**1 stage** (*in a theatre*)
**sur scène** on stage
**mettre une pièce en scène** to stage a play
**mise en scène de Spielberg** directed by Spielberg
**2 scene**
**des scènes de panique** scenes of panic
**faire une scène** to throw a fit

**sceptique** *masc & fem adjective*
**sceptical**

le **schéma** *masc noun*
**diagram**

la **scie** *fem noun*
**saw**

♂ la **science** *fem noun*
**science**
**Ma matière préférée, c'est la science.** Science is my favourite subject.

les **sciences naturelles** *plural fem noun*
**biology**

**scientifique** *masc & fem adjective*
▷ see **scientifique** *noun*
**scientific**

le & la **scientifique** *masc & fem noun*
▷ see **scientifique** *adj*
**scientist**
**Elle est scientifique.** She's a scientist.

♂ **scolaire** *masc & fem adjective*
**school**
**les vacances scolaires** the school holidays
**le livret scolaire** school report

la **scolarité** *fem noun*
**schooling, education**

le **Scorpion** *masc noun*
**Scorpio**
**Delphine est Scorpion.** Delphine is a Scorpio.

**WORD TIP** Signs of the zodiac do not take an article: *un* or *une*.

le **Scotch**® *masc noun*
**Sellotape**®

le **scout** *masc noun*
**boy scout**

la **scoute** *fem noun*
**girl guide**

le **scrutin** *masc noun*
1 **ballot** (*process of voting*)
2 **polls** (*in an election*)

le **sculpteur** *masc noun*, la **sculpteuse** *fem*
**sculptor**

la **sculpture** *fem noun*
**sculpture**

le & la **SDF** *masc & fem noun*
(*= sans domicile fixe*) **with no fixed address**
**les SDF** the homeless

**se, s'** *reflexive pronoun*
1 **yourself** (*oneself*)
**se faire mal** to hurt yourself
2 **himself**
**Il se regarde.** He's looking at himself.
3 **herself**
**Elle s'est fait une salade.** She made herself a salad.
4 **itself**
**Le chien s'est fait mal.** The dog has hurt itself.
5 **themselves**
**Ils s'amusent beaucoup.** They're really enjoying themselves.
6 **each other**
**Ils s'envoient des textos.** They send each other text messages.
7 **se brosser les dents** to brush your teeth
**Il faut se dépêcher.** We have to hurry up.

**WORD TIP** *se* becomes *s'* before *a, e i, o, u* or *silent h*.

♂ la **séance** *fem noun*
1 **session** (*for discussions, treatment*)
**une séance d'aromathérapie** an aromatherapy session
2 **showing** (*of a film*)
**la séance de vingt heures** the eight o'clock showing

le **seau** *masc noun*, les **seaux** *plural*
**bucket**

♂ **sec** *masc adjective*, **sèche** *fem*
1 **dry**
**pour les peaux sèches** for dry skin
2 **dried**
**des abricots secs** dried apricots

le **sèche-cheveux** *invariable masc noun*
**hair dryer**

le **sèche-linge** *masc noun*
**tumble dryer**

le **sèche-mains** *masc noun*
**hand dryer**

**sécher** *verb* [1]
1 **to dry**
2 (*informal*) **to skip** (*a class, school*)

♂ la **sécheresse** *fem noun*
**drought**

**second** *masc adjective*, **seconde** *fem*
▷ see **second** *noun*
**second**
**la seconde fois** the second time

le **second** *masc noun* ▷ see **second** *adj*
**second floor**
**J'habite au second.** I live on the second floor.
**Il est arrivé en second.** He arrived second.

♂ **secondaire** *masc & fem adjective*
**secondary**

la **seconde** *fem noun*
1 **second** (*in time*)
2 **second class**
**voyager en seconde** to travel second class
3 (*the French equivalent of*) **Year 11**
**J'entre en seconde cette année.** I'm going into Year 11 this year.

**secouer** *verb* **[1]**
**to shake**
secouer la tête to shake your head

**secourir** *verb* **[29]**
1 **to rescue** (*a person in difficulty*)
2 **to give first aid to** (*an accident victim*)

le **secourisme** *masc noun*
**first aid**

**secouriste** *masc & fem noun*
**first aider**

♪ le **secours** *masc noun*
1 **help**
Au secours! Help!
2 les premiers secours first aid
3 une sortie de secours an emergency exit

**secret** *masc adjective*, **secrète** *fem*
▷ see **secret** *noun*
**secret**

le **secret** *masc noun* ▷ see **secret** *adj*
**secret**
en secret in secret

♪ le & la **secrétaire** *masc & fem noun*
1 **secretary**
Elle est secrétaire. She's a secretary.
2 un secrétaire a writing desk

le **secrétariat** *masc noun*
**secretary's office**

le **secteur** *masc noun*
**sector**
dans le secteur privé in the private sector
dans le secteur public in the public sector

la **sécu** *fem noun*
(*informal*) (= *Sécurité sociale*) **Social Security**

la **sécurité** *fem noun*
1 **safety**
la sécurité routière road safety
2 être en sécurité to be safe
se sentir en sécurité to feel safe
3 **security**
la sécurité de l'emploi job security
un problème avec le système de sécurité a problem with the security system

la **Sécurité sociale** *fem noun*
**Social Security** (*the welfare system in France*)

**séduisant** *masc adjective*, **séduisante** *fem*
**attractive** (*person, idea*)

le **seigle** *masc noun*
**rye**
le pain de seigle rye bread

le **seigneur** *masc noun*
**lord**
le Seigneur the Lord

le **sein** *masc noun*
**breast**
avoir un cancer du sein to have breast cancer

♪ **seize** *number*
**sixteen**
Corinne a seize ans. Corinne's sixteen.
le seize juillet the sixteenth of July

♪ **seizième** *number*
**sixteenth**

♪ le **séjour** *masc noun*
**stay**
pendant votre séjour en France during your stay in France

♪ le **sel** *masc noun*
**salt**
une pincée de sel a pinch of salt

la **sélection** *fem noun*
1 **selection**
2 **choice** (*of products*)
3 **team**

**sélectionner** *verb* **[1]**
**to select**

le **self** *masc noun*
(*informal*) **self-service restaurant**
• le **self-service** (*informal*) self-service restaurant

la **selle** *fem noun*
**saddle**

**selon** *preposition*
**according to**
Selon la météo, il va pleuvoir. According to the forecast, it's going to rain.

♪ la **semaine** *fem noun*
**week**
cette semaine this week
la semaine dernière last week
la semaine prochaine next week
une fois par semaine once a week
une semaine de vacances a week's holiday
une semaine sur deux every other week
10£ d'argent de poche par semaine £10 pocket money a week
Elle est payée à la semaine. She's paid by the week.

**semblable** *masc & fem adjective*
**similar**

**semblant** *masc noun*
faire semblant de faire quelque chose to pretend to do something
Elle fait semblant de ne pas entendre. She's pretending not to hear.

**sembler** *verb* **[1]**
**to seem**
**La maison semble vide.** The house seems empty.

la **semelle** *fem noun*
**sole** (*of a shoe*)

**semer** *verb* **[1]**
**to sow** (*seeds*)

le **semestre** *masc noun*
**semester**

le **semi-remorque** *masc noun*
**articulated truck**

le **sens** *masc noun*
1 **direction**
**dans les deux sens** in both directions
**dans le sens Calais-Paris** in the Calais-Paris direction
**sens dessus dessous** upside down
2 **meaning**
**le sens d'un mot** the meaning of a word

la **sensation** *fem noun*
1 **feeling**
**une sensation agréable** a nice feeling
2 **sensation**
**Le film a fait sensation à Cannes.** The film was a sensation at Cannes.

**sensationnel** *masc adjective*, **sensationnelle** *fem*
**sensational**

le **sens commun** *masc noun*
**common sense**

le **sens de l'humour** *masc noun*
**sense of humour**

**sensé** *masc adjective*, **sensée** *fem*
**sensible**

**sensibiliser** *verb* **[1]**
**sensibiliser quelqu'un à quelque chose** to increase somebody's awareness of something (*a problem*)
**une campagne pour sensibiliser les gens au racisme** a campaign to increase people's awareness of racism

la **sensibilité** *fem noun*
**sensitivity**

**sensible** *masc & fem adjective*
1 **sensitive** *masc & fem*
**C'est une fille très sensible.** She's a very sensitive girl.
2 **noticeable**
**une différence sensible** a noticeable difference

**WORD TIP** *Sensible* does not mean *sensible* in English: for the meaning of *sensible* ▷ **sage**.

**sensiblement** *adverb*
**noticeably**

le **sens interdit** *masc noun*
1 **no entry sign**
2 **one-way street**

le **sens unique** *masc noun*
**one-way street**

le **sentier** *masc noun*
**path**
- le **sentier de randonnée** long-distance footpath (*a marked route for ramblers*)

le **sentiment** *masc noun*
1 **feeling**
**J'ai le sentiment que...** I have a feeling that...
2 (*endings for a formal letters*) **Veuillez accepter l'expression de mes sentiments respectueux.** Yours sincerely, Yours faithfully

**sentimental** *masc adjective*, **sentimentale** *fem*, **sentimentaux** *masc pl* **sentimentales** *fem pl*
**sentimental**

**sentir** *verb* **[58]**
1 **to smell**
**Ça sent bon!** That smells good!
**Ce fromage sent fort.** There's a strong smell from that cheese.
2 **to smell of**
**Ça sent les roses.** It smells of roses.
3 **to feel**
**Je ne sens rien.** I can't feel anything.
**Je sens qu'elle est sincère.** I feel that she's sincere.

se **sentir** *reflexive verb* ⓔ
**to feel**
**Tu te sens mieux?** Are you feeling better?
**Je ne me sens pas bien.** I don't feel well.

**séparé** *masc adjective*, **séparée** *fem*
1 **separated**
**Mes parents sont séparés.** My parents are separated.
2 **separate**
**dans une chambre séparée** in a separate bedroom

**séparément** *adverb*
**separately**

**séparer** *verb* **[1]**
**to separate**

se **séparer** *reflexive verb* ⓔ
1 **to separate**
**Mes parents se sont séparés.** My parents have separated.

♪ **sept** *number*
**seven**
**Yasmine a sept ans.** Yasmine's seven.
**Il est sept heures.** It's seven o'clock.
**le sept mars** the seventh of March

♪ **septante** *number*
**seventy** (*Used in Belgium and Switzerland, for soixante-dix.*)
**septante-sept** seventy-seven

♪ le **septembre** *masc noun*
**September**
**en septembre, au mois de septembre** in September
**fin septembre** at the end of September

**WORD TIP** Months of the year and days of the week start with small letters in French.

♪ **septième** *masc & fem adjective*
▷ see **septième** *noun*
**seventh**

♪ le **septième** *masc noun*
▷ see **septième** *adj*
**seventh floor**
**J'habite au septième.** I live on the seventh floor.

**sera**, **serai**, **seras**, **serez** *verb* ▷ **être**

la **série** *fem noun*
**series**
**une série australienne** an Australian series

**sérieusement** *adverb*
**seriously**

♪ **sérieux** *masc adjective*, **sérieuse** *fem*
▷ see **sérieux** *noun*
1 **serious**
**Vraiment? Tu es sérieux?** Really? Are you serious?
2 **responsible**
**Aurélie est une jeune fille sérieuse.** Aurélie is a responsible young woman.
3 **reliable**
**Il est tout à fait sérieux.** He's completely reliable.
4 **conscientious**
**des élèves sérieux** conscientious students

**WORD TIP** *sérieux* does not mean *serious* in English: for the meaning of *serious* ▷ **grave**.

le **sérieux** *masc noun* ▷ see **sérieux** *adj*
**prendre quelque chose au sérieux** to take something seriously
**Il prend tout au sérieux.** He takes everything seriously.

le **serin** *masc noun*
**canary**

**séronégatif** *masc adjective*, **séronégative** *fem*
**HIV-negative**

**serons**, **seront** *verb* ▷ **être**

**séropositif** *masc adjective*, **séropositive** *fem*
**HIV-positive**

le **serpent** *masc noun*
**snake**

la **serpillière** *fem noun*
**floorcloth**

la **serre** *fem noun*
**greenhouse**
**l'effet de serre** the greenhouse effect

**serré** *masc adjective*, **serrée** *fem*
1 **tight** (*clothes, budget*)
2 **close** (*match, competition*)

**serrer** *verb* **[1]**
1 **to grip**
2 **serrer la main à quelqu'un** to shake somebody's hand
**Nous nous sommes serré la main.** We shook hands.
3 **serrer quelqu'un dans ses bras** to hug somebody
**Il a serré sa fille dans ses bras.** He hugged his daughter.
4 **serrer les poings** to clench your fists
5 **to tighten** (*a screw, a belt*)
6 **to be too tight**
**Mes chaussures me serrent.** My shoes are too tight.
7 **to push closer together**
**Serrez les tables.** Move the tables closer together.

se **serrer** *reflexive verb* ❻
**to squeeze up**
**Serrez-vous un peu!** Squeeze up a bit!

la **serrure** *fem noun*
**lock**

♪ le **serveur** *masc noun*
**waiter**

♪ la **serveuse** *fem noun*
**waitress**

♪ le **service** *masc noun*
1 **favour**
**Je peux te demander un service?** Can I ask a favour?
2 **service** (*on bus or train routes*)
**service de dimanche** Sunday service
3 **être en service** to be working
**Est-ce que l'ascenseur est en service?** Is the lift working?
**être hors service** to be out of order ⏩

**4 duty**
**Je suis de service ce soir.** I am on duty this evening.
**5 service** (*charge*)
**service non compris** service not included
**6 department** (*in a town hall, a hospital*)
**le service des urgences** the casualty department
• le **service après-vente** after-sales service
• le **service clientèle** customer services
• le **service militaire** national service

la **serviette** *fem noun*
**1 towel**
**2 table napkin**
**3 briefcase**
• la **serviette hygiénique** sanitary towel

**servir** *verb* [71]
**1 to serve** (*in a shop*)
**Merci, on me sert.** Thank you, I'm being served.
**2 to serve** (*with food, drink*)
**Est-ce que je peux vous servir du poulet?** Can I give you some chicken?
**'Servir frais'** 'Serve chilled'
**3 to serve** (*in tennis*)
**À toi de servir!** Your service!
**4 servir à quelque chose** to be used for something
**À quoi ça sert?** What's it for?

se **servir** *reflexive verb* ⓔ
**1 to help yourself** (*at a meal*)
**Sers-toi de riz.** Help yourself to rice.
**2 to be served** (*food, drink*)
**Ce vin se sert frais.** This wine should be served chilled.
**3 se servir de quelque chose** to use something
**Je sais me servir d'un scanneur.** I know how to use a scanner.

**ses** *adjective* ▷ **son**

le **set de table** *masc noun*
**place mat**

**seul** *masc adjective*, **seule** *fem*
**1 only**
**la seule personne** the only person
**être le seul à faire quelque chose** to be the only one to do something
**J'étais le seul à aimer le film.** I was the only one who liked the film.
**2 alone**
**Il ne faut pas y aller seul.** You mustn't go there alone.
**3 se sentir seul** to feel lonely
**Au début, Julie s'est sentie très seule.** In the beginning, Julie felt very lonely.
**4 tout seul** all by yourself
**Sophie sait s'habiller toute seule.** Sophie can get dressed all by herself.

**seulement** *adverb*
**1 only**
**trois fois seulement** only three times
**seulement une vingtaine d'élèves** only about twenty students
**2 Si seulement je l'avais su.** If only I'd known.

**sévère** *masc & fem adjective*
**strict**

le **sexe** *masc noun*
**1 sex**
**2 genitals**

**sexuel** *masc adjective*, **sexuelle** *fem*
**sexual**

le **shampooing** *masc noun*
**shampoo**

le **short** *masc noun*
**(pair of) shorts**

**si** *adverb* ▷ **see si** *conj*
**1 so**
**Tu chantes si bien!** You sing so well!
**2 yes** (*when you are contradicting somebody*)
**'Tu ne viens pas avec nous?' — 'Si!'** 'You're not coming with us?' — 'Yes I am!'

**si, s'** *conjunction* ▷ **see si** *adv*
**1 if**
**si tu veux** if you like
**Demande-lui si elle vient avec nous.** Ask her if she's coming with us.
**2 s'il te plaît, s'il vous plaît** please

**WORD TIP** *si* becomes *s'* before *il* or *ils*.

la **Sicile** *fem noun*
**Sicily**

le **sida** *masc noun*
(*= syndrome immuno-déficitaire acquis*) **AIDS**

le **siècle** *masc noun*
**century**

le **siège** *masc noun*
**1 seat**
**2 head office** (*of a company*)
**3 siege** (*of a castle, a town*)
• le **siège social** head office

le **sien** *masc pronoun*, la **sienne** *fem*, les **siens** *masc pl*, les **siennes** *fem pl*
**1 his**
**J'ai prêté mon vélo à Mahmoud. Le sien est chez lui.** I've lent Mahmoud my bike. His is at home.
**'Est-ce que ces chaussures sont à Antoine?' — 'Oui, ce sont les siennes.'** 'Are these shoes Antoine's?' — 'Yes, they're his.'

**2 hers**
**J'ai prêté mon vélo à Anaïs. Le sien est chez elle.** I've lent Anaïs my bike. Hers is at home.
**'Est-ce que ces chaussures sont à Natalie?' — 'Oui, ce sont les siennes.'** 'Are these shoes Natalie's?' — 'Yes, they're hers.'

**WORD TIP** The article and pronoun change in French when they refer to fem and plural nouns.

la **sieste** *fem noun*
**nap**
faire la sieste to have a nap

**siffler** *verb* **[1]**
**to whistle**

le **sifflet** *masc noun*
**whistle**

le **signal** *masc noun*, les **signaux** *plural*
**signal**

**signaler** *verb* **[1]**
**1** signaler à quelqu'un que ... to point out (to somebody) that ...
**Je te signale que tu me dois de l'argent.** I'd like to point out that you owe me some money.
**2 to report** (*a theft, an incident*)
**3 to indicate** (*roadworks, danger*)

la **signalisation** *fem noun*
**signalling, signals**
• la **signalisation routière** road signs and markings

la **signature** *fem noun*
**signature**

le **signe** *masc noun*
**sign**
**C'est bon signe.** It's a good sign.
**faire signe à quelqu'un** to wave to someone
**Je te faisais signe du bus.** I was waving to you from the bus.
**faire signe à quelqu'un de faire quelque chose** to beckon somebody to do something
**Il m'a fait signe de m'asseoir.** He beckoned me to sit down.
**Tu es de quel signe?** What star sign are you?
• le **signe astrologique** star sign

**signer** *verb* **[1]**
**to sign**
N'oublie pas de signer le chèque. Don't forget to sign the cheque.

se **signer** *reflexive verb* **❻**
**to cross oneself**

la **signification** *fem noun*
**meaning**

**signifier** *verb* **[1]**
**to mean**
Qu'est-ce que ça signifie? What does that mean?

♪ le **silence** *masc noun*
**silence**
en silence in silence

**silencieux** *masc adjective*, **silencieuse** *fem*
**silent**

la **silhouette** *fem noun*
**1 silhouette**
**2 figure**

la **similarité** *fem noun*
**similarity**

♪ **simple** *masc & fem adjective*
▷ see **simple** *noun*
**simple**

♪ le **simple** *masc noun* ▷ see **simple** *adj*
**singles** (*in tennis*)

**simplement** *adverb*
**simply**

la **simplicité** *fem noun*
**simplicity**

**simplifier** *verb* **[1]**
**to simplify**

**simuler** *verb* **[1]**
**to simulate** (*a situation*)

**simultané** *masc adjective*, **simultanée** *fem*
**simultaneous**
en simultané simultaneously

**sincère** *masc & fem adjective*
**sincere**

la **sincérité** *fem noun*
**sincerity**

le **singe** *masc noun*
**monkey**
un grand singe an ape

le **singulier** *masc noun*
**singular**
au singulier in the singular

**sinistre** *masc & fem adjective*
▷ see **sinistre** *noun*
**1 sinister**
**2 gloomy**

le **sinistre** *masc noun* ▷ see **sinistre** *adj*
**accident, disaster** (*a fire, a flood*)

**sinistré** *masc adjective*, **sinistrée** *fem*
▷ see **sinistré** *noun*
**stricken**
les familles sinistrées the families stricken by the disaster

le **sinistré** *masc noun*, la **sinistrée** *fem*
▷ see **sinistré** *adj*
**disaster victim**

**sinon** *conjunction*
**otherwise**

la **sirène** *fem noun*
1 **siren**
une sirène d'alarme a fire alarm
2 **mermaid**

le **sirop** *masc noun*
1 **syrup**
sirop pectoral cough mixture
2 **cordial** (*drink*)
sirop de menthe mint cordial

le **site** *masc noun*
**site**, **area**
- le **site classé** conservation area
- le **site Internet** web site
- le **site pittoresque** beauty spot
- le **site touristique** place of interest (*for visitors*)
- le **site web** web site

**sitôt** *adverb*
**as soon as**
sitôt dit, sitôt fait no sooner said than done

la **situation** *fem noun*
1 **situation**
2 **job**

**situer** *verb* [1]
être situé to be situated
L'hôtel est situé au bord de la mer. The hotel is situated by the sea.

se **situer** *reflexive verb* Ⓔ
1 **to be situated in**
L'appartement se situe en plein centre-ville. The flat is right in the town centre.
2 **to be set**
Le film se situe au Japon. The film is set in Japan.

**six** *number*
**six**
Théo a six ans. Théo's six.
Il est six heures. It's six o'clock.
le six juillet the sixth of July

**sixième** *adjective* ▷ see **sixième** *masc noun, fem noun*
**sixth**

le **sixième** *masc noun* ▷ see **sixième** *adj, fem noun*
**sixth floor**
C'est au sixième. It's on the sixth floor.

la **sixième** *fem noun* ▷ see **sixième** *adj, masc noun*
(*the French equivalent of*) **Year 7**

le **skate** *masc noun*
1 **skateboarding**
2 **skateboard**

le **ski** *masc noun*
1 **ski**
2 **skiing**
- le **ski de fond** cross-country skiing
- le **ski de piste** downhill skiing

**skier** *verb* [1]
**to ski**
skier hors piste to ski off-piste

le **skieur** *masc noun*, la **skieuse** *fem*
**skier**

le **slip** *masc noun*
1 **underpants**
2 **knickers**
- le **slip de bain** trunks

la **Slovaquie** *fem noun*
**Slovakia**

la **Slovénie** *fem noun*
**Slovenia**

le **SMIC** *masc noun*
(*= salaire minimum interprofessionnel de croissance*) **guaranteed minimum wage**

le **SMS** *masc noun*
**text message**
J'ai envoyé un SMS à David. I texted David.

le **snack** *masc noun*
**snack bar**

la **SNCF** *fem noun*
(*= Société nationale des chemins de fer français*) **French national railways**

**snob** *fem & masc adjective* ▷ see **snob** *noun*
1 **snobbish** (*person*)
2 **posh** (*restaurant*)

le & la **snob** *masc & fem noun* ▷ see **snob** *adj*
**snob**

**sobre** *masc & fem adjective*
**sober**

**sociable** *masc & fem adjective*
**sociable**

**social** *masc adjective*, **sociale** *fem*, **sociaux** *masc pl*, **sociales** *fem pl*
**social**

**socialiste** *masc & fem adjective*
**socialist**

la **société** *fem noun*
1 **society**
dans notre société in our society
2 **company**
Il travaille pour une grande société. He works for a big company.

Ⓔ means the verb takes être to form the perfect

- la **société anonyme** public company
- la **société de consommation** consumer society

la **sociologie** *fem noun*
**sociology**

la **socquette** *fem noun*
**ankle sock**

le **soda**
**soda**

♪ la **sœur** *fem noun*
1 **sister**
**ma grande sœur** my big sister, my older sister
**J'ai deux sœurs et un frère.** I have two sisters and a brother.
2 **sister**
**Sœur Emmanuelle** Sister Emmanuelle
**une sœur** a nun

**soi** *pronoun*
1 **one, oneself**
**la confiance en soi** self-confidence
**la maîtrise de soi** self-control
2 **itself**
**Le sujet n'est pas très intéressant en soi.** The subject is not very interesting in itself.

**soi-disant** *masc adjective*, **soi-disante** *fem*
1 **so-called**
**Tom est le soi-disant champion.** Tom's the so-called champion.
2 **supposedly**
**Elle est soi-disant malade.** She's supposedly ill.

la **soie** *fem noun*
**silk**
**un foulard en soie** a silk scarf
**le papier de soie** tissue paper

♪ la **soif** *fem noun*
**thirst**
**avoir soif** to be thirsty
**J'ai soif.** I'm thirsty

**soigné** *masc adjective*, **soignée** *fem*
**neat** (*piece of work, writing*)
**Sophie a une écriture soignée.** Sophie has neat writing.

**soigner** *verb* **[1]**
1 **to treat** (*a wound, a patient*)
2 **to look after** (*a person, an animal*)
3 **to take care over** (*appearance, writing*)

**soigneusement** *adverb*
**carefully**

**soi-même** *pronoun*
**yourself, oneself**
**Il faut le faire soi-même.** You have to do it yourself.

le **soin** *masc noun*
1 **care**
**avec soin** carefully
2 **prendre soin de quelque chose** to take care of something
**Prends soin de tes nouveaux habits!** Take care of your new clothes!
3 **les soins** treatment
**les premiers soins** first aid

♪ le **soir** *masc noun*
**evening, night**
**ce soir** tonight
**hier soir** last night
**demain soir** tomorrow night
**le soir du 15 mai** on the evening of 15 May
**à six heures du soir** at six in the evening
**Je sors tous les samedis soirs.** I go out every Saturday night.
**À ce soir!** See you tonight!

♪ la **soirée** *fem noun*
1 **evening**
**pendant la soirée** during the evening
**Ils ont passé la soirée à bavarder.** They spent the evening chatting.
2 **party**
**Elle donne une petite soirée.** She's having a little party.
3 **Bonne soirée!** Have a nice evening!
- la **soirée dansante** dance

**sois** *verb* ▷ **être**
**Sois gentil!** Be good!

**soit** *conjunction*
**soit... soit...** either... or...
**soit demain, soit jeudi** either tomorrow or Thursday

la **soixantaine** *fem noun*
1 **about sixty**
**une soixantaine de personnes** about sixty people
2 **avoir la soixantaine** to be in your sixties
**Il a bien la soixantaine.** He's in his sixties at least.

♪ **soixante** *number*
**sixty**

♪ **soixante-dix** *number*
**seventy**
**soixante-dix-huit** seventy-eight

le **soja** *masc noun*
**soya bean**
**la sauce de soja** soy sauce

le **sol** *masc noun*
1 **floor**
2 **ground**
3 **soil**
4 (*Music*) **G** (*the note*)

**solaire** *masc & fem adjective*
**1 solar**
**2 sun**

le **soldat** *masc noun*
**soldier**

♪ le **solde** *masc noun*
**1 balance** (*of a bank account*)
**2** les soldes the sales

**soldé** *masc adjective*, **soldée** *fem*
**reduced**

la **sole** *fem noun*
**sole** (*the fish*)

♪ le **soleil** *masc noun*
**sun**
au soleil in the sun
Il y a du soleil. It's sunny.
Sophie a attrapé un coup de soleil. Sophie's got sunburnt.

**solide** *masc & fem adjective*
**1 solid**
**2 strong**

le & la **soliste** *masc & fem noun*
**soloist**

**solitaire** *masc & fem adjective*
**solitary**

la **solitude** *fem noun*
**1 solitude**
**2 loneliness**

la **solution** *fem noun*
**solution**

**sombre** *masc & fem adjective*
**dark**

le **somme** *masc noun* ▷ see **somme** *fem noun*
**nap**

la **somme** *fem noun* ▷ see **somme** *masc noun*
**sum** (*of money*)

le **sommeil** *masc noun*
**sleep**
avoir sommeil to feel sleepy
J'ai sommeil. I feel sleepy.

**sommes** *verb* ▷ **être**

le **sommet** *masc noun*
**summit**

le & la **somnambule** *masc & fem noun*
**sleepwalker**

**son** *masc adjective*, **sa** *fem*, **ses** *pl*
▷ see **son** *noun*
**1 his**
son fils his son
sa fille his daughter
ses enfants his children
**2 her**
son fils her son
sa fille her daughter
ses enfants her children
**3 its**
sa patte its paw
son collier its collar
**4 one's, your**
Chacun son tour! Wait your turn!

le **son** *masc noun* ▷ see **son** *adj*
**1 sound**
**2 volume** (*for radios, a hi-fi*)
**3 bran**

♪ le **sondage** *masc noun*
**survey**
• le **sondage d'opinion** opinion poll

**sonner** *verb* **[1]**
**1 to ring**
Le téléphone sonne. The phone's ringing.
**2 strike**
L'horloge sonne les heures. The clock strikes on the hour.

la **sonnerie** *fem noun*
**1 bell**
la sonnerie d'alarme the alarm bell
**2 ringtone**

la **sonnette** *fem noun*
**1 bell**
la sonnette d'alarme the alarm bell
**2 doorbell**

la **sono** *fem noun*
(*informal*) **sound system**

**sophistiqué** *masc adjective*, **sophistiquée** *fem*
**sophisticated**

le **sorbet** *masc noun*
**sorbet**
un sorbet au cassis a blackcurrant sorbet

le **sorcier** *masc noun*
**wizard**

la **sorcière** *fem noun*
**witch**

le **sort** *masc noun*
**fate**

**WORD TIP** *sort* does not mean *sort* in English; for the meaning of *sort* ▷ **sorte**.

la **sorte** *fem noun*
**1 sort**
toutes sortes d'activités all sorts of activities
C'est une sorte de poudre. It's a sort of powder.
**2** en quelque sorte in a way

♪ la **sortie** *fem noun*
1 **exit**
**Où se trouve la sortie?** Where's the exit?
2 **outing**
**Demain nous allons en sortie avec l'école.** Tomorrow we're going on a school outing.
3 **launch** (*of a new product*)
4 **release** (*of a film*)
5 **publication** (*of a book*)
• la **sortie de secours** emergency exit

♪ **sortir** *verb* **[72]**
1 Ⓔ **to go out**
**Elle est sortie en courant.** She ran out.
2 Ⓔ **to come out**
**Son nouveau film sortira en mai.** Her new film is coming out in May.
3 Ⓔ **to go out** (*for pleasure*)
**Mes parents sortent peu.** My parents don't go out much.
**Tu sors ce soir?** Are you going out tonight?
4 **sortir avec quelqu'un** Ⓔ **to be going out with someone**
**Thibault sort avec ma sœur.** Thibault's going out with my sister.
5 **to take out**
**J'ai oublié de sortir le chien.** I forgot to take the dog out.

**WORD TIP** When you say what you *take out* etc, use *avoir* in the perfect tense.

se **sortir** *reflexive verb* Ⓔ
**s'en sortir** to manage
**Je m'en sortirai d'une manière ou d'une autre.** I'll manage one way or another.

la **sottise** *fem noun*
1 **silliness**
2 **a silly remark**
**Il dit des sottises.** He talks nonsense.
3 **faire une sottise** to do something silly
**Arthur a fait une sottise.** Arthur's done something silly.

le **sou** *masc noun*
**penny**
**Il n'a pas un sou.** He's broke.
**une machine à sous** a fruit machine

le **souci** *masc noun*
1 **worry**
**se faire du souci** to worry
**Je me fais du souci pour Chantal.** I'm worried about Chantal.
2 **problem**
**J'ai d'autres soucis à présent.** I've got other problems just now.
3 **marigold**
**un parterre de soucis** a bed of marigolds

**soucieux** *masc adjective*, **soucieuse** *fem*
**worried**

♪ la **soucoupe** *fem noun*
**saucer**

♪ **soudain** *masc adjective*, **soudaine** *fem*
▷ see **soudain** *adv*
**sudden**
**une réaction soudaine** a sudden reaction

♪ **soudain** *adverb* ▷ see **soudain** *adj*
**suddenly**

le **souffle** *masc noun*
**breath**
**Laisse-moi reprendre mon souffle!** Let me catch my breath!
**être à bout de souffle** to be out of breath
**Après la course, il était à bout de souffle.** After the race he was out of breath.
**couper le souffle à quelqu'un** to take someone's breath away
**Ce spectacle fantastique vous coupe le souffle.** This fantastic show takes your breath away.

le **soufflé** *masc noun*
**soufflé**
**un soufflé au fromage** a cheese soufflé

**souffler** *verb* **[1]**
1 **to blow**
2 **to blow out** (*a candle*)
3 **to whisper**
4 **to tell**

la **souffrance** *fem noun*
1 **suffering**
2 **misery**

**souffrir** *verb* **[73]**
**to suffer**
**Elle a beaucoup souffert.** She has suffered a lot.
**souffrir de quelque chose** to suffer from something
**Il souffre du dos.** He suffers from back problems.
**Elle souffre d'asthme.** She suffers from asthma.
**Est-ce qu'il souffre?** Is he in pain?

le **souhait** *masc noun*
**wish**
**À tes souhaits!** Bless you! (*when somebody sneezes*)

**souhaiter** *verb* **[1]**
**to wish**
**souhaiter quelque chose à quelqu'un** to wish somebody something
**Je te souhaite bonne chance.** I wish you luck. ⏩

Il souhaite se marier. He'd like to get married.

**soûl** *masc adjective*, **soûle** *fem*
**drunk**

le **soulagement** *masc noun*
**relief**
à mon grand soulagement to my great relief

**soulever** *verb* **[50]**
1 **to lift**
Je n'arrive pas à soulever ta valise. I can't lift your case.
2 **to raise** (*problems, objections*)
Personne n'a soulevé la question. Nobody raised the question.

le **soulier** *masc noun*
**shoe**

**souligner** *verb* **[1]**
1 **to underline**
2 **to emphasize**

le **soupçon** *masc noun*
1 **suspicion**
2 **spot**, **drop** (*of food, drink*)
juste un soupçon de lait just a drop of milk

**soupçonner** *verb* **[1]**
**to suspect**
soupçonner quelqu'un de faire quelque chose to suspect somebody of doing something
Elle le soupçonne de voler. She suspects him of stealing.

la **soupe** *fem noun*
**soup**
la soupe aux oignons onion soup

**souper** *verb* **[1]**
**to have supper**

le **soupir** *masc noun*
**sigh**
pousser un soupir de soulagement to let out a sigh of relief

**soupirer** *verb* **[1]**
**to sigh**

**souple** *masc & fem adjective*
1 **supple** (*person*)
2 **flexible** (*system*)
3 **soft** (*hair*)

la **source** *fem noun*
1 **spring**
l'eau de source spring water
2 **source**
Quelle est la source de tes ennuis? What's the source of your problems?

le **sourcil** *masc noun*
**eyebrow**

**sourd** *masc adjective*, **sourde** *fem*
1 **deaf**
Ne crie pas, je ne suis pas sourd! Don't shout, I'm not deaf!
2 **dull**, **muffled** (*noise*)

**souriant** *masc adjective*, **souriante** *fem*
**cheerful**

le **sourire** *masc noun* ▷ see **sourire** *verb*
**smile**
faire un sourire à quelqu'un to give somebody a smile
Le bébé m'a fait un joli sourire. The baby gave me a lovely smile.

**sourire** *verb* **[68]** ▷ see **sourire** *noun*
**to smile**
Il ne sourit jamais. He never smiles.
sourire à quelqu'un to smile at somebody
Elle lui a souri. She smiled at him.

la **souris** *fem noun*
**mouse** (*the animal, for a computer*)

**sous** *preposition*
1 **under**, **underneath**
Il est caché sous la table. He's hiding under the table.
sous terre underground
2 **during**
sous l'Occupation during the Occupation
3 Anne est sous antibiotiques. Anne is on antibiotics.

**sous-entendu** *masc adjective*, **sous-entendue** *fem* ▷ see **sous-entendu** *noun*
**implied**

le **sous-entendu** *masc noun* ▷ see **sous-entendu** *adj*
**innuendo**

**sous-estimer** *verb* **[1]**
**to underestimate**

**sous-marin** *masc adjective*, **sous-marine** *fem* ▷ see **sous-marin** *noun*
**underwater**
la plongée sous-marine deep-sea diving

le **sous-marin** *masc noun* ▷ see **sous-marin** *adj*
**submarine**

le **sous-sol** *masc noun*
**basement**
au sous-sol in the basement

la **sous-tasse** *fem noun*
**saucer**

♪ le **sous-titre** *masc noun*
**subtitle**
**un film avec des sous-titres en français** a film with French subtitles

la **soustraction** *fem noun*
**subtraction**

le **sous-vêtement** *masc noun*
**underwear**

**soutenir** *verb* **[77]**
1 **to support**
**Je soutiens la pétition.** I support the petition.
**Il a besoin qu'on lui soutienne le moral.** He needs cheering up.
2 **to withstand** (*a shock, an attack*)

**souterrain** *masc adjective*, **souterraine** *fem*
**underground**
**un passage souterrain** an underground passage, a subway (*under a street*)

le **soutien** *masc noun*
**support**
**J'ai besoin de ton soutien moral.** I need your moral support.
• le **soutien scolaire** learning support

le **soutien-gorge** *masc noun*, les **soutiens-gorge** *plural*
**bra**

le **soutif** *masc noun*
(*informal*) **bra**

♪ le **souvenir** *masc noun* ▷ **see se souvenir** *verb*
1 **memory**
**mes souvenirs de Londres** my memories of London
**Je n'ai aucun souvenir de l'avoir rencontrée.** I have no memory of meeting her.
2 **souvenir**
**C'est un souvenir de mon voyage en Chine.** It's something I brought back from my trip to China.

se **souvenir** *reflexive verb* Ⓔ **[81]**
▷ **see souvenir** *noun*
**se souvenir de quelqu'un, quelque chose** to remember somebody *or* something
**Je me souviens d'elle.** I remember her.
**Il se souvient très bien de sa première école.** He remembers his first school very well.

♪ **souvent** *adverb*
**often**
**Je ne la vois pas très souvent.** I don't see her very often.
**Il faut manger des légumes le plus souvent possible.** You must eat vegetables as often as possible.

**spacieux** *masc adjective*, **spacieuse** *fem*
**spacious**

les **spaghettis** *plural masc noun*
**spaghetti**
**des spaghettis à la bolognaise** spaghetti bolognese

♪ le **sparadrap** *masc noun*
**sticking plaster**

le **speaker** *masc noun*, la **speakerine** *fem*
**announcer**

♪ **spécial** *masc adjective*, **spéciale** *fem*, **spéciaux** *masc pl*, **spéciales** *fem pl*
1 **special**
**les effets spéciaux** special effects
**'Que fais-tu ce week-end?' — 'Rien de spécial.'** 'What are you doing this weekend?' — 'Nothing special.'
2 **odd**
**Stan est vraiment très spécial.** Stan's really very odd.

**spécialement** *adverb*
**specially**
**Elle est venue spécialement pour te voir.** She came especially to see you.

se **spécialiser** *reflexive verb* Ⓔ **[1]**
**to specialize**
**Elle se spécialise dans la génétique.** She's specializing in genetics.

le & la **spécialiste** *masc & fem noun*
**specialist**

♪ la **spécialité** *fem noun*
**speciality**

**spécifier** *verb* **[1]**
**to specify**

♪ le **spectacle** *masc noun*
1 **show**
**Nous allons au spectacle.** We're going to see a show.
**un spectacle son et lumière** a son et lumière
2 **sight**
**un spectacle familier** a familiar sight

**spectaculaire** *masc & fem adjective*
**spectacular**

♪ le **spectateur** *masc noun*, la **spectatrice** *fem*
1 **member of the audience**
**Les spectateurs ont applaudi frénétiquement.** The audience applauded wildly. ▸▸

**2 spectator**
**Il y avait 30 000 spectateurs au match de football.** There were 30,000 spectators at the football match.

la **spéléologie** *fem noun*
**potholing**

**spirituel** *masc adjective*, **spirituelle** *fem*
**1 witty**
**2 spiritual**

la **splendeur** *fem noun*
**splendour**

**splendide** *masc & fem adjective*
**splendid**

**sponsoriser** *verb* **[1]**
**to sponsor**

**spontané** *masc adjective*, **spontanée** *fem*
**spontaneous**

le **sport** *masc noun*
**sport, sports**
**J'aime le sport.** I like sport.
**Il fait beaucoup de sport.** He does a lot of sport.
**Que fais-tu comme sport?** What sport do you do?
**Camille est bonne en sport.** Camille is good at sports.
**les sports d'hiver** winter sports
**Le foot est un sport d'équipe.** Football is a team sport.

**sportif** *masc adjective*, **sportive** *fem*
▷ see **sportif** *noun*
**1 sports**
**un club sportif** a sports club
**un journaliste sportif** a sports correspondent
**2 sporty**
**Émeline n'est pas sportive.** Émeline is not sporty.

le **sportif** *masc noun*, la **sportive** *fem*
▷ see **sportif** *adj*
**sportsman, sportswoman**
**une sportive de haut niveau** a top sportswoman

le **spot** *masc noun*
**spotlight**
• le **spot publicitaire** commercial

le **square** *masc noun*
**park** (*public garden*)
**La nounou emmène les enfants au square.** The nanny is taking the children to the park.

le **squelette** *masc noun*
**skeleton**

**stable** *masc & fem adjective*
**stable**
**L'échelle n'est pas stable.** The ladder isn't stable.
**Il a trouvé un emploi stable.** He's found a steady job.

le **stade** *masc noun*
**stadium**
**Le nouveau stade accueille 80 000 personnes.** The new stadium can seat 80,000 people.

le **stage** *masc noun*
**1 course**
**suivre un stage , faire un stage , aller en stage** to go on a course
**un stage de formation** a training course
**J'ai suivi un stage intensif de français de trois mois.** I went on a 3-month intensive French course.
**2 un stage professionnel, un stage pratique** work experience
**Elle fait un stage dans un supermarché.** She's doing work experience in a supermarket.

le & la **stagiaire** *masc & fem noun*
**trainee**

le **stand** *masc noun*
**1 stand** (*in a market, an exhibition*)
**2 stall** (*in a fairground*)

le **standard** *masc noun*
**switchboard**
**Il faut passer par le standard.** You have to go through the switchboard.

le & la **standardiste** *masc & fem noun*
**switchboard operator**

le **standing** *masc noun*
**un appartement de standing** a luxury flat

la **star** *fem noun*
**star** (*in a film, show*)

le **starter** *masc noun*
**choke** (*in a car*)

la **station** *fem noun*
**1 station**
**une station de métro** an underground station
**Nous descendons à la station Péreire.** We get off at Péreire.
**2 une station de taxis** a taxi rank
**3 resort**
**une station de ski** a ski resort
**une station balnéaire** a seaside resort
**une station thermale** a spa
**4 une station de radio** a radio station
• la **station de travail** (computer) work station

**stationnaire** *masc & fem adjective*
1 **stationary**
2 **stable**

♪ le **stationnement** *masc noun*
**parking**
'Stationnement interdit' 'No parking'

♪ **stationner** *verb* [1]
**to park**
'Défense de stationner' 'No parking'

la **station-service** *fem noun*, les **stations-service** *plural*
**service station, filling station**

la **statistique** *fem noun*
**statistics**

la **statue** *fem noun*
**statue**

le **statut** *masc noun*
1 **statute**
2 **status**

le **steak** *masc noun*
**steak**
un steak-frites steak and chips
un steak haché a hamburger
du steak haché minced beef

**stéréo** *invariable masc & fem adjective*
▷ see **stéreo** *noun*
**stereo**

la **stéréo** *fem noun* ▷ see **stéreo** *adj*
**stereo**
en stéréo in stereo

**stérile** *masc & fem adjective*
**sterile**

**stériliser** *verb* [1]
**to sterilize**

le **steward** *masc noun*
**flight attendant** (*male*)

**stimulant** *masc adjective*, **stimulante** *fem*
**stimulating**

le **stock** *masc noun*
**stock**
en stock in stock

le **stop** *masc noun*
1 **stop sign**
2 **hitchhiking**
faire du stop to hitchhike
**Nous allons faire l'Espagne en stop.** We're going to hitchhike round Spain.

**stopper** *verb* [1]
**to stop**

le **store** *masc noun*
1 **blind**
2 **awning**

le **strapontin** *masc noun*
**fold-down seat**

la **stratégie** *fem noun*
**strategy**

**stratégique** *masc & fem adjective*
**strategic**

le **stress** *masc noun*
**stress**

**stressant** *masc adjective*, **stressante** *fem*
**stressful**
un travail stressant a stressful job

**stressé** *masc adjective*, **stressée** *fem*
**stressed**
**Je suis très stressé en ce moment.** I'm stressed out at the moment.

**strict** *masc adjective*, **stricte** *fem*
1 **strict**
Le prof est très strict. The teacher is very strict.
2 **severe**
une coiffure stricte a severe hairstyle

**studieux** *masc adjective*, **studieuse** *fem*
**studious**

le **studio** *masc noun*
1 **studio flat**
**Il habite dans un studio.** He lives in a studio flat.
2 **studio**
les studios de cinéma film studios

**stupéfait** *masc adjective*, **stupéfaite** *fem*
**astounded**

les **stupéfiants** *plural masc noun*
**narcotics**

la **stupeur** *fem noun*
**astonishment**

**stupide** *masc & fem adjective*
**stupid**

la **stupidité** *fem noun*
**stupidity**

le **style** *masc noun*
**style**
un style de vie a lifestyle
**C'est bien son style!** That's just like him!

le & la **styliste** *masc & fem noun*
**designer**

♪ le **stylo** *masc noun*
**pen**
- le **stylo bille** ball-point pen
- le **stylo à encre** fountain pen
- le **stylo feutre** felt-tip pen
- le **stylo plume** fountain pen

**su** *verb* ▷ **savoir** *verb*

**subir** *verb* **[2]**
1 **to be subjected to** *(violence, pressure)*
2 **to suffer** *(a defeat, discrimination)*
3 **to undergo** *(an operation)*

**subitement** *adverb*
**suddenly**

le **subjonctif** *masc noun*
**subjunctive**
au subjonctif in the subjunctive

**substituer** *verb* **[1]**
**to substitute**

**subtil** *masc adjective*, **subtile** *fem*
**subtle**

la **subvention** *fem noun*
**subsidy**

le **succès** *masc noun*
**success**
**C'est un grand succès!** It's a great success!
**avoir du succès auprès de quelqu'un** to be a favourite with somebody
**La nouvelle BD a du succès auprès des jeunes.** The new comic book is a favourite with young people.

la **succursale** *fem noun*
**branch** *(of a company)*

**sucer** *verb* **[61]**
**to suck**

la **sucette** *fem noun*
**lollipop**

♪ le **sucre** *masc noun*
1 **sugar**
**un chewing-gum sans sucre** sugar-free chewing-gum
2 **un sucre** a lump of sugar
**Tu veux combien de sucres dans ton café?** How many sugars do you take in your coffee?
- le **sucre cristallisé** granulated sugar
- le **sucre glace** icing sugar
- le **sucre en morceaux** sugar lumps
- le **sucre en poudre** caster sugar
- le **sucre roux** brown sugar

♪ **sucré** *masc adjective*, **sucrée** *fem*
**sweet**
**C'est trop sucré pour moi.** It's too sweet for me.
**sucré au miel** sweetened with honey
**non sucré** unsweetened

les **sucreries** *plural fem noun*
**sweet things**

♪ **sud** *invariable masc & fem adjective*
▷ see **sud** *noun*
1 **south**
**la côte sud** the south coast
2 **southern**
**la région sud** the southern area

**WORD TIP** *sud* never changes.

♪ le **sud** *masc noun* ▷ see **sud** *adj*
**south**
**le sud de la France** southern France
**un vent du sud** a south wind
**Je suis du sud d'Angleterre.** I'm from the south of England.
**J'habite dans le sud (de l'Écosse).** I live in the south (of Scotland).
**C'est au sud de Paris.** It's south of Paris.

**sud-africain** *masc adjective*, **sud-africaine** *fem* ▷ see **Sud-africain** *noun*
**South African**

le **Sud-Africain** *masc noun*, la **Sud-Africaine** *fem* ▷ see **sud-africain** *adj*
**South African**

**sud-américain** *masc adjective*, **sud-américaine** *fem* ▷ see **Sud-américain** *noun*
**South American**

le **Sud-Américain** *masc noun*, la **Sud-Américaine** *fem* ▷ see **sud-américain** *adj*
**South American**

**sud-est** *invariable masc & fem adjective*
▷ see **sud-est** *noun*
**south-east**

le **sud-est** *masc noun* ▷ see **sud-est** *adj*
**south-east**
**le sud-est de l'Angleterre** south-east England

**sud-ouest** *invariable masc & fem adjective*
▷ see **sud-ouest** *noun*
**south-west**

le **sud-ouest** *masc noun* ▷ see **sud-ouest** *adj*
**south-west**
**le sud-ouest de l'Irlande** south-west Ireland

la **Suède** *fem noun*
**Sweden**

**suédois** *masc adjective*, **suédoise** *fem*
▷ see **Suédois** *masc noun*
**Swedish**

un **Suédois** *masc noun*, une **Suédoise** *fem*
▷ see **suédois** *adj*
1 **Swede** (*person from Sweden*)
les Suédois the Swedes
2 le suédois Swedish (*the language*)

**suer** *verb* [1]
**to sweat**

la **sueur** *fem noun*
**sweat**
Je suis en sueur. I'm sweating.

**suffire** *verb* [74]
1 **to be enough**
**Un kilo d'abricots suffit pour faire une tarte.** One kilo of apricots is enough to make a tarte.
**Ça suffit!** That's enough!
2 **il suffit de faire ...** all you have to do is ...
**Il suffit de nous téléphoner.** All you have to do is give us a call.

**suffisamment** *adverb*
**enough**
**Nous ne sommes pas suffisamment informés.** We don't have enough information.
**Il n'y a pas suffisamment de verres.** There aren't enough glasses.

**suffisant** *masc adjective*, **suffisante** *fem*
**sufficient**
**100 euros, c'est bien suffisant!** 100 euros, that's quite enough!

**suffoquer** *verb* [1]
**to suffocate**

**suggérer** *verb* [24]
**to suggest**

la **suggestion** *fem noun*
**suggestion**

se **suicider** *reflexive verb* Ⓔ [1]
**to commit suicide**

**suis** *verb* ▷ **être, suivre**

**suisse** *masc & fem adjective* ▷ see **Suisse** *noun*
**Swiss**
**un mot suisse** a Swiss word
**la cuisine suisse** Swiss cooking

**WORD TIP** Adjectives never have capitals in French, even for nationality or regional origin.

un & une **Suisse** *masc & fem noun*
▷ see **suisse** *adj*
1 **Swiss** (*person*)
**les Suisses romands** the French-speaking Swiss
**les Suisses allemands** the German-speaking Swiss
2 **la Suisse** Switzerland
**Verbier est en Suisse.** Verbier is in Switzerland.
**la Suisse romande** French-speaking Switzerland
**la Suisse allemande** German-speaking Switzerland

**WORD TIP** Countries and regions in French take *le*, *la*, or *les*.

la **suite** *fem noun*
1 **rest**
**Je te raconterai la suite plus tard.** I'll tell you the rest later.
**Et on connaît la suite.** And we all know what happened next.
2 **continuation**
**'Suite page 67.'** 'Continued on page 67.'
**Regardez la suite jeudi.** Watch the next instalment on Thursday.
3 **suite** (*in a hotel*)
4 **in succession**
**trois fois de suite** three times in succession
5 **tout de suite** straightaway
**J'arrive tout de suite.** I'll be right there.
6 **par la suite** later
**On s'est rendu compte par la suite que c'était une erreur.** We realized later that it was a mistake.

**suivant** *masc adjective*, **suivante** *fem*
▷ see **suivant** *noun*
1 **following**
**le jour suivant** the following day
2 **next**
**le chapitre suivant** the next chapter

le **suivant** *masc noun*, la **suivante** *fem*
▷ see **suivant** *adj*
**next one**
**pas ce lundi mais le suivant** not this Monday but the next
**Au suivant!** Next please!

**suivre** *verb* [75]
1 **to follow**
**Suivez-moi!** Follow me!
**Tu devrais suivre ses conseils.** You should follow his advice.
**Elle ne suit jamais la recette.** She nevers follows the recipe.
**Il a décidé de suivre un régime.** He decided to go on a diet.
2 **'À suivre'** 'To be continued'
3 **to keep up**
**Luc n'arrive pas à suivre en maths.** Luc can't keep up in maths.
**Je suis l'actualité.** I keep up with the news.
4 **suivre un cours** to do a course
**Éric suit un cours d'informatique.** Éric is doing a computing course. ⏩

5 **to pay attention** (*at school*)
**Alexis ne suit pas en classe, il bavarde trop.** Alexis is not paying attention in class, he chatters too much.

6 **to follow** (*to understand*)
**Je ne te suis pas, c'est trop compliqué!** I don't follow you, it's too complicated!

7 **faire suivre** to forward
**J'ai fait suivre ton email.** I forwarded your email.
**Il fait suivre son courrier à sa nouvelle adresse.** He has his mail forwarded to his new address.

le **sujet** *masc noun*
1 **subject**
**un sujet de conversation** a topic of conversation
**au sujet de quelque chose** about something
**C'est au sujet de votre sœur.** It's about your sister.
**C'est à quel sujet?** What's it about?
2 **question**
**un sujet d'examen** an exam question
**un sujet d'histoire** a history question
**une dissertation sur sujet libre** an essay on a subject of your choice

♂ **super** *invariable masc & fem adjective* ▷ see **super** *adv*
(*informal*) **great**
**Mais c'est super!** But that's great!
**Ses parents sont super!** Her parents are great!

♂ **super** *adverb* ▷ see **super** *adj*
**really**
**C'est super bon!** It's really good!

la **superficie** *fem noun*
**area**

**superficiel** *masc adjective*, **superficielle** *fem*
**superficial**

**supérieur** *masc adjective*, **supérieure** *fem* ▷ see **supérieur** *noun*
1 **upper**
**l'étage supérieur** the upper floor
2 **greater**
**à une vitesse supérieure** at a faster speed
**à une température supérieure** at a higher temperature
3 **superior**, **better** (*work, quality*)
**Cet album est de loin supérieur à l'autre.** This album's much better than the other one.

le **supérieur** *masc noun*, la **supérieure** *fem* ▷ see **supérieur** *adj*
**superior**

le **superlatif** *masc noun*
**superlative**

♂ le **supermarché** *masc noun*
**supermarket**
**Nous faisons nos courses au supermarché.** We do our shopping in the supermarket.

**superposer** *verb* [1]
1 **to stack up** (*chairs, boxes*)
**des lits superposés** bunk beds
2 **to superimpose** (*an image*)

**superstitieux** *masc adjective*, **superstitieuse** *fem*
**superstitious**

la **superstition** *fem noun*
**superstition**

♂ le **supplément** *masc noun*
1 **extra charge**
**Le vin est en supplément.** Wine is extra.
**Il y a un supplément de 5 euros pour le plateau de fruits de mer.** The seafood platter is 5 euros extra.
2 **supplement** (*in a newspaper*)

**supplémentaire** *masc & fem adjective*
1 **additional**
**des dépenses supplémentaires** extra expenses
2 **les heures supplémentaires** overtime

le **supplice** *masc noun*
**torture**

**supplier** *verb* [1]
**to beg**

le **support** *masc noun*
**support**
**un support audiovisuel** an audiovisual aid

**supportable** *masc & fem adjective*
**bearable**

**supporter** *verb* [1]
1 **to stand**
**Je ne supporte pas cette musique.** I can't stand this music.
**Elle ne supporte pas d'attendre.** She can't stand waiting.
2 **to withstand**
**Les plantes ont bien supporté le gel.** The plants withstood the frost.
**Il supporte mal les longs voyages en voiture.** Long car journeys are too much for him.
3 **to support** (*a weight*)

se **supporter** *reflexive verb* Ⓔ
**to stand each other**
**Ils ne peuvent plus se supporter.** They can't stand each other any longer.

**supposer** *verb* [1]
**to suppose**
**Je suppose que tu n'as toujours pas fini.** I suppose you still haven't finished.

**supprimer** *verb* [1]
1 **to delete**
**J'ai supprimé un paragraphe de ma dissertation.** I deleted a paragraph in my essay.
2 **to cut**
**Ils ont supprimé la dernière scène du film.** They cut the last scene of the film.
**La direction a supprimé dix emplois.** Management cut ten jobs.
3 **to cancel**
**Ils ont supprimé le train de 14 heures.** They cancelled the 2 o'clock train.

♪ **sur** *preposition*
1 **on**
**Le chat est sur ton lit.** The cat's on your bed.
**Il l'a écrit sur un morceau de papier.** He wrote it on a piece of paper.
**un débat sur le racisme** a discussion on racism
**Le cinéma est sur la droite.** The cinema's on the right.
2 **over**
**un pont sur la Tamise** a bridge over the Thames
**sur une période de trois ans** over a three-year period
3 **by** (*in measurements*)
**La pièce mesure deux mètres sur trois.** The room is two metres by three.
4 **out of**
**trois élèves sur cinq** three pupils out of five
**J'ai eu douze sur vingt en géographie.** I got twelve out of twenty in geography.

♪ **sûr** *masc adjective*, **sûre** *fem*
1 **sure**
Tu es sûr? Are you sure?
**Oui, bien sûr!** Yes, of course!
**Elle est sûre qu'il viendra.** She's sure that he'll come.
2 **sûr de soi, de lui, d'elle ...** self-confident
**Elle est très sûre d'elle.** She's very self-confident.
3 **safe**
**en lieu sûr** in a safe place

**surcharger** *verb* [52]
**to overload**

la **surdité** *fem noun*
**deafness**

la **surdose** *fem noun*
**overdose** (*of medicine*)

**sûrement** *adverb*
1 **certainly**
**Sûrement pas!** Certainly not!
2 **most probably**
**Tu as sûrement entendu la nouvelle.** You've most probably heard the news.

la **sûreté** *fem noun*
**safety**

le **surf** *masc noun*
1 **surfing**
**faire du surf** to go surfing
2 **netsurf** (*on Internet*)

la **surface** *fem noun*
1 **surface**
2 **area**
**Je calcule la surface du triangle.** I'm working out the area of the triangle.
3 **une grande surface** a hypermarket
• la **surface de réparation** penalty area

le **surf des neiges** *masc noun*
**snowboarding**
**Vanessa va faire du surf des neiges.** Vanessa's going snowboarding.

♪ **surfer** *verb* [1]
1 **to go surfing**
2 **to surf**
**surfer sur Internet** to surf the Net

le **surfeur** *masc noun*, la **surfeuse** *fem*
1 **surfer** (*on the sea*)
2 **netsurfer** (*on Internet*)

**surgelé** *masc adjective*, **surgelée** *fem*
▷ see **surgelé** *noun*
**frozen**
**les légumes surgelés** frozen vegetables

le **surgelé** *masc noun* ▷ see **surgelé** *adj*
**les surgelés** frozen food

**sur-le-champ** *adverb*
**right away**

le **surlendemain** *masc noun*
**two days later**
**Elle est arrivée le surlendemain.** She arrived two days later.

**surmonter** *verb* [1]
**to overcome**

**surnaturel** *masc adjective*, **surnaturelle** *fem*
**supernatural**

le **surnom** *masc noun*
**nickname**

**surnommer** *verb* **[1]**
**to nickname**

**surpeuplé** *masc adjective*, **surpeuplée** *fem*
**overpopulated**

**surprenant** *masc adjective*, **surprenante** *fem*
**surprising**

**surprendre** *verb* **[64]**
1 **to surprise**
**J'ai été agréablement surprise.** I was pleasantly surprised.
**Ça m'a beaucoup surpris.** I found that really surprising.
2 **surprendre quelqu'un en train de faire quelque chose** to catch somebody doing something
**Je l'ai surprise en train de lire mon courrier.** I caught her reading my mail.
3 **se laisser surprendre par quelque chose** to get caught by something
**Il s'est laissé surprendre par la marée montante.** He got caught by the rising tide.

**surpris** *masc adjective*, **surprise** *fem*
**surprised**
**Je suis surpris de te voir.** I'm surprised to see you.

la **surprise** *fem noun*
**surprise**
**Quelle surprise!** What a surprise!
**Ne dis rien, c'est une surprise!** Don't say a word, it's a surprise!
**À ma grande surprise, elle a accepté.** To my great surprise she agreed.
**Il y avait un invité surprise.** There was a surprise guest.
**faire une surprise à quelqu'un** to give somebody a surprise
**Nous allons faire une surprise à nos parents.** We're going to give our parents a surprise.
• la **surprise-partie** surprise party

**surréaliste** *masc & fem adjective*
▷ see **surréaliste** *noun*
**surreal**

le & la **surréaliste** *masc & fem noun*
▷ see **surréaliste** *adj*
**surrealist**

♪**surtout** *adverb*
1 **especially**
**Il y a beaucoup de touristes, surtout en été.** There is a lot of tourists, especially in the summer.
2 **above all**
**Il faut surtout rester calme.** Above all, we must stay calm.

le **surveillant** *masc noun*, la **surveillante** *fem*
**supervisor** (*In a school, responsible for maintaining school discipline outside the classroom.*)

**surveiller** *verb* **[1]**
1 **to watch, to keep an eye on**
**Est-ce que tu peux surveiller mon sac?** Can you keep an eye on my bag?
2 **surveiller une maison** to keep a house under surveillance
3 **to supervise** (*work, progress*)
**surveiller le travail des élèves** to supervise the students' work
4 **surveiller un examen** to invigilate an exam
5 **watch**
**Je surveille ma ligne.** I'm watching my figure.
**Surveille ton langage!** Watch your language!

le **survêtement** *masc noun*
**tracksuit**

la **survie** *fem noun*
**survival**

le **survivant** *masc noun*, la **survivante** *fem*
**survivor**

**survivre** *verb* **[82]**
**to survive**
**survivre à quelque chose** to survive something
**Elle a survécu au tsunami.** She survived the tsunami.

**survoler** *verb* **[1]**
**to fly over**

**suspect** *masc adjective*, **suspecte** *fem*
▷ see **suspect** *noun*
**suspicious**

le **suspect** *masc noun*, la **suspecte** *fem*
▷ see **suspect** *adj*
**suspect**

le **suspense** *masc noun*
**suspense** (*as in a thriller*)

la **suture** *fem noun*
**un point de suture** a stitch (*in a wound*)

**svelte** *masc & fem adjective*
**slender**

♪la **SVP** *abbreviation*
(*= s'il vous plaît*) **please**

le **sweat** *masc noun* ▷ **sweatshirt**

le **sweatshirt** *masc noun*
**sweatshirt**

la **syllabe** *fem noun*
**syllable**

le **symbole** *masc noun*
**symbol**

**symbolique** *masc & fem adjective*
**symbolic**
un geste symbolique a token gesture

♪ **sympa** *invariable masc & fem adjective*
(*informal*) **nice**
Je le trouve très sympa, ton copain. He's really nice, your boyfriend.

la **sympathie** *fem noun*
J'ai beaucoup de sympathie pour elle. I like her a lot.

**sympathique** *masc & fem*
**nice**
C'est un type sympathique. He's a nice guy.

**sympathiser** *verb* **[1]**
sympathiser avec quelqu'un to get on well with someone
Il sympathise avec le nouvel élève. He gets on well with the new student.

le **symptôme** *masc noun*
**symptom**

la **synagogue** *fem noun*
**synagogue**

le **syndicat** *masc noun*
**trade union**
- le **syndicat d'initiative** tourist information office

**synthétique** *masc & fem*
**synthetic**

le **synthétiseur** *masc noun*
**synthesizer**

le **système** *masc noun*
**system**

# Tt

**t'** *abbreviation: te* ▷ **te** *pronoun*

**WORD TIP** *te* becomes *t'* before a word beginning with *a, e, i, o, u* or *silent h.*

**ta** *fem adjective* ▷ **ton**

♪ le **tabac** *masc noun*
1 **tobacco**
2 un bureau de tabac a tobacconist's

♪ la **table** *fem noun*
**table**
Léa met la table. Léa's laying the table.
À table! Dinner's ready!
- la **table de chevet** bedside table
- la **table de nuit** bedside table

♪ le **tableau** *masc noun*
1 **painting**
un tableau de Renoir a painting by Renoir
2 **table, chart**
un tableau horaire a timetable
- le **tableau d'affichage** notice board
- le **tableau noir** blackboard

la **tablette** *fem noun*
**bar**
une tablette de chocolat a bar of chocolate

**WORD TIP** *tablette* does not mean *tablet* in English; for the meaning of *tablet* ▷ **comprimé**.

le **tableur** *masc noun*
**spreadsheet**

le **tablier** *masc noun*
**apron**

le **tabouret** *masc noun*
**stool**

la **tache** *fem noun*
1 **stain**
2 **spot**
- les **taches de rousseur** *fem pl* freckles

la **tâche** *fem noun*
**task**
- les **tâches ménagères** *fem pl* household chores

**tacher** *verb* **[1]**
**to stain**

le **tacle** *masc noun*
**tackle** (*in soccer*)

le **tact** *masc noun*
**tact**

la **tactique** *fem noun*
**tactics**

la **taie d'oreiller** *fem noun*
**pillowcase**

♪ la **taille** *fem noun*
1 **size**
**la taille au-dessus** the next size up
**la taille au-dessous** the next size down
**Quelle taille faites-vous?** What size are you?
**'Taille unique'** 'One size'
2 **height**
**une personne de taille moyenne** a person of average height
3 **waist**

le **taille-crayon** *masc noun*, les **taille-crayons** *plural*
**pencil sharpener**

**tailler** *verb* [1]
1 **to cut**
2 **to carve** (*wood*)
3 **to prune** (*a tree*)
4 **to sharpen** (*a pencil*)

le **tailleur** *masc noun*
1 **suit** (*for a woman*)
2 **tailor**
**être assis en tailleur** to be sitting cross-legged

se **taire** *reflexive verb* Ⓔ [76]
**to stop talking**
**Taisez-vous!** Be quiet!

le **talent** *masc noun*
**talent**
**Il a du talent.** He's talented

♪ le **talon** *masc noun*
1 **heel** (*of your foot, a shoe*)
**chaussures à talons hauts** high-heeled shoes
2 **stub** (*of a ticket*)

le **tambour** *masc noun*
**drum**

le **tambourin** *masc noun*
**tambourine**

la **Tamise** *fem noun*
**la Tamise** the Thames

le **tampon** *masc noun*
**stamp**
• le **tampon à récurer** scouring pad
• le **tampon hygiénique** tampon

**tamponneuse** *fem adjective*
**les autos tamponneuses** the dodgems

**tandis que** *conjunction*
**while**

**tant** *adverb*
1 **so much**
**J'ai tant mangé!** I've eaten so much!
**ce qu'elle avait tant voulu** what she had wanted so much
2 **tant de** so much, so many
**tant d'argent** so much money
**tant d'amis** so many friends
3 **Tant pis.** Never mind.
4 **Tant mieux.** It's just as well.
5 **tant que** while
**Allons se promener tant qu'il fait beau!** Let's go for a walk while it's nice!
6 **tant que** as long as
**Je reste dehors tant qu'il y aura du soleil.** I'm staying outside as long as there's some sunshine.

♪ la **tante** *fem noun*
**aunt**

**tantôt** *adverb*
**sometimes**

**taper** *verb* [1]
1 **taper quelqu'un** to hit somebody
**Lydia m'a tapé.** Lydia hit me.
2 **taper à la machine** to type
3 **taper des mains** to clap your hands
4 **taper à quelque chose** to knock on something
**Il y a quelqu'un qui tape à la porte.** There's someone knocking at the door.

se **taper** *reflexive verb* Ⓔ
**se taper dessus** to knock each other about

le **tapis** *invariable masc noun*
**carpet**
• le **tapis de souris** mousemat

le **tapis roulant** *masc noun*
1 **moving walkway**
2 **carousel** (*for airport luggage*)
3 **conveyor belt**

**tapisser** *verb* [1]
**to wallpaper**

la **tapisserie** *fem noun*
1 **tapestry**
2 **wallpaper**

**taquiner** *verb* [1]
**to tease**

♪ **tard** *adverb*
**late**
**Il est tard.** It's late.
**trop tard** too late
**plus tard** later

**tardif** *masc adjective*, **tardive** *fem*
**late**

♪ le **tarif** *masc noun*
1 **rate**
**le tarif horaire** the hourly rate

Ⓔ means the verb takes être to form the perfect

2 **fare**
le plein tarif full fare
le tarif réduit reduced fare
à tarif réduit at a reduced price
3 **price list**
tarif des consommations price list (*in a French cafe*)

ℰ la **tarte** *fem noun*
**tart**
une tarte aux abricots an apricot tart

ℰ la **tartine** *fem noun*
**slice of bread and butter**
une tartine de confiture a slice of bread and jam

**tartiner** *verb* [1]
**to spread** (*on bread*)

le **tas** *invariable masc noun*
1 **pile**
un tas de bois a pile of wood
2 (*informal*) **un tas de quelque chose** stacks of something
J'ai un tas de choses à faire ce soir. I've got stacks of things to do tonight.

ℰ la **tasse** *fem noun*
**cup**
une tasse de thé a cup of tea

la **taupe** *fem noun*
**mole** (*the animal*)

la **taupinière** *fem noun*
**molehill**

le **taureau** *masc noun*, les **taureaux** *plural*
▷ see **Taureau** *masc noun*
**bull**

le **Taureau** *masc noun* ▷ see **taureau** *masc noun*
**Taurus**
Camille est Taureau. Camille is a Taurus.

**WORD TIP** Signs of the zodiac do not take an article: *un* or *une*.

le **taux** *invariable masc noun*
**rate**
le taux de natalité the birth rate
• le **taux de change** exchange rate

la **taxe** *fem noun*
**tax**
la boutique hors taxes the duty-free shop

le **taxi** *masc noun*
**taxi**
appeler un taxi to call a taxi
On a pris un taxi. We took a taxi.

**tchèque** *masc & fem adjective*
**Czech**
la République tchèque the Czech Republic

**te** *pronoun*
1 (*as a direct object*) **you**
Elle te taquine. She's teasing you.
Il ne t'aime pas. He doesn't like you.
2 (*as an indirect object*) **(to) you**
Écoute, elle te parle! Listen, she's talking to you!
Il t'a expliqué le problème? Did he explain the problem to you?
3 (*with reflexive verbs*) **yourself**
Tu te lèves à quelle heure? What time do you get up? (*se lever is a reflexive verb*)
4 **(for) yourself**
Tu t'es acheté un jean? Did you buy yourself a pair of jeans?

**WORD TIP** *te* becomes *t'* before *a, e, i, o, u* or silent *h*.

le **technicien** *masc noun*, la **technicienne** *fem*
**technician**

**technique** *masc & fem adjective*
▷ see **technique** *noun*
**technical**

la **technique** *fem noun*
▷ see **technique** *adj*
**technique**

la **technologie** *fem noun*
**technology**

le **tee-shirt** *masc noun*
**T-shirt**

le **teint** *masc noun*
**complexion**
avoir le teint clair to have a fair complexion
avoir le teint mat to have olive skin

le **teinturier** *masc noun*, la **teinturière** *fem*
**dry-cleaner's**

**tel** *masc adjective*, **telle** *fem*
1 **such**
un tel talent such talent
une telle aventure such an adventure
de tels mensonges such lies
Je n'ai jamais rien vu de tel. I've never seen anything like it.
2 **tel que** such as
les animaux tels que le lion et le tigre animals such as the lion and the tiger
les grandes villes telles que Paris et Lyon big cities such as Paris and Lyons
3 **rien de tel que ...** nothing like ...
Il n'y a rien de tel qu'un bon repas. There's nothing like a good meal.
4 **tel quel** as it is
Servir le saumon tel quel. Serve the salmon just as it is. ▸▸

J'ai acheté la veste telle quelle. I bought the jacket just as it was.

♪ la **télé** *fem noun*
(*informal*) **telly**
à la télé on telly
- la **télécabine** cable car
- la **télécarte**® phonecard
- la **télécommande** remote control
- la **télécopie** fax
- le **télécopieur** fax machine
- le **télégramme** telegram
- le **téléphérique** cable car

♪ le **téléphone** *masc noun*
**telephone**
au téléphone on the phone
un numéro de téléphone a phone number
- le **téléphone portable** mobile phone

♪ **téléphoner** *verb* **[1]**
**to phone**
téléphoner à quelqu'un to phone somebody
Je vais téléphoner à Nicolas. I'm going to phone Nicolas.

**téléphonique** *masc & fem adjective*
une cabine téléphonique a phone box

le **télésiège** *masc noun*
**chairlift**

♪ le **téléspectateur** *masc noun*, la **téléspectatrice** *fem*
**viewer** (*of TV programme*)

♪ le **téléviseur** *masc noun*
**television (set)**

♪ la **télévision** *fem noun*
**television**
Nous regardons la télévision. We're watching television.
- la **télévision par câble** cable television
- la **télévision par satellite** satellite television

**telle** *fem adjective* ▷ **tel**

**tellement** *adverb*
1 **so**
C'est tellement compliqué. It's so complicated.
2 **so much**
Il a tellement plu. It rained so much.
'Tu aimes lire?' — 'Pas tellement.' 'Do you like reading?' — 'Not much.'
3 tellement de so much, so many
J'ai tellement de travail. I've got so much work.
Il y avait tellement de monde. There were so many people there.

**tels** *plural masc adjective*, **telles** *fem pl* ▷ **tel**

le **témoignage** *masc noun*
1 **story** (*of a person's life*)
le témoignage d'une adolescente africaine an African teenager's story
2 **account**
selon les témoignages de quelques passants according to accounts given by some passers-by
3 **evidence** (*used in court*)

**témoigner** *verb* **[1]**
**to give evidence**

le **témoin** *masc noun*
**witness**

♪ la **température** *fem noun*
**temperature**
La température est de 20°C. The temperature is 20°C.
Martine est malade, elle a de la température. Martine is ill, she has a temperature.
prendre la température de quelqu'un to take somebody's temperature
L'infirmière m'a pris la température. The nurse took my temperature.

la **tempête** *fem noun*
**storm**

le **temple** *masc noun*
1 **temple**
2 **(Protestant) church**

**temporaire** *masc & fem adjective*
**temporary**

♪ le **temps** *invariable masc noun*
1 **weather**
le mauvais temps the bad weather
par temps de pluie in rainy weather
Quel temps fait-il? What's the weather like?
2 **time**
Je n'ai pas le temps. I haven't got time.
Il nous reste combien de temps? How much time have we got left?
Il est temps de partir. It's time to go.
mettre du temps pour faire quelque chose to take time to do something
Ça a mis beaucoup de temps. It took a long time.
Il met beaucoup de temps à s'habiller. He takes his time to get dressed.
passer son temps à faire quelque chose to spend your time doing something
Elle passe son temps à écouter de la musique. She spends her time listening to music.
perdre son temps to waste your time
Tu perds ton temps. You're wasting your

time.
**Il était temps!** About time too!
**à temps** in time, on time
**de temps en temps** from time to time
**en même temps** at the same time
**un travail à plein temps** a full-time job
**un travail à temps partiel** a part-time job
3 **tense** *(of a verb)*

la **tendance** *fem noun*
1 **tendency**
**Elle a une tendance à l'étourderie.** She can be a bit absent-minded.
**avoir tendance à faire quelque chose** to tend to do something
**Il a tendance à croire tout ce qu'on dit.** He tends to believe everything you say.
2 **trend**

**tendre** *masc & fem adjective*
▷ see **tendre** *verb*
1 **tender**
**de la viande tendre** tender meat
2 **soft**
**C'est un dur au cœur tendre.** He's got a soft heart beneath that tough exterior.

**tendre** *verb* [3] ▷ see **tendre** *adj*
1 **to stretch** *(something elastic)*
2 **to hold out**
**tendre quelque chose à quelqu'un** to hold something out to somebody
**Elle m'a tendu un crayon.** She held out a pencil to me.
3 **tendre le bras** to reach out

la **tendresse** *fem noun*
**tenderness**

**tendu** *masc adjective*, **tendue** *fem*
**tense**

♪ **tenir** *verb* [77]
1 **to hold**
**Peux-tu tenir la corde?** Can you hold the rope?
**Elle tenait l'enfant par la main.** She was holding the child by the hand.
2 **to run** *(a business)*
**Mon oncle tient un restaurant.** My uncle runs a restaurant.
3 **to keep**
**'Tenir hors de la portée des enfants'** 'Keep away from children'
4 **to take up**
**tenir de la place** to take up space
5 **to fit**
**Nous ne tiendrons pas tous à table.** We won't all fit around the table.
6 **tenir à faire quelque chose** to be determined to do something
**Je tiens à le finir aujourd'hui.** I'm determined to finish it today.
7 **Tiens!** Oh!

se **tenir** *reflexive verb* ⓔ
1 **to hold**
**Tiens-toi à la rampe!** Hold the banister!
2 **to stand**
**Elle se tenait devant l'entrée.** She was standing by the entrance.
**Tiens-toi droit!** Stand up straight!
3 *(meeting)* **to be held**
**La réunion se tiendra à 19 heures.** The meeting will be held at 7 pm.

le **tennis** *invariable masc noun*
**tennis**
**Victor joue au tennis.** Victor plays tennis.
**un terrain de tennis, un court de tennis** a tennis court
• le **tennis de table** table tennis

la **tension** *fem noun*
1 **tension** *(of a rope)*
2 **blood pressure**

**tentant** *masc adjective*, **tentante** *fem*
**tempting**

la **tentation** *fem noun*
**temptation**

la **tentative** *fem noun*
**attempt**

♪ la **tente** *fem noun*
**tent**
**une tente pour 6 personnes** a six-man tent
**monter la tente** to pitch the tent

**tenter** *verb* [1]
1 **to attempt**
**tenter de faire quelque chose** to try to do something
**Il a tenté de s'échapper.** He tried to escape.
2 **to tempt**

la **tenue** *fem noun*
1 **clothes**
**changer de tenue** to change clothes
**en tenue décontractée** wearing casual clothes
**la tenue de sport** sports kit
**'Tenue correcte exigée'** 'Appropriate clothing must be worn' *(in a church, a museum)*
2 **behaviour**
**Sa tenue en classe est irréprochable.** Her behaviour in class is impeccable.

le **terme** *masc noun*
1 **word**
**un terme technique** a technical term ⏩

French-English

2 **end**
à court terme short-term
à long terme long-term
3 les termes the terms

**WORD TIP** *terme* does not mean *school term* in English; for the meaning of *term* ▷ **trimestre**

la **terminale** *fem noun*
(*the French equivalent of*) **Year 13**

**terminer** *verb* [1]
**to finish**
'Avez-vous terminé?' — 'Oui, merci.' 'Have you finished?' — 'Yes, thanks.'

se **terminer** *reflexive verb* Ⓔ
**to end**
La réunion s'est terminée à 18 heures. The meeting ended at 6 pm.

le **terminus** *invariable masc noun*
**terminus**

♂ le **terrain** *masc noun*
1 **land**, **ground**
du terrain marécageux some marshy land
2 **plot of land**
un terrain à bâtir a site (*for building on*)
3 **ground**, **pitch** (*for sports*)
un nouveau terrain de sport a new sports ground
- le **terrain de camping** campsite
- le **terrain de football** football pitch
- le **terrain de golf** golf course
- le **terrain de jeu(x)** playground

la **terrasse** *fem noun*
**terrace**
Je me suis assis à la terrasse d'un café. I sat at a table outside a cafe.

la **terre** *fem noun*
1 **ground**
Il était à terre. He was lying on the ground.
2 **soil**
La terre ici est fertile. The soil here is rich.
3 **land** (*not sea*)
4 par terre on the floor, on the ground
Le verre est tombé par terre. The glass fell on the floor.
5 **earth**
vivre sur terre to live on earth
6 la Terre the Earth
- la **terre cuite** terracotta

♂ **terrible** *masc & fem adjective*
1 **terrible**
des événements terribles terrible events
2 (*informal*) **terrific**
Le concert était terrible! The concert was terrific!

**terrifiant** *masc adjective*, **terrifiante** *fem*
**terrifying**

**terrifier** *verb* [1]
**terrify**

la **terrine** *fem*
1 **(round) bowl** (*for cooking*)
2 terrine de canard terrine of duck

le **territoire** *masc noun*
1 **territory**
2 **country**

le **terrorisme** *masc noun*
**terrorism**

le & la **terroriste** *masc & fem noun*
**terrorist**

**tes** *plural adjective* ▷ **ton your**

le **test** *masc noun*
**test**

**WORD TIP** *test* does not mean *a school test* in English; for the meaning of *test* ▷ **contrôle**.

le **testament** *masc noun*
**will**

**tester** *verb* [1]
**to test**

le **tétanos** *invariable masc noun*
**tetanus**

le **têtard** *masc noun*
**tadpole**

♂ la **tête** *fem noun*
1 **head**
Tu t'es cogné la tête. You banged your head.
Elle a mal à la tête. She has a headache.
se laver la tête to wash your hair
2 **face**
Pourquoi fait-il cette tête? Why is he pulling such a face?
3 **mind**
J'ai quelque chose en tête. I've got something in mind.
4 faire la tête to sulk
Il fait la tête car il n'est pas invité. He's sulking because he isn't invited.
5 en tête à tête in private
un dîner en tête à tête an intimate dinner for two
6 **top**
Tu es en tête de la liste. You're first on the list.
7 **front** (*of a train*)
les deux wagons de tête the two front coaches

**têtu** *masc adjective*, **têtue** *fem*
**stubborn**



Ⓔ means the verb takes être to form the perfect

le **texte** *masc noun*
**text**

le **texto**® *masc noun*
**text message**
**envoyer un texto à quelqu'un** to text somebody
**Jeanne m'a envoyé un texto pour dire qu'elle arrive.** Jeanne texted me to say she's on her way.

le **TGV**® *masc noun*
(*= train à grande vitesse*) **high-speed train**

la **thalassothérapie** *fem noun*
**sea-water treatment** (*at a health spa*)

le **thé** *masc noun*
**tea**
**un thé au lait** tea with milk
**un thé au citron** a lemon tea
**une tasse de thé** a cup of tea
**Je vais faire du thé.** I'll make some tea.
**Deux thés, s'il vous plaît!** Two teas please!
**un salon de thé** a tea room
- le **thé à la bergamote** Earl Grey tea
- le **thé vert** green tea

le **théâtre** *masc noun*
1 **theatre**
**Demain, nous allons au théâtre.** Tomorrow we're going to the theatre.
**une pièce de théâtre** a play
**un coup de théâtre** a dramatic turn of events
2 **plays**
**le théâtre de Molière** Molière's plays
3 **drama**
**une école de théâtre** a drama school
**Lou fait du théâtre.** Lou's in a drama group.

la **théière** *fem noun*
**teapot**

le **thème** *masc noun*
**subject**

la **théorie** *fem noun*
**theory**

la **thérapie** *fem noun*
1 **(medical) treatment**
2 **therapy**

**thermal** *masc adjective*, **thermale** *fem*, **thermaux** *masc pl*, **thermales** *fem pl*
**thermal**
**une station thermale** a spa

le **thermomètre** *masc noun*
**thermometer**

le or la **thermos**® *invariable masc & fem noun*
**vacuum flask**

le **thon** *masc noun*
**tuna**

le **tibia** *masc noun*
**Il a reçu un coup de pied dans les tibias.** He got a kick in the shins.

le **tic** *masc noun*
**nervous twitch**

le **ticket** *masc noun*
**ticket**
- le **ticket de caisse** till receipt
- le **ticket de métro** underground ticket
- le **ticket de quai** platform ticket

**tiède** *masc & fem adjective*
1 **warm**
2 **lukewarm**

le **tien** *masc pronoun*, la **tienne** *fem*, les **tiens** *masc pl*, les **tiennes** *fem pl*
**yours**
**Est-ce que ce stylo est le tien?** Is this pen yours?
**J'ai laissé ma moto chez moi. On va prendre la tienne.** I left my motorbike at home. We'll take yours.
**Je n'aime pas ces baskets. Je préfère les tiens.** I don't like those trainers. I prefer yours.
**Ces chaussures, ce sont les tiennes, n'est-ce pas?** Those shoes - they're yours, aren't they?

**WORD TIP** The article and pronoun change in French when they refer to fem and plural nouns.

**tiens** *verb* ▷ **tenir**

**tiers** *masc adjective*, **tierce** *fem* ▷ see **tiers** *noun*
**third**

le **tiers** *masc noun* ▷ see **tiers** *adj*
**third**
**les deux tiers de la population** two-thirds of the population

le **tiers-monde** *masc noun*
**Third World**

le **tigre** *masc noun*
**tiger**

le **tilleul** *masc noun*
1 **lime tree**
2 **herbal tea** (*made from lime flowers*)

le **timbre** *masc noun*
**stamp**
**un timbre tarif rapide** a first-class stamp
**un timbre tarif lent** a second-class stamp
**un timbre à 55 centimes** a 55-cent stamp
**Je voudrais un timbre pour la Grande-Bretagne.** I'd like a stamp for Great Britain.

**timide** *masc & fem adjective*
**shy**

la **timidité** *fem noun*
**shyness**

le **tir** *masc noun*
1 **shooting**
2 **shot** (*in football*)
• le **tir à l'arc** archery

le **tirage** *masc noun*
**draw**
**le tirage de la loterie** the lottery draw
**le tirage au sort** the draw

le **tire-bouchon** *masc noun*
**corkscrew**

la **tirelire** *fem noun*
**money box**

**tirer** *verb* **[1]**
1 **to pull**
**Le bébé tire les cheveux.** The baby pulls my hair.
**Il m'a tiré par le bras.** He pulled my arm.
**'Tirez'** 'Pull' (*on doors*)
2 **to draw**
**tirer les rideaux** to draw the curtains
**tirer au sort** to draw lots
**tirer des conclusions** to draw conclusions
3 **to fire** (*a gun*)
4 **to shoot** (*in ball games*)

le **tiret** *masc noun*
**dash**

le **tiroir** *masc noun*
**drawer**

la **tisane** *fem noun*
**herbal tea**

le **tissu** *masc noun*
**material, fabric**

**WORD TIP** *tissu* does not mean *a tissue* in English; for the meaning of *tissue* ▷ **kleenex**®

le **titre** *masc noun*
1 **title**
**le titre du livre** the book title
2 **headline**
**les gros titres** the headlines
**les titres de l'actualité** the news headlines
• le **titre de transport** travel ticket

**tituber** *verb* **[1]**
**to stagger**

le **toast** *masc noun*
1 **piece of toast**
2 **toast** (*in champagne*)

le **toboggan** *masc noun*
**slide**

**WORD TIP** *toboggan* does not mean *toboggan* in English; for the meaning of *toboggan* ▷ **luge**.

**toi** *pronoun*
1 **you** (*as opposed to anybody else*)
**C'était toi!** It was you!
**chez toi** at your house
**Elle pense à toi.** She's thinking of you.
2 (*after prepositions like* **avec** *or* **sans** *and in comparisons*) **you**
**Je peux venir avec toi?** Can I come with you?
**C'est pour toi.** It's for you.
**Louis est plus grand que toi.** Louis is taller than you.
3 **à toi** yours (*belonging to you*)
**J'ai vu des amis à toi.** I saw some friends of yours.
**Ce n'est pas a toi.** That's not yours.
4 (*for emphasis*) **you**
**Toi, tu restes là.** You stay there.
**C'est toi qui as oublié.** You're the one who forgot.
**C'est à toi de jouer.** It's your turn to play.

la **toile** *fem noun*
1 **cloth**
2 **canvas**
3 **painting**
**une toile de Picasso** a painting by Picasso
4 **la toile** the web (*Internet*)
• la **toile d'araignée** cobweb

la **toilette** *fem noun*
1 **wash**
**faire sa toilette** to have a wash
**les produits de toilette** toiletries
2 **outfit**
**Je me suis acheté une nouvelle toilette.** I've bought a new outfit.

**WORD TIP** *toilette* does not mean *toilet* in English; for the meaning of toilet ▷ **toilettes**.

les **toilettes** *plural fem noun*
**toilet**
**Où sont les toilettes, s'il vous plaît?** Where are the toilets please?
**les toilettes pour dames** the ladies
**les toilettes pour hommes** the gents

**toi-même** *pronoun*
**yourself**
**Est-ce que tu l'as fait toi-même?** Did you make it yourself?

le **toit** *masc noun*
**roof**

**tolérant** *masc adjective*, **tolérante** *fem*
**tolerant**

**tolérer** *verb* **[24]**
**to tolerate**

♪ la **tomate** *fem noun*
**tomato**
**des tomates en salade, une salade de tomates** a tomato salad
**la sauce tomate** tomato sauce

la **tombe** *fem noun*
**grave**

le **tombeau** *masc noun*, les **tombeaux** *plural*
**tomb**

♪ **tomber** *verb* Ⓔ **[1]**
1 **to fall**
**Attention, tu vas tomber!** Careful, you'll fall!
**La chaise est tombée.** The chair fell over.
**Lucy est tombée à l'eau.** Lucy fell into the water.
**La nuit tombe.** It's getting dark.
2 **tomber malade** to fall ill
**Je suis tombé malade pendant les vacances.** I fell ill during the holidays.
**tomber amoureux de quelqu'un** to fall in love with somebody
**Nadjette est tombée amoureuse de Kevin.** Nadjette fell in love with Kevin.
3 **to come**
**C'est tombé au bon moment.** It came at the right time.
4 **faire tomber quelqu'un, quelque chose** to knock somebody, something over
**J'ai fait tomber le vase.** I knocked the vase over.
5 **laisser tomber** to drop
**J'ai laissé tomber mon porte-monnaie.** I've dropped my purse.
6 **laisser tomber** to give up *(an activity)*
**Elle a laissé tomber l'espagnol.** She's given up Spanish.
**Laisse tomber!** Forget it!
**laisser tomber quelqu'un** to drop somebody
**Il a laissé tomber sa petite amie.** He dumped his girlfriend.

**WORD TIP** When you use *faire* or *laisser* before *tomber* to talk about the past, use *avoir* in the perfect tense.

**ton** *masc adjective*, **ta** *fem*, **tes** *plural*
▷ see **ton** *noun*
**your**
**ton frère** your brother
**ta sœur** your sister
**tes amis** your friends
**tes yeux** your eyes

le **ton** *masc noun* ▷ see **ton** *adj*
1 **tone of voice**
**Ne me parle pas sur ce ton!** Don't speak to me in that tone of voice!
2 **shade**
**des tons de bleu** shades of blue

la **tonalité** *fem noun*
1 **tone** *(of voice)*
2 *(Telephones)* **dialling tone**

la **tondeuse** *fem noun*
**lawnmower**

**tondre** *verb* **[3]**
1 **to mow** *(a lawn)*
2 **to clip** *(a dog, a horse)*

les **tongs** *plural fem noun*
**flip-flops**

**tonique** *masc & fem adjective*
1 **tonic** *(drink)*
2 **lively** *(child)*

la **tonne** *fem noun*
1 **tonne** *(1,000 kg)*
2 **ton**
**J'ai des tonnes de choses à faire.** I've got tons of things to do.

le **tonneau** *masc noun*, les **tonneaux** *plural*
**barrel**

le **tonnerre** *masc noun*
**thunder**
**un coup de tonnerre** a clap of thunder

le **tonton** *masc noun*
*(informal)* **uncle**

le **tonus** *invariable masc noun*
1 **energy** *(for a person)*
**avoir du tonus** to be dynamic
2 **tone** *(for your muscles)*

la **toque** *fem noun*
1 **chef's hat**
2 **cap** *(for a jockey)*

le **torchon** *masc noun*
1 **tea towel**
2 *(informal)* **rag** *(newspaper)*
3 *(informal)* **messy piece of work**
**La prof a dit que je lui ai rendu un torchon.** The teacher said that the piece of work I handed in was a real mess.

**tordre** *verb* **[3]**
1 **to twist** *(your arm, your wrist)*
**tordre le bras à quelqu'un** to twist somebody's arm
**Il m'a tordu le bras.** He twisted my arm.
2 **to wring out** *(the washing, a towel)*
3 **to bend** *(metal, a bumper)*

se **tordre** *reflexive verb* Ⓔ
**to twist**
se tordre le bras to twist your arm
**Je me suis tordu la cheville.** I twisted my ankle.

**tordu** *masc adjective*, **tordue** *fem*
**bent**

la **tornade** *fem noun*
**tornado**

le **torrent** *masc noun*
**mountain stream**

le **torse** *masc noun*
**chest**

♪le **tort** *masc noun*
**avoir tort** to be wrong
**Je crois que tu as tort.** I think you're wrong.
**avoir tort de faire quelque chose** to be wrong to do something
**Il a tort de dire ça.** He's wrong to say that.

le **torticolis** *invariable masc noun*
**stiff neck**
**avoir un torticolis** to have a stiff neck

se **tortiller** *reflexive verb* Ⓔ [1]
**to wriggle**

la **tortue** *fem noun*
**tortoise**

la **torture** *fem noun*
**torture**

**torturer** *verb* [1]
**to torture**

♪**tôt** *adverb*
1 **early**
**On va partir tôt.** We're leaving early.
2 **soon**
**Je viendrai le plus tôt possible.** I'll come as soon as possible.
**tôt ou tard** sooner or later
**au plus tôt** at the earliest
(*informal*) **'J'ai fini.' — 'Eh bien, ce n'est pas trop tôt!'** 'I've finished.' — 'About time too!'

**total** *masc adjective*, **totale** *fem*, **totaux** *masc pl*, **totales** *fem pl* ▷ see **total** *noun*
**total**

le **total** *masc noun*, les **totaux** *plural* ▷ see **total** *adj*
**total**
**au total** in total

**totalement** *adverb*
**totally**

la **totalité** *fem noun*
**la totalité du groupe** the whole group

**touchant** *masc adjective*, **touchante** *fem*
**touching**

la **touche** *fem noun*
1 **key** (*on a keyboard*)
2 **button** (*on a machine*)
**Appuyez sur la touche.** Press the button.
3 **la (ligne de) touche** the touchline
**Le ballon est sorti en touche.** The ball went into touch.

♪**toucher** *verb* [1]
1 **to touch**
**Ne touche pas à ma peinture.** Don't touch my painting.
2 **to touch** (*emotionally*)
**Cette histoire m'a beaucoup touché.** That story really touched me.
3 **to affect, to concern**
**Ce problème nous touche tous.** This problem affects us all.
4 **to get** (*money, wages*)
**Il touche 350 euros par semaine.** He's getting 350 euros a week.

**touffu** *masc adjective*, **touffue** *fem*
**bushy**

♪**toujours** *adverb*
1 **always**
**comme toujours** as always
**pour toujours** forever
**Il est toujours en retard.** He's always late.
2 **still**
**Nous habitons toujours au même endroit.** We're still living in the same place.
**Ton paquet n'est toujours pas arrivé.** Your parcel still hasn't arrived.

le **tour** *masc noun* ▷ see **tour** *fem noun*
1 **faire le tour de quelque chose** to go round something
**faire le tour des magasins** to go round all the shops
**faire le tour du monde** to go round the world
2 **walk**
**On va faire un petit tour.** We'll go for a little walk.
3 **ride**
**Allons faire un tour à vélo!** Let's go for a bike ride!
4 **drive**
**Nous avons fait un tour en voiture dans la campagne.** We went for a drive in countryside.
5 **turn**
**C'est ton tour de jouer.** It's your turn to play.
**À qui le tour?** Whose turn is it?

6 **trick**
**un tour de cartes** a card trick

**WORD TIP** *un tour* does not mean *a tour* in English; for the meaning of *tour* ▷ **visite, voyage organisé**.

la **tour** *fem noun* ▷ see **tour** *masc noun*
1 **tower**
**la tour Eiffel** the Eiffel Tower
2 **tower block**
3 **castle**, **rook** (*in chess*)

***tour***

On a construit la Tour Eiffel en 1889 pour les 100 ans de la Révolution française.

le **tourbillon** *masc noun*
1 **whirlwind**
2 **whirlpool**

le **tourisme** *masc noun*
**tourism**
- le **tourisme solidaire** responsible tourism

le & la **touriste** *masc & fem noun*
**tourist**

**touristique** *masc & fem adjective*
**un guide touristique** a tourist guide(book)
**une ville touristique** a town which attracts tourists

le **tournant** *masc noun*
1 **bend** (*in a road*)
2 **turning-point**

la **tournée** *fem noun*
1 **round** (*by a postman, a baker*)
2 **round** (*of drinks*)
**C'est ma tournée.** It's my round.
3 **tour** (*by a performer*)
**être en tournée** to be on tour
**Le groupe est en tournée au Japon.** The band is on tour in Japan.

𝄞 **tourner** *verb* [1]
1 **to turn**
**Tournez à gauche à l'église.** Turn left at the church.
**J'ai tourné la tête et je l'ai vu.** I looked around and I saw him.
2 **to go round and round**
**Leur discussion tourne en rond.** Their discussion is going round in circles.
3 **to shoot** (*a film*)
**Ils tournent un film dans notre école.** There're shooting a film in our school.
4 **mal tourner** to go badly
**La soirée a mal tourné.** The evening went badly.
**Son frère a mal tourné.** His brother turned out badly.

se **tourner** *reflexive verb* ⓔ
1 **to turn**
**Elle s'est tournée vers moi.** She turned to face me.
2 **to turn round**
**Tourne-toi, je me change!** Turn around, I'm getting changed!

le **tournevis** *invariable masc noun*
**screwdriver**

le **tournoi** *masc noun*
**tournament**
**le Tournoi des Six Nations** the Six Nations Championship (*in rugby*)

**tous** *adjective, pronoun* ▷ **tout**

la **Toussaint** *fem noun*
**All Saints' Day** (*1 November*)

**tousser** *verb* [1]
**to cough**

𝄞 **tout** *masc adjective*, **toute** *fem* **tous** *masc pl* **toutes** *fem pl* ▷ see **tout** *adv, pron*
1 **all**
**Il a mangé tout le pain.** He ate all the bread.
**Tous les garçons jouent au tennis.** All the boys play tennis.
**Toutes les filles jouent au foot.** All the girls play football.
**Toute la classe est punie.** The whole class is punished.
**tout le monde** everybody
**Ils sont invités tous les deux.** They are both invited.
**Elles sont invitées toutes les deux.** They are both invited.
**Elle a voyagé en Europe pendant toute une année.** She travelled through Europe for a whole year.
2 **any**
**'Service à toute heure'** 'Service at any time'
3 **every**
**Je me lève à 6 heures tous les jours.** I get up at 6 am every day.
**Prenez un comprimé toutes les quatre heures.** Take one pill every four hours.
**Ils se voient tous les mois.** They see each other every month.
**toutes directions** all directions

**WORD TIP** *tout* changes when it refers to fem and plural nouns.

𝄞 **tout** *adverb* ▷ see **tout** *adj, pron*
1 **very**
**tout droit** straight ahead
**tout petit** very small
2 **all**
**Je suis tout mouillé.** I'm all wet.
**Elle est toute seule.** She's all alone.

**tout** *masc pronoun*, **toute** *fem*, **tous** *masc pl*, **toutes** *fem pl* ▷ see **tout** *adj, adv*
1 **everything**
Ils ont tout pris. They took everything.
Tout va bien. Everything's fine.
2 **all**
C'est tout? Is that all?
J'en compte 14 en tout. I count 14 in all.
3 **all**
Allons-y tous ensemble! Let's all go together!
Écoutez-moi tous! Listen to me, all of you!
Elles étaient toutes là. They were all there.
4 pas du tout not at all

**WORD TIP** *Tous* becomes *toutes* when it refers to fem people or things.

**tout à coup** *adverb*
**suddenly**

**tout à fait** *adverb*
1 **absolutely**
Elle avait tout à fait raison. She was absolutely right.
'Tu es d'accord?' — 'Tout à fait.' 'Do you agree?' — 'Absolutely.'
2 **quite**
Je n'ai pas tout à fait fini. I haven't quite finished.
Ce n'est pas tout à fait pareil. It's not quite the same thing.

**tout à l'heure** *adverb*
**a little while**
Je l'ai vu tout à l'heure. I saw him a little while ago.
À tout à l'heure! See you later!

**tout de même** *adverb*
1 **all the same**
C'est tout de même bizarre. All the same, it's odd.
2 **honestly**
Tout de même, tu exagères! Honestly! You're going a bit far.

**tout de suite** *adverb*
**at once, straight away**
Fais-le tout de suite! Do it at once!

**toute** *adjective, pronoun* ▷ **tout**

**toutefois** *adverb*
**however**

**toutes** *adjective, pronoun* ▷ **tout**

la **toux** *invariable fem noun*
**cough**

le & la **toxicomane** *masc & fem noun*
**drug addict**

**toxique** *masc & fem adjective*
**toxic**

le **trac** *masc noun*
(*informal*)
1 **stage fright**
2 **nerves**

la **trace** *fem noun*
1 **les traces** tracks
des traces de pas footprints
2 **mark**
des traces de doigts fingermarks

**tracer** *verb* **[61]**
**to draw**

**WORD TIP** *tracer* does not mean *to trace (somebody)* in English; for the meaning of *to trace* ▷ **retrouver, localiser**.

le **tracteur** *masc noun*
**tractor**

la **tradition** *fem noun*
**tradition**

**traditionnel** *masc adjective*, **traditionnelle** *fem*
**traditional**

le **traducteur** *masc noun*, la **traductrice** *fem*
**translator**

la **traduction** *fem noun*
**translation**

**traduire** *verb* **[26]**
**to translate**
Je traduis un article en français. I'm translating an article into French.

le **trafic** *masc noun*
1 **dealing** (*usually illegal*)
le trafic de drogue drug dealing
2 **traffic** (*by air, sea, rail*)

le **trafiquant** *masc noun*, la **trafiquante** *fem*
**dealer** (*in drugs, arms*)

**tragique** *masc & fem adjective*
**tragic**

**trahir** *verb* **[2]**
**to betray**

la **trahison** *fem noun*
1 **betrayal**
2 **treason**

le **train** *masc noun*
1 **train**
en train by train
le train de dix heures the ten o'clock train
Le train pour Nice partira du quai 1. The train for Nice will be leaving from platform 1.
Le train est à l'heure. The train is on time.

Le train a une heure de retard. The train is an hour late.
2 être en train de faire quelque chose to be doing something
Je suis en train de faire mes devoirs. I'm doing my homework.

**train**

Le TGV (« train à grande vitesse ») roule depuis 1981. Il va très vite ! Son record : plus de 500 km/h (300 mph). Il fait Paris-Marseille en 3 heures.

**traîner** *verb* **[1]**
1 **to drag** (*your feet, a bag*)
2 **to hang around**
3 **to lie around**
4 **to dawdle**
5 **to drag on** (*time, classes*)

**WORD TIP** *traîner* does not mean *to train (in sport)* in English; for the meaning of *train* ▷ **s'entraîner**.

**traire** *verb* **[78]**
**to milk**

le **trait** *masc noun*
1 **line**
Tirez un trait en bas de page. Draw a line at the end of the page.
2 **trait**
C'est un trait de caractère bien français. It's a typically French trait.
3 les traits features (*of your face*)
Il avait les traits tirés. He looked tired and drawn.
4 d'un seul trait in one go
Il a bu son verre d'un seul trait. He drank his glass down in one go.
• le **trait d'union** hyphen

le **traité** *masc noun*
**treaty**

le **traitement** *masc noun*
1 **treatment**
Henri est sous traitement. Henri's undergoing treatment.
2 **processing**
le traitement de texte word processing
3 **salary**

**traiter** *verb* **[1]**
1 **to treat**
Il la traite très mal. He treats her very badly.
le médecin qui me traite the doctor who's treating me
2 **to deal with** (*a question, a problem*)
3 traiter quelqu'un de quelque chose to call someone something
Il m'a traité de menteur. He called me a liar.
Il l'a traitée de tricheuse. He called her a cheat.

le **traiteur** *masc noun*
**caterer**

ɗ le **trajet** *masc noun*
1 **journey**
un trajet de deux heures a two-hour journey
2 **route**

le **trampoline** *masc noun*
**trampoline**
faire du trampoline to do trampolining

le **tramway** *masc noun*
1 **tram**
2 **tramway**

**tranchant** *masc adjective*, **tranchante** *fem*
**sharp**

ɗ la **tranche** *fem noun*
1 **slice**
deux tranches de jambon two slices of ham
Il faut couper le saucisson en tranches. You have to slice up the sausage.
2 **phase** (*of work*)
3 **period** (*of time*)

**trancher** *verb* **[1]**
1 **to slice**
2 **to come to a decision**

ɗ **tranquille** *masc & fem adjective*
1 **quiet**
une rue tranquille a quiet street
Tiens-toi tranquille! Keep still!
2 Laisse-moi tranquille! Leave me alone!
3 ne pas être tranquille to worry
Maman n'est pas tranquille si je n'appelle pas. Mum worries if I don't ring.
Sois tranquille, je ne dirai rien! Don't worry, I won't say anything!

la **tranquillité** *fem noun*
**peace**

le **transat** *masc noun*
(*informal*) **deck chair**

**transférer** *verb* **[24]**
**to transfer** (*an employee, a player*)

le **transfert** *masc noun*
**transfer** (*of an employee, a footballer*)

**transformer** *verb* **[1]**
**to change**
Ils ont tout transformé dans leur salon. They've changed everything in their sitting room.
transformer quelque chose en quelque chose to turn something into something
Nous avons transformé le garage en salle de jeux. We've turned the garage into a playroom.



French-English
a b c d e f g h i j k l m n o p q r s t u v w x y z

se **transformer** *reflexive verb* ⓔ
**to change**

la **transfusion** *fem noun*
**transfusion**
**une transfusion sanguine** a blood transfusion

le **transistor** *masc noun*
**transistor**

**transmettre** *verb* [11]
1 **transmettre quelque chose à quelqu'un** to pass something on to somebody
**Je leur ai transmis tes instructions.** I passed your instructions on to them.
**Il m'a transmis un virus par email.** He passed a virus on to me through my email.
2 **to transmit**
**transmettre des chaînes de télévision par satellite** to transmit TV channels by satellite

la **transpiration** *fem noun*
**sweat**

**transpirer** *verb* [1]
**to sweat**

la **transplantation** *fem noun*
1 **transplant** (*medical*)
2 **transplantation** (*of plants*)

♪le **transport** *masc noun*
**transport**
**un mode de transport** a means of transport
**le transport par route** road transport
**le transport des déchets nucléaires** the transport of nuclear waste
• les **transports en commun** public transport

**transporter** *verb* [1]
1 **to transport**
2 **to carry**

la **trappe** *fem noun*
**trap door**

**WORD TIP** *trappe* does not mean *trap* in English; for the meaning of *trap* ▷ **piège**.

♪le **travail** *masc noun*, les **travaux** *pl*
1 **work**
**J'ai beaucoup de travail à faire.** I've got a lot of work to do.
2 **job**
**un travail à mi-temps** a part-time job
**Sylvie cherche un travail.** Sylvie's looking for a job.
**Ma mère a cessé le travail.** My mother stopped work.
3 **les travaux** work
**des travaux de construction** building work
4 **des travaux** roadworks
**On ne peut pas passer à cause des travaux.** We can't drive through because of the roadworks.
• les **travaux dirigés** classwork
• les **travaux manuels** arts and crafts
• les **travaux ménagers** housework

♪**travailler** *verb* [1]
1 **to work**
**Nous travaillons dur.** We're working hard.
**Jacques travaille dans l'édition.** Jacques works in publishing.
**Dominique travaille comme secrétaire.** Dominique works as a secretary.
**travailler quelque chose** to work on something
**Il faut que je travaille mon français.** I must work on my French.
**Va travailler ton piano!** Go and practise your piano!
2 **travailler quelqu'un** to bother somebody
**Qu'est-ce qui te travaille?** What's bothering you?
**C'est ça qui me travaille.** That's what's bothering me.

**travailleur** *masc adjective*, **travailleuse** *fem* ▷ see **travailleur** *noun*
**hard-working**

le **travailleur** *masc noun*, la **travailleuse** *fem* ▷ see **travailleur** *adj*
**worker**

**travailliste** *masc & fem adjective*
**Labour** (*in British politics*)
**le parti travailliste** the Labour party

les **travaux** *plural masc noun* ▷ **travail**

le **travers** *invariable masc noun*
1 **à travers quelque chose** through something
**passer à travers les mailles du filet** to slip through the net
**Quelqu'un regardait à travers les rideaux.** Somebody was looking through the curtains.
2 **à travers quelque chose** across something
**Elles ont marché à travers la campagne.** They walked across country.
**Il voyage à travers le monde.** He travels all over the world.
3 **de travers** crooked
**Le tableau est de travers.** The picture's crooked.
4 **de travers** wrongly
**Tout va de travers aujourd'hui.** Everything is going wrong today.

a b c d e f g h i j k l m n o p q r s t u v w x y z

la **traversée** *fem noun*
**crossing**
**une traversée de l'Atlantique** an Atlantic crossing
**Nous avons fait une bonne traversée.** We had a good crossing.

♪ **traverser** *verb* **[1]**
**1 to cross**
**Regardez avant de traverser la rue.** Look before you cross the road.
**Allez, on traverse!** Let's cross over!
**2 to go through**
**Ils ont traversé la France pour aller en Italie.** They went through France on the way to Italy.
**La pluie a traversé ma veste.** The rain's gone right through my jacket.
**Ils ont traversé une crise.** They went through a crisis.

**trébucher** *verb* **[1]**
**to stumble**

le **trèfle** *masc noun*
**1 clover**
**un trèfle à quatre feuilles** a four-leaved clover
**2 clubs** (*in cards*)
**la dame de trèfle** the queen of clubs

♪ **treize** *invariable number*
**thirteen**
**à treize heures** at one pm
**le treize juillet** the thirteenth of July
**Aurélie a treize ans.** Aurélie's thirteen.

♪ **treizième** *number*
**thirteenth**

le **tremblement de terre** *masc noun*
**earthquake**

**trembler** *verb* **[1]**
**to shake**
**Elle tremble de tout son corps.** She's shaking all over.
**La terre a encore tremblé en Inde.** There's been another earthquake in India.

**trempé** *masc adjective*, **trempée** *fem*
**soaked**

**tremper** *verb* **[1]**
**to soak**

le **tremplin** *masc noun*
**springboard**

la **trentaine** *fem noun*
**about thirty**
**une trentaine de personnes** about thirty people
**Elle a la trentaine.** She's in her thirties.

♪ **trente** *invariable number*
**thirty**
**le trente juillet** the thirtieth of July
**Elle a trente ans.** She's thirty.

♪ **très** *adverb*
**very**
**Ils sont très heureux.** They are very happy.
**Il est très amoureux.** He's very much in love.
**Nous sommes très en avance.** We're very early.
**Je vais très bien.** I'm very well.
**J'ai très faim.** I'm very hungry.

le **trésor** *masc noun*
**treasure**

la **tresse** *fem noun*
**plait**

**triangulaire** *masc & fem adjective*
**triangular**

la **tribu** *fem noun*
**tribe**

le **tribunal** *masc noun*, les **tribunaux** *plural*
**court**
**paraître devant le tribunal** to appear in court (*on a charge*)

**tricher** *verb* **[1]**
**to cheat**
**Il m'a accusé d'avoir triché.** He accused me of cheating.

**tricolore** *masc & fem adjective*
**three-coloured**
**le drapeau tricolore** the French flag (*in three vertical bands of blue, white, and red*)

le **tricot**
**knitting**
**faire du tricot** to do knitting

**tricoter** *verb* **[1]**
**to knit**

**trier** *verb* **[1]**
**to sort (out)**
**Hier soir, nous avons trié toutes les photos.** Last night we sorted out all the photographs.

♪ le **trimestre** *masc noun*
**term**
**au premier trimestre** in the first term

**trinidadien** *masc adjective*, **trinidadienne** *fem*
▷ see **Trinidadien** *noun*
**Trinidadian**

le **Trinidadien** *masc noun*, la **Trinidadienne** *fem*
▷ see **trinidadien** *adj*
**Trinidadian** *(person)*

la **Trinité** *fem noun*
l'île de la Trinité Trinidad

le **triomphe** *masc noun*
**triumph**

**triompher** *verb* [1]
**to triumph**

les **tripes** *plural fem noun*
**tripe** *(for eating)*

le **triple** *masc noun*
**three times as much**
**Ça m'a coûté le triple.** It cost me three times as much.

**tripler** *verb* [1]
**to treble**

les **triplés** *plural masc noun*
**triplets**

**triste** *masc & fem adjective*
1 **sad**
**Tu as l'air triste.** You look sad.
**Ne sois pas triste!** Don't be sad!
2 **sorry** *(state, sight)*
**Ton anorak est dans un triste état.** Your anorak's in a sorry state.

la **tristesse** *fem noun*
**sadness**

le **trognon** *masc noun*
1 **core** *(of an apple, a pear)*
2 **stalk** *(of a lettuce)*

**trois** *invariable number*
**three**
**à trois heures** at three o'clock
**le trois mars** the third of March
**Tom a trois ans.** Tom's three.

**troisième** *masc & fem adjective*
▷ see **troisième** *noun*
**third**
• le **troisième âge** the elderly

la **troisième** *fem noun*
▷ see **troisième** *adj*
**Year 10** *(in the French system)*

le **trombone** *masc noun*
1 **trombone**
2 **paperclip**

la **trompe** *fem noun*
**trunk** *(of an elephant)*

**tromper** *verb* [1]
**to deceive**

se **tromper** *reflexive verb* ⓔ
**to make a mistake**
**Il se trompe souvent.** He often makes mistakes.
**se tromper de quelque chose** to get something wrong
**Vous vous êtes trompé de numéro.** You've got the wrong number.

la **trompette** *fem noun*
**trumpet**
**Charlotte joue de la trompette.** Charlotte plays the trumpet.

le **tronc** *masc noun*
**trunk** *(of a tree)*

la **tronçonneuse** *fem noun*
**chainsaw**

**trop** *adverb*
1 **too**
**C'est trop loin.** It's too far.
**C'est beaucoup trop cher.** It's far too expensive.
2 **too much**
**J'ai trop mangé.** I've eaten too much.
**Tu m'en as donné trop.** You've given me too much.
3 **trop de** too much, too many
**J'ai acheté trop de pain.** I bought too much bread.
**Tu as mangé trop de bonbons.** You've eaten too many sweets.
**Il y a trop de monde.** There are too many people.
4 **de trop** too many, too much
**Il y a une chaise de trop.** There's one chair too many.
**Il y a dix euros de trop.** That's ten euros too much.

le **trottoir** *masc noun*
**pavement**
**Reste sur le trottoir.** Stay on the pavement.
**le bord du trottoir** the kerb

le **trou** *masc noun*
**hole**
**le trou dans la couche d'ozone** the hole in the ozone layer
• le **trou de la serrure** keyhole

**troublant** *masc adjective*, **troublante** *fem*
**disturbing**

**trouer** *verb* [1]
**to make a hole in**
**des chaussettes trouées** socks with holes in them
**J'ai troué mon jean neuf.** I put a hole in my new jeans.

la **trouille** *fem noun*
(*informal*) **fear**
**avoir la trouille** to be scared
**Elle a la trouille du prof.** She's scared of the teacher.

la **troupe** *fem noun*
1 **troop** (*of soldiers*)
2 **troop** (*of tourists, children*)
3 **flock** (*of birds*)
• la **troupe de théâtre** theatre company

le **troupeau** *masc noun*, les **troupeaux** *plural*
1 **herd** (*of cattle*)
2 **flock** (*of sheep*)

♪ la **trousse** *fem noun*
**pencil case**
• la **trousse de maquillage** make-up bag
• la **trousse de secours** first-aid kit

le **trousseau** *masc noun*, les **trousseaux** *plural*
**bunch**
**un trousseau de clés** a bunch of keys

♪ **trouver** *verb* [1]
1 **to find**
**J'ai trouvé un portefeuille dans le bus.** I found a wallet on the bus.
**As-tu trouvé ton passeport?** Did you find your passport?
**Il a trouvé son chemin.** He found his way.
**Savez-vous où je peux trouver des ciseaux?** Do you know where I can find a pair of scissors?
2 **trouver que ...** to think that ...
**Moi, je trouve que c'est intéressant.** I think it's interesting.
**Ah bon, tu trouves?** Really, do you think so?
**J'ai trouvé le film passionnant.** I thought the film was wonderful.

se **trouver** *reflexive verb* ⓔ
1 **to be** (*in a place*)
**Cette semaine elle se trouve à Montpellier.** She's in Montpellier this week.
**Le musée se trouve près de la mairie.** The museum is next to the town hall.
2 **to find yourself**
**Trouve-toi quelque chose à faire!** Find yourself something to do!

♪ le **truc** *masc noun*
1 (*informal*) **thing**
**un petit truc en bois** a little thing made of wood
**Qu'est-ce que c'est que ce truc?** What on earth is that thing?
**Il y a un truc qui ne va pas.** Something's wrong.
**Le jazz, ce n'est pas mon truc.** Jazz just isn't my thing.
2 **trick**
**Il doit y avoir un truc.** There must be a trick to it.

♪ la **truite** *fem noun*
**trout**

**TSVP** *abbreviation*
(= *tournez s'il vous plaît*) **PTO, please turn over**

**TTC** *abbreviation*
(= *toutes taxes comprises*) **inclusive of tax**

**tu** *pronoun*
**you** (*singular*)
**Toi, tu restes ici.** You stay here.
**Tu as fait tes devoirs?** Have you done your homework?

**WORD TIP** *tu* is used to speak to a family member, a person you know well or a person of your own age; otherwise *vous* is used.

le **tube** *masc noun*
1 **tube**
2 (*informal*) **hit** (*in pop music*)
**un des tubes de l'été dernier** one of last summer's hits

**tuer** *verb* [1]
**to kill**

se **tuer** *reflexive verb* ⓔ
1 **to be killed**
**Elle s'est tuée dans un accident de voiture.** She was killed in a car accident.
2 **to kill yourself**

**tue-tête** *in phrase*
**crier à tue-tête** to shout at the top of your voice

la **tuile** *fem noun*
1 **tile** (*on a roof*)
2 **thin almond biscuit**

la **Tunisie** *fem noun*
**Tunisia**

**tunisien** *masc adjective*, **tunisienne** *fem*
▷ see **Tunisien** *noun*
**Tunisian**

le **Tunisien** *masc noun*, la **Tunisienne** *fem*
▷ see **tunisien** *adj*
**Tunisian**

♪ le **tunnel** *masc noun*
**tunnel**
**le tunnel sous la Manche** the Channel Tunnel

**turc** *masc adjective*, **turque** *fem*
▷ see **Turc** *noun*
**Turkish**

a b c d e f g h i j k l m n o p q r s t u v w x y z

le **Turc** *masc noun*, la **Turque** *fem*
▷ see **turc** *adj*
1 **Turk**
les Turcs the Turks
2 le turc Turkish (*the language*)

la **Turquie** *fem noun*
**Turkey**

le **tuteur** *masc noun*, la **tutrice** *fem*
1 **guardian**
2 **tutor**

**tutoyer** *verb* [39]
**tutoyer quelqu'un** to use 'tu' with somebody
**Il ne faut pas tutoyer ton professeur.** You shouldn't use 'tu' with your teacher.
**On peut se tutoyer?** Can we use 'tu' with each other?
**Tu peux me tutoyer.** You can say 'tu' to me. ▷ **tu**

le **tuyau** *masc noun*, les **tuyaux** *pl*
1 **pipe** (*for water, drainage, etc*)
2 (*informal*) **tip** (*a helpful hint*)
**Tu as des tuyaux pour les examens?** Do you have any exam tips?

- le **tuyau d'arrosage** hosepipe

la **TVA** *fem noun*
(= *taxe à la valeur ajoutée*) **VAT, value added tax**

le **type** *masc noun*
1 **kind**
**Quel type de papier?** What type of paper?
2 (*informal*) **guy**
**un drôle de type** a strange guy
**Je le connais, c'est le type qui m'a vendu la moto.** I know him, he's the guy who sold me the motorbike.

**typique** *masc & fem adjective*
**typical**

**tyranniser** *verb* [1]
**to tyrannize**

**tzigane** *masc & fem adjective*
▷ see **tzigane** *noun*
**gypsy**

le & la **tzigane** *masc & fem noun*
▷ see **tzigane** *adj*
**gypsy**

# U u

un **ulcère** *masc noun*
**ulcer**

**un** *masc determiner*, **une** *fem*, **des** *pl*
▷ see **un** *number, pron*
1 (*with masc singular nouns*) **a, an**
**un film** a film
**un animal** an animal
2 (*with fem singular nouns*) **a, an**
**une moto** a motorbike
**une orange** an orange
▷ **de, des**

**un** *masc pronoun*, **une** *fem*, **uns** *masc pl*, **unes** *fem pl* ▷ see **un** *determiner, number*
**one**
**l'un d'entre nous** one of us
**l'une d'entre les filles** one of the girls
**Les uns pensent que ...** Some think that ...
**l'un(e) et l'autre** the one and the other
**L'un est français et l'autre est allemand.** One's French and the other's German.
**l'un(e) ou l'autre** either of them
**Prends l'une ou l'autre, ça n'a pas d'importance.** Take either of them, it doesn't matter.

**WORD TIP** *l'un* changes to *l'une* when used for a fem noun, to *les uns* when used for masc plural nouns, and to *les unes* when used for fem plural nouns.

**un** *masc number*, **une** *fem*
▷ see **un** *determiner, pronoun*
**one**
**Il y a un paquet pour moi et deux pour toi.** There's one parcel for me and two for you.
**un par un** one by one
**trente et une personnes** thirty-one people
**un jour sur deux** every other day

**uni** *masc adjective*, **unie** *fem*
1 **close-knit** (*family, group*)
2 **plain** (*not patterned*)
**un tissu uni** a plain fabric

♂ un **uniforme** *masc noun*
**uniform**
**Dans mon école, on ne porte pas d'uniforme.** In my school we don't wear a uniform.

une **union** *fem noun*
**union**
**l'ex-Union soviétique** the former Soviet Union
- l'**Union européenne** European Union

♪ **unique** *masc & fem adjective*
1 **only**
**Elle est fille unique.** She's an only child.
**Il est fils unique.** He's an only child.
**C'est l'unique solution à tous tes problèmes.** That's the only solution to all your problems.
2 **single**
'Prix unique' 'All one price'
3 **unique**
**C'est une occasion unique de le rencontrer.** This is a unique opportunity to meet him.
**Ce musée est unique au monde.** This museum is unique in the world.

**uniquement** *adverb*
**only**

une **unité** *fem noun*
1 **unity**
2 **unit** (*of currency, measurement*)

un **univers** *invariable masc noun*
1 **universe**
2 **world**
**l'univers de Dali** Dali's world

**universitaire** *masc & fem adjective*
1 **university** (*degree, town*)
2 **academic** (*work*)

une **université** *fem noun*
**university**
**Audrey est à l'université.** Audrey is at university.
**Je voudrais aller à l'université.** I would like to go to university.

un **urbanisme** *masc noun*
**town planning**

une **urgence** *fem noun*
1 **urgency**
**Il y a urgence!** It's urgent!
2 **d'urgence** immediately, at once
**Il faut téléphoner d'urgence.** You must phone at once.
3 **emergency**
**Je te donne mon numéro de portable en cas d'urgence.** I'll give you my mobile number in case of emergency.
4 **les urgences, le service des urgences** accident and emergency (*in a hospital*)
**On l'a emmené aux urgences.** He was taken to casualty.

♪ **urgent** *masc adjective*, **urgente** *fem*
**urgent**
**Je dois lui parler, c'est urgent!** I must speak to him, it's urgent!

les **USA** *plural masc noun*
**USA**
**Patsy habite aux USA.** Patsy lives in the USA.
**Mon père va en voyage d'affaires aux USA.** My father is going on a business trip to the USA.

**WORD TIP** Countries and regions in French take *le, la* or *les*.

un **usage** *masc noun*
**use**
**hors d'usage** out of order
**L'usage d'une calculatrice est interdit à l'examen.** The use of a calculator is forbidden in the exam.
**'À usage externe'** 'For external use only'

**usagé** *masc adjective*, **usagée** *fem*
1 **worn**
2 **used**

un **usager** *masc noun*
**user**
**un usager de la route** a road user
**les usagers des transports en commun** the users of public transport

**usé** *masc adjective*, **usée** *fem*
**worn** (*shoes, clothing, tyre*)

**user** *verb* **[1]**
**to wear out** (*shoes, clothing*)

♪ une **usine** *fem noun*
**factory**
**Mon frère travaille dans une usine.** My brother works in a factory.

un **ustensile** *masc noun*
**utensil**

♪ **utile** *masc & fem adjective*
**useful**
**un renseignement utile** a useful piece of information
**se rendre utile** to make oneself useful
**Si tu veux te rendre utile, mets-moi la table!** If you'd like to make yourself useful, lay the table for me!

**utilisable** *masc & fem adjective*
**usable**

un **utilisateur** *masc noun*, une **utilisatrice** *fem*
**user**

♪ **utiliser** *verb* [1]
**to use**
**J'utilise un dictionnaire pour vérifier l'orthographe d'un mot nouveau.** I use a dictionary to check the spelling of a new word.

l'**utilité** *fem noun*
**use**
**'Tu n'as pas de portable?' — 'Non, je n'en ai pas l'utilité.'** 'You don't have a mobile phone?' — 'No, I have no use for one.'

# V v

**va** *verb* ▷ **aller**

♪ les **vacances** *plural fem noun*
**holidays**
**les vacances scolaires** the school holidays
**les grandes vacances** the summer holidays
**être en vacances** to be on holiday
**Nous sommes en vacances pendant deux semaines.** We're on holiday for two weeks.
**aller en vacances** to go on holiday
**Nous allons en vacances en Irlande.** We're going on holiday to Ireland.
**Bonnes vacances!** Have a good holiday!

le **vacancier** *masc noun*, la **vacancière** *fem*
**holidaymaker**

le **vacarme** *masc noun*
**din**

la **vaccination** *fem noun*
**vaccination**

**vacciner** *verb* [1]
**to vaccinate**
**se faire vacciner** to be vaccinated
**Je me suis fait vacciner contre le tétanos.** I've been vaccinated against tetanus.

♪ **vache** *masc & fem adjective*
▷ **see vache** *noun*
(*informal*) **mean**
**être vache avec quelqu'un** to be mean to somebody
**Il a été vache avec elle.** He was mean to her.

♪ la **vache** *fem noun* ▷ **see vache** *adj*
1 **cow**
2 (*informal*) **Oh, la vache!** Wow!

**vachement** *adverb*
(*informal*) **really**
**C'était vachement bien!** It was really good!

le **vagabond** *masc noun*, la **vagabonde** *fem*
**tramp**

le **vagin** *masc noun*
**vagina**

**vague** *masc & fem adjective*
▷ **see vague** *noun*
**vague**

la **vague** *fem noun* ▷ **see vague** *adj*
**wave** (*in the sea*)
- la **vague de chaleur** heatwave

**vain** *masc adjective*, **vaine** *fem*
1 **useless**
2 **en vain** in vain

**WORD TIP** *vain* does not mean *vain* in English: for the meaning of *vain* ▷ **vaniteux**.

**vaincre** *verb* [79]
1 **to defeat** (*an enemy*)
2 **to overcome** (*an illness*)

le **vainqueur** *masc noun*
**winner**

**vais** *verb* ▷ **aller**

le **vaisseau** *masc noun*, les **vaisseaux** *plural*
**vessel**
- le **vaisseau spatial** spaceship

♪ la **vaisselle** *fem noun*
**dishes**
**faire la vaisselle** to wash up
**C'est ton tour de faire la vaisselle.** It's your turn to wash up.

**valable** *masc & fem adjective*
**valid**

le **valet** *masc noun*
**jack**
**le valet de pique** the jack of spades

la **valeur** *fem noun*
**value**
**des objets de valeur** valuables

**valider** *verb* [1]
**to stamp** (*a ticket*)





Ⓔ means the verb takes être to form the perfect

♪ la **valise** *fem noun*
**suitcase**
faire ses valises to pack
Je n'ai pas encore fait mes valises! I haven't packed yet!

la **vallée** *fem noun*
**valley**

**valoir** *verb* [80]
1 **to be, to cost**
Ça vaut combien? How much is that?
Combien valent ces bottes? How much are those boots?
2 ça vaut la peine de faire quelque chose it's worth doing something
Ça vaut la peine d'essayer. It's worth trying.
Ça ne vaut pas la peine d'y aller. It's not worth going.
3 il vaut mieux faire quelque chose it's better to do something
Il vaut mieux demander la permission. It's better to ask permission.

la **valse** *fem noun*
**waltz**

le **vandalisme** *masc noun*
**vandalism**

♪ la **vanille** *fem noun*
**vanilla**
une glace à la vanille a vanilla ice cream

**vaniteux** *masc adjective*, **vaniteuse** *fem*, **vaniteux** *masc pl*, **vaniteuses** *fem pl*
**vain**

se **vanter** *reflexive verb* ⓔ [1]
**to boast**

♪ la **vapeur** *fem noun*
**steam**
faire cuire quelque chose à la vapeur to steam something
Je fais cuire les légumes à la vapeur. I steam the vegetables.

la **varicelle** *fem noun*
**chickenpox**

♪ **varié** *masc adjective*, **variée** *fem*
1 **varied**
un menu varié a varied menu
2 **various**
sous des formes variées in various forms

**varier** *verb* [1]
**to vary**

la **variété** *fem noun*
1 **variety**
2 **popular music**
un spectacle de variétés a variety show

**vas** *verb* ▷ **aller**

le **vase** *masc noun*
**vase**

**vaste** *masc & fem adjective*
**huge**
un vaste choix a huge selection

**vaudrait** *verb* ▷ **valoir**

**vaut** *verb* ▷ **valoir**

**va-vite** *adverb*
à la va-vite in a rush

♪ le **veau** *masc noun*, les **veaux** *plural*
1 **calf**
2 **veal**

**vécu** *verb* ▷ **vivre**

♪ la **vedette** *fem noun*
**star**
un enfant vedette a child star

**végétal** *masc adjective*, **végétale** *fem*, **végétaux** *masc pl*, **végétales** *fem pl*
**vegetable**
l'huile végétale vegetable oil

**végétalien** *masc adjective*, **végétalienne** *fem*
**vegan**

♪ **végétarien** *masc adjective*, **végétarienne** *fem*
▷ see **végétarien** *noun*
**vegetarian**
Elle est végétarienne. She's a vegetarian.

♪ le **végétarien** *masc noun*, la **végétarienne** *fem*
▷ see **végétarien** *adj*
**vegetarian**

♪ le **véhicule** *masc noun*
**vehicle**

♪ la **veille** *fem noun*
la veille the day before
la veille de Noël Christmas Eve

le **veinard** *masc noun*, la **veinarde** *fem*(*informal*)
Petit veinard! You lucky little devil!

la **veine** *fem noun*
1 **vein**
2 (*informal*) **luck**
Il a de la veine. He's lucky.

♪ le **vélo** *masc noun*
**bike**
Je suis venu à vélo. I came by bike.
faire du vélo to go cycling
Le dimanche matin, je fais du vélo. On Sunday mornings I go cycling.
• le **vélo tout terrain** mountain bike

le **vélomoteur** *masc noun*
**moped**

le **velours** *invariable masc noun*
**velvet**
une écharpe en velours a velvet scarf
• le **velours côtelé** corduroy

le **velouté** *masc noun*
**cream soup**
un velouté de champignons cream of mushroom soup

les **vendanges** *plural fem noun*
**grape harvest**

**mini-info vendanges**
Des étudiants du monde entier viennent faire les vendanges en France début septembre.

♂ le **vendeur** *masc noun*, la **vendeuse** *fem*
1 **shop assistant**
2 **salesperson**
3 **seller**

♂ **vendre** *verb* [3]
**to sell**
vendre quelque chose à quelqu'un to sell something to somebody
J'ai vendu mon ordinateur à Céline. I've sold my computer to Céline.
'À vendre' 'For sale'

♂ le **vendredi** *masc noun*
1 **Friday**
vendredi dernier last Friday
vendredi prochain next Friday
Nous sommes vendredi aujourd'hui. It's Friday today.
2 **on Friday**
À vendredi! See you on Friday!
3 **on Fridays**
'Fermé le vendredi' 'Closed on Fridays'
4 tous les vendredis every Friday
Tous les vendredis, je fais de l'athlétisme. Every Friday I do athletics.

**WORD TIP** Months of the year and days of the week start with small letters in French.

• le **vendredi saint** Good Friday

**vénéneux** *masc adjective*, **vénéneuse** *fem*
**poisonous** (*plant*)

la **vengeance** *fem noun*
**revenge**

se **venger** *reflexive verb* Ⓔ [52]
**to have your revenge**

**venimeux** *masc adjective*, **venimeuse** *fem*
**poisonous** (*snake, spider*)

♂ **venir** *verb* Ⓔ [81]
1 **to come**
Il vient de Provence. He comes from Provence.
Elles sont venues mardi. They came on Tuesday.
Viens voir! Come and see!
Venez nous aider! Come and help us!
2 faire venir quelqu'un to send for somebody
Il faut faire venir le médecin. We must send for the doctor.
3 venir de faire quelque chose to have just done something
Ils viennent d'arriver. They've just arrived.
Elle venait de partir. She had just left.

♂ le **vent** *masc noun*
**wind**
Il y a du vent. It's windy.

♂ la **vente** *fem noun*
**sale**
être en vente to be for sale
Leur maison est en vente. Their house is for sale.
Il travaille au service des ventes. He works in the sales department.
• la **vente aux enchères** auction sale

le **ventilateur** *masc noun*
**(electric) fan**

♂ le **ventre** *masc noun*
**stomach**
avoir mal au ventre to have stomach ache
Lili a mal au ventre. Lili's got stomach ache.

**venu** *verb* ▷ **venir**

le **ver** *masc noun*
**worm**

le **verbe** *masc noun*
**verb**

le **verger** *masc noun*
**orchard**

le **verglas** *invariable masc noun*
**black ice**

♂ **vérifier** *verb* [1]
**to check**
vérifier que ... to check that ...
Il vérifie que ses réponses sont correctes. He's checking that his answers are correct.

**véritable** *masc & fem adjective*
**real**

la **vérité** *fem noun*
**truth**
Dis-moi la vérité. Tell me the truth.
À la vérité ... To tell the truth ...





Ⓔ means the verb takes être to form the perfect

**vernir** *verb* **[2]**
**to varnish**

le **vernis** *masc noun*
**varnish**
- le **vernis à ongles** nail varnish

♪ le **verre** *masc noun*
1 **glass**
une table en verre a glass table
2 **glass** *(to drink from)*
un verre de vin a glass of wine
3 **drink**
**Tu veux prendre un verre?** Do you want to go for a drink?
4 **lens** *(for glasses)*

le **verrou** *masc noun*
**bolt** *(on a door)*

**verrouiller** *verb* **[1]**
**to bolt** *(a door)*

la **verrue** *fem noun*
**wart**

♪ le **vers** *invariable masc noun* ▷ **see vers** *prep*
**line** *(of poetry)*

♪ **vers** *preposition* ▷ **see vers** *noun*
1 **towards**
**Tu vas vers la mairie ...** You go towards the town hall ...
2 **near**
**Ils habitent vers Tours.** They live near Tours.
3 **about** *(in time)*
**Il arrivera vers midi.** He'll arrive about twelve.

le **Verseau** *masc noun*
**Aquarius**
**Catherine est Verseau.** Catherine is an Aquarius.

**WORD TIP** Signs of the zodiac do not take an article: *un* or *une*.

le **versement** *masc noun*
**payment**

**verser** *verb* **[1]**
1 **to pour** *(a drink)*
2 **to pay in** *(at a bank, etc)*
3 **to shed** *(tears, blood)*

♪ la **version** *fem noun*
1 **version**
2 **translation** *(into your own language)*
- la **version originale** original version *(of a film)*

le **verso** *masc noun*
**back** *(of a piece of paper)*
voir au verso see overleaf

♪ **vert** *masc adjective*, **verte** *fem*
**green**
le feu vert the green light

**vertical** *masc adjective*, **verticale** *fem*, **verticaux** *masc pl*, **verticales** *fem pl*
**vertical**

le **vertige** *masc noun*
**vertigo** *(dizziness)*
avoir le vertige to be scared of heights

la **verveine** *fem noun*
**herbal tea** *(with verbena)*

♪ la **veste** *fem noun*
**jacket**

**WORD TIP** *veste* does not mean *vest* in English; for the meaning of *vest* ▷ **maillot de corps**.

le **vestiaire** *masc noun*
1 **cloakroom** *(in a theatre)*
2 **changing room** *(in a gym)*

♪ le **vestibule** *masc noun*
**hall**

♪ le **vêtement** *masc noun*
**garment**
les vêtements clothes

le & la **vétérinaire** *masc & fem noun*
**vet**

♪ **veuf** *masc adjective*, **veuve** *fem* ▷ **see veuf** *noun*, **veuve** *noun*
**Le directeur est veuf.** The headmaster is a widower.
**Ma voisine est veuve.** My neighbour is a widow.

♪ le **veuf** *masc noun* ▷ **see veuf** *adj*
**a widower**

♪ la **veuve** *fem noun* ▷ **see veuf** *adj*
**widow**

**vexer** *verb* **[1]**
**to upset**

♪ la **viande** *fem noun*
**meat**
la viande rouge red meat

**vibrer** *verb* **[1]**
**to vibrate**

la **victime** *fem noun*
**victim**

la **victoire** *fem noun*
**victory**

♪ **vide** *masc & fem adjective* ▷ **see vide** *noun*
**empty**

♪ le **vide** *masc noun* ▷ **see vide** *adj*
1 **space**
dans le vide in space, into space
2 **vacuum**
du café emballé sous vide vacuum-packed coffee

French–English

le **vide-greniers** *invariable masc noun*
**car boot sale**

♪ **vidéo** *invariable masc & fem adjective*
▷ see **vidéo** *noun*
**video**
une cassette vidéo a video cassette
une caméra vidéo a video camera
un jeu vidéo a video game

♪ la **vidéo** *fem noun* ▷ see **vidéo** *adj*
**video**

le **vidéoclip** *masc noun*
**music video**

le **vidéoclub** *masc noun*
**video shop**

**vider** *verb* [1]
**to empty**

♪ la **vie** *fem noun*
**life**
la vie urbaine city life
leur mode de vie their lifestyle
C'est la vie! That's life!
être en vie to be alive
**Il est encore en vie.** He's still alive.

**vieil** *adjective* ▷ **vieux**

le **vieillard** *masc noun*, la **vieillarde** *fem*
1 un vieillard an old man
les veillards old people
2 une vieillarde an old woman ▷ **vieux** *noun*

**vieille** *fem adjective* ▷ **vieux**

la **vieillesse** *fem noun*
**old age**

**vieillir** *verb* [2]
**to age**

**vierge** *masc & fem adjective*
▷ see **vierge** *noun*
1 **virgin**
2 **blank**
une cassette vierge a blank cassette

la **vierge** *fem noun* ▷ see **vierge** *adj*
**virgin**
la Sainte Vierge the Virgin Mary

la **Vierge** *fem noun, noun*
**Virgo**
**Nicolas est du signe de la Vierge.** Nicolas is a Virgo.

**WORD TIP** Signs of the zodiac do not take an article: *un* or *une*.

♪ **vieux**, **vieil** *masc adjective*, **vieille** *fem*
▷ see **vieux** *noun*
**old**
un vieux tableau an old picture
un vieil arbre an old tree
une vieille dame an old lady
**Cléo est plus vieille que Bess.** Cléo is older than Bess.
**Oscar est moins vieux qu'Hugo.** Oscar is younger than Hugo.

**WORD TIP** *vieux* becomes *vieil* before *a, e, i, o, u* or *silent h*.

♪ le **vieux** *masc noun*, la **vieille** *fem*
▷ see **vieux** *adj*
un vieux an old man
une vieille an old woman
les vieux old people

**WORD TIP** It's more polite to use *un vieil homme*, *une vieille femme* or *les personnes âgées* to refer to elderly people in French.

**vif** *masc adjective*, **vive** *fem*
1 **alive**
2 **lively** (*colours, discussion*)
3 **brisk** (*gesture, action*)

la **vigne** *fem noun*
1 **vine**
2 **vineyard**

le **vigneron** *masc noun*, la **vigneronne** *fem*
**winegrower**

la **vignette** *fem noun*
1 **tax disc** (*for cars*)
2 **label** (*on prescribed medicines*)

le **vignoble** *masc noun*
**vineyard**

♪ **vilain** *masc adjective*, **vilaine** *fem*
1 **ugly**
une vilaine robe an ugly dress
2 **naughty**
**Liliane est vilaine.** Liliane is naughty.
3 **nasty**
**Il a attrapé un vilain rhume.** He's caught a nasty cold.

la **villa** *fem noun*
**villa**

♪ le **village** *masc noun*
**village**
dans un village in a village

♪ la **ville** *fem noun*
**town**, **city**
une grande ville a city
**Ce matin, je vais en ville.** This morning I'm going into town.

♪ le **vin** *masc noun*
**wine**
du vin blanc white wine
du vin rouge red wine
du vin rosé rosé wine
du vin pétillant sparkling wine
• le **vin chaud** mulled wine





a b c d e f g h i j k l m n o p q r s t u v w x y z

𝄞 le **vinaigre** *masc noun*
**vinegar**

la **vinaigrette** *fem noun*
**French dressing**

𝄞 **vingt** *number*
**twenty**
le vingt juillet the twentieth of July
à vingt heures at 8 pm
vingt-trois twenty-three
Marion a vingt ans. Marion's twenty.

la **vingtaine** *fem noun*
**about twenty**
Elle a la vingtaine. She's about twenty.
une vingtaine de personnes about twenty people

𝄞 **vingtième** *masc & fem adjective*
**twentieth**

le **viol** *masc noun*
**rape**

**violemment** *adverb*
**violently**

la **violence** *fem noun*
**violence**

**violent** *masc adjective*, **violente** *fem*
**violent**

**violer** *verb* **[1]**
**to rape**

**violet** *masc adjective*, **violette** *fem*
**purple**

la **violette** *fem noun*
**violet** (*the flower*)

le **violon** *masc noun*
**violin**
jouer du violon to play the violin

le **violoncelle** *masc noun*
**cello**
jouer du violoncelle to play the cello

le **virage** *masc noun*
**bend** (*in the road*)

la **virgule** *fem noun*
1 **comma**
2 (*Maths*) **decimal point**
sept virgule trois seven point three

le **virus** *invariable masc noun*
**virus**
le virus du sida the Aids virus

la **vis** *invariable fem noun* ▷ **see vis** *verb*
**screw**

**vis** *verb* ▷ **see vis** *noun* ▷ **vivre**

le **visa** *masc noun*
**visa**

𝄞 le **visage** *masc noun*
**face**

**viser** *verb* **[1]**
1 **to aim** (*with a weapon*)
2 **to aim for** (*a target, a result*)
une campagne qui vise les jeunes a campaign aimed at young people
viser à faire quelque chose to aim to do something
Cette loi vise à protéger les minorités. This law aims to protect minorities.

la **visibilité** *fem noun*
**visibility**

**visible** *masc & fem adjective*
1 **visible**
2 **obvious**

la **visite** *fem noun*
**visit**
rendre visite à quelqu'un to visit somebody
Demain, nous allons rendre visite à ma grand-mère. Tomorrow we're going to visit my grandmother.

𝄞 **visiter** *verb* **[1]**
**to visit** (*a place*)
Je voudrais visiter le Louvre. I'd like to visit the Louvre.

le **visiteur** *masc noun*, la **visiteuse** *fem*
**visitor**

**vit** *verb* ▷ **vivre**

la **vitamine** *fem noun*
**vitamin**

𝄞 **vite** *adverb*
1 **fast**
Tu conduis trop vite. You drive too fast.
2 **quick**
Vite! Le bus arrive! Quick! Here's the bus!
3 **soon**
Elle a vite compris. She soon understood.

la **vitesse** *fem noun*
1 **speed**
en vitesse quickly
Elle est partie à toute vitesse. She rushed off.
2 **gear** (*in a car*)
en deuxième vitesse in second gear

le **vitrail** *masc noun*, les **vitraux** *plural*
**stained glass window**

la **vitre** *fem noun*
1 **window pane**
2 **window** (*of a car, a train*)

𝄞 la **vitrine** *fem noun*
**shop window**
faire les vitrines to go window-shopping

**vivant** *masc adjective*, **vivante** *fem*
1 **living**
Il est vivant. He's alive.
2 **lively**
**C'est un enfant très vivant.** He's a very lively child.

**vive** *fem adjective* ▷ see **vive** *excl* ▷ **vif**

**vive** *exclamation* ▷ see **vive** *adj*
Vive le roi! Long live the king!

**vivement** *adverb*
1 **strongly**
2 **Vivement samedi!** I can't wait for Saturday!

**vivre** *verb* [82]
1 **to live**
**Ils vivent ensemble.** They live together.
2 **to live through**
**Elle a vécu une période difficile.** She's been through a difficult period.
**Ils vivent une vie tranquille.** They lead a quiet life.

le **vocabulaire** *masc noun*
**vocabulary**

le **vœu** *masc noun*, les **vœux** *plural*
1 **wish**
**faire un vœu** to make a wish
**Meilleurs vœux!** Best wishes! (*especially at New Year*)
2 **vow**
**faire un vœu** to make a vow

la **vogue** *fem noun*
**fashion**
**en vogue** in fashion

**voici** *adverb*
1 **here is, here are**
**Voici l'addition.** Here's the bill.
**Voici les clés.** Here are the keys.
2 **this is, these are**
**Voici ma sœur.** This is my sister.
**Voici mes copines.** These are my friends.

**WORD TIP** *voici* never changes

la **voie** *fem noun*
1 **way**
2 **track** (*for trains*)
**la voie ferrée** the railway track
3 **lane** (*on a main road*)
**une autoroute à trois voies** a three-lane motorway

**voilà** *adverb*
1 **there is, there are**
**Voilà ta trousse, là-bas sur la table.** There's your pencil case, over there on the table.
**La voilà!** There she is!
2 **here is, here are**
**Voilà ton jus d'orange.** Here's your orange juice.
**Voilà tes frites.** Here are your chips.
**Voilà Anna qui arrive.** Here comes Anna now.
3 **Voilà pourquoi elle est triste.** That's why she's sad.
**Voilà comment ça se fait.** That's how it's done.
**Voilà, c'est tout.** Right, that's all.

**WORD TIP** *voilà* never changes

le **voile** *masc noun* ▷ see **voile** *fem noun*
**veil, headscarf**

la **voile** *fem noun* ▷ see **voile** *masc noun*
1 **sail** (*of a boat*)
2 **sailing**
**faire de la voile** to go sailing

le **voilier** *masc noun*
**sailing boat**

**voir** *verb* [13]
1 **to see**
**Je te vois.** I can see you.
**Je vois mon médecin à 11 heures.** I'm seeing the doctor at 11 am.
**Il va voir son copain.** He's going to see his friend.
**Je viendrai te voir un de ces jours.** I'll come and see you one of these days.
**Oui, je vois...** Yes, I see...
**Peut-être, on verra.** Maybe, we'll see.
**Voir page 50.** See page 50.
2 **faire voir quelque chose à quelqu'un** to show somebody something
**Je te ferai voir mes photos.** I'll show you my photos.

se **voir** *reflexive verb* Ⓔ
1 **to show**
**La tache ne se verra pas.** The stain won't show.
2 **to see each other**
**Ils se voient à Noël.** They see each other at Christmas.

le **voisin** *masc noun*, la **voisine** *fem*
**neighbour**
**chez les voisins** at the neighbours'

le **voisinage** *masc noun*
**neighbourhood**

la **voiture** *fem noun*
1 **car**
**en voiture** by car
2 **carriage** (*on a train*)
**la voiture de première classe** the first-class carriage

♪ la **voix** *invariable fem noun*
**1 voice**
**lire à haute voix** to read out loud
**2 vote**
**Samuel a eu 10 voix et Manon 17.** Samuel got 10 votes and Manon got 17.

♪ le **vol** *masc noun*
**1 flight**
**le vol pour Edimbourg** the flight to Edinburgh
**Il y a deux heures de vol.** It's a two-hour flight.
**2 theft**
**un vol à main armée** an armed robbery

la **volaille** *fem noun*
**poultry**

**volant** *masc adjective*, **volante** *fem*
▷ see **volant** *noun*
**flying**

le **volant** *masc noun* ▷ see **volant** *adj*
**1 steering wheel**
**être au volant** to be driving
**2 shuttlecock**

le **volcan** *masc noun*
**volcano**

la **volée** *fem noun*
**1** *(Sport)* **volley**
**2 flock** *(of birds)*

♪ **voler** *verb* **[1]**
**1 to steal**
**voler quelque chose à quelqu'un** to steal something from someone
**Quelqu'un m'a volé mon passeport.** Somebody's stolen my passport.
**se faire voler quelque chose** to have something stolen
**Il s'est fait voler son vélo.** He's had his bicycle stolen.
**2 voler quelqu'un** to rob somebody
**Ils volent leurs clients.** They're robbing their customers.
**3 to fly**
**L'avion volait juste au-dessus de leurs têtes.** The plane was flying just above their heads.

le **volet** *masc noun*
**shutter**

♪ le **voleur** *masc noun*, la **voleuse** *fem*
**thief**

le **volley** *masc noun*
**volleyball**
**jouer au volley** to play volleyball

**WORD TIP** *volley* does not mean *volley (in tennis)* in English; for the meaning of *volley* ▷ **volée.**

le & la **volontaire** *masc & fem noun*
**volunteer**

la **volonté** *fem noun*
**1 will**
**2 willpower**
**3 à volonté** unlimited
**'Pizza à volonté'** 'As much pizza as you want'

**volontiers** *adverb*
**gladly**
**'Volontiers!'** 'I'd love to!'

♪ **vomir** *verb* **[2]**
**to be sick**
**Elle a envie de vomir.** She's feeling sick.

♪ **vos** *plural masc & fem adjective*
**your**
**vos cahiers** your notebooks
**vos amies françaises** your French friends

**WORD TIP** Use *vos* for *your* with plural French nouns. ▷ **votre**

**voter** *verb* **[1]**
**to vote**

♪ **votre** *masc & fem adjective*, **vos** *pl*
**your**
**votre professeur** your teacher
**votre voiture** your car

**WORD TIP** Use *votre* for *your* with singular French nouns. ▷ **vos**

le **vôtre** *masc pronoun*, la **vôtre** *fem*, les **vôtres** *pl*
**1 yours**
**un pays comme le vôtre** a country like yours
**une maison comme la vôtre** a house like yours
**mes parents et les vôtres** my parents and yours
**'Ces photos sont à vous?' — 'Non, ce sont les vôtres.'** 'Are these photos yours?' — 'No, they're yours.'
**2** *(as a toast)* **À la vôtre!** Cheers!

**WORD TIP** The article and pronoun change in French when they refer to fem and plural nouns.

♪ **vouloir** *verb* **[14]**
**1 to want**
**Je veux du chocolat.** I want some chocolate.
**vouloir faire quelque chose** to want to do something
**Veux-tu venir avec nous?** Do you want to come with us?
**Il n'a pas voulu venir.** He didn't want to come.
**2 to like**
**si tu veux** if you like
**Je voudrais un verre d'eau.** I'd like a glass of water. ▸▸

Elle voudrait visiter Versailles. She'd like to go to Versailles.

3 **Voulez-vous m'excuser?** Would you excuse me?
**Veux-tu fermer la porte?** Would you shut the door?

4 **bien vouloir quelque chose** not to mind something
**Je voudrais bien de la confiture.** I wouldn't mind some jam.

5 **bien vouloir faire quelque chose** to be happy to do something
**Je veux bien le faire.** I'm happy to do it.

6 **vouloir dire** to mean
**Qu'est-ce que tu veux dire?** What do you mean?

7 **en vouloir à quelqu'un** to bear a grudge against somebody
**Elle en veut à ses parents.** She's never forgiven her parents.

**voulu** *verb* ▷ **vouloir**

♪ **vous** *pronoun*

1 (*plural speaking to more than one person*) **you**
**Vous avez fait vos devoirs?** Have you done your homework?
**Elle va vous aider.** She's going to help you.

2 (*polite form of vous for one or more persons*) **you**
**Vous voulez du vin, monsieur?** Would you like some wine, sir?
**Je vais vous montrer le chemin.** I'll show you the way.

3 (*after prepositions like* **avec** *or* **contre** *and in comparisons*) **you**
**Je viens avec vous.** I'm coming with you.
**Ils sont plus âgés que vous.** They're older than you.

4 (*as a direct object*) **you**
**Elle vous aide.** She helps you.
**Elle vous a aidés.** She helped you. (*to several people*)
**Elle vous a aidé.** She helped you. (*politely to one person*)

5 (*as an indirect object*) **(to) you**
**Je vous écrirai.** I'll write to you.
**Je vous ai donné mon adresse.** I've given you my address.

6 **à vous** yours
**Ceci est à vous.** This is yours.
**Ce sont des amis à vous?** Are they friends of yours?

7 (*with reflexive verbs*) **Vous vous levez à sept heures.** You get up at seven o'clock.

8 (*polite form with reflexive verbs*) **yourself, yourselves**
**Ne vous coupez pas!** Don't cut yourself!

9 **chez vous** at your house

**vous-même** *pronoun*
**yourself**
**Vous me l'avez dit vous-même.** You told me yourself.

**WORD TIP** This is the polite form to one person.

**vous-mêmes** *plural pronoun*
**yourselves**
**Est-ce que vous l'avez fait vous-mêmes?** Did you make it yourselves?

**WORD TIP** This is the plural form used to speak to several people.

**vouvoyer** *verb* [39]
**vouvoyer quelqu'un** to use 'vous' to somebody
**Il faut vouvoyer le professeur.** You should use 'vous' to the teacher. ▷ **tutoyer**

se **vouvoyer** *reflexive verb* Ⓔ
**to use the polite 'vous' form to**
**Après tant d'années, ils continuent à se vouvoyer.** After all these years, they still say 'vous' to each other. (*Use* **vous** *to people you don't know well, especially adults. You may be asked to use* **tu** *when you get to know someone well.*)

♪ le **voyage** *masc noun*

1 **trip**
**On fait un voyage en Chine.** We're going on a trip to China.
**Bon voyage!** Have a good trip!

2 **journey**
**un voyage de 10 000 kilomètres** a 10,000-kilometre journey

♪ **voyager** *verb* [52]
**to travel**
**Il a beaucoup voyagé.** He's travelled a lot.

le **voyageur** *masc noun*, la **voyageuse** *fem*
**passenger**

la **voyelle** *fem noun*
**vowel**

le **voyou** *masc noun*
**hooligan**

**vrac** *adverb*
**acheter des olives en vrac** to buy olives loose (*not packaged*)

♪ **vrai** *masc adjective*, **vraie** *fem*
**real, genuine**
**un vrai diamant** a real diamond
**C'est vrai?** Really?

**vraiment** *adverb*
**really**

**vraisemblable** *adjective*
**likely**

le **VTT** *masc noun*
(= *vélo tout-terrain*) **mountain bike**

**vu** *masc adjective*, **vue** *fem* ▷ **see vu** *verb*
1 **être mal vu** to be disapproved of
**Il est plutôt mal vu.** People don't think much of him.
**C'est mal vu de faire beaucoup de bruit.** They don't like people making a lot of noise.
2 **être bien vu** to be well thought of
**Elle est très bien vue à l'école.** People at the school think highly of her.
3 **Bien vu!** Good point!

**vu** *verb* ▷ **see vu** *adj* ▷ **voir**

la **vue** *fem noun*
1 **eyesight**
**Tu as une bonne vue.** You've got good eyesight.
2 **sight**
**à première vue** at first sight
**connaître quelqu'un de vue** to know somebody by sight
**Je le connais de vue.** I know him by sight.
**perdre quelqu'un de vue** to lose touch with somebody
**Nous l'avons perdue de vue.** We've lost touch with her.
3 **view**
**une chambre avec vue sur le lac** a room with a view of the lake

**vulgaire** *masc & fem adjective*
1 **vulgar**
**Ne sois pas si vulgaire!** Don't be so vulgar!
2 **common**

# W w

le **wagon** *masc noun*
1 **railway carriage**
**Nos places sont dans le wagon numéro 2.** Our seats are in carriage number 2.
2 **waggon**
- le **wagon-lit** sleeper (*on a train*)
- le **wagon-restaurant** dining car

le **walkman** *masc noun*
**walkman**

**wallon** *masc adjective*, **wallonne** *fem*
▷ **see Wallon** *noun*
**Walloon** (*from French-speaking Belgium*)

**WORD TIP** Adjectives never have capitals in French, even for nationality or regional origin.

le **Wallon** *masc noun*, la **Wallonne** *fem*
▷ **see wallon** *adj*
1 **Walloon** (*French-speaking Belgian*)
**les Wallons** the Walloons
2 **le wallon** Walloon (*the language of Wallonia, Belgium*)
**Je parle wallon.** I speak Walloon.

**WORD TIP** Languages never have capitals in French.

les **WC** *plural masc noun*
**toilet**
**Où sont les WC?** Where's the toilet?
**J'ai besoin d'aller aux WC.** I need to go to the toilet.
**Il est aux WC.** He's in the loo.

le **web** *masc noun*
**the web**
**un site web** a website

le **weekend** *masc noun*
**weekend**

le **western** *masc noun*
**western**
**Il n'aime que les vieux westerns.** He only likes old westerns.

la **xénophobie** *fem noun*
**xenophobia**
**continuer [1] la lutte contre la xénophobie** to continue the fight against xenophobia

le **xylophone** *masc noun*
**xylophone**
**Simon joue du xylophone.** Simon plays the xylophone.

# Y y

♪ **y** *pronoun*

1 **there** (*not always translated*)
**J'y vais demain.** I'm going there tomorrow.
**Ils vont faire une fête. Tu y vas?** They're going to have a party. Are you going?
**N'y va pas!** Don't go!

2 **il y a** there is, there are
**Il y a un café à côté.** There's a cafe next door.
**Il y a des poissons dans l'étang.** There are some fish in the pond.
**Il y a de la limonade dans le frigo.** There's some lemonade in the fridge.
**Des cerises? Il n'y en a pas.** Cherries? There aren't any.
**Il n'y en a plus.** There are none left.

3 (*y is used for the preposition* **à** *with verbs like* **penser à, croire à, réfléchir à** *and is translated in different ways*)
**J'y pense.** I'm thinking about it.
**Tu n'y peux rien.** You can't do anything about it.
**Laisse-moi y réfléchir.** Let me have a think about it.
**Il n'y comprend rien.** He doesn't understand a thing.
**Attends, j'y viens.** Just wait, I'm coming to that point.
**Le Père Noël? Tu y crois?** Father Christmas? Do you believe in him?

♪ le **yaourt** *masc noun*
**yoghurt**
- le **yaourt aux fruits** fruit yoghurt
- le **yaourt nature** natural yogurt

♪ les **yeux** *plural masc noun*
**eyes**
▷ **œil**

le **yoga** *masc noun*
**yoga**

# Z z

**zapper** *verb* **[1]**
**to channel-hop** (*with a TV*)

le **zèbre** *masc noun*
**zebra**

le **zéro** *masc noun*
1 **zero** (*when counting*)
**Elle a le moral à zéro.** She's really depressed.
2 **nil**
**Ils ont gagné deux à zéro.** They won two nil.
3 **love** (*in tennis*)
**15 zéro.** 15 love

le **zeste** *masc noun*
**peel** (*of oranges, lemons*)

**zézayer** *verb* **[59]**
**to lisp**

le **zigzag** *masc noun*
**zigzag**
**une route en zigzag** a winding road
**faire des zigzags** to zigzag

**zinzin** *invariable adjective*
**crazy**

le **zodiaque** *masc noun*
**zodiac**
**Quel est ton signe du zodiaque?** What sign of the zodiac are you?

la **zone** *fem noun*
1 **zone**, **area**
2 **la zone** the slums
**un enfant de la zone** a child who grew up in the slums
- la **zone euro** eurozone
- la **zone industrielle** industrial estate
- la **zone piétonne** pedestrian area

le **zoo** *masc noun*
**zoo**

**zoologique** *masc & fem adjective*
**zoological**

**zut** *exclamation*
(*informal*) **damn!**

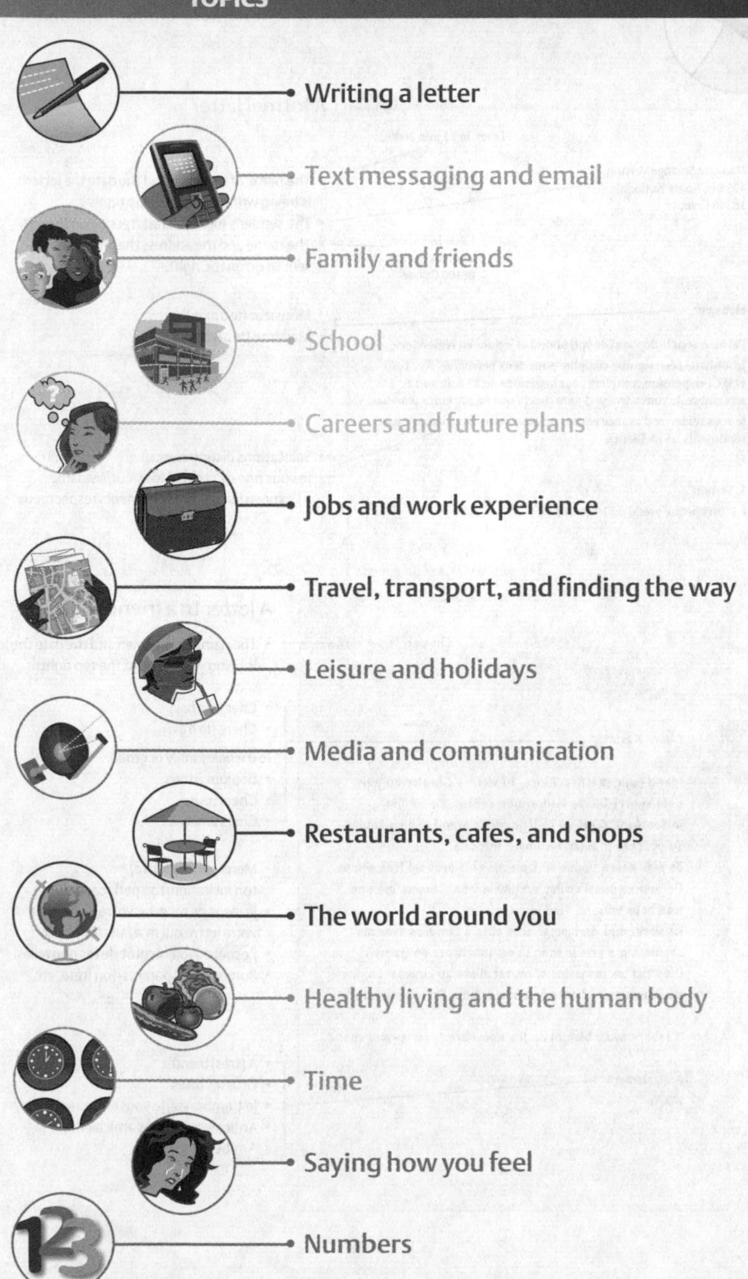

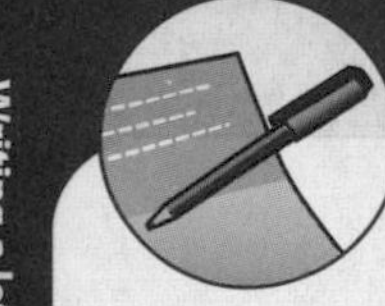

# Writing a letter

## A formal letter

Levet, le 22 juin 2006

Madame Solange Vernon
125 bis, Route Nationale
18340 Levet

Hôtel Le Repos
Chemin des Lys
06100 Grasse

Monsieur,

J'ai bien reçu le dépliant de votre hôtel et je vous en remercie.

Je souhaite réserver une chambre pour deux personnes avec bain et WC, en pension complète pour la période du 27 août au 12 septembre. Je vous adresse ci-joint un chèque de 100 euros d'arrhes.

Je vous remercie d'avance et vous prie de croire, Monsieur, en mes sentiments les meilleurs.

S. Vernon

P.J.: un chèque postal de 100 euros

- The name of the town and the date the letter is being written go at the top right.
- The sender's name and address go on the left.
- The name and the address the letter is being sent to go on the right.

- Monsieur (*to a man*)
- Madame (*to a woman*)

- Salutations distinguées.
- Je vous prie de croire, Monsieur/Madame, à l'expression de mes sentiments respectueux.

## A letter to a friend

Chester, le 23 avril

Chère Karima,

Merci pour ta lettre. Alors, tu viens à Chester en juin, c'est super! Tu vas visiter mon collège. Ça va être intéressant. C'est un collège assez grand et bien équipé. Tu pourras m'aider avec mon français.
Je suis assez bonne en français et le prof est très sympa.
On pourra aussi visiter un peu la ville. Chester est une très belle ville.
Le week-end dernier, je suis allée à Londres avec ma copine. On a pris le train (c'est une heure en train).
On a fait les magasins et on est allées au cinéma. Là, il y a beaucoup de choses à voir et à faire. On y va en juin?

J'espère avoir bientôt de tes nouvelles ... écris-moi vite!

Amicalement
Marie

- The name of the town and the date the letter is being written go at the top right.

- Cher (*to a boy*)
- Chère (*to a girl*)

***To a whole family or group:***

- Bonjour à tous,
- Chers tous,
- Chers amis,

- Merci pour ta lettre/ton invitation/ton petit cadeau.
- Je viens de recevoir votre invitation/votre lettre qui m'a fait très plaisir.
- J'espère avoir bientôt de tes nouvelles.
- Bonjour à tes parents/ton frère, etc.

- À (très) bientôt
- Grosses bises
- Je t'embrasse/Je vous embrasse
- Amicalement/Très amicalement
- Amitiés

## Text messaging and email

### Text messaging

- Certain words or syllables can be represented by letters or numbers that sound the same but take up less space, e.g. *2m1 = demain.*
- Accents are often left out. The syllables -pé and -té can be replaced by the letters P and T, etc.
- Another way of shortening words is to leave out certain letters, especially vowels. For example, *bonjour* becomes *bjr* and *quand* becomes *qd*.
- Emoticons are very popular, e.g. :-) = sourire, :-( = pas content, ;-D = je rigole.

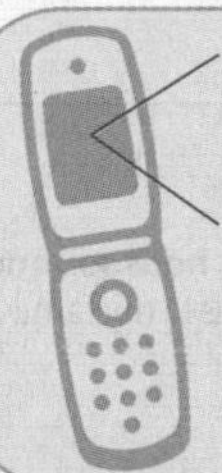

**slt cv? G vu ton fr IR. Il est 5pa.**
Salut, ça va ? J'ai vu ton frère hier. Il est sympa.

**Bsr. TOK? On va au 6né ou au kfé 2m1?**
Bonsoir. Tu es OK? On va au ciné ou au café demain?

| Abbreviation | Full Word | Abbreviation | Full Word | Abbreviation | Full Word |
|---|---|---|---|---|---|
| 100 | sans | fet | fête | MSG | message |
| 5pa | sympa | frR | frère | pb | problème |
| 6né | cinéma | G | j'ai | pk | pourquoi |
| @+ | à plus tard | IR | hier | pr | pour |
| @2m1 | à demain | jamé | jamais | qd | quand |
| ap | après | jenémar | j'en ai marre | ri1 | rien |
| aprM, AM | après -midi | je t'M | je t'aime | rstp | répond s'il te plaît |
| bi1to | bientôt | ke | que | seur | sœur |
| bjr | bonjour | kfé | café | slt cv? | salut ça va ? |
| bsr | bonsoir | ki | qui | strC | stressé |
| C | c'est | koi29 | quoi de neuf | svp | s'il vous plaît |
| cad | c'est à dire | l8 | lui | tjr | toujours |
| dak | d'accord | L | elle | TOK | t'es OK? |
| d1gue | dingue | mat1 | matin | TOQP | t'es occupé? |
| dzolé | désolé | MDR | mort de rire | vs | vous |

### Email

un mail, un email, un courriel = an email
une adresse électronique = an email address
une boîte de réception = to delete a message
envoyer un email = to send an email
recevoir un email = to receive an email
une pièce jointe = an attachment
un arobase = an *at* sign
un site web = a website
cliquer (sur) = to click (on)

Pierre,

Salut! Je viens de passer l'après-midi au Cybercafé de la Rue de la République et j'ai trouvé un site génial: www.quoideneuf.com. Tu devrais l'ajouter à ta liste de sites favoris. Tu choisis la ville dans laquelle tu te trouves sur la page d'accueil, et le site te donne l'adresse de tous les cafés et les restaurants, le programme des cinémas et des concerts, etc. On peut cliquer sur le nom des bars pour obtenir une photo qui indique où ils se trouvent. Envoie-moi un mail quand tu y auras jeté un coup d'œil.

@ +
Tim

P.J.: Est-ce que tu peux faire suivre ce message à Marc? Je voulais le lui envoyer en copie, mais je ne trouve plus son adresse, j'ai effacé son dernier message de ma boîte de réception. Je suis sûr que ça l'intéressera aussi.

# Family and friends

## Relationships

**Dans ma famille, nous sommes cinq.**
There are five of us in my family.
**Il y a ...**
There are ...
- **mes parents.**
- my parents.
- **mon père/ma mère.**
- my father/my mother.
- **mon beau-père/ma belle-mère.**
- my stepfather/my stepmother.

**Il/Elle a ...**
He/She has ...
- **des enfants.**
- children.
- **un fils/une fille.**
- a son/a daughter.

**J'ai ...**
I have ...
- **un frère/une sœur.**
- a brother/a sister.
- **un demi-frère/une demi-sœur.**
- a half-brother/a half-sister.
- **un jumeau/une jumelle.**
- a twin brother/a twin sister.

**Je suis fils unique.**
I'm an only child (*boy speaking*).
**Je suis fille unique.**
I'm an only child (*girl speaking*).
**Je m'entends bien/Je ne m'entends pas avec ...**
I get on well/I don't get on well with ...
- **mes grands-parents.**
- my grandparents.
- **ma grand-mère/mon grand-père.**
- my grandmother/my grandfather.
- **mon oncle/ma tante.**
- my uncle/my aunt.
- **mon cousin** (*boy*)**/ma cousine** (*girl*).
- my cousin.

## Status

**Il/Elle est ...**
He/she is ...
- **célibataire.** single.
- **fiancé(e).** engaged.
- **marié(e).** married.
- **veuf/veuve.** a widower/a widow.
- **séparé(e).** separated.
- **divorcé(e).** divorced.
- **mort(e).** dead.

**Ma meilleure amie s'appelle ...** (*for a girl*)
**Mon meilleur ami s'appelle ...** (*for a boy*)
My best friend's name is ...

## Descriptions

**Il/Elle est ...**
He/she is ...
- **grand(e).** tall.
- **petit(e).** short.
- **blond(e).** blond.
- **brun(e).** dark-haired.
- **sympa.** really nice.
- **pénible.** a pain.

**J'ai un copain/une copine, qui a quinze ans ...**
I have a friend who is fifteen years old ...
**et qui adore le sport/les jeux vidéo.**
and who loves sport/video games.

# School

Ma matière préférée, c'est ...
My favourite subject is ...

**le français** French | **les sciences** science | **le dessin** art

**l'anglais** English | **la chimie** chemistry | **la musique** music

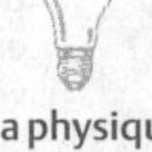

**l'allemand** German | **la physique** physics | **l'EPS** PE

**l'espagnol** Spanish | **la biologie** biology | **l'informatique** computing

**la technologie** technology | **l'histoire-géo** history and geography

**Je vais à l'école à pied.** I walk to school.
**Mon école s'appelle ...** My school is called ...
**Je suis en troisième.** I'm in Year 10.
**Il y a 25 élèves dans ma classe.**
There are 25 pupils in my class.
**Les cours commencent à neuf heures.**
Lessons start at nine o'clock.
**Un cours dure 45 minutes.**
A lesson lasts 45 minutes.
**Lundi, à neuf heures, j'ai maths.**
On Mondays at nine o'clock I have maths.
**À midi, je mange à la cantine.**
At lunchtime, I have lunch at the canteen.
**Je fais anglais et espagnol.**
I do English and Spanish.
**Je suis fort en ...** (*boy speaking*)
**Je suis forte en ...** (*girl speaking*)
I'm good at ...
**Je suis faible en ...** I'm not very good at ...
**Je prépare un examen qui s'appelle ...**
I'm working towards an exam called ...
**On a beaucoup de devoirs.**
We have a lot of homework.

## Classroom instructions

**Entrez!** Come in!
**Sortez vos cahiers.**
Take out your exercise book.
**Ouvrez vos livres, page 23.**
Open your books at page 23.
**En silence, s' il vous plaît.**
In silence, please.
**Écoutez bien.** Listen carefully.
**Écoutez et répétez.** Listen and repeat.
**Travaillez avec un partenaire.**
Work with a partner.
**Lisez le premier paragraphe.**
Read the first paragraph.
**Écrivez une description.**
Write a description.
**Cherchez les mots dans le dictionnaire.**
Look up the words in the dictionary.

## Classroom objects

**un manuel** a textbook
**un cahier** an exercise book
**un crayon** a pencil
**un bic** a ballpoint pen
**un feutre** a felt-tip pen
**une règle** a ruler
**une gomme** a rubber
**un taille-crayons** a pencil sharpener
**des ciseaux** scissors
**une calculatrice** a calculator

## Careers and future plans

**Cette année, je prépare le GCSE.**
This year, I'm studying for my GCSEs.
**L'année prochaine, je vais passer 8 examens.**
Next year, I'll be taking 8 exams.
**Après, j'aimerais bien ...**
Then, I'd like to ...
**Plus tard, je voudrais ...**
Later on, I'd like to ...
**J'ai l'intention de ...** I plan to ...
**Je veux...** I want to ...

**Mon ambition, c'est de/d'...**
My ambition is to ...
- **faire des études.** study.
- **aller à l'université.** go to university.
- **préparer un diplôme.** work for a diploma.
- **faire un apprentissage.** do an apprenticeship.
- **faire un stage.** go on a work placement.
- **trouver un emploi.** find a job.
- **aller à l'étranger.** go abroad.
- **être professeur/médecin.** become a teacher/a doctor.
- **travailler ...** work ...
  - **en plein air.** outdoors.
  - **dans le tourisme.** in tourism.

**Pour moi, le métier idéal, c'est ...**
For me, the ideal job is ...
**... parce que ...**
... because ...
- **c'est intéressant.** it's interesting.
- **c'est bien payé.** it's well paid.
- **j'aime ça.** I like it.

**Quand j'aurai [trente] ans ...**
When I'm [thirty] ...
- **je serai marié(e).** I'll be married.
- **j'aurai une famille.** I'll have a family.
- **j'irai en vacances.** I'll go on holiday.

**Mon ambition, c'est de/d'...**
My ambition is to...

**faire des études**
study

**aller à l'étranger**
go abroad

**travailler avec des enfants**
work with children

**travailler en plein air**
work outdoors

**être médecin**
be a doctor

**être coiffeur/ coiffeuse**
be a hairdresser

**être secrétaire**
be a secretary

**être comptable**
be an accountant

**être mécanicien/ mécanicienne**
be a car mechanic

abc
**être professeur**
be a teacher

# Jobs and work experience

## Writing a CV

- Remember the order of the information:
  —personal details
  —education
  —work experience
  —language skills (whether spoken or written), computer skills and membership of any clubs or voluntary organizations.
- Check your spelling and grammar—if possible, get a French person to help you with this.
- In France, it is quite usual to include a passport-sized photo with your job application.
- Always handwrite a covering letter—it's quite common for French companies to use a graphologist (handwriting expert).

**Lucy Belmont**

**Adresse**
34, Darlington Street
London NW4 5RT
tél: 0208 203 5687

Née le 30 juillet 1990, à Londres
Nationalité britannique

**Formation**
Préparation des A levels (équivalent du baccalauréat)
options: anglais, français, allemand, géographie, histoire, musique

| | |
|---|---|
| depuis 2006 | Owen's Sixth Form Centre (lycée) |
| 2006 | 8 GCSEs (équivalent du Brevet des Collèges)<br>options: mathématiques, sciences, anglais, français, allemand, géographie, histoire, musique |
| 2001–2006 | Ashworth Secondary School (collège) |

**Expérience professionnelle**

| | |
|---|---|
| 2006 | Emploi d'été:<br>stage dans un journal local |
| 2005 | Emploi d'été:<br>vendeuse en magasin |
| 2004 | baby-sitting |

**Divers**
Langues étrangères:
français (bonnes connaissances orales et écrites), allemand (bonnes connaissances), espagnol (notions)

Informatique:
bonne connaissance de Microsoft Word

Qualités personnelles:
calme, responsable, sociable, énergique

Centres d'intérêt:
les voyages, les langues, la lecture, la musique, le cinéma

Membre de l'orchestre et du groupe de théâtre du lycée

**Je voudrais ...**
I'd like to ...
- **travailler dans un magasin.** work in a shop.
- **faire du baby-sitting.** do babysitting.
- **faire du jardinage.** do gardening.
- **laver des voitures.** wash cars.

**J'ai déjà travaillé dans ...**
I've already worked in ...
- **un bureau.** an office.
- **une usine.** a factory.
- **une station-service.** a filling-station.
- **un supermarché.** a supermarket.

**J'ai distribué des journaux.**
I did a paper round.
**pendant un mois/un an** for a month/a year

**J'ai de l'expérience.** I have experience.
**Je n'ai jamais travaillé.** I've never worked.
**C'était intéressant.** It was interesting.
**J'ai trouvé le travail ...** I found the job
- **passionnant.** fascinating.
- **fatigant.** tiring.
- **bien payé.** well paid.
- **mal payé.** badly paid.

**J'ai gagné ...** I earned ...
- **7 euros de l' heure** 7 euros an hour.
- **150 euros par mois** 150 euros a month.

**J'ai ...**
I have ...
- **un job d'été.** a summer job.
- **un emploi à plein temps.** a full time job.
- **un emploi à temps partiel.** a part-time job.

**L'année dernière, j'ai fait un stage.**
Last year I did work experience.
**C'était intéressant.**
It was interesting.

**un employé** an employee (*man*)
**une employée** an employee (*woman*)
**un employeur** an employer
**le salaire** the salary/wages
**les horaires** the hours
**les qualifications** the qualifications
**la lettre de motivation** covering letter
**le CV** CV

## Travel, transport, and finding the way

**Je vais...**
I'm going...

**en avion**
by plane

**en train**
by train

**en voiture**
by car

**en bus**
by bus

**en bateau**
by ship

**à vélo**
by bike

**en car**
by coach

**en taxi**
by taxi

**à moto**
on a motorbike

**partir/le départ** to leave/departure
**arriver/l'arrivée** to arrive/arrival
**voyager/un voyage** to travel/a journey
**les bagages** luggage

**On se retrouve ...?** Shall we meet ...?
- **à l'aéroport.** at the airport.
- **au port.** at the port.
- **à la gare.** at the station.
- **à la gare routière.** at the bus station.

**Je voudrais ...**
I'd like ...
- **un aller-simple/un aller-retour pour Paris, s'il vous plaît.**
- a single/a return to Paris, please.
- **acheter un billet.**
- to buy a ticket.
- **réserver une place.**
- to reserve a seat.
- **consulter l'horaire.**
- to check the timetable.

**Le train part de quel quai?**
What platform does the train leave from?

**Où est l'arrêt de bus?**
Where is the bus stop?

**La station de métro est tout près.**
The underground station is close by.

**L'année dernière, je suis allé(e) en Espagne.**
Last year, I went to Spain.

**On a voyagé en car.**
We travelled by coach.

**Je ne suis jamais allé(e) à l'étranger.**
I have never been abroad.

Mon passe-temps préféré, c'est ...
My favourite pastime is ...

**nager**
going swimming

**faire du tourisme**
going sight-seeing

**faire de la voile**
going sailing

**Mon passe-temps préféré, c'est ...**
My favourite pastime is ...
- **sortir avec des copains.** going out with friends.
- **aller en ville.** going into town.
- **faire les magasins.** going shopping.
- **aller à des concerts.** going to concerts.
- **lire.** reading.
- **écouter de la musique.** listening to music.
- **regarder la télévision.** watching TV.
- **jouer sur une console.** playing on a games console.

**Si on allait au parc?**
Shall we go to the park?
**On se retrouve à la salle de gym!**
Let's meet up at the gym!
**J'aimerais mieux aller au stade.**
I'd rather go to the stadium.
**Rendez-vous ...**
See you ...
- **au cinéma!** at the cinema!
- **à la disco(thèque)!** at the disco!

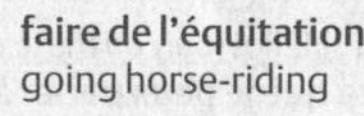

**faire de l'équitation**
going horse-riding

**Pendant les vacances, je vais ...**
During the holidays, I stay ...
- **à l'hôtel.** in a hotel.
- **dans une auberge de jeunesse.** in a youth hostel.
- **dans un gîte rural.** in a holiday home in the country.
- **dans un terrain de camping.** on a campsite.
- **au bord de la mer.** by the sea.
- **à la montagne.** in the mountains.
- **à la campagne.** in the country.
- **à la plage.** at the beach.

**faire du ski**
going skiing

**faire des promenades**
going for walks

**L'été dernier, je suis allé en France.**
Last summer, I went to France. (*boy speaking*)
**L'été dernier, je suis allée en France.**
Last summer, I went to France. (*girl speaking*)
**Cette année, je reste à la maison.**
This year, I'll stay at home.
**Tous les étés, je vais au Maroc.**
Every summer, I go to Morocco.
**L'été prochain, je vais aller à Paris.**
Next summer, I'll be going to Paris.

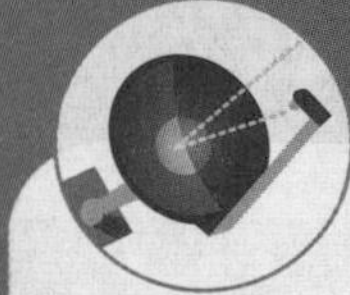

# Media and communication

## Top 10 media gadgets

**une télévision (grand écran)** a (wide screen) TV
**une antenne parabolique** a satellite dish
**un lecteur MP3** an MP3 player
**un lecteur DVD** a DVD player
**une console de jeux** a games console
**un ordinateur portable** laptop computer
**un appareil photo numérique** a digital camera
**un caméscope** a video camera
**une chaîne hi-fi** a music system
**un (téléphone) portable** a mobile phone

## Television and cinema

**regarder la télé** to watch TV
**Qu'est-ce qu'il y a comme émission?** What programmes are on?
**Il y a ...** There's ...
- **une émission sportive.** a sports programme.
- **un documentaire.** a documentary.
- **un feuilleton.** a soap.
- **un jeu.** a game show.
- **les infos.** the news.

**C'est sur quelle chaîne?** What channel is it on?
**Ma série préférée, c'est ...** My favourite series is ...
**aller au cinéma** to go to the cinema
**On passe ...** They're showing ...
- **un film policier.** a detective film.
- **un dessin animé.** a cartoon.
- **une comédie.** a drama/a comedy.
- **un film d'horreur/d'épouvante.** a horror film.

**J'ai vu Star Wars récemment.** I saw Star Wars recently.

## On the telephone

**Allô!** Hallo! (*only on the telephone*)
**Est-ce que je peux parler à ... ?** Can I speak to ... ?
**Qui est à l'appareil?** Who's calling?
**Ne quittez pas.** Hold on.
**Je peux laisser un message?** Can I leave a message?
**Je rappellerai plus tard.** I'll call back later.

## Radio, newspapers and magazines

**écouter la radio** to listen to the radio
**Je lis le journal tous les jours.** I read the newspaper every day.
**Mon magazine/mon journal préféré, c'est...** My favourite magazine/newspaper is ...

## Restaurants, cafes, and shops

**Je fais des courses ...**
I go shopping (for food) ...

**à la pâtisserie**
at the cake shop

**à la pharmacie**
at the chemist's

### At the restaurant/cafe

**Je voudrais réserver ...** I'd like to reserve ...
**une table pour quatre personnes.**
a table for four people.
**Vous désirez?** What would you like?
**Je voudrais...**
I'd like...
- **un café.** a coffee.
- **un thé.** a cup of tea.
- **un jus d'orange.** an orange juice.

**Vous avez des glaces à la vanille?**
Have you got any vanilla ice cream?
**Comme entrée, je prends ...**
For a starter, I'll have ...
- **la soupe à l'oignon.** onion soup.
- **la salade de tomates.** tomato salad.

**à la boucherie**
at the butcher's

**à la charcuterie**
at the delicatessen

**au marché**
at the market

**à la boulangerie**
at the baker's

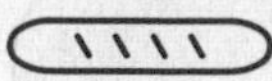

**au supermarché**
at the supermarket

**Comme plat principal, je voudrais ...**
For the main course, I'd like ...
- **le coq au vin.** chicken in wine sauce.
- **le gigot d'agneau.** leg of lamb.

**avec ...** with
- **des petits pois.** peas.
- **des frites.** chips.

**Comme dessert, je voudrais ...**
For dessert, I'd like ...
- **la tarte aux poires.** pear tart.
- **la mousse au chocolat.** chocolate mousse.

**Comme boisson, je vais prendre ...**
To drink, I'll have ...
- **de l'eau minérale.** mineral water.
- **du vin (blanc/rouge).** (white/red) wine.

**L'addition, s'il vous plaît.** The bill, please.
**C'est combien?** How much is it?

## The world around you

**Tu habites ...**
Do you live ...
- **dans le centre-ville?** in the city centre?
- **dans la banlieue?** in the suburbs?
- **à la campagne?** in the country?
- **au bord de la mer?** at the sea-side?
- **à la montagne?** in the mountains?

**J'habite dans le nord/sud/est/ouest/centre de ...**
I live in the north/south/east/west/centre of ...
**C'est une ville industrielle/moderne/animée.**
It's an industrial/a modern/a lively town.
**C'est un village agricole/calme/touristique.**
It's a farming/quiet/touristy village.

**Dans ma ville, il y a ...**
In my town there is/are ...
- **des magasins.** shops.
- **des restaurants.** restaurants.
- **des hôtels.** hotels.
- **des cafés.** cafes.
- **un musée.** a museum.
- **une église.** a church.
- **une piscine.** a swimming pool.
- **un cinéma.** a cinema.
- **un théâtre.** a theatre.

**au rez-de-chaussée**
on the ground floor
**au premier étage**
on the first floor

**J'habite dans ...**
I live in ...
- **une maison.** a house.
- **un appartement au deuxième étage.** a flat on the second floor.

**Chez moi, c'est petit/grand/moderne/ancien.**
My home is small/big/modern/old.

**Il y a ...**
There is ...

**une cuisine**
a kitchen

**un salon/un séjour**
a lounge/a living room

**une salle à manger**
a dining room

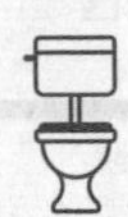

**des WC/des toilettes**
a toilet

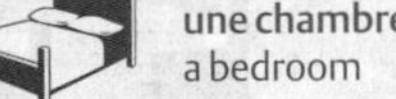

**une chambre**
a bedroom

**une salle de bains**
a bathroom

**un bureau**
an office/a study

**un garage**
a garage

**un jardin**
a garden

# Healthy living and the human body



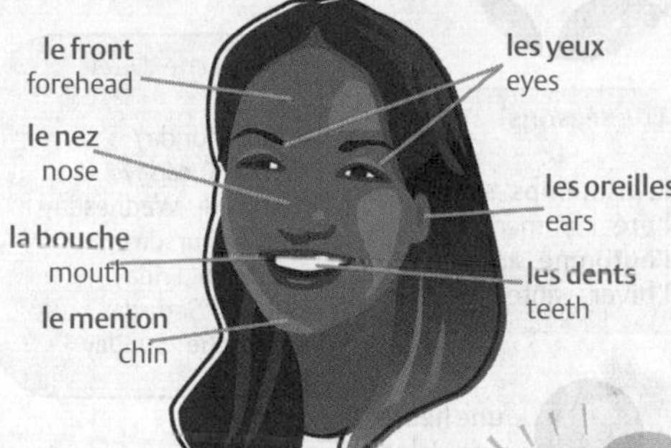

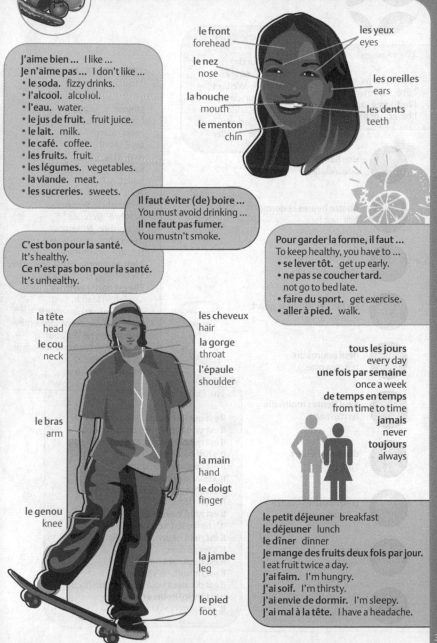

**J'aime bien ...** I like ...
**Je n'aime pas ...** I don't like ...
- **le soda.** fizzy drinks.
- **l'alcool.** alcohol.
- **l'eau.** water.
- **le jus de fruit.** fruit juice.
- **le lait.** milk.
- **le café.** coffee.
- **les fruits.** fruit.
- **les légumes.** vegetables.
- **la viande.** meat.
- **les sucreries.** sweets.

**Il faut éviter (de) boire ...**
You must avoid drinking ...
**Il ne faut pas fumer.**
You mustn't smoke.

**C'est bon pour la santé.**
It's healthy.
**Ce n'est pas bon pour la santé.**
It's unhealthy.

**Pour garder la forme, il faut ...**
To keep healthy, you have to ...
- **se lever tôt.** get up early.
- **ne pas se coucher tard.** not go to bed late.
- **faire du sport.** get exercise.
- **aller à pied.** walk.

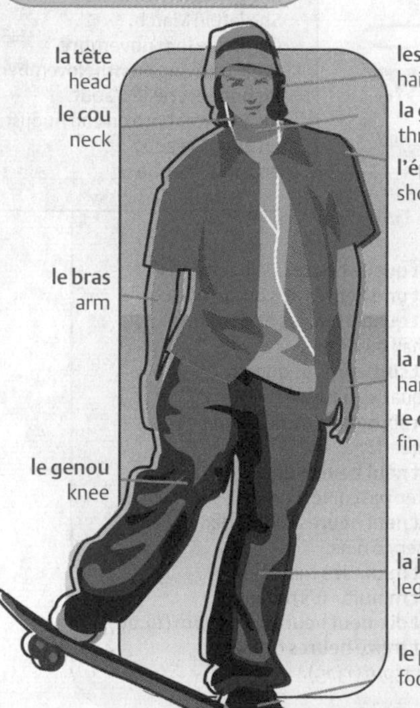


**tous les jours**
every day
**une fois par semaine**
once a week
**de temps en temps**
from time to time
**jamais**
never
**toujours**
always

**le petit déjeuner** breakfast
**le déjeuner** lunch
**le dîner** dinner
**Je mange des fruits deux fois par jour.**
I eat fruit twice a day.
**J'ai faim.** I'm hungry.
**J'ai soif.** I'm thirsty.
**J'ai envie de dormir.** I'm sleepy.
**J'ai mal à la tête.** I have a headache.

## Time

### The seasons

**le printemps** spring
**l'été** summer
**l'automne** autumn
**l'hiver** winter

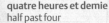

### Days of the Week

**lundi** Monday
**mardi** Tuesday
**mercredi** Wednesday
**jeudi** Thursday
**vendredi** Friday
**samedi** Saturday
**dimanche** Sunday

### Months

**janvier** January
**février** February
**mars** March
**avril** April
**mai** May
**juin** June
**juillet** July
**août** August
**septembre** September
**octobre** October
**novembre** November
**décembre** December
NB: in + month = **en**
**Mon anniversaire est en février.**
My birthday is in February.
**Elle est partie en mars.**
She left in March.
**On arrive le 11 novembre.**
We're arriving on 11th November.
**Richard est né le 2 août.**
Richard was born on 2nd August.
**en 2007** in 2007
**en 1999** in 1999

**une heure**
one o'clock

**quatre heures et demie**
half past four

**six heures et quart**
quarter past six

**six heures moins le quart**
quarter to six

**neuf heures dix**
ten past nine

**neuf heures moins dix**
ten to nine

**dix-neuf heures**
7pm (19.00)

**treize heures quinze**
1.15pm (13.15)

**midi**
midday

**minuit**
midnight

### The Time

**Il est quelle heure?** What time is it?
**Il est une heure.** It's one o'clock.
**Il est quatre heures et demie.**
It's half past four.
**Il est six heures et quart.**
It's quarter past six.
**Il est six heures moins le quart.**
It's quarter to six.
**Il est neuf heures dix.**
It's ten past nine.
**Il est neuf heures moins dix.**
It's ten to nine.
**Il est midi.** It's midday.
**Il est minuit.** It's midnight.
**Il est dix-neuf heures.** It's 7pm (19.00).
**Il est treize heures quinze.**
It's 1.15pm (13.15).

# Saying how you feel

**être triste**
to be sad

**être heureux (boy) /heureuse (girl)**
to be happy

**être fâché (boy) /fâchée (girl)**
to be angry

**être amoureux (boy) /amoureuse (girl)**
to be in love

**avoir sommeil**
to be tired

**avoir peur**
to be afraid

**avoir froid**
to be cold

**avoir chaud**
to be hot

**avoir faim**
to be hungry

## Numbers

One is *une* in French when it agrees with a feminine noun, so *un crayon* but *une table*, *une des tables*, *vingt et une tables*, etc

| | | | | |
|---|---|---|---|---|
| 0 | zéro | | | |
| 1 | un (*sometimes* une) | 1st | 1er | premier (*fem* première) |
| 2 | deux | 2nd | 2e | second (*fem* seconde) *or* deuxième |
| 3 | trois | 3rd | 3e | troisième |
| 4 | quatre | 4th | 4e | quatrième |
| 5 | cinq | 5th | 5e | cinquième |
| 6 | six | 6th | 6e | sixième |
| 7 | sept | 7th | 7e | septième |
| 8 | huit | 8th | 8e | huitième |
| 9 | neuf | 9th | 9e | neuvième |
| 10 | dix | 10th | 10e | dixième |
| 11 | onze | 11th | 11e | onzième |
| 12 | douze | 12th | 12e | douzième |
| 13 | treize | 13th | 13e | treizième |
| 14 | quatorze | 14th | 14e | quatorzième |
| 15 | quinze | 15th | 15e | quinzième |
| 16 | seize | 16th | 16e | seizième |
| 17 | dix-sept | 17th | 17e | dix-septième |
| 18 | dix-huit | 18th | 18e | dix-huitième |
| 19 | dix-neuf | 19th | 19e | dix-neuvième |
| 20 | vingt | 20th | 20e | vingtième |
| 21 | vingt et un | 21st | 21e | vingt et unième |
| 22 | vingt-deux | 22nd | 22e | vingt-deuxième |
| 30 | trente | 30th | 30e | trentième |
| 40 | quarante | 40th | 40e | quarantième |
| 50 | cinquante | 50th | 50e | cinquantième |
| 60 | soixante | 60th | 60e | soixantième |

70 is *soixante-dix* and 80 is *quatre-vingts*.
*Quatre-vingts* loses the -s when another number joins it.

| | | | | |
|---|---|---|---|---|
| 70 | soixante-dix | 70th | 70e | soixante-dixième |
| 71 | soixante et onze | 71st | 71e | soixante et onzième |
| 80 | quatre-vingts | 80th | 80e | quatre-vingtième |
| 81 | quatre-vingt-un | 81st | 81e | quatre-vingt-unième |
| 82 | quatre-vingt-deux | 82nd | 82e | quatre-vingt-deuxième |
| 90 | quatre-vingt-dix | 90th | 90e | quatre-vingt-dixième |
| 91 | quatre-vingt-onze | 91st | 91e | quatre-vingt-onzième |
| 92 | quatre-vingt-douze | 92nd | 92e | quatre-vingt-douzième |
| 99 | quatre-vingt-dix-neuf | 99th | 99e | quatre-vingt-dix-neuvième |
| 100 | cent | 100th | 100e | centième |
| 101 | cent un | 101st | 101e | cent et unième |
| 102 | cent deux | 102nd | 102e | cent-deuxième |
| 200 | deux cents | 200th | 200e | deux centième |
| 201 | deux cent un | 201st | 201e | deux cent et unième |
| 202 | deux cent deux | 202nd | 202e | deux cent deuxième |

When writing longer numbers French uses a space or a full stop instead of a comma—for example, 1 000 or 1.000 rather than 1,000.

| | | | | |
|---|---|---|---|---|
| 1 000 | mille | 1000th | 1 000e | millième |
| 1 001 | mille un | 1001st | 1 001e | mille et unième |
| 1 002 | mille deux | 1002nd | 1 002e | mille deuxième |
| 2 000 | deux mille | 2000th | 2 000e | deux millième |
| 1 000 000 | un million | 1000000th | 1 000 000e | millionième |

# Model regular verbs



# Main irregular verbs

## [1] aimer
### to like *or* to love

| Present | | Present subjunctive | |
|---|---|---|---|
| j' | aim**e** | j' | aim**e** |
| tu | aim**es** | tu | aim**es** |
| il | aim**e** | il | aim**e** |
| nous | aim**ons** | nous | aim**ions** |
| vous | aim**ez** | vous | aim**iez** |
| ils | aim**ent** | ils | aim**ent** |

| Perfect | | Imperfect | |
|---|---|---|---|
| j' | ai aim**é** | j' | aim**ais** |
| tu | as aim**é** | tu | aim**ais** |
| il | a aim**é** | il | aim**ait** |
| nous | avons aim**é** | nous | aim**ions** |
| vous | avez aim**é** | vous | aim**iez** |
| ils | ont aim**é** | ils | aim**aient** |

| Future | | Conditional | |
|---|---|---|---|
| j' | aimer**ai** | j' | aimer**ais** |
| tu | aimer**as** | tu | aimer**ais** |
| il | aimer**a** | il | aimer**ait** |
| nous | aimer**ons** | nous | aimer**ions** |
| vous | aimer**ez** | vous | aimer**iez** |
| ils | aimer**ont** | ils | aimer**aient** |

**Imperative**
aim**e**
aim**ons**
aim**ez**

**Past participle**
aim**é**

Verb tables

## [2] finir
**to finish**

### Present
| | |
|---|---|
| je | finis |
| tu | finis |
| il | finit |
| nous | finissons |
| vous | finissez |
| ils | finissent |

### Present subjunctive
| | |
|---|---|
| je | finisse |
| tu | finisses |
| il | finisse |
| nous | finissions |
| vous | finissiez |
| ils | finissent |

### Perfect
| | |
|---|---|
| j' | ai fini |
| tu | as fini |
| il | a fini |
| nous | avons fini |
| vous | avez fini |
| ils | ont fini |

### Imperfect
| | |
|---|---|
| je | finissais |
| tu | finissais |
| il | finissait |
| nous | finissions |
| vous | finissiez |
| ils | finissaient |

### Future
| | |
|---|---|
| je | finirai |
| tu | finiras |
| il | finira |
| nous | finirons |
| vous | finirez |
| ils | finiront |

### Conditional
| | |
|---|---|
| je | finirais |
| tu | finirais |
| il | finirait |
| nous | finirions |
| vous | finiriez |
| ils | finiraient |

### Imperative
finis
finissons
finissez

### Past participle
fini

## [3] attendre
**to wait**

**Present**

| | |
|---|---|
| j' | attends |
| tu | attends |
| il | attend |
| nous | attendons |
| vous | attendez |
| ils | attendent |

**Present subjunctive**

| | |
|---|---|
| j' | attende |
| tu | attendes |
| il | attende |
| nous | attendions |
| vous | attendiez |
| ils | attendent |

**Perfect**

| | |
|---|---|
| j' | ai attendu |
| tu | as attendu |
| il | a attendu |
| nous | avons attendu |
| vous | avez attendu |
| ils | ont attendu |

**Imperfect**

| | |
|---|---|
| j' | attendais |
| tu | attendais |
| il | attendait |
| nous | attendions |
| vous | attendiez |
| ils | attendaient |

**Future**

| | |
|---|---|
| j' | attendrai |
| tu | attendras |
| il | attendra |
| nous | attendrons |
| vous | attendrez |
| ils | attendront |

**Conditional**

| | |
|---|---|
| j' | attendrais |
| tu | attendrais |
| il | attendrait |
| nous | attendrions |
| vous | attendriez |
| ils | attendraient |

**Imperative**

attends
attendons
attendez

**Past participle**

attendu

## [4] se laver
## to wash (oneself)

### Present

| | |
|---|---|
| je | me lave |
| tu | te laves |
| il | se lave |
| nous | nous lavons |
| vous | vous lavez |
| ils | se lavent |

### Present subjunctive

| | |
|---|---|
| je | me lave |
| tu | te laves |
| il | se lave |
| nous | nous lavions |
| vous | vous laviez |
| ils | se lavent |

### Perfect

| | |
|---|---|
| je | me suis lavé |
| tu | t'es lavé |
| il | s'est lavé |
| nous | nous sommes lavés |
| vous | vous êtes lavé(s) |
| ils | se sont lavés |

### Imperfect

| | |
|---|---|
| je | me lavais |
| tu | te lavais |
| il | se lavait |
| nous | nous lavions |
| vous | vous laviez |
| ils | se lavaient |

### Future

| | |
|---|---|
| je | me laverai |
| tu | te laveras |
| il | se lavera |
| nous | nous laverons |
| vous | vous laverez |
| ils | se laveront |

### Conditional

| | |
|---|---|
| je | me laverais |
| tu | te laverais |
| il | se laverait |
| nous | nous laverions |
| vous | vous laveriez |
| ils | se laveraient |

### Imperative

lave-toi
lavons-nous
lavez-vous

### Past participle

lavé

## [5] avoir
## to have

### Present

| | |
|---|---|
| j' | ai |
| tu | as |
| il | a |
| nous | avons |
| vous | avez |
| ils | ont |

### Present subjunctive

| | |
|---|---|
| j' | aie |
| tu | aies |
| il | ait |
| nous | ayons |
| vous | ayez |
| ils | aient |

### Perfect

| | |
|---|---|
| j' | ai **eu** |
| tu | as **eu** |
| il | a **eu** |
| nous | avons **eu** |
| vous | avez **eu** |
| ils | ont **eu** |

### Imperfect

| | |
|---|---|
| j' | avais |
| tu | avais |
| il | avait |
| nous | avions |
| vous | aviez |
| ils | avaient |

### Future

| | |
|---|---|
| j' | aurai |
| tu | auras |
| il | aura |
| nous | aurons |
| vous | aurez |
| ils | auront |

### Conditional

| | |
|---|---|
| j' | aurais |
| tu | aurais |
| il | aurait |
| nous | aurions |
| vous | auriez |
| ils | auraient |

### Imperative

aie
ayons
ayez

### Past participle

eu

## [6] être
### to be

**Present**

| | |
|---|---|
| je | suis |
| tu | es |
| il | est |
| nous | sommes |
| vous | êtes |
| ils | sont |

**Present subjunctive**

| | |
|---|---|
| je | sois |
| tu | sois |
| il | soit |
| nous | soyons |
| vous | soyez |
| ils | soient |

**Perfect**

| | |
|---|---|
| j' | ai **été** |
| tu | as **été** |
| il | a **été** |
| nous | avons **été** |
| vous | avez **été** |
| ils | ont **été** |

**Imperfect**

| | |
|---|---|
| j' | étais |
| tu | étais |
| il | était |
| nous | étions |
| vous | étiez |
| ils | étaient |

**Future**

| | |
|---|---|
| je | serai |
| tu | seras |
| il | sera |
| nous | serons |
| vous | serez |
| ils | seront |

**Conditional**

| | |
|---|---|
| je | serai |
| tu | serais |
| il | serait |
| nous | serions |
| vous | seriez |
| ils | seraient |

**Imperative**

sois
soyons
soyez

**Past participle**

été

## [7] aller
## to go

### Present

| | |
|---|---|
| je | vais |
| tu | vas |
| il | va |
| nous | allons |
| vous | allez |
| ils | vont |

### Present subjunctive

| | |
|---|---|
| j' | aille |
| tu | ailles |
| il | aille |
| nous | aillions |
| vous | ailliez |
| ils | aillent |

### Perfect

| | |
|---|---|
| je | suis allé |
| tu | es allé |
| il | est allé |
| nous | sommes allés |
| vous | êtes allé(s) |
| ils | sont allés |

### Imperfect

| | |
|---|---|
| j' | allais |
| tu | allais |
| il | allait |
| nous | allions |
| vous | alliez |
| ils | allaient |

### Future

| | |
|---|---|
| j' | irai |
| tu | iras |
| il | ira |
| nous | irons |
| vous | irez |
| ils | iront |

### Conditional

| | |
|---|---|
| j' | irais |
| tu | irais |
| il | irait |
| nous | irions |
| vous | iriez |
| ils | iraient |

### Imperative

va
allons
allez

### Past participle

allé

## [8] devoir
## to have to

### Present
je **dois**
tu **dois**
il **doit**
nous **devons**
vous **devez**
ils **doivent**

### Present subjunctive
je **doive**
tu **doives**
il **doive**
nous **devions**
vous **deviez**
ils **doivent**

### Perfect
j' ai **dû**
tu as **dû**
il a **dû**
nous avons **dû**
vous avez **dû**
ils ont **dû**

### Imperfect
je **devais**
tu **devais**
il **devait**
nous **devions**
vous **deviez**
ils **devaient**

### Future
je **devrai**
tu **devras**
il **devra**
nous **devrons**
vous **devrez**
ils **devront**

### Conditional
je **devrais**
tu **devrais**
il **devrait**
nous **devrions**
vous **devriez**
ils **devraient**

### Imperative
**dois**
**devons**
**devez**

### Past participle
**dû**

## [9] dire
## to say

### Present

| | |
|---|---|
| je | **dis** |
| tu | **dis** |
| il | **dit** |
| nous | **disons** |
| vous | **dites** |
| ils | **disent** |

### Present subjunctive

| | |
|---|---|
| je | **dise** |
| tu | **dises** |
| il | **dise** |
| nous | **disions** |
| vous | **disiez** |
| ils | **disent** |

### Perfect

| | |
|---|---|
| j' | ai **dit** |
| tu | as **dit** |
| il | a **dit** |
| nous | avons **dit** |
| vous | avez **dit** |
| ils | ont **dit** |

### Imperfect

| | |
|---|---|
| je | **disais** |
| tu | **disais** |
| il | **disait** |
| nous | **disions** |
| vous | **disiez** |
| ils | **disaient** |

### Future

| | |
|---|---|
| je | dirai |
| tu | diras |
| il | dira |
| nous | dirons |
| vous | direz |
| ils | diront |

### Conditional

| | |
|---|---|
| je | dirais |
| tu | dirais |
| il | dirait |
| nous | dirions |
| vous | diriez |
| ils | diraient |

### Imperative

dis
disons
dites

### Past participle

dit

## [10] faire
## to do *or* to make

| Present | | Present subjunctive | |
|---|---|---|---|
| je | fais | je | fasse |
| tu | fais | tu | fasses |
| il | fait | il | fasse |
| nous | faisons | nous | fassions |
| vous | faites | vous | fassiez |
| ils | font | ils | fassent |

| Perfect | | Imperfect | |
|---|---|---|---|
| j' | ai **fait** | je | faisais |
| tu | as **fait** | tu | faisais |
| il | a **fait** | il | faisait |
| nous | avons **fait** | nous | faisions |
| vous | avez **fait** | vous | faisiez |
| ils | ont **fait** | ils | faisaient |

| Future | | Conditional | |
|---|---|---|---|
| je | ferai | je | ferai |
| tu | feras | tu | ferais |
| il | fera | il | ferait |
| nous | ferons | nous | ferions |
| vous | ferez | vous | feriez |
| ils | feront | ils | feraient |

**Imperative**
fais
faisons
faites

**Past participle**
fait

## [11] mettre
### to put

**Present**

| | |
|---|---|
| je | mets |
| tu | mets |
| il | met |
| nous | mettons |
| vous | mettez |
| ils | mettent |

**Present subjunctive**

| | |
|---|---|
| je | mette |
| tu | mettes |
| il | mette |
| nous | mettions |
| vous | mettiez |
| ils | mettent |

**Perfect**

| | |
|---|---|
| j' | ai **mis** |
| tu | as **mis** |
| il | a **mis** |
| nous | avons **mis** |
| vous | avez **mis** |
| ils | ont **mis** |

**Imperfect**

| | |
|---|---|
| je | mettais |
| tu | mettais |
| il | mettait |
| nous | mettions |
| vous | mettiez |
| ils | mettaient |

**Future**

| | |
|---|---|
| je | mettrai |
| tu | mettras |
| il | mettra |
| nous | mettrons |
| vous | mettrez |
| ils | mettront |

**Conditional**

| | |
|---|---|
| je | mettrais |
| tu | mettrais |
| il | mettrait |
| nous | mettrions |
| vous | mettriez |
| ils | mettraient |

**Imperative**

mets
mettons
mettez

**Past participle**

mis

## [12] pouvoir
## to be able

### Present

| | |
|---|---|
| je | **peux** |
| tu | **peux** |
| il | **peut** |
| nous | pouvons |
| vous | pouvez |
| ils | **peuvent** |

### Present subjunctive

| | |
|---|---|
| je | **puisse** |
| tu | **puisses** |
| il | **puisse** |
| nous | **puissions** |
| vous | **puissiez** |
| ils | **puissent** |

### Perfect

| | |
|---|---|
| j' | ai **pu** |
| tu | as **pu** |
| il | a **pu** |
| nous | avons **pu** |
| vous | avez **pu** |
| ils | ont **pu** |

### Imperfect

| | |
|---|---|
| je | pouvais |
| tu | pouvais |
| il | pouvait |
| nous | pouvions |
| vous | pouviez |
| ils | pouvaient |

### Future

| | |
|---|---|
| je | **pourrai** |
| tu | **pourras** |
| il | **pourra** |
| nous | **pourrons** |
| vous | **pourrez** |
| ils | **pourront** |

### Conditional

| | |
|---|---|
| je | **pourrais** |
| tu | **pourrais** |
| il | **pourrait** |
| nous | **pourrions** |
| vous | **pourriez** |
| ils | **pourraient** |

### Imperative

The imperative of *pouvoir* is not used

### Past participle

**pu**

## [13] voir
## to see

| Present | | Present subjunctive | |
|---|---|---|---|
| je | vois | je | voie |
| tu | vois | tu | voies |
| il | voit | il | voie |
| nous | **voyons** | nous | **voyions** |
| vous | **voyez** | vous | **voyiez** |
| ils | voient | ils | voient |

| Perfect | | Imperfect | |
|---|---|---|---|
| j' | ai **vu** | je | **voyais** |
| tu | as **vu** | tu | **voyais** |
| il | a **vu** | il | **voyait** |
| nous | avons **vu** | nous | **voyions** |
| vous | avez **vu** | vous | **voyiez** |
| ils | ont **vu** | ils | **voyaient** |

| Future | | Conditional | |
|---|---|---|---|
| je | **verrai** | je | **verrais** |
| tu | **verras** | tu | **verrais** |
| il | **verra** | il | **verrait** |
| nous | **verrons** | nous | **verrions** |
| vous | **verrez** | vous | **verriez** |
| ils | **verront** | ils | **verraient** |

**Imperative**

vois
**voyons**
**voyez**

**Past participle**

**vu**

## [14] vouloir
## to want

### Present

| | |
|---|---|
| je | **veux** |
| tu | **veux** |
| il | **veut** |
| nous | voul<u>ons</u> |
| vous | voul<u>ez</u> |
| ils | **veulent** |

### Present subjunctive

| | |
|---|---|
| je | **veuille** |
| tu | **veuilles** |
| il | **veuille** |
| nous | voul<u>ions</u> |
| vous | voul<u>iez</u> |
| ils | **veuillent** |

### Perfect

| | |
|---|---|
| j' | ai voul<u>u</u> |
| tu | as voul<u>u</u> |
| il | a voul<u>u</u> |
| nous | avons voul<u>u</u> |
| vous | avez voul<u>u</u> |
| ils | ont voul<u>u</u> |

### Imperfect

| | |
|---|---|
| je | voul<u>ais</u> |
| tu | voul<u>ais</u> |
| il | voul<u>ait</u> |
| nous | voul<u>ions</u> |
| vous | voul<u>iez</u> |
| ils | voul<u>aient</u> |

### Future

| | |
|---|---|
| je | **voudrai** |
| tu | **voudras** |
| il | **voudra** |
| nous | **voudrons** |
| vous | **voudrez** |
| ils | **voudront** |

### Conditional

| | |
|---|---|
| je | **voudrais** |
| tu | **voudrais** |
| il | **voudrait** |
| nous | **voudrions** |
| vous | **voudriez** |
| ils | **voudraient** |

### Imperative

**veuille**
**veuillons**
**veuillez**

### Past participle

voul<u>u</u>

# Other irregular verbs

abréger
acheter
acquérir
appeler
apprendre
s'asseoir
battre
boire
bouillir
céder
conclure
conduire
connaître
coudre
courir
couvrir
craindre
créer
croire
croître
cueillir
cuire
dormir
écrire
employer
envoyer
essuyer
faillir
falloir
fuir
geler
haïr
interdire
jeter
joindre
lever
lire
manger
mentir
mourir
naître
offrir
paraître
partir
payer
peindre
placer
plaire
pleuvoir
prendre
prévoir
recevoir
résoudre
rire
rompre
savoir
servir
sortir
souffrir
suffire
suivre
taire
tenir
traire
vaincre
valoir
venir
vivre

## Irregular verb forms

This list shows the main forms of other irregular verbs. The number before the infinitve is the number given after verbs in the dictionary which follow this pattern. **1** = Present **2** = Past participle **3** = Imperfect **4** = Future

### [15] abréger
**1** j'abrège, nous abrégons, ils abrègent
**2** abrégé
**3** j'abrégeais
**4** j'abrégerai

### [16] acheter
**1** j'achète, nous achetons, Ils achètent
**2** acheté
**3** j'achetais
**4** j'achèterai

### [17] acquérir
**1** j'acquiers, il acquiert, nous acquérons, vous acquérez, ils acquièrent
**2** acquis
**3** j'acquérais
**4** j'acquerrai

### [18] appeler
**1** j'appelle, nous appelons
**2** appelé
**3** j'appelais
**4** j'apellerai

### [19] apprendre
**1** j'apprends, nous apprenons, vous apprenez, ils apprennent
**2** appris
**3** j'apprenais
**4** j'apprendrai

### [20] s'asseoir
**1** je m'assieds, nous nous asseyons, vous vous asseyez, ils s'asseyent
**2** assis
**3** je m'asseyais
**4** je m'assiérai

### [21] battre
**1** je bats, il bat, nous battons
**2** battu
**3** je buvais
**4** je battrai

### [22] boire
**1** je bois, nous buvons, ils boivent
**2** bu
**3** je buvais
**4** je boirai

### [23] bouillir
**1** je bous, nous bouillons
**2** bouilli
**3** je bouillais
**4** je bouillirai

### [24] céder
**1** je cède, nous cédons, ils cèdent
**2** cédé
**3** je cédais
**4** je céderai

### [25] conclure
**1** je conclus, nous concluons
**2** conclu
**3** je concluais
**4** je conclurai

### [26] conduire
**1** je conduis, nous conduisons
**2** conduit
**3** je conduisais
**4** je conduirai

### [27] connaître
**1** je connais, nous connaissons
**2** connu
**3** je connaissais
**4** je connaîtrai

[28] **coudre**
1 je couds, nous cousons, vous cousez, ils cousent
2 cousu
3 je cousais
4 je coudrai

[29] **courir**
1 je cours, nous courons
2 couru
3 je courais
4 je courrai

[30] **couvrir**
1 je couvre, nous couvrons
2 couvert
3 je couvrais
4 je couvrirai

[31] **craindre**
1 je crains, nous craignons
2 craint
3 je craignais
4 je craindrai

[32] **créer**
1 je crée, nous créons
2 crée
3 je créais
4 je créerai

[33] **croire**
1 je crois, nous croyons, ils croient
2 cru
3 je croyais
4 je croirai

[34] **croître**
1 je croîs, nous croissons
2 crû, crue
3 je croissais
4 je croîtrai

[35] **cueillir**
1 je cueille, nous cueillons
2 cueilli
3 je cueillais
4 je cueillerai

[36] **cuire**
1 je cuis, nous cuisons, ils cuisent
2 cuit
3 je cuisais
4 je cuirai

[37] **dormir**
1 je dors, nous dormons
2 dormi
3 je dormais
4 je dormirai

[38] **écrire**
1 écris, nous écrivons
2 écrit
3 j'écrivais
4 j'écrirai

[39] **employer**
1 j'emploie, nous employons, vous employez, ils emploient
2 employé
3 j'employais
4 j'emploierai

[40] **envoyer**
1 j'envoie, nous envoyons, vous envoyez, ils envoient
2 envoyé
3 j'envoyais
4 j'enverrai

[41] **essuyer**
1 j'essuie, nous essuyons, vous essuyez, ils essuient
2 essuyé
3 j'essuyais
4 j'essuierai

[42] **faillir**
1 je faille
2 failli

[43] **falloir**
1 il faut
2 fallu
3 il fallait
4 il faudra

[44] **fuir**
1 je fuis, nous fuyons, ils fuient
2 fui
3 je fuyais
4 je fuirai

[45] **geler**
1 je gèle, nous gelons, vous gelez, ils gèlent
2 gelé
3 je gelais
4 je gèlerai

[46] **haïr**
1 je hais, nous haïssons, ils haïssent
2 haï
3 je haïssais
4 je haïrai

[47] **interdire**
1 j'interdis, nous interdisons, vous interdisez
2 interdit
3 j'interdisais
4 j'interdirai

[48] **jeter**
1 je jette, nous jetons, ils jettent
2 jeté
3 je jetais
4 je jetterai

[49] **joindre**
1 je joins, nous joignons
2 joint
3 je joignais
4 je joindrai

[50] **lever**
1 je lève, nous levons, ils lèvent
2 levé
3 je levais
4 je lèverai

[51] **lire**
1 je lis, nous lisons
2 lu
3 je lisais
4 je lirai

[52] **manger**
1 je mange, nous mangeons
2 mangé
3 je mangeais
4 je mangerai

[53] **mentir**
1 je mens, nous mentons
2 menti
3 je mentais
4 je mentirai

[54] **mourir**
1 je meurs, nous mourons, ils meurent
2 mort
3 je mourais
4 je mourrai

[55] **naître**
1 je nais, il naît, nous naissons
2 né
3 je naissais
4 je naîtrai

**[56] offrir**
1 j'offre, nous offrons
2 offert
3 j'offrais
4 j'offrirai

**[57] paraître**
1 je parais, il paraît, nous paraissons
2 paru
3 je paraissais
4 je paraîtrai

**[58] partir**
1 je pars, nous partons
2 parti
3 je partais
4 je partirai

**[59] payer**
1 je paie/je paye, nous payons, vous payez, ils paient/ils payent
2 payé
3 je payais
4 je paierai/je payerai

**[60] peindre**
1 je peins, nous peignons
2 peint
3 je peignais
4 je peindrai

**[61] placer**
1 je place, nous plaçons
2 placé
3 je plaçais
4 je placerai

**[62] plaire**
1 je plais, il plaît, nous plaisons
2 plu
3 je plaisais
4 je plairai

**[63] pleuvoir**
1 il pleut
2 plu
3 il pleuvait
4 il pleuvra

**[64] prendre**
1 je prends, nous prenons, ils prennent
2 pris
3 je prenais
4 je prendrai

**[65] prévoir**
1 je prévois, nous prévoyons, nous prévoyez, ils prévoient
2 prévu
3 je prévoyais
4 je prévoirai

**[66] recevoir**
1 je reçois, il reçoit, ils reçoivent
2 reçu
3 je recevais
4 je recevrai

**[67] résoudre**
1 je résous, nous résolvons, nous résolvez, ils résolvent
2 résolu
3 je résolvais
4 je résoudrai

**[68] rire**
1 je ris, nous rions
2 ri
3 je riais
4 je rirai

**[69] rompre**
1 je romps, il rompt, nous rompons
2 rompu
3 je rompais
4 je romprai

## Other irregular verbs

[70] **savoir**
1 je sais, nous savons, ils savent
2 su
3 je savais
4 je saurai

[71] **servir**
1 je sers, nous servons
2 servi
3 je servais
4 je servirai

[72] **sortir**
1 je sors, nous sortons
2 sorti
3 je sortais
4 je sortirai

[73] **souffrir**
1 je souffre, nous souffrons
2 souffert
3 je souffrais
4 je souffrirai

[74] **suffire**
1 je suffis, nous suffisons
2 suffi
3 je suffisais
4 je suffirai

[75] **suivre**
1 je suis, nous suivons
2 suivi
3 je suivais
4 je suivrai

[76] **se taire**
1 je me tais, nous nous taisons
2 tu
3 je me taisais
4 je me tairai

[77] **tenir**
1 je tiens, nous tenons, ils tiennent
2 tenu
3 je tenais
4 je tiendrai

[78] **traire**
1 je trais, nous trayons, ils traient
2 trait
3 je trayais
4 je trairai

[79] **vaincre**
1 je vaincs, il vainc, nous vainquons
2 vaincu
3 je vainquais

[80] **valoir**
1 je vaux, il vaut, nous valons
2 valu
3 je valais
4 je vaudrai

[81] **venir**
1 je viens, nous venons, ils viennent
2 venu
3 je venais
4 je viendrai

[82] **vivre**
1 je vis, nous vivons
2 vécu
3 je vivais
4 je vivrai

# A a

♪ **a**, **an** *determiner*

**1** (*before a masc singular noun*) **un**
**a shop** un magasin
**a tree** un arbre
**a man** un homme

**2** (*before a fem singular noun*) **une**
**a house** une maison
**a school** une école
**a woman** une femme

**3** (*showing how much, how many, how often*) **five euros a kilo** cinq euros le kilo
**fifty kilometres an hour** cinquante kilomètres à l'heure
**three times a day** trois fois par jour
**I do athletics twice a week.** Je fais de l'athlétisme deux fois par semaine.

**4** (*when saying what you do*) **She's a dentist.** Elle est dentiste.
**I'm a student.** Je suis étudiant (*boy speaking*), Je suis étudiante (*girl speaking*).

**WORD TIP** *a* before an occupation is not translated into French.

to **abandon** *verb*
**abandonner [1]**

**abbey** *noun*
une **abbaye** *fem*
**Westminster Abbey** l'Abbaye de Westminster

**abbreviation** *noun*
une **abréviation** *fem*

**ability** *noun*
la **capacité** *fem*
**the ability to do something** la capacité de faire quelque chose

♪ **able** *adjective*
**to be able to do something** pouvoir **[12]** faire quelque chose
**I wasn't able to sleep.** Je n'ai pas pu dormir.

to **abolish** *verb*
**abolir [2]**

**abortion** *noun*
un **avortement** *masc*
**She had an abortion.** Elle s'est fait avorter.

♪ **about** *preposition* ▷ see **about** *adv*

**1** (*telling the story of*) **sur**
**a book about a rock band** un livre sur un groupe de rock
**What's the film about?** De quoi le film parle-t-il?

**2** (*concerning*) **au sujet de**
**He wants to talk to you about your exam.** Il veut te parler au sujet de ton examen.
(*emails, letters, messages*) **What's it about?** De quoi s'agit-il?
**It's about the school trip.** Il s'agit du voyage scolaire.

**3** **to talk about something** parler de quelque chose
**What's she talking about?** De quoi parle-t-elle?

♪ **about** *adverb* ▷ see **about** *prep*

**1** (*nearly*) **environ**
**There are about twenty people here.** Il y a environ vingt personnes ici.

**2** (*talking about the time*) **vers**
**at about three o'clock** vers trois heures

**3** **to be about to do something** être **[6]** sur le point de faire quelque chose
**She's just about to leave.** Elle est sur le point de partir.

♪ **above** *preposition*

**1** **au-dessus de**
**the shelf above the TV** l'étagère au-dessus de la télévision

**2** **above all** surtout
**Above all, wait for me.** Surtout, attendez-moi!

♪ **abroad** *adverb*
**à l'étranger**
**They live abroad.** Ils vivent à l'étranger.
**to go abroad** aller ❷ **[7]** à l'étranger
**I'd like to go abroad next summer.** J'aimerais aller à l'étranger l'été prochain.

**abseiling** *noun*
la **descente en rappel** *fem*

**absent** *adjective*
**absent** *masc*, **absente** *fem*
**He was absent yesterday.** Il était absent hier.

**absolute** *adjective*
**complet** *masc*, **complète** *fem*
**The party was an absolute disaster.** La fête a été un désastre complet.

♪ **absolutely** *adverb*
**absolument**
**You're absolutely right.** Tu as tout à fait raison.
**Absolutely not!** Pas du tout!

**abuse** *noun* ▷ see **abuse** *verb*
1 (*of drugs, alcohol*) l'**abus** *masc*
2 (*violence*) le **mauvais traitement** *masc*
3 (*insulting words*) les **injures** *fem plural*

to **abuse** *verb* ▷ see **abuse** *noun*
to abuse somebody maltraiter [1] quelqu'un

to **accelerate** *verb*
**accélérer** [24]

**accelerator** *noun*
un **accélérateur** *masc*

**accent** *noun*
un **accent** *masc*
She has a French accent. Elle a l'accent français.

to **accept** *verb*
**accepter** [1]

**acceptable** *adjective*
**acceptable** *masc & fem*

**access** *noun* ▷ see **access** *verb*
un **accès** *masc*

to **access** *verb* ▷ see **access** *noun*
to access the file accéder [24] au fichier

**accessory** *noun*
un **accessoire** *masc*

**accident** *noun*
1 (*something bad*) un **accident** *masc*
a car accident un accident de voiture
a road accident un accident de la route
to have an accident avoir [5] un accident
2 (*chance*) un **hasard** *masc*
by accident par hasard
I found it by accident. Je l'ai trouvé par hasard.

**accident & emergency** *noun*
(*Medicine*) **les urgences** *fem plural*

**accidentally** *adverb*
1 (*without meaning to*) **accidentellement**
I accidentally sent this email. J'ai envoyé cet email accidentellement.
2 (*by chance*) **par hasard**
Amy accidentally discovered that ... Amy a découvert par hasard que ...

to **accommodate** *verb*
**recevoir** [66]
The centre accommodates sixty people. Le centre reçoit soixante personnes.

**accommodation** *noun*
le **logement** *masc*
We are looking for accommodation. Nous cherchons un logement.

to **accompany** *verb*
to accompany somebody accompagner [1] quelqu'un

**according to** *phrase*
**selon**
According to Laura they've split up. Selon Laura ils ne sont plus ensemble.

**accordion** *noun*
un **accordéon** *masc*

**account** *noun*
1 (*in a bank, shop, post office*) le **compte** *masc*
to open an account ouvrir un compte
I have twenty pounds in my account. J'ai vingt livres sur mon compte.
2 (*of an event*) le **compte rendu** *masc*
3 on account of something à cause de quelque chose
There are no buses on account of the strike. Il n'y a pas de bus à cause de la grève.
4 to take something into account tenir compte de quelque chose
You have to take travel expenses into account. Il faut tenir compte des frais de voyage.

**accountant** *noun*
le & la **comptable** *masc & fem*
She's an accountant. Elle est comptable.

**accuracy** *noun*
la **précision** *fem*

**accurate** *adjective*
**précis** *masc*, **précise** *fem*

to **accuse** *verb*
to accuse somebody of doing something accuser [1] quelqu'un d'avoir fait quelque chose
She accused me of stealing her CD. Elle m'a accusé d'avoir volé son CD.
He is accused of killing many people. On l'accuse d'avoir tué beaucoup de gens.

**accustomed to** *adjective*
to be accustomed to something être [6] habitué à quelque chose
She is accustomed to life in the city. Elle est habituée à la vie en ville.

**ace** *adjective* ▷ see **ace** *noun*
(*informal*) **super** *masc & fem invariable*
He's an ace drummer. C'est un super batteur.

**ace** *noun* ▷ see **ace** *adj*
un **as** *masc*
the ace of hearts l'as de cœur

to **ache** *verb*
My head aches. J'ai mal à la tête.
My feet are aching. J'ai mal aux pieds.

to **achieve** *verb*
**accomplir [2]**
**She's achieved great things.** Elle a accompli de grandes choses.

**achievement** *noun*
la **réussite** *fem*
**It's a great achievement.** C'est une grande réussite.

**acid** *noun*
un **acide** *masc*
- **acid rain** les pluies acides *fem pl*

**acne** *noun*
l'**acné** *fem*

**acorn** *noun*
le **gland** *masc*

**acrobat** *noun*
un & une **acrobate** *masc & fem*

♪ **across** *preposition*
1 (*to the other side of*)
**to walk across something** traverser **[1]** quelque chose
**We walked across the park.** On a traversé le parc.
2 (*on the other side of*) **de l'autre côté de**
**the house across the canal** la maison de l'autre côté du canal
3 (*opposite*) **across from** en face de
**She was sitting across from me.** Elle était assise en face de moi.

**act** *noun* ▷ see **act** *verb*
un **acte** *masc*

♪ to **act** *verb* ▷ see **act** *noun*
1 (*in plays, films*) **jouer [1]**
**He acts in the Bond films.** Il joue dans les films de James Bond.
2 (*to take action*) **agir [2]**
**They acted quickly.** Ils ont agi rapidement.

**acting** *noun*
le **jeu** *masc*
**She wants to go into acting.** Elle veut devenir actrice.
**The acting was terrible.** Les acteurs jouaient très mal.

**action** *noun*
une **action** *fem*
- **action replay** le replay

**active** *adjective*
**actif** *masc*, **active** *fem*

♪ **activity** *noun*
une **activité** *fem*
**They have lots of sports activities.** Ils ont beaucoup d'activités sportives.
- **activity holiday** les vacances sportives

**actor** *noun*
un **acteur** *masc*
**your favourite actor** ton acteur préféré

**actress** *noun*
une **actrice** *fem*
**my favourite actress** mon actrice préférée

**actual** *adjective*
1 (*exact*) **exact** *masc*, **exacte** *fem*
**I don't remember the actual words.** Je ne me rappelle pas les mots exacts.
2 (*real*) **the actual house where he was born** la maison même où il est né

♪ **actually** *adverb*
1 (*in fact*) **en fait**
**Actually, I've changed my mind.** En fait, j'ai changé d'avis.
2 (*really and truly*) **vraiment**
**Did she actually say that?** Est-ce qu'elle a vraiment dit ça?

**acute** *adjective*
1 (*intense*) **vif** *masc*, **vive** *fem*
**The pain was acute.** La douleur était vive.
2 (*Grammar*) **an acute accent** un accent aigu (*as in café*)

♪ **ad** *noun*
1 (*on television*) la **pub** *fem* (*informal*)
**That ad annoys me.** Cette pub m'agace.
2 (*in a newspaper*) une **annonce** *fem*
**to put an ad in the paper** mettre une annonce dans le journal
**the small ads** les petites annonces

**AD** *abbreviation*
**après Jésus-Christ**, **apr. J-C**
**in 400 AD** en quatre cents après Jésus-Christ

to **adapt** *verb*
1 **to adapt something for something** adapter **[1]** quelque chose pour quelque chose
**The book has been adapted for television.** Le livre a été adapté pour la télévision.
2 **to adapt to something** s'adapter **[1]** Ⓔ à quelque chose
**She has adapted well to the new school.** Elle s'est bien adaptée à la nouvelle école.

**adaptor** *noun*
un **adaptateur** *masc*

♪ to **add** *verb*
**ajouter [1]**
**Add three eggs.** Ajoutez trois œufs.
- **to add something up additionner [1] quelque chose**
**Add up the scores.** Additionnez les points.

**addict** *noun*
1 (*drug addict*) le **drogué** *masc*, la **droguée** *fem*
2 (*fan*) un & une **accro** *masc & fem*
She's a telly addict. C'est une accro de la télé.

**addicted** *adjective*
1 to be addicted to drugs avoir une dépendance à la drogue
She's addicted to heroine. Elle a une dépendance à l'héroïne.
2 (*to sweets, junk food*) to be addicted to something être [6] accro de quelque chose (*informal*)
I'm addicted to chocolate. Je suis accro de chocolat.

**addition** *noun*
(*adding up*) l'**addition** *fem*
in addition to something en plus de quelque chose

**additional** *adjective*
**supplémentaire** *masc & fem*

**additive** *noun*
un **additif** *masc*

**address** *noun*
une **adresse** *fem*
an email address une adresse électronique
What's your address? Quelle est ton adresse?
to change your address changer [52] d'adresse
• **address book** le carnet d'adresses

**adhesive** *adjective* ▷ see **adhesive** *noun*
**collant** *masc*, **collante** *fem*
some adhesive tape du ruban adhésif

**adhesive** *noun* ▷ see **adhesive** *adjective*
la **colle** *fem*

**adjective** *noun*
un **adjectif** *masc*

to **adjust** *verb*
1 to adjust something régler [24] quelque chose
to adjust the screen régler l'écran.
2 to adjust to something s'adapter [1] Ⓔ à quelque chose
He didn't adjust to the changes. Il ne s'est pas adapté aux changements.

**adjustable** *adjective*
**réglable** *masc & fem*

**administration** *noun*
une **administration** *fem*

**admiral** *noun*
un **amiral** *masc*

**admiration** *noun*
l'**admiration** *fem*

to **admire** *verb*
**admirer** [1]
I admire her a lot. Je l'admire beaucoup.

**admission** *noun*
une **entrée** *fem*
'No admission' 'Entrée interdite'
'Admission free' 'Entrée gratuite'

to **admit** *verb*
1 (*to confess*) **reconnaître** [27]
She admits that she lied. Elle reconnaît qu'elle a menti.
I admit I was wrong. Je reconnais que j'ai eu tort.
2 to be admitted to hospital être [6] hospitalisé
She was admitted to hospital. Elle a été hospitalisée.

**adolescence** *noun*
l'**adolescence** *fem*

**adolescent** *noun*
un **adolescent** *masc*, une **adolescente** *fem*

to **adopt** *verb*
**adopter** [1]

**adopted** *adjective*
**adoptif** *masc*, **adoptive** *fem*

**adoption** *noun*
une **adoption** *fem*

to **adore** *verb*
**adorer** [1]

**Adriatic Sea** *noun*
the Adriatic Sea la mer Adriatique

**adult** *adjective* ▷ see **adult** *noun*
**adulte** *masc & fem*
the adult population la population adulte

**adult** *noun* ▷ see **adult** *adj*
un & une **adulte** *masc & fem*

**advance** *noun* ▷ see **advance** *verb*
le **progrès** *masc*
advances in technology les progrès de la technologie

to **advance** *verb* ▷ see **advance** *noun*
**progresser** [1]
Technology has advanced a lot in ten years. La technologie a beaucoup progressé en dix ans.

**advanced** *adjective*
**avancé** *masc*, **avancée** *fem*

**advantage** *noun*
un **avantage** *masc*
There are several advantages. Il y a

plusieurs avantages.
**to take advantage of something** profiter [1] de quelque chose
**We took advantage of the good weather and got a tan.** Nous avons profité du beau temps et nous avons bronzé.

**Advent** *noun*
l'**Avent** *masc*

**adventure** *noun*
une **aventure** *fem*

**adventurous** *adjective*
**aventureux** *masc*, **aventureuse** *fem*

**adverb** *noun*
un **adverbe** *masc*

**advert** *noun* ▷ **advertisement**

♪ to **advertise** *verb*
1 **to advertise something in the newspaper** mettre [11] une annonce pour quelque chose dans le journal
**I saw a bike advertised in the paper.** J'ai vu une annonce pour un vélo dans le journal.
2 **to advertise a product** faire [10] de la publicité pour un produit

**advertisement** *noun*
1 *(on TV)* la **publicité** *fem*
2 *(in a newspaper)* une **annonce** *fem*
3 *(small ad)* une **petite annonce** *fem*

**advertising** *noun*
la **publicité** *fem*
**I'd like to work in advertising.** J'aimerais travailler dans la publicité.

♪ **advice** *noun*
les **conseils** *masc plural*
**a piece of advice** un conseil
**She gave us some good advice.** Elle nous a donné de bons conseils.
**to ask for advice about something** demander [1] des conseils à propos de quelque chose
**Ask for advice about the exam.** Demande des conseils à propos de l'examen.

♪ to **advise** *verb*
**to advise somebody to do something** conseiller [1] à quelqu'un de faire quelque chose
**I advised my brother to leave.** J'ai conseillé à mon frère de partir.
**I advised her not to wait.** Je lui ai conseillé de ne pas attendre.

**adviser** *noun*
le **conseiller** *masc*, la **conseillère** *fem*

**aerial** *noun*
une **antenne** *fem*

**aerobics** *noun*
l'**aérobic** *masc*
**to do aerobics** faire [10] de l'aérobic

**aeroplane** *noun*
un **avion** *masc*
**We went by aeroplane.** Nous avons voyagé en avion.

**aerosol** *noun*
**an aerosol can** une bombe aérosol

**affair** *noun*
1 *(event)* une **affaire** *fem*
**international affairs** les affaires internationales
2 *(romance)* une **liaison** *fem*

♪ to **affect** *verb*
**toucher** [1]
**the people most affected by the floods** les gens les plus touchés par les inondations
**The changes don't affect us yet.** Les changements ne nous concernent pas encore.

**affectionate** *adjective*
**affectueux** *masc*, **affectueuse** *fem*

♪ to **afford** *verb*
**to afford something** avoir [5] les moyens d'acheter quelque chose
**They can afford it.** Ils ont les moyens de l'acheter.
**They can't afford it.** Ils n'ont pas les moyens de l'acheter.
**to be able to afford to do something** avoir les moyens de faire quelque chose
**They can afford to go out a lot.** Ils ont les moyens de sortir beaucoup.

♪ **afraid** *adjective*
1 **to be afraid of something** avoir [5] peur de quelque chose
**She's afraid of dogs.** Elle a peur des chiens.
2 *(when giving bad news)* **I'm afraid ...** Je suis désolé mais ...
**I'm afraid there are no seats left.** Je suis désolée mais il ne reste plus de places.

**Africa** *noun*
l'**Afrique** *fem*

**African** *adjective* ▷ see **African** *noun*
**africain** *masc*, **africaine** *fem*

**African** *noun* ▷ see **African** *adj*
un **Africain** *masc*, une **Africaine** *fem*

♪ **after** *adverb, preposition, conjunction*
**après**
**after 10 o'clock** après dix heures
**after lunch** après le déjeuner
**after school** après l'école
**the day after tomorrow** après-demain ▸▸

the day after le lendemain
soon after peu après
**After I had tidied my room, I watched TV.** Après avoir rangé ma chambre, j'ai regardé la télévision.
**After I've done my homework, I'll call you.** Quand j'aurai fait mes devoirs, je t'appellerai.
**The dog ran after us.** Le chien nous a couru après.

**after all** *adverb*
**après tout**
**After all, she's only six.** Elle n'a que six ans après tout.

**afternoon** *noun*
un & une **après-midi** *invariable masc & fem*
**this afternoon** cet après-midi
**every afternoon** tous les après-midi
**at four o'clock in the afternoon** à quatre heures de l'après-midi
**on Saturday afternoon** samedi après-midi
**on Saturday afternoons** le samedi après-midi

**afters** *noun*
le **dessert** *masc*

**after-shave** *noun*
un **après-rasage** *masc*

**afterwards** *adverb*
**après**
**shortly afterwards** peu de temps après

**again** *adverb*
1 (*one more time*) **encore une fois**
**Try again.** Essaie encore une fois.
**I've forgotten it again.** Je l'ai encore oublié.
**Oh no, not again!** Ah non, pas encore!
2 (*once more*) **de nouveau**
**She's ill again.** Elle est de nouveau malade.
3 (*with verbs*) **to start again** recommencer
**I'm going to do it again.** Je vais le refaire.
**I phoned her again yesterday.** Je lui ai retéléphoné hier.
**I've told him again and again.** Je lui ai dit et redit.

**against** *preposition*
**contre**
**the fight against racism** la lutte contre le racisme
**I'm against the idea.** Je suis contre l'idée.
**They're playing against Scotland.** Ils jouent contre l'Écosse.

**age** *noun*
1 un **âge** *masc*
**at the age of fifteen** à l'âge de quinze ans
**She's the same age as me.** Elle a le même âge que moi.
**to be under age** être [6] mineur
**Those boys are under age.** Ces garçons sont mineurs.
2 **... for ages** Ça fait une éternité que ...
**I haven't seen Johnny for ages.** Ça fait une éternité que je n'ai pas vu Johnny.
**We've lived here for ages.** Ça fait une éternité que nous habitons ici.

**aged** *adjective*
**âgé de** *masc*, **âgée de** *fem*
**a girl aged eleven** une fille âgée de onze ans

**aggressive** *adjective*
**agressif** *masc*, **agressive** *fem*

**ago** *adverb*
**an hour ago** il y a une heure
**three days ago** il y a trois jours
**five years ago** il y a cinq ans
**a long time ago** il y a longtemps
**How long ago was it?** C'était il y a combien de temps?

to **agree** *verb*
1 **to agree with somebody** être [6] d'accord avec quelqu'un
**I agree with Sophie.** Je suis d'accord avec Sophie.
**I really don't agree.** Je ne suis pas du tout d'accord.
2 **to agree to do something** accepter [1] de faire quelque chose
**Steve has agreed to help us.** Steve a accepté de nous aider.

**agreement** *noun*
un **accord** *masc*
**an agreement between France and Britain** un accord entre la France et la Grande-Bretagne

**agricultural** *adjective*
**agricole** *masc & fem*

**agriculture** *noun*
l'**agriculture** *fem*

**ahead** *adverb*
1 **straight ahead** tout droit
2 **Go straight ahead until you get to the crossroads.** Allez tout droit jusqu'au carrefour.
3 **Go ahead!** (*polite form*) Allez-y!, (*familiar form*) Vas-y!
**Go ahead, try it. It's good.** Vas-y, goûte! C'est bon.

**aid** *noun*
une **aide** *fem*
**to give aid to developing countries** donner de l'aide aux pays en voie de développement

a concert in aid of the homeless un concert au profit des sans-abri

**AIDS** *noun*
le **sida** *masc* (*short for syndrome immunodéficitaire acquis*)
to have AIDS avoir le sida

**aim** *noun* ▷ see **aim** *verb*
un **objectif** *masc*
to achieve our aims atteindre [60] nos objectifs
Their aim is to control pollution. Leur objectif est de contrôler la pollution.

to **aim** *verb* ▷ see **aim** *noun*
1 to aim to do something avoir [5] l'intention de faire quelque chose
We're aiming to finish it today. Nous avons l'intention de le finir aujourd'hui.
2 to aim a gun at somebody braquer [1] un revolver sur quelqu'un
She aimed the pistol at him. Elle a braqué le revolver sur lui.
an advertising campaign aimed at young people une campagne publicitaire qui vise les jeunes

♪ **air** *noun*
1 l'**air** *masc*
in the open air en plein air
We're going to get some fresh air. Nous sortons prendre l'air.
2 by air en avion
We came by air. Nous sommes venus en avion.
- **airbag** un airbag
- **air-conditioned** climatisé *masc*, climatisée *fem*
- **air-conditioning** la climatisation

**air force** *noun*
l'**armée de l'air** *fem*
My brother's in the air force. Mon frère est dans l'armée de l'air.

**air hostess** *noun*
une **hôtesse de l'air**
She's an air hostess. Elle est hôtesse de l'air.

**airline** *noun*
la **compagnie aérienne**

**airmail** *noun*
by airmail par avion

♪ **airport** *noun*
un **aéroport** *masc*
to pick somebody up at the airport aller Ⓔ [7] chercher quelqu'un à l'aéroport

**alarm** *noun*
une **alarme** *fem*
to set off the alarm déclencher [1] l'alarme ▷ **burglar alarm, fire alarm**
- **alarm clock** le réveil

**album** *noun*
un **album** *masc*
a photo album un album photos

**alcohol** *noun*
l'**alcool** *masc*
There's no alcohol in it. Il n'y a pas d'alcool dedans.
- **alcohol abuse** l'abus d'alcool *masc*

**alcoholic** *adjective* ▷ see **alcoholic** *noun*
**alcoolisé** *masc*, **alcoolisée** *fem*

**alcoholic** *noun* ▷ see **alcoholic** *adj*
un & une **alcoolique** *masc & fem*
She's an alcoholic. C'est une alcoolique.
- **alcoholic drink** la boisson alcoolisée

**alert** *adjective*
**vif** *masc*, **vive** *fem*

**A levels** *plural noun*
le **baccalauréat** *masc*, le **bac** *masc* (*informal*)
(*Students take 'le bac' at the same age as A levels are taken in Britain. You can explain A levels briefly as follows: Les A levels sont répartis en deux niveaux, AS et A2. On passe les examens AS au bout d'une année de préparation, généralement dans quatre ou cinq matières. On passe les examens A2 l'année suivante, dans un plus petit nombre de matières, en choisissant parmi celles qui ont déjà fait l'objet d'un examen AS. La meilleure note que l'on peut obtenir est A et la note la plus basse est N. Les A levels permettent de s'inscrire à l'université.*)
▷ **baccalauréat**

**Algeria** *noun*
l'**Algérie** *fem*

**alien** *noun*
un & une **extra-terrestre** *masc & fem*
Bart is kidnapped by aliens. Bart est enlevé par des extra-terrestres.

**alike** *adjective*
(*in behaviour, attitudes*) **pareil** *masc*, **pareille** *fem*
to look alike se ressembler Ⓔ [1]
The brothers look very alike. Les frères se ressemblent beaucoup.

♪ **alive** *adjective*
**vivant** *masc*, **vivante** *fem*
She was still alive. Elle était encore vivante.

♪ **all** *adjective, adverb, pronoun*
1 (*with masc singular nouns*) **tout**
all my money tout mon argent
He complains all the time. Il se plaint ▸▸

English–French

tout le temps.
**We're doing all the work!** C'est nous qui faisons tout le travail!
2 (*with fem singular nouns*) **toute**
**all day** toute la journée
**I was at home all week.** J'ai passé toute la semaine à la maison.
3 (*with masc plural nouns*) **tous**
**all the boys** tous les garçons
**They all got your text.** Ils ont tous reçu ton texto.
**All of us decided to leave.** Nous avons tous décidé de partir.
4 (*with fem plural nouns*) **toutes**
**all the girls** toutes les filles
**all my holidays** toutes mes vacances
5 (*everything*) **tout**
**Is that all?** C'est tout?
**I spent it all.** J'ai tout dépensé.
6 (*completely*) **tout** *masc*, **toute** *fem*
**to be all wet** être [6] tout mouillé
7 (*in scores*) **partout**
**They're two all.** Il y a deux partout.
- **all along** depuis le début
- **all over** (*everywhere*) partout

**allergic** *adjective*
**allergique** *masc & fem*
**to be allergic to something** être [6] allergique à quelque chose

**allergy** *noun*
une **allergie** *fem*
**to have an allergy to something** être [6] allergique à quelque chose
**I have an allergy to cats.** Je suis allergique aux chats.

**alligator** *noun*
un **alligator** *masc*

to **allow** *verb*
1 **to allow somebody to do something** permettre [11] à quelqu'un de faire quelque chose
**The teacher allows them to go out.** Le professeur leur permet de sortir.
2 **to be allowed to do something** avoir [5] le droit de faire quelque chose
**I'm allowed to go out during the week.** J'ai le droit de sortir en semaine.
**It's not allowed.** C'est interdit.

**all right** *adverb*
1 (*yes*) **d'accord**
**'Come round to my house at six.' — 'All right.'** 'Passe chez moi à six heures.' - 'D'accord.'
2 (*fine, well*) **bien**
**Is everything all right?** Est-ce que tout va bien?
**She's all right now.** Elle va bien maintenant.
**Are you all right?** Ça va?
3 (*not bad*) **pas mal**
**The meal was all right.** Le repas n'était pas mal.
4 (*allowable*) **Is it all right to ...** Est-ce qu'on peut ...?
**Is it all right to leave the door open?** Est-ce qu'on peut laisser la porte ouverte?

**almond** *noun*
une **amande** *fem*

**almost** *adverb*
**presque**
**almost every day** presque tous les jours
**almost everybody** presque tout le monde
**She's almost five.** Elle a presque cinq ans.

**alone** *adjective, adverb*
1 (*on your own*) **seul** *masc*, **seule** *fem*
**I'm all alone.** Je suis tout seul (*boy speaking*), Je suis toute seule (*girl speaking*).
**She hates travelling alone.** Elle déteste voyager seule.
2 (*in peace*) **to leave somebody alone** laisser [1] quelqu'un tranquille
**She wants to be left alone.** Elle veut qu'on la laisse tranquille.
3 (*undisturbed*) **to leave something alone** ne pas toucher [1] à quelque chose
**Leave those CDs alone!** Ne touche pas à ces CD!

**along** *preposition*
1 (*showing where*) **le long de**
**There are trees along the road.** Il y a des arbres tout le long de la route.
2 (*with to come, to go*) **avec quelqu'un**
**Would you like to come along?** Est-ce que tu veux venir avec nous?

**aloud** *adverb*
**à haute voix**
**He read the poem aloud.** Il a lu le poème à haute voix.

**alphabet** *noun*
l'**alphabet** *masc*

**alphabetical** *adjective*
**alphabétique** *masc & fem*
**in alphabetical order** par ordre alphabétique

**Alps** *plural noun*
**the Alps** les Alpes *fem plural*

**already** *adverb*
**déjà**
**They've already left.** Ils sont déjà partis.
**It's six o'clock already!** Il est déjà six heures!

**alright** *adverb* ▷ **all right**

**Alsatian** *noun*
le **berger allemand** (*dog*)

♪ **also** *adverb*
1 (*as well*) **aussi**
I've also invited Karen. J'ai aussi invité Karen.
She also plays the piano. Elle joue aussi du piano.
2 (*in addition*) **en plus**
It's too cold. Also, I've got homework to do. Il fait trop froid. En plus, j'ai des devoirs à faire.

to **alter** *verb*
**changer [52]**

**alternative** *adjective*
▷ see **alternative** *noun*
**autre**
an alternative solution une autre solution

**alternative** *noun* ▷ see **alternative** *adj*
la **possibilité** *fem*
There are several alternatives. Il y a plusieurs possibilités.

**alternative medicine** *noun*
la **médecine douce**

**although** *conjunction*
**bien que**
Although she's ill, she wants to go to school. Bien qu'elle soit malade, elle veut aller en cours.

**altitude** *noun*
l'**altitude** *fem*

**altogether** *adverb*
**en tout**
I've spent thirty pounds altogether. J'ai dépensé trente livres en tout.
Altogether, there were five of us. Nous étions cinq en tout.

**aluminium** *noun*
l'**aluminium** *masc*

♪ **always** *adverb*
**toujours**
I always phone her on Saturdays. Je lui téléphone toujours le samedi.

**am** *verb* ▷ **be**

♪ **a.m.** *adverb*
**du matin**
at eight a.m. à huit heures du matin ▷ **p.m.**

**amateur** *noun*
un **amateur** *masc*

to **amaze** *verb*
**surprendre [64]**
What amazes me is how easy it is. Ce qui me surprend, c'est que c'est si facile.

**amazed** *adjective*
**stupéfait** *masc*, **stupéfaite** *fem*
He was amazed to see her. Il était stupéfait de la voir.
I'm amazed that ... Ça m'étonne que ...
I'm amazed that you still speak to him. Ça m'étonne que tu lui parles encore.

**amazement** *noun*
la **stupéfaction** *fem*
He looked at us in amazement. Il nous a regardés avec stupéfaction.

**amazing** *adjective*
1 (*surprising*) **extraordinaire**
She has an amazing number of friends. Elle a un nombre extraordinaire d'amis.
He told me an amazing story. Il m'a raconté une histoire extraordinaire.
2 (*very good*) **fantastique**
Your dress is amazing! Ta robe est fantastique!
She's got an amazing tan. Elle a un bronzage fantastique.

**ambassador** *noun*
un **ambassadeur** *masc*, une **ambassadrice** *fem*

**ambition** *noun*
une **ambition** *fem*

**ambitious** *adjective*
**ambitieux** *masc*, **ambitieuse** *fem*

**ambulance** *noun*
une **ambulance** *fem*
• **ambulance driver** un ambulancier, une ambulancière

**amenities** *plural noun*
les **équipements** *masc plural*

**America** *noun*
l'**Amérique** *fem*
in America en Amérique
to America en Amérique

**WORD TIP** Countries and regions in French take *le*, *la* or *les*.

**American** *adjective* ▷ see **American** *noun*
**américain** *masc*, **américaine** *fem*

**WORD TIP** Adjectives never have capitals in French, even for nationality or regional origin.

**American** *noun* ▷ see **American** *adj*
un **Américain** *masc*, une **Américaine** *fem*
the Americans les Américains



a b c d e f g h i j k l m n o p q r s t u v w x y z

**ammunition** *noun*
la **munition** *fem*

**among**, **amongst** *preposition*
1 (*with*) **parmi**
I found it amongst my books. Je l'ai trouvé parmi mes livres.
2 (*between*) **entre**
You can decide amongst yourselves. Vous pouvez décider entre vous.

**amount** *noun*
1 (*of food, effort, time*) la **quantité** *fem*
an enormous amount of time énormément de temps
an enormous amount of bread une énorme quantité de pain
2 (*of money*) la **somme** *fem*
a large amount of money une grosse somme d'argent

**amp** *noun*
1 (*in electricity*) une **ampère** *masc*
2 (*amplifier*) un **ampli** *masc* (*informal*)

**amplifier** *noun*
un **amplificateur** *masc*

to **amuse** *verb*
**amuser [1]**
The teacher is not amused. La prof ne trouve pas ça drôle.

**amusement arcade** *noun*
la **salle de jeux électroniques** *fem*

**amusing** *adjective*
**amusant** *masc*, **amusante** *fem*

**an** *determiner*
**un** (*masculine*), **une** (*feminine*)
▷ **a**

to **analyse** *verb*
**analyser [1]**

**analysis** *noun*
une **analyse** *fem*

**ancestor** *noun*
un & une **ancêtre** *masc & fem*

**anchor** *noun*
une **ancre** *fem*

**ancient** *adjective*
1 (*historic*) **ancien** *masc*, **ancienne** *fem*
an ancient abbey une abbaye ancienne
2 (*very old*) **très vieux** *masc*, **très vieille** *fem*
an ancient pair of jeans un très vieux jean
3 (*Greece, Rome*) **antique**
ancient Greece la Grèce antique

♂ **and** *conjunction*
1 **et**
Ben and Amy Ben et Amy
Rosie and me Rosie et moi
your shoes and socks tes chaussures et tes chaussettes
2 louder and louder de plus en plus fort
faster and faster de plus en plus rapide

**angel** *noun*
un **ange** *masc*

**anger** *noun*
la **colère** *fem*

**angle** *noun*
un **angle** *masc*

♂ **angry** *adjective*
to be angry être **[6]** en colère
The teacher was angry. La prof était en colère.
to be angry with somebody être **[6]** en colère contre quelqu'un
I'm not angry with you. Je ne suis pas en colère contre toi.
to get angry se fâcher ⓔ **[1]**
He gets angry easily. Il se fâche facilement.

**animal** *noun*
un **animal** *masc* (*pl* les **animaux**)

**ankle** *noun*
la **cheville** *fem*
to break your ankle se casser ⓔ **[1]** la cheville

**anniversary** *noun*
un **anniversaire** *masc*
a wedding anniversary un anniversaire de mariage

to **announce** *verb*
**annoncer [61]**
to announce the winner annoncer le gagnant

**announcement** *noun*
une **annonce** *fem*
to make an announcement faire **[10]** une annonce

to **annoy** *verb*
**agacer [61]**
She really annoys me! Vraiment elle m'agace!

**annoyed** *adjective*
**fâché** *masc*, **fâchée** *fem*
to get annoyed se fâcher ⓔ **[1]**
I got annoyed. Je me suis fâché.
He's very annoyed with us! Il est très fâché contre nous!

**annoying** *adjective*
**agaçant** *masc*, **agaçante** *fem*
I find that very annoying. Je trouve ça très agaçant.

**annual** *adjective*
**annuel** *masc*, **annuelle** *fem*

**anorak** *noun*
un **anorak** *masc*

**anorexia** *noun*
l'**anorexie** *fem*

ℰ **another** *adjective*
1 (*different*) **un autre** *masc*, **une autre** *fem*
**Would you like another ice cream?** Voulez-vous une autre glace?
2 (*more of the same*) **encore**
**another two years** encore deux ans
**She had another coffee.** Elle a pris un autre café.
**We need another three chairs.** Il nous faut encore trois chaises.

ℰ **answer** *noun* ▷ see **answer** *verb*
1 (*to a question*) la **réponse** *fem*
**the right answer** la bonne réponse
**the wrong answer** la mauvaise réponse
2 (*to a problem*) la **solution** *fem*
**That's not the answer!** Ce n'est pas une solution!

ℰ to **answer** *verb* ▷ see **answer** *noun*
1 **répondre [3]**
**He's afraid to answer.** Il a peur de répondre.
**Answer the question.** Réponds à la question.
**You didn't answer my email.** Tu n'as pas répondu à mon mail.
**to answer somebody** répondre à quelqu'un
**She answered me immediately.** Elle m'a tout de suite répondu.

**answering machine** *noun*
le **répondeur** *masc*
**to leave a message on the answering machine** laisser [1] un message sur le répondeur

**ant** *noun*
la **fourmi** *fem*

**Antarctic** *noun*
l'**Antarctique** *masc*
**in the Antarctic** dans l'Antarctique

**antibiotic** *noun*
un **antibiotique** *masc*
**to be on antibiotics** être [6] sous antibiotiques

**antique** *adjective* ▷ see **antique** *noun*
**ancien** *masc*, **ancienne** *fem*
**an antique table** une table ancienne

**antique** *noun* ▷ see **antique** *adj*
1 (*piece of furniture*) le **meuble ancien**
2 **antiques** (*for collectors*) les antiquités *fem plural*

**antiseptic** *noun*
un **antiseptique** *masc*

**anxious** *adjective*
**inquiet** *masc*, **inquiète** *fem*
**to get anxious** s'inquiéter **[24]**

ℰ **any** *adjective, adverb, pronoun*
1 (*before a masc singular noun*) **du**
**Is there any butter?** Y a-t-il du beurre?
**Is there any cake left?** Est-ce qu'il reste du gâteau?
2 (*before a fem singular noun*) **de la**
**Is there any flour?** Y a-t-il de la farine?
3 (*before singular nouns beginning with **a, e, i, o, u** or silent **h***) **de l'**
**Do you have any money?** Avez-vous de l'argent?
**Is there any oil?** Y a-t-il de l'huile?
4 (*before plural nouns*) **des**
**Are there any eggs?** Y a-t-il des œufs?
**Do you have any stamps?** Est-ce que tu as des timbres?
5 (*saying no, not*) **de**
**There isn't any flour.** Il n'y a pas de farine.
**There aren't any eggs.** Il n'y a pas d'œufs.
6 (*when **any** is by itself without a noun*) **en**
**I don't want any.** Je n'en veux pas.
**Don't you have any?** Tu n'en as pas?
7 **not ... any more** ne ... plus
**There isn't any more butter.** Il n'y a plus de beurre.
**She doesn't eat meat any more.** Elle ne mange plus de viande.

ℰ **anybody**, **anyone** *pronoun*
1 (*in questions and after if*) **quelqu'un**
**Is anybody in?** Est-ce qu'il y a quelqu'un?
**If anybody wants water, it's ...** Si quelqu'un veut de l'eau, elle ...
**Does anybody want some tea?** Qui veut du thé?
2 **not ... anybody** ne ... personne
**He doesn't talk to anybody.** Il ne parle à personne.
**There isn't anybody in the office.** Il n'y a personne dans le bureau.
3 (*anybody at all*) **n'importe qui**
**I'm not giving it to anybody.** Je ne vais pas le donner à n'importe qui.

**anyhow** *adverb* ▷ **anyway**

**anyone** *pronoun* ▷ **anybody**

**anything** *pronoun*

1 *(in questions and after if)* **quelque chose**
**Is there anything I can do to help?** Est-ce que je peux faire quelque chose pour t'aider?
**If you find out anything, tell me.** Si tu découvres quelque chose, dis-le-moi.

2 **not ... anything** ne ... rien
**There isn't anything on the table.** Il n'y a rien sur la table.
**I can't understand anything!** Je ne comprends rien!
**She hasn't said anything to me.** Elle ne m'a rien dit.

3 *(anything at all)* **n'importe quoi**
**Anything could happen.** Il pourrait arriver n'importe quoi.

**anyway**, **anyhow** *adverb*
**de toute façon**
**Anyway, I'll ring you.** De toute façon, je t'appellerai.

**anywhere** *adverb*

1 *(in questions)* **quelque part**
**Have you seen my keys anywhere?** Est-ce que tu as vu mes clés quelque part?
**Are you going anywhere tomorrow?** Est-ce que tu vas quelque part demain?

2 **not ... anywhere** ne ... nulle part
**I can't find my keys anywhere.** Je ne trouve mes clés nulle part .
**You're not going anywhere tonight!** Tu ne sors pas ce soir!

3 *(anywhere at all)* **n'importe où**
**Put your cases down anywhere.** Pose tes valises n'importe où.

**apart** *adjective, adverb*

1 *(separate)* **séparé** *masc*, **séparée** *fem*
**We don't like being apart.** Nous n'aimons pas être séparés.

2 *(indicating distance)* **to be two metres apart** être **[6]** à deux mètres l'un de l'autre

3 **apart from** à part, sauf
**Apart from Jack, everybody was there.** À part Jack, tout le monde était là.
**I eat everything apart from shellfish.** Je mange de tout sauf des fruits de mer.

**apartment** *noun*
un **appartement** *masc*
**an apartment on the fourth floor** un appartement au quatrième étage
• **apartment block** un immeuble *masc*

**ape** *noun*
le **(grand) singe** *masc*

to **apologize** *verb*
**s'excuser [1]** Ⓔ
**I apologize.** Je m'excuse.
**to apologize for something** s'excuser de quelque chose
**He apologizes for his behaviour.** Il s'excuse de son comportement.
**to apologize to someone** s'excuser auprès de quelqu'un
**She apologized to Peter.** Elle s'est excusée auprès de Peter.

**apology** *noun*
**an apology** des excuses *fem plural*
**I owe you an apology.** Je te dois des excuses.

**apostrophe** *noun*
une **apostrophe** *fem*

**apparently** *adverb*
**apparemment**
**Apparently they know each other.** Apparemment, ils se connaissent.

**appeal** *noun* ▷ **see appeal** *verb*
un **appel** *masc*
**an appeal for help** un appel à l'aide

to **appeal** *verb* ▷ **see appeal** *noun*

1 **to appeal for something** lancer **[61]** un appel pour quelque chose
**They appealed for a million euros.** Ils ont lancé un appel pour un million d'euros.

2 *(to interest)* **to appeal to somebody** tenter **[1]** quelqu'un
**Horror films don't appeal to me.** Les films d'épouvante ne me tentent pas.

to **appear** *verb*

1 *(to turn up)* **apparaître** Ⓔ **[57]**
**Sophie appeared at the door.** Sophie est apparue à la porte.

2 **to appear on TV** passer Ⓔ **[1]** à la télévision
**the day I appeared on TV** le jour où je suis passé à la télévision

3 *(to seem)* **paraître [57]**
**It appears that somebody has stolen the key.** Il paraît que quelqu'un a volé la clé.

**appendicitis** *noun*
l'**appendicite** *fem*

**appendix** *noun*
un **appendice** *masc*
**I've had my appendix out.** Je me suis fait opérer de l'appendicite.

**appetite** *noun*
l'**appétit** *masc*

to **applaud** *verb*
**applaudir [2]**

**applause** *noun*
les **applaudissements** *masc plural*

♪**apple** *noun*
la **pomme** *fem*
- **apple juice** le jus de pomme
- **apple tart** la tarte aux pommes
- **apple tree** le pommier

**applicant** *noun*
le **candidat** *masc*, la **candidate** *fem*

**application** *noun*
(*for a job*) **la candidature** *fem*
- **application form** le dossier de candidature

to **apply** *verb*
1 **to apply for something** poser [1] sa candidature à quelque chose
**He has applied for the job.** Il a posé sa candidature au poste.
**I'm applying for that sailing course.** Je fais une demande d'inscription à ce cours de voile.
2 **to apply to somebody** s'appliquer Ⓔ [1] à quelqu'un
**The rule doesn't apply to students.** La règle ne s'applique pas aux élèves.

**appointment** *noun*
le **rendez-vous** *masc*
**to make an appointment at the dentist's** prendre rendez-vous chez le dentiste

**apprentice** *noun*
un **apprenti** *masc*, une **apprentie** *fem*

**apprenticeship** *noun*
un **apprentissage** *masc*

to **approach** *verb*
1 **to approach something** s'approcher [1] Ⓔ de quelque chose
**We are approaching the stadium.** Nous nous approchons du stade.
2 **to approach somebody** s'approcher [1] Ⓔ de quelqu'un
**Do not approach him.** Ne t'approche pas de lui.

**approval** *noun*
l'**approbation** *fem*

to **approve** *verb*
**to approve of somebody** apprécier [1] quelqu'un
**They don't approve of her boyfriend.** Ils n'apprécient pas son copain.

**apricot** *noun*
un **abricot** *masc*
- **apricot jam** la confiture d'abricots

♪**April** *noun*
**avril** *masc*
**in April** en avril
- **April Fool** le poisson d'avril
- **April Fool's Day** le premier avril

**WORD TIP** Months of the year and days of the week start with small letters in French.

**apron** *noun*
le **tablier** *masc*

**aquarium** *noun*
un **aquarium** *masc*

**Aquarius** *noun*
**Verseau** *masc*
**Lucy's Aquarius.** Lucy est Verseau.

**WORD TIP** Signs of the zodiac do not take an article: *un* or *une*.

**Arab** *adjective* ▷ **see Arab** *noun*
**arabe** *masc & fem*
**the Arab countries** les pays arabes

**Arab** *noun* ▷ **see Arab** *adj*
un & une **Arabe** *masc & fem*

**Arabic** *noun*
(*the language*) l'**arabe** *masc*

**arch** *noun*
une **arche** *fem*

**archaeologist** *noun*
un & une **archéologue** *masc & fem*

**archaeology** *noun*
l'**archéologie** *fem*

**archbishop** *noun*
un **archevêque** *masc*

**architect** *noun*
un & une **architecte** *masc & fem*

**architecture** *noun*
l'**architecture** *fem*

**Arctic** *noun*
l'**Arctique** *masc*
**in the Arctic** dans l'Arctique

**are** *verb* ▷ **be**

**area** *noun*
1 (*part of a town*) le **quartier** *masc*
**a nice area** un beau quartier
**a rough area** un quartier mal fréquenté
2 (*region*) la **région** *fem*
**in the Leeds area** dans la région de Leeds

to **argue** *verb*
1 **se disputer** Ⓔ [1]
**We never argue.** Nous ne nous disputons jamais.
2 **to argue about something** discuter [1] de quelque chose ⏩

**They're arguing about the result.** Ils sont en train de discuter du résultat.

**argument** *noun*
la **dispute** *fem*
**to have an argument** se disputer Ⓔ [1]
**Julie and Emma had an argument.** Julie et Emma se sont disputées.

**Aries** *noun*
**Bélier** *masc*
**Rachel's Aries.** Rachel est Bélier.

**WORD TIP** Signs of the zodiac do not take an article: *un* or *une*.

**arithmetic** *noun*
l'**arithmétique** *fem*

**arm** *noun*
le **bras** *masc*
**to fold your arms** croiser [1] les bras
**They went off arm in arm.** Ils sont partis bras dessus bras dessous.
**to break your arm** se casser Ⓔ [1] le bras
**She's broken her arm.** Elle s'est cassé le bras.

**armchair** *noun*
le **fauteuil** *masc*

**armed** *adjective*
**armé** *masc*, **armée** *fem*

**armpit** *noun*
une **aisselle** *fem*

**army** *noun*
une **armée** *fem*
**to join the army** s'engager Ⓔ [1] dans l'armée
**He joined the army.** Il s'est engagé dans l'armée.

**around** *adverb, preposition*
1 (*with time*) **vers**
**at around midnight** vers minuit
**We'll arrive around ten.** On va arriver vers dix heures.
2 (*with ages, amounts*) **environ**
**She's around fifteen.** Elle a environ quinze ans.
**We need around six kilos.** Il nous faut environ six kilos.
**It costs around ten euros.** Ça coûte environ dix euros.
3 (*surrounding*) **autour de**
**the countryside around Edinburgh** la campagne autour d'Édimbourg
4 (*near*) **Is Phil around?** Est-ce que Phil est là?
**Is there a post office around here?** Est-ce qu'il y a un bureau de poste près d'ici?
**There was nobody around.** Il n'y avait personne.
5 (*wrapped around*) **autour de**
**She had a scarf around her neck.** Elle avait une écharpe autour du cou.

to **arrange** *verb*
**to arrange to do something** prévoir [65] de faire quelque chose
**We've arranged to see a film on Saturday.** Nous avons prévu de voir un film samedi.
**I haven't arranged anything yet.** Je n'ai encore rien prévu.

**arrangement** *noun*
**arrangements** les préparatifs *masc plural*
**the arrangements for the trip** les préparatifs pour le voyage
**to make arrangements to do something** s'arranger Ⓔ [52] pour faire quelque chose

**arrest** *noun* ▷ see **arrest** *verb*
**to be under arrest** être [6] en état d'arrestation

to **arrest** *verb* ▷ see **arrest** *noun*
**arrêter** [1]
**They're going to arrest her.** Ils vont l'arrêter.

**arrival** *noun*
l'**arrivée** *fem*

to **arrive** *verb*
**arriver** Ⓔ [1]
**They arrive in Poitiers at 3 p.m.** Ils arrivent à Poitiers à quinze heures.

**arrow** *noun*
la **flèche** *fem*

**art** *noun*
1 **l'art** *masc*
**modern art** l'art moderne
2 (*school subject*) le **dessin** *masc*

**artery** *noun*
une **artère** *fem*

**art gallery** *noun*
(*public*) le **musée des beaux arts** *masc*

**artichoke** *noun*
un **artichaut** *masc*

**article** *noun*
1 (*in a newspaper, magazine*) un **article** *masc*
**a magazine article** un article de magazine
2 (*Grammar*) un **article** *masc*
**the definite article** l'article défini (*in French these are le, la, les*)
**the indefinite article** l'article indéfini (*in French these are un, une, des*)

**artificial** *adjective*
**artificiel** *masc*, **artificielle** *fem masc pl*

**artist** *noun*
un & une **artiste** *masc & fem*
**She's an artist.** C'est une artiste.

**artistic** *adjective*
**artistique** *masc & fem*

**art school** *noun*
une **école de beaux arts**

♪ **as** *adverb, conjunction, preposition*
1 (*like*) **comme**
**as you know** comme vous le savez
**as I told you** comme je t'avais dit
**as usual** comme d'habitude
2 (*because*) **puisque**
**As there were no trains, we took the bus.** Puisqu'il n'y avait pas de trains, nous avons pris le bus.
3 **as ... as** aussi ... que
**He's as tall as his brother.** Il est aussi grand que son frère.
4 **as much ... as** autant de ... que
**You have as much time as I do.** Tu as autant de temps que moi.
5 **as many ... as** autant de ... que
**We have as many problems as he does.** Nous avons autant de problèmes que lui.
6 **as long as** pourvu que
**We'll go tomorrow, as long as it's a nice day.** On va y aller demain, pourvu qu'il fasse beau.
7 **as soon as possible** dès que possible
8 **to work as something** travailler [1] comme quelque chose
**He works as a taxi driver.** Il travaille comme chauffeur de taxi.

**ashes** *plural noun*
les **cendres** *fem plural*

**ashamed** *adjective*
**to be ashamed** avoir [5] honte
**I was so ashamed!** J'avais tellement honte!

**ashtray** *noun*
le **cendrier** *masc*

**Asia** *noun*
l'**Asie** *fem*

**Asian** *adjective* ▷ see **Asian** *noun*
1 (*from Asia generally*) **asiatique** *masc & fem*
2 (*from India*) **indien** *masc*, **indienne** *fem*
3 (*from Pakistan*) **pakistanais** *masc*, **pakistanaise** *fem*

**Asian** *noun* ▷ see **Asian** *adj*
1 (*from the Far East*) un & une **Asiatique** *masc & fem*
2 (*from India*) un **Indien** *masc*, une **Indienne** *fem*
3 (*from Pakistan*) un **Pakistanais** *masc*, une **Pakistanaise** *fem*

♪ **to ask** *verb*
1 **demander** [1]
**You can ask at reception.** Tu peux demander à l'accueil.
**to ask somebody something** demander quelque chose à quelqu'un
**I'll ask him where he lives.** Je lui demanderai où il habite.
**to ask for something** demander quelque chose
**I asked for three coffees.** J'ai demandé trois cafés.
**to ask somebody for something** demander quelque chose à quelqu'un
**Did you ask her for the DVD?** Est-ce que tu lui as demandé le DVD?
**to ask somebody to do something** demander à quelqu'un de faire quelque chose
**Ask Jake to give you a hand.** Demande à Jake de te donner un coup de main.
2 **to ask somebody a question** poser [1] une question à quelqu'un
**I asked you a question!** Je t'ai posé une question!
3 (*to invite*) **inviter** [1]
**They've asked us to a party at their house.** Ils nous ont invités à une fête chez eux.
**Adam's asked Julie out on Friday.** Adam a invité Julie à sortir avec lui vendredi.

♪ **asleep** *adjective*
**to be asleep** dormir [37]
**The baby's asleep.** Le bébé dort.
**to fall asleep** s'endormir ❷ [37]
**She's fallen asleep!** Elle s'est endormie!

**asparagus** *noun*
une **asperge** *fem*

**aspirin** *noun*
l'**aspirine** *fem*

**assembly** *noun*
(*at school*) le **rassemblement** *masc*

**assignment** *noun*
(*at school*) le **devoir** *masc*
**I finished my assignment on Paris.** J'ai fini mon devoir sur Paris.

**assistance** *noun*
l'**aide** *fem*

**assistant** *noun*
1 un **assistant** *masc*, une **assistante** *fem*
2 **a shop assistant** un vendeur, une vendeuse

**association** *noun*
une **association** *fem*

English–French

**assorted** *adjective*
**variés** *masc plural*, **variées** *fem plural*
**assorted colours** des couleurs variées

**assortment** *noun*
le **mélange** *masc*

to **assume** *verb*
**supposer** [1]
**I assume she's coming too.** Je suppose qu'elle vient aussi.

to **assure** *verb*
**assurer** [1]

**asterisk** *noun*
un **astérisque** *masc*

**asthma** *noun*
l'**asthme** *masc*
**She has asthma.** Elle a de l'asthme.

**astonishing** *adjective*
**étonnant** *masc*, **étonnante** *fem*

**astrologer** *noun*
un & une **astrologue** *masc & fem*

**astrology** *noun*
l'**astrologie** *fem*

**astronaut** *noun*
un & une **astronaute** *masc & fem*

**astronomer** *noun*
un & une **astronome** *masc & fem*

**astronomy** *noun*
l'**astronomie** *fem*

**at** *preposition*
1 (*saying where*) **à**
**at home** à la maison
**at school** à l'école
**at my office** à mon bureau
**at the market** au marché
**at meetings** aux réunions

**WORD TIP** *à + le* becomes *au*; *à + les* becomes *aux*.

2 (*at person's house, office*) **chez**
**at Emma's house** chez Emma
**at her brother's** chez son frère
**at the hairdresser's** chez le coiffeur
3 (*talking about time*) **à**
**at eight o'clock** à huit heures
4 **at night** la nuit
**at the weekend** le week-end
**She's never there at weekends.** Elle n'est jamais là le week-end.
5 **at last** enfin
**He's found a job at last.** Il a enfin trouvé un emploi.
6 (*@ in emailing*) une **arobase** *fem*
**jane-dot-smith@easyconnect-dot-com** jane-point-smith-arobase-easyconnect-point-com

**athlete** *noun*
un & une **athlète** *masc & fem*

**athletic** *adjective*
**athlétique** *masc & fem*

**athletics** *noun*
l'**athlétisme** *masc*

**Atlantic** *noun*
l'**Atlantique** *masc*
**to sail across the Atlantic** traverser [1] l'Atlantique à la voile.

**atlas** *noun*
un **atlas** *masc*

**atmosphere** *noun*
l'**atmosphère** *fem*

**atom** *noun*
un **atome** *masc*

**atomic** *adjective*
**atomique**

to **attach** *verb*
**attacher** [1]

**attached** *adjective*
**to be attached to something** être [6] attaché à quelque chose
**The chain is attached to the wall.** La chaîne est attachée au mur.

**attachment** *noun*
la **pièce jointe** *fem*
**to open the attachment** ouvrir [30] la pièce jointe

**attack** *noun* ▷ see **attack** *verb*
une **attaque** *fem*

to **attack** *verb* ▷ see **attack** *noun*
1 (*armies, in sport*) **attaquer** [1]
2 (*muggers*) **agresser** [1]
**He was attacked in the street.** Il s'est fait agresser dans la rue.

**attacker** *noun*
un **agresseur** *masc*

**attempt** *noun* ▷ see **attempt** *verb*
la **tentative** *fem*
**at the first attempt** à la première tentative

to **attempt** *verb* ▷ see **attempt** *noun*
**to attempt to do something** essayer [59] de faire quelque chose
**She's attempting to break the record.** Elle essaie de battre le record.

**attendance** *noun*
(*at meetings*) la **présence** *fem*
**school attendance** la fréquentation scolaire



Ⓔ means the verb takes être to form the perfect

a b c d e f g h i j k l m n o p q r s t u v w x y z

**attention** *noun*
l'**attention** *fem*
to pay attention faire attention
**I wasn't paying attention.** Je ne faisais pas attention.

**attic** *noun*
le **grenier** *masc*
in the attic au grenier

**attitude** *noun*
une **attitude** *fem*
**He's got an attitude problem.** Son attitude lui vaut des problèmes

to **attract** *verb*
**attirer [1]**
to attract attention attirer l'attention

**attraction** *noun*
une **attraction** *fem*

**attractive** *adjective*
**séduisant** *masc*, **séduisante** *fem*

**aubergine** *noun*
une **aubergine** *fem*

**auction** *noun*
la **vente aux enchères**

**audience** *noun*
le **public** *masc*
a lively audience un public animé

♪ **August** *noun*
**août** *masc*
in August en août

**WORD TIP** Months of the year and days of the week start with small letters in French.

**aunt**, **auntie** *noun*
la **tante** *fem*
my aunt Ruth ma tante Ruth

**au pair** *noun*
une **jeune fille au pair** *fem*, un **jeune homme au pair** *masc*
**I'm looking for a job as an au pair.** Je cherche un emploi de jeune fille au pair.

**Australia** *noun*
l'**Australie** *fem*
in Australia en Australie
to Australia en Australie

**WORD TIP** Countries and regions in French take *le, la* or *les*.

**Australian** *adjective*
▷ see **Australian** *noun*
**australien** *masc*, **australienne** *fem*

**WORD TIP** Adjectives never have capitals in French, even for nationality or regional origin.

**Australian** *noun* ▷ see **Australian** *adj*
un **Australien** *masc*, une **Australienne** *fem*
the Australians les Australiens

**Austria** *noun*
l'**Autriche** *fem*

**Austrian** *adjective* ▷ see **Austrian** *noun*
**autrichien** *masc*, **autrichienne** *fem*

**Austrian** *noun* ▷ see **Austrian** *adj*
un **Autrichien** *masc*, une **Autrichienne** *fem*

**author** *noun*
un **auteur** *masc*

**autobiography** *noun*
une **autobiographie** *fem*

**automatic** *adjective*
**automatique** *masc & fem*

**automatically** *adverb*
**automatiquement**

♪ **autumn** *noun*
l'**automne** *masc*
in autumn en automne
next autumn l'automne prochain
last autumn l'automne dernier

**availability** *noun*
la **disponibilité** *fem*

**available** *adjective*
**disponible** *masc & fem*
**The film is not available on DVD yet.** Le film n'est pas encore disponible en DVD.

**avalanche** *noun*
une **avalanche** *fem*

**avenue** *noun*
une **avenue** *fem*

**average** *adjective* ▷ see **average** *noun*
**moyen** *masc*, **moyenne** *fem*
the average age l'âge moyen
the average height la hauteur moyenne

**average** *noun* ▷ see **average** *adj*
la **moyenne** *fem*
on average en moyenne
above average au-dessus de la moyenne
below average au-dessous de la moyenne

**avocado** *noun*
un **avocat** *masc*

to **avoid** *verb*
**éviter [1]**
**She's avoiding us.** Elle nous évite.
to avoid doing something éviter de faire quelque chose
**I avoid speaking to him.** J'évite de lui parler.

**awake** *adjective*
to be awake être [6] réveillé
**Is Chloë awake?** Est-ce que Chloë ▸▸

est réveillée?
**I was awake all night.** Je n'ai pas dormi de la nuit.

**award** *noun*
le **prix** *masc*
**to win an award** remporter [1] un prix

**aware** *adjective*
**to be aware of something** être [6] au courant de quelque chose
**I wasn't aware of the problem.** Je n'étais pas au courant du problème.

**away** *adverb*
1 (*describing distances*) **It's two kilometres away.** C'est à deux kilomètres d'ici.
**How far away is it?** C'est à quelle distance d'ici?
**It's not far away.** Ce n'est pas loin d'ici.
2 (*absent*) **to be away** être [6] absent
**while he was away** pendant qu'il était absent
**She'll be away next week.** Elle sera absente la semaine prochaine.
3 (*with verbs*) **to give something away** donner quelque chose
**to go away** partir Ⓔ [58]
**Go away!** Va-t'en!
**to put something away** ranger [52] quelque chose
**to run away** partir Ⓔ [58] en courant
• **away match** le match à l'extérieur

**awful** *adjective*
1 (*no good*) **affreux** *masc*, **affreuse** *fem*
**The weather was awful!** Le temps était affreux!
**It tastes awful.** C'est dégoûtant.
2 (*ill*) **I feel awful.** Je ne me sens pas bien du tout.
**You look awful.** Tu as très mauvaise mine.
3 (*embarrassed, unhappy*) **I feel awful about it.** Ça m'ennuie vraiment.
4 (*to say how much, many, etc*) **an awful lot of something** énormément de quelque chose
**It costs an awful lot of money.** Ça coûte énormément d'argent.
**He knows an awful lot of people.** Il connaît énormément de gens.

**awkward** *adjective*
1 (*problem, situation*) **difficile** *masc & fem*
**It's an awkward situation.** C'est une situation difficile.
2 (*person*) **difficile** *masc & fem*
**She's really awkward.** Elle est vraiment difficile.

**axe** *noun*
la **hache** *fem*

# B b

**baby** *noun*
le **bébé** *masc*

**to babysit** *verb*
**faire [10] du baby-sitting**

**babysitter** *noun*
le & la **baby-sitter** *masc & fem*

**babysitting** *noun*
le **baby-sitting** *masc*

**bachelor** *noun*
le **célibataire** *masc*

**back** *adjective* ▷ see **back** *adv, verb, noun*
1 (*wheel, seat*) **arrière**
**the back seat of the car** le siège arrière de la voiture
2 (*door, gate, etc*) **de derrière**
**the back gate** la porte de derrière
**the back garden** le jardin de derrière

**back** *adverb* ▷ see **back** *adj, verb, noun*
1 (*showing movement to and from places*) **rentrer** Ⓔ [1]
**to go back** rentrer
**Lucy's gone back home.** Lucy est rentrée chez elle.
**to go back to school** rentrer à l'école
**When do we go back to school?** Quand est-ce qu'on rentre à l'école?
**to come back from a place** rentrer
**They've come back from Normandy.** Ils sont rentrés de Normandie.
**We went by bus and walked back.** Nous avons pris le bus pour y aller et nous sommes rentrés à pied.
2 (*showing where someone is now*)
**to be back** être [6] rentré
**Emma's not back yet.** Emma n'est pas encore rentrée.



Ⓔ means the verb takes être to form the perfect

Hannah's back at work. Hannah a repris le travail.
3 to give something back to somebody rendre [3] quelque chose à quelqu'un
I gave him back his cassettes. Je lui ai rendu ses cassettes.
Give it back! Rends-le-moi!

♪ to **back** *verb* ▷ see **back** *adj, adv, noun*
1 (*a candidate*) **soutenir [77]**
2 (*a horse*) **parier [1] sur**
• **to back up**
1 (*Computing*) **to back up a file** sauvegarder [1] un fichier sur disquette
**You must back up your work.** Il faut sauvegarder votre travail.
2 (*in an argument, discussion*) **to back somebody up** soutenir [77] quelqu'un
**Josh backed me up.** Josh m'a soutenu.

♪ **back** *noun* ▷ see **back** *adj, adv, verb*
1 (*of a person, animal, hand*) le **dos** *masc*
**Write your name on the back of the sheet.** Écrivez votre nom au dos du papier.
2 (*of a car, a plane, a building*) l'**arrière** *masc*
**There are seats at the back.** Il y a des places à l'arrière.
**There's a garden at the back of our house.** Il y a un jardin à l'arrière de notre maison.
3 (*of a room*) le **fond** *masc*
**Tom was at the back of the room.** Tom était au fond de la salle.
4 (*of a chair, sofa*) le **dossier** *masc*
5 (*in football, etc*) un **arrière** *masc*
**the left back** l'arrière gauche
• **backache** le mal de dos
• **backbone** la colonne vertébrale

**back door** *noun*
1 (*of a building*) la **porte de derrière**
2 (*of a car*) la **portière arrière**

**background** *noun*
1 (*of a person*) le **milieu** *masc*
2 (*of events, a situation*) le **contexte** *masc*
3 (*of a picture, view*) un **arrière-plan** *masc*
**in the background** les arbres à l'arrière-plan
• **background music** *noun* la musique d'ambiance

**backhand** *noun*
le **revers** *masc*

**backing** *noun*
1 (*on sticky-backed plastic*) le **revêtement intérieur**
2 (*moral support*) le **soutien** *masc*

**backpack** *noun*
le **sac à dos**

**backpacking** *noun*
**to go backpacking** partir Ⓔ [58] en randonnée
**I'm going backpacking in August.** En août je pars en randonnée.

♪ **backside** *noun*
le **derrière** *masc*

**backstage** *adverb*
**to go backstage** aller Ⓔ [7] dans les coulisses

**backstroke** *noun*
le **dos crawlé**

**back to front** *adverb*
**à l'envers**

**backup** *noun*
1 (*support*) le **soutien** *masc*
2 (*in computing*) la **sauvegarde** *fem*
**a backup disk** un disque de sauvegarde

**backwards** *adverb*
(*to lean, fall*) **en arrière**

**bacon** *noun*
1 (*streaky*) le **lard** *masc*
2 (*smoked*) le **bacon** *masc*
**bacon and eggs** les œufs au bacon

♪ **bad** *adjective*
1 (*not good*) **mauvais** *masc*, **mauvaise** *fem*
**a bad meal** un mauvais repas
**a bad experience** une mauvaise expérience
**His new film's not bad.** Son nouveau film n'est pas mauvais.
**to be bad at something** être [6] mauvais en quelque chose
**I'm bad at physics.** Je suis mauvais en physique (*boy speaking*), Je suis mauvaise en physique (*girl speaking*).
**Smoking is bad for your health.** Fumer est mauvais pour la santé.
2 (*serious*) **grave** *masc & fem*
**a bad accident** un accident grave
**a bad cold** un gros rhume
3 (*rotten*) **pourri** *masc*, **pourrie** *fem*
**a bad apple** une pomme pourrie
**to go bad** se gâter Ⓔ [1]
**This meat has gone bad.** La viande s'est gâtée.
4 (*naughty*) **vilain** *masc*, **vilaine** *fem*
**Bad dog!** Vilain!
5 (*rude*) **grossier** *masc*, **grossière** *fem*
**bad language** un langage grossier

**badge** *noun*
le **badge** *masc*

**badly** *adverb*
1 (*not well*) **mal**
I slept badly. J'ai mal dormi.
He writes very badly. Il écrit très mal.
to go badly se passer ⓔ [1] mal
The exam went badly. L'examen s'est mal passé.
2 (*damaged*) **sérieusement**
My bike was badly damaged. Mon vélo a été sérieusement endommagé.
3 (*injured*) to be badly hurt
être [6] grièvement blessé
Her sister was badly hurt. Sa sœur a été grièvement blessée.

**bad-mannered** *adjective*
**mal élevé** *masc*, **mal élevée** *fem*

**badminton** *noun*
le **badminton** *masc*
to play badminton jouer [1] au badminton

**bag** *noun*
le **sac** *masc*

**baggage** *noun*
les **bagages** *masc plural*
- **baggage allowance** la franchise de bagages
- **baggage reclaim** la réception des bagages

**bagpipes** *plural noun*
la **cornemuse** *fem*
to play the bagpipes jouer [1] de la cornemuse

**bags** *plural noun*
les **bagages** *masc plural*
to pack your bags faire [10] ses bagages

**Bahamas** *plural noun*
the Bahamas les Bahamas *fem pl*
We had a holiday in the Bahamas. Nous avons passé les vacances aux Bahamas.

to **bake** *verb*
1 (*a dish, vegetables*) **faire [10] cuire**
2 (*a cake, bread*) **faire [10]**
I like baking cakes. J'aime faire des gâteaux.

**baked** *adjective*
(*fish, fruit, vegetables*) **au four**
a baked potato une pomme de terre au four
- **baked beans** les haricots blancs à la sauce tomate

**baker** *noun*
le **boulanger** *masc*, la **boulangère** *fem*
I bought croissants at the baker's. J'ai acheté des croissants à la boulangerie.
to go to the baker's aller ⓔ [7] à la boulangerie

**bakery** *noun*
la **boulangerie** *fem*

**balance** *noun*
1 (*of a person*) l'**équilibre** *masc*
to lose your balance perdre [3] l'équilibre
2 (*of a bank account*) le **solde** *masc*

**balcony** *noun*
le **balcon** *masc*

**bald** *adjective*
**chauve** *masc & fem*

**ball** *noun*
1 (*for tennis, golf*) la **balle** *fem*
2 (*for football, volleyball*) le **ballon** *masc*
3 (*of string, wool*) la **pelote** *fem*

**ballet** *noun*
le **ballet** *masc*
- **ballet dancer** le danseur de ballet, la danseuse de ballet

**balloon** *noun*
1 (*for a party*) le **ballon** *masc*
2 (*hot air*) la **montgolfière** *fem*

**ballot** *noun*
le **scrutin** *masc*

**ballpoint pen** *noun*
le **stylo à bille**

**ban** *noun* ▷ see **ban** *verb*
une **interdiction** *fem*
a ban on smoking une interdiction de fumer

to **ban** *verb* ▷ see **ban** *noun*
**interdire [47]**

**banana** *noun*
la **banane** *fem*

**band** *noun*
1 (*musical*) le **groupe** *masc*
a rock band un groupe de rock
a jazz band un orchestre de jazz
2 (*for your head*) le **bandeau** *masc*

**bandage** *noun* ▷ see **bandage** *verb*
le **bandage** *masc*

to **bandage** *verb* ▷ see **bandage** *noun*
**faire [10] un bandage à**
She will bandage your arm. Elle te fera un bandage au bras.

**bang** *noun* ▷ see **bang** *verb, excl*
1 (*noise*) le **boum** *masc*
2 (*of a door, shutter, window*) le **claquement** *masc*

to **bang** *verb* ▷ see **bang** *noun, excl*
1 (*to hit*) **taper [1] sur** (*a drum*)
He banged his fist on the table. Il a tapé du poing sur la table.

2 (*to knock*) **cogner [1]**
to bang your head se cogner ⓔ la tête
to bang into heurter [1]
I banged into the table. J'ai heurté la table.
3 (*to slam*) **claquer [1]**
to bang the door claquer la porte

**bang** *exclamation* ▷ see **bang** *noun, verb*
(*like a gun*) **pan!**

**Bangladesh** *noun*
le **Bangladesh** *masc*
in Bangladesh au Bangladesh

**Bangladeshi** *adjective*
▷ see **Bangladeshi** *noun*
**du Bangladesh**

**Bangladeshi** *noun*
▷ see **Bangladeshi** *adj*
**Bangladais** *masc*, **Bangladaise** *fem*

**bangle** *noun*
le **bracelet** *masc*

**banisters** *(plural) noun*
la **rampe (d'escalier)**

♪ **bank** *noun*
1 (*for money*) la **banque** *fem*
I'm going to the bank. Je vais à la banque.
2 (*of a river, lake*) le **bord** *masc*
- **bank account** le compte bancaire
- **bank balance** le solde bancaire
- **bank card** la carte bancaire
- **bank holiday** le jour férié
- **banknote** le billet de banque
- **bank statement** le relevé de compte

to **baptize** *verb*
**baptiser [1]**

♪ **bar** *noun* ▷ see **bar** *verb*
1 (*selling drinks*) le **bar** *masc*
Her brother works in a bar. Son frère travaille dans un bar.
2 (*the counter*) le **comptoir** *masc*
3 (*a block of something*) la **barre** *fem*
a metal bar une barre en métal
a bar of chocolate une tablette de chocolat
a bar of soap une savonnette
4 (*in music*) la **mesure** *fem*

♪ to **bar** *verb* ▷ see **bar** *noun*
(*to block*) **barrer [1]**
to bar someone's way barrer le passage à quelqu'un
A tall man barred my way. Un homme grand m'a barré le passage.

**Barbadian** *adjective*
▷ see **Barbadian** *noun*
**de la Barbade**

**Barbadian** *noun* ▷ see **Barbadian** *adj*
**Barbadien** *masc*, **Barbadienne** *fem*

**Barbados** *noun*
la **Barbade** *fem*
to be in Barbados être [6] à la Barbade
to go to Barbados aller à la Barbade

**barbecue** *noun* ▷ see **barbecue** *verb*
le **barbecue** *masc*

to **barbecue** *verb* ▷ see **barbecue** *noun*
**faire [10] griller au barbecue**
to barbecue a chicken faire griller un poulet au barbecue

**bare** *adjective*
**nu** *masc*, **nue** *fem*

**barefoot** *adjective*
to be barefoot être [6] nu-pieds
to walk barefoot marcher pieds nus

**bargain** *noun*
une **affaire** *fem*
It's a bargain! C'est une bonne affaire!

**barge** *noun*
la **péniche** *fem*

**bark** *noun* ▷ see **bark** *verb*
1 (*of a dog*) l'**aboiement** *masc*
2 (*of a tree*) une **écorce** *fem*

to **bark** *verb* ▷ see **bark** *noun*
**aboyer [39]**

**barley** *noun*
l'**orge** *masc*

**barmaid** *noun*
la **barmaid** *fem*

**barman** *noun*
le **barman** *masc*

**barn** *noun*
la **grange** *fem*

**barometer** *noun*
le **baromètre** *masc*

**barrel** *noun*
le **tonneau** *masc* (*pl* les **tonneaux**)

**barrier** *noun*
la **barrière** *fem*

**base** *noun*
la **base** *fem*

**baseball** *noun*
le **base-ball** *masc*

**based** *adjective*
to be based on something être [6] fondé sur quelque chose
The film is based on a true story. Le film est tiré d'une histoire vraie.

ℰ **basement** *noun*
le **sous-sol** *masc*
in the basement au sous-sol

**bash** *noun* ▷ see **bash** *verb*
1 (*a knock*) la **bosse** *fem*
It's got a bash on the wing. L'aile est cabossée.
2 (*a try*) to have a bash essayer**[59]** un coup
I'll have a bash. Je vais essayer un coup.

to **bash** *verb* ▷ see **bash** *noun*
**cogner[1]**
I bashed my head. Je me suis cogné la tête.

**basic** *adjective*
1 (*at the bottom level*) **de base**
basic knowledge des connaissances de base
her basic salary son salaire de base
2 (*essential*) **essentiel** *masc*, **essentielle** *fem*
the basic facts les faits essentiels
3 (*not luxurious*) **rudimentaire** *masc & fem*

**basically** *adverb*
1 (*essentially*) **au fond**
It's basically all right. Au fond, ça va.
2 (*to be honest*) **à vrai dire**
Basically, I don't want to go. À vrai dire, je ne veux pas y aller.

**basics** *noun*
les **rudiments** *masc plural*

**basin** *noun*
(*washbasin*) le **lavabo** *masc*

**basis** *noun*
la **base** *fem*

ℰ **basket** *noun*
1 (*for shopping*) le **panier** *masc*
2 (*other*) la **corbeille** *fem*

**basketball** *noun*
le **basketball** *masc*
to play basketball jouer**[1]** au basketball

**bass** *noun*
la **basse** *fem*
to play bass jouer**[1]** de la basse
- **bass drum** la grosse caisse
- **bass guitar** la guitare basse

**bassoon** *noun*
le **basson** *masc*
to play the bassoon jouer**[1]** du basson

**bat** *noun*
1 (*for cricket, baseball*) la **batte** *fem*
2 (*for table tennis*) la **raquette** *fem*
3 (*the animal*) la **chauve-souris** *fem*

**batch** *noun*
1 (*of books, orders*) le **lot** *masc*
2 (*of cakes*) la **fournée** *fem*

ℰ **bath** *noun*
1 (*act of washing*) le **bain** *masc*
I was in the bath. J'étais dans mon bain.
I'm going to have a bath. Je vais prendre un bain.
2 (*bathtub*) la **baignoire** *fem*
The bath's pink. La baignoire est rose.

to **bathe** *verb*
1 (*a wound*) **laver[1]**

ℰ **bathroom** *noun*
la **salle de bains** (*pl* les **salles de bains**)

**baths** *plural noun*
la **piscine** *fem*

**bath towel** *noun*
la **serviette de bain**

**batter** *noun*
(*for frying*) la **pâte à frire**
pancake batter la pâte à crêpes

**battery** *noun*
1 (*for a torch, radio*) la **pile** *fem*
2 (*for a car*) la **batterie** *fem*

**battle** *noun*
la **bataille** *fem*

**bay** *noun*
1 (*on the coast*) la **baie** *fem*
2 (*for coaches*) la **travée** *fem*

**B.C.** *abbreviation*
(*short for before Christ*) av. J-C

ℰ to **be** *verb*
1 (*showing where or how something is*) **être[6]**
Gita is in the kitchen. Gita est dans la cuisine.
Where is the butter? Où est le beurre?
I'm tired. Je suis fatigué (*boy speaking*), Je suis fatiguée (*girl speaking*).
I saw the film when we were in France. J'ai vu le film quand nous étions en France.
2 (*with jobs and professions*) **être[6]**
Mum's a teacher. Ma mère est professeur.
He's a taxi driver. Il est chauffeur de taxi.

**WORD TIP** *a* before the name of the job is not translated into French.

3 (*telling the time*) **être[6]**
It's three o'clock. Il est trois heures.
It's half past five. Il est cinq heures et demie.
4 (*days of the week and dates*) What day is it today? Nous sommes quel jour aujourd'hui?
It's Tuesday today. On est mardi aujourd'hui.
It's the tenth of May. On est le dix mai.
5 (*talking about age*) **avoir[5]**
How old are you? Quel âge as-tu?

I'm fifteen. J'ai quinze ans.
Harry's twenty. Harry a vingt ans.
6 (*cold, hot, hungry*) **avoir [5]**
to be hot avoir chaud
I'm hot. J'ai chaud.
to be cold avoir froid
I'm cold. J'ai froid.
to be hungry avoir faim
I'm hungry. J'ai faim.
7 (*with weather expressions*) **faire [10]**
It's cold today. Il fait froid aujourd'hui.
It's a nice day. Il fait beau.
8 to have been to a place être [6] allé à un endroit
I've never been to Paris. Je ne suis jamais allé à Paris (*boy speaking*), Je ne suis jamais allée à Paris (*girl speaking*).
Have you ever been to Greece? Est-ce que tu as jamais été en Grèce?
9 (*with -ed forms of verbs*) to be loved être [6] aimé
Jackson is adored by his fans. Jackson est adoré par ses fans.
The president has been assassinated. Le président a été assassiné.

**beach** *noun*
la **plage** *fem*
on the beach sur la plage
The children are playing on the beach. Les enfants jouent sur la plage.
to go to the beach aller Ⓔ [7] à la plage
Let's go to the beach! Allons à la plage!

**bead** *noun*
la **perle** *fem*

**beak** *noun*
le **bec** *masc*

**beam** *noun*
1 (*of light*) le **rayon** *masc*
2 (*for a roof*) la **poutre** *fem*

**bean** *noun*
un **haricot** *masc*
green beans les haricots verts

**bear** *noun* ▷ see **bear** *verb*
un **ours** *masc*

to **bear** *verb* ▷ see **bear** *noun*
1 (*something bad*) **supporter [1]**
I can't bear him. Je ne peux pas le supporter.
• to **bear up**
**tenir [77] le coup**
'How's your mum?' — 'She's bearing up.' 'Comment va ta mère?' — 'Elle tient le coup.'

**beard** *noun*
la **barbe** *fem*

**bearded** *adjective*
**barbu** *masc*, **barbue** *fem*

**beast** *noun*
1 (*an animal*) la **bête** *fem*
2 (*a person*) le **chameau** *masc*

**beat** *noun* ▷ see **beat** *verb*
le **rythme** *masc*

to **beat** *verb* ▷ see **beat** *noun*
1 (*an army, other players*) **battre [21]**
We beat them! On les a battus!
2 (*eggs, mixture*) **battre [21]**
Beat the eggs. Battez les œufs.
• **to beat somebody up**
**tabasser [1] quelqu'un**

**beautician** *noun*
un **esthéticien** *masc*, une **esthéticienne** *fem*

**beautiful** *adjective*
**beau** *masc*, **bel** *masc*, **belle** *fem*, **beaux** *masc pl*, **belles** *fem pl*
a beautiful day un beau jour
a beautiful girl une belle fille
beautiful pictures de beaux tableaux
a beautiful place un bel endroit

**WORD TIP** *beau, belle etc go before the noun. bel is for singular masc nouns starting with a, e, i, o, u or silent h-.*

**beautifully** *adverb*
1 (*to behave, write, play*) **admirablement**
2 (*decorated, set*) **magnifiquement**
She dresses beautifully. Elle s'habille toujours avec beaucoup de goût.

**beauty** *noun*
la **beauté** *fem*
• **beauty spot** le site pittoresque

**because** *conjunction*
**parce que**
I'm late because I missed the bus. Je suis en retard parce que j'ai raté le bus.
because of à cause de
because of the accident à cause de l'accident
I got into trouble because of you. C'est à cause de toi que j'ai des ennuis.

to **become** *verb*
**devenir** Ⓔ **[81]**

**bed** *noun*
1 (*for sleeping*) le **lit** *masc*
to make the bed faire le lit
a double bed un grand lit
in bed au lit
Are the children in bed? Les enfants sont-ils au lit?
to go to bed aller Ⓔ [7] se coucher ▸▸

**I usually go to bed at 11 o'clock.** D'habitude, je me couche à onze heures.

2 (*for flowers*) le **parterre** *masc*

- **bedclothes** les couvertures

**bedding** *noun*

la **literie** *fem*

**bedroom** *noun* ▷ see **bedroom** *adjective*

la **chambre** *fem*

**bedside** *noun*

le **chevet** *masc*

**a bedside table** une table de chevet

**bedsit** *noun*

la **chambre meublée**

**bedspread** *noun*

le **dessus-de-lit** *masc*

**bedtime** *noun*

**It's bedtime.** C'est l'heure d'aller se coucher.

**bee** *noun*

une **abeille** *fem*

**beech** *noun*

un **hêtre** *masc*

**beef** *noun*

le **bœuf** *masc*

**We had beef for dinner.** On a mangé du bœuf au dîner.

- **beefburger** un hamburger *masc*

**beer** *noun*

la **bière** *fem*

**Two beers, please.** Deux bières, s'il vous plaît.

**a beer can** une canette de bière

**beetle** *noun*

le **scarabée** *masc*

**beetroot** *noun*

la **betterave** *fem*

**before** *adverb* ▷ see **before** *conj, prep*

1 (*already*) **déjà**

**I've seen him before.** Je l'ai déjà vu.

**I had seen the film before.** J'avais déjà vu le film.

2 (*earlier*) **the day before** la veille

**the day before the wedding** la veille du mariage

**the day before yesterday** avant-hier

**the week before** la semaine d'avant

**before** *preposition* ▷ see **before** *adv, conj*

**avant**

**before Monday** avant lundi

**He left before me.** Il est parti avant moi.

**There's a to be done before the exams.** On a beaucoup à faire avant les examens.

**before** *conjunction* ▷ see **before** *adv, prep*

1 **before doing something** avant de faire quelque chose

**I closed the windows before I left.** J'ai fermé les fenêtres avant de partir.

2 **avant que**

**Phone me before they leave.** Appelle-moi avant qu'ils s'en aillent.

**Oh, before I forget ...** Avant que j'oublie ...

**WORD TIP** *avant que* is followed by a verb in the subjunctive.

**beforehand** *adverb*

**à l'avance**

**Phone beforehand.** Appelle à l'avance.

to **beg** *verb*

1 (*for money*) **mendier [1]**

2 (*somebody*) **supplier [1]**

**to beg somebody to do something** supplier quelqu'un de faire quelque chose

**She begged me not to leave.** Elle m'a supplié de ne pas partir.

to **begin** *verb*

**commencer [61]**

**Lessons begin at nine.** Les cours commencent à neuf heures.

**words beginning with P** les mots qui commencent par un P

**to begin to do something** commencer à faire quelque chose

**I'm beginning to understand.** Je commence à comprendre.

**It began to rain.** Il a commencé à pleuvoir.

**beginner** *noun*

le **débutant** *masc*, la **débutante** *fem*

**beginning** *noun*

le **début** *masc*

**at the beginning** au début

**We went away at the beginning of the holidays.** Nous sommes partis au début des vacances.

**behalf** *noun*

**on behalf of** pour

**The headmaster spoke on behalf of the school.** Le directeur a parlé pour l'école.

to **behave** *verb*

**se comporter** ⓔ **[1]**

**He behaved badly.** Il s'est mal comporté.

**She behaved even worse.** Elle s'est comportée encore plus mal.

**to behave yourself** être **[6]** sage

**Behave yourselves!** Soyez sages!

**behaviour** *noun*

le **comportement** *masc*

♪ **behind** *adverb* ▷ see **behind** *noun, prep*
(*to forget*) **to leave something behind**
oublier **[1]** quelque chose
**I left my phone behind on the train.** J'ai oublié mon portable dans le train.

♪ **behind** *preposition* ▷ see **behind** *adv, noun*
1 (*in a place*) **derrière**
**behind them** derrière eux
**He hid behind the sofa.** Il s'est caché derrière le canapé.
2 (*in class, at school*)
**to be behind** avoir **[5]** du retard
**Joe's behind in Maths.** Joe a du retard en math.

♪ **behind** *noun* ▷ see **behind** *adv, prep*
le **derrière** *masc*

**beige** *adjective*
**beige** *masc & fem*

**Belgian** *adjective* ▷ see **Belgian** *noun*
**belge** *masc & fem*
**Belgian chocolates** des chocolats belges

**WORD TIP** Adjectives never have capitals in French, even for nationality.

♪ **Belgian** *noun* ▷ see **Belgian** *adj*
un **Belge** *masc*, une **Belge** *fem*

♪ **Belgium** *noun*
la **Belgique**
**to be in Belgium** être **[6]** en Belgique
**to go to Belgium** aller Ⓔ **[7]** en Belgique

**belief** *noun*
la **conviction** *fem*
**his political beliefs** ses convictions politiques

♪ to **believe** *verb*
**croire [33]**
**I believe you.** Je te crois.
**They believed what I said.** Ils ont cru ce que j'ai dit.
**I don't believe you!** Ce n'est pas vrai!
**to believe in something** croire à quelque chose
**Do you believe in ghosts?** Tu crois aux fantômes?
**to believe in God** croire en Dieu
**I believe in God.** Je crois en Dieu.

**bell** *noun*
1 (*in a church*) la **cloche** *fem*
2 (*on a door*) la **sonnette** *fem*
**Ring the bell!** Appuyez sur la sonnette!

♪ to **belong** *verb*
1 (*to be somebody's*) **to belong to somebody**
appartenir **[81]** à quelqu'un
**That watch belongs to Nick.** Cette montre-là appartient à Nick.
2 (*to be part of something*) **to belong to a club**
faire **[10]** partie d'un club
**Paul belongs to a tennis club.** Paul fait partie d'un club de tennis.
3 (*to be kept somewhere*) **aller** Ⓔ **[7]**
**That chair belongs in the study.** Cette chaise va dans le bureau.
**Where does this vase belong?** Ce vase va où?

**belongings** *plural noun*
les **affaires** *fem plural*
**All my belongings are at my dad's.** Toutes mes affaires sont chez mon père.

♪ **below** *adverb, preposition*
1 (*under something else*) **au-dessous de** (*quelque chose*)
**below the window** au-dessous de la fenêtre
**She lives in the flat below yours.** Elle habite l'appartement au-dessous du tien.
2 (*underneath*) **de dessous**
**She lives in the flat below.** Elle habite l'appartement de dessous.

♪ **belt** *noun*
la **ceinture** *fem*

**bench** *noun*
le **banc** *masc*

**bend** *noun* ▷ see **bend** *verb*
1 (*in a road*) le **virage** *masc*
2 (*in a river*) la **courbe** *fem*

to **bend** *verb* ▷ see **bend** *noun*
1 (*your arm, your leg, a wire*) **plier [1]**
**to bend down** se pencher Ⓔ **[1]**
2 (*roads, paths*) **tourner [1]**
**The road bends to the right.** La route tourne à droite.

**beneath** *preposition*
**sous**
**beneath the window** sous la fenêtre
**She lives in the flat beneath yours.** Elle habite l'appartement sous le tien.

**benefit** *noun*
un **avantage** *masc*

**bent** *adjective*
**tordu** *masc*, **tordue** *fem*

**beret** *noun*
le **béret** *masc*

**berry** *noun*
la **baie** *fem*

**berth** *noun*
la **couchette** *fem*

**beside** *preposition*
**à côté de**
**She was sitting beside me.** Elle était assise à côté de moi.

**besides** *adverb*
1 (*anyway*) **d'ailleurs**
**Besides, it's too late.** D'ailleurs, il est trop tard.

**best** *adjective, adverb* ▷ see **best** *noun*
1 (*with nouns*) **meilleur** *masc*, **meilleure** *fem*
**That's the best car.** Cette voiture-là est la meilleure.
**She's my best friend.** C'est ma meilleure amie.
**He's my best friend.** C'est mon meilleur ami.
**The best thing to do is to phone them.** La meilleure chose à faire, c'est de leur téléphoner.
2 (*with verbs*) **le mieux**
**Harry plays best.** Harry joue le mieux.
**I like Paris best.** C'est Paris que je préfère.
**best of all** mieux que tout
**I like Science best of all.** J'aime les sciences plus que tout.

**best** *noun* ▷ see **best** *adj, adv*
le **meilleur** *masc*, la **meilleure** *fem*
**It's the best.** C'est le meilleur.
**It's the best I can do.** Je ne peux pas faire mieux.
**All the best!** (*good luck*) Bonne chance!, (*cheers*) À ta santé!
**He's the best at tennis.** C'est lui le meilleur au tennis.
**to do your best to do something** faire **[10]** de son mieux pour faire quelque chose
**I did my best to help her.** J'ai fait de mon mieux pour l'aider.
- **best man** le garçon d'honneur

**bet** *noun* ▷ see **bet** *verb*
le **pari** *masc*

to **bet** *verb* ▷ see **bet** *noun*
**parier [1]**
**He bet on the winning horse.** Il a parié sur le cheval gagnant.
**I bet you he'll forget!** Je te parie qu'il va oublier!

**better** *adjective, adverb* ▷ see **better** *noun*
1 (*showing improvement*) **mieux**
**This pen writes better.** Ce stylo écrit mieux.
**even better** encore mieux
**to get better** s'améliorer ⓔ **[1]**
**My French is getting better.** Mon français s'améliore.
2 (*in comparisons*) **It works better than the other one.** Il fonctionne mieux que l'autre.
**He's better at English than French.** Il est meilleur en anglais qu'en français.
**It's even better than before.** C'est encore mieux qu'avant.
3 (*less ill*) **to be better** aller ⓔ **[7]** mieux
**He's a bit better today.** Il va un peu mieux aujourd'hui.
**to feel better** se sentir ⓔ **[58]** mieux
**I feel better.** Je me sens mieux.
4 (*to say you must do something*) **You had better do something.** Tu ferais mieux de faire quelque chose.
**I'd better go now.** Je dois partir maintenant.
**He'd better not go.** Il ferait mieux de ne pas y aller.
**You had better phone at once.** Tu ferais mieux d'appeler tout de suite.

**better** *noun* ▷ see **better** *adj, adv*
**the sooner the better** le plus vite possible
**I need to see you, and the sooner the better.** Je dois te voir, et le plus vite possible.
**so much the better** tant mieux
**If Will can come, so much the better.** Si Will peut venir, tant mieux.

**better off** *adjective*
1 (*richer*) **plus riche** *masc & fem*
**They're better off than us.** Ils sont plus riches que nous.
2 (*more comfortable*) **mieux** *masc & fem*
**You'd be better off in bed.** Tu serais mieux au lit.

**between** *preposition*
**entre**
**between London and Dover** entre Londres et Douvres
**between the two** entre les deux
**I'll get there between 5 and 6 o'clock.** J'arriverai entre cinq et six heures.

to **beware** *verb*
**Beware of the dog!** Chien méchant!

**beyond** *preposition*
1 (*in time and space*) **au-delà de**
**They went beyond the village.** Ils sont allés au-delà du village.

**Bible** *noun*
**the Bible** la Bible

**bicycle** *noun*
le **vélo** *masc*
**by bicycle** à vélo

I come to school by bicycle. Je viens à l'école à vélo.
- **bicycle lane** la piste cyclable
- **bicycle rack** le parc à bicyclettes

♪ **bidet** *noun*
le **bidet** *masc*

♪ **big** *adjective*
1 (*place, person, clothing*) **grand** *masc*, **grande** *fem*
a big garden un grand jardin
a big city une grande ville
my big sister ma grande sœur
It's too big for me. C'est trop grand pour moi.
2 (*animal, car, box*) **gros** *masc*, **grosse** *fem*
a big dog un gros chien
a big car une grosse voiture
a big mistake une grosse erreur

**WORD TIP** *grand* and *gros* go before the noun.

**bigheaded** *adjective*
to be bigheaded avoir **[5]** la grosse tête

**big toe** *noun*
le **gros orteil**

♪ **bike** *noun*
1 (*with pedals*) le **vélo** *masc*
by bike à vélo
to go for a bike ride se promener Ⓔ **[1]** à vélo
He came by bike. Il est venu à vélo.
2 (*with motor*) la **moto** *fem*

**bikini** *noun*
le **bikini** *masc*

**bilingual** *adjective*
**bilingue** *masc & fem*

♪ **bill** *noun*
1 (*in a restaurant*) une **addition** *fem*
Can we have the bill, please? L'addition, s'il vous plaît.
2 (*for gas, electricity, etc*) la **facture** *fem*

**billiards** *noun*
le **billard** *masc*
to play billiards jouer **[1]** au billard

**billion** *noun*
le **milliard** *masc*

**bin** *noun*
la **poubelle** *fem*

♪ **binoculars** *noun*
les **jumelles** *fem plural*

**biochemistry** *noun*
la **biochimie** *fem*

**biography** *noun*
la **biographie** *fem*

**biologist** *noun*
le & la **biologiste** *masc & fem*

♪ **biology** *noun*
la **biologie** *fem*

♪ **bird**
un **oiseau** *masc* (*pl* **les oiseaux**)
- **bird flu** la grippe aviaire
- **bird sanctuary** la réserve ornithologique

**birdwatching** *noun*
to go birdwatching observer **[1]** les oiseaux

**Biro**® *noun*
le **bic**® *masc*

♪ **birth** *noun*
la **naissance** *fem*
- **birth certificate** un acte de naissance
- **birth control** la contraception

♪ **birthday** *noun*
un **anniversaire** *masc*
a birthday present un cadeau d'anniversaire
Happy birthday! Joyeux anniversaire!

♪ **birthday party** *noun*
1 (*children's*) le **goûter d'anniversaire**
2 (*adult's*) la **soirée d'anniversaire**

♪ **biscuit** *noun*
le **biscuit** *masc*

**bishop** *noun*
un **évêque** *masc*

♪ **bit** *noun*
1 (*of bread, cheese, wood*) le **morceau** *masc*
a bit of coal un morceau de charbon
2 (*of string, paper, garden*) le **bout** *masc*
a bit of string un bout de ficelle
with a little bit of garden avec un petit bout de jardin
3 (*a small amount*)
a bit un peu
a bit hot un peu chaud
a bit early un peu trop tôt
Wait a bit! Attends un peu!
a bit of un peu de
a bit of sugar un peu de sucre
a bit of news une nouvelle
bit by bit petit à petit
With a bit of luck we will win. Avec un peu de chance, nous gagnerons.
4 (*of a book, film, etc*) le **passage** *masc*
This bit is brilliant! Ce passage est génial!
5 (*piece*) **to fall to bits** tomber Ⓔ **[1]** en morceaux
My old diary fell to bits. Mon vieux journal est tombé en morceaux.

**bite** *noun* ▷ see **bite** *verb*
1 (*snack*) le **morceau** *masc*
I'll just have a bite before I go. Je vais juste manger un morceau avant de partir.
2 (*insect's*) la **piqûre** *fem*
a mosquito bite une piqûre de moustique
3 (*dog's*) la **morsure** *fem*

to **bite** *verb* ▷ see **bite** *noun*
1 (*person, dog*) **mordre** [3]
2 (*insect*) **piquer** [1]
3 to bite your nails se ronger ⓔ [52] les ongles

**bitter** *adjective*
(*taste*) **amer** *masc*, **amère** *fem*

**black** *noun* ▷ see **black** *adj*
le **noir** *masc*

**black** *adjective* ▷ see **black** *noun*
1 (*colour*) **noir** *masc*, **noire** *fem*
a black cat un chat noir
my black jacket ma veste noire
a black coffee un café noir
to turn black noircir [2]
The plant turned black. La plante a noirci.
2 (*skin*) a Black man un Noir
a Black woman une Noire
- **blackberry** la mûre
- **blackbird** le merle
- **blackboard** le tableau noir
- **blackcurrant** le cassis
- **black eye** un œil au beurre noir
- **black pudding** le boudin noir

**blade** *noun*
la **lame** *fem*

**blame** *noun* ▷ see **blame** *verb*
la **responsabilité** *fem*
to take the blame for something prendre [64] la responsabilité de quelque chose

to **blame** *verb* ▷ see **blame** *noun*
to blame someone for something tenir [77] quelqu'un responsable de quelque chose
They blamed him for the accident. Ils l'ont tenu responsable de l'accident.
She is to blame for it. Elle en est responsable.

**blank** *adjective* ▷ see **blank** *noun*
1 (*page, piece of paper, cheque*) **blanc** *masc*, **blanche** *fem*
2 (*tape, disk*) **vierge** *masc & fem*
3 (*screen*) **vide** *masc & fem*

**blank** *noun* ▷ see **blank** *adj*
le **blanc** *masc*

**blanket** *noun*
la **couverture** *fem*

**blast** *noun*
1 (*an explosion*) une **explosion** *fem*
2 (*of air*) le **souffle** *masc*
3 (*of sounds*) at full blast à plein volume
She plays her CDs at full blast. Elle met ses CD à plein volume.

**blaze** *noun* ▷ see **blaze** *verb*
un **incendie** *masc*

to **blaze** *verb* ▷ see **blaze** *noun*
**brûler** [1]

**bleach** *noun*
l'**eau de javel** *fem*

to **bleed** *verb*
**saigner** [1]

**blend** *noun*
le **mélange** *masc*

**blender** *noun*
le **mixer** *masc*

to **bless** *verb*
**bénir** [2]
Bless you! À tes souhaits! (*after a sneeze*)

**blind** *adjective* ▷ see **blind** *noun*
**aveugle** *masc & fem*
to go blind perdre la vue

**blind** *noun* ▷ see **blind** *adj*
(*in a window*) le **store** *masc*

**blindness** *noun*
la **cécité** *fem*

to **blink** *verb*
**cligner** [1] **des yeux**

**blister** *noun*
une **ampoule** *fem*

**blizzard** *noun*
la **tempête de neige**

**blob** *noun*
la **goutte** *fem*

**block** *noun* ▷ see **block** *verb*
1 (*building*)
a block of flats un immeuble
an office block un immeuble de bureaux
2 (*square group of buildings*) le **pâté de maisons**
We drove round the block. Nous avons fait le tour du pâté de maisons.

to **block** *verb* ▷ see **block** *noun*
1 (*an exit, road*) **bloquer** [1]
2 (*a drain, hole*) **boucher** [1]
The sink's blocked. L'évier est bouché.

**blonde** *adjective*
**blond** *masc*, **blonde** *fem*

**blood** *noun*
le **sang** *masc*

- **blood test** la prise de sang

**blossom** *noun*
les **fleurs** *fem plural*
to be in blossom être [6] en fleurs

**blot** *noun*
la **tache** *fem*

**blotchy** *adjective*
(*skin*) **marbré** *masc*, **marbrée** *fem*

♪ **blouse** *noun*
le **chemisier** *masc*

♪ **blow** *noun* ▷ see **blow** *verb*
le **coup** *masc*

♪ to **blow** *verb* ▷ see **blow** *noun*
1 (*wind, person*) **souffler [1]**
to blow your nose se moucher ⓔ [1]
2 (*explosion*) **to blow a hole in something** faire un trou dans quelque chose
**The bomb blew a hole in the wall.** La bombe a fait un trou dans le mur.
- **to blow something out** (*a candle*) **souffler [1]**, (*flames*) **éteindre [60]**
- **to blow up** (*to explode*) **exploser [1]**
**The plane blew up.** L'avion a explosé.
- **to blow something up** (*a balloon, tyre*) **gonfler [1]**, (*a building*) **faire [10] sauter**

**blow-dry** *noun*
le **brushing** *masc*

♪ **blue** *adjective* ▷ see **blue** *noun*
**bleu** *masc*, **bleue** *fem*
blue eyes les yeux bleus

**blue** *noun* ▷ see **blue** *adj*
1 le **bleu** *masc*
2 (*Music*) the blues le blues
- **bluebell** la jacinthe des bois

**blunder** *noun*
la **gaffe** *fem*

**blunt** *adjective*
1 (*knife, scissors*) **émoussé** *masc*, **émoussée** *fem*
2 (*pencil*) **mal taillé** *masc*, **mal taillée** *fem*
3 (*person*) **brusque** *masc & fem*

**blurred** *adjective*
1 (*view, colours*) **indistinct** *masc*, **indistincte** *fem*
2 (*photo*) **flou** *masc*, **floue** *fem*

to **blush** *verb*
**rougir [2]**

**board** *noun*
1 (*plank*) la **planche** *fem*
2 (*blackboard*) le **tableau noir**
3 (*whiteboard*) le **tableau blanc**
4 (*notice board*) le **panneau d'affichage**
5 (*for a board game*) le **jeu** *masc*
a chess board un échiquier
6 (*accommodation in a hotel*)
full board la pension complète
half board la demi-pension
7 (*on a boat*) **on board** à bord
**We were on board the ferry.** Nous étions à bord du ferry.

**boarder** *noun*
(*in a school*) l'**interne** *masc & fem*

**board game** *noun*
le **jeu de société** (*pl* les **jeux de société**)

**boarding** *noun*
l'**embarquement** *masc*
- **boarding card** la carte d'embarquement
- **boarding school** un internat

to **boast** *verb*
**se vanter** ⓔ **[1]**

♪ **boat** *noun*
1 (*in general*) le **bateau** *masc*
2 (*sailing boat*) le **voilier** *masc*
3 (*rowing boat*) la **barque** *fem*

♪ **body** *noun*
1 (*of a person, animal*) le **corps** *masc*
2 (*dead body*) le **cadavre** *masc*
- **bodybuilding** le culturisme
- **bodyguard** le garde du corps

**bodyboard** *noun*
le **bodyboard** *masc*

♪ **boil** *noun* ▷ see **boil** *verb*
1 (*swelling*) le **furoncle** *masc*
2 (*in cooking*) **Bring the water to the boil.** Portez l'eau à ébullition.

♪ to **boil** *verb* ▷ see **boil** *noun*
**bouillir [23]**
**The water's boiling.** L'eau bout.
to boil something faire [10] bouillir quelque chose
**I'm going to boil some water.** Je vais faire bouillir de l'eau.
to boil an egg faire cuire un œuf
- **boil over déborder [1]**

**boiled egg** *noun*
un **œuf à la coque**

**boiler** *noun*
la **chaudière** *fem*

**boiling** *adjective*
1 (*water*) **bouillant** *masc*, **bouillante** *fem*
2 (*weather*)
**It's boiling hot today!** Il fait une chaleur infernale aujourd'hui!

**bolt** *noun* ▷ see **bolt** *verb*
le **verrou** *masc*

to **bolt** *verb* ▷ see **bolt** *noun*
**verrouiller [1]**

**bomb** *noun* ▷ see **bomb** *verb*
la **bombe** *fem*

to **bomb** *verb* ▷ see **bomb** *noun*
**bombarder [1]**

**bombing** *noun*
1 (*in a war*) le **bombardement** *masc*
2 (*terrorist attack*) un **attentat à la bombe**

**bone** *noun*
1 (*of a person, animal*) un **os** *masc*
2 (*of a fish*) une **arête** *fem*

**bonfire** *noun*
1 (*for rubbish*) le **feu de jardin**
2 (*for a celebration*) le **feu de joie**

**bonnet** *noun*
(*of a car*) le **capot** *masc*

**bony** *adjective*
1 (*fish*) **plein d'arêtes** *masc*, **pleine d'arêtes** *fem*
2 (*body*) **anguleux** *masc*, **anguleuse** *fem*
3 (*knee*) **osseux** *masc*, **osseuse** *fem*

to **boo** *verb*
**huer [1]**

♪ **book** *noun* ▷ see **book** *verb*
1 (*that you read*) le **livre** *masc*
**a book about dinosaurs** un livre sur les dinosaures
**a biology book** un livre de biologie
2 (*that you write in*) le **cahier** *masc*
3 (*of cheques, stamps, etc*) le **carnet** *masc*
• **bookcase** la bibliothèque

♪ to **book** *verb* ▷ see **book** *noun*
**réserver [1]**
**I booked a table for 8 o'clock.** J'ai réservé une table pour vingt heures.

♪ **booking** *noun*
(*for holidays, etc*) la **réservation** *fem*
• **booking office** le bureau de location

♪ **booklet** *noun*
la **brochure** *fem*

**bookshelf** *noun*
une **étagère** *fem*

♪ **bookshop** *noun*
la **librairie** *fem*

**boom** *noun*
1 (*of thunder*) le **grondement** *masc*
2 (*time of prosperity*) le **boom** *masc*

♪ **boot** *noun*
1 (*for football, climbing, skiing*) la **chaussure** *fem*
**walking boots** des chaussures de randonnée
2 (*short fashion boot*) le **bottine** *fem*
3 (*knee-high boots, wellingtons*) la **botte** *fem*
4 (*of a car*) le **coffre** *masc*

**border** *noun*
(*between countries*) la **frontière** *fem*

**bore** *noun*
1 (*person*) **raseur** *masc*, **raseuse** *fem* (*informal*)
2 (*nuisance*)
**What a bore!** Quelle barbe!

**bored** *adjective*
**to be bored** s'ennuyer Ⓔ **[41]**
**I'm bored.** Je m'ennuie.
**to get bored** s'ennuyer

♪ **boring** *adjective*
**ennuyeux** *masc*, **ennuyeuse** *fem*
**It's boring at school.** On s'ennuie en cours.

♪ **born** *adjective*
**né** *masc*, **née** *fem*
**to be born** naître Ⓔ **[55]**
**I was born on 12 June in Chester.** Je suis né le douze juin à Chester (*boy speaking*), Je suis née le douze juin à Chester (*girl speaking*).

to **borrow** *verb*
**emprunter [1]**
**Can I borrow your bike?** Je peux emprunter ton vélo?
**to borrow something from someone** emprunter quelque chose à quelqu'un
**I'll borrow some money from Dad.** Je vais emprunter de l'argent à papa.

♪ **boss** *noun*
le **patron** *masc*, la **patronne** *fem*

**bossy** *adjective*
**autoritaire** *masc & fem*

**both** *pronoun*
1 (*when you talk about people*) **tous les deux** *masc*, **toutes les deux** *fem*
**They both came.** Ils sont venus tous les deux (*2 boys or a boy and a girl.*)
**Both my sisters were there.** Mes sœurs y étaient toutes les deux.
2 (*when you talk about things*) **les deux**
**both my feet** mes deux pieds
**They have both been sold.** Les deux sont vendus.
3 **both ... and ...**
**I like to go to the seaside both in winter and in summer.** J'aime aller à la mer en hiver comme en été.

♪ **bother** *noun* ▷ see **bother** *verb*
l'**ennui** *masc*
**I've had a lot of bother with the car.** J'ai eu beaucoup d'ennuis avec la voiture.
**It's too much bother.** C'est trop de tracas.



Ⓔ means the verb takes être to form the perfect

**I answered the question without any bother.** J'ai répondu à la question sans aucune difficulté.

🔑to **bother** *verb* ▷ see **bother** *noun*

1 (*to disturb*) **déranger [52]**
**I'm sorry to bother you.** Je suis désolé de vous déranger (*boy speaking*), Je suis désolée de vous déranger (*girl speaking*).

2 (*to worry*) **inquiéter [24]**
**That doesn't bother me at all.** Ça ne m'inquiète pas du tout.
**Don't bother about the change.** Ne t'inquiète pas pour la monnaie.

3 (*to take the trouble*) **prendre la peine**
**She didn't even bother to come.** Elle n'a même pas pris la peine de venir.
**Don't bother!** Ce n'est pas la peine!

🔑**bottle** *noun*
la **bouteille** *fem*
- **bottle bank** le conteneur à verre
- **bottle opener** un ouvre-bouteille (*pl* les ouvre-bouteilles)

🔑**bottom** *adjective* ▷ see **bottom** *noun*

1 (*lowest*) **inférieur** *masc*, **inférieure** *fem*
**the bottom shelf** le rayon inférieur

2 (*division, team, place*) **dernier** *masc*, **dernière** *fem*
**His team is in bottom place in the league.** Son équipe se trouve à la dernière place du championnat.

3 (*sheet, blanket*) **de dessous**
**Change the bottom sheet.** Changez le drap de dessous.

4 (*flat*) **du rez-de-chaussée**
**I live in the bottom flat.** J'habite l'appartement du rez-de-chaussée.

🔑**bottom** *noun* ▷ see **bottom** *adjective*

1 (*of a hill, wall, steps*) le **pied** *masc*
**She was waiting at the bottom of the hill.** Elle attendait au pied de la colline.

2 (*of a bag, bottle, hole, pond, garden*) le **fond** *masc*
**The car was at the bottom of the lake.** La voiture se trouvait au fond du lac.

3 (*of a page*) le **bas** *masc*
**at the bottom of the page** en bas de la page

4 (*buttocks*) le **derrière** *masc*

to **bounce** *verb*
**rebondir [2]**

**bouncer** *noun*
(*in a club*) le **videur** *masc*

**bound** *adjective*
**He's bound to be late.** Il va sûrement être en retard.
**That was bound to happen.** Cela devait arriver.

**boundary** *noun*
la **limite** *fem*

**bow** *noun*

1 (*in a shoelace, ribbon*) le **nœud** *masc*

2 (*for a violin*) un **archet** *masc*

3 (*for archery*) un **arc** *masc*
**a bow and arrow** un arc et une flèche

🔑**bowl** *noun* ▷ see **bowl** *verb*

1 (*to eat from*) le **bol** *masc*

2 (*larger, for salad, mixing*) le **saladier** *masc*

3 (*for washing up*) la **cuvette** *fem*

🔑to **bowl** *verb* ▷ see **bowl** *noun*
(*a ball*) **lancer [61]**

**bowler** *noun*
(*in cricket*) le **lanceur** *masc*, la **lanceuse** *fem*

**bowling** *noun*
(*tenpin*) le **bowling** *masc*
**to go bowling** jouer **[1]** au bowling

🔑**box** *noun*

1 (*container*) la **boîte** *fem*
**a box of chocolates** une boîte de chocolats

2 **a cardboard box** un carton

3 (*in printed form*) la **case** *fem*

**boxer** *noun*

1 (*fighter*) le **boxeur** *masc*

2 (*dog*) le **boxer** *masc*
- **boxer shorts** le caleçon

**boxing** *noun*
la **boxe** *fem*
**a boxing match** un match de boxe

**Boxing Day** *noun*
**le lendemain de Noël**

**box office** *noun*
le **guichet** *masc*

🔑**boy** *noun*
le **garçon** *masc*
**a little boy** un petit garçon

🔑**boyfriend** *noun*
le **copain** *masc*

**bra** *noun*
le **soutien-gorge** *masc*

**brace** *noun*
(*for teeth*) un **appareil** *masc*

**bracelet** *noun*
le **bracelet** *masc*

**bracket** *noun*
la **parenthèse** *fem*
**in brackets** entre parenthèses

English–French

**brain** *noun*
le **cerveau** *masc* (*pl* les **cerveaux**)
• **brainwave** une idée géniale

**brake** *noun* ▷ see **brake** *verb*
le **frein** *masc*

to **brake** *verb* ▷ see **brake** *noun*
**freiner[1]**

**bramble** *noun*
la **ronce** *fem*

**branch** *noun*
1 (*of a tree*) la **branche** *fem*
2 (*of a shop*) la **succursale** *fem*
3 (*of a bank*) une **agence** *fem*

**brand** *noun*
la **marque** *fem*

**brand new** *adjective*
**tout neuf** *masc*, **toute neuve** *fem*

**brandy** *noun*
le **cognac** *masc*

**brass** *noun*
le **laiton** *masc*, le **cuivre jaune**
**a brass candlestick** un chandelier en cuivre jaune
• **brass band** la fanfare

**brave** *adjective*
**courageux** *masc*, **courageuse** *fem*

**bravery** *noun*
le **courage** *masc*

**Brazil** *noun*
le **Brésil** *masc*

**Brazilian** *adjective* ▷ see **Brazilian** *noun*
**brésilien** *masc*, **brésilienne** *fem*

**Brazilian** *noun* ▷ see **Brazilian** *adj*
le **Brésilien** *masc*, la **Brésilienne** *fem*

**bread** *noun*
le **pain** *masc*
**a loaf of bread** un pain
**a slice of bread** une tranche de pain

**break** *noun* ▷ see **break** *verb*
1 (*short rest*) la **pause** *fem*
**fifteen minutes' break** une pause de quinze minutes
**to take a break** faire**[10]** une pause
**Let's take a break for five minutes.** Faisons une pause de cinq minutes.
2 (*in school*) la **récréation** *fem*
3 (*holiday*) les **vacances** *fem plural*
**the Christmas break** les vacances de Noël

to **break** *verb* ▷ see **break** *noun*
1 (*a plate, vase*) **casser[1]**
**He broke a glass.** Il a cassé un verre.
2 (*by itself - window, cup, eggs*) **se casser** Ⓔ **[1]**
**The eggs broke.** Les œufs se sont cassés.
3 (*an arm, leg, tooth*) **se casser** Ⓔ **[1]**
**to break your arm** se casser le bras
**I broke my arm.** Je me suis cassé le bras.
4 (*a record*) **battre[21]**
**The French swimmer broke the record.** Le nageur français a battu le record.
5 **to break a promise** ne pas tenir**[77]** sa promesse
**You broke your promise.** Tu n'as pas tenu ta promesse.
**to break the rules** ne pas respecter**[1]** le règlement
**You mustn't break the rules.** Il faut respecter le règlement.
• **to break down tomber** Ⓔ **[1] en panne**
**The car broke down.** La voiture est tombée en panne.
• **to break in** (*thief*) **entrer** Ⓔ **[1] par effraction**
**Someone broke in and stole our TV.** Quelqu'un est entré et nous a volé la télé.
• **to break out**
1 (*fire*) **se déclarer** Ⓔ **[1]**
2 (*fight, storm*) **éclater[1]**
3 (*prisoner*) **s'évader** Ⓔ **[1]**
• **to break up**
1 (*family, couple*) **se séparer** Ⓔ **[1]**
2 (*crowd, clouds*) **se disperser** Ⓔ **[1]**
3 (*from school*) **We break up on Thursday.** Les cours finissent jeudi.

**breakdown** *noun*
1 (*of a vehicle*) la **panne** *fem*
**We had a breakdown on the motorway.** Nous sommes tombés en panne sur l'autoroute.
2 (*in talks, negotiations*) la **rupture** *fem*
3 (*mental*) la **dépression** *fem*
**to have a breakdown** faire**[10]** une dépression
**She had a breakdown after the accident.** Après l'accident, elle a fait une dépression.
• **breakdown truck** le camion de dépannage

**breakfast** *noun*
le **petit déjeuner** *masc*

**break-in** *noun*
le **cambriolage** *masc*

**breast** *noun*
1 (*of a woman*) le **sein** *masc*
2 (*of a chicken*) le **blanc** *masc*
• **breaststroke** la brasse

**breath** *noun*
1 (*when you breathe in*) le **souffle** *masc*
**out of breath** à bout de souffle

a b c d e f g h i j k l m n o p q r s t u v w x y z

to get your breath reprendre [64] son souffle
2 (*when you breathe out*) l'**haleine** *fem*
to have bad breath avoir [5] mauvaise haleine

to **breathe** *verb*
**respirer** [1]

**breathing** *noun*
la **respiration** *fem*

**breed** *noun* ▷ see **breed** *verb*
(*of dog, cat, etc*) la **race** *fem*

to **breed** *verb* ▷ see **breed** *noun*
1 (*animals*) **élever** [50]
2 (*to have young*) **se reproduire** Ⓔ [26]

**breeze** *noun*
la **brise** *fem*

to **brew** *verb*
1 (*tea*) **préparer** [1]
2 (*beer*) **brasser** [1]

**brewery** *noun*
la **brasserie** *fem*

**brick** *noun*
la **brique** *fem*

♪ **bride** *noun*
la **mariée** *fem*
the bride and groom les mariés *masc plural*

♪ **bridegroom** *noun*
le **marié** *masc*

**bridesmaid** *noun*
la **demoiselle d'honneur**

♪ **bridge** *noun*
1 (*on a river*) le **pont** *masc*
a bridge over the Seine un pont sur la Seine
2 (*card game*) le **bridge** *masc*
to play bridge jouer [1] au bridge

**bridle** *noun*
la **bride** *fem*

**brief** *adjective*
**bref** *masc*, **brève** *fem*

**briefcase** *noun*
la **serviette** *fem*

**briefly** *adverb*
**brièvement**

**briefs** *plural noun*
le **slip** *masc*

**bright** *adjective*
1 (*colour, light*) **vif** *masc*, **vive** *fem*
bright green le vert vif
Try to look on the bright side. Essayez de voir le bon côté des choses.
2 (*sunshine*) **éclatant** *masc*, **éclatante** *fem*
3 (*clever*) **intelligent** *masc*, **intelligente** *fem*
She's very bright. Elle est très intelligente.

to **brighten up** *verb*
(*weather, day*) **s'éclaircir** Ⓔ [3]
The weather's brightening up. Le temps s'éclaircit.

**brilliant** *adjective*
1 (*very clever*) **brillant** *masc*, **brillante** *fem*
a brilliant surgeon un chirurgien brillant
He's brilliant at maths. Il est très doué en maths.
2 (*wonderful*) **génial** *masc*, **géniale** *fem*, **géniaux** *masc pl*, **géniales** *fem pl*
The party was brilliant! La fête était géniale!

♪ to **bring** *verb*
1 (*something you carry*) **apporter** [1]
They brought a present. Ils ont apporté un cadeau.
Bring your camera! Apporte ton appareil photo!
Bring the garden chairs in. Rentrez les chaises de jardin.
2 (*a person, animal*) **amener** [50]
She's bringing all the children. Elle va amener tous les enfants.
- **to bring something back rapporter** [1] **quelque chose**
She brought me back a present. Elle m'a rapporté un cadeau.
- **to bring somebody up** (*children*) **élever** [50] **quelqu'un**
He was brought up by his aunt. Il a été élevé par sa tante.

♪ **Britain**, **Great Britain** *noun*
la **Grande-Bretagne** *fem*
Britain's amabassadeur l'ambassadeur de la Grande-Bretagne
to go to Britain aller Ⓔ [7] en Grande-Bretagne
to be in Britain être [6] en Grande-Bretagne
They came to Britain in 1995. Ils sont arrivés en Grande-Bretagne en 1995.
We have lived in Britain for three years. Nous vivons en Grande-Bretagne depuis trois ans.

♪ **British** *adjective* ▷ see **British** *pl noun*
**britannique** *masc & fem*
the British Isles les îles Britanniques

**WORD TIP** Adjectives never have capitals in French, even for nationality.

♪ **British** *plural noun* ▷ see **British** *adj*
the British les Britanniques *masc & fem plural*

English–French

**Brittany** *noun*
la **Bretagne** *fem* (*a region of north-west France*)
to be in Brittany être [6] en Bretagne
to go to Brittany aller ⓔ [7] en Bretagne

**broad** *adjective*
**large** *masc & fem*
- **broad bean** la fève

**broadcast** *noun* ▷ see **broadcast** *verb*
une **émission** *fem*

♪ to **broadcast** *verb* ▷ see **broadcast** *noun*
(*a programme*) **diffuser** [1]

**broccoli** *noun*
le **brocoli** *masc*

♪ **brochure** *noun*
la **brochure** *fem*

**broke** *adjective*
to be broke être [6] fauché

**broken** *adjective*
**cassé** *masc*, **cassée** *fem*
The phone's broken. Le téléphone est cassé.
My car has broken down. Ma voiture est en panne.

**bronchitis** *noun*
la **bronchite** *fem*
to have bronchitis avoir [5] une bronchite

**brooch** *noun*
la **broche** *fem*

**broom** *noun*
1 (*for sweeping*) le **balai** *masc*
2 (*plant*) le **genêt** *masc*

♪ **brother** *noun*
le **frère** *masc*
my little brother mon petit frère
- **brother-in-law** le beau-frère (*pl* les beaux-frères)

♪ **brown** *adjective*
1 (*colour*) **marron** *invariable adjective*
my brown jacket ma veste marron
your brown shoes tes chaussures marron
light brown marron clair
dark brown marron foncé
2 (*tanned in the sun*) **bronzé** *masc*, **bronzée** *fem*
to go brown bronzer [1]
I go brown easily. Je bronze facilement.
3 (*hair*) **châtain** *invariable adjective*

**WORD TIP** *châtain* and *marron* do not change in the feminine or plural

- **brown bread** le pain complet
- **brown sugar** le sucre roux

**bruise** *noun*
1 (*on a person*) le **bleu** *masc*
2 (*on fruit*) la **tache** *fem*

♪ **brush** *noun* ▷ see **brush** *verb*
1 (*for hair, clothes, shoes*) la **brosse** *fem*
my hair brush ma brosse à cheveux
2 (*for sweeping*) le **balai** *masc*
3 (*for painting*) le **pinceau** *masc*

♪ to **brush** *verb* ▷ see **brush** *noun*
1 (*the floor, clothes*) **brosser** [1]
2 (*your hair, teeth*) **se brosser** ⓔ [1]
to brush your hair se brosser les cheveux
to brush your teeth se brosser les dents
She brushed her hair. Elle s'est brossé les cheveux.

**Brussels** *noun*
**Bruxelles**
- **Brussels sprout** le chou de Bruxelles

**bubble** *noun*
la **bulle** *fem*
- **bubble bath** le bain moussant

**bucket** *noun*
le **seau** *masc* (*pl* les **seaux**)

**buckle** *noun*
la **boucle** *fem*

**Buddhism** *noun*
le **bouddhisme** *masc*

**Buddhist** *noun*
le & la **bouddhiste** *masc & fem*

**WORD TIP** Adjectives and nouns of religion start with a small letter in French

**budget** *noun*
le **budget** *masc*

**budgie** *noun*
la **perruche** *fem*

♪ **buffet** *noun*
le **buffet** *masc*
- **buffet car** la voiture-buffet

**bug** *noun*
1 (*insect*) la **bestiole** *fem* (*informal*)
2 (*germ*) le **microbe** *masc*
a stomach bug une gastroentérite
3 (*in a computer*) le **virus** *masc*

to **build** *verb*
**construire** [26]

**builder** *noun*
le **maçon** *masc*

♪ **building** *noun*
1 (*house, church, etc.*) le **bâtiment** *masc*
2 (*with offices, flats*) un **immeuble** *masc*
- **building site** le chantier
- **building society** la société d'investissement et de crédit immobilier

**built-up** *adjective*
**urbanisé** *masc*, **urbanisée** *fem*
a built-up area une agglomération

**bulb** *noun*
1 (*for a light*) une **ampoule** *fem*
2 (*that you plant*) un **oignon** *masc*

**bull** *noun*
le **taureau** *masc* (*pl* les **taureaux**)

**bulldozer** *noun*
le **bulldozer** *masc*

♪**bullet** *noun*
la **balle** *fem*

**bulletin** *noun*
le **bulletin** *masc*

**bully** *noun* ▷ see **bully** *verb*
la **brute** *fem*
He's a bully. C'est une brute.

to **bully** *verb* ▷ see **bully** *noun*
**tyranniser [1]**

**bum** *noun*
le **derrière** *masc*

**bump** *noun* ▷ see **bump** *verb*
1 (*that sticks up*) la **bosse** *fem*
a bump on the head une bosse à la tête
a bump in the road une bosse sur la route
2 (*jolt*) la **secousse** *fem*
3 (*noise*) le **bruit sourd**

to **bump** *verb* ▷ see **bump** *noun*
1 (*to bang*) **cogner [1]**
I bumped my head. Je me suis cogné la tête.
She bumped into the wall. Elle est rentrée dans le mur.
2 to bump into somebody croiser **[1]** quelqu'un
I bumped into Sue in the supermarket. J'ai croisé Sue au supermarché.

**bumper** *noun*
le **pare-chocs** *masc*

**bumpy** *adjective*
1 (*road*) **accidenté** *masc*, **accidentée** *fem*
2 (*plane landing*) **agité** *masc*, **agitée** *fem*

**bun** *noun*
1 (*for a burger*) le **petit pain** *masc*
2 (*sugary*) le **petit cake** *masc*

**bunch** *noun*
1 (*of flowers*) le **bouquet** *masc*
2 (*of carrots, radishes*) la **botte** *fem*
3 (*of keys*) le **trousseau** *masc*
4 (*of grapes*) la grappe *fem*

**bundle** *noun*
le **tas** *masc*

**bungalow** *noun*
le **pavillon** *masc*

**bunk** *noun*
(*on a train, boat*) la **couchette** *fem*
• **bunk beds** les lits superposés *masc pl*

**bureau** *noun*
une **agence** *fem*

**burger** *noun*
le **hamburger** *masc*

**burglar** *noun*
le **cambrioleur** *masc*, la **cambrioleuse** *fem*
• **burglar alarm** la sonnerie d'alarme

♪**burglary** *noun*
le **cambriolage** *masc*

**burn** *noun* ▷ see **burn** *verb*
la **brûlure** *fem*

to **burn** *verb* ▷ see **burn** *noun*
1 (*paper, wood, etc.*) **brûler [1]**
2 (*to burn yourself*) **se brûler** Ⓔ **[1]**
She burnt herself on the grill. Elle s'est brûlée au gril.
3 (*by accident*) **laisser [1] brûler**
Mum's burnt her cake. Maman a laissé brûler son gâteau.
4 (*in the sun*) I burn easily. J'attrape facilement des coups de soleil.

**burnt** *adjective*
**brûlé** *masc*, **brûlée** *fem*

♪**burst** *adjective* ▷ see **burst** *verb*
**crevé** *masc*, **crevée** *fem*
a burst tyre un pneu crevé

♪to **burst** *verb* ▷ see **burst** *adj*
1 (*balloon, tyre*) **crever [50]**
2 (*to do something suddenly*) **to burst out laughing** éclater **[1]** de rire
Jo burst out laughing. Jo a éclaté de rire.
to burst into tears fondre **[3]** en larmes
The baby burst into tears. Le bébé a fondu en larmes.
to burst into flames prendre **[64]** feu
The bus burst into flames. Le bus a pris feu.

to **bury** *verb*
**enterrer [1]**

♪**bus** *noun*
1 (*public transport*) un **autobus** *masc*, le **bus** *masc*
a bus ticket un ticket de bus
I get the bus to school. Je prends le bus pour aller à l'école.
2 (*coach*) le **car** *masc*
I usually go to London by bus. D'habitude je vais à Londres en car.
• **bus driver** le conducteur de bus, la conductrice de bus

**bush** *noun*
le **buisson** *masc*

**business** *noun*
1 (*commercial dealings*) les **affaires** *fem plural*
**a business letter** une lettre d'affaires
**to be in business** être [6] dans les affaires
**Her father's in business.** Son père est dans les affaires.
**He's in Leeds on business.** Il est à Leeds en voyage d'affaires.
**She's in the insurance business.** Elle travaille dans les assurances.
2 (*company*) une **entreprise** *fem*
**small businesses** les petites entreprises
- **business class** la classe affaires
- **businessman** un homme d'affaires
- **business trip** le voyage d'affaires
- **businesswoman** une femme d'affaires

**bus lane** *noun*
le **couloir d'autobus**

**bus pass** *noun*
la **carte de bus**

**bus route** *noun*
la **ligne d'autobus**

**bus shelter** *noun*
un **Abribus®** *masc*

**bus station** *noun*
la **gare routière**

**bus stop** *noun*
l'**arrêt de bus**

**bust** *noun*
la **poitrine** *fem*
**bust size** le tour de poitrine

**busy** *adjective*
1 (*person*) **occupé** *masc*, **occupée** *fem*
**He's busy.** Il est occupé.
**to be busy doing something** être [6] en train de faire quelque chose
**Dad's busy washing the car.** Papa est en train de laver la voiture.
2 (*day, week*) **chargé** *masc*, **chargée** *fem*
**a busy day** une journée chargée
3 (*street, shop*) **très fréquenté** *masc*, **très fréquentée** *fem*
**The shops were busy.** Il y avait beaucoup de monde dans les magasins.
4 (*phone*) **occupé** *masc*, **occupée** *fem*
**The line's busy.** La ligne est occupée.

**but** *conjunction*
**mais**
**not Thursday but Friday** pas jeudi mais vendredi
**Max is small but strong.** Max est petit mais fort.
**I'll try, but it's difficult.** J'essaierai, mais c'est difficile.

**butcher** *noun*
le **boucher** *masc*, la **bouchère** *fem*
**He's a butcher.** Il est boucher.
**I'm going to the butcher's.** Je vais chez le boucher.
**Where is the nearest butcher's?** Où est la boucherie la plus proche?

**butter** *noun* ▷ see **butter** *verb*
le **beurre** *masc*
- **buttercup** le bouton-d'or
- **butterfly** le papillon

to **butter** *verb* ▷ see **butter** *noun*
**beurrer [1]**

**button** *noun*
le **bouton** *masc*
**Press the record button.** Appuyez sur la touche d'enregistrement.
- **buttonhole** la boutonnière

**buy** *noun* ▷ see **buy** *verb*
**a good buy** une bonne affaire
**a bad buy** une mauvaise affaire

to **buy** *verb* ▷ see **buy** *noun*
**acheter [16]**
**I bought the tickets.** J'ai acheté les billets.
**to buy something for somebody** acheter quelque chose pour quelqu'un
**Sarah bought him a sweater.** Sarah lui a acheté un pull.
**to buy something from someone** acheter quelque chose à quelqu'un
**I bought my bike from Tom.** J'ai acheté mon vélo à Tom.

**buyer** *noun*
un **acheteur** *masc*, une **acheteuse** *fem*

to **buzz** *verb*
(*flies, bees*) **bourdonner [1]**

**buzzer** *noun*
la **sonnerie** *fem*

**by** *preposition*
1 (*using, because of*) **par**
**by telephone** par téléphone
**by mistake** par erreur
**The hamster was eaten by the dog.** Le hamster a été mangé par le chien.
**to take somebody by the hand** prendre quelqu'un par la main
**Lucy took me by the hand.** Lucy m'a pris par la main.
2 (*when saying how you travel*) **en**
**Ravi came by bus.** Ravi est venu en bus.
**They are leaving by train.** Ils partent en train.

I come to school by car. Je viens à l'école en voiture.

3 (*near a place*) **à côté de**
**She was sitting by the fire.** Elle était assise à côté du feu.
**I'd love to live by the sea.** J'aimerais bien habiter au bord de la mer.
**His family lives close by.** Sa famille habite tout près.

4 (*before a time*) **avant**
**Kevin was back by four.** Kevin est rentré avant quatre heures.

5 (*with myself, yourself, etc*) **tout seul** *masc*, **toute seule** *fem*
**by yourself** tout seul (*boy, man*), toute seule (*girl, woman*)
**I was by myself.** J'étais tout seul (*boy speaking*), J'étais toute seule (*girl speaking*).
**She did it by herself.** Elle l'a fait toute seule.

6 **to go by** passer ⓔ **[1]**
**A car went by.** Une voiture est passée.

**bye** *exclamation*
**au revoir**
**Bye for now!** À bientôt!

**bypass** *noun*
la **rocade** *fem*

# C c

**cab** *noun*
le **taxi** *masc*

♪ **cabbage** *noun*
le **chou** *masc* (*pl* les **choux**)

**cabin** *noun*
la **cabine** *fem*

♪ **cable** *noun*
1 (*electrical*) le **câble** *masc*
2 (*TV*) la **télévision par câble**
**They've got cable.** Ils ont le câble.
- **cable car** le téléphérique *masc*
- **cable TV** la télévision par câble

**cactus** *noun*
le **cactus** *masc*

♪ **cafe** *noun*
le **café** *masc*

**cage** *noun*
la **cage** *fem*

♪ **cake** *noun*
le **gâteau** *masc* (*pl* les **gâteaux**)
**a piece of cake** un morceau de gâteau
**a birthday cake** un gâteau d'anniversaire

to **calculate** *verb*
**calculer [1]**

**calculation** *noun*
le **calcul** *masc*
**to do some calculations** faire **[10]** des calculs

**calculator** *noun*
la **calculatrice** *fem*

**calendar** *noun*
le **calendrier** *masc*

♪ **calf** *noun*
1 (*animal*) le **veau** *masc* (*pl* les **veaux**)
2 (*of your leg*) le **mollet** *masc*

♪ **call** *noun* ▷ see **call** *verb*
un **appel** *masc*
**Thanks for your call.** Merci de votre appel.
**I've had several calls.** J'ai eu plusieurs appels.
**There was a call for you.** Quelqu'un t'a téléphoné.
**I got a phone call from her.** J'ai eu un coup de téléphone d'elle.

♪ to **call** *verb* ▷ see **call** *noun*
1 (*to phone*) **appeler [18]**
**to call a taxi** appeler un taxi
**Let's call a taxi!** Appelons un taxi!
**to call the doctor** appeler le médecin
**Call this number.** Appelez ce numéro.

2 (*to name*) **appeler [18]**
**They've called the baby Rachel.** Ils ont appelé le bébé Rachel.

3 **to be called ...** s'appeler ⓔ **[18]** ...
**She's called Salma.** Elle s'appelle Salma.
**I've got a brother called Josh.** J'ai un frère qui s'appelle Josh.
**What's he called?** Comment s'appelle-t-il?
**It's called 'babyfoot'.** Ça s'appelle un 'babyfoot'.
**What's it called in French?** Ça s'appelle comment en français? ⏩

**4** (*to insult*) **to call somebody something** traiter **[1]** quelqu'un de quelque chose
**She called him an idiot.** Elle l'a traité d'imbécile.

**5** (*to wake up*) **réveiller [1]**
**Call me at eight o'clock.** Réveille-moi à huit heures.

• to **call back**
**rappeler [18]**
**I'll call back later.** Je rappellerai plus tard.
**He won't call her back.** Il ne va pas la rappeler.

• to **call in**
**passer [1]** Ⓔ
**She called in briefly yesterday.** Elle est passée rapidement hier.

**call box** *noun*
la **cabine téléphonique**

**calm** *adjective* ▷ see **calm** *verb*
**calme** *masc & fem*
**The sea is calm.** La mer est calme.
**We remained calm.** Nous sommes restés calmes.

to **calm** *verb* ▷ see **calm** *noun*
**calmer [1]**

• to **calm down**
**1** **se calmer** Ⓔ **[1]**
**He's calmed down.** Il s'est calmé.
**2** **to calm somebody down** calmer quelqu'un
**I tried to calm her down.** J'ai essayé de la calmer.

**calmly** *adverb*
**calmement**

**calorie** *noun*
la **calorie** *fem*

**camcorder** *noun*
le **caméscope** *masc*

**camel** *noun*
le **chameau** *masc* (*pl* les **chameaux**)

**camera** *noun*
**1** (*for photos*) un **appareil photo** (*pl* les **appareils photo**)
**2** (*for film, TV*) la **caméra** *fem*
• **cameraman** le caméraman *masc*

**camp** *noun* ▷ see **camp** *verb*
le **camp** *masc*

to **camp** *verb* ▷ see **camp** *noun*
**camper [1]**
**We camped in the forest.** Nous avons campé dans la forêt.

**campaign** *noun*
la **campagne** *fem*
**an advertising campaign** une campagne publicitaire

**camper van** *noun*
le **camping-car** *masc*

**camping** *noun*
le **camping** *masc*
**to go camping** faire **[10]** du camping
**We're going camping in Italy.** Nous allons faire du camping en Italie.

**campsite** *noun*
le **terrain de camping**

**can** *noun* ▷ see **can** *verb*
**1** (*for food, drinks*) la **boîte** *fem*
**a can of tuna** une boîte de thon
**2** (*for beer*) la **canette** *fem*
**3** (*for petrol, oil*) le **bidon** *masc*

**can** *verb* ▷ see **can** *noun*
**1** (*to be able to do something*) **pouvoir [12]**
**You can leave your bag here.** Tu peux laisser ton sac ici.
**They cannot believe it.** Ils ne peuvent pas le croire.
**They couldn't come.** Ils n'ont pas pu venir.
**2** (*to know how to do something*) **savoir [70]**
**She can drive.** Elle sait conduire.
**I can't swim.** Je ne sais pas nager.
**Can you play the guitar?** Tu sais jouer de la guitare?
**3** (*when* **can** *is not translated in French*)
**Can you hear me?** Est-ce que tu m'entends?
**I can't see him.** Je ne le vois pas.
**Can you understand?** Tu comprends?
**I can't remember.** Je ne me souviens pas.
**4** (*to ask for, to offer help*) **pouvoir [12]**
**Can you open the door, please?** Est-ce que tu peux ouvrir la porte, s'il te plaît?
**Can I help you?** Est-ce que je peux t'aider?
▷ **could**

**Canada** *noun*
le **Canada** *masc*
**to be in Canada** être **[6]** au Canada
**to go to Canada** aller Ⓔ **[7]** au Canada

**WORD TIP** Countries and regions in French take *le*, *la* or *les*.

***Canada***

The second largest French-speaking city in the world is Montreal, in Canada.

**Canadian** *adjective* ▷ see **Canadian** *noun*
**canadien** *masc*, **canadienne** *fem*

**WORD TIP** Adjectives never have capitals in French, even for nationality or regional origin.

**Canadian** *noun* ▷ see **Canadian** *adjective*
le **Canadien** *masc*, la **Canadienne** *fem*



Ⓔ means the verb takes être to form the perfect

**canal** *noun*
le **canal** *masc* (*pl* les **canaux**)

**canary** *noun*
le **canari** *masc*

to **cancel** *verb*
**annuler [1]**
**to cancel a concert** annuler un concert

**cancer** *noun*
le **cancer** *masc*
**lung cancer** le cancer du poumon
**to have cancer** avoir **[5]** le cancer

**Cancer** *noun*
**Cancer** *masc*
**I'm Cancer.** Je suis Cancer.

**WORD TIP** Signs of the zodiac do not take an article: *un* or *une*.

**candidate** *noun*
le **candidat** *masc*, la **candidate** *fem*

**candle** *noun*
la **bougie** *fem*

**candyfloss** *noun*
la **barbe à papa**

**canned** *adjective*
**en conserve**
**canned tuna** le thon en conserve

**cannon** *noun*
le **canon** *masc*

**cannot** *verb* ▷ **can** *verb*

**canoe** *noun*
le **canoë** *masc*

**canoeing** *noun*
**to go canoeing** faire **[10]** du canoë

**can-opener** *noun*
un **ouvre-boîtes** *masc* (*pl* les **ouvre-boîtes**)

♪ **canteen** *noun*
la **cantine** *fem*
**to eat in the canteen** manger **[52]** à la cantine.

**canvas** *noun*
la **toile** *fem*

**cap** *noun*
1 (*hat*) la **casquette** *fem*
**a baseball cap** une casquette de baseball
2 (*on a bottle, tube*) le **bouchon** *masc*

**capable** *adjective*
**capable** *masc & fem*
**a capable girl** une fille capable
**We're quite capable of doing it.** Nous sommes bien capables de le faire.

**capital** *noun*
1 (*city*) la **capitale** *fem*
**Paris is the capital of France.** Paris est la capitale de la France.
2 (*letter*) la **majuscule** *fem*
**in capitals** en majuscules

**capitalism** *noun*
le **capitalisme** *masc*

**Capricorn** *noun*
**Capricorne** *masc*
**Linda's Capricorn.** Linda est Capricorne.

**WORD TIP** Signs of the zodiac do not take an article: *un* or *une*.

to **capsize** *verb*
**chavirer [1]**
**to capsize a boat** faire **[10]** chavirer un bateau

**captain** *noun*
le **capitaine** *masc*

**captivity** *noun*
**in captivity** en captivité
**They're kept in captivity.** Ils sont gardés en captivité.

to **capture** *verb*
1 (*an animal, a person*) **capturer [1]**
2 (*a town, a castle*) **prendre [64]**

♪ **car** *noun*
la **voiture** *fem*
**in the car** dans la voiture
**The car was parked here.** La voiture était garée ici.
**We're going by car.** Nous y allons en voiture.

**caramel** *noun*
le **caramel** *masc*

♪ **caravan** *noun*
la **caravane** *fem*
**a caravan holiday** des vacances en caravane

**car crash** *noun*
un **accident de voiture**

♪ **card** *noun*
1 (*for playing games*) la **carte** *fem*
**a pack of cards** un jeu de cartes
**a game of cards** une partie de cartes
**to play cards** jouer **[1]** aux cartes
2 (*for birthdays, etc*) la **carte** *fem*
**I sent her a card from Nice.** Je lui ai envoyé une carte de Nice.
▷ **birthday card, postcard**

**cardboard** *noun*
le **carton** *masc*
• **cardboard box** le carton

**cardigan** *noun*
le **cardigan** *masc*

**cardphone** *noun*
le **téléphone à carte**

**care** *noun* ▷ see **care** *verb*
1 (*doing your best*) le **soin** *masc*
with great care avec beaucoup de soin
to take care to do something prendre **[64]** soin de faire quelque chose
I take care to eat well. Je prends soin de bien manger. ▷ **medical care**
2 to take care of somebody (*to look after*) s'occuper ⓔ **[1]** de quelqu'un
She takes care of us. Elle s'occupe de nous.
3 to take care of something (*to sort out*) s'occuper ⓔ **[1]** de quelque chose
I'll take care of the present. Je vais m'occuper du cadeau.
4 to take care (when) doing something (*to watch out*) faire **[10]** attention en faisant quelque chose
Take care typing the password. Fais attention en tapant le mot de passe.
5 Bye, take care! Salut! À bientôt!

to **care** *verb* ▷ see **care** *noun*
1 to care about something se soucier ⓔ **[1]** de quelque chose
They don't care about recycling. Ils ne se soucient pas du recyclage.
2 She doesn't care. Ça lui est égal.
I couldn't care less! Ça m'est complètement égal!
Who cares! On s'en fiche! (*informal*)
3 to care about somebody aimer **[1]** quelqu'un
They don't care about me. Ils ne m'aiment pas.

**career** *noun*
la **carrière** *fem*

**careful** *adjective*
**prudent** *masc*, **prudente** *fem*
to be careful faire **[10]** attention
Be careful! Fais attention!
to be careful not to do something faire **[10]** attention de ne pas faire quelque chose
Be careful not to bang your head. Fais attention de ne pas te cogner la tête.

**carefully** *adverb*
1 (*paying attention*) **attentivement**
Read the questions carefully. Lisez attentivement les questions.
2 (*with great care*) **avec précaution**
3 (*to avoid mistakes*) **soigneusement**

**careless** *adjective*
1 (*person*) to be careless ne pas faire **[10]** attention à ce qu'on fait
She's very careless. Elle ne fait pas attention à ce qu'elle fait.
2 (*piece of work*) **peu soigné** *masc*, **peu soignée** *fem*
This is careless work. C'est du travail peu soigné.
careless mistakes des fautes d'inattention

**caretaker** *noun*
le **gardien** *masc*, la **gardienne** *fem*

**car ferry** *noun*
le **ferry** *masc*

**car hire** *noun*
la **location de voitures**

**Caribbean** *noun*
the Caribbean les Caraïbes *fem plural*
the Caribbean Sea la mer des Caraïbes
to be in the Caribbean être **[6]** aux Caraïbes
to go to the Caribbean aller ⓔ **[7]** aux Caraïbes

**carnation** *noun*
un **œillet** *masc*

**carnival** *noun*
le **carnaval** *masc* (*pl* les **carnavals**)

**car park** *noun*
le **parking** *masc*

**carpenter** *noun*
le **menuisier** *masc*
He's a carpenter. Il est menuisier.

**carpentry** *noun*
la **menuiserie** *fem*

**carpet** *noun*
1 (*fitted*) la **moquette** *fem*
2 (*large rug*) le **tapis** *masc*

**car phone** *noun*
le **téléphone de voiture**

**car radio** *noun*
un **autoradio** *masc*

**carriage** *noun*
(*of a train*) la **voiture** *fem*

**carrier bag** *noun*
le **sac en plastique**

**carrot** *noun*
la **carotte** *fem*

to **carry** *verb*
1 (*vehicles, planes*) **transporter [1]**
The coach was carrying schoolchildren. Le car transportait des élèves.
• to **carry on**

continuer **[1]**
**to carry on doing something** continuer à faire quelque chose
**They carried on talking.** Ils ont continué à parler.

**carrycot** *noun*
le **porte-bébé** *invariable masc*

**carsick** *adjective*
**to be carsick** être **[6]** malade en voiture

**cart** *noun*
la **charrette** *fem*

**carton** *noun*
1 (*of cream, yoghurt*) le **pot** *masc*
2 (*of milk, orange*) la **brique** *fem*

**cartoon** *noun*
1 (*film*) le **dessin animé**
2 (*comic strip*) la **bande dessinée**, **la BD**
3 (*amusing drawing*) le **dessin humoristique**

**cartridge** *noun*
(*for a pen, a video*) la **cartouche** *fem*

to **carve** *verb*
(*meat*) **découper [1]**

**case** *noun*
1 (*suitcase*) la **valise** *fem*
**to pack a case** faire une valise
2 (*large wooden crate*) la **caisse** *fem*
3 (*for your glasses, etc*) un **étui** *masc*
4 (*situation*) le **cas** *masc*
**In that case, I'm not going.** En ce cas, je n'y vais pas.
**In any case, it's too late.** De toute façon, c'est trop tard.

**cash** *noun*
1 (*money in general*) l'**argent** *masc*
**I haven't got any cash on me.** Je n'ai pas d'argent.
2 (*notes and coins*) les **espèces** *fem plural*
**I paid £50 in cash.** J'ai payé cinquante livres en espèces.
- **cash desk** la caisse
- **cash dispenser** le guichet automatique

**cashier** *noun*
le **caissier** *masc*, la **caissière** *fem*

**cash point** *noun*
le **distributeur automatique**

**cassette** *noun*
la **cassette** *fem*

**cast** *noun*
**the cast** les acteurs *masc plural*

**castle** *noun*
le **château** *masc* (*pl* les **châteaux**)
**a medieval castle** un château du Moyen Âge

**casual** *adjective*
**décontracté** *masc*, **décontractée** *fem*
- **casual clothes** les vêtements décontractés *masc pl*

**casualty** *noun*
1 (*in an accident, explosion*) la **victime** *fem*
**many casualties** plusieurs victimes
2 (*in a crash*) le **blessé** *masc*, la **blessée** *fem*
3 **to be in casualty** être **[6]** aux urgences

**cat** *noun*
1 le **chat** *masc*
**a big black cat** un gros chat noir
2 (*female*) la **chatte** *fem*

**catalogue** *noun*
le **catalogue** *masc*

**catastrophe** *noun*
la **catastrophe** *fem*

**catch** *noun* ▷ **see catch** *verb*
(*on a window, door*) la **fermeture** *fem*

to **catch** *verb* ▷ **see catch** *noun*
1 (*a ball, a person, an animal*) **attraper [1]**
**Jack caught a mouse.** Jack a attrapé une souris.
**You can't catch me!** Tu ne m'attraperas pas!
**I caught hold of a branch.** J'ai attrapé une branche.
2 **to catch somebody doing something** attraper quelqu'un en train de faire quelque chose
**They caught her stealing.** On l'a attrapée en train de voler.
**to get caught doing something** se faire Ⓔ **[10]** attraper en train de faire quelque chose
**He got caught copying.** Il s'est fait attraper en train de copier.
3 (*a bus, plane, train*) **prendre [64]**
4 (*an illness*) **attraper [1]**
**I've caught a cold.** J'ai attrapé un rhume.
5 **to catch your finger in something** se prendre Ⓔ **[64]** les doigts dans quelque chose
**I caught my finger in the door.** Je me suis pris le doigt dans la porte.
6 ▷ **fire**
- **to catch up with somebody rattraper [1] quelqu'un**

**category** *noun*
la **catégorie** *fem*

**catering** *noun*
la **restauration** *fem*

**caterpillar** *noun*
la **chenille** *fem*

English–French

**cathedral** *noun*
la **cathédrale** *fem*
Wells cathedral la cathédrale de Wells

**Catholic** *noun,, adjective*
un & une **catholique** *masc & fem*

**WORD TIP** Adjectives and nouns of religion start with a small letter in French

**cattle** *plural noun*
le **bétail** *masc singular*

**caught** ▷**catch** *verb*

**cauliflower** *noun*
le **chou-fleur** *masc* (*pl* les **choux-fleurs**)

**cause** *noun* ▷ see **cause** *verb*
1 (*of fire, accident, problem*) la **cause** *fem*
**the main causes of pollution** les causes principales de la pollution
2 (*charity, political goal*) la **cause** *fem*
**a good cause** une bonne cause

to **cause** *verb* ▷ see **cause** *noun*
1 (*problems, damage*) **causer[1]**
**to cause trouble** créer**[32]** des problèmes
**Stop causing trouble!** Arrête de créer des problèmes!
2 (*chaos, disease*) **provoquer[1]**
**It caused delays.** Ça a provoqué des retards.

**caution** *noun*
la **prudence** *fem*

**cautious** *adjective*
**prudent** *masc*, **prudente** *fem*

**cave** *noun*
la **grotte** *fem*

**caving** *noun*
la **spéléologie** *fem*
**to go caving** faire**[10]** de la spéléologie

**CD** *noun*
le **CD** *masc*
**to put a CD on** mettre**[11]** un CD

**WORD TIP** *CD* never changes.

- **CD player** la platine laser

**CD-ROM** *noun*
le **CD-ROM** *masc*
**I've got it on CD-ROM.** Je l'ai sur CD-ROM.

**WORD TIP** *CD-ROM* never changes.

**ceiling** *noun*
le **plafond** *masc*

to **celebrate** *verb*
**fêter[1]**
**I'm celebrating my birthday.** Je fête mon anniversaire.

**celebrity** *noun*
la **célébrité** *fem*
**to become a celebrity** devenir Ⓔ **[81]** une célébrité

**celery** *noun*
le **céleri** *masc*

**cell** *noun*
la **cellule** *fem*

**cellar** *noun*
la **cave** *fem*

**cello** *noun*
le **violoncelle** *masc*
**to play the cello** jouer**[1]** du violoncelle

**cement** *noun*
le **ciment** *masc*

**cemetery** *noun*
le **cimetière** *masc*

**cent** *noun*
1 (*in euro system*) le **centime** *masc* (*usual term*), le **cent** (*official term*)
2 (*in dollar system*) le **cent** *masc*

**centenary** *noun*
le **centenaire** *masc*

**centigrade** *adjective*
**centigrade**
**ten degrees centigrade** dix degrés centigrade

**centimetre** *noun*
le **centimètre** *masc*

**central** *adjective*
**central** *masc*, **centrale** *fem*, **centraux** *masc plural*, **centrales** *fem plural*
**in central London** dans le centre de Londres

- **central heating** le chauffage central

**centre** *noun*
1 (*middle*) le **centre** *masc*
**in the centre of the forest** au centre de la forêt
2 (*of a town, city*) le **centre-ville** *masc*
**right in the centre** en plein centre-ville
3 ▷**shopping centre, leisure centre, sports centre**

**century** *noun*
le **siècle** *masc*
**in the twenty-first century** au vingt-et-unième siècle

**cereal** *noun*
**(breakfast) cereal** les céréales *fem plural* pour le petit déjeuner
**I have cereal for breakfast.** Je prends des céréales au petit déjeuner.



Ⓔ means the verb takes être to form the perfect

**ceremony** *noun*
la **cérémonie** *fem*

♪ **certain** *adjective*
**certain** *masc*, **certaine** *fem*
**a certain number of people** un certain nombre de personnes
**to be certain that ...** être **[6]** sûr que ...
**Lucy's certain that you're wrong.** Lucy est sûre que tu as tort.
**Nobody knows for certain.** Personne ne sait au juste.
**I can't say for certain.** Je ne sais pas au juste.

**certainly** *adverb*
**certainement**
**certainly not** certainement pas

♪ **certificate** *noun*
1 (*document, qualification*) le **certificat** *masc*
2 (*award for a skill*) le **brevet** *masc*
3 **an 18-certificate film** un film interdit aux moins de 18 ans

♪ **chain** *noun*
la **chaîne** *fem*
**a gold chain** une chaîne en or

♪ **chair** *noun*
1 (*in class, at dining table*) la **chaise** *fem*
2 (*armchair*) le **fauteuil** *masc*
• **chair lift** le télésiège

**chalet** *noun*
1 (*in the mountains*) le **chalet** *masc*
2 (*in a holiday camp*) le **bungalow** *masc*

**chalk** *noun*
la **craie** *fem*

**challenge** *noun*
1 (*that excites you*) le **défi** *masc*
**We rose to the challenge and beat them.** Nous avons relevé le défi et nous les avons battus.
2 (*test*) une **épreuve** *fem*
**The exam was a challenge for him.** L'examen l'a mis à l'épreuve.

♪ **champion** *noun*
le **champion** *masc*, la **championne** *fem*
**She was world champion at 17.** Elle a été championne du monde à 17 ans.

♪ **chance** *noun*
1 (*opportunity*) une **occasion** *fem*
**to have the chance to do something** avoir **[5]** l'occasion de faire quelque chose
**If you have the chance to go there ...** Si tu as l'occasion d'y aller ...
**I didn't get the chance to go.** Je n'ai pas eu l'occasion d'y aller.
2 (*hope*)
**not to stand a chance of doing something** n'avoir **[5]** aucune chance de faire quelque chose
**We don't stand a chance of beating them.** Nous n'avons aucune chance de les battre.
3 (*luck*)
**by chance** par hasard
**You haven't seen him, by any chance?** Tu ne l'as pas vu, par hasard?
4 (*risk*)
**to take a chance** prendre **[64]** un risque
**I'm not taking any chances.** Je ne prends pas de risques.

♪ **change** *noun* ▷ see **change** *verb*
1 (*something new, different*) le **changement** *masc*
**a change of plan** un changement de programme
**I've made some changes to my room.** J'ai fait des changements dans ma chambre.
**Take a change of clothes.** Prends des vêtements de rechange.
**to do something for a change** faire **[10]** quelque chose pour changer
**Let's go to the ice rink for a change!** Allons à la patinoire pour changer!
**It makes a change from burgers.** Ça change un peu des hamburgers.
2 (*cash*) la **monnaie** *fem*
**I don't have any change.** Je n'ai pas de monnaie.
**The machine doesn't give change.** La machine ne rend pas la monnaie.

♪ to **change** *verb* ▷ see **change** *noun*
1 (*to transform completely*) **changer [52]**
**It changed my life.** Cela m'a changé la vie.
**Amy will never change.** Amy ne changera jamais.
**Josh has changed a lot.** Josh a beaucoup changé.
2 (*to switch from one thing to another*) **changer [52] de**
**I must change my jeans.** Je dois changer de jean.
**They changed places.** Ils ont changé de place.
**We changed trains in Paris.** Nous avons changé de train à Paris.
**to change your mind** changer **[52]** d'avis
**Well, I've changed my mind.** Eh bien, j'ai changé d'avis.
3 (*to exchange in a shop*) **échanger [52]**
**to change something for something** échanger quelque chose contre quelque chose
**Can I change it for the larger size?** Puis-je l'échanger contre la taille au-dessus? ▸▸

4 (*to change your clothes*) **se changer** Ⓔ **[52]**
John's gone up to change. John est monté se changer.
Go and get changed. Va te changer.

5 (*money*) **changer [52]**
to change some money changer de l'argent

**changing room** *noun*
1 (*in pool, club*) le **vestiaire** *masc*
2 (*in a shop*) le **salon d'essayage**

**channel** *noun*
1 (*on TV*) la **chaîne** *fem*
to change channels changer **[52]** de chaîne
2 the Channel la Manche
• **Channel Islands** les îles Anglo-Normandes
• **Channel Tunnel** le tunnel sous la Manche

**chaos** *noun*
la **pagaille** *fem* (*informal*)
It was chaos! C'était la pagaille!

**chapel** *noun*
la **chapelle** *fem*

**chapter** *noun*
le **chapitre** *masc*
in chapter two au chapitre deux

**character** *noun*
1 (*personality*) le **caractère** *masc*
She's got character. Elle a du caractère.
2 (*somebody in a book, play, film*) le **personnage** *masc*

**characteristic** *adjective*
**caractéristique** *masc & fem*

**charcoal** *noun*
(*for burning*) le **charbon de bois**

**charge** *noun* ▷ see **charge** *verb*
1 (*payment*) les **frais** *masc plural*
to pay a booking charge payer **[59]** des frais de réservation
free of charge gratuit
There's no charge. C'est gratuit.
2 to be in charge être **[6]** responsable
Who's in charge? Qui est responsable?
I'm in charge of the money. Je suis responsable de l'argent.

to **charge** *verb* ▷ see **charge** *noun*
1 (*to ask a specific sum*) **prendre [64]**
They charge twenty euros an hour. Ils prennent vingt euros de l'heure.
How much do you charge? Vous prenez combien?
2 (*to ask people to pay*) **faire [10] payer**
They don't charge, it's free. Ils ne font pas payer, c'est gratuit.
They charged me for the phone call. Il m'ont fait payer l'appel téléphonique.
3 to charge somebody with something inculper **[1]** quelqu'un de quelque chose
to be charged with murder être **[6]** inculpé de meurtre

**charity** *noun*
une **organisation caritative**

**charm** *noun*
le **charme** *masc*

**charming** *adjective*
**charmant** *masc*, **charmante** *fem*

**chart** *noun*
1 (*table*) le **tableau** *masc*
Our names are on the chart. Nos noms sont dans le tableau.
2 (*for weather*) the weather chart la carte du temps
3 the charts le hit-parade *masc*
number one in the charts numéro un au hit-parade

**chase** *noun* ▷ see **chase** *verb*
a car chase une poursuite en voiture

to **chase** *verb* ▷ see **chase** *noun*
(*a person, an animal*) **pourchasser [1]**
They chased us for a long time. Ils nous ont longtemps pourchassés.
• to **chase somebody away**
**chasser [1] quelqu'un**

**chat** *noun* ▷ see **chat** *verb*
la **conversation** *fem*
to have a chat with somebody bavarder **[1]** avec quelqu'un
I was having a chat with my friends. Je bavardais avec mes copains.
• **chatroom** le chatroom
• **chat show** le talk-show

to **chat** *verb* ▷ see **chat** *noun*
**causer [1]**
• to **chat somebody up**
**draguer [1] quelqu'un** (*informal*)
He's trying to chat her up. Il essaie de la draguer.

to **chatter** *verb*
1 (*to gossip*) **bavarder [1]**
2 (*with cold*) My teeth are chattering. Je claque des dents.

**chatty** *adjective*
**bavard** *masc*, **bavarde** *fem*

**cheap** *adjective*
1 (*low in price*) **pas cher** *masc*, **pas chère** *fem*
a cheap holiday des vacances pas chères
Wow! That's really cheap! Ça alors! Ce n'est vraiment pas cher!



Ⓔ means the verb takes être to form the perfect

2 (*shoddy*) **de mauvaise qualité**
It won't last. It's cheap. Ça ne va pas durer. C'est de la mauvaise qualité.

♪ **cheaper** *adjective*
**moins cher** *masc*, **moins chère** *fem*
This ring is cheaper than the others. Cette bague est moins chère que les autres.
It's cheaper to go by bus. Ça revient moins cher d'y aller en bus.

**cheapest** *adjective*
**le moins cher** *masc*, **la moins chère** *fem*
the cheapest CDs les CD les moins chers

**cheaply** *adverb*
**pas cher**
You can eat cheaply there. On y mange pour pas cher.

**cheap rate** *adjective*
(*phone call*) **à tarif réduit**

**cheat** *noun* ▷ see **cheat** *verb*
le **tricheur** *masc*, la **tricheuse** *fem*

to **cheat** *verb* ▷ see **cheat** *noun*
**tricher [1]**
to cheat in an exam tricher à un examen

♪ **check** *noun* ▷ see **check** *verb*
le **contrôle** *masc*
a passport check un contrôle des passeports

♪ to **check** *verb* ▷ see **check** *noun*
(*to make sure*) **vérifier [1]**
He checked the time. Il a vérifié l'heure.
Check the spelling. Vérifie l'orthographe.
Check that they're all back. Vérifiez qu'ils sont tous rentrés.
to check with somebody demander [1] à quelqu'un
Check with your father. Demande à ton père.
• to **check in**
1 (*at the airport*) **enregistrer [1]**
2 (*at a hotel*) **arriver** ⓔ **[1] à l'hôtel**
• to **check out**
(*of a hotel*) **quitter [1] l'hôtel**

♪ **check-in** *noun*
l'**enregistrement** *masc*

♪ **checkout** *noun*
la **caisse** *fem*

**check-up** *noun*
un **examen médical**

**cheek** *noun*
1 (*part of face*) la **joue** *fem*
2 (*nerve*)
What a cheek! Quel culot! (*informal*)

**cheeky** *adjective*
1 (*playful*) **coquin** *masc*, **coquine** *fem*
2 (*rude*) **impoli** *masc*, **impolie** *fem*

♪ to **cheer** *verb*
(*to shout hurray*) **applaudir [2]**
• to **cheer somebody on**
**encourager [52] quelqu'un**
• to **cheer up**
**reprendre [64] courage**
Cheer up! Courage!
That's to cheer you up. Ça c'est pour te remonter le moral.

**cheerful** *adjective*
**gai** *masc*, **gaie** *fem*

♪ **cheers** *noun*
1 (*when you have a drink*)
Cheers! À la vôtre!
2 (*when you say thanks*)
Cheers! Merci!

♪ **cheese** *noun*
le **fromage** *masc*
blue cheese le fromage bleu
a cheese sandwich un sandwich au fromage

♪ **chef** *noun*
le **chef cuisinier**
She's a chef. Elle est chef cuisinier.

**chemical** *noun* ▷ see **chemical** *adjective*
le **produit chimique**

**chemical** *adjective* ▷ see **chemical** *noun*
**chimique** *masc & fem*

♪ **chemist** *noun*
1 (*selling medicines*) le **pharmacien** *masc*, la **pharmacienne** *fem*
2 a chemist's une pharmacie
at the chemist's à la pharmacie
3 (*scientist*) le & la **chimiste** *masc & fem*

♪ **chemistry** *noun*
la **chimie** *fem*

♪ **cheque** *noun*
le **chèque** *masc*
to pay by cheque payer par chèque
to write a cheque faire un chèque
traveller's cheque le chèque de voyage
• **chequebook** le carnet de chèques

♪ **cherry** *noun*
la **cerise** *fem*
• **cherry tree** le cerisier

♪ **chess** *noun*
les **échecs** *masc plural*
to play chess jouer [1] aux échecs
• **chessboard** un échiquier
• **chess set** le jeu d'échecs

**chest** *noun*
1 (*part of the body*) la **poitrine** *fem*
2 (*box*) le **coffre** *masc*
• **chest of drawers** la commode

**chestnut** *noun*
le **marron** *masc*

to **chew** *verb*
(*food, gum*) **mâcher [1]**

**chewing gum** *noun*
le **chewing-gum** *masc*

**chick** *noun*
(*of a hen*) le **poussin** *masc*

**chicken** *noun*
le **poulet** *masc*
roast chicken du poulet rôti
a chicken sandwich un sandwich au poulet

**chickenpox** *noun*
la **varicelle** *fem*

**chief** *noun*
le **chef** *masc*
the chief of police le préfet de police

**child** *noun*
un & une **enfant** *masc & fem*
a two-year old child un enfant de deux ans
I'm an only child. Je suis enfant unique.

**childish** *adjective*
**puéril** *masc*, **puérile** *fem*

**childminder** *noun*
la **nourrice** *fem*

**chill** *noun*
1 (*in weather*) la **fraîcheur** *fem*
2 (*illness*) le **coup de froid**

**chilli** *noun*
le **piment** *masc*

to **chill out** *verb*
**décompresser [1]** (*informal*)

**chilly** *adjective*
**froid** *masc*, **froide** *fem*
to be chilly faire [10] froid

**chimney** *noun*
la **cheminée** *fem*

**chimpanzee** *noun*
le **chimpanzé** *masc*

**chin** *noun*
le **menton** *masc*

**China** *noun*
la **Chine** *fem*
to be in China être [6] en Chine
to go to China aller ⓔ [7] en Chine

**china** *noun*
la **porcelaine** *fem*

**Chinese** *adjective* ▷ see **Chinese** *noun*
**chinois** *masc*, **chinoise** *fem*

**Chinese** *noun* ▷ see **Chinese** *adjective*
1 (*person*) le **Chinois** *masc*, la **Chinoise** *fem*
the Chinese les Chinois
2 (*language*) le **chinois** *masc*

**chip** *noun*
1 (*fried potato*) la **frite** *fem*
steak and chips le steak frites
2 (*microchip*) la **puce** *fem*

**chocolate** *noun*
le **chocolat** *masc*
a bar of chocolate une tablette de chocolat
a box of chocolates une boîte de chocolats
a chocolate ice cream une glace au chocolat ▷ **hot chocolate**

**choice** *noun*
le **choix** *masc*
a difficult choice un choix difficile
to have a choice avoir [5] le choix
You have a choice of two colours. Vous avez le choix entre deux couleurs.

**choir** *noun*
(*in a school*) la **chorale** *fem*
to sing in a choir faire [10] partie d'une chorale

to **choke** *verb*
1 (*on food, drink*) **s'étouffer** ⓔ **[1]**
to choke on a bone s'étouffer avec une arête
2 (*on smoke, fumes*) **étouffer [1]**

to **choose** *verb*
**choisir [2]**
Alice chose the present. Alice a choisi le cadeau.
I can't choose between the red and the blue. Je n'arrive pas à choisir entre le rouge et le bleu.
It's hard to choose from all these colours. Il est difficile de choisir parmi toutes ces couleurs.
There isn't much to choose from. Il y a très peu de choix.

**chop** *noun* ▷ see **chop** *verb*
la **côtelette** *fem*
a lamb chop une côtelette d'agneau

to **chop** *verb* ▷ see **chop** *noun*
(*food*) **hacher [1]**

**chopstick** *noun*
la **baguette** *fem*

**chord** *noun*
un **accord** *masc*



ⓔ means the verb takes être to form the perfect

**chorus** *noun*
le **refrain** *masc*

**Christ** *noun*
le **Christ** *masc*

**christening** *noun*
le **baptême** *masc*

**Christian** *noun* ▷ see **Christian** *adj*
le **chrétien** *masc*, la **chrétienne** *fem*

**WORD TIP** Adjectives and nouns of religion start with a small letter in French.

**Christian** *adjective* ▷ see **Christian** *noun*
**chrétien** *masc*, **chrétienne** *fem*
- **Christian name** le prénom
  ▷ **first name**

♂ **Christmas** *noun*
**Noël** *masc*
at Christmas à Noël
Happy Christmas! Joyeux Noël!
What did you get for Christmas? Qu'est-ce que tu as eu à Noël?
We go to their house for Christmas. Nous allons chez eux pour Noël.
- **Christmas card** la carte de Noël
- **Christmas carol** le chant de Noël
- **Christmas cracker** le diablotin
- **Christmas Day** le jour de Noël
- **Christmas dinner** le repas de Noël
- **Christmas Eve** la veille de Noël
- **Christmas present** le cadeau de Noël
- **Christmas tree** le sapin de Noël

**chunk** *noun*
(*of wood, bread*) le **morceau** *masc*

♂ **church** *noun*
une **église** *fem*
to go to church aller ⓔ [7] à l'église
- **churchyard** le cimetière

**chute** *noun*
(*in a pool, playground*) le **toboggan** *masc*

♂ **cider** *noun*
le **cidre** *masc*

**cigar** *noun*
le **cigare** *masc*

♂ **cigarette** *noun*
la **cigarette** *fem*
- **cigarette stub** le mégot

♂ **cinema** *noun*
le **cinéma** *masc*
Let's go to the cinema. Allons au cinéma.
What's on at the cinema? Qu'est-ce qu'on joue au cinéma?

♂ **circle** *noun*
le **cercle** *masc*
I drew a circle. J'ai dessiné un cercle.
to sit in a circle s'asseoir ⓔ [20] en cercle
to go round in circles tourner [1] en rond

**circuit** *noun*
1 (*for athletes*) la **piste** *fem*
2 (*for cars*) le **circuit** *masc*

**circumference** *noun*
(*Grammar*) la **circonférence** *fem*

**circumflex** *noun*
un **accent circonflexe**

**circumstances** *plural noun*
les **circonstances** *fem plural*

♂ **circus** *noun*
le **cirque** *masc*
to go to the circus aller ⓔ [7] au cirque
- **circus act** le numéro de cirque

**city** *noun*
la **(grande) ville** *fem*
the city of Paris la ville de Paris
- **city centre** le centre-ville *masc*

**civilian** *noun*
le **civil** *masc*, la **civile** *fem*

**civilization** *noun*
la **civilisation** *fem*

**civil servant** *noun*
le & la **fonctionnaire** *masc & fem*
She's a civil servant. Elle est fonctionnaire.

**civil service** *noun*
la **fonction publique**

**civil war** *noun*
la **guerre civile**

to **claim** *verb*
to claim that ... prétendre [3] que ...
She claims that I'm telling lies. Elle prétend que je dis des mensonges.

to **clap** *verb*
1 (*at a performance*) **applaudir [2]**
Everyone clapped. Tout le monde a applaudi.
2 to clap your hands battre [21] des mains

**clapping** *noun*
les **applaudissements** *masc plural*

**clarinet** *noun*
la **clarinette** *fem*
to play the clarinet jouer [1] de la clarinette

to **clash** *verb*
1 (*rivals*) **s'affronter** ⓔ **[1]**
Fans clashed outside the stadium. Les supporters se sont affrontés devant le stade.
to clash with somebody se heurter ⓔ [1] à quelqu'un ▸▸

They clashed with the police. Ils se sont heurtés à la police.

2 (*colours*) **jurer [1]**
The skirt and shirt clash. La jupe jure avec la chemise.

**class** *noun*

1 (*of students, pupils*) la **classe** *fem*
She's in the same class as me. Elle est dans la même classe que moi.
There are fifteen boys in my class. Il y a quinze garçons dans ma classe.

2 (*lesson*) le **cours** *masc*
an art class un cours de dessin
I was chatting in class. Je bavardais en cours.

**classic** *adjective*
**classique** *masc & fem*

**classical** *adjective*
**classique** *masc & fem*
- **classical music** la musique classique

**classmate** *noun*
le & la **camarade de classe**

**classroom** *noun*
la **salle de classe**

**claw** *noun*

1 (*of a cat, dog*) la **griffe** *fem*

2 (*of a crab*) la **pince** *fem*

**clay** *noun*
(*for modelling*) l'**argile** *fem*

**clean** *adjective* ▷ see **clean** *verb*

1 (*not dirty*) **propre** *masc & fem*
My hands are clean. J'ai les mains propres.
Your room isn't clean. Ta chambre n'est pas propre.
to keep something clean ne pas salir **[2]** quelque chose
Keep your trainers clean. Ne salis pas tes baskets.

2 (*not polluted*) **pur** *masc*, **pure** *fem*

to **clean** *verb* ▷ see **clean** *adjective*
**nettoyer [39]**
She's cleaning her room. Elle est en train de nettoyer sa chambre.
I cleaned the car. J'ai nettoyé la voiture.
to clean your teeth se laver Ⓔ **[1]** les dents

**cleaner** *noun*

1 (*cleaning lady*) la **femme de ménage**

2 (*of public places*) l'**agent de nettoyage** *masc*

3 ▷ **dry cleaner**

**cleaning** *noun*
to do the cleaning faire **[10]** le ménage

**cleanser** *noun*
(*for the face*) le **démaquillant** *masc*

**clear** *adjective* ▷ see **clear** *verb*

1 (*that you can see through*) **transparent** *masc*, **transparente** *fem*

2 (*cloudless*) **clair** *masc*, **claire** *fem*
The sky was clear. Le ciel était clair.

3 (*easy to understand*) **clair** *masc*, **claire** *fem*
a clear example un exemple clair
Is that clear? Est-ce que c'est clair?
It wasn't very clear. Ce n'était pas très clair.
It's clear he's lying. Il est clair qu'il ment.

to **clear** *verb* ▷ see **clear** *adj*

1 (*papers, rubbish, clothes*) to clear something out of something enlever **[50]** quelque chose de quelque chose
I cleared my stuff out of the room. J'ai enlevé mes affaires de la chambre.

2 (*a table, a room*) **débarrasser [1]**
Can I clear the table? Puis-je débarrasser la table?

3 (*a road, path*) **dégager [52]**

4 (*fog, snow*) **se dissiper** Ⓔ **[1]**
(*your throat*) to clear your throat se racler Ⓔ **[1]** la gorge
- to **clear something out**
(*a cupboard, a room*) **vider [1] quelque chose**

**clearly** *adverb*
(*to think, speak, hear*) **clairement**

**clementine** *noun*
la **clémentine** *fem*

**clever** *adjective*

1 **intelligent** *masc*, **intelligente** *fem*
clever children des enfants intelligents

2 (*ingenious*) **astucieux** *masc*, **astucieuse** *fem*
a clever idea une idée astucieuse

**click** *noun* ▷ see **click** *verb*

1 (*noise*) le **petit bruit sec**
I heard a click. J'ai entendu un petit bruit sec.

2 (*with mouse*) le **clic** *masc*
a double-click un double-clic

to **click** *verb* ▷ see **click** *noun*

1 (*using a mouse*) **cliquer [1]**
Click on the icon. Cliquer sur l'icône.

2 (*with a person*) **sympathiser [1]** (*informal*)

**cliff** *noun*
la **falaise** *fem*

**climate** *noun*
le **climat** *masc*
a mild climate un climat doux
- **climate change** le changement climatique

Ⓔ means the verb takes être to form the perfect

to **climb** *verb*
1 (*a hill, stairs*) **monter [1]**
I climbed the stairs in the dark. J'ai monté l'escalier dans le noir.
2 (*a mountain*) **faire [10] l'escalade de**
They climbed Mont Blanc. Ils ont fait l'escalade du Mont Blanc.

**climber** *noun*
un & une **alpiniste** *masc & fem*

♪ **climbing** *noun*
l'**escalade** *fem*
to go climbing faire [10] de l'escalade

**clinic** *noun*
le **centre médical** (*pl* les **centres médicaux**)

**clip** *noun* ▷ see **clip** *verb*
1 (*from a film*) un **extrait** *masc*
a clip from the film un extrait du film
2 (*for your hair*) la **barrette** *fem*

to **clip** *verb* ▷ see **clip** *noun*
(*a hedge*) **couper [1]**

**cloakroom** *noun*
le **vestiaire** *masc*

♪ **clock** *noun*
1 (*large*) une **horloge** *fem*
the town hall clock l'horloge de la mairie
2 (*smaller*) la **pendule** *fem*
to put the clocks back reculer [1] les pendules
to put the clocks forward an hour avancer [61] les pendules d'une heure
3 ▷ **alarm clock, o'clock**
• **clock radio** le radio-réveil
• **clockwise** (*to turn*) dans le sens des aiguilles d'une montre

♪ **close** *adverb,, adjective* ▷ see **close** *noun, verb*
1 (*near*) **près**
not very close pas tout près
The school's very close. L'école est tout près.
She lives close by. Elle habite tout près.
to be close to something être [6] près de quelque chose
The shop's close to the cinema. Le magasin est près du cinéma.
2 (*friend, relation*) **proche** *masc & fem*
They're very close. Ils sont très proches l'un de l'autre.
I'm close to my Dad. Je suis proche de mon père.
3 (*result, match*) **serré** *masc*, **serrée** *fem*
It was a close match. C'était un match serré.

♪ to **close** *verb* ▷ see **close** *adj, adv, noun*
1 (*by itself*) **se fermer** Ⓔ **[1]**
The door closed. La porte s'est fermée.
• to **close down**
**fermer [1]**
The school's closing down. L'école ferme.
They closed the club down. Ils ont fermé le club.

♪ **closed** *adjective*
**fermé** *masc*, **fermée** *fem*
Too late, it's closed! Trop tard, c'est fermé!

**closely** *adverb*
(*to examine, look at*) **de près**

**closing date** *noun*
la **date limite**

**closing-down sale** *noun*
la **liquidation** *fem*

♪ **closing time** *noun*
l'**heure de fermeture**

**cloth** *noun*
1 (*for the floor*) la **serpillière** *fem*
2 (*for polishing*) le **chiffon** *masc*
3 (*for sewing, dressmaking*) le **tissu** *masc*

♪ **clothes** *plural noun*
les **vêtements** *masc plural*
some great clothes des vêtements super
to put your clothes on s'habiller Ⓔ [1]
I put my clothes on. Je me suis habillé (*boy speaking*). Je me suis habillée (*girl speaking*).
to take your clothes off se déshabiller Ⓔ [1]
to change your clothes se changer Ⓔ [52]
I had to change my clothes. J'ai dû me changer.
• **clothes line** la corde à linge
• **clothes peg** la pince à linge

**clothing** *noun*
les **vêtements** *masc plural*

**cloud** *noun*
le **nuage** *masc*

♪ **cloudy** *adjective*
**nuageux** *masc*, **nuageuse** *fem*
to become cloudy se couvrir Ⓔ [30]
The weather was cloudy. Le temps était couvert.

**clove** *noun*
1 (*spice*) le **clou de girofle**
2 a clove of garlic une gousse d'ail

**clown** *noun*
le **clown** *masc*

♪ indicates key words

**club** *noun*
1 (*association*) le **club** *masc*
to be in a club faire [10] partie d'un club
2 (*in cards*) le **trèfle** *masc*
the four of clubs le quatre de trèfle
3 (*in golf*) le **club** *masc*

**clue** *noun*
1 (*in problems*) un **indice** *masc*
Look for clues. Cherchez des indices.
Give me a clue. Aide-moi.
(*understanding*) I haven't a clue. Je n'en ai pas la moindre idée.
2 (*in a crossword*) la **définition** *fem*
to work out a clue comprendre [64] une définition

**clumsy** *adjective*
**maladroit** *masc*, **maladroite** *fem*

to **clutch** *verb*
**tenir [77] fermement**

**coach** *noun*
1 (*bus*) le **car** *masc*
on the coach dans le car
We travelled to Metz by coach. Nous sommes allés à Metz en car.
to go on a coach trip faire [10] une excursion en car
Our class is going on a coach trip. Notre classe va faire une excursion en car.
2 (*in sports*) un **entraîneur** *masc*, une **entraîneuse** *fem*
3 (*railway carriage*) le **wagon** *masc*
- **coach station** la gare routière

**coal** *noun*
le **charbon** *masc*
- **coal mine** la mine de charbon
- **coal miner** le mineur

**coast** *noun*
la **côte** *fem*
We went to the coast. Nous sommes allés sur la côte.

**coat** *noun*
1 (*clothing*) le **manteau** *masc* (*pl* les **manteaux**)
2 (*layer*) la **couche** *fem*
a coat of red paint une couche de peinture rouge
- **coat hanger** le cintre

**cobweb** *noun*
la **toile d'araignée**

**cock**, **cockerel** *noun*
le **coq** *masc*

**cocoa** *noun*
1 (*drink*) le **chocolat (chaud)**
2 (*powder*) le **cacao** *masc*

**coconut** *noun*
la **noix de coco**

**cod** *noun*
le **cabillaud** *masc*

**code** *noun*
1 (*set of rules*) le **code** *masc*
the highway code le code de la route
2 (*in phone number*) un **indicatif** *masc*
the code for Bristol l'indicatif pour Bristol

**coffee** *noun*
le **café** *masc*
a cup of coffee un café
a black coffee un café
a white coffee un café au lait
- **coffee break** la pause-café
- **coffee machine** la cafetière électrique

**coffin** *noun*
le **cercueil** *masc*

**coin** *noun*
la **pièce de monnaie**
a pound coin une pièce d'une livre
a two-euro coin une pièce de deux euros

**coincidence** *noun*
la **coïncidence** *fem*

**Coke®** *noun*
le **coca** *masc*
Two Cokes®, please. Deux cocas, s'il vous plaît.

**cold** *adjective* ▷ see **cold** *noun*
1 (*weather, places*)
to be cold faire [10] froid
It's cold today. Il fait froid aujourd'hui.
It was very cold outside. Il faisait très froid dehors.
2 (*the feeling*)
to be cold avoir [5] froid
I'm cold. J'ai froid.
I'm very cold. J'ai très froid.
I was too cold. J'avais trop froid.
Your hands are cold. Tu as les mains froides.

**cold** *noun* ▷ see **cold** *adj*
1 (*cold weather*) le **froid** *masc*
out in the cold dehors dans le froid
2 (*illness*) le **rhume** *masc*
to have a cold être [6] enrhumé
to get a cold s'enrhumer [1]
I got a cold. Je me suis enrhumé (*boy speaking*), Je me suis enrhumée (*girl speaking*).
- **cold sore** le bouton de fièvre

to **collapse** *verb*
1 (*walls, rooves*) **s'écrouler** Ⓔ **[1]**
2 (*buildings*) **s'effondrer** Ⓔ **[1]**

**collar** *noun*
1 *(on a shirt)* le **col** *masc*
2 *(for a dog)* le **collier** *masc*
· **collarbone** la clavicule *fem*

**colleague** *noun*
le & la **collègue** *masc & fem*

♪ to **collect** *verb*
1 *(as a hobby)* **collectionner [1]**
**She collects phone cards.** Elle collectionne les télécartes.
2 *(a person)* **aller ⓔ [7] chercher**
**He collects the children from school.** Il va chercher les enfants à l'école.
**I'll come and collect you.** Je vais venir te chercher.
3 *(a thing)* **passer ⓔ [1] prendre**
**I'll collect my jacket later.** Je passerai prendre ma veste plus tard.
4 *(fares, money)* **encaisser [1]**
5 *(to gather up)* **ramasser [1]**
**Who collected the exercise books?** Qui a ramassé les cahiers?

**collection** *noun*
1 *(of stamps, CDs, posters)* la **collection** *fem*
2 *(of money)* la **collecte** *fem*
**We'll organize a collection.** Nous ferons une collecte.

**college** *noun*
1 *(school)* le **collège** *masc*
2 *(for higher education)* un **établissement d'études supérieures**
**to go to college** faire **[10]** des études supérieures

**collision** *noun*
la **collision** *fem*

to **colour** *verb* ▷ see **colour** *noun*
1 *(with paints, crayons)* **colorier [1]**
**I've coloured the sky pink.** J'ai colorié le ciel en rose.
2 **to get your hair coloured** se faire ⓔ **[10]** faire une couleur

♪ **colour** *noun* ▷ see **colour** *verb*
la **couleur** *fem*
**What colour is it?** C'est de quelle couleur?
**What colour is your bag?** De quelle couleur est ton sac?
**What colour are her eyes?** Elle a les yeux de quelle couleur?
**Do you have it in a different colour?** Est-ce que vous l'avez dans une autre couleur?
· **colour blind** *adjective* daltonien *masc*, daltonienne *fem*
· **colour film** la pellicule couleur (*pl* les pellicules couleur)

**colourful** *adjective*
*(picture, display)* **aux couleurs vives**

**colouring book** *noun*
un **album à colorier**

**column** *noun*
la **colonne** *fem*

♪ **comb** *noun* ▷ see **comb** *verb*
le **peigne** *masc*

♪ to **comb** *verb* ▷ see **comb** *noun*
**to comb your hair** se peigner ⓔ **[1]**

**combination** *noun*
la **combinaison** *fem*

to **combine** *verb*
1 *(two or more things)* **combiner [1]**
2 *(colours, tastes)* **se combiner ⓔ [1]**

♪ to **come** *verb*
1 *(to a place)* **venir ⓔ [81]**
**Come quick!** Viens vite!
**Come and see!** Venez voir!
**Did Jess come to school?** Est-ce que Jess est venue à l'école?
**Do you want to come to my house?** Tu veux venir chez moi?
**She came on holiday with us.** Elle est venue en vacances avec nous.
**Peter comes from Scotland.** Peter vient d'Écosse.
2 *(to arrive)* **arriver ⓔ [1]**
**Coming!** J'arrive!
**The bus is coming.** Le bus arrive.
**as soon as the train comes** dès que le train arrive
3 *(to collect)* **to come for somebody** passer ⓔ **[1]** prendre quelqu'un
**My father's coming for me.** Mon père passe me prendre.
4 **Come on!** Allez!
**Come on, hurry up!** Allez, dépêche-toi!
· to **come apart**
1 *(drawers, boxes, machines)* **se casser ⓔ [1]**
2 *(books, seams)* **se déchirer ⓔ [1]**
· to **come back**
**revenir ⓔ [81]**
**Come back!** Reviens!
**to come back home** rentrer ⓔ **[1]**
· to **come down**
**descendre ⓔ [3]**
**Come down right now!** Descends tout de suite!
· to **come down something**
*(a street, a hill, the stairs)* **descendre ⓔ [3] quelque chose**
**Max is coming down the stairs.** Max descend l'escalier. ▸▸

- to **come in**

1 **entrer** Ⓔ **[1]**
Come in! Entrez!
**He came in through the window.** Il est entré par la fenêtre.
2 **The tide is coming in.** La marée monte.

- to **come off**

1 *(buttons, handle)* **se détacher** Ⓔ **[1]**
2 *(stains, dirt)* **partir** Ⓔ **[58]**

- to **come out**

1 **sortir** Ⓔ **[72]**
**Are you coming out with us?** Est-ce que tu sors avec nous?
2 *(book, CD, film, game)* **sortir** Ⓔ **[72]**
3 *(sun, moon)* **se montrer** Ⓔ **[1]**

- to **come round**

**passer** Ⓔ **[1]**
**I'll come round later.** Je passerai plus tard.

- to **come up**

**monter** Ⓔ **[1]**
**Can you come up a moment?** Peux-tu monter un instant?

- to **come up something**

*(a street, a hill, the stairs)* **monter [1] quelque chose**
**They came up the stairs.** Ils ont monté l'escalier.

**comedian** *noun*
le **comique** *masc*, l'**actrice comique** *fem*

**comedy** *noun*
la **comédie** *fem*

🗝 **comfortable** *adjective*
1 *(chair, bed)* **confortable** *masc & fem*
**This bed's comfortable.** Ce lit est confortable.
**I'm quite comfortable here.** Je suis bien là.
2 *(at ease)* **à l'aise**
**I'm not too comfortable.** Je ne suis pas très à l'aise.

**comfortably** *adverb*
**confortablement**

🗝 **comic** *noun*
*(magazine)* une **bande dessinée** *fem*
- **comic strip** la bande dessinée

**command** *noun*
un **ordre** *masc*

**comment** *noun*
*(in a conversation)* la **remarque** *fem*
**He made a rude comment about you.** Il a fait une remarque impolie sur toi.

**commentary** *noun*
le **reportage en direct**
**the match commentary** le reportage du match

**commentator** *noun*
le **commentateur** *masc*, la **commentatrice** *fem*
**a sports commentator** un commentateur sportif

**commercial** *adjective*
▷ see **commercial** *noun*
**commercial** *masc*, **commerciale** *fem*, **commerciaux** *masc plural*, **commerciales** *fem plural*

**commercial** *noun*
▷ see **commercial** *adj*
le **spot publicitaire**

to **commit** *verb*
**to commit a crime** commettre **[11]** un crime

**committee** *noun*
le **comité** *masc*

**common** *adjective*
1 *(happening a lot)* **courant** *masc*, **courante** *fem*
**a common problem** un problème courant
**It's not very common.** Ce n'est pas très courant.
2 *(interests, activities)* **in common** en commun
**We don't have a lot in common.** On n'a pas grand-chose en commun.
- **common sense** le bon sens

to **communicate** *verb*
**communiquer [1]**

**communication** *noun*
1 *(being in contact)* la **communication** *fem*
2 *(telephone, fax etc)*
**communications** les communications *fem plural*

**communion** *noun*
la **communion** *fem*

**communism** *noun*
le **communisme** *masc*

**community** *noun*
la **communauté** *fem*
**to be part of the community** faire **[10]** partie de la communauté

to **commute** *verb*
**to commute between Oxford and London** faire **[10]** le trajet entre Oxford et Londres tous les jours

**commuter** *noun*
le **banlieusard** *masc*, la **banlieusarde** *fem*

**compact disc** *noun*
le **disque compact**
- **compact disc player** la platine laser

Ⓔ means the verb takes être to form the perfect

**company** *noun*
1 (*business*) la **société** *fem*
**an insurance company** une société d'assurances
2 (*group*) la **compagnie** *fem*
**a theatre company** une compagnie théâtrale
3 **to keep somebody company** tenir [77] compagnie à quelqu'un
**I'll keep you company.** Je vais te tenir compagnie.

♪ to **compare** *verb*
**comparer** [1]
**to compare the French with the English** comparer les Français aux Anglais
**I compared my photo with hers.** J'ai comparé ma photo à la sienne.
**compared with something** par rapport à quelque chose
**Our house is small compared with yours.** Notre maison est petite par rapport à la tienne.

**comparison** *noun*
la **comparaison** *fem*
**in comparison with England** par rapport à l'Angleterre

♪ **compartment** *noun*
le **compartiment** *masc*

**compass** *noun*
la **boussole** *fem*

**compatible** *adjective*
(*printer, scanner, webcam*) **compatible** *masc & fem*

to **compete** *verb*
**to compete in something** participer [1] à quelque chose
**I competed in the relay race.** J'ai participé à la course de relais.
**to compete for first prize** se disputer Ⓔ [1] le premier prix

**competition** *noun*
1 (*event*) le **concours** *masc*
**to take part in a competition** participer [1] à un concours
2 (*the drive to win*) la **concurrence** *fem*
**There's a lot of competition.** Il y a beaucoup de concurrence.

**competitor** *noun*
le **concurrent** *masc*, la **concurrente** *fem*

to **complain** *verb*
**se plaindre** Ⓔ [31]
**He's always complaining!** Il se plaint sans arrêt!
**to complain about something** se plaindre de quelque chose

**complaint** *noun*
la **plainte** *fem*
**to make a complaint** se plaindre Ⓔ [31]

♪ **complete** *adjective* ▷ see **complete** *verb*
1 (*entire, full*) **complet** *masc*, **complète** *fem*
**the complete collection** la collection complète
2 (*total, utter*) **total** *masc*, **totale** *fem*
**a complete disaster** un désastre total
**a complete nightmare** un vrai cauchemar

♪ to **complete** *verb* ▷ see **complete** *adj*
(*to finish*) **compléter** [24]
**Complete the sentence.** Complétez la phrase.

♪ **completely** *adverb*
**complètement**

**complexion** *noun*
le **teint** *masc*
**to have a pale complexion** avoir [5] le teint pâle

**complicated** *adjective*
**compliqué** *masc*, **compliquée** *fem*
**to get complicated** se compliquer Ⓔ [1]

**compliment** *noun*
le **compliment** *masc*
**to pay somebody a compliment** faire [10] un compliment à quelqu'un

to **compose** *verb*
(*music, score*) **composer** [1]

**composer** *noun*
le **compositeur** *masc*, la **compositrice** *fem*

**comprehension** *noun*
la **compréhension** *fem*
**a comprehension test** un test de compréhension

**compromise** *noun*
le **compromis** *masc*

♪ **compulsory** *adjective*
**obligatoire** *masc & fem*

♪ **computer** *noun*
un **ordinateur** *masc*
**to work on computer** travailler sur ordinateur
**He's got his homework on computer.** Il a des devoirs sur ordinateur.
**The computers are down.** Les ordinateurs sont en panne.
- **computer engineer** le technicien en informatique, la technicienne en informatique
- **computer game** le jeu électronique ⏩

(*pl* les jeux électroniques)
- **computer programmer** le programmeur, la programmeuse
- **computer science** l'**informatique** *fem*

**computing** *noun*
l'**informatique** *fem*

**conceited** *adjective*
**vaniteux**, *masc*, **vaniteuse** *fem*

to **concentrate** *verb*
**se concentrer** Ⓔ **[1]**
I can't concentrate. Je n'arrive pas à me concentrer.
I was concentrating on the film. Je me concentrais sur le film.

**concentration** *noun*
la **concentration** *fem*

**concern** *noun* ▷ see **concern** *verb*
(*worry*) une **inquiétude** *fem*
It's causing concern. C'est inquiétant.

to **concern** *verb* ▷ see **concern** *noun*
1 (*to affect*) **concerner [1]**
The environment concerns us all. L'environnement nous concerne tous.
2 (*showing your opinion*)
as far as I'm concerned, ... en ce qui me concerne, ...

**concerned** *adjective*
**inquiet** *masc*, **inquiète** *fem*
We're very concerned. Nous sommes très inquiets.

♪ **concert** *noun*
le **concert** *masc*
to go to a concert aller Ⓔ **[7]** à un concert
I got tickets for the concert. J'ai acheté des billets pour le concert.
- **concert hall** la salle de concert

**conclusion** *noun*
la **conclusion** *fem*

**concrete** *noun*
le **béton** *masc*
a concrete floor un sol en béton

to **condemn** *verb*
**condamner [1]**

♪ **condition** *noun*
1 (*state*) la **condition** *fem*
in good condition en bonne condition
The bike was in good condition. Le vélo était en bonne condition.
in bad condition en mauvaise condition
The tyres are in bad condition. Les pneus sont en mauvaise condition.
2 (*state of the weather*) **weather conditions** les conditions météorologiques
3 (*when you make a deal*) la **condition** *fem*
Ok, but on one condition - you tidy up. D'accord, mais à une condition: c'est toi qui ranges.
on condition that ... à condition que ...
I'll go on condition that you come too. J'irai à condition que tu viennes aussi.

**conditional** *noun*
le **conditionnel** *masc*

**conditioner** *noun*
un **après-shampooing** *masc*

**condom** *noun*
le **préservatif** *masc*

**conduct** *noun* ▷ see **conduct** *verb*
la **conduite** *fem*
good conduct la bonne conduite

to **conduct** *verb* ▷ see **conduct** *noun*
(*an orchestra, a choir*) **diriger [52]**

**conductor** *noun*
(*of an orchestra*) le **chef d'orchestre**

**cone** *noun*
1 (*for ice cream*) le **cornet** *masc*
2 (*for traffic*) la **balise** *fem*

**confectionery** *noun*
la **confiserie** *fem*

**conference** *noun*
la **conférence** *fem*

to **confess** *verb*
**avouer [1]**

**confession** *noun*
la **confession** *fem*

**confidence** *noun*
1 (*faith in somebody else*) la **confiance** *fem*
I don't have confidence in them. Je n'ai pas confiance en eux.
2 (*self-confidence*) l'**assurance** *fem*
to be lacking in confidence manquer **[1]** d'assurance
to have lots of confidence être **[6]** très assuré
Emma has lots of confidence. Emma est très assurée.

♪ **confident** *adjective*
1 (*sure of yourself*) **assuré** *masc*, **assurée** *fem*
2 (*optimistic*) **sûr** *masc*, **sûre** *fem*
They're confident that we'll win. Ils sont sûrs que nous allons gagner.

to **confirm** *verb*
(*a date, a time*) **confirmer [1]**



Ⓔ means the verb takes être to form the perfect

♪ to **confuse** *verb*
1 (*to mix up*) **confondre [69]**
**It's easy to confuse the two words.** Il est facile de confondre les deux mots.
**I always confuse him with his brother.** Je le confonds toujours avec son frère.
2 (*to bother, upset*) **troubler [1]**
**The whole thing confuses me.** Tout ça me trouble.

♪ **confused** *adjective*
**confus** *masc*, **confuse** *fem*
**a confused story** une histoire confuse
**I'm completely confused!** Là je n'y comprends plus rien!

**confusing** *adjective*
**pas clair** *masc*, **pas claire** *fem*
**The message is confusing.** Le message n'est pas clair.

**confusion** *noun*
la **confusion** *fem*

to **congratulate** *verb*
**féliciter [1]**
**I congratulated her on winning.** Je l'ai félicitée d'avoir gagné.

♪ **congratulations** *plural noun*
les **félicitations** *fem plural*
**Congratulations!** Félicitations!

**conjurer** *noun*
le **prestidigitateur** *masc*, la **prestidigitatrice** *fem*

to **connect** *verb*
1 (*a computer, printer, TV*) **brancher [1]**
2 (*Internet*) **connecter [1]**
**We're not connected yet.** Nous ne sommes pas encore connectés.
3 (*the parts, wires, etc*) **raccorder [1]**

**connection** *noun*
1 (*between two ideas, events*) le **rapport** *masc*
**I don't see the connection.** Je ne vois pas le rapport.
2 (*between trains or planes*) la **correspondance** *fem*
**We'll miss our connection.** Nous allons rater notre correspondance.
3 (*electrical*) le **contact** *masc*
**a faulty connection** un mauvais contact

**conscience** *noun*
la **conscience** *fem*
**to have a guilty conscience** avoir **[5]** mauvaise conscience

**conscious** *adjective*
**conscient** *masc*, **consciente** *fem*

**consequence** *noun*
la **conséquence** *fem*
**as a consequence** par conséquent

**conservation** *noun*
(*of nature, environment*) la **protection** *fem*

**conservative** *adjective*
**conservateur** *masc*, **conservatrice** *fem*

**Conservative** *noun*
le **conservateur** *masc*
**the Conservative Party** le parti conservateur

**conservatory** *noun*
la **véranda** *fem*

to **consider** *verb*
**to consider doing something** envisager **[52]** de faire quelque chose
**I'm considering changing schools.** J'envisage de changer d'école.

**considerable** *adjective*
**considérable** *masc & fem*

**considerate** *adjective*
**gentil** *masc*, **gentille** *fem*

**consideration** *noun*
la **considération** *fem*
**You must take holidays into consideration.** Il faut prendre les vacances en considération.

**considering** *preposition*
**étant donné**
**Considering that Tom did it all himself, it's great.** Étant donné que Tom a tout fait lui-même, c'est génial.

to **consist** *verb*
**to consist of** être **[6]** composé de
**This dish consists of vegetables and rice.** Ce plat est composé de légumes et de riz.

**consonant** *noun*
la **consonne** *fem*

**constant** *adjective*
**permanent** *masc*, **permanente** *fem*

**constipated** *adjective*
**constipé** *masc*, **constipée** *fem*

to **construct** *verb*
**construire [26]**

**consulate** *noun*
le **consulat** *masc*

to **consult** *verb*
**consulter [1]**
**The students were consulted.** On a consulté les étudiants.

**consumer** *noun*
le **consommateur** *masc*, la **consommatrice** *fem*

**consumption** *noun*
la **consommation** *fem*

**contact** *noun* ▷ see **contact** *verb*
1 (*communication*) le **contact** *masc*
**We've lost contact.** Nous avons perdu contact.
**to be in contact with somebody** être [6] en contact avec quelqu'un
**Are you still in contact with Marie?** Est-ce que tu es toujours en contact avec Marie?
2 (*person you know*) la **connaissance** *fem*

to **contact** *verb* ▷ see **contact** *noun*
**contacter** [1]
**I'll contact you tomorrow.** Je te contacterai demain.

**contact lens** *noun*
la **lentille de contact** (*pl* les **lentilles de contact**)
**to wear contact lenses** porter [1] des lentilles de contact

to **contain** *verb*
**contenir** [77]
**It contains salt.** Ça contient du sel.

**container** *noun*
(*for food, for small objects*) le **récipient** *masc*

to **contaminate** *verb*
**contaminer** [1]
**The water has been contaminated.** L'eau a été contaminée.

**contents** *plural noun*
(*of a suitcase, bag, box*) le **contenu** *masc*

**contest** *noun*
le **concours** *masc*

**contestant** *noun*
le **concurrent** *masc*, la **concurrente** *fem*

**continent** *noun*
le **continent** *masc*
**on the Continent** en Europe continentale

**continental** *adjective*
**a continental holiday** des vacances en Europe continentale

♪ to **continue** *verb*
**continuer** [1]
**We continued our journey.** Nous avons continué notre voyage.
**to continue doing something** continuer de faire quelque chose
**Mark continued chatting.** Mark a continué de bavarder.

**continuous** *adjective*
**continu** *masc*, **continue** *fem*
• **continuous assessment** le contrôle continu

**contraception** *noun*
la **contraception** *fem*

**contraceptive** *noun*
le **contraceptif** *masc*

**contract** *noun*
le **contrat** *masc*

to **contradict** *verb*
**contredire** [47]

**contradiction** *noun*
la **contradiction** *fem*

**contrary** *noun*
**on the contrary** au contraire
**On the contrary, she's funny.** Au contraire, elle est marrante.

**contrast** *noun*
le **contraste** *masc*

to **contribute** *verb*
1 (*money*) **donner** [1]
2 (*in class, in discussion*) **participer** [1]

**contribution** *noun*
(*to charity, for a good cause*) le **don** *masc*
**to make a contribution** faire [10] un don

**control** *noun* ▷ see **control** *verb*
(*of a crowd*) le **contrôle** *masc*
**Max lost control of his motorbike.** Max a perdu le contrôle de sa moto.
**Everything's under control.** Tout va bien.
**The fire was out of control.** On ne maîtrisait plus l'incendie.

to **control** *verb* ▷ see **control** *noun*
1 (*a crowd, animals, a fire*) **maîtriser** [1]
**They can't control the fans.** Ils ne maîtrisent plus les supporters.
2 (*yourself*) **to control yourself** se contrôler ⓔ [1]
**I couldn't control myself.** Je n'arrivais plus à me contrôler.

**controversial** *adjective*
(*decision, choice*) **discutable** *masc & fem*

♪ **convenient** *adjective*
1 (*appliance*) **pratique** *masc & fem*
**The microwave is very convenient.** Le micro-ondes est très pratique.
2 (*plan*) **to be convenient for somebody** convenir [81] à quelqu'un
**It's not convenient for me.** Ça ne me convient pas.
**If it's more convenient for you, ...** Si ça vous convient mieux, ...



ⓔ means the verb takes être to form the perfect

3 (*place*) **bien situé** *masc*, **bien située** *fem*
It's convenient for the shops. C'est bien situé par rapport aux magasins.

**convent** *noun*
le **couvent** *masc*

**conventional** *adjective*
(*person*) **conformiste** *masc & fem*

**conversation** *noun*
la **conversation** *fem*
**a conversation in French** une conversation en français

to **convert** *verb*
**transformer [1]**
**to convert a garage into a games room** transformer un garage en salle de jeux

to **convince** *verb*
**convaincre [79]**
**I couldn't convince them.** Je n'ai pas pu les convaincre.
**I'm convinced that Jack's wrong.** Je suis convaincu que Jack a tort.

**convincing** *adjective*
**convaincant** *masc*, **convaincante** *fem*

♪ **cook** *noun* ▷ see **cook** *verb*
le **cuisinier** *masc*, la **cuisinière** *fem*
**She's a cook.** Elle est cuisinière.

♪ to **cook** *verb* ▷ see **cook** *noun*
1 (*to prepare food*) **faire [10] la cuisine**
**I like cooking.** J'aime faire la cuisine.
**Dad never cooks.** Papa ne fait jamais la cuisine.
2 (*vegetables, pasta*) **faire [10] cuire**
**Cook the carrots for five minutes.** Faire cuire les carottes pendant cinq minutes.
3 (*a meal*) **préparer [1]**
**Zoë's cooking supper.** Zoë est en train de préparer le dîner.
4 (*food*) **cuire [36]**
**It's cooked.** C'est cuit.
**The stew's cooking.** Le ragoût est en train de cuire.

♪ **cooker** *noun*
la **cuisinière** *fem*

**cookery** *noun*
la **cuisine** *fem*
• **cookery book** le livre de cuisine

♪ **cooking** *noun*
la **cuisine** *fem*
**French cooking** la cuisine française
**to do the cooking** faire [10] la cuisine

♪ **cool** *adjective* ▷ see **cool** *noun, verb*
1 (*food, drink*) **frais** *masc*, **fraîche** *fem*
**a cool drink** une boisson fraîche
**to keep something cool** tenir [77] quelque chose au frais
2 (*the weather, a place*) **to be cool** faire [10] frais
**It's cool at night.** Il fait frais la nuit.
3 (*laid-back*) **décontracté** *masc*, **décontractée** *fem*
4 (*sophisticated*) **branché** *masc*, **branchée** *fem*
**It looks cool.** Ça fait branché.
**She's so cool!** Elle est vraiment branchée!
5 (*great*) **super** *masc & fem*
**a cool bike** un vélo super
**Cool!** Super!
**That's cool!** C'est cool!
**Your parents are cool.** Tes parents sont cool.

to **cool** *verb* ▷ see **cool** *adj, noun*
(*a liquid*) **refroidir [2]**
• **to cool down**
(*food, hot drinks*) **se refroidir** Ⓔ **[2]**
**It's cooling down.** Ça se refroidit.

♪ **cool** *noun* ▷ see **cool** *adj, verb*
1 (*coldness*) la **fraîcheur** *fem*
**Stay in the cool.** Reste au frais.
2 (*calm*) le **sang-froid** *masc*
**I lost my cool.** J'ai perdu mon sang-froid.
**She always keeps her cool.** Elle garde toujours son sang-froid.

to **cooperate** *verb*
**coopérer [24]**
**He won't cooperate with anyone.** Il ne veut coopérer avec personne.

♪ **cop** *noun*
le **flic** *masc* (*informal*)

to **cope** *verb*
1 (*with a new situation*) **se débrouiller** Ⓔ **[1]**
**She's coping well.** Elle se débrouille bien.
2 (*with a difficult situation*) **faire [10] face à**
**He can't cope with school any more.** Il n'arrive plus à faire face à l'école.

**copper** *noun*
le **cuivre** *masc*

**copy** *noun* ▷ see **copy** *verb*
1 (*photocopy*) la **copie** *fem*
**ten copies of the worksheet** dix copies de la feuille d'exercices
2 (*of a book*) un **exemplaire** *masc*
**the very last copy** le tout dernier exemplaire

to **copy** *verb* ▷ see **copy** *noun*
1 (*a document, file*) **copier [1]**
**Copy the file onto a disk.** Copiez le fichier sur disquette.
**He copied Amy's project.** Il a copié le dossier d'Amy. ▸▸

2 (*a person*) **copier sur**
She copies you. Elle copie sur toi.

**cord** *noun*
(*on a blind*) le **cordon** *masc*

**cordless phone** *noun*
le **téléphone sans fil**

**core** *noun*
(*of an apple, pear*) le **trognon** *masc*

**cork** *noun*
(*in a bottle*) le **bouchon** *masc*
• **corkscrew** le tire-bouchon

**corn** *noun*
1 (*wheat*) le **blé** *masc*
2 (*sweetcorn*) le **maïs** *masc*

**corner** *noun*
le **coin** *masc*
**at the corner of the street** au coin de la rue
**out of the corner of your eye** du coin de l'œil
**just round the corner** tout près

**cornflakes** *noun*
les **corn-flakes** *masc plural*

**Cornwall** *noun*
la **Cornouailles** *fem*
**in Cornwall** en Cornouailles

**corpse** *noun*
le **cadavre** *masc*

**correct** *adjective* ▷ see **correct** *verb*
1 (*true*) **exact** *masc*, **exacte** *fem*
**Yes, that's correct.** Oui, c'est exact.
2 (*right*) **bon** *masc*, **bonne** *fem*
**the correct result** le bon résultat
**the correct answers** les bonnes réponses

to **correct** *verb* ▷ see **correct** *adj*
(*a mistake, a typo*) **corriger [52]**

**correction** *noun*
la **correction** *fem*

**correctly** *adverb*
(*to fill in, write, pronounce*) **correctement**

**corridor** *noun*
le **couloir** *masc*

**Corsica** *noun*
**la Corse** *fem*
**to be in Corsica** être **[6]** en Corse
**to go to Corsica** aller Ⓔ **[7]** en Corse

**cosmetics** *plural noun*
les **produits de beauté**

**cost** *noun* ▷ see **cost** *verb*
le **prix** *masc*
**the cost of a new computer** le prix d'un nouvel ordinateur

to **cost** *verb* ▷ see **cost** *noun*
**coûter [1]**
**How much does it cost?** Ça coûte combien?
**The tickets cost £10.** Les billets coûtent dix livres.
**It doesn't cost much to hire bikes.** Ça ne coûte pas cher de louer des vélos.

**costume** *noun*
le **costume** *masc*

**cosy** *adjective*
(*room*) **douillet** *masc*, **douillette** *fem*
**It's cosy by the fire.** On est bien à côté du feu.

**cot** *noun*
le **lit d'enfant**

**cottage** *noun*
la **petite maison**

**cotton** *noun*
1 (*fabric*) le **coton** *masc*
**a cotton shirt** une chemise en coton
2 (*thread*) le **fil de coton**
• **cotton wool** la ouate

**couch** *noun*
le **canapé** *masc*

**cough** *noun* ▷ see **cough** *verb*
la **toux** *fem*
**to have a cough** tousser **[1]**

to **cough** *verb* ▷ see **cough** *noun*
**tousser [1]**

**could** *verb*
1 (*able to do something*) **They couldn't believe it.** Ils ne pouvaient pas le croire.
**They asked if he could pay.** Ils ont demandé s'il pouvait payer.
**I did everything I could.** J'ai fait tout ce que j'ai pu.
2 (*knowing how to do something*) **She could drive at fifteen.** Elle savait conduire à quinze ans.
**I couldn't even swim.** Je ne savais même pas nager.
3 (*when 'could' is not translated in French*) **I could hear the police car.** J'entendais la voiture de police.
**They could smell gas.** Ça sentait le gaz.
**She couldn't see anything.** Elle ne voyait rien.
**I could understand some French.** Je comprenais un peu de français.
4 (*to ask for, to offer help*) **Could I speak to David?** Pourrais-je parler à David?
**You could phone him.** Tu pourrais lui téléphoner.



Ⓔ means the verb takes être to form the perfect

**council** *noun*
le **conseil** *masc*
the town council le conseil municipal

♪ to **count** *verb*
1 (*to add up*) **compter [1]**
I counted my money. J'ai compté mon argent.
That makes eight, not counting Mel. Ça fait huit, sans compter Mel.
2 (*to be treated as*) **être [6] considéré comme**
Teenagers count as adults. Les adolescents sont considérés comme des adultes.
3 (*to be allowed*) **compter [1]**
That doesn't count. Ça ne compte pas.

**counter** *noun*
1 (*in a shop, cafe*) le **comptoir** *masc*
2 (*in a post office, bank*) le **guichet** *masc*
3 (*in a big store*) le **rayon** *masc*
the cheese counter le rayon fromagerie
4 (*for board games*) le **jeton** *masc*

♪ **country** *noun*
1 (*France, England, etc*) le **pays** *masc*
foreign countries les pays étrangers
from another country d'un autre pays
2 (*countryside*) la **campagne** *fem*
a country road une route de campagne
a holiday in the country des vacances à la campagne
• **countryside** la campagne

**county** *noun*
le **comté** *masc*

♪ **couple** *noun*
1 (*pair*) le **couple** *masc*
a young couple from London un jeune couple de Londres
2 (*one or two*)
a couple of students deux ou trois étudiants
a couple of times deux ou trois fois
I've got a couple of things to do. J'ai deux ou trois choses à faire.

**courage** *noun*
le **courage** *masc*

**courgette** *noun*
la **courgette** *fem*

**courier** *noun*
1 (*travel courier*) un **accompagnateur** *masc*, une **accompagnatrice** *fem*
2 (*delivery service*) le **coursier** *masc*
by courier par coursier

♪ **course** *noun*
1 (*set of lessons*) le **cours** *masc*
a computer course un cours d'informatique
I'm going on a course. Je vais suivre un cours.
2 (*part of a meal*) le **plat** *masc*
For the main course, there's chicken. Comme plat principal, il y a du poulet.
3 (*certainly*) **of course** bien sûr
Of course not! Bien sûr que non!
He's forgotten, of course. Il a oublié, bien sûr.
4 ▷ **golf course**

**court** *noun*
1 (*for tennis, squash*) le **court** *masc*
2 (*for basketball*) le **terrain** *masc*
• **courtyard** la cour

♪ **cousin** *noun*
le **cousin** *masc*, la **cousine** *fem*
my cousin Janet ma cousine Janet ▷ **first cousin**

♪ **cover** *noun* ▷ see **cover** *verb*
1 (*for a book, magazine*) la **couverture** *fem*
2 (*for a duvet, cushion*) la **housse** *fem*
3 (*cover version*) la **version** *fem*
a cover of a French hit une version d'un tube français

♪ to **cover** *verb* ▷ see **cover** *noun*
1 (*to protect*) **couvrir [30]**
Cover the wound. Couvrez la blessure.
to be covered in something être [6] couvert de quelque chose
She was covered in spots. Elle était couverte de boutons.
2 (*with leaves, snow, fabric*) **recouvrir [30]**
covered with snow recouvert de neige

♪ **cow** *noun*
la **vache** *fem*

**coward** *noun*
le & la **lâche** *masc & fem*

**cowboy** *noun*
le **cowboy** *masc*

**crab** *noun*
le **crabe** *masc*

**crack** *noun* ▷ see **crack** *verb*
1 (*in a wall, cup*) la **fêlure** *fem*
2 (*cracking noise*) le **craquement** *masc*
I heard a crack. J'ai entendu un craquement.

to **crack** *verb* ▷ see **crack** *noun*
1 (*a plate, the ice*) **fêler [1]**
2 (*to break*) **casser [1]**
You cracked the eggs! Tu as cassé les œufs!
3 (*to split by itself*) **se fêler** Ⓔ **[1]**
The ice is starting to crack. La glace commence à se fêler.

**cracker** *noun*
1 (*biscuit*) le **cracker** *masc*
2 (*Christmas cracker*) le **diablotin** *masc*

to **crackle** *verb*
(*fire*) **crépiter [1]**

**crafts** *noun*
(*at school*) les **travaux manuels**

**crafty** *adjective*
**ingénieux** *masc*, **ingénieuse** *fem*

**cramp** *noun*
la **crampe** *fem*
a cramp in your leg une crampe à la jambe

**crane** *noun*
la **grue** *fem*

to **crash** *verb* ▷ see **crash** *noun*
1 (*cars, planes*) **s'écraser** Ⓔ **[1]**
The plane crashed. L'avion s'est écrasé.
2 to crash into rentrer Ⓔ **[1]** dans
They crashed into a tree. Ils sont rentrés dans un arbre.

**crash** *noun* ▷ see **crash** *verb*
1 (*accident*) un **accident** *masc*
a car crash un accident de voiture
2 (*of broken glass*) le **fracas** *masc*
• **crash course** le cours intensif
• **crash helmet** le casque *masc*

♂ **crate** *noun*
1 (*for bottles, china*) la **caisse** *fem*
2 (*for fruit*) le **cageot** *masc*

**crawl** *noun* ▷ see **crawl** *verb*
(*in swimming*) le **crawl** *masc*

to **crawl** *verb* ▷ see **crawl** *noun*
1 (*person, baby*) **marcher [1] à quatre pattes**
2 (*cars in a traffic jam*) **rouler [1] au pas**

**crayon** *noun*
1 (*wax*) le **crayon gras**
2 (*coloured pencil*) le **crayon de couleur**

**craze** *noun*
la **vogue** *fem*
the craze for rollerblades la vogue des rollers

♂ **crazy** *adjective*
**fou** *masc*, **folle** *fem*
She's crazy! Elle est folle!
to go crazy devenir Ⓔ **[81]** fou

to **creak** *verb*
1 (*door*) **grincer [61]**
2 (*floorboard*) **craquer [1]**

♂ **cream** *noun*
la **crème** *fem*
strawberries and cream des fraises à la crème
• **cream cheese** le fromage à tartiner

**creased** *adjective*
**froissé** *masc*, **froissée** *fem*

to **create** *verb*
(*problems*) **créer [32]**

**creative** *adjective*
**créatif** *masc*, **créative** *fem*

**creature** *noun*
la **créature** *fem*

**crèche** *noun*
la **crèche** *fem*

**credit** *noun*
le **crédit** *masc*
We bought it on credit. On l'a acheté à crédit.
• **credit card** la carte de crédit

**creepy** *adjective*
a creepy film un film qui donne la chair de poule

**crew** *noun*
1 (*on a ship, plane*) un **équipage** *masc*
2 (*rowing, filming*) une **équipe** *fem*
• **crew cut** les cheveux en brosse

**cricket** *noun*
1 (*game*) le **cricket** *masc*
to play cricket jouer **[1]** au cricket
2 (*insect*) le **grillon** *masc*
• **cricket bat** la batte de cricket

**crime** *noun*
1 (*illegal act*) le **crime** *masc*
2 (*trend within society*) la **criminalité** *fem*

**criminal** *noun*
le **criminel** *masc*, la **criminelle** *fem*

**crimson** *adjective*
**pourpre** *masc & fem*

**crisis** *noun*
la **crise** *fem*

♂ **crisp** *adjective* ▷ see **crisp** *noun*
**croustillant** *masc*, **croustillante** *fem*

♂ **crisp** *noun* ▷ see **crisp** *adj*
la **chip** *fem*
a packet of crisps un paquet de chips

**critical** *adjective*
**critique** *masc & fem*
She's too critical. Elle est trop critique.

**criticism** *noun*
la **critique** *fem*

to **criticize** *verb*
**critiquer [1]**

**crockery** *noun*
la **vaisselle** *fem*

**crocodile** *noun*
le **crocodile** *masc*

**crook** *noun*
(*criminal*) un **escroc** *masc*

**crooked** *adjective*
(*picture, hat*) **to be crooked** être [6] de travers

**crop** *noun*
la **récolte** *fem*

**cross** *noun* ▷ see **cross** *adj, verb*
la **croix** *fem*
a silver cross une croix en argent

♂ **cross** *adjective* ▷ see **cross** *noun, verb*
**fâché** *masc*, **fâchée** *fem*
She's very cross. Elle est très fâchée.
I'm cross with you. Je suis fâché contre toi.
to get cross se fâcher Ⓔ [1]
My mum got cross. Ma mère s'est fâchée.

♂ to **cross** *verb* ▷ see **cross** *noun, adj*
1 (*a road, a river*) **traverser** [1]
Watch out crossing the road. Faites attention en traversant la rue.
2 (*your fingers, legs*) **croiser** [1]
I'll keep my fingers crossed. Je croise les doigts.
3 (*a border*) **passer** Ⓔ [1]
to cross into Italy passer en Italie
4 (*to meet each other*) **se croiser** Ⓔ [1]
• to **cross out something**
(*a mistake, your name*) **rayer** [59] **quelque chose**

**cross-Channel** *adjective*
(*ferry*) **transmanche** *invariable adjective*

**cross-country** *noun*
le **cross** *masc*
• **cross-country skiing** le ski de fond

♂ **crossing** *noun*
la **traversée** *fem*
a Channel crossing une traversée transmanche ▷ **level crossing, pedestrian crossing**

**cross-legged** *adjective*
to sit cross-legged être [6] assis en tailleur

♂ **crossroads** *noun*
le **carrefour** *masc*
at the crossroads au carrefour

**crossword** *noun*
les **mots croisés**
to do the crossword faire [10] les mots croisés

to **crouch** *verb*
**s'accroupir** [2]

**crow** *noun* ▷ see **crow** *verb*
le **corbeau** *masc*

to **crow** *verb* ▷ see **check** *noun*
(*cockerels*) **chanter** [1]

♂ **crowd** *noun* ▷ see **crowd** *verb*
la **foule** *fem*
in the crowd dans la foule
a crowd of 5,000 une foule de cinq mille personnes
to avoid the crowds éviter [1] la foule

**crowded** *adjective*
**bondé** *masc*, **bondée** *fem*
The hall was crowded. La salle était bondée.

**crown** *noun*
la **couronne** *fem*

**cruel** *adjective*
**cruel** *masc*, **cruelle** *fem*

**cruelty** *noun*
la **cruauté** *fem*

**cruise** *noun*
la **croisière** *fem*
They're on a cruise. Ils font une croisière.

**crumb** *noun*
la **miette** *fem*

to **crumple** *verb*
**froisser** [1]

to **crunch** *verb*
(*an apple*) **croquer** [1]

**crunchy** *adjective*
**croquant** *masc*, **croquante** *fem*

to **crush** *verb*
**écraser** [1]

**crust** *noun*
la **croûte** *fem*

**crusty** *adjective*
(*bread*) **croustillant** *masc*, **croustillante** *fem*

**crutch** *noun*
la **béquille** *fem*
He's on crutches. Il marche avec des béquilles.

♂ **cry** *noun* ▷ see **cry** *verb*
le **cri** *masc*

♂ to **cry** *verb* ▷ see **cry** *noun*
1 (*to weep*) **pleurer** [1]
Don't cry. Ne pleure pas.
to make somebody cry faire [10] pleurer quelqu'un
They made me cry. Ils m'ont fait pleurer. ▸▸

2 (*to call out*) **crier [1]**
to cry out loudly crier fort
to cry for help appeler [18] au secours

**crystal** *noun*
le **cristal** *masc*

**cub** *noun*
1 (*young animal*) le **petit** *masc*
2 (*scout*) le **louveteau** *masc*

**Cuba** *noun*
la **Cuba** *fem*
to be in Cuba être [6] à Cuba
to go to Cuba aller ⓔ [7] à Cuba

**Cuban** *noun*
un **Cubain** *masc*, une **Cubaine** *fem*

**Cuban** *adjective*
**cubain** *masc*, **cubaine** *fem*

**cube** *noun*
le **cube** *masc*
an ice cube un glaçon

**cubicle** *noun*
1 (*in a changing room*) la **cabine** *fem*
2 (*in a public toilet*) le **cabinet** *masc*

**cuckoo** *noun*
le **coucou** *masc*

**cucumber** *noun*
le **concombre** *masc*

**cuddle** *noun*
to give somebody a cuddle faire [10] un câlin à quelqu'un
She gave him a cuddle. Elle lui a fait un câlin.

**cue** *noun*
(*in billiards, etc*) la **queue de billard**

**cuff** *noun*
(*on a shirt*) la **manchette** *fem*

**cul-de-sac** *noun*
une **impasse** *fem*

**culture** *noun*
la **culture** *fem*

**cunning** *adjective*
**rusé** *masc*, **rusée** *fem*

♪ **cup** *noun*
1 (*for drinking*) la **tasse** *fem*
a cup of tea une tasse de thé
2 (*trophy*) la **coupe** *fem*
the World Cup la Coupe du Monde
• **cupboard** le placard
• **cup final** la finale de la coupe
• **cup tie** le match de coupe

**cure** *noun* ▷ see **cure** *verb*
le **remède** *masc*
a cure for warts un remède contre les verrues

to **cure** *verb* ▷ see **cure** *noun*
(*a sick person*) **guérir [2]**

**curiosity** *noun*
la **curiosité** *fem*
I asked out of curiosity. J'ai demandé par curiosité.

**curious** *adjective*
**curieux** *masc*, **curieuse** *fem*

**curl** *noun* ▷ see **curl** *verb*
la **boucle** *fem*

to **curl** *verb* ▷ see **curl** *noun*
(*your hair*) **friser [1]**

**curly** *adjective*
**bouclé** *masc*, **bouclée** *fem*
curly hair les cheveux bouclés

**currant** *noun*
le **raisin de Corinthe**

♪ **currency** *noun*
(*money*) les **devises** *fem plural*

**current** *noun* ▷ see **adjective** *adj*
(*of electricity, in sea*) le **courant** *masc*

**current** *adjective* ▷ see **current** *noun*
(*present-day*) **actuel** *masc*, **actuelle** *fem*
• **current affairs** l'actualité *fem*

**curriculum** *noun*
le **programme** *masc*

**curry** *noun*
le **curry** *masc*
chicken curry le curry de poulet

♪ **cursor** *noun*
le **curseur** *masc*

♪ **curtain** *noun*
le **rideau** *masc* (*pl* les **rideaux**)

**cushion** *noun*
le **coussin** *masc*

**custard** *noun*
1 (*runny*) la **crème anglaise**
2 (*baked*) le **flan** *masc*

**custom** *noun*
la **coutume** *fem*

♪ **customer** *noun*
le **client** *masc*, la **cliente** *fem*
full of customers plein de clients

♪ **customs** *plural noun*
la **douane** *fem singular*
We went through customs. Nous sommes passés à la douane.



ⓔ means the verb takes être to form the perfect

- **customs hall** la douane *fem*
- **customs officer** le douanier *masc*

ℰ **cut** *noun* ▷ see **cut** *verb*

1 (*injury*) la **coupure** *fem*
2 (*haircut*) la **coupe** *fem*

ℰ to **cut** *verb* ▷ see **cut** *noun*

1 (*with scissors, a knife*) **couper [1]**
I've cut the bread. J'ai coupé le pain.
Cut the pizza in half. Coupe la pizza en deux.
to cut yourself se couper Ⓔ [1]
Ruth's cut her finger. Ruth s'est coupé le doigt.
2 (*with lawnmower*) **tondre [3]**
I cut the grass. J'ai tondu le gazon.
3 to get your hair cut se faire Ⓔ [10] couper les cheveux
Sophie's had her hair cut. Sophie s'est fait couper les cheveux.
4 (*on computer*) **couper [1]**
I cut the image and pasted it into the file. J'ai coupé l'image et je l'ai collée dans le fichier.
5 (*prices*) **baisser [1]**

- to **cut something down**
(*a tree*) **abattre [21] quelque chose**
- to **cut something out**

1 (*a photo, an article*) **découper [1] quelque chose**
2 (*sugar, salt*) **supprimer [1] quelque chose**

- to **cut something up**
(*carrots, a chicken*) **couper [1] quelque chose**

**cutlery** *noun*
les **couverts** *masc plural*

**CV** *noun*
le **CV** *masc*

to **cycle** *verb*
**faire [10] du vélo**
I enjoy cycling. J'aime faire du vélo.
I cycle to school every day. Tous les jours, je vais à l'école à vélo.

**cycle lane** *noun*
la **piste cyclable**

**cycle race** *noun*
la **course cycliste**

ℰ **cycling** *noun*
le **cyclisme** *masc*
to go on a cycling holiday faire [10] du cyclotourisme

**mini-info** ***cycling***

The *Tour de France* cycle race takes place in France every summer. The 4,000 kilometre route changes every year but always finishes in Paris. The previous day's winner wears a special yellow jersey.

ℰ **cyclist** *noun*
le & la **cycliste** *masc & fem*

**cylinder** *noun*
le **cylindre** *masc*

# D d

ℰ **dad** *noun*

1 (*in general*) le **père** *masc*
Anna's dad le père d'Anna
Dad works in a bank. Mon père travaille dans une banque.
2 (*within the family*) **papa** *masc*
Dad's not home yet. Papa n'est pas encore rentré.

**daffodil** *noun*
la **jonquille** *fem*

**daily** *adjective* ▷ see **daily** *adv*
**quotidien** *masc*, **quotidienne** *fem*
a daily newspaper un journal quotidien

**daily** *adverb* ▷ see **daily** *adj*
**quotidiennement**
She visits him daily. Elle lui rend visite tous les jours.

**dairy products** *plural noun*
les **produits laitiers** *masc plural*
Connor is allergic to dairy products. Connor est allergique aux produits laitiers.

**dam** *noun*
le **barrage** *masc*

ℰ to **damage** *verb* ▷ see **damage** *noun*

1 (*a car, building*) **endommager [52]** ▸▸

**2** (*your health*) **s'abîmer [1]** Ⓔ
**You're going to damage your eyesight.** Tu vas t'abîmer la vue.

**damage** *noun* ▷ see **damage** *verb*
les **dégâts** *masc plural*

**damn** *noun* ▷ see **damn** *excl*
(*informal*) **not to give a damn** s'en ficher
**He doesn't give a damn.** Il s'en fiche complètement.

**damn** *exclamation* ▷ see **damn** *noun*
(*informal*) **damn!** zut!

**damp** *adjective* ▷ see **damp** *noun*
**humide** *masc & fem*

**damp** *noun* ▷ see **damp** *adj*
l'**humidité** *fem*

♪ **dance** *noun* ▷ see **dance** *verb*
**1** (*like salsa, waltz*) la **danse** *fem*
**a folk dance** une danse traditionnelle
**2** (*party*) la **soirée dansante**

♪ to **dance** *verb* ▷ see **dance** *noun*
**danser [1]**

**dancer** *noun*
le **danseur** *masc*, la **danseuse** *fem*

**dancing** *noun*
la **danse** *fem*
**I like dancing.** J'aime danser.
• **dancing class** le cours de danse

**dandruff** *noun*
les **pellicules** *fem plural*

**danger** *noun*
le **danger** *masc*
**to be in danger** être **[6]** en danger
**The world is in danger.** Le monde est en danger.

♪ **dangerous** *adjective*
**dangereux** *masc*, **dangereuse** *fem*
**to be dangerous to do something** être **[6]** dangereux de faire quelque chose
**It's dangerous to drive fast.** Il est dangereux de conduire vite.

**Danish** *adjective* ▷ see **Danish** *noun*
**danois** *masc*, **danoise** *fem*

**Danish** *noun* ▷ see **Danish** *adj*
(*language*) le **danois** *masc*

to **dare** *verb*
**1 to dare to do something** oser **[1]** faire quelque chose
**I didn't dare to suggest it.** Je n'ai pas osé le suggérer.
**2** (*in orders*) **Don't you dare tell her I'm here!** Je t'interdis de lui dire que je suis là!
**3 I dare you!** Chiche! (*informal*)
**I dare you to drink it all!** Chiche que tu bois tout!

**daring** *adjective*
**osé** *masc*, **osée** *fem*
**a daring choice** un choix osé

**dark** *adjective* ▷ see **dark** *noun*
**1** (*colour*) **foncé** *masc*, **foncée** *fem*
**a dark blue skirt** une jupe bleu foncé
**2** (*night*) **It's dark already.** Il fait nuit déjà.
**It gets dark around five.** La nuit commence à tomber vers cinq heures.
**3** (*hair, skin*) **brun** *masc*, **brune** *fem*
**She has dark brown hair.** Elle est brune.
**4** (*room*) **sombre** *masc & fem*
**It's dark in here.** Il fait sombre ici.

**dark** *noun* ▷ see **dark** *adj*
**in the dark** dans l'obscurité
**after dark** après la tombée de la nuit
**My little brother's afraid of the dark.** Mon petit frère a peur du noir.

**darkness** *noun*
l'**obscurité** *fem*
**in darkness** dans l'obscurité

**darling** *noun*
**chéri** *masc*, **chérie** *fem*
**See you later, darling!** À tout à l'heure, chéri!

**dart** *noun*
la **fléchette** *fem*
**to play darts** jouer **[1]** aux fléchettes

**data** *plural noun*
les **données** *fem plural*

**database** *noun*
la **base de données**

♪ **date** *noun*
**1** (*in time*) la **date** *fem*
**What's the date today?** Nous sommes le combien aujourd'hui?
**to fix a date for something** fixer **[1]** une date pour quelque chose
**They've fixed a date for their wedding.** Ils ont fixé la date de leur mariage.
**2** (*to go out with somebody*) **to have a date with somebody** sortir Ⓔ **[72]** avec quelqu'un
**Laura's got a date with Mick tonight.** Laura sort avec Mick ce soir.
**3** (*fruit*) la **datte** *fem*
• **date of birth** la date de naissance

♪ **daughter** *noun*
la **fille** *fem*
**Tina's daughter** la fille de Tina

**daughter-in-law** *noun*
la **belle-fille** *fem* (*pl* les **belles-filles**)

**dawn** *noun*
**l'aube** *fem*

♪ **day** *noun*
1 le **jour** *masc*
**three days later** trois jours plus tard
**the day I met my girlfriend** le jour où j'ai rencontré ma copine
2 *(as a period of time)* la **journée** *fem*
**It rained all day.** Il a plu toute la journée.
3 *(when you refer to the weather)* **It's a nice day.** Il fait beau.
4 *(in expressions)* **the day after** le lendemain
**the day after tomorrow** après-demain
5 **the day before** la veille
**the day before yesterday** avant-hier
• **day off** le jour de congé
**When's your day off?** Quel est ton jour de congé?

♪ **dead** *adjective* ▷ see **dead** *adv*
**mort** *masc*, **morte** *fem*
**Her mother's dead.** Sa mère est morte.
**The cat's dead.** Le chat est mort.

**dead** *adverb* ▷ see **dead** *adj*
1 *(very, really)* **vachement**
**It's dead easy.** C'est vachement facile.
2 *(completely)* **absolument**
**You're dead right.** Tu as absolument raison.
**dead on time** à l'heure pile
• **dead end** une impasse
• **deadline** la date limite

♪ **deaf** *adjective*
**sourd** *masc*, **sourde** *fem*

**deafening** *adjective*
**assourdissant** *masc*, **assourdissante** *fem*

**deal** *noun* ▷ see **deal** *verb*
1 *(buying and selling)* une **affaire** *fem*
**It's a good deal.** C'est une bonne affaire.
2 *(agreement)* le **marché** *masc*
**It's a deal!** Marché conclu!
**I'll make a deal with you.** Je ferai un marché avec toi.
3 **a great deal of something** beaucoup de quelque chose
**a great deal of money** beaucoup d'argent
**I don't have a great deal of time.** Je n'ai pas beaucoup de temps.

to **deal** *verb* ▷ see **deal** *noun*
*(in cards)* **donner** [1]
• **to deal with something**
**s'occuper** [1] **de quelque chose**
**I'll deal with it.** Je m'en occuperai.
**I dealt with the repairs.** Je me suis occupé des réparations.

♪ **dear** *adjective*
1 *(in letters)* **cher** *masc*, **chère** *fem*
Dear Sylvie Chère Sylvie
2 *(expensive)* **cher** *masc*, **chère** *fem*
**That's dear.** Ça coûte cher.

**death** *noun*
la **mort** *fem*
**after his father's death** après la mort de son père
**I was bored to death.** Je m'ennuyais à mourir.
**I'm sick to death of it!** J'en ai vraiment marre! *(informal)*
• **death penalty** la peine de mort

**debate** *noun* ▷ see **debate** *verb*
le **débat** *masc*

to **debate** *verb* ▷ see **debate** *noun*
**débattre** [21]

**debt** *noun*
la **dette** *fem*
**to get into debt** s'endetter ❷ [1]
**Students are getting into too much debt.** Les étudiants s'endettent trop.

**decade** *noun*
la **décennie** *fem*

**decaffeinated** *adjective*
**décaféiné** *masc*, **décaféinée** *fem*

to **deceive** *verb*
**tromper** [1]

**December** *noun*
**décembre** *masc*
**in December** en décembre

**WORD TIP** Months of the year and days of the week start with small letters in French.

**decent** *adjective*
*(adequate)* **convenable** *masc & fem*
**a decent salary** un salaire convenable
**a decent meal** un bon repas

♪ to **decide** *verb*
**décider** [1]
**I haven't decided yet.** Je n'ai pas encore décidé.
**to decide to do something** décider de faire quelque chose
**She's decided to buy a car.** Elle a decidé d'acheter une voiture.
**She's decided not to look for a job.** Elle a décidé de ne pas chercher de petit boulot.

**decimal** *adjective*
**décimal** *masc*, **décimale** *fem*, **décimaux** *masc pl*, **décimales** *fem pl* ▶▶

- **decimal point** la virgule

**WORD TIP** In French a comma is used for a dot in decimals.

**decision** *noun*
la **décision** *fem*
**the right decision** la bonne décision
**the wrong decision** la mauvaise décision
**to take a decision** prendre **[64]** une décision

**deck** *noun*
**1** (*on a ship*) le **pont** *masc*
**2** (*on a bus, plane*) un **étage** *masc*
- **deckchair** le transat

to **declare** *verb*
**déclarer [1]**

to **decorate** *verb*
**1 décorer [1]**
**I love decorating the Christmas tree.** J'aime décorer le sapin de Noël.
**2** (*paint*) **peindre [60]**
**Dad is going to decorate the kitchen.** Papa va peindre la cuisine.

**decoration** *noun*
la **décoration** *fem*

**decorator** *noun*
le **peintre-décorateur** *masc*, la **peintre-décoratrice** *fem*

**decrease** *noun*
la **diminution** *fem*
**a decrease in the number of marriages** une diminution du nombre de mariages

to **decrease** *verb*
**diminuer [1]**

to **deduct** *verb*
**déduire [26]**

**deep** *adjective*
**profond** *masc*, **profonde** *fem*
**a deep hole** un trou profond
**a hole two metres deep** un trou de deux mètres de profondeur
**The river is very deep.** La rivière est très profonde.
**How deep is the swimming pool?** Quelle est la profondeur de la piscine?
- **deep end** (*of a swimming pool*) le grand bassin
- **deep freeze** le congélateur

**deeply** *adverb*
**profondément**

**deer** *noun*
(*male*) le **cerf** *masc*, (*female*) la **biche** *fem*

**defeat** *noun* ▷ see **defeat** *verb*
la **défaite** *fem*

to **defeat** *verb* ▷ see **defeat** *noun*
**battre [21]**

**defect** *noun*
le **défaut** *masc*

**defence** *noun*
la **défense** *fem*

to **defend** *verb*
**défendre [3]**

**defender** *noun*
le **défenseur** *masc*

to **define** *verb*
**définir [2]**

**definite** *adjective*
**1** (*clear*) **net** *masc*, **nette** *fem*
**a definite change** un net changement
**a definite improvement** une nette amélioration
**2** (*certain*) **sûr** *masc*, **sûre** *fem*
**It's not definite yet.** Ce n'est pas encore sûr.
**3** (*exact*) **précis** *masc*, **précise** *fem*
**a definite answer** une réponse précise
**I don't have a definite idea of what I want.** Je n'ai pas une idée précise de ce que je veux.
- **definite article** l'article défini *masc*

**definitely** *adverb*
**1** (*when giving your opinion*) **sans aucun doute**
**The blue one is definitely the biggest.** Le bleu est sans aucun doute le plus grand.
**Your French is definitely better than mine.** Ton français est sans aucun doute meilleur que le mien.
**'Do you like this one better?' — 'Definitely!'** 'Tu préfères celui-ci?' — 'Sans aucun doute!'
**2** (*certainly*) **She's definitely going to be there.** Elle va y être, c'est sûr.
**I'm definitely not going.** C'est décidé, je n'y vais pas.

**definition** *noun*
la **définition** *fem*

♪ **degree** *noun*
**1** (*in temperatures, angles*) le **degré** *masc*
**thirty degrees** trente degrés
**2** (*qualification*) **a university degree** un diplôme universitaire

♪ **delay** *noun* ▷ see **delay** *verb*
le **retard** *masc*
**a two-hour delay** un retard de deux heures

♪ to **delay** *verb* ▷ see **delay** *noun*
**1** (*to make late*) **retarder [1]**
**The flight was delayed by bad weather.** Le vol a été retardé par le mauvais temps.

2 (*to postpone*) **différer [24]**
**The decision has been delayed until Thursday.** La décision a été différée jusqu'à jeudi.

to **delete** *verb*
**effacer [61]**

**deliberate** *adjective*
**délibéré** *masc*, **délibérée** *fem*

**deliberately** *adverb*
**exprès**
**He left it there deliberately.** Il a fait exprès de le laisser là.

**delicate** *adjective*
**délicat** *masc*, **délicate** *fem*

**delicatessen** *noun*
une **épicerie fine**

**delicatessen**

*Charcuteries* were originally pork butchers. Modern *charcuteries* are delicatessens selling a range of cooked meats, pâtés, quiches or pizzas and salads. Many have a range of ready-cooked, takeaway meals— from *choucroute* to *couscous*.

♪ **delicious** *adjective*
**délicieux** *masc*, **délicieuse** *fem*

♪ **delighted** *adjective*
**ravi** *masc*, **ravie** *fem*
**I'm delighted to hear you can come.** Je suis ravi d'apprendre que tu peux venir (*boy speaking*), Je suis ravie d'apprendre que tu peux venir (*girl speaking*).
**They're delighted with their new car.** Ils sont ravis de leur nouvelle voiture.

to **deliver** *verb*
1 (*goods*) **livrer [1]**
**They're delivering the computer tomorrow.** Ils vont livrer l'ordinateur demain.
2 (*mail*) **distribuer [1]**

**delivery** *noun*
la **livraison** *fem*

**demand** *noun* ▷ see **demand** *verb*
la **demande** *fem*

to **demand** *verb* ▷ see **demand** *noun*
**exiger [52]**

**democracy** *noun*
la **démocratie** *fem*

**democratic** *adjective*
**démocratique** *masc & fem*

to **demolish** *verb*
**démolir [2]**

to **demonstrate** *verb*
1 (*a product, a machine, etc*) **faire [10] la démonstration de**
2 (*to protest*) **manifester [1]**
**to demonstrate against something** manifester contre quelque chose
**Millions of people demonstrated against the war.** Des millions de gens ont manifesté contre la guerre.

**demonstration** *noun*
1 (*of a product, a machine, etc*) la **démonstration** *fem*
2 (*protest*) la **manifestation** *fem*

**demonstrator** *noun*
le **manifestant** *masc*, la **manifestante** *fem*

**denim** *noun*
le **jean** *masc*
**a denim jacket** un blouson en jean

**Denmark** *noun*
**Danemark** *masc*
**in Denmark** au Danemark
**to Denmark** au Danemark

**dense** *adjective*
**dense** *masc & fem*

**dent** *noun* ▷ see **dent** *verb*
la **bosse** *fem*

to **dent** *verb* ▷ see **dent** *noun*
**cabosser [1]**

**dental** *adjective*
**dentaire** *masc & fem*
**dental floss** du fil dentaire
**a dental appointment** un rendez-vous chez le dentiste
- **dental hygiene** l'hygiène dentaire *fem*
- **dental surgeon** le chirurgien-dentiste, la chirurgienne-dentiste

♪ **dentist** *noun*
le & la **dentiste** *masc & fem*
**My mum's a dentist.** Ma mère est dentiste.

to **deny** *verb*
**nier [1]**

**deodorant** *noun*
le **déodorant** *masc*

to **depart** *verb*
**partir ⓔ [58]**

♪ **department** *noun*
1 (*in a shop*) le **rayon** *masc*
**the men's department** le rayon hommes
2 (*in schools*) le **département** *masc*
**the language department** le département de langues étrangères
- **department store** le grand magasin

English-French

a b c d e f g h i j k l m n o p q r s t u v w x y z

**departure** *noun*
le **départ** *masc*
- **departure lounge** la salle d'embarquement

to **depend** *verb*
It depends. Ça dépend.
to depend on something dépendre [3] de quelque chose
It depends on the price. Ça dépend du prix.
It depends on what you want. Ça dépend de ce que tu veux.

**deposit** *noun*
1 (*with a booking*) les **arrhes** *fem plural*
to pay a deposit verser des arrhes
We paid a deposit of 50 euros. Nous avons versé des arrhes de 50 euros.
2 (*for hiring something*) la **caution** *fem*
3 (*on a bottle*) la **consigne** *fem*

**depressed** *adjective*
**déprimé** *masc*, **déprimée** *fem*

**depressing** *adjective*
**déprimant** *masc*, **déprimante** *fem*

**depth** *noun*
la **profondeur** *fem*

**deputy** *noun*
**adjoint** *masc*, **adjointe** *fem*
- **deputy head** le directeur adjoint, la directrice adjointe

to **descend** *verb*
**descendre** Ⓔ [3]

to **describe** *verb*
**décrire** [38]

**description** *noun*
la **description** *fem*

**desert** *noun*
le **désert** *masc*
in the desert dans le désert
- **desert island** une île déserte

to **deserve** *verb*
**mériter** [1]

**design** *noun* ▷ see **design** *verb*
1 (*artistic*) le **design** *masc*
fashion design le stylisme
2 (*pattern*) le **motif** *masc*
a floral design un motif floral
3 (*technological*) la **conception** *fem*
the design of the plane la conception de l'avion

to **design** *verb* ▷ see **design** *noun*
1 (*costumes, clothes, scenery*) **créer** [32]
2 (*a machine, a plane, a system*) **concevoir** [66]

**designer** *noun*
1 (*in fashion*) le & la **styliste** *masc & fem*
2 (*in graphics*) le & la **graphiste** *masc & fem*

**desire** *noun* ▷ see **desire** *verb*
le **désir** *masc*

to **desire** *verb* ▷ see **desire** *noun*
**désirer** [1]

**desk** *noun*
1 (*in an office, at home*) le **bureau** *masc*
the information desk le bureau des renseignements
the reception desk la réception
2 (*at school*) la **table** *fem*

**despair** *noun* ▷ see **despair** *verb*
le **désespoir** *masc*

to **despair** *verb* ▷ see **despair** *noun*
to despair of doing something désespérer [24] de faire quelque chose
We despaired of ever finishing this project. Nous nous désespérions de ne jamais finir ce projet.

**desperate** *adjective*
1 **désespéré** *masc*, **désespérée** *fem*
a desperate attempt une tentative désespérée
2 to be desperate to do something avoir [5] très envie de faire quelque chose
I'm desperate to see you. J'ai très envie de te voir.

to **despise** *verb*
**mépriser** [1]

**dessert** *noun*
le **dessert** *masc*
What's for dessert? Qu'est-ce qu'il y a comme dessert?
For dessert, we have ... Comme dessert, nous avons ...

**destination** *noun*
la **destination** *fem*

to **destroy** *verb*
**détruire** [26]

**destruction** *noun*
la **destruction** *fem*

**detached house** *noun*
le **maison individuelle**

**detail** *noun*
le **détail** *masc*

**detailed** *adjective*
**détaillé** *masc*, **détaillée** *fem*

**detective** *noun*
un **inspecteur de police**, une **inspectrice de police**
a private detective le détective, la détective



Ⓔ means the verb takes être to form the perfect

• **detective story** le roman policier

**detention** *noun*
la **retenue** *fem*

**detergent** *noun*
le **détergent** *masc*

**determined** *adjective*
**résolu** *masc*, **résolue** *fem*
**He's determined to leave.** Il est résolu de partir.

**determiner** *noun*
(*Grammar*) le **déterminant** *masc*

**WORD TIP** In English these are *a, an* and *the*. In French they are *un, une, des* and *le, la, les*.

**detour** *noun*
le **détour** *masc*

to **develop** *verb*
1 (*a film*) **faire [10] développer**
**I got the film developed.** J'ai fait développer la pellicule.
2 (*people, children*) **se développer** Ⓔ **[1]**
**how children develop** comment les enfants se développent

**developing country** *noun*
le **pays en voie de développement**

**development** *noun*
le **développement** *masc*

**devil** *noun*
le **diable** *masc*

**devoted** *adjective*
**dévoué** *masc*, **dévouée** *fem*

**dew** *noun*
la **rosée** *fem*

**diabetes** *noun*
le **diabète** *masc*

**diabetic** *adjective, noun*
**diabétique** *masc & fem*
**to be diabetic** être [6] diabétique
**Diane is diabetic.** Diane est diabétique.
**Jack is a diabetic.** Jack est diabétique.

**diagnosis** *noun*
le **diagnostic** *masc*

**diagonal** *adjective*
**diagonal** *masc*, **diagonale** *fem*, **diagonaux** *masc pl*, **diagonales** *fem pl*

**diagram** *noun*
le **schéma** *masc*

to **dial** *verb*
**composer [1] le numéro**
**Dial 999.** Composez le 999.
**Dial 00 33 for France.** Faîtes le 00 33 pour la France.

**dialling tone** *noun*
la **tonalité** *fem*

**dialogue** *noun*
le **dialogue** *masc*

**diameter** *noun*
le **diamètre** *masc*

**diamond** *noun*
1 (*jewel*) le **diamant** *masc*
2 (*shape*) le **losange** *masc*
3 (*in cards*) le **carreau** *masc*
**the jack of diamonds** le valet de carreau

**diarrhoea** *noun*
la **diarrhée** *fem*
**to have diarrhoea** avoir [5] la diarrhée
**The baby had diarrhoea.** Le bébé avait la diarrhée.

**diary** *noun*
1 (*for appointments*) un **agenda** *masc*
**I've noted it in my diary.** Je l'ai marqué dans mon agenda.
2 (*of what you do*) le **journal intime**
**to keep a diary** tenir [77] un journal
**Do you keep a diary?** Est-ce que tu tiens un journal?

**dice** *noun*
le **dé** *masc*
**Throw the dice!** Jette le dé!

**dictation** *noun*
la **dictée** *fem*

**dictionary** *noun*
le **dictionnaire** *masc*
**to look up a word in the dictionary** chercher [1] un mot dans le dictionnaire
**You can look it up in your dictionary.** Tu peux le chercher dans ton dictionnaire.

**did** *verb* ▷ **do**

to **die** *verb*
1 **mourir** Ⓔ **[54]**
**My grandmother died in January.** Ma grand-mère est morte en janvier.
2 **to be dying to do something** mourir d'envie de faire quelque chose
**I'm dying to see them!** Je meurs d'envie de les voir!

• **to die out**
**disparaître [27]**

**diesel** *noun*
le **gazole** *masc*
**a diesel car** une voiture diesel
**a diesel engine** un moteur diesel

**diet** *noun*
1 (*what you eat*) une **alimentation** *fem*
I try to have a healthy diet. J'essaye d'avoir une alimentation saine.
2 (*for slimming*) le **régime** *masc*
a salt-free diet un régime sans sel
to be on a diet être [6] au régime
She's on a diet. Elle est au régime.

**difference** *noun*
1 la **différence** *fem*
the difference between the two la différence entre les deux
What's the difference between adopt and adapt? Quelle est la différence entre adopter et adapter?
2 to make a difference changer [52] quelque chose
It makes a difference. Ça change quelque chose.
It makes no difference. Ça ne change rien.

**different** *adjective*
**différent** *masc*, **différente** *fem*
The sisters are very different. Les sœurs sont très différentes.
to be different from somebody être [6] différent de quelqu'un
She's very different from her sister. Elle est très différente de sa sœur.

**difficult** *adjective*
**difficile** *masc & fem*
It's very difficult. C'est très difficile.
to be difficult to do something être [6] difficile de faire quelque chose
It's difficult to decide. Il est difficile de décider.

**difficulty** *noun*
1 la **difficulté** *fem*
2 to have difficulty doing something avoir [5] du mal à faire quelque chose
I had difficulty answering the questions. J'ai eu du mal à répondre aux questions.

to **dig** *verb*
(*a hole*) **creuser** [1]
The dog had dug a deep hole. Le chien avait creusé un trou profond.

**digestion** *noun*
la **digestion** *fem*

**digital** *adjective*
**numérique** *masc & fem*
a digital recording un enregistrement numérique
a digital watch une montre à affichage numérique

**dim** *adjective*
1 (*weak*) a dim light une lumière faible
2 (*not clever*) She's a bit dim. Elle est un peu bouchée.

**dimension** *noun*
la **dimension** *fem*

**din** *noun*
le **vacarme** *masc*
What a din! Quel vacarme!

**dinghy** *noun*
a sailing dinghy un dériveur *masc*
a rubber dinghy un canot pneumatique

**dining room** *noun*
la **salle à manger**

**dinner** *noun*
1 (*in the evening*) le **dîner** *masc*
Mum invited him to dinner. Maman l'a invité à dîner.
2 (*at midday*) le **déjeuner** *masc*
to have school dinners déjeuner [1] à la cantine
• **dinner time** *noun*
1 (*at midday*) **l'heure du déjeuner**
2 (*in the evening*) **l'heure du dîner**

**dinosaur** *noun*
le **dinosaure** *masc*

**diploma** *noun*
le **diplôme** *masc*

**direct** *adjective* ▷ see **direct** *adv, verb*
**direct** *masc*, **directe** *fem*
a direct flight un vol direct

**direct** *adverb* ▷ see **direct** *adj, verb*
**directement**
The bus goes direct to the airport. Le bus va directement à l'aéroport.

to **direct** *verb* ▷ see **direct** *adj, adv*
1 (*a film, a programme*) **réaliser** [1]
2 (*a play*) **mettre** [11] **en scène**
3 (*the traffic*) **régler** [24]

**direction** *noun*
1 (*the way you go*) la **direction** *fem*
in the other direction dans l'autre direction
2 (*instructions*) to ask somebody for directions demander [1] son chemin à quelqu'un
We asked a woman for directions. Nous avons demandé notre chemin à une dame.
Directions for use Mode d'emploi

**directly** *adverb*
**directement**

**director** *noun*
1 (*of a company*) le **directeur** *masc*, la **directrice** *fem*
2 (*of a film, programme*) le **réalisateur** *masc*, la **réalisatrice** *fem*

3 (*of a play*) le **metteur en scène**

♪ **directory** *noun*
l'**annuaire** *masc*
to be ex-directory être [6] sur la liste rouge
We are ex-directory. Nous sommes sur la liste rouge.

**dirt** *noun*
la **saleté** *fem*

♪ **dirty** *adjective*
**sale** *masc & fem*
a dirty sweater un pull sale
My hands are dirty. J'ai les mains sales.
Your trainers are dirty. Tes baskets sont sales.
to get something dirty salir [2] quelque chose
I got my jeans dirty. J'ai sali mon jean.
to get dirty se salir Ⓔ [2]
Trainers get dirty quickly. Les baskets se salissent vite.

**disability** *noun*
l'**infirmité** *fem*
Does he have a disability? Est-il infirme?

**disabled** *adjective*
**handicapé** *masc*, **handicapée** *fem*
to work with disabled people travailler [1] avec les handicapés

**disadvantage** *noun*
1 le **désavantage** *masc*
2 to be at a disadvantage être [6] désavantagé
Without experience you're at a disadvantage. Sans expérience, on est désavantagé.

to **disagree** *verb*
**ne pas être [6] d'accord**
I disagree. Je ne suis pas d'accord.
I disagree with you. Je ne suis pas d'accord avec toi.

to **disappear** *verb*
**disparaître [27]**

**disappearance** *noun*
la **disparition** *fem*

♪ **disappointed** *adjective*
**déçu** *masc*, **déçue** *fem*
I was disappointed with my results. J'ai été déçu par mes résultats.

**disappointment** *noun*
la **déception** *fem*

**disaster** *noun*
le **désastre** *masc*
It was a complete disaster. Ça a été un désastre complet.

**disastrous** *adjective*
**désastreux** *masc*, **désastreuse** *fem*

**disc** *noun*
1 (*in general*) le **disque** *masc*
a compact disc un disque compact
2 a slipped disc une hernie discale
3 (*for a vehicle*) a tax disc la vignette *fem*

**discipline** *noun*
la **discipline** *fem*

**disc-jockey** *noun*
le **disc-jockey** *masc*

♪ **disco** *noun*
1 (*party*) la **soirée disco**
They're having a disco. Ils font une soirée disco.
2 (*club*) la **discothèque** *fem*

to **disconnect** *verb*
1 (*the telephone, electricity*) **couper [1]**
2 (*a cooker, a fridge*) **débrancher [1]**

**discount** *noun*
la **réduction** *fem*

to **discourage** *verb*
**décourager [52]**

to **discover** *verb*
**découvrir [30]**

**discovery** *noun*
la **découverte** *fem*

**discreet** *adjective*
**discret** *masc*, **discrète** *fem*

**discrimination** *noun*
la **discrimination** *fem*
racial discrimination la discrimination raciale

♪ to **discuss** *verb*
to discuss something discuter [1] de quelque chose
to discuss the problem discuter du problème
I'm going to discuss it with Phil. Je vais en discuter avec Phil.

**discussion** *noun*
la **discussion** *fem*

**disease** *noun*
la **maladie** *fem*

**disgraceful** *adjective*
**scandaleux** *masc*, **scandaleuse** *fem*

**disguise** *noun* ▷ see **disguise** *verb*
le **déguisement** *masc*
to be in disguise être [6] déguisé
Nobody recognised him because he was in disguise. Personne ne l'a reconnu parce qu'il était déguisé.



a b c d e f g h i j k l m n o p q r s t u v w x y z

to **disguise** *verb* ▷ see **disguise** *noun*
**déguiser [1]**
He was disguised as a woman. Il était déguisé en femme.

**disgust** *noun*
le **dégoût** *masc*

**disgusted** *adjective*
**dégoûté** *masc*, **dégoûtée** *fem*

♂ **disgusting** *adjective*
**dégoûtant** *masc*, **dégoûtante** *fem*

♂ **dish** *noun*
1 (*plate, food*) le **plat** *masc*
a large white dish un grand plat blanc
my favourite dish. mon plat favori.
2 to do the dishes faire [10] la vaisselle
It's my turn to do the dishes. C'est à moi de faire la vaisselle.
3 (*TV*) une **antenne parabolique**
• **dishcloth** le torchon

**dishonest** *adjective*
**malhonnête** *masc & fem*

**dishonesty** *noun*
la **malhonnêteté** *fem*

♂ **dishwasher** *noun*
la **lave-vaisselle** *invariable masc*

**disinfectant** *noun*
le **désinfectant** *masc*

♂ **disk** *noun*
le **disque** *masc*
the hard disk le disque dur
• **disk drive** une unité de disque

♂ **diskette** *noun*
la **disquette** *fem*

to **dislike** *verb*
**ne pas aimer [1]**
I dislike sport. Je n'aime pas le sport.
She dislikes Becky. Elle n'aime pas Becky.

to **dismiss** *verb*
(*employees*) **licencier [1]**

**disobedient** *adjective*
**désobéissant** *masc*, **désobéissante** *fem*

to **disobey** *verb*
1 (*a person*) **désobéir à [2]**
2 (*the rules*) **enfreindre [60]**

**display** *noun* ▷ see **display** *verb*
1 une **exposition** *fem*
a handicrafts display une exposition d'artisanat
to be on display être [6] exposé
2 (*in a shop*) a window display une vitrine
3 (*of fireworks*) un feu d'artifice
There will be a firework display in the square. Il y aura un feu d'artifice dans la place.

to **display** *verb* ▷ see **display** *noun*
**exposer [1]**

**disposable** *adjective*
**jetable** *masc & fem*

**dispute** *noun*
la **dispute** *fem*

to **disqualify** *verb*
**disqualifier [1]**

to **disrupt** *verb*
**perturber [1]**

to **dissolve** *verb*
**dissoudre [67]**

♂ **distance** *noun*
la **distance** *fem*
It's within walking distance. On peut y aller à pied.
from a distance de loin
I didn't recognise Adam from a distance. Je n'ai pas reconnu Adam de loin.
in the distance au loin
We saw the fire in the distance. Nous avons vu l'incendie au loin.

**distant** *adjective*
**lointain** *masc*, **lointaine** *fem*

**distinct** *adjective*
**net** *masc*, **nette** *fem*

**distinctly** *adverb*
**distinctement**
It's distinctly odd. C'est vraiment bizarre.

to **distract** *verb*
**distraire [78]**

to **distribute** *verb*
**distribuer [1]**

**district** *noun*
1 (*in a town*) le **quartier** *masc*
a poor district of Paris un quartier pauvre de Paris
2 (*in the country*) la **région** *fem*

to **disturb** *verb*
**déranger [52]**
Do not disturb. Ne pas déranger.
Sorry to disturb you. Je suis désolé de vous déranger.

**ditch** *noun* ▷ see **ditch** *verb*
le **fossé** *masc*

to **ditch** *verb* ▷ see **ditch** *noun*
(*informal*) to ditch somebody plaquer [1] quelqu'un
I ditched him. Je l'ai plaqué.

**dive** *noun* ▷ see **dive** *verb*
le **plongeon** *masc*

to **dive** *verb* ▷ see **dive** *noun*
**plonger [52]**

**diver** *noun*
le **plongeur** *masc*, la **plongeuse** *fem*

**diversion** *noun*
(*on the roads*) la **déviation** *fem*

to **divide** *verb*
**diviser [1]**

**diving** *noun*
la **plongée** *fem*
**to go diving** faire [10] de la plongée
**Let's go diving!** Faisons de la plongée!
· **diving board** le plongeoir

**division** *noun*
la **division** *fem*

**divorce** *noun* ▷ see **divorce** *verb*
le **divorce** *masc*

to **divorce** *verb* ▷ see **divorce** *noun*
**divorcer [61]**
**They divorced last year.** Ils ont divorcé l'année dernière.

**divorced** *adjective*
**divorcé** *masc*, **divorcée** *fem*
**My parents are divorced.** Mes parents sont divorcés.

**DIY** *noun*
le **bricolage** *masc*
**to do DIY** faire [10] du bricolage
**Dad doesn't like doing DIY.** Mon père n'aime pas le bricolage.
**a DIY shop** un magasin de bricolage

**dizzy** *adjective*
**I feel dizzy.** J'ai la tête qui tourne.

**DJ** *noun*
le **disc-jockey** *masc*

to **do** *verb*
1 (*to carry out*) **faire [10]**
**What are you doing?** Qu'est-ce que tu fais?
**I'm doing my homework.** Je fais mes devoirs.
**What have you done with the hammer?** Qu'est-ce que tu as fait du marteau?
2 (*to make sentences with* **no, not**) ne ... pas
**I do not like mushrooms, I don't like mushrooms.** Je n'aime pas les champignons.
**She does not like spinach, She doesn't like spinach.** Elle n'aime pas les épinards.
**You did not shut the door, You didn't shut the door.** Tu n'as pas fermé la porte.
**It doesn't matter.** Ça ne fait rien.
3 (*when* **do** *refers to another verb, it is not translated*) **'Do you live here?' — 'Yes, I do.'** 'Est-ce que tu habites ici?' — 'Oui.'
**She has more money than I do.** Elle a plus d'argent que moi.
**'I live in Chester.' — 'So do I.'** 'J'habite à Chester.' — 'Moi aussi.'
**'I didn't phone Gemma.' — 'Neither did I.'** 'Je n'ai pas appelé Gemma.'—'Moi non plus.'
4 (*used to form questions*) **Do you want some strawberries?** Est-ce que tu veux des fraises?, Veux-tu des fraises?
**When does it start?** Quand est-ce que ça commence?
**How did you open it?** Comment l'as-tu ouvert?
5 (*in question tags*) **don't you?, doesn't he?** etc. n'est-ce pas?
**You know Bill, don't you?** Tu connais Bill, n'est-ce pas?
**She left on Thursday, didn't she?** Elle est partie jeudi, n'est-ce pas?
6 (*to say enough*) **That'll do.** Ça ira.
**Fifteen will do.** Avec quinze ça suffit.
7 (*to concern*) **It has to do with money.** Il s'agit d'argent.
**It has nothing to do with her.** Ça ne la regarde pas.
· **could do with something**
**avoir [5] besoin de**
**I could do with a rest.** J'ai bien besoin de me reposer.
· **to do something up**
1 (*your shoes*) **lacer [61]**
2 (*a jacket, cardigan*) **boutonner [1]**
3 (*a house*) **retaper [1]**
· **to do without something**
**se passer Ⓔ [1] de quelque chose**
**We did without butter.** Nous nous sommes passés de beurre.

**doctor** *noun*
le **médecin** *masc*
**Her mother's a doctor.** Sa mère est médecin.

**document** *noun*
le **document** *masc*

**documentary** *noun*
le **documentaire** *masc*

**dodgems** *plural noun*
**the dodgems** les autos tamponneuses *fem plural*

**dog** *noun*
le **chien** *masc*, (*female*) la **chienne** *fem*

**do-it-yourself** *noun*
le **bricolage** *masc*

English–French

a b c d e f g h i j k l m n o p q r s t u v w x y z

**dole** *noun*
les **allocations chômage**
to be on the dole être [6] au chômage
Ken is on the dole. Ken est au chômage.

**doll** *noun*
la **poupée** *fem*

**dollar** *noun*
le **dollar** *masc*

**dolphin** *noun*
le **dauphin** *masc*

**Dominican** *adjective*
▷ see **Dominican** *noun*
**dominicain** *masc*, **dominicaine** *fem*

**Dominican** *noun* ▷ see **Dominican** *adj*
le **Dominicain** *masc*, la **Dominicaine** *fem*

**Dominican Republic** *noun*
la **République dominicaine**

**domino** *noun*
le **domino** *masc*
to play dominoes jouer [1] aux dominos
Do you want to play dominoes? Tu veux jouer aux dominos?

**don't** ▷ **do**

**donation** *noun*
le **don** *masc*

**donkey** *noun*
un **âne** *masc*

**door** *noun*
1 (*of a house*) la **porte** *fem*
Could you open the door? Tu peux ouvrir la porte?
Please shut the door! Ferme la porte, s'il te plaît!
2 (*of a car*) la **portière** *fem*

**doorbell** *noun*
la **sonnerie** *fem*
to ring the doorbell sonner [1] à la porte
There's the doorbell! On sonne!

**dormitory** *noun*
le **dortoir** *masc*

**dot** *noun*
1 (*written*) le **point** *masc*
2 (*on fabric*) le **pois** *masc*
3 on the dot pile
The train arrived at ten on the dot. Le train est arrivé à dix heures pile.

**double** *adjective* ▷ see **double** *adv*
1 (*twice as much*) **double**
a double whisky un double whisky
a double helping of chips une double portion de frites
2 (*for two people*) a double room une chambre pour deux personnes
a double bed un grand lit

**double** *adverb* ▷ see **double** *adj*
1 **le double**
double the time le double du temps
I paid double the price. J'ai payé le double du prix.
- **double bass** la contrebasse
- **double-decker bus** un autobus à impériale
- **double-glazing** le double vitrage

**doubles** *noun*
(*in tennis, squash*) le **double** *masc*
to play a game of doubles faire [10] un double
We played a game of doubles. Nous avons fait un double.

**doubt** *noun* ▷ see **doubt** *verb*
le **doute** *masc*
There's no doubt about it. Il n'y a aucun doute là-dessus.
I have my doubts. J'ai des doutes.

to **doubt** *verb* ▷ see **doubt** *noun*
to doubt something douter [1] de quelque chose
I doubt it. J'en doute.
I doubt that ... douter que ... (*+ subjunctive*)
I doubt that they'll do it. Je doute qu'ils le fassent.

**doubtful** *adjective*
**pas sûr** *masc*, **pas sûre** *fem*
It's doubtful. Ce n'est pas sûr.
1 to be doubtful about doing something hésiter [1] à faire quelque chose
I'm doubtful about inviting them together. J'hésite à les inviter ensemble.

**dough** *noun*
la **pâte** *fem*

**doughnut** *noun*
le **beignet** *masc*

**Dover** *noun*
**Douvres**
the ferry from Dover to Calais le ferry qui relie Douvres à Calais

**down** *adverb, preposition*
1 (*below*) **en bas**
He's down in the cellar. Il est en bas dans la cave.
2 (*showing movement*) She came down . Elle est descendue.
She was walking down the street. Elle descendait la rue.
She sat down on the sofa. Elle s'est assise

sur le canapé.
**Jenny ran down the stairs.** Jenny a descendu l'escalier en courant.
**Paul went down to the kitchen.** Paul est descendu dans la cuisine.
**3** (*nearby*) à côté
**There's a chemist's just down the road.** Il y a une pharmacie juste à côté.

♂ **downstairs** *adjective, adverb*
**1** (*showing where*) **en bas**
**She's downstairs in the sitting-room.** Elle est en bas dans le salon.
**The dog sleeps downstairs.** Le chien dort en bas.
**2** (*showing belonging*) **du dessous**
**Who lives in the downstairs flat?** Qui habite l'appartement du dessous?
**Have you met the people downstairs?** As-tu rencontré les voisins du dessous?

to **doze** *verb*
**sommeiller [1]**

**dozen** *noun*
la **douzaine** *fem*
**a dozen eggs** une douzaine d'œufs

**drag** *noun* ▷ see **drag** *verb*
(*informal*) **What a drag!** Quelle barbe!
**She's a bit of a drag.** Elle n'est pas marrante.

to **drag** *verb* ▷ see **drag** *noun*
(*informal*) **traîner [1]**

**dragon** *noun*
le **dragon** *masc*

**drain** *noun* ▷ see **drain** *verb*
un **égout** *masc*

to **drain** *verb* ▷ see **drain** *noun*
(*vegetables, pasta*) **égoutter [1]**

**drama** *noun*
**1** (*in theatre*) l'**art dramatique** *masc*
**2** (*fuss*)
(*informal*) **He made a big drama out of it.** Il en a fait tout un cinéma.

**dramatic** *adjective*
**spectaculaire** *masc & fem*

**draught** *noun*
le **courant d'air**

**draughts** *noun*
les **dames** *fem plural*
**to play draughts** jouer **[1]** aux dames
**Grandad taught me to play draughts.** Mon grand-père m'a appris à jouer aux dames.

♂ **draw** *verb* ▷ see **draw** *noun*
**1** (*a picture, an object*) **dessiner [1]**
**She can draw really well.** Elle dessine vraiment bien.
**I can't draw horses.** Je ne sais pas dessiner les chevaux.
**2** **to draw a picture** faire **[10]** un dessin
**3** (*the curtains*) **tirer [1] les rideaux**
**Shall I draw the curtains?** Tu veux que je tire les rideaux?
**4** (*a crowd*) **attirer [1] une foule de spectateurs**
**The concert drew a big crowd.** Le concert a attiré une foule de spectateurs.
**5** (*Sports*) **faire [10] match nul**
**We drew three all.** Nous avons fait match nul trois à trois.
**6** **to draw lots** tirer **[1]** au sort
**They drew lots for the winner.** Ils ont tiré le gagnant au sort.

♂ **draw** *noun* ▷ see **draw** *verb*
**1** (*Sports*) le **match nul**
**It was a draw.** Ils ont fait match nul.
**2** (*in a lottery*) le **tirage au sort**
• **drawback** un inconvénient *masc*

**drawer** *noun*
le **tiroir** *masc*

♂ **drawing** *noun*
le **dessin** *masc*
• **drawing pin** la punaise

**dreadful** *adjective*
**affreux** *masc*, **affreuse** *fem*

**dreadfully** *adverb*
**terriblement**
**I was dreadfully late.** J'étais terriblement en retard.
**I'm dreadfully sorry.** Je suis vraiment navré.

**dream** *noun* ▷ see **dream** *verb*
le **rêve** *masc*
**my dream holiday** mes vacances de rêve
**to have a dream** faire **[10]** un rêve
**I had a horrible dream.** J'ai fait un rêve horrible.

to **dream** *verb* ▷ see **dream** *noun*
**rêver [1]**
**to dream about something** rêver de quelque chose
**I was dreaming about the sea.** Je rêvais de la mer.

**drenched** *adjective*
**trempé** *masc*, **trempée** *fem*
**to get drenched** se faire **Ⓔ [10]** tremper
**We got drenched.** On s'est fait tremper.

♂ **dress** *noun* ▷ see **dress** *verb*
la **robe** *fem*

♪ to **dress** *verb* ▷ see **dress** *noun*
to dress a child habiller [1] un enfant
I dressed Billy while mum ... J'ai habillé Billy pendant que maman ...
• **to dress up**
**se déguiser** Ⓔ [1]
Nick dressed up as a vampire. Nick s'est déguisé en vampire.

♪ **dressed** *adjective*
1 **habillé** *masc*, **habillée** *fem*
Is he dressed yet? Est-ce qu'il est habillé?
to be dressed in something être [6] habillé de quelque chose
She was dressed in black trousers and a yellow shirt. Elle était habillée d'un pantalon noir et d'une chemise jaune.
2 to get dressed s'habiller Ⓔ [1]
I got dressed quickly. Je me suis vite habillé (*boy speaking*), Je me suis vite habillée (*girl speaking*).

**dressing gown** *noun*
la **robe de chambre**

**dressing table** *noun*
la **coiffeuse** *fem*

**drier** *noun*
1 (*for hair*) le **sèche-cheveux**
2 (*for clothes*) le **sèche-linge**

**drill** *noun*
la **perceuse** *fem*

♪ **drink** *noun* ▷ see **drink** *verb*
la **boisson** *fem*
a hot drink une boisson chaude
a cold drink une boisson fraîche
1 Would you like a drink? Tu veux boire quelque chose?
to go out for a drink aller Ⓔ [7] prendre un pot
Let's go out for a drink! Allons prendre un pot!

♪ to **drink** *verb* ▷ see **drink** *noun*
**boire** [22]
What would you like to drink? Qu'est-ce que tu veux boire?
He drank a glass of water. Il a bu un verre d'eau.

♪ **drive** *noun* ▷ see **drive** *verb*
1 (*to a house*) une **allée** *fem*
2 (*in a car*) to go for a drive faire [10] un tour en voiture
We went for a drive. Nous avons fait un tour en voiture.

♪ to **drive** *verb* ▷ see **drive** *noun*
1 (*a car, a bus*) **conduire** [26]
to drive a car conduire une voiture
Can you drive? Tu sais conduire?
Yes, I can drive. Oui, je sais conduire.
Suzie drives very fast. Suzie conduit très vite.
I'd like to learn to drive. J'aimerais apprendre à conduire.
2 (*to go by car*) **aller** Ⓔ [7] **en voiture**
We drove to Toulouse. Nous sommes allés à Toulouse en voiture.
3 to drive somebody to a place emmener [50] quelqu'un à un endroit en voiture
She drove me to the station. Elle m'a emmené en voiture à la gare.
to drive somebody home raccompagner [1] quelqu'un
Peter drove me home. Peter m'a raccompagnée.
4 to drive somebody mad rendre [3] quelqu'un fou *masc*, rendre quelqu'un folle *fem*
She drives me mad! Elle me rend fou! (*boy speaking*), Elle me rend folle! (*girl speaking*).

♪ **driver** *noun*
1 (*of a car*) le **conducteur** *masc*, la **conductrice** *fem*
2 (*of a taxi, a bus*) le **chauffeur** *masc*

**driving instructor** *noun*
le **moniteur d'auto-école**, la **monitrice d'auto-école**

**driving lesson** *noun*
la **leçon de conduite**

♪ **driving licence** *noun*
le **permis de conduire**

**driving school** *noun*
l'**école de conduite** *fem*

**driving test** *noun*
l'**examen du permis de conduire** *masc*
to take your driving test passer [1] son permis
I'm going to take my driving test soon. Je vais bientôt passer mon permis.
to pass your driving test avoir [5] son permis
Misha's passed her driving test. Misha a eu son permis.

**drop** *noun* ▷ see **drop** *verb*
la **goutte** *fem*

♪ to **drop** *verb* ▷ see **drop** *noun*
1 to drop something laisser [1] tomber quelque chose
I dropped my glasses. J'ai laissé tomber mes lunettes.
I'm dropping history next year. Je vais laisser tomber l'histoire l'année prochaine.
Drop it! Laisse tomber!

2 (*a person*) **déposer [1]**
**Could you drop me at the station?** Est-ce que tu peux me déposer à la gare?

**drought** *noun*
la **sécheresse** *fem*

to **drown** *verb*
**se noyer ⓔ [39]**
**She drowned in the lake.** Elle s'est noyée dans le lac.
**He nearly drowned.** Il a failli se noyer.

**drug** *noun*
1 (*medicine*) le **médicament** *masc*
2 (*illegal*) **drugs** la drogue *fem*
**soft drugs** les drogues douces
**hard drugs** les drogues dures
**to take drugs** se droguer ⓔ **[1]**
**He used to take drugs.** Il se droguait.
- **drug abuse** l'usage des stupéfiants *masc*
- **drug addict** le & la toxicomane
- **drug addiction** la toxicomanie

**drum** *noun*
1 le **tambour** *masc*
2 **the drums** la batterie
**Baz plays the drums.** Baz joue de la batterie.
- **drum kit** la batterie

**drummer** *noun*
le **batteur** *masc*, la **batteuse** *fem*

**drunk** *adjective* ▷ see **drunk** *noun*
**ivre** *masc & fem*

**drunk** *noun* ▷ see **drunk** *adj*
un & une **ivrogne** *masc & fem*

**dry** *adjective* ▷ see **dry** *verb*
1 (*clothes, paint, etc*) **sec** *masc*, **sèche** *fem*
**My hair's dry.** J'ai les cheveux secs.
2 (*weather*) **a dry day** un jour de soleil
**in wet weather** quand il fait beau
**It's going to be wet tomorrow.** Il va faire beau demain.

to **dry** *verb* ▷ see **dry** *adj*
1 **sécher [24]**
**She let the towels dry in the sun.** Elle a laissé sécher les serviettes au soleil.
**to dry the washing** faire **[10]** sécher le linge
**I dried the washing.** J'ai fait sécher le linge.
2 **to dry your hair** se sécher ⓔ **[1]** les cheveux
3 (*to wipe dry*) **essuyer [41]**
**Can you dry the dishes, please?** Peux-tu essuyer la vaisselle, s'il te plaît?
**to dry your hands** s'essuyer ⓔ **[41]** les mains
**Dry your hands carefully!** Essuie-toi bien les mains!
- **dry cleaner's** la teinturerie

**dryer** *noun* ▷ **drier**

**dual carriageway** *noun*
la **route à quatre voies**

**dubbed** *adjective*
**a dubbed film** un film doublé

**duck** *noun*
le **canard** *masc*

**due** *adjective, adverb*
1 **due to** en raison de
**The match has been cancelled due to bad weather.** Le match a été annulé en raison du mauvais temps.
2 **to be due to do something** devoir **[8]** faire quelque chose
**We're due to leave on Thursday.** Nous devons partir jeudi.
**Pria's due back soon.** Pria doit bientôt revenir.

**duke** *noun*
le **duc** *masc*

**dull** *adjective*
1 (*day, weather*) **maussade** *masc & fem*
**dull weather** un temps maussade
**It's dull today.** Il fait un temps maussade aujourd'hui.
2 (*boring*) **ennuyeux** *masc*, **ennuyeuse** *fem*

**dumb** *adjective*
**bête** *masc & fem*
**He asked some dumb questions.** Il a posé des questions bêtes.

to **dump** *verb*
1 (*rubbish*) **jeter [48]**
2 (*a boyfriend, a girlfriend*) **plaquer [1]**
**She's dumped her boyfriend.** Elle a plaqué son copain.

**dune** *noun*
la **dune** *fem*

**dungarees** *plural noun*
la **salopette** *fem*

**dungeon** *noun*
le **cachot** *masc*

**Dunkirk** *noun*
**Dunkerque**

**during** *preposition*
**pendant**
**during the night** pendant la nuit
**I saw her during the holidays.** Je l'ai vue pendant les vacances.

**dusk** *noun*
**at dusk** à la nuit tombante

**dust** *noun* ▷ see **dust** *verb*
la **poussière** *fem*

English–French

to **dust** *verb* ▷ see **dust** *noun*
**épousseter [48]**

**dustbin** *noun*
la **poubelle** *fem*
Put the bag in the dustbin. Jette le sac à la poubelle.

**dustman** *noun*
un **éboueur** *masc*

**dusty** *adjective*
**poussiéreux** *masc*, **poussiéreuse** *fem*

**Dutch** *adjective* ▷ see **Dutch** *noun*
**hollandais** *masc*, **hollandaise** *fem*

**Dutch** *noun* ▷ see **Dutch** *adj*
1 (*the people*) the Dutch les Hollandais *masc plural*, les Hollandaises *fem plural*
2 (*the language*) le **hollandais** *masc*

**duty** *noun*
1 le **devoir** *masc*
to have a duty to do something avoir **[5]** le devoir de faire quelque chose
You have a duty to inform us. Vous avez le devoir de nous informer.
2 to be on duty être **[6]** de service
Dad is on duty at the weekend. Papa est de service pendant le week-end.
to be on night duty être **[6]** de service de nuit
She's on night duty next week. Elle est de service de nuit la semaine prochaine.
to be off duty ne pas être de service
I'm off duty tonight. Je ne suis pas de service ce soir.

**duty-free** *adjective*
**hors taxes** *masc & fem*
the duty-free shops les boutiques hors taxes
duty-free purchases les achats hors taxes

**duvet** *noun*
la **couette** *fem*
- **duvet cover** la housse de couette

**DVD** *noun*
le **DVD** *invariable masc*
- **DVD player** le lecteur DVD
- **DVD recorder** un enregistreur DVD

**dwarf** *noun*
le **nain** *masc*, la **naine** *fem*

**dye** *noun* ▷ see **dye** *verb*
la **teinture** *fem*

to **dye** *verb* ▷ see **dye** *noun*
**teindre [60]**
to dye your hair se teindre Ⓔ **[60]** les cheveux
I'm going to dye my hair pink. Je vais me teindre les cheveux en rose.

**dynamic** *adjective*
**dynamique** *masc & fem*

**dyslexia** *noun*
la **dyslexie** *fem*

**dyslexic** *adjective*
**dyslexique** *masc & fem*

# E e

**each** *adjective* ▷ see **each** *pron*
**chaque** *masc & fem*
each time chaque fois
5 euros for each child cinq euros pour chaque enfant

**each** *pronoun* ▷ see **each** *adj*
**chacun** *masc*, **chacune** *fem*
My sisters each have a computer. Mes sœurs ont chacune un ordinateur.
She gave us a pound each. Elle nous a donné une livre chacun.
The posters cost ten pounds each. Les affiches coûtent dix livres chacune.
I have a present for each of you. J'ai un cadeau pour chacun de vous.
We each got a present. Chacun de nous a reçu un cadeau.

**each other** *pronoun*
They love each other. Ils s'aiment.
We write to each other every day. Nous nous écrivons chaque jour.
Do you see each other often? Est-ce que vous vous voyez souvent?

**WORD TIP** *each other* is usually translated with a reflexive verb in French.

**eagle** *noun*
un **aigle** *masc*

**ear** *noun*
une **oreille** *fem*



Ⓔ means the verb takes être to form the perfect

**earache** *noun*
une **otite** *fem*
**to have earache** avoir **[5]** une otite

**earlier** *adverb*
1 (*a while ago*) **tout à l'heure**
**He phoned earlier.** Il a appelé tout à l'heure.
2 (*not as late*) **plus tôt**
**I started earlier this time.** J'ai commencé plus tôt cette fois.
**We had seen him earlier in the day.** Nous l'avions vu plus tôt dans la journée.

𝄞 **early** *adverb* ▷ see **early** *adj*
1 (*in the day*) **tôt**
**early in the morning** tôt le matin
**It's too early.** Il est trop tôt.
**John gets up early.** John se lève tôt.
2 (*for an appointment*) **en avance**
**to be early** être **[6]** en avance
**Alice likes to be early.** Alice aime être en avance.

𝄞 **early** *adjective* ▷ see **early** *adv*
1 (*one of the first*) **premier** *masc*, **première** *fem*
**in the early months** pendant les premiers mois
**I'm getting the early train.** Je prends le premier train.
2 (*before the usual time*) **tôt**
**I had an early lunch.** J'ai déjeuné tôt.
**Jane's having an early night.** Jane va se coucher tôt.
**We're making an early start.** Nous partons tôt.
3 (*in expressions*) **in the early afternoon** en début d'après-midi
**in the early hours** au petit matin

to **earn** *verb*
(*money*) **gagner [1]**
**He earns seven pounds an hour.** Il gagne sept livres de l'heure.

**earnings** *plural noun*
le **salaire** *masc*

**earphones** *noun*
les **écouteurs** *masc plural*

**earring** *noun*
la **boucle d'oreille**

**earth** *noun*
la **terre** *fem*
**life on earth** la vie sur terre
**What on earth are you doing?** Mais qu'est-ce que tu fais là?
- **earthquake** le tremblement de terre

**easily** *adverb*
1 (*without difficulty*) **facilement**
2 (*by far*) **de loin**
**Pete's easily the best.** Pete est de loin le meilleur.

𝄞 **east** *adjective, adverb* ▷ see **east** *noun*
**est**
**the east side of the city** le côté est de la ville
**an east wind** un vent d'est
**a town east of Bordeaux** une ville à l'est de Bordeaux
**We're going east.** Nous allons vers l'est.

**WORD TIP** *est* never changes.

𝄞 **east** *noun* ▷ see **east** *adj, adv*
l'**est** *masc*
**in the east** à l'est
**in the east of Scotland** dans l'est de l'Écosse

**Easter** *noun*
**Pâques**
**They're coming at Easter.** Ils viennent à Pâques.
**Happy Easter!** Joyeuses Pâques!
- **Easter Day** le dimanche de Pâques
- **Easter egg** un œuf de Pâques

**Eastern Europe** *noun*
l'**Europe de l'Est** *fem*

𝄞 **easy** *adjective*
**facile** *masc & fem*
**an easy exam** un examen facile
**It's easy!** C'est facile!
**It was easy to make.** C'était facile à faire.

𝄞 to **eat** *verb*
1 **manger [52]**
**He was eating a croissant.** Il mangeait un croissant.
**We're going to have something to eat.** On va manger quelque chose.
2 (*a meal*) **prendre [64]**
**We were eating breakfast.** Nous prenions le petit déjeuner.
3 **to eat out** manger au restaurant
**Let's eat out tonight.** Mangeons au restaurant ce soir.

**echo** *noun* ▷ see **echo** *verb*
un **écho** *masc*

to **echo** *verb* ▷ see **echo** *noun*
**retentir [2]**

**eclipse** *noun*
(*of the sun, moon*) une **éclipse** *fem*

**ecological** *adjective*
**écologique** *masc & fem*

**ecologist** *noun*
un & une **écologiste** *masc & fem*

**ecology** *noun*
l'**écologie** *fem*

**economic** *adjective*
1 (*relating to economics*) **économique** *masc & fem*
2 (*profitable*) **rentable** *masc & fem*

**economical** *adjective*
1 (*person*) **économe** *masc & fem*
2 (*method*) **économique** *masc & fem*

**economics** *noun*
l'**économie** *fem*
to study economics étudier l'économie

**economy** *noun*
une **économie** *fem*

**eczema** *noun*
l'**eczéma** *masc*

**edge** *noun*
1 le **bord** *masc*
the edge of the table le bord de la table
at the edge of the lake au bord du lac
2 to be on edge être[6] énervé
She was all on edge. Elle était vraiment énervée.

**edible** *adjective*
**comestible** *masc & fem*

**Edinburgh** *noun*
**Édimbourg**

to **edit** *verb*
**éditer**[1]

**editor** *noun*
1 (*of a newspaper*) le **rédacteur en chef**, la **rédactrice en chef**
2 (*of texts*) le **correcteur** *masc*, la **correctrice** *fem*
3 (*Computers*) un **éditeur** *masc*

to **educate** *verb*
(*a student*) **instruire**[26]

**education** *noun*
une **éducation** *fem*

**educational** *adjective*
**éducatif** *masc*, **éducative** *fem*
educational toys des jouets éducatifs

**effect** *noun*
un **effet** *masc*
the effect of the accident l'effet de l'accident
brilliant special effects des effets spéciaux sensationnels
to have an effect on somebody avoir[5] un effet sur quelqu'un
It had a good effect on the whole family. Cela a eu un bon effet sur toute la famille.

**effective** *adjective*
**efficace** *masc & fem*

**efficient** *adjective*
**efficace** *masc & fem*

**effort** *noun*
un **effort** *masc*
to make an effort faire[10] un effort
David made an effort to help us. David a fait un effort pour nous aider.
He didn't even make the effort to go. Il n'a même pas fait l'effort d'y aller.

**e.g.** *abbreviation*
(*for: for example*) **par ex, par exemple**

**egg** *noun*
un **œuf** *masc*
a dozen eggs une douzaine d'œufs
a fried egg un œuf au plat
two boiled eggs deux œufs à la coque
a hard-boiled egg un œuf dur
scrambled eggs les œufs brouillés
- **egg-cup** le coquetier
- **eggshell** la coquille d'œuf
- **egg-white** le blanc d'œuf
- **egg-yolk** le jaune d'œuf

**eight** *number*
**huit**
Maya's eight. Maya a huit ans.

**eighteen** *number*
**dix-huit**
Jason's eighteen. Jason a dix-huit ans.

**eighth** *adjective*
1 **huitième** *masc & fem*
on the eighth floor au huitième étage
2 (*in dates*) the eighth of July le huit juillet

**eighty** *number*
**quatre-vingts**
eighty-five quatre-vingt-cinq

**WORD TIP** The *s* of *-vingts* is omitted when another number follows.

**Éire** *noun*
**la République d'Irlande**

**either** *pronoun* ▷ see **either** *conj*
1 (*one or the other*) **l'un ou l'autre** *masc*, **l'une ou l'autre** *fem*
Choose either. Choisis l'un ou l'autre.
I don't like either of them. Je n'aime ni l'un ni l'autre.
2 (*both*) **les deux** *masc & fem*
Either is possible. Tous les deux sont possibles.

**either** *conjunction* ▷ see **either** *pron*
1 (*when you give alternatives*)
either ... or ou ... ou
either Thursday or Friday ou jeudi ou vendredi

I'll take either Susie or Judy. J'accompagnerai ou Susie ou Judy.
2 (*in negative statements*) **non plus**
He doesn't want to either. Il ne veut pas non plus.
I don't know them either. Je les connais pas non plus.

**elastic** *adjective* ▷ see **elastic** *noun*
**élastique** *masc & fem*

**elastic** *noun* ▷ see **elastic** *adj*
l'**élastique** *masc*
• **elastic band** un élastique *masc*

♪ **elbow** *noun*
le **coude** *masc*

♪ **elder** *adjective*
**aîné** *masc*, **aînée** *fem*
her elder brother son frère aîné
his elder sister sa sœur aînée

**elderly** *adjective*
**âgé** *masc*, **âgée** *fem*
the elderly les personnes âgées

♪ **eldest** *adjective*
**aîné** *masc*, **aînée** *fem*
her eldest brother son frère aîné
his eldest sister sa sœur aînée

to **elect** *verb*
(*a leader, a politician*) **élire [51]**

♪ **election** *noun*
une **élection** *fem*
in the elections aux élections
to win an election gagner aux élections
They lost the election. Ils ont perdu aux élections.

**electric** *adjective*
**électrique** *masc & fem*

**electrical** *adjective*
**électrique** *masc & fem*

**electrician** *noun*
un **électricien** *masc*, une **électricienne** *fem*

♪ **electricity** *noun*
l'**électricité** *fem*
the electricity bill la facture d'électricité
to turn off the electricity couper [1] le courant.

**electronic** *adjective*
**électronique** *masc & fem*
• **electronic mail** le courrier électronique

**electronics** *noun*
l'**électronique** *fem*

♪ **elegant** *adjective*
**élégant** *masc*, **élégante** *fem*

**element** *noun*
un **élément** *masc*

**elephant** *noun*
un **éléphant** *masc*

♪ **eleven** *number*
1 **onze**
Josh is eleven. Josh a onze ans.
2 (*a team*) a football eleven une équipe de football

**eleventh** *adjective*
1 **onzième** *masc & fem*
on the eleventh floor au onzième étage
2 (*in dates*) the eleventh of May le onze mai

to **eliminate** *verb*
**éliminer [1]**

**else** *adverb*
1 **d'autre**
somebody else, anybody else quelqu'un d'autre
Pick somebody else. Choisis quelqu'un d'autre.
Did you see anybody else? As-tu vu quelqu'un d'autre?
nothing else, anything else rien d'autre
I don't want anything else. Je ne veux rien d'autre.
2 something else, anything else autre chose
Would you like something else? Désirez-vous autre chose?
3 somewhere else, anywhere else ailleurs
Do you want to go anywhere else? Est-ce que tu veux aller ailleurs?
4 or else sinon
Hurry, or else we'll be late. Dépêche-toi, sinon nous serons en retard.

♪ to **email** *verb* ▷ see **email** *noun*
**envoyer [40] un mail**
Email me! Envoie-moi un mail!

♪ **email** *noun* ▷ see **email** *verb*
1 (*a message*) le **mail**, un **email**
Did you get my email? As-tu reçu mon mail?
2 (*system*) le **courrier électronique**
• **email address** une adresse électronique

**embarrassed** *adjective*
**gêné** *masc*, **gênée** *fem*

**embarrassing** *adjective*
**gênant** *masc*, **gênante** *fem*

**embarrassment** *noun*
l'**embarras** *masc*

**embassy** *noun*
une **ambassade** *fem*
the French Embassy l'ambassade de France

English–French

a b c d e f g h i j k l m n o p q r s t u v w x y z

**embroidery** *noun*
la **broderie** *fem*

**emergency** *noun*
le **cas d'urgence**
**It's an emergency!** C'est urgent!
**In an emergency, break the glass.** En cas d'urgence, casser la vitre.
- **emergency exit** la sortie de secours
- **emergency landing** un atterrissage forcé

**emotion** *noun*
une **émotion** *fem*

**emotional** *adjective*
1 (*person*) **ému** *masc*, **émue** *fem*
2 (*speech, occasion*) **chargé d'émotion** *masc*, **chargée d'émotion** *fem*

**emperor** *noun*
un **empereur** *masc*

**emphasis** *noun*
un **accent** *masc*
**to put the emphasis on** mettre[11] l'accent sur

to **emphasize** *verb*
1 (*to highlight*) **mettre[11] l'accent sur**
2 (*to stress a point*) **insister[1] sur le fait que**

**empire** *noun*
un **empire** *masc*
**the Roman Empire** l'Empire Romain

to **employ** *verb*
**employer[39]**

**employee** *noun*
le **salarié** *masc*, la **salariée** *fem*

**employer** *noun*
un **employeur** *masc*, une **employeuse** *fem*

**employment** *noun*
le **travail** *masc*

**empress** *noun*
une **impératrice** *fem*

**empty** *adjective* ▷ see **empty** *verb*
**vide** *masc & fem*
**an empty bottle** une bouteille vide
**The room was empty.** La pièce était vide.

to **empty** *verb* ▷ see **empty** *adj*
**vider[1]**
**I emptied the teapot into the sink.** J'ai vidé la théière dans l'évier.

to **enclose** *verb*
(*in a letter*) **joindre[49]**
**Please find enclosed a cheque.** Veuillez trouver ci-joint un chèque.

**encore** *noun*
le **bis** *masc*
**to give an encore** jouer[1] un bis

to **encourage** *verb*
**encourager[52]**
**to encourage somebody to do something** encourager quelqu'un à faire quelque chose
**She encouraged me to try again.** Elle m'a encouragé à recommencer.

**encouragement** *noun*
un **encouragement** *masc*

**encouraging** *adjective*
**encourageant** *masc*, **encourageante** *fem*

**encyclopedia** *noun*
une **encyclopédie** *fem*

**end** *noun* ▷ see **end** *verb*
1 (*last part*) la **fin** *fem*
**at the end of the film** à la fin du film
**I was exhausted by the end of the day.** J'étais épuisé à la fin de la journée.
**In the end I went home.** Finalement je suis rentré chez moi.
**Sally's coming at the end of June.** Sally viendra fin juin.
2 (*in a book, a film*) **'The End'** 'Fin'
3 (*of a table, garden, stick, road*) le **bout** *masc*
**Hold the other end.** Tiens l'autre bout.
**She lives at the end of the street.** Elle habite au bout de la rue.
4 (*in tennis, football*) le **côté** *masc*
**We change ends at half-time.** Nous changeons de côté à la mi-temps.

to **end** *verb* ▷ see **end** *noun*
1 (*to put an end to*) **mettre[11] fin à**
**They've ended the strike.** Ils ont mis fin à la grève.
2 (*to come to an end*) **se terminer[1]**
**The day ended with a dance.** La journée s'est terminée par un bal.
- **to end up**
**to end up doing something** finir[2] par faire quelque chose
**We ended up taking a taxi.** Nous avons fini par prendre un taxi.
**to end up somewhere** se retrouver[1] quelque part
**Mark ended up in San Francisco.** Mark s'est retrouvé à San Francisco.

**endangered** *adjective*
**menacé** *masc*, **menacée** *fem*
**an endangered species** une espèce en voie d'extinction

**ending** *noun*
la **fin** *fem*

**endless** *adjective*
**interminable** *masc & fem*

**enemy** *noun*
un **ennemi** *masc*, une **ennemie** *fem*
to make enemies se faire ⓔ [10] des ennemis

**energetic** *adjective*
**énergique** *masc & fem*

**energy** *noun*
l'**énergie** *fem*

♪ **engaged** *adjective*
1 (*to be married*) **fiancé** *masc*, **fiancée** *fem*
Kate's engaged. Kate est fiancée.
They're engaged. Ils sont fiancés.
They're going to get engaged. Ils vont se fiancer.
2 (*phones, toilets*) **occupé** *masc*, **occupée** *fem*
It's engaged, I'll ring later. C'est occupé, j'appellerai plus tard.

**engagement** *noun*
(*to marry*) les **fiançailles** *fem plural*
• **engagement ring** la bague de fiançailles

♪ **engine** *noun*
1 (*in a car*) le **moteur** *masc*
2 (*pulling a train*) la **locomotive** *fem*

♪ **engineer** *noun*
1 (*repair person*) le **technicien** *masc*
2 (*graduate*) un **ingénieur** *masc*

**engineering** *noun*
l'**ingénierie** *fem*
to study engineering faire [10] des études d'ingénieur

♪ **England** *noun*
l'**Angleterre** *fem*
in England en Angleterre
Richard lives in England. Richard vit en Angleterre.
to England en Angleterre
He came to England in 1999. Il est venu en Angleterre en 1999.
I'm from England. Je suis anglais (*boy speaking*), Je suis anglaise (*girl speaking*).

**WORD TIP** Countries and regions in French take *le*, *la* or *les*.

♪ **English** *adjective* ▷ see **English** *noun*
1 (*of or from England*) **anglais** *masc*, **anglaise** *fem*
the English team l'équipe anglaise
2 (*of the English language*) **d'anglais**
an English lesson un cours d'anglais
our English teacher notre professeur d'anglais

**WORD TIP** Adjectives never have capitals in French, even for nationality or regional origin.

♪ **English** *noun* ▷ see **English** *adj*
1 (*the people*) the English les Anglais *masc plural*
2 (*the language*) l'**anglais** *masc*
Do you speak English? Parlez-vous anglais?
He answered in English. Il a répondu en anglais.

**WORD TIP** Languages never have capitals in French.

• **English Channel** la Manche
• **Englishman** un Anglais
• **Englishwoman** une Anglaise

♪ to **enjoy** *verb*
1 **aimer** [1]
Did you enjoy the party? As-tu aimé la soirée?
We really enjoyed the concert. Nous avons beaucoup aimé le concert.
2 **to enjoy doing something** aimer [1] faire quelque chose
I enjoy swimming. J'aime nager.
3 **to enjoy yourself** s'amuser [1]
We really enjoyed ourselves. Nous nous sommes bien amusés.
Did you enjoy yourself? Tu t'es bien amusé?
Enjoy your meal! Bon appétit!

**enjoyable** *adjective*
**agréable** *masc & fem*

to **enlarge** *verb*
(*a photo*) **agrandir** [2]

**enlargement** *noun*
(*of a photo*) un **agrandissement** *masc*

**enormous** *adjective*
**énorme** *masc & fem*

♪ **enough** *adverb, pronoun*
1 **assez**
There's enough for everyone. Il y en a assez pour tout le monde.
That's enough. Ça suffit.
2 (*followed by a noun*) **assez de**
enough water assez d'eau
Is there enough bread? Est-ce qu'il y a assez de pain?
3 (*following an adjective or adverb*) **assez**
This jacket's big enough for you. Cette veste est assez grande pour toi.
Am I walking slowly enough? Est-ce que je marche assez lentement?

to **enquire** *verb*
**se renseigner** [1]
to enquire about the trains se renseigner sur les trains

**enquiry** *noun*
la **demande de renseignements**
**to make enquiries about something** demander [1] des renseignements sur quelque chose

to **enrol** *verb*
**s'inscrire** [38]
**to enrol on a course** s'inscrire à un cours

to **enter** *verb*
1 (*to go inside*) **entrer** Ⓔ [1] **dans**
**We all entered the church.** Nous sommes tous entrés dans l'église.
2 **to enter for something** s'inscrire [38] à quelque chose
**I'm going to enter for seven GCSEs.** Je vais m'inscrire à sept épreuves de GCSE.

to **entertain** *verb*
**divertir** [2]
**Find something to entertain the children.** Trouve quelque chose pour divertir les enfants.

**entertaining** *adjective*
**amusant** *masc*, **amusante** *fem*

**entertainment** *noun*
les **distractions** *fem plural*
**There wasn't much entertainment at night.** Il n'y avait pas beaucoup de distractions le soir.

**enthusiasm** *noun*
l'**enthousiasme** *masc*

**enthusiast** *noun*
**passionné** *masc*, **passionnée** *fem*
**He's a rugby enthusiast.** C'est un passionné de rugby.

**enthusiastic** *adjective*
**enthousiaste** *masc & fem*

**entire** *adjective*
**entier** *masc*, **entière** *fem*
**The entire class went to the theatre.** La classe entière est allée au théâtre.

**entirely** *adverb*
**complètement**

**entrance** *noun*
une **entrée** *fem*

**entry** *noun*
(*the way in*) une **entrée** *fem*
**'No entry'** 'Défense d'entrer'
• **entry phone** un interphone *masc*

**envelope** *noun*
une **enveloppe** *fem*

**envious** *adjective*
**envieux** *masc*, **envieuse** *fem*
**to be envious of** être [6] jaloux de
**She's envious of my results.** Elle est jalouse de mes résultats.

**environment** *noun*
l'**environnement** *masc*

**environmental** *adjective*
**écologique** *masc & fem*

**environment-friendly** *adjective*
**écologique** *masc & fem*

**envy** *noun*
l'**envie** *fem*

**epidemic** *noun*
une **épidémie** *fem*

**epileptic** *noun*
un & une **épileptique** *masc & fem*

**episode** *noun*
un **épisode** *masc*

**equal** *adjective* ▷ **see equal** *verb*
**égal** *masc*, **égale** *fem*, **égaux** *masc pl*, **égales** *fem pl*
**in equal quantities** en quantités égales

to **equal** *verb* ▷ **see equal** *adj*
**égaler** [1]

**equality** *noun*
l'**égalité** *fem*

to **equalize** *verb*
(*in a contest, match*) **égaliser** [1]

**equally** *adverb*
(*to share, divide up*) **en parts égales**

**equator** *noun*
l'**équateur** *masc*

to **equip** *verb*
**équiper** [1]
**Joe's well equipped for the hike.** Joe est bien équipé pour la randonnée.
**to be equipped with something** être [6] équipé de quelque chose

**equipment** *noun*
1 (*for sport*) l'**équipement** *masc*
2 (*in an office, a lab*) le **matériel** *masc*
**laboratory equipment** le matériel de laboratoire

**equivalent** *adjective*
**to be equivalent to something** être [6] équivalent à quelque chose
**Grade A is equivalent to 16 out of 20.** Un A est équivalent à 16 sur 20.

**error** *noun*
1 (*in spelling, typing*) la **faute** *fem*
**a spelling error** une faute d'orthographe
2 (*in maths, on a PC*) une **erreur** *fem*
• **error message** le message d'erreur



Ⓔ means the verb takes être to form the perfect

**escalator** *noun*
un **escalier mécanique**

**escape** *noun* ▷ see **escape** *verb*
(*from prison*) une **évasion** *fem*

**escape** *verb* ▷ see **escape** *noun*
1 (*person*) **s'évader [1]**
**an escaped prisoner** un évadé
2 (*animal*) **s'échapper [1]**

**escort** *noun*
l'**escorte** *fem*
**a police escort** une escorte de police

♂**especially** *adjective*
1 (*above all*) **surtout**
**There are lots of tourists, especially in August.** Il y a beaucoup de touristes, surtout en août.
2 (*unusually*) **particulièrement**
**'Was it funny?' — 'Not especially'.** 'C'était drôle?' — 'Pas particulièrement'.

**essay** *noun*
la **rédaction** *fem*
**an essay on pollution** une rédaction sur la pollution

**essential** *adjective*
**essentiel** *masc*, **essentielle** *fem*
**It's essential to reply quickly.** Il est essentiel de répondre vite.

**establishment** *noun*
un **établissement** *masc*

**estate** *noun*
1 (*housing estate*) la **cité** *fem*
2 (*car*) le **break** *masc*
3 (*big house and grounds*) le **domaine** *masc*
• **estate agent** un agent immobilier
• **estate agency** une agence immobilière

**estimate** *noun* ▷ see **estimate** *verb*
1 (*quote for work*) le **devis** *masc*
2 (*rough guess*) une **estimation** *fem*

to **estimate** *verb* ▷ see **estimate** *noun*
**évaluer [1]**

**etc** *abbreviation*
**etc**

**ethnic** *adjective*
**ethnique** *masc & fem*
**an ethnic minority** une minorité ethnique

**EU** *noun*
(*short for European Union*) la **UE** *fem*, l'**Union européenne** *fem*

**euro** *noun*
un **euro** *masc*
**The euro is divided into cents.** L'euro est divisé en centimes.

**Europe** *noun*
l'**Europe** *fem*
**to travel outside Europe** voyager en dehors de l'Europe

**European** *adjective* ▷ see **European** *noun*
**européen** *masc*, **européenne** *fem*

**European** *noun* ▷ see **European** *adj*
un **Européen** *masc*, une **Européenne** *fem*
• **European Union** l'Union européenne *fem*

**eurozone** *noun*
la **zone euro**

to **evacuate** *verb*
**faire [10] évacuer**
**The police evacuated the building.** La police a fait évacuer l'immeuble.

to **evaporate** *verb*
**s'évaporer [1]**

♂**eve** *noun*
la **veille** *fem*
**Christmas Eve** la veille de Noël
**New Year's Eve** la Saint-Sylvestre

♂**even** *adverb* ▷ see **even** *adj*
1 (*when you talk about something surprising*) **même**
**Even Lisa didn't like it.** Même Lisa ne l'a pas aimé.
**He did it without even asking.** Il l'a fait sans même demander.
**even if** même si
**Even if they arrive now, we'll be late.** Même s'ils arrivent maintenant, nous serons en retard.
**I don't like animals, not even dogs.** Je n'aime pas les animaux, même pas les chiens.
**even so** quand même
**Even so, we had a good time.** Nous nous sommes bien amusés quand même.
2 (*in comparisons*) **encore plus**
**Her suitcase was even bigger.** Sa valise était encore plus grande.
**Omar drove even faster.** Omar est allé encore plus vite.
**I like this song even more than the last.** J'aime cette chanson encore plus que la dernière.

♂**even** *adjective* ▷ see **even** *adv*
1 (*surface, layer*) **régulier** *masc*, **régulière** *fem*
2 (*number*) **pair** *masc*, **paire** *fem*
**Six is an even number.** Six est un numéro pair.
3 (*with the same score*) **à égalité**
**Lee and Barry are even.** Lee et Barry sont à égalité.

English–French

**evening** *noun* ▷ see **evening** *adj*
1 le **soir** *masc*
at six o'clock in the evening à six heures du soir
See you this evening! À ce soir!
Let's eat out tomorrow evening! Allons manger au restaurant demain soir!
I saw the film on Thursday evening. J'ai vu le film jeudi soir.
I'd spoken to him the evening before. Je lui avais parlé la veille au soir.
Bill watches TV every evening. Bill regarde la télé tous les soirs.
I work in the evenings. Je travaille le soir.
2 (*from beginning to end*) la **soirée** *fem*
an evening with Madonna une soirée avec Madonna
Did you go out during the evening? Est-ce que tu es sorti pendant la soirée?

**evening** *adjective* ▷ see **evening** *noun*
**du soir**
the evening meal le repas du soir
• **evening class** le cours du soir

**event** *noun*
1 (*happening*) un **événement** *masc*
an important event un événement important
2 (*in athletics*) une **épreuve** *fem*
track events les épreuves de vitesse

**eventful** *adjective*
**mouvementé** *masc*, **mouvementée** *fem*

**eventually** *adverb*
**finalement**

**ever** *adverb*
1 (*at any time*) **jamais**
Have you ever been to France? As-tu jamais été en France?
Haven't you ever noticed that? Tu n'as jamais remarqué ça?
Nobody ever came. Personne n'est jamais venu.
I hardly ever see her. Je ne la vois presque jamais.
It was hotter than ever. Il faisait plus chaud que jamais.
2 (*always*) **toujours**
Harry was as cheerful as ever. Harry était toujours aussi gai.
Dad's the same as ever. Papa est toujours le même.
3 ever since depuis
And it's been raining ever since. Et depuis il pleut tout le temps.

**every** *adjective*
1 (*all*) **tous** *masc plural*, **toutes** *fem plural*
Every house has a garden. Toutes les maisons ont un jardin.
He sees her every day. Il la voit tous les jours.
I've seen every one of his films. J'ai vu tous ses films.
2 (*showing repetition*) every other week une semaine sur deux
every now and then de temps en temps
to stop every ten kilometres s'arrêter tous les dix kilomètres
It rains every time we go there. Il pleut chaque fois qu'on y va.

**everybody**, **everyone** *pronoun*
1 **tout le monde**
Everybody knows she likes Sam. Tout le monde sait qu'elle aime bien Sam.
2 everybody else tous les autres
We stayed but everyone else left. Nous sommes restés mais tous les autres sont partis.

**everything** *pronoun*
**tout**
Everything is ready. Tout est prêt.
Everything's fine. Tout va bien.
Everything you said was true. Tout ce que tu as dit était vrai.
everything else tout le reste

**everywhere** *adverb*
**partout**
There were tourists everywhere. Il y avait des touristes partout.
Everywhere she went, people recognised her. Partout où elle allait, les gens la reconnaissaient.
I've looked everywhere else. J'ai cherché partout ailleurs.

**evidently** *adverb*
**manifestement**

**evil** *adjective* ▷ see **evil** *noun*
**mauvais** *masc*, **mauvaise** *fem*

**evil** *noun* ▷ see **evil** *adj*
le **mal** *masc*

**exact** *adjective*
**exact** *masc*, **exacte** *fem*
the exact amount la somme exacte
It's the exact opposite. C'est exactement le contraire.

**exactly** *adverb*
**exactement**
Yes, exactly. Oui, exactement.
They're exactly the same age. Ils ont exactement le même âge.





a b c d e f g h i j k l m n o p q r s t u v w x y z

to **exaggerate** *verb*
**exagérer [24]**

**exaggeration** *noun*
une **exagération** *fem*

♪ **exam** *noun*
un **examen** *masc*
a history exam un examen d'histoire
to take an exam passer **[1]** un examen
to pass an exam réussir **[2]** un examen
I passed all my exams. J'ai réussi tous mes examens.
to fail an exam échouer **[1]** à un examen
Adam failed the Latin exam. Adam a échoué à l'examen de latin.

**examination** *noun*
un **examen** *masc*

to **examine** *verb*
**examiner [1]**

**examiner** *noun*
un **examinateur** *masc*, une **examinatrice** *fem*

♪ **example** *noun*
un **exemple** *masc*
for example par exemple
Simple dishes, for example, omelettes ... Des plats simples, par exemple, l'omelette ...
to set a good example donner l'exemple

♪ **excellent** *adjective*
**excellent** *masc*, **excellente** *fem*

♪ **except** *preposition*
1 **sauf**
except in March sauf au mois de mars
except when it rains sauf quand il pleut
I train every day except Tuesday. Je m'entraîne tous les jours sauf le mardi.
2 except for sauf
We all went except for Liz. Nous y sommes tous allés sauf Liz.

**exception** *noun*
une **exception** *fem*
without exception sans exception
with the exception of à l'exception de

♪ **exchange** *noun* ▷ see **exchange** *verb*
1 un **échange** *masc*
in exchange for the shoes en échange des chaussures
2 (*an exchange visit*) un **échange**
I went on an exchange to France. J'ai fait un échange en France.

♪ **exchange** *verb* ▷ see **exchange** *noun*
**échanger [52]**
Can I exchange this sweatshirt for a smaller one? Puis-je échanger ce sweatshirt contre le même la taille au-dessous?

**exchange rate** *noun*
le **taux de change**

to **excite** *verb*
**exciter [1]**

**excited** *adjective*
**excité** *masc*, **excitée** *fem*
The children are excited. Les enfants sont excités.
to get excited s'exciter **[1]**
They get excited when they hear the car. Ils s'excitent quand ils entendent la voiture.

**excitement** *noun*
l'**excitation** *fem*

♪ **exciting** *adjective*
**passionnant** *masc*, **passionnante** *fem*
a really exciting film un film vraiment passionnant

**exclamation mark** *noun*
le **point d'exclamation**

**excursion** *noun*
une **excursion** *fem*

**excuse** *noun* ▷ see **excuse** *verb*
une **excuse** *fem*
I've got a good excuse. J'ai une bonne excuse.

♪ to **excuse** *verb* ▷ see **excuse** *noun*
**excuser [1]**
Excuse me! Excuse-moi!
Excuse me! Excusez-moi! (*formal*)

to **execute** *verb*
**exécuter [1]**

♪ **exercise** *noun*
un **exercice** *masc*
a maths exercise un exercice de maths
physical exercise l'exercice physique
- **exercise bike** le vélo d'appartement
- **exercise book** le cahier

**exhaust (pipe)** *noun*
le **pot d'échappement**

♪ **exhausted** *adjective*
**épuisé** *masc*, **épuisée** *fem*

**exhaust fumes** *plural noun*
le **gaz d'échappement**

**exhibition** *noun*
une **exposition** *fem*

to **exist** *verb*
**exister [1]**

♪ **exit** *noun*
la **sortie** *fem*

English–French

a b c d e f g h i j k l m n o p q r s t u v w x y z

to **expand** *verb*
**s'agrandir** [2]
**The town is expanding.** La ville se développe.

to **expect** *verb*
1 *(guests, a baby)* **attendre** [3]
**We're expecting thirty people.** Nous attendons trente personnes.
2 *(something to happen)* **s'attendre** [3] **à**
**I didn't expect that.** Je ne m'attendais pas à ça.
**I didn't expect it at all.** Je ne m'y attendais pas du tout.
3 *(to suppose)* **imaginer** [1]
**I expect she'll bring her boyfriend.** J'imagine qu'elle amènera son copain.
**Yes, I expect so.** Oui, j'imagine.

**expedition** *noun*
une **expédition** *fem*

to **expel** *verb*
**to be expelled** se faire Ⓔ [10] renvoyer
**Lee has been expelled.** Lee s'est fait renvoyer.

**expenses** *plural noun*
les **frais** *masc plural*

**expensive** *adjective*
**cher** *masc*, **chère** *fem*
**expensive trainers** des baskets chers
**an expensive meal** un repas cher
**the most expensive CDs** les CD les plus chers
**Those shoes are too expensive for me.** Ces chaussures sont trop chères pour moi.

**experience** *noun*
une **expérience** *fem*

**experienced** *adjective*
**expérimenté** *masc*, **expérimentée** *fem*

**experiment** *noun*
une **expérience** *fem*
**Let's do an experiment!** Faisons une expérience!

**expert** *noun*
le & la **spécialiste** *masc & fem*
**He's a computer expert.** C'est un spécialiste en informatique.

**expiry date** *noun*
la **date d'expiration**

to **explain** *verb*
**expliquer** [1]
**Can you explain it to me?** Tu peux me l'expliquer?

**explanation** *noun*
une **explication** *fem*

to **explode** *verb*
**exploser** [1]

to **explore** *verb*
**explorer** [1]

**explosion** *noun*
une **explosion** *fem*

**export** *noun* ▷ see **export** *verb*
une **exportation** *fem*
**the chief export** le premier produit d'exportation

to **export** *verb* ▷ see **export** *noun*
**exporter** [1]
**France exports a lot of cars.** La France exporte beaucoup de voitures.

**exposure** *noun*
*(of a film)* la **pose** *fem*
**a 24-exposure film** une pellicule de vingt-quatre poses

**express** *adjective* ▷ see **express** *noun, verb*
1 *(train)* **rapide** *masc & fem*
2 *(letter)* **exprès** *masc*, **expresse** *fem*

**express** *noun* ▷ see **express** *adj, verb*
le **rapide** *masc*
**to take the express** prendre [64] le rapide

to **express** *verb* ▷ see **express** *adj, noun*
1 **exprimer** [1]
2 **to express yourself** s'exprimer
**She expresses herself well.** Elle s'exprime bien.

**expression** *noun*
une **expression** *fem*

to **extend** *verb*
*(a house, room, etc)* **agrandir** [2]

**extension** *noun*
1 *(to a house)* un **agrandissement** *masc*
2 *(telephone)* le **poste** *masc*
**Can I have extension 4055, please?** Est-ce que je peux avoir le poste quarante-cinquante-cinq, s'il vous plaît? *(The French say telephone numbers in pairs.)*
3 *(extension lead)* la **rallonge** *fem*
• **extension number** le numéro de poste

**exterior** *adjective*
**extérieur** *masc*, **extérieure** *fem*

**extinct** *adjective*
1 *(species)* **disparu** *masc*, **disparue** *fem*
2 *(volcano)* **éteint** *masc*, **éteinte** *fem*

to **extinguish** *verb*
**éteindre** [60]

**extinguisher** *noun*
(*for fires*) un **extincteur** *masc*

**extra** *adjective* ▷ see **extra** *adv*
**supplémentaire** *masc & fem*
**extra homework** des devoirs supplémentaires
**at no extra charge** sans supplément
**I paid extra.** J'ai payé un supplément.

**extra** *adverb* ▷ see **extra** *adj*
**extra hot** très chaud
**extra large** très grand

♂ **extraordinary** *adjective*
**extraordinaire** *masc & fem*

**extra-special** *adjective*
**exceptionnel** *masc*, **exceptionnelle** *fem*

**extra time** *noun*
(*in football*) la **prolongation** *fem*
**to go into extra time** jouer [1] les prolongations

**extreme** *adjective* ▷ see **extreme** *noun*
**extrême** *masc & fem*

**extreme** *noun* ▷ see **extreme** *adj*
un **extrême** *masc*
**to go to extremes** pousser [1] les choses à l'extrême

♂ **extremely** *adverb*
**extrêmement**

♂ **eye** *noun*
un **œil** *masc* (*pl* **les yeux**)
**my left eye** mon œil gauche
**a girl with blue eyes** une fille aux yeux bleus
**Shut your eyes!** Ferme les yeux!
**to keep an eye on something** surveiller [1] quelque chose
**Could you keep an eye on my bag?** Tu peux surveiller mon sac?
**to make eyes at somebody** faire [10] les yeux doux à quelqu'un
**She's making eyes at my boyfriend.** Elle fait les yeux doux à mon copain.

- **eyebrow** le sourcil
- **eyelash** le cil
- **eyelid** la paupière
- **eyeliner** un eye-liner
- **eye make-up** le maquillage pour les yeux
- **eye shadow** le fard à paupières
- **eyesight** la vue

# F f

**fabric** *noun*
(*cloth*) le **tissu** *masc*

**fabulous** *adjective*
**sensationnel** *masc*, **sensationnelle** *fem*

♂ **face** *noun* ▷ see **face** *verb*
1 (*of a person*) le **visage** *masc*
**You've got chocolate on your face.** Tu as du chocolat sur le visage.
2 **to pull a face** faire [10] une grimace
**Lucy tasted it and pulled a face.** Lucy l'a goûté et a fait une grimace.
3 (*of a clock, watch*) le **cadran** *masc*

♂ **to face** *verb* ▷ see **face** *noun*
1 (*a person*) **faire [10] face à**
**She faced her attacker.** Elle a fait face à son agresseur.
2 (*to look onto*) **The house faces the park.** La maison donne sur le jardin public.
3 (*to stand the idea of*) **avoir [5] le courage de**
**I can't face going back.** Je n'ai pas le courage de rentrer.

- **face up to something** **faire [10] face à quelque chose**
**You have to face up to the fact that you're going to fail.** Tu dois faire face au fait que tu vas échouer.
- **face cloth** le gant de toilette

**facilities** *plural noun*
1 **The school has good sports facilities.** L'école dispose de bonnes installations sportives.
2 **The flat has cooking facilities.** L'appartement a une cuisine équipée.

**fact** *noun*
le **fait** *masc*
**The fact is that we lost the match.** Le fait est que nous avons perdu le match.
**in fact** en fait
**In fact, he's right.** En fait, il a raison.
**Is that a fact?** Vraiment?

♂ **factory** *noun*
une **usine** *fem*

English–French

**to fade** *verb*
1 (*fabrics*) **se décolorer[1]**
**faded jeans** un jean délavé
2 (*colours*) **passer[1]**
**The colours have faded.** Les couleurs ont passé.

**to fail** *verb*
1 (*an exam*) **rater[1]**
**I failed my driving test.** J'ai raté mon permis.
2 (*students*) **échouer[1]**
**Three students failed.** Trois étudiants ont échoué.
3 (*to be unable to do*) **to fail to do something** ne pas réussir**[2]** à faire quelque chose
**He failed to finish the exam.** Il n'a pas réussi à terminer l'épreuve.
4 **without fail** sans faute
**Ring me without fail!** Appelle-moi sans faute!

**failure** *noun*
1 (*in general*) un **échec** *masc*
**It was a terrible failure.** C'était un échec terrible.
2 (*breakdown*) la **panne** *fem*
**There was a power failure.** Il y avait une panne de courant.

**faint** *adjective* ▷ see **faint** *verb*
1 **to feel faint** se sentir**[58]** mal
**I feel faint.** Je me sens mal.
2 (*smell, taste*) **léger** *masc*, **légère** *fem*
**a faint smell of gas** une légère odeur de gaz
**I haven't the faintest idea.** Je n'en ai pas la moindre idée.
3 (*voice, sound*) **faible** *masc & fem*

**faint** *verb* ▷ see **faint** *adj*
**s'évanouir[2]**
**Lisa fainted.** Lisa s'est évanouie.

**fair** *adjective* ▷ see **fair** *noun*
1 (*even-handed*) **juste** *masc & fem*
**It's not fair!** Ce n'est pas juste!
2 (*hair*) **blond** *masc*, **blonde** *fem*
**He's fair-haired.** Il a les cheveux blonds.
3 (*skin*) **clair** *masc*, **claire** *fem*
**people with fair skin** les gens qui ont la peau claire
4 (*quite good*) **assez bon** *masc*, **assez bonne** *fem*
**Her history is fair.** Elle est assez bonne en histoire.
5 (*weather*) **If it's fair we'll go out.** S'il ne pleut pas, nous irons nous promener.

**fair** *noun* ▷ see **fair** *adj*
la **foire** *fem*
• **fairground** le champ de foire

**fairly** *adverb*
(*quite*) **assez**
**She's fairly happy.** Elle est assez contente.

**fairy** *noun*
la **fée** *fem*
• **fairy tale** le conte de fées

**faith** *noun*
1 (*trust*) la **confiance** *fem*
**I have faith in him.** J'ai confiance en lui.
2 (*in God*) la **foi** *fem*

**faithful** *adjective*
**fidèle** *masc & fem*

**faithfully** *adverb*
(*in a letter ending to someone you don't know*) **Yours faithfully,** Veuillez agréer l'expression de mes sentiments distingués.

**fake** *adjective* ▷ see **fake** *noun*
**faux** *masc*, **fausse** *fem*
**a fake passport** un faux passeport

**fake** *noun* ▷ see **fake** *adj*
le **faux** *masc* (*pl* les **faux**)
**The diamonds are fakes.** Les diamants sont des faux.

**fall** *noun* ▷ see **fall** *verb*
la **chute** *fem*
**to have a fall** tomber Ⓔ **[1]**
**Granny had a fall.** Mamie est tombée.

**fall** *verb* ▷ see **fall** *noun*
1 (*people, things*) **tomber** Ⓔ **[1]**
**Mind, you'll fall!** Attention, tu vas tomber!
**Tony fell off his bike.** Tony est tombé de son vélo.
**Katie fell downstairs.** Katie est tombée dans l'escalier.
**My jacket fell on the floor.** Ma veste est tombée par terre.
2 (*temperature*) **descendre** Ⓔ **[3]**
**The temperature fell to minus eleven last night.** La température est descendue à moins onze cette nuit.
3 (*prices*) **baisser[1]**

**false** *adjective*
**faux** *masc*, **fausse** *fem*
**a false alarm** une fausse alerte
• **false teeth** le dentier

**fame** *noun*
la **renommée** *fem*

**familiar** *adjective*
**familier** *masc*, **familière** *fem*
**Your face is familiar.** Votre visage m'est familier.

Ⓔ means the verb takes être to form the perfect

♂ **family** *noun*
la **famille** *fem*
**a family of six** une famille de six personnes
**the Barnes family** la famille Barnes
**Ben's one of the family.** Ben fait partie de la famille.
• **family name** le nom de famille

♂ **famous** *adjective*
**célèbre** *masc & fem*

**fan** *noun*
1 (*of a team*) le **supporter** *masc*
**Matt's a Chelsea fan.** Matt est un supporter de Chelsea.
2 (*of a star, a band*) le & la **fan** *masc & fem*
**Sophie's an Oasis fan.** Sophie est une fan de Oasis.
3 (*electric*) le **ventilateur** *masc*
4 (*hand-held*) l'**éventail** *masc*

**fanatic** *noun*
le & la **fanatique** *masc & fem*

**fancy** *adjective* ▷ see **fancy** *noun, verb*
1 (*equipment*) **sophistiqué** *masc*, **sophistiquée** *fem*
2 (*clothes*) **chic** *masc & fem*
3 (*price*) **cher** *masc*, **chère** *fem*

**fancy** *noun* ▷ see **fancy** *adj, verb*
**to take someone's fancy** faire [10] envie à quelqu'un
**The cake took his fancy.** Le gâteau lui a fait envie.

to **fancy** *verb* ▷ see **fancy** *adj, noun*
1 (*to want*) **Do you fancy a coffee?** Tu veux un café?
**Do you fancy going to see the film?** Ça te dirait d'aller voir le film?
2 (*a person*) **I really fancy him.** Il me plaît beaucoup.
3 (*expressing surprise*) **Fancy that!** Pas possible!
**Fancy you being here!** Tiens donc, toi ici!

**fancy dress** *noun*
**in fancy dress** déguisé *masc*, déguisée *fem*
**a fancy-dress party** une soirée déguisée

♂ **fantastic** *adjective*
**génial** *masc*, **géniale** *fem*, **géniaux** *masc pl*, **géniales** *fem pl*
**a fantastic holiday** des vacances géniales
**Really? That's fantastic!** Vraiment? C'est génial!

♂ **far** *adjective, adverb*
1 **loin**
**It's not far.** Ce n'est pas loin.
**Is it far to Cambridge?** Est-ce que Cambridge est loin d'ici?
**How far is it to Bristol?** Bristol est à quelle distance d'ici?
**as far as** jusqu'à
**He took us as far as Newport.** Il nous a emmenés jusqu'à Newport.
2 **by far** de loin
**the prettiest by far** de loin le plus joli
3 (*much*) **beaucoup**
**You're working is far better.** Tu travailles beaucoup mieux.
**This bike goes far faster.** Ce vélo va beaucoup plus vite.
**There were far too many people in the lift.** Il y avait beaucoup trop de monde dans l'ascenseur.
4 **so far** jusqu'ici
**So far everything's going well.** Jusqu'ici tout va bien.
5 **as far as I know** pour autant que je sache

♂ **fare** *noun*
1 (*on a bus, in the metro*) le **prix du ticket**
2 (*on a train, plane*) le **prix du billet**
**half fare** le demi-tarif *masc*
**full fare** le plein tarif *masc*
**What's the return fare to Cardiff?** Quel est le prix d'un aller-retour à Cardiff?

**Far East** *noun*
l'**Extrême-Orient** *masc*

♂ **farm** *noun*
la **ferme** *fem*

♂ **farmer** *noun*
un **agriculteur** *masc*, une **agricultrice** *fem*

**farmhouse** *noun*
la **ferme** *fem*

**farming** *noun*
l'**agriculture** *fem*

**farthest** *adjective* ▷ see **farthest** *adv*
**le plus éloigné** *masc*, **la plus éloignée** *fem*

**farthest** *adverb* ▷ see **farthest** *adj*
**le plus loin**

**fascinating** *adjective*
**fascinant** *masc*, **fascinante** *fem*

**fashion** *noun*
1 la **mode** *fem*
**in fashion** à la mode
**Short skirts are in fashion.** Les jupes courtes sont à la mode.
2 **out of fashion** démodé *masc*, démodée *fem*
**Cowboy boots are out of fashion.** Les bottes de cow-boy sont démodées.

**fashionable** *adjective*
**à la mode**

**fashion model** *noun*
le **mannequin** *masc*

English-French

a b c d e f g h i j k l m n o p q r s t u v w x y z

**fashion show** *noun*
la **présentation de collection**

**fast** *adjective* ▷ see **fast** *adv*
1 **rapide** *masc & fem*
a fast car une voiture rapide
2 (*clocks, watches*) **My watch is fast.** Ma montre avance.
**You're ten minutes fast.** Ta montre avance de dix minutes.

**fast** *adverb* ▷ see **fast** *adj*
1 **vite**
He swims fast. Il nage vite.
2 **to be fast asleep** être [6] profondément endormi
**The baby was fast asleep.** Le bébé était profondément endormi.
- **fast food** le fast-food *masc*
- **fast forward** l'avance rapide *fem*

**fat** *adjective* ▷ see **fat** *noun*
**gros** *masc*, **grosse** *fem*
a fat man un gros monsieur
a fat woman une grosse femme
to get fat grossir
**I'm getting a bit fat.** Je grossis.

**fat** *noun* ▷ see **fat** *adj*
1 (*on your body*) la **graisse** *fem*
2 (*on meat*) le **gras** *masc*
3 (*in food*) les **matières grasses** *fem pl*

**fatal** *adjective*
(*accident*) **mortel** *masc*, **mortelle** *fem*

**father** *noun*
le **père** *masc*
my father's office le bureau de mon père
- **Father Christmas** le père Noël
- **father-in-law** le beau-père

**Father's Day** *noun*
la **fête des Pères**

**fault** *noun*
1 (*responsibility*) la **faute** *fem*
**It's Stephen's fault.** C'est la faute de Stephen.
**It's not my fault.** Ce n'est pas ma faute.
2 (*defect*) le **défaut** *masc*
**There's a fault in this sweater.** Il y a un défaut dans ce pull.
3 (*in tennis*) la **faute** *fem*

**favour** *noun*
1 (*kindness*) le **service** *masc*
**to do somebody a favour** rendre service à quelqu'un
**Can you do me a favour?** Peux-tu me rendre service?
**to ask somebody a favour** demander un service à quelqu'un
**Can I ask you a favour?** Puis-je te demander un service?
2 **to be in favour of something** être [6] pour quelque chose
**I'm in favour of introducing identity cards.** Je suis pour l'introduction des cartes d'identité.

**favourite** *adjective*
**préféré** *masc*, **préférée** *fem*
**my favourite band** mon groupe préféré

**fax** *noun* ▷ see **fax** *verb*
le **fax** *masc*

to **fax** *verb* ▷ see **fax** *noun*
**faxer** [1]
**Fax me the details!** Faxez-moi les renseignements!

**fear** *noun* ▷ see **fear** *verb*
la **peur** *fem*

to **fear** *verb* ▷ see **fear** *noun*
**craindre** [31]
**He fears the worst.** Il craint le pire.

**feather** *noun*
la **plume** *fem*

**feature** *noun*
1 (*of a car, a mobile phone*) la **caractéristique** *fem*
2 (*of your face*) le **trait** *masc*

**February** *noun*
**février** *masc*
**in February** en février

**WORD TIP** Months of the year and days of the week start with small letters in French.

**fed up** *adjective*
**I'm fed up.** J'en ai marre. (*informal*)
**I'm fed up with working every day.** J'en ai marre de travailler tous les jours.

to **feed** *verb*
**donner** [1] **à manger à**
**Have you fed the dog?** Est-ce que tu as donné à manger au chien?

to **feel** *verb*
1 (*tired, well*) **se sentir** [58]
**I feel tired.** Je me sens fatigué.
**I don't feel well.** Je ne me sens pas bien.
2 (*a pain*) **sentir** [58]
**I didn't feel a thing.** Je n'ai rien senti.
3 (*afraid, cold*) **to feel afraid** avoir [5] peur
**She felt afraid to move.** Elle avait peur de bouger.
**to feel cold** avoir [5] froid
**Do you feel cold?** As-tu froid?
4 **to feel like doing something** avoir [5] envie de faire quelque chose

I feel like going to the cinema. Je ai envie d'aller au cinéma.
5 (*to touch*) **toucher [1]**
Feel this! It's really soft. Touche! C'est vraiment doux.

**feeling** *noun*
1 (*mental*) le **sentiment** *masc*
**a feeling of embarrassment** un sentiment de gêne
**to show your feelings** montrer [1] ses sentiments
**Oliver never shows his feelings.** Oliver ne montre jamais ses sentiments.
**to hurt somebody's feelings** blesser [1] quelqu'un
**You hurt her feelings.** Tu l'as blessée.
2 (*physical*) la **sensation** *fem*
**a dizzy feeling** une sensation de vertige
3 (*idea*) une **impression** *fem*
**I have the feeling James doesn't like me.** J'ai l'impression que James ne m'aime pas.

**felt-tip (pen)** *noun*
le **feutre** *masc*

**female** *adjective* ▷ see **female** *noun*
1 (*person, population*) **féminin** *masc*, **féminine** *fem*
2 (*animal, insect*) **femelle** *masc & fem*

**female** *noun* ▷ see **female** *adj*
(*of a species*) la **femelle** *fem*

**feminine** *adjective* ▷ see **feminine** *noun*
**féminin** *masc*, **féminine** *fem*
a feminine noun un nom féminin

**feminine** *noun* ▷ see **feminine** *adj*
(*Grammar*) le **féminin** *masc*
**in the feminine** au féminin

**feminist** *noun*
le & la **féministe** *masc & fem*

**fence** *noun*
la **clôture** *fem*

**fern** *noun*
la **fougère** *fem*

**ferry** *noun*
le **ferry** *masc*

**fertilizer** *noun*
l'**engrais** *masc*

**festival** *noun*
le **festival** *masc*

to **fetch** *verb*
**aller** Ⓔ **[7] chercher**
**Tom's fetching the children.** Tom est allé chercher les enfants.
**Fetch me the other knife!** Va me chercher l'autre couteau!

**fever** *noun*
la **fièvre** *fem*

ℰ **few** *adjective, pronoun*
1 (*followed by a noun*) **peu de**
**few people think that ...** peu de gens pensent que...
**Very few houses have a swimming-pool.** Très peu de maisons ont une piscine.
2 **a few** quelques
**a few weeks earlier** quelques semaines plus tôt
**I'll be ready in a few minutes.** Je serai prêt dans quelques minutes.
3 (*by itself*) **a few** quelques-uns *masc*, quelques-unes *fem*
**Have you any tomatoes? We want a few for the salad.** Avez-vous des tomates? Nous en voulons quelques-unes pour la salade.
4 **quite a few** pas mal de
**There were quite a few tourists.** Il y avait pas mal de touristes.

ℰ **fewer** *adjective*
**moins de**
**There are fewer tourists this year.** Il y a moins de touristes cette année.

ℰ **fiancé** *noun*
le **fiancé** *masc*

ℰ **fiancée** *noun*
la **fiancée** *fem*

**fiction** *noun*
les **romans** *masc plural*
**I read a lot of fiction.** Je lis beaucoup de romans.

ℰ **field** *noun*
1 (*on a farm*) le **champ** *masc*
**a field of wheat** un champ de blé
2 (*for sport*) le **terrain** *masc*
3 (*of work, study*) le **domaine** *masc*

**fierce** *adjective*
1 (*animal, person*) **féroce** *masc & fem*
2 (*storm, battle*) **violent** *masc*, **violente** *fem*

ℰ **fifteen** *number*
**quinze**
**Laura's fifteen.** Laura a quinze ans.

**fifth** *adjective*
1 **cinquième** *masc & fem*
**on the fifth floor** au cinquième étage
2 (*in dates*) **the fifth of January** le cinq janvier

**fifty** *number*
**cinquante**
**My uncle's fifty.** Mon oncle a cinquante ans.

**fig** *noun*
la **figue** *fem*

English–French

**fight** *noun* ▷ see **fight** *verb*
1 (*in the street*) la **bagarre** *fem*
2 (*in boxing*) le **combat** *masc*
3 (*against illness*) la **lutte** *fem*

**fight** *verb* ▷ see **fight** *noun*
1 (*to have a fight*) **se battre [21]**
**They were fighting.** Ils se battaient.
2 (*to quarrel*) **se disputer [1]**
**They're always fighting.** Ils sont toujours en train de se disputer.
3 (*against cancer*) **lutter [1] contre**

**fighting** *noun*
1 (*in the street*) la **bagarre** *fem*
2 (*in a war*) le **combat** *masc*

𝄞 **figure** *noun*
1 (*number*) le **chiffre** *masc*
**a four-figure number** un nombre de quatre chiffres
2 (*body shape*) la **ligne** *fem*
**Swimming is good for your figure.** La natation, c'est bon pour la ligne.
3 (*person*) le **personnage** *masc*
**a familiar figure** un personnage familier
4 (*diagram*) la **figure** *fem*

**file** *noun* ▷ see **file** *verb*
1 (*for records*) le **dossier** *masc*
2 (*ring binder*) le **classeur** *masc*
3 (*cardboard folder*) la **chemise** *fem*
4 (*on a computer*) le **fichier** *masc*
5 **a nail file** une lime

to **file** *verb* ▷ see **file** *verb*
1 (*a document*) **classer [1]**
2 **to file your nails** se limer **[1]** les ongles

𝄞 to **fill** *verb*
(*a bottle, jar*) **remplir [2]**
**She filled my glass.** Elle a rempli mon verre.
**a smoke-filled room** une pièce remplie de fumée
• **to fill in**
(*a form*) **remplir [2] quelque chose**
• **to fill in for someone**
**remplacer [61] quelqu'un**

**filling** *noun*
1 (*for a sandwich*) la **garniture** *fem*
2 (*of meat, vegetables*) la **farce** *fem*
3 (*in a chocolate, pastry*) **with an apricot filling** fourré à l'abricot
4 (*in a tooth*) le **plombage** *masc*

𝄞 **film** *noun*
1 (*in a cinema*) le **film** *masc*
**the new film about Picasso** le nouveau film au sujet de Picasso
**Shall we go and see a film?** Si on allait voir un film?
2 (*for a camera*) la **pellicule** *fem*
**a 24-exposure colour film** une pellicule couleur de 24 poses

**film star** *noun*
la **vedette de cinéma**

**filter** *noun*
le **filtre** *masc*

𝄞 **filthy** *adjective*
**dégoûtant** *masc*, **dégoûtante** *fem*

**fin** *noun*
la **nageoire** *fem*

**final** *adjective* ▷ see **final** *noun*
**dernier** *masc*, **dernière** *fem*
**the final instalment** le dernier épisode
**the final result** le résultat final

**final** *noun* ▷ see **final** *adj*
(*Sports*) la **finale** *fem*

𝄞 **finally** *adverb*
**finalement**

𝄞 to **find** *verb*
**trouver [1]**
**Did you find your passport?** As-tu trouvé ton passeport?
**I can't find my keys.** Je ne trouve pas mes clefs.
• **to find out**
(*to enquire*) **se renseigner** Ⓔ **[1]**
**I don't know, I'll find out.** Je ne sais pas, je me renseignerai.
**to find something out** découvrir **[30]** quelque chose
**Luke found out the truth.** Luke a découvert la vérité.

**fine** *adjective* ▷ see **fine** *noun*
1 (*in good health*) **bien** *invariable masc & fem*
**'How are you?' — 'Fine, thanks'.** 'Comment ça va?' — 'Très bien merci.'
2 (*very good*) **excellent** *masc*, **excellente** *fem*
**She's a fine athlete.** C'est une excellente athlète.
3 (*convenient*) **très bien** *invariable masc & fem*
**Ten o'clock? Yes, that's fine.** Dix heures? Oui, très bien.
**Friday will be fine.** Vendredi sera très bien.
4 (*weather, day*) **beau** *masc*, **belle** *fem*
**a fine day** une belle journée
5 (*cloth, silk*) **fin** *masc*, **fine** *fem*
**in fine wool** en laine fine

**fine** *noun* ▷ see **fine** *adj*
1 (*in general*) l'**amende** *fem*
2 (*for parking, speeding*) la **contravention** *fem*



Ⓔ means the verb takes être to form the perfect

a b c d e f g h i j k l m n o p q r s t u v w x y z

♂ **finger** *noun*
le **doigt** *masc*
**I'll keep my fingers crossed for you.** Je croise les doigts pour toi.
• **fingernail** l'ongle *masc*

**finish** *noun* ▷ see **finish** *verb*
1 (*end*) la **fin** *fem*
2 (*in a race*) l'**arrivée** *fem*

♂ to **finish** *verb* ▷ see **finish** *noun*
1 (*to stop*) **finir [2]**
**I've finished.** J'ai fini.
**When does school finish?** À quelle heure finit l'école?
2 (*to come to the end of*) **terminer [1]**
**Have you finished the book?** Est-ce que tu as terminé le livre?
3 **to finish doing something** finir **[2]** de faire quelque chose
**Have you finished telephoning?** As-tu fini de téléphoner?
• **to finish with something**
**finir avec quelque chose**
**Have you finished with the computer?** As-tu fini avec l'ordinateur?

**finishing line** *noun*
la **ligne d'arrivée**

**Finland** *noun*
la **Finlande** *fem*

**Finnish** *adjective* ▷ see **Finnish** *noun*
**finlandais** *masc*, **finlandaise** *fem*

**Finnish** *noun* ▷ see **Finnish** *adj*
(*the language*) le **finnois** *masc*

♂ **fire** *noun* ▷ see **fire** *verb*
1 (*for heating*) le **feu** *masc*
**to light a fire** allumer un feu
**Dad lit a fire.** Papa a allumé un feu.
**She was sitting by the fire.** Elle était assise près du feu.
2 **to catch fire** prendre **[64]** feu
**The newspaper caught fire.** Le journal a pris feu.
3 (*accidental*) un **incendie** *masc*
**a fire in a factory** un incendie dans une usine

♂ **fire** *verb* ▷ see **fire** *noun*
1 (*to shoot*) **tirer [1]**
**The soldiers were firing.** Les soldats tiraient.
**to fire at somebody** tirer sur quelqu'un
**Someone had fired at them.** Quelqu'un avait tiré sur eux.
2 (*a gun*) **décharger**
• **fire alarm** une alarme incendie
• **fire brigade** les pompiers *masc plural*
• **fire engine** la voiture des pompiers
• **fire escape** un escalier de secours
• **fire extinguisher** un extincteur
• **fire fighter** le pompier
• **fireplace** la cheminée
• **fire station** la caserne de pompiers
• **firework** le feu d'artifice (*pl* les feux d'artifice)
**There will be a firework display.** Il y aura un feu d'artifice.

**firm** *adjective* ▷ see **firm** *noun*
**ferme** *masc & fem*

**firm** *noun* ▷ see **firm** *adj*
(*business*) une **entreprise** *fem*

♂ **first** *adjective, adverb*
1 (*in order*) **premier** *masc*, **première** *fem*
**the first of May** le premier mai
**I met him for the first time yesterday.** Je l'ai rencontré hier pour la première fois.
**Susan's the first.** Susan est la première.
**I came first in the 200 metres.** Je suis arrivé premier aux 200 mètres (*boy speaking*), Je suis arrivée première aux 200 mètres (*girl speaking*).
2 (*to begin with*) **d'abord**
**First, I'm going to have a shower.** D'abord je vais prendre une douche.
3 **at first** au début
**At first he was shy.** Au début il était timide.

**first aid** *noun*
les **premiers secours** *masc plural*
• **first-aid kit** la trousse de secours

**first class** *adjective*
1 (*ticket, carriage, hotel*) **de première classe**
**a first-class compartment** un compartiment de première classe
**He always travels first class.** Il voyage toujours en première.
2 (*stamp, letter*) **au tarif rapide**
**six first-class stamps** six timbres au tarif rapide

**first floor** *noun*
le **premier étage** *masc*
**on the first floor** au premier étage

**firstly** *adverb*
**premièrement**

♂ **first name** *noun*
le **prénom** *masc*

**fir tree** *noun*
le **sapin** *masc*

♂ **fish** *noun* ▷ see **fish** *verb*
le **poisson** *masc*
**Do you like fish?** Aimez-vous le poisson?

♂ indicates key words

English–French

to **fish** *verb* ▷ see **fish** *noun*
**pêcher** [1]
**Dad was fishing for trout.** Papa pêchait la truite.
- **fish and chips** le poisson frit avec des frites

**fisherman** *noun*
le **pêcheur** *masc*

**fishing** *noun*
la **pêche** *fem*
**I love fishing.** J'adore la pêche.
**to go fishing** aller ❷ [7] à la pêche
**Tom's gone fishing.** Tom est allé à la pêche.
- **fishing rod** la canne à pêche
- **fishing tackle** le matériel de pêche

**fist** *noun*
le **poing** *masc*

**fit** *adjective* ▷ see **fit** *noun, verb*
(*healthy*) **en forme**
**I feel really fit.** Je me sens vraiment en forme.
**to keep fit** se maintenir [81] en forme
**I'm trying to keep fit.** J'essaie de me maintenir en forme.

**fit** *noun* ▷ see **fit** *adj, verb*
1 (*of rage*) **to have a fit** piquer une crise
**Your dad'll have a fit when he sees your tattoo!** Ton père va piquer une crise quand il va voir ton tatouage!
2 (*illness*) **an epileptic fit** une crise d'épilepsie

**fit** *verb* ▷ see **fit** *adj, noun*
1 (*clothes*) **être** [6] **à la taille**
**This skirt doesn't fit me.** Cette jupe n'est pas à ma taille.
2 (*shoes*) **être** [6] **à la pointure de**
3 (*to go into*) **aller** ❷ [7] **dans**
**Will my cases fit in the car?** Est-ce que mes valises iront dans la voiture?
**The key doesn't fit in the lock.** La clé ne va pas dans la serrure.
4 (*to install*) **installer** [1]
**They've fitted an alarm.** Ils ont installé une alarme.

**fitness** *noun*
la **forme** *fem*
**fitness training** les exercices de mise en forme

**fitted carpet** *noun*
la **moquette** *fem*

**fitted kitchen** *noun*
la **cuisine intégrée**

**fitting room** *noun*
la **cabine d'essayage**

**five** *number*
**cinq**
**Beth's five.** Beth a cinq ans.
**It's five o'clock.** Il est cinq heures.

to **fix** *verb*
1 (*a machine*) **réparer** [1]
**Rob's fixed the computer.** Rob a réparé l'ordinateur.
2 (*a date, a price*) **fixer** [1]
**to fix a date** fixer une date
**They've fixed a date for the wedding.** Ils ont fixé une date pour le mariage.
**at a fixed price** à prix fixe
3 (*a meal*) **préparer** [1]
**I'll fix supper.** Je vais préparer le dîner.

**fizzy** *adjective*
**gazeux** *masc*, **gazeuse** *fem*
**fizzy water** l'eau gazeuse

**flag** *noun*
le **drapeau** *masc* (*pl* les **drapeaux**)

***flag***

The French flag (*le Tricolore*) has three vertical stripes: blue, white and red. It dates from the French Revolution (1794), combining the colours of Paris (blue/red) with that of the king (white).

**flame** *noun*
la **flamme** *fem*

**flamingo** *noun*
le **flamant rose**

**flan** *noun*
la **tarte** *fem*
**an onion flan** une tarte à l'oignon

to **flap** *verb*
**battre** [21]
**The bird flapped its wings.** L'oiseau battait des ailes.

**flash** *noun* ▷ see **flash** *verb*
1 (*bright light*) **a flash of lightning** un éclair
2 (*short time*) **in a flash** en un clin d'œil
**He was ready in a flash.** Il était prêt en un clin d'œil.
3 (*for a camera*) le **flash** *masc*

to **flash** *verb* ▷ see **flash** *noun*
1 (*lights*) **clignoter** [1]
2 **to flash by** passer [1] comme un éclair
**The ambulance flashed by.** L'ambulance est passée comme un éclair.
3 **to flash your headlights** faire [10] des appels de phares
- **flashback** le flash-back *masc*



❷ means the verb takes être to form the perfect

**flask** *noun*
1 (*insulated bottle*) le or la **thermos**® *masc or fem*
2 (*of spirits*) le **flacon** *masc*

♪ **flat** *adjective* ▷ **see flat** *noun*
**plat** *masc*, **plate** *fem*
flat shoes des chaussures plates
a flat landscape un paysage plat
a flat tyre un pneu crevé

♪ **flat** *noun* ▷ **see flat** *adj*
un **appartement** *masc*
a third-floor flat un appartement au troisième étage
• **flatmate** le & la colocataire *masc & fem*

to **flatter** *verb*
**flatter [1]**

**flattering** *adjective*
**flatteur** *masc*, **flatteuse** *fem*

♪ **flavour** *noun* ▷ **see flavour** *verb*
1 (*taste*) le **goût** *masc*
The sauce had no flavour. La sauce n'avait aucun goût.
2 (*of a drink, an ice cream*) le **parfum** *masc*
What flavour of ice cream would you like? Tu veux quel parfum de glace?

to **flavour** *verb* ▷ **see flavour** *noun*
**parfumer [1]**
vanilla-flavoured parfumé à la vanille

**flea** *noun*
la **puce** *fem*
• **flea market** le marché aux puces

**fleet** *noun*
1 (*of ships*) la **flotte** *fem*
2 (*of vehicles*) le **parc** *masc*

**flesh** *noun*
la **chair** *fem*

**flex** *noun*
le **fil** *masc*

**flexible** *adjective*
**flexible** *masc & fem*

♪ **flight** *noun*
1 le **vol** *masc*
a charter flight un vol charter
The flight from Moscow is delayed. Le vol de Moscou est retardé.
2 a flight of stairs un escalier
four flights of stairs quatre étages
• **flight attendant**
1 (*male*) le **steward**
2 (*female*) une **hôtesse de l'air**

to **fling** *verb*
**lancer [61]**

**flipper** *noun*
(*for a swimmer*) la **palme** *fem*

to **flirt** *verb*
**flirter [1]**

to **float** *verb*
**flotter [1]**

**flood** *noun* ▷ **see flood** *verb*
1 (*of water*) une **inondation** *fem*
the floods in the south les inondations au sud
to be in floods of tears verser [1] des torrents de larmes
Rosie was in floods of tears. Rosie versait des torrents de larmes.
2 (*of letters, complaints*) le **déluge** *masc*

to **flood** *verb* ▷ **see flood** *noun*
**inonder [1]**
• **floodlight** le projecteur

♪ **floor** *noun*
1 (*wooden*) le **plancher** *masc*
to sweep the floor balayer
I've swept the kitchen floor. J'ai balayé la cuisine.
Your glasses are on the floor. Tes lunettes sont par terre.
2 (*concrete*) le **sol** *masc*
3 (*storey*) un **étage** *masc*
on the second floor au deuxième étage

**floppy disk** *noun*
la **disquette** *fem*

**florist** *noun*
le & la **fleuriste** *masc & fem*

**flour** *noun*
la **farine** *fem*

to **flow** *verb*
**couler [1]**

♪ **flower** *noun* ▷ **see flower** *verb*
la **fleur** *fem*
a bunch of flowers un bouquet

to **flower** *verb* ▷ **see flower** *noun*
**fleurir [2]**

♪ **flu** *noun*
la **grippe** *fem*
to have flu avoir [5] la grippe
Sally has flu. Sally a la grippe.

**fluent** *adjective*
She speaks fluent Italian. Elle parle couramment l'italien.

**fluently** *adverb*
**couramment**

**fluid** *noun*
le **liquide** *masc*

to **flush** *verb*
to flush the toilet tirer [1] la chasse

**flute** *noun*
la **flûte** *fem*
to play the flute jouer [1] de la flûte
Jo plays the flute. Jo joue de la flûte.

**fly** *noun* ▷ see **fly** *verb*
la **mouche** *fem*
• **fly spray** la bombe insecticide

𝄞 to **fly** *verb* ▷ see **fly** *noun*
1 (*birds, bees, planes*) **voler [1]**
2 (*in a plane*) **prendre [64] l'avion**
We flew to Edinburgh. Nous sommes allés à Édimbourg en avion.
We flew from Gatwick. Nous sommes partis de Gatwick.
3 (*a kite*) **faire [10] voler**
4 (*time*) **passer ⓔ [1] très vite**

**foam** *noun*
1 (*foam rubber*) la **mousse** *fem*
a foam mattress un matelas mousse
2 (*on a drink*) la **mousse** *fem*

**focus** *noun* ▷ see **focus** *verb*
to be in focus être [6] au point
to be out of focus être flou
All the photos were out of focus. Toutes les photos étaient floues.

to **focus** *verb* ▷ see **focus** *noun*
(*a camera*) **mettre [11] au point**

𝄞 **fog** *noun*
le **brouillard** *masc*

**foggy** *adjective*
(*weather*) **brumeux** *masc*, **brumeuse** *fem*
It was foggy. Il y avait du brouillard.

**fold** *noun* ▷ see **fold** *verb*
le **pli** *masc*

to **fold** *verb* ▷ see **fold** *noun*
1 **plier [1]**
to fold something up plier quelque chose
I folded up the towels. J'ai plié les serviettes.
2 to fold your arms croiser [1] les bras

**folder** *noun*
la **chemise** *fem*

**folding** *adjective*
**pliant** *masc*, **pliante** *fem*
a folding table une table pliante

to **follow** *verb*
(*a person, advice, a path*) **suivre [75]**
Follow me! Suivez-moi!
You must follow the instructions. Il faut suivre les instructions.
Do you follow me? Vous me suivez?

**following** *adjective*
**suivant** *masc*, **suivante** *fem*
the following year l'année suivante

**fond** *adjective*
to be fond of somebody aimer beaucoup quelqu'un
I'm very fond of him. Je l'aime beaucoup.

𝄞 **food** *noun*
1 (*to keep you alive*) la **nourriture** *fem*
to buy food acheter à manger
I like French food. J'aime la cuisine française.
2 (*stocks*) les **provisions** *fem plural*
We bought food for the holiday. Nous avons acheté des provisions pour les vacances.
• **food poisoning** une intoxication alimentaire

**fool** *noun*
un **idiot** *masc*, une **idiote** *fem*

𝄞 **foot** *noun*
1 le **pied** *masc*
on foot à pied
Hannah came on foot. Hannah est venue à pied.
2 (*the bottom*) at the foot of the stairs en bas de l'escalier

𝄞 **football** *noun*
1 (*game*) le **football** *masc*
to play football jouer [1] au football
George loves playing football. George aime beaucoup jouer au football.
2 (*ball*) le **ballon de football**

**footballer** *noun*
le **joueur de football**, la **joueuse de football**

**footpath** *noun*
le **sentier** *masc*

**footprint** *noun*
une **empreinte** *fem*

**footstep** *noun*
le **pas** *masc*

𝄞 **for** *preposition*
1 (*in general*) **pour**
a present for my mother un cadeau pour ma mère
petrol for the car de l'essence pour la voiture
sausages for lunch des saucisses pour le déjeuner
It's for cleaning. C'est pour nettoyer.
What's it for? C'est pour quoi faire?
What's the French for 'bee'? Comment dit-on 'bee' en français?

2 (*in time expressions in the past or future*) **pendant**
**I studied French for six years.** J'ai étudié le français pendant six ans (*but I no longer do*).
**I'll be away for four days.** Je serai absent pendant quatre jours.
3 (*in time expressions continuing into the present*) **depuis**
**I've been waiting here for an hour.** J'attends ici depuis une heure (*and am still waiting*).
**My brother's been living in Paris for three years.** Mon frère habite à Paris depuis trois ans (*and is still living there*).
4 (*with prices*) **I sold my bike for fifty pounds.** J'ai vendu mon vélo cinquante livres.

to **forbid** *verb*
**défendre [3]**
**to forbid somebody to do something** défendre [3] à quelqu'un de faire quelque chose
**I forbid you to go out.** Je te défends de sortir.

**forbidden** *adjective*
**défendu** *masc*, **défendue** *fem*

**force** *noun* ▷ see **force** *verb*
la **force** *fem*

to **force** *verb* ▷ see **force** *noun*
**forcer [61]**
**to force somebody to do something** forcer quelqu'un à faire quelque chose
**No-one forced you to go.** Personne ne t'a forcé à y aller.

**forefinger** *noun*
un **index** *masc*

**foreground** *noun*
le **premier plan** *masc*
**in the foreground** au premier plan

**forehead** *noun*
le **front** *masc*

**foreign** *adjective*
**étranger** *masc*, **étrangère** *fem*
**in a foreign country** dans un pays étranger

**foreigner** *noun*
un **étranger** *masc*, une **étrangère** *fem*

to **foresee** *verb*
**prévoir [65]**

**forest** *noun*
la **forêt** *fem*

**forever** *adverb*
1 **pour toujours**
**I'd like to stay here forever.** J'aimerais rester là pour toujours.
2 (*non-stop*) **sans arrêt**
**He's forever asking questions.** Il pose des questions sans arrêt.

**forgery** *noun*
1 (*painting*) un **faux** *masc*
2 (*signature, banknote*) une **contrefaçon** *fem*

to **forget** *verb*
**oublier [1]**
**I forget his name.** J'oublie son nom.
**We've forgotten the bread!** Nous avons oublié le pain!
**to forget to do something** oublier de faire quelque chose
**I forgot to phone.** J'ai oublié d'appeler.
**to forget about something** oublier quelque chose
**I forgot all about it.** Je l'ai complètement oublié.

to **forgive** *verb*
**pardonner [1] à**
**to forgive somebody** pardonner à quelqu'un
**I forgave him.** Je lui ai pardonné.
**to forgive somebody for doing something** pardonner à quelqu'un d'avoir fait quelque chose
**I forgave her for losing my ring.** Je lui ai pardonné d'avoir perdu ma bague.

**fork** *noun*
la **fourchette** *fem*

**form** *noun* ▷ see **form** *verb*
1 (*for applications*) le **formulaire** *masc*
**to fill in a form** remplir un formulaire
**I've filled in the forms.** J'ai rempli les formulaires.
2 (*shape, type*) la **forme** *fem*
**in the form of a letter** sous forme de lettre
3 **to be on form** être [6] en forme
**Mandy was on good form.** Mandy était en pleine forme.
4 (*school class*) la **classe** *fem*

to **form** *verb* ▷ see **form** *noun*
**former [1]**

**formal** *adjective*
(*invitation, event, complaint*) **officiel** *masc*, **officielle** *fem*

**format** *noun*
le **format** *masc*

**former** *adjective*
**ancien** *masc*, **ancienne** *fem*
**a former pupil** un ancien élève

**formula** *noun*
la **formule** *fem*

English–French

a b c d e f g h i j k l m n o p q r s t u v w x y z

**fortnight** *noun*
**quinze jours** *masc plural*
**We're going to Spain for a fortnight.** Nous allons passer quinze jours en Espagne.

**fortress** *noun*
la **forteresse** *fem*

**fortunate** *adjective*
**to be fortunate** avoir **[5]** de la chance
**You were very fortunate.** Tu avais bien de la chance.

**fortunately** *adverb*
**heureusement**

**fortune** *noun*
la **fortune** *fem*
**to make a fortune** gagner **[1]** beaucoup d'argent
**Will makes a fortune at the bank.** Will gagne beaucoup d'argent à la banque.

**forty** *number*
**quarante**
**My aunt's forty.** Ma tante a quarante ans.

**forward** *adverb* ▷ **see forward** *noun*
**to move forward** avancer
**Move forward a little!** Avancez un peu!

**forward** *noun* ▷ **see forward** *adv*
(*in sport*) un **avant** *masc*

**foster child** *noun*
un **enfant adoptif**, une **enfant adoptive**

**foul** *adjective* ▷ **see foul** *noun*
**infect** *masc*, **infecte** *fem*
**The weather's foul.** Il fait un temps infect.

**foul** *noun* ▷ **see foul** *adj*
(*Sports*) la **faute** *fem*

**fountain** *noun*
la **fontaine** *fem*
- **fountain pen** un stylo à encre

**four** *number*
**quatre**
**Simon's four.** Simon a quatre ans.
**It's four o'clock.** Il est quatre heures.
**Sam was on all fours looking for his contact lens.** Sam était à quatre pattes pour chercher sa lentille de contact.

**fourteen** *number*
**quatorze**
**Susie's fourteen.** Susie a quatorze ans.

**fourth** *adjective*
1 **quatrième** *masc & fem*
**on the fourth floor** au quatrième étage
2 (*in dates*) **the fourth of July** le quatre juillet

**fox** *noun*
le **renard** *masc*

**fracture** *noun*
la **fracture** *fem*

♪ **fragile** *adjective*
**fragile** *masc & fem*

**frame** *noun*
1 (*of a picture*) le **cadre** *masc*
2 (*of a door*) un **encadrement** *masc*

♪ **franc** *noun*
le **franc** *masc* (*Switzerland's money; name of the money used in France, Belgium and Luxembourg before the euro; 100 French francs = 15.24 euros*)

♪ **France** *noun*
la **France** *fem*
**I like France.** J'aime la France.
**in France** en France
**They live in France.** Ils vivent en France.
**to France** en France
**She's going to France.** Elle part en France.
**Nadine's from France.** Nadine est française.

**WORD TIP** Countries and regions in French take *le, la* or *les.*

**frantic** *adjective*
1 (*very upset*) **fou** *masc*, **folle** *fem*
**Mum was frantic with worry.** Maman était folle d'inquiétude.
2 (*efforts, search*) **désespéré** *masc*, **désespérée** *fem*

**freckle** *noun*
la **tache de rousseur**

♪ **free** *adjective* ▷ **see free** *verb*
1 (*when you don't pay*) **gratuit** *masc*, **gratuite** *fem*
**The bus is free.** Le bus est gratuit.
**a free ticket** un billet gratuit
2 (*not occupied*) **libre** *masc & fem*
**Are you free on Thursday?** Es-tu libre jeudi?
3 **sugar-free** sans sucre
**lead-free** sans plomb

to **free** *verb* ▷ **see free** *adj*
**libérer [24]**

**freedom** *noun*
la **liberté** *fem*

**free gift** *noun*
le **cadeau** *masc* (*pl* les **cadeaux**)

**free kick** *noun*
le **coup franc**

♪ to **freeze** *verb*
1 (*in a freezer*) **congeler [45]**
**frozen peas** des petits pois congelés
2 (*in cold weather*) **geler [45]**
**It's freezing outside.** Il gèle dehors.

♪ **freezer** *noun*
le **congélateur** *masc*

**freezing** *adjective* ▷ see **freezing** *noun*
**I'm freezing.** Je suis gelé.
**It's freezing outside.** Il fait très froid dehors.

**freezing** *noun* ▷ see **freezing** *adj*
**zéro** *masc*
**Three degrees below freezing.** Trois degrés en-dessous de zéro.

♪ **French** *adjective* ▷ see **French** *noun*
1 **français** *masc*, **française** *fem*
**Jean-Marc is French.** Jean-Marc est français.
**Élodie is French.** Élodie est française.
2 (*teacher, lesson*) **de français**
**the French class** le cours de français

**WORD TIP** Adjectives never have capitals in French, even for nationality or regional origin.

♪ **French** *noun* ▷ see **French** *adj*
1 (*the language*) le **français** *masc*
**to speak French** parler français
**Say it in French.** Dis-le en français.
**to learn French** apprendre **[64]** le français
**Adam's learning French.** Adam apprend le français.
2 (*the people*) **the French** les Français *masc plural*
**most of the French** la plupart des Français
- **French bean** le haricot vert
- **French dressing** la vinaigrette
- **French fries** les frites *fem pl*
- **Frenchman** un Français
- **French stick** la baguette
- **Frenchwoman** une Française

**mini-info** ***French***
160 million people around the world speak French as their main language.

**frequent** *adjective*
**fréquent** *masc*, **fréquente** *fem*

**frequently** *adverb*
**souvent**

♪ **fresh** *adjective*
**frais** *masc*, **fraîche** *fem*
**fresh eggs** des œufs frais
**I'm going out for some fresh air.** Je vais prendre l'air.

♪ **Friday** *noun*
le **vendredi** *masc*
**next Friday** vendredi prochain
**last Friday** vendredi dernier
**on Friday** vendredi
**I'll phone you on Friday evening.** Je t'appellerai vendredi soir.
**on Fridays** le vendredi
**closed on Fridays** fermé le vendredi
**I see her every Friday.** Je la vois tous les vendredis.
**Good Friday** le Vendredi saint

**WORD TIP** Months of the year and days of the week start with small letters in French.

**fridge** *noun*
le **frigo** *masc*
**Put it in the fridge.** Mets-le au frigo.

♪ **friend** *noun*
un **ami** *masc*, une **amie** *fem*
**a friend of mine** un ami à moi (*a boy*), une amie à moi (*a girl*)
**to make friends** se faire ⓔ **[10]** des amis
**You'll soon make new friends.** Tu te feras vite de nouveaux amis.
**He made friends with Danny.** Il est devenu ami avec Danny.

**friendly** *adjective*
**sympathique** *masc & fem*

**friendship** *noun*
l'**amitié** *fem*

**fries** *plural noun*
les **frites** *fem plural*

**fright** *noun*
la **peur** *fem*
**to get a fright** avoir **[5]** peur
**I got such a fright.** J'ai eu tellement peur.
**You gave me a fright!** Tu m'as fait peur!

to **frighten** *verb*
**effrayer [59]**

♪ **frightened** *adjective*
**to be frightened** avoir **[5]** peur
**Martin's frightened of snakes.** Martin a peur des serpents.

**frightening** *adjective*
**effrayant** *masc*, **effrayante** *fem*

**fringe** *noun*
la **frange** *fem*

**frog** *noun*
la **grenouille** *fem*

♪ **from** *preposition*
**de**
**a letter from Tina** une lettre de Tina
**100 metres from the cinema** à cent mètres du cinéma
**from Monday to Friday** du lundi jusqu'au vendredi
**He comes from Dublin.** Il vient de Dublin.
**two years from now** d'ici deux ans ▸▸

from seven o'clock onwards à partir de sept heures

**WORD TIP** *de + le gives du. de + les gives des. de + a, e, i, o, u gives d'.*

**front** *adjective* ▷ see **front** *noun*
1 **de devant**
his front paw sa patte de devant
in the front row au premier rang
2 **avant**
the front seat (*of a car*) le siège avant
the front wheel la roue avant

**front** *noun* ▷ see **front** *adj*
1 (*of a building, garment*) le **devant** *masc*
2 (*of a car*) l'**avant** *masc*
He was sitting in the front. Il était assis à l'avant.
3 (*of a train, queue*) la **tête** *fem*
There are seats at the front of the train. Il y a des places en tête du train.
4 (*of a card, envelope*) le **recto** *masc*
The address is on the front. L'adresse est au recto.
5 (*in a theatre, cinema, class*) le **premier rang** *masc*
seats at the front des places au premier rang
6 in front of devant
in front of the TV devant la télé
Jack sat in front of me. Jack s'est assis devant moi.
• **front door** la porte d'entrée

**frontier** *noun*
la **frontière** *fem*

**frost** *noun*
le **gel** *masc*

**frosty** *adjective*
1 (*weather*)
It's frosty this morning. Il gèle ce matin.
2 (*windscreen, grass*) **couvert de givre** *masc*, **couverte de givre** *fem*

to **frown** *verb*
**froncer [61] les sourcils**
He frowned at us. Il nous a regardés en fronçant les sourcils.

**frozen** *adjective*
1 (*fingers, ground, lake*) **gelé** *masc*, **gelée** *fem*
2 (*food*) **surgelé** *masc*, **surgelée** *fem*

**fruit** *noun*
les **fruits** *masc plural*
I like fruit. J'aime les fruits.
a piece of fruit un fruit
fruit juice le jus de fruits
We bought cheese and fruit. Nous avons acheté du fromage et des fruits.
• **fruit machine** la machine à sous
• **fruit salad** la salade de fruits

**frustrated** *adjective*
**frustré** *masc*, **frustrée** *fem*

**frustrating** *adjective*
**frustrant** *masc*, **frustrante** *fem*

to **fry** *verb*
**faire [10] frire**
a fried egg un œuf au plat
We fried the fish. Nous avons fait frire les poissons.

**frying pan** *noun*
la **poêle** *fem*

**fuel** *noun*
(*for vehicles, planes*) le **carburant** *masc*

**full** *adjective*
1 (*in general*) **plein** *masc*, **pleine** *fem*
This glass is full. Ce verre est plein.
The train was full of tourists. Le train était plein de touristes.
I'm full. J'ai assez mangé.
2 (*hotels, flights*) **complet** *masc*, **complète** *fem*
3 (*in expressions*) at full speed à toute vitesse
at full volume à plein volume
Write your name out in full. Écris ton nom en toutes lettres.
• **full stop** le point

**full-time** *adjective* ▷ see **full time** *noun*
**à plein temps**
a full-time job un travail à plein temps

**full time** *noun* ▷ see **full-time** *adj*
(*in sport*) la **fin du match**

**fully** *adverb*
**entièrement**

**fun** *noun*
le **plaisir** *masc*
Skiing is fun. C'est amusant de faire du ski.
I do it for fun. Je le fais pour m'amuser.
to have fun s'amuser
Have fun! Amusez-vous bien!
We had lots of fun. Nous nous sommes beaucoup amusés.
to make fun of somebody se moquer ⓔ [1] de quelqu'un
They all made fun of her. Ils se sont tous moqués d'elle.

**funds** *plural noun*
les **fonds** *masc plural*

**funeral** *noun*
l'**enterrement** *masc*

**funfair** *noun*
la **fête foraine**

**funny** *adjective* (key word)
1 (*when you laugh*) **drôle** *masc & fem*
**How funny you are!** Que tu es drôle!
2 (*strange*) **bizarre** *masc & fem*
**a funny noise** un bruit bizarre
**That's funny, I'm sure I paid.** C'est bizarre, je suis certain d'avoir payé.

**fur** *noun*
1 (*animal's*) les **poils** *masc plural*
2 (*for coats*) la **fourrure** *fem*
**a fur coat** un manteau de fourrure

**furious** *adjective*
**furieux** *masc*, **furieuse** *fem*
**She's furious with Steve.** Elle est furieuse contre Steve.

**furniture** *noun* (key word)
les **meubles** *masc plural*
**a piece of furniture** un meuble
**I want to buy some furniture.** Je veux acheter des meubles.

**further** *adverb*
**plus loin**
**further than the station** plus loin que la gare
**ten kilometres further on** dix kilomètres plus loin
**further forward** plus en avant
**further back** plus en arrière

**fuse** *noun*
le **fusible** *masc*

**fuss** *noun*
**to make a fuss** faire **[10]** toute une histoire
**He made a fuss about the bill.** Il a fait toute une histoire à propos de l'addition.

**fussy** *adjective*
**difficile** *masc & fem*
**to be fussy about something** être **[6]** difficile sur quelque chose
**He's fussy about what he eats.** Il est difficile sur ce qu'il mange.

**future** *noun*
1 **l'avenir** *masc*
**in future** à l'avenir
**Be more careful in future!** Faites plus attention à l'avenir!
**in the future** dans l'avenir
**In the future we'll all have electric cars.** Dans l'avenir on aura tous les voitures électriques.
2 (*Grammar*) le **futur** *masc*
**a verb in the future** un verbe au futur

# G g

**gadget** *noun*
le **gadget** *masc*

to **gain** *verb*
1 **gagner [1]**
**We have nothing to gain.** Nous n'avons rien à gagner.
**in order to gain time** pour gagner du temps
2 **to gain speed** prendre **[64]** de la vitesse
**The car behind is gaining speed.** La voiture de derrière prend de la vitesse.
**to gain weight** prendre **[64]** du poids
**Hayley's gained five kilos.** Hayley a pris cinq kilos.

**galaxy** *noun*
la **galaxie** *fem*
**a galaxy of film stars** une constellation de vedettes

**gale** *noun*
le **vent violent**

**gallery** *noun*
**an art gallery** (*public*) un musée, (*private*) une galerie

to **gamble** *verb*
**jouer [1]**

**gambling** *noun*
le **jeu** *masc*

**game** *noun*
1 (*in general*) le **jeu** *masc*
**children's games** les jeux d'enfant
**a game of chance** un jeu de hasard
**a board game** un jeu de société
2 (*of cards*) la **partie de cartes**
**Let's have a game of cards.** Faisons une partie de cartes.
3 le **match** *masc*
**a game of football** un match de foot
4 **games** le sport *masc*
**Jack's very good at games.** Jack est très bon en sport.

**gang** *noun*
1 *(of friends)* la **bande** *fem*
**All the gang were there.** Toute la bande y était.
2 *(of criminals)* le **gang** *masc*

**gangster** *noun*
le **gangster** *masc*

**gap** *noun*
1 *(hole)* le **trou** *masc*
2 *(in time)* un **intervalle** *masc*
**a two-year gap** un intervalle de deux ans
3 *(difference)* la **différence** *fem*
**an age gap** une différence d'âge
- **gap year** une année sabbatique avant d'entrer à l'université

**garage** *noun*
le **garage** *masc*

**garden** *noun*
le **jardin** *masc*

**gardener** *noun*
le **jardinier** *masc*
**Paul wants to be a gardener.** Paul veut être jardinier.

**gardening** *noun*
le **jardinage** *masc*

**garlic** *noun*
l'**ail** *masc*
- **garlic mayonnaise** l'aïoli *masc*

**garment** *noun*
le **vêtement** *masc*

**gas** *noun*
le **gaz** *masc*
- **gas cooker** la cuisinière à gaz
- **gas fire** un appareil de chauffage au gaz
- **gas meter** le compteur à gaz

**gate** *noun*
1 *(in a garden)* le **portail** *masc*
2 *(in a field)* la **barrière** *fem*
3 *(at the airport)* la **porte** *fem*

to **gather** *verb*
1 *(people)* **se rassembler** Ⓔ **[1]**
**A crowd gathered.** Une foule s'est rassemblée.
2 *(fruit, vegetables, flowers)* **cueillir [35]**
3 *(to understand)* **As far as I can gather ...** Autant que je sache ...

**gay** *adjective*
**homosexuel** *masc*, **homosexuelle** *fem*

to **gaze** *verb*
**to gaze at something** regarder **[1]** quelque chose
**Joe was gazing longingly at the cake.** Joe regardait le gâteau avec convoitise.

**GCSEs** *plural noun*
*(You can explain GCSEs briefly as follows: Ce sont des examens que l'on passe à environ 16 ans dans un certain nombre de matières (12 au maximum). La meilleure note que l'on peut obtenir est A-star et la note la plus basse est N. Une fois qu'ils ont obtenu leurs GCSEs, de nombreux étudiants se préparent pour les A levels)*
▷ **A levels**

**gear** *noun*
1 *(in a car)* la **vitesse** *fem*
**to change gear** changer de vitesse
2 *(equipment)* le **matériel** *masc*
**camping gear** du matériel de camping
3 *(things)* les **affaires** *fem plural*
**I've left all my gear at Gary's.** J'ai laissé toutes mes affaires chez Gary.
- **gear lever** le levier de vitesses

**gel** *noun*
**hair gel** le gel pour les cheveux

**Gemini** *noun*
les **Gémeaux** *masc plural*
**Stuart's Gemini.** Stuart est Gémeaux.

**WORD TIP** Signs of the zodiac do not take an article: *un* or *une*.

**gender** *noun*
*(of a word)* le **genre** *masc*
**What is the gender of 'maison'?** Quel est le genre de 'maison'?

**general** *adjective* ▷ see **general** *noun*
**général** *masc*, **générale** *fem*, **généraux** *masc pl*, **générales** *fem pl*
**in general** en général
**I like fantasy books in general.** J'aime les romans fantastiques en général.
- **general election** les élections législatives
- **general knowledge** les connaissances générales

**general** *noun* ▷ see **general** *adj*
le **général** *masc* (*pl* les **généraux**)
**General Jackson** le général Jackson

**generally** *adverb*
**généralement**

**generation** *noun*
la **génération** *fem*

**generator** *noun*
le **générateur** *masc*

**generous** *adjective*
**généreux** *masc*, **généreuse** *fem*

**genetics** *noun*
la **génétique** *fem*

**Geneva** *noun*
**Genève**
**to Geneva** à Genève
**We went to Geneva in 1999.** Nous sommes allés à Genève en 1999.
**in Geneva** à Genève
**Sally works in Geneva.** Sally travaille à Genève.
**Lake Geneva** le lac Léman

**genius** *noun*
le **génie** *masc*
**Lisa, you're a genius!** Lisa, tu es un génie!

♪ **gentle** *adjective*
**doux** *masc*, **douce** *fem*

♪ **gentleman** *noun*
le **monsieur** *masc* (*pl* les **messieurs**)
**ladies and gentlemen** mesdames et messieurs

♪ **gently** *adverb*
**doucement**

**gents** *noun*
1 les **toilettes** *fem plural* **(pour hommes)**
**Where's the gents?** Où sont les toilettes?
2 (*men's toilets*) **'Messieurs'**

**genuine** *adjective*
1 (*real*) **véritable** *masc & fem*
**a genuine diamond** un véritable diamant
2 (*authentic*) **authentique** *masc & fem*
**a genuine signature** une signature authentique
3 (*person*) **sincère** *masc & fem*
**She's very genuine.** Elle est très sincère.

♪ **geography** *noun*
la **géographie** *fem*

**geology** *noun*
la **géologie** *fem*

**geometry** *noun*
la **géométrie** *fem*

**germ** *noun*
le **microbe** *masc*

**German** *adjective* ▷ **see German** *noun*
**allemand** *masc*, **allemande** *fem*
**a German car** une voiture allemande

**German** *noun* ▷ **see German** *adj*
1 un **Allemand** *masc*, une **Allemande** *fem*
**the Germans** les Allemands
2 (*the language*) l'**allemand** *masc*
**I speak German.** Je parle allemand.

**Germany** *noun*
l'**Allemagne** *fem*
**to Germany** en Allemagne
**in Germany** en Allemagne

♪ to **get** *verb*
1 (*to receive*) **avoir [5]**
**I got a bike for my birthday.** J'ai eu un vélo pour mon anniversaire.
**I got your letter yesterday.** J'ai eu ta lettre hier.
**I got fifteen for my French homework.** J'ai eu quinze pour mon devoir de français.
2 (*to have*) **have got** avoir **[5]**
**He's got lots of money.** Il a beaucoup d'argent.
**She's got long hair.** Elle a les cheveux longs.
3 (*to fetch*) **chercher [1]**
**I'll go and get some bread.** J'irai chercher du pain.
**I'll get your bag for you.** Je te chercherai ton sac.
4 (*to obtain*) **trouver [1]**
**Maya's got a job.** Maya a trouvé un emploi.
**Where did you get that jacket?** Où est-ce que tu as trouvé cette veste?
5 **to have got to do something** devoir **[8]** faire quelque chose
**I've got to phone before midday.** Je dois appeler avant midi.
6 **to get to somewhere** arriver Ⓔ **[1]** quelque part
**I rang when we got to London.** J'ai téléphoné quand nous sommes arrivés à Londres.
**to get here**, , **to get there** arriver Ⓔ **[1]**
**We got here this morning.** Nous sommes arrivés ce matin.
**What time did they get there?** Ils sont arrivés à quelle heure?
7 (*to become*) **commencer [61] à être**
**I'm getting tired.** Je commence à être fatigué (*boy speaking*), Je commence à être fatiguée (*girl speaking*).
**It's getting late.** Il se fait tard.
**It's getting dark.** Il commence à faire nuit.
**I'm getting hungry.** Je commence à avoir faim.
8 **to get something done** faire **[10]** faire quelque chose
**I'm getting my hair cut this afternoon.** Je vais me faire couper les cheveux cet après-midi.

• **to get back**
**rentrer** Ⓔ **[1]**
**Mum gets back at six.** Maman rentre à six heures.

• **to get something back**
**récupérer [24] quelque chose**
**Did you get your books back?** Est-ce que tu as récupéré tes livres? ⏩

English–French

- **to get into something**
  (*a car, lorry, taxi*) **monter Ⓔ [1] dans quelque chose**
  He got into the car. Il est monté dans la voiture.
- **to get off something**
  **descendre Ⓔ [3] de quelque chose**
  We got off the train at Bristol. Nous sommes descendus du train à Bristol.
- **to get on**
  **aller Ⓔ [7]**
  How's Amanda getting on? Comment va Amanda?
- **to get on something**
  (*a bus, train, plane*) **monter Ⓔ [1] dans quelque chose**
  She got on the train at Reading. Elle est montée dans le train à Reading.
- **to get on with somebody**
  **s'entendre [3] avec quelqu'un**
  Sita doesn't get on with her brother. Sita ne s'entend pas avec son frère.
- **to get out of something**
  (*a car, lorry, taxi*) **descendre Ⓔ [3] de quelque chose**
  Laura got out of the car. Laura est descendue de la voiture.
- **to get something out**
  **sortir [72] quelque chose**
  Robert got his guitar out. Robert a sorti sa guitare.
- **to get together**
  **se voir Ⓔ [13]**
  We must get together soon. Il faut qu'on se voie bientôt.
- **to get up**
  **se lever Ⓔ [50]**
  I get up at seven. Je me lève à sept heures.

**ghost** *noun*
le **fantôme** *masc*

**giant** *adjective* ▷ see **giant** *noun*
**énorme** *masc & fem*
a giant lorry un énorme camion

**giant** *noun* ▷ see **giant** *adj*
le **géant** *masc*, la **géante** *fem*

**giddy** *adjective*
to feel giddy avoir [5] la tête qui tourne
I'm feeling giddy. J'ai la tête qui tourne.

♪**gift** *noun*
1 le **cadeau** *masc* (*pl* les **cadeaux**)
a Christmas gift un cadeau de Noël
2 (*talent*) to have a gift for something avoir [5] un don pour quelque chose
Jenny has a real gift for languages. Jenny a vraiment un don pour les langues.

**gifted** *adjective*
**doué** *masc*, **douée** *fem*

**gig** *noun*
le **concert de rock**

**gigabyte** *noun*
le **gigaoctet** *masc*
a twenty gigabyte hard disk un disque dur de 20 gigaoctets

**gigantic** *adjective*
**gigantesque** *masc & fem*

**gin** *noun*
le **gin** *masc*

**ginger** *noun*
le **gingembre** *masc*

**gipsy** *noun*
1 (*in general*) le **bohémien** *masc*, la **bohémienne** *fem*
2 (*from Spain*) le **gitan** *masc*, la **gitane** *fem*
3 (*from Eastern Europe*) le & la **tzigane** *masc & fem*

**giraffe** *noun*
la **girafe** *fem*

♪**girl** *noun*
1 (*in general*) la **fille** *fem*
three boys and four girls trois garçons et quatre filles
a little girl une petite fille
when I was a little girl quand j'étais petite
2 (*teenager, young woman*) une **jeune fille** *fem*
an eighteen-year-old girl une jeune fille de dix-huit ans

♪**girlfriend** *noun*
la **copine** *fem*
Darren's gone out with his girlfriend. Darren est sorti avec sa copine.
Lizzie and her girlfriends have gone to the cinema. Lizzie et ses copines sont allées au cinéma.

♪to **give** *verb*
**donner [1]**
to give something to somebody, , to give somebody something donner quelque chose à quelqu'un
She gave her address to me. Elle m'a donné son adresse.
Give me the key. Donne-moi la clé.
Yasmin's dad gave her the money. Le père de Yasmin lui a donné l'argent.
- **to give something away**
  **donner quelque chose**
  She's given away all her books. Elle a donné tous ses livres.



Ⓔ means the verb takes être to form the perfect

- **to give something back to somebody**
  **rendre [3] quelque chose à quelqu'un**
  I gave her back the keys. Je lui ai rendu les clés.
- **to give in**
  **céder [24]**
  My mum said no but she gave in in the end. Maman a dit non, mais elle a fini par céder.
- **to give up**
  **abandonner [1]**
  I give up! J'abandonne!
- **to give up doing something**
  **arrêter [1] de faire quelque chose**
  She's given up smoking. Elle a arrêté de fumer.

**glacier** *noun*
le **glacier** *masc*

**glad** *adjective*
**content** *masc*, **contente** *fem*
I'm glad to hear he's better. Je suis content d'apprendre qu'il va mieux (*boy speaking*)
I'm glad to be back. Je suis contente d'être de retour (*girl speaking*).

**glamorous** *adjective*
1 (*life*) **luxueux** *masc*, **luxueuse** *fem*
2 (*job*) **prestigieux** *masc*, **prestigieuse** *fem*
3 (*woman*) **élégant** *masc*, **élégante** *fem*

**glance** *noun* ▷ see **glance** *verb*
un **coup d'œil** *masc*

**glance** *verb* ▷ see **glance** *noun*
to glance at something jeter **[48]** un coup d'œil à quelque chose
Sara glanced at the envelope. Sara a jeté un coup d'œil à l'enveloppe.

**glass** *adjective* ▷ see **glass** *noun*
**en verre**
a glass table une table en verre

**glass** *noun* ▷ see **glass** *adj*
le **verre** *masc*
a glass of water un verre d'eau

**glasses** *plural noun*
les **lunettes** *fem plural*
to wear glasses porter des lunettes
Does Katie wear glasses? Est-ce que Katie porte des lunettes?

**glider** *noun*
le **planeur** *masc*

**global** *adjective*
**mondial** *masc*, **mondiale** *fem*, **mondiaux** *masc pl*, **mondiales** *fem pl*

**global warming** *noun*
le **réchauffement de la planète**

**globe** *noun*
le **globe** *masc*

**gloomy** *adjective*
1 (*expression*) **lugubre** *masc & fem*
2 (*weather*) **déprimant** *masc*, **déprimante** *fem*

**glory** *noun*
la **gloire** *fem*

**glove** *noun*
le **gant** *masc*
a pair of gloves une paire de gants
- **glove compartment** la boîte à gants

**glue** *noun*
la **colle** *fem*

**go** *noun* ▷ see **go** *verb*
1 (*turn*) **Whose go is it?** C'est à qui de jouer?
**It's my go.** C'est à moi de jouer.
2 (*a try*) **to have a go at doing something**
essayer **[59]** de faire quelque chose
**I'll have a go at mending it for you.** Je vais essayer de te le réparer.

**to go** *verb* ▷ see **go** *noun*
1 (*in general*) **aller** Ⓔ **[7]**
**We're going to London tomorrow.** Nous allons à Londres demain.
**Mark's gone to the dentist's.** Mark est allé chez le dentiste.
**Beth's gone home.** Beth est rentrée chez elle.
**to go for a walk** aller Ⓔ **[7]** se promener
**We went for a walk on the beach.** Nous sommes allés nous promener sur la plage.
2 **to be going to do something** aller Ⓔ **[7]** faire quelque chose
**I'm going to make some coffee.** Je vais faire du café.
**He was going to phone me.** Il allait m'appeler.
3 (*to leave*) **partir** Ⓔ **[58]**
**Pam's already gone.** Pam est déjà partie.
**We're going on holiday tomorrow.** Nous partons en vacances demain.
4 (*parties, meetings, events*) **se passer [1]**
**Did the party go well?** Est-ce que la soirée s'est bien passée?
- **to go away**
  **s'en aller** Ⓔ **[7]**
  **He's going away.** Il s'en va.
  **She's gone away.** Elle est partie.
  **Go away!** Va-t'en!
- **to go back**
  1 **retourner** Ⓔ **[1]**
  **I'm going back to France in March.** En mars je retourne en France. ▸▸

a b c d e f g h i j k l m n o p q r s t u v w x y z

English–French

I'm not going back there again! Je n'y retourne plus!

2 (*to home, school, office*) **rentrer** Ⓔ [1]
**She went back home.** Elle est rentrée chez moi.

• **to go down**

1 **descendre** Ⓔ [3]
**She's gone down to the kitchen.** Elle est descendue dans la cuisine.
**to go down the stairs** descendre l'escalier
**You go down the stairs, then turn left.** Vous descendez l'escalier puis vous tournez à gauche.

2 (*prices, temperature*) **baisser** [1]
**Prices have gone down.** Les prix ont baissé.

3 (*tyres, balloons, etc*) **se dégonfler** Ⓔ [1]

• **to go in**

**entrer** Ⓔ [1]
**He went in and shut the door.** Il est entré et il a fermé la porte.

• **to go into something**

1 (*person*) **entrer** Ⓔ [1] **dans quelque chose**
**Fran went into the kitchen.** Fran est entrée dans la cuisine.

2 (*thing*) **rentrer** Ⓔ [1] **dans quelque chose**
**This file won't go into my bag.** Ce classeur ne rentre pas dans mon sac.

• **to go off**

1 **exploser** [1]
**A bomb went off in the city centre.** Une bombe a explosé dans le centre-ville.

2 (*alarm clocks*) **sonner** [1]
**My alarm clock went off at six.** Mon réveil a sonné à six heures.

3 (*fire alarms, burglar alarms*) **se déclencher** Ⓔ [1]
**The fire alarm went off.** L'alarme d'incendie s'est déclenchée.

• **to go on**

1 (*to happen*) **se passer** Ⓔ [1]
**What's going on?** Qu'est-ce qui se passe?

2 (*to continue*) **to go on doing something** continuer [1] à faire quelque chose
**She went on talking.** Elle a continué à parler.

3 **to go on about something** ne pas arrêter [1] de parler de quelque chose
**Rob's always going on about his dog.** Rob n'arrête pas de parler de son chien.

• **to go out**

1 **sortir** Ⓔ [72]
**I'm going out tonight.** Je sors ce soir.
**She went out of the kitchen.** Elle est sortie de la cuisine.

2 (*light, fire*) **s'éteindre** Ⓔ [60]
**The light went out.** La lumière s'est éteinte.

• **to go out with somebody sortir** Ⓔ [72] **avec quelqu'un**
**Anna's going out with my brother.** Anna sort avec mon frère.

• **to go past something**

**passer** Ⓔ [1] **devant quelque chose**
**We went past your house.** Nous sommes passés devant chez toi.

• **to go round**

**to go round to somebody's house** aller Ⓔ [7] chez quelqu'un
**I went round to Imran's last night.** Je suis allé chez Imran hier soir.

• **to go round something**

1 (*a building, garden, park*) **faire [10] le tour de quelque chose**

2 (*a museum, monument*) **visiter** [1] **quelque chose**

• **to go through something**

**passer** Ⓔ [1] **par quelque chose**
**This train goes through Dijon.** Ce train passe par Dijon.
**You can go through my office.** Tu peux passer par mon bureau.

• **to go up**

1 (*people*) **monter** Ⓔ [1]
**She's gone up to her room.** Elle est montée dans sa chambre.
**to go up the stairs** monter l'escalier
**I saw someone going up the stairs.** J'ai vu quelqu'un qui montait l'escalier.

2 (*prices*) **augmenter** [1]
**The price of petrol has gone up.** Le prix de l'essence a augmenté.

**goal** *noun*
le **but** *masc*
**to score a goal** marquer un but
**Adam scored two goals!** Adam a marqué deux buts!
**We won by three goals to two.** On a gagné trois buts à deux.
• **goalkeeper** le gardien de but

**goat** *noun*
la **chèvre** *fem*
**goat's cheese** le fromage de chèvre

**god** *noun* ▷ see **God** *noun*
le **dieu** *masc* (*pl* les **dieux**)

**God** *noun* ▷ see **god** *noun*
le **Dieu** *masc*
**to believe in God** croire en Dieu
**Do you believe in God?** Est-ce que tu crois en Dieu?
• **goddaughter** la filleule *fem*

**goddess** *noun*
la **déesse** *fem*

**godfather** *noun*
le **parrain** *masc*

**godmother** *noun*
la **marraine** *fem*

**godson** *noun*
le **filleul** *masc*

**goggles** *plural noun*
les **lunettes** *fem plural*
**swimming goggles** les lunettes de plongée
**skiing goggles** les lunettes de ski

**go-karting** *noun*
le **karting** *masc*
**to go go-karting** faire [10] du karting
**I love to go go-karting with my friends.** J'aime bien faire du karting avec mes amis.

**gold** *adjective* ▷ see **gold** *noun*
**en or**
**a gold bracelet** un bracelet en or

**gold** *noun* ▷ see **gold** *adj*
l'**or** *masc*
- **goldfish** le poisson rouge

**golf** *noun*
le **golf** *masc*
**to play golf** jouer [1] au golf
**More young people are playing golf.** De plus en plus de jeunes jouent au golf.

**golf club** *noun*
*(place, stick)* le **club de golf**

**golf course** *noun*
le **terrain de golf**

**golfer** *noun*
le **golfeur** *masc*, la **golfeuse** *fem*

♪ **good** *adjective*
1 *(in general)* **bon** *masc*, **bonne** *fem*
**She's a good teacher.** C'est un bon professeur.
**The cherries are very good.** Les cerises sont très bonnes.
2 **to be good for you** être [6] bon pour la santé
**Tomatoes are good for you.** Les tomates sont bonnes pour la santé.
3 **to be good at something** être [6] bon *masc* en quelque chose, être bonne *fem* en quelque chose
**She's good at art.** Elle est bonne en dessin.
4 *(well-behaved)* **sage** *masc & fem*
**Be good!** Sois sage!
5 *(kind)* **gentil** *masc*, **gentille** *fem*
**She's been very good to me.** Elle a été très gentille avec moi.
6 **for good** pour de bon
**I've stopped smoking for good.** J'ai arrêté de fumer pour de bon.
- **good afternoon** bonjour
- **goodbye** au revoir
- **good evening** bonsoir
- **Good Friday** le Vendredi saint

**good-looking** *adjective*
**beau** *masc*, **belle** *fem*, **beaux** *masc pl*, **belles** *fem pl*
**Maria's boyfriend is really good-looking.** Le copain de Maria est très beau.

**good morning** *exclamation*
**bonjour**

**goodness** *exclamation*
**mon Dieu!**
**For goodness sake!** Au nom du ciel!

**good night** *exclamation*
**bonne nuit**

**goods** *plural noun*
les **marchandises** *fem plural*
- **goods train** le train de marchandises

**goose** *noun*
une **oie** *fem*
- **goose pimples** la chair de poule

**gorgeous** *adjective*
**superbe** *masc & fem*
**a gorgeous dress** une robe superbe
**It's a gorgeous day.** Il fait un temps superbe.

**gorilla** *noun*
le **gorille** *masc*

**gorse** *noun*
les **ajoncs** *masc plural*

**gosh** *exclamation*
**ça alors!**

**gossip** *noun* ▷ see **gossip** *verb*
1 *(person)* le **bavard** *masc*, la **bavarde** *fem*
2 *(news)* les **nouvelles** *fem plural*
**What's the latest gossip?** Quoi de neuf?

**gossip** *verb* ▷ see **gossip** *noun*
**bavarder** [1]

**government** *noun*
le **gouvernement** *masc*

to **grab** *verb*
1 **saisir** [2]
**She grabbed my arm.** Elle m'a saisi par le bras.
2 *(to take away)* **to grab something from somebody** arracher [1] quelque chose à quelqu'un
**He grabbed the book from me.** Il m'a arraché le livre.

**graceful** *adjective*
**élégant** *masc*, **élégante** *fem*

English-French

**grade** *noun*
(*mark*) la **note** *fem*
to get good grades avoir [5] de bonnes notes
Kat always gets good grades. Kat a toujours de bonnes notes.

**gradual** *adjective*
**progressif** *masc*, **progressive** *fem*

**gradually** *adverb*
**petit à petit**
The weather got gradually better. Le temps s'est amélioré petit à petit.

**graffiti** *plural noun*
les **graffiti** *masc plural*

**grain** *noun*
le **grain** *masc*

**grammar** *noun*
la **grammaire** *fem*

**grammar school** *noun*
1 (*from age 11 to 15*) le **collège** *masc*
2 (*from age 15 to 18*) le **lycée** *masc*

**grammatical** *adjective*
a grammatical error une faute de grammaire

♪ **gramme** *noun*
le **gramme** *masc*

**gran** *noun*
la **mamie** *fem*

♪ **grandchildren** *plural noun*
les **petits-enfants** *masc plural*

**granddad** *noun*
le **papy** *masc*

♪ **granddaughter** *noun*
la **petite-fille** *fem*

♪ **grandfather** *noun*
le **grand-père** *masc*

**grandma** *noun*
la **mamie** *fem*

♪ **grandmother** *noun*
la **grand-mère** *fem*

**grandpa** *noun*
le **papi** *masc*

♪ **grandparents** *plural noun*
les **grands-parents** *masc plural*

♪ **grandson** *noun*
le **petit-fils** *masc*

**granny** *noun*
la **mamie** *fem*

♪ **grape** *noun*
a grape un grain de raisin
to buy some grapes acheter du raisin
Do you like grapes? Est-ce que tu aimes le raisin?
a bunch of grapes une grappe de raisin

**grapefruit** *noun*
le **pamplemousse** *masc*

**graph** *noun*
le **graphique** *masc*

**graphic designer** *noun*
le & la **graphiste** *masc & fem*

**graphics** *noun*
la **visualisation graphique**

to **grasp** *verb*
**saisir** [2]

♪ **grass** *noun*
1 l'**herbe** *fem*
Ben was sitting on the grass. Ben était assis dans l'herbe.
2 (*lawn*) la **pelouse** *fem*
to cut the grass tondre la pelouse
Could you cut the grass this afternoon? Pourrais-tu tondre la pelouse cet après-midi?
• **grasshopper** la sauterelle

to **grate** *verb*
**râper** [1]
grated cheese du fromage râpé

**grateful** *adjective*
**reconnaissant** *masc*, **reconnaissante** *fem*

**grater** *noun*
la **râpe** *fem*

**grave** *noun*
1 (*burial site*) la **tombe** *fem*
2 (*Grammar*) un **accent grave** (*as in grève*)

**gravel** *noun*
les **gravillons** *masc plural*

**graveyard** *noun*
le **cimetière** *masc*

**gravity** *noun*
la **pesanteur** *fem*

**gravy** *noun*
la **sauce (au jus de rôti)**

**grease** *noun*
la **graisse** *fem*

♪ **greasy** *adjective*
**gras** *masc*, **grasse** *fem*
to have greasy skin avoir [5] la peau grasse
I hate greasy food. Je déteste la nourriture grasse.

♪ **great** *adjective*
1 **grand** *masc*, **grande** *fem*
a great poet un grand poète

2 (*terrific*) **génial** *masc*, **géniale** *fem*, **géniaux** *masc pl*, **géniales** *fem pl*
It was a great party! Ça a été une soirée géniale!
Great! Génial!
3 a great deal of something beaucoup de quelque chose
a great deal of money beaucoup d'argent
a great many beaucoup de
There are a great many things still to be done. Il reste encore beaucoup de choses à faire.

**Great Britain** *noun*
la **Grande-Bretagne** *fem*
to Great Britain en Grande-Bretagne
Many tourists come to Great Britain. Beaucoup de touristes viennent en Grande-Bretagne.
in Great Britain en Grande-Bretagne
There are beautiful places to visit in Great Britain. Il y a des beaux endroits à visiter en Grande-Bretagne.
to be from Great Britain être [6] britannique
Todd's grandparents were from Great Britain. Les grands-parents de Todd étaient britanniques.

**WORD TIP** Countries and regions in French take *le*, *la* or *les*.

**Greece** *noun*
la **Grèce** *fem*
to go to Greece aller ❷ [7] en Grèce
to be in Greece être [6] en Grèce

**greedy** *adjective*
(*with food*) **gourmand** *masc*, **gourmande** *fem*

**Greek** *noun* ▷ see **Greek** *adj*
1 (*person*) un **Grec** *masc*, une **Grecque** *fem*
2 (*the language*) le **grec** *masc*

**Greek** *adjective* ▷ see **Greek** *noun*
**grec** *masc*, **grecque** *fem*

♪ **green** *adjective* ▷ see **green** *noun*
1 **vert** *masc*, **verte** *fem*
a green door une porte verte
2 **écologiste** *masc & fem*
the Green Party le parti écologiste

♪ **green** *noun* ▷ see **green** *adj*
1 (*colour*) le **vert** *masc*
a pale green un vert pâle
2 (*vegetables*) greens les légumes verts
3 (*Politics*) the Greens les Verts *masc plural*

**greengrocer** *noun*
le **marchand de fruits et légumes**

**greenhouse** *noun*
la **serre** *fem*
• **greenhouse effect** l'effet de serre *masc*

**greetings** *plural noun*
Season's Greetings! Meilleurs vœux! *masc plural*
• **greetings card** la carte de vœux

♪ **grey** *adjective*
**gris** *masc*, **grise** *fem*
a grey skirt une jupe grise
to have grey hair avoir [5] les cheveux gris

**greyhound** *noun*
le **lévrier** *masc*

**grid** *noun*
1 (*grating*) la **grille** *fem*
2 (*network*) le **réseau** *masc* (*pl* les **réseaux**)

**grief** *noun*
le **chagrin** *masc*

**grill** *noun* ▷ see **grill** *verb*
(*of a cooker*) le **gril** *masc*

to **grill** *verb* ▷ see **grill** *noun*
to grill something faire [10] griller quelque chose
I grilled the sausages. J'ai fait griller les saucisses.

**grim** *adjective*
**sinistre** *masc & fem*

**grin** *noun* ▷ see **grin** *verb*
le **sourire** *masc*

to **grin** *verb* ▷ see **grin** *noun*
**sourire** [68]

**grip** *noun* ▷ see **grip** *verb*
la **prise** *fem*

to **grip** *verb* ▷ see **grip** *noun*
**serrer** [1]

**grit** *noun*
(*for roads*) les **gravillons** *masc pl*

**groan** *noun* ▷ see **groan** *verb*
1 (*of pain*) le **gémissement** *masc*
2 (*of disgust, boredom*) le **grognement** *masc*

to **groan** *verb* ▷ see **groan** *noun*
1 (*in pain*) **gémir** [2]
2 (*in disgust, boredom*) **grogner** [1]

♪ **grocer** *noun*
un **épicier** *masc*, une **épicière** *fem*
My dad's a grocer. Mon père est épicier.

♪ **groceries** *plural noun*
les **provisions** *fem pl*
to buy some groceries faire [10] ses provisions

**grocer's** *noun*
une **épicerie** *fem*
**I met Jake in the grocer's.** J'ai rencontré Jake à l'épicerie.

**groom** *noun*
(*bridegroom*) le **marié** *masc*
**the bride and groom** les jeunes mariés

**gross** *adjective*
1 **a gross injustice** une injustice flagrante
2 **a gross error** une erreur grossière
3 (*disgusting*) **dégoûtant** *masc*, **dégoûtante** *fem*
**The food was gross!** La nourriture était dégoûtante!

**ground** *adjective* ▷ see **ground** *noun, verb*
**moulu** *masc*, **moulue** *fem*
**ground coffee** du café moulu

**ground** *noun* ▷ see **ground** *adj, verb*
1 la **terre** *fem*
**to sit on the ground** s'asseoir par terre
**The children were sitting on the ground.** Les enfants étaient assis par terre.
**to throw something on the ground** jeter quelque chose par terre
**Jim threw the book on the ground.** Jim a jeté le livre par terre.
2 (*for sport*) le **terrain** *masc*
**a football ground** un terrain de foot

to **ground** *verb* ▷ see **ground** *adj, noun*
**priver** [1] **quelqu'un de sorties**
**You're grounded for a week!** Tu es privé de sorties pendant une semaine!

**ground floor** *noun*
le **rez-de-chaussée** *masc*
**They live on the ground floor.** Ils habitent au rez-de-chaussée.

**group** *noun*
le **groupe** *masc*

to **grow** *verb*
1 (*plant, hair*) **pousser** [1]
**Your hair's grown!** Tes cheveux ont poussé!
2 (*person*) **grandir** [2]
**My little sister's grown a lot this year.** Ma petite sœur a beaucoup grandi cette année.
3 (*numbers*) **augmenter** [1]
**The number of students has grown.** Le nombre d'étudiants a augmenté.
4 (*a plant, fruit, vegetables*) **faire** [10] **pousser**
**Our neighbours grow strawberries.** Nos voisins font pousser des fraises.
5 **to grow a beard** se laisser Ⓔ [1] pousser la barbe
6 **to grow old** vieillir [2]
**Granddad's growing old.** Papy vieillit.
• **to grow up**
**grandir** [2]
**The children are growing up.** Les enfants grandissent.
**She grew up in Scotland.** Elle a grandi en Écosse.

to **growl** *verb*
**grogner** [1]

**grown-up** *noun*
l'**adulte** *masc & fem*

**growth** *noun*
la **croissance** *fem*

**grudge** *noun*
**to bear a grudge against somebody** en vouloir à quelqu'un
**She bears me a grudge.** Elle m'en veut.

**gruesome** *adjective*
**horrible** *masc & fem*

to **grumble** *verb*
**se plaindre** Ⓔ [31]
**She's always grumbling.** Elle est toujours en train de se plaindre.
**to grumble about something** se plaindre de quelque chose
**Stop grumbling about the weather.** Arrête de te plaindre du temps.

**guarantee** *noun* ▷ see **guarantee** *verb*
la **garantie** *fem*
**a year's guarantee** une garantie d'un an

**guarantee** *verb* ▷ see **guarantee** *noun*
**garantir** [2]

**guard** *noun* ▷ see **guard** *verb*
1 **a prison guard** un gardien de prison
2 (*on a train*) le **chef de train**
3 **a security guard** un vigile

to **guard** *verb* ▷ see **guard** *noun*
**surveiller** [1]
• **guard dog** le chien de garde

**guardian** *noun*
(*of child*) le **tuteur** *masc*, la **tutrice** *fem*

**guess** *noun* ▷ see **guess** *verb*
**Have a guess!** Devine!
**It's a good guess.** Tu as deviné.

to **guess** *verb* ▷ see **guess** *noun*
**deviner** [1]
**Guess who I saw last night!** Devine qui j'ai vu hier soir!
**You'll never guess!** Tu ne devineras jamais!

**guest** *noun*
1 un **invité** *masc*, une **invitée** *fem*
**We've got guests coming tonight.** Nous avons des invités ce soir.
2 (*in a hotel*) le **client** *masc*, la **cliente** *fem*
3 (*in somebody's home*) **a paying guest** un hôte payant

**guesthouse** *noun*
la **pension de famille**

ɗ **guide** *noun*
1 (*person, book*) le **guide** *masc*
2 (*girl guide*) la **guide** *fem*
- **guidebook** le guide
- **guide dog** le chien d'aveugle
- **guideline** une indication

**guilty** *adjective*
**coupable** *masc & fem*
**to feel guilty** se sentir ❷ [58] coupable
**It wasn't my fault but I feel guilty.** Ce n'était pas ma faute mais je me sens coupable.

**guinea pig** *noun*
1 (*pet*) le **cochon d'Inde**
2 (*in an experiment*) le **cobaye** *masc*
**They want me to be a guinea pig.** Ils veulent que je serve de cobaye.

**guitar** *noun*
la **guitare** *fem*
**to play the guitar** jouer [1] de la guitare
**I can play the guitar.** Je sais jouer de la guitare.
**on the guitar** à la guitare

**guitarist** *noun*
le & la **guitariste** *masc & fem*

**gum** *noun*
1 (*in your mouth*) la **gencive** *fem*
2 (*chewing gum*) le **chewing-gum** *masc*

**gun** *noun*
1 le **revolver** *masc*
2 (*rifle*) le **fusil** *masc*

**gust** *noun*
**a gust of wind** une rafale de vent

**gutter** *noun*
(*in the street*) le **caniveau** *masc* (*pl* les **caniveaux**)

**guy** *noun*
le **type** *masc* (*informal*)
**a guy from Newcastle** un type qui vient de Newcastle
**He's a nice guy.** C'est un type sympa.
- **guy rope** la corde d'attache

ɗ **gym** *noun*
la **gym** *fem*
**to go to the gym** aller ❷ [7] à la gym
**Alex goes to the gym three times a week.** Alex va à la gym trois fois par semaine.

**gymnasium** *noun*
le **gymnase** *masc*

**gymnast** *noun*
le & la **gymnaste** *masc & fem*

**gymnastics** *noun*
la **gymnastique** *fem*

**gym shoe** *noun*
la **chaussure de gym**

# H h

ɗ **habit** *noun*
une **habitude** *fem*
**It's a bad habit.** C'est une mauvaise habitude.
**to be in the habit of doing something** avoir [5] l'habitude de faire quelque chose

**haddock** *noun*
un **églefin** *masc*
**smoked haddock** le haddock

**hail** *noun*
la **grêle** *fem*

**hailstone** *noun*
le **grêlon** *masc*

**hailstorm** *noun*
une **averse de grêle**

ɗ **hair** *noun*
1 (*one hair on your head*) un **cheveu**
2 (*one hair on your body*) un **poil**
3 (*those on your head*) **les cheveux** *masc plural*
**to have short hair** avoir [5] les cheveux courts
**Lucy has long hair.** Lucy a les cheveux longs.
**She's brushing her hair.** Elle se brosse les cheveux.
**Gita washes her hair every day.** Gita se lave les cheveux tous les jours. ⏩

She's had her hair cut. Elle s'est fait couper les cheveux.
- **hairbrush** la brosse à cheveux
- **haircut** la coupe

**hairdresser** *noun*
le **coiffeur** *masc*, la **coiffeuse** *fem*
She's a hairdresser. Elle est coiffeuse.
Mum's at the hairdresser's. Maman est chez le coiffeur.

**hairdrier** *noun*
le **sèche-cheveux** *masc*

**hairgel** *noun*
le **gel pour les cheveux**

**hairgrip** *noun*
la **pince à cheveux**

**hair remover** *noun*
la **crème dépilatoire**

**hairslide** *noun*
la **barrette** *fem*

**hairspray** *noun*
la **laque** *fem*

**hairstyle** *noun*
la **coiffure** *fem*

**hairy** *adjective*
**poilu** *masc*, **poilue** *fem*

**Haiti** *noun*
**Haïti** *masc*

**WORD TIP** Unlike other names of countries, *Haïti* does not take *le* or *la*.

**Haitian** *adjective* ▷ see **Haitian** *noun*
**haïtien** *masc*, **haïtienne** *fem*

**Haitian** *noun* ▷ see **Haitian** *adj*
un **Haïtien** *masc*, une **Haïtienne** *fem*

♂**half** *noun*
1 (*of something*) la **moitié** *fem*
half an apple la moitié d'une pomme
half of the money la moitié de l'argent
You've only eaten half of it. Tu n'en as mangé que la moitié.
half the people la moitié des gens
2 (*as a fraction*) **demi**
three and a half trois et demi
She's five and a half. Elle a cinq ans et demi.
to cut something in half couper **[1]** quelque chose en deux
3 (*when telling the time*) **demi** *masc*, **demie** *fem*
half an hour une demi-heure
an hour and a half une heure et demie
It's half past three. Il est trois heures et demie.
4 (*in weights and measures*) **demi** *masc*, **demie** *fem*
half a litre un demi-litre
half a cup une demi-tasse
a litre and a half un litre et demi

**half hour** *noun*
la **demi-heure** *fem*
every half hour toutes les demi-heures

**half-price** *adjective, adverb*
**à moitié prix**
half-price CDs des CD à moitié prix
I bought it half price. Je l'ai acheté à moitié prix.

**half time** *noun*
la **mi-temps** *fem*
at half time à la mi-temps

**halfway** *adverb*
1 (*in distance*) **à mi-chemin**
halfway between Paris and Dijon à mi-chemin entre Paris et Dijon
2 (*in time*) to be halfway through something avoir **[5]** à moitié fini quelque chose
I'm halfway through my homework. J'ai à moitié fini mes devoirs.

♂**hall** *noun*
1 (*in a house*) une **entrée** *fem*
2 (*for meetings, events*) la **salle** *fem*
the village hall la salle des fêtes

**Hallowe'en** *noun*
**la veille de la Toussaint** (*Hallowe'en is not celebrated in France.*)

♂**ham** *noun*
le **jambon** *masc*
a slice of ham une tranche de jambon
a ham sandwich un sandwich au jambon

**hamburger** *noun*
un **hamburger** *masc*

**hammer** *noun*
le **marteau** *masc* (*pl* les **marteaux**)

**hammock** *noun*
un **hamac** *masc*

**hamster** *noun*
un **hamster** *masc*

♂**hand** *noun* ▷ see **hand** *verb*
1 (*part of the body*) la **main** *fem*
to have something in your hand avoir **[5]** quelque chose à la main
to hold somebody's hand tenir **[77]** quelqu'un par la main
They were holding hands. Ils se tenaient par la main.
2 (*help*) a hand un coup de main
Can you give me a hand? Est-ce que tu peux me donner un coup de main?
Do you need a hand? Est-ce que tu as besoin d'un coup de main?

3 (*of a watch, clock*) une **aiguille** *fem*
the hour hand l'aiguille des heures

♪ to **hand** *verb* ▷ see **hand** *noun*
**passer [1]**
I handed him the keys. Je lui ai passé les clés.
- **to hand something in**
**rendre [3] quelque chose**
I've handed in my homework. J'ai rendu mon devoir.
- **to hand something out**
**distribuer [1] quelque chose**
Claire handed out the exercise books. Claire a distribué les cahiers.
- **handbag** le sac à main (*pl* les sacs à main)
- **handcuffs** les menottes *fem pl*

**handful** *noun*
**poignée** *fem*
a handful of something une poignée de quelque chose

**handicapped** *adjective*
**handicapé** *masc*, **handicapée** *fem*

♪ **handkerchief** *noun*
le **mouchoir** *masc*

**handle** *noun* ▷ see **handle** *verb*
1 (*of a door, drawer*) la **poignée** *fem*
2 (*of a knife, tool*) le **manche** *masc*
3 (*of a frying pan, saucepan*) la **queue** *fem*
4 (*of a cup, basket*) une **anse** *fem*

to **handle** *verb* ▷ see **handle** *noun*
1 **s'occuper [1] de**
Gina handles the accounts. Gina s'occupe de la comptabilité.
Leave it to me, I can handle it. Laisse-moi faire, je peux m'en occuper.
She's good at handling people. Elle a un bon contact avec les gens.

**handlebars** *plural noun*
le **guidon** *masc*

**hand luggage** *noun*
les **bagages à main** *masc plural*

**handmade** *adjective*
**fait à la main** *masc*, **faite à la main** *fem*

♪ **handsome** *adjective*
**beau** *masc*, **belle** *fem*, **beaux** *masc pl*, **belles** *fem pl*
He's a handsome guy. C'est un beau type.

**handwriting** *noun*
l'**écriture** *fem*

♪ **handy** *adjective*
1 (*useful*) **pratique** *masc & fem*
This bag's very handy. Ce sac est très pratique.
2 (*nearby*) **sous la main**
I keep a notebook handy. Je garde un calepin sous la main.

♪ to **hang** *verb*
1 (*to be hanging*) **être [6] accroché**
A painting was hanging on the wall. Une peinture était accrochée au mur.
A light hung from the ceiling. Une lumière pendait du plafond.
2 (*a picture, a painting*) **accrocher [1]**
We hung the mirror on the wall. Nous avons accroché le miroir au mur.
- **to hang around**
**traîner [1]**
We were hanging around in the street. On traînait dans la rue.
- **to hang on**
**attendre [3]**
Hang on a second! Attends une seconde!
- **to hang up**
(*on the phone*) **raccrocher [1]**
She hung up on me. Elle m'a raccroché au nez.
Do not hang up. Ne quittez pas.
- **to hang something up**
**accrocher [1] quelque chose**
Hang your coat up. Accroche ton manteau.

**hang-gliding** *noun*
le **deltaplane** *masc*
to go hang-gliding faire **[10]** du deltaplane

**hangover** *noun*
la **gueule de bois**
to have a hangover avoir **[5]** la gueule de bois

to **happen** *verb*
**se passer ❷ [1]**
What's happening? Qu'est-ce qui se passe?
It happened in June. Ça s'est passé en juin.
What happened at school? Qu'est-ce qui s'est passé à l'école?

**happily** *adverb*
1 (*cheerfully*) **joyeusement**
2 (*willingly*) **volontiers**
I'll happily do it for you. Je le ferai pour toi volontiers.

**happiness** *noun*
le **bonheur** *masc*

♪ **happy** *adjective*
**heureux** *masc*, **heureuse** *fem*
a happy child un enfant heureux
a happy family une famille heureuse
Happy Birthday! Bon anniversaire!

♪ **harbour** *noun*
le **port** *masc*

♪ indicates keywords

ꝺ **hard** *adjective* ▷ see **hard** *adv*

1 (*not soft*) **dur** *masc*, **dure** *fem*
to go hard durcir
The cheese has gone hard. Le fromage a durci.

2 (*difficult*) **difficile** *masc & fem*
a hard question une question difficile
It's hard to know ... Il est difficile de savoir ...

ꝺ **hard** *adverb* ▷ see **hard** *adj*

1 to work hard travailler dur
He works hard. Il travaille dur.

2 to try hard faire [10] beaucoup d'efforts

- **hard-boiled egg** un œuf dur
- **hard disk** le disque dur

**hardly** *adverb*

1 **à peine**
I can hardly hear him. Je l'entends à peine.

2 (*in expressions*) hardly any presque pas de
There's hardly any milk. Il n'y a presque pas de lait.
hardly ever presque jamais
I hardly ever see them. Je ne les vois presque jamais.
hardly anyone presque personne
There was hardly anyone there. Il n'y avait presque personne.

**hare** *noun*
le **lièvre** *masc*

**harm** *noun* ▷ see **harm** *verb*
**mal**
It won't do you any harm. Ça ne te fera pas de mal.

to **harm** *verb* ▷ see **harm** *noun*
to harm somebody faire [10] du mal à quelqu'un
They did not harm him. Ils ne lui ont pas fait de mal.

**harmful** *adjective*
**nuisible** *masc & fem*

**harmless** *adjective*
**inoffensif** *masc*, **inoffensive** *fem*

**harvest** *noun*
la **récolte** *fem*

ꝺ **hat** *noun*
le **chapeau** *masc* (*pl* les **chapeaux**)

ꝺ to **hate** *verb*
**détester** [1]
I hate spiders. Je déteste les araignées.

**hatred** *noun*
la **haine** *fem*

ꝺ to **have** *verb*

1 (*to possess*) **avoir** [5]
Anna has three brothers. Anna a trois frères.
How many sisters do you have? Tu as combien de sœurs?
We've got a dog. Nous avons un chien.
What have you got in your hand? Qu'est-ce que tu as dans la main?

2 (*in English past tenses with have, had + -ed words - some French verbs take* **avoir**) I've finished. J'ai fini.
Have you seen the film? Est-ce que tu as vu le film?
We had already eaten. Nous avions déjà mangé.

3 (*some French verbs take* **être**) Rosie hasn't arrived yet. Rosie n'est pas encore arrivée.
He had left. Il était parti.
They have sat down. Ils se sont assis.

4 to have to do something devoir [8] faire quelque chose
I have to phone Nathalie. Je dois appeler Nathalie.

5 (*food, a drink, a shower*) **prendre** [64]
We had a coffee. Nous avons pris un café.
I'll have an omelette. Je prends une omelette.
I'm going to have a shower. Je vais prendre une douche.

6 (*with meals*) to have breakfast prendre [64] le petit déjeuner
to have lunch déjeuner [1]
to have dinner dîner [1] (*in the evening*)

7 to have something done se faire Ⓔ [10] faire quelque chose
I'm going to have my hair cut. Je vais me faire couper les cheveux.

**WORD TIP** Verbs taking *être* for the *-ed* tenses in English do not have direct objects: *Je suis arrivé.* = I have arrived. *Il est entré.* = He has come in. Reflexive verbs (with *se*) also take *être* in the tenses where English uses *have, had*: *Elle s'est lavée.* = She has washed herself.

**hawk** *noun*
le **faucon** *masc*

**hay** *noun*
le **foin** *masc*

- **hay fever** le rhume des foins

**hazelnut** *noun*
la **noisette** *fem*

ꝺ **he** *pronoun*
**il**
He's a student. Il est étudiant.
He lives in Manchester. Il habite à Manchester.
He's a musician. C'est un musicien.

Who is he? C'est qui?
Here he is! Le voici!
There he is! Le voilà!

♪ **head** *noun* ▷ see **head** *verb*

1 (*part of your body*) la **tête** *fem*
He has a cap on his head. Il a une casquette sur la tête.
at the head of the queue en tête de queue

2 (*of a school*) le **directeur** *masc*, la **directrice** *fem*

3 (*when tossing a coin*) **'Heads or tails?' — 'Heads.'** 'Pile ou face?' — 'Face.'

to **head** *verb* ▷ see **head** *noun*

• **to head for something**
**se diriger** Ⓔ **[52] vers quelque chose**
Liz headed for the door. Liz s'est dirigée vers la porte.

**headache** *noun*
I've got a headache. J'ai mal à la tête.

**headlight** *noun*
le **phare** *masc*

**headline** *noun*
le **gros titre**

**headmaster** *noun*
le **directeur** *masc*

**headmistress** *noun*
la **directrice** *fem*

**headphones** *plural noun*
le **casque** *masc singular*

**headquarters** *noun*
1 (*of an organization*) le **siège social**
2 (*military*) le **quartier général**

**headteacher** *noun*
le **directeur** *masc*, la **directrice** *fem*

♪ **health** *noun*
la **santé** *fem*
• **health centre** le centre médico-social

**healthy** *adjective*
1 (*person*) **en bonne santé**
to be healthy être [6] en bonne santé
2 (*diet*) **sain** *masc*, **saine** *fem*

**heap** *noun*
le **tas** *masc*

♪ to **hear** *verb*
1 (*a sound, a noise*) **entendre [3]**
I can hear you. Je t'entends.
I can't hear anything. Je n'entends rien.
2 (*some news*) **apprendre [64]**
I hear you've bought a dog. J'apprends que tu as acheté un chien.
• **to hear about something**
**entendre [3] parler de quelque chose**
Have you heard about the concert? As-tu entendu parler du concert?
• **to hear of something**
**entendre parler de quelque chose**
She's never heard of crêpes. Elle ne sait pas ce que c'est qu'une crêpe.

**hearing aid** *noun*
le **Sonotone**® *masc*

**heart** *noun*
1 (*part of the body*) le **cœur** *masc*
to learn something by heart apprendre [64] quelque chose par cœur
2 (*in cards*) le **cœur** *masc*
the jack of hearts le valet de cœur
• **heart attack** la crise cardiaque

♪ **heat** *noun* ▷ see **heat** *verb*
la **chaleur** *fem*

♪ to **heat** *verb* ▷ see **heat** *noun*
**chauffer [1]**
to heat the house with gas chauffer la maison au gaz
The soup's heating. La soupe est en train de chauffer.
• **to heat something up faire [10] chauffer quelque chose**
I'll heat up the soup. Je vais faire chauffer la soupe.

**heater** *noun*
le **radiateur** *masc*

**heather** *noun*
la **bruyère** *fem*

♪ **heating** *noun*
le **chauffage** *masc*

**heatwave** *noun*
la **vague de chaleur**

**heaven** *noun*
le **paradis** *masc*

♪ **heavy** *adjective*
(*weight, weather, defeat*) **lourd** *masc*, **lourde** *fem*
My rucksack's heavy. Mon sac à dos est lourd.
heavy rain de fortes pluies
heavy traffic une circulation dense
• **heavy metal** le hard rock

**hedge** *noun*
la **haie** *fem*

**hedgehog** *noun*
un **hérisson** *masc*

♪ **heel** *noun*
le **talon** *masc*

English-French

a b c d e f g h i j k l m n o p q r s t u v w x y z

**height** *noun*
1 (*of a person*) la **taille** *fem*
**a man of average height** un homme de taille moyenne
2 (*of a building*) la **hauteur** *fem*
3 (*of a mountain*) l'**altitude** *fem*

**helicopter** *noun*
un **hélicoptère** *masc*

**hell** *noun*
l'**enfer** *masc*
**It's hell here!** C'est infernal ici!

**hello** *exclamation*
1 (*polite*) **bonjour!**
2 (*informal*) **salut!**
3 (*on the telephone*) **allô!**

**helmet** *noun*
le **casque** *masc*

**help** *noun* ▷ see **help** *verb*
l'**aide** *fem*
**Do you need any help?** Est-ce que tu as besoin d'aide?

to **help** *verb* ▷ see **help** *noun*
1 **aider [1]**
**to help somebody to do something** aider [1] quelqu'un à faire quelque chose
**Can you help me move the table?** Peux-tu m'aider à déplacer la table?
2 **Help yourself!** Sers-toi!
**Help yourselves to vegetables.** Prenez des légumes.
3 **Help!** Au secours!

**helper** *noun*
un & une **aide** *masc & fem*

**helpful** *adjective*
(*person*) **serviable** *masc & fem*

**helping** *noun*
la **portion** *fem*
**Would you like a second helping of chips?** Est-ce que tu veux encore des frites?

**hem** *noun*
un **ourlet** *masc*

**hen** *noun*
la **poule** *fem*

**her** *pronoun* ▷ see **her** *adj*
1 (*as a direct object*) **la**
**I know her.** Je la connais.
**I don't know her.** Je ne la connais pas.
**I saw her last week.** Je l'ai vue la semaine dernière.
**Watch her!** Regarde-la!
**Don't forget her.** Ne l'oublie pas.

**WORD TIP** *la* as a direct object becomes *l'* before *a, e, i, o, u* or *silent h*.

2 (*as the indirect object*) **lui**
**Give the book to her.** Donne-lui le livre.
**Can you write to her?** Est-ce que tu peux lui écrire?
**I gave her my address.** Je lui ai donné mon adresse.
**Don't give her my number.** Ne lui donne pas mon numéro.

**WORD TIP** *lui* as an indirect object never changes.

3 (*after prepositions*) **elle**
**I'll go with her.** J'irai avec elle.
**We left without her.** Nous sommes partis sans elle.
**It's a present for her.** C'est un cadeau pour elle.

**WORD TIP** *elle* is used after prepositions like *avec* or *sans*.

4 (*in comparisons*) **elle**
**I'm older than her.** Je suis plus âgé qu'elle.

**her** *adjective* ▷ see **her** *pron*
1 (*with masc singular nouns*) **son**
**her brother** son frère
**her computer** son ordinateur
2 (*with fem singular nouns*) **sa**
**her sister** sa sœur
**her house** sa maison
**What's her address?** Quelle est son adresse?
3 (*with plural nouns*) **ses**
**her friends** ses amis
4 (*with parts of the body*) **le, la, les**
**She's washing her hands.** Elle se lave les mains.
**She had a glass in her hand.** Elle avait un verre à la main.

**WORD TIP** Use *son* with fem nouns beginning with *a, e, i, o, u* or *silent h*.

**herb** *noun*
l'**herbe** *fem*

**herd** *noun*
le **troupeau** *masc* (*pl* les **troupeaux**)

**here** *adverb*
1 (*close to the speaker*) **ici**
**Leave it here.** Laisse-le ici.
**Come here.** Viens ici.
**We're in here in the kitchen.** Nous sommes ici dans la cuisine.
2 (*in this general area*) **ici**
**the shops around here** les magasins par ici
**It's sunnier over here.** Il fait plus de soleil ici.
**The cashpoint's not far from here.** Le guichet automatique n'est pas loin d'ici.
**Is Tom here?** Est-ce que Tom est là?
**He isn't here at the moment.** Il n'est pas là en ce moment.

3 (*when you point things out*) **here is** voici, voilà
**Here's my address.** Voici mon adresse.
**Look, here comes Ben now.** Tiens, voilà Ben qui arrive.
**here are** voici, voilà
**Here are the photos.** Voici les photos.
**And here they are!** Et les voilà!

**hero** *noun*
un **héros** *masc*

**heroin** *noun*
l'**héroïne** *fem*

**heroine** *noun*
une **héroïne** *fem*

**herring** *noun*
un **hareng** *masc*

♪ **hers** *pronoun*
1 (*for masc singular nouns*) **le sien**
**I took my hat and she took hers.** J'ai pris mon chapeau et elle a pris le sien.
2 (*for fem singular nouns*) **la sienne**
**I gave her my address and she gave me hers.** Je lui ai donné mon adresse et elle m'a donné la sienne.
3 (*for masc plural nouns*) **les siens**
**I invited my parents and Karen invited hers.** J'ai invité mes parents et Karen a invité les siens.
4 (*for fem plural nouns*) **les siennes**
**I showed her my photos and she showed me hers.** Je lui ai montré mes photos et elle m'a montré les siennes.
5 (*belonging to her*) **à elle**
**It's hers.** C'est à elle.
**Is that hers?** C'est à elle, ça?
**The green one's hers.** Le vert est à elle.

**herself** *pronoun*
1 **se**
**She's going to hurt herself.** Elle va se blesser.
**She enjoyed herself.** Elle s'est amusée.

**WORD TIP** *se* becomes *s'* before *a, e, i, o, u* or *silent h*. *amusée* agrees with *se*, which refers to *elle*.

2 (*for emphasis*) **elle-même**
**She said it herself.** Elle l'a dit elle-même.
3 (*on her own*) **by herself** toute seule
**She did it by herself.** Elle l'a fait toute seule.

to **hesitate** *verb*
**hésiter [1]**

**heterosexual** *adjective*
**hétérosexuel** *masc*, **hétérosexuelle** *fem*

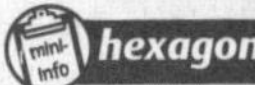
***hexagon***
France is sometimes nicknamed *l'Hexagone*, because of its six-sided shape.

♪ **hi** *exclamation*
(*informal*) **salut!**

**hiccups** *plural noun*
**to have the hiccups** avoir **[5]** le hoquet

**hidden** *adjective*
**caché** *masc*, **cachée** *fem*

to **hide** *verb*
1 (*to hide yourself*) **se cacher** Ⓔ **[1]**
**She hid behind the door.** Elle s'est cachée derrière la porte.
2 (*something*) **cacher [1]**
**Who's hidden the chocolate?** Qui a caché le chocolat?

**hide-and-seek** *noun*
**to play hide-and-seek** jouer **[1]** à cache-cache

**hi-fi** *noun*
la **chaîne hi-fi**

♪ **high** *adjective*
1 (*in general*) **haut** *masc*, **haute** *fem*
**a high shelf** une étagère haute
**The wall is very high.** Le mur est très haut.
**The wall is two metres high.** Le mur fait deux mètres de hauteur.
**How high is the Eiffel Tower?** Quelle est la hauteur de la tour Eiffel?
2 (*numbers, prices, temperatures*) **élevé** *masc*, **élevée** *fem*
**The prices are very high.** Les prix sont très élevés.
3 (*speed*) **grand** *masc*, **grande** *fem*
**at high speed** à grande vitesse
**high winds** des vents forts
4 (*voice, note*) **aigu** *masc*, **aiguë** *fem*
**a high voice** une voix aiguë

**higher education** *noun*
l'**enseignement supérieur** *masc*

**Highers, Advanced Highers** *plural noun*
le **baccalauréat** *masc*, le **bac** *masc* (*informal*) (*the exam taken at the end of secondary school*)

**high-heeled** *adjective*
**à hauts talons**
**high-heeled shoes** des chaussures à hauts talons

**high jump** *noun*
le **saut en hauteur**

**highly** *adverb*
**extrêmement**

to **hijack** *verb*
**to hijack a plane** détourner **[1]** un avion

**hijacker** *noun*
le **pirate de l'air**

English–French

**hijacking** *noun*
le **détournement** *masc*

**hike** *noun*
la **randonnée** *fem*
to go on a hike faire [10] une randonnée

**hiker** *noun*
le **randonneur** *masc*, la **randonneuse** *fem*

**hiking** *noun*
la **randonnée** *fem*

**hilarious** *adjective*
**hilarant** *masc*, **hilarante** *fem*

**hill** *noun*
1 (*in the landscape*) la **colline** *fem*
**You can see the hills.** On voit les collines.
2 (*steep slope*) le **coteau** *masc* (*pl* les **coteaux**)
**the houses on the hill** les maisons sur le coteau
3 (*sloping street, road*) **to go up the hill** monter
**You go up the hill as far as the church ...** Vous montez jusqu'à l'église ...

**him** *pronoun*
1 (*as a direct object*) **le**
**I know him.** Je le connais.
**I don't know him.** Je ne le connais pas.
**I saw him last week.** Je l'ai vu la semaine dernière.
**Watch him!** Regarde-le!
**Don't forget him.** Ne l'oublie pas.

**WORD TIP** *le* as a direct object becomes *l'* before *a, e, i, o, u* or *silent h*.

2 (*as an indirect object*) **lui**
**Give the book to him.** Donne-lui le livre.
**Can you write to him?** Est-ce que tu peux lui écrire?
**I gave him my address.** Je lui ai donné mon adresse.
**Don't give him my number.** Ne lui donne pas mon numéro.

**WORD TIP** *lui* as an indirect object never changes.

3 (*after prepositions*) **lui**
**I'll go with him.** J'irai avec lui.
**We left without him.** Nous sommes partis sans lui.
**It's a present for him.** C'est un cadeau pour lui.

**WORD TIP** *lui* is used after prepositions like *avec* or *sans*.

4 (*in comparisons*) **lui**
**She's older than him.** Elle est plus âgée que lui.

**himself** *pronoun*
1 **se**
**He's going to hurt himself.** Il va se blesser.
**He enjoyed himself.** Il s'est beaucoup amusé.

**WORD TIP** *se* becomes *s'* before *a, e, i, o, u* or *silent h. amusé* above, agrees with *se*, which refers to *il*.

2 (*for emphasis*) **lui-même**
**He said it himself.** Il l'a dit lui-même.
3 (*on his own*) **by himself** tout seul
**He did it by himself.** Il l'a fait tout seul.

**Hindu** *adjective*
**hindou** *masc*, **hindoue** *fem*

**WORD TIP** Adjectives and nouns of religion start with a small letter in French.

**hip** *noun*
la **hanche** *fem*

**hippie** *noun*
le & la **hippy** *masc & fem*

**hippopotamus** *noun*
un **hippopotame** *masc*

**hire** *noun* ▷ see **hire** *verb*
la **location** *fem*
car hire la location de voitures
for hire à louer

**to hire** *verb* ▷ see **hire** *noun*
**louer** [1]
**We always hire a car.** Nous louons toujours une voiture.

**his** *adjective* ▷ see **his** *pron*
1 (*with masc singular nouns*) **son**
**his brother** son frère
**his computer** son ordinateur
2 (*with fem singular nouns*) **sa**
**his sister** sa sœur
**his house** sa maison
**What's his address?** Quelle est son adresse?
3 (*with plural nouns*) **ses**
**his friends** ses amis
4 (*with parts of the body*) **le, la, les**
**He's washing his hands.** Il se lave les mains.
**He had a glass in his hand.** Il avait un verre à la main.

**WORD TIP** Use *son* with fem nouns beginning with *a, e, i, o, u* or *silent h*.

**his** *pronoun* ▷ see **his** *adj*
1 (*for masc singular nouns*) **le sien**
**I took my hat and he took his.** J'ai pris mon chapeau et il a pris le sien.
2 (*for fem singular nouns*) **la sienne**
**I gave him my address and he gave me his.** Je lui ai donné mon adresse et il m'a donné la sienne.
3 (*for masc plural nouns*) **les siens**
**I've invited my parents and Steve's invited**

his. J'ai invité mes parents et Steve a invité les siens.
4 (*for fem plural nouns*) **les siennes**
I showed him my photos and he showed me his. Je lui ai montré mes photos et il m'a montré les siennes.
5 (*belonging to him*) **à lui**
It's his. C'est à lui.
Is that his? C'est à lui, ça?
The green car's his. La voiture verte est à lui.

**historic** *adjective*
**historique** *masc & fem*

♪**history** *noun*
une **histoire** *fem*

**hit** *noun* ▷ see **hit** *verb*
1 (*song*) le **tube** *masc*
their latest hit leur dernier tube
2 (*success*) le **succès** *masc*
The film was a huge hit. Le film a eu un succès fou.

♪to **hit** *verb* ▷ see **hit** *noun*
1 **frapper [1]**
to hit the ball frapper la balle
2 to hit your head on something se cogner Ⓔ [1] la tête contre quelque chose
3 (*to go into*) **heurter [1]**
The car hit a tree. La voiture a heurté un arbre.
4 to be hit by a car être [6] renversé par une voiture
She was hit by a car. Elle a été renversée par une voiture.

**hitch** *noun* ▷ see **hitch** *verb*
le **problème** *masc*

to **hitch** *verb* ▷ see **hitch** *noun*
to hitch a lift faire [10] du stop
Harry hitched a lift home. Harry est rentré en stop.

♪to **hitchhike** *verb*
**faire [10] du stop**
We hitchhiked for a week. Nous avons fait du stop pendant une semaine.
We hitchhiked to Dijon. Nous sommes allés à Dijon en stop.

**hitchhiker** *noun*
un **auto-stoppeur** *masc*, une **auto-stoppeuse** *fem*

♪**hitchhiking** *noun*
l'**auto-stop** *masc*

**HIV-negative** *adjective*
**séronégatif** *masc*, **séronégative** *fem*

**HIV-positive** *adjective*
**séropositif** *masc*, **séropositive** *fem*

♪**hobby** *noun*
le **passe-temps** *masc*
My favourite hobby is skiing. Mon passe-temps préféré, c'est le ski.

**hockey** *noun*
le **hockey** *masc*
to play hockey jouer [1] au hockey
• **hockey stick** la crosse de hockey

to **hold** *verb*
1 (*in your hands*) **tenir [77]**
Can you hold the torch? Est-ce que tu peux tenir la lampe?
2 (*to contain*) **contenir [77]**
a jug which holds a litre un pichet qui contient un litre
3 (*a meeting, an event*) tenir [77]
A meeting was held in the village hall. On a tenu une réunion dans la salle des fêtes.
4 (*when telephoning*) Hold the line. Ne quittez pas.
• **to hold on**
(*to wait*) **attendre [3]**
Hold on! Attends!, (*on the telephone*) Ne quittez pas!
• **to hold somebody up**
**retenir [77] quelqu'un**
I was held up at the dentist's. J'ai été retenu chez le dentiste.
• **to hold something up**
**lever [50] quelque chose**
He held up his glass. Il a levé son verre.

**hold-up** *noun*
1 (*delay*) le **retard** *masc*
2 (*traffic jam*) le **bouchon** *masc*
3 (*robbery*) le **hold-up** *masc*

**hole** *noun*
le **trou** *masc*

♪**holiday** *noun*
1 (*non-working day*) **a public holiday** un jour férié
Monday's a holiday. Lundi est férié.
2 (*time for relaxation*) les **vacances** *fem plural*
the school holidays les vacances scolaires
Where are you going for your holiday? Où est-ce que vous partez en vacances?
Leyla is away on holiday. Leyla est en vacances.
to go on holiday partir Ⓔ [58] en vacances
When are you going on holiday? Quand est-ce que tu pars en vacances?
Have a good holiday! Bonnes vacances!
3 (*from work*) le **congé** *masc*
I'm taking two days' holiday. Je prends deux jours de congé.
• **holiday home** la résidence secondaire

♪ indicates key words



English-French

a b c d e f g h i j k l m n o p q r s t u v w x y z

**Holland** *noun*
la **Hollande** *fem*
**They went to Holland at Easter.** Ils sont allés en Hollande à Pâques.
**Laura works in Holland.** Laura travaille en Hollande.

**WORD TIP** Countries and regions in French take *le, la* or *les*.

**hollow** *adjective*
**creux** *masc*, **creuse** *fem*

**holly** *noun*
le **houx** *masc*

**holy** *adjective*
**saint** *masc*, **sainte** *fem*

**home** *noun* ▷ see **home** *adv*
la **maison** *fem*
**I was at home.** J'étais à la maison.
**We stayed at home.** Nous sommes restés à la maison.
**Make yourself at home!** Fais comme chez toi!

**home** *adverb* ▷ see **home** *noun*
1 **chez ...**
**I'll call on my way home.** Je passerai te voir en rentrant chez moi.
**Susie came home with us.** Susie est venue chez nous.

**WORD TIP** You show whose home with *chez moi* my house, *chez toi* your house, *chez Emma* Emma's house, etc.

2 **to get home** rentrer Ⓔ [1]
**We got home at midnight.** Nous sommes rentrés à minuit.

**homeless** *noun*
**the homeless** les sans-abri *masc plural*

**homemade** *adjective*
**fait maison** *masc* **faite maison** *fem*
**homemade cakes** des gâteaux faits maison

**home match** *noun*
le **match à domicile**

**homeopathic** *adjective*
**homéopathique** *masc & fem*

**homesick** *adjective*
**to be homesick** avoir [5] le mal du pays
**I'm homesick.** J'ai le mal du pays.

**homework** *noun*
les **devoirs** *masc plural*
**I did my homework.** J'ai fait mes devoirs.
**my French homework** mes devoirs de français

**homosexual** *adjective*
**homosexuel** *masc*, **homosexuelle** *fem*

**honest** *adjective*
**honnête** *masc & fem*

**honestly** *adverb*
**franchement**

**honesty** *noun*
l'**honnêteté** *fem*

**honey** *noun*
le **miel** *masc*

**honeymoon** *noun*
le **voyage de noces**
**They're going to Paris on their honeymoon.** Ils partent à Paris en voyage de noces.

**honeysuckle** *noun*
le **chèvrefeuille** *masc*

**honour** *noun*
un **honneur** *masc*

**hood** *noun*
la **capuche** *fem*

**hook** *noun*
1 le **crochet** *masc*
2 **to take the phone off the hook** décrocher le téléphone

**hooligan** *noun*
le **voyou** *masc*

**hooray** *exclamation*
**hourra!**

**Hoover**® *noun*
un **aspirateur** *masc*

to **hoover** *verb*
**passer [1] l'aspirateur**
**I hoovered my bedroom.** J'ai passé l'aspirateur dans ma chambre.

**hope** *noun* ▷ see **hope** *verb*
un **espoir** *masc*
**to give up hope** perdre l'espoir
**They gave up hope of finding her.** Ils ont perdu l'espoir de lui trouver.

to **hope** *verb* ▷ see **hope** *noun*
**espérer [24]**
**We hope you'll be able to come.** Nous espérons que vous pourrez venir.
**Hoping to see you on Friday.** En espérant te voir vendredi.
**I hope so.** Je l'espère.
**I hope not.** J'espère que non.

**hopefully** *adverb*
**avec un peu de chance**
**Hopefully, the film won't have started.** Avec un peu de chance, le film n'aura pas commencé.





a b c d e f g h i j k l m n o p q r s t u v w x y z

**hopeless** *adjective*
**nul** *masc*, **nulle** *fem*
I'm hopeless at maths. Je suis nul en maths.

**horizon** *noun*
l'**horizon** *masc*

**horizontal** *adjective*
**horizontal** *masc*, **horizontale** *fem*, **horizontaux** *masc pl*, **horizontales** *fem pl*

**horn** *noun*
1 (*of an animal*) la **corne** *fem*
2 (*of a car*) le **klaxon** *masc*
to sound your horn klaxonner
3 (*musical instrument*) le **cor** *masc*
to play the horn jouer [1] du cor

**horoscope** *noun*
un **horoscope** *masc*

♪ **horrible** *adjective*
1 (*weather, experience*) **affreux** *masc*, **affreuse** *fem*
The weather was horrible. Il a fait un temps affreux.
2 (*person*) **désagréable** *masc & fem*
She's really horrible! Elle est vraiment désagréable!
He was horrible to me. Il a été désagréable avec moi.

**horrific** *adjective*
**terrible** *masc & fem*

**horror** *noun*
l'**horreur** *fem*
• **horror film** le film d'épouvante

♪ **horse** *noun*
le **cheval** *masc* (*pl* les **chevaux**)

**horse chestnut** *noun*
1 (*tree*) le **marronnier** *masc*
2 (*nut*) le **marron** *masc*

**horse racing** *noun*
les **courses hippiques** *fem plural*

**horseshoe** *noun*
le **fer à cheval**

**hose** *noun*
le **tuyau** *masc* (*pl* les **tuyaux**)

**hosepipe** *noun*
le **tuyau d'arrosage**

♪ **hospital** *noun*
un **hôpital** *masc* (*pl* les **hôpitaux**)
to be in hospital être [6] à l'hôpital
Nina was in hospital for three weeks. Nina était à l'hôpital pendant trois semaines.
to be taken into hospital être hospitalisé *masc*, être hospitalisée *fem*

**hospitality** *noun*
l'**hospitalité** *fem*

**host** *noun*
1 un **hôte** *masc*, une **hôtesse** *fem*
2 (*in exchanges*) **host family** la famille d'accueil
My host family is very nice. Ma famille d'accueil est très sympathique.

**hostage** *noun*
un **otage** *masc*

**hostel** *noun*
le **foyer** *masc*

**hostess** *noun*
une **hôtesse** *fem*
an air hostess une hôtesse de l'air

♪ **hot** *adjective*
1 (*food, drink*) **chaud** *masc*, **chaude** *fem*
a hot drink une boisson chaude
hot meals des repas chauds
Be careful, the plates are hot! Fais attention, les assiettes sont très chaudes!
2 (*weather, places*) **to be hot** faire [10] chaud
It's hot today. Il fait chaud aujourd'hui.
It won't be too hot. Il ne fera pas trop chaud.
It was very hot in the kitchen. Il faisait très chaud dans la cuisine.
3 (*the feeling*) **to be hot** avoir [5] chaud
I'm hot. J'ai chaud.
I'm very hot. J'ai très chaud.
I'm too hot. J'ai trop chaud.
Your hands are hot. Tu as les mains chaudes.
4 (*spicy*) **épicé** *masc*, **épicée** *fem*
• **hot dog** un hot-dog

♪ **hotel** *noun*
un **hôtel** *masc*

♪ **hour** *noun*
une **heure** *fem*
an hour ago il y a une heure
two hours later deux heures plus tard
We waited for three hours. Nous avons attendu trois heures.
There's a train every hour. Il y a un train toutes les heures.
an hour and a half une heure et demie
to be paid by the hour être [6] payé à l'heure

**hourly** *adjective, adverb*
1 (*every hour*) **toutes les heures**
There is an hourly bus. Il y a un bus toutes les heures.
2 (*by the hour*) **à l'heure**
We're paid on an hourly basis. On nous paye à l'heure.

English–French

**house** *noun*
1 la **maison** *fem*
to buy a house acheter une maison
2 **at somebody's house** chez quelqu'un
**I'm at Jake's house.** Je suis chez Jake.
**I'm going to Hannah's house.** Je vais chez Hannah.
- **housewife** la femme au foyer

**housework** *noun*
le **ménage** *masc*
**to do the housework** faire [10] le ménage

**how** *adverb*
1 (*asking in what way*) **comment**
**How are you?** Comment allez-vous?
**How did you do it?** Comment l'as-tu fait?
2 (*asking about quantity*) **how much, how many** combien
**How much is it?** Ça coûte combien?
**How much money do you have?** Tu as combien d'argent?
**How many brothers do you have?** Tu as combien de frères?
3 (*asking general questions*) **How old are you?** Quel âge as-tu?
**How far is it?** C'est à quelle distance d'ici?
**How long will it take?** Ça va prendre combien de temps?
**How long have you known her?** Tu la connais depuis combien de temps?

**however** *adverb*
**cependant**

**hug** *noun*
**to give somebody a hug** serrer [1] quelqu'un dans ses bras
**She gave me a hug.** Elle m'a serré dans ses bras.
**They gave each other a hug.** Ils se sont serrés dans ses bras.

**huge** *adjective*
**immense** *masc & fem*

to **hum** *verb*
**fredonner** [1]

**human** *adjective*
**humain** *masc*, **humaine** *fem*
- **human being** un être humain

**humour** *noun*
l'**humour** *masc*
**to have a sense of humour** avoir [5] le sens de l'humour

**hundred** *number*
1 (*exactly 100*) **cent**
**a hundred people** cent personnes
**two hundred** deux cents
**two hundred and ten** deux cent dix

**WORD TIP** *cent* does not take an *-s* when another number follows it.

2 (*around 100*) **about a hundred** une centaine
**about a hundred people** une centaine de personnes
**hundreds of people** des centaines de personnes

**Hungary** *noun*
la **Hongrie** *fem*

**WORD TIP** Countries and regions in French take *le*, *la* or *les*.

**hunger** *noun*
la **faim** *fem*

**hungry** *adjective*
**to be hungry** avoir [5] faim
**I'm hungry.** J'ai faim.

to **hunt** *verb*
1 (*an animal*) **chasser** [1]
2 (*a person*) **rechercher** [1]

**hunting** *noun*
la **chasse** *fem*
**fox-hunting** la chasse au renard

**hurricane** *noun*
un **ouragan** *masc*

**hurry** *noun* ▷ see **hurry** *verb*
**to be in a hurry** être [6] pressé *masc*, être pressée *fem*
**He's always in a hurry.** Il est toujours pressé.
**Dina was in a hurry.** Dina était pressée.

to **hurry** *verb* ▷ see **hurry** *noun*
**se dépêcher** ⓔ [50]
**I must hurry.** Je dois me dépêcher.
**He hurried home.** Il s'est dépêché de rentrer chez lui.
**She hurried to catch the bus.** Elle s'est dépêchée d'attraper le bus.
**Hurry up!** Dépêche-toi!, Dépêchez-vous! (*formal or plural form*)

**hurt** *adjective* ▷ see **hurt** *verb*
**blessé** *masc*, **blessée** *fem*
**Three people were hurt.** Trois personnes ont été blessées.

to **hurt** *verb* ▷ see **hurt** *adj*
1 (*to injure*) **to hurt somebody** faire [10] mal à quelqu'un
**You're hurting me!** Tu me fais mal!
**That hurts!** Ça fait mal!
2 (*to give pain*) **My back hurts.** J'ai mal au dos.
3 **to hurt yourself** se faire ⓔ [10] mal
**Did you hurt yourself?** Est-ce que tu t'es fait mal?



ⓔ means the verb takes être to form the perfect

♪ **husband** *noun*
le **mari** *masc*

**hygienic** *adjective*
**hygiénique** *masc & fem*

**hymn** *noun*
le **cantique** *masc*

♪ **hypermarket** *noun*
un **hypermarché** *masc*

**hyphen** *noun*
le **trait d'union**

to **hypnotize** *verb*
**hypnotiser** [1]

# I i

♪ **I** *pronoun*
1 (*before the verb*) **je, j'**
**I'm Scottish.** Je suis écossais (*boy speaking*), Je suis écossaise (*girl speaking*).
**I have two sisters.** J'ai deux sœurs.
**I live in London.** J'habite à Londres.
**I'm learning French.** J'apprends le français.
2 (*in other positions*) **moi**
**my brother and I** mon frère et moi
**I'm the person who ...** C'est moi qui ...
**Tom and I left before you.** Tom et moi sommes partis avant vous.
**Here I am at last!** Me voici enfin!

**WORD TIP** *je* becomes *j'* before *a, e, i, o, u* or a silent *h.*

♪ **ice** *noun*
1 (*frozen water*) la **glace** *fem*
2 (*on the roads*) le **verglas** *masc*
3 (*in a drink*) les **glaçons** *masc plural*
• **iceberg** *noun* un iceberg

**ice cream** *noun*
la **glace** *fem*
**a chocolate ice cream** une glace au chocolat

**ice-cube** *noun*
le **glaçon** *masc*

**ice hockey** *noun*
le **hockey sur glace**

**ice rink** *noun*
la **patinoire** *fem*

**ice-skating** *noun*
**to go ice-skating** faire [10] du patin à glace
**We went ice-skating on Saturday.** Nous avons fait du patin à glace samedi.

**icing** *noun*
le **glaçage** *masc*

**icon** *noun*
une **icône** *fem*

**icy** *adjective*
1 (*road*) **verglacé** *masc*, **verglacée** *fem*
2 (*very cold*) **glacial** *masc*, **glaciale** *fem*
**an icy wind** un vent glacial

♪ **idea** *noun*
une **idée** *fem*
**What a good idea!** Quelle bonne idée!
**I have an idea.** J'ai une idée.
**I have no idea.** Je n'en ai aucune idée.

**ideal** *adjective*
**idéal** *masc*, **idéale** *fem*, **idéaux** *masc pl*, **idéales** *fem pl*

**identical** *adjective*
**identique** *masc & fem*
**identical twins** des vrais jumeaux

♪ **identification** *noun*
une **identification** *fem*

to **identify** *verb*
**identifier** [1]

♪ **identity card** *noun*
la **carte d'identité**

mini-info **identity card**

By law, all French people must carry an identity card, called *une carte d'identité.*

♪ **idiot** *noun*
un **idiot** *masc*, une **idiote** *fem*

**idiotic** *adjective*
**bête** *masc & fem*

**i.e.** *abbreviation*
**c-à-d** (*short for c'est-à-dire*)

♪ **if** *conjunction*
1 **si, s'**
**If Sophie's there, he'll be happy.** Si Sophie est là, il sera content.
**If it rains, we won't go.** S'il pleut, nous n'irons pas.
**If I won the lottery, I would buy a flat.** ▸▸

Si je gagnais la loterie, j'achèterais un appartement.
if not sinon
2 if only ... si seulement ...
If only you'd told me, I would have helped you. Si seulement tu me l'avais dit, je t'aurais aidé.
3 even if même si
We're going out, even if it snows. On sort, même s'il neige.
4 if I were you ... à ta place ...
If I were you, I'd forget about it. À ta place je n'y penserais plus.

**WORD TIP** *si* becomes *s'* before *il* and *ils*.

to **ignore** *verb*
1 (*a person*) **ignorer [1]**
2 (*what somebody says*) **ne pas écouter [1]**
3 Ignore it. Ne fais pas attention.

**ill** *adjective*
**malade** *masc & fem*
I feel ill. Je ne me sens pas bien.
to be taken ill tomber ⓔ [1] malade
Her grandmother has been taken ill. Sa grand-mère est tombée malade.

**illegal** *adjective*
**illégal** *masc*, **illégale** *fem*, **illégaux** *masc pl*, **illégales** *fem pl*

**illness** *noun*
la **maladie** *fem*

**illusion** *noun*
une **illusion** *fem*

**illustrated** *adjective*
**illustré** *masc*, **illustrée** *fem*

**illustration** *noun*
une **illustration** *fem*

**image** *noun*
une **image** *fem*

**imagination** *noun*
l'**imagination** *fem*
to show imagination faire [10] preuve d'imagination
Joe shows real imagination. Joe fait preuve de beaucoup d'imagination.

to **imagine** *verb*
**imaginer [1]**
Imagine that you're very rich. Imagine que tu es très riche.
You can't imagine how hard it was! Tu ne peux pas t'imaginer combien c'était difficile!

to **imitate** *verb*
**imiter [1]**

**imitation** *noun*
une **imitation** *fem*

**immediate** *adjective*
**immédiat** *masc*, **immédiate** *fem*

**immediately** *adverb*
**immédiatement**
I rang them immediately. Je les ai appelés immédiatement.
immediately before the party juste avant la soirée

**immigrant** *noun*
un **immigré** *masc*, une **immigrée** *fem*

**immigration** *noun*
l'**immigration** *fem*

**impact** *noun*
un **impact** *masc*

**impatience** *noun*
l'**impatience** *fem*

**impatient** *adjective*
1 **impatient** *masc*, **impatiente** *fem*
2 to get impatient with somebody s'impatienter [1] contre quelqu'un

**impatiently** *adverb*
**avec impatience**

**imperfect** *noun*
(*Grammar*) l'**imparfait** *masc*
in the imperfect à l'imparfait

**import** *noun* ▷ see **import** *verb*
le **produit importé**

to **import** *verb* ▷ see **import** *noun*
**importer [1]**
wine imported from France du vin importé de France

**importance** *noun*
l'**importance** *fem*

**important** *adjective*
**important** *masc*, **importante** *fem*
It's not important. Ça n'a pas d'importance.

**impossible** *adjective*
**impossible** *masc & fem*
It's impossible to find a telephone. Il est impossible de trouver un téléphone.

**impressed** *adjective*
**impressionné** *masc*, **impressionnée** *fem*

**impression** *noun*
une **impression** *fem*
to make a good impression on somebody faire [10] bonne impression sur quelqu'un
He made a good impression on me. Il a fait bonne impression sur moi.



ⓔ means the verb takes être to form the perfect

I got the impression that ... J'avais l'impression que ...

**impressive** *adjective*
**impressionnant** *masc*, **impressionnante** *fem*
**an impressive performance** une interprétation impressionante

to **improve** *verb*
1 (*a design, grades etc*) **améliorer [1]**
**I'm trying to improve my grades.** J'essaye d'améliorer mes notes.
2 (*to get better*) **s'améliorer [1]**
**The weather is improving.** Le temps s'améliore.

**improvement** *noun*
1 (*change for the better*) une **amélioration** *fem*
2 (*gradual progress*) les **progrès** *masc plural*

♪ **in** *adverb, preposition*
1 (*in general*) **dans**
**in the kitchen** dans la cuisine
**in the newspaper** dans le journal
**in my class** dans ma classe
**I was in the bath.** J'étais dans mon bain.
2 (*in named towns, places*) **à**
**in Dover** à Douvres
**in town** en ville
**a house in the country** une maison à la campagne
**in the sun** au soleil
3 (*dressed in*) **à**
**the girl in the pink blouse** la fille à la chemise rose
**dressed in white** habillé en blanc (*boy*), habillée en blanc (*girl*)
4 (*in languges, countries*) **en**
**in French** en français
**in France** en France
**in Portugal** au Portugal

**WORD TIP** *en* is used for fem countries, *au* for most masc countries

5 (*in time expressions*)
**in May** en mai
**in 2006** en deux mil six
**in winter** en hiver
**in summer** en été
**in autumn** en automne
**in spring** au printemps
**in the morning** le matin
**at eight in the morning** à huit heures du matin
**in the night** pendant la nuit
**I'll phone you in ten minutes.** Je t'appellerai dans dix minutes.
**She did it in five minutes.** Elle l'a fait en cinq minutes.
6 (*with biggest, greatest, etc*) **de**
**the tallest boy in the class** le garçon le plus grand de la classe
**the biggest city in the world** la ville la plus grande du monde
7 (*at home*) **to be in** être **[6]** là
**Mick's not in at the moment.** Mick n'est pas là en ce moment.
8 (*in expressions*) **in the photo** sur la photo
**in the rain** sous la pluie
9 (*with verbs*) **to come in** entrer Ⓔ **[1]**
**to run in** entrer Ⓔ en courant
**to go in** entrer Ⓔ

**incident** *noun*
un **incident** *masc*

♪ to **include** *verb*
**comprendre [64]**
**service included** service compris
**Dinner is included in the price.** Le dîner est compris dans le prix.

♪ **including** *preposition*
**(y) compris**
**including Sundays** y compris les dimanches
**£50 including VAT** cinquante livres TVA comprise
**not including Sundays** sans compter les dimanches
**everyone, including children** tout le monde, y compris les enfants

**income** *noun*
le **revenu** *masc*
• **income tax** l'impôt sur le revenu *masc*

**inconvenient** *adjective*
1 (*place, arrangement*) **incommode** *masc & fem*
2 (*time*) **inopportun** *masc*, **inopportune** *fem*

**increase** *noun* ▷ see **increase** *verb*
une **augmentation** *fem*

♪ to **increase** *verb* ▷ see **increase** *noun*
**augmenter [1]**
**The price has increased by £10.** Le prix a augmenté de dix livres.

**incredible** *adjective*
**incroyable** *masc & fem*

**incredibly** *adverb*
**extrêmement**
**The film's incredibly boring.** Le film est extrêmement ennuyeux.

**indeed** *adverb*
1 (*for emphasis*) **vraiment**
**I'm very hungry indeed.** J'ai vraiment très faim.
**Thank you very much indeed.** Merci beaucoup. ▸▸

2 (*certainly*) **bien sûr**
'Can you hear his radio?' — 'Indeed I can!'
'Tu entends sa radio?' — 'Bien sûr que oui!'

**indefinite article** *noun*
(*Grammar*) **l'article indéfini** *masc*

**independence** *noun*
**l'indépendance** *fem*

**independent** *adjective*
**indépendant** *masc*, **indépendante** *fem*

**index** *noun*
un **index** *masc*
• **index finger** l'index *masc*

**India** *noun*
**l'Inde** *fem*
in India en Inde

**Indian** *adjective* ▷ see **Indian** *noun*
**indien** *masc*, **indienne** *fem*

**Indian** *noun* ▷ see **Indian** *adj*
un **Indien** *masc*, une **Indienne** *fem*

to **indicate** *verb*
**indiquer** [1]

**indigestion** *noun*
une **indigestion** *fem*
to have indigestion avoir [5] une indigestion

**indirect** *adjective*
**indirect** *masc*, **indirecte** *fem*

**individual** *adjective*
▷ see **individual** *noun*
1 (*portion, contribution*) **individuel** *masc*, **individuelle** *fem*
2 individual tuition des cours particuliers

**individual** *noun* ▷ see **individual** *adj*
un **individu** *masc*

**indoor** *adjective*
**couvert** *masc*, **couverte** *fem*
an indoor swimming pool une piscine couverte

**indoors** *adverb*
**à l'intérieur**
It's cooler indoors. Il fait plus frais à l'intérieur.
to go indoors rentrer Ⓔ [1]
Shall we go indoors? On rentre?

**industrial** *adjective*
**industriel** *masc*, **industrielle** *fem*
• **industrial estate** la zone industrielle

♪ **industry** *noun*
une **industrie** *fem*
the advertising industry l'industrie de la publicité

**inefficient** *adjective*
**inefficace** *masc & fem*

**inevitable** *adjective*
**inévitable** *masc & fem*

**inexperienced** *adjective*
**inexpérimenté** *masc*, **inexpérimentée** *fem*

**infant school** *noun*
une **école maternelle**

**infected** *adjective*
1 (*wound*) **infecté** *masc*, **infectée** *fem*
2 (*person, blood*) **contaminé** *masc*, **contaminée** *fem*

**infection** *noun*
une **infection** *fem*
an eye infection une infection de l'œil
a throat infection une angine

**infectious** *adjective*
**contagieux** *masc*, **contagieuse** *fem*

**infinitive** *noun*
(*Grammar*) **l'infinitif** *masc*
in the infinitive à l'infinitif

**inflammable** *adjective*
**inflammable** *masc & fem*

**inflatable** *adjective*
**pneumatique** *masc & fem*

to **inflate** *verb*
(*a mattress, a boat*) **gonfler** [1]

**inflation** *noun*
**l'inflation** *fem*

**influence** *noun* ▷ see **influence** *verb*
une **influence** *fem*
to be a good influence on somebody avoir [5] une bonne influence sur quelqu'un
My brother was a good influence on me. Mon frère a eu une bonne influence sur moi.

to **influence** *verb* ▷ see **influence** *noun*
**influencer** [61]

to **inform** *verb*
**informer** [1]
to inform somebody that ... informer quelqu'un du fait que ...
They informed us that there was a problem. Ils nous ont informés du fait qu'il y avait un problème.
to inform somebody of something informer quelqu'un de quelque chose
Please inform us of any change of address. Prière de nous informer de tout changement de domicile.

**informal** *adjective*
1 (*meal, event*) **simple** *masc & fem*
2 (*phrase, expression*) **familier** *masc*, **familière** *fem*

♪ **information** *noun*
les **renseignements** *masc plural*
a piece of information un renseignement
I need information on flights to Paris. J'ai besoin de renseignements sur les vols vers Paris.
• **information desk** le bureau des renseignements
• **information technology** l'informatique *fem*

**ingredient** *noun*
un **ingrédient** *masc*

**inhabitant** *noun*
un **habitant** *masc*, une **habitante** *fem*

**inhaler** *noun*
un **inhalateur** *masc*

**initials** *plural noun*
les **initiales** *fem plural*
Write your initials here. Mettez vos initiales ici.

**initiative** *noun*
une **initiative** *fem*

**injection** *noun*
la **piqûre** *fem*
The doctor gave me an injection. Le médecin m'a fait une piqûre.

♪ to **injure** *verb*
**blesser [1]**
No one was injured. Il n'y avait pas de blessés.

**injured** *adjective*
**blessé** *masc*, **blessée** *fem*

**injury** *noun*
la **blessure** *fem*

**ink** *noun*
l'**encre** *fem*

**in-laws** *noun*
les **beaux-parents** *masc plural*

**inner** *adjective*
**intérieur** *masc*, **intérieure** *fem*

**innocent** *adjective*
**innocent** *masc*, **innocente** *fem*

**inscription** *noun*
une **inscription** *fem*

♪ **insect** *noun*
un **insecte** *masc*
an insect bite une piqûre d'insecte
• **insect repellent** un insectifuge

to **insert** *verb*
**insérer [24]**

♪ **inside** *adverb* ▷ see **inside** *noun, prep*
**à l'intérieur**
She's inside, I think. Elle est à l'intérieur, je crois.
to go inside entrer Ⓔ **[1]**
He went inside. Il est entré.

♪ **inside** *preposition* ▷ see **inside** *adv, noun*
**à l'intérieur de**
inside the cinema à l'intérieur du cinéma
inside the house à l'intérieur de la maison

**inside** *noun* ▷ see **inside** *adv, prep*
**l'intérieur** *masc*
the inside of the box l'intérieur de la boîte

**inside out** *adverb*
**à l'envers**
Your sweater's inside out. Tu as mis ton pull à l'envers.

**insincere** *adjective*
**peu sincère** *masc & fem*

to **insist** *verb*
1 (*to demand*) **insister [1]**
if you insist puisque tu insistes
to insist on doing something insister pour faire quelque chose
He insisted on paying. Il a insisté pour payer.
2 to insist that affirmer **[1]** que
Rob insisted I was wrong. Rob a affirmé que j'avais tort.

**inspector** *noun*
un **inspecteur** *masc*, une **inspectrice** *fem*

to **install** *verb*
**installer [1]**

**instalment** *noun*
1 (*of a story, serial*) un **épisode** *masc*
2 (*payment*) le **versement** *masc*

**instance** *noun*
for instance par exemple

**instant** *adjective* ▷ see **instant** *noun*
1 (*coffee, soup*) **instantané** *masc*, **instantanée** *fem*
2 (*milk*) **en poudre**
3 (*effect, success*) **immédiat** *masc*, **immédiate** *fem*

**instant** *noun* ▷ see **instant** *adj*
un **instant** *masc*
in an instant dans un instant
Come here this instant! Viens ici tout de suite!

**instantly** *adverb*
**immédiatement**

**instead** *adverb*
1 **I couldn't go, so Lisa went instead.** Je ne pouvais pas y aller, donc Lisa est allée à ma place.
2 **instead of** au lieu de
**Instead of pudding I had cheese.** J'ai pris le fromage au lieu du dessert.
**Instead of playing tennis we went swimming.** Au lieu de jouer au tennis nous sommes allés à la piscine.

**instinct** *noun*
l'**instinct** *masc*

**institute** *noun*
un **institut** *masc*

**institution** *noun*
une **institution** *fem*

to **instruct** *verb*
**to instruct somebody to do something** donner [1] l'ordre à quelqu'un de faire quelque chose
**The teacher instructed us to stay together.** Le professeur nous a donné l'ordre de rester en groupe.

**instructions** *plural noun*
les **instructions** *fem plural*
**'Instructions for use.'** 'Mode d'emploi.'
**Follow the instructions on the packet.** Suivez les instructions sur l'emballage.

**instructor** *noun*
le **moniteur** *masc*, la **monitrice** *fem*
**my skiing instructor** mon moniteur de ski

**instrument** *noun*
un **instrument** *masc*
**to play an instrument** jouer [1] d'un instrument

**insult** *noun* ▷ see **insult** *verb*
une **insulte** *fem*

to **insult** *verb* ▷ see **insult** *noun*
**insulter** [1]

**insurance** *noun*
l'**assurance** *fem*
**travel insurance** l'assurance voyage
**Do you have medical insurance?** Est-ce que vous avez une assurance maladie?

**intelligence** *noun*
l'**intelligence** *fem*

**intelligent** *adjective*
**intelligent** *masc*, **intelligente** *fem*

to **intend** *verb*
1 **vouloir** [14]
**as I intended** comme je le voulais
2 **to intend to do something** avoir [5] l'intention de faire quelque chose
**We intend to spend the night in Rome.** Nous avons l'intention de passer la nuit à Rome.

**intensive** *adjective*
**intensif** *masc*, **intensive** *fem*

**intensive care** *noun*
**in intensive care** en réanimation

**intention** *noun*
une **intention** *fem*
**I have no intention of paying.** Je n'ai aucune intention de payer.

**interest** *noun* ▷ see **interest** *verb*
1 (*hobby*) le **centre d'intérêt**
**What are your interests?** Quels sont vos centres d'intérêt?
2 (*enthusiasm*) un **intérêt** *masc*
**to take an interest in something** s'intéresser [1] à quelque chose
**He has an interest in jazz.** Il s'intéresse au jazz.
**Katie has no interest in politics.** Katie ne s'intéresse pas à la politique.
3 (*on a loan*) les **intérêts** *masc plural*

to **interest** *verb* ▷ see **interest** *noun*
**intéresser** [1]
**That doesn't interest me.** Ça ne m'intéresse pas.

**interested** *adjective*
**to be interested in something** s'intéresser Ⓔ [1] à quelque chose
**Sean's very interested in cars.** Sean s'intéresse beaucoup aux voitures.

**interesting** *adjective*
**intéressant** *masc*, **intéressante** *fem*

to **interfere** *verb*
**to interfere with something** toucher [1] quelque chose
**to interfere in something** se mêler Ⓔ [1] de quelque chose
**He always interferes in everything.** Il se mêle de tout.

**interior** *adjective*
**intérieur** *masc*, **intérieure** *fem*
• **interior designer** un & une architecte d'intérieur

**international** *adjective*
**international** *masc*, **internationale** *fem*, **internationaux** *masc pl*, **internationales** *fem pl*

**Internet** *noun*
l'**Internet** *masc*
**to find something on the Internet** trouver [1] quelque chose sur Internet



Ⓔ means the verb takes être to form the perfect

Jack's on the Internet all the time. Jack est tout le temps sur Internet
- **Internet café** le cybercafé
- **Internet service provider** le fournisseur d'accèss Internet

to **interpret** *verb*
1 (*act as an interpreter*) **faire [10] l'interprète**
2 (*a remark, an action*) **interpréter [1]**

**interpreter** *noun*
un & une **interprète** *masc & fem*

to **interrupt** *verb*
**interrompre [69]**

**interruption** *noun*
une **interruption** *fem*

**interval** *noun*
(*in a play, concert*) un **entracte** *masc*

♪ **interview** *noun* ▷ see **interview** *verb*
1 (*for a job*) un **entretien** *masc*
**a job interview** un entretien
2 (*in a newspaper, on TV, radio*) une **interview** *fem*

♪ to **interview** *verb* ▷ see **interview** *noun*
(*on TV, radio, etc*) **interviewer [1]**

**interviewer** *noun*
(*on TV, radio, etc*) un **intervieweur** *masc*, une **intervieweuse** *fem*

♪ **into** *preposition*
1 (*showing movement*) **dans**
**He's gone into the bank.** Il est entré dans la banque.
**Mum's gone into town.** Maman est allée en ville.
**We got into the car.** Nous sommes montés dans la voiture.
**Get into bed !** Va au lit!
2 (*showing change*) **en**
**to translate into French** traduire **[26]** en français
**to change pounds into euros** changer **[52]** des livres sterling en euros
3 **to be into something** être **[6]** fana de quelque chose
**Pete's really into Afro music.** Pete est vraiment fana de musique africaine.

to **introduce** *verb*
**présenter [1]**
**She introduced me to her brother.** Elle m'a présenté à son frère.
**Can I introduce you to my mother?** Je te présente ma mère.

**introduction** *noun*
1 (*in a book*) une **introduction** *fem*
2 (*of a person*) la **présentation** *fem*

**intuition** *noun*
l'**intuition** *fem*

to **invade** *verb*
**envahir [2]**

**invalid** *noun*
le & la **malade** *masc & fem*

**invasion** *noun*
une **invasion** *fem*

to **invent** *verb*
**inventer [1]**

**invention** *noun*
une **invention** *fem*

**inventor** *noun*
un **inventeur** *masc*, une **inventrice** *fem*

**inverted commas** *plural noun*
(*Grammar*) les **guillemets** *masc plural*
**in inverted commas** entre guillemets

**investigation** *noun*
une **enquête** *fem*
**an investigation into the fire** une enquête sur l'incendie

**invisible** *adjective*
**invisible** *masc & fem*

**invitation** *noun*
une **invitation** *fem*
**an invitation to dinner** une invitation à dîner

♪ to **invite** *verb*
**inviter [1]**
**Kirsty invited me to lunch.** Kirsty m'a invité à déjeuner (*boy speaking*)
**He's invited me out on Tuesday.** Il m'a invitée à sortir avec lui mardi (*girl speaking*).

**invoice** *noun*
la **facture** *fem*

to **involve** *verb*
1 (*to require*) **nécessiter [1]**
**It involves a lot of work.** Cela nécessite beaucoup de travail.
2 (*to affect*) **concerner [1]**
**Two cars were involved.** Deux voitures étaient concernées.
3 **to be involved in something** participer **[1]** à quelque chose
**I am involved in the new project.** Je participe au nouveau projet.

**Iran** *noun*
l'**Iran** *masc*

**Iraq** *noun*
l'**Iraq** *masc*

**Ireland** *noun*
**l'Irlande** *fem*
in Ireland en Irlande
**We went to Ireland at Christmas.** Nous sommes allés en Irlande à Noël.
**the Republic of Ireland** la République d'Irlande

**WORD TIP** Countries and regions in French take *le, la* or *les.*

**Irish** *noun* ▷ see **Irish** *adj*
1 (*the people*) **the Irish** les Irlandais *masc plural*
2 (*the language*) **l'irlandais** *masc*

**WORD TIP** Languages never have capitals in French.

**Irish** *adjective* ▷ see **Irish** *noun*
**irlandais** *masc*, **irlandaise** *fem*

**WORD TIP** Adjectives never have capitals in French, even for nationality or regional origin.

- **Irishman** un Irlandais
- **Irish Sea** la mer d'Irlande
- **Irishwoman** une Irlandaise

**iron** *noun* ▷ see **iron** *verb*
1 (*the metal*) **le fer** *masc*
2 (*for clothes*) **le fer à repasser**

to **iron** *verb* ▷ see **iron** *noun*
**repasser [1]**

**ironing** *noun*
**le repassage** *masc*
**to do the ironing** faire [10] le repassage
- **ironing board** la planche à repasser

**ironmonger's** *noun*
**la quincaillerie** *fem*

**irregular** *adjective*
**irrégulier** *masc*, **irrégulière** *fem*

**irresponsible** *adjective*
**irresponsable** *masc & fem*

**irritable** *adjective*
**irritable** *masc & fem*

to **irritate** *verb*
**irriter [1]**

**irritating** *adjective*
**irritant** *masc*, **irritante** *fem*

**Islam** *noun*
(*Religion*) **l'islam** *masc*

**WORD TIP** Adjectives and nouns of religion start with a small letter in French.

**Islamic** *adjective*
**islamique** *masc & fem*

**island** *noun*
**une île** *fem*

**isolated** *adjective*
**isolé** *masc*, **isolée** *fem*

**Israel** *noun*
**Israël** *masc*

**WORD TIP** Unlike other names of countries *Israël* does not take *l', la* or *les.*

**Israeli** *adjective* ▷ see **Israeli** *noun*
**israélien** *masc*, **israélienne** *fem*

**Israeli** *noun* ▷ see **Israeli** *adj*
un **Israélien** *masc*, une **Israélienne** *fem*

**issue** *noun* ▷ see **issue** *verb*
1 (*discussion point*) **la question** *fem*
**a political issue** une question politique
2 (*of a magazine*) **le numéro** *masc*

**IT**
(*Computers*) **l'informatique** *fem*

**it** *pronoun*
1 (*referring to masc singular nouns, as subject*) **il**
**'Where's my bag?' — 'It's in the kitchen.'** 'Où est mon sac?' — 'Il est dans la cuisine.'
2 (*referring to fem singular nouns, as subject*) **elle**
**'How old is your TV?' — 'It's five years old.'** 'Quel âge a ta télévision?' — 'Elle a cinq ans.'
3 (*referring to masc singular nouns, as object*) **le**
**His new book? I know it.** Son nouveau livre? Je le connais.
**I like the CD. Can I borrow it?** J'aime bien le CD. Je peux l'emprunter?
4 (*referring to fem singular nouns, as object*) **la**
**His address? I know it.** Son addresse? Je la connais.
**Where's my key? I've lost it.** Où est ma clé? Je l'ai perdue.
5 (*when the gender is not given*) **Yes, it's true.** Oui, c'est vrai.
**It's a bit strange.** C'est un peu bizarre.
**It doesn't matter.** Ça ne fait rien.
6 **Who is it?** Qui c'est?
**It's me.** C'est moi.
**What is it?** Qu'est-ce que c'est?
**It's a ring.** C'est une bague.
7 (*when talking about the weather and clock time*) **il**
**It's raining.** Il pleut.
**It's a nice day.** Il fait beau.
**It's two o'clock.** Il est deux heures.
8 (*after prepositions like to or of*) **Jake's having a party. I'm going to it.** Jake fait une fête. J'y vais.
**I'm going to think about it.** Je vais y réfléchir.
**I've had enough of it.** J'en ai assez.

**WORD TIP** *le* and *la* become *l'* before *a, e, i, o, u* or *silent h,* when used as objects.

**Italian** *adjective* ▷ see **Italian** *noun*
1 **italien** *masc*, **italienne** *fem*
Italian food la cuisine italienne
2 *(teacher, lesson)* **d'italien** *masc & fem*
my Italian class mon cours d'italien

**Italian** *noun* ▷ see **Italian** *adjective*
1 *(person)* un **Italien** *masc*, une **Italienne** *fem*
2 *(the language)* l'**italien** *masc*

**italics** *noun*
l'**italique** *masc*
in italics en italique

**Italy** *noun*
l'**Italie** *fem*
in Italy en Italie
to Italy en Italie

to **itch** *verb*
1 *(hands, arm, etc)* **My back is itching.** J'ai le dos qui me démange.
2 *(clothes, material)* **This sweater itches.** Ce pull me gratte.

**item** *noun*
un **article** *masc*

**its** *adjective*
1 *(for masc and fem nouns beginning with **a, e, i, o, u** or silent h)* **son**
**The dog has lost its collar.** Le chien a perdu son collier.
its ear son oreille *(**oreille** is feminine)*
2 *(for fem nouns)* **sa**
**The dog's in its kennel.** Le chien est dans sa niche.
3 *(for plural nouns)* **ses**
its toys ses jouets
**Its eyes were shining.** Ses yeux brillaient.

**itself** *pronoun*
1 **se, s'**
**The cat is washing itself.** Le chat se lave.
**The animal injured itself.** L'animal s'est blessé.
2 **all by itself** tout seul
**He left the dog all by itself.** Il a laissé le chien tout seul.

**WORD TIP** *se* becomes before *a, e, i, o, u* or *silent h*.

**ivy** *noun*
le **lierre** *masc*

# Jj

**jack** *noun*
1 *(in cards)* le **valet** *masc*
2 *(for a car)* le **cric** *masc*

♪ **jacket** *noun*
la **veste** *fem*
- **jacket potato** la pomme de terre en robe des champs

**jackpot** *noun*
le **gros lot**
to win the jackpot gagner [1] le gros lot

**jagged** *adjective*
**dentelé** *masc*, **dentelée** *fem*

**jail** *noun* ▷ see **jail** *verb*
la **prison** *fem*

to **jail** *verb* ▷ see **jail** *noun*
**emprisonner [1]**

♪ **jam** *noun*
1 *(for eating)* la **confiture** *fem*
raspberry jam la confiture de framboises
2 *(in traffic)* un **embouteillage** *masc*

**Jamaica** *noun*
la **Jamaïque** *fem*

**Jamaican** *adjective* ▷ see **Jamaican** *noun*
**jamaïquain** *masc*, **jamaïquaine** *fem*

**Jamaican** *noun* ▷ see **Jamaican** *adj*
un **Jamaïquain** *masc*, une **Jamaïquaine** *fem*

**jammed** *adjective*
**coincé** *masc*, **coincée** *fem*

♪ **January** *noun*
**janvier** *masc*
in January en janvier

**WORD TIP** Months of the year and days of the week start with small letters in French.

**Japan** *noun*
le **Japon** *masc*
in Japan au Japon

**Japanese** *adjective* ▷ see **Japanese** *noun*
**japonais** *masc*, **japonaise** *fem*
a Japanese car une voiture japonaise

**Japanese** *noun* ▷ see **Japanese** *adj*
1 *(person)* un **Japonais** *masc*, une **Japonaise** *fem*
the Japanese les Japonais ⏩

2 (*the language*) le **japonais** *masc*
I speak Japanese. Je parle japonais.

**jar** *noun*
1 (*small*) le **pot** *masc*
a jar of jam un pot de confiture
2 (*large*) le **bocal** *masc* (*pl* les **bocaux**)

**javelin** *noun*
le **javelot** *masc*

**jaw** *noun*
la **mâchoire** *fem*

**jazz** *noun*
le **jazz** *masc*
- **jazz band** un orchestre de jazz

**jealous** *adjective*
**jaloux** *masc*, **jalouse** *fem*

**jealousy** *noun*
la **jalousie** *fem*

**jeans** *noun*
le **jean** *masc*
a pair of jeans un jean

**mini-info *jeans***
Jeans (a singular word in French: *le jean*, or *le blue-jean*) are made of the strong cotton material that originally came from the French town of Nîmes— *de Nîmes* was shortened to 'denim'.

**jelly** *noun*
la **gelée** *fem*

**jellyfish** *noun*
la **méduse** *fem*

**jersey** *noun* ▷ see **Jersey** *noun*
1 (*pullover*) le **pull** *masc*
2 (*for sport*) le **maillot** *masc*

**Jersey** *noun* ▷ see **jersey** *noun*
**Jersey** *fem* (*in the Channel Islands*)

**WORD TIP** Unlike other names of islands, *Jersey* does not take *le* or *la*.

**Jesus** *noun*
**Jésus** *masc*
Jesus Christ Jésus-Christ

**jet** *noun*
le **jet** *masc*
- **jet lag** le décalage horaire
- **jet-ski** le jet-ski

**jetty** *noun*
la **jetée** *fem*

**Jew** *noun*
un **juif** *masc*, une **juive** *fem*

**WORD TIP** Adjectives and nouns of religion start with a small letter in French.

**jewel** *noun*
le **bijou** *masc* (*pl* les **bijoux**)

**jeweller** *noun*
le **bijoutier** *masc*, la **bijoutière** *fem*
- **jeweller's shop** la bijouterie

**jewellery** *noun*
les **bijoux** *masc pl*

**Jewish** *adjective*
**juif** *masc*, **juive** *fem*

**WORD TIP** Adjectives and nouns of religion start with a small letter in French.

**jigsaw** *noun*
le **puzzle** *masc*

♪ **job** *noun*
1 (*paid work*) un **emploi** *masc*
a job as a secretary un emploi comme secrétaire
He's got a job at the supermarket. Il a un emploi au supermarché.
What's your job? Qu'est-ce que vous faites comme travail?
to be out of a job être [6] sans emploi
I'm out of a job right now. En ce moment je suis sans emploi.
2 (*a task*) le **travail** *masc*
It's not an easy job. Ce n'est pas un travail facile.
She made a good job of it. Elle a fait un bon travail.

**jobless** *adjective*
**sans emploi**

**jockey** *noun*
le **jockey** *masc*

to **jog** *verb*
to go jogging faire [10] du jogging
She goes jogging every day. Elle fait du jogging tous les jours.

to **join** *verb*
1 (*parts, ends*) **joindre [49]**
2 (*to become a member of*) **s'inscrire [38] à**
I've joined the judo club. Je me suis inscrit au club de judo.
3 (*to meet up with*) **rejoindre [49]**
I'll join you later. Je te rejoins tout à l'heure.
- **to join in**
**participer [1]**
Ruth never joins in. Ruth ne participe jamais.
- **to join in something**
**participer [1] à quelque chose**
Won't you join in the game? Veux-tu participer au jeu?

**joiner** *noun*
le **menuisier** *masc*, la **menuisière** *fem*

**joint** *adjective* ▷ see **joint** *noun*
the joint winners les lauréats ex aequo

**joint** *noun* ▷ see **joint** *adj*
1 (*of meat*) le **rôti** *masc*
2 (*in your body*) une **articulation** *fem*

**joke** *noun* ▷ see **joke** *verb*
(*a funny story*) la **plaisanterie** *fem*
to tell a joke raconter une plaisanterie

to **joke** *verb* ▷ see **joke** *noun*
**plaisanter [1]**
You're joking! Tu plaisantes!

**joker** *noun*
1 (*in cards*) le **joker** *masc*
2 (*in class*) le **farceur** *masc*, la **farceuse** *fem*

**Jordan** *noun*
la **Jordanie** *fem*

**journalism** *noun*
le **journalisme** *masc*

♂ **journalist** *noun*
le & la **journaliste** *masc & fem*
Sean's dad is a journalist. Le père de Sean est journaliste.

♂ **journey** *noun*
1 (*long distance*) le **voyage** *masc*
our journey to Morocco notre voyage au Maroc
2 (*to work, school*) le **trajet** *masc*
a bus journey un trajet en bus
My journey to school takes half an hour. Le trajet à l'école dure trente minutes.

**joy** *noun*
la **joie** *fem*

**joy-riding** *noun*
le **rodéo à la voiture volée**

**joystick** *noun*
(*for computer games*) la **manette de jeu**

**Judaism** *noun*
le **judaïsme** *masc*

**WORD TIP** Adjectives and nouns of religion start with a small letter in French.

**judge** *noun* ▷ see **judge** *verb*
le **juge** *masc*

to **judge** *verb* ▷ see **judge** *noun*
1 (*a time, a distance*) **estimer [1]**
2 (*a person*) **juger [52]**

**judgement** *noun*
le **jugement** *masc*

**judo** *noun*
le **judo** *masc*
She does judo. Elle fait du judo.

**jug** *noun*
le **pot** *masc*

to **juggle** *verb*
**jongler [1]**

**juggler** *noun*
le **jongleur** *masc*, la **jongleuse** *fem*

♂ **juice** *noun*
le **jus** *masc*
Two orange juices, please. Deux jus d'orange, s'il vous plaît.

**juicy** *adjective*
**juteux** *masc*, **juteuse** *fem*

**jukebox** *noun*
le **jukebox** *masc*

♂ **July** *noun*
**juillet** *masc*
in July en juillet

**WORD TIP** Months of the year and days of the week start with small letters in French.

**jumble sale** *noun*
la **vente de charité**

**jumbo jet** *noun*
le **gros-porteur** *masc*

**jump** *noun* ▷ see **jump** *verb*
le **saut** *masc*
a parachute jump un saut en parachute

♂ to **jump** *verb* ▷ see **jump** *noun*
**sauter [1]**

♂ **jumper** *noun*
le **pull** *masc*

**junction** *noun*
1 (*of roads*) le **carrefour** *masc*
2 (*of motorways*) un **échangeur** *masc*
3 (*on a railway*) le **nœud ferroviaire**

♂ **June** *noun*
**juin** *masc*
in June en juin

**WORD TIP** Months of the year and days of the week start with small letters in French.

**jungle** *noun*
la **jungle** *fem*

♂ **junior** *adjective* ▷ see **junior** *noun*
**primaire** *masc & fem*
a junior school une école primaire

♂ **junior** *noun* ▷ see **junior** *adj*
un & une **élève du primaire**
the juniors les élèves du primaire

**junk** *noun*
(*useless things*) le **bric-à-brac** *masc*
• **junk food** la nourriture industrielle
• **junk shop** la brocante

**jury** *noun*
le **jury** *masc*



English–French
a b c d e f g h i j k l m n o p q r s t u v w x y z

**just** *adverb*
1 (*immediately, simply*) **juste**
**just before midday** juste avant midi
**just after the church** juste après l'église
**just for fun** juste pour rire
2 **to have just done something** venir Ⓔ **[81]** juste de faire quelque chose
**Tom has just arrived.** Tom vient juste d'arriver.
**Helen had just called.** Helen venait juste d'appeler.
3 (*right now*) **I'm just finishing my homework.** Je suis en train de finir mes devoirs.
**I'm just coming!** J'arrive!
4 (*only*) **ne ... que**
**It's just for you.** Ce n'est que pour toi.
**There's just me and Justine.** Il n'y a que Justine et moi.
**Just a moment, please.** Un moment, s'il vous plait.
5 (*exactly*) **exactement**
**It's just what I need.** C'est exactement ce que je veux.

**justice** *noun*
la **justice** *fem*

to **justify** *verb*
**justifier [1]**

# Kk

**kangaroo** *noun*
le **kangourou** *masc*

**karaoke** *noun*
le **karaoké** *masc*

**karate** *noun*
le **karaté** *masc*
• **karate chop** *noun*
le coup de karaté

**kebab** *noun*
la **brochette** *fem*

**keen** *adjective*
1 **passionnée** *fem*, **passionné** *masc*
**She's a keen photographer.** C'est une photographe passionnée.
**I'm keen to see it.** J'ai envie de le voir.
**You don't look very keen.** Tu n'as pas l'air très enthousiaste.
2 **to be keen on something** aimer bien quelque chose
**I'm keen on tennis.** J'aime bien le tennis.
3 **to be keen on doing something** avoir **[5]** très envie de faire quelque chose
**I'm not keen on camping.** Je n'ai pas très envie de faire du camping.
4 **to be keen on someone** être **[6]** très attiré par quelqu'une (*boy by a girl*), être très attirée par quelqu'un (*girl by a boy*)
**He is keen on her.** Il est très attiré par elle.
**She is keen on him.** Elle est très attirée par lui.

to **keep** *verb*
1 (*a letter, a seat*) **garder [1]**
**I kept the letter.** J'ai gardé la lettre.
**Will you keep my seat?** Tu peux garder ma place?
**They kept her in hospital.** Ils l'ont gardée à l'hôpital.
2 (*a promise, a secret*) **to keep a promise** tenir **[77]** sa promesse
**He kept his promise.** Il a tenu sa promesse.
**to keep a secret** garder un secret
**He kept it to himself.** Il l'a gardé pour soi.
3 (*to stay*) **rester** Ⓔ **[1]**
**Keep calm!** Restez calme!
4 (*to store*) **ranger**
**I keep my bike in the garage.** Je range mon vélo dans le garage.
• **to keep on**
**continuer [1]**
**Keep straight on.** Continuez tout droit.
**She kept on talking.** Elle a continué à parler.
**He keeps on ringing me up.** Il n'arrête pas de m'appeler.
• **to keep out**
**Keep out!** Ne pas entrer!
• **to keep up**
1 (*to be as good as the rest*) **suivre [75]**
**He can't keep up in chemistry.** Il ne suit pas bien en chimie.
2 (*to continue*) **continuer [1]**
**Keep up the good work!** Continuez comme ça!

**keep fit** *noun*
la **gymnastique d'entretien** *fem*

**kennel** *noun*
1 (*for one dog*) la **niche** *fem*
2 **kennels** (*for boarding*) le **chenil** *masc*

**kerb** *noun*
le **bord du trottoir** *masc*

**ketchup** *noun*
le **ketchup** *masc*

**kettle** *noun*
la **bouilloire** *fem*
**to put the kettle on** mettre [11] l'eau à chauffer
**The kettle's boiling.** L'eau bout.

**key** *noun*
1 (*for a lock*) la **clé** *fem*
**a bunch of keys** un trousseau de clés
2 (*on a piano, a computer*) la **touche** *fem*
3 (*in music*) le **ton** *masc*
**What key is it in?** Dans quel ton est-il?
**It is in the key of C minor.** Il est en Do mineur.

**keyboard** *noun*
(*of a piano, a computer*) le **clavier** *masc*
**the numeric keyboard** le clavier numérique
**... and on the keyboards, Jean-Baptiste ...** et au clavier, Jean-Baptiste

**keyhole** *noun*
le **trou de serrure** *masc*

**keyring** *noun*
le **porte-clés** *masc*

♪ **kick** *noun* ▷ see **kick** *verb*
1 (*from a person, a horse*) le **coup de pied** *masc*
**to give somebody a kick** donner [1] un coup de pied à quelqu'un
**He gave him a good kick.** Il lui a donné un bon coup de pied.
2 (*in football*) le **tir** *masc*
**a free kick** un coup franc
**Rooney took a kick at goal.** Rooney a tiré vers le but.
3 **to get a kick out of something** prendre [64] plaisir à faire quelque chose
**She gets a kick out of it.** Elle prend plaisir à faire ça.

to **kick** *verb* ▷ see **kick** *noun*
**donner [1] un coup de pied**
**She kicked him.** Elle lui a donné un coup de pied.
**to kick the ball** donner un coup de pied dans le ballon
**Jean-Luc kicked the ball over the goalpost.** Jean-Luc a envoyé le ballon par-dessus le poteau de but d'un coup de pied.

**kick-off** *noun*
le **coup d'envoi** *masc*
**What time's the kick-off?** À quelle heure on décolle?

**kid** *noun* ▷ see **kid** *verb*
1 (*child*) le & la **gosse** *masc & fem* (*informal*)
**Dad's looking after the kids.** Papa s'occupe des gosses.
2 (*young goat*) le **chevreau** *masc*, la **chevrette** *fem*

**kid** *noun* ▷ see **kid** *verb*
**rigoler [1]**
**I'm only kidding!** Je rigole!
**You've got to be kidding!** Tu veux rire!

to **kidnap** *verb*
**enlever [50]**
**He was kidnapped.** Il a été enlevé.

**kidnapper** *noun*
le **kidnappeur** *masc*, la **kidnappeuse** *fem*

**kidney** *noun*
1 (*part of the body*) le **rein** *masc*
2 (*food*) le **rognon** *masc*

to **kill** *verb*
1 (*to cause death to*) **tuer [1]**
**He killed the wasp.** Il a tué la guêpe.
**She was killed in an accident.** Elle a été tuée dans un accident.
**My feet are killing me.** J'ai mal aux pieds.
2 **to kill oneself** se suicider Ⓔ [1]
**He killed himself.** Il s'est suicidé.

**killer** *noun*
(*murderer*) le **meurtrier** *masc*, la **meurtrière** *fem*

♪ **kilo** *noun* ▷ see **kilogramme** *noun*
le **kilo** *masc*
**a kilo of sugar** un kilo de sucre
**five euros a kilo** cinq euros le kilo

**kilogramme** *noun* ▷ see **kilo** *noun*
le **kilogramme** *masc*

♪ **kilometre** *noun*
le **kilomètre** *masc* (*All road distances in France and Belgium are measured in kilometres.*)

♪ **kind** *adjective* ▷ see **kind** *noun*
**gentil** *masc*, **gentille** *fem*
**Marion was very kind to me.** Marion a été très gentille avec moi.
**That's very kind of you.** C'est très gentil de votre part.

**kind** *noun* ▷ see **kind** *adj*
la **sorte** *fem*
**all kinds of people** toutes sortes de gens
**He's kind of cute.** Il est plutôt mignon.

**kindness** *noun*
la **gentillesse** *fem*

English-French

a b c d e f g h i j k l m n o p q r s t u v w x y z

**king** *noun*
le **roi** *masc*
King George le roi Georges
the king of hearts le roi de cœur

**WORD TIP** *le* is used with names of kings and a small letter is used for *roi* in French.

**kingdom** *noun*
le **royaume** *masc*
the United Kingdom le Royaume-Uni
the animal kingdom le règne animal

**kiosk** *noun*
1 (*for newspapers, snacks*) le **kiosque** *masc*
2 (*phonebox*) la **cabine** *fem*

**kipper** *noun*
un **hareng fumé** *masc*

**kiss** *noun* ▷ see **kiss** *verb*
le **baiser** *masc*
to give somebody a kiss embrasser quelqu'un
• **the kiss of life** le bouche-à-bouche

to **kiss** *verb* ▷ see **kiss** *noun*
**embrasser [1]**
Kiss me! Embrasse-moi!
We kissed each other. Nous nous sommes embrassés.

**kit** *noun*
1 (*set of tools*) la **trousse** *fem*
a tool kit une trousse à outils
2 (*clothes*) les **affaires** *fem plural*
Where's my football kit? Où sont mes affaires de foot?
3 (*for making models, furniture*) le **kit** *masc*
a hands-free kit un kit mains libres conducteur

**kitchen** *noun*
la **cuisine** *fem*
the kitchen table la table de la cuisine
• **kitchen foil** le papier d'aluminium
• **kitchen roll** l'essuie-tout *masc*

**kite** *noun*
(*toy*) le **cerf-volant** *masc*
to fly a kite faire **[10]** voler un cerf-volant

**kitten** *noun*
le **chaton** *masc*
to have kittens avoir **[5]** des chatons

**kiwi fruit** *noun*
le **kiwi** *masc*

**knack** *noun*
le **don** *masc*
I think I've got the knack of it. Je crois que j'en ai attrapé le tour de main.

**knee** *noun*
le **genou** *masc* (*pl* les **genoux**)
on hands and knees à quatre pattes

to **kneel** *verb*
**se mettre** Ⓔ **[11] à genoux**

**knickers** *plural noun*
la **petite culotte** *fem*

**knife** *noun*
le **couteau** *masc* (*pl* les **couteaux**)
a bread knife un couteau à pain
a sharp knife un couteau tranchant

**knight** *noun*
1 (*in chess*) le **cavalier** *masc*
2 (*in history*) le **chevalier** *masc*

to **knit** *verb*
**tricoter [1]**

**knitting** *noun*
le **tricot** *masc*

**knob** *noun*
le **bouton** *masc*

**knock** *noun* ▷ see **knock** *verb*
le **coup** *masc*
a knock on the head un coup à la tête
a knock at the door un coup à la porte

to **knock** *verb* ▷ see **knock** *noun*
1 (*to bang*) **cogner [1]**
I knocked my arm on the table. Je me suis cogné le bras contre la table.
2 (*on the door*) **frapper [1]**
I'll knock on the door around 7.30. Je frapperai à ta porte vers 7 h 30.
• **to knock down**
1 (*a pedestrian, child*) **renverser [1]**
She was knocked down by a car. Elle a été renversée par une voiture.
2 (*an old building*) **démolir [2]**
• **to knock out**
1 (*in boxing*) **assommer [1]**
2 (*in competitions*) **éliminer [1]**
They were knocked out in the first round. Ils ont été éliminé au premier tour.

**knocker** *noun*
un **heurtoir** *masc*

**knot** *noun*
le **nœud** *masc*
to tie a knot in something nouer **[1]** quelque chose

to **know** *verb*
1 (*a fact, something*) **savoir [70]**
Do you know where Tim is? Tu sais où est Tim?
I know they've moved house. Je sais qu'ils ont déménagé.

Yes, I know. Oui, je sais.
You never know! On ne sait jamais!
Who knows? Va savoir!
to know how to do something savoir [70] faire quelque chose
Steve knows how to make couscous. Steve sait faire du couscous.
Liz knows how to mend it. Liz sait le réparer.

2 (*a person, a place, a book, some music*) **connaître [27]**
Do you know the Jacksons? Est-ce que tu connais les Jackson?
all the people I know tous les gens que je connais
Yes, I know Paris. Oui, je connais Paris.
I know him. Je le connais.
I don't know his mother. Je ne connais pas sa mère.

• **to know about**

1 (*a situation, a person*) être [6] au courant de quelque chose
She knows about the situation. Elle est au courant de la situation.
Do you know about Mark? Est-que vous êtes au courant pour Mark?

2 (*how things work*) s'y connaître Ⓔ [27] en quelque chose
She knows about computers Elle s'y connaît en informatique.

**knowledge** *noun*
la **connaissance** *fem*
It's common knowledge. C'est de notoriété publique.

**knuckle** *noun*
l'**articulation des doigts** *fem*

**Koran** *noun*
(*Religion*) le **Coran** *masc*
a verse of the Koran un verset du Coran
to follow the teachings of the Koran suivre le Coran

**kosher** *adjective*
**casher** *masc & fem*
a kosher restaurant un restaurant casher

# L l

**lab** *noun*
le **labo** *masc* (*informal*)

**label** *noun*
une **étiquette** *fem*

**laboratory** *noun*
le **laboratoire** *masc*

**Labour** *noun*
**les travaillistes** *masc pl*
the Labour Party le parti travailliste

**lace** *noun*
1 (*for a shoe*) le **lacet** *masc*
2 (*material*) la **dentelle** *fem*

**lad** *noun*
le **gars** *invariable masc*

**ladder** *noun*
une **échelle** *fem*

**ladies** *noun*
1 (*lavatory*) les **toilettes** *fem pl*
2 (*on a sign*) 'Ladies' 'Dames'

♪ **lady** *noun*
la **dame** *fem*
ladies and gentlemen mesdames et messieurs

**lager** *noun*
la **bière blonde**

**laid-back** *adjective*
**décontracté** *masc*, **décontractée** *fem*

♪ **lake** *noun*
le **lac** *masc*
Lake Geneva le lac Léman

♪ **lamb** *noun*
un **agneau** *masc* (*pl* les **agneaux**)

♪ **lamp** *noun*
la **lampe** *fem*
• **lamp-post** le réverbère

♪ **land** *noun* ▷ see **land** *verb*
1 (*from the sea*) la **terre** *fem*
2 (*property*) le **terrain** *masc*
a piece of land un terrain
They've bought some land there. Ils ont acheté du terrain là-bas.

to **land** *verb* ▷ see **land** *noun*
1 (*planes, passengers*) **atterrir [2]**
2 (*from a ship*) **débarquer [1]**

**landing** *noun*
1 (*on the stairs*) le **palier** *masc*
2 (*of a plane*) un **atterrissage** *masc*
3 (*from a boat*) le **débarquement** *masc*

**landlady** *noun*
la **propriétaire** *fem*

**landlord** *noun*
le **propriétaire** *masc*

**landmark** *noun*
le **point de repère**

**landscape** *noun*
le **paysage** *masc*

**lane** *noun*
1 (*country road*) le **chemin** *masc*
2 (*of a motorway*) la **voie** *fem*

♪ **language** *noun*
1 (*French, Italian, etc*) la **langue** *fem*
**a foreign language** une langue étrangère
**She speaks three languages.** Elle parle trois langues.
2 (*way of speaking*) le **langage** *masc*
**bad language** le langage grossier
• **language lab** le laboratoire de langues
• **language school** une école de langue

**lap** *noun*
1 (*your knees*) les **genoux** *masc pl*
**The cat was on my lap.** Le chat était sur mes genoux.
2 (*in races*) le **tour de piste**
**They're on the last lap.** Ils font le dernier tour.
• **laptop** le portable

♪ **large** *adjective*
1 (*in general*) **grand** *masc*, **grande** *fem*
**a large number** un grand nombre
**a large crowd** une grande foule
**Do you have a larger size?** Vous avez la taille au-dessus?
2 (*piece, part, animal*) **gros** *masc*, **grosse** *fem*
**a large piece of cake** un gros morceau de gâteau
**a large amount of money** une grosse somme d'argent
**a large family** une famille nombreuse

**laser** *noun*
le **laser** *masc*
• **laser beam** le rayon laser
• **laser printer** une imprimante à laser
• **laser surgery** la chirurgie au laser

♪ **last** *adjective* ▷ see **last** *adv, verb*
1 (*after the noun*) **dernier** *masc*, **dernière** *fem*
**last week** la semaine dernière
**last month** le mois dernier
2 (*before the noun*) , **dernier** *masc*, **dernière** *fem*
**the last time I played tennis** la dernière fois que j'ai joué au tennis

♪ **last** *adverb* ▷ see **last** *adj, verb*
1 (*in final position*) **en dernier**
**Mark arrived last.** Mark est arrivé en dernier.
**At last!** Enfin!
2 (*most recently*) **I last saw her in May.** La dernière fois que je l'ai vue c'était en mai.

♪ to **last** *verb* ▷ see **last** *adj, adv*
**durer** [1]
**How long does it last?** Ça dure combien de temps?
**It lasts two hours.** Ça dure deux heures.

♪ **late** *adjective, adverb*
1 **en retard**
**I was late.** J'étais en retard.
**They arrived late.** Ils sont arrivés en retard.
**We were late for the film.** Nous étions en retard pour le film.
2 (*buses, trains*) **to be late** avoir [5] du retard
**The train was an hour late.** Le train a eu une heure de retard.
3 (*in the day*) **tard**
**late last night** tard hier soir
**I got up late.** Je me suis levé tard.
**It's getting late.** Il se fait tard.

**lately** *adverb*
**ces derniers temps**

♪ **later** *adverb*
**plus tard**
**I'll explain later.** J'expliquerai plus tard.
**See you later!** À tout à l'heure!

**latest** *adjective* ▷ see **latest** *noun*
**dernier** *masc*, **dernière** *fem*
**the latest news** les dernières nouvelles
**her latest album** son dernier album

**latest** *noun* ▷ see **latest** *adj*
**at the latest** au plus tard
**the latest in audio equipment** le dernier cri en matière d'équipement hi-fi

**laugh** *noun* ▷ see **laugh** *verb*
1 le **rire** *masc*
2 **I did it for a laugh.** Je l'ai fait pour rigoler.

♪ to **laugh** *verb* ▷ see **laugh** *noun*
1 **rire** [68]
**Everybody laughed.** Tout le monde a ri.
2 **to laugh at somebody** se moquer Ⓔ [1] de quelqu'un
**They laughed at me.** Ils se sont moqués de moi.
**Don't laugh!** Ne te moque pas!

Ⓔ means the verb takes être to form the perfect

**launch** *noun* ▷ see **launch** *verb*
1 (*of a product, a rocket*) le **lancement** *masc*
2 (*boat*) la **vedette** *fem*

to **launch** *verb* ▷ see **launch** *noun*
1 (*a product, a spacecraft*) **lancer [61]**
2 (*a ship*) **mettre [11] à l'eau**

**launderette** *noun*
la **laverie automatique**

**laundry** *noun*
1 (*in a hotel*) la **laverie** *fem*
2 (*shop*) la **blanchisserie** *fem*

**lavatory** *noun*
les **toilettes** *fem pl*

**law** *noun*
1 (*rules*) la **loi** *fem*
**It's against the law.** C'est interdit.
2 (*subject of study*) le **droit** *masc*

♪ **lawn** *noun*
la **pelouse** *fem*
**to mow the lawn** tondre [3] la pelouse
• **lawnmower** la tondeuse

**lawyer** *noun*
un **avocat** *masc*, une **avocate** *fem*

♪ to **lay** *verb*
1 **to lay the table** mettre [11] la table
**I usually lay the table.** D'habitude c'est moi qui mets la table.
2 (*rugs, newspaper*) **étaler [1]**
**We laid newspaper on the floor.** Nous avons étalé du papier journal par terre.
3 (*your hand, bricks*) **poser [1]**
• **lay-by** une aire de stationnement

**layer** *noun*
la **couche** *fem*

**laziness** *noun*
la **paresse** *fem*

♪ **lazy** *adjective*
**paresseux** *masc*, **paresseuse** *fem*
**Don't be so lazy!** Ne sois pas si paresseux!

**lead** *noun* ▷ see **lead** *verb*
1 **to be in the lead** être [6] en tête
**Harry's in the lead.** Harry est en tête.
2 (*cable*) le **fil** *masc*
3 (*for a dog*) la **laisse** *fem*
4 (*metal*) le **plomb** *masc*

to **lead** *verb* ▷ see **lead** *noun*
1 **to lead to a place** mener [50] à quelque chose
**The path leads to the sea.** Le chemin mène à la mer.
2 **to lead to something** entraîner [1] quelque chose
**It could lead to difficulties.** Ça pourrait entraîner des difficultés.
3 **to be leading** être [6] en tête
**Who's leading?** Qui est en tête?

♪ **leader** *noun*
1 (*of a political party, a gang*) le **chef** *masc*
2 (*in a competition*) le **premier** *masc*, la **première** *fem*

**lead-free petrol** *noun*
l'**essence sans plomb** *fem*

**lead singer** *noun*
le **chanteur principal**, la **chanteuse principale**

**leaf** *noun*
la **feuille** *fem*

♪ **leaflet** *noun*
le **dépliant** *masc*

**league** *noun*
le **championnat** *masc*

**leak** *noun* ▷ see **leak** *verb*
la **fuite** *fem*
**a gas leak** une fuite de gaz

to **leak** *verb* ▷ see **leak** *noun*
(*bottles, roof*) **fuir [44]**
**The roof is leaking!** Le toit fuit!

to **lean** *verb*
1 **to lean on something** s'appuyer ⓔ [41] sur quelque chose
**She was leaning on my arm.** Elle s'appuyait sur mon bras.
2 **to lean something against something** appuyer [41] quelque chose contre quelque chose
**to lean the ladder against the tree** Appuyer l'échelle contre l'arbre
3 (*person*) **se pencher** ⓔ **[1]**
**to lean out of the window** se pencher par la fenêtre

to **leap** *verb*
**sauter [1]**
**to leap over something** franchir [2] quelque chose d'un bond
• **leap year** une année bissextile

♪ to **learn** *verb*
**apprendre [64]**
**Sally's learning Russian.** Sally apprend le russe.
**We learned a lot.** On a appris beaucoup de choses.
**to learn how to do something** apprendre [64] à faire quelque chose
**I want to learn to drive.** Je veux apprendre à conduire.

English–French

**learner** *noun*
un **apprenant** *masc*, une **apprenante** *fem*
Alex is a fast learner. Alex apprend vite.
• **learner driver** un & une élève d'auto-école

**least** *adverb, adjective, pronoun*
1 (*followed by an adjective*) **the least** le moins, la moins, les moins
**the least expensive hotel** l'hôtel le moins cher
**the least expensive car** la voiture la moins chère
2 (*followed by a noun*) **the least** le moins de
**I've got the least food.** C'est moi qui ai le moins de nourriture.
3 (*after verb*) **(the) least** le moins
**I like the blue shirt least.** C'est la chemise bleue que j'aime le moins.
4 (*with numbers*) **at least** au moins
**at least twenty people** au moins vingt personnes
5 (*at any rate*) **at least** du moins
**At least, I think she's a teacher.** Du moins, je crois qu'elle est professeur.

**leather** *noun*
le **cuir** *masc*
**a leather jacket** un blouson en cuir

to **leave** *verb*
1 (*to go away*) **partir** Ⓔ **[58]**
**They leave tomorrow.** Ils vont partir demain.
**He has already left.** Il est déjà parti.
**We left at six.** Nous sommes partis à six heures.
2 (*a place*) **quitter [1]**
**I left the office at five.** J'ai quitté le bureau à cinq heures.
**John left school at sixteen.** John a quitté l'école à seize ans.
3 (*to go out of*) **sortir** Ⓔ **[72] de**
**She left the cinema at ten.** Elle est sortie du cinéma à dix heures.
4 (*to put, to put off*) **laisser [1]**
**You can leave your coats in the hall.** Vous pouvez laisser vos manteaux dans l'entrée.
**I left it till the last minute.** Je l'ai laissé jusqu'à la dernière minute.
5 (*to forget*) **oublier [1]**
**He left his bag on the train.** Il a oublié son sac dans le train.
**to leave something behind** laisser quelque chose
**Don't leave your mobile behind.** Ne laisse pas ton portable.
6 **to be left** rester Ⓔ **[1]**
**There are two pancakes left.** Il reste deux crêpes.
**We have ten minutes left.** Il nous reste dix minutes.
• **to leave something out**
**omettre [11] quelque chose**
**You left out that information.** Tu as omis cette information.

**lecture** *noun*
1 (*for the public*) la **conférence** *fem*
2 (*at university*) le **cours magistral** (*pl* les **cours magistraux**)

**lecturer** *noun*
le **professeur à l'université**

**leek** *noun*
le **poireau** *masc* (*pl* les **poireaux**)

**left** *adjective* ▷ see **left** *noun*
**gauche** *masc & fem*
**his left foot** son pied gauche

**left** *noun* ▷ see **left** *adj*
la **gauche** *fem*
**on my left** à ma gauche
**to drive on the left** conduire **[26]** à gauche
**Turn left at the church.** Tournez à gauche à l'église.

to **left-click** *verb*
**to left-click on the icon** cliquer **[1]** sur l'icône en appuyant sur le bouton gauche de la souris

**left-hand** *adjective*
**the left-hand side** la gauche

**left-handed** *adjective*
**gaucher** *masc*, **gauchère** *fem*

**left luggage office** *noun*
la **consigne** *fem*

**leftovers** *plural noun*
les **restes** *masc pl*

**leg** *noun*
1 (*of a person, horse*) la **jambe** *fem*
**my left leg** ma jambe gauche
**My leg hurts.** J'ai mal à la jambe.
**to break your leg** se casser Ⓔ **[1]** la jambe
2 (*of other animals*) la **patte** *fem*
3 (*of a table, chair*) le **pied** *masc*
4 (*in cooking*) **a leg of chicken** une cuisse de poulet
**a leg of lamb** un gigot

**legal** *adjective*
**légal** *masc*, **légale** *fem*, **légaux** *masc pl*, **légales** *fem pl*

**legend** *noun*
la **légende** *fem*

**leggings** *plural noun*
le **caleçon** *masc*



Ⓔ means the verb takes être to form the perfect

**legible** *adjective*
**lisible** *masc & fem*

♪ **leisure** *noun*
les **loisirs** *masc pl*
**in my leisure time** pendant mes loisirs

♪ **leisure activities** *plural noun*
les **loisirs** *masc pl*
**What sort of leisure activities are there?** Qu'est-ce qu'il y a comme loisirs?

**leisure centre** *noun*
le **centre de loisirs**

♪ **lemon** *noun*
le **citron** *masc*
**a lemon yoghurt** un yaourt au citron

♪ **lemonade** *noun*
la **limonade** *fem*
**a can of lemonade** une boîte de limonade

**lemon juice** *noun*
le **jus de citron**

♪ to **lend** *verb*
**to lend something to somebody** prêter **[1]** quelque chose à quelqu'un
**I lent my bike to Janet.** J'ai prêté mon vélo à Janet.
**I'm lending Dan some money.** Je prête de l'argent à Dan.
**Will you lend it to me?** Veux-tu me le prêter?

**length** *noun*
la **longueur** *fem*
**What length is the garden?** Quelle est la longueur du jardin?
**It's 20 metres in length.** Il est long de 20 mètres.

♪ **lens** *noun*
1 (*in a camera*) un **objectif** *masc*
2 (*in spectacles*) le **verre** *masc*
3 (*contact lenses*) **to wear lenses** porter des lentilles de contact

**Lent** *noun*
le **Carême** *masc*

**lentil** *noun*
la **lentille** *fem*

**Leo** *noun*
le **Lion** *masc*
**I'm a Leo.** Je suis Lion.

**WORD TIP** Signs of the zodiac do not take an article: *un* or *une*.

**leotard** *noun*
le **justaucorps** *invariable masc*

**lesbian** *noun*
la **lesbienne** *fem*

♪ **less** *adjective, adverb, pronoun*
1 (*before a noun*) **moins de**
**less traffic** moins de circulation
**less energy** moins d'énergie
**I have less time now.** J'ai moins de temps maintenant.
2 (*before adjectives, adverbs*) **moins**
**less interesting** moins intéressant
**less quickly than us** moins vite que nous
3 (*after a verb*) **moins**
**Richard eats less.** Richard mange moins.
**She travels less.** Elle voyage moins.
4 (*in amounts*) **less than** moins de
**less than three hours** moins de trois heures
**less than a kilo** moins d'un kilo
5 (*in comparisons*) **less than** moins que
**You spend less than me.** Tu dépenses moins que moi.

♪ **lesson** *noun*
1 (*class*) le **cours** *masc*
**the history lesson** le cours d'histoire
2 (*in a series*) la **leçon** *fem*
**a driving lesson** une leçon de conduite
3 **That taught them a lesson!** Ça leur a servi de leçon!

♪ to **let** *verb*
1 **to let somebody do something** laisser **[1]** quelqu'un faire quelque chose
**She lets me borrow her bike.** Elle me laisse lui emprunter son vélo.
**Will you let me go alone?** Tu me laisses y aller toute seule?
**Let me help you.** Laisse-moi t'aider.
**Let me see it.** Fais voir.
2 (*as a suggestion*) **Let's go!** Allons-y!
**Let's not talk about it.** N'en parlons pas.
**Let's eat out.** Si on allait manger au restaurant?
3 **to let go of somebody** lâcher **[1]** quelqu'un
**Let go of me!** Lâche-moi!
4 (*a house, a flat*) **louer [1]**
**'Flat to let.'** 'Appartement à louer.'

- **to let somebody in**
**faire [10] entrer quelqu'un**
- **to let something off**
1 (*fireworks*) **tirer [1] quelque chose**
2 (*a bomb*) **faire [10] exploser quelque chose**
- **to let somebody off something**
**dispenser [1] quelqu'un de quelque chose**
**He let me off my homework.** Il m'a dispensé de mes devoirs.
- **to let somebody out**
**laisser [1] sortir quelqu'un**
**She won't let us out.** Elle ne va pas nous laisser sortir.

**lethal** *adjective*
**mortel** *masc*, **mortelle** *fem*

♪ **letter** *noun*
1 (*sent by post*) **la lettre** *fem*
**I wrote her a letter.** Je lui ai écrit une lettre.
2 (*in the alphabet*) **la lettre** *fem*
**a word with five letters** un mot de cinq lettres
• **letterbox** la boîte à lettres

**lettuce** *noun*
la **salade** *fem*
**two lettuces** deux salades

**leukaemia** *noun*
la **leucémie** *fem*

**level** *adjective* ▷ see **level** *noun*
1 (*shelf, floor*) **droit** *masc*, **droite** *fem*
2 (*ground*) **plat** *masc*, **plate** *fem*

**level** *noun* ▷ see **level** *adj*
le **niveau** *masc* (*pl* les **niveaux**)
**at street level** au niveau de la rue
• **level crossing** le passage à niveau

**lever** *noun*
le **levier** *masc*

**liar** *noun*
le **menteur** *masc*, la **menteuse** *fem*

**liberal** *adjective*
**libéral** *masc*, **libérale** *fem*, **libéraux** *masc pl*, **libérales** *fem pl*

**Liberal Democrats** *plural noun*
le **parti libéral-démocrate**

**liberty** *noun*
la **liberté** *fem*

**Libra** *noun*
la **Balance** *fem*
**Sean's a Libra.** Sean est Balance.

**WORD TIP** Signs of the zodiac do not take an article: *un* or *une*.

**librarian** *noun*
le & la **bibliothécaire** *masc & fem*

♪ **library** *noun*
la **bibliothèque** *fem*

♪ **licence** *noun*
1 (*for driving, fishing*) le **permis** *masc*
2 (*for a TV*) la **redevance** *fem*

to **lick** *verb*
**lécher** [24]
**to lick your fingers** se lécher Ⓔ [24] les doigts

**lid** *noun*
le **couvercle** *masc*
**to take off the lid** enlever [50] le couvercle

**lie** *noun* ▷ see **lie** *verb*
le **mensonge** *masc*
**to tell lies** mentir [53]

♪ to **lie** *verb* ▷ see **lie** *noun*
1 **to lie on something** être [6] allongé sur quelque chose
**Alice was lying on the sofa.** Alice était allongée sur le canapé.
**My coat lay on the bed.** Mon manteau était sur le lit.
2 (*not to tell the truth*) **mentir** [53]
**I know when she's lying.** Je sais quand elle ment.
**He lied to them.** Il leur a menti.
• **to lie down**
1 (*to sleep*) **se coucher** Ⓔ [1]
2 (*to relax*) **s'allonger** Ⓔ [52]

**lieutenant** *noun*
le **lieutenant** *masc*

♪ **life** *noun*
la **vie** *fem*
**all her life** toute sa vie
**That's life!** C'est la vie!
**to save somebody's life** sauver [1] la vie à quelqu'un
**You saved my life.** Tu m'as sauvé la vie.
• **lifebelt** la bouée de sauvetage
• **lifeboat** le canot de sauvetage

**lifeguard** *noun*
le **maître nageur**

**life jacket** *noun*
le **gilet de sauvetage**

**lifestyle** *noun*
le **style de vie**

♪ **lift** *noun* ▷ see **lift** *verb*
1 (*between floors*) un **ascenseur** *masc*
**Let's take the lift.** Prenons l'ascenseur.
2 (*a ride*) **to give somebody a lift home** déposer [1] quelqu'un chez soi
**Tom gave me a lift home.** Tom m'a déposé chez moi.
**Could you give us a lift to the station?** Tu pourrais nous déposer à la gare?

♪ to **lift** *verb* ▷ see **lift** *noun*
**soulever** [50]
**He lifted the box.** Il a soulevé le carton.

♪ **light** *adjective* ▷ see **light** *noun, verb*
1 (*not heavy*) **léger** *masc*, **légère** *fem*
**a light sweater** un pull léger
**a light meal** un repas léger
**a light breeze** une brise légère
2 **to get light** faire [10] jour
**It gets light at six.** Il fait jour à six heures.
3 (*in colour*) **clair** *masc & fem*

Ⓔ means the verb takes être to form the perfect

**light** *noun* ▷ see **light** *adj, verb*
1 (*electric*) la **lumière** *fem*
**to turn on the light** allumer [1] la lumière
**to turn off the light** éteindre [3] la lumière
2 (*streetlight*) le **réverbère** *masc*
3 (*headlight*) le **phare** *masc*
**His lights aren't on.** Il n'a pas allumé ses phares.
4 (*indicator on a machine*) le **voyant** *masc*
5 (*at cross-roads*) **les feux** *masc pl*
**The lights were green.** Le feu était au vert.
**She didn't stop at the lights.** Elle ne s'est pas arrêtée au feu.
6 (*match*) **Have you got a light?** Tu as du feu?

to **light** *verb* ▷ see **light** *adj, noun*
1 (*an oven, a cigarette*) **allumer** [1]
**to light a fire** faire [10] un feu
2 (*a match*) **craquer** [1]
• **light bulb** une ampoule

**lighter** *noun*
le **briquet** *masc*

**lighthouse** *noun*
le **phare** *masc*

**lightning** *noun*
les **éclairs** *masc pl*
**a flash of lightning** un éclair
**The tree was struck by lightning.** L'arbre a été frappé par la foudre.

**light switch** *noun*
un **interrupteur** *masc*

**like** *conjunction, preposition* ▷ see **like** *verb*
1 (*in descriptions*) **comme**
**like me** comme moi
**like this** comme ça
**like a dog** comme un chien
**like I said** comme j'ai dit
**something like that** quelque chose comme ça
**You're just like my sister!** Tu es exactement comme ma sœur!
2 **to look like somebody** ressembler [1] à quelqu'un
**Katie looks like her father.** Katie ressemble à son père.
3 (*in questions*) **What's it like?** C'est comment?
**What's she like?** Elle est comment?
**What was the weather like?** Quel temps faisait-il?

to **like** *verb* ▷ see **like** *conj, prep*
1 (*saying what you enjoy*) **aimer [1] (bien)**
**I like fish.** J'aime bien le poisson.
**I don't like snakes.** Je n'aime pas les serpents.
**Do you like the campsite?** Il te plaît le camping?
**I really like it.** Ça me plaît beaucoup.
**to like somebody** aimer [1] bien quelqu'un
**I like Peter.** J'aime bien Peter.
2 **to like doing something,** aimer [1] (bien) faire quelque chose
**Mum likes travelling.** Maman aime bien voyager.
**I like to write stories.** J'aime bien écrire des histoires.
3 **to like something best** préférer [24] quelque chose
**I like Spielberg films best.** Je préfère les films de Spielberg.
4 (*talking about what you want*) **What would you like to eat?** Qu'est-ce que tu veux manger?
**I'd like some soup.** Je voudrais de la soupe.
**Would you like a coffee?** Est-ce que tu voudrais un café?
**I'd like a hot chocolate.** Je voudrais un chocolat chaud.

**likely** *adjective*
**probable** *masc & fem*
**It's not very likely.** Ce n'est pas très probable.

**lilac** *noun*
le **lilas** *masc*

**lily** *noun*
le **lys** *masc*

**lime** *noun*
le **citron vert**

**limit** *noun*
la **limitation** *fem*
**the speed limit** la limitation de vitesse

**line** *noun*
1 (*on paper*) la **ligne** *fem*
**a straight line** une ligne droite
**to draw a line** tirer [1] un trait
2 (*for telephones*) la **ligne** *fem*
**Hold the line, please!** Ne quittez pas!
3 (*electric cable*) la **ligne** *fem*
**All the lines are down.** Toutes les lignes ont été abattues.

**linen** *noun*
le **lin** *masc*

**lining** *noun*
la **doublure** *fem*

**link** *noun* ▷ see **link** *verb*
1 (*connection*) le **rapport** *masc*
**Is there a link between the two?** Quel est le rapport entre les deux?
2 (*on a web page*) le **lien** *masc*
**Click on the link.** Cliquez sur le lien.

to **link** *verb* ▷ see **link** *noun*
(*two places*) **relier [1]**
**the motorway which links Cardiff to London** l'autoroute qui relie Cardiff à Londres

**lion** *noun*
le **lion** *masc*

**lip** *noun*
la **lèvre** *fem*
• **lipstick** le rouge à lèvres

**liquid** *adjective, noun*
le **liquide** *masc*

**liquidizer** *noun*
le **mixer** *masc*

**list** *noun*
la **liste** *fem*
**the shopping list** la liste des courses
**to make a list** faire **[10]** une liste

♪ to **listen** *verb*
**écouter [1]**
**I wasn't listening.** Je n'écoutais pas.
**to listen to something** écouter **[1]** quelque chose
**Listen to me.** Écoute-moi.
**Listen to the music.** Écoutez la musique.
**You're not listening to me.** Tu ne m'écoutes pas.

**listener** *noun*
(*Radio*) un **auditeur** *masc*, une **auditrice** *fem*

**literally** *adverb*
**littéralement**

**literature** *noun*
la **littérature** *fem*

♪ **litre** *noun*
le **litre** *masc*
**a litre of milk** un litre de lait

**litter** *noun*
les **détritus** *masc pl*
• **litter bin** la poubelle *fem*

♪ **little** *adjective, pronoun*
1 (*small*) **petit** *masc*, **petite** *fem*
**a little boy** un petit garçon
**a little break** une petite pause
**my little brother** mon petit frère
**little by little** petit à petit
2 (*not much*) **peu de**
**They have little money.** Ils ont peu d'argent.
**We have very little time.** Nous avons très peu de temps.
3 **a little** un peu (de)
**It's a little late.** C'est un peu tard.
**We have a little money.** Nous avons un peu d'argent.
**a little more** un peu plus de
**Could I have a little more cake?** Je peux prendre encore un peu de gâteau?
• **little finger** le petit doigt

♪ **live** *adjective* ▷ see **live** *verb*
1 (*broadcast*) **en direct**
**a live concert** un concert en direct
2 (*animals*) **vivant** *masc*, **vivante** *fem*
**live animals.** des animaux vivants

♪ to **live** *verb* ▷ see **live** *adj*
1 (*in a house, town, country*) **habiter [1]**
**We live at number 57.** Nous habitons au numéro cinquante-sept.
**Shazia lives in Newcastle.** Shazia habite Newcastle, Shazia habite à Newcastle.
**They live in a flat.** Ils habitent dans un appartement.
**They live in France.** Ils habitent en France.
**We're living in the country now.** Nous habitons à la campagne maintenant.
**He's not living at home any more.** Il n'habite plus chez ses parents.
2 (*to be alive, stay alive, spend your life*) **vivre [82]**
**They live together.** Ils vivent ensemble.
**I like living here.** J'aime bien vivre ici.
**to live on something** vivre de quelque chose
**They live on fruit.** Ils vivent de fruits.

**lively** *adjective*
(*party, restaurant*) **animé** *masc*, **animée** *fem*
**a very lively street** une rue très animée

**liver** *noun*
le **foie** *masc*

**living** *noun*
la **vie** *fem*
**What do they do for a living?** Qu'est-ce qu'ils font dans la vie?
**to earn a living** gagner **[1]** sa vie
• **living room** la salle de séjour

**lizard** *noun*
le **lézard** *masc*

♪ **load** *noun* ▷ see **load** *verb*
1 (*on a lorry*) le **chargement** *masc*
2 **a bus-load of tourists** un autobus plein de touristes
3 **loads of** des tas de
**We bought loads of things.** Nous avons acheté des tas de choses.
**They've got loads of money.** Ils sont bourrés de fric.

♪ to **load** *verb* ▷ see **load** *noun*
**charger [52]**
**a lorry loaded with wood** un camion

chargé de bois
**to load a program** charger un programme

**loaf** *noun*
le **pain** *masc*
**a loaf of bread** un pain

**loan** *noun* ▷ see **loan** *verb*
le **prêt** *masc*

to **loan** *verb* ▷ see **loan** *noun*
**prêter [1]**

**lobster** *noun*
le **homard** *masc*

**local** *adjective* ▷ see **local** *noun*
(*shops, school, pool*) **du coin**
**the local library** la bibliothèque du coin
**the local newspaper** le journal local

**local** *noun* ▷ see **local** *adj*
1 (*pub, bar*) le **pub du coin**
2 **the locals** les gens du coin

**locality** *noun*
la **région** *fem*

**lock** *noun* ▷ see **lock** *verb*
1 (*for a door, cupboard*) la **serrure** *fem*
2 (*for a bike, steering wheel*) un **antivol** *masc*
3 (*on a canal*) une **écluse** *fem*

to **lock** *verb* ▷ see **lock** *noun*
**to lock the door** fermer **[1]** la porte à clé
**All the doors are locked.** Toutes les portes sont fermées à clé.

**locker** *noun*
le **casier** *masc*
• **locker room** le vestiaire

**lodger** *noun*
le & la **locataire** *masc & fem*

**loft** *noun*
le **grenier** *masc*

**log** *noun*
la **bûche** *fem*

**logical** *adjective*
**logique** *masc & fem*

**lollipop** *noun*
la **sucette** *fem*

**London** *noun*
**Londres**
**to London** à Londres
**a day in London** une journée à Londres

**Londoner** *noun*
le **Londonien** *masc*, la **Londonienne** *fem*

**loneliness** *noun*
la **solitude** *fem*

♪**lonely** *adjective*
1 **seul** *masc*, **seule** *fem*
**to feel lonely** se sentir Ⓔ **[53]** seul
**I felt lonely at first.** Au début je me sentais seul (*boy speaking*), Au début je me sentais seule (*girl speaking*).
2 (*place*) **isolé** *masc*, **isolée** *fem*
**a lonely farmhouse** une ferme isolée

♪**long** *adjective, adverb* ▷ see **long** *verb*
1 (*in general*) **long** *masc*, **longue** *fem*
**a long film** un film long
**a long dress** une robe longue
**The pool's 50 metres long.** La piscine fait 50 mètres de long.
2 **a long way** loin *masc & fem*
**It's quite a long way.** C'est assez loin.
**It's a long way to the pool.** La piscine est loin d'ici.
3 (*in time expressions*) **all day long** toute la journée
**all night long** toute la nuit
**It's an hour long.** Ça dure une heure.
**a long time** longtemps
**He stayed for a long time.** Il est resté longtemps.
**I've been here for a long time.** Je suis là depuis longtemps.
4 (*with ago*) **long ago, a long time ago** il y a longtemps
**They lived here long ago.** Ils habitaient ici il y a longtemps.
**It happened a long time ago.** Cela s'est passé il y a longtemps.
5 **How long?** Combien de temps?
**How long did it last?** Ça a duré combien de temps?
**How long have you been here?** Tu es là depuis combien de temps?

to **long** *verb* ▷ see **long** *adj, adv*
1 **to long to do something** avoir **[5]** très envie de faire quelque chose
**I'm longing to see you.** J'ai très envie de te voir.
2 **to long for something** attendre **[3]** quelque chose avec impatience
**I'm longing for the holidays.** J'attends les vacances avec impatience.

**long-distance call** *noun*
un **appel interurbain**

**long-distance runner** *noun*
le **coureur de fond**, la **coureuse de fond**

**longer** *adverb*
no longer ne ... plus
**I no longer know.** Je ne sais plus.
**They no longer live here.** Ils n'habitent plus ici.

**long jump** *noun*
le **saut en longueur**

**loo** *noun*
les **toilettes** *fem pl*
**Where's the loo?** Où sont les toilettes?

**look** *noun* ▷ see **look** *verb*
1 (*glance*) le **coup d'œil**
**to have a look at something** jeter [1] un coup d'œil à quelque chose
**Could you have a look at my homework?** Tu peux jeter un coup d'œil à mes devoirs?
2 **to have a look round** faire [10] un tour
**We had a look round the town.** On a fait un tour en ville.
**Let's have a look round the shops.** Si on faisait les magasins?

to **look** *verb* ▷ see **look** *noun*
1 **regarder** [1]
**to look out of the window** regarder par la fenêtre
**I wasn't looking.** Je ne regardais pas.
2 **to look at something** regarder [1] quelque chose
**Martin was looking at the photos.** Martin regardait les photos.
3 (*to seem*) **avoir** [5] **l'air + adjective**
**Melanie looks pleased.** Melanie a l'air contente.
**The salad looks delicious.** La salade a l'air délicieuse.
4 (*to look like*) **What does the house look like?** Comment est la maison?
**It looks like a palace.** On dirait un palais.
**They look like each other.** Ils se ressemblent.
**It looks like rain.** On dirait qu'il va pleuvoir.
**to look like somebody** ressembler [1] à quelqu'un
**Alicia looks like her sister.** Alicia ressemble à sa sœur.
• **to look after**
1 **to look after somebody** s'occuper [1] de quelqu'un
**Dad's looking after the baby.** Papa s'occupe du bébé.
2 **to look after something** surveiller [1] quelque chose
**Can you look after my suitcase?** Tu peux surveiller ma valise?
• **to look for something**
**chercher** [1] **quelque chose**
**I'm looking for the keys.** Je cherche les clés.
• **to look forward to something**
(*a party, a holiday*) **attendre** [3] **quelque chose avec impatience**
**I'm looking forward to your visit.** J'attends ta visite avec impatience.
• **to look onto something**
**donner** [1] **sur quelque chose**
**My room looks onto the garden.** Ma chambre donne sur le jardin.
• **to look round**
**se retourner** Ⓔ [1]
**I looked round to see.** Je me suis retourné pour voir.
• **to look up**
**lever** [1] **les yeux**
**When I looked up, she was gone.** Quand j'ai levé les yeux, elle n'était plus là.
• **to look up something**
**chercher** [1] **quelque chose**
**Look it up in the dictionary.** Cherche-le dans le dictionnaire.

**loony** *adjective* (*informal*)
**dingue** *masc & fem* (*informal*)
**a loony idea** une idée dingue

**loose** *adjective*
1 (*screw, knot*) **desserré** *masc*, **desserrée** *fem*
2 (*trousers, jacket, dress*) **ample** *masc & fem*

**lorry** *noun*
le **camion** *masc*
• **lorry driver** le routier

to **lose** *verb*
1 (*a game, glasses*) **perdre** [3]
**We lost.** Nous avons perdu.
**We lost the match.** Nous avons perdu le match.
**Sam's lost his watch.** Sam a perdu sa montre.
2 **to lose your way** se perdre Ⓔ [3]
**We lost our way in the suburbs.** Nous nous sommes perdus dans la banlieue.

**loss** *noun*
la **perte** *fem*

**lost** *adjective*
**perdu** *masc*, **perdue** *fem*
**Are you lost?** Vous êtes perdus?
**I'm lost.** Je suis perdu.
**to get lost** se perdre Ⓔ [3]
**I got lost on the way.** Je me suis perdu en route.

**lost property** *noun*
les **objets trouvés**
• **lost property office** le bureau des objets trouvés



Ⓔ means the verb takes être to form the perfect

**lot** *noun*
1 **a lot** beaucoup
**Josh eats a lot.** Josh mange beaucoup.
**He's a lot better.** Il va beaucoup mieux.
**She's a lot nicer.** Elle est beaucoup plus sympa.
**Thanks a lot!** Merci beaucoup!
2 **a lot of, lots of** beaucoup de
**a lot of coffee** beaucoup de café
**lots of people** beaucoup de gens
**lots of friends** beaucoup d'amis
**a lot of money** beaucoup d'argent

**WORD TIP** *beaucoup de* becomes *beaucoup d'* before *a, e, i, o, u* or *silent h*.

**lottery** *noun*
la **loterie** *fem*
**to win the lottery** gagner [1] à la loterie
• **lottery ticket** le ticket de loto

**loud** *adjective*
1 **fort** *masc*, **forte** *fem*
**in a loud voice** d'une voix forte
**a little louder** un peu plus fort
2 **out loud** à haute voix
**Ellie read the letter out loud.** Ellie a lu la lettre à haute voix.

**loudly** *adverb*
**fort**

**loudspeaker** *noun*
le **haut-parleur** *masc* (*pl* les **haut-parleurs**)

to **love** *verb* ▷ see **love** *noun*
1 (*a person*) **aimer [1]**
**I love you.** Je t'aime.
**They love each other.** Ils s'aiment.
2 (*a place, a suggestion*) **aimer [1] beaucoup**
**She loves London.** Elle aime beaucoup Londres.
**I'd love to come.** J'aimerais beaucoup venir.
3 (*an activity, a thing*) **adorer [1]**
**Sophie loves seafood.** Sophie adore les fruits de mer.
**to love doing something** adorer faire quelque chose
**I love dancing.** J'adore danser.

**love** *noun* ▷ see **love** *verb*
1 l'**amour** *masc*
**Gina sends her love.** Gina t'embrasse.
**to be in love with somebody** être [6] amoureux *masc* , amoureuse *fem* de quelqu'un
**She's in love with Jake.** Elle est amoureuse de Jake.
**He's in love with Liz.** Il est amoureux de Liz.
**to fall in love with somebody** tomber ❷ [1] amoureux, amoureuse de quelqu'un
**Pete fell in love with her.** Pete est tombé amoureux d'elle.
(*in letters*) **With love from Charlie** Amitiés, Charlie
**Lots of love, ...** Grosses bises, ...
2 (*in tennis*) le **zéro** *masc*
**15 love** 15 à zéro
• **love affair** la liaison *fem*
• **love story** une histoire d'amour

**lovely** *adjective*
1 (*to look at*) **joli** *masc*, **jolie** *fem*
**a lovely dress** une jolie robe
**It's a lovely village.** C'est un joli village.
2 (*weather*) **It's a lovely day.** Il fait très beau.
**We had lovely weather.** Il a fait très beau.
3 (*food, meals*) **délicieux** *masc*, **délicieuse** *fem*
**That was really lovely!** C'était vraiment délicieux!
4 **a lovely surprise** une belle surprise
5 (*person*) **très aimable** *masc & fem*

**lover** *noun*
1 (*in general*) le & la **partenaire** *masc & fem*
2 (*married man's*) la **maîtresse** *fem*
3 (*married woman's*) un **amant** *masc*

**low** *adjective*
**bas** *masc*, **basse** *fem*
**a low table** une table basse
**at a low price** à prix bas
**in a low voice** à voix basse

**lower** *adjective* ▷ see **lower** *verb*
**inférieur** *masc*, **inférieure** *fem*

to **lower** *verb* ▷ see **lower** *adj*
(*lights, prices, sound*) **baisser [1]**

**low-fat milk** *noun*
le **lait écrémé**

**luck** *noun*
la **chance** *fem*
**Good luck!** Bonne chance!
**Bad luck!** Pas de chance!
**with a bit of luck** avec un peu de chance

**luckily** *adverb*
**heureusement**
**luckily for them** heureusement pour eux

**lucky** *adjective*
**to be lucky** avoir [5] de la chance
**We were lucky.** Nous avons eu de la chance.
**That's my lucky number.** C'est mon numéro porte-bonheur.

**luggage** *noun*
les **bagages** *masc pl*
**My luggage is in the boot.** Mes bagages sont dans le coffre.

**lump** *noun*
1 (*of earth*) la **motte** *fem*
2 (*swelling*) la **grosseur** *fem*
3 (*in sauce, gravy*) le **grumeau** *masc* (*pl* les **grumeaux**)

**lunch** *noun*
le **déjeuner** *masc*
to have lunch déjeuner **[1]**
**We had lunch in Boulogne.** Nous avons déjeuné à Boulogne.
- **lunch break** la pause-déjeuner
- **lunch hour** l'heure du déjeuner *fem*

**lung** *noun*
le **poumon** *masc*

**Luxembourg** *noun*
1 (*country*) le **Luxembourg** *masc*
to go to Luxembourg aller ⓔ **[7]** au Luxembourg
2 (*city*) **Luxembourg**
in Luxembourg à Luxembourg

**luxurious** *adjective*
**luxueux** *masc*, **luxueuse** *fem*

**luxury** *noun*
le **luxe** *masc*
a luxury hotel un hôtel de luxe

**lyrics** *plural noun*
les **paroles** *fem pl*

# Mm

**mac** *noun*
un **imper** *masc* (*informal*)

**macaroni** *noun*
les **macaronis** *masc pl*

**machine** *noun*
la **machine** *fem*

**machinery** *noun*
les **machines** *fem pl*

**mackerel** *noun*
le **maquereau** *masc* (*pl* les **maquereaux**)

**mad** *adjective*
1 (*crazy*) **fou** *masc*, **folle** *fem*
**She's completely mad!** Elle est complètement folle!
2 (*angry*) **furieux** *masc*, **furieuse** *fem*
**My mum will be mad!** Ma mère sera furieuse!
3 **to be mad about something** adorer **[1]** quelque chose
**Fiona's mad about horses.** Fiona adore les chevaux.

**madam** *noun*
**madame** *fem*

**madman** *noun*
le **fou** *masc*

**madness** *noun*
la **folie** *fem*

**magazine** *noun*
le **magazine** *masc*

**maggot** *noun*
un **asticot** *masc*

**magic** *adjective* ▷ see **magic** *noun*
1 (*supernatural*) **magique** *masc & fem*
2 (*great*) **super** *invariable adj*

**magic** *noun* ▷ see **magic** *adj*
la **magie** *fem*

**magician** *noun*
1 (*wizard*) le **magicien** *masc*
2 (*conjurer*) le **prestidigitateur** *masc*

**magnet** *noun*
un **aimant** *masc*

**magnificent** *adjective*
**magnifique** *masc & fem*

**magnifying glass** *noun*
la **loupe** *fem*

**mahogany** *noun*
l'**acajou** *masc*

**maiden name** *noun*
le **nom de jeune fille**

**mail** *noun*
1 (*post*) le **courrier** *masc*
2 (*email*) le **courrier électronique**

**mail order** *noun*
**to buy something by mail order** acheter **[1]** quelque chose par correspondance

**main** *adjective*
**principal** *masc*, **principale** *fem*, **principaux** *masc pl*, **principales** *fem pl*
the main entrance l'entrée principale



ⓔ means the verb takes être to form the perfect

The main thing is to eat well. Le principal, c'est de bien manger.
- **main course** le plat principal

**mainly** *adverb*
**principalement**

**main road** *noun*
la **route principale**

**maize** *noun*
le **maïs** *masc*

**major** *adjective* ▷ see **major** *noun*
**majeur** *masc*, **majeure** *fem*

**major** *noun* ▷ see **major** *adj*
le **commandant** *masc*

**Majorca** *noun*
**Majorque** *fem*

**WORD TIP** Unlike other names of islands, *Majorque* does not take *le* or *la*.

**majority** *noun*
la **majorité** *fem*

**malicious** *adjective*
**malveillant** *masc*, **malveillante** *fem*

𝄞 to **make** *verb* ▷ see **make** *noun*
1 (*in general*) **faire [10]**
**She made her bed.** Elle a fait son lit.
**I'm making an omelette.** Je fais une omelette.
**Two and three make five.** Deux et trois font cinq.
**to make friends** se faire Ⓔ **[10]** des amis
**I've made some friends.** Je me suis fait des amis.
**to make a meal** préparer **[1]** un repas
**to make a phone call** passer **[1]** un coup de fil
2 **to make somebody do something** faire **[10]** faire quelque chose à quelqu'un
**He made me wait.** Il m'a fait attendre.
**She makes me laugh.** Elle me fait rire.
3 (*to produce*) **fabriquer [1]**
**They make computers.** Ils fabriquent des ordinateurs.
**'Made in France'** 'Fabriqué en France'
4 **to make somebody happy, sad** rendre **[3]** quelqu'un heureux, triste
**Her comments made us proud.** Ses remarques nous ont rendus fiers.
**It makes me nervous.** Ça m'angoisse.
5 (*to earn*) **gagner [1]**
**He makes forty pounds a day.** Il gagne quarante livres par jour.
**to make a living** gagner **[1]** sa vie
6 **to make somebody do something** obliger **[52]** quelqu'un à faire quelque chose
**She made him return the money.** Elle l'a obligé à rendre l'argent.
7 **I can't make it tonight.** Je ne peux pas venir ce soir.
- to **make something up**
1 (*an excuse, a story*) **inventer [1] quelque chose**
2 **to make it up** se réconcilier Ⓔ **[1]**
**They've made it up.** Ils se sont réconciliés.

**make** *noun* ▷ see **make** *verb*
la **marque** *fem*
**What make is your bike?** De quelle marque est ton vélo?

𝄞 **make-up** *noun*
le **maquillage** *masc*
**to wear make-up** se maquiller Ⓔ **[1]**
**I don't wear make-up.** Je ne me maquille pas.
**to put on (your) make-up** se maquiller

**male** *adjective*
1 (*animal*) **mâle** *masc*
2 (*sex, gender*) **masculin** *masc*, **masculine** *fem*
- **male chauvinist** le macho

**mall** *noun*
le **centre commercial**

**Malta** *noun*
**Malte** *fem*

**WORD TIP** Unlike other names of islands, *Malte* does not take *le* or *la*.

**mammal** *noun*
le **mammifère** *masc*

𝄞 **man** *noun*
un **homme** *masc*
**modern man** l'homme moderne

to **manage** *verb*
1 (*a business*) **diriger [52]**
2 (*to cope*) **se débrouiller** Ⓔ **[1]**
**I can manage.** Je me débrouille.
3 **to manage to do something** réussir **[2]** à faire quelque chose
**He managed to open the door.** Il a réussi à ouvrir la porte.

**management** *noun*
1 (*of a business*) la **gestion** *fem*
2 (*the people in charge*) la **direction** *fem*

𝄞 **manager** *noun*
1 (*of a company, bank*) le **directeur** *masc*, la **directrice** *fem*
2 (*of a shop, restaurant*) le **gérant** *masc*, la **gérante** *fem*
3 (*in sport, entertainment*) le **manager** *masc*

**manageress** *noun*
la **gérante** *fem*

**managing director** *noun*
le **directeur général**, la **directrice générale**

**mandarin orange** *noun*
la **mandarine** *fem*

**mango** *noun*
la **mangue** *fem*

**maniac** *noun*
le **fou** *masc*, la **folle** *fem*

**mankind** *noun*
l'**humanité** *fem*

**man-made** *adjective*
(*fibre*) **synthétique** *masc & fem*

**manners** *plural noun*
**to have good manners** être [6] poli
**It's bad manners to talk like that.** Ce n'est pas poli de parler comme ça.

**mansion** *noun*
le **manoir** *fem*

**mantelpiece** *noun*
la **cheminée** *fem*

**manual** *noun*
le **manuel** *masc*

to **manufacture** *verb*
**fabriquer** [1]

**manufacturer** *noun*
le **fabricant** *masc*

**manure** *noun*
le **fumier** *masc*

**many** *adjective, pronoun*
1 **beaucoup de**
**Many people came.** Beaucoup de gens sont venus.
**many of them** beaucoup d'entre eux
**Are there many left?** Est-ce qu'il en reste beaucoup?
**not many** pas beaucoup de
**There weren't many young people.** Il n'y avait pas beaucoup de jeunes.
**Onions? There aren't many left.** Des oignons? Il n'en reste pas beaucoup.
2 **very many** beaucoup de
**There aren't very many seats.** Il n'y a pas beaucoup de places.
3 **so many** (*such a lot of*) tant de
**so many places to visit** tant d'endroits à visiter
**I have so many things to do!** J'ai tant de choses à faire!
4 **so many** (*as many*) autant de
**I've never eaten so many sweets!** Je n'ai jamais mangé autant de bonbons!
**as many as** autant que
**Take as many as you like.** Prends autant que tu veux.
**I've got as many friends as he has.** J'ai autant d'amis que lui.
5 **too many** trop (de)
**too many people** trop de monde
**I have too many things to do.** J'ai trop de choses à faire.
**That's far too many!** C'est beaucoup trop!
6 **how many?** combien?
**How many are there?** Il y en a combien?
**How many are there left?** Il en reste combien?
**How many sisters do you have?** Tu as combien de sœurs?

**map** *noun*
1 (*of a country, region*) la **carte** *fem*
**a road map** une carte routière
2 (*of a city*) le **plan** *masc*
**Can you point it out on the map?** Pouvez-vous l'indiquer sur le plan?

**marathon** *noun*
le **marathon** *masc*

**marble** *noun*
1 (*the stone*) le **marbre** *masc*
2 (*in a game*) la **bille** *fem*
**to play marbles** jouer [1] aux billes

to **march** *verb* ▷ see **march** *noun*
1 (*demonstrators*) **défiler** [1]
2 (*soldiers*) **marcher** [1]

**march** *noun* ▷ see **march** *verb*
la **manifestation** *fem*
**a peace march** une manifestation pour la paix

**March** *noun*
**mars** *masc*
**in March** en mars

**WORD TIP** Months of the year and days of the week start with small letters in French.

**mare** *noun*
la **jument** *fem*

**margarine** *noun*
la **margarine** *fem*

**margin** *noun*
la **marge** *fem*

**marijuana** *noun*
la **marijuana** *fem*

to **mark** *verb* ▷ see **mark** *noun*
1 (*to correct*) **corriger** [52]
**The teacher marks our homework.** Le professeur corrige nos devoirs.
2 (*to stain*) **marquer** [1]
3 (*in sport*) **marquer** [1]

**mark** *noun* ▷ see **mark** *verb*
1 (*for school work*) la **note** *fem*
I got a good mark. J'ai eu une bonne note.
What mark did you get for French? Tu as eu combien en français?
2 (*stain*) la **tache** *fem*
to leave a mark faire une tache

**market** *noun*
le **marché** *masc*
to go to the market aller Ⓔ [7] au marché

**marketing** *noun*
le **marketing** *masc*

**marmalade** *noun*
la **confiture d'oranges amères**

**maroon** *adjective*
**bordeaux** *invariable adj*

**marriage** *noun*
le **mariage** *masc*

**married** *adjective*
**marié** *masc*, **mariée** *fem*
a married couple un couple marié

to **marry** *verb*
1 to marry somebody épouser [1] quelqu'un
She married a Frenchman. Elle a épousé un Français.
2 to get married se marier Ⓔ [1]
They got married in July. Ils se sont mariés en juillet.

**marvellous** *adjective*
**merveilleux** *masc*, **merveilleuse** *fem*
The weather's marvellous. Il fait un temps merveilleux.

**marzipan** *noun*
la **pâte d'amandes**

**mascara** *noun*
le **mascara** *masc*

**masculine** *adjective*
▷ see **masculine** *noun*
**masculin** *masc*, **masculine** *fem*
a masculine noun un nom masculin

**masculine** *noun* ▷ see **masculine** *adj*
(*Grammar*) le **masculin** *masc*
in the masculine au masculin

to **mash** *verb*
(*vegetables*) **écraser** [1]

**mashed potatoes** *plural noun*
la **purée de pommes de terre**

**mask** *noun*
le **masque** *masc*

**mass** *noun*
1 (*amount*) la **masse** *fem*
2 (*lots*) masses of beaucoup de
masses of money beaucoup d'argent
There's masses left over. Il en reste beaucoup.
3 (*Church*) la **messe** *fem*
to go to mass aller Ⓔ [7] à la messe

**massacre** *noun*
le **massacre** *masc*

**massage** *noun*
le **massage** *masc*

**massive** *adjective*
**énorme** *masc & fem*

to **master** *verb*
(*a skill, a technique*) **maîtriser** [1]
• **master bedroom** la chambre principale
• **masterpiece** le chef-d'œuvre (*pl* les chefs-d'œuvre)

**mat** *noun*
1 (*doormat*) le **paillasson** *masc*
2 a table mat un set de table

to **match** *verb* ▷ see **match** *noun*
to match something être [6] assorti à quelque chose
The jacket matches the skirt. La veste est assortie à la jupe.

**match** *noun* ▷ see **match** *verb*
1 (*for lighting a fire*) une **allumette** *fem*
2 (*in sport*) le **match** *masc* (*pl* les **matchs**)
a football match un match de foot
United won the match. United a gagné le match.
We lost the match 3-0. Nous avons perdu le match trois à zéro.

**matching** *adjective*
(*curtains, clothes*) **assorti** *masc*, **assortie** *fem*

**mate** *noun*
**copain** *masc*, **copine** *fem* (*informal*)
She's my best mate. C'est ma meilleure copine.
to go out with your mates sortir Ⓔ [2] avec les copains

**material** *noun*
1 (*fabric*) le **tissu** *masc*
2 (*information*) la **documentation** *fem*
some material for my project de la documentation pour mon dossier

**mathematics** *noun*
les **mathématiques** *fem pl*

**maths** *noun*
les **maths** *fem pl*
Anna's good at maths. Anna est forte en maths.

♪ to **matter** *verb* ▷ see **matter** *noun*
**être [6] important**
**to matter to somebody** être [6] important pour quelqu'un
**It matters a lot to me.** C'est très important pour moi.
**It doesn't matter.** Ça n'a pas d'importance.
**Don't worry, it doesn't matter.** Ne t'inquiète pas, ça ne fait rien.
**It doesn't matter if it rains.** Ça ne fait rien s'il pleut.

**matter** *noun* ▷ see **matter** *verb*
**What's the matter?** Qu'est-ce qu'il y a?
**What's the matter with you?** Qu'est-ce que tu as?
**What's the matter with Emily?** Qu'est-ce qu'elle a, Emily?

**mattress** *noun*
le **matelas** *masc*
**a foam mattress** un matelas de mousse

**mature** *adjective*
**mûr** *masc*, **mûre** *fem*
**to be mature for your age** être [6] mûr pour son âge

**maximum** *adjective*
▷ see **maximum** *noun*
**maximum** *invariable adj*
**the maximum temperature** la température maximum
**a maximum speed of 70 mph** une vitesse maximum de 110km/h

**maximum** *noun* ▷ see **maximum** *adj*
le **maximum** *masc*
**a maximum of four hours a day** un maximum de quatre heures par jour
**a maximum of 30 students** 30 élèves au maximum

**May** *noun*
**mai** *masc*
**in May** en mai

**WORD TIP** Months of the year and days of the week start with small letters in French.

**may** *verb*
1 (*when you suggest a possibility*) **She may be ill.** Elle est peut-être malade.
**We may go to Spain.** Nous irons peut-être en Espagne.
**They may have left.** Ils sont peut-être partis.
2 (*when you ask politely*) **May I close the door?** Est-ce que je peux fermer la porte?

♪ **maybe** *adverb*
**peut-être**
**maybe not** peut-être pas
**Maybe I'm wrong.** J'ai peut-être tort.
**Maybe he's forgotten.** Il a peut-être oublié.
**Maybe they've got lost.** Ils se sont peut-être perdus.

**May Day** *noun*
**le Premier Mai**

**mayonnaise** *noun*
la **mayonnaise** *fem*

**mayor** *noun*
le **maire** *masc*

**mayoress** *noun*
la **mairesse** *fem*

♪ **me** *pronoun*
1 (*as object*) **me**, **m'** (*before a, e, i, o, u or silent h*)
**She knows me.** Elle me connaît.
**Can you help me, please?** Est-ce que tu peux m'aider, s'il te plaît?
**Can you give me your address?** Peux-tu me donner ton adresse?
**Can you give it to me?** Peux-tu me la donner?
2 (*after prepositions like* **avec, sans**) **moi**
**I took her with me.** Je l'ai emmenée avec moi.
**They left without me.** Ils sont partis sans moi.
**That parcel's for me.** Ce paquet est pour moi.
3 (*in commands*) **moi**
**Listen to me!** Écoute-moi!
**Excuse me!** Excusez-moi!
**Give me the key.** Donne-moi la clé.
4 (*in comparisons*) **moi**
**She's older than me.** Elle est plus âgée que moi.
**He's not as smart as me.** Il n'est pas aussi intelligent que moi.
5 **Me too!** Moi aussi!

**meadow** *noun*
le **pré** *masc*

♪ **meal** *noun*
le **repas** *masc*
**a family meal** un repas de famille
**to go out for a meal** aller ⓔ [7] manger au restaurant

♪ to **mean** *verb* ▷ see **mean** *adj*
1 **vouloir [14] dire**
**What do you mean?** Qu'est-ce que tu veux dire?
**What does that mean?** Qu'est-ce que ça veut dire?
**It means that we don't pay.** Ça veut dire que nous ne payons pas.
**That's not what I meant.** Ce n'est pas ce que je voulais dire.





a b c d e f g h i j k l m n o p q r s t u v w x y z

**2** **to mean to do something** avoir **[5]** l'intention de faire quelque chose
**I meant to phone you.** J'avais l'intention de t'appeler.
**I didn't mean to annoy her.** Je n'ai pas voulu la contrarier.
**I didn't mean it.** Je ne l'ai pas fait exprès.
**3** **to be meant to do something** devoir **[8]** faire quelque chose
**You were meant to be here at six.** Tu devais être là à six heures.

**mean** *adjective* ▷ see **mean** *verb*
**1** (*with money*) **radin** *masc*, **radine** *fem* (*informal*)
**2** (*unkind*) **méchant** *masc*, **méchante** *fem*
**to be mean to somebody** être **[6]** méchant avec quelqu'un
**She was mean to you.** Elle a été méchante avec toi.

**meaning** *noun*
le **sens** *masc*

**means** *noun*
**1** le **moyen** *masc*
**a means of transport** un moyen de transport
**a means of doing something** un moyen de faire quelque chose
**I have no means of checking.** Je n'ai aucun moyen de vérifier.
**2** **by all means** certainement
**'Can I come in?' — 'By all means, do.'** 'Je peux entrer?' — 'Certainement.'

**meantime** *noun*
**for the meantime** pour le moment
**in the meantime** pendant ce temps
**In the meantime, I looked it up on the Internet.** Pendant ce temps, je l'ai cherché sur Internet.

**meanwhile** *adverb*
**pendant ce temps**
**Meanwhile, she was waiting at the station.** Pendant ce temps, elle attendait à la gare.

**measles** *noun*
la **rougeole** *fem*

to **measure** *verb*
**mesurer [1]**

**measurements** *plural noun*
**1** (*of a room, an object*) les **dimensions** *fem pl*
**2** (*for clothes*) les **mensurations** *fem pl*
**my chest measurement** mon tour de poitrine
**my waist measurement** mon tour de taille

**meat** *noun*
la **viande** *fem*
**Georgia doesn't eat meat.** Georgia ne mange pas de viande.

**Mecca** *noun*
la **Mecque** *fem*

**mechanic** *noun*
le **mécanicien** *masc*
**He's a mechanic.** Il est mécanicien.

**mechanical** *adjective*
**mécanique** *masc & fem*

**medal** *noun*
la **médaille** *fem*
**the gold medal** la médaille d'or

to **meddle** *verb*
**to meddle in something** se mêler Ⓔ **[1]** à quelque chose
**He meddles in people's business.** Il se mêle aux affaires des autres.

**media** *noun*
**the media** les médias *masc pl*

**medical** *adjective* ▷ see **medical** *noun*
**médical** *masc*, **médicale** *fem*, **médicaux** *masc pl*, **médicales** *fem pl*
**a medical student** un étudiant en médecine

**medical** *noun* ▷ see **medical** *adj*
la **visite médicale**
**to have a medical** passer **[1]** une visite médicale

**medicine** *noun*
**1** (*remedy*) le **médicament** *masc*
**some cough medicine** un médicament pour la toux
**2** (*medical studies*) la **médecine** *fem*
**to study medicine** faire **[10]** des études de médecine

**medieval** *adjective*
**médiéval** *masc*, **médiévale** *fem*, **médiévaux** *masc pl*, **médiévales** *fem pl*
**medieval castles** des châteaux médiévaux
**medieval knights** des chevaliers du Moyen Âge

**Mediterranean** *noun*
**the Mediterranean** la Méditerranée

**medium** *adjective*
**moyen** *masc*, **moyenne** *fem*
**He's about medium height.** Il est de taille moyenne.
- **medium-sized** (*school, building*) de taille moyenne

♪ to **meet** *verb*
1 (*by chance*) **rencontrer [1]**
**I met them outside the pool.** Je les ai rencontrés devant la piscine.
2 (*by arrangement*) **retrouver [1]**
**I'll meet you there at six.** Je t'y retrouverai à six heures.
3 (*to get to know*) **faire [10] la connaissance de**
**I met some French people.** J'ai fait la connaissance de quelques Français.
**Tom, have you met Oliver?** Tom, est-ce que tu connais Oliver?
4 (*at a station, airport*) **venir Ⓔ [81] chercher**
**He's meeting me at the station.** Il vient me chercher à la gare.

♪ **meeting** *noun*
la **réunion** *fem*
**She's in a meeting.** Elle est en réunion.

**megabyte** *noun*
le **mégaoctet** *masc*

**melody** *noun*
la **mélodie** *fem*

♪ **melon** *noun*
le **melon** *masc*

to **melt** *verb*
1 **fondre [3]**
**It melts in your mouth.** Ça fond dans la bouche.
2 **to melt something** faire **[10]** fondre quelque chose
**Melt the butter.** Faites fondre le beurre.

**member** *noun*
le **membre** *masc*
**to be a member of something** être **[6]** membre de quelque chose

**Member of Parliament** *noun*
le **député** *masc*

**membership** *noun*
l'**adhésion** *fem*
- **membership card** la carte de membre
- **membership fee** la cotisation

**memorial** *noun*
**a war memorial** un monument aux morts

to **memorize** *verb*
**to memorize something** apprendre **[64]** quelque chose par cœur
**to memorize your verb endings** apprendre ses conjugaisons

**memory** *noun*
1 (*person's, computer's*) la **mémoire** *fem*
**You have a good memory!** Tu as bonne mémoire!
**I have a bad memory.** Je n'ai pas de mémoire.
2 (*of the past*) le **souvenir** *masc*
**I've good memories of my stay.** J'ai de bons souvenirs de mon séjour.

to **mend** *verb*
**réparer [1]**

**meningitis** *noun*
la **méningite** *fem*

**mental** *adjective*
**mental** *masc*, **mentale** *fem*, **mentaux** *masc pl*, **mentales** *fem pl*
**a mental illness** une maladie mentale
**a mental hospital** un hôpital psychiatrique

to **mention** *verb*
**mentionner [1]**
**She mentioned your name.** Elle a mentionné ton nom.
**Mention three French regions.** Mentionne trois régions françaises.

♪ **menu** *noun*
le **menu** *masc*
**a set menu** un menu
**a children's menu** un menu pour enfants
**on the menu** au menu
**I'm having the €15 menu.** Je prends le menu à 15€ .

**mercy** *noun*
la **pitié** *fem*

to **merge** *verb*
1 (*roads*) **se rejoindre Ⓔ [49]**
2 (*the data*) **fusionner [1]**

**meringue** *noun*
la **meringue** *fem*

**merit** *noun*
le **mérite** *masc*

**mermaid** *noun*
la **sirène** *fem*

**merry** *adjective*
(*happy*) **joyeux** *masc*, **joyeuse** *fem*
**Merry Christmas!** Joyeux Noël!
- **merry-go-round** le manège

**mess** *noun*
le **désordre** *masc*
**My things are in a mess.** Mes affaires sont dans le désordre.
**to make a mess** mettre **[11]** du désordre
**What a mess!** Quelle pagaille! (*informal*)
- to **mess about**
**faire [10] l'imbécile**
- to **mess about with something**
(*with matches, alcohol*) **jouer [1] avec quelque chose**

• to **mess something up** (*files, belongings*) **mettre [11] la pagaille dans quelque chose**

**message** *noun*
le **message** *masc*
a phone message un message téléphonique
to leave a message laisser [1] un message
**He didn't leave a message.** Il n'a pas laissé de message.

**messenger** *noun*
le **messager** *masc*

**messy** *adjective*
1 a messy job un travail salissant
2 messy handwriting une écriture peu soignée

**metal** *noun*
le **métal** *masc* (*pl* les **métaux**)

**meter** *noun*
1 (*for electricity, gas, in a taxi*) le **compteur** *masc*
2 (*parking meter*) le **parcmètre** *masc*

**method** *noun*
la **méthode** *fem*
• **method of transport** le moyen de transport

**Methodist** *noun*
le & la **méthodiste** *masc & fem*

**WORD TIP** Adjectives never have capitals in French, even for religions.

♪ **metre** *noun*
le **mètre** *masc*
a 50-metre pool une piscine de 50 mètres
**The hedge is two metres high.** La haie fait deux mètres de haut.

**metric** *adjective*
**métrique** *masc & fem*

**Mexican** *adjective* ▷ see **Mexican** *noun*
**mexicain** *masc*, **mexicaine** *fem*

**Mexican** *noun* ▷ see **Mexican** *adj*
un **Mexicain** *masc*, une **Mexicaine** *fem*

**Mexico** *noun*
le **Mexique** *masc*
in Mexico au Mexique
to Mexico au Mexique

**microphone** *noun*
le **microphone** *masc*

**microscope** *noun*
le **microscope** *masc*

**microwave (oven)** *noun*
le **(four à) micro-ondes**
**Heat it up in the microwave.** Fais-le chauffer au micro-ondes.

♪ **midday** *noun*
**midi** *masc*
at midday à midi
**The shops close at midday.** Les magasins ferment à midi.

♪ **middle** *noun*
1 le **milieu** *masc*
in the middle of the night au milieu de la nuit
in the middle of the room au milieu de la pièce
2 **to be in the middle of doing something** être [6] en train de faire quelque chose
**I was in the middle of washing my hair.** J'étais en train de me laver les cheveux.
• **middle-aged** d'un certain âge
• **middle-class** de la classe moyenne
• **Middle East** le Moyen-Orient
• **middle finger** le majeur

**midge** *noun*
le **moucheron** *masc*

♪ **midnight** *noun*
**minuit** *masc*
at midnight à minuit
**It was almost midnight.** Il était presque minuit.

**Midsummer's Day** *noun*
**la Saint Jean**

**midwife** *noun*
la **sage-femme** *fem* (*pl* les **sages-femmes**)

♪ **might** *verb*
**'Will you phone him?' — 'I might.'** 'Est-ce que tu vas l'appeler?' — 'Peut-être.'
**I might invite Jess.** J'inviterai peut-être Jess.
**He might have forgotten.** Il a peut-être oublié.

**migraine** *noun*
la **migraine** *fem*

**mike** *noun*
le **micro** *masc* (*informal*)

**mild** *adjective*
**doux** *masc*, **douce** *fem*
**It's mild today.** Il fait doux aujourd'hui.

**mile** *noun*
le *masc* (*to convert miles to kilometres, multiply by 8 and divide by 5*)
**The village is ten miles from Newhaven.** Le village est à seize kilomètres de Newhaven.
**We walked for miles.** On a marché pendant des kilomètres.

**mileage** *noun*
le **kilométrage** *masc*
**What's the mileage on the car?** Elle a combien de kilomètres, la voiture?

**military** *adjective*
**militaire** *masc & fem*

to **milk** *verb* ▷ see **milk** *noun*
(*a cow*) **traire [78]**

**milk** *noun* ▷ see **milk** *verb*
le **lait** *masc*
full-cream milk le lait entier
skimmed milk le lait écrémé
semi-skimmed milk le lait demi-écrémé
- **milk chocolate** le chocolat au lait
- **milkman** le laitier
- **milk round** la tournée de laitier
- **milk shake** le milk-shake

**millennium** *noun*
le **millénaire** *masc*

**millimetre** *noun*
le **millimètre** *masc*

**million** *noun*
le **million** *masc*
a million people un million de personnes
two million people deux millions de personnes

**WORD TIP** Use *de* after million in French.

**millionth** *adjective*
**millionième** *masc & fem*

**millionaire** *noun*
le & la **millionnaire** *masc & fem*

to **mimic** *verb*
**imiter [1]**

**mince** *noun*
la **viande hachée** *fem*

to **mind** *verb* ▷ see **mind** *noun*
1 (*to keep an eye on*) **surveiller [1]**
Can you mind my bag for me? Est-ce que tu peux surveiller mon sac?
2 (*to be bothered by*) I don't mind the heat. La chaleur ne me dérange pas.
Do you mind if ...? Est-ce que cela vous dérange si ...?
Do you mind if I close the door? Est-ce que cela vous dérange si je ferme la porte?
3 (*to be careful*) Mind the step! Attention à la marche!
Mind your fingers! Attention à tes doigts!
4 (*to care*) Never mind! Peu importe!
'What shall we do?' — 'I don't mind.' 'Qu'est-ce qu'on va faire?' — 'Ça m'est égal.'

**mind** *noun* ▷ see **mind** *verb*
1 un **esprit** *masc*
to have a logical mind avoir **[5]** l'esprit logique.
It never even crossed my mind! Ça ne m'est même pas venu à l'esprit!
It's on my mind. Ça me préoccupe.
to have a lot on your mind être **[6]** très préoccupé
2 to change your mind changer **[52]** d'avis
I've changed my mind. J'ai changé d'avis.
3 to make up your mind se décider Ⓔ **[1]**
I can't make up my mind. Je n'arrive pas à me décider.

**mine** *noun* ▷ see **mine** *pron*
la **mine** *fem*
a coal mine une mine de charbon

**mine** *pronoun* ▷ see **mine** *noun*
1 (*for masc singular nouns*) **le mien**
She took her bag and I took mine. Elle a pris son sac et j'ai pris le mien.
2 (*for fem singular nouns*) **la mienne**
She gave me her address and I gave her mine. Elle m'a donné son adresse et je lui ai donné la mienne.
3 (*for masc plural nouns*) **les miens**
Karen's invited her parents and I've invited mine. Karen a invité ses parents et j'ai invité les miens.
4 (*for fem plural nouns*) **les miennes**
She showed me her photos and I showed her mine. Elle m'a montré ses photos et je lui ai montré les miennes.
5 (*belonging to me*) **à moi**
It's mine. C'est à moi.
The green one's mine. Le vert est à moi.

**miner** *noun*
le **mineur** *masc*

**mineral water** *noun*
l'**eau minérale**
two bottles of mineral water deux bouteilles d'eau minérale

**miniature** *adjective*
▷ see **miniature** *noun*
**miniature** *masc & fem*

**miniature** *noun* ▷ see **miniature** *adj*
la **miniature** *fem*

**minibus** *noun*
le **minibus** *masc*

**minimum** *adjective*
▷ see **minimum** *noun*
**minimum** *invariable adj*
the minimum age l'âge minimum
minimum safety measures des mesures de sécurité minimum
the minimum amount le minimum



Ⓔ means the verb takes être to form the perfect

**minimum** *noun* ▷ see **minimum** *adj*
le **minimum** *masc*
**a minimum of 10 minutes a day** un minimum de 10 minutes par jour
**a minimum of eight people** un minimum de huit personnes
**I did the minimum.** J'ai fait le minimum.

**miniskirt** *noun*
la **mini-jupe** *fem*

**minister** *noun*
1 (*in a government*) le **ministre** *masc*
**the minister of health** le ministre de la santé
2 (*in a church*) le **pasteur** *masc*

**ministry** *noun*
le **ministère** *masc*

**minor** *adjective*
**mineur** *masc*, **mineure** *fem*

**minority** *noun*
la **minorité** *fem*

**mint** *noun*
1 (*herb*) la **menthe** *fem*
2 (*sweet*) le **bonbon à la menthe**

**minus** *preposition*
**moins**
**Seven minus three is four.** Sept moins trois égale quatre.
**It was minus five last night.** Il a fait moins cinq la nuit dernière.

**minute** *adjective* ▷ see **minute** *noun*
**minuscule** *masc & fem*

♪ **minute** *noun* ▷ see **minute** *adj*
la **minute** *fem*
**at the last minute** à la dernière minute
**Just a minute!** Une minute!
**It's five minutes' walk from here.** C'est à cinq minutes à pied d'ici.
**We'll be ready in two minutes.** Nous serons prêts dans deux minutes.

**miracle** *noun*
le **miracle** *masc*

♪ **mirror** *noun*
1 la **glace** *fem*
**He looked at himself in the mirror.** Il s'est regardé dans la glace.
2 (*in a car*) le **rétroviseur** *masc*

to **misbehave** *verb*
**se conduire** Ⓔ **[26] mal**

**mischief** *noun*
**to get up to mischief** faire **[10]** des bêtises
**He's always getting up to mischief.** Il fait toujours des bêtises.

**mischievous** *adjective*
**coquin** *masc*, **coquine** *fem*

**miser** *noun*
un & une **avare** *masc & fem*

**miserable** *adjective*
1 (*unhappy*) **malheureux** *masc*, **malheureuse** *fem*
**He's miserable without her.** Il est malheureux sans elle.
**I feel really miserable.** Je n'ai vraiment pas le moral.
**It's miserable weather.** Il fait un sale temps.
2 (*pay, salary*) **de misère**
**They're paid a miserable wage.** Ils gagnent un salaire de misère.

**misery** *noun*
la **souffrance** *fem*

**misfortune** *noun*
1 (*unfortunate event*) le **malheur** *masc*
2 (*bad luck*) la **malchance**
**She had the misfortune of losing her passport.** Elle a eu la malchance de perdre son passeport.

to **misjudge** *verb*
1 (*an amount, a distance*) **mal évaluer [1]**
**I misjudged the distance.** J'ai mal évalué la distance.
2 (*a person*) **mal juger [52]**
**Everybody had misjudged her.** Tout le monde l'avait mal jugée.

to **mislay** *verb*
(*the keys, money, passport*) **égarer [1]**

**misleading** *adjective*
**trompeur** *masc*, **trompeuse** *fem*
**a misleading advertisement** une publicité trompeuse

♪ to **miss** *verb*
1 (*a bus, a target, an event*) **rater [1]**
**She missed her train.** Elle a raté son train.
**The ball missed the goal.** Le ballon a raté le but.
**Missed!** Raté!
2 (*a class*) **manquer [1]**
**He's missed several classes.** Il a manqué plusieurs cours.
3 **to miss an opportunity** manquer une occasion
**It's an opportunity not to be missed!** C'est une occasion à ne pas manquer!
4 **to be missed by somebody** manquer **[1]** à quelqu'un
**He'll be missed.** Il va nous manquer.
**I miss you.** Tu me manques. ⏩

She's missing her sister. Sa sœur lui manque.
I miss France. La France me manque.

**WORD TIP** The subject of the verb *manquer* is the thing or person that you miss.

**Miss** *noun*
**Mademoiselle** *fem*
**Miss Jones** Mademoiselle Jones, Mlle Jones (*usual written form*)

**missile** *noun*
le **missile** *masc*

**missing** *adjective*
1 **manquant** *masc*, **manquante** *fem*
**the missing pieces** les pièces manquantes
2 **to be missing** manquer [1]
**What's missing?** Qu'est-ce qui manque?
**There's a plate missing.** Il manque une assiette.
**There are three forks missing.** Il manque trois fourchettes.
3 **to go missing** disparaître [27]
**Several computers have gone missing.** Plusieurs ordinateurs ont disparu.
**Three people are missing.** Trois personnes ont disparu.

**missionary** *noun*
le & la **missionnaire** *masc & fem*

**mist** *noun*
la **brume** *fem*

to **mistake** *verb* ▷ see **mistake** *noun*
**to mistake somebody for somebody else** prendre [64] quelqu'un pour quelqu'un d'autre
**I mistook you for your brother.** Je vous ai pris pour votre frère.

**mistake** *noun* ▷ see **mistake** *verb*
1 (*in a calculation, judgement*) une **erreur** *fem*
**by mistake** par erreur
**It was my mistake.** C'était une erreur de ma part.
2 (*in spelling, typing*) la **faute** *fem*
**a spelling mistake** une faute d'orthographe
**You've made lots of mistakes.** Tu as fait beaucoup de fautes.
3 (*to be wrong*) **to make a mistake** se tromper Ⓔ [1]
**I've made a mistake.** Je me suis trompé (*boy speaking*), Je me suis trompée (*girl speaking*).

**mistaken** *adjective*
**to be mistaken** se tromper Ⓔ [1]

**mistletoe** *noun*
le **gui** *masc*

**misty** *adjective*
**brumeux** *masc*, **brumeuse** *fem*
**a misty morning** un matin brumeux
**It's misty this morning.** Il y a de la brume ce matin.

to **misunderstand** *verb*
**mal comprendre** [64]
**I misunderstood.** J'ai mal compris.

**misunderstanding** *noun*
le **malentendu** *masc*
**There's been a misunderstanding.** Il y a eu un malentendu.

to **mix** *verb* ▷ see **mix** *noun*
1 **mélanger** [52]
**Mix the ingredients together.** Mélangez les ingrédients.
**Oil and water don't mix.** L'eau et l'huile ne se mélangent pas.
2 **to mix with people** fréquenter [1] des gens
**I don't like the kind of people she mixes with.** Je n'aime pas trop les gens qu'elle fréquente.
**They're mixing with the local people.** Ils se mêlent aux gens du coin.

- to **mix up**

1 **to mix something up** mélanger [52] quelque chose
**You've mixed up my files!** Tu as mélangé mes fichiers!
**to get something mixed up** mélanger [52] quelque chose
**You've got it all mixed up!** Tu mélanges tout!
2 **to get mixed up in something** se trouver Ⓔ [1] mêlé à quelque chose
**He got mixed up in a fight.** Il s'est trouvé mêlé à une bagarre.
3 **to mix somebody up with somebody else** confondre [69] quelqu'un avec quelqu'un d'autre
**I get her mixed up with her sister.** Je la confonds avec sa sœur.

**mix** *noun* ▷ see **mix** *verb*
1 le **mélange** *masc*
**a good mix of people** un bon mélange de gens

**mixed** *adjective*
**varié** *masc*, **variée** *fem*
**a mixed programme** un programme varié

- **mixed salad** la salade composée
- **mixed school** une école mixte

**mixer** *noun*
le **batteur électrique**

**mixture** *noun*
le **mélange** *masc*
**It's a mixture of jazz and rock.** C'est un mélange de jazz et de rock.

**mix-up** *noun*
la **confusion** *fem*
**a mix-up with the names** une confusion sur les noms

to **moan** *verb*
1 (*to complain*) **râler [1]** (*informal*)
**Stop moaning!** Arrête de râler!
**She was moaning about you.** Elle râlait contre toi.
2 (*to make a low noise*) **gémir [2]**

**mobile home** *noun*
le **mobile home**

**mobile phone** *noun*
le **téléphone portable**
**to call somebody on their mobile** appeler quelqu'un au portable

to **mock** *verb*
**to mock somebody** se moquer ⓔ [1] de quelqu'un
**They're mocking us.** Ils se moquent de nous.
**Don't mock!** Ne te moque pas de moi!

**mock exam** *noun*
un **examen blanc**

**model** *noun*
1 (*in a series*) le **modèle** *masc*
**the latest model** le dernier modèle
2 (*fashion worker*) le **mannequin** (*man or woman*)
**She's a top model.** Elle est top-modèle.
3 (*of a plane, car*) le **modèle réduit**
**He makes models.** Il fait des modèles réduits.
4 (*scale model*) la **maquette** *fem*
**a model of the prototype** une maquette du prototype
- **model aeroplane** le modèle réduit d'avion
- **model railway** le chemin de fer miniature
- **model village** le village miniature

**modem** *noun*
le **modem** *masc*

**moderate** *adjective*
**modéré** *masc*, **modérée** *fem*

♪ **modern** *adjective*
**moderne** *masc & fem*
**I like modern buildings.** J'aime les bâtiments modernes.
**life in the modern world** la vie dans le monde contemporain

to **modernize** *verb*
**moderniser [1]**
**It needs to be modernized.** Il a besoin d'être modernisé.

**modern languages** *plural noun*
les **langues vivantes** *fem pl*

**modest** *adjective*
**modeste** *masc & fem*

to **modify** *verb*
**modifier [1]**

**moisture** *noun*
l'**humidité** *fem*

**moisturizer** *noun*
1 (*lotion*) le **lait hydratant**
2 (*cream*) la **crème hydratante**

**mole** *noun*
1 (*animal*) la **taupe** *fem*
2 (*on skin*) le **grain de beauté**

♪ **moment** *noun*
1 un **instant** *masc*
**He'll be here in a moment.** Il sera là dans un instant.
**It could happen at any moment.** Ça pourrait se produire à tout instant.
2 **at the moment** en ce moment
**She's studying at the moment.** Elle étudie en ce moment.
**You rang at just the right moment.** Tu as téléphoné au bon moment.

**Monaco** *noun*
**Monaco** *masc*
**to go to Monaco** aller ⓔ [7] à Monaco

**WORD TIP** *Monaco* does not take *le* or *la*.

♪ **monarchy** *noun*
la **monarchie** *fem*

**monastery** *noun*
le **monastère** *masc*

♪ **Monday** *noun*
le **lundi** *masc*
**on Monday** lundi
**last Monday** lundi dernier
**next Monday** lundi prochain
**every Monday** tous les lundis
**on Mondays** le lundi ▶▶

English–French

a b c d e f g h i j k l m n o p q r s t u v w x y z

I'm going out on Monday. Je sors lundi.
See you on Monday! À lundi!

**WORD TIP** Months of the year and days of the week start with small letters in French.

**money** *noun*
l'**argent** *masc*
to make money gagner [1] de l'argent
I've got enough money. J'ai assez d'argent.
I've got no money left. Je n'ai plus d'argent.
to get money back (*in a shop*) être [6] remboursé
They gave me my money back. Ils m'ont remboursé.
• **money box** la tirelire

**mongrel** *noun*
le **chien bâtard**

**monitor** *noun*
(*Computers*) le **moniteur** *masc*

**monk** *noun*
le **moine** *masc*

**monkey** *noun*
le **singe** *masc*

**monotonous** *adjective*
(*voice, music*) **monotone** *masc & fem*

**monster** *noun*
le **monstre** *masc*

**month** *noun*
le **mois** *masc*
last month le mois dernier
next month le mois prochain
this month ce mois-ci
every month tous les mois
in the month of May au mois de mai
in two months' time dans deux mois
at the end of the month à la fin du mois

**monthly** *adjective*
**mensuel** *masc*, **mensuelle** *fem*

**monument** *noun*
le **monument** *masc*

**mood** *noun*
l'**humeur** *fem*
to be in a good mood être [6] de bonne humeur
Paul's in a good mood. Paul est de bonne humeur.
to be in a bad mood être de mauvaise humeur
Sally's in a bad mood. Sally est de mauvaise humeur.

**moody** *adjective*
**lunatique** *masc & fem*

**moon** *noun*
1 la **lune** *fem*
to put a man on the moon envoyer [40] un homme sur la lune
2 to be over the moon être [6] aux anges
She's over the moon about winning. Elle est aux anges depuis qu'elle a gagné.
• **moonlight** le clair de lune

**moor** *noun*
la **lande** *fem*
the Yorkshire moors les landes du Yorkshire

**moped** *noun*
la **mobylette** *fem*

**moral** *adjective* ▷ see **moral** *noun*
**moral** *masc*, **morale** *fem*, **moraux** *masc pl*, **morales** *fem pl*

**moral** *noun* ▷ see **moral** *adj*
la **morale** *fem*
the moral of the story la morale de l'histoire

**morale** *noun*
le **moral** *masc*
Our morale is high. Notre moral est bon.
It will raise the team's morale. Ça va remonter le moral à l'équipe.

**morals** *noun*
la **moralité** *fem*

**more** *adjective, adverb, pronoun*
1 (*with verbs*) **plus**
She's studying more. Elle étudie plus.
I train more in the summer. Je m'entraîne plus en été.
2 (*before a noun*) **plus de**
more time plus de temps
more money plus d'argent
We need more light. Il nous faut plus de lumière.
Would you like some more milk? Voulez-vous encore du lait?
Is there any more pasta? Il reste encore des pâtes?
3 (*for a noun*) **plus**
I'll have some more. J'en prendrai un peu plus.
Do you want some more? Tu en veux encore?
I don't want any more. Je n'en veux plus.
We need more. Il nous en faut plus.
4 (*before an adjective or adverb*) **plus**
more entertaining plus amusant
more difficult plus difficile
more slowly plus lentement
more easily plus facilement

5 more than (*in amounts*) plus de
**more than a hundred people** plus de cent personnes
**more than a thousand pounds** plus de mille livres
6 more than (*in comparisons*) plus que
**She eats more than me.** Elle mange plus que moi.
**The game's more interesting than the film.** Le jeu est plus intéressant que le film.
7 **more and more** de plus en plus
**It's getting more and more expensive.** Ça coûte de plus en plus cher.
**It takes more and more time.** Ça prend de plus en plus de temps.
8 **more or less** plus ou moins
**It's more or less finished.** C'est plus ou moins fini.

**morning** *noun*
1 (*early in the day*) le **matin** *masc*
**this morning** ce matin
**tomorrow morning** demain matin
**yesterday morning** hier matin
**in the morning** le matin
**on Friday mornings** le vendredi matin
**She works in the mornings.** Elle travaille le matin.
**at six o'clock in the morning** à six heures du matin
2 (*as period of time*) la **matinée** *fem*
**sometime during the morning** au cours de la matinée
**I spent the morning reading.** J'ai passé la matinée à lire.

**Morocco** *noun*
le **Maroc** *masc*
**in Morocco** au Maroc

**mortgage** *noun*
le **crédit (immobilier)**

**Moscow** *noun*
**Moscou**

**Moslem** *noun*
le **musulman** *masc*, la **musulmane** *fem*

**WORD TIP** Adjectives never have capitals in French, even for religions.

**mosque** *noun*
la **mosquée** *fem*

**mosquito** *noun*
le **moustique** *masc*
**a mosquito bite** une piqûre de moustique
**I got bitten by mosquitoes.** Je me suis fait piquer par des moustiques.

**most** *adjective, adverb, pronoun*
1 (*followed by a plural noun*) **la plupart de**
**Most of my friends live in London.** La plupart de mes amis habitent à Londres.
**Most children like chocolate.** La plupart des enfants aiment le chocolat.
**Most people go home at 6 p.m.** La plupart des gens rentrent chez eux à 18 heures.
2 (*followed by a singular noun*) **presque tout, presque toute**
**They've eaten most of the chocolate.** Ils ont mangé presque tout le chocolat.
**I spent most of the day in bed.** J'ai passé presque toute la journée au lit.
3 **most of the time** la plupart du temps
**They quarrel most of the time.** Ils se disputent la plupart du temps.
4 (*followed by an adjective*) **the most** le plus, la plus, les plus
**the most interesting film** le film le plus intéressant
**the most exciting story** l'histoire la plus passionnante
**the most boring books** les livres les plus ennuyeux
5 (*followed by a noun*) **the most** le plus de
**I've got the most time.** C'est moi qui ai le plus de temps.
6 (*after a verb*) **(the) most** le plus
**I like Paris the most.** C'est Paris que j'aime le plus.
**What I hate most is the noise.** Ce que je déteste le plus, c'est le bruit.

**moth** *noun*
1 (*large insect*) le **papillon de nuit**
2 (*clothes moth*) la **mite**

**mother** *noun*
la **mère** *fem*
**my mother** ma mère
**Kate's mother** la mère de Kate

**mother-in-law** *noun*
la **belle-mère** *fem* (*pl* les **belles-mères**)

**Mother's Day** *noun*
**la fête des Mères** (*the last Sunday in May*)

**motivated** *adjective*
**motivé** *masc*, **motivée** *fem*

**motivation** *noun*
la **motivation** *fem*

**motor** *noun*
le **moteur** *masc*
- **motorbike** la moto
- **motorboat** le bateau à moteur
- **motorcyclist** le & la motocycliste

**motorist** *noun*
un & une **automobiliste** *masc & fem*

**motor racing** *noun*
la **course automobile**

**motorway** *noun*
une **autoroute** *fem*
**to take the motorway** prendre **[64]** l'autoroute

***motorway***

France has 9,000 kilometres of motorways, numbered: A1, A2, etc. (A = *autoroute*). Some also have names, like the motorway to the south: *l'Autoroute du soleil*. You have to pay a toll to use many French motorways.

**mouldy** *adjective*
**moisi** *masc*, **moisie** *fem*

**mountain** *noun*
la **montagne** *fem*
**in the mountains** à la montagne
**We spent a week in the mountains.** Nous avons passé une semaine à la montagne.
- **mountain bike** le VTT (= *vélo tout-terrain*)

***mountain***

The highest mountain in Europe is Mont Blanc (4 897m) in the French Alps.

**mountaineer** *noun*
un & une **alpiniste** *masc & fem*

**mountaineering** *noun*
l'**alpinisme** *masc*
**to go mountaineering** faire **[10]** de l'alpinisme

**mountainous** *adjective*
**montagneux** *masc*, **montagneuse** *fem*

**mouse** *noun*
(*the animal, for computers*) la **souris** *fem*
- **mouse mat** (*Computers*) le tapis de souris
- **mousetrap** la souricière

**mousse** *noun*
la **mousse** *fem*
**chocolate mousse** la mousse au chocolat

**moustache** *noun*
la **moustache** *fem*
**a man with a moustache** un moustachu

**mouth** *noun*
la **bouche** *fem*
- **mouthful** la bouchée
- **mouth organ** un harmonica

to **move** *verb* ▷ see **move** *noun*
1 (*people, things*) **bouger [52]**
**Don't move!** Ne bouge pas!
**The dog wasn't moving.** Le chien ne bougeait pas.
2 (*a piece of furniture, a car*) **déplacer [61]**
**I can't move the wardrobe.** Je n'arrive pas à déplacer l'armoire.
3 (*your personal items, a bag, a phone*) enlever **[50]** quelque chose
**Can you move your bag, please?** Est-ce que tu peux enlever ton sac, s'il te plaît?
**Someone's moved my things.** Quelqu'un a enlevé mes affaires.
**Move the chairs out of the way.** Enlève les chaises de là.
4 (*traffic*) **avancer [61]**
**The traffic was moving slowly.** La circulation avançait lentement.
5 (*vehicles*) **rouler [1]**
**The cars were moving at high speed.** Les voitures roulaient à grande vitesse.
6 (*to go to a new address*) **déménager [52]**
**We're moving house on Tuesday.** Nous déménageons mardi.
**They've moved to France.** Ils se sont installés en France.
7 (*to make space, get out of the way*) **Move up a bit.** Pousse-toi un peu.
**Move your head, I can't see!** Pousse ta tête, je ne vois rien!
- to **move forward**
**s'avancer [61]**
**He moved forward a step.** Il s'est avancé d'un pas.
- to **move in**
**emménager [52]**
**They've just moved in.** Ils viennent d'emménager.
- to **move out**
**déménager [52]**
**We're moving out soon.** Nous déménageons bientôt.

**move** *noun* ▷ see **move** *verb*
1 (*to a different address*) le **déménagement** *masc*
2 (*in games*) **Your move!** À toi de jouer!

**movement** *noun*
1 (*of waves, of trees, of your body*) le **mouvement** *masc*
2 (*group, organization*) le **mouvement** *masc*
**the peace movement** le mouvement pour la paix

**movie** *noun*
1 (*film*) le **film** *masc*
2 **the movies** le cinéma
**I love going to the movies.** J'aime beaucoup aller au cinéma.

**moving** *adjective*
1 (*vehicle*) **en marche**
**a moving vehicle** un véhicule en marche
2 (*experience, story*) **émouvant** *masc*, **émouvante** *fem*



(e) means the verb takes être to form the perfect

to **mow** *verb*
**tondre [3]**
**to mow the lawn** tondre la pelouse

**mower** *noun*
la **tondeuse à gazon**

**MP** *noun*
le **député** *masc*
**She's an MP.** Elle est député.

♪ **Mr** *noun*
**Monsieur** (*abbreviated to M.*)
**Mr Angus Brown** M. Angus Brown

♪ **Mrs** *noun*
**Madame** (*abbreviated to Mme*)
**Mrs Mary Hendry** Mme Mary Hendry

**Ms** *noun*
**Madame** (*abbreviated to **Mme***) (*Ms has no equivalent in French, but **Madame** is used for all women.*)

♪ **much** *adjective, adverb, pronoun*
1 **beaucoup**
**She doesn't eat much.** Elle ne mange pas beaucoup.
**We don't go out much.** Nous ne sortons pas beaucoup.
**much more** beaucoup plus
**much shorter** beaucoup plus court
**much easier** beaucoup plus facile
**It's much more fun.** C'est beaucoup plus marrant.
2 **beaucoup de**
**We don't have much time.** Nous n'avons pas beaucoup de temps.
**Is there much left?** Est-ce qu'il en reste beaucoup?
3 **not much** pas beaucoup
**'Do you have any homework?' — 'Yes, but not much.'** 'Est-ce que tu as des devoirs?' — 'Oui, mais pas beaucoup.'
4 **very much** (*a lot*) beaucoup
**Thanks very much.** Merci beaucoup.
**I don't train very much.** Je ne m'entraîne pas beaucoup.
5 **very much** (*a lot of*) beaucoup de
**There isn't very much milk.** Il n'y a pas beaucoup de lait.
6 (*such a lot*) **so much** tellement
**I have so much to do!** J'ai tellement de choses à faire!
7 (*all of that*) **so much** autant
**You shouldn't have given me so much.** Tu n'aurais pas dû m'en donner autant.
8 **as much as** autant que
**You can take as much as you like.** Tu peux en prendre autant que tu veux.
**I spent as much money as you did.** J'ai dépensé autant d'argent que toi.
9 **too much** trop (de)
**too much money** trop d'argent
**That's far too much!** C'est beaucoup trop!
10 **how much?** combien?
**How much is it?** Ça coûte combien?
**How much money do you have?** Tu as combien d'argent?
**How much time do you have left?** Il te reste combien de temps?

**mud** *noun*
la **boue** *fem*

**muddle** *noun*
1 le **désordre** *masc*
**to be in a muddle** être **[6]** en désordre
**to leave something in a muddle** laisser **[1]** quelque chose en désordre
2 **to get into a muddle** s'embrouiller **[1]**
**We got into a muddle.** Nous nous sommes embrouillés.

**muddy** *adjective*
1 (*path, road*) **boueux** *masc*, **boueuse** *fem*
2 (*shoes, clothes*) **couvert de boue** *masc*, **couverte de boue** *fem*
**My boots are all muddy.** Mes bottes sont couvertes de boue.

to **mug** *verb* ▷ see **mug** *noun*
**agresser [1]**
**The old lady was mugged.** La vieille dame a été agressée.
**to get mugged** se faire ❷ **[10]** agresser
**My brother got mugged in the park.** Mon frère s'est fait agresser au parc.

**mug** *noun* ▷ see **mug** *verb*
la **grande tasse** *fem*
**a mug of coffee** une grande tasse de café

**mugging** *noun*
une **agression** *fem*

**multiplication** *noun*
la **multiplication** *fem*

to **multiply** *verb*
**multiplier [1]**

♪ **mum, mummy** *noun*
1 (*mother*) la **mère** *fem*
**Jim's mum** la mère de Jim
**I'll ask my mum.** Je vais demander à ma mère.
2 (*within the family, as a name*) la **maman** *fem*
**Mum's not back yet.** Maman n'est pas encore rentrée.

**mumps** *noun*
les **oreillons** *masc pl*

to **murder** *verb* ▷ see **murder** *noun*
**assassiner [1]**

**murder** *noun* ▷ see **murder** *verb*
le **meurtre** *masc*
to be accused of murder être [6] accusé de meurtre

**murderer** *noun*
un **assassin** *masc*

**muscle** *noun*
le **muscle** *masc*

**muscular** *adjective*
**musclé** *masc*, **musclée** *fem*

**museum** *noun*
le **musée** *masc*
to go to the museum aller Ⓔ [7] au musée
I can't stand museums! J'ai horreur des musées!

**mushroom** *noun*
le **champignon** *masc*
a mushroom pizza une pizza aux champignons

**music** *noun*
la **musique** *fem*
classical music la musique classique
reggae music le reggae
I prefer pop music. J'aime mieux la musique pop.

**musical** *noun* ▷ see **musical** *adj*
la **comédie musicale**

**musical** *adjective* ▷ see **musical** *noun*
to be musical être [6] musicien
Lauren's musical. Lauren est musicienne.
They're a very musical family. Ils sont très musiciens dans la famille.

**musical instrument** *noun*
un **instrument de musique**
to play a musical instrument jouer [1] d'un instrument de musique

**musician** *noun*
le **musicien** *masc*, la **musicienne** *fem*
He wants to be a musician. Il veut être musicien.

**Muslim** *noun*
le **Musulman** *masc*, la **Musulmane** *fem*

**mussel** *noun*
la **moule** *fem*

**must** *verb*
1 (*to have to*) **falloir** [43] (*only used with the **il faut** form*)
We must leave now. Il faut partir maintenant.
We mustn't forget Jake. Il ne faut pas oublier Jake.
I must tell you something. Il faut que je te dise quelque chose.
2 (*if you assume something to be true*) **devoir** [8]
You must be tired. Tu dois être fatigué.
It must be five o'clock. Il doit être cinq heures.
They must have forgotten. Ils ont dû oublier.

**mustard** *noun*
la **moutarde** *fem*

to **mutter** *verb*
**marmonner** [1]

**my** *adjective*
1 (*with masc singular nouns*) **mon**
my brother mon frère
my book mon livre
my computer mon ordinateur
2 (*with fem singular nouns*) **ma**
my sister ma sœur
my house ma maison
Here's my address. Voici mon adresse.

**WORD TIP** Use *mon* with feminine nouns beginning with *a, e, i, o, u* or *silent h*.

3 (*with plural nouns*) **mes**
my children mes enfants
my friends mes amis
my sisters mes sœurs
4 (*with parts of the body*) **le**, **la**, **les**
I'm washing my hands. Je me lave les mains.
I had a glass in my hand. J'avais un verre à la main.
My eyes are sore. J'ai mal aux yeux.

**myself** *pronoun*
1 **me**, **m'** (*before a, e, i, o, u or silent h*)
I've hurt myself. Je me suis blessé.
I'm really enjoying myself. Je m'amuse beaucoup.
2 (*for emphasis*) **moi-même**
I said it myself. Je l'ai dit moi-même.
3 (*on my own*) **by myself** tout seul (*boy speaking*), toute seule (*girl speaking*)
I did it by myself. Je l'ai fait tout seul.

**mysterious** *adjective*
**mystérieux** *masc*, **mystérieuse** *fem*
mysterious noises des bruits mystérieux

**mystery** *noun*
1 (*puzzle*) le **mystère** *masc*
It's a mystery to me how they won. Je ne comprends vraiment pas comment ils ont gagné.
2 (*book*) le **roman policier**

**myth** *noun*
le **mythe** *masc*

**mythology** *noun*
la **mythologie** *fem*

a b c d e f g h i j k l m n o p q r s t u v w x y z

# N n

to **nail** *verb* ▷ see **nail** *noun*
**clouer [1]**
a sign nailed to the gate un panneau cloué à la barrière

**nail** *noun* ▷ see **nail** *verb*
1 (*on fingers, toes*) un **ongle** *masc*
2 (*for wood*) le **clou** *masc*
• **nailbrush** la brosse à ongles
• **nailfile** la lime à ongles
• **nail scissors** les ciseaux à ongles

**naked** *adjective*
**nu** *masc*, **nue** *fem*

♪ **name** *noun*
1 (*person's*) le **nom** *masc*
What's your name? Comment vous appelez-vous?
My name is Debbie. Je m'appelle Debbie.
2 (*of a book, film*) le **titre** *masc*

***names***

The most common surname in France is *Martin*.

**nap** *noun*
le **petit somme** *masc*
to have a nap faire **[10]** un petit somme

**napkin** *noun*
la **serviette** *fem*

♪ **narrow** *adjective*
**étroit** *masc*, **étroite** *fem*
the narrow streets les rues étroites
The trousers are too narrow. Le pantalon est trop étroit.

♪ **nasty** *adjective*
1 (*mean*) **méchant** *masc*, **méchante** *fem*
That was a nasty thing to do. Ça, c'était méchant.
to be nasty to somebody être **[6]** méchant avec quelqu'un
The girls are nasty to her. Les filles sont méchantes avec elle.
2 (*unpleasant*) **désagréable** *masc & fem*
a nasty job une tâche désagréable
a nasty cold un gros rhume
3 (*food, smell*) **mauvais** *masc*, **mauvaise** *fem*
The soup tastes nasty. La soupe a mauvais goût.

**nation** *noun*
la **nation** *fem*

**national** *adjective*
**national** *masc*, **nationale** *fem*, **nationaux** *masc pl*, **nationales** *fem pl*
• **national anthem** un hymne national

**nationality** *noun*
la **nationalité** *fem*
What nationality are you? Vous êtes de quelle nationalité?

**national park** *noun*
le **parc national** (*pl* les **parcs nationaux**)

**Nativity** *noun*
la **nativité** *fem*

♪ **natural** *adjective*
1 (*from nature*) **naturel** *masc*, **naturelle** *fem*
the planet's natural resources les ressources naturelles de la planète
2 (*understandable*) **normal** *masc*, **normale** *fem*
It's natural to be curious. Il est normal d'être curieux.

**naturally** *adverb*
**naturellement**
Naturally, he said no. Naturellement, il a refusé.

♪ **nature** *noun*
la **nature** *fem*
• **nature reserve** la réserve naturelle

**naughty** *adjective*
**vilain** *masc*, **vilaine** *fem*
a naughty little girl une vilaine petite fille

**nausea** *noun*
la **nausée** *fem*

**navel** *noun*
le **nombril** *masc*

to **navigate** *verb*
**naviguer [1]**

**navy** *noun*
1 la **marine** *fem*
to join the navy s'engager **[52]** dans la marine
My uncle's in the navy. Mon oncle est dans la marine.
2 (*colour*) le **bleu marine** *masc*

**navy-blue** *adjective*
**bleu marine** *invariable adj*
navy-blue gloves des gants bleu marine

♪ **near** *adjective* ▷ see **near** *adv, prep*
**proche** *masc & fem*
the nearest phone booth la cabine téléphonique la plus proche
The supermarket is quite near. Le supermarché est assez proche.

English–French

**near** *adverb, preposition* ▷ see **near** *adj*
1 **près**
**I live quite near.** J'habite tout près.
**to come nearer** s'approcher [1]
**As the bull came nearer, …** Comme le taureau s'approchait de plus en plus, …
2 **near (to) something** près de quelque chose
**It's near the station.** C'est près de la gare.
**Is there a cafe near here?** Est-ce qu'il y a un café près d'ici?
**We live near Edinburgh.** Nous habitons près d'Édimbourg.

**nearby** *adverb*
**tout près**

**nearly** *adverb*
**presque**
**nearly empty** presque vide
**I've nearly finished.** J'ai presque fini.
**I nearly forgot.** J'ai failli oublier.

**neat** *adjective*
1 (*room, house*) **bien rangé** *masc*, **bien rangée** *fem*
2 (*appearance, writing*) **soigné** *masc*, **soignée** *fem*
**She always looks neat.** Elle est toujours soignée.

**neatly** *adverb*
**avec soin**

**necessary** *adjective*
**nécessaire** *masc & fem*
**That's not necessary.** Cela n'est pas nécessaire.
**If necessary, they'll collect us.** Si besoin est, ils viendront nous chercher.

**neck** *noun*
1 (*of a person*) le **cou** *masc*
2 (*of a top, a shirt*) une **encolure** *fem*

**necklace** *noun*
le **collier** *masc*

**nectarine** *noun*
la **nectarine** *fem*

to **need** *verb* ▷ see **need** *noun*
1 **to need something, somebody** avoir [5] besoin de quelqu'un, quelque chose
**We need bread.** Nous avons besoin de pain.
**Is that everything you need?** C'est tout ce qu'il vous faut?
**That's all I need.** C'est tout ce qu'il me faut.
2 **to need to do something** devoir [8] faire quelque chose
**We need to call Paul.** Nous devons appeler Paul.
3 **I don't need to go now.** Je ne suis pas obligé d'y aller maintenant.
**We needn't wait.** Nous ne sommes pas obligés d'attendre.

**need** *noun* ▷ see **need** *verb*
**There's no need, I've done it.** Inutile, c'est fait.
**There's no need to wait.** Inutile d'attendre.

**needle** *noun*
une **aiguille** *fem*

**negative** *adjective* ▷ see **negative** *noun*
**négatif** *masc*, **négative** *fem*

**negative** *noun* ▷ see **negative** *adj*
1 (*of photos*) le **négatif** *masc*
2 (*Grammar*) la **forme négative**

**neglected** *adjective*
**mal entretenu** *masc*, **mal entretenue** *fem*

**neighbour** *noun*
le **voisin** *masc*, la **voisine** *fem*
**I'm going round to the neighbours'.** Je vais chez les voisins.

**neighbourhood** *noun*
le **quartier** *masc*
**to live in a good neighbourhood** habiter [1] un quartier agréable
**It's a tough neighbourhood.** C'est un quartier dur.

**neither** *conjunction*
1 **neither … nor** ne … ni … ni
**I have neither the time nor the money.** Je n'ai ni le temps ni l'argent.
2 (*when there is no verb*) **ni l'un ni l'autre** (*ni l'une … with feminine nouns*)
**'Which do you like?' — 'Neither.'** 'Lequel aimes-tu?' — 'Ni l'un ni l'autre.'
3 (*in replies*) **Neither do I.** Moi non plus.
**'I don't like fish.' — 'Neither do I.'** 'Je n'aime pas le poisson.' — 'Moi non plus.'
**'I didn't like the film.' — 'Neither did we.'** 'Je n'ai pas aimé le film.' — 'Nous non plus.'

**WORD TIP** *non plus* can be used for 'nor do they', etc *eux non plus*, etc.

**nephew** *noun*
le **neveu** *masc* (*pl* les **neveux**)

**nerve** *noun*
1 (*in the body*) le **nerf** *masc*
**He gets on my nerves.** Il me tape sur les nerfs.
2 (*daring*) le **courage** *masc*
**You've got a nerve!** Tu as un sacré culot!

**nervous** *adjective*
**nerveux** *masc*, **nerveuse** *fem*
**nervous students** des élèves nerveux
• **nervous breakdown** la dépression nerveuse




a b c d e f g h i j k l m n o p q r s t u v w x y z

**nest** *noun*
le **nid** *masc*
a bird's nest un nid d'oiseau

**net** *noun*
1 (*for fishing, in tennis*) le **filet** *masc*
2 (*in football*) les **filets** *masc pl*
3 the Net l'Internet *masc*
to look something up on the Net chercher [1] quelque chose sur Internet
We can look it up on the Net. On peut le chercher sur Internet.
• **netball** le netball

**Netherlands** *noun*
the Netherlands les Pays-Bas *masc pl*

**nettle** *noun*
une **ortie** *fem*

**network** *noun*
le **réseau** *masc* (*pl* les **réseaux**)
a television network un réseau de télévision

**neutral** *adjective*
**neutre** *masc & fem*
neutral colours des couleurs neutres

**never** *adjective*
1 (*when used with a verb*) **ne ... jamais**
Ben never smokes. Ben ne fume jamais.
I've never seen the film. Je n'ai jamais vu le film.
2 (*when used alone*) **jamais**
'Have you ever been to Spain?' — 'Never.' 'Est-ce que tu es déjà allé en Espagne?' — 'Jamais.'
3 (*in expressions*) Never again. Plus jamais.
Never mind! Peu importe!

**WORD TIP** *ne* comes before the verb or verb group, including pronouns, with *jamais* coming after. ▷ **nobody, not, nothing**.

**new** *adjective*
1 (*different, unknown to you*) **nouveau** *masc*, **nouvel** *masc*, **nouvelle** *fem*, **nouveaux** *masc pl*, **nouvelles** *fem pl*
my new coat mon nouveau manteau
a new album un nouvel album
Liam's new girlfriend la nouvelle copine de Liam
our new neighbours les nouveaux voisins

**WORD TIP** *nouveau*, etc come before the noun; *nouvel* is used before *a, e, i, o, u* or silent *h*.

2 (*brand new*) **neuf** *masc*, **neuve** *fem*
a new house une maison neuve
It's a new bike. C'est un vélo neuf.

**newcomer** *noun*
le **nouveau venu** *masc* (*pl* les **nouveaux venus**), la **nouvelle venue** *fem* (*pl* les **nouvelles venues**)

**news** *plural noun*
1 (*in conversation*) la **nouvelle** *fem*, les **nouvelles** *fem pl*
a piece of news une nouvelle
She got some bad news. Elle a eu une mauvaise nouvelle.
I've got good news. J'ai de bonnes nouvelles.
2 (*on the radio, TV*) le **journal** *masc*, les **informations** *fem pl*
the midday news le journal de midi
They're watching the news. Ils regardent le journal.

**newsagent** *noun*
le **marchand de journaux**
at the newsagent's chez le marchand de journaux

**newspaper** *noun*
le **journal** *masc* (*pl* les **journaux**)
I read it in the newspaper. Je l'ai lu dans le journal.

**newsreader** *noun*
le **présentateur** *masc*, la **présentatrice** *fem*

**New Year** *noun*
**le Nouvel An**
Happy New Year! Bonne Année!
• **New Year's Day** le jour de l'An
• **New Year's Eve** la Saint-Sylvestre

**New Zealand** *noun*
la **Nouvelle-Zélande** *fem*
in New Zealand en Nouvelle-Zélande
to go to New Zealand aller ⓔ [7] en Nouvelle-Zélande

**WORD TIP** Countries and regions in French take *le, la* or *les*.

**New Zealander** *noun*
un **Néo-Zélandais** *masc*, une **Néo-Zélandaise** *fem*
the New Zealanders les Néo-Zélandais

**WORD TIP** Adjectives never have capitals in French, even for nationality or regional origin.

**next** *adjective* ▷ see **next** *adv*
1 (*in the future*) **prochain** *masc*, **prochaine** *fem*
next week la semaine prochaine
next Thursday jeudi prochain
next year l'année prochaine
The next train is at ten. Le prochain train est à dix heures.
2 (*in a series*) **suivant** *masc*, **suivante** *fem*
the next page la page suivante
the next day le lendemain
3 (*office, room*) **voisin** *masc*, **voisine** *fem*

English–French

♂ **next** *adverb* ▷ see **next** *adj*
1 (*afterwards*) **ensuite**
**What did he say next?** Qu'est-ce qu'il a dit ensuite?
2 (*now*) **maintenant**
**What shall we do next?** Qu'est-ce qu'on fait maintenant?
3 **next to** à côté de
**the girl next to Emma** la fille à côté d'Emma

**next door** *adverb*
**à côté**
**Who lives next door?** Qui habite à côté?

♂ **nice** *adjective*
1 (*place, time*) **agréable** *masc & fem*
**I had a nice evening.** J'ai passé une soirée agréable.
**Have a nice time!** Amusez-vous bien!
2 (*clothes*) **joli** *masc*, **jolie** *fem*
**I bought a nice ring.** J'ai acheté une jolie bague.
3 (*people*) **sympathique** *masc & fem*
**Amy's really nice.** Amy est vraiment sympathique.
4 **to be nice to somebody** être[6] gentil avec quelqu'un
**She's been very nice to us.** Elle a été très gentille avec nous.
5 (*taste, drink*) **bon** *masc*, **bonne** *fem*
**a nice meal** un bon repas
**a nice cup of tea** une bonne tasse de thé
6 (*weather*) **to be nice** faire[10] beau
**It's a nice day.** Il fait beau.
**The weather was nice.** Il a fait beau.

**WORD TIP** *joli* and *bon* come before the noun.

**nickname** *noun*
le **surnom** *masc*
**My nickname is Mizz.** On m'a surnommé Mizz.

♂ **niece** *noun*
la **nièce** *fem*

♂ **night** *noun*
1 (*before bedtime*) le **soir** *masc*
**tomorrow night** demain soir
**on Saturday night** samedi soir
**I saw Jason last night.** J'ai vu Jason hier soir.
2 (*after bedtime*) la **nuit** *fem*
**in the middle of the night** au milieu de la nuit
**It's cold at night.** Il fait froid la nuit.
**We stayed the night at Rachel's.** Nous avons couché chez Rachel.
• **night club** la boîte de nuit

**nightie** *noun*
la **chemise de nuit**

**nightmare** *noun*
le **cauchemar** *masc*
**to have a nightmare** faire[10] un cauchemar

**nil** *noun*
le **zéro** *masc*
**They won four-nil.** Ils ont gagné quatre à zéro.

**nine** *number*
**neuf**
**Jake's nine.** Jake a neuf ans.

**nineteen** *number*
**dix-neuf**
**Kate's nineteen.** Kate a dix-neuf ans.

**nineteenth** *adjective*
1 **dix-neuvième** *masc & fem*
2 (*in dates*) **the nineteenth of September** le dix-neuf septembre

**ninetieth** *adjective*
**quatre-vingt-dixième** *masc & fem*
**It's his ninetieth birthday.** Il fête ses quatre-vingt-dix ans.

**ninety** *number*
**quatre-vingt-dix**
**My great-uncle is ninety.** Mon grand-oncle a quatre-vingt-dix ans.

**ninth** *adjective*
1 **neuvième** *masc & fem*
**on the ninth floor** au neuvième étage
2 (*in dates*) **the ninth of June** le neuf juin

♂ **no** *adverb* ▷ see **no** *adj*
**non**
**'Are you hungry?' — 'No.'** 'Tu as faim?' — 'Non.'
**No, thank you.** Non merci.

♂ **no** *adjective* ▷ see **no** *adv*
1 (*in general*) **pas de**
**No problem!** Pas de problème!
**No way!** Pas question!
2 (*on notices*) **'No smoking'** 'Défense de fumer'
**'No parking'** 'Stationnement interdit'
3 (*with a verb*) **ne ... pas de**
**We've got no bread.** Nous n'avons pas de pain.
**He has no friends.** Il n'a pas d'amis.

**WORD TIP** *ne* comes before the verb, or verb group, and *pas de* comes after it. *Ne* becomes *n'* before *a, e, i, o, u* or silent *h*.

♂ **nobody** *pronoun*
1 (*without a verb*) **personne**
**'Who's there?' — 'Nobody.'** 'Qui est là?' — 'Personne.'

2 (*with a verb*) **ne ... personne**
There's nobody in the classroom. Il n'y a personne dans la salle de classe.
Nobody knows me. Personne ne me connaît.
Nobody answered. Personne n'a répondu.

**WORD TIP** *ne* comes before the verb or verb group, including pronouns, with *personne* coming after. ▷ **never**, **not**, **nothing**.

to **nod** *verb*
**hocher [1] la tête**

♪ **noise** *noun*
le **bruit** *masc*
too much noise trop de bruit
to make a noise faire **[10]** du bruit
I heard strange noises. J'ai entendu des bruits bizarres.

♪ **noisy** *adjective*
**bruyant** *masc*, **bruyante** *fem*
It's too noisy here. Ici c'est trop bruyant.

♪ **none** *pronoun*
1 (*not one*) **aucun** *masc*, **aucune** *fem*
'How many students failed the exam?' — 'None.' 'Combien d'étudiants ont raté l'examen?' — 'Aucun.'
2 (*with a verb*) **ne ... aucun** (*aucune with feminine nouns*)
None of the girls knows him. Aucune des filles ne le connaît.
None of these biros works. Aucun de ces bics ne marche.
3 (*no more*) **ne ... plus**
There's none left. Il n'y en a plus.
There are none left. Il n'y en a plus.

**WORD TIP** *ne* comes before the verb or verb group, including pronouns, no matter where *aucun* or *aucune* appears in the sentence. *... plus* follows the verb or verb group. *ne* becomes *n'* before *a, e, i, o, u* or silent *h*. ▷ **nothing**, **nobody**, **not**.

**nonsense** *noun*
les **bêtises** *fem pl*
to talk nonsense dire **[47]** des bêtises

♪ **non-smoker** *noun*
le **non-fumeur**, la **non-fumeuse**

**non-stop** *adjective* ▷ see **non-stop** *adv*
(*train, bus service*) **direct**

**non-stop** *adverb* ▷ see **non-stop** *adj*
**sans arrêt**
She talks non-stop. Elle parle sans arrêt.

**noodles** *plural noun*
les **nouilles** *fem pl*

♪ **noon** *noun*
**midi** *masc*
at (twelve) noon à midi

♪ **no one**, **no-one** *pronoun* ▷ **nobody**

♪ **nor** *conjunction*
1 **neither ... nor ne ... ni ... ni**
I have neither the time nor the money. Je n'ai ni le temps ni l'argent.
2 (*in replies*) **Nor do I.** Moi non plus.
'I don't like fish.' — 'Nor do I.' 'Je n'aime pas le poisson.' — 'Moi non plus.'
'I wasn't invited.' — 'Nor were we.' 'Je n'ai pas été invité.' — 'Nous non plus.'

**WORD TIP** *ne* becomes *n'* before *a, e, i, o, u* or silent *h*. *non plus* can be used for 'nor do they', etc, *eux non plus*, etc.

♪ **normal** *adjective*
1 (*natural*) **normal** *masc*, **normale** *fem*, **normaux** *masc pl*, **normales** *fem pl*
a normal reaction une réaction normale
That's normal. C'est normal.
2 (*usual*) **habituel** *masc*, **habituelle** *fem*
my normal work mon travail habituel
We'll come at the normal time. On viendra à l'heure habituelle.

**normally** *adverb*
**normalement**

**Normandy** *noun*
la **Normandie** *fem*
in Normandy en Normandie

♪ **north** *adjective, adverb* ▷ see **north** *noun*
**nord** *invariable adj*
the north side le côté nord
a north wind un vent du nord
north of Paris au nord de Paris
We're going north. Nous allons vers le nord.

**WORD TIP** *nord* never changes.

♪ **north** *noun* ▷ see **north** *adj, adv*
le **nord** *masc*
in the north au nord
in the north of France dans le nord de la France

**North America** *noun*
l'**Amérique du Nord** *fem*
in North America en Amérique du Nord

**North American** *adjective* ▷ see **North American** *noun*
**nord-américain** *masc*, **nord-américaine** *fem*

**North American** *noun* ▷ see **North American** *adj*
un **Nord-Américain** *masc*, une **Nord-Américaine** *fem*

**northeast** *adjective*
▷ see **northeast** *noun*
in northeast England au nord-est de l'Angleterre

**northeast** *noun*
▷ see **northeast** *adjective*
le **nord-est** *masc*

**Northern Ireland** *noun*
l'**Irlande du Nord** *fem*
in Northern Ireland en Irlande du Nord

**WORD TIP** Countries and regions in French take *le, la,* or *les.*

**Northern Irish** *adjective*
**d'Irlande du Nord**
I'm Northern Irish. Je suis d'Irlande du Nord.

**North Pole** *noun*
the North Pole le pôle Nord

**North Sea** *noun*
the North Sea la mer du Nord

**northwest** *adjective*
▷ see **northwest** *noun*
in northwest Scotland au nord-ouest de l'Écosse

**northwest** *noun* ▷ see **northwest** *adj*
le **nord-ouest** *masc*

**Norway** *noun*
la **Norvège** *fem*

**Norwegian** *adjective*
▷ see **Norwegian** *noun*
**norvégien** *masc*, **norvégienne** *fem*

**Norwegian** *noun* ▷ see **Norwegian** *adj*
1 (*person*) un **Norvégien** *masc*, une **Norvégienne** *fem*
2 (*the language*) le **norvégien** *masc*

**nose** *noun*
le **nez** *masc*
to blow your nose se moucher Ⓔ [1]

**nostril** *noun*
la **narine** *fem*

**not** *adverb*
1 (*without a verb*) **pas**
not bad pas mal
not yet pas encore
not on Saturdays pas le samedi
Not me! Pas moi!
Not again! Pas encore!
2 (*when used with a verb*) **ne ... pas**
I don't know. Je ne sais pas.
It's not my watch. Ce n'est pas ma montre.
It doesn't matter. Ça ne fait rien.
I haven't replied. Je n'ai pas répondu.
Will didn't phone. Will n'a pas appelé.
They won't come. Ils ne viendront pas.
We decided not to wait. Nous avons décidé de ne pas attendre. (*ne pas comes before an infinitive.*)

**WORD TIP** *ne* comes before the verb or verb group, including pronouns, with *pas* coming after. *ne* becomes *n'* before *a, e, i, o, u* or silent *h.* ▷ **never, nobody, nothing**.

**note** *noun*
1 (*message*) le **mot** *masc*
She left me a note. Elle m'a laissé un mot.
2 (*in order to remember*) la **note** *fem*
to take notes prendre [64] des notes
to make a note of something noter [1] quelque chose
I made a note of the date. J'ai noté la date.
3 (*banknote*) le **billet** *masc*
a ten-pound note un billet de dix livres
4 (*in music*) la **note** *fem*
• **notebook** le carnet
• **notepad**
le **bloc-notes** (*pl* les **blocs-notes**)

**nothing** *pronoun*
1 (*without a verb*) **rien**
'What did you buy?' — 'Nothing.' 'Qu'est-ce que tu as acheté?' — 'Rien.'
'What's going on?' — 'Nothing.' 'Qu'est-ce qui se passe?' — 'Rien.'
2 nothing + adjective rien de ( *+ adjective*)
nothing new rien de nouveau
There's nothing interesting on TV. Il n'y a rien d'intéressant à la télé.
3 (*with a verb as object*) **ne ... rien**
She knows nothing. Elle ne sait rien.
I heard nothing. Je n'ai rien entendu.
There's nothing left. Il ne reste rien.
We've got nothing to do. On n'a rien à faire.
I've decided to do nothing. J'ai décidé de ne rien faire.
4 (*with a verb as subject*) Nothing has changed. Rien n'a changé.
Nothing's happening. Il ne se passe rien.

**WORD TIP** *ne* comes before the verb or verb group, including pronouns, no matter where *rien* appears in the sentence. *ne* becomes *n'* before *a, e, i, o, u* or silent *h.* ▷ **never, nobody, not**

**to notice** *verb* ▷ see **notice** *noun*
**remarquer [1]**
I noticed the box. J'ai remarqué la boîte.
to notice that ... remarquer que ...
Did you notice that she was talking? Est-ce que tu as remarqué qu'elle parlait?

**notice** *noun* ▷ see **notice** *verb*
1 (*sign*) le **panneau** *masc* (*pl* les **panneaux**)
It's written on the notice. C'est marqué sur le panneau.

2 (*advertisement*) une **annonce** *fem*
3 to take no notice ne pas faire [10] attention
You never take any notice. Tu ne fais jamais attention.
Don't take any notice of her! Ne fais pas attention à elle!

**noticeable** *adjective*
**visible** *masc & fem*

**noticeboard** *noun*
le **panneau d'affichage**

**nought** *noun*
le **zéro** *masc*

**noun** *noun*
le **nom** *masc*

♂ **novel** *noun*
le **roman** *masc*

**novelist** *noun*
le **romancier** *masc*, la **romancière** *fem*

**November** *noun*
**novembre** *masc*
in November en novembre

**WORD TIP** Months of the year and days of the week take a small letter in French.

♂ **now** *adverb*
1 (*in general*) **maintenant**
Where is he now? Où est-il maintenant?
I have two cats now. J'ai deux chats maintenant.
Bye for now. À bientôt.
2 (*this minute*) **just now** en ce moment
I'm busy just now. Je suis occupé en ce moment.
3 (*a minute ago*) **just now**
I saw Jack just now. Je viens de voir Jack.
4 **right now** tout de suite
5 **to be doing something right now** être [6] en train de faire quelque chose
I'm reading your text right now. Je suis en train de lire ton texto.
6 **now and then** de temps en temps

**WORD TIP** *venir de + infinitive verb* is for very recent actions. *être en train de + infinitive verb* is for actions as they happen.

**nowadays** *adverb*
**de nos jours**
Nowadays people use computers. De nos jours, on se sert des ordinateurs.

♂ **nowhere** *adverb*
**nulle part**
nowhere in France nulle part en France
There's nowhere to play ball. Il n'y a aucun endroit pour jouer au ballon.

**nuclear** *adjective*
**nucléaire** *masc & fem*
a nuclear power station une centrale nucléaire

**nude** *adjective*
**nu** *masc*, **nue** *fem*
in the nude nu

**nuisance** *noun*
That's a nuisance. Ça, c'est embêtant.
She's a nuisance. Elle est pénible.

**numb** *adjective*
1 (*with cold*) **engourdi** *masc*, **engourdie** *fem*
My foot's numb. J'ai le pied engourdi.
2 (*without feeling*) **insensible** *masc & fem*

♂ **number** *noun*
1 (*of a house, a phone, an account, in a list*) le **numéro** *masc*
my mobile number mon numéro de portable
What's your number? Ton numéro de téléphone, c'est quoi?
2 (*written figure*) le **chiffre** *masc*
the third number is a 7 le troisième chiffre est un 7
3 (*amount*) le **nombre** *masc*
a large number of visitors un grand nombre de visiteurs
• **number plate** la plaque d'immatriculation

**nun** *noun*
la **religieuse** *fem*

♂ **nurse** *noun*
un **infirmier** *masc*, une **infirmière** *fem*
Janet's a nurse Janet est infirmière.

**nursery** *noun*
1 (*for children*) la **crèche** *fem*
2 (*for plants*) la **pépinière** *fem*
• **nursery school** une école maternelle

**nursing** *noun*
la **profession d'infirmière, d'infirmier** (*for a male nurse*)
to go into nursing devenir ❷ [81] infirmière (*female nurse*), infirmier (*male nurse*)

**nut** *noun*
1 (*walnut*) la **noix** *fem*
2 (*almond*) une **amande** *fem*
3 (*peanut*) la **cacahuète** *fem*
4 (*for a bolt*) un **écrou** *masc*

**nylon** *noun*
le **nylon** *masc*
made of nylon en nylon

English–French

# O o

**oak** *noun*
le **chêne** *masc*

**oar** *noun*
la **rame** *fem*

**oasis** *noun*
une **oasis** *fem*

**oats** *noun*
l'**avoine** *fem*

**obedient** *adjective*
**obéissant** *masc*, **obéissante** *fem*

to **obey** *verb*
1 (*a person*) **obéir [2] à**
You must obey your team leader. Il faut que tu obéisses à ton chef d'équipe.
2 **to obey the rules** respecter [1] le règlement
You must obey the rules. Il faut que tu respectes le règlement.

to **object** *verb* ▷ see **object** *noun*
**soulever [50] des objections**

**object** *noun* ▷ see **object** *verb*
un **objet** *masc*

**objection** *noun*
une **objection** *fem*

**oblong** *adjective*
**rectangulaire** *masc & fem*

**oboe** *noun*
le **hautbois** *masc*
to play the oboe jouer [1] du hautbois

**obscene** *adjective*
**obscène** *masc & fem*

**obsessed** *adjective*
**obsédé** *masc*, **obsédée** *fem*
Kat's obsessed with her diet. Kat est obsédée par son régime.

**obsession** *noun*
une **obsession**
She has an obsession with cleanliness. Elle est obsédée par la propreté.

**obstacle** *noun*
un **obstacle** *masc*

**obstinate** *adjective*
**têtu** *masc*, **têtue** *fem*

to **obstruct** *verb*
(*the traffic, a person*) **gêner [1]**

to **obtain** *verb*
**obtenir [77]**

**obvious** *adjective*
**évident** *masc*, **évidente** *fem*

**obviously** *adverb*
1 (*of course*) **bien sûr**
'Do you want to come too?' — 'Obviously.' 'Veux-tu venir avec nous?' — 'Bien sûr.'
2 (*visibly*) **manifestement**
The house is obviously empty. La maison est manifestement vide.

**occasion** *noun*
une **occasion** *fem*
a special occasion une grande occasion

**occasionally** *adverb*
**de temps en temps**
I see her occasionally. Je la vois de temps en temps.

**occupation** *noun*
1 (*job*) la **profession** *fem*
2 (*of a country*) l'**occupation** *fem*

**occupied** *adjective*
**occupé** *masc*, **occupée** *fem*

to **occur** *verb*
1 (*to happen*) **avoir [5] lieu**
The accident occurred on Monday. L'accident a eu lieu lundi.
2 (*to come to mind*) **It occurs to me that ...** Il me vient à l'esprit que ...
It never occurred to me. Cela ne m'est pas venu à l'idée.

**ocean** *noun*
un **océan** *masc*

**o'clock** *adverb*
It's one o'clock. Il est une heure.
Jane's arriving at ten o'clock. Jane arrive à dix heures.

**October** *noun*
**octobre** *masc*
Alex's birthday is in October. L'anniversaire d'Alex est en octobre.

**WORD TIP** Months of the year and days of the week start with small letters in French.

**octopus** *noun*
la **pieuvre** *fem*

**odd** *adjective*
1 (*strange*) **bizarre** *masc & fem*
an odd flavour un goût bizarre
That's odd. C'est bizarre.

**2** (*in numbers*) **impair** *masc*, **impaire** *fem*
**Three is an odd number.** Trois est un chiffre impair.

𝄞 **of** *preposition*
**1** (*in general*) **de**
**a kilo of tomatoes** un kilo de tomates
**the end of my work** la fin de mon travail
**two of us** deux d'entre nous
**2** (*in dates*) **the sixth of June** le six juin
**3** **made of** en
**a bracelet made of silver** un bracelet en argent
**4** (*followed by* the) **the name of the flower** le nom de la fleur
**the beginning of the concert** le début du concert
**the parents of the children** les parents des enfants
**5** **of it, of them** en
**We ate a lot of it.** Nous en avons mangé beaucoup.
**He's selling three of them.** Il en vend trois.

**WORD TIP** *en* goes before the verb.

**off** *adjective, adverb, preposition*
**1** (*electrical things*) **éteint** *masc*, **éteinte** *fem*
**Is the telly off?** Est-ce que la télé est éteinte?
**Could you turn off the light?** Est-ce que tu peux éteindre la lumière?
**2** (*tap, water, gas*) **fermé** *masc*, **fermée** *fem*
**The tap's off.** Le robinet est fermé.
**3** (*when supply is cut*) **coupé** *masc*, **coupée** *fem*
**The gas and electricity were off.** Le gaz et l'électricité étaient coupés.
**4** **to be off** s'en aller Ⓔ **[7]**
**I'm off.** Je m'en vais.
**5** **a day off** un jour de congé
**to be off sick** être **[6]** malade
**Maya's off school today.** Maya n'est pas à l'école aujourd'hui.
**6** (*cancelled*) **annulé** *masc*, **annulée** *fem*
**The match is off.** Le match est annulé.
**7** (*in prices*) **'20% off shoes'** '20% de remise sur les chaussures'

**offence** *noun*
**1** (*crime*) **le délit** *masc*
**2** **to take offence** s'offenser **[1]**

to **offer** *verb* ▷ see **offer** *noun*
**1** (*a present, reward, job*) **offrir [56]**
**He offered her a chair.** Il lui a offert une chaise.
**2** **to offer to do something** proposer **[1]** de faire quelque chose
**Ben offered to drive me to the station.** Ben m'a proposé de me conduire à la gare.

**offer** *noun* ▷ see **offer** *verb*
**1** une **offre** *fem*
**a job offer** une offre d'emploi
**2** **'On special offer'** 'En promotion'

𝄞 **office** *noun*
le **bureau** *masc* (*pl* les **bureaux**)
**He's at the office.** Il est au bureau.

**officer** *noun*
un **officier** *noun*

**official** *adjective*
**officiel** *masc*, **officielle** *fem*

**off-licence** *noun*
le **magasin de vins et de spiritueux**

**offside** *adjective*
(*player*) **hors jeu**

𝄞 **often** *adverb*
**souvent**
**He's often late.** Il est souvent en retard.
**Do you see Rosie often?** Est-ce que tu vois Rosie souvent?

𝄞 **oil** *noun*
**1** (*in general*) l'**huile** *fem*
**2** (*crude oil*) le **pétrole** *masc*
- **oil painting** la peinture à l'huile
- **oil rig** la plateforme pétrolière
- **oil slick** la marée noire
- **oil tanker** le pétrolier

**ointment** *noun*
la **pommade** *fem*

𝄞 **okay** *adjective*
**1** **d'accord**
**Okay, tomorrow at ten.** D'accord, demain à dix heures.
**2** (*all right*) **pas mal**
**The film was okay.** Le film n'était pas mal.
**3** (*not ill*) **Are you okay?** Ça va?
**I'm okay now.** Ça va mieux maintenant.
**4** (*person*) **sympa** *invariable adj*
**Daisy's okay.** Daisy est sympa.

**WORD TIP** *sympa* never changes.

𝄞 **old** *adjective*
**1** (*in general*) **vieux** *masc*, **vieil** *masc*, **vieille** *fem*, **vieux** *masc pl*, **vieilles** *fem pl*
**an old man** un vieux monsieur
**an old lady** une vieille dame
**an old tree** un vieil arbre
**2** (*when talking about age*) **a two-year-old child** un enfant de deux ans
**old people** les personnes âgées
**How old are you?** Tu as quel âge?
**James is ten years old.** James a dix ans.
**3** (*when comparing ages*) **my older sister** ma sœur aînée ▸▸

She's older than me. Elle est plus âgée que moi.
He's a year older than me. Il a un an de plus que moi.

4 (*previous*) **ancien** *masc*, **ancienne** *fem*
It's their old address. C'est leur ancienne adresse.

**WORD TIP** *ancien* and *ancienne* come before the noun.

- **old age** la vieillesse
- **old age pensioner** le retraité (*man*), la retraitée (*woman*)

**old-fashioned** *adjective*

1 (*clothes, music, style*) **démodé** *masc*, **démodée** *fem*

2 (*person*) **vieux jeu**
My parents are so old-fashioned. Mes parents sont si vieux jeu.

**olive** *noun*
une **olive** *fem*
- **olive oil** l'huile d'olive *fem*

**Olympic Games**, **Olympics** *plural noun*
les **Jeux Olympiques** *masc pl*

mini-info **Olympic Games**
A Frenchman, Baron Pierre de Coubertin, organised the first modern Olympic Games in 1896.

**omelette** *noun*
une **omelette** *fem*
a cheese omelette une omelette au fromage

**on** *adjective* ▷ see **on** *prep*

1 (*TV, light, oven*) **to be on** être[6] allumé *masc*, allumée *fem*
All the lights were on. Toutes les lumières étaient allumées.

2 (*machine*) **être[6] en marche**
The dishwasher is on. Le lave-vaisselle est en marche.

3 (*showing*) What's on on TV? Qu'est-ce qu'il y a à la télé?
What's on at the cinema? Qu'est-ce qui passe au cinéma?

**on** *preposition* ▷ see **on** *adj*

1 (*saying where*) **sur**
on the desk sur le bureau
on the beach sur la plage

2 (*saying when*) **on 21st March** le 21 mars
He's arriving on Tuesday. Il arrive mardi.
It's shut on Saturdays. C'est fermé le samedi.
On rainy days I take the train. Quand il pleut je prend le train.

3 (*on buses, trains*) She arrived on the bus. Elle est arrivée en bus.
I met Jackie on the bus. J'ai vu Jackie dans le bus.
I slept on the plane. J'ai dormi dans l'avion.
Let's go on our bikes! Allons-y à vélo!

4 (*with activities*) **on holiday** en vacances
**to be on strike** être en grève

5 (*with media*) **on TV** à la télé
**on the radio** à la radio
**on video** en vidéo

**once** *adverb*

1 **une fois**
once a day une fois par jour
more than once plus d'une fois
I've tried once already. J'ai déjà essayé une fois.
Try once more. Essaie encore une fois.

2 (*without delay*) **at once** tout de suite
The doctor came at once. Le médecin est venu tout de suite.

3 (*at the same time*) **at once** à la fois
I can't do two things at once. Je ne peux pas faire deux choses à la fois.

**one** *number* ▷ see **one** *pron*
**un** *masc*, **une** *fem*
one son un fils
one apple une pomme
at one o'clock à une heure

**one** *pronoun* ▷ see **one** *number*

1 **on**
One never knows. On ne sait jamais.

2 **this one** celui-ci *masc*, celle-ci *fem*
I like that bike, but this one's cheaper. J'aime bien ce vélo-là, mais celui-ci est moins cher.
Do you want the red dress or this one? Veux-tu la robe rouge ou celle-ci?
**these ones** ceux-ci *masc*, celles-ci *fem*
I'd like these CDs but my brother wants these ones. Je voudrais ces CD mais mon frère veut ceux-ci.
'Which shoes do you like best?' — 'I like these ones.' 'Quelles chaussures préfères-tu?' — 'J'aime celles-ci.'

3 **that one** celui-là *masc*, celle-là *fem*
'Which video?' — 'That one.' 'Quelle vidéo?' — 'Celle-là.'
**those ones** ceux-là *masc pl*, celles-là *fem pl*
And as for the earrings, I prefer those ones. Et quant aux boucles d'oreille, je préfère celles-là.

4 **which one?** lequel? *masc*, laquelle? *fem*
'She borrowed a skirt from me.' — 'Which one?' 'Elle m'a emprunté une jupe.' — 'Laquelle?'

'My foot's hurting.' — 'Which one?' 'J'ai mal au pied.' — 'Auquel?'

**WORD TIP** *à+ lequel* become *auquel.*

**one's** *adjective*
(*before a masc noun*) **son**, (*before a fem noun*) **sa**, (*before a plural noun*) **ses**
**One does one's best.** On fait de son mieux.
**to wash one's hands** se laver Ⓔ **[1]** les mains

**oneself** *pronoun*
1 **to wash oneself** se laver Ⓔ **[1]**
**to hurt oneself** se blesser Ⓔ **[1]**
2 (*for emphasis*) **soi-même**
**One has to do everything oneself.** Il faut tout faire soi-même.
3 **by oneself** tout seul *masc*, toute seule *fem*

♪ **one-way street** *noun*
le **sens unique**

♪ **onion** *noun*
un **oignon** *masc*

♪ **only** *adjective* ▷ see **only** *adv, conj*
1 (*one*) **seul** *masc*, **seule** *fem*
**the only free seat** la seule place libre
**It was the only thing to do.** C'était la seule chose à faire.
2 (*children*) **an only child** un enfant unique
**I'm an only child.** Je suis enfant unique.

♪ **only** *adverb, conjunction* ▷ see **only** *adj*
1 (*with a verb*) **ne ... que**
**They've only got two bedrooms.** Ils n'ont que deux chambres.
**Anne's only free on Fridays.** Anne n'est libre que le vendredi.
**There are only three left.** Il n'en reste que trois.
2 (*just*) **seulement**
**'How long did they stay?' — 'Only two days.'** 'Ils sont restés combien de temps?' — 'Deux jours seulement.'

**onto** *preposition*
**sur**

♪ to **open** *verb* ▷ see **open** *adj, noun*
1 (*a door, a box*) **ouvrir [30]**
**Can you open the door?** Est-ce que tu peux ouvrir la porte?
**The bank opens at nine.** La banque ouvre à neuf heures.
**What time do you open?** Vous ouvrez à quelle heure?
2 (*by itself*) **s'ouvrir [30]**
**The door opened slowly.** La porte s'est ouverte lentement.

♪ **open** *adjective* ▷ see **open** *noun, verb*
**ouvert** *masc*, **ouverte** *fem*
**The door's open.** La porte est ouverte.
**Are the shops still open?** Est-ce que les magasins sont toujours ouverts?

**open** *noun* ▷ see **open** *adj, verb*
**in the open** en plein air
**I love eating in the open.** J'adore manger en plein air.

**open-air** *adjective*
**en plein air**
**an open-air swimming pool** une piscine en plein air

**opening** *noun*
1 (*space*) une **ouverture** *fem*
2 (*opportunity*) une **occasion** *fem*
3 (*for a job*) un **débouché** *masc*

**opera** *noun*
un **opéra** *masc*

to **operate** *verb*
(*medically*) **opérer [24]**

**operation** *noun*
une **opération** *fem*
**to have an operation** se faire Ⓔ **[10]** opérer
**She's had an operation.** Elle s'est fait opérer.

♪ **opinion** *noun*
un **avis** *masc*
**in my opinion** à mon avis
• **opinion poll** le sondage

**opponent** *noun*
un & une **adversaire** *masc & fem*

**opportunity** *noun*
une **occasion** *fem*
**to have the opportunity of doing something** avoir **[5]** l'occasion de faire quelque chose

**opposed** *adjective*
**to be opposed to something** être **[6]** opposé à quelque chose

♪ **opposite** *adjective* ▷ see **opposite** *adv, noun, prep*
1 (*direction, side, view*) **opposé** *masc*, **opposée** *fem*
**She went off in the opposite direction.** Elle est partie dans la direction opposée.
2 (*facing*) **d'en face**
**Joe lives in the house opposite.** Joe habite dans la maison d'en face.

English–French

**opposite** *adverb, preposition* ▷ see **opposite** *adj, noun*
1 **en face**
They live opposite. Ils habitent en face.
2 **en face de**
The school's opposite the station. L'école est en face de la gare.

**opposite** *noun* ▷ see **opposite** *adj, adv, prep*
le **contraire** *masc*

**opposition** *noun*
l'**opposition** *fem*

**optician** *noun*
un **opticien** *masc*, une **opticienne** *fem*

**optimistic** *adjective*
**optimiste** *masc & fem*

**option** *noun*
le **choix** *masc*
We have no option. Nous n'avons pas le choix.

**optional** *adjective*
**facultatif** *masc*, **facultative** *fem*
an optional course un cours facultatif

**or** *conjunction*
1 (*in general*) **ou**
today or Tuesday? aujourd'hui ou mardi?
Is he English or French? Il est anglais ou français?
2 (*after not*) **ni**
not in June or July ni en juin ni en juillet
I don't have a cat or a dog. Je n'ai ni chat ni chien.
3 (*or else*) **sinon**
Phone Mum, or she'll worry. Appelle maman, sinon elle va s'inquiéter.

**oral** *noun*
(*an exam*) un **oral** *masc* (*pl* les **oraux**)
the French oral l'oral de français

**orange** *adjective* ▷ see **orange** *noun*
**orange** *invariable adj*
my orange socks mes chaussettes orange

**WORD TIP** *orange* never changes.

**orange** *noun* ▷ see **orange** *adj*
(*the fruit*) une **orange** *fem*
an orange juice un jus d'orange

**orchestra** *noun*
un **orchestre** *masc*

to **order** *verb* ▷ see **order** *noun*
1 (*in a restaurant, shop*) **commander [1]**
2 (*a taxi*) **réserver [1]**

**order** *noun* ▷ see **order** *verb*
1 (*arrangement*) l'**ordre** *masc*
in the right order dans le bon ordre
in the wrong order dans le mauvais ordre
in alphabetical order dans l'ordre alphabétique
2 (*for buying*) la **commande** *fem*
Can I take your orders? Puis-je prendre vos commandes?
3 out of order en panne
The lift is out of order again. L'ascenseur est de nouveau en panne.
4 in order to do something pour faire quelque chose
We hurried in order to be on time. Nous nous sommes dépêchés pour arriver à l'heure.

**ordinary** *adjective*
**ordinaire** *masc & fem*

**organ** *noun*
1 (*musical instrument*) un **orgue** *masc*
to play the organ jouer de l'orgue
2 (*of the body*) un **organe** *masc*

**organic** *adjective*
(*food*) **biologique** *masc & fem*

**organization** *noun*
une **organisation** *fem*

to **organize** *verb*
**organiser [1]**

**orienteering** *noun*
la **course d'orientation**

**original** *adjective*
**original** *masc*, **originale** *fem* , **originaux** *masc pl*, **originales** *fem pl*
the original version la version originale

**originally** *adverb*
**à l'origine**
Originally we wanted to take the car. À l'origine, nous voulions prendre la voiture.

**Orkneys** *plural noun*
the Orkneys les Orcades *fem pl*

**ornament** *noun*
le **bibelot** *masc*

**orphan** *noun*
un **orphelin** *masc*, une **orpheline** *fem*

**ostrich** *noun*
une **autruche** *fem*

**other** *adjective, pronoun*
1 **autre** *masc & fem*
the other day l'autre jour
the other two cars les deux autres voitures
Where are the others? Où sont les autres?
Give me the other one. Donne-moi l'autre.

2 (*in expressions*) **every other week** une semaine sur deux
**somebody or other** quelqu'un
**something or other** quelque chose
**somewhere or other** quelque part

**otherwise** *adverb, conjunction*
1 (*or else*) **sinon**
**I'll phone home, otherwise they'll worry.** Je vais appeler chez moi, sinon ils vont s'inquiéter.
2 (*in other ways*) **à part ça**
**The flat's a bit small but otherwise it's lovely.** L'appartement n'est pas très grand mais à part ça il est très bien.

**ought** *verb* **[8]**
**I ought to go now.** Je devrais partir maintenant.
**They ought to know the address.** Ils devraient connaître l'adresse.
**You oughtn't to have any problems.** Vous ne devriez pas avoir des problèmes.

**WORD TIP** *ought* is translated by the conditional tense of *devoir*: *je devrais, tu devrais* etc.

**our** *adjective*
1 (*with singular nouns*) **notre**
**our house** notre maison
**our family** notre famille
**Do you like our garden?** Est-ce que tu aimes notre jardin?
2 (*with plural nouns*) **nos**
**our parents** nos parents
3 (*with parts of the body*) **le**, **la**, **les**
**We're washing our hands.** Nous nous lavons les mains.

**ours** *pronoun*
1 (*for masc singular nouns*) **le nôtre**
**Their garden's bigger than ours.** Leur jardin est plus grand que le nôtre.
2 (*for fem singular nouns*) **la nôtre**
**Their house is smaller than ours.** Leur maison est plus petite que la nôtre.
3 (*for plural nouns*) **les nôtres**
**They've invited their friends and we've invited ours.** Ils ont invité leurs amis et nous avons invité les nôtres.
4 (*belonging to us*) **à nous**
**It's ours.** C'est à nous.
**The green one's ours.** Le vert est à nous.
**Will is a friend of ours.** Will est un ami à nous.

**ourselves** *pronoun*
1 **nous** (*second nous in these examples*)
**We introduced ourselves.** Nous nous sommes présentés.
**We really enjoyed ourselves.** Nous nous sommes bien amusés.
2 (*for emphasis*) **nous-mêmes**
**In the end we did it ourselves.** Finalement nous l'avons fait nous-mêmes.

**out** *adjective* ▷ see **out** *adv*
**éteint** *masc*, **éteinte** *fem*
**Are all the lights out?** Est-ce que toutes les lumières sont éteintes?

**out** *adverb* ▷ see **out** *adj*
1 (*outside*) **It's cold out there.** Il fait froid dehors.
**out in the rain** sous la pluie
**They're out in the garden.** Ils sont dans le jardin.
2 (*showing movement*) **to go out** sortir ⓔ **[72]**
**She went out an hour ago.** Elle est sortie il y a une heure.
**to go out of the room** sortir de la pièce
**Are you going out this evening?** Est-ce que tu sors ce soir?
3 (*out of something*) **to drink out of a glass** boire **[22]** dans un verre
**He threw it out of the window.** Il l'a jeté par la fenêtre.
**She took the photo out of her bag.** Elle a pris la photo dans son sac.
4 (*not at home*) **to be out** être **[6]** sorti *masc*, sortie *fem*
**Mrs Barnes is out.** Madame Barnes est sortie.

**outdoor** *adjective*
1 (*activity, sport*) **de plein air**
2 (*cinema, theatre, restaurant*) **en plein air**

**outdoors** *adverb*
**en plein air**

**outing** *noun*
la **sortie** *fem*

**out-of-date** *adjective*
1 (*not valid*) **périmé** *masc*, **périmée** *fem*
**My passport's out-of-date.** Mon passeport est périmé.
2 (*old-fashioned*) **démodé** *masc*, **démodée** *fem*
**This music is so out-of-date!** Cette musique est tellement démodée!

**outside** *adjective, adverb, noun, preposition*
1 (*wall*) **extérieur** *masc*, **extérieure** *fem*
2 (*outside surface*) l'**extérieur** *masc*
**It's blue on the outside.** C'est bleu à l'extérieur.
3 (*in the open*) **dehors**
**It's cold outside.** Il fait froid dehors.
4 (*a cafe, theatre*) **devant**
**I'll meet you outside the cinema.** On se retrouve devant le cinéma.

**outskirts** *noun*
la **périphérie** *fem*
**on the outskirts of Glasgow** à la périphérie de Glasgow

**outstanding** *adjective*
**exceptionnel** *masc*, **exceptionnelle** *fem*

**oven** *noun*
le **four** *masc*
**I've put it in the oven.** Je l'ai mis au four.

**over** *adjective* ▷ see **over** *adv, prep*
**terminé** *masc*, **terminée** *fem*
**when the meeting's over** quand la réunion sera terminée
**It's all over now.** C'est terminé maintenant.

**over** *adverb, preposition* ▷ see **over** *adj*
1 (*above*) **au-dessus de**
**There's a mirror over the sideboard.** Il y a un miroir au-dessus du buffet.
2 (*showing movement*) **par-dessus**
**She jumped over the fence.** Elle a sauté par-dessus la clôture.
3 **over here** par ici
**The drinks are over here.** Les boissons sont par ici.
4 **over there** là-bas
**She's over there.** Elle est là-bas.
5 (*with numbers*) **plus de**
**It will cost over a hundred pounds.** Ça coûtera plus de cent livres.
**He's over sixty.** Il a plus de soixante ans.
6 (*during*) **pendant**
**over the weekend** pendant le week-end
**over Christmas** à Noël
7 (*in expressions*) **over the phone** par téléphone
**all over the place** partout

**overcast** *adjective*
**couvert** *masc*, **couverte** *fem*
**The sky was overcast.** Le ciel était couvert.

**overcrowded** *adjective*
**bondé** *masc*, **bondée** *fem*
**an overcrowded room** une pièce bondée

**overdose** *noun*
1 (*of drugs*) une **overdose** *fem*
2 (*of medicine*) la **surdose** *fem*

to **overflow** *verb*
**déborder [1]**

**overseas** *adverb*
**à l'étranger**
**Dave works overseas.** Dave travaille à l'étranger.

to **oversleep** *verb*
**se réveiller** Ⓔ **[1] trop tard**
**Matt overslept this morning.** Matt s'est réveillé trop tard ce matin.

to **overtake** *verb*
(*cars*) **doubler [1]**

**overtime** *noun*
**to work overtime** faire **[10]** des heures supplémentaires
**Dad works a lot of overtime.** Papa fait beaucoup d'heures supplémentaires.

**overweight** *adjective*
**trop gros** *masc*, **trop grosse** *fem*

to **owe** *verb*
**devoir [8]**
**to owe somebody something** devoir quelque chose à quelqu'un
**I owe Rick ten pounds.** Je dois dix livres à Rick.

**owing** *adjective*
1 **owing to** en raison de
**The school is closed owing to the snow.** L'école est fermée en raison des chutes de neige.

**owl** *noun*
le **hibou** *masc* (*pl* les **hiboux**)

to **own** *verb* ▷ see **own** *adj*
**posséder [24]**

**own** *adjective* ▷ see **own** *verb*
1 **propre** *masc & fem*
**my own computer** mon propre ordinateur
**I've got my own room.** J'ai une chambre à moi.

**WORD TIP** *propre* comes before the noun when it means *own*.

2 **on your own** tout seul *masc*, toute seule *fem*
**Amy did it on her own.** Amy l'a fait toute seule.

**owner** *noun*
le & la **propriétaire** *masc & fem*

**oxygen** *noun*
l'**oxygène** *masc*

**oyster** *noun*
une **huître** *fem*

**ozone layer** *noun*
la **couche d'ozone**
**a hole in the the ozone layer** un trou dans la couche d'ozone

Ⓔ means the verb takes être to form the perfect

# P p

**pace** *noun*
**1** (*step*) le **pas** *masc*
**2** (*the speed you walk at*) une **allure** *fem*
**They were walking at a brisk pace.** Ils marchaient à vive allure.

**Pacific** *noun*
**the Pacific Ocean** l'océan Pacifique *masc*

𝄞 to **pack** *verb* ▷ see **pack** *noun*
**1** **faire [10] ses bagages**
**I've packed.** J'ai fait mes bagages.
**2** **to pack your case** faire sa valise
**I'll pack my case.** Je ferai ma valise.
**Have you packed your trainers?** Est-ce que tu as mis tes baskets dans la valise?

**pack** *noun* ▷ see **pack** *verb*
**1** le **paquet** *masc*
**2** **a pack of cards** un jeu de cartes

𝄞 **package** *noun*
le **paquet** *masc*
**A package came in the post.** Un paquet est arrivé par la poste.

**package holiday**, **package tour** *noun*
le **voyage organisé**
**to go on a package holiday to Greece** aller Ⓔ [7] en Grèce en voyage organisé

**packed** *adjective*
**bondé** *masc*, **bondée** *fem*
**The hall was packed.** La salle était bondée.
**The beach is packed with tourists in summer.** La plage est pleine de touristes en été.
• **packed lunch** le panier-repas

𝄞 **packet** *noun*
**1** le **paquet** *masc*
**a packet of biscuits** un paquet de biscuits
**2** (*bag*) le **sachet** *masc*

**packing** *noun*
**to do your packing** faire [10] ses bagages

**pad** *noun*
(*of paper*) le **bloc-notes** *masc*

**paddle** *noun*
(*for a canoe*) la **pagaie** *fem*

**padlock** *noun*
le **cadenas** *masc*

𝄞 **page** *noun*
la **page** *fem*
**on page seven** à la page sept

𝄞 **pain** *noun*
**1** la **douleur** *fem*
**to have a pain in ...** avoir [5] mal à ...
**I've got a pain in my leg.** J'ai mal à la jambe.
**The pain's gone.** Je n'ai plus mal.
**2** **to be a pain in the neck** être [6] pénible
**She's a real pain in the neck!** Elle est vraiment pénible!

**painful** *adjective*
**douloureux** *masc*, **douloureuse** *fem*

**painkiller** *noun*
un **analgésique** *masc*

to **paint** *verb* ▷ see **paint** *noun*
**peindre [60]**
**to paint the walls blue** peindre les murs en bleu
**The door is painted red.** La porte est peinte en rouge.

**paint** *noun* ▷ see **paint** *verb*
la **peinture** *fem*
**two pots of paint** deux pots de peinture
**'Wet paint'** 'Peinture fraîche'
• **paintbrush** le pinceau (*pl* les pinceaux)

**painter** *noun*
le **peintre** *masc*

𝄞 **painting** *noun*
**1** (*picture*) le **tableau** *masc* (*pl* les **tableaux**)
**a painting by Bacon** un tableau de Bacon
**2** (*the activity*) la **peinture**
**I love painting.** J'adore la peinture.

𝄞 **pair** *noun*
**1** (*in general*) la **paire** *fem*
**a pair of socks** une paire de chaussettes
**a pair of scissors** une paire de ciseaux
**a pair of jeans** un jean
**2** **to work in pairs** travailler [1] en groupes de deux
**We're working in pairs.** Nous travaillons en groupes de deux.

**Pakistan** *noun*
le **Pakistan** *masc*

**Pakistani** *adjective* ▷ see **Pakistani** *noun*
**pakistanais** *masc*, **pakistanaise** *fem*

**Pakistani** *noun* ▷ see **Pakistani** *adj*
un **Pakistanais** *masc*, une **Pakistanaise** *fem*

**palace** *noun*
le **palais** *masc*
**the Palace of Versailles** le palais de Versailles

**pale** *adjective*
**pâle** *masc & fem*
**pale green** vert pâle
**She looks very pale.** Elle est très pâle.
**to go pale** pâlir **[2]**

**palm** *noun*
1 (*of your hand*) la **paume** *fem*
2 (*tree*) le **palmier** *masc*

**pan** *noun*
1 (*saucepan*) la **casserole** *fem*
**a pan of water** une casserole d'eau
2 (*frying-pan*) la **poêle** *fem*
**Heat some oil in a pan.** Faire chauffer de l'huile dans une poêle.

**pancake** *noun*
la **crêpe** *fem*
**pancakes with jam** des crêpes à la confiture

**panda** *noun*
le **panda** *masc*

**panel** *noun*
1 (*in a TV show*) les **invités** *masc pl*
**Let me introduce our panel.** Je vous présente nos invités.
2 (*for walls*) le **panneau** *masc* (*pl* les **panneaux**)
**a wooden panel** un panneau en bois

to **panic** *verb* ▷ see **panic** *noun*
**s'affoler [1]**
**I panicked.** Je me suis affolé.
**Don't panic!** Pas de panique!

**panic** *noun* ▷ see **panic** *verb*
la **panique** *fem*
**She's in a complete panic.** Elle est complètement affolée.
**to cause panic** provoquer **[1]** la panique

**pannier** *noun*
la **sacoche** *fem*

**panther** *noun*
la **panthère** *fem*

**panties** *noun*
la **petite culotte**

**pantomime** *noun*
le **spectacle pour enfants**

**pants** *plural noun*
le **slip** *masc*
**a pair of pants** un slip

**paper** *noun*
1 le **papier** *masc*
**a sheet of paper** une feuille de papier
2 (*made of paper*) **a paper cup** un gobelet en carton
3 (*newspaper*) le **journal** *masc* (*pl* les **journaux**)
**the Sunday papers** les journaux de dimanche
• **paperback** le livre de poche
• **paper towel** un essuie-tout (*pl* les essuie-tout)

**parachute** *noun*
le **parachute** *masc*

**parachuting** *noun*
le **parachutisme** *masc*
**to go parachuting** faire **[10]** du parachutisme

**parade** *noun*
le **défilé** *masc*
**There are street parades.** Il y a des défilés dans la rue.

**paradise** *noun*
le **paradis** *masc*

**paraffin** *noun*
le **pétrole** *masc*

**paragraph** *noun*
le **paragraphe** *masc*
**I wrote a paragraph in French.** J'ai écrit un paragraphe en français.

**parallel** *adjective*
**parallèle** *masc & fem*
**parallel lines** des lignes parallèles

**paralysed** *adjective*
**paralysé** *masc*, **paralysée** *fem*

**parcel** *noun*
le **paquet** *masc*

**pardon** *exclamation*
**Pardon?** Pardon?

**parent** *noun*
le **parent** *masc*
**a parents' evening** une réunion pour les parents d'élèves
**My parents are Scottish.** Mes parents sont écossais.

**Paris** *noun*
**Paris**
**to live in Paris** habiter à Paris
**to go to Paris** aller ⓔ **[7]** à Paris

**Parisian** *adjective* ▷ see **Parisian** *noun*
**parisien** *masc*, **parisienne** *fem*

**WORD TIP** Adjectives never have capitals in French, even for nationality or regional origin.

**Parisian** *noun* ▷ see **Parisian** *adj*
un **Parisien** *masc*, une **Parisienne** *fem*

to **park** *verb* ▷ see **park** *noun*

1 **se garer** Ⓔ **[1]**
**Can we park here?** Est-ce qu'on peut se garer ici?

2 (*a car*) **garer [1]**
**Where did you park the car?** Où avez-vous garé la voiture?

♪ **park** *noun* ▷ see **park** *verb*

1 le **parc** *masc*
**We're going for a walk in the park.** On va se promener dans le parc.

2 **a car park** un parking

**mini-info park**

There are two great theme parks (*parcs d'attractions* or *parcs de loisirs*) in the Paris region: Disneyland Paris at Marne-la-Vallée and Parc Astérix, based on the cartoon character, at Plailly.

**parking** *noun*
le **stationnement** *masc*
**'No parking'** 'Stationnement interdit'
- **parking meter** le parcmètre
- **parking ticket** la contravention

**parliament** *noun*
le **parlement** *masc*

**parrot** *noun*
le **perroquet** *masc*

**parsley** *noun*
le **persil** *masc*

♪ **part** *noun*

1 la **partie** *fem*
**part of the garden** une partie du jardin
**the funniest part of the film** le passage le plus drôle du film

2 **to be part of something** faire **[10]** partie de quelque chose
**It's part of my homework.** Ça fait partie de mes devoirs.

3 **to take part in something** participer **[1]** à quelque chose
**I didn't take part in the competition.** Je n'ai pas participé au concours.

4 (*in a play*) le **rôle** *masc*
**I play the part of Juliet.** Je joue le rôle de Juliet.

**particular** *adjective*
**particulier** *masc*, **particulière** *fem*
**nothing in particular** rien de particulier
**I don't like that particular song.** Je n'aime pas cette chanson-là.

**particularly** *adverb*

1 (*very much*) **particulièrement**
**It's not particularly interesting.** Ce n'est pas particulièrement intéressant.

2 (*in particular*) **surtout**
**Particularly as it was our last day.** Surtout que c'était notre dernier jour.

**parting** *noun*
(*in your hair*) la **raie** *fem*

**partly** *adverb*
**en partie**
**That's partly why we missed the train.** C'est en partie pourquoi nous avons raté notre train.

**partner** *noun*

1 (*in games, in life*) le **partenaire** *masc*
**Who's your partner?** Ton partenaire, c'est qui?

2 (*in business*) un **associé** *masc*, une **associée** *fem*

**partridge** *noun*
la **perdrix** *fem*

**part-time** *adjective, adverb*
**à temps partiel**
**part-time work** le travail à temps partiel
**to work part-time** travailler **[1]** à temps partiel
**She works part-time.** Elle travaille à temps partiel.

♪ **party** *noun*

1 (*in general*) la **fête** *fem*
**a Christmas party** une fête de Noël
**We've been invited to a party.** Nous sommes invités à une fête.
**There's a party at Josh's.** Il y a une fête chez Josh.

2 (*formal evening event*) la **soirée** *fem*

3 (*group*) le **groupe** *masc*
**a party of schoolchildren** un groupe d'élèves
**a rescue party** une équipe de secours

4 (*in politics*) le **parti** *masc*
**a political party** un parti politique
- **party game** le jeu de société (*pl* les jeux de société)

♪ to **pass** *verb* ▷ see **pass** *noun*

1 (*a place, building*) **passer [1]** Ⓔ **devant**
**We passed your house.** Nous sommes passés devant chez toi.

2 (*a car*) **doubler [1]**
**A truck tried to pass us.** Un camion a essayé de nous doubler.

3 **to pass something to somebody** passer quelque chose à quelqu'un
**Could you pass me the paper?** Peux-tu me passer le journal?
**She passed me a plate.** Elle m'a passé une assiette.
**Pass the ball!** Passe-moi le ballon! ▸▸

4 (*time*) **passer [1]**
The time passed slowly. Le temps passait lentement.
5 (*in an exam*) **être [6] reçu**
to pass an exam être reçu à un examen
Did you pass? Est-ce que tu as été reçu?

**pass** *noun* ▷ see **pass** *verb*
1 (*to let you in*) le **laissez-passer** *masc* (*pl* les **laissez-passer**)
2 (*for transport*) la **carte** *fem*
a bus pass une carte de bus
3 (*in the mountains*) le **col** *masc*

**passage** *noun*
1 (*corridor*) le **couloir** *masc*
2 (*text*) le **passage** *masc*
Read the passage aloud. Lis le passage à haute voix.

**passenger** *noun*
1 (*in a car, plane, ship*) le **passager** *masc*, la **passagère** *fem*
2 (*in trains, buses*) le **voyageur** *masc*, la **voyageuse** *fem*

**passerby** *noun*
le **passant** *masc*, la **passante** *fem*

**passion** *noun*
la **passion** *fem*

**passionate** *adjective*
**passionné** *masc*, **passionnée** *fem*

**passive** *noun*
(*Grammar*) le **passif** *masc*

**Passover** *noun*
la **Pâque juive**

**passport** *noun*
le **passeport** *masc*
an EU passport un passeport de l'UE
They check passports at the border. Ils contrôlent les passeports à la frontière.

**password** *noun*
le **mot de passe**
What's your password? Quel est ton mot de passe?
to change your password changer [52] ton mot de passe.

**past** *adjective* ▷ see *adv, noun, prep*
1 (*recent*) **dernier** *masc*, **dernière** *fem*
in the past few weeks pendant les dernières semaines
2 (*over*) **fini** *masc*, **finie** *fem*
Winter is past. L'hiver est fini.

**past** *noun* ▷ see **past** *adj, adv, prep*
1 (*the old days*) le **passé** *masc*
in the past dans le passé
2 (*Grammar*) the past (tense) le passé
a verb in the past un verbe au passé

**past** *adverb, preposition* ▷ see **past** *adj, noun*
1 to go past something passer ⓔ [1] devant quelque chose
We went past the school. Nous sommes passés devant l'école.
Peter went past on his bike. Peter est passé sur son vélo.
2 (*the other side of*) **après**
It's just past the post office. C'est juste après la poste.
3 (*in time expressions*) ten past six six heures dix
half past four quatre heures et demie
a quarter past two deux heures et quart

**pasta** *noun*
les **pâtes** *fem pl*

to **paste** *verb*
**coller [1]**
to paste cards into a notebook coller des cartes dans un carnet
to cut and paste a table couper-coller un tableau

**pasteurized** *adjective*
**pasteurisé** *masc*, **pasteurisée** *fem*

**pastry** *noun*
1 (*dough*) la **pâte** *fem*
to make pastry faire [10] une pâte
2 (*small cake*) la **pâtisserie** *fem*

**patch** *noun*
1 (*for mending*) la **pièce** *fem*
2 (*of snow, ice*) la **plaque** *fem*
patches of black ice des plaques de verglas
3 (*of fog*) la **nappe** *fem*
fog patches des nappes de brouillard
4 (*of blue sky*) le **coin** *masc*

**path** *noun*
1 (*track*) le **chemin** *masc*
a path through the wood un chemin à travers le bois
2 (*very narrow*) le **sentier** *masc*
a mountain path un sentier de montagne

**pathetic** *adjective*
**lamentable** *masc & fem*
That's so pathetic! C'est vraiment lamentable!

**patience** *noun*
1 la **patience** *fem*
2 (*card game*) la **réussite** *fem*

**patient** *adjective* ▷ see **patient** *noun*
**patient** *masc*, **patiente** *fem*
She's very patient. Elle est très patiente.
Be patient! Patience!



ⓔ means the verb takes être to form the perfect

**patient** *noun* ▷ see **patient** *adj*
le **patient** *masc*, la **patiente** *fem*

**patiently** *adverb*
**avec patience**

**patio** *noun*
la **terrasse** *fem*
on the patio sur la terrasse

**patrol** *noun*
la **patrouille** *fem*
to be out on patrol être [6] de patrouille
- **patrol car** la voiture de police

**pattern** *noun*
1 (*on wallpaper, fabric*) le **motif** *masc*
a pattern with stripes un motif à rayures
2 (*for dressmaking*) le **patron** *masc*

**pause** *noun*
1 (*in a conversation*) le **silence** *masc*
2 (*in an activity*) la **pause** *fem*

𝄞 **pavement** *noun*
le **trottoir** *masc*
on the pavement sur le trottoir

**paw** *noun*
la **patte** *fem*

**pawn** *noun*
le **pion** *masc*

𝄞 to **pay** *verb* ▷ see **pay** *noun*
1 **payer** [59]
**I'm paying.** C'est moi qui paie.
**Are they paying for you?** Est-ce qu'ils paient pour toi?
**You have to pay cash.** Il faut payer comptant.
2 **to pay for something** payer [59] quelque chose
**Sophie paid for the pizzas.** Sophie a payé les pizzas.
**It's all paid for.** C'est tout payé.
3 **to pay by credit card** régler [24] par carte de crédit
**to pay by cheque** régler par chèque
4 **to pay somebody back** rembourser [1] quelqu'un
**I haven't paid them back yet.** Je ne les ai pas encore remboursés.
5 **to pay attention** faire [10] attention
**We weren't paying attention.** On ne faisait pas attention.
6 **to pay a visit to somebody** rendre [3] visite à quelqu'un
**I'm paying a visit to my cousins.** Je rends visite à mes cousins.
- **paydesk** la caisse

**pay** *noun* ▷ see **pay** *verb*
le **salaire** *masc*

**payment** *noun*
1 le **paiement** *masc*
**to make a payment of £50** faire un paiement de 50 livres sterling
2 (*of a bill*) le **règlement** *masc*

**pay phone** *noun*
le **téléphone public**
**I'm looking for a pay phone.** Je cherche un téléphone public.

**PC** *noun*
le **PC** *masc*

𝄞 **pea** *noun*
le **petit pois** *masc*
**I don't eat peas.** Je ne mange pas de petits pois.

𝄞 **peace** *noun*
1 la **paix** *fem*
**They're trying to make peace.** Ils essaient de faire la paix.
2 (*of a place*) **peace and quiet** la tranquillité

**peaceful** *adjective*
1 (*tranquil*) **paisible** *masc & fem*
**It's a peaceful place.** C'est un endroit paisible.
2 (*without conflict*) **pacifique** *masc & fem*
**to find a peaceful solution** trouver une solution pacifique

𝄞 **peach** *noun*
la **pêche** *fem*
**a kilo of peaches** un kilo de pêches

**peacock** *noun*
le **paon** *masc*

**peak** *noun*
(*of a mountain*) le **pic** *masc*
- **peak period** la période de pointe
- **peak rate** (*Telephones*) le tarif rouge

**peak time** *noun*
(*for traffic*) les **heures de pointe** *fem pl*
**at peak time** aux heures de pointe

**peanut** *noun*
la **cacahuète** *fem*
- **peanut butter** le beurre de cacahuètes

𝄞 **pear** *noun*
la **poire** *fem*
**The pears are ripe.** Les poires sont mûres.

**pearl** *noun*
la **perle** *fem*

𝄞 **peasant** *noun*
le **paysan** *masc*, la **paysanne** *fem* (*The word* paysan *is less old-fashioned than* **peasant**.)

**pebble** *noun*
1 (*on the road*) le **caillou** *masc* (*pl* les **cailloux**)
2 (*on a beach*) le **galet** *masc*
a pebble beach une plage de galets

**peculiar** *adjective*
**bizarre** *masc & fem*
**a peculiar noise** un bruit bizarre

to **pedal** *verb* ▷ see **pedal** *noun*
**pédaler[1]**

**pedal** *noun* ▷ see **pedal** *verb*
la **pédale** *fem*

**pedal boat** *noun*
le **pédalo®** *masc*

♪ **pedestrian** *noun*
le **piéton** *masc*, la **piétonne** *fem*
**It's dangerous for pedestrians.** C'est dangereux pour les piétons.
• **pedestrian crossing** le passage pour piétons
• **pedestrian precinct** la zone piétonne

**pee** *noun*
le **pipi** *masc* (*informal*)
**to have a pee** faire**[10]** pipi

to **peel** *verb* ▷ see **peel** *noun*
**éplucher[1]**
**Peel the potates.** Éplucher les pommes de terre.

**peel** *noun* ▷ see **peel** *verb*
1 (*of an apple*) la **peau** *fem*
2 (*of an orange*) une **écorce** *fem*

to **peer** *verb*
**to peer at something** regarder**[1]** quelque chose attentivement
**He was peering at the screen.** Il regardait l'écran attentivement.

**peg** *noun*
1 (*hook*) la **patère** *fem*
2 **a clothes peg** une pince à linge
3 **a tent peg** un piquet de tente

♪ **pen** *noun*
le **stylo** *masc*
**a felt pen** un stylo-feutre
**I lent her my red pen.** Je lui ai prêté mon stylo rouge.

**penalty** *noun*
1 (*a fine*) une **amende** *fem*
2 (*in football*) le **penalty** *masc*
**to take a penalty** tirer**[1]** un penalty
**to give a penalty** siffler**[1]** un penalty
3 (*in rugby*) la **pénalité** *fem*
• **penalty area** la surface de réparation

**pence** *plural noun*
les **pence** *masc pl*

♪ **pencil** *noun*
le **crayon** *masc*
**coloured pencils** les crayons de couleur
**I wrote it in pencil first.** Je l'ai écrit au crayon d'abord.
• **pencil case** la trousse
• **pencil sharpener** le taille-crayon

**pendant** *noun*
le **pendentif** *masc*

♪ **penfriend** *noun*
le **correspondant** *masc*, la **correspondante** *fem*
**I'd like to have a French penfriend.** J'aimerais avoir un correspondant français.
**My penfriend's name is Maryse.** Ma correspondante s'appelle Maryse.

**penguin** *noun*
le **pingouin** *masc*

**penis** *noun*
le **pénis** *masc*

**penknife** *noun*
le **canif** *masc*

**penny** *noun*
le **penny** *masc*

**pension** *noun*
la **pension** *fem*

**pensioner** *noun*
le **retraité** *masc*, la **retraitée** *fem*

♪ **people** *plural noun*
1 les **gens** *masc pl*
**people round here** les gens d'ici
**most people** la plupart des gens
**They're nice people.** Ce sont des gens sympathiques.
**I enjoy working with people.** J'aime travailler avec les gens.
2 (*when you count them*) les **personnes** *fem pl*
**ten people** dix personnes
**several people** plusieurs personnes
**How many people have you invited?** Tu as invité combien de personnes?
3 **people say that ...** on dit que ...
**People say he's very rich.** On dit qu'il est très riche.

**pepper** *noun*
1 (*spice*) le **poivre** *masc*
2 (*vegetable*) le **poivron** *masc*
**a green pepper** un poivron vert
• **peppermill** le moulin à poivre

**peppermint** *noun*
1 (*herb*) la **menthe** *fem*
2 (*sweet*) le **bonbon à la menthe**
• **peppermint tea** le thé à la menthe

**per** *preposition*
**par**
**It costs ten pounds per person.** Ça coûte dix livres par personne.

**per cent** *adverb*
**pour cent**
**sixty per cent of students** soixante pour cent des étudiants

**percentage** *noun*
le **pourcentage** *masc*

**percussion** *noun*
la **percussion** *fem*
**to play percussion** jouer des percussions

ℰ **perfect** *adjective* ▷ see **perfect** *noun*
1 (*flawless*) **parfait** *masc*, **parfaite** *fem*
**She speaks perfect French.** Elle parle un français parfait.
**The weather's perfect.** Il fait un temps parfait.
2 (*ideal*) **idéal** *masc*, **idéale** *fem*, **idéaux** *masc pl*, **idéales** *fem pl*
**It's the perfect place for a picnic.** C'est l'endroit idéal pour un pique-nique.
**We've found the perfect solution.** Nous avons trouvé la solution idéale.

**perfect** *noun* ▷ see **perfect** *adj*
(*Grammar*) le **parfait** *masc*
**in the perfect** au parfait

**perfectly** *adverb*
**parfaitement**

to **perform** *verb*
1 (*a piece of music, play*) **jouer [1]**
2 (*a song*) **chanter [1]**

ℰ **performance** *noun*
1 (*show*) le **spectacle** *masc*
**The performance starts at eight.** Le spectacle commence à huit heures.
2 (*acting, playing a role*) une **interprétation** *fem*
**a wonderful performance of Macbeth** une superbe interprétation de Macbeth

**performer** *noun*
un **artiste** *masc*, une **artiste** *fem*

ℰ **perfume** *noun*
le **parfum** *masc*
**I bought her some perfume.** Je lui ai acheté du parfum.

ℰ **perhaps** *adverb*
**peut-être**
**Perhaps it's in the drawer?** Il est peut-être dans le tiroir?
**Perhaps he's missed the train.** Il a peut-être raté le train.

ℰ **period** *noun*
1 (*length of time*) la **période** *fem*
**a two-year period** une période de deux ans
**the holiday period** la période des vacances
**over a period of three weeks** pendant trois semaines
2 (*a lesson*) le **cours** *masc*
**a forty-five-minute period** un cours de quarante-cinq minutes
**I have a double period of French.** J'ai deux cours de français à la suite.
3 (*menstruation*) les **règles** *fem pl*
**during your period** pendant vos règles

**perm** *noun*
la **permanente** *fem*
**to have a perm** se faire ⓔ **[10]** faire une permanente

**permanent** *adjective*
**permanent** *masc*, **permanente** *fem*

**permanently** *adverb*
**en permanence**
**They're going to stay there permanently.** Ils vont rester là définitivement.

**permission** *noun*
la **permission** *fem*
**to ask permission** demander **[1]** la permission
**Let's ask permission first.** Demandons la permission d'abord.
**to get permission to do something** obtenir **[77]** la permission de faire quelque chose
**We didn't get permission to go out.** Nous n'avons pas obtenu la permission de sortir.

ℰ to **permit** *verb* ▷ see **permit** *noun*
**permettre [11]**
**Her parents will not permit it.** Ses parents ne le permettrons pas.
**to permit somebody to do something** permettre à quelqu'un de faire quelque chose
**They are not permitted to go out at night.** On ne les permet pas de sortir le soir.
**Smoking is not permitted.** Il est interdit de fumer.
**Weather permitting, we'll go camping.** Si le temps le permet, on va faire du camping.

**permit** *noun* ▷ see **permit** *verb*
(*for fishing*) le **permis** *masc*

ℰ **person** *noun*
la **personne** *fem*
**There's room for one more person.** Il y a de la place pour une autre personne.
**He's the sort of person who always complains.** C'est le genre de personne qui se plaint toujours. ▸▸

English–French

to do something in person faire quelque chose en personne
He wrote to me in person. Il m'a écrit en personne.

**personal** *adjective*
**personnel** *masc*, **personnelle** *fem*
personal belongings les affaires personnelles
my personal appearance mon apparence
She's got personal problems. Elle a des problèmes personnels.

**personality** *noun*
1 (*a person's character*) la **personnalité** *fem*
to have a strong personality avoir **[5]** une forte personnalité
2 (*a celebrity*) la **vedette** *fem*
a TV personality une vedette de la télévision

**personally** *adverb*
**personnellement**
Personally, I'm against it.
Personnellement, je suis contre.

**personal stereo** *noun*
le **baladeur** *masc*

**perspiration** *noun*
la **transpiration** *fem*

to **perspire** *verb*
**transpirer [1]**

♪ to **persuade** *verb*
**persuader [1]**
to persuade somebody to do something persuader quelqu'un de faire quelque chose
Can you persuade them to come too? Est-ce que tu peux les persuader de venir aussi?
We persuaded Tim to sing. Nous avons persuadé Tim de chanter.

**pessimistic** *adjective*
**pessimiste** *masc & fem*

**pest** *noun*
(*annoying person*) le **casse-pieds** *masc*, la **casse-pieds** *fem*
She can be a pest. Elle peut être casse-pieds.

to **pester** *verb*
**harceler [45]**
to pester somebody for something harceler quelqu'un pour obtenir quelque chose
They pester people for money. Ils harcèlent les gens pour obtenir de l'argent.

♪ **pet** *noun*
1 un **animal de compagnie** (*pl* les **animaux de compagnie**)
Do you have a pet? Avez-vous un animal de compagnie?
I've got a pet dog. J'ai un chien.
They're not allowed pets. Ils n'ont pas le droit d'avoir des animaux.
2 (*favourite person*) le **chouchou** *masc*, la **chouchoute** *fem*
Julie's the teacher's pet. Julie est la chouchoute du prof.

**petal** *noun*
le **pétale** *masc*

**pet name** *noun*
le **petit nom** *masc*

♪ **petrol** *noun*
l'**essence** *fem*
unleaded petrol l'essence sans plomb
to fill up with petrol faire **[10]** le plein d'essence
to run out of petrol tomber Ⓔ **[1]** en panne d'essence
We ran out of petrol. Nous sommes tombés en panne d'essence.
• **petrol station** la station-service

**petticoat** *noun*
le **jupon** *masc*

**pharmacist** *noun*
le **pharmacien** *masc*, la **pharmacienne** *fem*

**pharmacy** *noun*
la **pharmacie** *fem*

**pheasant** *noun*
le **faisan** *masc*

**philosophy** *noun*
la **philosophie** *fem*

♪ to **phone** *verb* ▷ see **phone** *noun*
1 **téléphoner [1]**
while I was phoning pendant que je téléphonais
It's quicker to phone. Ça va plus vite de téléphoner.
Phone up and ask for information. Téléphone et demande-leur des renseignements.
2 to phone somebody appeler **[18]** quelqu'un
I'll phone you later. Je t'appellerai plus tard.
It's too late to phone her. Il est trop tard pour l'appeler.

♪ **phone** *noun* ▷ see **phone** *verb*
le **téléphone** *masc*
She's on the phone. Elle est au téléphone.
to be on the phone to somebody être **[6]** au téléphone avec quelqu'un
I was on the phone to Claire. J'étais au téléphone avec Claire.

a b c d e f g h i j k l m n o p q r s t u v w x y z



Ⓔ means the verb takes être to form the perfect

Can you book by phone? Est-ce qu'on peut réserver par téléphone?
Nobody answered the phone. Personne n'a répondu au téléphone.

♪ **phone book** *noun*
un **annuaire** *masc*
Look it up in the phone book. Cherche dans l'annuaire.

♪ **phone box** *noun*
la **cabine téléphonique**
the nearest phone box la cabine téléphonique la plus proche

♪ **phone call** *noun*
un **appel** *masc*
Phone calls are free. Les appels sont gratuits.
May I make a phone call? Puis-je téléphoner?

♪ **phone card** *noun*
la **télécarte** *fem*
Do you sell phone cards? Est-ce que vous vendez les télécartes?

**phone number** *noun*
le **numéro de téléphone**
to get somebody's phone number prendre [64] le numéro de téléphone de quelqu'un

♪ **photo** *noun*
la **photo** *fem*
to take a photo prendre [64] une photo
to take a photo of somebody prendre quelqu'un en photo
Could you take a photo of us? Pourriez-vous nous prendre en photo?
I took a photo of their house J'ai pris leur maison en photo.
I'd like to get some photos developed. Je voudrais faire développer des photos.

**photocopier** *noun*
la **photocopieuse** *fem*

to **photocopy** *verb*
▷ see **photocopy** *noun*
**photocopier [1]**

**photocopy** *noun* ▷ see **photocopy** *verb*
la **photocopie** *fem*
I made a few photocopies. J'ai fait quelques photocopies.

to **photograph** *verb*
▷ see **photograph** *noun*
**photographier [1]**

**photograph** *noun*
▷ see **photograph** *verb*
la **photo** *fem*
to take a photograph prendre [64] une photo
to take a photograph of somebody prendre quelqu'un en photo
He took a photograph of the family. Il a pris la famille en photo.

**photographer** *noun*
le & la **photographe** *masc & fem*

**photography** *noun*
la **photographie** *fem*
I'm interested in photography. Je m'intéresse à la photographie.

♪ **phrase** *noun*
une **expression** *fem*
a French expression une expression française
• **phrase-book** le manuel de conversation

**physical** *adjective*
**physique** *masc & fem*

**physicist** *noun*
le **physicien** *masc*, la **physicienne** *fem*

♪ **physics** *noun*
la **physique** *fem*
She's good at physics. Elle est bonne en physique.

**physiotherapist** *noun*
le & la **kinésithérapeute** *masc & fem*

**physiotherapy** *noun*
la **kinésithérapie** *fem*

**pianist** *noun*
le & la **pianiste** *masc & fem*

♪ **piano** *noun*
le **piano** *masc*
a piano lesson une leçon de piano
to play the piano jouer du piano
I know how to play it on the piano. Je sais le jouer au piano.

♪ to **pick** *verb* ▷ see **pick** *noun*
1 (*to choose*) **choisir [2]**
Pick a card. Choisis une carte.
We picked a good present. Nous avons choisi un bon cadeau.
2 (*for a team*) **sélectionner [1]**
I've been picked for Saturday. J'ai été sélectionné pour samedi.
3 (*fruit, flowers*) **cueillir [35]**
I like picking strawberries. J'aime cueillir les fraises.
• **to pick something up**
1 (*lift*) **prendre [64] quelque chose**
She picked up her bag and went out. Elle a pris son sac et elle est sortie.
2 (*collect together*) **ramasser [1] quelque chose**
Could you pick up the toys? Est-ce que tu peux ramasser les jouets? ▸▸

3 (*to collect*) **venir** Ⓔ **[81] chercher quelque chose**
I'll pick up the keys tomorrow. Je viendrai chercher les clés demain.
4 (*learn*) **apprendre [64] quelque chose**
I picked up a few words of French. J'ai appris quelques mots de français.
You'll soon pick it up. Tu vas vite l'apprendre.
• **to pick somebody up**
**venir** Ⓔ **[81] chercher quelqu'un**
My mum's picking me up at six. Ma mère vient me chercher à six heures.

**pick** *noun* ▷ see **pick** *verb*
Take your pick! Choisis!

**pickpocket** *noun*
le **pickpocket** *masc*

**picnic** *noun*
le **pique-nique** *masc*
to have a picnic pique-niquer [1]
We went for a picnic by the lake. Nous sommes allés pique-niquer au bord du lac.

**picture** *noun*
1 (*a painting*) le **tableau** *masc* (*pl* les **tableaux**)
a picture by Matisse un tableau de Matisse
It's a lovely picture. C'est un beau tableau.
to paint a picture of something peindre quelque chose
He painted a picture of a horse. Il a peint un cheval.
2 (*a drawing*) le **dessin** *masc*
She draws brilliant pictures. Elle fait des dessins superbes.
to draw a picture of something dessiner quelque chose
Can you draw a picture of the house? Est-ce que tu peux dessiner la maison?
3 (*in a book*) une **illustration** *fem*
a book with lots of pictures un livre avec beaucoup d'illustrations
4 (*the cinema*) the pictures le cinéma
I love going to the pictures. J'adore aller au cinéma.

**pie** *noun*
1 (*sweet*) la **tarte** *fem*
an apple pie une tarte aux pommes
2 (*savoury*) la **tourte** *fem*
a meat pie une tourte à la viande

**piece** *noun*
1 (*a bit*) le **morceau** *masc* (*pl* les **morceaux**)
a big piece of cheese un gros morceau de fromage
2 (*that you fit together*) la **pièce** *fem*
the pieces of a jigsaw les pièces d'un puzzle
There was a piece missing. Il manquait une pièce.
to take something to pieces démonter [1] quelque chose
He took the radio to pieces. Il a démonté la radio.
The vase was smashed to pieces. Le vase était cassé en mille morceaux.
3 a piece of furniture un meuble
a piece of fruit un fruit
a piece of good news une bonne nouvelle
a useful piece of information un renseignement utile
We have four pieces of luggage. Nous avons quatre valises.
That's a piece of luck! C'est un coup de chance!
4 (*coin*) la **pièce** *fem*
a ten-pence piece une pièce de dix pence

**pier** *noun*
la **jetée** *fem*

**pierced** *adjective*
**percé** *masc*, **percée** *fem*
to have pierced ears avoir [5] les oreilles percées
I'm having my ears pierced. Je me fais percer les oreilles.

**pig** *noun*
le **cochon** *masc*

**pigeon** *noun*
le **pigeon** *masc*

**piggy bank** *noun*
la **tirelire** *fem*

**pigsty** *noun*
la **porcherie** *fem*
Your room is a pigsty. Ta chambre est une vraie porcherie.

**pigtail** *noun*
la **natte** *fem*

to **pile** *verb* ▷ see **pile** *noun*
to be piled with something être [6] recouvert de quelque chose
The table was piled with plates. La table était recouverte d'assiettes.
• **to pile up**
1 (*leaves, rubbish*) **s'entasser [1]**
The rubbish is starting to pile up. Les ordures commencent à s'entasser.
2 (*work, problems*) **s'accumuler [1]**
• **to pile something up**
1 (*neatly*) **empiler [1] quelque chose**
I piled the books up on the shelf. J'ai empilé les livres sur l'étagère.
2 (*in a heap*) **entasser [1] quelque chose**

**pile** *noun* ▷ see **pile** *verb*
1 (*a neat stack*) la **pile** *fem*
a pile of plates une pile d'assiettes
2 (*a heap*) le **tas** *masc*
a pile of dirty shirts un tas de chemises sales

**pilgrimage** *noun*
le **pèlerinage** *masc*
to go on a pilgrimage faire [10] un pèlerinage

**pill** *noun*
1 (*tablet*) le **comprimé** *masc*
2 the pill la pilule
to be on the pill prendre [64] la pilule

**pillar** *noun*
le **pilier** *masc*
- **pillar box** la boîte aux lettres

**pillow** *noun*
un **oreiller** *masc*
- **pillowcase** la taie d'oreiller

**pilot** *noun*
le **pilote** *masc*
an airline pilot un pilote de ligne
a fighter pilot un pilote de chasse

**pimple** *noun*
le **bouton** *masc*
He's got pimples. Il a des boutons.

to **pin** *verb* ▷ see **pin** *noun*
to pin something to something accrocher [1] quelque chose à quelque chose
I pinned the balloons to the door. J'ai accroché les ballons à la porte.
- **to pin something up**
1 (*a notice*) **accrocher** [1]
Can you pin up the ad? Est-ce que tu peux accrocher l'annonce?
2 (*a hem*) **épingler** [1]

**pin** *noun* ▷ see **pin** *verb*
1 (*for sewing*) une **épingle** *fem*
2 a three-pin plug une prise à trois fiches

**PIN** *noun*
(*personal identification number*) le **code confidentiel**
I've forgotten my PIN. J'ai oublié le code confidentiel.

**pinball** *noun*
le **flipper** *masc*
to play pinball jouer au flipper
a pinball machine un flipper

to **pinch** *verb* ▷ see **pinch** *noun*
1 (*nip*) **pincer** [61]
to pinch somebody pincer quelqu'un
Stop pinching me! Arrête de me pincer!
She pinched my arm. Elle m'a pincé le bras.
2 (*steal*) **piquer** [1] (*informal*)
Somebody's pinched my bike. On m'a piqué mon vélo.

**pinch** *noun* ▷ see **pinch** *verb*
la **pincée** *fem*
a pinch of salt une pincée de sel

**pine** *noun*
le **pin** *masc*
- **pineapple** un ananas
- **pine cone** la pomme de pin
- **pine needles** les aiguilles de pin
- **pine nuts** les pignons de pin
- **pine tree** le pin

**ping-pong** *noun*
le **ping-pong** *masc*
to play ping-pong jouer au ping-pong

**pink** *adjective*
**rose** *masc & fem*
a pink skirt une jupe rose

**pip** *noun*
(*in a fruit*) le **pépin** *masc*

**pipe** *noun*
1 (*for gas, water*) le **tuyau** *masc* (*pl* les **tuyaux**)
The pipes have burst. Les tuyaux ont éclaté.
2 (*for smoking*) la **pipe** *fem*
He smokes a pipe. Il fume la pipe.

**pirate** *noun*
le **pirate** *masc*

**pirated** *adjective*
**piraté** *masc*, **piratée** *fem*
a pirated video une vidéo piratée

**Pisces** *noun*
les **Poissons** *masc pl*
Valerie is Pisces. Valerie est Poissons.

**WORD TIP** Signs of the zodiac do not take an article: *un* or *une*.

**pistachio** *noun*
la **pistache** *fem*

**pit** *noun*
la **fosse** *fem*

to **pitch** *verb* ▷ see **pitch** *noun*
to pitch a tent dresser [1] une tente

**pitch** *noun* ▷ see **pitch** *verb*
le **terrain** *masc*
a football pitch un terrain de foot
The pitch was flooded. Le terrain a été inondé.

**pitch dark** *adjective*
**tout noir** *masc*, **toute noire** *fem*
It was pitch dark outside. Dehors, il faisait tout noir.

to **pity** *verb* ▷ see **pity** *noun*
**to pity somebody** plaindre **[31]** quelqu'un
**I pity them.** Je les plains.

♪ **pity** *noun* ▷ see **pity** *verb*
1 (*a shame*) le **dommage** *masc*
**That's a pity!** C'est dommage!
**It would be a pity to miss the film.** Ce serait dommage de rater le film.
**It's a pity she's not coming.** C'est dommage qu'elle ne vienne pas.
2 (*feeling of sympathy*) la **pitié** *fem*
**to take pity on** avoir **[5]** pitié de
**They took pity on me.** Ils ont eu pitié de moi.

**pizza** *noun*
la **pizza** *fem*
**a mushroom pizza** une pizza aux champignons

to **place** *verb* ▷ see **place** *noun*
**mettre [11]**
**He placed his cup on the table.** Il a mis sa tasse sur la table.

♪ **place** *noun* ▷ see **place** *verb*
1 (*location*) un **endroit** *masc*
**in a warm place** dans un endroit chaud
**a wonderful place** un endroit merveilleux
**a good place to have a picnic** un bon endroit pour pique-niquer
**It's my favourite place.** C'est mon endroit préféré.
**Bath is a nice place to live.** Bath est agréable à vivre.
**all over the place** partout
**We looked all over the place for the keys.** On a cherché les clés partout.
**There was water all over the place.** Il y avait de l'eau partout.
2 (*a space*) la **place** *fem*
**a place for the car** une place pour la voiture
**Is there a place for me?** Y a-t-il une place pour moi?
**Will you keep my place?** Veux-tu me garder ma place?
**to change places** changer de place
**I changed places with Jessica.** J'ai changé de place avec Jessica.
3 (*in a race*) la **place** *fem*
**in first place** à la première place
4 (*house*) **chez quelqu'un**
**at your place** chez toi
**Come to my place.** Viens chez moi.
**We'll go round to Hassan's place.** On ira chez Hassan.
5 **to take place** avoir **[5]** lieu
**The competition will take place at four.** Le concours aura lieu à seize heures.

**plain** *noun* ▷ see **plain** *adj*
la **plaine** *fem*

♪ **plain** *adjective* ▷ see **plain** *noun*
1 (*not fussy*) **simple** *masc & fem*
**plain cooking** une cuisine simple
2 (*not patterned*) **uni** *masc*, **unie** *fem*
**plain curtains** des rideaux unis
3 (*unflavoured*) **nature** *invariable adj*
**some plain yoghurt** du yaourt nature

**WORD TIP** As an adjective, *nature* never changes.

**plait** *noun*
la **natte** *fem*

♪ to **plan** *verb* ▷ see **plan** *noun*
1 **to plan to do something** avoir **[5]** l'intention de faire quelque chose
**We're planning to leave early.** Nous avons l'intention de partir tôt.
**Jack was planning to look for a job.** Jack avait l'intention de chercher un travail.
2 (*make plans for*) **préparer [1]**
**Mr Smith's planning a trip to Italy.** M. Smith prépare un voyage en Italie.
**I'm planning a surprise for my parents.** Je prépare une surprise à mes parents.
3 (*organize*) **organiser [1]**
**I need to plan my day.** J'ai besoin d'organiser ma journée.
**She loves planning the holiday.** Elle aime organiser les vacances.
4 (*a house, garden*) **concevoir [66]**
**a well-planned kitchen** une cuisine bien conçue

♪ **plan** *noun* ▷ see **plan** *verb*
1 (*idea, scheme*) le **projet** *masc*
**my plans for the future** mes projets d'avenir
**What are your plans for this summer?** Quels sont vos projets pour cet été?
**I don't have any plans yet.** Je n'ai pas encore de projets.
**She's got plans tonight.** Elle a prévu quelque chose pour ce soir.
**to go according to plan** se passer ⓔ **[1]** comme prévu
**Everything went according to plan.** Tout s'est passé comme prévu.
2 (*a map*) le **plan** *masc*
**a plan of the city** un plan de la ville

♪ **plane** *noun*
un **avion** *masc*
**to catch a plane to Paris** prendre **[64]** un avion pour Paris
**We went by plane.** Nous avons pris l'avion.
**I nearly missed my plane.** J'ai failli rater mon avion.

**planet** *noun*
la **planète** *fem*

**plank** *noun*
la **planche** *fem*

to **plant** *verb* ▷ see **plant** *noun*
**planter** [1]
**We planted some tomatoes.** Nous avons planté des tomates.

♪ **plant** *noun* ▷ see **plant** *verb*
la **plante** *fem*
**a house plant** une plante d'intérieur
**to water the plants** arroser [1] les plantes

**plaster** *noun*
1 (*sticking plaster*) le **pansement adhésif**
**She put a plaster on my hand.** Elle m'a mis un pansement à la main.
2 (*to heal a fracture*) le **plâtre** *masc*
**to have your leg in plaster** avoir la jambe dans le plâtre
**My arm was in plaster for a month.** J'avais le bras dans le plâtre pendant un mois.
3 (*for walls*) le **plâtre** *masc*

**plastic** *noun*
le **plastique** *masc*
**a plastic bag** un sac en plastique
**The table is made of plastic.** La table est en plastique.

♪ **plate** *noun*
une **assiette** *fem*
**paper plates** des assiettes en carton

♪ **platform** *noun*
1 (*in a station*) le **quai** *masc*
**at platform three** au quai numéro trois
**the train arriving at platform six** le train qui entre en gare quai numéro six
2 (*for lecturing or performing on*) une **estrade** *fem*

♪ to **play** *verb* ▷ see **play** *noun*
1 **jouer** [1]
**I play with my little sister.** Je joue avec ma petite sœur.
**The children were playing with matches.** Les enfants jouaient avec des allumettes.
**They play all kinds of music.** Ils jouent toutes sortes de musique.
**I don't play pop music.** Je ne joue pas de musique pop.
2 (*in sport*) **jouer** [1] **à**
**to play tennis** jouer au tennis
**Who wants to play football?** Qui veut jouer au football?
**I was playing cards.** Je jouais aux cartes.
3 (*in music*) **jouer** [1] **de**
**to play the violin** jouer du violon
**She plays the drums.** Elle joue de la batterie.
**Can you play the flute?** Tu sais jouer de la flûte?
4 (*a CD, DVD, video*) **mettre** [11]
**Play me your new CD.** Mets-moi ton nouveau CD.
5 (*a trick*) **jouer** [1]
**to play a trick on somebody** jouer un tour à quelqu'un
**They played a trick on me.** Ils m'ont joué un tour.
6 (*a part, role*) **jouer** [1]
**Who's playing Hamlet?** Qui joue Hamlet?
**She plays the doctor in the film.** Elle joue le rôle du médecin dans le film.

♪ **play** *noun* ▷ see **play** *verb*
la **pièce** *fem*
**a play by Molière** une pièce de Molière
**to put on a play** monter [1] une pièce
**Our school is putting on a play.** Notre école monte une pièce.
**I'm acting in the play.** Je joue dans la pièce.

♪ **player** *noun*
1 (*in sport*) le **joueur** *masc*, la **joueuse** *fem*
**a football player** un joueur de foot
**a tennis player** un joueur de tennis
**She's my favourite player.** C'est ma joueuse préférée.
2 (*musician*) le **musicien** *masc*, la **musicienne** *fem*

**playground** *noun*
la **cour de récréation** *fem*

**playgroup** *noun*
la **halte-garderie** *fem*

**playing card** *noun*
la **carte à jouer**

**playing field** *noun*
le **terrain de sport**

**playroom** *noun*
la **salle de jeux**

**plaza** *noun*
**a shopping plaza** un centre commercial

♪ **pleasant** *adjective*
**agréable** *masc & fem*
**I spent a pleasant day there.** J'y ai passé une journée agréable.

♪ **please** *adverb*
1 **s'il vous plaît**
**Two coffees, please.** Deux cafés, s'il vous plaît.
**Follow me, please.** Voulez-vous me suivre?
2 (*less formal*) **s'il te plaît**
**Could you turn the TV off, please?** Est-ce que tu peux éteindre la télé, s'il te plaît?

**pleased** *adjective*
**content** *masc*, **contente** *fem*
**I was really pleased!** J'étais vraiment content! (*boy speaking*), J'étais vraiment contente! (*girl speaking*).
**to be pleased with something** être **[6]** content de quelque chose
**She's very pleased with her present.** Elle est très contente de son cadeau.
**He was quite pleased with himself!** Il était assez content de soi!
**Pleased to meet you!** Enchanté! (*boy speaking*), Enchantée! (*girl speaking*).

**pleasure** *noun*
le **plaisir** *masc*

**plenty** *pronoun*
1 (*lots*) **beaucoup**
**plenty of something** beaucoup de quelque chose
**There's plenty of bread.** Il y a beaucoup de pain.
**He's got plenty of money.** Il a beaucoup d'argent.
**We have plenty of friends here.** Nous avons beaucoup d'amis ici.
2 (*quite enough*) **We've got plenty of time to chat.** Nous avons largement le temps de bavarder.
**Thanks, that's plenty!** Merci, ça suffit!

**pliers** *noun*
la **pince** *fem*
**a pair of pliers** une pince

**plot** *noun*
(*of a film, novel*) une **intrigue** *fem*
**I couldn't follow the plot.** Je n'ai pas réussi à suivre l'intrigue.

to **plough** *verb*
**labourer [1]**

**plug** *noun*
1 (*electrical*) la **prise** *fem*
2 (*in a bath, sink*) la **bonde** *fem*
**to pull out the plug** retirer la bonde

**plum** *noun*
la **prune** *fem*
**a plum tart** une tarte aux prunes

**plumber** *noun*
le **plombier** *masc*
**He's a plumber.** Il est plombier.

**plump** *adjective*
**potelé** *masc*, **potelée** *fem*

to **plunge** *verb*
**plonger [52]**
**He plunged into the river.** Il a plongé dans la rivière.

**plural** *noun*
(*Grammar*) le **pluriel** *masc*
**a noun in the plural** un nom au pluriel

**plus** *preposition*
**plus**
**three children plus the dog** trois enfants plus le chien

**p.m.** *adverb*
1 (*French people usually use the 24-hour clock to refer to times after midday*) **at two p.m.** à quatorze heures
**at nine p.m.** à vingt-et-une heures
2 (*You can also use 'de l'après-midi' for times up to 6 p.m. and 'du soir' for times after that*) **at two p.m.** à deux heures de l'après-midi
**at nine p.m.** à neuf heures du soir

**poached egg** *noun*
un **œuf poché**

**pocket** *noun*
la **poche** *fem*
**to have your hands in your pockets** avoir **[5]** les mains dans les poches
**to put your hand in your pocket** mettre **[11]** sa main dans sa poche
- **pocket money** l'argent de poche

**poem** *noun*
le **poème** *masc*
**I've written a poem.** J'ai écrit un poème.

**poet** *noun*
le **poète** *masc*

**poetry** *noun*
la **poésie** *fem*
**to write poetry** écrire **[38]** de la poésie

to **point** *verb* ▷ see **point** *noun*
1 (*to give directions*) **indiquer [1]**
**to point to something** indiquer quelque chose
**a sign pointing to the station** un flèche qui indiquait la gare
2 (*with your finger*) **montrer [1] du doigt**
**to point at somebody** montrer quelqu'un du doigt
**Don't point at her.** Ne la montre pas du doigt.
**He pointed at one of the children.** Il a montré l'un des enfants du doigt.
- **to point out something**

1 (*a building, a sight, an object*) **montrer [1]**
**James pointed out the cathedral to us.** James nous a montré la cathédrale.
2 (*to make it clear*) **to point out that ...** signaler **[1]** que ...
**I'd like to point out that I'm paying.** Je vous signale que c'est moi qui paie.

He pointed out that it was a mistake. Il a fait remarquer que c'était une erreur.

**𝄞 point** *noun* ▷ see **point** *verb*

1 *(tip)* la **pointe** *fem*
the point of a nail la pointe d'un clou
I removed it with the point of the knife. Je l'ai enlevé avec la pointe du couteau.

2 *(in time)* le **moment** *masc*
at that point à ce moment-là
At that point, the police arrived. À ce moment-là, la police est arrivée.

3 *(in a discussion, argument)*
to get the point comprendre **[64]**
I don't get the point. Je ne comprends pas.
That's not the point. Il ne s'agit pas de ça.
Let's stick to the point. Restons dans le sujet.
That's a good point! C'est vrai!
I see your point but ... Je vois ce que tu veux dire mais ...
what's the point of doing...? ça sert à quoi de faire...?
What's the point of waiting? Ça sert à quoi d'attendre?
there's no point in doing... ça ne sert à rien de faire...
There's no point in phoning, he's out. Ça ne sert à rien d'appeler, il est sorti.

4 *(in somebody's personality)* le **point** *masc*
her strong point son point fort
It's one of her weak points. C'est un de ses points faibles.
It's not my strong point! Ce n'est pas mon point fort!

5 *(in scoring)* le **point** *masc*
fifteen points to eleven quinze points à onze

6 *(in decimals)* **virgule**
6 point 4 six virgule quatre *(This is how you say it aloud.)*

**WORD TIP** When writing in French, a comma is used for the decimal point: 6,75.

**pointless** *adjective*
**inutile** *masc & fem*
The whole thing is pointless! Tout ça, c'est inutile!
it's pointless to do (something) il est inutile de faire (quelque chose)
It's pointless to keep on walking. Il est inutile de continuer à marcher.

**𝄞 point of view** *noun*
le **point de vue**
from my point of view de mon point de vue
Everyone has a point of view. Chacun a son point de vue.

to **poison** *verb* ▷ see **poison** *noun*
**empoisonner [1]**
to poison the water empoisonner l'eau

**poison** *noun* ▷ see **poison** *verb*
le **poison** *masc*
That's poison. C'est du poison.

**poisonous** *adjective*

1 *(chemical, gas)* **toxique** *masc & fem*
poisonous gases des gaz toxiques

2 *(toadstool, berry)* **vénéneux** *masc*, **vénéneuse** *fem*
poisonous mushrooms des champignons vénéneux

3 *(snake, insect)* **venimeux** *masc*, **venimeuse** *fem*

**poker** *noun*

1 *(for fire)* le **tisonnier** *masc*

2 *(card game)* le **poker** *masc*
to play poker jouer **[1]** au poker

**Poland** *noun*
la **Pologne** *fem*

**polar bear** *noun*
un **ours polaire**

**pole** *noun* ▷ see **Pole** *noun*

1 *(for a tent)* le **mât** *masc*
One of the poles snapped. Un des mâts s'est cassé.

2 *(for skiing)* le **bâton** *masc*

3 the North Pole le pôle Nord
the South Pole le pôle Sud

**Pole** *noun* ▷ see **pole** *noun*
un **Polonais** *masc*, une **Polonaise** *fem*
the Poles les Polonais

**𝄞 police** *noun*
the police la police
to join the police entrer **Ⓔ [1]** dans la police
Somebody called the police. Quelqu'un a appelé la police.
The police are coming. La police arrive.

- **police car** la voiture de police
- **police dog** le chien policier
- **policeman** un agent de police
- **police record** le casier judiciaire
- **police station** le commissariat de police
- **police van** le fourgon cellulaire
- **policewoman** la femme policier

**policy** *noun*

1 *(plan of action)* la **politique** *fem*

2 *(document)* la **police** *fem*

to **polish** *verb* ▷ see **polish** *noun*
*(shoes, furniture)* **cirer [1]**

**polish** *noun* ▷ see **polish** *verb*

1 *(for furniture)* la **cire** *fem*

2 *(for shoes)* le **cirage** *masc*

**Polish** *adjective* ▷ see **Polish** *noun*
**polonais** *masc*, **polonaise** *fem*

**Polish** *noun* ▷ see **Polish** *adj*
(*the language*) le **polonais**
▷ **Pole**.

**polite** *adjective*
**poli** *masc*, **polie** *fem*
**a polite girl** une jeune fille polie
**to be polite to somebody** être poli avec quelqu'un
**They weren't very polite to us.** Ils n'étaient pas très polis avec nous.

**political** *adjective*
**politique** *masc & fem*
**the political situation** la situation politique

**politician** *noun*
un **homme politique** *masc*, une **femme politique** *fem*

**politics** *noun*
la **politique** *fem*
**I'm very interested in politics.** La politique m'intéresse beaucoup.

to **pollute** *verb*
**polluer [1]**
**It pollutes the atmosphere.** Ça pollue l'atmosphère.

**polluted** *adjective*
**pollué** *masc*, **polluée** *fem*
**to become polluted** devenir Ⓔ **[81]** pollué

**pollution** *noun*
la **pollution** *fem*
**The fish die because of pollution.** Les poissons meurent à cause de la pollution.

**polo-necked** *adjective*
**à col roulé**
**a polo-necked jumper** un pull à col roulé

**polythene bag** *noun*
le **sac en plastique**

**pond** *noun*
1 (*large*) un **étang** *masc*
2 (*smaller*) la **mare** *fem*
3 (*in a garden*) le **bassin** *masc*

**pony** *noun*
le **poney** *masc*
• **ponytail** la queue de cheval

**poodle** *noun*
le **caniche** *masc*

**pool** *noun*
1 (*swimming pool*) la **piscine** *fem*
**The pool's closed.** La piscine est fermée.
2 (*in the country*) un **étang** *masc*
3 (*puddle*) la **flaque** *fem*
**There were pools of water everywhere.** Il y avait des flaques d'eau partout.
4 (*game*) le **billard américain**
**Who wants a game of pool?** Qui veut jouer au billard américain?
5 **the football pools** le loto sportif
**to do the pools** jouer au loto sportif

**poor** *adjective*
1 **pauvre** *masc & fem*
**a poor area** un quartier pauvre
**a poor family** une famille pauvre
**poor people** les pauvres
**Poor Jane's failed her exam.** La pauvre Jane a raté son examen.
**You poor thing!** Mon pauvre! (*to a boy*), Ma pauvre! (*to a girl*)
2 (*bad*) **mauvais** *masc*, **mauvaise** *fem*
**a poor mark** une mauvaise note
**This is poor work.** C'est du mauvais travail.
**The weather was pretty poor.** Le temps était plutôt mauvais.

to **pop** *verb* ▷ see **pop** *noun*
**to pop into a shop** faire **[10]** un saut dans un magasin
**I'll just pop into the post office.** Je vais juste faire un saut au bureau de poste.
**I popped home to eat.** J'ai mangé en vitesse à la maison.
**She'll pop by tomorrow.** Elle va passer en vitesse demain.

**pop** *noun* ▷ see **pop** *verb*
(*music*) le **pop** *masc*
**She can't stand pop.** Elle ne supporte pas le pop.

**pop concert** *noun*
le **concert de pop**

**popcorn** *noun*
le **pop-corn** *masc*

**pope** *noun*
le **pape** *masc*

**poppy** *noun*
le **coquelicot** *masc*

**pop song** *noun*
la **chanson pop**

**pop star** *noun*
la **pop star**

**popular** *adjective*
**populaire** *masc & fem*
**a popular actor** un acteur populaire
**a popular hobby among young people** un passe-temps répandu chez les jeunes
**to be popular** avoir **[5]** beaucoup d'amis
**She's very popular.** Elle a beaucoup d'amis.

He's very popular with the girls. Il a beaucoup de succès auprès des filles.

**population** *noun*
la **population** *fem*
most of the population la majorité de la population

**porch** *noun*
le **porche** *masc*

♂ **pork** *noun*
le **porc** *masc*
a pork chop une côtelette de porc
I don't eat pork. Je ne mange pas de porc.

**porridge** *noun*
le **porridge** *masc*

♂ **port** *noun*
le **port** *masc*
a fishing port un port de pêche
The ferry was in port. Le ferry était au port.

**portable computer** *noun*
(*Computers*) un **ordinateur portable**

**portable DVD player** *noun*
le **lecteur DVD portable**

**porter** *noun*
1 (*at a station, airport*) le **porteur** *masc*
2 (*in a hotel*) le **portier** *masc*

**portion** *noun*
la **portion** *fem*
half a portion une demi-portion
a portion of chips une portion de frites

**portrait** *noun*
le **portrait** *masc*

**Portugal** *noun*
le **Portugal** *masc*

**Portuguese** *adjective*
▷ see **Portuguese** *noun*
**portugais** *masc*, **portugaise** *fem*

**Portuguese** *noun* ▷ see **Portuguese** *adj*
1 un **Portugais** *masc*, une **Portugaise** *fem*
the Portuguese les Portugais
2 (*the language*) le **portugais** *masc*

**posh** *adjective*
**chic** *invariable adj*
a posh house une maison chic
a posh area un quartier chic

**WORD TIP** *chic* never changes.

**position** *noun*
1 (*where something is*) la **position** *fem*
to get into position se mettre ❷ [11] en place
2 (*in a competition*) la **position** *fem*
in third position en troisième position

♂ **positive** *adjective*
1 (*very sure*) **sûr** *masc*, **sûre** *fem*
I'm positive he's left. Je suis sûr qu'il est parti.
2 (*enthusiastic*) **positif** *masc*, **positive** *fem*
a positive reaction une réaction positive
to stay positive rester ❷ [1] positif
Try to be more positive. Essaie d'être plus positif.

to **possess** *verb*
**posséder [24]**

**possessions** *plural noun*
les **affaires** *fem pl*
They lost all their possessions. Ils ont perdu toutes leurs affaires.

**possibility** *noun*
la **possibilité** *fem*
That's another possibility. C'est une autre possibilité.
There are a number of possibilities. Il y a plusieurs possibilités.

♂ **possible** *adjective*
**possible** *masc & fem*
if possible si possible
as quickly as possible le plus vite possible
I'll do it as quickly as possible. Je le ferai le plus vite possible.
It's quite possible. C'est tout à fait possible.
Is it possible to book online? Est-ce qu'il est possible de réserver en ligne?
It's not yet possible. Ce n'est pas encore possible.

**possibly** *adverb*
1 (*maybe*) **peut-être**
'Are they back already?' — 'Possibly.' 'Est-ce qu'ils sont déjà rentrés?' — 'Peut-être.'
2 (*to express a strong feeling*) I can't possibly arrive before Thursday. Je ne peux vraiment pas arriver avant jeudi.
You can't possibly say that! Mais tu ne peux vraiment pas dire ça!

♂ to **post** *verb* ▷ see **post** *noun*
to post a letter mettre [11] une lettre à la poste
Post that as soon as possible. Mets ça à la poste le plus vite possible.

♂ **post** *noun* ▷ see **post** *verb*
1 la **poste** *fem*
to send something by post envoyer quelque chose par la poste
I sent her the CD by post. Je lui ai envoyé le CD par la poste.
2 (*letters*) le **courrier** *masc*
Is there any post for me? Y a-t-il du courrier pour moi? ➤➤

You haven't got any post. Tu n'as pas de courrier.
3 (*job*) le **poste** *masc*
He was offered a post abroad. On lui a proposé un poste à l'étranger.
4 (*pole*) le **poteau** *masc*

**postbox** *noun*
la **boîte aux lettres**
The postboxes are yellow. Les boîtes aux lettres sont jaunes.

♪ **postcard** *noun*
la **carte postale**
to send postcards envoyer des cartes postales

**postcode** *noun*
le **code postal**

♪ **poster** *noun*
1 (*for decoration*) le **poster** *masc*
I've got posters all over my room. J'ai des posters partout dans ma chambre.
2 (*advertising*) une **affiche** *fem*
I saw a poster for the concert. J'ai vu une affiche pour le concert.
We're putting up posters at school. On met des affiches à l'école.

♪ **postman** *noun*
le **facteur** *masc*
Has the postman been? Est-ce que le facteur est passé?

♪ **post office** *noun*
la **poste** *fem*
I'm looking for the post office. Je cherche la poste.
The post office is on the right. La poste est à droite.

to **postpone** *verb*
to postpone something remettre [11] quelque chose à plus tard
The trip was postponed until August. On a remis l'excursion au mois d'août.

**postwoman** *noun*
la **factrice** *fem*

**pot** *noun*
1 (*jar*) le **pot** *masc*
a pot of honey un pot de miel
three pots of paint trois pots de peinture
2 (*teapot*) la **théière** *fem*
I'll make a pot of tea. Je vais faire du thé.
3 (*pan*) la **casserole** *fem*
to put away the pots and pans ranger [52] les casseroles

♪ **potato** *noun*
la **pomme de terre**
fried potatoes les pommes de terre sautées
some mashed potatoes de la purée
• **potato crisps** les chips *masc pl*

**pottery** *noun*
la **poterie** *fem*
a piece of pottery une poterie
to make pottery fabriquer [1] des poteries

♪ **pound** *noun*
1 (*money*) la **livre** *fem*
fourteen pounds quatorze livres
How much is that in pounds? C'est combien en livres sterling?
2 (*in weight*) la **livre** *fem*
a pound of apples une livre de pommes

♪ to **pour** *verb*
1 (*a liquid*) **verser [1]**
I poured the milk into the pan. J'ai versé le lait dans la casserole.
2 (*a drink*) **servir [71]**
to pour the tea servir le thé
to pour somebody a drink servir à boire à quelqu'un
I poured him a drink. Je lui ai servi à boire.
3 to be pouring with rain pleuvoir [63] à verse
It's pouring. Il pleut à verse.

♪ **poverty** *noun*
la **pauvreté** *fem*
to fight against poverty lutter [1] contre la pauvreté

**powder** *noun*
la **poudre** *fem*

♪ **power** *noun*
1 (*electricity*) le **courant** *masc*
They've turned on the power. Ils ont mis le courant.
2 (*energy*) l'**énergie** *fem*
nuclear power l'énergie nucléaire
3 (*over other people*) le **pouvoir** *masc*
to have a lot of power avoir beaucoup de pouvoir
to be in power être [6] au pouvoir
He wants to stay in power. Il veut rester au pouvoir.

**power cut** *noun*
la **coupure de courant**

**powerful** *adjective*
**puissant** *masc*, **puissante** *fem*
a powerful computer un ordinateur puissant

**power point** *noun*
la **prise de courant**

**power station** *noun*
la **centrale électrique**

**practical** *adjective*
**pratique** *masc & fem*
**to be a practical person** avoir **[5]** l'esprit pratique
· **practical joke** la farce

**practically** *adverb*
**pratiquement**
**They've practically all gone.** Ils sont pratiquement tous partis.

♪ **practice** *noun*
1 (*for sport*) l'**entraînement** *masc*
**hockey practice** l'entraînement de hockey
2 (*for an instrument*) **to do your piano practice** travailler **[1]** son piano
**I've got to do some flute practice.** Je dois travailler ma flûte.
3 **to be out of practice** être **[6]** rouillé
**She's a bit out of practice.** Elle est un peu rouillée.

♪ to **practise** *verb*
1 (*music, a language*) **travailler [1]**
**an opportunity to practise my French** une occasion pour travailler mon français
**She's practising the violin.** Elle est en train de travailler son violon.
2 (*in a sport*) **s'entraîner [1]**
**The team practises on Wednesdays.** L'équipe s'entraîne le mercredi.
**I've got to practise for the match.** Je dois m'entraîner pour le match.

to **praise** *verb*
**to praise somebody for something** féliciter **[1]** quelqu'un de quelque chose
**They praised her for her achievement.** Ils l'ont félicitée de son succès.

**pram** *noun*
le **landau** *masc*

**prawn** *noun*
la **crevette** *fem*

to **pray** *verb*
**prier [1]**

**prayer** *noun*
la **prière** *fem*

**precaution** *noun*
la **précaution** *fem*
**to take precautions** prendre ses précautions

**precinct** *noun*
**a shopping precinct** un quartier commerçant
**a pedestrian precinct** une zone piétonne

**precious** *adjective*
**précieux** *masc*, **précieuse** *fem*
**precious stones** les pierres précieuses

**precise** *adjective*
**précis** *masc*, **précise** *fem*
**at 2 a.m. to be precise** à deux heures du matin, pour être précis

**precisely** *adverb*
**précisément**
**at eleven o'clock precisely** à onze heures précises
**That's precisely why they don't get on.** C'est précisément pour ça qu'ils ne s'entendent pas bien.

**preface** *noun*
la **préface** *fem*

♪ to **prefer** *verb*
**préférer [24]**
**Which dress do you prefer?** Tu préfères quelle robe?
**I prefer the red one.** Je préfère la rouge.
**to prefer something to something** préférer quelque chose à quelque chose
**I prefer coffee to tea.** Je préfère le café au thé.
**to prefer to do something** préférer faire quelque chose
**I'd prefer to go to the gym.** Je préfère aller au gymnase.
**She prefers swimming.** Elle préfère la natation.

**pregnancy** *noun*
la **grossesse** *fem*

**pregnant** *adjective*
**enceinte** *fem*

**prejudice** *noun*
le **préjugé** *masc*
**a prejudice** un préjugé
**to fight against racial prejudice** lutter contre les préjugés raciaux

**prejudiced** *adjective*
**to be prejudiced** avoir **[5]** des préjugés

**preliminary** *adjective*
**préliminaire** *masc & fem*

**première** *noun*
(*of a play, film*) la **première** *fem*

**prep** *noun*
les **devoirs** *masc pl*
**my English prep** mes devoirs d'anglais

**preparation** *noun*
1 la **préparation** *fem*
2 (*for a trip, event*) **preparations** les préparatifs *masc pl*
**the preparations for something** les préparatifs pour quelque chose
**our preparations for Christmas** nos préparatifs pour Noël

♪ to **prepare** *verb*
**préparer [1]**
**to prepare for something** se préparer Ⓔ à quelque chose
**We're preparing for the exam.** Nous nous préparons à l'examen.
**Prepare yourselves!** Préparez-vous!
**to prepare somebody for something** préparer quelqu'un à quelque chose
**I wasn't prepared for the shock.** On ne m'a pas préparé au choc.

**prepared** *adjective*
**prêt** *masc*, **prête** *fem*
**to be prepared to do something** être **[6]** prêt à faire quelque chose
**I'm prepared to pay half.** Je suis prêt à en payer la moitié.
**We weren't prepared to wait.** Nous n'étions pas prêts à attendre.
**to be prepared for something** s'attendre **[3]** à quelque chose
**I was prepared for the worst.** Je m'attendais au pire.

**preposition** *noun*
(*Grammar*) la **préposition** *fem*

**prep school** *noun*
une **école primaire privée**

to **prescribe** *verb*
**prescrire [38]**
**He prescribed antibiotics for me.** Il m'a prescrit des antibiotiques.

**prescription** *noun*
une **ordonnance** *fem*
**on prescription** sur ordonnance
**I got it on prescription.** Je l'ai eu sur ordonnance.

**presence** *noun*
la **présence** *fem*
**in my presence** en ma présence

**presence of mind** *noun*
la **présence d'esprit**

to **present** *verb* ▷ see **present** *noun, adj*
1 (*a prize*) **remettre [11]**
**Who's going to present the prizes?** Qui va remettre les prix?
**to present somebody with something** remettre quelque chose à quelqu'un
**He presented me with the cup.** Il m'a remis la coupe.
2 (*on TV, radio*) **présenter [1]**
**She presents the programme every year.** Elle présente l'émission chaque année.

♪ **present** *adjective* ▷ see **present** *noun, verb*
1 (*attending a class, ceremony*) **présent** *masc*, **présente** *fem*
**Is Jenny present?** Est-ce que Jenny est présente?
**to be present at something** assister **[1]** à quelque chose
**Fifty people were present at the funeral.** Cinquante personnes ont assisté à l'enterrement.
2 (*existing now*) **actuel** *masc*, **actuelle** *fem*
**the present situation** la situation actuelle
3 **at the present time** actuellement

♪ **present** *noun* ▷ see **present** *adj, verb*
1 (*gift*) le **cadeau** *masc* (*pl* les **cadeaux**)
**to give somebody a present** offrir **[56]** un cadeau à quelqu'un
**We gave Rashid a present.** Nous avons offert un cadeau à Rashid.
**to give something to somebody as a present** offrir **[56]** quelque chose à quelqu'un
**I'll give him the CD as a present.** Je vais lui offrir le CD.
2 (*at the moment*) **for the present** pour le moment
**That's all for the present.** C'est tout pour le moment
3 (*Grammar*) le **présent** *masc*
**in the present (tense)** au présent

**presenter** *noun*
(*on TV*) le **présentateur** *masc*, la **présentatrice** *fem*

**presently** *adverb*
(*soon*) **bientôt**

♪ **president** *noun*
le **président** *masc*, la **présidente** *fem*
**the first woman president** la première présidente
**to run for president** être **[6]** candidat à la présidence
**She wants to run for president.** Elle veut être candidate à la présidence.

♪ to **press** *verb* ▷ see **press** *noun*
1 (*to push*) **appuyer [41]**
**You have to press here to open it.** Il faut appuyer ici pour l'ouvrir.
**Press hard.** Appuyez fort.
2 (*a button, switch, pedal*) **appuyer [41] sur**
**I pressed the bell.** J'ai appuyé sur la sonnette.
**Don't press that button.** N'appuie pas sur ce bouton.

**press** *noun* ▷ see **press** *verb*
the press la presse
the tabloid press la presse populaire

**press conference** *noun*
la **conférence de presse**

**pressure** *noun*
la **pression** *fem*
She did it under pressure from the others. Elle l'a fait sous la pression des autres.
to put pressure on somebody faire [10] pression sur quelqu'un
They put pressure on him. Ils ont fait pression sur lui.
- **pressure gauge** un indicateur de pression
- **pressure group** le groupe de pression

♪ to **pretend** *verb*
to pretend to do something faire [10] semblant de faire quelque chose
I pretended to be asleep. J'ai fait semblant de dormir.
He's pretending not to hear. Il fait semblant de ne pas entendre.
Let's pretend that we missed class. Faisons semblant d'avoir manqué le cours.

**pretty** *adverb* ▷ see **pretty** *adj*
**plutôt**
It was pretty stupid. C'était plutôt bête.
The exam's pretty easy. L'examen est plutôt facile.

♪ **pretty** *adjective* ▷ see **pretty** *adv*
**joli** *masc*, **jolie** *fem*
a pretty village un joli village
They've got pretty things in that shop. Ils ont de jolies choses dans ce magasin.

**WORD TIP** *joli goes before the noun.*

♪ to **prevent** *verb*
to prevent somebody from doing something empêcher [1] quelqu'un de faire quelque chose
It's preventing me from having fun. Ça m'empêche de m'amuser.
There's nothing to prevent you from leaving. Rien ne vous empêche de partir.

**previous** *adjective*
**précédent** *masc*, **précédente** *fem*
during the previous week pendant la semaine précédente

**previously** *adverb*
**auparavant**

♪ **price** *noun*
le **prix** *masc*
the price per kilo le prix du kilo
Prices are high. Les prix sont élevés.
to go up in price augmenter [1]
CDs have gone up in price. Les CD ont augmenté.
- **price list** la liste des prix
- **price ticket** une étiquette

to **prick** *verb*
**piquer** [1]
to be pricked by thorns se faire Ⓔ [10] piquer par des épines
to prick your finger se piquer Ⓔ le doigt
I pricked my finger with the needle. Je me suis piqué le doigt avec l'aiguille.

**pride** *noun*
la **fierté** *fem*

**priest** *noun*
le **prêtre** *masc*

♪ **primary school** *noun*
une **école primaire**
the local primary school l'école primaire du quartier

♪ **primary (school) teacher** *noun*
un **instituteur** *masc*, une **institutrice** *fem*
My mother's a primary teacher. Ma mère est institutrice.

♪ **prime minister** *noun*
le **Premier ministre** *masc*
the Prime Minister of France le Premier ministre de la France

**prince** *noun*
le **prince** *masc*
Prince William le prince William

**princess** *noun*
la **princesse** *fem*
Princess Anne la princesse Anne

♪ **principal** *noun* ▷ see **principal** *adj*
(*of a college*) le **directeur** *masc*, la **directrice** *fem*
at the principal's office au bureau du directeur

**principal** *adjective* ▷ see **principal** *noun*
(*main*) **principal** *masc*, **principale** *fem*, **principaux** *masc pl*, **principales** *fem pl*
one of the principal reasons une des raisons principales

**principle** *noun*
le **principe** *masc*
on principle par principe
That's true in principle. Cela est vrai en principe.
It's against my principles. C'est contraire à mes principes.

**print** *noun*
1 (*printed letters*) **les caractères** *masc pl*
in small print en petits caractères ▸▸

2 (*a photo*) le **tirage** *masc*
a colour print un tirage en couleur

♪ **printer** *noun*
une **imprimante** *fem*
a laser printer une imprimante à laser

**print-out** *noun*
la **copie papier**

**prison** *noun*
la **prison** *fem*
in prison en prison

**prisoner** *noun*
le **prisonnier** *masc*, la **prisonnière** *fem*
to take somebody prisoner faire quelqu'un prisonnier
She was taken prisoner. On l'a fait prisonnière.
• **prisoner of war** le prisonnier de guerre, la prisonnière de guerre

♪ **private** *adjective*
1 **privé** *masc*, **privée** *fem*
a private school une école privée
'Private property' 'Propriété privée'
in private en privé
Can we talk to you in private? Est-ce qu'on peut vous parler en privé?
It's my private business. Ce sont mes affaires personnelles.
2 (*one-to-one*) **particulier** *masc*, **particulière** *fem*
to have private lessons prendre **[64]** des cours particuliers
She has private lessons in music. Elle prend des cours particuliers de musique.

**privately** *adverb*
**en privé**

♪ **prize** *noun*
le **prix** *masc*
to win a prize gagner un prix
I won first prize. J'ai gagné le premier prix.
• **prize-giving** la distribution des prix
• **prizewinner** le gagnant, la gagnante

**probable** *adjective*
**probable** *masc & fem*
one of the probable effects un des effets probables

**probably** *adverb*
**probablement**
I'll probably be late. Je serai probablement en retard.

♪ **problem** *noun*
le **problème** *masc*
a serious problem un grave problème
What's the problem? Quel est le problème?
No problem! Pas de problème!
I had a bit of a problem. J'ai eu un petit problème.

**process** *noun*
1 le **processus** *masc*
2 to be in the process of doing something être en train de faire quelque chose
We're in the process of making dinner. Nous sommes en train de préparer le repas.

**procession** *noun*
1 (*in parade*) le **défilé** *masc*
2 (*at religious festival*) la **procession** *fem*

to **produce** *verb* ▷ see **produce** *noun*
**produire [26]**
I produced my passport. J'ai produit mon passeport.
It produces a lot of heat. Ça produit beaucoup de chaleur.
He has produced some fine work. Il a produit un beau travail.

**produce** *noun* ▷ see **produce** *verb*
les **produits** *masc pl*
organic produce les produits biologiques

**producer** *noun*
(*of a film, programme*) le **producteur** *masc*, la **productrice** *fem*
a famous film producer un célèbre producteur de cinéma

♪ **product** *noun*
le **produit** *masc*
a range of products une gamme de produits
to import cheap products importer des produits bon marché

**production** *noun*
1 (*of a film, opera*) la **production** *fem*
She's in charge of the production. Elle est responsable de la production.
2 (*of a play*) la **mise en scène** *fem*
a new production of Hamlet une nouvelle mise en scène de Hamlet
3 (*by a factory*) la **production** *fem*
That motorbike has gone out of production. On ne fabrique plus cette moto.
• **production line** la chaîne de fabrication

**profession** *noun*
la **profession** *fem*

**professional** *noun*
▷ see **professional** *adj*
le **professionnel** *masc*, la **professionnelle** *fem*
They're professionals. Ce sont des professionnels.





Ⓔ means the verb takes être to form the perfect

**professional** *adjective*
▷ see **professional** *noun*
**professionnel** *masc*, **professionnelle** *fem*
**professional players** les joueurs professionnels
**She's a professional singer.** C'est une chanteuse professionnelle.

**professor** *noun*
le **professeur** *masc*

**profile** *noun*
le **profil** *masc*

**profit** *noun*
le **bénéfice** *masc*
**to make a profit** faire **[10]** un bénéfice
**We sold the cakes at a profit.** Nous avons fait un bénéfice sur la vente des gâteaux.

**profitable** *adjective*
**rentable** *masc & fem*

**program** *noun* ▷ see **programme** *noun*
**a computer program** un programme informatique

♪ **programme** *noun* ▷ see **program** *noun*
1 (*on TV, radio*) une **émission** *fem*
**a popular TV programme** une émission télévisée grand public
2 (*for a play, event*) le **programme** *masc*
**Could I see the programme?** Est-ce que je peux voir le programme?

**programmer** *noun*
le **programmateur** *masc*, la **programmatrice** *fem*

♪ **progress** *noun*
1 le **progrès** *masc*
**That's progress!** C'est ça le progrès!
**to make progress** faire **[10]** des progrès
**I'm making progress in French.** Je fais des progrès en français.
2 **to be in progress** être en cours
**Talks are in progress.** Les négociations sont en cours.

♪ **project** *noun*
1 (*at school*) le **dossier** *masc*
**a project on something** un dossier sur quelque chose
**my project on the rain forest** mon dossier sur la forêt tropicale
2 (*a plan*) le **projet** *masc*
**Our school is taking part in the project.** Notre école participe au projet.
**a project to do something** un projet pour faire quelque chose
**a project to build a bridge** un projet pour construire un pont
• **project manager** le directeur de projet, la directrice de projet

**projector** *noun*
le **projecteur** *masc*

♪ to **promise** *verb* ▷ see **promise** *noun*
**to promise to do something** promettre **[11]** de faire quelque chose
**I've promised to be home by ten.** J'ai promis de rentrer avant dix heures.
**I promise I'll phone when I get there.** Je t'appelle quand j'y arriverai, je le promets.

♪ **promise** *noun* ▷ see **promise** *verb*
la **promesse** *fem*
**to make a promise** faire **[10]** une promesse
**She's always making promises.** Elle fait toujours des promesses.
**to break a promise** manquer **[1]** à sa promesse
**I never break a promise.** Je ne manque jamais à ma promesse.
**It's a promise!** C'est promis!

to **promote** *verb*
**to be promoted** être **[6]** promu
**She's been promoted.** Elle a été promue.

**promotion** *noun*
la **promotion** *fem*
**to get a promotion** être **[6]** promu

**prompt** *adjective*
**rapide** *masc & fem*
**a prompt reply** une réponse rapide

**promptly** *adjective*
1 (*at once*) **immédiatement**
**He promptly fell off again.** Il est retombé immédiatement.
2 (*quickly*) **rapidement**
**Please reply promptly.** Répondez rapidement s'il vous plaît.
3 **Lessons begin promptly at nine o'clock.** Les cours commencent à neuf heures précises.

**pronoun** *noun*
(*Grammar*) le **pronom** *masc*

♪ to **pronounce** *verb*
**prononcer [61]**
**It's hard to pronounce.** C'est difficile à prononcer.
**I can't pronounce the word.** Je ne peux pas prononcer le mot.
**How do you pronounce it?** Ça se prononce comment?

**pronunciation** *noun*
la **prononciation** *fem*
**Your pronunciation is good.** Tu as une bonne prononciation.

♂ **proof** *noun*
la **preuve** *fem*
**They still have no proof.** Ils n'ont toujours aucune preuve.
**I've got proof.** J'ai des preuves.
**There's no proof that ...** Rien ne prouve que ...
**There's no proof that it's dangerous.** Rien ne prouve que c'est dangereux.

**propaganda** *noun*
la **propagande** *fem*

**propeller** *noun*
une **hélice** *fem*

♂ **proper** *adjective*
1 (*real, genuine*) **vrai** *masc*, **vraie** *fem*
**a proper doctor** un vrai médecin
**I need a proper meal.** J'ai besoin d'un vrai repas.
**We haven't had a proper holiday.** Nous n'avons pas eu de vraies vacances.
2 (*correct*) **bon** *masc*, **bonne** *fem*
**the proper tools** les bons outils
**That's not the proper answer.** Ce n'est pas la bonne réponse.
**The TV wasn't in its proper place.** La télé n'était pas à sa place.

**WORD TIP** The adjectives *vrai* and *bon* come before the noun.

♂ **properly** *adverb*
**comme il faut**
**Hold it properly.** Tiens-le comme il faut.
**Is it properly wrapped?** Est-ce que c'est emballé comme il faut?

**property** *noun*
1 la **propriété** *fem*
**'Private property'** 'Propriété privée'
2 (*belongings*) les **affaires** *fem pl*
**my personal property** mes affaires personnelles
**to be somebody's property** appartenir **[81]** à quelqu'un
**It's not your property.** Cela ne t'appartient pas.

**proposal** *noun*
la **proposition** *fem*

to **propose** *verb*
1 (*suggest*) **proposer [1]**
2 **to propose (marriage) to somebody** demander quelqu'un en mariage
**He proposed to her.** Il l'a demandée en mariage.

**prostitute** *noun*
la **prostituée** *fem*
**a male prostitute** un prostitué

♂ to **protect** *verb*
**protéger [15]**
**to protect the environment** protéger l'environnement
**to protect somebody from something** protéger quelqu'un contre quelque chose
**to protect children from drugs** protéger les enfants contre la drogue

**protection** *noun*
la **protection** *fem*

**protein** *noun*
la **protéine** *fem*

♂ to **protest** *verb* ▷ see **protest** *noun*
1 (*to grumble*) **protester [1]**
**We protested, but it was pointless.** Nous avons protesté, mais c'était inutile.
2 (*demonstrate*) **manifester [1]**
**They're protesting against poverty.** Ils manifestent contre la pauvreté.

**protest** *noun* ▷ see **protest** *verb*
1 (*opposition*) la **protestation** *fem*
**in spite of their protests** malgré leurs protestations
**to do something in protest against something** faire quelque chose en signe de protestation contre quelque chose
2 (*a demonstration*) la **manifestation** *fem*
**a street protest** une manifestation
**to organize a protest** organiser **[1]** une manifestation

**Protestant** *adjective*
▷ see **Protestant** *noun*
**protestant** *masc*, **protestante** *fem*

**Protestant** *noun* ▷ see **Protestant** *adj*
le **protestant** *masc*, la **protestante** *fem*

**WORD TIP** Adjectives never have capitals in French, even for religions.

**protester** *noun*
le **manifestant** *masc*, la **manifestante** *fem*

**protest march** *noun*
la **manifestation** *fem*

♂ **proud** *adjective*
**fier** *masc*, **fière** *fem*
**to be proud of something** être **[6]** fier de quelque chose
**She's proud of her garden.** Elle est fière de son jardin.
**to be proud of yourself** être **[6]** fier de soi
**I was very proud of myself.** J'étais très fier de moi.

♂ to **prove** *verb*
**prouver [1]**
**What does it prove?** Qu'est-ce que ça prouve?

That doesn't prove anything. Ça ne prouve rien.
to prove that ... prouver que ...
It proves that we're right. Ça prouve que nous avons raison.

**proverb** *noun*
le **proverbe** *masc*

to **provide** *verb*
**fournir [2]**
Are meals provided? Est-ce que les repas sont fournis?
to provide somebody with something fournir quelque chose à quelqu'un
It provides people with work. Ça fournit du travail aux gens.
to provide training assurer [1] la formation

♪ **provided** *conjunction*
**à condition que**
provided you do it now à condition que tu le fasses maintenant

**province** *noun*
la **province** *fem*

**prune** *noun*
le **pruneau** *masc* (*pl* les **pruneaux**)

**ps** *abbreviation*
(*in a letter*) **P.S.**

**psychiatrist** *noun*
le & la **psychiatre** *masc & fem*
He's a psychiatrist. Il est psychiatre.

**psychological** *adjective*
**psychologique** *masc & fem*

**psychologist** *noun*
le & la **psychologue** *masc & fem*
She's a psychologist Elle est psychologue.

**psychology** *noun*
la **psychologie** *fem*

**PTO** *abbreviation*
**TSVP** (*= tournez s'il vous plaît*)

**pub** *noun*
le **pub** *masc*
They went to the pub. Ils sont allés au pub.

♪ **public** *adjective* ▷ see **public** *noun*
1 **public** *masc*, **publique** *fem*
public opinion l'opinion publique
2 the public library la bibliothèque municipale
• **public address system** la sonorisation

♪ **public** *noun* ▷ see **public** *adj*
the public le public
open to the public ouvert au public
in public en public

♪ **public holiday** *noun*
le **jour férié**
January 1 is a public holiday. Le premier janvier est férié.

**publicity** *noun*
la **publicité** *fem*

**public school** *noun*
une **école privée**

**public transport** *noun*
les **transports en commun** *masc pl*

to **publish** *verb*
**publier [1]**

**publisher** *noun*
un **éditeur** *masc*

♪ **pudding** *noun*
le **dessert** *masc*
What's for pudding? Qu'est-ce qu'il y a comme dessert?
For pudding we've got strawberries. Comme dessert nous avons des fraises.

**puddle** *noun*
la **flaque** *fem*

**Puerto Rico** *noun*
**Porto Rico** *fem*

**WORD TIP** Unlike other names of islands, *Porto Rico* does not take *le* or *la*.

**puff** *noun*
(*of smoke*) la **bouffée** *fem*
• **puff pastry** la pâte feuilletée

♪ to **pull** *verb*
1 **tirer [1]**
Pull hard! Tire fort!
to pull a rope tirer sur une corde
to pull the chain tirer sur la chasse d'eau
She was pulling me by the arm. Elle me tirait par le bras.
to pull something out of something tirer quelque chose de quelque chose
He pulled a mobile out of his pocket. Il a tiré un portable de sa poche.
to pull somebody out of something sortir [72] quelqu'un de quelque chose
They pulled me out of the water. Ils m'ont sorti de l'eau.
We pulled the sledge up the hill. Nous avons monté la côte en tirant la luge.
2 to pull faces faire [10] des grimaces
• **to pull away**
(*car, bus*) **démarrer [1]**
As the bus was pulling away, ... Comme le bus démarrait, ...
• **to pull something down**
(*a blind*) **baisser [1]**
Pull down the blind. Baissez le store. ▸▸

- **to pull in**
  (*at the roadside*) **s'arrêter [1]**
  **We pulled in to have a rest.** Nous nous sommes arrêtés pour nous reposer.
- **to pull through**
  (*after an accident, illness*) **s'en sortir ❷ [2]**
  **Luckily, she pulled through.**
  Heureusement, elle s'en est sortie.

**pullover** *noun*
le **pull-over** *masc*, le **pull** *masc*

**pulse** *noun*
le **pouls** *masc*
**The doctor took my pulse.** Le médecin a pris mon pouls.

to **pump** *verb* ▷ see **pump** *noun*
**pomper [1]**
**They were pumping the water out of the cellar.** Ils pompaient l'eau de la cave.
- **to pump something up**
  (*a tyre*) **gonfler [1]**
  **The tyres need to be pumped up.** Il faut gonfler les pneus.

**pump** *noun* ▷ see **pump** *verb*
1 (*for tyres*) la **pompe** *fem*
**a bicycle pump** une pompe à vélo
2 (*shoe*) la **ballerine** *fem*
**ballet pumps** des ballerines

**pumpkin** *noun*
la **citrouille** *fem*

to **punch** *verb* ▷ see **punch** *noun*
1 **to punch somebody** donner [1] un coup de poing à quelqu'un
**He punched me.** Il m'a donné un coup de poing.
2 (*a ticket*) **composter [1]**
**Don't forget to punch your tickets.**
N'oubliez pas de composter vos billets.

**punch** *noun* ▷ see **punch** *verb*
1 (*a blow*) le **coup de poing**
**a punch on the nose** un coup de poing dans le nez
**to give somebody a punch** donner un coup de poing à quelqu'un
2 (*drink*) le **punch** *masc*
**We had some punch.** Nous avons bu du punch.

**punctual** *adjective*
**ponctuel** *masc*, **ponctuelle** *fem*

**punctuation** *noun*
la **ponctuation** *fem*
**punctuation errors** des erreurs de ponctuation
- **punctuation mark** le signe de ponctuation

**puncture** *noun*
la **crevaison** *fem*
**to get a puncture** crever [1]
**I got a puncture on the way.** J'ai crevé en route.

to **punish** *verb*
**punir [2]**
**to punish somebody for doing something** punir quelqu'un pour avoir fait quelque chose
**We'll be punished for missing class.** On va nous punir pour avoir séché le cours.

**punishment** *noun*
la **punition** *fem*

♪ **pupil** *noun*
un **élève** *masc*, une **élève** *fem*
**They're good pupils.** Ce sont de bons élèves.

**puppet** *noun*
la **marionnette** *fem*

**puppy** *noun*
le **chiot** *masc*
**a labrador puppy** un chiot labrador

**pure** *adjective*
**pur** *masc*, **pure** *fem*

♪ **purple** *adjective*
**violet** *masc*, **violette** *fem*
**She's got purple hair.** Elle a les cheveux violets.

♪ **purpose** *noun*
1 **on purpose** exprès
**to do something on purpose** faire exprès de faire quelque chose
**He closed the door on purpose.** Il a fait exprès de fermer la porte.
**Did she do it on purpose?** Est-ce qu'elle l'a fait exprès?
**I didn't do it on purpose.** Je ne l'ai pas fait exprès.
2 (*aim*) le **but** *masc*
**to have a purpose in life** avoir un but dans la vie
**What's the purpose of this meeting?** Quel est le but de cette réunion?

to **purr** *verb*
**ronronner [1]**

♪ **purse** *noun*
le **porte-monnaie** *masc* (*pl* les **porte-monnaie**)
**My purse was stolen.** On m'a volé mon porte-monnaie.



❷ means the verb takes être to form the perfect

♪ to **push** *verb* ▷ see **push** *noun*

1 **pousser [1]**
He pushed me. Il m'a poussé.
Can you help me to push the table? Tu peux m'aider à pousser la table?

2 (*a bell, button*) **appuyer [41] sur**
Push the red button. Appuyez sur le bouton rouge.

3 to push somebody to do something pousser [1] quelqu'un à faire quelque chose
His teacher's pushing him to learn German. Son prof le pousse à apprendre l'allemand.

• **to push somebody around**
**bousculer [1] quelqu'un**
Stop pushing me around. Arrête de me bousculer.

• **to push something away**
**repousser [1] quelque chose**
I pushed my plate away. J'ai repoussé mon assiette.

• **to push on**
(*with a journey, task*) **continuer [1]**
We pushed on for another hour. Nous avons continué pendant une heure encore.

**push** *noun* ▷ see **push** *verb*
to give something a push pousser [1] quelque chose
We had to give the car a push. Nous avons dû pousser la voiture.

**pushchair** *noun*
la **poussette** *fem*

♪ to **put** *verb*

1 (*to place*) **mettre [11]**
Put your suitcases here. Mettez vos valises ici.
I didn't put the cream in the fridge. Je n'ai pas mis la crème au frigo.
Where did you put my skirt? Où est-ce que tu as mis ma jupe?

2 (*to write*) **écrire [38]**
Put your address here. Écris ton adresse ici.

• **to put something away**
**ranger [52] quelque chose**
I put the shopping away. J'ai rangé les courses.

• **to put something back**

1 **remettre [11] quelque chose**
Put it back in the drawer. Remets-le dans le tiroir.

2 (*to postpone*) **remettre [11]**
The trip has been put back until Thursday. La sortie a été remise à jeudi.

• **to put something down**
**poser [1] quelque chose**
She put the plant down on the floor. Elle a posé la plante par terre.

• **to put somebody off**

1 **décourager [52] quelqu'un**
The experience hasn't put me off. L'expérience ne m'a pas découragé.
to be put off se décourager ❷ [52]
She's easily put off. Elle se décourage facilement.
Don't be put off! Ne te décourage pas!

2 to put somebody off something dégoûter [1] quelqu'un de quelque chose
It really put me off meat! Ça m'a vraiment dégoûté de la viande!

• **to put something off**

1 (*a class, match*) **remettre [11]**
He's put off my lesson till Thursday. Il a remis ma leçon à jeudi.

2 (*a light, TV*) **éteindre [60]**
Don't forget to put off the TV. N'oublie pas d'éteindre la télé.

• **to put something on**

1 (*clothing, make-up, music*) **mettre [11]**
I'll just put my shoes on. Je vais juste mettre mes chaussures.
He's put on his favourite CD. Il a mis son CD préféré.

2 (*a light, the heating*) **allumer [1]**
Who put the lamp on? Qui a allumé la lampe?

3 (*a play*) **monter [1]**
We're putting on a French play. Nous sommes en train de monter une pièce française.

• **to put something out**

1 (*a bin, the rubbish*) **sortir [72]**
Have you put the rubbish out? Est-ce que tu as sorti les ordures?

2 (*a fire, light, cigarette*) **éteindre [60]**
I've put the lights out. J'ai éteint la lumière.

3 to put out your hand tendre [3] la main

• **to put somebody through to passer [52] quelqu'un à**
Could you put me through to the secretary? Pourriez-vous me passer la secrétaire?

• **to put something up**

1 (*your hand*) **lever [50]**
I put up my hand. J'ai levé la main.

2 (*a picture, poster*) **mettre [11]**
I've put up some photos in my room. J'ai mis des photos dans ma chambre.

3 (*a notice*) **afficher [1]**

4 (*the price*) **augmenter [1]**
They've put up the price of the tickets. Ils ont augmenté le prix des billets. ⏩

- **to put somebody up** (*for the night*) **héberger [52] quelqu'un**
  **Can you put me up on Friday?** Est-ce que tu peux m'héberger vendredi?
- **to put up with something supporter [1] quelque chose**
  **We can't put up with this situation any more.** Nous ne pouvons plus supporter cette situation.
  **I don't know how she puts up with it.** Je ne sais pas comment elle le supporte.

**puzzle** *noun*
(*jigsaw*) le **puzzle** *masc*
- **puzzle book** le livre de jeux

**puzzled** *adjective*
**perplexe** *masc & fem*
**He looked puzzled.** Il avait l'air perplexe.

**pyjamas** *plural noun*
le **pyjama** *masc singular*
**a pair of pyjamas** un pyjama
**Where are my pyjamas?** Où est mon pyjama?

**pylon** *noun*
le **pylône** *masc*

**Pyrenees** *noun*
**the Pyrenees** les Pyrénées *fem pl*

# Q q

**qualification** *noun*
1 (*exam pass, degree*) le **diplôme** *masc*
2 (*in general*) **qualifications** qualifications *fem pl*
**vocational qualifications** les qualifications professionnelles

**qualified** *adjective*
1 (*experienced, trained*) **qualifié** *masc*, **qualifiée** *fem*
2 (*having a degree, diploma*) **diplômé** *masc*, **diplômée** *fem*

to **qualify** *verb*
1 (*in sport*) **se qualifier** Ⓔ **[1]**
**Our team qualified for the semifinal.** Notre équipe s'est qualifiée pour la demi-finale.
2 **to qualify for something** avoir **[5]** droit à
**I qualify for a reduction.** J'ai droit à une réduction.
3 (*to get a qualification*) **obtenir [77] son diplôme**
**She qualified as a nurse.** Elle a obtenu son diplôme d'infirmière.
- **qualifying match** le match de qualification

**quality** *noun*
la **qualité** *fem*
**good quality clothes** des vêtements de bonne qualité
**It's poor quality.** C'est de la mauvaise qualité.

**quantity** *noun*
la **quantité** *fem*
**They grow large quantities of vegetables.** Ils cultivent de grandes quantités de légumes.

**WORD TIP** *quantité* is followed by *de* before a noun.

to **quarrel** *verb* ▷ see **quarrel** *noun*
**se disputer** Ⓔ **[1]**

**quarrel** *noun* ▷ see **quarrel** *verb*
la **dispute** *fem*
**to have a quarrel** se disputer Ⓔ **[1]**

**quarry** *noun*
la **carrière** *fem*

**quarter** *noun*
1 le **quart** *masc*
**A quarter of the class is ill.** Le quart de la classe est malade.
**Three quarters of the class are absent.** Les trois quarts de la classe sont absents.
2 (*talking about time*) le **quart**
**a quarter to ten** dix heures moins le quart
**a quarter past ten** dix heures et quart
**a quarter of an hour** un quart d'heure
**three quarters of an hour** trois quarts d'heure
- **quarter-final** le quart de finale

**quartet** *noun*
le **quatuor** *masc*

**quay** *noun*
le **quai** *masc*

**Quebec** *noun*
le **Québec**

**WORD TIP** Countries and regions in French take *le*, *la* or *les*.

**Quebecker** *noun*
le **Québecois**, la **Québecoise**

**queen** *noun*
la **reine** *fem*
**Queen Elizabeth** la reine Elizabeth
**the Queen of Spain** la reine d'Espagne

**WORD TIP** *la* is used with names of queens and a small letter is used for *reine* in French.

**query** *noun*
la **question** *fem*

to **question** *verb* ▷ see **question** *noun*
**interroger [52]**

**question** *noun* ▷ see **question** *verb*
1 (*query*) la **question** *fem*
**You haven't answered my question.** Tu n'as pas répondu à ma question.
**to ask somebody a question** poser [1] une question à quelqu'un
**I asked her a question.** Je lui ai posé une question.
2 (*matter*) la **question**
**It's a question of time.** C'est une question de temps.
**It's out of the question!** C'est hors de question!
• **question mark** le point d'interrogation

**questionnaire** *noun*
le **questionnaire** *masc*

to **queue** *verb* ▷ see **queue** *noun*
**faire [10] la queue**
**We queued for hours.** Nous avons fait la queue pendant des heures.

**queue** *noun* ▷ see **queue** *verb*
1 (*of people*) la **queue** *fem*
2 (*of cars*) la **file** *fem*

**quick** *adjective*
1 **rapide** *masc & fem*
**We had a quick lunch** Nous avons déjeuné rapidement
**It's quicker on the motorway.** C'est plus rapide par l'autoroute.
2 (*as an order*) **Quick! There's the bus!** Vite! Voilà le bus!
**Be quick!** Dépêche-toi!, Dépêchez-vous!

**quickly** *adverb*
**vite**
**I ate too quickly.** J'ai mangé trop vite.
**Come quickly!** Viens vite!, Venez vite!

**quiet** *adjective*
1 (*person, class*) **silencieux** *masc*, **silencieuse** *fem*
**The children are very quiet.** Les enfants sont très silencieux.
**Keep quiet.** Tais-toi (*to one person*)., Taisez-vous (*to two or more people*).
2 (*in character*) **réservé** *masc*, **réservée** *fem*
**Zoë's a quiet girl.** Zoë est une fille réservée.
3 (*voice, music*) **doux** *masc*, **douce** *fem*
**She was speaking in a quiet voice.** Elle parlait à voix basse.
4 (*street, evening, life*) **tranquille** *masc & fem*
**a quiet area** un quartier tranquille

**quietly** *adverb*
1 (*to move*) **sans bruit**
**to get up quietly** se lever Ⓔ [50] sans bruit
2 (*to speak, sing*) **doucement**
**to talk quietly** parler doucement
3 (*to read, play*) **en silence**
**to work quietly** travailler en silence

**quilt** *noun*
la **couette** *fem*

to **quit** *verb*
1 (*school*) **quitter [1]**
**to quit doing something** arrêter [1] de faire quelque chose
2 (*from a computer game*) **sortir** Ⓔ **[72]**

**quite** *adverb*
1 (*in general*) **assez, plutôt**
**I draw quite well.** Je dessine assez bien.
**It's quite cold outside.** Il fait assez froid dehors.
**It's quite expensive.** C'est plutôt cher.
**That's quite a good idea.** C'est une assez bonne idée.
**quite often** assez souvent
**You're quite right!** Tu as tout à fait raison!
2 **not quite** pas tout à fait
**That's not quite true.** Ce n'est pas tout à fait vrai.
3 **quite a lot of** pas mal de
**quite a lot of homework** pas mal de devoirs
**We have quite a lot of friends.** Nous avons pas mal d'amis.

**quiz** *noun*
le **quiz** *masc*
**a TV quiz show** un jeu télévisé

**quotation** *noun*
la **citation** *fem*
• **quotation marks** les guillemets *masc pl*
**in quotation marks** entre guillemets

to **quote** *verb* ▷ see **quote** *noun*
**citer [1]**

**quote** *noun* ▷ see **quote** *verb*
1 (*from a book*) la **citation** *fem*
2 **in quotes** entre guillemets

English–French

# R r

**rabbi** *noun*
le **rabbin** *masc*

♫**rabbit** *noun*
le **lapin** *masc*
- **rabbit hutch** le clapier

**rabies** *noun*
la **rage** *fem*

to **race** *verb* ▷ see **race** *noun*
to race against somebody faire **[10]** la course avec quelqu'un

**race** *noun* ▷ see **race** *verb*
1 (*sports event*) la **course** *fem*
a cycle race une course cycliste
She came third in the race. Elle est arrivée troisième dans la course.
to have a race faire **[10]** la course
Two children were having a race. Deux enfants faisaient la course.
2 (*ethnic group*) la **race** *fem*
the human race la race humaine
- **race relations** les relations inter-raciales *fem pl*
- **race riots** les émeutes raciales *fem pl*

**racer** *noun*
(*bike*) le **vélo de course**

**racehorse** *noun*
le **cheval de course**

**racetrack** *noun*
1 (*for horses*) le **champ de course**
2 (*for cars*) le **circuit** *masc*
3 (*for cycles*) la **piste** *fem*

**racial** *adjective*
**racial** *masc*, **raciale** *fem*, **raciaux** *masc pl*, **raciales** *fem pl*
racial discrimination la discrimination raciale

**racing** *noun*
les **courses** *fem pl*
He's watching the racing. Il regarde les courses.
- **racing car** la voiture de course
- **racing driver** le pilote de course

**racism** *noun*
le **racisme** *masc*

**racist** *adjective* ▷ see **racist** *noun*
**raciste** *masc & fem*
a racist comment une réflexion raciste

**racist** *noun* ▷ see **racist** *adjective*
le & la **raciste** *masc & fem*

**rack** *noun*
1 (*for luggage*) le **porte-bagages** *masc* (*pl* les **porte-bagages**)
2 (*for bicycles*) le **parc à bicyclettes**

**racket** *noun*
1 (*for tennis, badminton*) la **raquette** *fem*
Here's your tennis racket. Voici ta raquette de tennis.
2 (*noise*) le **vacarme** *masc*
The boys were making a racket. Les garçons faisaient du vacarme.
3 (*swindle*) l'**escroquerie** *fem*

**radar** *noun*
le **radar** *masc*
by radar au radar

**radiation** *noun*
la **radiation** *fem*
- **radiation sickness** le mal des rayons
- **radiation therapy** la radiothérapie

**radiator** *noun*
le **radiateur** *masc*

♫**radio** *noun*
la **radio** *fem*
to listen to the radio écouter **[1]** la radio
I was listening to the radio when he arrived. J'écoutais la radio quand il est arrivé.
to hear something on the radio entendre **[3]** quelque chose à la radio
I think I heard it on the radio. Je crois que je l'ai entendu à la radio.
to be on the radio passer ⓔ **[1]** à la radio
She was on the radio. Elle est passée à la radio.

**radioactive** *adjective*
**radioactif** *masc*, **radioactive** *fem*

**radio-controlled** *adjective*
(*toy*) **téléguidé** *masc*, **téléguidée** *fem*

**radio station** *noun*
la **station de radio**

**radish** *noun*
le **radis** *masc*

**radius** *noun*
le **rayon** *masc*
all houses within a 10-kilometre radius toutes les maisons dans un rayon de 10 kilomètres

**raffle** *noun*
la **tombola** *fem*

a b c d e f g h i j k l m n o p q r s t u v w x y z



ⓔ means the verb takes être to form the perfect

**raft** *noun*
le **radeau** *masc*

**rag** *noun*
le **chiffon** *masc*

**rage** *noun*
1 la **colère** *fem*
**to be in a rage** être [6] furieux
**She's in a rage.** Elle est furieuse.
**He flew into a rage.** Il s'est mis dans une colère noire.
2 **to be all the rage** faire [10] fureur
**It's all the rage now.** Ça fait fureur à présent.

**raging** *adjective*
**to be raging** être [6] fou de rage (*boy*), être [6] folle de rage (*girl*)

to **raid** *verb* ▷ see **raid** *noun*
1 (*robbers*) **attaquer** [1]
2 (*police*) **faire** [10] **une rafle dans**

**raid** *noun* ▷ see **raid** *verb*
1 (*on a bank*) le **hold-up** *masc*
2 (*by the police*) la **rafle** *fem*

**rail** *noun*
1 **to go by rail** prendre [64] le train
2 (*on a balcony, bridge*) la **balustrade** *fem*
3 (*on stairs*) la **rampe** *fem*
4 (*for a train*) le **rail** *masc*
**The train went off the rails.** Le train a déraillé.

**railing** *noun*, **railings** *pl*
la **grille** *fem*

**rail strike** *noun*
la **grève des cheminots**

♪ **railway** *noun*
1 (*the system*) le **chemin de fer**
**the railways** les chemins de fer
2 (*from one place to another*) **a railway line** une ligne de chemin de fer
**the railway line between London and Oxford** la ligne entre Londres et Oxford
3 **an accident on the railway line** un accident sur la voie ferrée
- **railway carriage** le wagon
- **railway track** la voie ferrée

♪ **railway station** *noun*
la **gare** *fem*

♪ **rain** *noun* ▷ see **rain** *verb*
la **pluie** *fem*
**in the rain** sous la pluie
**I like walking in the rain.** J'aime bien me promener sous la pluie.
**when the rain stopped** quand il s'est arrêté de pleuvoir
- **rainbow** un arc-en-ciel (*pl* les arcs-en-ciel)
- **raincoat** un imperméable
- **raindrop** la goutte de pluie
- **rainfall** le niveau de précipitations
- **rain forest** la forêt tropicale

♪ to **rain** *verb* ▷ see **rain** *noun*
**pleuvoir** [63]
**It's raining.** Il pleut.
**It's going to rain.** Il va pleuvoir.
**It rained all night.** Il a plu toute la nuit.

♪ **rainy** *adjective*
**pluvieux** *masc*, **pluvieuse** *fem*
**a rainy day** un jour pluvieux

to **raise** *verb*
1 (*to lift up*) **lever** [50]
**She raised her head.** Elle a levé la tête.
**Raise your hands, please!** Levez la main, s'il vous plaît!
2 (*so as to be heard*) **to raise your voice** parler [1] plus fort
3 (*a price, a salary*) **augmenter** [1]
4 **The school is raising money for computers.** L'école collecte des fonds pour acheter des ordinateurs.
5 (*a child, a family*) **élever**
**I was raised in Scotland.** J'ai été élevé en Écosse (*boy speaking*), J'ai été élevée en Écosse (*girl speaking*).
**Helen was raised by her grandmother.** Helen a été élevée par sa grand-mère.
6 **to raise the alarm** donner [1] l'alarme

**raisin** *noun*
le **raisin sec**

**rake** *noun*
le **râteau** *masc* (*pl* les **râteaux**)

**rally** *noun*
1 (*public gathering*) le **rassemblement** *masc*
2 (*for sport*) le **rallye** *masc*
3 (*in tennis*) un **échange** *masc*

**rambler** *noun*
le **randonneur** *masc*, la **randonneuse** *fem*

**rambling** *noun*
la **randonnée** *fem*
**to go rambling** faire [10] une randonnée

**ramp** *noun*
la **rampe** *fem*

**ranch** *noun*
le **ranch** *masc*

**range** *noun*
1 (*of activities, prices*) la **gamme** *fem*
**We offer a range of sports activities.** Nous vous proposons une gamme d'activités sportives.
**The computer is top of the range.** C'est un ordinateur haut de gamme. ⏩

2 (*of colours, products*) le **choix** *masc*
**They have a very large range of CDs.** Ils ont un très grand choix de CD.
3 (*of mountains*) la **chaîne** *fem*

to **ransack** *verb*
**fouiller [1] dans**

to **rap** *verb* ▷ see **rap** *noun*
**to rap at the door** frapper **[1]** à la porte

**rap** *noun* ▷ see **rap** *verb*
le **rap** *masc*
- **rap music** la musique rap
- **rap singer** le chanteur rap, la chanteuse rap

to **rape** *verb* ▷ see **rape** *noun*
**violer [1]**

**rape** *noun* ▷ see **rape** *verb*
le **viol** *masc*

**rare** *adjective*
1 **rare** *masc & fem*
**a rare bird** un oiseau rare
2 (*meat*) **saignant** *masc*, **saignante** *fem*
**I like my steak rare.** J'aime le steak saignant.
**a bit too rare** un peu trop saignant
**a medium-rare steak** un steak à point

**rarely** *adverb*
**rarement**

**rash** *adjective* ▷ see **rash** *noun*
**irréfléchi** *masc*, **irréfléchie** *fem*
**a rash decision** une décision irréfléchie

**rash** *noun* ▷ see **rash** *adj*
les **rougeurs** *fem pl*
**I've got a rash on my arms.** J'ai des rougeurs sur les bras.
**to come out in a rash** se couvrir Ⓔ **[30]** de rougeurs
**I came out in a rash.** Je me suis couvert de rougeurs.

**raspberry** *noun*
la **framboise** *fem*
**raspberry jam** la confiture de framboises
**a raspberry tart** une tarte aux framboises
**raspberry-flavoured yoghurt** le yaourt à la framboise

**rat** *noun*
le **rat** *masc*

**rate** *noun*
1 (*charge*) le **tarif** *masc*
**a special rate** un tarif spécial
**an hourly rate** un tarif horaire
**Children travel at a reduced rate.** Les enfants bénéficient d'un tarif réduit.
2 (*level*) le **taux** *masc*
**the birth rate** le taux de natalité
**the high crime rate** le taux élevé de criminalité
3 **at any rate** en tout cas
**I hope I've passed, at any rate.** En tout cas, j'espère avoir réussi.

**rather** *adverb*
1 **plutôt**
**It's rather expensive.** C'est plutôt cher.
2 **rather a lot of** pas mal de
**I've got rather a lot of homework to do.** J'ai pas mal de devoirs à faire.
3 **rather than** plutôt que
**Go there in summer rather than winter.** Allez-y en été plutôt qu'en hiver.
4 (*showing preference*) **I'd rather go to the cinema.** Je préférerais aller au cinéma.
**Would you rather stay here?** Est-ce que tu préférerais rester ici?
**I'd rather walk than wait for the bus.** Je préférerais aller à pied plutôt que d'attendre le bus.

**rave** *noun*
(*party*) le **rave** *masc*

**raw** *adjective*
**cru** *masc*, **crue** *fem*
**raw fish** le poisson cru
- **raw materials** les matières premières *fem*

**ray** *noun*
1 le **rayon** *masc*
**rays of sunshine** des rayons de soleil
2 (*fish*) la **raie** *fem*

**razor** *noun*
le **rasoir** *masc*
- **razor blade** la lame de rasoir

**RE** *noun*
**l'éducation religieuse** *fem*

to **reach** *verb* ▷ see **reach** *noun*
1 **arriver** Ⓔ **[1] à quelque chose**
**When you reach the church, turn left.** Quand vous arrivez à l'église, tournez à gauche.
2 **to reach a decision** arriver Ⓔ **[1]** à une décision
**The committee still hasn't reached a decision.** Le comité n'est pas encore arrivé à une décision.
**to reach the final** parvenir Ⓔ **[81]** en finale
**The defending champions didn't reach the final.** Les tenants du titre ne sont pas parvenus en finale.
3 (*a particular age, level*) **atteindre [60]**
**when you reach the age of 18** quand on atteint la majorité

Ⓔ means the verb takes être to form the perfect

**reach** *noun* ▷ see **reach** *verb*
la **portée** *fem*
out of reach hors de portée
within reach (*of your hand*) à portée de main
We've rented a villa within easy reach of the sea. Nous avons loué une villa à proximité de la mer.

to **react** *verb*
**réagir [2]**
How did you react? Comment est-ce que tu as réagi?

**reaction** *noun*
la **réaction** *fem*

& to **read** *verb*
**lire [51]**
What are you reading at the moment? Qu'est-ce que tu lis en ce moment?
I didn't read the instructions. Je n'ai pas lu les instructions.
I'd like to read that book again. J'aimerais relire ce livre.
- **to read something out**
**lire [51] quelque chose à haute voix**
He read out the list. Il a lu la liste à haute voix.
- **to read up on something**
**étudier [1] quelque chose**
I have to read up on the subject. Je dois étudier le sujet.

& **reading** *noun*
la **lecture** *fem*
I don't much like reading. Je n'aime pas beaucoup la lecture.

& **ready** *adjective*
1 **prêt** *masc*, **prête** *fem*
Jane's not ready yet. Jane n'est pas encore prête.
Dinner's ready! À table!
to be ready to do something être [6] prêt à faire quelque chose
Are you ready to leave? Est-ce que tu es prêt à partir?
2 to get ready se préparer ❷ [1]
I need to get ready. Je dois me préparer.
to get ready to do something se préparer à faire quelque chose
I'm getting ready to go out. Je me prépare à sortir.
3 to get something ready préparer [1] quelque chose
I'll get your room ready. Je vais préparer ta chambre.
- **ready-made meal** le plat préparé

& **real** *adjective*
**vrai** *masc*, **vraie** *fem*
They're real diamonds. Ce sont de vrais diamants.
That's the real reason. Ça, c'est la vraie raison.
He's a real bore. C'est un vrai casse-pieds.
Is that his real name? Est-ce que c'est son vrai nom?
His real name is Jack. Son vrai nom, c'est Jack.
Her real father is dead. Son vrai père est mort.
She's a real friend. C'est une véritable amie.

**WORD TIP** *vrai* comes before the noun.

**realistic** *adjective*
**réaliste** *masc & fem*

**reality** *noun*
la **réalité** *fem*

& to **realize** *verb*
1 **to realize something** se rendre ❷ [3] compte de quelque chose
when I realized my mistake quand je me suis rendu compte de mon erreur
They don't realize how hard it is. Ils ne se rendent pas compte de la difficulté.
Do you realize what time it is? Tu te rends compte de l'heure qu'il est?
I hadn't realized. Je ne m'en étais pas rendu compte.
to realize (that) ... se rendre compte que ...
I didn't realize he was French. Je ne m'étais pas rendu compte qu'il était français.
2 (*an ambition, a dream*) **réaliser [1]**

& **really** *adverb*
**vraiment**
The film was really good. Le film était vraiment très bon.
Is it really midnight? Est-ce qu'il est vraiment minuit?
not really pas vraiment
'Are you pleased?' — 'Not really.' 'Tu es content?' — 'Pas vraiment.'
I really don't know. Je ne sais vraiment pas.
Really? C'est vrai?

to **rearrange** *verb*
1 (*a room, a house*) **réaménager [52]**
2 (*your plans*) **modifier [1]**

**rear** *adjective* ▷ see **rear** *noun*
**arrière** *masc & fem*
(*of a car*) the rear door la portière arrière

English-French

a b c d e f g h i j k l m n o p q **r** s t u v w x y z

**rear** *noun* ▷ see **rear** *adj*
(*of a building*) l'**arrière** *masc*
**to get on at the rear of the train** monter [1] en queue de train

**reason** *noun*
la **raison** *fem*
**the reason why ...** la raison pour laquelle ...
**I nearly forgot the reason why I phoned.** J'ai presque oublié la raison pour laquelle j'appelais.
**That's the reason why I'm not going.** C'est pourquoi je n'y vais pas.
**What's the reason for the delay?** Quelle est la raison du retard?

**reasonable** *adjective*
**raisonnable** *masc & fem*
**Be reasonable!** Sois raisonnable!

to **reassure** *verb*
**rassurer** [1]

**reassuring** *adjective*
**rassurant** *masc*, **rassurante** *fem*

**rebel** *noun*
le & la **rebelle** *masc & fem*

**rebellion** *noun*
la **rébellion** *fem*, la **révolte** *fem*

to **rebuild** *verb*
**reconstruire** [26]

**receipt** *noun*
le **reçu** *masc*
**I've kept the receipt.** J'ai gardé le reçu.

to **receive** *verb*
**recevoir** [66]

**receiver** *noun*
le **combiné** *masc*
**to pick up the receiver** décrocher [1]

**recent** *adjective*
**récent** *masc*, **récente** *fem*
**It's quite a recent discovery.** C'est une découverte assez récente.

**recently** *adverb*
**récemment**

**reception** *noun*
1 la **réception** *fem*
**a big wedding reception** une grande réception de mariage
**at (the) reception** à la réception
**He's waiting at reception.** Il attend à la réception.
2 (*for a mobile phone*) la **réception** *fem*
**The reception is good.** La réception est bonne.

**receptionist** *noun*
le & la **réceptionniste** *masc & fem*
**She's a receptionist.** Elle est réceptionniste.

**recipe** *noun*
la **recette** *fem*
**the recipe for risotto** la recette du risotto
**Can I have the recipe for this cake?** Est-ce que je peux avoir la recette de ce gâteau?

to **reckon** *verb*
**penser** [1]
**I reckon it's a good idea.** Je pense que c'est une bonne idée.
**What do you reckon?** Qu'est-ce que tu en penses?

to **recognize** *verb*
**reconnaître** [27]
**She recognized my voice.** Elle a reconnu ma voix.
**I didn't recognize him.** Je ne l'ai pas reconnu.
**to recognize each other** se reconnaître Ⓔ [27]
**We recognized each other immediately.** Nous nous sommes reconnus tout de suite.

to **recommend** *verb*
**to recommend something to somebody** recommander [1] quelque chose à quelqu'un
**I recommend the fish soup.** Je vous recommande la soupe de poisson.
**Can you recommend a dentist?** Est-ce que vous pouvez me recommander un dentiste?
**They recommended the hotel to us.** Ils nous ont recommandé l'hôtel.

**recommendation** *noun*
la **recommandation** *fem*

to **record** *verb* ▷ see **record** *noun*
**enregistrer** [1]
**They're recording a new album.** Ils sont en train d'enregistrer un nouvel album.

**record** *noun* ▷ see **record** *verb*
1 le **record** *masc*
**She broke the record.** Elle a battu le record.
**It's a world record.** C'est le record mondial.
**the hottest summer on record** l'été le plus chaud qu'on ait jamais enregistré
**We finished it in record time.** Nous l'avons terminé en un temps record.
2 **to keep a record of something** noter [1] quelque chose
**Could you please keep a record of the results?** Est-ce que tu peux noter les résultats?



Ⓔ means the verb takes être to form the perfect

3 le **disque** *masc*
a huge record collection une énorme collection de disques
4 (*office files*) le **dossier** *masc*
I'll just check your records. Je vais juste vérifier votre dossier.

**recorder** *noun*
1 la **flûte à bec**
to play the recorder jouer [1] de la flûte à bec
2 a DVD recorder un enregistreur DVD
a video recorder un magnétoscope

**record-holder** *noun*
le **recordman** *masc*, la **recordwoman** *fem*

♪ **recording** *noun*
un **enregistrement** *masc*

**record player** *noun*
le **tourne-disque** *masc*

to **recover** *verb*
**se remettre** ⓔ **[11]**
to recover from something se remettre de quelque chose
I'm still recovering from flu. Je me remets encore de la grippe.

**recovery** *noun*
(*from an illness*) le **rétablissement** *masc*
He's made a full recovery. Il s'est complètement rétabli.
• **recovery vehicle** le camion de dépannage

**rectangle** *noun*
le **rectangle** *masc*

**rectangular** *adjective*
**rectangulaire** *masc & fem*

to **recycle** *verb*
**recycler [1]**

♪ **red** *adjective*
1 **rouge** *masc & fem*
a red shirt une chemise rouge
a bright red car une voiture rouge vif
to go red rougir [2]
He went red when he saw her. Il a rougi quand il l'a vue.
2 (*hair*) **roux** *masc*, **rousse** *fem*
to have red hair avoir [5] les cheveux roux
Rachel has red hair. Rachel a les cheveux roux.
• **red card** le carton rouge

**Red Cross** *noun*
the Red Cross la Croix-Rouge

**redcurrant** *noun*
la **groseille** *fem*
redcurrant jelly la gelée de groseilles

to **redecorate** *verb*
**refaire [10]**
They've had the kitchen redecorated. Ils ont fait refaire la cuisine.

to **redo** *verb*
**refaire [10]**

to **reduce** *verb*
**réduire [68]**
They've reduced all the bags by 20%. Ils ont réduit tous les sacs de 20%.
to reduce your speed ralentir [2]

♪ **reduction** *noun*
la **réduction** *fem*

**redundancy** *noun*
1 (*a lost job*) le **licenciement** *masc*
2 (*unemployment*) le **chômage** *masc*

**redundant** *adjective*
to be made redundant être [6] licencié

**reel** *noun*
(*of cotton*) la **bobine** *fem*

to **refer** *verb*
to refer to someone, something parler [1] de quelqu'un, quelque chose
She's referring to you. Elle parle de toi.
Did he refer to the trip? Est-ce qu'il a parlé de l'excursion?

**referee** *noun*
un **arbitre** *masc*

**reference** *noun*
(*for a job, course*) les **références** *fem pl*
to give somebody a reference fournir [2] des références à quelqu'un
• **reference book** un ouvrage de référence

**refill** *noun*
(*for a pen, a lighter*) la **recharge** *fem*

to **reflect** *verb*
**refléter [24]**

**reflection** *noun*
1 (*in a mirror*) une **image** *fem*
2 (*thought*) la **réflexion** *fem*
on reflection à la réflexion

**reflex** *noun*
le **réflexe** *masc*

**reflexive** *adjective*
(*Grammar*) **réfléchi** *masc*, **réfléchie** *fem*
a reflexive verb un verbe pronominal

**refreshing** *adjective*
**rafraîchissant** *masc*, **rafraîchissante** *fem*

**refreshment** *noun*
le **rafraîchissement** *masc*

**refrigerator** *noun*
le **réfrigérateur** *masc*

**refuge** *noun*
le **refuge** *masc*
to take refuge in something se réfugier Ⓔ [1] dans quelque chose

**refugee** *noun*
le **réfugié** *masc*, la **réfugiée** *fem*

to **refund** *verb* ▷ see **refund** *noun*
**rembourser [1]**

**refund** *noun* ▷ see **refund** *verb*
le **remboursement** *masc*
to get a refund se faire Ⓔ [10] rembourser

**refusal** *noun*
le **refus** *masc*

to **refuse** *verb* ▷ see **refuse** *noun*
**refuser [1]**
I refused. J'ai refusé.
to refuse to do something refuser de faire quelque chose

**refuse** *noun* ▷ see **refuse** *verb*
(*rubbish*) les **ordures** *fem pl*

**regards** *plural noun*
les **amitiés** *fem pl*
'Regards to your parents.' 'Mes amitiés à vos parents.'

**reggae** *noun*
le **reggae** *masc*

♪ **region** *noun*
la **région** *fem*

**regional** *adjective*
**régional** *masc*, **régionale** *fem*, **régionaux** *masc pl*, **régionales** *fem pl*

♪ to **register** *verb* ▷ see **register** *noun*
**s'inscrire [38]**
I've registered for the class. Je me suis inscrit au cours.

**register** *noun* ▷ see **register** *verb*
(*in school*) le **cahier des absences**
to take the register faire [10] l'appel

**registered letter** *noun*
la **lettre recommandée**

**registration number** *noun*
le **numéro d'immatriculation**

to **regret** *verb*
**regretter [1]**
to regret doing something regretter d'avoir fait quelque chose

**regular** *adjective*
**régulier** *masc*, **régulière** *fem*

**regularly** *adverb*
**régulièrement**

♪ **regulation** *noun*
le **règlement** *masc*
It's against regulations. C'est contraire au règlement.

**rehearsal** *noun*
la **répétition** *fem*

to **rehearse** *verb*
**répéter [24]**

to **reheat** *verb*
**réchauffer [1]**

**reign** *noun*
le **règne** *masc*

**rein** *noun*
la **rêne** *fem*

**reindeer** *noun*
le **renne** *masc*

to **reject** *verb*
**rejeter [48]**

**related** *adjective*
1 (*person, language*) **apparenté** *masc*, **apparentée** *fem*
2 (*connected*) **lié** *masc*, **liée** *fem*
a work-related accident un accident lié au travail

♪ **relation** *noun*
le **parent** *masc*, la **parente** *fem*
a close relation un parent proche
my relations ma famille
I met all her relations. J'ai rencontré toute sa famille.
There were just relations and close friends. Il n'y avait que la famille et des amis proches.
Rashid's got relations in France. Rashid a de la famille en France.

**relationship** *noun*
les **relations** *fem pl*
to have a good relationship with somebody s'entendre [3] très bien

**relative** *noun*
le **membre de la famille**
We've invited a few relatives. Nous avons invité quelques membres de la famille.
All my relatives were there. Il y avait toute ma famille.

**relatively** *adverb*
**relativement**

♪ to **relax** *verb*
**se détendre** Ⓔ **[3]**
to relax by doing something se détendre en faisant quelque chose
I relax by playing squash. Je me détends en jouant au squash.

I'm going to relax and watch telly tonight. Je vais me détendre en regardant la télé ce soir.

**relaxation** *noun*
la **détente** *fem*
a form of relaxation une détente

**relaxed** *adjective*
**détendu** *masc*, **détendue** *fem*

**relaxing** *adjective*
**reposant** *masc*, **reposante** *fem*

**relay race** *noun*
la **course de relais**

to **release** *verb* ▷ see **release** *noun*
1 (*a CD, a DVD*) **sortir [72]**
2 (*a prisoner*) **libérer [24]**

**release** *noun* ▷ see **release** *verb*
1 (*film, CD*) la **nouveauté** *fem*
2 (*of a prisoner, a hostage*) la **libération** *fem*

**relevant** *adjective*
**pertinent** *masc*, **pertinente** *fem*

ℰ **reliable** *adjective*
(*person, car*) **fiable** *masc & fem*
She's extremely reliable. Elle est très fiable.

**relief** *noun*
1 le **soulagement** *masc*
2 (*aid*) l'**aide** *fem*
famine relief l'aide aux victimes de la famine

to **relieve** *verb*
**soulager [52]**

**relieved** *adjective*
**soulagé** *masc*, **soulagée** *fem*
I was relieved to hear you'd arrived. J'ai été soulagé d'apprendre que tu étais arrivé.

**religion** *noun*
la **religion** *fem*

**religious** *adjective*
1 (*person*) **croyant** *masc*, **croyante** *fem*
2 (*art, music*) **religieux** *masc*, **religieuse** *fem*

**reluctant** *adj*
**réticent** *masc*, **réticente** *fem*
to be reluctant to do something être peu disposé à faire quelque chose

ℰ to **rely** *verb*
to rely on somebody compter **[1]** sur quelqu'un
I'm relying on you for Saturday. Je compte sur toi pour samedi.
You can't rely on them. On ne peut pas compter sur eux.

ℰ to **remain** *verb*
**rester** Ⓔ **[1]**
She remained calm. Elle est restée calme.
That remains to be seen. Ça reste à voir.

**remains** *plural noun*
les **restes** *masc pl*

**remark** *noun*
la **remarque** *fem*
an odd remark une remarque bizarre
to make remarks about somebody faire des réflexions sur quelqu'un

**remarkable** *adjective*
**remarquable** *masc & fem*

**remarkably** *adverb*
**remarquablement**

ℰ to **remember** *verb*
1 **se souvenir** Ⓔ **[81]**
I don't remember. Je ne me souviens pas.
2 to remember something se souvenir Ⓔ **[81]** de quelque chose
Do you remember his name? Est-ce que tu te souviens de son nom?
I can't remember the number. Je ne me souviens pas du numéro.
3 to remember somebody se souvenir Ⓔ **[81]** de quelqu'un
I remember Lucy well. Je me souviens très bien de Lucy.
4 (*to recall*) to remember doing something se souvenir Ⓔ **[81]** d'avoir fait quelque chose
I remember switching off the TV. Je me souviens d'avoir éteint la télévision.
5 (*not to forget*) to remember to do something ne pas oublier **[1]** de faire quelque chose
Remember to shut the door. N'oublie pas de fermer la porte.

ℰ to **remind** *verb*
1 **rappeler [18]**
to remind somebody to do something rappeler à quelqu'un de faire quelque chose
Remind your father to pick me up. Rappelle à ton père de venir me chercher.
Remind me to buy some milk. Rappelle-moi d'acheter du lait.
2 to remind somebody of something faire **[10]** penser quelqu'un à quelque chose
It reminds me of Paris. Ça me fait penser à Paris.
He reminds me of Frank. Il me fait penser à Frank.
Oh, that reminds me ... Tiens, à ce propos...

**remote** *adjective*
**isolé** *masc*, **isolée** *fem*
• **remote control** la télécommande



English-French

a b c d e f g h i j k l m n o p q r s t u v w x y z

English–French

to **remove** *verb*
**enlever [50]**
**He removed the packaging.** Il a enlevé l'emballage.
**It's for removing stains.** C'est pour enlever les taches.

to **renew** *verb*
**renouveler [18]**

**renewable** *adjective*
(*form of energy*) **renouvelable** *masc & fem*

♪ to **rent** *verb* ▷ see **rent** *noun*
**louer [1]**
**Simon's rented a flat.** Simon a loué un appartement.
**We rented a house in Brittany.** Nous avons loué une maison en Bretagne.

♪ **rent** *noun* ▷ see **rent** *verb*
le **loyer** *masc*

♪ **rental** *noun*
la **location** *fem*

to **reorganize** *verb*
**réorganiser [1]**

♪ to **repair** *verb* ▷ see **repair** *noun*
**réparer [1]**
**to get something repaired** faire **[10]** réparer quelque chose
**We got the television repaired.** Nous avons fait réparer la télévision.

**repair** *noun* ▷ see **repair** *verb*
la **réparation** *fem*

to **repay** *verb*
**rembourser [1]**
**to repay somebody something** rembourser quelque chose à quelqu'un

♪ to **repeat** *verb* ▷ see **repeat** *noun*
1 **répéter [24]**
**Repeat after me.** Répétez après moi.
2 (*at school*) **redoubler [1]**
**She has to repeat a year.** Elle doit redoubler.

**repeat** *noun* ▷ see **repeat** *verb*
(*of a TV programme*) la **reprise** *fem*

**repeatedly** *adverb*
**à plusieurs reprises**

**repertoire** *noun*
le **répertoire** *masc*

**repetitive** *adjective*
**répétitif** *masc*, **répétitive** *fem*

♪ to **replace** *verb*
**remplacer [61]**
**I replaced the broken plate.** J'ai remplacé l'assiette cassée.
**to be replaced by something** être **[6]** remplacé par quelque chose
**Records have been replaced by CDs.** Les disques ont été remplacés par les CD.
**Replace each noun with the correct pronoun.** Remplace chaque nom par le pronom qui convient.

**replacement** *noun*
1 (*person*) le **remplaçant** *masc*, la **remplaçante** *fem*
2 **to find a replacement for something** remplacer **[6]** quelque chose
**The chain broke and I couldn't find a replacement for it.** La chaîne s'est cassée et je n'ai pas pu la remplacer.

to **replay** *verb*
1 (*a game*) **rejouer [1]**
2 (*a DVD, a video*) **repasser [1]**

♪ to **reply** *verb* ▷ see **reply** *noun*
**répondre [3]**
**to reply to something** répondre à quelque chose
**I still haven't replied to the letter.** Je n'ai toujours pas répondu à la lettre.

♪ **reply** *noun* ▷ see **reply** *verb*
la **réponse** *fem*
**We're still waiting for a reply.** Nous attendons toujours une réponse.
**I didn't get a reply to my letter.** Je n'ai pas reçu de réponse à ma lettre.
(*on the telephone*) **There's no reply.** Ça ne répond pas.

♪ to **report** *verb* ▷ see **report** *noun*
1 (*a problem, an accident*) **signaler [1]**
**We've reported the theft.** Nous avons signalé le vol.
**There's nothing to report.** Il n'y a rien à signaler.
**Two people were reported dead.** On a signalé deux morts.
2 **to report somebody to somebody** dénoncer **[1]** quelqu'un à quelqu'un
**They reported him to the teacher.** Ils l'ont dénoncé au professeur.
3 (*to present yourself*) **se présenter** Ⓔ **[1]**
**I had to report to reception.** Je devais me présenter à la réception.
4 **to report on something** faire **[10]** un reportage sur quelque chose
**the journalists reporting on the conflict** les journalistes qui font des reportages sur le conflit

♪ **report** *noun* ▷ see **report** *verb*
1 (*description, account*) le **compte rendu** *masc*, le **rapport** *masc*

a b c d e f g h i j k l m n o p q **r** s t u v w x y z

to write a report faire [10] un compte rendu
Write a report on today's events. Fais un compte rendu des événements d'aujourd'hui.
2 (*school report*) le **bulletin scolaire**
3 (*on the news*) le **reportage**

**reporter** *noun*
le & la **journaliste** *masc & fem*
She's a reporter. Elle est journaliste.

to **represent** *verb*
**représenter [1]**

**representative** *noun*
le **représentant** *masc*, la **représentante** *fem*

to **reproach** *verb* ▷ see **reproach** *noun*
to reproach somebody faire [10] des reproches à quelqu'un

**reproach** *noun* ▷ see **reproach** *verb*
le **reproche** *masc*

**reproduction** *noun*
la **reproduction** *fem*

**reptile** *noun*
le **reptile** *masc*

**republic** *noun*
la **république** *fem*

**reputation** *noun*
la **réputation** *fem*
The town has a bad reputation. La ville a mauvaise réputation.
Claire has a reputation for honesty. Claire a la réputation d'être honnête.

to **request** *verb* ▷ see **request** *noun*
**demander [1]**

**request** *noun* ▷ see **request** *verb*
la **demande** *fem*
I've got a special request. J'ai quelque chose à te demander.
on request sur demande
prices on request tarifs sur demande

to **rescue** *verb* ▷ see **rescue** *noun*
**sauver [1]**
They rescued the dog. Ils ont sauvé le chien.

♪ **rescue** *noun* ▷ see **rescue** *verb*
le **secours** *masc*
to come to somebody's rescue venir ❷ [81] au secours de quelqu'un
A policeman came to the woman's rescue. Un agent de police est venu au secours de la dame.
Jack to the rescue! Jack à la rescousse!
• **rescue operation** une opération de sauvetage
• **rescue party** une équipe de secours
• **rescue worker** le & la secouriste

to **research** *verb* ▷ see **research** *noun*
to research into something faire [10] des recherches sur quelque chose
to be well researched être [6] bien documenté

**research** *noun* ▷ see **research** *verb*
la **recherche** *fem*
to do research into something faire [10] des recherches sur quelque chose
She wants to do research into autism. Elle veut faire des recherches sur l'autisme.

**resemblance** *noun*
la **ressemblance** *fem*
There's a strong resemblance between them. Ils se ressemblent beaucoup.
a family resemblance un air de famille

to **resemble** *verb*
**ressembler [1] à**
She resembles her aunt. Elle ressemble à sa tante.

to **resent** *verb*
to resent somebody en vouloir [14] à quelqu'un
She resents me because I won, not her. Elle m'en veut parce que c'est moi qui ai gagné et pas elle.

♪ **reservation** *noun*
la **réservation** *fem*
to make a reservation faire [10] une réservation
Have you made a reservation? Avez-vous fait une réservation?
We don't have a reservation. Nous n'avons pas fait de réservation.

♪ to **reserve** *verb* ▷ see **reserve** *noun*
**réserver [1]**
This table is reserved. Cette table est réservée.

**reserve** *noun* ▷ see **reserve** *verb*
1 (*supply*) la **réserve** *fem*
We have some in reserve. Nous en avons en réserve.
2 (*for wildlife*) la **réserve** *fem*
a nature reserve une réserve naturelle
3 (*person*) le **remplaçant** *masc*, la **remplaçante** *fem*
Ella's on the reserve team. Ella fait partie de l'équipe de réserve.

**reserved** *adjective*
**réservé** *masc*, **réservée** *fem*

**reservoir** *noun*
le **réservoir** *masc*

English–French

**resident** *noun*
le **résident** *masc*, la **résidente** *fem*

**residential** *adjective*
**résidentiel** *masc*, **résidentielle** *fem*

to **resign** *verb*
**démissionner [1]**

**resignation** *noun*
la **démission** *fem*

to **resist** *verb*
**résister [1] à**

to **resit** *verb*
**repasser [1]**

♪ **resort** *noun*
1 (*for holidays*) le **lieu de villégiature**
**a popular holiday resort** un lieu de villégiature très visité
**a ski resort** une station de ski
**a seaside resort** une station balnéaire
2 **as a last resort** en dernier recours
**I'll call her only as a last resort.** Je ne l'appellerai qu'en dernier recours.

to **respect** *verb* ▷ see **respect** *noun*
**respecter [1]**

**respect** *noun* ▷ see **respect** *verb*
le **respect** *masc*
**out of respect for** par respect pour

**respectable** *adjective*
**respectable** *masc & fem*

**respectful** *adjective*
**respectueux** *masc*, **respectueuse** *fem*

**responsibility** *noun*
la **responsabilité** *fem*

♪ **responsible** *adjective*
1 (*to blame*) **responsable** *masc & fem*
**to be responsible for something** être **[6]** responsable de quelque chose
**He's responsible for the delay.** Il est responsable du retard.
2 (*in charge*) **responsable** *masc & fem*
**Kirsty's responsible for booking the rooms.** Kirsty est responsable de la réservation des chambres.
**to make somebody responsible for doing something** charger **[52]** quelqu'un de faire quelque chose
**They made me responsible for collecting the money.** On m'a chargé de collecter l'argent.
3 (*reliable*) **sérieux** *masc*, **sérieuse** *fem*
**Daniel's not very responsible.** Daniel n'est pas très sérieux.
4 **to have a responsible job** avoir **[5]** un poste à responsabilités

♪ **to rest** *verb* ▷ see **rest** *noun*
**se reposer ⓔ [1]**
**Try to rest.** Essaie de te reposer.

♪ **rest** *noun* ▷ see **rest** *verb*
1 (*the remainder*) **the rest** le reste *masc*
**the rest of the bread** le reste du pain
**the rest of the day** le reste de la journée
2 (*the others*) **the rest** les autres *masc pl*
**The rest have gone home.** Les autres sont rentrés.
**What about the rest of them?** Et les autres?
3 (*from work*) le **repos** *masc*,
**ten days' complete rest** dix jours de repos complet
**to have a rest** se reposer ⓔ **[1]**
**You need to have a rest.** Tu as besoin de te reposer.
4 (*a break*) la **pause** *fem*
**to stop for a rest** faire **[10]** une pause
**We stopped for a rest at two o'clock.** Nous avons fait une pause à deux heures.

♪ **restaurant** *noun*
le **restaurant** *masc*
**a Chinese restaurant** un restaurant chinois
**We had a meal in a restaurant.** Nous avons mangé au restaurant.

**restful** *adjective*
**reposant** *masc*, **reposante** *fem*

**restless** *adjective*
**nerveux** *masc*, **nerveuse** *fem*

to **restore** *verb*
1 (*order, peace*) **rétablir [2]**
**It will restore his confidence.** Ça va lui redonner confiance.
2 (*a building, a work of art*) **restaurer [1]**

to **restrain** *verb*
1 (*a person*) **retenir [77]**
2 (*a crowd*) **contenir [77]**

to **restrict** *verb*
**limiter [1]**

**restriction** *noun*
la **limitation** *fem*

♪ **result** *noun*
1 le **résultat** *masc*
**the exam results** les résultats des examens
**Laura's just got her results.** Laura vient d'avoir ses résultats.
2 **as a result** par conséquent
**As a result we missed the ferry.** Par conséquent nous avons raté le ferry.

to **retire** *verb*
(*older person*) **prendre [64] sa retraite**
**holidays for retired people** des vacances pour les retraités





a b c d e f g h i j k l m n o p q r s t u v w x y z

**retirement** *noun*
la **retraite** *fem*

♪ to **return** *verb* ▷ see **return** *noun*
1 (*to come back*) **revenir** Ⓔ **[81]**
**He returned ten minutes later.** Il est revenu dix minutes plus tard.
2 (*to go back*) **retourner** Ⓔ **[1]**
**when they return to school** quand ils retournent à l'école
**He won't be returning to France.** Il ne va pas retourner en France.
3 (*to get home*) **rentrer** Ⓔ **[1]**
**to return from holiday** rentrer de vacances
4 (*to give back*) **rendre [3]**
**Gemma hasn't returned the DVD yet.** Gemma n'a pas encore rendu le DVD.
5 (*to a shop*) **rapporter [1]**
**I had to return the shoes.** J'ai dû rapporter les chaussures.
6 (*a phone call*) **to return somebody's call** rappeler **[18]** quelqu'un
**She never returns my calls.** Elle ne me rappelle jamais.
- **return fare** le prix d'un billet aller-retour
- **return ticket** le billet aller-retour
- **return trip** le voyage de retour

♪ **return** *noun* ▷ see **return** *verb*
1 le **retour** *masc*
**on my return** à mon retour
**the return to normal** le retour à la normale
2 **in return for something** en échange de quelque chose
**in return for his help** en échange de son aide
3 **Many happy returns!** Bon anniversaire!

**reunion** *noun*
la **réunion** *fem*
**a class reunion** une réunion d'anciens élèves

to **reunite** *verb*
**réunir [2]**

to **reveal** *verb*
**révéler [24]**

**revenge** *noun*
la **vengeance** *fem*
**to get your revenge** se venger Ⓔ **[52]**

to **reverse** *verb* ▷ see **reverse** *noun*
1 (*car, bus*) **faire [10] marche arrière**
**The truck was reversing.** Le camion faisait marche arrière.
**Dad reversed the car out of the garage.** Papa a sorti la voiture du garage en marche arrière.
2 **to reverse the charges** faire **[10]** un appel en PCV

**reverse** *noun* ▷ see **reverse** *verb*
1 (*of a coin*) le **revers** *masc*
2 (*of a page*) le **dos** *masc*
3 (*the opposite*) le **contraire** *masc*
4 (*gear in car*) la **marche arrière**

to **review** *verb* ▷ see **review** *noun*
**faire [10] la critique de**
**The film was well reviewed.** Le film a eu une bonne critique.

**review** *noun* ▷ see **review** *verb*
(*of a play, a book, a film*) la **critique** *fem*

to **revise** *verb*
**réviser [1]**

**revision** *noun*
la **révision** *fem*
**to do your revision** faire **[10]** ses révisions
**I still haven't done my revision.** Je n'ai pas encore fait mes révisions.

to **revive** *verb*
**ranimer [1]**

**revolting** *adjective*
**infect** *masc*, **infecte** *fem*

**revolution** *noun*
la **révolution** *fem*

**revolving door** *noun*
la **porte à tambour**

to **reward** *verb* ▷ see **reward** *noun*
**récompenser [1]**

♪ **reward** *noun* ▷ see **reward** *verb*
la **récompense** *fem*
**They're offering a reward of £50.** On offre 50 livres de récompense.
**as a reward for something** en récompense de quelque chose
**as a reward for all their work** en récompense de tout leur travail

**rewarding** *adjective*
**enrichissant** *masc*, **enrichissante** *fem*

to **rewind** *verb*
**rembobiner [1]**

**rhinoceros** *noun*
le **rhinocéros** *masc*

**rhubarb** *noun*
la **rhubarbe** *fem*

**rhyme** *noun*
la **rime** *fem*

**rhythm** *noun*
le **rythme** *masc*

**rib** *noun*
la **côte** *fem*

English-French

a b c d e f g h i j k l m n o p q r s t u v w x y z

English–French

**ribbon** *noun*
le **ruban** *masc*

**rice** *noun*
le **riz** *masc*
**chicken and rice** du poulet avec du riz
**rice pudding** le riz au lait

**rich** *adjective*
**riche** *masc & fem*
**We're not very rich.** Nous ne sommes pas très riches.
**the rich and the poor** les riches et les pauvres

**rid** *adjective*
**to get rid of something** se débarrasser Ⓔ [1] de quelque chose
**We got rid of the car.** Nous nous sommes débarrassés de la voiture.
**Can't you get rid of them?** Tu ne peux pas te débarrasser d'eux?

**riddle** *noun*
la **devinette** *fem*

to **ride** *verb* ▷ see **ride** *noun*
1 **to ride a bike** faire [10] du vélo
**Sam's learning to ride a bike.** Sam apprend à faire du vélo.
2 **to ride a horse** monter Ⓔ [1] à cheval
**I've never ridden a horse.** Je ne suis jamais monté à cheval (*boy speaking*), Je ne suis jamais montée à cheval (*girl speaking*).
**to learn to ride** apprendre [64] à monter à cheval

**ride** *noun* ▷ see **ride** *verb*
1 le **tour à vélo**
**to go for a (bike) ride** faire [10] un tour à vélo
**We went for a ride in the park.** Nous avons fait un tour à vélo au parc.
2 la **promenade à cheval**
**to go for a ride** faire [10] une promenade à cheval
**You can go for rides at the weekend.** On peut faire des promenades le week-end.

**rider** *noun*
1 (*on a horse*) le **cavalier** *masc*, la **cavalière** *fem*
2 (*on a bike*) le & la **cycliste** *masc & fem*
3 (*on a motorbike*) le & la **motocycliste** *masc & fem*

**ridiculous** *adjective*
**ridicule** *masc & fem*

**riding** *noun*
l'**équitation** *fem*
**to go riding** faire [10] de l'équitation
**We went riding every day.** Nous avons fait de l'équitation tous les jours.

- **riding lesson** la leçon d'équitation
- **riding school** le centre équestre

**rifle** *noun*
le **fusil** *masc*

**right** *adjective* ▷ see **right** *adv, noun*
1 (*not left*) **droit** *masc*, **droite** *fem*
**my right hand** ma main droite
2 (*correct*) **bon** *masc*, **bonne** *fem*
**the right answer** la bonne réponse
**the right amount of sugar** la bonne quantité de sucre
**Is this the right address?** Est-ce que c'est la bonne adresse?
3 **to be right** avoir [5] raison
**I'm right.** J'ai raison.
**You're absolutely right.** Tu as tout à fait raison.
4 (*morally*) **to be right to do something** bien faire [10] de faire quelque chose
**You're right to stay at home.** Tu fais bien de rester chez toi.
**He was right not to say anything.** Il a bien fait de ne rien dire.

**right** *adverb* ▷ see **right** *adj, noun*
1 (*direction*) **à droite**
**Turn right at the junction.** Tournez à droite au carrefour.
2 (*correctly*) **comme il faut**
**If you do it right, you'll learn faster.** Si tu le fais comme il faut, tu apprendras plus vite.
**I'm not doing it right.** Je ne le fais pas comme il faut.
3 (*exactly*) **tout**
**right at the beginning** tout au début
**right in the middle of the street** en plein milieu de la rue
**My keys were right at the bottom of my bag.** Mes clés étaient tout au fond de mon sac.
**The headmaster wants to see you right now.** Le directeur veut te voir tout de suite.
4 (*okay*) **bon**
**Right, let's go!** Bon, allons-y!

**right** *noun* ▷ see **right** *adj, adv*
1 (*not left*) la **droite** *fem*
**on the right** à droite
**to drive on the right** rouler [1] à droite
**The supermarket is on the right.** Le supermarché est à droite.
**on my right** à ma droite
**Becky sat on my right.** Becky était assise à ma droite.
2 (*to do something*) le **droit** *masc*
**the right to strike** le droit de grève
**human rights** les droits de l'homme
**to have the right to do something** avoir [5]

a b c d e f g h i j k l m n o p q **r** s t u v w x y z



Ⓔ means the verb takes être to form the perfect

le droit de faire quelque chose
You have no right to say that. Tu n'as pas le droit de dire ça.

to **right-click** *verb* ▷ see **right-click** *noun*
to right-click on the icon cliquer [1] sur l'icône en appuyant sur le bouton droit de la souris

**right-click** *noun* ▷ see **right-click** *verb*
le **clic sur le bouton droit de la souris**

**right-hand** *adjective*
on the right-hand side à droite

**right-handed** *adjective*
**droitier** *masc*, **droitière** *fem*

**rind** *noun*
1 (*on fruit*) la **peau** *fem*
2 (*on cheese*) la **croûte** *fem*

♪ to **ring** *verb* ▷ see **ring** *noun*
1 (*bell, phone*) **sonner [1]**
The phone rang. Le téléphone a sonné.
2 (*to phone*) **appeler [18]**
Ring me when you get back. Appelle-moi quand tu rentres.
I tried to ring you. J'ai essayé de t'appeler.
to ring for something appeler quelque chose
Could you ring for a taxi? Est-ce que tu peux appeler un taxi?
• **to ring back**
**rappeler [18]**
I'll ring you back later. Je te rappellerai tout à l'heure.
• **to ring off**
**raccrocher [1]**
• **ring road** la rocade

**ring** *noun* ▷ see **ring** *verb*
1 (*on the phone*) to give somebody a ring appeler [18] quelqu'un
2 (*for your finger*) la **bague** *fem*
3 (*circle*) le **cercle** *masc*
4 There was a ring at the door. On a sonné à la porte.

**ringtone** *noun*
la **sonnerie** *fem*

to **rinse** *verb*
**rincer [61]**

**riot** *noun*
une **émeute** *fem*

**rioting** *noun*
les **émeutes** *fem pl*

to **rip** *verb*
**déchirer [1]**
• **to rip something apart**
**déchiqueter [1] quelque chose**
• **to rip somebody off**
**arnaquer** (*informal*) **[1] quelqu'un**
to get ripped off se faire Ⓔ [10] arnaquer
• **to rip something open**
**déchirer [1] quelque chose**

**ripe** *adjective*
**mûr** *masc*, **mûre** *fem*

**rip-off** *noun*
une **arnaque** *fem* (*informal*)
It's a total rip-off! C'est de l'arnaque!

♪ to **rise** *verb* ▷ see **rise** *noun*
1 (*sun*) **se lever** Ⓔ **[50]**
2 (*prices, temperatures*) **augmenter [1]**
Prices are rising fast. Les prix augmentent rapidement.
Temperatures are still rising. Les températures augmentent encore.
3 (*water, path*) **monter** Ⓔ **[1]**

**rise** *noun* ▷ see **rise** *verb*
1 la **hausse** *fem*
2 a pay rise une augmentation

to **risk** *verb* ▷ see **risk** *noun*
**risquer [1]**
She even risked her life. Elle a même risqué sa vie.
to risk doing something risquer de faire quelque chose
He risks getting suspended from school. Il risque d'être exclu du lycée.
I don't want to risk it. Je ne veux pas prendre le risque.

♪ **risk** *noun* ▷ see **risk** *verb*
le **risque** *masc*
to take risks prendre [10] des risques
You take too many risks. Tu prends trop de risques.

**rival** *noun*
le **rival** *masc* (*pl* les **rivaux**), la **rivale** *fem*

♪ **river** *noun*
1 la **rivière** *fem*
We picnicked on the edge of a river. Nous avons pique-niqué au bord d'une rivière.
2 le **fleuve** *masc*
the rivers of Europe les fleuves d'Europe

**WORD TIP** *fleuve* is only used for a river which flows directly into the sea like the Thames in Britain or the Seine in France.

• **river bank** la berge

**Riviera** *noun*
the French Riviera la Côte d'Azur

English–French

**road** *noun*
1 la **route** *fem*
the road to London la route de Londres
Is this the right road for Bradford? C'est bien la route pour Bradford?
2 (*in a town*) la **rue** *fem*
on the other side of the road de l'autre côté de la rue
The bus stop's on the other side of the road. L'arrêt de bus est de l'autre côté de la rue.
3 across the road en face
They live just across the road from us. Ils habitent juste en face de chez nous.
4 (*to success, disaster*) la **voie** *fem*
to be on the road to success être [6] sur la voie du succès
• **road accident** un accident de la route
• **road map** la carte routière
• **road rage** la violence au volant

**roadside** *noun*
by the roadside au bord de la route

**road sign** *noun*
le **panneau de signalisation** (*pl* les **panneaux de signalisation**)

**roadworks** *noun*
les **travaux** *masc pl*

**roast** *adjective* ▷ see **roast** *noun*
**rôti** *masc*, **rôtie** *fem*
roast potatoes les pommes de terre rôties
roast beef le rôti de bœuf

**roast** *noun* ▷ see **roast** *adj*
le **rôti** *masc*

to **rob** *verb*
1 (*a person*) **voler [1]**
2 (*a bank*) **dévaliser [1]**

**robber** *noun*
le **voleur** *masc*, la **voleuse** *fem*

**robbery** *noun*
le **vol** *masc*
a bank robbery un hold-up

**robot** *noun*
le **robot** *masc*

**rock** *noun*
1 (*large stone*) le **rocher** *masc*
2 (*material*) la **roche** *fem*
3 (*music*) le **rock** *masc*
a rock band un groupe de rock
a rock concert un concert rock
to dance rock and roll danser [1] le rock

**rock climbing** *noun*
l'**escalade** *fem*
to go rock climbing faire [10] de l'escalade

**rocket** *noun*
1 la **fusée** *fem*
2 (*in salad*) la **roquette** *fem*

**rocking horse** *noun*
le **cheval à bascule**

**rock star** *noun*
la **rock-star** *fem*

**rocky** *adjective*
**rocailleux** *masc*, **rocailleuse** *fem*

**rod** *noun*
(*for fishing*) la **canne à pêche**

**role** *noun*
le **rôle** *masc*

to **roll** *verb* ▷ see **roll** *noun*
1 (*ball, coin, pen*) **rouler [1]**
The coins rolled everywhere. Les pièces ont roulé partout.
The pen rolled off the table. Le stylo est tombé de la table.
2 to roll around on the grass se rouler (e) [1] dans l'herbe
3 to roll your eyes rouler [1] des yeux
Why are you rolling your eyes? Pourquoi est-ce que tu roules des yeux?
4 to roll something into a ball rouler [1] quelque chose en boule
I rolled my sweater into a ball. J'ai roulé mon pull en boule.
• **to roll something out**
(*pastry*) **étendre [3] quelque chose**
• **to roll something up**
1 (*a carpet, a newspaper, a sleeping bag*) **rouler [1] quelque chose**
2 (*your sleeves*) **retrousser [1] quelque chose**
Ross rolled up his sleeves. Ross a retroussé ses manches.

**roll** *noun* ▷ see **roll** *verb*
1 le **rouleau** *masc* (*pl* les **rouleaux**)
a roll of fabric un rouleau de tissu
a toilet roll un rouleau de papier hygiénique
a roll of film une pellicule
2 le **petit pain**
six bread rolls six petits pains
a ham roll un sandwich au jambon

**roller** *noun*
1 (*for paint*) le **rouleau** *masc* (*pl* les **rouleaux**)
2 (*for hair*) le **bigoudi** *masc*
3 (*for surfers*) le **rouleau** (*pl* les **rouleaux**)
• **rollerblades** les rollers *masc pl*



(e) means the verb takes être to form the perfect

- **rollercoaster** les montagnes russes *fem pl*
- **roller skates** les patins à roulettes *masc pl*

**Roman Catholic** *adjective* ▷ see **Roman Catholic** *noun*
**catholique** *masc & fem*

**Roman Catholic** *noun* ▷ see **Roman Catholic** *adj*
le & la **catholique** *masc & fem*

**WORD TIP** Adjectives never have capitals in French, even for religions.

**Romania** *noun*
la **Roumanie**

**Romanian** *adjective* ▷ see **Romanian** *noun*
**roumain** *masc*, **roumaine** *fem*

**Romanian** *noun* ▷ see **Romanian** *adj*
un **Roumain** *masc*, une **Roumaine** *fem*

**romantic** *adjective*
**romantique** *masc & fem*

**roof** *noun*
le **toit** *masc*
- **roof rack** la galerie

**rook** *noun*
1 (*in chess*) la **tour** *fem*
2 (*bird*) le **freux** *masc*

♪ **room** *noun*
1 la **pièce** *fem*
**Mum's in the other room.** Maman est dans l'autre pièce.
**She lives in a three-room flat.** Elle habite dans un appartement de trois pièces.
2 (*bedroom*) la **chambre** *fem*
**Leila's in her room.** Leila est dans sa chambre.
3 (*space*) la **place** *fem*
**There's very little room.** Il y a très peu de place.
**Is there enough room for two?** Est-ce qu'il y a assez de place pour deux?
**There's no room left.** Il n'y a plus de place.
**to make room for something** faire **[10]** de la place pour quelque chose
**I have to make room for the table.** Je dois faire de la place pour la table.
- **roommate** le & la camarade de chambre

**root** *noun*
la **racine** *fem*

**rope** *noun*
la **corde** *fem*

♪ **rose** *noun*
la **rose** *fem*
- **rosebush** le rosier

to **rot** *verb*
**pourrir [2]**

**rota** *noun*
le **tableau de service**

**rotten** *adjective*
(*fruit, wood, weather*) **pourri** *masc*, **pourrie** *fem*

**rough** *adjective*
1 (*scratchy, bumpy*) **rugueux** *masc*, **rugueuse** *fem*
2 (*vague*) **approximatif** *masc*, **approximative** *fem*
**a rough idea** une idée approximative
3 (*stormy*) **agité** *masc*, **agitée** *fem*
4 **to have a rough time** traverser **[1]** une période difficile
5 **to sleep rough** dormir **[2]** à la dure
**They're sleeping rough on the streets.** Ils dorment à la dure dans les rues.

**roughly** *adverb*
**à peu près**
**roughly ten per cent** à peu près dix pour cent

**round** *adverb* ▷ see **round** *adj, noun, prep*
1 **to go round to somebody's house** aller Ⓔ **[7]** chez quelqu'un
**We invited Josh round for lunch.** Nous avons invité Josh à déjeuner.
2 **It's sunny all the year round.** Il y a du soleil toute l'année.

**round** *preposition* ▷ see **round** *adj, adv, noun*
1 **autour de**
**round the city** autour de la ville
2 **to go round the shops** faire **[10]** les magasins
**to go round a museum** visiter **[1]** un musée
**It's just round the corner.** C'est juste au coin de la rue.
**There aren't many shops round here.** Il n'y a pas beaucoup de magasins par ici.

♪ **round** *adjective* ▷ see **round** *adv, noun, prep*
**rond** *masc*, **ronde** *fem*
**a round table** une table ronde
**a round face** un visage rond

**round** *noun* ▷ see **round** *adj, adv, prep*
1 (*in a tournament*) la **manche** *fem*
2 (*of cards*) la **partie** *fem*
3 **a round of drinks** une tournée

**roundabout** *noun*
1 (*for traffic*) le **rond-point** *masc* (*pl* les **ronds-points**)
2 (*in fairground*) le **manège** *masc*

**round trip** *noun*
un **aller-retour**

**route** *noun*
1 (*that you plan*) un **itinéraire** *masc*
**The best route is via Calais.** Le meilleur itinéraire passe par Calais.
**They went by another route.** Ils ont pris un autre chemin.
2 (*of a bus, race*) le **parcours** *masc*
**The 13 takes the same route.** Le numéro 13 suit le même parcours.

**routine** *noun*
la **routine** *fem*

**route** *noun*
1 (*that you plan*) un **itinéraire** *masc*
**The best route is via Calais.** Le meilleur itinéraire passe par Calais.
**They went by another route.** Ils ont pris un autre chemin.
2 (*of a bus, race*) le **parcours** *masc*
**The 13 takes the same route.** Le numéro 13 suit le même parcours.

**row** *verb* ▷ see **row** *noun*
**ramer [1]**
**We rowed across the lake.** Nous avons traversé le lac à la rame.

**row** *noun* ▷ see **row** *verb*
1 (*quarrel*) la **dispute** *fem*
**to have a row** se disputer Ⓔ **[1]**
**I had a row with my parents.** Je me suis disputé avec mes parents.
2 (*noise*) le **vacarme** *masc*
3 (*of houses*) la **rangée** *fem*
4 (*of seats*) le **rang** *masc*

**rowing** *noun*
l'**aviron** *masc*
**to go rowing** faire **[10]** de l'aviron
• **rowing boat** la barque

**royal** *adjective*
**royal** *masc*, **royale** *fem*, **royaux** *masc pl*, **royales** *fem pl*
**the royal family** la famille royale

**to rub** *verb*
**frotter [1]**
**to rub your eyes** se frotter Ⓔ les yeux
• **to rub something out**
**effacer [61] quelque chose**

**rubber** *noun*
1 (*eraser*) la **gomme** *fem*
2 (*material*) le **caoutchouc** *masc*
• **rubber band** un élastique

**rubbish** *adjective* ▷ see **rubbish** *noun*
**nul** *masc*, **nulle** *fem*
**The film was rubbish.** Le film était nul.
**I'm rubbish at maths.** Je suis nul en maths.

**rubbish** *noun* ▷ see **rubbish** *adj*
1 (*for the bin*) les **ordures** *fem pl*
2 (*nonsense*) les **bêtises** *fem pl*
**to talk rubbish** dire **[9]** des bêtises
• **rubbish bin** la poubelle

**rucksack** *noun*
le **sac à dos**
**I put on my rucksack.** J'ai mis mon sac à dos.

**rude** *adjective*
1 (*impolite*) **impoli** *masc*, **impolie** *fem*
**That's rude.** C'est impoli.
2 (*crude*) **grossier** *masc*, **grossière** *fem*
**a rude joke** une plaisanterie grossière
**a rude word** un gros mot

**rug** *noun*
1 le **tapis** *masc*
2 (*blanket*) la **couverture** *fem*

**rugby** *noun*
le **rugby** *masc*
**a rugby match** un match de rugby
**to play rugby** jouer **[1]** au rugby

**to ruin** *verb* ▷ see **ruin** *noun*
1 (*clothes, shoes, a carpet, a book*) **abîmer [1]**
**to ruin your eyesight** s'abîmer **[1]** la vue
2 (*a day, a holiday*) **gâcher [1]**
**It ruined my evening.** Ça m'a gâché la soirée.
3 (*to make poor*) **ruiner [1]**

**ruin** *noun* ▷ see **ruin** *verb*
la **ruine** *fem*
**The house was in ruins.** La maison était en ruines.

**to rule** *verb* ▷ see **rule** *noun*
1 (*king, queen*) **régner [24] sur**
2 (*political party*) **gouverner [1]**

**rule** *noun* ▷ see **rule** *verb*
1 la **règle** *fem*
**the rules of the game** les règles du jeu
**a grammar rule** une règle de grammaire
2 (*in an organization*) le **règlement**
**the school rules** le règlement de l'école
**It's against the rules.** C'est contraire au règlement.



Ⓔ means the verb takes être to form the perfect

3 as a rule en général
As a rule, I don't eat fish. En général, je ne mange pas de poisson.

**ruler** *noun*
la **règle** *fem*

**rum** *noun*
le **rhum** *masc*

to **rummage** *verb*
**fouiller [1]**

**rumour** *noun*
la **rumeur** *fem*

♪ to **run** *verb* ▷ see **run** *noun*
1 **courir [29]**
I ran ten kilometres. J'ai couru dix kilomètres.
He ran across the pitch. Il a traversé le terrain en courant.
I ran down the stairs. J'ai descendu l'escalier en courant.
Somebody was running after us. Quelqu'un nous courait après.
2 (*to organize*) **organiser [1]**
Who's running this concert? Qui organise ce concert?
3 (*a business*) **diriger [52]**
My parents run a small company. Mes parents dirigent une petite entreprise.
4 (*train, bus*) **circuler [1]**
The buses don't run on Sundays. Les bus ne circulent pas le dimanche.
5 to run a bath faire [10] couler un bain
I'll run you a bath. Je vais te faire couler un bain.

• **to run away**
1 **s'enfuir [44]**
The thieves ran away. Les voleurs se sont enfuis.
2 (*child, teenager*) **faire [10] une fugue**
She ran away from home. Elle a fait une fugue.

• **to run into something**
**rentrer Ⓔ [1] dans quelque chose**
The car ran into a lamppost. La voiture est rentrée dans un réverbère.

• **to run out of something**
We've run out of bread. Il ne reste plus de pain.
I'm running out of money. Je n'ai presque plus d'argent.

• **to run somebody over**
**écraser [1] quelqu'un**
to get run over se faire Ⓔ [10] écraser

**run** *noun* ▷ see **run** *verb*
1 to go for a run aller Ⓔ [7] courir
2 (*in cricket*) le **point** *masc*
3 in the long run à long terme

**runner** *noun*
le **coureur** *masc*, la **coureuse** *fem*

**runner-up** *noun*
le **second** *masc*, la **seconde** *fem*

**running** *adjective* ▷ see **running** *noun*
1 running water l'eau courante
2 (*in a row*) **de suite**
three days running trois jours de suite

**running** *noun* ▷ see **running** *adj*
la **course à pied**
to take up running se mettre Ⓔ [11] à la course à pied

**runway** *noun*
la **piste** *fem*

to **rush** *verb* ▷ see **rush** *noun*
1 (*to hurry*) **se dépêcher Ⓔ [1]**
2 (*to make a person hurry*) **bousculer [1]**
3 (*to run*) **se précipiter Ⓔ [1]**
She rushed into the street. Elle s'est précipitée dans la rue.
4 to rush somebody to hospital emmener [50] quelqu'un d'urgence à l'hôpital

**rush** *noun* ▷ see **rush** *verb*
to be in a rush être [6] pressé
There's no rush. Ça ne presse pas.

**rush hour** *noun*
les **heures de pointe** *fem pl*
in the rush hour aux heures de pointe

**Russia** *noun*
la **Russie** *fem*
in Russia en Russie
to Russia en Russie

**Russian** *adjective* ▷ see **Russian** *noun*
**russe** *masc & fem*

**Russian** *noun* ▷ see **Russian** *adj*
1 un & une **Russe** *masc & fem*
the Russians les Russes
2 (*the language*) le **russe** *masc*

**rust** *noun*
la **rouille** *fem*

**rusty** *adjective*
**rouillé** *masc*, **rouillée** *fem*

**rye** *noun*
le **seigle** *masc*
rye bread le pain de seigle

English–French

# S s

**Sabbath** *noun*
1 (*Christian*) le **dimanche** *masc*
2 (*Jewish*) le **sabbat** *masc*

**WORD TIP** Months of the year and days of the week start with small letters in French.

**sack** *noun*
le **sac** *masc*
sacks of corn des sacs de maïs

**sacred** *adjective*
**sacré** *masc*, **sacrée** *fem*

**sacrifice** *noun*
le **sacrifice** *masc*
to make sacrifices faire **[10]** des sacrifices

♪ **sad** *adjective*
1 (*unhappy*) **triste** *masc & fem*
She looks sad. Elle a l'air triste.
to make somebody sad rendre **[3]** quelqu'un triste
It makes me sad. Ça me rend triste.
2 (*pathetic*) **nul** *masc*, **nulle** *fem*
You're so sad! Vous êtes vraiment nuls!

**saddle** *noun*
la **selle** *fem*

**saddlebag** *noun*
la **sacoche** *fem*

**sadly** *adverb*
1 **tristement**
2 (*unfortunately*) **malheureusement**
Sadly, they never saw him again. Malheureusement, ils ne l'ont jamais revu.

♪ **safe** *adjective* ▷ see **safe** *noun*
1 (*unharmed*) **hors de danger**
The children are safe. Les enfants sont hors de danger.
to feel safe se sentir Ⓔ **[58]** en sécurité
I don't feel safe here. Je ne me sens pas en sécurité ici.
2 (*not dangerous*) **pas dangereux** *masc*, **pas dangereuse** *fem*
It's a safe activity. Cette activité n'est pas dangereuse.
Is it safe to swim here? Est-ce qu'on peut se baigner ici sans danger?
The paths are safe. Les sentiers ne sont pas dangereux.
Your bag is safe there. Ton sac ne risque rien là.

**safe** *noun* ▷ see **safe** *adj*
le **coffre-fort** (*pl* les **coffres-forts**)

**safety** *noun*
la **sécurité** *fem*
safety on the roads la sécurité routière
- **safety belt** la ceinture de sécurité
- **safety pin** une épingle de nourrice

**Sagittarius** *noun*
le **Sagittaire** *masc*
Debbie's Sagittarius. Debbie est Sagittaire.

**WORD TIP** Signs of the zodiac do not take an article: *un* or *une*.

**to sail** *verb* ▷ see **sail** *noun*
to sail around the world faire **[10]** le tour du monde en bateau

**sail** *noun* ▷ see **sail** *verb*
la **voile** *fem*

**sailing** *noun*
la **voile** *fem*
She does a lot of sailing. Elle fait beaucoup de voile.
We went sailing in Corsica. Nous avons fait de la voile en Corse.
- **sailing boat** le voilier
- **sailing club** le club de voile

**sailor** *noun*
le **marin** *masc*

**saint** *noun*
le **saint** *masc*, la **sainte** *fem*

**salad** *noun*
la **salade** *fem*
a tomato salad une salade de tomates
- **salad dressing** la vinaigrette

♪ **salami** *noun*
le **saucisson** *masc*

**salary** *noun*
le **salaire** *masc*

♪ **sale** *noun*
1 (*selling*) la **vente** *fem*
the sale of the house la vente de la maison
on sale at the post office en vente au bureau de poste
'For sale' 'À vendre'
2 the sales les soldes *fem pl*
There's a sale on. Il y a des soldes.
I bought it in the sales. Je l'ai acheté en solde.
- **sales assistant** le vendeur, la vendeuse
- **salesman** le représentant
- **saleswoman** la représentante

a b c d e f g h i j k l m n o p q r **s** t u v w x y z



Ⓔ means the verb takes être to form the perfect

**saliva** *noun*
la **salive** *fem*

**salmon** *noun*
le **saumon** *masc*

♪ **salt** *noun*
le **sel** *masc*

♪ **salty** *adjective*
**salé** *masc*, **salée** *fem*

♪ **same** *adjective*
1 **même** *masc & fem*
the same thing la même chose
the same people les mêmes gens
**We arrived at the same time.** Nous sommes arrivés en même temps.
2 the same pareil *masc*, pareille *fem*
**It's not the same.** Ce n'est pas pareil.
**The two bikes are the same.** Les deux vélos sont pareils.
3 the same as comme
**We did the same as everyone else.** On a fait comme tous les autres.

**sample** *noun*
un **échantillon** *masc*

**sand** *noun*
le **sable** *masc*

♪ **sandal** *noun*
la **sandale** *fem*
a pair of sandals une paire de sandales

**sand castle** *noun*
le **château de sable** (*pl* les **châteaux de sable**)

**sand dune** *noun*
la **dune** *fem*

**sandpaper** *noun*
le **papier de verre**

♪ **sandwich** *noun*
le **sandwich** *masc*
a ham sandwich un sandwich au jambon

**sanitary towel** *noun*
la **serviette hygiénique**

**Santa Claus** *noun*
**le père Noël**
to believe in Santa Claus croire **[33]** au père Noël

**sarcasm** *noun*
le **sarcasme** *masc*

**sarcastic** *adjective*
**sarcastique** *masc & fem*
sarcastic comments des remarques sarcastiques

**sardine** *noun*
la **sardine** *fem*

**satchel** *noun*
le **cartable** *masc*

♪ **satellite** *noun*
la **satellite** *masc*
to be transmitted by satellite être **[6]** transmis par satellite
- **satellite dish** une antenne parabolique
- **satellite television** la télévision par satellite

**satisfactory** *adjective*
**satisfaisant** *masc*, **satisfaisante** *fem*

♪ **satisfied** *adjective*
**satisfait** *masc*, **satisfaite** *fem*
satisfied customers des clients satisfaits
**The teacher wasn't satisfied.** La prof n'était pas satisfaite.
to be satisfied with something être **[6]** satisfait de quelque chose
**He's satisfied with my progress.** Il est satisfait de mes progrès.

to **satisfy** *verb*
**satisfaire [10]**

**satisfying** *adjective*
1 (*pleasing*) **satisfaisant** *masc*, **satisfaisante** *fem*
a satisfying result un résultat satisfaisant
2 (*meal*) **consistant** *masc*, **consistante** *fem*

♪ **Saturday** *noun*
le **samedi** *masc*
last Saturday samedi dernier
next Saturday samedi prochain
every Saturday tous les samedis
on Saturdays le samedi
**I'm going out on Saturday.** Je sors samedi.
**See you on Saturday!** À samedi!

**WORD TIP** Months of the year and days of the week start with small letters in French.

**sauce** *noun*
la **sauce** *fem*
in tomato sauce à la sauce tomate

♪ **saucepan** *noun*
la **casserole** *fem*

♪ **saucer** *noun*
la **soucoupe** *fem*

♪ **sausage** *noun*
1 la **saucisse** *fem*
2 (*salami*) le **saucisson** *masc*

♪ to **save** *verb*
1 (*to rescue*) **sauver [1]**
to save somebody's life sauver la vie à quelqu'un
**The doctors saved his life.** Les médecins lui ont sauvé la vie. ▸▸

English-French

2 (*money, food*) **mettre [11] de côté**
**I've saved £60.** J'ai mis soixante livres de côté.
**I walk to school to save money.** Je vais à l'école à pied pour économiser de l'argent.
3 **to save time** gagner **[1]** du temps
**We took a taxi to save time.** On a pris un taxi pour gagner du temps.
4 (*work, a document*) **sauvegarder [1]**
**Always save your documents.** Il faut toujours sauvegarder tes documents.
5 (*a penalty, a shot*) **arrêter [1]**
• **to save up**
**mettre [11] de l'argent de côté**
**I'm saving up to go to Spain.** Je mets de l'argent de côté pour aller en Espagne.

**savings** *plural noun*
les **économies** *fem pl*
• **savings account** la compte d'épargne

**savoury** *adjective*
**salé** *masc*, **salée** *fem*
**I prefer savoury things to sweet things.** J'aime mieux les choses salées que les choses sucrées.

**saw** *noun*
la **scie** *fem*
**to cut wood with a saw** scier **[1]** du bois

**saxophone** *noun*
le **saxophone** *masc*
**to play the saxophone** jouer **[1]** du saxophone

to **say** *verb*
1 **dire [9]**
**What did you say?** Qu'est-ce que tu as dit?
**to say that ...** dire que ...
**She says (that) she's tired.** Elle dit qu'elle est fatiguée.
**They say (that) there's no class.** Ils disent qu'il n'y a pas de cours.
**How do you say 'money' in French?** Comment dire 'money' en français?
**I didn't know what to say.** Je ne savais quoi dire.
2 **to say something again** répéter **[24]** quelque chose
**Could you say it again, please?** Pouvez-vous répéter, s'il vous plaît?
3 (*in expressions*) **let's say** disons
**Let's say, 15 cm.** Disons, quinze centimètres.
**as they say** comme on dit
**'À bientôt', as they say in French.** 'À bientôt', comme on dit en français.

**saying** *noun*
le **dicton** *masc*

**scab** *noun*
la **croûte** *fem*

**scale** *noun*
1 (*of a map, a model*) l'**échelle** *fem*
**a large-scale map** une carte à grande échelle
2 (*extent*) l'**ampleur** *fem*
**to estimate the scale of the disaster** évaluer l'ampleur du désastre
3 (*in music*) la **gamme** *fem*
**to practise your scales** faire **[10]** ses gammes
4 (*of a fish*) une **écaille** *fem*

**scales** *noun*
1 (*for food*) la **balance** *fem*
2 (*for people*) le **pèse-personne** *masc*

**scallop** *noun*
la **coquille Saint-Jacques**

**scalp** *noun*
le **cuir chevelu**

to **scan** *verb*
**scanner [1]**
**to scan a photograph** scanner une photo

**scandal** *noun*
le **scandale** *masc*

**Scandinavia** *noun*
la **Scandinavie** *fem*

**Scandinavian** *adjective*
**scandinave** *masc & fem*

**scanner** *noun*
le **scanner** *masc*

**scar** *noun*
la **cicatrice** *fem*

**scarce** *adjective*
**rare** *masc & fem*
**to become scarce** devenir Ⓔ **[81]** rare
**Water is scarce.** L'eau est rare.

**scarcely** *adverb*
**à peine**
**She scarcely spoke to us.** Elle nous a parlé à peine.

to **scare** *verb* ▷ see **scare** *noun*
**to scare somebody** faire **[10]** peur à quelqu'un
**You scared me!** Tu m'as fait peur!

**scare** *noun* ▷ see **scare** *verb*
1 la **panique** *fem*
**It caused a scare.** Cela a provoqué une panique.
**We got quite a scare.** Nous avons vraiment eu peur.
2 **a bomb scare** une alerte à la bombe

a b c d e f g h i j k l m n o p q r s t u v w x y z

**scarecrow** *noun*
un **épouvantail** *masc*

**scared** *adjective*
**to be scared** avoir **[5]** peur
**I'm scared!** J'ai peur!
**to be scared of something** avoir **[5]** peur de quelque chose
**She's scared of spiders.** Elle a peur des araignées.
**He's scared of his grandmother.** Il a peur de sa grand-mère.
**to be scared of doing something** avoir **[5]** peur de faire quelque chose
**I'm scared of failing the exam.** J'ai peur d'échouer l'examen.

**scarf** *noun*
**1** (*silky*) le **foulard** *masc*
**2** (*long, warm*) une **écharpe** *fem*

**scary** *adjective*
**effrayant** *masc*, **effrayante** *fem*
**a scary experience** une expérience effrayante
**It's quite scary.** Ça fait plutôt peur.

**scene** *noun*
**1** (*of an incident, a crime*) le **lieu** *masc*
**the scene of the crime** le lieu du crime
**to be at the scene** être **[6]** sur les lieux
**The police were at the scene.** La police était sur les lieux.
**2** (*world*) le **monde** *masc*
**on the music scene** dans le monde de la musique
**3** **scenes of violence** des incidents violents

**scenery** *noun*
**1** (*landscape*) le **paysage** *masc*
**2** (*theatrical*) les **décors** *masc pl*

**scent** *noun*
le **parfum** *masc*

**scented** *adjective*
**parfumé** *masc*, **parfumée** *fem*

**schedule** *noun*
le **programme** *masc*
**We have a tight schedule.** Nous avons un programme serré.

**scheme** *noun*
le **projet** *masc*
**It's a scheme to solve traffic problems.** C'est un projet pour résoudre les problèmes de circulation.

**scholarship** *noun*
la **bourse** *fem*
**to win a scholarship** gagner **[1]** une bourse

**school** *noun*
une **école** *fem*
**at school** à l'école
**to go to school** aller **@** **[7]** à l'école
**She goes to the same school as me.** Elle va à la même école que moi.
**I take the bus to school.** Je prends le bus pour aller à l'école.
**I'm going to change schools.** Je vais changer d'école.
**There's no school on Friday.** Il n'y a pas de classe vendredi.
- **schoolbag** le cartable
- **schoolbook** le livre scolaire
- **schoolboy** un écolier
- **schoolchildren** les écoliers *masc pl*
- **schoolfriend** le & la camarade de classe
- **schoolgirl** une écolière
- **school trip** le voyage scolaire
- **school uniform** un uniforme scolaire
- **school year** une année scolaire

**science** *noun*
la **science** *fem*
**the science teacher** le prof des sciences
**I like science.** J'aime la science.

**science fiction** *noun*
la **science-fiction** *fem*
**science fiction films** les films de science-fiction

**scientific** *adjective*
**scientifique** *masc & fem*
**a scientific experiment** une expérience scientifique

**scientist** *noun*
le & la **scientifique** *masc & fem*

**scissors** *plural noun*
les **ciseaux** *masc pl*

to **scoff** *verb*
(*to eat*) **bouffer [1]** (*informal*)
**He's scoffed everything!** Il a tout bouffé!

**scoop** *noun*
(*of ice cream*) la **boule** *fem*
**How many scoops would you like?** Vous voulez combien de boules?
**Two scoops of vanilla.** Deux boules de vanille.

**scooter** *noun*
**1** (*motor scooter*) le **scooter** *masc*
**2** (*for a child*) la **trottinette** *fem*

♪ to **score** *verb* ▷ see **score** *noun*
**marquer [1]**
She scored twice. Elle a marqué deux buts.
to score a goal marquer un but
Ollie scored a goal. Ollie a marqué un but.
I scored three points. J'ai marqué trois points.

**score** *noun* ▷ see **score** *verb*
le **score** *masc*
The score was five two. Le score était cinq à deux.
to keep score compter [1] les points

**Scorpio** *noun*
le **Scorpion** *masc*
Jessica's Scorpio. Jessica est Scorpion.

**WORD TIP** Signs of the zodiac do not take an article: *un* or *une*.

♪ **Scot** *noun*
un **Écossais** *masc*, une **Écossaise** *fem*
the Scots les Écossais *masc pl*

♪ **Scotland** *noun*
l'**Écosse** *fem*
in Scotland en Écosse
to go to Scotland aller Ⓔ [7] en Écosse
Pauline's from Scotland. Pauline est écossaise.

**WORD TIP** Countries and regions in French take *le*, *la* or *les*.

**Scots** *adjective*
**écossais** *masc*, **écossaise** *fem*
a Scots accent un accent écossais

**WORD TIP** Adjectives never have capitals in French, even for nationality or regional origin.

**Scotsman** *noun*
un **Écossais** *masc*

**Scotswoman** *noun*
une **Écossaise** *fem*

♪ **Scottish** *adjective*
**écossais** *masc*, **écossaise** *fem*
a Scottish dance une danse écossaise
Scottish people les Écossais

**WORD TIP** Adjectives never have capitals in French, even for nationality or regional origin.

**scout** *noun*
le **scout** *masc*

**scrambled eggs** *noun*
les **œufs brouillés**

**scrap** *noun*
1 (*of cloth, food*) le **bout** *masc*
a scrap of paper un bout de papier
some scraps of bread quelques bouts de pain
2 (*a fight*) la **bagarre** *fem*
a scrap in the playground une bagarre dans la cour
• **scrapbook** un album

to **scrape** *verb*
1 **gratter [1]**
2 to scrape your knees s'écorcher [1] les genous

to **scratch** *verb* ▷ see **scratch** *noun*
1 to scratch (yourself) se gratter Ⓔ [1]
to scratch your head se gratter Ⓔ [1] la tête
2 (*the paintwork*) **érafler [1]**

**scratch** *noun* ▷ see **scratch** *verb*
1 (*on your skin*) une **égratignure** *fem*
2 (*on a surface*) la **rayure** *fem*
3 (*from the start*) from scratch
We had to start from scratch. Nous avons dû partir de zéro.

♪ to **scream** *verb* ▷ see **scream** *noun*
**crier [1]**
to scream with fright crier de peur

**scream** *noun* ▷ see **scream** *verb*
le **cri** *masc*

♪ **screen** *noun*
un **écran** *masc*
on the screen à l'écran
on the computer screen sur l'écran d'ordinateur

to **screw** *verb* ▷ see **screw** *noun*
**visser [1]**
to screw the top on a bottle visser le bouchon sur une bouteille.

**screw** *noun* ▷ see **screw** *verb*
la **vis** *fem*

**screwdriver** *noun*
le **tournevis** *masc*

to **scribble** *verb*
**griffonner [1]**

to **scrub** *verb*
(*a saucepan*) **récurer [1]**
to scrub your nails se brosser Ⓔ [1] les ongles

**scuba diving** *noun*
la **plongée sous-marine**
to go scuba diving faire [10] la plongée sous-marine

**sculptor** *noun*
le **sculpteur** *masc*, la **sculpteuse** *fem*

**sculpture** *noun*
la **sculpture** *fem*

♪ **sea** *noun*
la **mer** *fem*
a holiday by the sea des vacances au bord de la mer

♪ **seafood** *noun*
les **fruits de mer**
I love seafood. J'adore les fruits de mer.

**seagull** *noun*
la **mouette** *fem*

to **seal** *verb* ▷ see **seal** *noun*
*(an envelope)* **coller [1]**
It wasn't sealed properly. Ce n'était pas bien collé.

**seal** *noun* ▷ see **seal** *verb*
*(animal)* le **phoque** *masc*

**seaman** *noun*
le **marin** *masc*

♪ to **search** *verb* ▷ see **search** *noun*
1 *(a house, a bag)* **fouiller [1]**
The police are searching the area. La police est en train de fouiller le quartier.
They searched us at the airport. Ils nous ont fouillé à l'aéroport.
2 *(for something, someone)* **chercher [1]**
They're still searching for the family. Ils cherchent encore la famille.
I've searched everywhere for the scissors. J'ai cherché les ciseaux partout.

**search** *noun* ▷ see **search** *verb*
1 la **fouille** *fem*
to carry out a search of something fouiller [1] quelque chose
2 *(Computers)* la **recherche**
to do a search effectuer [1] une recherche

**seashell** *noun*
le **coquillage** *masc*

**seasick** *adjective*
to be seasick avoir [5] le mal de mer

**seaside** *noun*
at the seaside au bord de la mer
We spent a week at the seaside. Nous avons passé une semaine au bord de la mer.
- **seaside resort** la station balnéaire

♪ **season** *noun*
la **saison** *fem*
the rugby season la saison de rugby
during the holiday season pendant la période des vacances
Strawberries are in season. C'est la saison des fraises.
- **season ticket** la carte d'abonnement

♪ **seat** *noun*
1 *(part of a chair)* le **siège** *masc*
the front seat le siège avant
the back seat le siège arrière
to be sitting in the front seat être [6] assis à l'avant.
Have a seat. Asseyez-vous.
2 *(that you book)* la **place** *fem*
to book a seat réserver [1] une place
I'd like a window seat. Je voudrais une place côté fenêtre.
There are no more seats. Il n'y a plus de places.

**seatbelt** *noun*
la **ceinture de sécurité**
to fasten your seatbelt attacher [1] sa ceinture de sécurité

**seaweed** *noun*
les **algues** *fem pl*

♪ **second** *adjective* ▷ see **second** *noun*
1 **deuxième** *masc & fem*
for the second time pour la deuxième fois
to come second arriver ⓔ [1] en deuxième position
2 *(in dates)* the second of July le deux juillet
3 the Second World War la Seconde Guerre mondiale

♪ **second** *noun* ▷ see **second** *adj*
la **seconde** *fem*
Can you wait a second? Est-ce que tu peux attendre une seconde?
It takes a few seconds. Ça prend quelques secondes.

♪ **secondary school** *noun*
1 le **collège** *masc (up to the end of the equivalent of Year 10)*
2 le **lycée** *masc (for the equivalent of Years 11 to 13)*

**second class** *adjective, adverb*
1 to travel second class voyager [52] en deuxième classe
a seat in second class une place en deuxième classe
2 *(average)* a second class team une équipe de niveau très moyen

♪ **secondhand** *adjective, adverb*
**d'occasion**
a secondhand bike un vélo d'occasion
I bought it secondhand. Je l'ai acheté d'occasion.

**secondly** *adverb*
**deuxièmement**

**secret** *adjective* ▷ see **secret** *noun*
**secret** *masc*, **secrète** *fem*

**secret** *noun* ▷ see **secret** *adj*
le **secret** *masc*
**to keep a secret** garder [1] un secret
**Can you keep a secret?** Est-ce que tu peux garder un secret?
**He sees her in secret.** Il la voit en secret.

**secretarial college** *noun*
une **école de secrétariat**

**secretary** *noun*
le & la **secrétaire** *masc & fem*
**She's a secretary.** Elle est secrétaire.

**secretly** *adverb*
**secrètement**

**sect** *noun*
la **secte** *fem*

**section** *noun*
1 la **partie** *fem*
**a section of the train** une partie du train
2 (*in a shop, a library*) le **rayon** *masc*
**in the children's section** au rayon enfants

**security** *noun*
la **sécurité** *fem*
• **security guard** le vigile

to **see** *verb*
1 (*in general*) **voir** [13]
**I saw Becky yesterday.** J'ai vu Becky hier.
**Have you seen the film?** Est-ce que tu as vu le film?
**Did you see that programme?** Est-ce que tu as vu cette émission?
**I'm going to see the doctor.** Je vais voir le médecin.
**'Can Luke come?' — 'We'll see.'** 'Est-ce que Luke peut venir?' — 'On verra.'
2 **to be able to see** voir [13]
**Can you see it?** Est-ce que tu le vois?
**I can't see anything.** Je ne vois rien.
3 (*saying goodbye*) **See you!** Salut!, À plus! (*informal*)
**See you on Saturday!** À samedi!
**See you soon!** À bientôt!
• to **see to something**
**s'occuper** [1] **de quelque chose**
**Could you see to the drinks, please?** Tu peux t'occuper des boissons, s'il te plaît?

**seed** *noun*
la **graine** *fem*
**to plant seeds** semer [50] des graines

to **seem** *verb*
1 **paraître** [57]
**it seems that ...** il paraît que ...
**It seems that he's left.** Il paraît qu'il est parti.
**It seems odd to me.** Ça me paraît bizarre.
2 (*to look, to appear to be*) **avoir** [5] **l'air**
**to seem shy** avoir l'air timide
**Amy seemed tired.** Amy avait l'air fatiguée.
**to seem to be ...** avoir [5] l'air d'être ...
**The pool seems to be closed.** La piscine a l'air d'être fermée.

**seesaw** *noun*
la **balançoire** *fem*

to **select** *verb*
**sélectionner** [1]
**to be selected for the team** être [6] sélectionné pour l'équipe

**selection** *noun*
la **sélection** *fem*

**self-confidence** *noun*
la **confiance en soi**
**He has a lot of self-confidence.** Il a beaucoup de confiance en lui.

**self-confident** *adjective*
**assuré** *masc*, **assurée** *fem*
**to be self-confident** être [6] sûr de soi

**self-conscious** *adjective*
**timide** *masc & fem*

**self-employed** *adjective*
**a self-employed person** un travailleur indépendant
**to be self-employed** travailler [1] à son compte

**selfish** *adjective*
**égoïste** *masc & fem*

to **sell** *verb*
**vendre** [3]
**Do you sell stamps?** Est-ce que vous vendez des timbres?
**The house has been sold.** La maison a été vendue.
**to sell something to somebody** vendre quelque chose à quelqu'un
**I sold him my bike.** Je lui ai vendu mon vélo.
• **sell-by date** la date limite de vente

**seller** *noun*
le **vendeur** *masc*, la **vendeuse** *fem*

**Sellotape**® *noun*
le **Scotch**® *masc*
**to stick something with Sellotape** scotcher [1] quelque chose (*informal*)

**semicircle** *noun*
le **demi-cercle** *masc*

**semicolon** *noun*
le **point-virgule** *masc*

**semi-detached house** *noun*
la **maison jumelée**
**We live in a semi-detached house.** Nous habitons dans une maison jumelée.

**semi-final** *noun*
la **demi-finale** *fem*

**semi-skimmed milk** *noun*
le **lait demi-écrémé**

♪ to **send** *verb*
**envoyer [40]**
**to send an email** envoyer un e-mail
**to send something to somebody** envoyer quelque chose à quelqu'un
**I sent her a Valentine card.** Je lui ai envoyé une carte de la Saint-Valentin.
**Send me a text.** Envoie-moi un texto.
- to **send somebody back**
**renvoyer [40] quelqu'un**
**She sent me back home.** Elle m'a renvoyé chez moi.
- to **send something back**
**renvoyer [40] quelque chose**
**I'm going to send the book back.** Je vais renvoyer le livre.

**sender** *noun*
un **expéditeur** *masc*, une **expéditrice** *fem*

**senior citizen** *noun*
une **personne âgée**

**sensation** *noun*
1 (*feeling*) la **sensation** *fem*
2 (*impact*) la **sensation** *fem*
**She caused a sensation.** Elle a fait sensation.

**sensational** *adjective*
**sensationnel** *masc*, **sensationnelle** *fem*

♪ **sense** *noun*
1 le **sens** *masc*
**It doesn't make sense.** Ça n'a pas de sens.
**That makes sense.** Ça paraît logique.
**to have the sense to do something** avoir [5] le bon sens de faire quelque chose
**She had the sense to tell me.** Elle a eu le bon sens de me le dire.
**I can't make sense of it.** Je ne le comprends pas.
- **sense of humour** le sens de l'humour
- **sense of smell** l'odorat *masc*
- **sense of touch** le toucher

♪ **sensible** *adjective*
**raisonnable** *masc & fem*
**He's very sensible.** Il est très raisonnable.
**It's a sensible decision.** C'est une décision raisonnable.

♪ **sensitive** *adjective*
**sensible** *masc & fem*
**I've got sensitive skin.** J'ai la peau sensible.
**She's very sensitive.** Elle est très sensible.

to **sentence** *verb* ▷ see **sentence** *noun*
**condamner [1]**
**to be sentenced to death** être [6] condamné à mort

♪ **sentence** *noun* ▷ see **sentence** *verb*
1 (*in writing*) la **phrase** *fem*
Écris une phrase en français. **Write a sentence in French.**
2 (*Law*) **the death sentence** la peine de mort

**sentimental** *adjective*
**sentimental** *masc*, **sentimentale** *fem*, **sentimentaux** *masc pl*, **sentimentales** *fem pl*

to **separate** *verb* ▷ see **separate** *adj*
1 **séparer [1]**
**The teacher separated them.** Le prof les a séparés.
2 (*couple*) **se séparer ❷ [1]**
**Her parents have separated.** Ses parents se sont séparés.

♪ **separate** *adjective* ▷ see **separate** *verb*
1 (*apart*) **à part**
**in a separate pile** dans une pile à part
**on a separate sheet of paper** sur une feuille à part
2 (*different*) **autre** *masc & fem*
**in a separate box** dans une autre boîte
**That's a separate problem.** C'est un autre problème.
3 **We have separate rooms.** Nous avons chacun notre chambre.

**separately** *adverb*
**séparément**

**separation** *noun*
la **séparation** *fem*

**September** *noun*
**septembre** *masc*
**in September** en septembre

**WORD TIP** Months of the year and days of the week start with small letters in French.

**sequel** *noun*
la **suite** *fem*
**in the film's sequel** dans la suite au film

**sequence** *noun*
1 (*of events*) la **série** *fem*
2 (*in a film*) la **séquence** *fem*

**sergeant** *noun*
1 (*in the police*) le **brigadier** *masc*
2 (*in the army*) le **sergent** *masc*

English–French

**serial** *noun*
le **feuilleton** *masc*
a TV serial un feuilleton télévisé
- **serial killer** un auteur de meurtres en série

**series** *noun*
la **série** *fem*
a television series une série télévisée
a series of strange events une série d'événements bizarres

**serious** *adjective*
1 (*illness, injury, mistake, problem*) **grave** *masc & fem*
a serious problem un grave problème.
It's not a serious mistake. Ce n'est pas une grave erreur.
2 (*earnest*) **sérieux** *masc*, **sérieuse** *fem*
a serious discussion une discussion sérieuse
Are you serious? Sérieusement?
to be serious about doing something avoir **[5]** vraiment l'intention de faire quelque chose
I'm serious about looking for a job. J'ai vraiment l'intention de chercher un travail.

**seriously** *adverb*
1 (*ill, injured*) **gravement**
She's seriously ill. Elle est gravement malade.
2 (*no joking*) **sérieusement**
Seriously, I have to go. Sérieusement, je dois partir.
3 to take somebody seriously prendre **[64]** quelqu'un au sérieux
She doesn't take me seriously. Elle ne me prend pas au sérieux.

**servant** *noun*
le & la **domestique** *masc & fem*

to **serve** *verb* ▷ see **serve** *noun*
1 (*food, a meal*) **servir [71]**
They served the fish with a lemon sauce. Ils ont servi le poisson accompagné d'une sauce au citron.
2 (*in tennis*) **servir [71]**
3 It serves him right! C'est bien fait pour lui!

**serve** *noun* ▷ see **serve** *verb*
(*in tennis*) le **service** *masc*
Whose serve is it? C'est à qui de servir?

to **service** *verb* ▷ see **service** *noun*
**réviser [1]**
to have your car serviced faire **[10]** réviser sa voiture

**service** *noun* ▷ see **service** *verb*
1 (*in a restaurants, hotels*) le **service** *masc*
room service le service de chambre
Is service included? Est-ce que le service est compris?
Service is not included. Le service n'est pas compris.
2 (*for the public*) le **service** *masc*
a bus service un service d'autobus
Call the emergency services! Appelle police-secours!
3 (*for cars*) la **révision** *fem*
4 (*in church*) un **office** *masc*

**service area** *noun*
une **aire de services**

**service charge** *noun*
le **service** *masc*
There's no service charge. Le service est compris.

**service station** *noun*
la **station-service** *fem* (*pl* les **stations-service**)

**serviette** *noun*
la **serviette** *fem*

**session** *noun*
la **séance** *fem*
a training session une séance d'entraînement
a recording session une séance d'enregistrement

to **set** *verb* ▷ see **set** *adj, noun*
1 (*a date, a time*) **fixer [1]**
They've set the date. Ils ont fixé la date.
2 (*a record*) **établir [2]**
She set a new world record. Elle a établi un nouveau record mondial.
3 (*the table, an alarm clock*) **mettre [11]**
Who's setting the table? Qui met la table?
I've set my alarm for seven. J'ai mis mon réveil à sept heures.
to set your watch régler **[24]** sa montre
4 (*sun*) **se coucher** Ⓔ **[1]**
- to **set off**
**partir** Ⓔ **[58]**
We're setting off at ten. Nous allons partir à dix heures.
- to **set off something**
1 (*a firework*) **faire [10] partir**
2 (*a bomb*) **faire [10] exploser**
3 (*an alarm*) **déclencher [1]**
- to **set out**
**partir** Ⓔ **[58]**
They set out for Calais yesterday. Ils sont partis pour Calais hier.

**set** *adjective* ▷ see **set** *noun, verb*
**fixe** *masc & fem*
at a set time à une heure fixe
There's a set menu. Il y a un menu.

Ⓔ means the verb takes être to form the perfect

a b c d e f g h i j k l m n o p q r s t u v w x y z

**set** *noun* ▷ see **set** *adj, verb*
1 (*games*) le **jeu** *masc* (*pl* les **jeux**)
a chess set un jeu d'échecs
2 a train set un petit train
3 (*in tennis*) le **set** *masc*

**settee** *noun*
le **canapé** *masc*

to **settle** *verb*
(*a bill, an argument*) **régler [24]**
**Have you settled the bill?** Est-ce que tu as réglé l'addition?

**seven** *number*
**sept**
**Lucy's seven.** Lucy a sept ans.

**seventeen** *number*
**dix-sept**
**Matt's seventeen.** Matt a dix-sept ans.

**seventeenth** *adjective*
1 **dix-sept** *masc & fem*
2 (*in dates*) **the seventeenth of June** le dix-sept juin

**seventh** *adjective*
1 **septième** *masc & fem*
**on the seventh floor** au septième étage
2 (*in dates*) **the seventh of July** le sept juillet

**seventies** *plural noun*
**the seventies** les années soixante-dix
**in the seventies** aux années soixante-dix

**seventieth** *adjective*
**soixante-dixième** *masc & fem*
**It's her seventieth birthday.** Elle fête ses soixante-dix ans.

**seventy** *number*
**soixante-dix**
**Grandma's seventy.** Ma grand-mère a soixante-dix ans.

**several** *adjective, pronoun*
**plusieurs** *masc & fem*
**several people** plusieurs personnes
**several times** plusieurs fois
**I've seen several of her films.** J'ai vu plusieurs de ses films.

**severe** *adjective*
1 (*serious*) **grave** *masc & fem*
**severe injuries** des blessures graves
2 (*weather*) **rigoureux** *masc*, **rigoureuse** *fem*
3 (*in manner*) **sévère** *masc & fem*

to **sew** *verb*
**coudre [28]**

**sewer** *noun*
un **égout** *masc*

**sewing** *noun*
la **couture** *fem*
• **sewing machine** la machine à coudre

**sex** *noun*
1 (*gender*) le **sexe** *masc*
2 (*intercourse*) les **rapports sexuels** *masc pl*
**to have sex with someone** coucher [1] avec quelqu'un
• **sex education** l'éducation sexuelle *fem*

**sexism** *noun*
le **sexisme** *masc*

**sexist** *adjective*
**sexiste** *masc & fem*
**sexist remarks** des propos sexistes

**sexual** *adjective*
**sexuel** *masc*, **sexuelle** *fem*
• **sexual harassment** le harcèlement sexuel

**sexuality** *noun*
la **sexualité** *fem*

**sexy** *adjective*
**sexy** *invariable adj*

**shade** *noun*
1 (*out of the sun*) l'**ombre** *fem*
**in the shade** à l'ombre
**The tent is in the shade.** La tente est à l'ombre.
2 (*of a colour*) le **ton** *masc*
**a paler shade** un ton plus pâle

**shadow** *noun*
une **ombre** *fem*

to **shake** *verb*
1 (*to tremble*) **trembler [1]**
**My hands are shaking.** J'ai les mains qui tremblent.
2 **to shake something** secouer [1] quelque chose
**Shake the bottle before you open it.** Secoue la bouteille avant de l'ouvrir.
**The event shook the world.** L'événement a secoué le monde entier.
3 **to shake hands with somebody** serrer [1] la main à quelqu'un
**She shook hands with me.** Elle m'a serré la main.
**We shook hands.** Nous nous sommes serré la main.

**shaken** *adjective*
**bouleversé** *masc*, **bouleversée** *fem*
**She looked shaken.** Elle avait l'air bouleversée.

**shall** *verb*
**Shall I come with you?** Tu veux que je t'accompagne?
**Shall we stop now?** Si on s'arrêtait maintenant?
**What shall we do?** Qu'est-ce qu'on fait?

**shallow** *adjective*
**peu profond** *masc*, **peu profonde** *fem*
**The water's very shallow here.** L'eau est très peu profonde ici.
- **shallow end** la partie la moins profonde de la piscine

**shambles** *noun*
la **pagaille** *fem* (*informal*)
**It was a complete shambles!** Ça a été la pagaille complète!

**shame** *noun*
1 **What a shame!** Quel dommage!
**It's a real shame.** C'est vraiment dommage.
**It's a shame that she can't come.** C'est dommage qu'elle ne puisse pas venir.
2 (*guilty thought*) la **honte** *fem*

**shampoo** *noun*
le **shampooing** *masc*
**I bought some shampoo.** J'ai acheté du shampooing.

**shamrock** *noun*
le **trèfle** *masc*

**shandy** *noun*
le **panaché** *masc*

**shape** *noun*
la **forme** *fem*
**in the shape of something** en forme de quelque chose
**a building in the shape of a boat** un bâtiment en forme de bateau

to **share** *verb* ▷ see **share** *noun*
1 (*a room, costs with one person*) **partager [52]**
**I'm sharing a room with Emma.** Je partage une chambre avec Emma.
2 (*between several people*) **se partager Ⓔ [52]**
**It will be quicker if we share the task.** Ça ira plus vite si nous nous partageons la tâche.
- to **share out something**
**partager [52] quelque chose**
**We shared out the pizza.** Nous avons partagé la pizza.

**share** *noun* ▷ see **share** *verb*
1 (*proportion*) la **part** *fem*
**the biggest share** la plus grande part
**your share of the bill** ta part de l'addition
**He paid his fair share.** Il a payé sa part.
2 (*in a company*) une **action** *fem*

**shark** *noun*
le **requin** *masc*

**sharp** *adjective*
1 (*scissors*) **bien aiguisé** *masc*, **bien aiguisée** *fem*
2 (*knife*) **tranchant** *masc*, **tranchante** *fem*
3 (*pencil*) **bien taillé** *masc*, **bien taillée** *fem*
4 (*bend*) **brusque** *masc & fem*
5 (*clever*) **intelligent** *masc*, **intelligente** *fem*

to **sharpen** *verb*
1 (*a pencil*) **tailler [1]**
2 (*a knife*) **aiguiser [1]**

**sharpener** *noun*
le **taille-crayon** *masc*

to **shave** *verb*
1 (*to have a shave*) **se raser Ⓔ [1]**
2 (*to shave something*) **to shave your beard** se raser la barbe
**to shave your legs** se raser Ⓔ **[1]** les jambes

**shaver** *noun*
le **rasoir** *masc*

**shaving cream** *noun*
la **crème à raser**

**shaving foam** *noun*
la **mousse à raser**

**she** *pronoun*
**elle**
**She's a student.** Elle est étudiante.
**She lives in Glasgow.** Elle habite à Glasgow.
**She's a teacher.** C'est un professeur.
**Who is she?** C'est qui?
**Here she is!** La voici!
**There she is!** La voilà!

**shed** *noun*
la **remise** *fem*

**sheep** *noun*
le **mouton** *masc*
- **sheepdog** le chien de berger (*pl* les chiens de berger)

**sheet** *noun*
1 (*for a bed*) le **drap** *masc*
2 (*of paper*) la **feuille** *fem*
**a sheet of wrapping paper** une feuille de papier-cadeau

**shelf** *noun*
1 (*in the home*) une **étagère** *fem*
**I have shelves in my room.** J'ai une étagère dans ma chambre.
2 (*in shops, fridges*) le **rayon** *masc*
**It's on the top shelf.** C'est au rayon le plus haut.

**shell** *noun*
1 (*of an egg, a nut*) la **coquille** *fem*
2 (*seashell*) le **coquillage** *masc*
3 (*explosive*) un **obus** *masc*
- **shellfish** les fruits de mer

**shelter** *noun*
1 l'**abri** *masc*
**in the shelter of a tree** à l'abri d'un arbre





Ⓔ means the verb takes être to form the perfect

to take shelter from something se mettre Ⓔ [11] à l'abri de quelque chose
They took shelter from the rain. Ils se sont mis à l'abri de la pluie.
2 a bus shelter un abribus®

**shepherd** *noun*
le **berger** *masc*

**sheriff** *noun*
le **shérif** *masc*

**Shetland Islands** *plural noun*
les **îles Shetland**

**shield** *noun*
le **bouclier** *masc*

to **shift** *verb* ▷ see **shift** *noun*
to shift something déplacer [61] quelque chose
Can you help me shift this table? Est-ce que tu peux m'aider à déplacer cette table?

**shift** *noun* ▷ see **shift** *verb*
le **service** *masc*
the night shift le service de nuit
to be on night shift être [6] de nuit

**shifty** *adjective*
**louche** *masc & fem*
He looks a bit shifty. Il a l'air un peu louche.

**shin** *noun*
le **tibia** *masc*

♪ to **shine** *verb*
**briller** [1]
The sun's shining again. Le soleil brille encore.
The tiles shone. Les carreaux brillaient.

**shiny** *adjective*
**brillant** *masc*, **brillante** *fem*
shiny hair des cheveux brillants

♪ **ship** *noun*
1 (*in general*) le **bateau** *masc*
a passenger ship un paquebot
2 (*naval ship*) le **navire** *masc*
- **shipbuilding** la construction navale
- **shipyard** le chantier naval

♪ **shirt** *noun*
1 (*man's*) la **chemise** *fem*
2 (*woman's*) le **chemisier** *masc*

to **shiver** *verb*
**frissonner** [1]
We were shivering with cold. On frissonnait de froid.

to **shock** *verb* ▷ see **shock** *noun*
**choquer** [1]
He likes to shock people. Il aime choquer les gens.

♪ **shock** *noun* ▷ see **shock** *verb*
1 le **choc** *masc*
It was a shock. Ça a été un choc.
It gave me a shock. J'ai eu un choc.
to be in shock être [6] en état de choc
2 (*electric*) la **décharge**
She got an electric shock. Elle a pris une décharge.

**shocked** *adjective*
**choqué** *masc*, **choquée** *fem*
We were shocked. Nous avons été choqués.

**shocking** *adjective*
**choquant** *masc*, **choquante** *fem*

♪ **shoe** *noun*
la **chaussure** *fem*
a pair of shoes une paire de chaussures
to take off your shoes enlever [50] ses chaussures
to put on your shoes mettre [11] ses chaussures
- **shoelace** le lacet
- **shoe polish** le cirage
- **shoe shop** le magasin de chaussures

♪ to **shoot** *verb*
1 (*to fire*) **tirer** [1]
She shot him in the leg. Elle lui a tiré une balle dans la jambe.
He shot himself in the head. Il s'est tiré une balle dans la tête.
2 (*to kill*) **abattre** [21]
He was shot by terrorists. Il a été abattu par des terroristes.
3 (*a film*) **tourner** [1]
The film was shot in Dublin. Le film a été tourné à Dublin.
4 (*in football, hockey*) **shooter** [1]
5 (*to execute*) **fusiller** [1]

**shooting** *noun*
1 (*as a sport*) le **tir** *masc*
2 (*murder*) le **meurtre** *masc*

♪ **shop** *noun*
1 le **magasin** *masc*
a shoe shop un magasin de chaussures
to go round the shops faire [10] les magasins
We went round the shops. On a fait les magasins.
2 to go to the shops aller Ⓔ [7] faire les courses
She's gone to the shops. Elle est allée faire les courses.
- **shop assistant** le vendeur, la vendeuse
- **shopkeeper** le commerçant, la commerçante ▸▸

- **shoplifter** le voleur à l'étalage, la voleuse à l'étalage
- **shoplifting** le vol à l'étalage

**shopping** *noun*
1 les **courses** *fem pl*
2 (*to buy food*) **to do the shopping** faire **[10]** des courses
**I've got a lot of shopping to do.** J'ai beaucoup de courses à faire.
3 (*for clothes, presents*) **to go shopping** faire **[10]** du shopping
**Mark hates going shopping.** Mark déteste faire du shopping.
- **shopping bag** le sac à provisions
- **shopping centre** le centre commercial
- **shopping mall** le centre commercial
- **shopping trolley** le chariot

**shop window** *noun*
la **vitrine** *fem*

**short** *adjective*
1 (*in length*) **court** *masc*, **courte** *fem*
**a short dress** une robe courte
**She has short hair.** Elle a les cheveux courts.
**She's quite short.** Ele est assez petite.
2 (*not lasting long*) **petit** *masc*, **petite** *fem*
**for a short while** pendant un petit moment
**I went for a short walk.** J'ai fait une petite promenade.
3 **to be short of something** ne pas avoir **[5]** beaucoup de quelque chose
**I'm short of money.** Je n'ai pas d'argent.

**shortage** *noun*
la **pénurie** *fem*

**shortbread** *noun*
le **sablé** *masc*

**short cut** *noun*
le **raccourci** *masc*
**to take a short cut** prendre **[64]** un raccourci

to **shorten** *verb*
1 (*a skirt, a sleeve*) **raccourcir [2]**
2 (*a stay, a journey*) **écourter [1]**

**shortly** *adverb*
**bientôt**

**shorts** *plural noun*
le **short** *masc*
**Where are my red shorts?** Où est mon short rouge?

**short-sighted** *adjective*
**myope** *masc & fem*

**short story** *noun*
la **nouvelle** *fem*

**shot** *noun*
1 (*from a gun*) le **coup de feu** *masc* (*pl* les **coups de feu**)
**There were shots.** Il y a eu des coups de feu.
2 (*photo*) la **photo** *fem*
**I took a few shots of the castle.** J'ai pris quelques photos du château.
- **shotgun** le fusil de chasse (*pl* les fusils de chasse)

**should** *verb*
1 (*ought to*) **devoir [8]**
**You should ask Farida.** Tu devrais demander à Farida.
**The pasta should be cooked now.** Les pâtes devraient être cuites maintenant.
2 (*with conditional*) **You should have checked.** Tu aurais dû vérifier.
**I shouldn't have told her.** Je n'aurais pas dû le lui dire.
3 (*in suggestions*) **I should forget it if I were you.** À ta place je l'oublierais.
4 (*expressing opinion, surprise*) **I should think he's forgotten.** À mon avis, il a oublié.
**'I had to apologize.' — 'I should think so too!'** 'J'ai dû m'excuser.' — 'Je pense bien!'

**shoulder** *noun*
une **épaule** *fem*
**Straighten your shoulders.** Redressez les épaules.
- **shoulder bag** le sac à bandoulière

to **shout** *verb* ▷ see **shout** *noun*
**crier [1]**
**Stop shouting!** Arrêtez de crier!
**There's no need to shout.** Ce n'est pas la peine de crier.
**to shout for help** crier au secours

**shout** *noun* ▷ see **shout** *verb*
le **cri** *masc*

**shovel** *noun*
la **pelle** *fem*

to **show** *verb* ▷ see **show** *noun*
**montrer [1]**
**to show something to somebody** montrer quelque chose à quelqu'un
**I'll show you my photos.** Je te montrerai mes photos.
**Show me what you found.** Montre-moi ce que tu as trouvé.
**to show somebody how to do something** montrer à quelqu'un comment on fait quelque chose
**He showed me how to download songs.** Il m'a montré comment on télécharge les chansons.
- to **show somebody around**

**faire [10] visiter quelqu'un**
**I'll show you around.** Je te ferai visiter.
**She showed me around the apartment.** Elle m'a fait visiter l'appartement.

• to **show off**
**frimer [1]** (*informal*)

**show** *noun* ▷ see **show** *verb*
1 (*on stage*) le **spectacle** *masc*
**We went to see a show.** Nous sommes allés voir un spectacle.
**We're putting on a show.** Nous montons un spectacle.
2 (*on TV*) une **émission**
**He has a TV show.** Il a une émission à la télé.
3 (*on exhibition*) **to be on show** être [6] exposé
**The photos are on show this week.** Les photos sont exposées cette semaine.

**shower** *noun*
1 (*in a bathroom*) la **douche** *fem*
**to have a shower** prendre **[64]** une douche
**I'll have a shower now.** Je prendrai maintenant ma douche.
2 (*of rain*) une **averse** *fem*
**There'll be showers.** Il y aura des averses.

**show-jumping** *noun*
le **saut d'obstacles**

**show-off** *noun*
le **frimeur** *masc*, la **frimeuse** *fem*

**shrimp** *noun*
la **crevette** *fem*

**shrine** *noun*
1 (*in a church*) un **autel** *masc*
2 (*for pilgrims*) le **lieu de pèlerinage**

to **shrink** *verb*
**rétrécir [2]**
**My jeans shrank.** Mon jean a rétréci.

**Shrove Tuesday** *noun*
le **mardi gras**

to **shrug** *verb*
**to shrug your shoulders** hausser [1] les épaules

to **shuffle** *verb*
**to shuffle the cards** battre **[21]** les cartes

to **shut** *verb* ▷ see **shut** *adj*
(*windows, shops, factories*) **fermer [1]**
**When do the shops shut?** Les magasins ferment à quelle heure?
**The shops shut at six.** Les magasins ferment à six heures.
**to shut the window** fermer la fenêtre

• to **shut up**
**se taire** Ⓔ **[76]**
**Shut up!** Tais-toi!

**shut** *adjective* ▷ see **shut** *verb*
**fermé** *masc*, **fermée** *fem*
**The shops are shut.** Les magasins sont fermés.
**The door's not shut properly.** La porte n'est pas bien fermée.

**shutter** *noun*
le **volet** *masc*

**shuttle** *noun*
la **navette** *fem*
**There's a shuttle service from the airport.** Il y a une navette de l'aéroport.

**shuttlecock** *noun*
le **volant** *masc*

**shy** *adjective*
**timide** *masc & fem*
**She's a bit shy.** Elle est un peu timide.
**He's too shy to say it in French.** Il n'ose pas le dire en français.

**shyness** *noun*
la **timidité** *fem*

**Sicily** *noun*
la **Sicile** *fem*

**sick** *adjective*
1 (*ill*) **malade** *masc & fem*
**She's sick today.** Elle est malade aujourd'hui.
**a sick joke** une plaisanterie malsaine
2 **to be sick** vomir **[2]**
**I was sick several times.** J'ai vomi plusieurs fois.
**to feel sick** avoir **[5]** mal au cœur
**I felt really sick.** J'ai eu vraiment mal au cœur.
3 **to be sick of something** en avoir **[5]** assez de quelque chose
**I'm sick of staying at home every night.** J'en ai assez de rester à la maison tous les soirs.

**sickness** *noun*
la **maladie** *fem*

**side** *noun*
1 le **côté** *masc*
**on the wrong side** du mauvais côté
**side by side** côte à côte
**on the other side of the street** de l'autre côté de la rue
**from one side to the other** d'un côté jusqu'à l'autre
2 (*of the road, pool*) le **bord** *masc*
**at the side of the road** au bord de la route
3 (*team*) une **équipe** *fem*
**She plays on our side.** Elle joue dans notre équipe.

• **side-effect** un effet secondaire ⏩

- **sideline** la ligne de touche
- **side street** la petite rue

**siege** *noun*
le **siège** *masc*

**sieve** *noun*
la **passoire** *fem*

to **sigh** *verb* ▷ see **sigh** *noun*
**pousser [1] un soupir**

**sigh** *noun* ▷ see **sigh** *verb*
le **soupir** *masc*

**sight** *noun*
1 *(vista)* le **spectacle** *masc*
**What a sight!** Quel spectacle!
**It was a marvellous sight.** C'était un spectacle merveilleux.
2 *(eyesight)* la **vue** *fem*
**to have poor sight** avoir **[5]** une mauvaise vue
**to know somebody by sight** connaître **[27]** quelqu'un de vue
3 **out of sight** caché
**We stayed out of sight.** Nous sommes restés cachés.
4 *(place to see)* **to see the sights** visiter **[1]** les attractions touristiques

**sightseeing** *noun*
le **tourisme** *masc*
**to do some sightseeing** faire **[10]** du tourisme
**Shall we do some sightseeing?** Si on faisait un peu de tourisme?

to **sign** *verb* ▷ see **sign** *noun*
*(documents)* **signer [1]**
**to sign a cheque** signer un chèque
**You need to sign there.** Il faut signer là.

**sign** *noun* ▷ see **sign** *verb*
1 *(notice)* le **panneau** *masc* (*pl* les **panneaux**)
2 *(trace, indication)* le **signe** *masc*
**It's a good sign.** C'est bon signe.
**There's no sign of life at Paul's.** Il n'y a aucun signe de vie chez Paul.
3 *(of the Zodiac)* le **signe** *masc*
**What sign are you?** Tu es de quel signe?

**signal** *noun*
le **signal** *masc* (*pl* les **signaux**)
**a danger signal** un signal de danger

**signature** *noun*
la **signature** *fem*

**significance** *noun*
l'**importance** *fem*

**significant** *adjective*
**important** *masc*, **importante** *fem*
**a significant victory** une victoire importante

**sign language** *noun*
le **langage par signes**
**to talk in sign language** communiquer **[1]** par signes

**signpost** *noun*
le **poteau indicateur** (*pl* les **poteaux indicateurs**)

**silence** *noun*
le **silence** *masc*
**Silence, please!** Silence, s'il vous plaît!

**silent** *adjective*
**silencieux** *masc*, **silencieuse** *fem*
**the silent streets** les rues silencieuses

**silicon chip** *noun*
la **puce électronique**

**silk** *adjective* ▷ see **silk** *noun*
**en soie**
**a silk shirt** une chemise en soie

**silk** *noun* ▷ see **silk** *adj*
la **soie** *fem*

**silky** *adjective*
**soyeux** *masc*, **soyeuse** *fem*

**silly** *adjective*
**idiot** *masc*, **idiote** *fem*
**It was a really silly thing to do.** C'était vraiment idiot.
**I said some silly things.** J'ai dit des bêtises.
**Don't be silly!** Ne dis pas de bêtises!

**silver** *adjective* ▷ see **silver** *noun*
**en argent**
**a silver chain** une chaîne en argent
**a silver medal** une médaille d'argent

**silver** *noun* ▷ see **silver** *adj*
l'**argent** *masc*

**SIM card** *noun*
la **carte SIM**

**similar** *adjective*
**semblable** *masc & fem*

**similarity** *noun*
la **ressemblance** *fem*

**simple** *adjective*
1 **simple** *masc & fem*
**It's so simple.** C'est tellement simple.
2 **facile** *masc & fem*
**It's a simple question.** C'est une question facile.

to **simplify** *verb*
**simplifier [1]**

**simply** *adverb*
**simplement**

**sin** *noun*
(*Religion*) le **péché** *masc*

♪ **since** *adverb, conjunction, preposition*
1 (*because*) **puisque**
**Since it was raining, the match was cancelled.** Puisqu'il pleuvait, le match a été annulé.
2 (*with a specific time*) **depuis**
**I have been in Paris since Saturday.** Je suis à Paris depuis samedi.
**I've been learning French since last year.** J'apprends le français depuis l'année dernière.
**I haven't seen her since Monday.** Je ne l'ai pas revue depuis lundi.
**Since when?** Depuis quand?
3 (*with a vague time*) **depuis que**
**Since I have known Jessica...** Depuis que je connais Jessica...
**Since I've been learning French...** Depuis que j'apprends le français...

**WORD TIP** When what you are talking about is still going on, use the present tense in French followed by *depuis* and the length of time.

**sincere** *adjective*
**sincère** *masc & fem*
**She seemed sincere.** Elle semblait sincère.

**sincerely** *adverb*
**sincèrement**
**He spoke sincerely.** Il a parlé sincèrement.
(*ending a formal letter*) **Yours sincerely, ...** Veuillez agréer, Monsieur, l'expression de mes sentiments les meilleurs (*Madame, if to a woman*)

♪ to **sing** *verb*
**chanter** [1]
**Everyone was singing on the way home.** Tout le monde chantait en rentrant.

♪ **singer** *noun*
le **chanteur** *masc*, la **chanteuse** *fem*
**my favourite female singer** ma chanteuse préférée
**He's a good singer.** Il chante bien.

♪ **singing** *noun*
1 le **chant** *masc*
**a singing lesson** une leçon de chant
2 **I like singing.** J'aime chanter.

♪ **single** *adjective* ▷ see **single** *noun*
1 (*not married*) **célibataire** *masc & fem*
**to stay single** rester Ⓔ [1] célibataire
**I'm staying single.** Je reste célibataire.
2 (*room, bed*) **a single room** une chambre pour une personne
**a single bed** un lit pour une personne
3 **not a single ...** pas un seul ... *masc*, pas une seule ... *fem*
**I haven't had a single reply.** Je n'ai pas reçu une seule réponse.

♪ **single** *noun* ▷ see **single** *adj*
un **aller simple**
**A single to Lyons, please.** Un aller simple pour Lyon, s'il vous plaît.

**single parent** *noun*
**to be a single parent** élever [50] ses enfants tout seul
**She's a single parent.** Elle élève ses enfants toute seule.
• **single-parent family** la famille monoparentale

**singles** *plural noun*
(*in tennis*) le **simple** *masc*
**the women's singles** le simple dames
**the men's singles** le simple messieurs

**singular** *noun*
le **singulier** *masc*
**a noun in the singular** un nom au singulier

to **sink** *verb* ▷ see **sink** *noun*
**couler** [1]
**The Titanic sank.** Le Titanic a coulé.
**to sink a ship** faire [10] couler un navire

♪ **sink** *noun* ▷ see **sink** *verb*
un **évier** *masc*

**sir** *noun*
le **monsieur** *masc*
**Yes, sir.** Oui, Monsieur.

**siren** *noun*
la **sirène** *fem*

♪ **sister** *noun*
la **sœur** *fem*
**my older sister** ma sœur aînée
**my youngest sister** ma sœur cadette
**my twin sister** ma jumelle

**sister-in-law** *noun*
la **belle-sœur** *fem* (*pl* les **belles-sœurs**)

♪ to **sit** *verb*
1 **s'asseoir** Ⓔ [20]
**I can sit on the floor.** Je peux m'asseoir par terre.
**Sit beside me.** Assieds-toi à côté de moi.
2 **to be sitting** être [6] assis
**Leila was sitting on the sofa.** Leila était assise sur le canapé.
3 **to sit an exam** passer [1] un examen
**She's sitting the exam today.** Elle passe l'examen aujourd'hui. ▸▸

- to **sit down**
 **s'asseoir [20]**
 He sat down on a chair. Il s'est assis sur une chaise.
 Do sit down. Asseyez-vous.

**sitcom** *noun*
la **comédie de situation** (*pl* les **comédies de situation**)

**site** *noun*
a building site un chantier
an archaeological site un site archéologique

♪**sitting room** *noun*
le **salon** *masc*

♪**situated** *adjective*
to be situated être [6] situé
The house is situated in a small village. La maison est située dans un petit village.

**situation** *noun*
la **situation** *fem*

**six** *number*
**six**
David's six. David a six ans.

**sixteen** *number*
**seize**
Shahnaz is sixteen. Shahnaz a seize ans.

**sixteenth** *adjective*
1 **seizième** *masc & fem*
2 (*in dates*) the sixteenth of January le seize janvier

**sixth** *adjective*
1 **sixième** *masc & fem*
on the sixth floor au sixième étage
2 (*in dates*) the sixth of July le six juillet

**sixtieth** *adjective*
**soixantième** *masc & fem*
It's his sixtieth birthday. Il fête ses soixante ans.

**sixty** *number*
**soixante**
She's sixty. Elle a soixante ans.

♪**size** *noun*
1 (*in general*) la **grandeur** *fem*
the size of the house. la grandeur de la maison.
It's the size of my bedroom. C'est de la grandeur de ma chambre.
2 (*precise measurements*) les **dimensions** *fem pl*
What size is the window? Quelles sont les dimensions de la fenêtre?
3 (*for clothes*) la **taille** *fem*
What size do you take? Quelle taille faites-vous?
I take a size 8. Je fais du 8.
4 (*for shoes*) la **pointure** *fem*
What size shoe do you take? Tu fais quelle pointure?
I take a size thirty-eight. Je fais du trente-huit.

to **skate** *verb* ▷ see **skate** *noun*
1 (*on ice*) **faire [10] du patin à glace**
2 (*on rollerskates*) **faire [10] du patin à roulettes**

**skate** *noun* ▷ see **skate** *verb*
le **patin** *masc*
an ice skate un patin à glace

**skateboard** *noun*
le **skateboard** *masc*

**skateboarding** *noun*
le **skateboard** *masc*
to do skateboarding faire [10] du skateboard

**skater** *noun*
le **patineur** *masc*, la **patineuse** *fem*

**skating** *noun*
1 (*on ice*) le **patin à glace**
2 (*on rollerskates*) le **patin à roulettes**

♪**skating rink** *noun*
la **patinoire** *fem*
Is there a skating rink here? Est-ce qu'il y a une patinoire ici?

**skeleton** *noun*
le **squelette** *masc*

**sketch** *noun*
1 (*drawing*) le **croquis** *masc*
2 (*comedy routine*) le **sketch** *masc*

♪to **ski** *verb* ▷ see **ski** *noun*
**faire [10] du ski**
I can ski. Je sais faire du ski.
I'm learning to ski. J'apprends à faire du ski.

**ski** *noun* ▷ see **ski** *verb*
le **ski** *masc*
to put on your skis mettre [11] ses skis

**ski boot** *noun*
la **chaussure de ski**

to **skid** *verb*
(*cars, bikes*) **déraper [1]**
The car skidded. La voiture a dérapé.

**skier** *noun*
le **skieur** *masc*, la **skieuse** *fem*

♪**skiing** *noun*
le **ski** *masc*
to go skiing faire [10] du ski
- **skiing holiday** les vacances de neige
- **skiing instructor** le moniteur de ski, la monitrice de ski

**ski lift** *noun*
le **remonte-pente** *masc* (*pl* les **remonte-pentes**)

**skill** *noun*
la **compétence** *fem*

**skimmed milk** *noun*
le **lait écrémé**

♪ **skin** *noun*
la **peau** *fem* (*pl* les **peaux**)
to have lovely skin avoir **[5]** une belle peau
She's got dark skin. Elle a la peau brune.
- **skinhead** le & la skinhead

**skinny** *adjective*
**maigre** *masc & fem*
a bit too skinny un peu trop maigre

to **skip** *verb* ▷ see **skip** *noun*
1 (*a meal, a chapter*) **sauter [1]**
2 to skip a lesson sécher un cours (*informal*)
3 (*with a rope*) **sauter [1] à la corde**

**skip** *noun* ▷ see **skip** *verb*
la **benne** *fem*

**ski pants** *plural noun*
le **fuseau** *masc singular*
I bought some ski pants. J'ai acheté un fuseau.

**skipping rope** *noun*
la **corde à sauter**

♪ **skirt** *noun*
la **jupe** *fem*
a long skirt une jupe longue
a mini-skirt une mini-jupe

**ski suit** *noun*
la **combinaison de ski**

**skittles** *plural noun*
les **quilles** *fem pl*
to play skittles jouer **[1]** aux quilles

**skull** *noun*
le **crâne** *masc*

♪ **sky** *noun*
le **ciel** *masc*
a cloudy sky un ciel nuageux
The sky is clear. Le ciel est clair.
- **skyscraper** le gratte-ciel (*pl* les gratte-ciel)

to **slam** *verb*
**claquer [1]**
I slammed the door. J'ai claqué la porte.

**slang** *noun*
l'**argot** *masc*

to **slap** *verb* ▷ see **slap** *noun*
to slap somebody donner **[1]** une claque à quelqu'un

**slap** *noun* ▷ see **slap** *verb*
la **claque** *fem*

**slate** *noun*
une **ardoise** *fem*

**slave** *noun*
un & une **esclave** *masc & fem*

**sledge** *noun*
la **luge** *fem*

**sledging** *noun*
to go sledging faire **[10]** de la luge

♪ to **sleep** *verb* ▷ see **sleep** *noun*
**dormir [37]**
She's sleeping. Elle dort.
Sleep well! Dors bien!
- to **sleep in**
**faire [10] la grasse matinée**
I like to sleep in on Saturdays. J'aime faire la grasse matinée le samedi.

♪ **sleep** *noun* ▷ see **sleep** *verb*
le **sommeil** *masc*
I had a good sleep. J'ai bien dormi.
We got no sleep. Nous n'avons pas dormi du tout.
to go to sleep s'endormir **[37]**
I couldn't get to sleep. Je n'arrivais pas à m'endormir.

♪ **sleeping bag** *noun*
le **sac de couchage**

**sleeping pill** *noun*
le **somnifère** *masc*

♪ **sleepy** *adjective*
to be sleepy avoir **[5]** sommeil
I feel sleepy. J'ai sommeil.
He was getting sleepy. Il commençait à avoir sommeil.

**sleet** *noun*
la **neige fondue**

**sleeve** *noun*
la **manche** *fem*
a long-sleeved jumper un pull à manches longues
a short-sleeved shirt une chemise à manches courtes
to roll up your sleeves retrousser **[1]** ses manches

to **slice** *verb* ▷ see **slice** *noun*
to slice something couper **[1]** quelque chose en tranches
I sliced the cheese. J'ai coupé le fromage en tranches.

♪ **slice** *noun* ▷ see **slice** *verb*
1 (*of bread, meat*) la **tranche** *fem*
two slices of ham deux tranches de jambon
2 (*of cake, pie*) la **part** *fem*
a slice of pizza une part de pizza

**slide** *noun*
1 (*photo*) la **diapositive** *fem*
2 (*for sliding down*) le **toboggan** *masc*

♪ **slight** *adjective*
**léger** *masc*, **légère** *fem*
a slight delay un léger retard
There is a slight problem. Il y a un léger problème.

**slightly** *adverb*
**légèrement**
He's slightly better. Il va un peu mieux.

to **slim** *verb* ▷ see **slim** *adj*
to be slimming faire [10] un régime
I'm slimming. Je fais un régime.

**slim** *adjective* ▷ see **slim** *verb*
**mince** *masc & fem*

**sling** *noun*
une **écharpe** *fem*

♪ to **slip** *verb* ▷ see **slip** *noun*
1 (*to fall*) **glisser** [1]
I slipped on the ice. J'ai glissé sur la glace.
Be careful not to slip. Attention de ne pas glisser.
2 (*to forget*) It had slipped my mind. J'avais oublié.

**slip** *noun* ▷ see **slip** *verb*
1 (*mistake*) une **erreur** *fem*
2 (*from the waist*) le **jupon** *masc*
3 (*full-length*) la **combinaison** *fem*

**slipper** *noun*
la **pantoufle** *fem*

**slippery** *adjective*
**glissant** *masc*, **glissante** *fem*

**slope** *noun*
la **pente** *fem*

**slot** *noun*
la **fente** *fem*

**slot machine** *noun*
1 (*for games*) la **machine à sous**
2 (*dispenser*) le **distributeur automatique**

♪ **slow** *adjective*
1 **lent** *masc*, **lente** *fem*
a slow train un train lent
2 (*clock, watch*) to be slow retarder [1]
My watch is slow. Ma montre retarde.

to **slow down** *verb*
**ralentir** [2]
The train is slowing down. Le train ralentit.

♪ **slowly** *adverb*
**lentement**
to work slowly travailler lentement
He got up slowly. Il s'est levé lentement.
Can you speak more slowly, please? Est-ce que vous pouvez parler plus lentement, s'il vous plaît?

**slug** *noun*
la **limace** *fem*

**slum** *noun*
le **quartier démuni**

**slush** *noun*
la **neige fondue**

**sly** *adjective*
**rusé** *masc*, **rusée** *fem*
to do something on the sly faire quelque chose en douce

to **smack** *verb* ▷ see **smack** *noun*
to smack somebody donner [1] une claque à quelqu'un

**smack** *noun* ▷ see **smack** *verb*
la **claque** *fem*

♪ **small** *adjective*
**petit** *masc*, **petite** *fem*
a small dog un petit chien
a small country town une petite ville de province

**WORD TIP** *petit* always goes before the noun.

♪ **smart** *adjective*
1 (*well-dressed*) **chic** (*doesn't change*)
a smart restaurant un restaurant chic
smart young women les jeunes femmes chic
2 (*clever*) **intelligent** *masc*, **intelligente** *fem*
She's a smart girl. Elle est très intelligente.
to try to be smart faire [10] le malin
Stop trying to be smart! Arrête de faire le malin!
• **smart card** la carte à puce

to **smash** *verb* ▷ see **smash** *noun*
1 (*a plate, a mirror*) **casser** [1]
They smashed a window. Ils ont cassé une vitre.
The windscreen was smashed. Le pare-brise était cassé.
2 (*by itself*) **se casser** ⓔ [1]
The vase fell and it smashed. Le vase est tombé et il s'est cassé.

**smash** *noun* ▷ see **smash** *verb*
a car smash un accident de voiture

**smashing** *adjective*
**formidable** *masc & fem*

♪ to **smell** *verb* ▷ see **smell** *noun*
1 (*in general*) **sentir [58]**
I can't smell anything. Je ne sens rien.
I can smell lavender. Ça sent la lavande.
2 (*to smell bad*) **sentir [58] mauvais**
The bins smell. Les poubelles sentent mauvais.
3 (*to smell good*) **sentir [58] bon**
That smells really good! Ça sent vraiment bon!

♪ **smell** *noun* ▷ see **smell** *verb*
une **odeur** *fem*
a nasty smell une mauvaise odeur
There's a smell of burning. Ça sent le brûlé.

**smelly** *adjective*
**qui sent mauvais**
her smelly dog son chien qui sent mauvais
to be smelly sentir [58] mauvais
My trainers are smelly. Mes baskets sentent mauvais.

♪ to **smile** *verb* ▷ see **smile** *noun*
**sourire [68]**
to smile at somebody sourire à quelqu'un
Everyone was smiling at James. Tout le monde souriait à James.

♪ **smile** *noun* ▷ see **smile** *verb*
le **sourire** *masc*
to give somebody a smile faire un sourire à quelqu'un
He gave me a big smile. Il m'a fait un gros sourire.

♪ to **smoke** *verb* ▷ see **smoke** *noun*
**fumer [1]**
She doesn't smoke. Elle ne fume pas.
He smokes a pipe. Il fume la pipe.

**smoke** *noun* ▷ see **smoke** *verb*
la **fumée** *fem*

**smoked** *adjective*
**fumé** *masc*, **fumée** *fem*
smoked salmon du saumon fumé

**smoker** *noun*
le **fumeur** *masc*, la **fumeuse** *fem*

**smoking** *noun*
'No smoking' 'Défense de fumer'
to give up smoking arrêter [1] de fumer
Adam has given up smoking. Adam a arrêté de fumer.

♪ **smooth** *adjective*
1 (*surfaces*) **lisse** *masc & fem*
to have smooth skin avoir la peau lisse
She's got smooth hair. Elle a les cheveux lisses.
2 (*person*) **mielleux** *masc*, **mielleuse** *fem*
He's too smooth. Il est trop mielleux.

**smug** *adjective*
**suffisant** *masc*, **suffisante** *fem*

to **smuggle** *verb*
to smuggle something faire [10] passer quelque chose en contrebande

**smuggler** *noun*
1 (*of goods*) le **contrebandier** *masc*, la **contrebandière** *fem*
2 (*of drugs, arms*) le **passeur**, la **passeuse**

**smuggling** *noun*
1 (*of goods*) la **contrebande** *fem*
2 (*of drugs, arms*) le **trafic** *masc*

**snack** *noun*
le **casse-croûte** *masc* (*pl* les **casse-croûte**)

**snack bar** *noun*
la **sandwicherie** *fem*, le **snack-bar** *masc*

**snail** *noun*
un **escargot** *masc*

**snails**

The French eat snails, but only occasionally: they are expensive! There are two edible varieties. You can get them in cans, frozen or in restaurants, often served with garlic butter.

**snake** *noun*
le **serpent** *masc*

to **snap** *verb* ▷ see **snap** *noun*
1 (*to break*) **se casser** Ⓔ **[1]**
The fishing rod snapped in two. La canne à pêche s'est cassée en deux.
2 **to snap your fingers** faire [10] claquer ses doigts
3 **to snap at somebody** être [6] agressif avec quelqu'un
She's always snapping at me. Elle est toujours agressive avec moi.

**snap** *noun* ▷ see **snap** *verb*
(*cards*) la **bataille** *fem*

**snapshot** *noun*
la **photo** *fem*

to **snarl** *verb*
**gronder [1]**

to **snatch** *verb*
**to snatch something from somebody** arracher [1] quelque chose à quelqu'un
He snatched my book from me. Il m'a arraché mon livre.
She had her bag snatched. On lui a arraché son sac.

to **sneak** *verb*
to sneak in entrer Ⓔ [1] furtivement
to sneak out sortir Ⓔ [72] furtivement
to sneak up on somebody s'approcher Ⓔ [1] de quelqu'un sans faire de bruit
He sneaked up on me. Il s'est approché de moi sans faire de bruit.

to **sneeze** *verb*
**éternuer** [1]
I can't stop sneezing. Je n'arrête pas d'éternuer.

to **sniff** *verb*
**renifler** [1]

**snob** *noun*
le & la **snob** *masc & fem*

**snobbery** *noun*
le **snobisme** *masc*

**snooker** *noun*
le **snooker** *masc*

**snooze** *noun*
le **somme** *masc*
to have a snooze faire [10] un petit somme

to **snore** *verb*
**ronfler** [1]

♪ to **snow** *verb* ▷ see **snow** *noun*
**neiger** [52]
It's snowing. Il neige.
It's going to snow. Il va neiger.
It snowed last night. Il a neigé cette nuit.

♪ **snow** *noun* ▷ see **snow** *verb*
la **neige** *fem*
a fall of snow une chute de neige

**snowball** *noun*
la **boule de neige** (*pl* les **boules de neige**)
to throw snowballs at each other se lancer Ⓔ [61] des boules de neige

**snowdrift** *noun*
la **congère** *fem*

**snowman** *noun*
le **bonhomme de neige** (*pl* les **bonshommes de neige**)

**snowy** *adjective*
**enneigé** *masc*, **enneigée** *fem*

♪ **so** *conjunction, adverb*
1 **tellement**
He's so lazy. Il est tellement paresseux.
She's so sweet! Elle est tellement mignonne!
so ... that ... tellement ... que ...
The coffee's so hot that I can't drink it. Le café est tellement chaud que je n'arrive pas à le boire.
2 not so (*+ adj*) moins (*+ adj*)
Our house is like yours, but not so big. Notre maison est comme la vôtre, mais moins grande.
I'm not so tired today. Je suis moins fatigué aujourd'hui.
3 so much tellement
I hate it so much! Je le déteste tellement!
4 so much, so many tellement de
I have so much work to do. J'ai tellement de travail à faire.
We've got so many problems. Nous avons tellement de problèmes.
5 (*therefore*) **donc**
He got up late, so he missed his train. Il s'est levé tard, donc il a raté son train.
6 (*starting a sentence*) **alors**
So, what's your name? Alors, tu t'appelles comment?
So, what shall we do? Alors, qu'est-ce qu'on fait?
So what? Et alors?
7 (*with be, do + I, you, he, she, we, etc*) **So am I, So was I.** Moi aussi.
So do I, So did I. Moi aussi.
'I live in Leeds.' — 'So do I.' 'J'habite à Leeds.' — 'Moi aussi.'
So do we. Nous aussi.
So does Zara. Zara aussi.
So do the French. Les Français aussi.
8 (*with think, hope + so*) **I think so.** Je crois.
We hope so. Nous espérons.

to **soak** *verb*
**tremper** [1]

**soaked** *adjective*
**trempé** *masc*, **trempée** *fem*
We got soaked. Nous avons été trempés.
to be soaked to the skin être [6] trempé jusqu'aux os

**soaking** *adjective*
**trempé** *masc*, **trempée** *fem*
It's soaking wet. C'est trempé.

♪ **soap** *noun*
le **savon** *masc*
a bar of soap un savon
- **soap opera** le feuilleton
- **soap powder** la lessive

**sober** *adjective*
to be sober ne pas avoir [5] bu
He's sober. Il n'a pas bu.

♪ **soccer** *noun*
le **football** *masc*

**sociable** *adjective*
**sociable** *masc & fem*
I'm quite sociable. Je suis assez sociable.

**social** *adjective*
**social** *masc*, **sociale** *fem*, **sociaux** *masc pl*, **sociales** *fem pl*
a social class une classe sociale
social groups des groupes sociaux

**socialism** *noun*
le **socialisme** *masc*

**socialist** *noun*
le & la **socialiste** *masc & fem*

**social security** *noun*
1 (*benefit*) l'**aide sociale** *fem*
to be on social security recevoir **[66]** de l'aide sociale
2 (*the system*) **la sécurité sociale**

**social worker** *noun*
le **travailleur social** (*pl* les **travailleurs sociaux**), la **travailleuse sociale**

**society** *noun*
la **société** *fem*
a multicultural society une société multiculturelle

**sociology** *noun*
la **sociologie** *fem*

♪ **sock** *noun*
la **chaussette** *fem*
a pair of socks une paire de chaussettes
my yellow socks mes chaussettes jaunes

**socket** *noun*
(*power point*) la **prise de courant** (*pl* les **prises de courant**)

♪ **sofa** *noun*
le **canapé** *masc*
a leather sofa un canapé en cuir
• **sofa bed** le canapé-lit *masc*

♪ **soft** *adjective*
1 (*in general*) **doux** *masc*, **douce** *fem*
a soft voice une voix douce
soft music une musique douce
I like soft fabrics. J'aime les tissus doux.
2 The butter's too soft. Le beurre est trop mou.
3 (*not strict*) **indulgent** *masc*, **indulgente** *fem*
• **soft drink** la boisson non alcoolisée
• **soft toy** la peluche
• **software** le logiciel

**soil** *noun*
la **terre** *fem*

**solar energy** *noun*
l'**énergie solaire** *fem*

**soldier** *noun*
le **soldat** *masc*
a woman soldier une femme soldat

**solicitor** *noun*
1 (*for legal disputes*) un **avocat** *masc*, une **avocate** *fem*
She's a solicitor. Elle est avocate.
2 (*for property*) le **notaire** *masc*

**solid** *adjective*
1 (*not flimsy*) **solide** *masc & fem*
a solid structure une structure solide
That shed looks solid. Cette remise a l'air solide.
2 (*pure*) **massif** *masc*, **massive** *fem*
a solid gold ring une bague en or massif

**solo** *adjective, adverb* ▷ see **solo** *noun*
**en solo**
a solo album un album en solo
to play solo jouer **[1]** en solo
I sing solo. Je chante en solo.

**solo** *noun* ▷ see **solo** *adj, adv*
le **solo** *masc*
a guitar solo un solo de guitare

**soloist** *noun*
le & la **soliste** *masc & fem*

**solution** *noun*
la **solution** *fem*

to **solve** *verb*
**résoudre [67]**
I think I've solved the problem. Je pense que j'ai résolu le problème.

♪ **some** *adjective, adverb, pronoun*
1 (*with masc singular nouns*) **du**
some paper du papier
Would you like some orange juice? Voulez-vous du jus d'orange?
2 (*with fem singular nouns*) **de la**
some meat de la viande
May I have some salad? Puis-je avoir de la salade?
3 (*with nouns beginning with a, e, i, o, u or silent h*) **de l'**
some help de l'aide
Can you lend me some money? Est-ce que tu peux me prêter de l'argent?
4 (*with plural nouns*) **des**
some friends des amis
I've bought some apples. J'ai acheté des pommes.
5 (*referring to something that has been mentioned*) **en**
'Would you like butter?' — 'Thanks, I've got some.' 'Veux-tu du beurre?' — 'Merci, j'en ai.'
He's eaten some of it. Il en a mangé un peu.
I'm going to have some more. Je vais en reprendre. ⏩

**6** some day un de ces jours
maybe some day un de ces jours, peut-être

**somebody**, **someone** *pronoun*
**quelqu'un**
**There's somebody in the garden.** Il y a quelqu'un dans le jardin.
**Somebody phoned this morning.** Quelqu'un a téléphoné ce matin.

**somehow** *adverb*
**d'une manière ou d'une autre**
**I've got to finish it somehow.** Je dois le finir d'une manière ou d'une autre.

**someone** *pronoun* ▷ **somebody**

**somersault** *noun*
**1** (*child's*) la **galipette** *fem*
**2** (*gymnast's*) le **roulade** *fem*
**3** (*diver's*) le **saut périlleux**

**something** *pronoun*
**1** **quelque chose**
**I've got something to tell you.** J'ai quelque chose à te dire.
**He had something to do.** Il avait quelque chose à faire.
**2** **something + adjective** quelque chose de (+ *adjective*)
**something pretty** quelque chose de joli
**I did something interesting today.** J'ai fait quelque chose d'intéressant aujourd'hui.
**There's something wrong.** Il y a quelque chose qui ne va pas.
**3** (*in expressions*) **Their house is really something!** Leur maison c'est vraiment quelque chose!
**a guy called Colin something or other** un type qui s'appelle Colin quelque chose

**sometime** *adverb*
**un de ces jours**
**Give me a ring sometime.** Appelle-moi un de ces jours.
**I'll ring you sometime next week.** Je t'appellerai dans le courant de la semaine prochaine.

**sometimes** *adverb*
**quelquefois**
**I sometimes take the train.** Quelquefois, je prends le train.

**somewhere** *adverb*
**quelque part**
**somewhere in Scotland** quelque part en Écosse
**I've left my bag somewhere.** J'ai posé mon sac quelque part.
**I've seen you before somewhere.** Je vous ai déjà vu quelque part.

**son** *noun*
le **fils** *masc*
**the eldest son** le fils aîné
**the adopted son** le fils adoptif

**song** *noun*
la **chanson** *fem*
**the song that won the contest** la chanson qui a gagné le concours

**son-in-law** *noun*
le **gendre** *masc*

**soon** *adverb*
**1** **bientôt**
**See you soon!** À bientôt!
**It will soon be the holidays.** C'est bientôt les vacances.
**I'll be back soon.** Je reviendrai bientôt.
**It's too soon.** C'est trop tôt.
**2** **as soon as ...** dès que ...
**as soon as she arrives** dès qu'elle arrivera
**as soon as possible** dès que possible
**I'll come as soon as possible.** Je viendrai dès que possible.

**sooner** *adverb*
**1** **plus tôt**
**We should have started sooner.** Nous aurions dû commencer plus tôt.
**2** **sooner or later** tôt ou tard
**It must be done sooner or later.** Il va falloir le faire tôt ou tard.

**soprano** *noun*
le & la **soprano** *masc & fem*

**sore** *adjective* ▷ see **sore** *noun*
**to have a sore throat** avoir **[5]** mal à la gorge
**My arm's sore.** J'ai mal au bras.

**sore** *noun* ▷ see **sore** *adj*
la **plaie** *fem*

**sorry** *adjective*
**1** (*in apologies*) **désolé** *masc*, **désolée** *fem*
**I'm really sorry.** Je suis vraiment désolé (*boy speaking*), Je suis vraiment désolée (*girl speaking*).
**2** **to be sorry you've done something** être **[6]** désolé d'avoir fait quelque chose
**I'm sorry I forgot your birthday** Je suis désolé d'avoir oublié ton anniversaire.
**3** **to say sorry** s'excuser **[1]**
**I wanted to say sorry.** Je voulais m'excuser.
**Sorry!** Excusez-moi!
**4** (*interrupting*) **Sorry to disturb you.** Je suis désolé de vous déranger.
**5** (*saying what politely*) **Sorry?** Comment?
**Sorry? Could you repeat that, please?** Comment? Pouvez-vous répéter s'il vous plaît?

**6** (*to pity*) to feel sorry for somebody plaindre **[31]** quelqu'un
I feel sorry for them. Je les plains.

to **sort** *verb* ▷ see **sort** *noun*
**classer [1]**
• to **sort something out**
**1** (*room, papers, belongings*) **mettre [11] de l'ordre dans**
**2** (*a problem, arrangements*) **s'occuper [1] de**
I'll sort out the tickets. Je m'en occuperai des billets.

𝄞 **sort** *noun* ▷ see **sort** *verb*
la **sorte** *fem*, le **genre** *masc*
a sort of une sorte de
what sort of ...? quelle sorte de ...
What sort of music do you like? Tu aimes quelle sorte de musique?
I don't like that sort of music. Je n'aime pas ce genre de musique.
I like all sorts of music. J'aime toutes sortes de musique.
It's a sort of hostel. C'est une sorte d'auberge.
He's not that sort of person. Ce n'est pas son genre.

**so-so** *adjective*
**moyen** *masc*, **moyenne** *fem*
'How was the film?' — 'So-so.' 'C'était comment le film?' — 'Moyen.'

**soul** *noun*
**1** (*person's*) une **âme** *fem*
**2** (*Music*) le **soul** *masc*

𝄞 to **sound** *verb* ▷ see **sound** *noun*
You sound bored. Tu as l'air ennuyé.
It sounds easy. Ça a l'air facile.
She sounded tired. Elle avait l'air fatiguée.
It sounds as if she's happy. Elle a l'air d'être heureuse.

𝄞 **sound** *noun* ▷ see **sound** *verb*
**1** (*noise*) le **bruit** *masc*
the sound of voices le bruit des voix
We left without making a sound. Nous sommes partis sans faire de bruit.
**2** (*volume*) le **volume** *masc*
to turn down the sound baisser **[1]** le volume
• **sound asleep** profondément endormi
• **sound card** la carte son
• **sound effect** un effet sonore
• **soundtrack** la bande sonore

𝄞 **soup** *noun*
la **soupe** *fem*
mushroom soup la soupe aux champignons
• **soup plate** une assiette creuse à soupe
• **soup spoon** la cuillère à soupe

**sour** *adjective*
**1** (*taste*) **aigre** *masc & fem*
**2** to go sour tourner **[1]**
The milk has gone sour. Le lait a tourné.

𝄞 **south** *adjective, adverb* ▷ see **south** *noun*
**sud** *invariable adj*
the south side le côté sud
a south wind un vent du sud
south of Paris au sud de Paris
We're going south. Nous allons vers le sud.

**WORD TIP** *sud* never changes.

𝄞 **south** *noun* ▷ see **south** *adj, adv*
le **sud** *masc*
in the south au sud
in the south of France dans le sud de la France

**South Africa** *noun*
l'**Afrique** *fem* **du Sud**
in South Africa en Afrique du Sud

**WORD TIP** Countries and regions in French take *le, la* or *les*.

**South African** *adjective* ▷ see **South African** *noun*
**sud-africain** *masc*, **sud-africaine** *fem*

**WORD TIP** Adjectives never have capitals in French, even for nationality or regional origin.

**South African** *noun* ▷ see **South African** *adj*
un **Sud-Africain** *masc*, une **Sud-Africaine** *fem*

**South America** *noun*
l'**Amérique** *fem* **du Sud**
in South America en Amérique du Sud

**southeast** *adjective*
▷ see **southeast** *noun*
in southeast England au sud-est de l'Angleterre

**southeast** *noun* ▷ see **southeast** *adj*
le **sud-est** *masc*

**South Pole** *noun*
le **pôle Sud**

**southwest** *adjective*
▷ see **southwest** *noun*
in southwest Scotland au sud-ouest de l'Écosse

**southwest** *noun* ▷ see **southwest** *adj*
le **sud-ouest** *masc*

**souvenir** *noun*
le **souvenir** *masc*

**soya** *noun*
le **soja** *masc*

**soy sauce** *noun*
la **sauce de soja**

ℰ **space** *noun*
1 (*room*) la **place** *fem*
Is there enough space? Est-ce qu'il y a de la place?
There's space for two. Il y a de la place pour deux.
2 (*gap*) un **espace** *masc*
Leave a space. Laissez un espace.
3 (*Astronomy*) l'**espace** *masc*
in space dans l'espace
She was staring into space. Elle regardait dans le vide.
• **spacecraft** le vaisseau spatial
• **space exploration** l'exploration *fem* de l'espace

**spade** *noun*
1 la **pelle** *fem*
2 (*in cards*) le **pique** *masc*
the queen of spades la reine de pique

**spaghetti** *noun*
les **spaghetti** *masc pl*

**Spain** *noun*
l'**Espagne** *fem*

**Spaniard** *noun*
un **Espagnol** *masc*, une **Espagnole** *fem*

**spaniel** *noun*
un **épagneul** *masc*

**Spanish** *adjective* ▷ see **Spanish** *noun*
**espagnol** *masc*, **espagnole** *fem*
Pedro is Spanish. Pedro est espagnol.

**Spanish** *noun* ▷ see **Spanish** *adj*
1 (*language*) l'**espagnol** *masc*
2 (*people*) the Spanish les Espagnols *masc pl*

**spanner** *noun*
la **clé anglaise**

to **spare** *verb* ▷ see **spare** *adj*
I can't spare the time. Je n'ai pas le temps.
Can you spare a moment? Est-ce que tu as un instant?

**spare** *adjective* ▷ see **spare** *verb*
**de rechange**
a spare battery une pile de rechange
I've got a spare ticket. J'ai un billet de trop.
There's a spare seat here. Il y a une place disponible ici.
• **spare part** la pièce de rechange
• **spare room** la chambre d'amis
• **spare time** le temps libre
• **spare wheel** la roue de secours

**sparkling** *adjective*
sparkling (mineral) water l'eau (minérale) pétillante
sparkling wine le vin mousseux

**sparrow** *noun*
le **moineau** *masc* (*pl* les **moineaux**)

ℰ to **speak** *verb*
1 **parler [1]**
Do you speak French? Est-ce que vous parlez français?
I can speak a little French. Je parle un peu français.
2 **to speak to somebody** parler [1] à quelqu'un
May I speak to Mrs Brown? Puis-je parler à Mrs Brown?
She's speaking to Ahmed. Elle parle à Ahmed.
**to speak to somebody about something** parler [1] de quelque chose à quelqu'un
Did you speak to Tom about the party? Est-ce que tu as parlé de la fête à Tom?
I'll speak to him about it. Je vais lui en parler.
3 **to speak to each other** se parler Ⓔ [1]
They speak to each other in Chinese. Ils se parlent en chinois.
4 (*on the phone*) **Who's speaking?** C'est qui à l'appareil?

**speaker** *noun*
1 (*on a music system*) une **enceinte** *fem*
2 (*at a public lecture*) le **conférencier** *masc*, la **conférencière** *fem*
3 (*of a language*) **a French speaker** un & une francophone
**an English speaker** un & une anglophone

**spear** *noun*
la **lance** *fem*

ℰ **special** *adjective*
**spécial** *masc*, **spéciale** *fem*, **spéciaux** *masc pl*, **spéciales** *fem pl*
the special effects les effets spéciaux
special training une formation spéciale
**to be on special offer** être [6] en promotion
They have it on special offer. Ils l'ont en promotion.
There's no special reason. Il n'y a pas de raison particulière.

**specialist** *noun*
le & la **spécialiste** *masc & fem*

to **specialize** *verb*
**to specialize in something** être [6] spécialisé dans quelque chose
They specialize in French cars. Ils sont spécialisés dans les voitures françaises.



Ⓔ means the verb takes être to form the perfect

**specially** *adverb*
1 (*in general*) **spécialement**
not specially pas spécialement
The songs were chosen specially for her. Les chansons ont été spécialement choisies pour elle.
2 (*specifically*) **exprès**
I came specially to see you. Je suis venu exprès pour te voir.
I copied this CD specially for you. J'ai copié ce CD exprès pour toi.

**species** *noun*
une **espèce** *fem*
an endangered species une espèce en voie de disparition

**specific** *adjective*
**précis** *masc*, **précise** *fem*

**spectacular** *adjective*
**spectaculaire** *masc & fem*

**spectator** *noun*
le **spectateur** *masc*, la **spectatrice** *fem*

**speech** *noun*
le **discours** *masc*
to make a speech faire [10] un discours

**speechless** *adjective*
**muet** *masc*, **muette** *fem*
to be speechless with rage rester Ⓔ [1] muet de colère

to **speed** *verb* ▷ see **speed** *noun*
**rouler [1] trop vite**
She was speeding. Elle roulait trop vite.
• to **speed up**
**accélérer [24]**

**speed** *noun* ▷ see **speed** *verb*
la **vitesse** *fem*
a twelve-speed bike un vélo à douze vitesses
What speed was he doing? Il roulait à quelle vitesse?
He was travelling at top speed. Il roulait à toute vitesse.

**speeding** *noun*
l'**excès de vitesse** *masc*
He was fined for speeding. Il a reçu une contravention pour excès de vitesse.

**speed limit** *noun*
la **limitation de vitesse**

to **spell** *verb* ▷ see **spell** *noun*
1 (*in writing*) **écrire [38]**
How do you spell it? Ça s'écrit comment?
It's spelt with an 'e'. Ça s'écrit avec un 'e'.
How do you spell your surname? Ça s'écrit comment, ton nom de famille?
2 (*out loud*) **épeler [18]**
I'll spell it for you. Je vais l'épeler pour vous.

**spell** *noun* ▷ see **spell** *verb*
(*of time*) la **période** *fem*
a cold spell une période de temps froid
sunny spells des belles éclaircies

**spell checker** *noun*
le **correcteur orthographique**

**spelling** *noun*
l'**orthographe** *fem*
a spelling mistake une faute d'orthographe

to **spend** *verb*
1 (*money*) **dépenser [1]**
I've spent all my money. J'ai dépensé tout mon argent.
How much money did you spend? Tu as dépensé combien d'argent?
to spend money on something dépenser de l'argent en quelque chose
I spend money on clothes. Je dépense de l'argent en vêtements.
2 (*time*) **passer [1]**
We spent three days in Paris. Nous avons passé trois jours à Paris.
to spend time doing something passer du temps à faire quelque chose
I spend my time sending texts. Je passe mon temps à envoyer des textos.

**spice** *noun*
une **épice** *fem*

**spicy** *adjective*
**épicé** *masc*, **épicée** *fem*

**spider** *noun*
une **araignée** *fem*

to **spill** *verb*
**renverser [1]**
to spill coffee on the carpet renverser du café sur la moquette

**spin** *noun*
le **tour** *masc*
to go for a spin aller Ⓔ [7] faire un tour
We went for a spin on our bikes. Nous sommes allés faire un tour à vélo.

**spinach** *noun*
les **épinards** *masc pl*

**spine** *noun*
la **colonne vertébrale**

**spiral** *noun*
la **spirale** *fem*

**spire** *noun*
la **flèche** *fem*

**spirit** *noun*
1 (*energy*) l'**énergie** *fem*
2 to get into the spirit of things se mettre Ⓔ [11] dans l'ambiance

**spirits** *noun*
1 (*alcohol*) les **alcools forts** *masc pl*
2 to be in good spirits être [6] de bonne humeur

to **spit** *verb*
**cracher** [1]

**spite** *noun*
1 in spite of something malgré quelque chose
We decided to go in spite of the rain. Nous avons décidé d'y aller malgré la pluie.
2 (*nastiness*) la **méchanceté** *fem*
He said that out of spite. Il a dit ça par méchanceté.

**spiteful** *adjective*
**méchant** *masc*, **méchante** *fem*

**splash** *noun*
1 (*noise*) le **plouf** *masc*
2 a splash of colour une touche de couleur

**splendid** *adjective*
**splendide** *masc & fem*

**splinter** *noun*
une **écharde** *fem*

to **split** *verb*
1 (*a log, a stone*) **fendre** [3]
to split a piece of wood fendre un morceau de bois
2 (*to come apart*) **se fendre** Ⓔ [3]
The lining has split. La doublure s'est fendue.
3 (*the cost, expense*) **partager** [52]
They split the money between them. Ils ont partagé l'argent entre eux.
• to **split up**
1 (*couples, groups*) **se séparer** Ⓔ [1]
Her parents have split up. Ses parents se sont séparés.
2 to split up with somebody rompre [69]
She's split up with her boyfriend. Elle a rompu avec son copain.

to **spoil** *verb*
1 (*an occasion, an event*) **gâcher** [1]
2 (*a child*) **gâter** [1]

**spoiled** *adjective*
**gâté** *masc*, **gâtée** *fem*

**spoilsport** *noun*
le & la **trouble-fête** *masc & fem*

**spoke** *noun*
(*of a wheel*) le **rayon** *masc*

**spokesman** *noun*
le **porte-parole** *masc* (*pl* les **porte-parole**)

**spokeswoman** *noun*
la **porte-parole** *masc* (*pl* les **porte-parole**)

**sponge** *noun*
une **éponge** *fem*
• **sponge bag** la trousse de toilette
• **sponge cake** la génoise

to **sponsor** *verb* ▷ see **sponsor** *noun*
**sponsoriser** [1]
to be sponsored by somebody être [6] sponsorisé par quelqu'un

**sponsor** *noun* ▷ see **sponsor** *verb*
le **sponsor** *masc*

**spontaneous** *adjective*
**spontané** *masc*, **spontanée** *fem*

**spooky** *adjective*
**sinistre** *masc & fem*
a spooky house une maison sinistre
a spooky story une histoire qui fait froid dans le dos

**spoon** *noun*
la **cuillère** *fem*

**spoonful** *noun*
la **cuillère** *fem*
a spoonful of cinnamon une cuillère de cannelle

**sport** *noun*
le **sport** *masc*
My favourite sport is tennis. Mon sport préféré, c'est le tennis.
to be good at sport être [6] bon en sport
to do a lot of sport faire [10] beaucoup de sport
Chloë does a lot of sport. Chloë fait beaucoup de sport.
• **sports bag** le sac de sport
• **sports car** la voiture de sport
• **sports centre** le centre sportif
• **sports club** le club sportif
• **sportsman** le sportif
• **sportswear** les vêtements de sport
• **sportswoman** la sportive

**sporty** *adjective*
**sportif** *masc*, **sportive** *fem*
Sarah's very sporty. Sarah est très sportive.

to **spot** *verb* ▷ see **spot** *noun*
**repérer** [24]
I spotted her in the crowd. Je l'ai repérée dans la foule.

♪ **spot** *noun* ▷ see **spot** *verb*
1 (*in a fabric design*) le **pois** *masc*
**a white scarf with black spots** une écharpe blanche aux pois noirs
2 (*pimple*) le **bouton** *masc*
**I've got spots.** J'ai des boutons.
**Amy was covered in spots.** Amy était couverte de boutons.
3 (*stain*) la **tache** *fem*
**You have a spot on your blouse.** Tu as une tache sur ta chemise.
4 (*in a theatre*) le **projecteur** *masc*
5 (*at home*) le **spot** *masc*
6 (*in expressions*) **on the spot**
**an on-the-spot repair** une réparation sur-le-champ.
**They have advisers on the spot.** Ils ont des conseillers sur place.

**spotless** *adjective*
**impeccable** *masc & fem*

**spotlight** *noun*
1 (*in theatre*) le **projecteur** *masc*
2 (*at home*) le **spot** *masc*

**spouse** *noun*
un **époux** *masc*, une **épouse** *fem*

to **sprain** *verb* ▷ see **sprain** *noun*
**to sprain your ankle** se faire Ⓔ **[10]** une entorse à la cheville

**sprain** *noun* ▷ see **sprain** *verb*
une **entorse** *fem*

to **spray** *verb* ▷ see **spray** *noun*
1 (*a liquid, flowers*) **vaporiser [1]**
2 (*a person*) **asperger [52]**
3 (*an oilslick*) **arroser [1]**

**spray** *noun* ▷ see **spray** *verb*
(*spray can*) la **bombe** *fem*
**a paint spray** une bombe de peinture

♪ to **spread** *verb* ▷ see **spread** *noun*
1 (*news, diseases, fire, panic*) **se propager** Ⓔ **[52]**
**The fire spread quickly.** L'incendie s'est propagée rapidement.
2 (*butter, jam, glue*) **étaler [1]**
3 (*a rumour*) **faire [10] circuler la rumeur**
**He's spreading a rumour that I'm going away.** Il fait circuler la rumeur que je pars.

**spread** *noun* ▷ see **spread** *verb*
la **pâte à tartiner**
**cheese spread** le fromage à tartiner

**spreadsheet** *noun*
le **tableur** *masc*

♪ **spring** *noun*
1 (*the season*) le **printemps** *masc*
**in the spring** au printemps
**next spring** le printemps prochain
**last spring** le printemps dernier
2 (*in a mattress, a seat*) le **ressort** *masc*
3 (*for water*) la **source** *fem*
• **spring-cleaning** le grand nettoyage de printemps
• **springtime** le printemps
• **spring water** l'eau de source *fem*

to **sprint** *verb* ▷ see **sprint** *noun*
**courir [2] à toute vitesse**
**I sprinted after the bus.** J'ai couru à toute vitesse après le bus.

**sprint** *noun* ▷ see **sprint** *verb*
le **sprint** *masc*

**sprinter** *noun*
le **sprinteur** *masc*, la **sprinteuse** *fem*

**sprout** *noun*
(*Brussels sprout*) le **chou de Bruxelles** (*pl* les **choux de Bruxelles**)

to **spy** *verb* ▷ see **spy** *noun*
**to spy on somebody** espionner **[1]** quelqu'un

**spy** *noun* ▷ see **spy** *verb*
un **espion** *masc*, une **espionne** *fem*

**spying** *noun*
l'**espionnage** *masc*

♪ **square** *adjective* ▷ see **square** *noun*
**carré** *masc*, **carrée** *fem*
**a square box** une boîte carrée
**three square metres** trois mètres carrés
**The room is four metres square.** La pièce fait quatre mètres carrés.

♪ **square** *noun* ▷ see **square** *adj*
1 (*shape*) le **carré**
**black and white squares** des carrés noirs et blancs
2 (*in a town, a village*) la **place** *fem*
**the village square** la place du village

to **squash** *verb* ▷ see **squash** *noun*
**écraser [1]**

**squash** *noun* ▷ see **squash** *verb*
1 (*drink*) le **sirop** *masc*
**orange squash** le sirop d'orange
2 (*the sport*) le **squash** *masc*
**to play squash** jouer au squash

to **squeak** *verb*
1 (*doors, hinges*) **grincer [61]**
2 (*people, animals*) **pousser [1] un petit cri**

to **squeeze** *verb*
1 (*someone's arm, hand*) **serrer [1]**
**to squeeze somebody's arm** serrer le bras à quelqu'un ⏩

**2** (*a toothpaste tube, a lemon*) **presser [1]**
to squeeze an orange presser une orange

**squid** *noun*
le **calmar** *masc*

**squirrel** *noun*
un **écureuil** *masc*

to **stab** *verb*
**poignarder [1]**

**stable** *adjective* ▷ see **stable** *noun*
**stable** *masc & fem*

**stable** *noun* ▷ see **stable** *adj*
une **écurie** *fem*

**stack** *noun*
**1** (*of plates, magazines*) **la pile** *fem*
**2** stacks of plein de
She's got stacks of CDs. Elle a plein de CD.

**stadium** *noun*
le **stade** *masc*
We train at the stadium. Nous nous entraînons au stade.

**staff** *noun*
**1** (*of a company*) le **personnel** *masc*
**2** (*in a school*) les **professeurs** *masc pl*

**stage** *noun*
**1** (*for performers*) la **scène** *fem*
on stage sur scène
The band came on stage. Le groupe est entré en scène.
**2** (*phase*) le **stade** *masc*
at this stage of the project à ce stade du projet

**staggered** *adjective*
(*amazed*) **stupéfié** *masc*, **stupéfiée** *fem*

to **stain** *verb* ▷ see **stain** *noun*
**tacher [1]**

**stain** *noun* ▷ see **stain** *verb*
la **tache** *fem*
to leave a stain faire [10] une tache
to remove a stain enlever [50] une tache

**stainless steel** *noun*
l'**inox** *masc*

**stairs** *noun*
l'**escalier** *masc*
to go up the stairs monter Ⓔ [1] l'escalier
to go down the stairs descendre Ⓔ [3] l'escalier
I met her on the stairs. Je l'ai croisée dans l'escalier.
She fell down the stairs. Elle est tombée dans l'escalier.

**staircase** *noun*
un **escalier** *masc*

**stale** *adjective*
(*bread*) **rassis** *masc*, **rassise** *fem*

**stalemate** *noun*
(*in chess*) le **pat** *masc*

**stall** *noun*
**1** (*in markets, fairs*) le **stand** *masc*
**2** (*in theatres*) the stalls l'orchestre *masc singular*

to **stammer** *verb* ▷ see **stammer** *noun*
**bégayer [59]**

**stammer** *noun* ▷ see **stammer** *verb*
to have a stammer bégayer [59]

to **stamp** *verb* ▷ see **stamp** *noun*
**1** (*a letter*) **affranchir [2]**
**2** to stamp your foot taper [1] du pied

**stamp** *noun* ▷ see **stamp** *verb*
le **timbre** *masc*
I have to buy stamps. Je dois acheter des timbres.
How much is a stamp for England? Un timbre pour l'Angleterre, c'est combien?

**stamp album** *noun*
un **album de timbres**

**stamp collection** *noun*
la **collection de timbres**

to **stand** *verb*
**1** **être [6] debout**
Several people were standing. Plusieurs personnes étaient debout.
**2** (*to put up with*) **supporter [1]**
I can't stand her. Je ne la supporte pas.
I can't stand waiting. Je ne supporte pas d'attendre.
**3** (*to be*) to be standing somewhere être [6] quelque part
They're still standing there. Ils sont toujours là.

- to **stand back**
**se reculer** Ⓔ **[1]**
Stand back from the road. Reculez-vous de la route.

- to **stand for something**
**être [6] l'abréviation de quelque chose**
'UN' stands for 'United Nations'. 'UN' est l'abréviation de 'United Nations'.

- to **stand up**
**se lever** Ⓔ **[50]**
Everybody stood up. Tout le monde s'est levé.

**standard** *adjective* ▷ see **standard** *noun*
**standard** *invariable adj*
the standard price le prix standard

**standard** *noun* ▷ see **standard** *adj*
le **niveau** *masc*
**to be of a high standard** être [6] d'un bon niveau
**They must reach the required standard.** Ils doivent atteindre le niveau exigé.

**Standard grades** *plural noun*
(*You can explain Standard grades as follows: Ce sont des examens que les lycéens écossais passent à l'âge d'environ 16 ans dans six ou sept matières. La meilleure note que l'on peut obtenir est 1 et la note la plus basse est 7. Une fois qu'ils ont obtenu leurs Standard grades, de nombreux étudiants se préparent pour les Highers.*)
▷ **Highers**

**standard of living** *noun*
le **niveau de vie**
**a higher standard of living** un niveau de vie supérieur

**stands** *plural noun*
la **tribune** *fem singular*
**a seat in the stands** une place à la tribune

to **staple** *verb* ▷ see **staple** *noun*
**agrafer [1]**

**staple** *noun* ▷ see **staple** *verb*
une **agrafe** *fem*

**stapler** *noun*
une **agrafeuse** *fem*

to **star** *verb* ▷ see **star** *noun*
**to star in a film** être [6] la vedette d'un film

♪ **star** *noun* ▷ see **star** *verb*
1 (*in the sky*) une **étoile** *fem*
2 (*personality*) une **vedette**
**He's a film star.** C'est une vedette de cinéma.

♪ to **stare** *verb*
**regarder [1] fixement**
**He was staring at me.** Il me regardait fixement.
**What are you staring at?** Qu'est-ce que tu regardes?

♪ **star sign** *noun*
le **signe astrologique**
**What star sign are you?** De quelle signe êtes-vous?

♪ to **start** *verb* ▷ see **start** *noun*
1 **commencer [61]**
**When does it start?** Ça commence à quelle heure?
**It starts at eight.** Ça commence à huit heures.
**I've started the book.** J'ai commencé le livre.
2 **to start doing something** commencer [61] à faire quelque chose
**I've started learning Spanish.** J'ai commencé à apprendre l'espagnol.
3 **to start again** recommencer
**We'll have to start all over again.** Il va falloir recommencer à zéro.
4 (*cars*) **démarrer [1]**
**The car won't start.** La voiture ne veut pas démarrer.
**She started the car.** Elle a fait démarrer la voiture.

♪ **start** *noun* ▷ see **start** *verb*
1 le **début** *masc*
**at the start** au début
**at the start of the book** au début du livre
**from the start** dès le début
2 **to make a start on something** commencer [61] à faire quelque chose
**I've made a start on my homework.** J'ai commencé à faire mes devoirs.
3 (*of a race*) le **départ** *masc*
4 **the start of the school year** la rentrée scolaire

♪ **starter** *noun*
une **entrée** *fem*
**What would you like as a starter?** Qu'est-ce que vous voulez comme entrée?
**I'd like the melon as a starter.** Je prendrai le melon comme entrée.

to **starve** *verb*
**mourir** Ⓔ **[54] de faim**
**I'm starving!** Je meurs de faim!

to **state** *verb* ▷ see **state** *noun*
1 (*an opinion, an intention*) **déclarer [1]**
2 (*your address, occupation*) **indiquer [1]**

♪ **state** *noun* ▷ see **state** *verb*
1 (*condition*) un **état** *masc*
**in a very bad state** en très mauvais état
2 (*in a country*) un **état** *masc*
3 (*in politics*) **the state** l'État
4 (*U.S.A.*) **the States** les États-Unis *masc pl*
**They live in the States.** Ils habitent aux États-Unis.

**stately home** *noun*
le **château** *masc* (*pl* les **châteaux**)

**statement** *noun*
la **déclaration** *fem*

♪ **station** *noun*
la **gare** *fem*
**the railway station** la gare
**the bus station** la gare routière
**She dropped me off at the station.** Elle m'a déposé à la gare.

**stationer's** *noun*
la **papeterie** *fem*

**stationery** *noun*
la **papeterie** *fem*

**statistics** *noun*
1 (*subject*) la **statistique** *fem*
2 (*figures*) the statistics les statistiques *fem pl*

**statue** *noun*
la **statue** *fem*

**status** *noun*
la **position** *fem*
social status la position sociale

♪ to **stay** *verb* ▷ see **stay** *noun*
1 (*in general*) **rester** Ⓔ **[1]**
I'll stay here. Je reste ici.
How long are you staying? Vous restez combien de temps?
I'll be staying here for two nights. Je reste deux nuits ici.
2 (*with periods of time*) passer **[1]**
We stayed in Nice for a week. Nous avons passé une semaine à Nice.
3 to stay with somebody aller Ⓔ **[7]** chez quelqu'un
We stayed with friends. Nous sommes allés chez des amis.
4 (*to be living temporarily*) **loger [52]**
Where are you staying? Où est-ce que vous logez?
We're staying at the youth hostel. Nous logeons à l'auberge de jeunesse.
• to **stay in**
**rester** Ⓔ **[1] à la maison**
I'm staying in tonight. Je reste à la maison ce soir.
• to **stay out**
to stay out late rentrer Ⓔ **[1]** tard
Don't stay out too late. Ne rentre pas trop tard.
• to **stay up**
to stay up late se coucher Ⓔ **[1]** tard

♪ **stay** *noun* ▷ see **stay** *verb*
le **séjour** *masc*
during our stay in Dijon pendant notre séjour à Dijon
Enjoy your stay! Bon séjour!

♪ **steady** *adjective*
1 (*job*) **stable** *masc & fem*
2 (*increase, decrease*) **régulier** *masc*, **régulière** *fem*
3 (*hand, voice*) **ferme** *masc & fem*
4 to hold something steady bien tenir **[77]** quelque chose
I held the ladder steady. J'ai bien tenu l'échelle.

**steak** *noun*
le **steack** *masc*
steak and chips un steack frites

♪ to **steal** *verb*
**voler [1]**
The purse was stolen. Le porte-monnaie a été volé.
to steal something from somebody voler quelque chose à quelqu'un
They stole money from us. Ils nous ont volé de l'argent.
My camera's been stolen. On m'a volé mon appareil photo.

**steam** *noun*
la **vapeur** *fem*
• **steam engine** la locomotive à vapeur
• **steam iron** le fer à vapeur

**steel** *noun*
l'**acier** *masc*
made of steel en acier

**steep** *adjective*
**raide** *masc & fem*

**steeple** *noun*
1 (*spire*) la **flèche** *fem*
2 (*bell tower*) le **clocher** *masc*

**steering wheel** *noun*
le **volant** *masc*

to **step** *verb* ▷ see **step** *noun*
to step into something entrer Ⓔ **[1]** dans quelque chose
I stepped into the office. Je suis entré dans le bureau.
• to **step back**
**faire [10] un pas en arrière**
• to **step forward**
**faire [10] un pas en avant**

♪ **step** *noun* ▷ see **step** *verb*
1 (*in walking*) le **pas** *masc*
to take a step forwards faire **[10]** un pas en avant
to take a step backwards faire **[10]** un pas en arrière
I heard steps. J'ai entendu des pas.
2 (*on stairs*) la **marche** *fem*
'Mind the step' 'Attention à la marche'

**stepbrother** *noun*
le **demi-frère** *masc* (*pl* les **demi-frères**)

**stepdaughter** *noun*
la **belle-fille** *fem* (*pl* les **belles-filles**)

**stepfather** *noun*
le **beau-père** *masc* (*pl* les **beaux-pères**)

**stepladder** *noun*
un **escabeau** *masc* (*pl* les **escabeaux**)

**stepmother** *noun*
la **belle-mère** *fem* (*pl* les **belles-mères**)

**stepsister** *noun*
la **demi-sœur** *fem* (*pl* les **demi-sœurs**)

**stepson** *noun*
le **beau-fils** *masc* (*pl* les **beaux-fils**)

**stereo** *noun*
la **chaîne stéréo** (*pl* les **chaînes stéréo**)

**stew** *noun*
le **ragoût** *masc*

**steward** *noun*
le **steward** *masc*

**stewardess** *noun*
une **hôtesse** *fem*

♪ to **stick** *verb* ▷ see **stick** *noun*
1 (*with glue*) **coller [1]**
I stuck it on with tape. Je l'ai collé avec du Scotch®.
2 (*to put*) **mettre [11]**
Stick them on my desk. Mets-les sur mon bureau.
3 **to stick out your tongue** tirer **[1]** la langue
• to **stick together**
1 (*to stay together*) **rester ⓔ [1] ensemble**
2 (*to be loyal*) **être [6] solidaire**

**stick** *noun* ▷ see **stick** *verb*
le **bâton** *masc*

**sticker** *noun*
un **autocollant** *masc*

**sticky** *adjective*
1 (*hands, fingers*) **poisseux** *masc*, **poisseuse** *fem*
2 (*paper, tape*) **adhésif** *masc*, **adhésive** *fem*

**sticky tape** *noun*
le **Scotch®** *masc*

♪ **stiff** *adjective*
1 **to feel stiff** avoir **[5]** des courbatures
**to have stiff legs** avoir des courbatures dans les jambes
**I was stiff all over.** J'avais des courbatures partout.
2 **to be bored stiff** s'ennuyer **[41]** à mourir
3 **to be scared stiff** être **[6]** mort de peur

**still** *adjective* ▷ see **still** *adv*
1 (*not moving*) **Sit still!** Tiens-toi tranquille!
**Keep still!** Ne bouge pas!
2 (*not fizzy*) **non-gazeux** *masc*, **non-gazeuse** *fem*

♪ **still** *adverb* ▷ see **still** *adj*
1 **toujours**
**I still go there.** J'y vais toujours.
**I've still not finished.** Je n'ai toujours pas fini.
**He's still working.** Il est toujours en train de travailler.
**Do you still live in Hull?** Est-ce que tu habites toujours à Hull?
2 **encore**
**There's still a lot of cake left.** Il reste encore beaucoup de gâteau.
**I've still got some money.** Il me reste encore de l'argent.
3 **better still** encore mieux

♪ to **sting** *verb* ▷ see **sting** *noun*
**piquer [1]**
**to be stung** se faire ⓔ **[10]** piquer
**I was stung by a bee.** Je me suis fait piquer par une abeille.

**sting** *noun* ▷ see **sting** *verb*
la **piqûre** *fem*

to **stink** *verb* ▷ see **stink** *noun*
**puer [1]**
**It stinks of cigarettes.** Ça pue la cigarette ici.

**stink** *noun* ▷ see **stink** *verb*
une **odeur** *fem*
**the stink of fish** l'odeur de poisson
**What a stink!** Ça pue!

♪ to **stir** *verb*
1 (*a liquid, a sauce*) **remuer [1]**
2 (*to move*) **bouger [52]**
**He was stirring in his sleep.** Il bougeait en dormant.
3 **to stir up trouble** faire **[10]** des histoires
**Why is she stirring up trouble?** Pourquoi est-ce qu'elle fait des histoires?

**stitch** *noun*
1 (*in sewing*) le **point** *masc*
2 (*in knitting*) la **maille** *fem*
3 (*for a wound*) le **point de souture** (*pl* les **points de souture**)
**I got ten stitches.** On m'a fait dix points de souture.
4 **to get a stitch** attraper **[1]** un point de côté

to **stock** *verb* ▷ see **stock** *noun*
**vendre [3]**
**They don't stock fireworks.** Ils ne vendent pas les feux d'artifice.
• to **stock up on something**
**s'approvisionner [1] en quelque chose**
**We must stock up on fruit.** Il faut s'approvisionner en fruits.

**stock** *noun* ▷ see **stock** *verb*
1 (*in store*) le **stock** *masc*
**in stock** en stock
**Do you have any others in stock?** Vous en avez d'autres en stock? ▸▸

2 (*supply*) la **réserve**
I always have a stock of pencils. J'ai toujours une réserve de crayons.
3 (*for cooking*) le **bouillon** *masc*
chicken stock le bouillon de poulet

**stock cube** *noun*
le **bouillon-cube** *masc*

**stock exchange** *noun*
la **Bourse (des valeurs)**

**stocking** *noun*
le **bas** *masc*
a pair of stockings une paire de bas

**stomach** *noun*
l'**estomac** *masc*

**stomach ache** *noun*
to have stomach ache avoir **[5]** mal au ventre

♂ **stone** *noun*
1 (*in general*) la **pierre** *fem*
a stone wall un mur en pierre
2 (*small*) le **caillou** *masc* (*pl* les **cailloux**)
to throw stones lancer **[61]** des cailloux
3 (*in fruit*) le **noyau** *masc* (*pl* les **noyaux**)
to remove the stone enlever **[50]** le noyau

**stool** *noun*
le **tabouret** *masc*

♂ to **stop** *verb* ▷ see **stop** *noun*
1 **s'arrêter** Ⓔ **[1]**
The music stopped. La musique s'est arrêtée.
Paul stopped in front of the shop. Paul s'est arrêté devant le magasin.
The train only stops once. Le train s'arrête une fois seulement.
Does the train stop in Dijon? Est-ce que le train s'arrête à Dijon?
2 (*a person, a car*) **arrêter [1]**
She stopped me in the street. Elle m'a arrêté dans la rue.
They're stopping the coach. Ils arrêtent le car.
3 **to stop doing something** arrêter **[1]** de faire quelque chose
Everyone stopped laughing. Tout le monde a arrêté de rire.
He's stopped smoking. Il a arrêté de fumer.
She never stops asking questions. Elle n'arrête pas de poser des questions.
4 **to stop somebody doing something** empêcher **[1]** quelqu'un de faire quelque chose
It stopped me sleeping. Ça m'a empêché de dormir.

♂ **stop** *noun* ▷ see **stop** *verb*
un **arrêt** *masc*
at the bus stop à l'arrêt de bus
the next stop le prochain arrêt

**stopwatch** *noun*
le **chronomètre** *masc*

to **store** *verb* ▷ see **store** *noun*
1 (*wine, food*) **garder [1]**
2 (*Computers*) **mémoriser [1]**

**store** *noun* ▷ see **store** *verb*
(*shop*) le **magasin** *masc*

♂ **storey** *noun*
un **étage** *masc*
a three-storey house une maison à trois étages
I live on the second storey. J'habite au deuxième étage.

**stork** *noun*
la **cigogne** *fem*

♂ **storm** *noun*
1 (*wind*) la **tempête** *fem*
a snowstorm une tempête de neige
2 (*thunderstorm*) un **orage** *masc*
There's going to be a storm. Il va y avoir de l'orage.

**stormy** *adjective*
**orageux** *masc*, **orageuse** *fem*

♂ **story** *noun*
1 (*a tale*) une **histoire** *fem*
a true story une histoire vécue
a ghost story une histoire de fantômes
to tell a story raconter **[1]** une histoire
to make up a story inventer **[1]** une histoire
2 (*in a newspaper*) un **article**
a front-page story un article à la une

**stove** *noun*
1 (*cooker*) la **cuisinière** *fem*
2 (*heater*) le **poêle** *masc*

♂ **straight** *adjective* ▷ see **straight** *adv*
1 **droit** *masc*, **droite** *fem*
a straight line une ligne droite
to have straight hair avoir **[5]** les cheveux raides
2 (*clear*) **clair** *masc*, **claire** *fem*
a straight answer une réponse claire

♂ **straight** *adverb* ▷ see **straight** *adj*
1 (*in direction*) **droit**
straight ahead tout droit
Go straight ahead. Continuez tout droit.
2 (*in time*) **directement**
He went straight to the doctor's. Il est allé directement chez le médecin.

3 straight away tout de suite
I called back straight away. J'ai rappelé tout de suite.

**straightforward** *adjective*
1 *(explanation, question)* **simple** *masc & fem*
2 *(honest)* **franc** *masc*, **franche** *fem*

to **strain** *verb* ▷ see **strain** *noun*
1 *(your back, eyes)* **se faire ⓔ [10] mal à**
2 *(a muscle)* **se froisser ⓔ [1]**
Dan strained a muscle during the match. Dan s'est froissé un muscle pendant le match.
3 *(rice, pasta)* **égoutter [1]**

**strain** *noun* ▷ see **strain** *verb*
le **stress** *masc*
the strain of the last few weeks le stress de ces dernières semaines
They're under a lot of strain. Ils sont stressés.

⚷ **strange** *adjective*
**bizarre** *masc & fem*
a strange situation une situation bizarre
It seems very strange to me. Ça me paraît très bizarre.

**stranger** *noun*
un **inconnu** *masc*, une **inconnue** *fem*
They were strangers. C'étaient des inconnus.

to **strangle** *verb*
**étrangler [1]**

**strap** *noun*
1 *(of a case, camera)* la **courroie** *fem*
2 *(of a shoulder bag)* la **bandoulière** *fem*
3 *(of a dress, a bra)* la **bretelle** *fem*
4 *(of a watch)* le **bracelet** *masc*
5 *(of a shoe)* la **lanière** *fem*

**strapless** *adjective*
*(dress, bra)* **sans bretelles**

**straw** *noun*
1 *(for drinking with)* la **paille** *fem*
2 *(material)* la **paille** *fem*
a straw hat un chapeau de paille

⚷ **strawberry** *noun*
la **fraise** *fem*
strawberry jam la confiture de fraises

**stray** *adjective*
a stray dog un chien perdu

**stream** *noun*
le **ruisseau** *masc (pl* les **ruisseaux***)*

⚷ **street** *noun*
la **rue** *fem*
The streets are always busy. Les rues sont toujours animées.
I met Ben in the street. J'ai croisé Ben dans la rue.
- **streetlamp** le réverbère
- **street map** le plan de la ville

**streetwise** *adjective*
**dégourdi** *masc*, **dégourdie** *fem*

⚷ **strength** *noun*
1 *(of a person)* la **force** *fem*
with all your strength de toutes ses forces
He pulled with all his strength. Il a tiré de toutes ses forces.
I hadn't got the strength to shout. Je n'ai pas eu la force de crier.
2 *(of a country)* la **puissance**
military strength la puissance militaire

to **stress** *verb* ▷ see **stress** *noun*
*(a point)* **souligner [1]**

**stress** *noun* ▷ see **stress** *verb*
le **stress** *masc*
to be under a lot of stress être [6] stressé

⚷ to **stretch** *verb*
1 *(fabrics, woollens)* **se déformer ⓔ [1]**
This jumper has stretched. Ce pull s'est déformé.
2 *(your muscles)* **étirer [1]**
to stretch out your arms étirer les bras
to stretch your legs se dégourdir ⓔ [2] les jambes
3 *(with your whole body)* **s'étirer ⓔ [1]**
4 *(shoes)* **s'élargir ⓔ [2]**

**stretcher** *noun*
le **brancard** *masc*

**stretchy** *adjective*
**élastique** *masc & fem*

**strict** *adjective*
**strict** *masc*, **stricte** *fem*

to **strike** *verb* ▷ see **strike** *noun*
1 *(to hit)* **frapper [1]**
2 *(clock)* **sonner [1]**
The clock struck six. L'horloge a sonné six heures.
3 *(workers)* **faire [10] grève**

⚷ **strike** *noun* ▷ see **strike** *verb*
la **grève** *fem*
to go on strike faire [10] grève
to be on strike être [6] en grève

**striker** *noun*
1 *(in football)* le **buteur** *masc*
2 *(worker)* le & la **gréviste** *masc & fem*

**striking** *adjective*
**frappant** *masc*, **frappante** *fem*
a striking resemblance une ressemblance frappante

**string** *noun*
1 *(for parcels)* la **ficelle** *fem*
2 *(for musical instruments)* la **corde** *fem*

to **strip** *verb* ▷ see **strip** *noun*
*(to undress)* **se déshabiller** ⓔ **[1]**

**strip** *noun* ▷ see **strip** *verb*
la **bande** *fem*

**strip cartoon** *noun*
la **bande dessinée**

**stripe** *noun*
la **rayure** *fem*

**striped** *adjective*
**rayé** *masc*, **rayée** *fem*

to **stroke** *verb* ▷ see **stroke** *noun*
**caresser [1]**

**stroke** *noun* ▷ see **stroke** *verb*
1 *(in swimming)* la **nage** *fem*
2 *(medical)* une **attaque** *fem*
**to have a stroke** avoir **[5]** une attaque
3 **to have a stroke of luck** avoir **[5]** un coup de chance

to **stroll** *verb* ▷ see **stroll** *noun*
**se promener** ⓔ **[50]**

**stroll** *noun* ▷ see **stroll** *verb*
**to go for a stroll** faire **[10]** une petite promenade

**strong** *adjective*
1 *(in general)* **fort** *masc*, **forte** *fem*
**She's as strong as you.** Elle est aussi forte que toi.
**There are strong currents.** Il y a des courants forts.
2 *(material)* **solide** *masc & fem*
**strong shoes** des chaussures solides
**Is the shelf strong enough?** Est-ce que l'étagère est assez solide?
3 *(country, state)* **puissant** *masc*, **puissante** *fem*

**strongly** *adverb*
1 *(to believe)* **fermement**
2 *(to support)* **fortement**
3 *(to advise, oppose)* **vivement**

to **struggle** *verb* ▷ see **struggle** *noun*
1 *(to get something)* **se battre** ⓔ **[21]**
**They have struggled to survive.** Ils se sont battus pour survivre.
2 *(physically)* **se débattre** ⓔ **[21]**
**I was struggling to stay awake.** Je me débattais pour rester éveillé.

**struggle** *noun* ▷ see **struggle** *verb*
la **lutte** *fem*
**a power struggle** une lutte pour le pouvoir
**the struggle for independence** la lutte pour l'indépendance

to **stub** *verb*
1 **to stub your toe on something** se cogner ⓔ **[1]** l'orteil contre quelque chose
2 **to stub a cigarette out** écraser **[1]** une cigarette

**stubborn** *adjective*
**têtu** *masc*, **têtue** *fem*

**stuck** *adjective*
1 *(jammed)* **coincé** *masc*, **coincée** *fem*
**The drawer's stuck.** Le tiroir est coincé.
2 **to get stuck** rester ⓔ **[1]** coincé
**We got stuck in the traffic.** Nous sommes restés coincés dans la circulation.

**stud** *noun*
1 *(on a belt, jacket)* le **clou** *masc*
2 *(on a boot)* le **clou** *masc*
3 *(earring)* la **boucle d'oreille**

**student** *noun*
un **étudiant** *masc*, une **étudiante** *fem*

**studio** *noun*
1 *(film, TV)* le **studio** *masc*
2 *(artist's)* un **atelier** *masc*
• **studio flat** le studio

to **study** *verb* ▷ see **study** *noun*
1 *(to revise)* **réviser [1]**
**He's studying for his exams.** Il est en train de réviser pour ses examens.
2 *(a subject)* **faire [10] des études de**
**She's studying medicine.** Elle fait des études de médecine.

**study** *noun* ▷ see **study** *verb*
le **bureau** *masc*

to **stuff** *verb* ▷ see **stuff** *noun*
1 *(to push)* **fourrer [1]**
**She stuffed some things into a backpack.** Elle a fourré quelques affaires dans un sac.
2 *(a chicken, vegetables)* **farcir [2]**
**stuffed aubergines** des aubergines farcies
3 **to be stuffed up** avoir **[5]** le nez bouché

**stuff** *noun* ▷ see **stuff** *verb*
1 *(personal belongings)* les **affaires** *fem pl*
**all my stuff** toutes mes affaires
**You can leave your stuff at my house.** Tu peux laisser tes affaires chez moi.
2 *(general things)* les **trucs** *masc pl*
**I put all that stuff in the attic.** J'ai mis tous ces trucs au grenier.
3 *(substance)* le **truc** *masc*
**some antiseptic stuff** un truc antiseptique

**stuffing** *noun*
la **farce** *fem*

ⓔ means the verb takes être to form the perfect

**stuffy** *adjective*
**étouffant** *masc*, **étouffante** *fem*

to **stumble** *verb*
**trébucher [1]**

**stunned** *adjective*
**stupéfait** *masc*, **stupéfaite** *fem*

**stunning** *adjective*
**sensationnel** *masc*, **sensationnelle** *fem*

**stunt** *noun*
(*in a film*) la **cascade** *fem*
- **stuntman** le cascadeur
- **stuntwoman** la cascadeuse

**stupid** *adjective*
**bête** *masc & fem*
**That was really stupid.** C'était vraiment bête.
**They're so stupid.** Ils sont tellement bêtes.
**to do something stupid** faire **[10]** une bêtise
**Don't do anything stupid.** Ne fais pas de bêtises.

**stutter** *noun* ▷ see **stutter** *verb*
**to have a stutter** bégayer **[59]**

to **stutter** *verb* ▷ see **stutter** *noun*
**bégayer [59]**

**style** *noun*
1 (*way*) le **style** *masc*
**a style of living** un style de vie
2 (*fashion*) la **mode** *fem*
**It's the latest style.** C'est la dernière mode.
**They have no sense of style.** Ils n'ont aucun sens de la mode.

**subject** *noun*
1 (*in general*) le **sujet** *masc*
**the subject of my talk** le sujet de mon exposé
**Can we change the subject?** Est-ce qu'on peut parler d'autre chose?
2 (*at school*) la **matière** *fem*
**My favourite subject is biology.** Ma matière préférée, c'est la biologie.

**submarine** *noun*
le **sous-marin** *masc* (*pl* les **sous-marins**)

**subscription** *noun*
un **abonnement** *masc*
**to take out a subscription to a magazine** s'abonner **[1]** à un magazine

**subsidy** *noun*
la **subvention** *fem*

**substance** *noun*
la **substance** *fem*

to **substitute** *verb* ▷ see **substitute** *noun*
**substituer [1]**

**substitute** *noun* ▷ see **substitute** *verb*
(*person*) le **remplaçant** *masc*, la **remplaçante** *fem*

**subtitled** *adjective*
**sous-titré** *masc*, **sous-titrée** *fem*

**subtitles** *plural noun*
les **sous-titres** *masc pl*

**subtle** *adjective*
**subtil** *masc*, **subtile** *fem*

to **subtract** *verb*
**soustraire [78]**

**suburb** *noun*
la **banlieue** *fem*
**a suburb of Edinburgh** une banlieue d'Édimbourg
**in the suburbs of London** dans la banlieue de Londres

**suburban** *adjective*
(*house, estate*) **de banlieue**
**large suburban estates** les cités de banlieue

**subway** *noun*
1 (*underpass*) le **passage souterrain**
2 (*in New York, Tokyo, etc*) le **métro**

to **succeed** *verb*
**réussir [2]**
**Will they succeed?** Est-ce qu'ils vont réussir?
**to succeed in doing something** réussir à faire quelque chose
**We've succeeded in contacting her.** Nous avons réussi à la contacter.

**success** *noun*
le **succès** *masc*
**a great success** un grand succès
**to have a lot of success** avoir **[5]** beaucoup de succès

**successful** *adjective*
**réussi** *masc*, **réussie** *fem*
**a successful operation** une opération réussie
**He's a successful writer.** C'est un écrivain à succès.

**successfully** *adverb*
**avec succès**

**such** *adverb*
1 **tellement**
**They're such nice people!** Ils sont tellement gentils!
**I've had such a busy day!** J'ai eu une journée tellement chargée! ▸▸

a b c d e f g h i j k l m n o p q r s t u v w x y z

It's such a long way. C'est tellement loin.
It's such a pity. C'est tellement dommage.

2 such a lot of tellement de
such a lot of homework tellement de devoirs

3 such as comme
in big cities such as Glasgow dans les grandes villes comme Glasgow

to **suck** *verb*
**sucer [61]**

**sudden** *adjective*
**soudain** *masc*, **soudaine** *fem*
a sudden noise un bruit soudain
all of a sudden tout d'un coup

♪ **suddenly** *adverb*
1 **tout d'un coup**
**Suddenly the light went out.** Tout d'un coup la lumière s'est éteinte.
2 **to die suddenly** mourir Ⓔ **[54]** subitement

**suede** *noun*
le **daim** *masc*

to **suffer** *verb*
**souffrir [73]**

**sufficiently** *adverb*
**suffisamment**

♪ **sugar** *noun*
le **sucre** *masc*
**Would you like sugar?** Est-ce que tu veux du sucre?

♪ to **suggest** *verb*
**suggérer [24]**
**to suggest to somebody that they should do something** suggérer à quelqu'un de faire quelque chose
**He suggested I should speak to you about it.** Il m'a suggéré de vous en parler.

**suggestion** *noun*
la **suggestion** *fem*

**suicide** *noun*
le **suicide** *masc*
**to commit suicide** se suicider Ⓔ **[1]**

♪ to **suit** *verb*
1 **to suit somebody** convenir **[81]** à quelqu'un
**Eight p.m., does that suit you?** Vingt heures, ça te convient?
**It doesn't suit me.** Ça ne me convient pas.
2 (*to look well on*) **to suit somebody** aller Ⓔ **[7]** (bien) à quelqu'un
**Does it suit me?** Est-ce que ça me va?
**Blue really suits you.** Le bleu te va bien.

♪ **suit** *noun* ▷ see **suit** *verb*
1 (*man's*) le **costume** *masc*
2 (*woman's*) le **tailleur** *masc*

**suitable** *adjective*
1 (*clothes, presents*) **approprié** *masc*, **appropriée** *fem*
**I don't have any suitable shoes.** Je n'ai pas de chaussures appropriées.
2 **to be suitable for somebody** convenir **[81]** à quelqu'un
**It's more suitable for children.** Ça convient mieux aux enfants.

♪ **suitcase** *noun*
la **valise** *fem*
**to pack your suitcase** faire **[10]** sa valise

to **sulk** *verb*
**bouder [1]**

**sum** *noun* ▷ see **sum** *verb*
1 (*quantity*) la **somme** *fem*
**a large sum of money** une grosse somme d'argent
2 (*calculation*) le **calcul** *masc*

to **summarize** *verb*
**résumer [1]**

**summary** *noun*
le **résumé** *masc*

♪ **summer** *noun*
l'**été** *masc*
**in summer** en été
**next summer** l'été prochain
**summer clothes** les vêtements d'été
**the summer holidays** les grandes vacances
**I'm going there for the summer.** J'y vais pour l'été.
**We went to Brittany last summer.** Nous sommes allés en Bretagne l'été dernier.

**summertime** *noun*
l'**été** *masc*
**in summertime** en été

**summit** *noun*
le **sommet** *masc*
**at the summit** au sommet

♪ **sun** *noun*
le **soleil** *masc*
**in the sun** au soleil
- **sunbathe** se bronzer Ⓔ **[1]**
- **sunblock** la crème écran total
- **sunburn** le coup de soleil

♪ **sunburned** *adjective*
**to get sunburned** attraper **[1]** un coup de soleil
**I got sunburned.** J'ai attrapé un coup de soleil.

Ⓔ means the verb takes être to form the perfect

**Sunday** *noun*
le **dimanche** *masc*
on Sunday dimanche
last Sunday dimanche dernier
next Sunday dimanche prochain
every Sunday tous les dimanches
on Sundays le dimanche
**The museum is closed on Sundays.** Le musée est fermé le dimanche.
**I'm going out on Sunday.** Je sors dimanche.
**See you on Sunday!** À dimanche!

**WORD TIP** Months of the year and days of the week start with small letters in French.

**sunflower** *noun*
le **tournesol** *masc*
• **sunflower oil** l'huile *fem* de tournesol

**sunglasses** *plural noun*
les **lunettes de soleil** *fem pl*

**sunlight** *noun*
le **soleil** *masc*

**sunny** *adjective*
1 to be sunny faire [10] du soleil
**It's very sunny.** Il fait du soleil.
**It's going to be sunny.** Il va faire du soleil.
2 (*place*) **ensoleillé** *masc*, **ensoleillée** *fem*
**in a sunny corner of the garden** dans un coin ensoleillé du jardin

**sunrise** *noun*
le **lever du soleil**

**sunroof** *noun*
le **toit ouvrant**

**sunset** *noun*
le **coucher du soleil**

**sunshine** *noun*
le **soleil** *masc*
in the sunshine au soleil

**sunstroke** *noun*
une **insolation** *fem*
to get sunstroke attraper [1] une insolation

**suntan** *noun*
le **bronzage** *masc*
to get a suntan bronzer [1]
• **suntan lotion** la lotion solaire

**super** *adjective*
**super** *invariable adj*, **formidable** *masc & fem*
**We had a super time!** C'était super!

**supermarket** *noun*
le **supermarché** *masc*

**supernatural** *adjective*
**surnaturel** *masc*, **surnaturelle** *fem*

**superstitious** *adjective*
**superstitieux** *masc*, **superstitieuse** *fem*

to **supervise** *verb*
**surveiller [1]**

**supervisor** *noun*
1 (*in a shop*) le & la **responsable** *masc & fem*
2 (*in a factory*) le **contremaître** *masc*

**supper** *noun*
le **dîner** *masc*
to have supper dîner [1]
**I had supper at Helen's.** J'ai dîné chez Helen.

**supplement** *noun*
le **supplément** *masc*
**There's a supplement.** Il y a un supplément à payer.
**There's no supplement.** Il n'y a pas de supplément.

**supplies** *plural noun*
les **provisions** *fem pl*

to **supply** *verb* ▷ see **supply** *noun*
**fournir [2]**
**The school supplies the paper.** C'est l'école qui fournit le papier.
**to supply somebody with something** fournir quelque chose à quelqu'un
**They supply us with the books.** Ils nous fournissent les livres.

**supply** *noun* ▷ see **supply** *verb*
1 (*stock*) les **réserves** *fem pl*
**food supplies** les réserves de nourriture
2 (*of oil, gas, electricity*) l'**alimentation** *fem*
3 to be in short supply être [6] difficile à trouver
**Work is in short supply.** Le travail est difficile à trouver.

**supply teacher** *noun*
le **suppléant** *masc*, la **suppléante** *fem*

to **support** *verb* ▷ see **support** *noun*
1 (*to back up*) **soutenir [77]**
**Her teachers have really supported her.** Ses professeurs l'ont vraiment soutenue.
2 (*a team*) **être [6] supporter de**
**Dave supports Liverpool.** Dave est supporter de Liverpool.
3 **to support a family** subvenir [81] aux besoins d'une famille

**support** *noun* ▷ see **support** *verb*
le **soutien** *masc*
**He has a lot of support.** Il a beaucoup de soutien.

English–French

**supporter** *noun*
le & la **supporter** *masc & fem*
a Rangers supporter un supporter de Rangers

to **suppose** *verb*
I suppose she's forgotten. Elle a sans doute oublié.
Suppose she doesn't come? Et si elle ne vient pas?

**supposed** *adjective*
to be supposed to do something être[6] censé faire quelque chose
You're supposed to wear a helmet. On est censé porter un casque.
We're not supposed to chat. Nous ne sommes pas censés bavarder.
He was supposed to be here at six. Il devait être là à six heures.

**sure** *adjective*
**sûr** *masc*, **sûre** *fem*
Are you sure? Tu es sûr?
Yes, I'm sure. Oui, j'en suis sûr.
Are you sure you've had enough to eat? Tu es sûr que tu as assez mangé?
Are you sure you saw her? Tu es sûr de l'avoir vue?
I'm sure I recognized her. Je suis sûr de l'avoir reconnue.
'Can you shut the door?' — 'Sure!' 'Peux-tu fermer la porte?' — 'Bien sûr!'

**surely** *adverb*
**quand même**
Surely you've checked! Tu as vérifié quand même!

to **surf** *verb* ▷ see **surf** *noun*
to surf the Net surfer[1] sur Internet

**surf** *noun* ▷ see **surf** *verb*
l'**écume** *fem*

**surface** *noun*
la **surface** *fem*
on the surface à la surface

**surfboard** *noun*
la **planche de surf** (*pl* les **planches de surf**)

**surfer** *noun*
1 (*in the sea*) le **surfeur** *masc*, la **surfeuse** *fem*
2 (*on the Internet*) un & une **internaute** *masc & fem*

**surfing** *noun*
le **surf** *masc*
to go surfing faire[10] du surf

**surgeon** *noun*
le **chirurgien** *masc*
She's a surgeon. Elle est chirurgien.

**surgery** *noun*
1 (*procedure*) la **chirurgie** *fem*
cosmetic surgery la chirurgie esthétique
to have surgery se faire Ⓔ [10] opérer
She had to have surgery. Elle a dû se faire opérer.
2 (*doctor's*) le **cabinet médical**
the dentist's surgery le cabinet dentaire

**surname** *noun*
le **nom de famille** (*pl* les **noms de famille**)
What's your surname? Quel est votre nom de famille?

to **surprise** *verb* ▷ see **surprise** *noun*
to surprise somebody faire[10] une surprise à quelqu'un
Let's surprise them. On va leur faire une surprise.

**surprise** *noun* ▷ see **surprise** *verb*
la **surprise** *fem*
What a surprise! Quelle surprise!
I want it to be a surprise. Je veux que ce soit une surprise.

**surprised** *adjective*
**étonné** *masc*, **étonnée** *fem*
I was surprised to see her. J'ai été étonné de la voir.

**surprising** *adjective*
**étonnant** *masc*, **étonnante** *fem*
I find that surprising. Je trouve ça étonnant.
It's not surprising. Ce n'est pas étonnant.

to **surrender** *verb* ▷ see **surrender** *noun*
1 (*soldiers*) **se rendre** Ⓔ [3]
2 (*country*) **capituler**[1]
3 (*a town, a castle*) **livrer**[1]

**surrender** *noun* ▷ see **surrender** *verb*
1 (*by a sportsman*) l'**abandon** *masc*
2 (*by an army*) la **capitulation** *fem*

to **surround** *verb*
1 (*police, enemy*) **encercler**[1]
Police have surrounded the building. La police a encerclé le bâtiment.
2 to be surrounded by something être[6] entouré de quelque chose
The house is surrounded by trees. La maison est entourée d'arbres.

**survey** *noun*
une **enquête** *fem*
to carry out a survey faire[10] une enquête



Ⓔ means the verb takes être to form the perfect

to **survive** *verb*
**survivre [82]**

**survivor** *noun*
le **survivant** *masc*, la **survivante** *fem*

to **suspect** *verb* ▷ see **suspect** *noun*
**soupçonner [1]**
**They're suspected of having stolen the money.** Ils sont soupçonnés d'avoir volé l'argent.

**suspect** *noun* ▷ see **suspect** *verb*
le **suspect** *masc*, la **suspecte** *fem*

to **suspend** *verb*
1 (*to hang*) **suspendre [3]**
**suspended in mid air** suspendu dans le vide
2 **to be suspended** (*from school*) être **[6]** exclu

**suspense** *noun*
le **suspense** *masc*

♪ **suspicious** *adjective*
1 (*wary*) **méfiant** *masc*, **méfiante** *fem*
**The locals are suspicious.** Les gens du coin sont méfiants.
**I'm suspicious of her.** Je me méfie d'elle.
2 (*worrying*) **suspect** *masc*, **suspecte** *fem*
**a suspicious parcel** un paquet suspect
3 (*person*) **louche** *masc & fem*
**He looks suspicious.** Il a l'air louche.

to **swallow** *verb* ▷ see **swallow** *noun*
**avaler [1]**

**swallow** *noun* ▷ see **swallow** *verb*
(*bird*) une **hirondelle** *fem*

**swan** *noun*
le **cygne** *masc*

♪ to **swap** *verb*
1 **échanger [52]**
**Do you want to swap?** Tu veux qu'on échange?
**to swap something for something** échanger quelque chose contre quelque chose
**I've swapped my bike for a computer.** J'ai échangé mon vélo contre un ordinateur.
2 **to swap places with somebody** changer **[52]** de place avec quelqu'un
**I swapped places with Rebecca.** J'ai changé de place avec Rebecca.

to **swear** *verb*
**utiliser [1] des gros mots**
**He swears a lot.** Il utilise beaucoup de gros mots.

**swearword** *noun*
le **gros mot**

to **sweat** *verb* ▷ see **sweat** *noun*
**transpirer [1]**

**sweat** *noun* ▷ see **sweat** *verb*
la **transpiration** *fem*

♪ **sweater** *noun*
le **pull** *masc*

**sweatshirt** *noun*
le **sweatshirt** *masc*, le **sweat** *masc*

**swede** *noun*
(*vegetable*) le **rutabaga** *masc*

**Swede** *noun* ▷ see **swede** *noun*
un **Suédois** *masc*, une **Suédoise** *fem*

**Sweden** *noun*
la **Suède** *fem*

**Swedish** *adjective* ▷ see **Swedish** *noun*
**suédois** *masc*, **suédoise** *fem*
▷ **Swede**.

**Swedish** *noun* ▷ see **Swedish** *adj*
(*language*) le **suédois** *masc*

to **sweep** *verb*
**balayer [59]**
**to sweep away the leaves** balayer les feuilles

♪ **sweet** *adjective* ▷ see **sweet** *noun*
1 (*food*) **sucré** *masc*, **sucrée** *fem*
**Avoid eating sweet things.** Évitez les choses sucrées.
2 (*kind*) **gentil** *masc*, **gentille** *fem*
**It was really sweet of him.** C'était vraiment gentil de sa part.
3 (*cute*) **mignon** *masc*, **mignonne** *fem*
**You look really sweet in that hat!** Tu es mignon avec ce chapeau!

**sweet** *noun* ▷ see **sweet** *adj*
1 (*wrapped*) le **bonbon** *masc*
2 (*dessert*) le **dessert** *masc*

**sweetcorn** *noun*
le **maïs** *masc*

to **swell** *verb*
**enfler [1]**

**swelling** *noun*
une **enflure** *fem*
**He has a swelling on his knee.** Il a le genou enflé.

to **swerve** *verb*
**faire [10] un écart**
**The car swerved to avoid the dog.** La voiture a fait un écart pour éviter le chien.

♂ to **swim** *verb* ▷ see **swim** *noun*
**nager [52]**
Can he swim? Est-ce qu'il sait nager?
He can't swim very well. Il ne sait pas très bien nager.
to swim across a lake traverser [1] un lac à la nage

♂ **swim** *noun* ▷ see **swim** *verb*
to go for a swim aller Ⓔ [7] se baigner Ⓔ
We went for a swim every morning. Nous sommes allés nous baigner tous les matins.

**swimmer** *noun*
le **nageur** *masc*, la **nageuse** *fem*

♂ **swimming** *noun*
la **natation** *fem*
to go swimming faire [10] de la natation
- **swimming cap** le bonnet de bain
- **swimming costume** le maillot de bain
- **swimming instructor** le maître-nageur (*pl* les maîtres-nageurs)
- **swimming pool** la piscine
- **swimming trunks** le maillot de bain

♂ **swimsuit** *noun*
le **maillot de bain**

**swindle** *noun*
l'**escroquerie** *fem*
What a swindle! Quelle escroquerie!

**swing** *noun*
la **balançoire** *fem*

**Swiss** *adjective* ▷ see **Swiss** *noun*
**suisse** *masc & fem*

**WORD TIP** Adjectives never have capitals in French, even for nationality or regional origin.

**Swiss** *noun* ▷ see **Swiss** *adj*
(*person*) un & une **Suisse** *masc & fem*
the Swiss les Suisses *masc pl*

♂ to **switch** *verb* ▷ see **switch** *noun*
(*change*) **changer [52] de**
to switch places changer de place
to switch from French to English passer [1] du français à l'anglais
- to **switch something off**
**éteindre [60] quelque chose**
I switched the light off. J'ai éteint la lumière.
- to **switch something on**
**allumer [1] quelque chose**
Can you switch on the computer? Est-ce que tu peux allumer l'ordinateur?

**switch** *noun* ▷ see **switch** *verb*
1 (*button type*) le **bouton** *masc*
2 (*up-down type*) un **interrupteur** *masc*

**Switzerland** *noun*
la **Suisse** *fem*
in Switzerland en Suisse
to Switzerland en Suisse

**WORD TIP** Countries and regions in French take *le*, *la* or *les*.

**swollen** *adjective*
**enflé** *masc*, **enflée** *fem*
My finger's swollen. J'ai le doigt enflé.

to **swop** *verb* ▷ **swap**

**sword** *noun*
une **épée** *fem*
- **swordfish** un espadon *masc*

**syllabus** *noun*
le **programme** *masc*
to be on the syllabus être [6] au programme

**symbol** *noun*
le **symbole** *masc*

**symbolic** *adjective*
**symbolique** *masc & fem*

**sympathetic** *adjective*
**compréhensif** *masc*, **compréhensive** *fem*
a sympathetic attitude une attitude compréhensive

to **sympathize** *verb*
to sympathize with somebody comprendre [64] quelqu'un
I sympathize with her. Je la comprends.

**sympathy** *noun*
la **compassion** *fem*
out of sympathy par compassion

**symphony** *noun*
la **symphonie** *fem*
- **symphony orchestra** un orchestre symphonique

**symptom** *noun*
le **symptôme** *masc*

**synagogue** *noun*
la **synagogue** *fem*

**synthesizer** *noun*
le **synthétiseur** *masc*

**synthetic** *adjective*
**synthétique** *masc & fem*

**syringe** *noun*
la **seringue** *fem*

**system** *noun*
le **système** *masc*



Ⓔ means the verb takes être to form the perfect

# T t

♪ **table** *noun*
la **table** *fem*
**on the table** sur la table
**to lay the table** mettre **[11]** la table
**to clear the table** débarrasser **[1]** la table
• **tablecloth** la nappe

**tablemat** *noun*
1 (*for individual plates*) le **set de table**
2 (*for a dish*) le **dessous-de-plat**

**tablespoon** *noun*
la **grande cuillère**

♪ **tablet** *noun*
le **comprimé** *masc*

**table tennis** *noun*
le **ping-pong**® *masc*
**to play table tennis** jouer **[1]** au ping-pong

**tabloid** *noun*
le **quotidien populaire**

to **tackle** *verb* ▷ see **tackle** *noun*
1 (*in football, hockey*) **tacler [1]**
2 (*in rugby*) **plaquer [1]**
3 (*a job, a problem*) **s'attaquer [1] à**

**tackle** *noun* ▷ see **tackle** *verb*
1 (*in football*) le **tacle** *masc*
2 (*in rugby*) le **plaquage** *masc*

**tactful** *adjective*
**plein de tact** *masc*, **pleine de tact** *fem*
**a tactful answer** une réponse pleine de tact

**tadpole** *noun*
le **têtard** *masc*

**tail** *noun*
la **queue** *fem*

♪ to **take** *verb*
1 (*in general*) **prendre [64]**
**I took the bus.** J'ai pris le bus.
**Who's taken my keys?** Qui a pris mes clefs?
**Take lots of photos.** Prenez beaucoup de photos.
**Did you take notes?** Est-ce que tu as pris des notes?
2 (*to a place*) **emmener [50]**
**She's taking Jack to the doctor's.** Elle emmène Jack chez le médecin.
3 (*to carry away*) **emporter [1]**
**She's taken some work home.** Elle a emporté du travail chez elle.
4 **to take something upstairs** monter **[1]** quelque chose
**Could you take these towels up?** Est-ce que tu peux monter ces serviettes?
5 **to take something downstairs** descendre **[3]** quelque chose
**Molly's taken the cups down.** Molly a descendu les tasses.
6 (*a credit card*) **accepter [1]**
**Do you take cheques?** Est-ce que vous acceptez les chèques?
7 (*an exam*) **passer [1]**
**She's taking her driving test.** Elle passe son permis.
8 (*to need*) **falloir [43]** (*falloir is used only in the il faut form.*) **It takes a lot of courage.** Il faut beaucoup de courage.
9 (*with clothes, shoes*) faire **[10]**
**What size shoe do you take?** Quelle pointure faites-vous?
**I take a size 36.** Je fais du 36.
• **to take something away**
(*fast food*) **emporter [1]**
**They have meals to take away.** Ils ont des plats à emporter.
• **to take something apart**
**démonter [1] quelque chose**
• **to take something back**
1 (*customers*) **rapporter [1] quelque chose**
**I have to take those shoes back.** Je dois rapporter ces chaussures.
2 (*shops*) **reprendre [64]**
• **to take off**
(*plane*) **décoller [1]**
• **to take something off**
1 (*clothes, shoes*) **enlever [50]**
2 (*to reduce*) **déduire [26]**
**She took five pounds off the price.** Elle a réduit le prix de cinq livres.
• **to take something out**
**sortir [72]**
**He took out his wallet.** Il a sorti son porte-feuille.
• **to take somebody out**
**to take somebody out somewhere** emmener **[50]** quelqu'un quelque part
**My mum took us out to the cinema.** Ma mère nous a emmenés au cinéma.
• **to take up something**
1 (*time, space*) **prendre [64]**
**The table takes up too much space.** La table prend trop de place.
2 (*the piano, tennis*) **se mettre ⓔ [11] à**
**Josh has taken up the guitar.** Josh s'est mis à la guitare.

**takeaway** *noun*
1 (*meal*) le **repas à emporter**
2 (*outlet*) le **restaurant qui fait des plats à emporter**

**tale** *noun*
une **histoire** *fem*

**talent** *noun*
le **talent** *masc*
**to have a talent for something** être [6] doué pour quelque chose

**talented** *adjective*
**doué** *masc*, **douée** *fem*

♪ to **talk** *verb*
1 **to talk about something** parler [1] de quelque chose
**What's she talking about?** De quoi est-ce qu'elle parle?
**She's talking about work.** Elle parle du travail.
**to talk to somebody about something** parler de quelque chose avec quelqu'un
**I was talking to Ibrahim about cars.** Je parlais de voitures avec Ibrahim.
2 (*to chat*) **bavarder** [1]
**They're always talking.** Ils sont toujours en train de bavarder.

♪ **talk** *noun* ▷ see **talk** *verb*
1 (*chat*) la **conversation** *fem*
**to have a talk about something** avoir [5] une conversation au sujet de quelque chose
**I had a talk with Matt about the concert.** J'ai eu une conversation avec Matt au sujet du concert.
2 **(peace) talks** les négociations (sur la paix)

♪ **tall** *adjective*
1 **grand** *masc*, **grande** *fem*
**She's very tall.** Elle est très grande.
**How tall are you?** Tu mesures combien?
**I'm 1.7 metres tall.** Je mesure un mètre soixante-dix.
2 (*building, wall, tree*) **haut** *masc*, **haute** *fem*

**tame** *adjective*
**apprivoisé** *masc*, **apprivoisée** *fem*

**tampon** *noun*
le **tampon** *masc*

**tan** *noun*
le **bronzage** *masc*

♪ to **tan** *verb*
**bronzer** [1]
**I tan easily.** Je bronze facilement.

**tank** *noun*
1 (*for petrol, water*) le **réservoir** *masc*
2 (*for fish*) un **aquarium** *masc*
3 (*military*) le **char** *masc*

**tanker** *noun*
1 (*ship*) le **navire-citerne** *invariable masc*
2 (*on road*) le **camion-citerne** *invariable masc*

**tanned** *adjective*
**bronzé** *masc*, **bronzée** *fem*

to **tap** *verb* ▷ see **tap** *noun*
**taper** [1]
**to tap on the window** taper sur la fenêtre
**to tap your feet** taper du pied

♪ **tap** *noun* ▷ see **tap** *verb*
1 (*for water, gas*) le **robinet** *masc*
**the hot tap** le robinet d'eau chaude
**to turn on the tap** ouvrir [30] le robinet
**to turn off the tap** fermer [1] le robinet
2 (*knock*) la **petite tape** *fem*

**tap-dancing** *noun*
les **claquettes** *fem pl*
**to do tap-dancing** faire [10] des claquettes

♪ to **tape** *verb* ▷ see **tape** *noun*
**enregistrer** [1]
**I want to tape the film.** Je veux enregistrer le film.

**tape** *noun* ▷ see **tape** *verb*
1 (*video, audio*) la **cassette** *fem*
2 (*adhesive*) le **scotch**®
• **tape recorder** le magnétophone

**tapestry** *noun*
la **tapisserie** *fem*

**target** *noun* ▷ see **target** *verb*
la **cible** *fem*

♪ **tart** *noun*
la **tarte** *fem*
**a raspberry tart** une tarte aux framboises

**tartan** *adjective*
**écossais** *masc*, **écossaise** *fem*

**task** *noun*
la **tâche** *fem*

to **taste** *verb* ▷ see **taste** *noun*
**goûter** [1]
**Do you want to taste?** Tu veux goûter?
**The steak tastes good.** Le bifteck a bon goût.
**The soup tasted horrible.** La soupe avait un goût infect.

♪ **taste** *noun* ▷ see **taste** *verb*
1 (*of food, drink*) le **goût** *masc*
**She hates the taste of garlic.** Elle déteste le goût d'ail.
2 (*what you like*) le **goût** *masc*
**Zoë has good taste in clothes.** Zoë s'habille avec goût.

That joke was in really bad taste. Cette blague était vraiment de mauvais goût.

**tasty** *adjective*
**savoureux** *masc*, **savoureuse** *fem*

**tattoo** *noun*
le **tatouage** *masc*

**Taurus** *noun*
**Taureau**
Joe's Taurus. Joe est Taureau.

**WORD TIP** Signs of the zodiac do not take an article: *un* or *une*.

**tax** *noun*
les **impôts** *masc pl*

**taxi** *noun*
le **taxi** *masc*
to take a taxi prendre **[64]** un taxi
Let's go by taxi. Allons-y en taxi.
- **taxi driver** le chauffeur de taxi
- **taxi rank** la station de taxis

♪ **tea** *noun*
1 le **thé** *masc*
a cup of tea une tasse de thé
2 (*evening meal*) le **dîner** *masc*
- **teabag** le sachet de thé

♪ to **teach** *verb*
1 to teach something to somebody
apprendre **[64]** quelque chose à quelqu'un
She's teaching me Italian. Elle m'apprend l'italien.
to teach somebody how to do something
apprendre à quelqu'un à faire quelque chose
Lee's teaching me to drive. Lee m'apprend à conduire.
2 **enseigner [1]**
Her mum teaches maths. Sa mère enseigne les maths.
She teaches children tennis. Elle enseigne le tennis aux enfants.

♪ **teacher** *noun*
1 (*in a secondary school*) le **professeur** *masc*
My mother's a biology teacher. Ma mère est professeur de biologie.
2 (*in a primary school*) un **instituteur** *masc*, une **institutrice** *fem*
She's a primary school teacher. Elle est institutrice.

**WORD TIP** *Le professeur* is used for both male and female teachers.

♪ **team** *noun*
une **équipe** *fem*
a football team une équipe de foot
Our team won. Notre équipe a gagné.
He wants to be in the team. Il veut faire partie de l'équipe.
- **team-mate** le coéquipier, la coéquipière
- **teamwork** le travail d'équipe

**teapot** *noun*
la **théière** *fem*

to **tear** *verb* ▷ see **tear** *noun*
**déchirer [1]**
You've torn the wrapping paper! Tu as déchiré le papier cadeau!
It tears easily. Ça se déchire facilement.
- **to tear something off**
(*a coupon, a label*) **détacher [1] quelque chose**
- **to tear something open**
**arracher [1] quelque chose**
She tore open the envelope. Elle a arraché l'enveloppe.
- **to tear something up**
**déchirer [1] quelque chose**
Tear the letter up. Déchire la lettre.

**tear** *noun* ▷ see **tear** *verb*
1 (*when you cry*) la **larme** *fem*
to burst into tears fondre **[3]** en larmes
2 (*in clothing*) un **accroc** *masc*

to **tease** *verb*
**taquiner [1]**

**teaspoon** *noun*
1 la **petite cuillère** *fem*
2 (*in recipes*) la **cuillère à café**

♪ **teatime** *noun*
l'**heure du dîner** *fem*

**tea towel** *noun*
le **torchon** *masc*

**technical** *adjective*
**technique** *masc & fem*

**technician** *noun*
le **technicien** *masc*, la **technicienne** *fem*
She's a technician. Elle est technicienne.

**technique** *noun*
la **technique** *fem*

**techno** *noun*
(*Music*) la **techno** *fem*

**technological** *adjective*
**technologique** *masc & fem*

**technology** *noun*
la **technologie** *fem*

♪ **teenage** *adjective*
1 **adolescent** *masc*, **adolescente** *fem*
a teenage son un fils adolescent
2 (*films, magazines*) **pour les jeunes**
a teenage magazine un magazine pour les jeunes

**teenager** *noun*
1 (*young person*) le & la **jeune** *masc & fem*
**a group of teenagers** une bande de jeunes
2 (*more precisely*) un **adolescent** *masc*, une **adolescente** *fem*

**teens** *plural noun*
l'**adolescence** *fem*
**She's in her teens.** C'est une adolescente.

**tee-shirt** *noun*
le **tee-shirt** *masc*

to **telephone** *verb* ▷ see **telephone** *noun*
**appeler**[18]
**I'll telephone Susie.** Je vais appeler Susie.

**telephone** *noun* ▷ see **telephone** *verb*
le **téléphone** *masc*
**He's on the telephone.** Il est au téléphone.
- **telephone call** le coup de téléphone
- **telephone card** la carte de téléphone
- **telephone directory** un annuaire
- **telephone kiosk** la cabine téléphonique
- **telephone number** le numéro de téléphone

**telescope** *noun*
le **télescope** *masc*

**television** *noun*
la **télévision** *fem*
**She's watching television.** Elle regarde la télévision.
**I saw it on television.** Je l'ai vu à la télévision.
- **television channel** la chaîne de télévision
- **television news** le journal télévisé
- **television programme** une émission de télévision

to **tell** *verb*
1 **to tell somebody something** dire[9] quelque chose à quelqu'un
**I've told Sarah.** Je l'ai dit à Sarah.
**Tell me the truth!** Dis-moi la vérité!
**You mustn't tell anyone.** Il ne faut le dire à personne.
2 **to tell somebody to do something** dire[9] à quelqu'un de faire quelque chose
**He told me to do it myself.** Il m'a dit de le faire moi-même.
**She told me not to wait.** Elle m'a dit de ne pas attendre.
3 **to tell somebody how to do something** expliquer[1] à quelqu'un comment faire quelque chose
**Joe will tell you how to save the file.** Joe va t'expliquer comment sauver le fichier.
**Can you tell me how to do it?** Est-ce que vous pouvez m'expliquer comment on le fait?
4 (*a story, a joke*) **raconter**[1]
**to tell somebody about something** raconter quelque chose à quelqu'un
**Tell me about your holiday.** Raconte-moi tes vacances.
5 (*to see*) **voir**[13]
**You can tell she's cross.** On voit bien qu'elle est fâchée.
**to tell somebody from somebody else** distinguer[1] quelqu'un de quelqu'un d'autre
**I can't tell them apart.** Je n'arrive pas à les distinguer.

**telly** *noun*
la **télé** *fem*
**to watch telly** regarder[1] la télé
**I saw her on telly.** Je l'ai vue à la télé.

**temper** *noun*
**to lose your temper** se mettre Ⓔ [11] en colère

**temperature** *noun*
1 la **température** *fem*
**The temperature is 25° Celsius.** La température est de 25°.
2 **to have a temperature** avoir[5] de la fièvre
**She took my temperature.** Elle m'a pris la température.

**temple** *noun*
le **temple** *masc*

**temporary** *adjective*
**temporaire** *masc & fem*

**temptation** *noun*
la **tentation** *fem*
**to resist the temptation** résister[1] à la tentation

**tempted** *adjective*
**tenté** *masc*, **tentée** *fem*
**to be tempted to do something** être[6] tenté de faire quelque chose

**tempting** *adjective*
**tentant** *masc*, **tentante** *fem*

**ten** *number*
**dix**
**Imran's ten.** Imran a dix ans.

to **tend** *verb*
**to tend to do something** avoir[5] tendance à faire
**He tends to talk a lot.** Il a tendance à beaucoup parler.

**tendency** *noun*
la **tendance** *fem*
**to have a tendency to do something** avoir[5] tendance à faire quelque chose

**tender** *adjective*
**tendre** *masc & fem*

**tennis** *noun*
le **tennis** *masc*
to play tennis jouer [1] au tennis
- **tennis ball** la balle de tennis
- **tennis court** le tennis
- **tennis player** le joueur de tennis, la joueuse de tennis
- **tennis racket** la raquette de tennis

**tenor** *noun*
le **ténor** *masc*

**tense** *adjective* ▷ see **tense** *noun*
(*atmosphere, person*) **tendu** *masc*, **tendue** *fem*
to get tense se crisper ❷ [1]

**tense** *noun* ▷ see **tense** *adj*
(*Grammar*) **the present tense** le présent
**the future tense** le futur

♪ **tent** *noun*
la **tente** *fem*
**to put up a tent** dresser [1] une tente
**to sleep in a tent** dormir [2] sous la tente

**tenth** *adjective*
1 **dixième** *masc & fem*
**on the tenth floor** au dixième étage
2 (*in dates*) **the tenth of April** le dix avril

♪ **term** *noun*
le **trimestre** *masc*
**during term** pendant le trimestre
**at the end of term** à la fin du trimestre

**terminal** *noun*
1 (*at an airport*) une **aérogare** *fem*
**at terminal two** à l'aérogare numéro deux
2 (*for ferries*) une **gare maritime**
3 (*Computers*) le **terminal** *masc* (*pl* les **terminaux**)

**terrace** *noun*
1 (*of a hotel*) la **terrasse** *fem*
2 (*at a stadium*) **the terraces** les gradins *masc pl*

♪ **terrible** *adjective*
**épouvantable** *masc & fem*
**The weather was terrible.** Il a fait un temps épouvantable.
**I feel terrible.** Je ne me sens pas bien du tout.

**terribly** *adverb*
(*badly*) **affreusement mal**
**I played terribly.** J'ai joué affreusement mal.

**terrific** *adjective*
1 (*impressive*) **épouvantable** *masc & fem*
**at a terrific speed** à une vitesse folle
2 (*exclamation*) **Terrific!** Formidable!

**terrified** *adjective*
**terrifié** *masc*, **terrifiée** *fem*

to **terrify** *verb*
**terrifier** [1]

**territory** *noun*
le **territoire** *masc*

**terrorism** *noun*
le **terrorisme** *masc*

**terrorist** *noun*
le & la **terroriste** *masc & fem*

to **test** *verb* ▷ see **test** *noun*
(*in school*) **contrôler** [1]
**to test somebody on something** interroger [52] quelqu'un sur quelque chose
**Can you test me on my verbs?** Tu peux m'interroger sur les verbes?

♪ **test** *noun* ▷ see **test** *verb*
1 (*in school*) le **contrôle** *masc*
**We've got a maths test tomorrow.** Nous avons un contrôle de maths demain.
2 (*of your skills, patience*) le **test** *masc*
**a personality test** un test de personnalité
3 (*medical*) une **analyse** *fem*
**a blood test** une analyse de sang
**an eye test** un examen des yeux

**test tube** *noun*
une **éprouvette** *fem*

♪ to **text** *verb*
**to text somebody** envoyer [40] un texto à quelqu'un
**I'll text you tomorrow.** Je t'enverrai un texto demain.

♪ **text** *noun*
1 (*of a book*) le **texte** *masc*
2 (*by mobile*) le **texto**®

**mini-info** ***texting***

Here are some common abbreviations to help you understand text messages in French: *jé = j'ai*, *Gt = j'étais*, *ya = il y a* and *parske = parce que*. Number 1 replaces the sounds *un*, *en* or *in* ( *b1 = bien*), 2 replaces *de* (*pa2koi = pas de quoi*).

**textbook** *noun*
le **manuel** *masc*

**text message** *noun*
le **texto** *masc*

♪ **than** *conjunction, preposition*
1 (*in comparisons*) **plus** + *adjective* + **que** (*except for irregular forms*)
**bigger than** plus grand que
**better than** meilleur que
**worse than** pire que ⏩

You're taller than her. Tu es plus grand qu'elle.
It's worse than ever. C'est pire que jamais.
2 (*for quantities*) **plus de** + *number*
more than 20 pounds plus de 20 livres
more than a year plus d'un an

to **thank** *verb*
**remercier[1]**
I forgot to thank you. J'ai oublié de vous remercier.

**thanks** *exclamation*
**merci**
Thanks a lot. Merci beaucoup.
No thanks. Non merci.
Thanks for helping us. Merci de nous avoir aidé.

**thank you** *exclamation*
**merci**
No thank you. Non merci.
Thank you for the card. Merci pour la carte.

**that** *adjective* ▷ see **that** *adv, conj, pron*
1 (*with masc singular nouns*) **ce**
that dog ce chien
2 (*with masc singular nouns starting a, e, i, o, u or silent h*) **cet**
that money cet argent
3 (*with fem singular nouns*) **cette**
that colour cette couleur
4 that one celui-là (*for masc nouns*)
'Which cake would you like?' — 'That one, please'. 'Tu veux quel gâteau?' — 'Celui-là, s'il te plaît'.
5 that one celle-là (*for fem nouns*)
I like all the jackets but I'm going to buy that one. J'aime toutes les vestes mais je vais acheter celle-là.

**WORD TIP** Add *-là* to a noun for emphasis: *cet homme-là* that *particular* man.

**that** *adverb* ▷ see **that** *adj, conj, pron*
The wall was that high. Le mur était haut comme ça.
It isn't all that good. Ce n'est pas si bon que ça.

**that** *conjunction, pronoun* ▷ see **that** *adj, adv*
1 **ce, c'** (*before e-*)
That's true. C'est vrai.
Is that true? C'est vrai?
What's that? Qu'est-ce que c'est?
Who's that? C'est qui?
Where's that? C'est où?
Is that Mandy? C'est Mandy?
2 **ça**
That smells good. Ça sent bon.
Did you see that? Tu as vu ça?
What does that mean? Ça veut dire quoi?
3 (*in place of a noun: subject*) **qui**
the book that is on the table le livre qui est sur la table
4 (*in place of a noun: object*) **que, qu'** (*a, e, i, o, u or silent h*)
the film that I liked the best le film que j'ai aimé le mieux
the house that he built la maison qu'il a construite
5 (*as a conjunction*) **que, qu'** (*a, e, i, o, u or silent h*)
I thought (that) you knew. Je croyais que tu le savais.
I knew (that) he was wrong. Je savais qu'il avait tort.

**WORD TIP** *that* is often left out in English, but *que* is always needed in French.

to **thaw** *verb*
**dégeler[45]**

**the** *determiner*
1 (*with masc singular nouns*) **le**
the cat le chat
the building le bâtiment
2 (*with fem singular nouns*) **la**
the table la table
the meeting la réunion
3 (*with singular nouns starting a, e, i, o, u or silent h*) **l'**
the engineer l'ingénieur *masc*
the nurse l'infirmière *fem*
the tree l'arbre *masc*
4 (*with plural nouns*) **les**
the holidays les vacances
the students les élèves
from the Netherlands des Pays-Bas
to go to the United States aller Ⓔ [7] aux États-Unis

**WORD TIP** ▷ **from, of** *de + le = du; de + la = de la; de + les = des.*
▷ **to** *à + le = au; à + la = à la; à + les = aux.*

**theatre** *noun*
**le théâtre** *masc*

**theft** *noun*
**le vol** *masc*

**their** *adjective*
1 (*with singular nouns*) **leur**
their flat leur appartement
their mother leur mère
2 (*with plural nouns*) **leurs**
their presents leurs cadeaux
their friends leurs amis
3 (*with parts of the body*) **le, la, les**
They're washing their hands. Elles se lavent les mains.

**theirs** *pronoun*

1 (*for masc singular nouns*) **le leur**
**Our garden's smaller than theirs.** Notre jardin est plus petit que le leur.

2 (*for fem singular nouns*) **la leur**
**Your house is bigger than theirs.** Ta maison est plus grande que la leur.

3 (*for plural nouns*) **les leurs**
**Our holidays are longer than theirs.** Nos vacances sont plus longues que les leurs.

4 (*belonging to them*) **à eux** (*male or mixed group*)
**He's a friend of theirs.** C'est un ami à eux.

5 (*belonging to them*) **à elles** (*all-female group*)
**The rackets are theirs.** Les racquettes sont à elles.

**them** *pronoun*

1 (*for plural nouns as direct object*) **les**
**I know them.** Je les connais.
**I saw them last week.** Je les ai vus la semaine dernière.
**Watch them!** Regarde-les!
**Give them to me.** Donne-les-moi.

2 (*for plural nouns as indirect object*) **leur**
**I gave them my address.** Je leur ai donné mon adresse.
**Give the book to them.** Donne-leur le livre.
**Can you write to them?** Est-ce que tu peux leur écrire?

3 (*after prepositions like* ***avec, sans***) **eux** (*male or mixed group*), **elles** (*all-female group*)
**I'll go with them.** J'irai avec eux.
**We left without them.** On est parti sans elles.

4 (*in comparisons*) **than them** qu'eux (*male or mixed group*), qu'elles (*all-female group*)
**He's older than them.** Il est plus âgé qu'eux.
**She's younger than them.** Elle est plus jeune qu'elles.

**theme** *noun*

la **thème** *fem*

- **theme park** le parc de loisirs

**themselves** *pronoun*

1 **se, s'**
**They all helped themselves.** Ils se sont tous servis.

2 (*for emphasis*) **eux-mêmes** (*male or mixed group*), **elles-mêmes** (*all-female group*)
**The boys can do it themselves.** Les garçons peuvent le faire eux-mêmes.
**The girls will tell you themselves.** Les filles vous le diront elles-mêmes.

**WORD TIP** *se* becomes *s'* before *a, e, i, o, u* or *silent h.*

**then** *adverb*

1 (*next*) **ensuite**
**I went to the post office and then the shops.** Je suis allé à la poste et ensuite aux magasins.

2 (*at that time*) **à l'époque**
**We were living in Leeds then.** Nous habitions à Leeds à l'époque.

3 (*in that case*) **alors**
**Then why worry?** Alors pourquoi s'inquiéter?

4 **by then** déjà

5 **from then on** à partir de ce moment-là

**theory** *noun*

la **théorie** *fem*

**there** *adverb, pronoun*

1 (*not far from the speaker*) **là**
**Put it there.** Mets-le là.
**They're in there.** Ils sont là.

2 **over there** là-bas

3 **down there** là-bas

4 **up there** là-haut

5 **y** (*referring to a place that was mentioned before*)
**We've never been there.** Nous n'y sommes jamais allés.
**Yes, I'm going there on Tuesday.** Oui, j'y vais mardi.

6 (*with facts and questions: singular*) **there is** il y a
**There's a cat in the garden.** Il y a un chat dans le jardin.
**There was no bread.** Il n'y avait pas de pain.
**Is there any milk?** Est-ce qu'il y a du lait?
(*: plural*) **there are** il y a
**Are there any seats?** Est-ce qu'il y a des places?
**There are plenty of seats.** Il y a beaucoup de places.

7 (*when you point things out*) **There she is!** La voilà!
**There they are!** Les voilà!

**therefore** *adverb*

**donc**

**thermometer** *noun*

le **thermomètre** *masc*

**these** *adjective, pronoun*

1 (*with plural nouns*) **ces**
**these books** ces livres
**these books here** ces livres-ci

2 (*for plural masc nouns*) **these (ones)** ceux-ci
**If you want some knives, take these.** Si tu veux des couteaux, prends ceux-ci.

3 (*for plural fem nouns*) **these (ones)** celles-ci
**If you want some plates, take these.** Si tu veux des assiettes, prends celles-ci.

**they** *pronoun*
1 (*for plural masc nouns*) **ils**
**'Where are the knives?' — 'They're in the drawer.'** 'Où sont les couteaux?' — 'Ils sont dans le tiroir.'
2 (*for plural fem nouns*) **elles**
**I bought some apples but they're not good.** J'ai acheté des pommes mais elles ne sont pas bonnes.

**thick** *adjective*
**épais** *masc*, **épaisse** *fem*
**a thick layer of snow** une couche épaisse de neige

**thief** *noun*
le **voleur** *masc*, la **voleuse** *fem*
**Look out for thieves.** Attention aux voleurs.

**thigh** *noun*
la **cuisse** *fem*

**thin** *adjective*
1 (*not fat*) **mince** *masc & fem*
**Joe's tall and thin.** Joe est grand et mince.
2 (*too thin*) **maigre** *masc & fem*
**to get thin** maigrir **[2]**

**thing** *noun*
1 (*in general*) la **chose** *fem*
**I've got lots of things to do.** J'ai beaucoup de choses à faire.
**How are things?** Comment ça va?
2 (*whatsit*) le **truc** *masc* (*informal*)
**that thing next to the hammer** ce truc à côté du marteau
3 (*belongings*) **things** les affaires *fem pl*
**I can't find my things.** Je ne trouve pas mes affaires.
4 **not ... a thing** ne ... rien
**I can't see a thing.** Je ne vois rien.

to **think** *verb*
1 (*to believe*) **croire [33]**
**I think he's already left.** Je crois qu'il est déjà parti.
**Do you think they'll come?** Tu crois qu'ils vont venir?
**No, I don't think so.** Non, je ne crois pas.
2 (*to have an opinion*) **penser [1]**
**What do you think of my new jacket?** Qu'est-ce que tu penses de ma nouvelle veste?
**What do you think of that?** Qu'en penses-tu?
3 **to think about somebody** penser **[1]** à quelqu'un
**I'm thinking about you.** Je pense à toi.
4 **to think of doing something** penser **[1]** faire quelque chose
**I'm thinking of buying a mobile.** Je pense acheter un portable.
5 (*to think carefully*) **réfléchir [2]**
**Let me think.** Laisse-moi réfléchir.
6 (*to imagine*) **imaginer [1]**
**Just think! We'll soon be in Spain!** Imagine! On va bientôt être en Espagne!

**third** *adjective* ▷ see **third** *noun*
1 **troisième** *masc & fem*
**on the third floor** au troisième étage
2 (*in dates*) **the third of March** le trois mars

**third** *noun* ▷ see **third** *adj*
le **tiers** *masc*
**a third of the population** un tiers de la population

**Third World** *noun*
le **tiers-monde** *masc*
**Third-World countries** les pays du tiers-monde

**thirst** *noun*
la **soif** *fem*

**thirsty** *adjective*
**to be thirsty** avoir **[5]** soif
**I'm very thirsty.** J'ai très soif.

**thirteen** *number*
**treize**
**My brother's thirteen.** Mon frère a treize ans.

**thirteenth** *adjective*
1 **treizième** *masc & fem*
**my thirteenth birthday** mon treizième anniversaire
2 (*in dates*) **the thirteenth of May** le treize mai

**thirty** *number*
**trente**
**My cousin is thirty.** Mon cousin a trente ans.

**thirtieth** *adjective*
1 **trentième** *masc & fem*
2 (*in dates*) **the thirtieth of October** le trente octobre

**this** *adjective* ▷ see **this** *pron*
1 (*with masc singular nouns*) **ce**
**this paintbrush** ce pinceau
2 (*with masc singular nouns beginning with* **a, e, i, o, u** *or silent* **h**) **cet**
**this tree** cet arbre
3 (*with fem singular nouns*) **cette**
**this cup** cette tasse
4 (*in place of masc nouns*) **this one** celui-ci
**If you need a pen you can use this one.** Si tu as besoin d'un stylo tu peux utiliser celui-ci.
5 (*in place of fem nouns*) **this one** celle-ci
**I like all the lamps but I'll take this one.**

Toutes les lampes me plaisent mais je prendrai celle-ci.

♪ **this** *pronoun* ▷ see **this** *adj*
1 (*with être*) **ce, c'** (*before e-*)
**This is painful!** C'est pénible!
**What's this?** Qu'est-ce que c'est?
**Who's this?** C'est qui?
2 (*introducing someone*) **This is ...** Je te présente ...
**This is my sister Carla.** Je te présente ma sœur Carla.
3 (*with other verbs*) **ça**
**I bought this in the sales.** J'ai acheté ça aux soldes.
**This means we've missed the train.** Ça veut dire qu'on a raté le train.

**thorn** *noun*
une **épine** *fem*

**thorough** *adjective*
1 (*search*) **minutieux** *masc*, **minutieuse** *fem*
2 (*person*) **consciencieux** *masc*, **consciencieuse** *fem*

**those** *adjective, pronoun*
1 (*with plural masc nouns*) **ces**
**those books** ces livres
**those books there** ces livres-là
2 (*for plural masc nouns*) **those (ones)** ceux-là
**If you want some knives, take those.** Si tu veux des couteaux, prends ceux-là.
3 (*for plural fem nouns*) **those (ones)** celles-là
**If you want some plates, take those.** Si tu veux des assiettes, prends celles-là.

**though** *adverb, conjunction*
1 (*although*) **bien que**
**Though it's cold, it's sunny.** Bien qu'il fasse froid, il y a du soleil.
2 (*however*) **pourtant**
**It was a good idea though.** Pourtant, c'était une bonne idée.

**thought** *noun*
1 (*thinking*) la **pensée** *fem*
2 (*idea*) une **idée**
**What a thought!** Quelle idée!

**thousand** *number*
**mille**
**a thousand** mille
**three thousand** trois mille
**five thousand euros** cinq mille euros
**thousands of tourists** des milliers de touristes

**WORD TIP** *mille* does not take an *-s* in the plural.

**thousandth** *adjective*
**millième** *masc & fem*

**thread** *noun*
le **fil** *masc*

**threat** *noun*
la **menace** *fem*

to **threaten** *verb*
**menacer [61]**
**to threaten to do something** menacer de faire quelque chose
**She's threatening to leave school.** Elle menace de quitter l'école.

**three** *number*
**trois**
**My little sister's three.** Ma petite sœur a trois ans.

**three-quarters** *noun*
les **trois-quarts** *masc pl*
**in three-quarters of an hour** en trois-quarts d'heure
**to be three-quarters full** être **[6]** plein aux trois-quarts

**thrilled** *adjective*
**ravi** *masc*, **ravie** *fem*
**She's thrilled with her presents.** Elle est ravie de ses cadeaux.

**thriller** *noun*
le **thriller** *masc*

♪ **throat** *noun*
la **gorge** *fem*
**Emma has a sore throat.** Emma a mal à la gorge.

**through** *adjective* ▷ see **through** *adv, prep*
(*train, service*) **direct** *masc*, **directe** *fem*

♪ **through** *adverb, preposition*
▷ see **through** *adj*
1 (*across*) **à travers**
**a path through the forest** un chemin à travers la forêt
**The police let us through.** La police nous a laissés passer.
2 (*by, via*) **par**
**I saw her through the window.** Je l'ai vue par la fenêtre.
**We went through the park.** Nous avons traversé le parc.
3 (*during*) **through the night** toute la nuit

**throughout** *preposition*
1 (*during the whole of*) **pendant tout** *masc*, **pendant toute** *fem*
**throughout the day** pendant toute la journée
2 (*all over*) **dans tout** *masc*, **dans toute** *fem*
**throughout the country** dans tout le pays
**known throughout the world** connu partout dans le monde

English–French

a b c d e f g h i j k l m n o p q r s **t** u v w x y z

♪ to **throw** *verb*
1 (*in general*) **jeter [48]**
I threw the letter into the bin. J'ai jeté la lettre dans la poubelle.
He threw it on the floor. Il l'a jeté par terre.
2 (*stones, a ball*) **lancer [61]**
to throw something to somebody lancer quelque chose à quelqu'un
Throw me the ball! Lance-moi le ballon!
• **to throw something away**
**jeter [48] quelque chose**
I've thrown away the old newspapers. J'ai jeté les vieux journaux.
• **to throw up**
**vomir [2]**

**thumb** *noun*
le **pouce** *masc*

**thunder** *noun*
le **tonnerre** *masc*
• **thunderstorm** un orage

**thundery** *adjective*
**orageux** *masc*, **orageuse** *fem*

♪ **Thursday** *noun*
le **jeudi**
last Thursday jeudi dernier
next Thursday jeudi prochain
every Thursday tous les jeudis
on Thursdays le jeudi
See you on Thursday! À jeudi!

**WORD TIP** Months of the year and days of the week start with small letters in French.

to **tick** *verb*
1 (*clock*) **faire [10] tic-tac**
2 (*on paper*) **cocher [1]**
Tick the box. Cochez la case.

♪ **ticket** *noun*
1 (*for planes, trains, films*) le **billet** *masc*
I have two tickets for the concert. J'ai deux billets pour le concert.
2 (*for the metro, buses, left luggage*) le **ticket** *masc*
a bus ticket un ticket de bus
3 (*a parking fine*) le **pv**
• **ticket inspector** le contrôleur
• **ticket office** le guichet

to **tickle** *verb*
**chatouiller [1]**

♪ **tide** *noun*
la **marée** *fem*

♪ to **tidy** *verb* ▷ see **tidy** *adj*
**ranger [52]**
I'll tidy up the kitchen. Je rangerai la cuisine.

**tidy** *adjective* ▷ see **tidy** *verb*
1 (*room*) **bien rangé** *masc*, **bien rangée** *fem*
2 (*piece of work, writing*) **soigné** *masc*, **soignée** *fem*
3 (*person*) **ordonné** *masc*, **ordonnée** *fem*

♪ to **tie** *verb* ▷ see **tie** *noun*
1 **nouer [1]**
2 to tie a knot in something faire [10] un nœud à quelque chose
I tied a knot in my scarf. J'ai fait un nœud à mon foulard.
• **to tie something up**
1 (*a parcel*) **ficeler [18] quelque chose**
2 (*a boat*) **amarrer [1] quelque chose**
3 (*an animal*) **attacher [1] quelque chose**

♪ **tie** *noun* ▷ see **tie** *verb*
1 la **cravate** *fem*
2 (*in games*) le **match nul** *masc*

**tiger** *noun*
le **tigre** *masc*

**tight** *adjective*
1 (*not comfortable*) **juste** *masc & fem*
The skirt's a bit tight. La jupe est un peu juste.
2 (*close-fitting*) **moulant** *masc*, **moulante** *fem*

to **tighten** *verb*
**serrer [1]**

**tightly** *adverb*
**fermement**

♪ **tights** *plural noun*
le **collant** *masc singular*
a pair of tights un collant

**tile** *noun*
1 (*on wall*) le **carreau** *masc* (*pl* les **carreaux**)
2 (*on roof*) la **tuile** *fem*

♪ **till** *conjunction, preposition*
▷ see **till** *noun*
1 **jusqu'à**
till now jusqu'à présent
2 not till ne ... pas avant
We won't be back till ten. Nous ne serons pas rentrés avant dix heures.

**till** *noun* ▷ see **till** *conj, prep*
la **caisse** *fem*

♪ **time** *noun*
1 (*on the clock*) l'**heure** *fem*
What time is it? Quelle heure est-il?
It's time for lunch. C'est l'heure du déjeuner.
to arrive on time arriver ⓔ [1] à l'heure
2 (*an amount of time*) le **temps** *masc*
We've got lots of time. Nous avons beaucoup de temps.
There's not much time left. Il ne reste plus beaucoup de temps.

I waited for a long time. J'ai attendu longtemps.
I see her from time to time. Je la vois de temps en temps.
3 (*moment*) le **moment** *masc*
Is this a good time to phone? Est-ce que c'est le bon moment pour vous appeler?
She'll arrive any time now. Elle devrait arriver d'un moment à l'autre.
4 (*in a series*) la **fois** *fem*
six times six fois
three times a year trois fois par an
the first, last time I saw you la première, dernière fois que je t'ai vu
5 to have a good time bien s'amuser [1]
Have a good time! Amusez-vous bien!
We had a really good time. Nous nous sommes très bien amusés.
6 (*in a person's life*) la **période**
the happiest time of her life la période la plus heureuse de sa vie

**time off** *noun*
1 (*free time*) le **temps libre**
2 (*holiday*) le **congé** *masc*

**timetable** *noun*
1 (*in school*) un **emploi du temps**
2 (*for trains, buses*) un **horaire**

✓**tin** *noun*
1 (*container*) la **boîte** *fem*
a tin of tomatoes une boîte de tomates
2 (*metal*) l'**étain** *masc*

**tinned** *adjective*
**en conserve**

**tin opener** *noun*
un **ouvre-boîtes** *masc* (*pl* les **ouvre-boîtes**)

**tiny** *adjective*
**minuscule** *masc & fem*

✓to **tip** *verb* ▷ see **tip** *noun*
1 to tip somebody donner [1] un pourboire à quelqu'un
We tipped the waiter. Nous avons donné un pourboire au garçon.
2 (*liquid*) **verser** [1]
I tipped it down the sink. Je l'ai versé dans l'évier.

✓**tip** *noun* ▷ see **tip** *verb*
1 (*of your finger, a pen*) le **bout** *masc*
on the tips of your toes sur la pointe des pieds
2 (*money*) le **pourboire** *masc*
a 10-euro tip un pourboire de 10 euros
3 (*hint*) le **tuyau** *masc* (*pl* les **tuyaux**)
She gave me some good tips. Elle m'a donné de bons tuyaux.
4 (*mess*) la **pagaille**
This place is a tip! C'est la pagaille ici!

**tiptoe** *noun*
la **pointe des pieds**

✓**tired** *adjective*
1 **fatigué** *masc*, **fatiguée** *fem*
We're tired. Nous sommes fatigués.
You look tired. Tu as l'air fatigué.
2 to be tired of something en avoir [5] assez de quelque chose
I'm tired of London. J'en ai assez de Londres.
to be tired of doing something en avoir assez de faire quelque chose
I'm tired of watching TV. J'en ai assez de regarder la télé.
3 to get tired se fatiguer Ⓔ [1]
She gets tired easily. Elle se fatigue facilement.
4 to get tired of something se lasser Ⓔ [1] de quelque chose
You get tired of it after a while. On s'en lasse au bout d'un moment.

**tiring** *adjective*
**fatigant** *masc*, **fatigante** *fem*

**tissue** *noun*
le **kleenex**®
• **tissue paper** le papier de soie

**title** *noun*
1 (*of a film, book, play*) le **titre**
2 (*in sport*) le **titre** *masc*
to win the world title remporter [1] le titre mondial

✓**to** *preposition*
1 (*a town, person*) **à**
Leah's gone to London. Leah est allée à Londres.
Give the book to Leila. Donne le livre à Leila.
2 (*with fem singular nouns*) **à**
Come to the pool. Viens à la piscine.
3 (*with masc singular nouns*) **au**
She's gone to the office. Elle est partie au bureau.
John works from Monday to Friday. John travaille du lundi au vendredi.
4 (*with singular nouns beginning with **a, e, i, o, u** or silent **h***) **à l'**
I'm going to school. Je vais à l'école.
5 (*with plural nouns*) **aux**
We've sent a letter to the parents. On a envoyé une lettre aux parents.
6 (*with fem country names*) **en**
to go to Spain aller en Espagne
7 (*with masc country names*) **au**
to go to Portugal aller au Portugal ▸▸

8 (*with plural country names*) **aux**
**to go to the United States** aller aux États-Unis
9 (*to somebody's house, shop, surgery*) **chez**
**to go to Paul's house** aller chez Paul
**I'm going to the dentist's.** Je vais chez le dentiste.
10 (*with verb infinitives*) **à**
**We're ready to go.** Nous sommes prêts à partir.
**I have a lot of homework to do.** J'ai beaucoup de devoirs à faire.
11 (*talking about the time*) **moins**
**It's ten to nine.** Il est neuf heures moins dix.
12 (*in order to*) **to do something** pour faire quelque chose
**We need money to pay for the tickets.** Nous avons besoin d'argent pour payer les billets.
13 (*towards*) **avec**
**They're mean to me.** Ils sont méchants avec moi.
**She's kind to animals.** Elle est gentille avec les animaux.

**toad** *noun*
le **crapaud** *masc*
• **toadstool** le champignon vénéneux

**toast** *noun*
1 le **pain grillé**
2 (*to someone's health*) le **toast** *masc*
**We drank a toast to the future.** Nous avons levé un verre à l'avenir.

**toaster** *noun*
le **grille-pain** *invariable masc*

**tobacco** *noun*
le **tabac** *masc*

**tobacconist's** *noun*
le **bureau de tabac**

**today** *noun*
**aujourd'hui** *masc*
**today's teenagers** les adolescents d'aujourd'hui
**What's the date today?** On est le combien aujourd'hui?
**Today's her birthday.** C'est son anniversaire aujourd'hui.

**toe** *noun*
le **doigt de pied**
**my big toe** mon gros orteil

**toffee** *noun*
le **caramel** *masc*

**together** *adverb*
1 (*with one another*) **ensemble**
**Kate and David arrived together.** Kate et David sont arrivés ensemble.
2 (*at the same time*) **en même temps**
**They all left together.** Ils sont tous partis en même temps.

**toilet** *noun*
les **toilettes** *fem pl*
**Where's the toilet?** Où sont les toilettes?
• **toilet paper** le papier hygiénique

**tolerant** *adjective*
**tolérant** *masc*, **tolérante** *fem*

**toll** *noun*
1 (*on a motorway, a bridge*) le **péage** *masc*
2 **death toll** le nombre de victimes
• **toll booth** le poste de péage
• **toll road** la route à péage

**tomato** *noun*
la **tomate** *fem*
**tomato soup** la soupe à la tomate
**tomato sauce** la sauce tomate

**tomorrow** *adverb*
**demain**
**tomorrow afternoon** demain après-midi
**tomorrow morning** demain matin
**tomorrow night** demain soir
**She's coming the day after tomorrow.** Elle arrive après-demain.

**ton** *noun*
la **tonne** *fem*
**She gets tons of letters.** Elle reçoit des tonnes de lettres.

**tone** *noun*
1 (*on an answerphone*) la **tonalité** *fem*
**Speak after the tone.** Parlez après la tonalité.
2 (*of a voice, letter*) le **ton** *masc*
**a tone of voice** un ton

**tongue** *noun*
la **langue** *fem*
**It's on the tip of my tongue.** Je l'ai sur le bout de la langue.

**tonic** *noun*
le **Schweppes®** *masc*
**a gin and tonic** un gin tonic

**tonight** *adverb*
1 (*this evening*) **ce soir**
**What are you doing tonight?** Qu'est-ce que tu fais ce soir?
**See you tonight!** À ce soir!
2 (*after bedtime*) **cette nuit**
**It's going to be cold tonight.** Il va faire froid cette nuit.

**tonsillitis** *noun*
une **angine** *fem*

♪**too** *adverb*
1 (*excessively*) **trop**
**too often** trop souvent
**It's too expensive.** C'est trop cher.
**You're too tired.** Tu es trop fatigué.
2 **too much, too many** trop (de)
**It takes too much time.** Ça prend trop de temps.
**There are too many accidents.** Il y a trop d'accidents.
**He eats too much.** Il mange trop.
3 (*also*) **aussi**
**Karen's coming too.** Karen vient aussi.
**Me too!** Moi aussi!

**tool** *noun*
un **outil** *masc*
• **tool box** la boîte à outils

♪**tooth** *noun*
la **dent** *fem*
**to brush your teeth** se brosser Ⓔ [1] les dents

**toothache** *noun*
le **mal de dents**
**to have toothache** avoir [5] mal aux dents
**I've got toothache.** J'ai mal aux dents.

**toothbrush** *noun*
la **brosse à dents**

**toothpaste** *noun*
le **dentifrice**

♪**top** *adjective* ▷ see **top** *noun*
1 (*step, floor*) **dernier** *masc*, **dernière** *fem*
**It's on the top floor.** C'est au dernier étage.
2 (*shelf, bunk*) **du haut**
**in the top bunk** dans le lit du haut
**in the top left-hand corner** en haut à gauche

♪**top** *noun* ▷ see **top** *adj*
1 (*of a page, a ladder, the stairs*) le **haut** *masc*
**at the top of the stairs** en haut de l'escalier
**from top to bottom** du haut en bas
**It's on top of the wardrobe.** C'est sur l'armoire.
2 (*of a container, box*) le **dessus** *masc*
3 (*of a mountain*) le **sommet** *masc*
4 (*lid for a pen*) le **capuchon** *masc*
5 (*lid for a bottle*) la **capsule** *fem*
6 (*clothing*) un **haut** *masc*
7 (*of a list, of the charts*) la **tête** *fem*
8 **Salma's top of the class.** Salma est la première de la classe.
9 (*to succeed*) **to get to the top** réussir [2]

**topic** *noun*
le **sujet** *masc*

**topping** *noun*
la **garniture** *fem*
**Which topping would you like on your pizza?** Vous voulez une pizza à quoi?

**torch** *noun*
la **lampe de poche**

**torn** *adjective*
**déchiré** *masc*, **déchirée** *fem*

**tornado** *noun*
la **tornade** *fem*

**tortoise** *noun*
la **tortue** *fem*

to **torture** *verb* ▷ see **torture** *noun*
**torturer** [1]

**torture** *noun* ▷ see **torture** *verb*
la **torture** *fem*

**Tory** *noun*
**conservateur** *masc*, **conservatrice** *fem*

♪**total** *adjective* ▷ see **total** *noun*
**total** *masc*, **totale** *fem*, **totaux** *masc pl*, **totales** *fem pl*
**What's the total cost?** Le prix total, c'est quoi?
**The party was a total failure.** La soirée était un échec total.

♪**total** *noun* ▷ see **total** *adj*
le **total** *masc*
**20 euros in total** 20 euros au total

**totally** *adverb*
**complètement**
**You're totally wrong.** Tu as complètement tort.
**I totally agree.** Je suis complètement d'accord.

♪to **touch** *verb* ▷ see **touch** *noun*
**toucher** [1]
**Don't touch my things!** Ne touche pas à mes affaires!

**touch** *noun* ▷ see **touch** *verb*
1 **to get in touch with somebody** prendre [64] contact avec quelqu'un
**to stay in touch with somebody** rester Ⓔ [1] en contact avec quelqu'un
2 **to lose touch with somebody** perdre [3] quelqu'un de vue
**We've lost touch.** On s'est perdu de vue.
3 **a touch of something** un petit peu de quelque chose
**a touch of vanilla** un petit peu de vanille

**touching** *adjective*
**touchant** *masc*, **touchante** *fem*

English–French

**tough** *adjective*
1 (*in general*) **dur** *masc*, **dure** *fem*
The meat's tough. La viande est dure.
Chris is a tough guy. Chris est un dur.
2 (*strong*) **robuste** *masc & fem*
a tough fabric un tissu robuste
3 (*strict*) **sévère** *masc & fem*
tough measures des mesures sévères
to be tough on somebody être [6] dur avec quelqu'un
4 (*too bad*) **tant pis**
That's just tough! Tant pis!

to **tour** *verb* ▷ see **tour** *noun*
1 (*holidaymakers*) **faire [10] du tourisme**
We toured around a bit. Nous avons fait un peu de tourisme.
2 (*performers*) **être [6] en tournée**
They're touring the States. Ils sont en tournée aux États-Unis.

**tour** *noun* ▷ see **tour** *verb*
1 (*around a place*) la **visite** *fem*
a guided tour of the city une visite guidée de la ville
to do a tour of something faire [1] la visite de quelque chose
We did a tour of the castle. Nous avons fait la visite du château.
2 (*by a band, theatre group*) la **tournée** *fem*
to go on tour partir Ⓔ [58] en tournée
The band is going on tour to Japan. Le groupe part en tournée au Japon.
- **tour guide** le & la guide

**tourism** *noun*
le **tourisme** *masc*

**tourist** *noun*
le & la **touriste** *masc & fem*
The town is popular with tourists. C'est une ville touristique.
- **tourist attraction** l'attraction touristique *fem*
- **tourist information office** le syndicat d'initiative
- **tourist trap** le piège à touristes

**tournament** *noun*
le **tournoi** *masc*

to **tow** *verb*
**remorquer [1]**
- **to tow something away**
(*breakdown truck*) **remorquer [1] quelque chose**

♪**towards** *preposition*
1 **en direction de**
She went off towards the park. Elle est partie en direction du parc.
They were coming towards us. Il s'approchaient de nous.
2 (*approximately*) **vers**
towards the end of the month vers la fin du mois
3 (*to*) **envers**
my attitude towards my parents mon attitude envers mes parents

♪**towel** *noun*
la **serviette** *fem*

**tower** *noun*
la **tour** *fem*
the Eiffel Tower la tour Eiffel
- **tower block** la tour

♪**town** *noun*
la **ville** *fem*
to go into town aller Ⓔ [7] en ville
- **town centre** le centre-ville
- **town hall** la mairie

**toxic** *adjective*
**toxique** *masc & fem*

♪**toy** *noun*
le **jouet** *masc*
a toy car une petite voiture
- **toyshop** le magasin de jouets

to **trace** *verb* ▷ see **trace** *noun*
1 (*a missing person*) **retrouver [1]**
2 (*a phone call*) **localiser [1]**

**trace** *noun* ▷ see **trace** *verb*
la **trace** *fem*
There was no trace of it. Il n'en restait aucune trace.

♪**track** *noun*
1 (*for athletics*) la **piste** *fem*
ten laps of the track dix tours de piste
2 (*for cars*) le **circuit**
3 (*path*) le **chemin** *masc*
4 (*song*) la **chanson** *fem*
This is my favourite track. C'est ma chanson préférée.
5 to be on the right track être [6] sur la bonne piste
I think we're on the right track. Je crois que nous sommes sur la bonne piste.
- **track and field** l'athlétisme *masc*
- **track suit** le survêtement

**tractor** *noun*
le **tracteur** *masc*

**trade** *noun*
1 (*job*) le **métier** *masc*
He's a plumber by trade. C'est un plombier de son métier.
2 (*business*) le **commerce**



Ⓔ means the verb takes être to form the perfect

**trademark** *noun*
la **marque**
a registered trademark une marque déposée

**tradition** *noun*
la **tradition** *fem*

**traditional** *adjective*
**traditionnel** *masc*, **traditionnelle** *fem*

♂ **traffic** *noun*
la **circulation** *fem*
The traffic's heavy. Il y a beaucoup de circulation.
- **traffic jam** un embouteillage
- **traffic lights** les feux *masc pl*
- **traffic warden** le gardien de la paix, la gardienne de la paix

**tragedy** *noun*
la **tragédie** *fem*

**tragic** *adjective*
**tragique** *masc & fem*

**trail** *noun*
le **sentier** *masc*
a nature trail un sentier écologique

**trailer** *noun*
la **remorque** *fem*
- **trailer tent** la tente-remorque

♂ to **train** *verb* ▷ see **train** *noun*
1 (*for a career*) **former [1]**
2 to train to be something suivre **[75]** une formation de quelque chose
He's training to be a plumber. Il suit une formation de plombier.
My mother trained as a teacher. Ma mère a reçu une formation de professeur.
3 (*for sport*) **s'entraîner [1]**
The team trains on Saturdays. L'équipe s'entraîne le samedi.

♂ **train** *noun* ▷ see **train** *verb*
le **train** *masc*
the train to Rouen le train pour Rouen
He's coming by train. Il prend le train.
We went to Rennes by train. Nous sommes allés à Rennes en train.

**train crash** *noun*
un **accident ferroviaire**

♂ **trainee** *noun*
le & la **stagiaire** *masc & fem*

**trainer** *noun*
1 (*shoe*) le **basket** *masc*
2 (*coach*) un **entraîneur** *masc*, une **entraîneuse** *fem*

♂ **training** *noun*
1 (*for a career*) la **formation** *fem*
2 (*for sport*) l'**entraînement** *masc*

**tram** *noun*
le **tramway** *masc*

**tramp** *noun*
le **clochard** *masc*, la **clocharde** *fem*

**trampoline** *noun*
le **trampoline** *masc*

to **transfer** *verb* ▷ see **transfer** *noun*
1 (*an employee, a player, data*) **transférer [1]**
2 (*money*) **virer [1]**

**transfer** *noun* ▷ see **transfer** *verb*
1 (*of money*) le **virement** *masc*
2 (*of an employee, a footballer*) le **transfert** *masc*
3 (*sticker*) la **décalcomanie** *fem*

to **transform** *verb*
**transformer [1]**

**transistor** *noun*
le **transistor** *masc*

to **translate** *verb*
**traduire [26]**
Translate the sentences into French. Traduisez les phrases en français.

**translation** *noun*
la **traduction** *fem*

**translator** *noun*
le **traducteur** *masc*, la **traductrice** *fem*

**transparent** *adjective*
**transparent** *masc*, **transparente** *fem*

**transplant** *noun*
1 (*operation*) la **transplantation** *fem*
2 (*organ*) le **transplant** *masc*

♂ **transport** *noun* ▷ see **transport** *verb*
le **transport** *masc*
public transport les transports en commun

to **trap** *verb* ▷ see **trap** *noun*
to be trapped être **[6]** coincé

**trap** *noun* ▷ see **trap** *verb*
le **piège** *masc*

♂ to **travel** *verb* ▷ see **travel** *noun*
**voyager [52]**
I love travelling abroad. J'aime beaucoup voyager à l'étranger.
He hates travelling by plane. Il déteste voyager par avion.

**travel** *noun* ▷ see **travel** *verb*
les **voyages** *masc pl*
some travel brochures des brochures de voyage
- **travel agency** une agence de voyages
- **travel agent** un agent de voyages

**traveller's cheque** *noun*
le **chèque-voyage** *masc* (*pl* les **chèques-voyage**)

**traveller** *noun*
1 (*in general*) le **voyageur** *masc*, la **voyageuse** *fem*
2 (*gypsy*) le & la **nomade** *masc & fem*

**travelling** *noun*
les **voyages** *masc pl*

**travel-sick** *adjective*
to get travel-sick souffrir **[73]** du mal de voyage

**travel-sickness** *noun*
le **mal de voyage**

**tray** *noun*
le **plateau** *masc* (*pl* les **plateaux**)

to **tread** *verb*
to tread on something marcher **[1]** sur quelque chose
Somebody trod on my toe. Quelqu'un m'a marché sur l'orteil.

**treasure** *noun*
le **trésor** *masc*

to **treat** *verb* ▷ see **treat** *noun*
1 (*in general*) **traiter [1]**
They treat me like an adult. Ils me traitent comme un adulte.
2 to treat somebody to something offrir **[56]** quelque chose à quelqu'un
I'll treat you to a drink. Je vous offre à boire.
to treat yourself to something s'offrir **[56]** quelque chose
I treated myself to a few CDs. Je me suis offert quelques CD.

**treat** *noun* ▷ see **treat** *verb*
1 (*something enjoyable*) le **petit plaisir**
I took them to the circus as a treat. Je les ai emmenés au cirque pour leur faire plaisir.
2 (*food*) la **gâterie** *fem*
It's a little treat. C'est une petite gâterie.

**treatment** *noun*
le **traitement** *masc*

**treaty** *noun*
le **traité** *masc*

**tree** *noun*
un **arbre** *masc*

to **tremble** *verb*
**trembler [1]**

**tremendous** *adjective*
**fantastique** *masc & fem*

**trend** *noun*
1 (*fashion*) la **mode** *fem*
2 (*tendency*) la **tendance** *fem*

**trendy** *adjective*
**branché** *masc*, **branchée** *fem*

**trial** *noun*
(*legal*) le **procès** *masc*
to go on trial passer **[1]** en jugement

**triangle** *noun*
le **triangle** *masc*

**triathlon** *noun*
le **triathlon** *masc*

**tribe** *noun*
la **tribu** *fem*

**tribute** *noun*
un **hommage** *masc*
to pay tribute to somebody rendre **[3]** hommage à quelqu'un

to **trick** *verb* ▷ see **trick** *noun*
**rouler [1]**
He tricked me! Il m'a roulé!

**trick** *noun* ▷ see **trick** *verb*
1 (*by a conjuror, as a joke*) le **tour** *masc*
to play a trick on somebody jouer un tour à quelqu'un
Rebecca played a trick on me. Rebecca m'a joué un tour.
2 to do the trick faire **[10]** l'affaire
That hat will do the trick. Ce chapeau fera l'affaire.

**tricky** *adjective*
**délicat** *masc*, **délicate** *fem*
It's a tricky situation. C'est une situation délicate.

to **trim** *verb*
**couper [1]**

**Trinidad** *noun*
**(l'île de) la Trinité**

**Trinidadian** *adjective* ▷ see **Trinidadian** *noun*
**trinidadien** *masc*, **trinidadienne** *fem*

**Trinidadian** *noun* ▷ see **Trinidadian** *adj*
un **Trinidadien** *masc*, une **Trinidadienne** *fem*

to **trip** *verb* ▷ see **trip** *noun*
**trébucher [1]**
to trip over something trébucher sur quelque chose

♪ **trip** *noun* ▷ see **trip** *verb*
le **voyage** *masc*
**a trip to Florida** un voyage en Floride
**a coach trip** un voyage en car
**a business trip** un voyage d'affaires
**a trip to Disneyworld** une visite à Disneyworld
**We went on a day-trip to France.** Nous avons fait une excursion d'une journée en France.

to **triple** *verb*
**tripler [1]**

**triumph** *noun*
le **triomphe** *masc*

♪ **trolley** *noun*
le **chariot** *masc*

**trombone** *noun*
le **trombone** *masc*
**to play the trombone** jouer **[1]** du trombone

**trophy** *noun*
le **trophée** *masc*

**tropical** *adjective*
**tropical** *masc*, **tropicale** *fem*, **tropicaux** *masc pl*, **tropicales** *fem pl*

to **trot** *verb*
**trotter [1]**

♪ **trouble** *noun*
1 (*problems*) les **problèmes** *masc pl*
**We've had trouble with the car.** Nous avons eu des problèmes avec la voiture.
2 (*personal problems*) les **ennuis** *masc pl*
**to be in trouble** avoir **[5]** des ennuis
**Steph's in trouble (with the school).** Steph a des ennuis (avec l'école).
**What's the trouble?** Qu'est-ce qui ne va pas?
3 **to have trouble doing something** avoir **[5]** du mal à faire quelque chose
**I had trouble finding a seat.** J'ai eu du mal à trouver une place.
4 **to go to a lot of trouble to do something** se donner **Ⓔ [1]** beaucoup de mal pour faire quelque chose
**She went to a lot of trouble to get the tickets.** Elle s'est donné beaucoup de mal pour avoir les billets.
**to be worth the trouble** valoir **[80]** la peine
**It's not worth the trouble.** Cela ne vaut pas la peine.

♪ **trousers** *plural noun*
le **pantalon** *masc singular*
**a new pair of trousers** un pantalon neuf

♪ **trout** *noun*
la **truite** *fem*

**truant** *noun*
**to play truant** faire **[10]** l'école buissonnière

♪ **truck** *noun*
le **camion** *masc*

♪ **true** *adjective*
**vrai** *masc*, **vraie** *fem*
**a true story** une histoire vraie
**Is that true?** C'est vrai?
**That's not true.** Ce n'est pas vrai.

**trump** *noun*
un **atout** *masc*
**Spades are trumps.** Atout pique.

**trumpet** *noun*
la **trompette** *fem*
**to play the trumpet** jouer **[1]** de la trompette

**trunk** *noun*
1 (*of a tree*) le **tronc** *masc*
2 (*elephant's*) la **trompe** *fem*
3 (*for clothes, belongings*) la **malle** *fem*

**trunks** *plural noun*
le **maillot de bain**
**my new swimming trunks** mon maillot de bain neuf

to **trust** *verb* ▷ see **trust** *noun*
**to trust somebody** faire **[10]** confiance à quelqu'un
**I trust her.** Je lui fais confiance.
**They don't trust each other.** Ils ne se font pas confiance.

**trust** *noun* ▷ see **trust** *verb*
la **confiance** *fem*

**truth** *noun*
la **vérité** *fem*
**She's telling the truth.** Elle dit la vérité.

♪ to **try** *verb* ▷ see **try** *noun*
**essayer [59]**
**to try to do something** essayer de faire quelque chose
**I'm trying to open the door.** J'essaie d'ouvrir la porte.
**Did you try calling her?** Est-ce que tu as essayé de l'appeler?
**I'm trying not to think about it.** J'essaie de ne pas y penser.
**to try hard to do something** faire **[10]** de gros efforts pour faire quelque chose
**She was trying hard to concentrate.** Elle faisait de gros efforts pour se concentrer.
• **to try something on**
**essayer [59] quelque chose**

**try** *noun* ▷ see **try** *verb*
1 to have a try essayer [59]
I'll have a try. J'essaierai.
It's worth a try. Cela vaut la peine d'essayer.
2 (*in rugby*) un **essai** *masc*
to score a try marquer [1] un essai

**T-shirt** *noun*
le **tee-shirt** *masc*

**tub** *noun*
le **pot** *masc*

**tube** *noun*
1 (*in general*) le **tube** *masc*
2 the Tube le métro (à Londres)

**Tuesday** *noun*
le **mardi** *masc*
last Tuesday mardi dernier
next Tuesday mardi prochain
every Tuesday tous les mardis
on Tuesdays le mardi
See you on Tuesday! À mardi!

**WORD TIP** Months of the year and days of the week start with small letters in French.

to **tug** *verb*
**tirer** [1]
to tug at something tirer sur quelque chose

**tuition** *noun*
les **cours** *masc pl*
piano tuition des cours de piano
private tuition des cours particuliers

**tumble-drier** *noun*
le **sèche-linge** *masc* (*pl* les **sèche-linge**)

**tumbler** *noun*
le **verre droit**

**tummy** *noun*
l'**estomac** *masc*

**tuna** *noun*
le **thon** *masc*

to **tune** *verb* ▷ see **tune** *noun*
(*musical instruments*) **accorder** [1]

**tune** *noun* ▷ see **tune** *verb*
1 un **air** *masc*
2 to sing in tune chanter [1] juste

**Tunisia** *noun*
la **Tunisie** *fem*

**Tunisian** *adjective* ▷ see **Tunisian** *noun*
**tunisien** *masc*, **tunisienne** *fem*

**Tunisian** *noun* ▷ see **Tunisian** *adj*
un **Tunisien**, une **Tunisienne**

♪ **tunnel** *noun*
le **tunnel** *masc*
the Channel Tunnel le tunnel sous la Manche

**mini-info** ***tunnel***
The Eurotunnel - linking Britain and France since 1994 - is the longest rail tunnel in the world.

**turban** *noun*
le **turban** *masc*

**turkey** *noun* ▷ see **Turkey** *noun*
la **dinde** *fem*

**Turkey** *noun*
la **Turquie** *fem*

**Turkish** *adjective* ▷ see **Turkish** *noun*
**turc** *masc*, **turque** *fem*

**Turkish** *noun* ▷ see **Turkish** *adj*
le **turc** *masc*

♪ to **turn** *verb* ▷ see **turn** *noun*
1 (*in general*) **tourner** [1]
Turn left at the next set of lights. Tournez à gauche aux prochains feux.
I turned to look out of the window. J'ai tourné la tête pour regarder par la fenêtre.
2 (*to become*) **devenir** Ⓔ [81]
She turned red. Elle est devenue rouge.
3 **to turn to somebody for something**
tourner [1] vers quelqu'un pour demander quelque chose
They turn to us for advice. Ils tournent vers nous pour demander des conseils.
• **to turn around**
**se retourner** Ⓔ [1]
When I turned around, I saw her. Quand je me suis retourné, je l'ai vue.
• **to turn something around**
**tourner** [1] **quelque chose**
Turn your chair around. Tourne ta chaise.
• **to turn back**
**faire** [10] **demi-tour**
We turned back. Nous avons fait demi-tour.
• **to turn something down**
1 (*a radio, the volume*) **baisser** [1] **quelque chose**
They won't turn the sound down. Ils ne veulent pas baisser le son.
2 (*an offer*) **rejeter** [1]
• **to turn something off**
1 (*a light, an oven, a TV, a radio*) **éteindre** [60] **quelque chose**
2 (*a tap*) **fermer** [1] **quelque chose**
• **to turn something on**
1 (*a light, an oven, a TV, a radio*) **allumer** [1] **quelque chose**

2 (*a tap*) **ouvrir [30] quelque chose**
- **to turn out**

**se terminer ⓔ [1]**
**The concert turned out well.** Le concert s'est bien terminé.
**The holiday turned out badly.** Les vacances se sont mal terminées.
- **to turn over**

1 (*by itself*) **se retourner ⓔ [1]**
2 (*a page, a steak*) **tourner [1]**
- **to turn up**

**arriver ⓔ [1]**
**They turned up an hour later.** Ils sont arrivés une heure plus tard.
- **to turn something up**

1 (*heating, gas*) **augmenter [1] quelque chose**
2 (*a radio, the volume*) **monter [1]**
**Can you turn up the volume?** Est-ce que tu peux monter le son?

**turn** *noun* ▷ **see turn** *verb*
1 (*in games, on a rota*) **le tour** *masc*
**It's your turn.** C'est ton tour.
**Whose turn is it?** C'est à qui le tour?
**We'll take turns.** On le fera, chacun à son tour.
**It's Jane's turn to wash up.** C'est à Jane de faire la vaisselle.
**to take turns doing something** faire **[10]** quelque chose à tour de rôle
**Mum and Dad took turns driving.** Ma mère et mon père ont conduit à tour de rôle.
2 (*in a road*) **le virage** *masc*
**the next turn on the left** la prochaine rue à gauche

**turning** *noun*
**le virage** *masc*
**Take the third turning on the left.** Prenez la troisième rue à gauche.

**turnip** *noun*
**le navet** *masc*

**turquoise** *adjective*
**turquoise** *masc & fem*

**turtle** *noun*
**la tortue marine**

**TV** *noun*
**la télé** *fem*
**I saw her on TV.** Je l'ai vue à la télé.

**tweezers** *noun*
**la pince à épiler**

**twelfth** *adjective*
1 **douzième** *masc & fem*
**on the twelfth floor** au douzième étage
2 (*in dates*) **the twelfth of May** le douze mai

**twelve** *number*
1 **douze**
**Daniel's twelve.** Daniel a douze ans.
2 **at twelve o'clock at night** à minuit
3 **at twelve noon** à midi

**twentieth** *adjective*
1 **vingtième** *masc & fem*
2 (*in dates*) **the twentieth of August** le vingt août

**twenty** *number*
**vingt**
**Marie's twenty.** Marie a vingt ans.
**twenty-one** vingt-et-un
**twenty-five** vingt-cinq

**twice** *adverb*
**deux fois**
**twice as many people** deux fois plus de personnes
**He eats twice as much as me.** Il mange deux fois plus que moi.
**It's twice as expensive here.** C'est deux fois plus cher ici.

🗝 to **twin** *verb* ▷ **see twin** *noun*
**to be twinned with** être **[6]** jumelé avec
**York is twinned with Dijon.** York est jumelée avec Dijon.

🗝 **twin** *noun* ▷ **see twin** *verb*
**le jumeau** *masc* (*pl* **les jumeaux**), **la jumelle** *fem*
**her twin sister** sa sœur jumelle
**Helen and Tim are twins.** Helen et Tim sont jumeaux.
- **twin town** la ville jumelle

to **twist** *verb*
**tordre [3]**
**to twist your ankle** se tordre ⓔ **[3]** la cheville

**two** *number*
**deux**
**Ben's two.** Ben a deux ans.

to **type** *verb* ▷ **see type** *noun*
**taper [1]**

**type** *noun* ▷ **see type** *verb*
**le type** *masc*
**What type of computer is it?** C'est quel type d'ordinateur?
**She's not my type.** Elle n'est pas mon genre.

**typical** *adjective*
**typique** *masc & fem*

🗝 **tyre** *noun*
**le pneu** *masc*
**a flat tyre** un pneu crevé

English–French

# U u

**UFO** *noun*
un **ovni** *masc*

**ugly** *adjective*
**laid** *masc*, **laide** *fem*

**UK** *noun*
(*= United Kingdom*) le **Royaume-Uni** *masc*
**They don't live in the UK.** Ils n'habitent pas au Royaume-Uni.

**WORD TIP** Countries and regions in French take *le*, *la* or *les*.

**ulcer** *noun*
un **ulcère** *masc*

**Ulster** *noun*
l'**Irlande** *fem* **du Nord**

**WORD TIP** Countries and regions in French take *le*, *la* or *les*.

**umbrella** *noun*
le **parapluie** *masc*

**umpire** *noun*
un **arbitre** *masc*

**UN** *noun*
(*= United Nations*) l'**ONU** *fem* (*= Organisation des Nations Unies*)

**unable** *adjective*
**to be unable to do something** ne pas pouvoir **[12]** faire quelque chose
**He's unable to come.** Il ne peut pas venir.
**I was unable to see him.** Je n'ai pas pu le voir.

**unacceptable** *adjective*
**inadmissible** *masc & fem*
**This is completely unacceptable.** Ceci est totalement inadmissible.

**unanimous** *adjective*
**unanime** *masc & fem*

**unattractive** *adjective*
(*person, place*) **peu attrayant** *masc*, **peu attrayante** *fem*

**unavoidable** *adjective*
**inévitable** *masc & fem*

**unbearable** *adjective*
**insupportable** *masc & fem*
**I find them unbearable.** Je les trouve insupportables.

**unbelievable** *adjective*
**incroyable** *masc & fem*

**uncertain** *adjective*
**incertain** *masc*, **incertaine** *fem*
**to be uncertain whether ...** ne pas être **[6]** sûr que ...
**I'm uncertain whether they're coming.** Je ne suis pas sûr qu'ils viennent.

**unchanged** *adjective*
**inchangé** *masc*, **inchangée** *fem*

**uncivilized** *adjective*
**barbare** *masc & fem*

**uncle** *noun*
un **oncle** *masc*
**my Uncle Bill** mon oncle Bill

**uncomfortable** *adjective*
1 (*shoes, chair*) **inconfortable** *masc & fem*
2 (*journey, situation*) **pénible** *masc & fem*
**to feel uncomfortable** se sentir Ⓔ **[2]** mal à l'aise.
**I'm feeling pretty uncomfortable.** Je me sens plutôt mal à l'aise.

**uncommon** *adjective*
**rare** *masc & fem*

**unconscious** *adjective*
**sans connaissance**
**Tessa's still unconscious.** Tessa est toujours sans connaissance.

**under** *preposition*
1 (*underneath*) **sous**
**Harry hid under the bed.** Harry s'est caché sous le lit.
**Perhaps it's under there.** C'est peut-être là-dessous.
2 (*less than*) **moins de**
**Tickets cost under £20.** Les billets coûtent moins de vingt livres.
**It's free for children under five.** C'est gratuit pour les enfants de moins de cinq ans.
**It took under two hours to get there.** Il a fallu moins de deux heures pour y aller.

**under-age** *adjective*
**to be under-age** être **[6]** mineur
**Jane can't go. She's under-age.** Jane ne peut pas y aller. Elle est mineure.

**underclothes** *plural noun*
les **sous-vêtements** *masc pl*

**undercooked** *adjective*
**pas assez cuit** *masc*, **pas assez cuite** *fem*

to **underestimate** *verb*
**sous-estimer [1]**

Ⓔ means the verb takes être to form the perfect



a b c d e f g h i j k l m n o p q r s t u v w x y z

**underground** *adjective*
▷ see **underground** *noun*
**souterrain** *masc*, **souterraine** *fem*
**an underground carpark** un parking souterrain

♪ **underground** *noun*
▷ see **underground** *adj*
le **métro** *masc*
**I saw her on the underground.** Je l'ai vue dans le métro.
**Shall we go by underground?** On prend le métro?

to **underline** *verb*
**souligner [1]**
**Underline all the adjectives.** Soulignez tous les adjectifs.

♪ **underneath** *adverb*
▷ see **underneath** *prep*
**dessous**
**Look underneath.** Cherche dessous.
**I was wearing a T-shirt underneath.** Je portais un tee-shirt dessous.

♪ **underneath** *preposition*
▷ see **underneath** *adv*
**sous**
**It's underneath these papers.** C'est sous ces papiers.

♪ **underpants** *plural noun*
le **slip** *masc*
**my underpants** mon slip

**underpass** *noun*
1 (*pedestrian*) le **passage souterrain**
2 (*for traffic*) le **passage inférieur**

♪ to **understand** *verb*
**comprendre [64]**
**Do you understand how it works?** Est-ce que tu comprends comment ça marche?
**I don't understand.** Je ne comprends pas.
**I couldn't understand what he was saying.** Je n'ai pas compris ce qu'il disait.
**They don't understand me.** Ils ne me comprennent pas.

**understandable** *adjective*
(*instructions, language*) **compréhensible** *masc & fem*
**You're upset. That's understandable.** Tu es contrarié. Ça se comprend.

**understanding** *adjective*
▷ see **understanding** *noun*
**compréhensif** *masc*, **compréhensive** *fem*
**He was very understanding.** Il a été très compréhensif.

**understanding** *noun*
▷ see **understanding** *adj*
la **compréhension** *fem*

**undertaker** *noun*
un **entrepreneur de pompes funèbres**
**at the undertaker's** aux pompes funèbres

**underwear** *noun*
les **sous-vêtements** *masc pl*

to **undo** *verb*
1 (*a button, a tie*) **défaire [10]**
2 (*a parcel, a zip*) **ouvrir [30]**

**undone** *adjective*
**to come undone** se défaire ⓔ **[10]**
**Your button's come undone.** Ton bouton s'est défait.

♪ to **undress** *verb*
**to get undressed** se déshabiller ⓔ **[1]**
**I got undressed.** Je me suis déshabillé (*boy speaking*), Je me suis déshabillée (*girl speaking*).

♪ **unemployed** *adjective*
▷ see **unemployed** *noun*
**au chômage**
**She's unemployed.** Elle est au chômage.

♪ **unemployed** *noun*
▷ see **unemployed** *adj*
**the unemployed** les chômeurs *masc pl*
**benefits to help the unemployed** des allocations pour les chômeurs

♪ **unemployment** *noun*
le **chômage** *masc*

**uneven** *adjective*
**irrégulier** *masc*, **irrégulière** *fem*

**unexpected** *adjective*
**imprévu** *masc*, **imprévue** *fem*
**an unexpected event** un événement imprévu

**unexpectedly** *adverb*
(*to happen, arrive*) **à l'improviste**

**unfair** *adjective*
**injuste** *masc & fem*
**It's unfair to young people.** C'est injuste pour les jeunes.
**It's unfair of them to do that.** Il est injuste qu'ils fassent ça.

**unfashionable** *adjective*
**démodé** *masc*, **démodée** *fem*

to **unfasten** *verb*
(*a belt, a button*) **défaire [10]**

English–French

**unfit** *adjective*
to be unfit ne pas être [6] en forme
I'm terribly unfit. Je ne suis pas du tout en forme.

to **unfold** *verb*
**déplier** [1]

**unforgettable** *adjective*
**inoubliable** *masc & fem*
**It was an unforgettable experience.** Cela a été une expérience inoubliable.

**unfortunate** *adjective*
1 **regrettable** *masc & fem*
**an unfortunate experience** une expérience regrettable
2 (*unlucky*) **malheureux** *masc*, **malheureuse** *fem*
**the unfortunate victims** les victimes malheureuses

**unfortunately** *adverb*
**malheureusement**
**He's not here unfortunately.** Il n'est pas là malheureusement.

**unfriendly** *adjective*
**pas très sympathique** *masc & fem*
**Some people are unfriendly.** Certaines personnes ne sont pas très sympathiques.

**unfurnished** *adjective*
**non meublé** *masc*, **non meublée** *fem*

**ungrateful** *adjective*
**ingrat** *masc*, **ingrate** *fem*

**unhappy** *adjective*
**malheureux** *masc*, **malheureuse** *fem*

**unhealthy** *adjective*
1 (*person*) **maladif** *masc*, **maladive** *fem*
2 (*food*) **malsain** *masc*, **malsaine** *fem*

**unhurt** *adjective*
**indemne** *masc & fem*
**to escape unhurt from an accident** sortir Ⓔ [72] indemne d'un accident

**uniform** *noun*
un **uniforme** *masc*
**She was in school uniform.** Elle était en uniforme scolaire.
**They don't wear a uniform.** Ils ne portent pas d'uniforme.

mini-info **uniform**
French pupils wear casual clothes to school as there is no school uniform.

**uninhabited** *adjective*
**inhabité** *masc*, **inhabitée** *fem*

**union** *noun*
(*a trade union*) le **syndicat** *masc*

**Union Jack** *noun*
le **drapeau du Royaume-Uni**

**unique** *adjective*
**unique** *masc & fem*

**unit** *noun*
1 (*for measuring, section in a book*) une **unité** *fem*
**a unit of measurement** une unité de mesure
2 (*for kitchen storage*) un **élément** *masc*
3 (*a hospital department*) le **service** *masc*
**the intensive care unit** le service des soins intensifs

to **unite** *verb*
**unir** [2]

**United Kingdom** *noun*
le **Royaume-Uni** *masc*

**WORD TIP** Countries and regions in French take *le, la* or *les*.

**United Nations** *noun*
l'**O.N.U.** (*Organisation des Nations Unies*)

**United States (of America)** *plural noun*
les **États-Unis** *masc pl*
**in the United States** aux États-Unis
**He's at college in the United States.** Il est à l'université aux États-Unis.
**to the United States** aux États-Unis
**Have you ever been to the United States?** Est-ce que tu es jamais allé aux États-Unis?

**WORD TIP** Countries and regions in French take *le, la* or *les*.

**universe** *noun*
l'**univers** *masc*

**university** *noun*
une **université** *fem*
**She's at university in London.** Elle est à l'université à Londres.
**to go to university** aller Ⓔ [7] à l'université
**Do you want to go to university?** Tu veux aller à l'université?
- **university education** la formation universitaire
- **university lecturer** un maître de conférences, une maîtresse de conférences
- **university professor** le professeur d'université
- **university town** la ville universitaire

**unjust** *adjective*
**injuste** *masc & fem*

Ⓔ means the verb takes être to form the perfect

**unkind** *adjective*
**pas gentil** *masc*, **pas gentille** *fem*
**He's unkind to animals.** Il n'est pas gentil avec les animaux.

**unknown** *adjective*
**inconnu** *masc*, **inconnue** *fem*

♪ **unleaded petrol** *noun*
**l'essence sans plomb** *fem*

♪ **unless** *conjunction*
unless ... à moins que ... ne ...
**I'm not going unless he phones.** Je ne vais pas à moins qu'il ne téléphone.
**She won't know unless you tell her.** Elle ne saura pas à moins que tu ne le lui dises.

**unlike** *preposition*
1 (*in contrast to*) **contrairement à**
**Unlike me, she hates dogs.** Contrairement à moi, elle déteste les chiens.
2 (*uncharacteristic of*) **It's unlike her to be late.** Ce n'est pas son genre d'être en retard.

**unlikely** *adjective*
**peu probable** *masc & fem*
**It's unlikely.** C'est peu probable.
**It's unlikely that we'll be going.** Il est peu probable que nous y allions.

**unlimited** *adjective*
**illimité** *masc*, **illimitée** *fem*
**an unlimited choice** un choix illimité

to **unload** *verb*
(*a lorry, a ship, goods*) **décharger [52]**

to **unlock** *verb*
**ouvrir [30]**
**The car's unlocked.** La voiture est ouverte.

♪ **unlucky** *adjective*
1 (*person*) **to be unlucky** ne pas avoir **[5]** de chance
**I was unlucky, it was shut.** Je n'ai pas eu de chance, c'était fermé.
2 (*colour, number*) **to be unlucky** porter **[1]** malheur
**Thirteen is an unlucky number.** Le treize porte malheur.

**unmarried** *adjective*
**célibataire** *masc & fem*

**unnatural** *adjective*
**anormal** *masc*, **anormale** *fem*, **anormaux** *masc pl*, **anormales** *fem pl*

**unnecessary** *adjective*
**inutile** *masc & fem*
**It's unnecessary to book.** Il est inutile de réserver.

to **unpack** *verb*
**défaire [10]**
**I unpacked my rucksack.** J'ai défait mon sac à dos.
**I'll just unpack and then I'll come down.** Je vais juste défaire ma valise et puis je descendrai.

**unpaid** *adjective*
1 (*bill*) **impayé** *masc*, **impayée** *fem*
2 (*work*) **non rémunéré** *masc*, **non rémunérée** *fem*

♪ **unpleasant** *adjective*
**désagréable** *masc & fem*
**an unpleasant trip** un voyage désagréable
**to be unpleasant to somebody** être **[6]** désagréable avec quelqu'un
**The waiter was unpleasant to us.** Le garçon a été désagréable avec nous.

to **unplug** *verb*
(*a computer, a TV, a kettle*) **débrancher [1]**

**unpopular** *adjective*
**impopulaire** *masc & fem*
**to make yourself unpopular** se rendre ⓔ **[3]** impopulaire

**unrealistic** *adjective*
**peu réaliste** *masc & fem*

**unreasonable** *adjective*
**pas raisonnable** *masc & fem*
**He's being really unreasonable.** Il n'est vraiment pas raisonnable.

**unrecognizable** *adjective*
**méconnaissable** *masc & fem*
**You're unrecognizable in that costume.** Tu es méconnaissable dans ce costume.

**unreliable** *adjective*
1 (*information, computer, car*) **peu fiable** *masc & fem*
2 **She's unreliable.** On ne peut pas compter sur elle.

to **unroll** *verb*
**dérouler [1]**

**unsafe** *adjective*
(*wiring, building*) **dangereux** *masc*, **dangereuse** *fem*

**unsatisfactory** *adjective*
**peu satisfaisant** *masc*, **peu satisfaisante** *fem*
**an unsatisfactory result** un résultat peu satisfaisant

to **unscrew** *verb*
**dévisser [1]**

**unshaven** *adjective*
**pas rasé** *masc*, **pas rasée** *fem*

**unsuccessful** *adjective*
**to be unsuccessful** ne pas réussir **[2]**
**I tried, but I was unsuccessful.** J'ai essayé mais je n'ai pas réussi.
**After a few unsuccessful attempts, I gave up.** Après quelques essais vains, j'ai abandonné.

**unsuitable** *adjective*
**inapproprié** *masc*, **inappropriée** *fem*

**untidy** *adjective*
**en désordre**
**The house is always untidy.** La maison est toujours en désordre.

to **untie** *verb*
*(a knot, a lace)* **défaire [10]**

**until** *preposition*
1 **jusqu'à**
**until Monday** jusqu'à lundi
**He's on holiday until the tenth.** Il est en vacances jusqu'au dix.
**until now** jusqu'à présent
**I didn't know about it until now.** Je n'étais pas au courant jusqu'à présent.
**until then** jusque-là
**There was no electricity until then.** Il n'y a pas eu d'électricité jusque-là.
2 **not until** pas avant
**not until September** pas avant septembre
**It won't be finished until Friday.** Ce ne sera pas fini avant vendredi.

**unusual** *adjective*
**peu commun** *masc*, **peu commune** *fem*
**You chose an unusual colour.** Tu as choisi une couleur peu commune.
**Storms are unusual in June.** Les orages au mois de juin sont rares.
**It's unusual for Matt to be absent.** Il est rare que Matt soit absent.

**unwilling** *adjective*
**to be unwilling to do something** ne pas vouloir faire quelque chose
**He's unwilling to wait.** Il ne veut pas attendre.

to **unwrap** *verb*
**déballer [1]**

**up** *preposition, adverb*
1 *(out of bed)* **to be up** être **[6]** levé
**Liz isn't up yet.** Liz n'est pas encore levée.
**to get up** se lever Ⓔ **[50]**
**I get up at seven.** Je me lève à sept heures.
**We got up at six.** Nous nous sommes levés à six heures.
2 *(not yet in bed)* **to be up late** se coucher Ⓔ **[1]** tard
**I was up late last night.** Je me suis couché tard hier soir *(boy speaking)*, Je me suis couchée tard hier soir *(girl speaking)*.
3 *(higher up)* **en haut**
**up at the top of the house** tout en haut de la maison
**Hands up!** Haut les mains!
**up here** ici
**It's up there.** C'est là-haut.
**We went up the road.** Nous avons remonté la rue.
**It's just up the street.** C'est tout près.
**He's working up in Glasgow.** Il travaille à Glasgow.
4 *(what's the matter?)* **What's up?** Qu'est-ce qui se passe?
**What's up with him?** Qu'est-ce qu'il a?
5 **up to** jusqu'à
**up to here** jusqu'ici
**You can invite up to fifty people.** Tu peux inviter jusqu'à cinquante personnes.
6 **to come up to somebody** s'approcher **[1]** de quelqu'un
**She came up to me.** Elle s'est approchée de moi.
7 **to be up to something** faire **[10]** quelque chose
**What's she up to?** Qu'est-ce qu'elle fait?
8 **It's up to you to decide.** C'est à toi de décider.
**It's not up to me.** Ce n'est pas à moi de décider.
9 *(finished, over)* **Time's up!** C'est l'heure!

to **update** *verb* ▷ see **update** *noun*
1 *(information, timetables)* **mettre [11] à jour**
2 *(style, decoration)* **moderniser [1]**

**update** *noun* ▷ see **update** *verb*
la **mise à jour**
**Here's an update on the delays.** Voici une mise à jour des retards.

**upheaval** *noun*
le **bouleversement** *masc*

**uphill** *adverb*
*(path)* **en montée**
**to walk uphill** marcher **[1]** en montée
**The road goes uphill to the square.** La route monte jusqu'à la place.

**upright** *adjective, adverb*
**droit** *masc*, **droite** *fem*
**Put it upright.** Mets-le droit.
**Try to stand upright.** Essaie de te tenir droit.

Ⓔ means the verb takes être to form the perfect

to **upset** *verb* ▷ see **upset** *adj, noun*
**contrarier [1]**
**You've upset your mother.** Tu as contrarié ta mère.
**I was upset by it.** Ça m'a contrarié.

**upset** *adjective* ▷ see **upset** *noun, verb*
**contrarié** *masc*, **contrariée** *fem*
**He's upset.** Il est contrarié.
**to get upset** se vexer ⓔ **[1]**
**They teased her and she got upset.** Ils l'ont taquinée et elle s'est vexée.

**upset** *noun* ▷ see **upset** *adj, verb*
**a stomach upset** une indigestion

**upside down** *adjective, adverb*
**à l'envers**

♪ **upstairs** *adverb*
**en haut**
**Mum's upstairs.** Maman est en haut.
**to go upstairs** monter ⓔ **[1]**
**He went upstairs to get a towel.** Il est monté chercher une serviette.

**up-to-date** *adjective*
1 (*clothes, equipment*) **moderne** *masc & fem*
2 (*information*) **à jour**
**The website's not up-to-date.** Le site web n'est pas à jour.

**upwards** *adverb*
(*to look, point*) **vers le haut**

**urban** *adjective*
**urbain** *masc*, **urbaine** *fem*

♪ **urgent** *adjective*
**urgent** *masc*, **urgente** *fem*
**Is it urgent?** C'est urgent?
**to be in urgent need of a doctor** avoir **[5]** un besoin urgent d'un médecin

**urgently** *adverb*
**d'urgence**
**She wants to see you urgently.** Elle veut te voir d'urgence.

♪ **us** *pronoun*
1 (*as a direct and indirect object*) **nous**
**She knows us.** Elle nous connaît.
**They saw us.** Ils nous ont vus.
**She hasn't spoken to us yet.** Elle ne nous a pas encore parlé.
**Can you point out the post office to us?** Pouvez-vous nous indiquer la poste?
**He gave us a cheque.** Il nous a donné un chèque.
2 (*in orders*) **nous**
**Wait for us!** Attendez-nous!
**Tell us the answer!** Dis-nous la réponse!
**Don't tell us!** Ne nous le dis pas!
3 (*after prepositions like avec, sans*) **nous**
**My gran lives with us.** Ma grand-mère habite avec nous.
**They went off without us.** Ils sont partis sans nous.
4 (*in comparisons*) **nous**
**They're older than us.** Ils sont plus âgés que nous.
**They're luckier than us.** Ils ont plus de chance que nous.

**US** *noun*
les **U.S.A.** *masc pl*

**USA** *noun*
les **U.S.A.** *masc pl*

**WORD TIP** Countries and regions in French take *le, la* or *les*.

♪ to **use** *verb* ▷ see **use** *noun*
**utiliser [1]**
**We used the dictionary.** Nous avons utilisé le dictionnaire.
**Use the information to fill in the gaps.** Utilise les renseignements pour remplir les blancs.
**May I use the phone?** Puis-je passer un coup de téléphone?
**to use something to do something** se servir ⓔ **[71]** de quelque chose pour faire quelque chose
**I used a knife to open the parcel.** Je me suis servi d'un couteau pour ouvrir le paquet.
**What did they use to decorate the garden?** Ils se sont servis de quoi pour décorer le jardin?
**to be used for doing something** servir **[71]** à faire quelque chose
**It's used for cleaning the screen.** Ça sert à nettoyer l'écran.
• to **use something up**
1 (*food, shampoo, petrol*) **consommer [1] quelque chose**
2 (*money*) **dépenser [1] quelque chose**

♪ **use** *noun* ▷ see **use** *verb*
1 **l'emploi** *masc*
**the instructions for use** le mode d'emploi
2 (*pointless*) **It's no use.** Ça ne sert à rien.
**it's no use doing** ça ne sert à rien de faire
**It's no use phoning.** Ça ne sert à rien de téléphoner.
**It's no use going on about it.** Ça ne sert à rien d'insister.
3 **to be of use** servir **[71]**
**It might be of some use.** Ça pourrait servir.

♪ **used** *adjective*
1 (*car, book*) **d'occasion**
**They want to buy a used car.** Ils veulent acheter une voiture d'occasion. ▸▸

2 **to be used to something** être [6] habitué à quelque chose
**She's used to life in France.** Elle est habituée à la vie en France.
**I'm not used to the noise.** Je ne suis pas habitué au bruit.
3 **to be used to doing something** avoir [5] l'habitude de faire quelque chose
**We're used to walking to school.** Nous avons l'habitude d'aller à l'école à pied.
**I'm not used to eating in restaurants.** Je n'ai pas l'habitude de manger au restaurant.
4 **to get used to (doing) something** s'habituer [1] à (faire) quelque chose
**I've got used to living here.** Je me suis habitué à habiter ici.
**You'll get used to it!** Tu t'y habitueras!

**used to** *verb*
**She used to smoke.** Elle fumait avant.
**They used to live in the country.** Ils habitaient à la campagne avant.
**He used not to cycle to school.** Il n'allait pas à l'école en vélo avant.

**useful** *adjective*
**utile** *masc & fem*
**a useful piece of information** un renseignement utile
**to be useful for doing something** être [6] utile pour faire quelque chose
**It's useful for storing CDs.** C'est utile pour ranger les CD.

**useless** *adjective*
**nul** *masc*, **nulle** *fem*
**This knife's useless.** Ce couteau est nul.
**You're completely useless!** Tu es complètement nul!
**I'm useless at art.** Je suis nul en dessin.

**user** *noun*
(*of a computer, product, book*) un **utilisateur** *masc*, une **utilisatrice** *fem*
**road users** les usagers de la route

**user-friendly** *adjective*
**convivial** *masc*, **conviviale** *fem*, **conviviaux** *masc pl*, **conviviales** *fem pl*

**usual** *adjective*
**habituel** *masc*, **habituelle** *fem*
**It's the usual problem.** C'est le problème habituel.
**as usual** comme d'habitude
**He was late as usual.** Il était en retard comme d'habitude.
**It's colder than usual.** Il fait plus froid que d'habitude.

**usually** *adverb*
**d'habitude**
**I usually leave at eight.** D'habitude je pars à huit heures.

**utensil** *noun*
un **ustensile** *masc*
**kitchen utensils** les ustensiles de cuisine

# Vv

**vacancy** *noun*
1 (*in a hotel*) **'Vacancies'** 'Chambres libres'
**'No vacancies'** 'Complet'
2 (*for employment*) **a job vacancy** un poste vacant

**vacant** *adjective*
**libre** *masc & fem*

to **vaccinate** *verb*
**vacciner** [1]

**vaccination** *noun*
la **vaccination** *fem*

to **vacuum** *verb* ▷ see **vacuum** *noun*
**passer** [1] **l'aspirateur**
**to vacuum my room** passer l'aspirateur dans ma chambre

**vacuum** *noun* ▷ see **vacuum** *verb*
le **vide** *masc*

**vacuum cleaner** *noun*
un **aspirateur**

**vagina** *noun*
le **vagin** *masc*

**vague** *adjective*
**vague** *masc & fem*

**vaguely** *adverb*
**vaguement**

**vain** *adjective*
1 **vaniteux** *masc*, **vaniteuse** *fem*
2 **in vain** en vain
**She tried in vain to wake him.** Elle a essayé en vain de le réveiller.

**Valentine's Day** *noun*
la **Saint-Valentin** *fem*

**valentine card** *noun*
la **carte de Saint-Valentin**

**valid** *adjective*
**valable** *masc & fem*
**This ticket's not valid at peak times.** Ce billet n'est pas valable en période de pointe.

**valley** *noun*
la **vallée** *fem*

**valuable** *adjective*
1 (*jewellery, painting*) **de valeur**
**some valuable jewels** des bijoux de valeur
**to be valuable** avoir **[5]** de la valeur
**That watch is very valuable.** Cette montre a une grande valeur.
2 (*appreciated*) **précieux** *masc*, **précieuse** *fem*
**He gave us some valuable information.** Il nous a donné des renseignements précieux.

to **value** *verb* ▷ see **value** *noun*
(*some help, an opinion, friendship*) **apprécier [1]**

**value** *noun* ▷ see **value** *verb*
la **valeur** *fem*

**van** *noun*
1 (*small*) la **fourgonnette** *fem*, la **camionnette** *fem*
2 (*large*) le **fourgon** *masc*, le **camion** *masc*

**vandal** *noun*
le & la **vandale** *masc & fem*

**vandalism** *noun*
le **vandalisme** *masc*

to **vandalize** *verb*
**vandaliser [1]**

𝆑 **vanilla** *noun*
la **vanille** *fem*
**a vanilla ice cream** une glace à la vanille

to **vanish** *verb*
**disparaître [27]**

**variety** *noun*
la **variété** *fem*

𝆑 **various** *adjective*
**plusieurs** *masc & fem*
**There are various ways of doing it.** Il y a plusieurs façons de le faire.
**We got letters from various people.** Nous avons reçu des lettres de plusieurs personnes.

to **vary** *verb*
**varier [1]**
**It varies a lot.** Ça varie beaucoup.
**It's good to vary the tasks.** Il est bien de varier les tâches.

**vase** *noun*
le **vase** *masc*

**VAT** *noun*
(*= Value Added Tax*) la **TVA** *fem* (*= Taxe à la valeur ajoutée*)

𝆑 **veal** *noun*
le **veau** *masc*

**vegan** *noun*
le **végétalien** *masc*, la **végétalienne** *fem*

𝆑 **vegetable** *noun*
le **légume** *masc*
**vegetable soup** la soupe aux légumes
**You don't eat enough vegetables.** Tu ne manges pas assez de légumes.

𝆑 **vegetarian** *noun, adjective*
le **végétarien** *masc*, la **végétarienne** *fem*
**a vegetarian recipe** une recette végétarienne
**He's vegetarian.** Il est végétarien.

𝆑 **vehicle** *noun*
le **véhicule** *masc*

**vein** *noun*
la **veine** *fem*

**velvet** *noun*
le **velours** *masc*

**vending machine** *noun*
le **distributeur automatique**

**ventilated** *adjective*
**aéré** *masc*, **aérée** *fem*

**ventilation** *noun*
l'**aération** *fem*

**verb** *noun*
(*Grammar*) le **verbe** *masc*
**a plural verb** un verbe au pluriel

**verdict** *noun*
le **verdict** *masc*

**verge** *noun*
1 (*roadside*) l'**accotement** *masc*
2 **to be on the verge of doing something** être **[6]** sur le point de faire quelque chose
**I was on the verge of leaving.** J'étais sur le point de partir.

𝆑 **version** *noun*
la **version** *fem*

English–French

a b c d e f g h i j k l m n o p q r s t u v w x y z

English–French

**versus** *preposition*
**contre**
Arsenal versus St Étienne Arsenal contre St Étienne

**vertical** *adjective*
**vertical** *masc*, **verticale** *fem*, **verticaux** *masc pl*, **verticales** *fem pl*

**vertigo** *noun*
le **vertige** *masc*

**very** *adverb* ▷ see **very** *adj*
**très**
a very funny film un film très drôle
You sang very well. Tu as très bien chanté.
They were driving very fast. Ils roulaient très vite.
very much beaucoup
I'm enjoying myself very much. Je m'amuse beaucoup.
You haven't changed very much. Tu n'as pas beaucoup changé.
very little très peu
It costs very little. Ça coûte très peu.

**very** *adjective* ▷ see **very** *adv*
(*the exact*) He found the very thing he was looking for. Il a trouvé exactement ce qu'il cherchait.
The very person I need! Exactement la personne qu'il me faut!

**vest** *noun*
le **maillot de corps**

**vet** *noun*
le & la **vétérinaire** *masc & fem*
She's a vet. Elle est vétérinaire.

**via** *preposition*
to go via somewhere passer **[1]** par quelque part
We went via Dover. Nous sommes passés par Douvres.

**vicar** *noun*
le **pasteur** *masc*

**vicious** *adjective*
1 (*dog*) **méchant** *masc*, **méchante** *fem*
The dog turned vicious. Le chien est devenu méchant.
2 (*attack*) **brutal** *masc*, **brutale** *fem*, **brutaux** *masc pl*, **brutales** *fem pl*

**victim** *noun*
la **victime** *fem*

**victory** *noun*
la **victoire** *fem*
a resounding victory une victoire écrasante

to **video** *verb* ▷ see **video** *noun*
(*a programme, a film*) **enregistrer [1]**
I'll video it for you. Je te l'enregistrerai.

**video** *noun* ▷ see **video** *verb*
1 (*recorded film*) la **vidéo** *fem*
We were watching a video. On regardait une vidéo.
I've got it on video. Je l'ai en vidéo.
2 (*cassette*) la **cassette vidéo** *fem*
I bought a couple of videos. J'ai acheté quelques cassettes vidéo.
3 (*video recorder*) le **magnétoscope** *masc*
- **video cassette** la cassette vidéo
- **video game** le jeu vidéo (*pl* les jeux vidéo)
- **video recorder** le magnétoscope
- **video shop** le vidéoclub

**view** *noun*
1 (*from a room*) la **vue** *fem*
a room with a view of the lake une chambre avec vue sur le lac
You're blocking my view. Tu me bouches la vue.
I climbed to the top to get a better view. Je suis monté jusqu'en haut pour mieux voir.
2 (*opinion*) un **avis** *masc*
in my view à mon avis
In your view, what does it mean? À ton avis, qu'est-ce que cela signifie?
from my point of view de mon point de vue

**viewer** *noun*
(*TV*) le **téléspectateur** *masc*, la **téléspectatrice** *fem*
Several viewers complained. Plusieurs téléspectateurs se sont plaints.

**viewpoint** *noun*
le **point de vue**
other viewpoints d'autres points de vue

**vigorous** *adjective*
**vigoureux** *masc*, **vigoureuse** *fem*

**vile** *adjective*
**abominable** *masc & fem*
The food was vile. La nourriture était abominable.

**villa** *noun*
la **villa** *fem*

**village** *noun*
le **village** *masc*
a fishing village un village de pêcheurs

**villager** *noun*
le **villageois** *masc*, la **villageoise** *fem*

**vine** *noun*
la **vigne** *fem*

**vinegar** *noun*
le **vinaigre** *masc*

**vineyard** *noun*
le **vignoble** *masc*

**violence** *noun*
la **violence** *fem*

♪ **violent** *adjective*
**violent** *masc*, **violente** *fem*
**a violent storm** une tempête violente
**I don't like violent films.** Je n'aime pas les films violents.

**violin** *noun*
le **violon** *masc*
**to play the violin** jouer [1] du violon
**Jo plays the violin.** Jo joue du violon.

**violinist** *noun*
le & la **violoniste** *masc & fem*

**virgin** *noun*
la **vierge** *fem*

**Virgo** *noun*
**Vierge**
**Sophie's Virgo.** Sophie est Vierge.

**WORD TIP** Signs of the zodiac do not take an article: *un* or *une*.

**virtually** *adverb*
**pratiquement**
**Virtually everyone was there.** Pratiquement tout le monde était là.

**virtual reality** *noun*
la **réalité virtuelle**

**virus** *noun*
le **virus** *masc*
**I got a nasty virus.** J'ai attrapé un sale virus.
**anti-virus software** un logiciel antivirus

**visa** *noun*
le **visa** *masc*

**visibility** *noun*
la **visibilité** *fem*
**Visibility was poor.** La visibilité était mauvaise.

**visible** *adjective*
**visible** *masc & fem*

♪ to **visit** *verb* ▷ see **visit** *noun*
1 (*a museum, a castle, a town*) **visiter [1]**
**We visited the Louvre.** On a visité le Musée du Louvre.
2 (*a person*) **aller** Ⓔ **[7] voir**
**We visited Auntie Pat at Christmas.** Nous sommes allés voir tante Pat à Noël.
**Come and visit us!** Viens nous voir!
**We're just visiting.** Nous sommes seulement de passage.

♪ **visit** *noun* ▷ see **visit** *verb*
1 (*by a friend, family, a VIP*) **la visite** *fem*
**an official visit** une visite officielle
**I really enjoyed your visit.** Ta visite m'a fait vraiment plaisir.
2 (*to a house, museum, site*) **la visite** *fem*
**They organized a visit to the castle.** On a organisé une visite du château.
3 (*stay*) **le séjour** *masc*
**my last visit to France** mon dernier séjour en France

**visitor** *noun*
1 (*guest*) **un invité** *masc*, **une invitée** *fem*
**We've got visitors tonight.** On a des invités ce soir.
2 (*tourist*) **le visiteur** *masc*, **la visiteuse** *fem*
**It's a guide for visitors.** C'est un guide pour les visiteurs.

**visual** *adjective*
**visuel** *masc*, **visuelle** *fem*

to **visualize** *verb*
(*a scene, a person*) **s'imaginer [1]**
**Try to visualize the scene.** Essaie de t'imaginer la scène.

**vital** *adjective*
**indispensable** *masc & fem*
**it's vital to do something** il est indispensable de faire quelque chose
**It's vital to book.** Il est indispensable de réserver.

**vitamin** *noun*
la **vitamine** *fem*

**vivid** *adjective*
(*colours*) **vif** *masc*, **vive** *fem*
**a poster in vivid colours** une affiche aux couleurs vives
**to have a vivid imagination** exagérer [1]
**He has a slightly vivid imagination.** Il exagère un peu.

**vocabulary** *noun*
le **vocabulaire** *masc*

**vocational** *adjective*
**professionnel** *masc*, **professionnelle** *fem*
• **vocational education** la formation professionnelle

**vodka** *noun*
le **vodka** *masc*

♪ **voice** *noun*
la **voix** *fem*
**Keep your voice down!** Baisse ta voix!
**Jasmine has a great voice.** Jasmine a une belle voix.
**His voice is breaking.** Sa voix mue.

**volcano** *noun*
le **volcan** *masc*

**volleyball** *noun*
**le volley-ball** *masc*
**to play volleyball** jouer **[1]** au volley-ball

**volume** *noun*
**le volume** *masc*
**Could you turn down the volume?** Est-ce que tu peux baisser le volume?

**voluntary** *adjective*
**1** (*not compulsory*) **volontaire** *masc & fem*
**2** **to do voluntary work** travailler **[1]** bénévolement
**I do voluntary work once a week.** Je travaille bénévolement une fois par semaine.

**volunteer** *noun*
**1** (*for a task*) **le & la volontaire** *masc & fem*
**2** (*doing charity work*) **le & la bénévole** *masc & fem*

**to vomit** *verb*
**vomir [2]**

**to vote** *verb* ▷ see **vote** *noun*
**voter [1]**
**Marie always votes Green.** Marie vote toujours pour les Verts.
**They voted against the changes.** Ils ont voté contre les changements.

**vote** *noun* ▷ see **vote** *verb*
**le vote** *masc*
**She got 20 votes.** Elle a obtenu 20 votes.

**voucher** *noun*
**1** (*for a discount, special offer*) **le bon** *masc*
**2** (*for a gift*) **le chèque-cadeau**
**a CD voucher** un chèque-cadeau pour CD

**vowel** *noun*
(*Grammar*) **la voyelle** *fem* (*the letters: a, e, i, o, u*)

**voyage** *noun*
**le voyage** *masc*
**a voyage across the Atlantic** un voyage à travers l'Atlantique

**vulgar** *adjective*
**vulgaire** *masc & fem*

# W w

**waffle** *noun*
**la gaufre** *fem*

**to wag** *verb*
**remuer [1]**

**wage** *noun*, **wages** *pl*
**le salaire** *masc*
**a weekly wage of £250** un salaire hebdomadaire de 250 livres

**waist** *noun*
**la taille** *fem*
- **waistcoat** le gilet
- **waist measurement** le tour de taille

**to wait** *verb* ▷ see **wait** *noun*
**1** **attendre [3]**
**They're waiting outside.** Ils attendent dehors.
**I've been waiting for an hour.** J'attends depuis une heure.
**2** **to wait for somebody, something** attendre **[3]** quelqu'un, quelque chose
**He's waiting for you.** Il t'attend.
**We're waiting for the train.** Nous attendons le train.
**3** **to keep somebody waiting** faire **[10]** attendre quelqu'un
**The dentist kept me waiting.** La dentiste m'a fait attendre.
**4** (*showing impatience*) **I can't wait for the holidays.** J'attends les vacances avec impatience.

**wait** *noun* ▷ see **wait** *verb*
**une attente** *fem*
**an hour's wait** une heure d'attente

**waiter** *noun*
**le serveur** *masc*

**waiting list** *noun*
**la liste d'attente**

**waiting room** *noun*
**la salle d'attente**

**waitress** *noun*
**la serveuse** *fem*

**to wake** *verb*
**1** (*somebody*) **réveiller [1]**
**Jess woke me at six.** Jess m'a réveillé à six heures.

2 (*to wake up*) **se réveiller** ⓔ **[1]**
**We woke at six.** Nous nous sommes réveillés à six heures.
**Wake up!** Réveille-toi!

♪ **Wales** *noun*
le **pays de Galles**
**in Wales** au pays de Galles
**to Wales** au pays de Galles
**We go to Wales every summer.** On va au pays de Galles tous les étés.

**WORD TIP** Countries and regions in French take *le*, *la* or *les*.

♪ to **walk** *verb* ▷ see **walk** *noun*
1 (*in general*) **marcher [1]**
**I like walking on sand.** J'aime marcher sur le sable.
2 (*to go for a walk*) **se promener** ⓔ **[50]**
**We walked around the old town.** Nous nous sommes promenés dans la vieille ville.
3 (*to go*) **aller** ⓔ **[7]**
**I'll walk to the station with you.** J'irai avec toi jusqu'à la gare.
4 (*to go on foot*) **aller** ⓔ **[7] à pied**
**We can walk there easily.** On peut y aller à pied sans problème.

♪ **walk** *noun* ▷ see **walk** *verb*
1 la **promenade** *fem*
**It's five minutes' walk from here.** C'est à cinq minutes à pied d'ici.
**I'm going to take the dog for a walk.** Je vais promener le chien.
**to go for a walk** faire **[10]** une promenade, se promener ⓔ **[50]**
**We went for a walk in the woods.** Nous avons fait une promenade dans la forêt.
**They've just been for a walk.** Ils sont sortis se promener.
2 (*stroll*) le **tour** *masc*

**walking** *noun*
(*hiking*) la **randonnée** *fem*
**We're going walking in Scotland.** Nous allons faire de la randonnée en Écosse.

**walking distance** *noun*
**to be within walking distance** être **[6]** à quelques minutes à pied

**walking stick** *noun*
la **canne** *fem*

**walkman**® *noun*
le **walkman**® *masc*

♪ **wall** *noun*
1 (*of a house*) le **mur** *masc*
2 (*of a city*) la **muraille** *fem*

♪ **wallet** *noun*
le **portefeuille** *masc*

**wallpaper** *noun*
le **papier peint**

**walnut** *noun*
la **noix** *fem* (*pl* les **noix**)

to **wander** *verb*
**to wander around a place** se balader ⓔ **[1]** quelque part
**We wandered around the town.** On s'est baladé en ville.

♪ to **want** *verb*
**vouloir [14]**
**I want a watch for Christmas.** Je veux une montre pour Noël.
**Do you want some coffee?** Tu veux du café?
**Who wants some ice cream?** Qui veut de la glace?
**to want to do something** vouloir faire quelque chose
**I want to go for a swim.** Je veux aller me baigner.
**What do you want to do?** Qu'est-ce que tu veux faire?

**war** *noun*
la **guerre** *fem*

♪ **wardrobe** *noun*
1 (*cupboard*) une **armoire** *fem*
2 (*clothes*) la **garde-robe** *fem*

**warehouse** *noun*
un **entrepôt** *masc*

♪ to **warm** *verb* ▷ see **warm** *adj*
(*the plates, water*) **chauffer [1]**
**Warm the plates.** Chauffez les assiettes.
• **to warm up**
1 (*after feeling cold*) **se réchauffer** ⓔ **[1]**
2 (*food*) **réchauffer [1]**
3 (*athletes*) **s'échauffer [1]**

♪ **warm** *adjective* ▷ see **warm** *verb*
1 (*food, drink*) **chaud** *masc*, **chaude** *fem*
**a warm drink** une boisson chaude
**to keep something warm** tenir **[77]** quelque chose au chaud
**I'll keep your dinner warm.** Je tiendrai ton dîner au chaud.
2 (*weather, places*) **to be warm** faire **[10]** chaud
**It was warmer yesterday.** Il faisait plus chaud hier.
**It's warm in the kitchen.** Il fait chaud dans la cuisine.
3 **to be warm** avoir **[5]** chaud
**I'm warm.** J'ai chaud.
4 (*welcome*) **chaleureux** *masc*, **chaleureuse** *fem*

English–French

**warmth** *noun*
la **chaleur** *fem*

to **warn** *verb*
1 (*to inform*) **prévenir [81]**
**I'm warning you, don't do it.** Je te préviens, ne le fais pas.
2 **to warn somebody not to do something** conseiller [1] à quelqu'un de ne pas faire quelque chose
**Ruth warned me not to go.** Ruth m'a conseillé de ne pas y aller.

**warning** *noun*
un **avertissement** *masc*

**wart** *noun*
la **verrue** *fem*

to **wash** *verb* ▷ see **wash** *noun*
1 (*clothes, car, floor*) **laver [1]**
**I've washed your jeans.** J'ai lavé ton jean.
2 (*yourself*) **se laver** Ⓔ **[1]**
**to wash your hands** se laver les mains
**I've washed my hands.** Je me suis lavé les mains.
**She's washing her hair.** Elle se lave les cheveux.
3 **to wash the dishes** faire [10] la vaisselle
• **to wash up**
**faire [10] la vaisselle**

**wash** *noun* ▷ see **wash** *verb*
1 **to give something a wash** laver [1] quelque chose
**My jeans need a wash.** Mon jean a besoin d'être lavé.
2 **to have a wash** se laver Ⓔ [1]

**washing** *noun*
1 (*dirty*) le **linge sale**
2 (*clean*) le **linge** *masc*
• **washing machine** la machine à laver
• **washing powder** la lessive

**washing-up** *noun*
la **vaisselle** *fem*
**Are you going to do the washing-up?** Tu vas faire la vaisselle?
• **washing-up liquid** le liquide à vaisselle

**wasp** *noun*
la **guêpe** *fem*

to **waste** *verb* ▷ see **waste** *noun*
1 (*food, money, paper*) **gaspiller [1]**
2 (*time*) **perdre [3]**
**You're wasting your time.** Tu perds ton temps.

**waste** *noun* ▷ see **waste** *verb*
1 (*of food, money*) le **gaspillage** *masc*
**It's a waste of money.** C'est de l'argent gaspillé.
2 (*of time*) la **perte** *fem*
**a waste of time** une perte de temps
3 (*household, industrial*) les **déchets** *masc pl*
• **wastepaper basket** la corbeille à papier

to **watch** *verb* ▷ see **watch** *noun*
1 (*to look at*) **regarder [1]**
**I like watching TV.** J'aime regarder la télé.
2 (*to keep a check on*) **surveiller [1]**
**You have to watch him.** Il faut le surveiller.
3 (*to be careful*) **faire [10] attention**
**Watch that step.** Fais attention à cette marche.
**Watch out!** Attention!

**watch** *noun* ▷ see **watch** *verb*
la **montre** *fem*
**My watch is fast.** Ma montre avance.
**My watch is slow.** Ma montre retarde.

to **water** *verb* ▷ see **water** *noun*
(*the plants*) **arroser [1]**

**water** *noun* ▷ see **water** *verb*
l'**eau** *fem*
**a glass of water** un verre d'eau

**watercolours** *noun*
la **peinture pour aquarelle**

**waterfall** *noun*
la **cascade** *fem*

**watering can** *noun*
un **arrosoir** *masc*

**watermelon** *noun*
la **pastèque** *fem*

**waterproof** *adjective*
**imperméable** *masc & fem*

**water-skiing** *noun*
le **ski nautique**
**to go water-skiing** faire [10] du ski nautique

to **wave** *verb* ▷ see **wave** *noun*
1 (*with your hand*) **saluer [1] de la main**
**to wave at somebody** saluer quelqu'un de la main
**They're waving at us.** Ils nous saluent de la main.
2 (*a flag, newspaper*) **agiter [1]**

**wave** *noun* ▷ see **wave** *verb*
1 (*in the sea*) la **vague** *fem*
2 (*with your hand*) le **signe** *masc*
**to give somebody a wave** faire [10] signe à quelqu'un

**wax** *noun*
la **cire** *fem*

**way** *noun*
1 (*route, road*) le **chemin** *masc*
**the way to town** le chemin pour aller en ville

a b c d e f g h i j k l m n o p q r s t u v **w** x y z



Ⓔ means the verb takes être to form the perfect

We met Chris on the way. Nous avons rencontré Chris en route.
I got a puncture on the way back. J'ai eu un pneu crevé sur le chemin de retour.
I'm on my way. J'arrive. ▷ **way in**, **way out**.

**2** (*direction*) la **direction** *fem*
Which way did they go? En quelle direction sont-ils partis?
They went that way. Ils sont partis par là.
Come this way. Venez par ici.

**3** (*manner*) la **façon** *fem*
a way of speaking une façon de parler
Is that the way to do it? Est-ce qu'on le fait comme ça?
Do it this way. Fais-le comme ceci.

**4** (*in expressions*) Is it the right way up? C'est à l'endroit?
It's the wrong way round. C'est à l'envers.
It's a long way. C'est loin.
No way! Pas question!
by the way à propos

- **way in** une entrée
- **way out** la sortie

**we** *pronoun*
**1** (*as subject*) **nous**
We live in Cardiff. Nous habitons Cardiff.
We're students. Nous sommes étudiants.
**2** (*informally*) **on**
We're going to the cinema tonight. On va au cinéma ce soir.

**weak** *adjective*
**1** (*not strong*) **faible** *masc & fem*
I feel weak. Je me sens faible.
**2** (*tea, coffee*) **léger** *masc*, **légère** *fem*
a cup of weak tea une tasse de thé léger

**wealth** *noun*
la **fortune** *fem*

**wealthy** *adjective*
**riche** *masc & fem*

**weapon** *noun*
une **arme** *fem*

to **wear** *verb*
**1** (*clothes, shoes, etc*) **porter [1]**
Tanya's wearing her new boots. Tanya porte ses nouvelles bottes.
**2** (*perfume, sun cream, jewellery*) **mettre [11]**
Are you wearing perfume? Est-ce que tu as mis du parfum?
to wear make-up se maquiller Ⓔ [1]

- **to wear something out**
(*clothes, shoes*) **user [1] quelque chose**

**weather** *noun*
le **temps** *masc*
What's the weather like? Quel temps fait-il?
The weather here is terrible. Il fait un temps affreux ici.
in fine weather quand il fait beau
The weather was cold. Il faisait froid.

**weather forecast** *noun*
la **météo** *fem*
according to the weather forecast ... selon la météo ...

**web** *noun*
**1** (*spider's*) la **toile** *fem*
**2** the Web le Web *masc*

- **webcam** le webcam
- **web designer** le concepteur de sites web, la conceptrice de sites web
- **website** le site web

***web***

Lots of expressions linked to the Internet (*Internet* or *le Net*) are based on English: *surfer le Net*, *un site web*, *un e-mail*, etc. When giving your e-mail address, @ = *arobase*, dot = *point*.

**wedding** *noun*
le **mariage** *masc*

**Wednesday** *noun*
le **mercredi** *masc*
on Wednesday mercredi
last Wednesday mercredi dernier
next Wednesday mercredi prochain
every Wednesday tous les mercredis
on Wednesdays le mercredi
See you on Wednesday! À mercredi!
I saw Mike last Wednesday. J'ai vu Mike mercredi dernier.

**WORD TIP** Months of the year and days of the week start with small letters in French.

**weed** *noun*
la **mauvaise herbe**

**week** *noun*
la **semaine** *fem*
this week cette semaine
She came back last week. Elle est rentrée la semaine dernière.
I'm on holiday next week. Je pars en vacances la semaine prochaine.
I'll see you in two weeks' time. Je te vois dans deux semaines.

**weekday** *noun*
le **jour de semaine**
on weekdays en semaine

**weekend** *noun*
le **week-end**
last weekend le week-end dernier
next weekend le week-end prochain ▸▸



English-French
a b c d e f g h i j k l m n o p q r s t u v w x y z

at weekends les week-end
They're coming for the weekend. Ils vont passer le week-end chez nous.
I'll do it at the weekend. Je le ferai pendant le week-end.
Have a nice weekend! Bon week-end!

**weekly** *adverb*
**une fois par semaine**

♪ to **weigh** *verb*
1 (*a suitcase, a person, ingredients*) **peser [50]**
I weigh 50 kilos. Je pèse cinquante kilos.
How much do you weigh? Tu pèses combien?
2 to weigh yourself se peser Ⓔ [1]

♪ **weight** *noun*
le **poids** *masc*
to put on weight prendre [64] du poids
She's put on weight. Elle a pris du poids.
to lose weight perdre [3] du poids
Have you lost weight? Est-ce que tu as perdu du poids?
- **weightlifting** l'haltérophilie *fem*
- **weight training** la musculation

**weird** *adjective*
**bizarre** *masc & fem*

to **welcome** *verb* ▷ see **welcome** *adj, noun*
**accueillir [35]**

♪ **welcome** *adjective* ▷ see **welcome** *noun, verb*
**bienvenu** *masc*, **bienvenue** *fem*
'Thank you!' — 'You're welcome!' 'Merci!' — 'De rien!'
Welcome to Chester! Bienvenue à Chester!

♪ **welcome** *noun* ▷ see **welcome** *adj, verb*
un **accueil** *masc*
a warm welcome un accueil chaleureux

♪ **well** *adverb* ▷ see **well** *noun*
1 (*in general*) **bien**
Henry played well. Henry a bien joué.
The operation went well. L'opération s'est bien passée.
Well done! Bravo!
2 (*to say how you feel*) to feel well se sentir Ⓔ [2] bien
I don't feel well. Je ne me sens pas bien.
I'm very well, thank you. Ça va très bien, merci.
3 as well aussi
Katie's coming as well. Katie vient aussi.
4 (*to start talking*) **alors**
Well, what's the problem? Alors, quel est le problème?
5 (*to say you agree*) very well très bien
Very well then, you can go. Très bien, tu peux y aller.
6 (*when hesitating*) (*informal*) **ben**
Well ... I'm not sure. Ben ... je ne suis pas sûr.

♪ **well-behaved** *adjective*
**sage** *masc & fem*

♪ **well-done** *adjective*
(*steak*) **bien cuit** *masc*, **bien cuite** *fem*

♪ **well-dressed** *adjective*
**bien habillé** *masc*, **bien habillée** *fem*

**wellington boot** *noun*
la **botte en caoutchouc**

**well-known** *adjective*
**célèbre** *masc & fem*

♪ **well-off** *adjective*
**aisé** *masc*, **aisée** *fem*

♪ **Welsh** *adjective* ▷ see **Welsh** *noun*
1 **gallois** *masc*, **galloise** *fem*
David is Welsh. David est gallois.
Rhiannon is Welsh. Rhiannon est galloise.
2 (*music, accent*) **gallois** *masc*, **galloise** *fem*
the Welsh team l'équipe galloise

**WORD TIP** Adjectives never have capitals in French, even for nationality or regional origin.

♪ **Welsh** *noun* ▷ see **Welsh** *adj*
1 (*people*) the Welsh les Gallois *masc pl*
2 (*language*) le **gallois** *masc*
to speak Welsh parler [1] gallois
to learn Welsh apprendre [64] le gallois

**WORD TIP** Languages never have capitals in French.

♪ **west** *adjective, adverb* ▷ see **west** *noun*
**ouest** *invariable adj*
the west side of the city le côté ouest de la ville
a west wind un vent d'ouest
a town west of Paris une ville à l'ouest de Paris
We're going west. Nous allons vers l'ouest.

**WORD TIP** *ouest* never changes.

♪ **west** *noun* ▷ see **west** *adj, adv*
l'**ouest** *masc*
in the west à l'ouest
in the west of Ireland dans l'ouest de l'Irlande

♪ **western** *noun*
(*film*) le **western** *masc*

**West Indian** *adjective* ▷ see **West Indian** *noun*
**antillais** *masc*, **antillaise** *fem*



Ⓔ means the verb takes être to form the perfect

**West Indian** *noun* ▷ see **West Indian** *adj*
un **Antillais** *masc*, une **Antillaise** *fem*

**West Indies** *plural noun*
les **Antilles** *fem pl*

♪ **wet** *adjective*
1 (*damp*) **mouillé** *masc*, **mouillée** *fem*
**The grass is wet.** L'herbe est mouillée.
**My hair's wet.** J'ai les cheveux mouillés.
**to get wet** se faire ⓔ [10] mouiller
**We got wet.** Nous nous sommes fait mouiller.
2 (*weather*) **a wet day** un jour de pluie
**in wet weather** quand il pleut
3 (*paint*) **frais** *masc*, **fraîche** *fem*
• **wet suit** la combinaison de plongée

**whale** *noun*
la **baleine** *fem*

♪ **what** *adjective, pronoun*
1 (*in questions: as object*) **qu'est-ce que**, **qu'** (*before a, e, i, o, u or silent h*)
**What's she doing?** Qu'est-ce qu'elle fait?
**What did you say?** Qu'est-ce que tu as dit?
**What is it?** Qu'est-ce que c'est?
**What's the matter?** Qu'est-ce qu'il y a?
2 (*in questions: as subject*) **qu'est-ce qui**
**What's happening?** Qu'est-ce qui se passe?
**What scared Joe?** Qu'est-ce qui a fait peur à Joe?
3 (*as object relative pronoun*) **ce que**, **qu'** (*before a, e, i, o, u or silent h*)
**Show me what you bought.** Montre-moi ce que tu as acheté.
**I'll tell him what we've done.** Je vais lui dire ce qu'on a fait.
4 (*as subject relative pronoun*) **ce qui**
**She told me what had happened.** Elle m'a dit ce qui était arrivé.
5 (*with nouns in questions*) **quel** *masc*, **quelle** *fem*
**What's your address?** Quelle est ton adresse?
**What colour is it?** C'est de quelle couleur?
**What make is it?** C'est quelle marque?
6 (*in exclamations*) **quel** *masc*, **quelle** *fem*
**What a bore!** Quelle barbe!
**What a strange idea!** Quelle idée bizarre!
7 (*when you don't hear, etc*) **What?** Comment?

**wheat** *noun*
le **blé** *masc*

**wheel** *noun*
la **roue** *fem*
• **wheelchair** le fauteuil roulant

♪ **when** *adverb, conjunction*
**quand**
**When's your birthday?** C'est quand, ton anniversaire?
**When is she arriving?** Quand est-ce qu'elle arrive?
**It was raining when I went out.** Il pleuvait quand je suis sorti.

♪ **where** *adverb, conjunction*
**où**
**Where do you live?** Tu habites où?
**Where are you going?** Où vas-tu?
**I don't know where they live.** Je ne sais pas où ils habitent.

**whether** *conjunction*
**si**
**I don't know whether he's back or not.** Je ne sais pas s'il est rentré ou non.

♪ **which** *adjective* ▷ see **which** *pron*
**quel** *masc*, **quelle** *fem*
**Which CD did you buy?** Quel CD as-tu acheté?
**Which jacket do you prefer?** Quelle veste préfères-tu?

♪ **which** *pronoun* ▷ see **which** *adj*
1 (*which one*) **lequel** *masc*, **laquelle** *fem*
**'I saw your brother.' — 'Which one?'** 'J'ai vu ton frère.' — 'Lequel?'
**'I saw your aunt.' — 'Which one?'** 'J'ai vu ta tante.' — 'Laquelle?'
**Which of these jackets is yours?** Laquelle de ces vestes est à toi?
2 (*which ones*) **lesquels** *masc pl*, **lesquelles** *fem pl*
**'I borrowed some CDs.' — 'Which ones?'** 'J'ai emprunté des CD.' — 'Lesquels?'
3 (*as subject relative pronoun*) **qui**
**the lamp which is on the table** la lampe qui est sur la table
4 (*as object relative pronoun*) **que**, **qu'** (*before a, e, i, o, u or silent h*)
**the book which you borrowed from me** le livre que tu m'as emprunté
**the books which you borrowed from me** les livres que tu m'as empruntés

♪ **while** *conjunction* ▷ see **while** *noun*
**pendant que**
**You can watch TV while I finish my homework.** Tu peux regarder la télé pendant que je finis mes devoirs.

♪ **while** *noun* ▷ see **while** *conj*
**a while** quelque temps
**a while ago** il y a quelque temps.
**for a while** pendant quelque temps
**in a little while** dans peu de temps

to **whip** *verb*
**fouetter** [1]
whipped cream la crème fouettée

**whiskers** *plural noun*
les **moustaches** *fem pl*

**whisky** *noun*
le **whisky** *masc*

to **whisper** *verb*
**chuchoter** [1]

to **whistle** *verb* ▷ see **whistle** *noun*
**siffler** [1]

**whistle** *noun* ▷ see **whistle** *verb*
le **sifflet** *masc*

**white** *noun* ▷ see **white** *adj*
le **blanc** *masc*

**white** *adjective* ▷ see **white** *noun*
**blanc** *masc*, **blanche** *fem*
a white shirt une chemise blanche
white wine le vin blanc
- **whiteboard** le tableau blanc
- **white coffee** le café au lait
- **white-water rafting** le rafting en eau vive

**who** *pronoun*
1 (*in questions*) **qui**
Who is it? Qui est-ce?
Who wants some chocolate? Qui veut du chocolat?
2 (*as subject relative pronoun*) **qui**
My friend who lives in Paris. Mon ami qui habite à Paris.
3 (*as object relative pronoun*) **que**, **qu'** (*before a, e, i, o, u or silent h*)
the friends who we invited les amis que nous avons invités, les amis qu'on a invités

**whole** *adjective* ▷ see **whole** *noun*
**tout** *masc*, **toute** *fem*
the whole time tout le temps
the whole family toute la famille
the whole world le monde entier

**whole** *noun* ▷ see **whole** *adj*
the whole of the cake le gâteau tout entier
the whole of the class la classe tout entière
for the whole of August pendant tout le mois d'août

**wholemeal bread** *noun*
le **pain complet** *masc*

**whom** *pronoun*
1 **que**, **qu'** (*before a, e, i, o, u or silent h*)
the person whom I saw la personne que j'ai vue
2 (*after a preposition*) **qui**
the person to whom I wrote la personne à qui j'ai écrit

**whose** *adjective, pronoun*
1 (*in questions*) **à qui**
Whose is this jacket? À qui est cette veste?
Whose shoes are these? À qui sont ces chaussures?
Whose is it? À qui c'est?
I know whose it is. Je sais à qui c'est.
2 (*relative pronoun*) **dont**
the man whose car has been stolen le monsieur dont la voiture a été volée
the ladies whose names I've forgotten les dames dont j'ai oublié le nom

**why** *adverb*
**pourquoi**
Why are they always late? Pourquoi est-ce qu'ils sont toujours en retard?
Why did she phone? Pourquoi a-t-elle appelé?

**wicked** *adjective*
1 (*witch, etc*) **méchant** *masc*, **méchante** *fem*
2 (*very good*) **génial** *masc*, **géniale** *fem*, **géniaux** *masc pl*, **géniales** *fem pl*
(*informal*) Wicked! Génial!

**wide** *adjective* ▷ see **wide** *adv*
1 **large** *masc & fem*
a piece of paper 20 cm wide une feuille de papier de vingt centimètres de large
The river is very wide. La rivière est très large.
2 (*ocean, choice*) **vaste** *masc & fem*
a wide range of games une vaste gamme de jeux

**wide** *adverb* ▷ see **wide** *adj*
1 to be wide open être [6] grand ouvert
2 to be wide awake être [6] complètement éveillé

**widow** *noun*
la **veuve** *fem*
She's a widow. Elle est veuve.

**widower** *noun*
le **veuf** *masc*
He's a widower. Il est veuf.

**width** *noun*
la **largeur** *fem*

**wife** *noun*
la **femme** *fem*

**wig** *noun*
la **perruque** *fem*

**wild** *adjective*
1 (*animal, plant, landscape*) **sauvage** *masc & fem*
2 (*idea, party, person*) **fou** *masc*, **folle** *fem*
The crowd went wild when she came on stage. Le public s'est déchaînée quand elle est entrée en scène.





a b c d e f g h i j k l m n o p q r s t u v w x y z

**wildlife** *noun*
la **faune** *fem*

**will** *verb*
1 (*talking about the future*) **He will be glad to see you.** Il sera content de te voir.
**There won't be a problem.** Il n'y aura pas de problème.
**I'll see you soon.** Je te reverrai bientôt.
**It won't rain.** Il ne pleuvra pas.
2 (*talking about the immediate future*) **I'll phone the doctor at once.** Je vais appeler le docteur tout de suite.
**What will you do?** Qu'est-ce que tu vas faire?
3 (*to make requests*) **Will you help me?** Est-ce que tu peux m'aider?
4 (*to say somebody won't do something*)
**He won't open the door.** Il ne veut pas ouvrir la porte.
**She won't speak to me.** Elle ne veut pas me parler.

**willing** *adjective*
**to be willing to do something** être[6] prêt à faire quelque chose

**willpower** *noun*
la **volonté** *fem*

♪ to **win** *verb* ▷ see **win** *noun*
**gagner**[1]
**I won!** J'ai gagné!
**Rovers won by two goals.** Rovers ont gagné de deux buts.

to **wind** *verb* ▷ see **wind** *noun*
1 (*a rope, a tape*) **enrouler**[1]
2 (*a clock*) **remonter**[1]
- **to wind something down**
(*a car window*) **baisser**[1]
- **to wind something up**
(*a car window*) **remonter**[1]

♪ **wind** *noun* ▷ see **wind** *verb*
le **vent** *masc*

**wind farm** *noun*
la **ferme d'éoliennes**

♪ **window** *noun*
1 (*in a building*) la **fenêtre** *fem*
**I was looking out of the window.** Je regardais par la fenêtre.
2 (*in a car, bus, train*) la **vitre** *fem*

♪ **windscreen** *noun*
le **pare-brise** *masc* (*pl* les **pare-brise**)
- **windscreen wiper** un essuie-glace

♪ **windsurfing** *noun*
la **planche à voile**
**We went windsurfing.** Nous avons fait de la planche à voile.

**windy** *adjective*
1 **to be windy** avoir[5] du vent
**It's windy today.** Il y a du vent aujourd'hui.
2 (*place*) **venteux** *masc*, **venteuse** *fem*

♪ **wine** *noun*
le **vin** *masc*

**wine**
France produces and exports more wine than any other country in the world.

**wing** *noun*
1 (*of a bird, plane*) une **aile** *fem*
2 (*in sport*) un **ailier** *masc*

**winner** *noun*
le **gagnant** *masc*, la **gagnante** *fem*

♪ **winter** *noun*
l'**hiver** *masc*
**in winter** en hiver
**next winter** l'hiver prochain
**last winter** l'hiver dernier
- **winter sports** les sports d'hiver *masc pl*

♪ to **wipe** *verb*
**essuyer**[41]
**I'll wipe the table.** Je vais essuyer la table.
**to wipe your eyes** s'essuyer[41] les yeux
**to wipe your feet** s'essuyer les pieds

**wire** *noun*
le **fil** *masc*

**wisdom** *noun*
la **sagesse**
- **wisdom tooth** la dent de sagesse

♪ **wise** *adjective*
**sage** *masc & fem*

to **wish** *verb* ▷ see **wish** *noun*
1 **si seulement ...**
**I wish he were here.** Si seulement il était ici.
**We wish we could go.** Si seulement on pouvait y aller.

**wish** *noun* ▷ see **wish** *verb*
le **vœu** *masc* (*pl* les **vœux**)
**to make a wish** faire[10] un vœu
**Best wishes** Meilleurs vœux

**witch** *noun*
la **sorcière** *fem*

♪ **with** *preposition*
1 (*in general*) **avec**
**with James** avec James
**with me** avec moi
**I bought it with my pocket money.** ▸▸

Je l'ai acheté avec mon argent de poche.
**Beat the eggs with a fork.** Battez les œufs avec une fourchette.

**2** (*in descriptions*) **au, aux**
**a girl with red hair** une fille aux cheveux roux
**the boy with glasses** le garçon aux lunettes

**3** (*because of*) **de**
**filled with water** rempli d'eau
**covered with mud** couvert de boue

♪ **without** *preposition*
**sans**
**without Charlotte** sans Charlotte
**without you** sans toi
**without sugar** sans sucre
**without a sweater** sans pull

**witness** *noun*
le **témoin** *masc*

**wizard** *noun*
le **magicien** *masc*

**wolf** *noun*
le **loup** *masc*

♪ **woman** *noun*
la **femme** *fem*
**a woman doctor** une femme médecin

to **wonder** *verb* ▷ see **wonder** *noun*
**se demander** Ⓔ **[1]**
**I wonder why.** Je me demande pourquoi.
**I wonder where Jake is.** Je me demande où est Jake.

**wonder** *noun* ▷ see **wonder** *verb*
la **merveille** *fem*
**No wonder you're tired.** Ce n'est pas étonnant si tu es fatigué.

**wonderful** *adjective*
**merveilleux** *masc*, **merveilleuse** *fem*
**a wonderful holiday** des vacances merveilleuses

♪ **wood** *noun*
le **bois** *masc*

**wooden** *adjective*
**en bois**

♪ **wool** *noun*
la **laine** *fem*

**woollen** *adjective*
**en laine**

♪ **word** *noun*
**1** le **mot** *masc*
**What's the French word for 'window'?** Comment dit-on 'window' en français?
**Mum had a word with my teacher.** Ma mère a parlé avec mon prof.

**2** (*of a song*) **the words** les paroles *fem pl*
**I've forgotten the words.** J'ai oublié les paroles.

• **word game** le jeu de lettres

♪ to **work** *verb* ▷ see **work** *noun*
**1** **travailler [1]**
**She works in an office.** Elle travaille dans un bureau.
**Leila works in advertising.** Leila travaille dans la publicité.
**She works as a librarian.** Elle travaille comme bibliothécaire.

**2** (*to operate*) **se servir** Ⓔ **[71] de**
**Can you work the video?** Est-ce que tu sais te servir du magnétoscope?

**3** (*to function*) **marcher [1]**
**The dishwasher's not working.** Le lave-vaisselle ne marche pas.

• **to work out**
**1** (*to exercise*) **s'entraîner [1]**
**2** (*to succeed*) **marcher [1]**

• **to work something out**
**1** (*the cost, a sum*) **calculer [1] quelque chose**
**2** (*to find*) **trouver [1] quelque chose**
**We'll work out how to get there.** On va trouver un moyen d'y aller.
**3** (*to understand*) **comprendre [64] quelque chose**
**I'm trying to work out how he did it.** J'essaie de comprendre comment il l'a fait.

♪ **work** *noun* ▷ see **work** *verb*
le **travail** *masc* (*pl* les **travaux**)
**I've got some work to do.** J'ai du travail à faire.
**That was a good piece of work.** C'était un bon travail.
**Mum's at work.** Maman est au travail.

**worked up** *adjective*
**to get worked up** s'énerver **[1]**

**worker** *noun*
**1** (*in general*) le **travailleur** *masc*, la **travailleuse** *fem*
**2** (*in a factory*) un **ouvrier** *masc*, une **ouvrière** *fem*

♪ **work experience** *noun*
**to do work experience** faire **[10]** un stage
**I did two weeks' work experience in an office.** J'ai fait un stage de deux semaines dans un bureau.



Ⓔ means the verb takes être to form the perfect

**working-class** *adjective*
**ouvrier** *masc*, **ouvrière** *fem*

**workstation** *noun*
le **poste de travail** (*pl* les **postes de travail**)

**world** *noun*
le **monde** *masc*
**the best team in the world** la meilleure équipe du monde

**World Cup** *noun*
the World Cup la Coupe du Monde

**world war** *noun*
la **guerre mondiale**
the Second World War la Seconde Guerre mondiale

**worm** *noun*
le **ver** *masc*

**worn out** *adjective*
1 (*person*) **épuisé** *masc*, **épuisée** *fem*
2 (*clothes, shoes*) **complètement usé** *masc*, **complètement usée** *fem*

♪ **worried** *adjective*
**inquiet** *masc*, **inquiète** *fem*
**She looks worried.** Elle a l'air inquiète.
**to be worried** s'inquiéter **[24]**
**They're worried.** Ils s'inquiètent.
**We're worried about Susan.** Nous nous inquiétons pour Susan.

♪ to **worry** *verb*
**s'inquiéter [24]**
**Don't worry!** Ne t'inquiète pas!
**There's nothing to worry about.** Il n'y a pas de quoi s'inquiéter.

♪ **worse** *adjective, adverb*
1 (*showing worsening*) **pire**
**even worse** encore pire
**to get worse** empirer **[1]**
**The weather's getting worse.** Le temps empire.
2 (*in comparisons*) **He's worse at English than French.** Il est pire en anglais qu'en français.
**You're worse than he is!** Tu es pire que lui!
**It's worse than before.** C'est pire qu'avant.
3 (*less ill*) **to feel worse** se sentir Ⓔ **[58]** plus malade
**I feel worse.** Je me sens plus malade.

**worst** *adjective, adverb*
1 (*with nouns*) **the worst** le plus mauvais *masc*, **la plus mauvaise** *fem*
**the worst day of my life.** la journée la plus mauvaise de ma vie
**It's the worst film I've ever seen.** C'est le film le plus mauvais que j'aie jamais vu.
**if the worst comes to the worst** au pire
2 (*with verbs*) **He plays the worst.** Il joue le moins bien.

**worth** *adjective*
1 **to be worth something** valoir **[80]** quelque chose
**How much is it worth?** Ça vaut combien?
**It's worth a lot of money.** Ça vaut beaucoup d'argent.
2 **to be worth doing something** valoir **[80]** la peine de faire quelque chose
**It's worth doing it.** Ça vaut la peine de le faire.

♪ **would** *verb*
1 (*to say what you'd like*) **I would like an omelette.** Je voudrais une omelette.
**I'd like to go to the cinema.** J'aimerais aller au cinéma.
**That would be a good idea.** Ce serait une bonne idée.
**If we asked her, she would help us.** Elle nous aiderait, si nous le lui demandions.
2 (*to make offers and requests*) **Would you like something to eat?** Voulez-vous quelque chose à manger?
**Would you like to come too?** Veux-tu venir aussi?
**Would you give me a hand?** Tu veux me donner un coup de main?
3 (*to show refusal*) **He wouldn't answer.** Il n'a pas voulu répondre.
**The car wouldn't start.** La voiture n'a pas voulu démarrer.

to **wound** *verb* ▷ see **wound** *noun*
**blesser [1]**
**seriously wounded** grièvement blessé

**wound** *noun* ▷ see **wound** *verb*
la **blessure** *fem*

to **wrap** *verb*
**emballer [1]**

**wrapping paper** *noun*
le **papier cadeau**

to **wreck** *verb*
1 (*a building, a car, a train*) **détruire [26]**
2 (*a plan, an occasion*) **gâcher [1]**

English–French

a b c d e f g h i j k l m n o p q r s t u v w x y z

**wrestler** *noun*
le **catcheur** *masc*, la **catcheuse** *fem*

**wrestling** *noun*
le **catch** *masc*

**wrist** *noun*
le **poignet** *masc*

♪ to **write** *verb*
**écrire [38]**
**She's writing her essay.** Elle est en train d'écrire sa rédaction.
**to write somebody a letter** écrire une lettre à quelqu'un
**I'll write them a letter.** Je leur écrirai une lettre.
**to write to somebody** écrire à quelqu'un
**I wrote to Jean yesterday.** J'ai écrit à Jean hier.
**to write to each other** s'écrire
**We write to each other regularly.** On s'écrit régulièrement.
- **to write something down**
**noter [1] quelque chose**

**writer** *noun*
un **écrivain** *masc*

♪ **wrong** *adjective*
1 (*not correct*) **mauvais** *masc*, **mauvaise** *fem*
**the wrong answer** la mauvaise réponse
**It's the wrong address.** Ce n'est pas la bonne adresse.
**to go the wrong way** se tromper ⓔ [1] de chemin
**I went the wrong way.** Je me suis trompé de chemin.
**Did you take the wrong bus?** Tu t'es trompé de bus?
**You've got the wrong number.** Vous vous êtes trompé de numéro.
2 (*mistaken*) **to be wrong** se tromper ⓔ [1]
**I was wrong.** Je me suis trompé.
**They were wrong.** Ils se sont trompés.
3 (*against the rules*) **What's wrong?** Qu'est-ce qu'il y a?
**There's nothing wrong.** Il n'y a rien.
4 (*false*) **faux** *masc*, **fausse** *fem*
**The information was wrong.** Les renseignements étaient faux.

# Xx

**xerox®** *noun* ▷ see **xerox®** *verb*
la **photocopie** *fem*

to **xerox®** *verb* ▷ see **xerox®** *noun*
**photocopier [1]**

**Xmas** *noun*
**Noël**

♪ **X-ray** *noun* ▷ see **X-ray** *verb*
la **radio** *fem*
**I saw the X-rays.** J'ai vu les radios.

to **X-ray** *verb* ▷ see **X-ray** *noun*
**faire [10] une radio de** (*part of the body*)
**They X-rayed her ankle.** Ils ont fait une radio de sa cheville.

# Yy

**yacht** *noun*
1 (*sailing boat*) le **voilier** *masc*
2 (*large luxury boat*) le **yacht** *masc*

to **yawn** *verb*
**bâiller [1]**
**I can't stop yawning.** Je n'arrête pas de bâiller.

♪ **year** *noun*
1 un **an** *masc*
**six years ago** il y a six ans
**I've known them for almost two years.** Je les connais depuis presque deux ans.
2 (*the whole period*) une **année** *fem*
**the whole year** toute l'année

a b c d e f g h i j k l m n o p q r s t u v w x y z

She spends part of the year in France. Elle passe une partie de l'année en France.
They lived in Moscow for years. Ils ont habité Moscou pendant des années.

**3** (*in the school system*) **I'm in Year 9.** Je suis en quatrième.
**I'm in Year 10.** Je suis en troisième.

**4** (*for someone's age*) **un an** *masc*
**a two-year-old child** un enfant de deux ans
**I'm fifteen years old.** J'ai quinze ans.

**WORD TIP** Always use *ans* in French even when in English you say your age without 'years' e.g. *I'm fifteen*.

**year**

French pupils start secondary school in *la sixième* (Year 7) and progress through *la cinquième* (Year 8), *la quatrième* (Year 9) to *la troisième* (Year 10). Then they change to a *lycée* for three years: *la seconde*, *la première* and *la terminale*.

**yearly** *adjective*
**annuel** *masc*, **annuelle** *fem*
**a yearly event** un événement annuel

to **yell** *verb*
**hurler [1]**
**You don't have to yell.** Tu n'es pas obligé de hurler.

**yellow** *adjective*
**jaune** *masc & fem*
**She's wearing yellow socks.** Elle porte des chaussettes jaunes.

**yes** *adverb*

**1** (*in general*) **oui**
**Yes, I know.** Oui, je sais.
**'Is Sam in his room?' — 'Yes, he is.'** 'Est-ce que Sam est dans sa chambre?' — 'Oui.'

**2** (*when **ne pas** is used in a question*) **si**
**'You don't want to go, do you?' — 'Yes, I do!'** 'Tu ne veux pas y aller, n'est-ce pas?' — 'Mais si!'
**'You haven't finished, have you?' — 'Yes, I have.'** 'Tu n'as pas fini?' — 'Si si.'

**yesterday** *adverb*
**hier**
**yesterday morning** hier matin
**yesterday afternoon** hier après-midi
**the day before yesterday** avant-hier
**I saw her yesterday.** Je l'ai vue hier.

**yet** *adverb*
**not yet** pas encore
**It's not ready yet.** Ce n'est pas encore prêt.
**I haven't finished yet.** Je n'ai pas encore fini.

**yoga** *noun*
le **yoga** *masc*

**yoghurt** *noun*
le **yaourt** *masc*
**a banana yoghurt** un yaourt à la banane

**yolk** *noun*
le **jaune d'œuf** (*pl* les **jaunes d'œuf**)

**you** *pronoun*

**1** (*informal form as a subject*) **tu**
**You look happy.** Tu as l'air content.
**Do you want to go to the cinema?** Tu veux aller au cinéma?

**2** (*as an object*) **te**
**I'll lend you my bike.** Je te prêterai mon vélo.
**I'll write to you.** Je t'écrirai.
**I've invited you.** Je t'ai invité.

**WORD TIP** *tu* becomes *t'* before a *a, e, i, o, u* or silent *h*.

**3** (*after prepositions like **avec, sans***) **toi**
**I'll go with you.** J'irai avec toi.
**Did they leave without you?** Est-ce qu'ils sont partis sans toi?
**I'm buying it for you.** Je l'achète pour toi.

**4** (*in comparisons*) **toi**
**He's older than you.** Il est plus âgé que toi.
**She's not as nice as you.** Elle n'est pas aussi sympa que toi.

**5** (*polite form: singular & plural*) **vous**
**You're very kind.** Vous êtes très gentil.
**Can you tell me where the station is, please?** Est-ce que vous pouvez m'indiquer la gare, s'il vous plaît?
**I can't help you, I'm sorry.** Je ne peux pas vous aider, je suis désolé.
**It's a present for you.** C'est un cadeau pour vous.
**They're older than you.** Ils sont plus âgés que vous.

**6** (*to more than one person*) **vous**
**I'll invite you all!** Je vous inviterai tous!
**Are you coming? You too?** Vous venez? Vous aussi?

**young** *adjective*
**jeune** *masc & fem*
**a young woman** une jeune femme
**She's the youngest in the class.** C'est elle la plus jeune de la classe.
**Tim's younger than me.** Tim est plus jeune que moi.
**Hannah's two years younger than me.** Hannah a deux ans de moins que moi.
**a young man** un jeune
**young people** les jeunes

**your** *adjective*

1 (*informal form: masc singular nouns*) **ton**
**your father** ton père
**your number** ton numéro

2 (*informal form: fem singular nouns*) **ta**
**your sister** ta sœur
**your skirt** ta jupe
**What's your address?** Quel est ton adresse?

**WORD TIP** Use *ton* with nouns beginning with *a, e, i, o, u* or *silent h*.

3 (*informal form: masc & fem plural nouns*) **tes**
**your cousins** tes cousins
**your friends** tes amis

4 (*formal form or to several people: masc & fem singular nouns*) **votre**
**your garden** votre jardin
**Thank you for your hospitality.** Merci pour votre hospitalité.

5 (*formal form or to several people: masc & fem plural nouns*) **vos**
**your children** vos enfants
**You can all bring your friends.** Vous pouvez tous amener vos amis.

**yours** *pronoun*

1 (*informal form: masc singular nouns*) **le tien**
**My brother's younger than yours.** Mon frère est plus jeune que le tien.

2 (*informal form: fem singular nouns*) **la tienne**
**I've got his address but not yours.** J'ai son adresse mais pas la tienne.

3 (*informal form: masc plural nouns*) **les tiens**
**There are my books. Where are yours?** Voilà mes livres. Où sont les tiens?

4 (*informal form: fem plural nouns*) **les tiennes**
**I don't like her photos, I prefer yours.** Je n'aime pas ses photos, je préfère les tiennes.

5 (*formal form or to several people: masc singular nouns*) **le vôtre**
**My son is younger than yours.** Mon fils est plus jeune que le vôtre.

6 (*formal form or to several people: fem singular nouns*) **la vôtre**
**My daughter is younger than yours.** Ma fille est plus jeune que la vôtre.

7 (*formal form or to several people: masc & fem plural nouns*) **les vôtres**
**My children are younger than yours.** Mes enfants sont plus jeunes que les vôtres.

8 (*belonging to you: informal*) **à toi**
**Is this pen yours?** Est-ce que ce stylo est à toi?

9 (*belonging to you: formal or with several people*) **à vous**
**Is this car yours?** Est-ce que cette voiture est à vous?

10 (*in letter endings*) **Yours, Cordialement.** (*informal*)
**Yours sincerely,** Veuillez agréer l'expression de mes sentiments distingués. (*formal*)

**yourself** *pronoun*

1 (*in reflexive verbs: informal*) **te**
**You'll hurt yourself.** Tu vas te faire mal.

2 (*in reflexive verbs: formal*) **vous**
**Are you enjoying yourself?** Est-ce que vous vous amusez?

3 (*for emphasis: informal*) **toi-même**
**Did you do it yourself?** Est-ce que tu l'as fait toi-même?

4 (*for emphasis: formal*) **vous-même**
**You said it yourself.** Vous l'avez dit vous-même.

5 **all by yourself** tout seul
**Amy, did you do it all by yourself?** Amy, tu l'as fait toute seule?

**yourselves** *pronoun*

1 (*in reflexive verbs*) **vous**
**Help yourselves.** Servez-vous.
**You can amuse yourselves.** Vous pouvez vous amuser.

2 (*for emphasis*) **vous-mêmes**
**Did you do it yourselves?** Est-ce que vous l'avez fait vous-mêmes?

**youth** *noun*

1 (*being young*) **la jeunesse** *fem*
**He travelled a lot in his youth.** Il a beaucoup voyagé dans sa jeunesse.

2 (*young people*) **les jeunes** *masc & fem pl*
**today's youth** les jeunes d'aujourd'hui

3 (*male teenager*) **le jeune** *masc*
**a group of youths** un groupe de jeunes

- **youth club** le club de jeunes
- **youth culture** la culture des jeunes
- **youth hostel** une auberge de jeunesse (*pl* les auberges de jeunesse)
- **youth worker** un éducateur, une éducatrice

**Yugoslavia** *noun*

**la Yougoslavie** *fem*
**the former Yugoslavia** l'ex-Yougoslavie





a b c d e f g h i j k l m n o p q r s t u v w x y z

# Z z

**zany** *adjective*
**loufoque** *masc & fem*

**zebra** *noun*
le **zèbre** *masc*
- **zebra crossing** le passage pour piétons

**zero** *noun*
le **zéro** *masc*

to **zigzag** *verb*
**zigzaguer [1]**

**zip** *noun*
la **fermeture éclair®**

**zodiac** *noun*
le **zodiaque** *masc*
**the signs of the zodiac** les signes du zodiaque

**zone** *noun*
la **zone** *fem*
the Euro zone la zone euro

**zoo** *noun*
le **zoo** *masc*

**zoom lens** *noun*
le **zoom** *masc*